ISBN 978-1-5277-8627-1
PIBN 10895527

1 MONTH OF
FREE
READING

at
www.ForgottenBooks.com

By purchasing this book you are eligible for one month membership to ForgottenBooks.com, giving you unlimited access to our entire collection of over 1,000,000 titles via our web site and mobile apps.

To claim your free month visit:

www.forgottenbooks.com/free895527

WAR OF THE REBELLION:

A COMPILATION OF THE

OFFICIAL RECORDS

OF THE

UNION AND CONFEDERATE ARMIES.

———

PREPARED, UNDER THE DIRECTION OF THE SECRETARY OF WAR, BY

The late Lieut. Col. ROBERT N. SCOTT, Third U. S. Artillery.

PURSUANT TO ACTS OF CONGRESS.

———

SERIES I—VOLUME XXIX—IN TWO PARTS.
PART II—CORRESPONDENCE, ETC.

———

WASHINGTON:
GOVERNMENT PRINTING OFFICE.
1890.

4.2249

PART II.–VOL. XXIX.

CORRESPONDENCE, ORDERS, AND RETURNS RELATING
SPECIALLY TO OPERATIONS IN NORTH CAROLINA,
VIRGINIA, WEST VIRGINIA, MARYLAND, AND PENN-
SYLVANIA, FROM AUGUST 4 TO DECEMBER 31, 1863.

UNION CORRESPONDENCE, ETC.

HDQRS. ARMY OF THE POTOMAC,
PROVOST-MARSHAL-GENERAL'S DEPARTMENT,
August 4, 1863.

Major-General HUMPHREYS,
Chief of Staff:

GENERAL: A most important expedition, conducted by Cline, attended by the highest results, has just returned. The party penetrated a considerable distance into Spotsylvania County, and from
their own observation and the employment of other agents, learned
the following, all of which was obtained in such a way as to make
the information of the first value:

The expedition was accompanied with much danger, on account of
the numerous bodies of cavalry who are scouring the country in pursuit of deserters. The number of these is very large, and has called
forth an extraordinary proclamation from Jeff. Davis, addressed to
the soldiers of the Confederate States, and attested by the Secretary
of State, in which a full pardon is extended to all who will return
within twenty days after the date of publication. All papers
throughout the Confederate States are required to publish the proclamation at the earliest moment, and for twenty days thereafter, and
to send·their bills to the private secretary of the President. Many
other facts tending to show the demoralization of their troops are
given, but the above is an index to them all.

All corn and other grains, bacon and cattle, and serviceable horses
are being gathered from the Northern Neck and other counties,
under orders from Richmond ; a special order being lately issued,
directing cavalry horses to be grazed on the oat-fields, and forage to
be given only to artillery and team horses.

One of our men went to Fredericksburg, and passed through
Cooke's brigade, which consists of four regiments and a battery of
Georgia troops. Lieutenant-General Ewell was seen personally at
Gordonsville five days ago, and there is a large force at Madison
Court-House, agreeing with our former reports. Pickett's division
of Longstreet's corps, lies opposite Kelly's Ford. The headquarters
of Fitzhugh Lee's brigade are at Chancellorsville, the brigade patrol-
ling the country and picketing the fords between the Rapidan and
Fredericksburg. The remainder of Longstreet's corps is between
Stevensburg and Slaughter's Mountain. A. P. Hill is between Stevensburg and Culpeper.

Lieutenant Martin, of the Forty-fifth Virginia, was heard in Fred-

ericksburg to state that a portion of Ewell's corps had been sent to
South Carolina, and we have evidence to show that besides Cooke's
brigade at Fredericksburg, another brigade has arrived at Gordonsville to replace those sent south. Our men were within the rebel
lines during the cavalry fight on Saturday. The troops in their
vicinity were entirely stampeded, and the citizens began leaving
their homes.

An extraordinary state of excitement is pervading all classes of
Southern society in regard to the late retreat of General Lee. A dis-
agreement has sprung up between himself and the Confederate cabi-
net, and General Lee has tendered his resignation. He desires to
retire to the line of the James River, and Mr. Davis urgently insists
upon his defending the line of the Rappahannock. Much recrimina-
tion exists in regard to the immense loss occasioned by the advance
into and retirement from Pennsylvania. All agree that the line of
the Rapidan will only be defended for the purpose of retarding our
movements.

The foregoing is not enlarged upon, being obtained from such
sources as to make it entirely reliable, the details thereof being personally communicated to the commanding general.

It is needless to say that our men were afoot, and that the foregoing location of the enemy's troops was, on their arrival this evening, two days old. Prior to their return there were indications of
the enemy's intention to retire beyond the Rapidan, fully confirmed
this evening, and forwarded in a special memorandum for the information of the general.

Very respectfully, your obedient servant,
GEO. H. SHARPE,
Colonel, and Deputy Provost-Marshal-General.

HEADQUARTERS FIRST CORPS, *August* 4, 1863.
(Received 6 p. m.)
Major-General HUMPHREYS,
Chief of Staff, Army of the Potomac:

An intercepted dispatch read by our signal officer is as follows:
General S. :

Orders to go just received; will do so at once. Enemy in same position.
C., *Colonel.*

A previously intercepted dispatch says :

Our left is left open by the withdrawal of Colonel Lomax.

Picket and artillery firing is now going on. Think enemy's movements will be developed soon. Will telegraph you. The enemy reported advancing.

JOHN NEWTON,
Major-General, Commanding.

HDQRS. THIRD BRIG., SECOND DIV., TWELFTH A. C.,
Near Ellis' Ford, Va., August 4, 1863.
Capt. THOMAS H. ELLIOTT, *Asst. Adjt. Gen. :*

CAPTAIN: I have the honor to report to the general commanding
that I have this morning examined the line of our pickets along the

river bank, which now connects with those of the Second Brigade of this division, forming a continuous line.

At Kemper's Ford, Colonel Ireland, One hundred and thirty-seventh New York Volunteers, has constructed a rifle-pit command ing the ford, and a large work, capable of containing his whole command, about 100 yards in rear.

About a dozen rebel cavalry have appeared to-day near Kemper's Ford, and Colonel Ireland has just reported to me that two regiments of rebel infantry have appeared about one-quarter of a mile above the ford.

I am, sir, very respectfully, your obedient servant,
GEO. S. GREENE,
Brigadier-General, Commanding Third Brigade.

HDQRS. FIRST BRIG., THIRD CAV. DIV., *August* 4, 1863.
(Received 11.45 a. m.)
Capt. J. L. GREENE,
Assistant Adjutant-General:

SIR: I have the honor to report all quiet along our picket line up to 1 o'clock last night. The occupation of Fredericksburg by the enemy's infantry and cavalry is fully confirmed. Captain Hamilton reported that he saw part of our Twelfth Corps crossing the Rappahannock at Kelly's Ford, and that the First and Third Corps, or parts of them, were already across the river at other points. If this be so, I do not think our pickets will be molested any more on the Rappahannock.

I think that in my hasty report of last night, I did not make it very clear as to what vedettes of Major Darlington were driven in. The attack was from the direction of Fredericksburg. The river at [or] near Fredericksburg is represented as fordable, and the enemy's force yesterday 6,000.

I shall do myself the honor to call at your headquarters this morning.

Very respectfully, your obedient servant,
EDWARD B. SAWYER,
Commanding Brigade.

WASHINGTON,
August 4, 1863.

Brigadier-General KING:

The major-general commanding desires that you send two parties of cavalry, of 60 or 70 men, to scout and beat up thoroughly the country in the vicinity of the Orange and Alexandria Railroad, one party taking the north and the other the south side. The party going south should call upon Stiles, the guide in Alexandria, through Lieutenant-Colonel Wells, provost-marshal-general.

No mercy need be shown to bushwhackers. These guerrillas must be destroyed.

J. H. TAYLOR,
Chief of Staff.

AUGUST 5, 1863—12.45 p. m.

Officer Commanding Fifth Corps:

The major-general commanding directs that a division of the Fifth Corps take position to hold Beverly Ford, where a regiment of the First Corps is now stationed. This regiment will be relieved by the division of the Fifth Corps as soon as it takes position.

A. A. HUMPHREYS,
Major-General, and Chief of Staff.

HDQRS. FIRST CAVALRY DIVISION, *August* 5, 1863.
(Received 9.30 p. m.)

Colonel ALEXANDER,
Chief of Staff, Cavalry Corps:

The enemy this morning at daylight attempted to advance his picket line, but failed. A few shots were exchanged. No harm done. All quiet now.

My horses are failing very fast. The grass is not good, and I have but little opportunity for grazing. Some of the dismounted men who went to Washington to be remounted have returned, and I learn that the officers and men are scattered all about the city.

JNO. BUFORD,
Brigadier-General of Volunteers.

HDQRS. SECOND BRIGADE, FIRST CAVALRY DIVISION,
Camp near Kelly's Ford, August 5, 1863—3.30 p. m.

Capt. T. C. BACON,
Assistant Adjutant-General, First Cavalry Division:

I have the honor to state that the party I sent to Barnett's Ford have returned. They were unable to cross, as the Rappahannock was not fordable at that point. Mountain Run is not fordable, and I will be unable to get to the Culpeper road with a sufficient number of men until the water has fallen. The rebel pickets are on the opposite side as yet.

The river is quite high at this point. One narrow pontoon bridge has been laid down and a *tête-de-pont* erected in front of it on this side. The sally-port is blockaded, and I cannot get my supply wagons across. General Slocum's troops are ordered not to allow us to pass ford or bridge without an order from him. The ford is almost impracticable for a loaded wagon. General Slocum's quarters are 1½ miles from here, and if I were attacked and crowded, I could not get my train off. I have therefore ordered it to remain on the north side of the river, and the troops to cross and supply themselves.

On my left a reconnaissance has developed the enemy's pickets along the base of the hills beyond the road from Brandy Station to the Germanna road. I will feel to the front as soon as the water is fordable.

Very respectfully, yours,

THOS. C. DEVIN,
Colonel, Commanding Brigade.

WASHINGTON, D. C.,
August 5, 1863—3.15 p. m.

Major-General MEADE,
 Warrenton, Va.:

 What is the strength of General Gordon's division?
H. W. HALLECK,
General-in-Chief.

HEADQUARTERS ARMY OF THE POTOMAC,
August 5, 1863—4.30 p. m.
(Received 5.10 p. m.)

Maj. Gen. H. W. HALLECK,
 General-in-Chief:

 On the return for July 31, the report of General Gordon's division is as follows:

	Aggregate.
Present for duty	3,708
Present	4,149
Present and absent	7,519

 This is the First Division, Eleventh Corps, and is not altogether the same division that General Gordon brought to this army.
GEO. G. MEADE,
Major-General, Commanding.

WASHINGTON, D. C.,
August 5, 1863—8.12 p. m.

Major-General MEADE,
 Warrenton, Va.:

 General Gordon's division will immediately come to Alexandria, where General Gordon will report by telegraph for further orders. All land transportation will be turned over to the quartermaster's department.
H. W. HALLECK,
General-in-Chief.

AUGUST 5, 1863.

Officer Commanding Eleventh Corps:

 Pursuant to orders received from the General-in-Chief, General Gordon's division will immediately proceed to Alexandria by railroad. When arrived there, General Gordon will be directed to report to Major-General Halleck by telegraph. You will please telegraph to General Ingalls, chief quartermaster, the number of troops for which transportation is required. Also take such measures as will effectually prevent other troops not belonging to from accompanying General Gordon's command. The land transportation will be turned in to Captain Peirce, assistant quartermaster, at Warrenton Junction.
S. WILLIAMS,
Assistant Adjutant-General.

HDQRS. ARMY OF THE POTOMAC, *August 5, 1863.*
(Received 9 p. m.)

Major-General HALLECK,
General-in-Chief:

Your orders with reference to General Gordon's division received, and the necessary instructions for the movement given. The division will be furnished with railroad transportation from Warrenton Junction to Alexandria.

GEO. G. MEADE, .
Major-General.

WASHINGTON, D. C.,
August 5, 1863.

Brigadier-General MEIGS,
Washington:

GENERAL: General Gordon's division, of about 4,000 men, has been ordered from the Army of the Potomac to Alexandria, to embark on steamers for Morris Island, S. C. Please have transportation ready for them. They are ordered to turn over all their land transportation to the quartermaster's department of the Army of the Potomac.

Very respectfully, your obedient servant,
H. W. HALLECK,
General-in-Chief.

WASHINGTON, D. C.,
August 5, 1863—12.50 p. m.

Major-General MEADE,
Army of the Potomac:

While waiting for re-enforcements from drafted men, the time should be availed of to recruit your animals; to collect all forage and provisions you can in the country, and to clean out all guerrilla bands and hostile inhabitants in the country occupied by our troops. I hope to send you by to-morrow an order in regard to transportation, based on the orders of Generals Scott, Taylor, and Wool, in Mexico, and General Grant's recent operations in Mississippi. An examination of these reports and orders prove that the transportation of the Army of the Potomac can be still further reduced to advantage. I forgot to inform you that General Griffin's resignation had been withdrawn, and its acceptance canceled.

H. W. HALLECK,
General-in-Chief.

WAR DEPARTMENT,
Washington, August 5, 1863—2 p. m.

Brig. Gen. H. H. LOCKWOOD,
Harper's Ferry, W. Va.:

Telegraph the number of your command of each arm.

H. W. HALLECK,
General-in-Chief.

HARPER'S FERRY, W. VA., *August 5*, 1863.
(Received 4.25 p. m.)

Maj. Gen. H. W. HALLECK,
General-in-Chief:

The number of this command present for duty is: Cavalry, six companies, 329 officers and men; heavy artillery, four companies, 442 officers and men; light artillery, three batteries, 356 officers and men; infantry, 3,446 officers and men. Of these, three regiments— the First Eastern Shore (Maryland) Volunteers, the Second Eastern Shore (Maryland) Volunteers, and the First Regiment Potomac Home Brigade (Maryland) Volunteers—were raised for special service in the State of Maryland, and decline crossing the Potomac. The regiments last named would possibly go to Leesburg or Winchester, Va. Two other regiments—Ninth and Tenth Maryland— are six-months' men, just raised and partially drilled.

HENRY H. LOCKWOOD,
Brigadier-General.

AUGUST 6, 1863—9.25 a. m.

Officer Commanding Eleventh Corps:

General Gordon's division must be held to mean the First Division of the Eleventh Corps. The General-in-Chief was informed before he issued the order that General Gordon's present command is not the same that he brought to this army. You are desired, however, to state, as soon as practicable, the regiments that composed the division that General Gordon joined us with, and, as far as possible, their strength.

S. WILLIAMS,
Assistant Adjutant-General.

HDQRS. SECOND DIV., FIFTH ARMY CORPS,
Camp at Beverly Ford, Va., August 6, 1863.

Colonel LOCKE,
Assistant Adjutant-General, Fifth Corps:

COLONEL: I have the honor to report my division in position commanding Beverly Ford. I have one regiment on the river bank; one brigade to its right and rear, about 900 yards; one brigade to its left and rear, about the same distance. One brigade about 1,000 yards in rear of these two, in support. My supply trains, &c., in rear of this last brigade.

R. B. AYRES,
Brigadier-General, Commanding.

P. S.—I have received a request from Major-General Newton, commanding First Corps, to relieve his pickets, as soon as convenient, as far as Rappahannock Station, and have replied that I am not instructed to relieve any troops, save the regiment of the First Corps stationed at and guarding the ford.

[Indorsement.]

AUGUST 6—11.30 p. m.

General Ayres to be informed that his course is a correct one.

S. W. [WILLIAMS.]

WESTON, *August 6, 1863.*

Colonel WILKINSON, *Commanding:*

One of Rowan's men just in from Glenville, where, in company with 9 citizens this morning, he killed 1 rebel and wounded 1. He says reliable men told him there were 300 of Jackson's men at Cedar Creek Mills, 6 miles from Glenville, gathering horses and cattle for Jackson's command, who they say is going to occupy Glenville. I give the report for what it is worth. From the many reports I hear, I think there are rebels near Glenville. I will press horses in a. m. for scout to Glenville, and when I can hear reliably will advise you.

C. J. HARRISON.

CINCINNATI, OHIO, *August 6, 1863.*
(Received 12.15 p. m.)

Maj. Gen. H. W. HALLECK,
General-in-Chief:

General Scammon is calling loudly for troops. He asks for four regiments. I do not see how I can help, but will do what I can.

A. E. BURNSIDE,
Major-General.

WAR DEPARTMENT,
Washington, August 6, 1863—1 p. m.

Major-General BURNSIDE,
Cincinnati, Ohio:

Why is General Scammon calling for troops from you? General Kelley, who commands in that department, asks for no re-enforcements.

H. W. HALLECK,
General-in-Chief.

BALTIMORE, MD., *August 6, 1863.*
(Received 3.10 p. m.)

Maj. Gen. H. W. HALLECK,
General-in-Chief:

The following telegram is just received from the captain in command at Drummondtown. One company of local cavalry is all the force left on the Eastern Shore, and, with that, I can give little protection, nor do anything considerable for prevention of rebel depredations or of contraband trade:

DRUMMONDTOWN, VA., *August 6, 1863.*

Major-General SCHENCK:

Light-house on Smith's Island much damaged by 9 men, purporting to be from Richmond. Light-reflectors, boats, &c., were taken. Damage, $2,000. They threaten Hog Island. Every man that could be spared from the line has been forwarded to reach Hog Island before their landing, and to scout both neighborhoods. I shall leave guards at both places. The mischief is done by rebels who left these counties, aided by friends here. We have captured 1 on the bay side. He asks if he will be exchanged. Is he not a spy?

W. P. LORD,
Captain.

ROBT. C. SCHENCK,
Major-General.

WASHINGTON, D. C.,
August 7, 1863—11.45 a. m.

Major-General SCHENCK,
Baltimore, Md.:

General Lockwood has only about 300 cavalry under his command.
If more troops are required to guard prisoners of war, they must
be taken from Baltimore and the railroad guard. Additional troops
cannot at present be sent to your department.

H. W. HALLECK,
General-in-Chief.

WAR DEPARTMENT,
Washington City, August 7, 1863.

Maj. Gen. GEORGE G. MEADE,
Commanding Army of the Potomac:

GENERAL : Great difficulty has been experienced in the regulation
of the subject of the transit of sutlers' merchandise to the Army of
the Potomac. These stores cannot be permitted to encumber the
railroads ; and by being transported over the other lines of communication from here to the army, where there is no safety from their
capture by guerrillas, opportunity is afforded for collusion with
them for the seizure of such goods, or where there is a real capture,
the merchandise is so much aid to the rebels. In either case, the
capture may be made the foundation of heavy claims for indemnifi-
cation hereafter.

The Secretary of War desires me to present for your consideration
the following suggestions upon the subject, with the view to the
determination of some proper system in the premises :

It is proposed that all sutlers present to you, before coming for or
sending for goods, a manifest, in which shall be set forth the goods
which they desire to bring to the army. In acting upon these manifests, you are to take into consideration the question of the probable
safety of the routes to the rear, so that there will be little risk of the
goods failing into the hands of the enemy, as well as how far the
character and quantity of merchandise sought to be introduced is
just and proper. If you approve the manifests, the goods may be
purchased, and upon their presentation at the office of the Quartermaster-General, the necessary permits may be given thereupon for
their passage to the army, provided there be no objection found to
the same. A certificate of sutlership will be required to accompany
the manifest of the sutler upon its presentation at the office of the
Quartermaster-General.

It is to be distinctly understood that no permits will be granted by
the Quartermaster-General for the transportation of sutlers' stores
upon the railroads, or other government means of conveyance. All
sutlers' goods, not covered with passes as herein provided, will be
liable to immediate confiscation by any commanding officer or provost-marshal, if sought to be introduced into the army.

No permits will be given to sutlers' agents unless they present
the sutler's certificate of office, accompanied by written evidence of
agency ; nor will any certificates be issued except the sutler elected
under the law be a citizen of the United States.

Be pleased, general, to report at your early convenience how far the suggestions herein made seem adapted to the circumstances of the case.

Very respectfully, your obedient servant,

JAS. A. HARDIE,
Assistant Adjutant-General.

AUGUST 7, 1863—6.15 p. m.

Brigadier-General CRAWFORD,
Commanding Fifth Corps:

The major-general commanding directs that the Fifth Corps be moved to-morrow morning to the vicinity of Beverly Ford; that as much of the artillery as can be placed in position on this side of the river be thus placed, and the remainder held ready to be transferred to the right bank, should it be required there. A bridge will be thrown across the Rappahannock in that vicinity to-morrow.

A. A. HUMPHREYS.

AUGUST 7, 1863—6.20 p. m.

Officer Commanding First Corps:

I am instructed by the major-general commanding to inform you that four batteries have been ordered to report to you from the Artillery Reserve—one 12-pounder and three rifled. Also that the Fifth Corps has been ordered to move to the vicinity of Beverly Ford to-morrow morning. The artillery will leave the park to-morrow morning at as early an hour as practicable.

A. A. HUMPHREYS,
Major-General, and Chief of Staff.

AUGUST 7, 1863—8 p. m.

Officer Commanding Eleventh Corps:

By direction of the major-general commanding, I transmit herewith a copy of the report* upon the inspection of the guards on the railroad from the vicinity of these headquarters to Manassas Junction, and am instructed to say that it exhibits a very unsatisfactory condition of the arrangements for protecting the road and an inefficient execution of the guard duties connected with it. The major-general commanding directs that you include that portion of the road from Warrenton Junction to Bealeton Station in the space protected by the Eleventh Corps, sending not less than a regiment to execute this duty, including the guard at the station.

I am instructed to say that the guard placed on the line of the road will be not less than 12 men to the mile, posted in groups of 3 or 4, and that at night these squads will keep up a constant patrol between the groups. Every bridge or culvert upon the road, how-

---

* Not found.

ever small, will be guarded.   The guard at Warrenton Junction will
be increased to the number recommended in the inspector's report.

The whole line of the road should be frequently inspected.   The
officer in command at Manassas Junction should ascertain the point
at which the guarding of the road by General King's command
ceases, and, if practicable, extend his protection to that point.   The
major-general commanding desires to know where the protection of
the road by General King's forces ceases.   He directs me to say that
guarding the road is esteemed a very important duty, and that its protection cannot be effective without strict vigilance on the part of
those to whom it is intrusted.

A. A. HUMPHREYS,
Major-General, and Chief of Staff.

HEADQUARTERS OF THE ARMY,
Washington, D. C., August 7, 1863.

Major-General MEADE,
    Commanding Army of the Potomac:

GENERAL: I inclose herewith a copy of General Orders, No. 274,
in advance of printed copies.   This order is based on that of General Taylor in moving from the Rio Grande on Monterey, but the
allowance is more liberal, and yet, I have no doubt, many will consider it niggardly, being so much below that formerly permitted to
the Army of the Potomac.   I am satisfied, however, from the experience of General Grant in Mississippi, and of General West in his
march from California to New Mexico, that there is no necessity for
the large trains heretofore allowed, and for which there is no parallel in European warfare.   I am satisfied, moreover, that when our
armies become accustomed to this allowance, it may be still further
reduced without any serious inconvenience.

One thing is certain, we must reduce our transportation or give up
all idea of competing with the enemy in the field.   Napoleon very
correctly estimated the effective strength of an army by its numbers
multiplied by its mobility; that is, 10,000 men who could march 20
miles per day as equal to 20,000 men who could march only 10 miles
per day.   Unless we can reduce our *impedimenta* very considerably,
we can equal the enemy only by a vast superiority in numbers.

While your army is inactive this matter should be thoroughly
studied, and the land transportation reduced to a much lower standard.   By comparison with other armies now in the field, and our
armies in the Mexican war, as well as with European armies in campaign, I am satisfied a very great reduction can be made in the transportation of the Army of the Potomac, and moreover, until this
reduction is actually made, we can expect no decided successes in the
field by that army, no matter how much heroic bravery it may exhibit on the battle-field.   I understand from General Ingalls that a
very great reduction of transportation has been made within the last
month.

During this extreme heat, troops and animals should be moved as
little as possible.

Very respectfully, your obedient servant,
H. W. HALLECK,
General-in-Chief.

[Inclosure.]

GENERAL ORDERS, ⎞ WAR DEPT., ADJT. GENERAL'S OFFICE,
No. 274.   ⎠   *Washington, August 7*, 1863.

I. The following is the maximum amount of transportation to be allowed in the field:

To headquarters of an army corps, 2 wagons or 8 pack animals.

To headquarters of a division or brigade, 1 wagon or 5 pack animals.

To field and staff of a regiment, 1 wagon or 4 pack animals.

To every 3 company officers, 1 pack animal.

To every 12 company officers, 1 wagon or 4 pack animals.

To every 2 staff officers not attached to any headquarters, 1 pack animal.

To every 10 staff officers not attached to any headquarters, 1 wagon or 4 pack animals.

To every 16 non-commissioned officers and privates, 1 pack animal.

To every 80 non-commissioned officers and privates, 1 wagon or 5 pack animals.

The above will include transportation for all personal baggage, mess-chests, cooking utensils, desks, papers, &c. The weight of officers' baggage in the field, specified in the Army Regulations, will be reduced so as to bring it within the foregoing schedule. All excess of transportation now with army corps, divisions, brigades, and regiments, or batteries, over the foregoing allowance, will be immediately turned in to the quartermaster's department, to be used in the trains. Commanding officers of corps, divisions, &c., will immediately cause inspections to be made, and will be held responsible for the strict execution of this order.

Commissary stores and forage will be transported by the trains. Where these are not convenient of access, and where troops act in detachments, the quartermaster's department will assign wagons or pack animals for that purpose; but the baggage of officers or of troops, or camp equipage, will not be permitted to be carried in the wagons or on the pack animals so assigned. The assignment of transportation for ammunition will be made in proportion to the amount ordered to be carried.

II. Cavalry horses are often broken down or injured by permitting the riders to carry extra baggage. Cavalry officers will be held responsible for the immediate removal of this evil.

The knapsacks of infantry soldiers will also be frequently inspected to see that they are properly packed and that nothing is carried in them except what is directed by regulations and orders.

III. In ordinary marches, where the troops can receive daily issues from the trains, they will be required to carry only two days' rations; but in the immediate vicinity of the enemy, and where the exigencies of the service render it necessary for troops to move without baggage or trains, the men may be required to carry with them from eight to twelve days' rations, as follows:

For eight days.

	Pounds.
Five days' beef or mutton, to be driven on the ho f or collected in the country passed over.	
Three days' cooked rations, in haversacks	5¼
Five days' rations of bread and small stores, in knapsacks	6
A change of underclothes, in knapsacks	2
A blanket	5¼
Total weight	19

For twelve days.

	Pounds.
Nine days' rations of meat, on the hoof.	
Three days' cooked rations, in haversacks	5¼
Nine days' rations of biscuit and small stores, in knapsacks	10¼
A change of underclothes, in knapsacks	2
A blanket	5¼
Total weight	23¼

The underclothing should be packed in the knapsacks next to the back.

One or two pack animals will march with each regiment, according to its size, to carry camp-kettles, rice, beans, &c. Where circumstances will permit, a wagon may be assigned to a brigade or division for this purpose.

Officers' servants are expected to carry rations for their officers and themselves. Those of mounted officers are expected to be mounted, and to be able to carry small forage for their animals. Long forage must be sought for in the country.

By increasing the ordinary meat ration and levying contributions of flour and meal in the country passed over, the bread and small rations carried as above by the soldier may be made to last from twenty to twenty-five days. In the proper season, the bread ration may be partially dispensed with by substituting green corn, which can be foraged in the fields. Movable columns in the field should be furnished with hand and horse mills for grinding the grain which they procure in the country.

Within one week after the receipt of this order at their respective headquarters, inspectors of armies and army corps will report directly to the Adjutant-General of the Army every violation of this order, certifying in their reports that they have thoroughly inspected the several commands, and have reported therein every deviation from this order in regard to allowance of transportation.

IV. The attention of all officers commanding forces in the field is called to the foregoing details, and they will adopt them as instructions in fitting out their command for movements which are to be made rapidly and without ordinary transportation.

This order will be published at the head of every regiment.

By order of the Secretary of War:

E. D. TOWNSEND,
Assistant Adjutant-General.

ALEXANDRIA, VA., *August 7*, 1863.
(Received 9.10 a. m.)

Maj. Gen. H. W. HALLECK,
General-in-Chief:

I sent a dispatch at 9 o'clock last night announcing my arrival here with my division. I am afraid the dispatch has miscarried. I have received no orders but to come to Alexandria. The division numbers, according to the last field return, a fortnight ago, 3,647 present for duty. A number have been reported sick since then.

GEO. H. GORDON,
Brigadier-General.

WAR DEPARTMENT,
Washington, August 7, 1863—9.40 a. m.

Brig. Gen. GEORGE H. GORDON,
Alexandria, Va.:

Your division will embark on transports for Morris Island, to re-enforce General Gillmore. The commissary and quartermaster's departments will furnish you with all necessary supplies. Your destination will not be made public until you are at sea.

H. W. HALLECK,
General-in-Chief.

FORT MONROE, *August 7, 1863—11.30 a. m.*
(Received 5.15 p. m.)

Hon. E. M. STANTON :

I have this moment returned from a reconnaissance toward Fort Darling, and your dispatch requiring immediate action to protect the Cherrystone Light-House, telegraph station, &c., has just this moment been received. The cable having been cut, I regret that steps had not been taken before to place the light-houses in this department under guard. I was not aware, owing to my recent arrival here, that they were in such a state. The necessary steps are being taken by General Potter to protect the remaining light-houses, and a force goes over with him to endeavor to catch the marauders.

I have the honor to be, your obedient servant,

J. G. FOSTER,
Major-General, Commanding.

CINCINNATI, OHIO, *August 7, 1863.*
(Received 12.25 p. m.)

Maj. Gen. H. W. HALLECK,
General-in-Chief:

General Scammon represents that a force largely superior to his own is pressing on him. I suppose he calls upon me because I have been in the habit of sending troops when needed in Western Virginia. After the receipt of your dispatch, I shall not assume the responsibility of sending troops out of my department without orders.

A. E. BURNSIDE,
Major-General.

WAR DEPARTMENT,
Washington, August 7, 1863—11.45 a. m.

Brigadier-General KELLEY,
West Virginia:

General Burnside telegraphs that General Scammon has applied to him for re-enforcements. What is the necessity of this; and is it made with your authority?

H. W. HALLECK,
General-in-Chief.

NEW CREEK, W. VA., *August* 7, 1863.
(Received 4.50 p. m.)

Brigadier-General CULLUM,
Chief of Staff:

On my arrival here yesterday I found a dispatch from General Scammon, in which he advised me that the enemy was concentrating a large force in his front, and that he feared an attack from toward Lewisburg, and asked for re-enforcements. I answered him that I had no troops to send him, but that I would relieve him from anxiety in the direction of Lewisburg and Huntersville, by a movement up this valley to Monterey; in answer to which I have just received the following dispatch. If a gunboat can be spared, I desire that one be sent to the Kanawha River:

CHARLESTON, W. VA.,
August 7, 1863—9 a. m.

Brigadier-General KELLEY:

Telegram received. The enemy is in small force at Lewisburg. There are rumors of his having gone to the Narrows of New River—probably a move indicating an advance on my right. Will keep you advised.

SCAMMON.

B. F. KELLEY,
Brigadier-General.

———

NEW CREEK, W. VA., *August* 7, 1863.
(Received 4.40 p. m.)

Brig. Gen. G. W. CULLUM,
Chief of Staff:

I left Hedgesville on Saturday, the 1st instant, and proceeded up the Valley of Back Creek to the Northwestern turnpike, and thence west by that road to Romney, which place my troops now occupy. My cavalry proceeded from Winchester, via Wardensville, to Moorefield. Found a portion of Imboden's force in this valley engaged in conscripting and gathering supplies. They have retreated up the valley. We captured on our march quite a number of guerrillas and horse thieves. Several hundred deserters from Lee's army have come in, and hundreds are yet secreted in the mountains, awaiting an opportunity to get inside our lines.

B. F. KELLEY,
Brigadier-General, Commanding Department.

———

HEADQUARTERS ARMY OF THE POTOMAC,
August 8, 1863—9.45 a. m.

Commanding Officer Cavalry Corps:

I am instructed by the major-general commanding to inquire by what authority the several cavalry commands arrest citizens, living within our lines, against whom there is no evidence of having been engaged in committing depredations or aiding those engaged in such practices, but who merely decline to take the oath of allegiance.

The general commanding directs that for the present such arrests will not be made, but will be limited to those engaged in the practice just referred to, and such others against whom there is suspicion of having been engaged in them, or of having been guilty of any disloyal act.

The mere fact of residence within the lines of this army, and an indisposition to take the oath of allegiance in a region alternately held by our troops and those of the enemy, should not in itself cause the arrest of an individual, unless there is some reason to believe that, directly or indirectly, the person is engaged in aiding those in arms against us.

Very respectfully, &c.,

A. A. HUMPHREYS,
Major-General, and Chief of Staff.

AUGUST 8, 1863—10.30 a. m.

Brigadier-General CRAWFORD,
Commanding Fifth Corps:

I omitted to mention in the instructions of last evening, under the impression that the order had been already given, that as soon as the bridge near Beverly Ford was finished, a sufficient force would be sent across the river to occupy a position that would serve as a bridge head. The remainder of the corps and such of the artillery as is not in position will be held in readiness to be thrown across the river to seize the heights in front, in the event of any movement on the part of the enemy rendering such operation necessary.

Very respectfully, your obedient servant,

A. A. HUMPHREYS,
Major-General, Chief of Staff.

AUGUST 8, 1863—10.30 a. m.

Major-General PLEASONTON,
Commanding Cavalry Corps:

The major-general commanding directs me to say that you are authorized to withdraw a portion of General Buford's command immediately in front of Rappahannock Station, leaving force enough for a strong picket, with reserves sufficient to hold the enemy in check, should he advance, until the infantry can come up to their support.

The portion of the cavalry withdrawn should be stationed at the nearest point to Rappahannock Station where water and grazing can be had, and be prepared to move to the front again upon notification of the presence of the enemy in such force as to require them to be there.

Very respectfully, your obedient servant,

A. A. HUMPHREYS,
Major-General, Chief of Staff.

AUGUST 8, 1863—11 a. m.

Major-General NEWTON,
Commanding First Corps:

The major-general commanding directs me to inform you that the Eleventh Corps has been ordered to guard the railroad from Warrenton Junction to Bealeton Station, including the guard at that station.

I am also instructed to say that as the cavalry pickets on your front on the south side of the Rappahannock, and as you have a force on that bank, the picketing of the river by your infantry on this side hardly seems necessary. General Buford is authorized to withdraw a portion of his cavalry to this side the river, leaving, however, a force sufficient for a strong picket, and reserves in your front sufficient to resist any attack until supported by the infantry. The portion withdrawn to this side (to the nearest point for grazing and water), is directed to hold itself in readiness to move to the front in the event of its being required there.

Very respectfully, your obedient servant,

A. A. HUMPHREYS, •
Major-General, and Chief of Staff.

AUGUST 8, 1863—5.30 p. m.

Officer Commanding First Corps:

I am instructed by the major-general commanding to say that it is not intended to relieve your pickets from Rappahannock Station to Wheatley's Ford by the pickets of any other corps; that part of the river is still to be covered by your corps, and the fords in that space heretofore guarded by your corps are still to be guarded by it.

The suggestion in reference to your pickets on this side the river had reference to the pickets or sentinels thrown out by the detachments guarding each ford, and was made subject to your own judgment. Along that part of the river where you have no force on the other side, you may still find them necessary.

A. A. HUMPHREYS,
Major-General, and Chief of Staff.

HEADQUARTERS FIFTH ARMY CORPS,
Beverly Ford, August 8, 1863. (Received 6 p. m.)

General HUMPHREYS,
Chief of Staff:

The engineers have thrown a bridge across the Rappahannock, some 200 yards above the ford. An infantry force was sent over to protect the outlet of the bridge. General Ayres thinks that General Meade designed the bridge to cross the river below or opposite Hamilton's house. The engineers did not come near me, and the first I knew of their presence was through General Garrard, who furnished the covering force for the bridge. I will throw the remainder of General Garrard's brigade on the right bank of the stream. A few cavalry pickets belonging to the enemy are hovering around. The woods are so dense that they can easily keep themselves hidden. I have three batteries in position and two in reserve, but the whole north bank of the river is commanded by the ground on the other side.

I am, sir, respectfully,

GEO. SYKES,
Major-General, Commanding.

RAPPAHANNOCK STATION, *August* 8, 1863.
(Received 3.30 p. m.)

General HUMPHREYS,
         Chief of Staff:

The following message was intercepted by our signal officers, 1.25 p. m., from rebel signal station to Taylor, rebel signal officer:

Please direct Colonel Worley [Corley?] to have the bridge planked.
                              C. [J. E. B.?] STUART,
                                              General.

The rebel signal officer was signaling toward Orange Court-House from Pony Mountain.

                              JOHN NEWTON,
                                Major-General.

———

RAPPAHANNOCK,
August 8, 1863.

Lieut. Col. C. ROSS SMITH,
         Cavalry Corps:

I have had a thorough inspection to-day of my picket line, extending from Hazel Run to Mountain Creek. My line is four times as strong as the rebel lines. I have reduced it. I attempted to communicate with General Gregg, and drove pickets 4 miles up Hazel Run without meeting any of his troops. I met with but little opposition. The rebels fired 50 shots, more or less, without a reply from me. A signal message (rebel) from General Stuart to Colonel S., south of Rapidan, says: "Plank the bridge as quickly as possible."

The Rapidan is very high. I do not believe there is any force this side of the Rapidan, save cavalry. They are ready to run west of Brandy Station. There is a brigade of horses grazing to-day at 12 m., probably Hampton's. There is no disposition to attack. Devin sees nothing this side of Mountain Run. In my front along the railroad the rebel pickets are strong.

                              JNO. BUFORD,
                                Brigadier-General.

———

HDQRS. ARMY OF THE POTOMAC, *August* 8, 1863.
(Received 7.35 p. m.)

Col. J. C. KELTON,
         Assistant Adjutant-General:

In answer to your telegram of this date, I would say that General Gordon brought to this army the One hundred and twenty-seventh, One hundred and forty-first, One hundred and forty-second, One hundred and forty-third, and One hundred and forty-fourth New York, and the Fortieth Massachusetts Volunteer Infantry, and took with him, when he left, the Forty-first, Fifty-fourth, One hundred and twenty-seventh, One hundred and forty-second, One hundred and forty-fourth, and One hundred and fifty-seventh New York; Twenty-fifth, Seventy-fifth, and One hundred and seventh Ohio; Seventy-fourth Pennsylvania, Fortieth Massachusetts, and Seventeenth Connecticut.

                              S. WILLIAMS,
                         Assistant Adjutant-General.

CIRCULAR.]　　　HEADQUARTERS ARMY OF THE POTOMAC,
August 8, 1863.

The commanding general invites the attention of corps commanders to the large number 'of officers and men reported in the tri-monthly report for July 31, 1863, under the headings hereinafter indicated, and he directs that an immediate investigation be made by officers on duty in inspector-general's department, and by others who may be detailed for the purpose, to ascertain generally upon what duties the officers and men accounted for on special, extra, or daily duty are engaged; when and how the officers and men reported on detached service within the army and without the army are employed, distinguishing between the two classes of absence; by what authority the officers and men reported absent with leave are so absent; whether the officers and men reported absent sick are so absent by competent authority, and how long the officers and men reported absent without authority have been so absent. It is desired that these reports should be made as full as possible, and forwarded at the earliest practicable moment, for the information of the commanding general.

On detached service.

Command.	Present.		Within the army.		Without the army.		With leave.		Sick.		Without leave.	
	Special duty, officers.	Daily duty, men.	Officers.	Men.	Officers.	Men.	Officers.	Men.	Officers.	Men.	Officers.	Men.
First Corps..........	58	1,052	108	1,962	98	668	24	230	247	5,536	18	306
Second Corps	59	684	124	1,836	103	622	26	80	328	7,627	27	483
Third Corps.........	62	899	150	2,411	117	558	48	211	304	8,021	25	629
Fifth Corps	58	1,188	138	1,540	174	497	19	161	170	3,050	20	604
Sixth Corps.........	42	1,254	123	2,200	106	484	11	104	105	3,548	16	471
Eleventh Corps	32	1,129	180	1,375	58	311	17	439	205	5,541	2	432
Twelfth Corps	31	787	95	1,102	54	286	24	332	118	3,450	4	214
Cavalry Corps	59	2,121	293	6,285	76	479	56	638	201	4,228	33	402
Artillery Reserve ...	1	110	7	145	14	38	2	17	11	320	......	33
Engineer Brigade...	......	61	9	761	1	60	......	10	......	38	......	43
Provost guard.......	5	159	6	93	15	84	7	63	20	423	4	101

By command of Major-General Meade:

S. WILLIAMS,
Assistant Adjutant-General.

———

WASHINGTON, D. C.,
August 8, 1863—1 p. m.

Major-General BROOKS,
　　Pittsburgh, Pa.:

Should General Scammon be hard pushed on the Kanawha, how many men can you send to re-enforce him?

H. W. HALLECK,
General-in-Chief.

PITTSBURGH, PA., *August 9, 1863.*
(Received 4 p. m.)

Major-General HALLECK:

Six companies six-months' cavalry can be sent at once. There are four regiments of three-months' militia here, and I have sent to inquire as to their willingness, but shall not hesitate to order them if they are needed. Some militia can be raised near Wheeling.

W. T. H. BROOKS,
Major-General.

RAPPAHANNOCK, *August 9, 1863.*
(Received between 2.30 and 3.30 p. m.)

General HUMPHREYS:

The following intercepted dispatch just received:

General LEE:

Yankee camps diminished about Warrenton and Waterloo; now appear on the railroad.

STUART,
General.

JOHN NEWTON,
Major-General.

CENTREVILLE,
August 9, 1863.

Major LA MOTTE,
Commanding Fairfax Station:

It is not impossible that Stuart may attempt such a raid in order to break up the railroad. Every precaution must be taken to guard against this, and the utmost vigilance exercised. The country south of the road in the vicinity of Accotink and Burke's Station should be constantly and thoroughly scouted. If you can find any trustworthy men, residents or others, familiar with the country, you are authorized to employ them for this purpose, in addition to your own troops.

RUFUS KING,
Brigadier-General, Commanding.

MARTINSBURG,
August 9, 1863.

Colonel McREYNOLDS,
Eutaw House:

Telegram received from Harper's Ferry. General Lockwood absent. His aide-de-camp says their cavalry were cut to pieces and scattered. Major Quinn is at Point of Rocks. He saw nothing of the enemy. The aide-de-camp wishes Quinn to remain until General Lockwood returns. I ordered Quinn back to this place unless absolutely necessary below. Let me know your address in Washington.

WILDES,
Lieutenant-Colonel, Commanding.

HEADQUARTERS,
Near Portsmouth, August 9, 1863.

Brigadier-General NAGLEE,
　　Norfolk:

I went to South Mills yesterday; returned this a. m. The three troops of cavalry under Captain Roberts, Eleventh Pennsylvania, arrived at South Mills from Camden Court-House late yesterday afternoon. There are no gunboats or troops on the Pasquotank. Citizens represent that there is a regiment of mounted infantry (State troops) in the counties bordering upon the Pasquotank. Captain Roberts' men, with few exceptions, have pistols only. His situation at South Mills is precarious, unless supported by infantry.

GEO. W. GETTY,
Brigadier-General.

FORT MONROE, VA., *August* 9, 1863—3.10 p. m.
(Received 6.30 a. m., 10th.)

Maj. Gen. H. W. HALLECK,
　　General-in-Chief:

I have the honor to report that General George H. Gordon's division, ordered here *en route* for South Carolina, has arrived. In order to water and ration the sea transports, the men were landed at Newport News. This, in addition to the above reason, was considered desirable, in order to deceive any possible spy of the enemy as to the destination of the troops. The First Brigade is now embarking on sea transports, and will sail this evening. General Potter, who was sent to ascertain what he could concerning the late destruction of light-houses on the coast, has returned. He established guards at Smith's Island, Hog Island, and Cherrystone. The result of his inquiries indicates that the destroying party were landed from sailing vessels lying off the lights. The character of the sailing vessels, whether sea-going or from the bay, could not be ascertained. The destroying party returned to their vessels, and so could not be overtaken and punished by General Potter.

J. G. FOSTER,
Major-General.

HEADQUARTERS ARMY OF THE POTOMAC,
August 10, 1863—10.30 a. m.

Maj. Gen. S. P. HEINTZELMAN,
　　Headquarters Defenses:

The following extract from the report of General Pleasonton is respectfully transmitted, for the information of Major-General Heintzelman, by direction of the major-general commanding:

He (General Kilpatrick) further reports that scouts report that numbers of deserters from General King's command, and the commands at Fairfax and Manassas, are joining Mosby for the purpose of plunder. It is thought some of Mosby's men are in the commands referred to, in the character of spies, influencing our men to desert.

A. A. HUMPHREYS,
Chief of Staff.

HEADQUARTERS ARMY OF THE POTOMAC,
August 10, 1863—7 p. m.

Commanding Officer Cavalry Corps:

I am directed by the major-general commanding to acknowledge the receipt of Brigadier-General Gregg's report* upon the detachments sent over to establish the picket line south of the Aestham River, and to say that it was unsatisfactory; for it was reported by General Gregg that the enemy picketed the south bank in force, and apprehensions were expressed by him that his outposts or pickets might be captured; yet a detachment of merely 1 officer and 16 men is sent from Welford's Ford to communicate with the right of Buford's picket line, 4 miles distant. Why so small a force was sent on this duty when Colonel [General] Gregg entertained the apprehensions referred to, in the opinion of the major-general commanding, requires explanation.

Very respectfully,

A. A. HUMPHREYS,
Major-General, and Chief of Staff.

[Inclosure.]

HEADQUARTERS CAVALRY CORPS,
August 10, 1863—8 a. m.

Major-General HUMPHREYS,
Chief of Staff:

GENERAL: The report from General Gregg, forwarded last night, is the latest received from him. General Kilpatrick reports all quiet along his picket line. A small squad of the enemy's cavalry showed themselves on the Falmouth road below United States Ford yesterday morning.

Two of Kilpatrick's men in disguise went into one of Mosby's rendezvous and found some 20 or 30 horses grazing. They made out they were Mosby's men. I have sent out a sufficient party to capture the concern. A second report from Kilpatrick just in states the squad of rebel cavalry captured a messenger, took him to Dumfries, and there paroled him. He sends in 6 prisoners; 2 are deserters from the rebel army.

He (General Kilpatrick) further reports that scouts report that numbers of deserters from General King's command, and the commands at Fairfax and Manasses, are joining Mosby for the purpose of plunder. It is thought some of Mosby's men are in the commands referred to, in the character of spies, influencing our men to desert.

General Merritt reports no change in front of Colonel Devin, or in the immediate front, as regards the enemy. Colonel Huey reports no change or occurrence worthy of note.

Very respectfully,

A. PLEASONTON,
Major-General, Commanding.

---

* See McIntosh's report of skirmish near Welford's Ford, Part I, p. 67.

HEADQUARTERS ARMY OF THE POTOMAC,
August 10, 1863.

Brigadier-General SLOCUM:

Respectfully forwarded for the information of Major-General Newton and Major-General Slocum:

SIGNAL STATION,
Watery Mountain, August 10, [1863]—8.10 a. m.

Captain NORTON,
Chief Signal Officer:

The enemy's camp smokes are plainly visible this morning, extending from the
vicinity of Raccoon Ford to a point due south from Watery Mountain. The main
body appears to be directly east of Clark's and Pony Mountains and south of Stevensburg, and between Culpeper and Raccoon Ford. Much smoke is seen at the
above-named places.

TAYLOR,
Signal Officer.

A. A. HUMPHREYS,
Major-General, and Chief of Staff.

———

HEADQUARTERS CAVALRY CORPS,
August 10, 1863—7.30 a. m.

Brigadier-General MERRITT,
Comdg. First Cav. Div., Rappahannock Station:

You will turn over all the surplus of good horses, after your division is mounted, to General Gregg and General Kilpatrick. You
will order Graham's battery to report to Captain Tidball, with the
Artillery Reserve. There was a battery sent up to relieve it.

C. ROSS SMITH,
Lieutenant-Colonel, and Chief of Staff.

———

HEADQUARTERS CAVALRY CORPS,
August 10, 1863.

Brigadier-General GREGG,
Commanding Second Cavalry Division:

GENERAL : The major-general commanding desires me to say you
need not persist in crossing until further orders.

C. ROSS SMITH,
Lieutenant-Colonel, and Chief of Staff

———

HEADQUARTERS CAVALRY CORPS,
August 10, 1863—2.30 p. m.

Brigadier-General MERRITT,
Comdg. First Cav. Div., Rappahannock Station:

The original order as regards your brigade will be carried out,
excepting as regards yourself. You will remain in command of
the division until General Buford's return.

C. ROSS SMITH,
Lieutenant-Colonel, and Chief of Staff.

HDQRS. DEF. OF WASHINGTON SOUTH OF POTOMAC,
August 10, 1863.

Lieut. Col. J. H. TAYLOR,
Asst. Adjt. Gen., Hdqrs. Dept. of Washington:

It is reported that one of our cavalry pickets was fired on last night while on duty near Falls Church. A Mr. Reed, resident of that place, says he knows that Mosby's headquarters are only about 5 miles from Falls Church, where he had about 40 men. My own cavalry force is not sufficient to send out a large enough party to verify this information and keep up the regular nightly patrols.

Very respectfully,

G. A. DE RUSSY,
Brigadier-General, Commanding.

————

HEADQUARTERS,
Near Portsmouth, August 10, 1863.

Brigadier-General NAGLEE,
Norfolk:

Is it intended that the cavalry expedition shall go by the way of Suffolk? A deserter from the Ninth Virginia has just come in. Reports no troops at Suffolk, or on the line of the Blackwater, excepting a few pickets on the Blackwater.

GEO. W. GETTY,
Brigadier-General.

————

WASHINGTON, D. C.,
August 10, 1863—9.30 a. m.

Major-General BURNSIDE,
Cincinnati, Ohio:

General Brooks, at Pittsburgh, is prepared to re-enforce General Scammon whenever necessary.

H. W. HALLECK,
General-in-Chief.

————

WAR DEPARTMENT,
Washington, August 10, 1863—10 a. m.

General KELLEY,
West Virginia:

General Brooks will be able to re-enforce General Scammon. Should it be necessary, make a requisition on General Brooks.

H. W. HALLECK,
General-in-Chief.

————

OFFICE PROVOST-MARSHAL-GENERAL,
August 10, 1863.

Maj. Gen. GEORGE G. MEADE,
Commanding Army of the Potomac:

GENERAL: In answer to the inquiry as to how newspapers are now supplied to the Army of the Potomac, I have the honor to report that, in accordance with the provisions of the circular of Major-General Hooker, of the 2d of June last, proposals for furnishing newspapers to the Army were received until 12 o'clock m. on the

12th of June, 1863, when these bids were opened in presence of the council of administration.

Mr. John M. Lamb was found to have offered the highest sum ($53.20 per day) for the privilege of supplying the army with newspapers and periodicals. He was accordingly sent for, and agreed to the following conditions, viz: That he would supply all papers called for within the army by the various commands composing it, ordered by commanders, or the news agents belonging to the corps, divisions, and brigades, respectively, at 5 cents per copy, periodicals and illustrated papers excepted.

The difficulties attendant upon the supply of the army during its movements necessarily interfered with all plans, but the necessity of making money enough to meet the monthly payment to the medical director has proved a sufficient stimulus to Mr. Lamb to bring his papers into camp whenever it has been possible.

Thus far, the system has worked far better than any that has preceeded it, the agents being obliged to furnish the papers called for and at fixed rates. The only complaints made to me are by newspaper agents and proprietors, who, by canvassing the troops themselves, have been able, heretofore, to make large individual profits.

At present, officers who desire the latest news by telegraph take Washington and Baltimore papers, while the rank and file, who want more local news, take Philadelphia or New York papers, according to the States from which they hail. The newsboys inform me that they make the most money on the Baltimore Clipper and Washington Chronicle.

All of which is respectfully submitted.

M. R. PATRICK,
Provost-Marshal-General.

GENERAL ORDERS, } HDQRS. MID. DEPT., 8TH ARMY CORPS,
No. 43.   }   *Baltimore, August* 10, 1863.

During the temporary absence of Major-General Schenck, the undersigned, in pursuance of instructions from the War Department, assumes command of the Middle Department, the Eighth Army Corps.

W. W. MORRIS,
Brevet Brigadier-General, U. S. Army, Commanding.

GENERAL ORDERS, }   HDQRS. DEPT. OF WEST VIRGINIA,
No. 2.   }   *Clarksburg, W. Va., August* 10, 1863.

I. The Department of West Virginia has been extended, by order of the War Department, so as to include all the State of Maryland west of the Monocacy River, and that portion of Virginia in the vicinity of Harper's Ferry.

II. Commanding officers will make out and forward to these headquarters, on the 5th, 15th, and 25th of each month, respectively, consolidated reports of their commands. The monthly return required by the Army Regulations will be furnished as soon after the expiration of the month as practicable.

By order of Brigadier-General Kelley:

THAYER MELVIN,
Assistant Adjutant-General.

Abstract from tri-monthly return of the Army of the Potomac, Maj. Gen. George G. Meade, U. S. Army, commanding, for August 10, 1863.

Command.	Present for duty.		Aggregate present.	Present for duty equipped.						Pieces of artillery.	Aggregate present and absent.
				Infantry.		Cavalry.		Artillery.			
	Officers.	Men.		Officers.	Men.	Officers.	Men.	Officers.	Men.		
General and staff..............	41	....	41	.....	....	...	....	...	....	...	62
Provost guard (Brig. Gen. Marsena R. Patrick).	72	971	1,192	.....	....	...	....	...	....	...	1,914
Engineer Brigade (Brig. Gen. Henry W. Benham).	36	808	1,021	...	....	...	....	...	....	...	1,389
Battalion U. S. Engineers (Capt. George H. Mendell).	7	308	382	.....	....	...	....	...	....	...	436
Guards and orderlies (Brig. Gen. Rufus Ingalls).	2	48	54	.....	....	...	....	...	....	...	75
Artillery Reserve (Brig. Gen. Robert O. Tyler).	76	1,718	1,934	15	265	2	49	50	1,400	80	2,965
Signal corps (Capt. Lemuel B. Norton).	6	....	6	.....	....	...	....	...	....	...	6
First Army Corps (Maj. Gen. John Newton).	483	6,380	8,552	453	5,823	2	48	16	509	23	17,451
Second Army Corps (Brig. Gen. William Hays).	469	6,868	8,738	416	5,629	...	...	14	514	22	19,627
Third Army Corps (Maj. Gen. William H. French).	655	11,546	14,105	591	9,013	...	...	28	741	42	25,939
Fifth Army Corps (Maj. Gen. George Sykes).	605	9,148	11,478	573	8,322	...	...	15	436	28	19,692
Sixth Army Corps (Maj. Gen. John Sedgwick).	791	11,721	14,387	739	10,715	5	110	26	771	42	20,866
Eleventh Army Corps (Maj. Gen. Oliver O. Howard).	349	5,697	7,504	321	4,952	5	40	8	541	25	12,716
Twelfth Army Corps (Maj. Gen. Henry W. Slocum).	404	7,125	8,887	369	6,735	...	....	11	361	20	14,477
Cavalry Corps (Maj. Gen. Alfred Pleasonton).	535	8,979	12,251	3	....	470	8,808	1	....	30	25,694
Total	4,531	71,312	90,522	3,480	51,454	484	9,055	164	5,273	312	163,329

Abstract from tri-monthly return of the Department of Washington, Maj. Gen. Samuel P. Heintzelman, U. S. Army, commanding, for August 10, 1863.

Command.	Present for duty.		Aggregate present.	Aggregate present and absent.	Pieces of artillery.
	Officers.	Men.			
Department headquarters............................	29	154	195	227	......
Artillery Camp of Instruction (Barry)................	45	1,251	1,454	1,725	60
Railway guard (Tracy).............................	24	688	908	924	......
District of Washington (Martindale)	119	2,397	3,424	4,301	......
Defenses North of the Potomac (Haskin)	201	5,064	6,839	7,250	414
Fort Washington, Md. (Merchant)	5	106	144	148	73
Defenses South of the Potomac (De Russy)...........	196	4,513	6,043	7,398	425
King's division....................................	126	2,222	2,674	3,399	6
Cavalry (Lowell)..................................	45	869	1,251	1,553	......
Provisional brigades (Casey).......................	11	220	251	256	......
District of Alexandria (Slough)....................	63	1,075	1,339	2,645	6
Camp Convalescent, &c. (McKelvey).................	93	3,240	7,417	7,789	......
Total..	957	21,799	31,934	37,565	984

Abstract from tri-monthly return of the Middle Department (Eighth Army Corps), Maj. Gen. Robert C. Schenck, U. S. Army, commanding, for August 10, 1863.

Command.	Present for duty.		Aggregate present.	Aggregate present and absent.	Pieces of artillery.
	Officers.	Men.			
Department staff	23	......	23	23	......
Second Separate Brigade (Bvt. Brig. Gen. W. W. Morris)	53	1,263	1,514	1,724	......
Defenses of Baltimore (Brig. Gen. E. B. Tyler)	27	781	890	1,101	......
Third Separate Brigade (Col. S. A. Graham)	72	1,033	1,248	1,455	......
Annapolis, Md. (Col. C. A. Waite)	11	258	297	407	......
Fort Delaware, Del. (Brig. Gen. A. Schoepf)	35	682	1,089	1,201	73
Total	221	4,017	5,061	5,911	73

Abstract from tri-monthly return of the Department of the Susquehanna, Maj. Gen. Darius N. Couch, U. S. Army, commanding, for August 10, 1863.

Command.	Present for duty.		Aggregate present.	Aggregate present and absent.	Pieces of artillery.
	Officers.	Men.			
Department headquarters	9	......	9	11	......
Chambersburg (Ferry)	45	1,141	1,264	1,527	4
Harrisburg (Stahel)	112	2,433	3,168	3,793	12
Huntingdon (McKeage)	49	880	937	1,147	....
Philadelphia (Cadwalader)	145	2,723	3,169	4,618	....
Pottsville (Whipple)	48	1,053	1,184	1,314	8
Reading (Sigel)	206	4,027	4,543	4,798	4
West Chester (Shorkley)	13	244	267	273	......
York (Palmer)	4	77	82	90	......
Total	631	12,583	14,643	17,571	28

Abstract from tri-monthly return of the Department of the Monongahela, Maj. Gen. William T. H. Brooks, U. S. Army, commanding, for August 10, 1863.

Command.	Present for duty.		Aggregate present.	Aggregate present and absent.
	Officers.	Men.		
Department headquarters	8	......	8	8
Burnesville, Ohio (Captain Deen)	3	90	98	101
Connellsville, Pa. (Lieutenant-Colonel Dale)	13	315	370	574
Pittsburgh, Pa. (Captain Churchill)	3	84	87	88
Pulaski, Pa. (Lieut. James M. Brown)	1	37	38	51
Wheeling, W. Va. (Capt. Wesley C. Thorp)	5	75	162	173
Total	33	601	758	995

Abstract from tri-monthly return of the Department of West Virginia, Brig. Gen. Benjamin F. Kelley, U. S. Army, commanding, for August 10, 1863.

Command.	Present for duty. Officers.	Present for duty. Men.	Aggregate present.	Aggregate present and absent.	Pieces of artillery.
Department staff	5	....	5	5	.....
Third Division (Scammon)	1:6	4,410	5,239	6,394	14
Averell's brigade	170	3,741	4,605	5,499	10
Campbell's brigade	59	1,632	1,825	2,298	6
Mulligan's brigade	79	1,669	1,841	2,423	6
Wilkinson's brigade	91	2,251	2,524	2,851	.....
Detachments a	81	1,833	2,075	2,276	.....
Total	681	15,536	18,114	21,746	36

a At Clarksburg, Green Spring Run, and New Creek.

Abstract from tri-monthly return of the Department of Virginia and North Carolina, Maj. Gen. John G. Foster, U. S. Army, commanding, for August 10, 1863.

Command.	Present for duty. Officers.	Present for duty. Men.	Aggregate present.	Aggregate present and absent.	Pieces of artillery.
Department headquarters	19	.....	19	19	.....
Fort Monroe, Va. (Roberts)	26	637	977	1,171	.....
Naglee's command a	405	8,039	10,504	16,674	62
Palmer's command b	432	7,693	10,283	c23,773	(d)
Total	883	16,369	21,783	41,637	62

a At Gloucester Point, Norfolk, Portsmouth, and Yorktown, Va.
b At Beaufort, New Berne, Plymouth, and Washington, N. C.
c Includes 10,065 reported as in Department of the South.
d Not reported in original.

HEADQUARTERS ARMY OF THE POTOMAC,
                                    August 11, 1863.
Hon. E. M. STANTON,
            Secretary of War:

I have to acknowledge the receipt of your letter of the 7th instant, in relation to the sale of newspapers in this army. I regret, in view of the authority vested in your hands, and your attention being called to the subject, that you did not indicate your wishes, in order that the same might be carried into effect. As, however, you are pleased still to commit this subject to my judgment as commanding general, I feel bound to say, after carefully examining into all that has occurred, that the present arrangement is, so far as I can see, the most just to the soldier and the fairest for the proprietors of journals.

There are two questions involved in the arrangement of the subject: (1) What journals shall be distributed in the army; and (2) by whom and upon what terms shall these journals be sold ?

The first question is in a manner political, and for the solution of which I am free to say I do not feel myself competent to decide from ignorance of the character of individual journals. It is one of great delicacy, and involving important questions touching the liberty of the press, and the rights of individuals, which it seems to me should be settled by higher and more competent authority than the commanding general of an army.

If left to my decision, I shall feel myself bound to be governed by the action of the Government with reference to other classes of citizens, and to decide that if the Government permit the publication and distribution of a journal among the citizens of the locality where it is published, that I have no right to deny the soldiers the same privilege which is acceded to their fellow-citizens at home. This, of course, is a very broad ground, and allows the circulation of all published journals. To adopt a different course, however, would be to virtually establish in this army a censorship of the press, which, as I remarked before, is impracticable for want of proper knowledge of the subject.

Having decided what journals should be circulated, the question next arises, By what mode shall their circulation be regulated and sanctioned ? You are aware that several methods have been adopted, and in succession abandoned as open to objections; among them one now proposed by Mr. Clark, in the letter referred to me, which is, that each journal should be represented by its own agent. The principal objection to this system is that it multiplies indefinitely the number of agents, and that it would be a constantly recurring question as to who should be the designated agent, unless, as Mr. Clark avers, he should be honored with the agency of the principal journals, which, so far as I can see, would then be establishing as much of a monopoly as now exists—only the monopoly would be in Mr. Clark's hands, and inure to the benefit of himself and friends, and not as now to the fund devoted to alleviating the sufferings of our sick and wounded.

It was the difficulty of deciding what journals should have agents, and the trouble of regulating and supervising so many different persons, which induced my predecessor, after much deliberation, and as I sincerely believe with an earnest desire to do justice to all parties, to adopt the present system, which was to give the agency for the whole army to one individual, requiring him to furnish such papers as are called for at a stipulated price, and, in order that all interested might have an opportunity to secure the position, it was determined to give it to the highest bidder, the proceeds of the contract to be turned over to the medical director to be expended for the benefit of the hospitals.

So far as I can judge from the examination I have made, this system has up to this time worked satisfactorily. I have heard no complaint of the character of Mr. Clark, except a letter received from the proprietor of the Daily Chronicle, in Washington, who averred that, owing to the cheapness of other journals, the agent did not procure as many of his papers as the officers and soldiers desired.

In regard to Mr. Clark's complaint, as well as his allegations against the character of the present agent, I beg leave to say whenever he substantiates either, by proper evidence and facts before the provost-marshal-general, the evils complained of will be immediately corrected, and the contract with the present agent annulled. With regard to the complaint, or rather objection, of the proprietor of the Daily Chronicle, I have advised him that the fact that the agent is compelled by the terms of his contract to supply such papers as are called for will be made public in orders, and a plan arranged by which each officer and man desiring his paper can register his name, and the agent will be compelled to procure and deliver a number equal to the demand thus indicated. By adopting this plan, I do not see how any monopoly can be injuriously established, and that each journal will be fairly and justly represented, its circulation being thus dependent on the will of the army.

So far, therefore, as my judgment is concerned, I should not be disposed to alter the present system, believing that the complaints made against it are based more on individual interests than on the general interests of the army.

As to who shall be the agent, I have no individual preference, and will most promptly discharge the present incumbent so soon as any reliable evidence is presented either that he is unworthy of employment from notoriously bad character, or that he fails to execute his contract in the most impartial manner and with the single object of giving satisfaction to the soldier.

At the same time, I shall be greatly relieved if you shall think proper to assume control of this subject, and you may rest assured whenever your wishes are distinctly indicated, they will be most promptly and cheerfully complied with. And if you should deem it of importance to designate another agent, the contract with the present incumbent will be at once revoked, and your nominee installed.

I inclose herewith a report * from the provost-marshal-general, showing the conditions upon which the present agent distributes papers, and the amount paid by him to the hospital fund.

Very respectfully, &c.,

GEO. G. MEADE,
Major-General, Commanding.

HEADQUARTERS CAVALRY CORPS,
August 11, [1863]—4 p. m.
(Received 5 p. m.)

Major-General HUMPHREYS,
Chief of Staff:

GENERAL: General Merritt reports that a party sent out by Colonel Devin had gone as far as the Rapidan. The enemy, about 100 strong, retreated before the advance of the party, but came back to his old position on the return of the party. The enemy's force extends as far east as Stevensburg, and his scouts and pickets move well down on the neck between the Rapidan and the Rappahannock. In front of Rappahannock Bridge everything remains the same.

Very respectfully,

A. PLEASONTON,
Major-General, Commanding.

---

* See p. 26.

HEADQUARTERS FIRST CAVALRY DIVISION,
August 11, 1863.

Col. C. ROSS SMITH,
    Chief of Staff, Headquarters Cavalry Corps:

Nothing new from the front. The lines are quiet and as previously reported. No horses have as yet been turned over by the Reserve Brigade since last report. General Kilpatrick's quartermaster looked through the lot to-day, but took none. Gregg has not been heard from. Cannot some order, requiring these horses to be taken, be sent to headquarters of Second and Third Divisions, or the horses be turned in to Catlett's Station, so that this brigade can get off?

    Very respectfully,

                    W. MERRITT,
    Brigadier-General of Volunteers, Comdg. Division.

HEADQUARTERS ARMY OF THE POTOMAC,
August 11, 1863.

Major-General SCHURZ,
    Commanding Eleventh Corps:

The major-general commanding directs me to say that in the course of conversation yesterday it was incidentally mentioned by General Wright that it was reported by his patrols toward Greenwich that they had seen nothing recently of the force at Greenwich. This was one of the points to be occupied by a regiment from the Eleventh Corps, which was to patrol toward New Baltimore and Bristoe Station.

    Very respectfully, your obedient servant,

                    A. A. HUMPHREYS,
    Major-General, and Chief Staff.

HDQRS. SECOND DIVISION, CAVALRY CORPS,
August 11, 1863.

Capt. A. J. COHEN,
    Assistant Adjutant-General, Cavalry Corps:

CAPTAIN: The communication from Major-General Humphreys, chief of staff, Army of the Potomac, addressed to Major-General Pleasonton, commanding Cavalry Corps, having been referred to me, I have the honor to submit the following reply:

When at Amissville, and on the 4th and 6th of this month, by direction of the major-general commanding the Cavalry Corps, reconnoitering parties were sent across the Aestham River, in the direction of Culpeper, to ascertain the position and movements of the enemy. Both these reconnaissances discovered the fact that the enemy's cavalry to the amount of a brigade occupied the country between Rixeyville and Culpeper. Other reconnaissances discovered that the enemy's cavalry to the amount of a brigade was in the vicinity of Sperryville. After these reconnaissances across the Aestham River, the fords at Oak Shade and Starke's were picketed by the enemy.

When, on the 9th, I received an order from Major-General Pleasonton to extend my line of pickets south of the Aestham River, crossing at Rixeyville, I did report that the enemy picketed the south bank in force. This had been ascertained from previous reconnaissances, and at the time of making such report the pickets were visible. I then expressed the opinion that a line of pickets established on the south bank of the Aestham River, in the very front of the enemy (there being but two points of crossing, Oak Shade Ford and Welford's, and this stream readily made unfordable by a heavy rain), would be greatly in danger of capture.

It not having been indicated to me at what point the left of my new line would connect with General Buford's right, I made application that such point be established. Beverly Ford was the point indicated. To Col. J. B. McIntosh, commanding First Brigade of this division, I sent an order to cross as directed from headquarters Cavalry Corps, and to employ his whole force for the purpose.* The order reached Colonel McIntosh at the river, where he had 250 men. In acknowledging the receipt of this order, Colonel McIntosh reported that it was impracticable to cross as directed, but that he had ordered a force to cross at Welford's Ford, to communicate with General Buford, and establish the left of the line as far as Welford's Ford. Having been officially informed that General Buford's pickets would be at Beverly Ford, and that General Sykes had put down a bridge and had infantry in front of Beverly Ford, a force of 40 men was sent across at Welford's Ford. The crossing was easily effected, and it was ten minutes after the departure of the lieutenant and 16 men before the enemy approached in superior force. Welford's Ford is 2½ miles from Beverly Ford.

It will be seen that the report made by me as to the enemy occupying and picketing the south bank of the river was made with reference to the point at which I was ordered to cross, viz, at Rixeyville Ford. Having been informed that General Buford's division was 1½ miles from Rappahannock Station, it was inferred that the enemy would not be so near the junction of the two rivers as at Welford's Ford. I did not direct the crossing of any portion of the command at Welford's Ford, nor did I know of it until it had been done, but when it was reported to me by Colonel McIntosh I fully approved of it. The force deployed by the enemy was but 18 men, and these fled at the approach of the force sent across. A personal examination of the fords at Rixeyville and Stark's Ford confirms me more fully as to the impracticability of crossing any ordinary force for picketing at either of these places, and also that a line of pickets established on the south bank of the Aestham River could not be maintained there without the support of the entire force at present under my command, stationed on the same side with the pickets. I must again refer to the report sent by me that the enemy picketed the south bank in force, and call attention to the fact that this report was made because of an order to cross at Rixeyville and referred to the south side of the river in that vicinity.

I would add that the lieutenant and 16 men returned yesterday, having communicated with General Buford's command, but could not return by the route they had taken.

This, the explanation of the acts of myself and subordinates in our attempts to execute an order so as to promote the best interests of the service, is respectfully submitted.

D. McM. GREGG,
Brigadier-General of Volunteers, Comdg. Second Division.

---

* For McIntosh's report, see p. 67, Part I.

WASHINGTON,
August 12, 1863—9 p. m.

General GEORGE G. MEADE,
  Commanding Army of the Potomac :

If you can conveniently leave your command, I would be glad to see you at the Department to-morrow, or at your earliest convenience, for the purpose of consultation. Please report whether you can come and when.

EDWIN M. STANTON,
Secretary of War.

GENERAL ORDERS, } HEADQUARTERS CAVALRY CORPS,
  No. 25.　}　*August* 12, 1863.

By direction of the major-general commanding Army of the Potomac, the Second Brigade of the Second Cavalry Division is hereby broken up, and will be distributed as follows :

Second New York Cavalry to the First Brigade, Third Division.

Fourth New York Cavalry to the Second Brigade, First Division.

The First Rhode Island, Sixth Ohio, and Eighth Pennsylvania Cavalry will be assigned by the division commander of the Second Division to the two brigades of that command, to equalize their numbers as much as possible.

By command of Major-General Pleasonton:

A. J. COHEN,
Assistant Adjutant-General.

HEADQUARTERS EIGHTEENTH ARMY CORPS,
New Berne, N. C., August 12, 1863.

Lieut. Col. SOUTHARD HOFFMAN,
  Assistant Adjutant-General.

COLONEL: I have the honor to inclose the communication in reference to the property stolen from Washington by various officers. The letter from Lieutenant-Colonel McChesney throws some light on the matter. Some of the things not enumerated by Colonel McChesney were doubtless taken without authority, but the precise amount cannot be ascertained. I inclose, also, copies of orders issued here since General Foster left this corps. With regard to the funds captured on the late raid, and placed in the hands of Lieutenant Cardner, I can only say that the whole matter was conducted in a very irregular manner. You inform me that this money ($2,600) had been turned over by Lieutenant Cardner to Colonel Lewis, who was to turn it over to General Potter. Why, then, did not Colonel Lewis do so? He was here for several days with General Potter, and as soon as General Potter left, he (Colonel Lewis) applied for and received a leave of absence to go direct to New York, taking the money with him. Besides, I think that the $2,600 was only a small portion of the amount of money captured. I think I can show that Lieutenant Cardner sold a considerable sum of money, either North Carolina State or Confederate money—as much as $1,100 to one person—all of which was money captured on that raid. The matter is in the hands of the provost-marshal, who will, I hope, be able to throw more light on this matter.

The order concerning horses was issued for the reason that there are hundreds upon hundreds of horses kept by citizens, traders, soldiers, &c., all of which are fed by the Government, while they are in no way in the service of the Government. No forage is brought here except such as is brought by the Government, and of course the quartermaster's department must feed all these animals. I wish to find out who are the owners, or pretended owners, of the animals, and where they get their forage.

A flag of truce came in yesterday, down the river, in charge of Major Whitford. The steamer Southfield received it, and, much to my surprise, permitted the officers with it to come to me. I sent them immediately back to the Southfield, and as soon as I could, I sent a steamer alongside of her to receive the officers and men who came with Whitford, and to return with them up the river this morning.

The dispatch brought was from General Martin, and unimportant, as it was only concerning some of Whitford's men, who are prisoners here, and who General Martin says were reported to be in irons.

Some women and children came in, too, to remain here, and one to go North. I never knew of their being here until they made their appearance before me. I should have felt obliged to refuse two of them admittance. One of them is a Northern woman from Massachusetts.

The canal I presume is fairly opened. About 200 men are stationed at Currituck Bridge. A small field-work is in process of construction, laid out by Lieutenant King, and there are two guns for the work, one a field piece and one a carronade. We are much in need of a boat to run through the canal. I hear that you have some suitable for that purpose at Norfolk or Fort Monroe. I go to-day to Hatteras to see how matters are there, and to regulate some difficulties that have arisen between the commanding officer, the quartermaster, and the surgeon of the post. Admiral Lee has been here, but he is now inspecting his force in the sounds. He will return in a few days. I shall send with this a supply of the latest Richmond papers.

I am, colonel, very respectfully, your obedient servant,

I. N. PALMER,
Brigadier-General, Commanding.

NORFOLK,
August 12, 1863.

General FOSTER.

The Governor [Peirpoint] called upon me last night, and, after a big effort to blind me, was taken up in handsome style. Admitted that the council were interfering with the military, and had failed at Washington, and concluded with me that he merely wished to suggest a certain policy which I will not order, namely, to at once confiscate all property unless the owners will take the oath of allegiance to the United States and to the State of Virginia. I have to-day issued the following order, which is as far as I will go. The Governor is too rabid.

NAGLEE.

[Inclosure]

SPECIAL ORDERS, } HDQRS. DEPT. OF VA., 7TH ARMY CORPS,
    No. 1.   }   Norfolk, Va., August 12, 1863.

The provost-marshals of the cities of Norfolk and Portsmouth will take possession of all houses owned by disloyal persons now within the rebel lines, and of all real property within said cities owned by disloyal persons, who take active part against the Government of the United States, or who violate the orders of the department; but no property shall be condemned until written evidence shall have been taken in the premises and be approved by the general commanding.

The fund created by the rental of the above property shall be appropriated exclusively toward the relief of the destitute families of officers and soldiers in the rebel army.

By command of Brigadier-General Naglee:

GEORGE H. JOHNSTON,
Assistant Adjutant-General.

GENERAL ORDERS, }   HDQRS. DEPT. OF VA. AND N. C.,
    No. 4.   }   August 12, 1863.

Maj. Gen. John J. Peck is hereby assigned to the command of the District of North Carolina and of the troops therein, and will be respected and obeyed accordingly.

By command of Major-General Foster :

SOUTHARD HOFFMAN,
Assistant Adjutant-General.

AUGUST 13, 1863.
(Received 9.40 p. m.)

Hon. E. M. STANTON,
    Secretary of War:

I will leave here at 12 m. and expect to be in the city and at the Department by 5 p. m. If this hour interferes with your arrangements, please leave word at what time I shall call.

GEO. G. MEADE,
Major-General, Commanding.

HEADQUARTERS,
August 13, [1863]—9 a. m.

Major-General SLOCUM,
    Commanding Twelfth Corps :

I am instructed by the major-general commanding to inform you that he is called to Washington, and that he deems it advisable that you should be at these headquarters until he returns. He leaves at 12 m.

A. A. HUMPHREYS,
Major-General, Chief of Staff.

HEADQUARTERS SECOND CAVALRY BRIGADE,
Hartwood Church, August 13, 1863.
(Received 11 a. m.)

Major-General PLEASONTON,
  Commanding Cavalry Corps:

I send you a copy of the Richmond Examiner of yesterday. By the editorial and official orders, you will readily perceive the hopelessness with which they regard their prospects. This feeling pervades their entire army. I learn this from two deserters who have just come in. They belong to the First Texas Infantry, Hood's division, Longstreet's corps. Their division is on picket from United States Ford to Fredericksburg. Pickett's division is on the left of Hood's division, and A. P. Hill's corps is on the left of Pickett. One week ago one of the deserters saw a portion if not all of Ewell's ammunition train crossing the Rapidan at the railroad bridge (from Culpeper), going south.

The rebel army is being re-enforced considerably by convalescents, but no conscripts have arrived. Desertions are frequent. Many more than do would desert was our army closer to them. Four more belonging to the company with those taken to-day wished to come over, but were afraid they could not "make the trip." They can tell nothing of their cavalry, except that they were told that 500 cavalry and a battery had crossed near Falmouth, and gone to a point on the Potomac about 20 miles below the mouth of the Potomac Creek, where they intended establishing a battery to annoy our boats on the Potomac. If this report proves to be true, I would like to go down the Neck with my command and drive them out or capture them.

The deserters report the rebel army as very much dispirited, and that it is the belief among the privates that Lee's army will fight us on the Peninsula (not news).

My patrols intercepted and captured the carrier of some letters from the South Branch of the Rappahannock. One of the letters was from the adjutant-general of General Garnett's command, which is now stationed at Orange Court-House. The letter was to a young lady on this side the river. Among other things the writer said he could not see her until after the next grand battle was fought, which would be soon, and which battle would be the last of the war and would produce peace. He also informed his correspondent that the war would soon close, "or, to use the words of the privates, it is about played out." This is his own language. Comparing the intelligence which I have received from three sources (Richmond paper, deserters, and this officer's letter), I find it is of one character, which fact adds to its reliability.

All quiet along my line to-day. Citizens whom I arrested several days ago and forwarded to the headquarters Cavalry Corps, have been paroled and returned to their homes. They regard their paroles no more than they do so much blank paper, and are as able to injure us by bushwhacking, &c., as they were before, if not more so. They are bolder and more defiant. They come into my camp among the men and boast of their paroles, and say they are for the Confederate Government, but will wait and see who comes off victor. Complaints have been made to me, and in some cases arrests have been made, but I am powerless to act in consequence of their paroles from the headquarters of the Army of the Potomac. I can suppress

bushwhacking, and render every man within the limits of my command practically loyal, if allowed to deal with them as I choose.
Very respectfully, &c.,

G. A. CUSTER,
Brigadier-General.

P. S.—I have forwarded the information obtained from the enemy to General Kilpatrick, but it is more direct to your headquarters than to his. I therefore send you a copy also, not doubting but that General Kilpatrick will do so likewise.

[Indorsement.]

HEADQUARTERS CAVALRY CORPS,
August 14, [1863]—10.15 a. m.
(Received 11 a. m.)

This communication is respectfully forwarded to headquarters Army of the Potomac, with the Richmond Examiner referred to. The captured letters were not sent. General Custer has been directed to forward them.

A. PLEASONTON,
Major-General, Commanding.

WAR DEPARTMENT,
Washington City, August 13, 1863—7 p. m.

Brig. Gen. S. WILLIAMS,
Headquarters Army of the Potomac:

Order at once the regular division in the Fifth Corps and the Vermont brigade in the Sixth Corps to Alexandria. Call on the Quartermaster's Department to furnish transportation by railroad, so as to forward these troops with as little delay as possible. No land transportation or supplies to accompany them.

GEO. G. MEADE,
Major-General, Commanding.

AUGUST 13, 1863—10.10 p. m.

Commanding Officer Sixth Corps:

The commanding general directs that the Vermont brigade of your corps proceed forthwith to Alexandria, there to receive further orders. The brigade will march at the earliest possible moment to Warrenton Junction, where railroad transportation will be provided for it. No land transportation or supplies will be taken by the brigade. Please acknowledge this dispatch at once, and report as soon as you can the number of officers and men for whom transportation will be required.

S. WILLIAMS,
Assistant Adjutant-General.

AUGUST 13, 1863—10.15 p. m.

Commanding Officer Fifth Corps:

The commanding general directs that the regular division of your corps proceed forthwith to Alexandria, there to receive further orders. The division will march as soon as possible to Rappahannock Station, where railroad transportation will be provided for it. No land transportation or supplies will accompany the division. Please acknowledge this dispatch, and report as soon as you can the number of officers and men for whom transportation will be required.

S. WILLIAMS,
Assistant Adjutant-General.

———

OFFICE PROVOST-MARSHAL-GENERAL,
August 13, 1863.

Col. G. H. SHARPE,
   Deputy Provost-Marshal-General, &c.:

COLONEL : At your suggestion, I have the honor to report in brief the manner in which goods have been brought to the Army of the Potomac by sutlers and traders during the time General Patrick has been acting as provost-marshal-general.

By referring to the circular issued November 7, 1862, and marked A, it will be seen that before goods could be brought to the army an invoice must be presented to this office for approval, or the goods attempted to be brought to the army would be liable to confiscation. Such instances, I may here add, were not a few. That system continued in force from the issuing of the circular, November 7, 1862, at which time goods were brought to the army in wagons, until the army went into winter quarters on the Rappahannock, when the following system went into effect :

A sutler wishing to bring goods to the army made up his invoice in conformity to the "Wilson bill," and for one month's supply. That invoice was approved by the commandant of his regiment and brigade, and latterly by command of the provost-marshal-general. Three sutlers, with their papers thus approved, could go to Washington, and there of the Quartermaster-General obtain permission to clear a vessel for Belle Plain or Aquia Creek. At these points were officers, acting under orders of the provost-marshal-general, who examined the goods and manifest accompanying the vessels. If found to agree, and no contraband goods discovered, the sutlers were permitted to land their goods.

The confiscations while the army lay at that point were not a few. Parties attempting to smuggle liquors and other contraband goods into the army, not only lost their goods, but were sent from the army not to return. The system last mentioned continued in effect until the army moved from the Rappahannock in June last, at which time sutlers were notified to go to the rear with their goods and teams, as they were not to be permitted to follow the army when on the move. Now that the army is stationary, and sutlers, if they come to it, will be obliged to have their goods in wagons, some plan should be hit upon preventing contraband goods from coming to the army.

I have carefully read the plan proposed by Colonel Hardie, assistant adjutant-general to Major-General Meade, and which, in the main, is the same as that followed by the army, in accordance with the circular marked A, and heretofore referred to. In those times, if I remember rightly, General Martindale gave the sutlers permission to come to the army from Washington, instead of the Quartermaster-General as proposed, and upon papers approved from this office. Again, by referring to the accompanying General Orders, No. 56, issued from headquarters of the army, you will discover that no public transportation is given the sutler or trader.

Such being the case, Colonel Hardie very properly suggests that some plan should be hit upon which in the future shall prevent the enemy from being supplied through the sutlers. Whether a mounted escort, at stated periods, is the best mode, others better qualified to judge will say. It would seem if the plan suggested by Colonel Hardie was followed, and which, by the way, does not materially differ from that heretofore followed in the army, the instances need be rare when imposition will be practiced, provided the inspecting officer at the Long Bridge, or at whatever point he is stationed, uses due vigilance and care in the exercise of his duties.

We have reason to believe that liquors are being brought to the army by sutlers and their employés. Whether properly or not, we have no means of knowing, as liquors now come to the army in accordance with a general order issued by General Martindale, a copy of which is herewith inclosed, marked D, from which it will be readily seen that we have not in our possession any record by which we can tell whether or not the liquors are brought upon proper papers.

The test of citizenship has never been applied to sutlers in this army, to my knowledge. The certificate accompanying is such as we give sutlers who are registered in our office upon what we deem proper papers. The certificate we require to be shown if we have any doubt as to whether the party applying for passes or favors is entitled to that for which he asks.

I have the honor to be, very respectfully, your obedient servant,

W. W. BECKWITH,
Captain, and Aide-de-Camp.

AUGUST 14, 1863—12.45 a. m.

Commanding Officer Fifth Corps:

I am instructed by the commanding general to say that the volunteer brigade attached to the regular division is to remain, and not accompany the division.

Please acknowledge.

S. WILLIAMS,
Assistant Adjutant-General.

HDQRS. CAVALRY CORPS, ARMY OF THE POTOMAC,
August 14, 1863—7.20 a. m.

Major-General HUMPHREYS,
Chief of Staff:

GENERAL: General Merritt reports the return of Colonel Devin. No new discoveries. Enemy's force in front about the same. In front of Merritt's pickets the enemy's [pickets] are in considerable force in cavalry.

Colonel Devin's signal officer read following dispatch of the enemy:

There is nothing new in our front. The enemy's fires seem to be increasing.

This dispatch was addressed to Colonel C.

General Kilpatrick reports he pickets 32 miles and patrols 14 more. The line he is required to occupy cannot be looked after with a less force.

I forward a copy of Colonel Mann's report of his scout after Mosby.*

Colonel Huey reports small scattering parties in the vicinity of Middleburg, Aldie, Salem, and surrounding country. He reports that White's guerrillas have joined Mosby.

The officer and 16 men supposed by General Gregg to be captured, have returned. I inclose communications from General Gregg† and Colonel McIntosh† relative to crossing the Aestham River. I shall call on General Gregg for further explanation.

Very respectfully,

A. PLEASONTON,
Major-General, Commanding.

HDQRS. ARMY OF THE POTOMAC, *August* 14, 1863—11 a. m.
(Received 11.10 a. m.)

Maj. Gen. GEORGE G. MEADE, *Washington, D. C.:*

The regular troops of Ayres' division (aggregating 2,000) are at Bealeton and the Vermont brigade (aggregating 2,000) are at Warrenton Junction. These troops are moving to Alexandria as fast as they are furnished with transportation by the railroad. Nothing new this morning.

S. WILLIAMS,
Assistant Adjutant-General.

HDQRS. CAVALRY CORPS, ARMY OF THE POTOMAC,
August 14, 1863—2.30 p. m.

Major-General HUMPHREYS, *Chief of Staff:*

GENERAL: I inclose a copy of a report* of a scout who has been on the south side of the Rappahannock, and brings important information. I have sent for the man himself, and will forward him to you; but as he belongs to the command out on picket, he may not arrive until to-morrow.

Taken in connection with other reports and information bearing on the same point, this dispatch is of the utmost importance. I have been satisfied the enemy was intending something on our left for some days past, and have desired a greater force of cavalry in that vicinity.

I would urge that this information be sent in cipher immediately to General Meade, that he may authorize a change in the present disposition of the cavalry, as well as other corps, our left flank being in no condition to receive an attack from the enemy's whole force, and we know from our own experience at Chancellorsville that an army entire can be crossed in a single night. United States Ford is evidently the point intended by the enemy to cross. From that point, and a night start, their cavalry could reach the vicinity of Washington before ours could, in any force, from its present location.

Very respectfully,

A. PLEASONTON,
Major-General, Commanding.

---

* Not found.   † See p. 33 and foot-note on p. 34.

HEADQUARTERS THIRD DIVISION CAVALRY CORPS,
August 14, 1863.
Captain COHEN,
Assistant Adjutant-General:

CAPTAIN: The inclosed communication is forwarded for the information of the major-general commanding Cavalry Corps.

I most respectfully suggest that the force now at Georgetown, under Major Cooke, can be safely reduced to one strong regiment, as the object of this force is but to watch and not to fight. I can then move to General Custer's assistance, with four regiments and the batteries, at any moment.

Respectfully submitted.

J. KILPATRICK,
Brigadier-General, Commanding.

[Inclosure.]

CAVALRY OUTPOST,
Falmouth Road, August 13, 1863.
Capt. JACOB L. GREENE,
Assistant Adjutant-General:

I have a scout of my own regiment who has just returned, having been across the river and in the camps of the enemy. He crossed half a mile below United States Ford. Had to swim the river. Found extensive camps. Longstreet's corps, 10,000 strong; also, 5,000 mounted men—mostly mounted infantry—armed with Enfield rifles; likewise some regular cavalry. He went through the camp as a member of the Fourth Virginia Cavalry. He saw some 500 negroes at work near United States Ford, cutting timber into logs from 10 to 30 feet in length. Report among the men in camp was that they were to cross in great force, getting in the rear of General Meade's army, and on to Washington. Said they were diverting General Meade to the left, while their forces come this way.

This man is a very square fellow; still I hardly know how much reliance to place in the report. He staid over some time; took dinner with them; saw large quantities of commissary stores. This report, taken with the remark in the private letter intercepted to-day—"the coming great battle"—may be of significance. Scout said the boys said this was to be their last great struggle. If successful, they would be recognized. If not, all was up.

W. D. MANN,
Colonel, Commanding.

HEADQUARTERS ARMY OF THE POTOMAC,
August 14, 1863—4.30 p. m.
Major-General MEADE,
Washington:

Dispatch from signal-officer at Watery Mountain:

A large cloud of smoke is rising between Orange Court-House and Gordonsville; very near the latter place. Can see the enemy's camp smoke south of Clark's Mountain. There is not so much smoke in vicinity of Culpeper as heretofore.

TAYLOR,
Signal Officer.

A. A. HUMPHREYS,
Chief of Staff.

HEADQUARTERS ARMY OF THE POTOMAC,
August 14, 1863—4.30 p. m.

Major-General MEADE,
Comdg. Army of the Potomac, War Dept., Washington :

The following report* is sent at the request of Major-General Pleasonton, who urges that it may be sent to General Meade immediately, so "that he may authorize a change in the present disposition of the cavalry as well as other corps."

This is not the opinion of Major-General Slocum, nor mine, excepting partially in respect to the Cavalry Corps. I can get nothing from Watery Mountain signal officer, although I have directed observations to be made in reference to this report and made repeated inquiries. Will keep you advised.

A. A. HUMPHREYS,
Major-General, Chief of Staff.

HEADQUARTERS ARMY OF THE POTOMAC,
August 14, 1863.

Maj. Gen. GEORGE G. MEADE,
Washington:

The following copy of a letter just received by me from General Williams is sent as corroboration of the dispatch transmitted 4.30 p. m.:

FAIRFAX STATION,
August 9, 1863.

DEAR BROTHER: A rebel raid on a large scale is intended through this s ction within a week or two. I have this information in a way that I consider reliable. It came from an officer in Stuart's cavalry, who, I think, has been stopping at Fairfax Court-House with his wife for some days, and left a day or two ago. It will probably come from Fredericksburg, by way of Dumfries and Occoquan, and strike the railroad at this point, with intention to destroy it to Manassas. Mosby, I think, is gone, as it was getting rather hot for him, but he has gained all the information desired of the positive strength of the forces guarding the railroads. Nothing can be easier than for 5,000 or 6,000 cavalry to sweep around Meade's army and gobble up the small forces along this road, destroy a large amount of stores at the various points, cars, locomotives, &c., and tear up the railroad itself, so as to take weeks to repair it, and compel Meade to detach a large force to defend it. Would it not be best to give General Heintzelman this information?

JOB HAWXHURST.

HUMPHREYS.

HDQRS. CAVALRY CORPS, ARMY OF THE POTOMAC,
August 14, 1863—7.15 p. m.   (Received 7.30 p. m.)

Major-General HUMPHREYS,
Chief of Staff :

GENERAL: Your dispatch of 7 p. m. received. Am I authorized to concentrate all the cavalry not on duty as picket guards? The commands are so scattered that it will take some time to concentrate any portion of them.

Very respectfully,

A. PLEASONTON,
Major-General, Commanding.

---

* Not found.

AUGUST 14, 1863—8 p. m.

Major-General PLEASONTON,
Commanding Cavalry Corps:

Major-General Slocum directs me to say, in answer to your dispatch of 7.15 p. m., that he is indisposed to make any material change in the disposition of the troops during the brief absence of General Meade, and intended merely to authorize the holding ready for concentration and movement all the cavalry not on duty as picket guards ; that is, all of Gregg's divison not on duty as pickets and supports of pickets should be concentrated at the most convenient point, all things considered, within the limits of his command, and held ready for general concentration and movement. The same of each of the other cavalry divisions.

Very respectfully, your obedient servant,
A. A. HUMPHREYS,
Major-General, Chief of Staff.

HDQRS. THIRD DIVISION, CAVALRY CORPS,
August 14, 1863.

Col. E. B. SAWYER,
Commanding First Brigade:

COLONEL: The general commanding directs me to say that the First Vermont must move at once to Thoroughfare Gap and relieve Major Cooke.

I am, colonel, very respectfully, your obedient servant,
L. G. ESTES,
Assistant Adjutant-General.

SECOND DIVISION, ELEVENTH CORPS,
August 11, 1863.

Maj. Gen. CARL SCHURZ,
Commanding Eleventh Corps:

GENERAL: In reply to communication relative to certain delays in stationing railroad guards, I present the following:

The instructions touching recent changes in the position of the One hundred and sixty-eighth New York Volunteers were issued to the commanding officer of the Second Brigade on the night of the 12th instant. Why that command failed to occupy the specified points I am yet unable to state. As soon as it was reported to me last night that the dispositions ordered were not made, I sent a strong detachment from the Second Brigade to Bristoe and Kettle Run, with instructions to frequently patrol, respectively, to Manassas Junction and Walnut Run, until relieved by the One hundred and sixty-eighth New York Volunteers, and for the accomplishment of this a staff officer was sent at an early hour to the commanding officer of the One hundred and sixty-eighth New York Volunteers.

I am, general, with proper respect,
A. VON STEINWEHR,
Brigadier-General, Second Division.

AUGUST 14, 1863.
(Received 11.45 p. m.)

General H. W. HALLECK:

I have directed the Eighth, One hundred and tenth, and One hundred and twenty-second Ohio, Third and Seventh Michigan, and First Minnesota Regiments to proceed to Alexandria to-day and report to you. These regiments are much weaker than I supposed at the time they were detached, numbering in the aggregate only 1,300 for duty. Other regiments will be promptly forwarded, but I understand that the road will not probably be able to transport to-day more men than are already ordered.

GEO. G. MEADE,
Major-General, Commanding.

———

AUGUST 14, 1863—11 p. m.
(Received 11.55 p. m.)

Major-General HALLECK:

Deserters from the enemy report the crossing at Fredericksburg of a regiment of cavalry with a battery of artillery, designed, it was said, to interfere with the navigation of the Potomac below Aquia—probably Mathias Point. Please notify the commanding officer of the Potomac flotilla, as, with the force reported at Fredericksburg, it would be risky for me to send after them.

GEO. G. MEADE,
Major-General, Commanding.

———

AUGUST 14, 1863—11.30 p. m.

Commanding Officer Sixth Corps:

The major-general commanding directs me to inform you that all the cavalry between the Hedgeman and Aestham Rivers will be immediately withdrawn, and that the observation and defense of the river on the front now held by you will be done solely by your corps, and that your pickets and supports and the disposition of your troops must be arranged accordingly. Should you deem it necessary to have more artillery to perfect the defense of any of the crossings, upon reporting the fact to these headquarters, it will be sent you from the reserve.

A. A. HUMPHREYS,
Major-General, and Chief of Staff.

———

CIRCULAR.]   HEADQUARTERS ARMY OF THE POTOMAC,
August 14, 1863.

The major-general commanding directs that corps and other independent commanders keep their trains in readiness to move at short notice, and make themselves acquainted with the roads leading to the flanks and rear, so as to be prepared in the event of a movement being ordered.

By command of Major-General Meade:

S. WILLIAMS,
Assistant Adjutant-General.

(Sent to Artillery Reserve, near Warrenton Junction; commanding officers Eleventh Corps, Warrenton Junction; Twelfth Corps, Kelly's Ford; Second Corps, Morrisville; Third Corps, via Bealeton; Fifth Corps, Rappahannock Station; Sixth Corps, Warrenton, and First Corps, Rappahannock Station.)

CIRCULAR.]   HEADQUARTERS ARMY OF THE POTOMAC,
August 14, 1863—10 p. m.

The major-general commanding directs that the troops keep three days' rations in the haversack, and be prepared to march at a moment's notice.

By command of Major-General Meade:

S. WILLIAMS,
Assistant Adjutant-General.

CENTREVILLE,
August 14, 1863—11 a. m.

Colonel GRIMSHAW,
Fairfax Station :

There is a current rumor that Stuart, with several thousand men, is preparing to make a dash at the Orange and Alexandria Railroad, with the view of breaking it up between Accotink and Manassas. Use your spies and scouts freely on the south side of the railroad toward Dumfries, so as to get timely notice of such an attempt, should it be made.

RUFUS KING,
Brigadier-General, Commanding.

POOLESVILLE, MD., *August 14, 1863.*
(Received 12.30 p. m.)

Maj. T. T. ECKERT :

About 6 or 8 cavalrymen rode through this place this morning, and went about 5 miles below here, toward Darnestown, and inquired for Colonel Dawson, revenue collector. He was not at home. They took 3 horses from his place. A little after 4 a. m. they returned, passing close by my office. Captain Means' officers say none of their men were out last night ; say also they heard that White was at Waterford, and intended crossing last night, but the report came too late for them to send out scouting parties. I am quite confident that it was a party of Confederates.

CHAS. DOUGLASS,
Telegraph Operator.

HEADQUARTERS EIGHTEENTH ARMY CORPS,
August 14, 1863.

Maj. Gen. J. G. FOSTER,
Comdg. Dept. of Virginia and North Carolina :

GENERAL : I have the honor to report my arrival, and that I have assumed command of the Eighteenth Army Corps, in pursuance of your instructions of the 12th instant. Brigadier-General Palmer reports everything quiet in North Carolina. To-morrow I shall proceed on a tour of inspection.

JOHN J. PECK, ·
Major-General.

HDQRS. DEPT. OF VIRGINIA, SEVENTH ARMY CORPS,
Norfolk, August 14, 1863.

Capt. JOHN C. LEE,
Ninety-ninth New York Volunteers:

CAPTAIN: You will take command of the army steam tug Curri-tuck, and forthwith proceed to the shore of this department referred to in the printed orders hereunto attached,* and which extends from the mouth of the Western Branch of the Elizabeth River to Pig Point. You will prevent all boats from approaching that shore nearer than the southern side of the main channel of the James and Elizabeth Rivers, and you will seize all boats that leave the shore. Your attention is especially directed to the capture and destruction of all boats that may attempt to enter or depart from the Nansemond River, and you will burn all boats found in that river. You will seize all boats that attempt to enter or depart from the Western Branch. You will, after the 15th instant, destroy all boats not numbered wherever found. You will report to these headquarters at least twice a week in person and by letter as much oftener as circumstances may require, sending promptly such information as you may deem important.

By command of Brigadier-General Naglee:
GEORGE H. JOHNSTON,
Assistant Adjutant-General.

HDQRS. DEPT. OF VIRGINIA, SEVENTH ARMY CORPS,
Norfolk, August 14, 1863.

Lieut. C. D. WILLARD,
Nineteenth Regiment Wisconsin Volunteers:

You will forthwith assume command of the army tug boat General Jesup and proceed to the Albemarle Sound, where you will watch constantly and closely the water courses that flow into it from Princess Anne, Currituck, and Camden Counties of this department. You will burn all boats that you find upon the Pasquotank River, and seize and destroy or send to this place all boats or other vessels that you find engaged in contraband trade. No fisheries will be allowed unless by special permission from these headquarters, and then you will satisfy yourself that all the restrictions that may be imposed are complied with. You will enforce the provisions of the special orders hereunto attached,* for which purpose you will communicate as often as necessary with the United States forces on the Pasquotank River. You will report, via the land forces above referred to, once a week to these headquarters, and more frequently if you have any important information to communicate.

By command of Brigadier-General Naglee:
[GEORGE H. JOHNSTON,]
· *Assistant Adjutant-General.*

---

* See sub-inclosure, p. 58.

GENERAL ORDERS, }   HDQRS. EIGHTEENTH ARMY CORPS,
No. 1.   }   *New Berne, N. C., August 14, 1863.*

In accordance with orders from headquarters Department of Virginia and North Carolina, the undersigned assumes command of the Eighteenth Army Corps. All existing orders and regulations will remain in force until modified or revoked.

The following officers are announced upon the staff of the major-general commanding:.

Maj. Benjamin B. Foster, assistant adjutant-general.
Surg. Daniel W. Hand, medical director.
Lieut. Col. Francis Darr, chief commissary of subsistence.
Capt. R. C. Webster, chief quartermaster.
Lieut. Charles R. Stirling, aide-de-camp.
Lieut. James D. Outwater, aide-de-camp.

The remainder of the staff will be announced in future orders.

JOHN J. PECK,
Major-General.

SPECIAL ORDERS, }   HDQRS. ARMY, ADJT. GENERAL'S OFFICE,
No. 361.   }   *Washington, August 14, 1863.*

*   *   *   *   *   *   *

V. Brig. Gen. A. N. Duffié, U. S. Volunteers, will report in person without delay for duty to Brig. Gen. B. F. Kelley, U. S. Volunteers, commanding, &c., West Virginia.

By command of Major-General Halleck:

E. D. TOWNSEND,
Assistant Adjutant-General.

HEADQUARTERS ARMY OF THE POTOMAC,
August 15, 1863—10.30 a. m.

Commanding Officer First Corps:

I am directed by the major-general commanding to inform you that information derived from scouts and other sources indicates a concentration of the enemy in the vicinity of the United States Ford. The purpose may be to turn the left of this army, or a cavalry raid only may be contemplated. To meet either of these projects, the cavalry has been concentrated, leaving a picket force only in your front.

The major-general commanding instructs me to say that his operations for the present will be defensive. Should either a raid or movement to turn the flank of the army be commenced, it will undoubtedly be accompanied by a demonstration upon that part of the river held by your corps. In the disposition of your force, that portion on the south bank of the river is to be regarded as subsidiary to or forming a subordinate part of the main defense which is to be made from this side of the river. You will, therefore, hold in view the necessity that may occur of your being forced to withdraw the troops on the south side to the north side of the river, and eventually of abandoning the line of the Rappahannock.

The major-general commanding thinks it due to you to communicate the information received at these headquarters, and to acquaint you with the contingencies that may arise.

Very respectfully, &c.,

A. A. HUMPHREYS,
Major-General, and Chief of Staff.

AUGUST 15, 1863.

Commanding Officer Fifth Corps:

Our cavalry in your front, immediate and advanced, is withdrawn and will not be replaced. We leave now no cavalry whatever on the Aestham River, nor on the Hedgeman River or Rappahannock above the fort near Beverly Ford, nor between those rivers. Cavalry scouts will move out constantly from Waterloo toward Little Washington and the mountains. Your front must be watched by your own pickets.

A. A. HUMPHREYS,
Major-General, and Chief of Staff.

AUGUST 15, 1863—6.30 p. m.

Commanding Officer Eleventh Corps:

Your dispatch relative to the number and arrangement of the force guarding the railroad depots and bridges from Bealcton to Union Mills (or vicinity) is received. The major-general commanding directs me to say that it was not intended to reduce the force of the railroad guard of 12 men per mile; that guard in groups of 4, one-quarter of a mile apart, is to be constantly maintained. In addition to the railroad guard, there is to be a guard for each railroad station and each bridge. The guard at Warrenton Junction should be not less than 100 men. The whole force of railroad guard, station guard, and depot guard should be from 800 to 900 men.

A. A. HUMPHREYS,
Major-General, and Chief of Staff.

HEADQUARTERS ARMY OF THE POTOMAC,
August 15, 1863—9.15 p. m.

Maj. Gen. H. W. SLOCUM,
Commanding Twelfth Army Corps:

The commanding general directs that the following regiments of your command procee to Alexandria to-morrow, under the command of Brig. Gen. Td H. Ruger, for service, with the nature of which you are acquainted, viz : Second Massachusetts, Third Wisconsin, Twenty-seventh Indiana, and Fifth, Seventh, Twenty-ninth, and Sixty-sixth Ohio Regiments. You will please also send the One hundred and seventh New York Regiment if you think it advisable to do so.

The regiments will march to Rappahannock Station, where railroad transportation will be furnished them. No supplies will be taken. The transportation now with the regiments will be turned over to Captain Peirce, assistant quartermaster, at his depot near these headquarters.

Please cause General Ruger to be informed that the Fourth and One hundred and twenty-sixth Ohio, Fifth Michigan, and Fourteenth Indiana Regiments are ordered to report to him at Alexandria. General Ruger, on arriving at Alexandria, will report by telegraph to the General-in-Chief for further instructions, and also by telegraph to the Quartermaster-General.

All men belonging to the regiments on daily or detached duty in the corps will accompany them. You are desired to report as soon as possible the number of officers and men for whom transportation will be required, and also when the command will probably reach Rappahannock Station.

Please acknowledge.

S. WILLIAMS,
Assistant Adjutant-General.

SPECIAL ORDERS, }   HDQRS. ARMY OF THE POTOMAC,
    No. 219.   {   *August* 15, 1863.

*   *   *   *   *   *   *

IV. The commanding general has learned that the wives of numerous officers and soldiers are now with this army. In view of the service the troops may at any moment be called upon to perform, the commanding general considers that the attention of the officers and men should be solely occupied with their public duties, and that the presence of their families is incompatible with the complete discharge of the same.

It is therefore directed that all families now with the army, other than those who as nurses or attached to the Sanitary Commission have special authority from the War Department or these headquarters to visit and remain with it, be forthwith removed beyond its lines. The commanding general regrets that it has become his unpleasant duty to issue an order of this character, but he trusts that its propriety will be recognized, and that it will not be necessary for him to recur to the subject.

By command of Major-General Meade:

S. WILLIAMS,
Assistant Adjutant-General.

SPECIAL ORDERS, }   HEADQUARTERS CAVALRY CORPS,
    No. 122.   {   *August* 15, 1863.

I. The Third (Reserve) Brigade of the First Division of this corps will turn over their horses, arms, and equipments to the respective staff officers of that division and proceed to Alexandria under the orders of Brigadier-General Merritt, who will report in person to Major-General Stoneman, Chief of Cavalry Bureau, Washington, for the purpose of being placed in depot to be filled up and remounted.

II. The commanding general of the First Cavalry Division will use the equipments, horses, and arms of the Third Brigade to mount and equip such men of his remaining brigades as require it. In case any surplus remains, it will be reported to these headquarters that it may be turned over to some other division.

III. The object of this order is to retain as many equipped and mounted men with this army as there are at present, including the Third Brigade, by mounting others before that command leaves. This requirement will be observed in the execution of this order.

IV. The batteries of horse artillery belonging to the Second Brigade (Tidball's), serving with corps, will be replaced by batteries from the First (or Robertson's) Brigade, after which Captain Tidball will report with his brigade to Brigadier-General Tyler, commanding Artillery Reserve.

V. To equalize the number of batteries in the brigades, the Ninth Michigan Battery is transferred to the Second Brigade Horse Artillery.

*   *   *   *   *   ..   ..

By command of Major-General Pleasonton:

A. J. ALEXANDER,
Assistant Adjutant-General.

WAR DEPARTMENT,
Washington, August 15, 1863—9.20 a. m.

Col. L. A. GRANT,
Alexandria, Va.:

You will embark your command on transports for New York, and, on arrival at Governor's Island, will report to General Canby.

H. W. HALLECK,
General-in-Chief.

WAR DEPARTMENT,
Washington, August 15, 1863—6.10 p. m.

Brigadier-General AYRES,
Alexandria, Va.:

It is expected that you will immediately embark your command on such transports as may be furnished by the Quartermaster's Department. There must be no delay.

H. W. HALLECK,
General-in-Chief.

POINT OF ROCKS, MD.,
August 15, 1863.

Hon. E. M. STANTON,
Secretary of War:

Longstreet (30,000 strong) and Fitz. Lee (10,000 strong) passed through Warrenton Saturday morning to re-enforce Early. Reliable. A larger force supposed to be following.

SAML. C. MEANS.

WASHINGTON, *August 15, 1863.*

Col. C. R. LOWELL, Jr.,
    Commanding Cavalry:

It is reported on authority which appears reliable that White is in the vicinity of Dranesville with a body of some 350 men. Can you make any expedition in that vicinity with sufficient force to attack if you succeed in finding the party? Captain Means, Independent Rangers, stationed at Point of Rocks, says he knows all the country from Dranesville to Aldie, and wishes to co-operate with you. Let me know when you can start, so that I can communicate with Means and appoint a rendezvous. Name some place at which [you?] can meet him and them.

J. H. TAYLOR,
Chief of Staff.

HEADQUARTERS ARMY OF THE POTOMAC,
August 16, 1863—10.30 a. m. (Received 11 a. m.)

Maj. Gen. H. W. HALLECK,
    General-in-Chief:

The following regiments will proceed to Alexandria to-day under the command of Brig. Gen. T. H. Ruger, viz: Second Massachusetts, Third Wisconsin, Twenty-seventh Indiana, Fifth Ohio, Seventh Ohio, Twenty-ninth Ohio, Sixty-sixth Ohio, Fourth Ohio, Fourteenth Indiana, Fifth Michigan, One hundred and twenty-sixth Ohio.

Aggregate strength of these regiments is about 3,800. General Ruger has been directed to report to you by telegraph on arriving at Alexandria, for further instructions, and also by telegraph to the Quartermaster-General for transportation.

The number of men already detached and who have left are as follows: August 14, regulars and Vermont brigade, under General Ayres, 4,000; August 15, regiments, 1,400*; August 16, Ruger's command, 3,800; making in all 9,200, which, when swollen by convalescents and men detached on extra duty (who will be sent as soon as possible), will make the aggregate force fully up to and over 10,000. I do not propose, without further orders, to send any more. I have sent you my best troops and some of my best officers.

GEO. G. MEADE,
Major-General, Commanding.

HDQRS. ARMY OF THE POTOMAC, *August* 16, 1863—1 p. m.
(Received 1.20 p. m.)

Maj. Gen. H. W. HALLECK,
    General-in-Chief:

It appears from later returns that the aggregate strength of the six regiments that left here yesterday for Alexandria was 1,800, instead of 1,400, as stated in my dispatch of this morning. Please correct my statement accordingly.

GEO. G. MEADE,
Major-General.

---

* See dispatch following.

WAR DEPARTMENT,
Washington, August 16, 1863—11.40 a. m.

Col. J. W. KEIFER,
    Alexandria, Va.:

You will embark your command on transports at Alexandria, for
Governor's Island, New York Harbor. On arrival, report to General Canby, commanding.

By order of Major-General Halleck:

J. C. KELTON,
    Assistant Adjutant-General.

WAR DEPARTMENT,
Washington, August 16, 1863—8.50 p. m.

Brig. Gen. THOMAS H. RUGER,
    Alexandria, Va.:

You will embark all troops of your command on transports, as
soon as furnished by the Quartermaster's Department, for Governor's
Island, New York Harbor, where you will report for duty to Brigadier-General Canby.

H. W. HALLECK,
    General-in-Chief.

HDQRS. DEPT. OF VIRGINIA AND NORTH CAROLINA,
    Fort Monroe, Va., August 16, 1863.

Hon. E. M. STANTON,
    Secretary of War, Washington, D. C.:

SIR: I have the honor herein to send the report of General Naglee
on the subject of the difference in opinion between himself and the
civil authorities at Portsmouth and Norfolk. I beg your careful
perusal of the paper, and request that instructions be sent me for my
guidance in the present case, and in such cases as may arise in the
future. The mayor and common council of Portsmouth passed an
ordinance taking possession of all property in the city belonging to
persons who refused to take the oath of allegiance to the United
States and to the new Government of Virginia, assuming the power
of confiscation, of collecting rents, &c., the money so collected to be
used to supply the wants of destitute families, and to defray the expenses of the city government. This order General Naglee refused
to sanction, on the ground that confiscations should be alone made
by the military authorities, and on the ground of the order of General Dix permitting the elected civil authorities to exercise their civil
functions so far only as it did not interfere with the enforcement
of martial law, "which is still continued throughout this military
department."

On lists furnished by the Lieutenant-Governor of the State, at the
request of General Naglee, he, General Naglee, issued rations to the
destitute families in Norfolk and Portsmouth, and still does so.

The difficulties of reconciling two powers in one town are apparent,
and I submit two courses for your consideration:

1. To allow the *status* of affairs to remain as at present, reserving,
however, to the military commandant the power of not approving

acts of the civil authorities which conflict with orders from the War Department.

2. To turn over the cities of Norfolk and Portsmouth entirely to the civil authorities, removing the United States troops beyond the city limits, establishing a cordon of soldiers beyond, so as to prevent ingress and egress, and carry out existing military orders, &c.

I have the honor to be, very respectfully, your obedient servant,

J. G. FOSTER, ·
Major-General, Commanding.

[Inclosure.]

HDQRS. DEPT. OF VIRGINIA, SEVENTH ARMY CORPS,
Norfolk, Va., August 15, 1863.

Maj. Gen. J. G. FOSTER:

GENERAL: Your favor of the 13th instant, inclosing a copy of that of the President of the United States of the 8th instant, is before me.

I regret that the efforts made by me to establish proper and friendly relations between myself and the civil authorities within this department should have been treated in so very unfriendly and unfair a manner by the mayor and common council of the city of Portsmouth, and that the representations made to the President are not in accordance with the facts.

From the tenor of the note of the President, he has been made to believe that there was some "difficulty at Norfolk and Portsmouth between the city authorities on the one side and our military on the other," and that they are "in serious conflict about the mode of providing for certain destitute families whose natural supporters are in the rebel army or have been killed in it." Now, general, with all due deference to the parties concerned, no such issue ever was made between the mayor and council and myself, and I never knew there ever existed any conflict between us upon any other subject until my attention was called to the resolutions passed by them. The facts are simply these:

On the 25th of July, I assumed command and made my headquarters at Norfolk as requested by you. On the same day the Lieutenant-Governor of the State of Virginia, Lieutenant-Governor Cowper, one of the committee sent to the President, called and informed me of the destitute condition of certain families who were suffering, and I immediately requested him to furnish me with proper lists, and that I would forthwith order them to be provided for, which was done. On the following day I was informed that the common council of Portsmouth, not of Norfolk, had passed the following ordinance:

Resolved, That the mayor be, and he is hereby authorized to collect rents for all houses, stores, and all other property owned by persons who refuse to take the oath of allegiance to the United States Government and the restored Government of Virginia, and that the proceeds be applied to relieve the wants of families in destitute circumstances and assist in defraying the expenses of the city government.

Adopted July 13, 1863.

WM. F. PARKER,
Clerk to Council.

And also another, repudiating certain obligations of that city, both of which were causing a great deal of excitement and alarm.

I immediately sought an interview with Mr. Daniel Collins, the mayor of the city of Portsmouth, with the purpose of a friendly exchange of opinion, intending thus to prevent any conflict with the authorities of Portsmouth. He admitted there was no authority of law for the ordinance, and that they could not legally enforce it and confiscate property and collect rents under it, but indicated that the military authorities were expected to enforce it. I replied that could not be; that there was no necessity of any violation of law; and that the property left vacant by the absence of owners in the rebel service should go into the charge of the provost-marshal, who could collect the rents, intending, as you will understand, that the Government should be thus in part reimbursed for the expenditures made for the destitute. This appeared to be entirely satisfactory to Mr. Collins, and he left me in a manner that led me to believe this subject was satisfactorily adjusted.

This comprises my whole and entire communication with the mayor and common council of the city of Portsmouth, and you may imagine my surprise, on the 1st of August, upon the perusal of the following resolutions:

Whereas by authority of writs of election issued by His Excellency Francis H. Peirpoint, Governor of Virginia, the citizens of Portsmouth did, on the 28th of May, 1863, elect civil officers, with a view to re-establish civil law; and whereas the said officers have been installed in office and recognized by the former military commander of this department, and in view of the fact, which we learn with regret, that the present commander of the Seventh Army Corps has seen proper to interfere, with a view to put aside certain acts of the city council. and believing that no commanding general, especially a non-resident, has a right to decide upon the constitutionality of any acts of this board when the courts of the Commonwealth are open to settle any grievances between the citizens and the civil authorities : Be it therefore

Resolved, First, that we refuse to recognize the authority of Brig. Gen. H. M. Naglee to decide any case of appeal from the action of this board.

Resolved, Second, that the mayor and other officers of the city government be required to enforce every act of this council, regardless of any orders emanating from the military authorities, and that in event of conflict of authority, an appeal shall be taken to His Excellency the Governor, to sustain and uphold the authority of the State and the city.

Adopted July 29, 1863.

WM. F. PARKER,
Clerk to Council.

Whereas the common council of this city did, on the 13th day of July, 1863, pass a resolution authorizing the collection of rents of all property owned by persons in rebellion against the United States Government, and persons who have failed to take the oath of allegiance to the United States Government and the restored Government of Virginia; and whereas the military authorities have usurped the powers vested in the courts of the Commonwealth and declared the action of the city council illegal, thus assuming the right to interfere in the execution of civil law; and whereas the right of military officers to interfere in civil matters cannot be tolerated, inasmuch as civil law existing only by and subject to the will of military officers does not exist at all:

Now, therefore, I, Daniel Collins, by virtue of authority vested in me by the common council of the city of Portsmouth, do hereby notify all persons occupying stores, halls, dwelling-houses, and other property owned by persons who have failed to take the oath of allegiance to the United States Government, to pay their rents to James Fleming, city collector. All persons who may be induced to pay their rents to the former owners or agents of said property are hereby notified that they will have to pay their rents over again, military orders to the contrary notwithstanding, and any person feeling aggrieved shall appeal to the civil courts of this Commonwealth for redress.

Given under my hand this 1st day of August, 1863.

DANIEL COLLINS,
Mayor.

Resolved, First, that a committee of three be appointed to wait on His Excellency Governor F. H. Peirpoint, and represent to him that the military commander of this department has interfered with the civil authorities, with a view to set aside certain acts of this board and decide upon points of civil law, when the courts of the Commonwealth are open to decide upon all civil questions.

Resolved, Second, that the committee, in conjunction with Governor Peirpoint, call upon His Excellency the President of the United States and on the honorable Secretary of War, and ask for the immediate removal of the commanding general of this department, and all other officers who have interfered with civil law; and also insist on a precise and exact adjustment of the boundaries between civil and military authorities.

Resolved, Third, that the committee be composed of his honor Daniel Collins, mayor of Portsmouth, his excellency Lieutenant-Governor L. C. P. Cowper, and James W. Brownley, H. D.

Adopted August 1, 1863.

WM. F. PARKER,
Clerk to Council.

I will for your further information advise you that General Getty issued an order on the 29th of July, of which I had no knowledge until the 2d or 3d of August, and which was as follows:

GENERAL ORDERS, }   PROVOST-MARSHAL'S OFFICE,
    No. 1.   }   *Portsmouth, Va., July 29, 1863.*

The resolution adopted at a meeting of the common council of the city of Portsmouth. held July 13, 1863, authorizing the mayor to "collect rents for all houses, stores, and all other property owned by persons who refuse to take the oath of allegiance," &c., is hereby suspended until the decision of the general commanding with reference to the same may be had, and while such decision is pending the mayor and other authorities of the city of Portsmouth will refrain from all further action under and by virtue of said resolution.

By command of Brigadier-General Getty:

HIRAM B. CROSBY,
Major, and Provost-Marshal.

And which, when referred to me, met with my approval.

On the 11th instant, Governor Peirpoint called upon me, referred to the letter of the President, and we compared views in relation to our respective civil and military positions. He admitted there was no difference of opinion, and that the council had no authority under their charter to condemn property and collect the rents. He, however, finally insisted that I should adopt as my rule of conduct the policy of the resolutions, and confiscate the property of every person that would not at once take the oath of allegiance to the Government of the United States and to the restored Government of Virginia. This I positively refused to do, which refusal, I regret to say, seemed to be received with an exhibition of much feeling, and in a very unfriendly manner.

The following is the order of Major-General Dix:

GENERAL ORDERS, }   HDQRS. DEPT. OF VIRGINIA, SEVENTH ARMY CORPS,
    No. 41.   }   *Fort Monroe, Va., June 16, 1863.*

I. The people of the county of Norfolk and of the cities of Norfolk and Portsmouth having held elections and chosen civil and judicial officers, with a view to the administration of civil and criminal law within those districts, it is hereby ordered that the authorities thus constituted be recognized and permitted to perform their functions, so far as may be compatible with the enforcement of martial law, which has been established in accordance with the usages of war, and which is still continued throughout this military department.

II. The jurisdiction of Maj. John A. Bolles, as provost judge, defined in General Orders, No. 6, dated 27th of June, 1862, is hereby enlarged, so as to include all military offenses not cognizable by courts-martial; but the provost court will not take cognizance of any capital offense, and an appeal may be taken in all cases to the commanding general of the department.

By command of Major-General Dix:

D. T. VAN BUREN,
Assistant Adjutant-General.

In which he "recognized" the civil authorities of Portsmouth so far as civil law "may be compatible with the enforcement of martial law." As we are situated, the control of the whole subject is with the military authorities, who may proclaim martial law whenever they may so determine. I am most happy to add that there has been no difference or "conflict" with the civil authorities of the city and county of Norfolk, and that our relations, both official and social, have been of the most agreeable and satisfactory character.

Since my interview with Governor Peirpoint above referred to, I have reviewed the subject, and I have issued the following order:

SPECIAL ORDERS, }   HDQRS. DEPT. OF VIRGINIA, SEVENTH ARMY CORPS,
No. 24.   }   *August* 12, 1863.

*   *   *   *   *   *   *

IX. The provost-marshals of the cities of Norfolk and Portsmouth will take possession of all houses owned by disloyal persons now within the rebel lines, and of all real property within said cities owned by disloyal persons who take an active part against the Government of the United States, or who violate the orders of this department; but no property shall be condemned until written evidence shall have been taken in the premises, and be approved by the general commanding.

X. The fund created by the rental of the above property shall be appropriated exclusively toward the relief of the destitute families of officers and soldiers in the rebel army.

By command of Brigadier-General Naglee:

GEORGE H. JOHNSTON,
Assistant Adjutant-General,

Which is now in force and which, in connection with special orders of August 1, herein inclosed, will indicate my policy, and which is as far as I can conscientiously go in the premises.

I regret the course pursued by the mayor of the city of Portsmouth. He has succeeded in doing just what I endeavored to avoid.

The persons in destitute condition, referred to by the President, were ordered to be taken care of immediately upon my arrival in Norfolk, and that subject was never one of difference, and, I believe, was never referred to by Mayor Collins at the only interview ever had between us.

Respectfully submitting the above report, let me request that it may be laid before the President in explanation of the subject.

I am, general, very respectfully, &c.,

HENRY M. NAGLEE,
Brigadier-General, Commanding.

[Sub-inclosure.]

SPECIAL ORDERS, }   HDQRS. DEPT. VA., 7TH ARMY CORPS,
No. —.   }   *Norfolk, Va., August* 1, 1863.

I. The following line is hereby established: Commencing at the mouth of the Western Branch of the Elizabeth River; thence, by the Western Branch, to the head of the same; thence, by Bowers' Hill, to the head of Deep Creek; thence, through the Dismal Swamp, to Lake Drummond; thence to the head of the Western Branch of the Pasquotank River, and thence, by the latter and the Pasquotank River, to Albemarle Sound.

II. Any person attempting to pass the above line will be arrested and severely punished.

III. Any person attempting to pass letters, information, or merchandise across the above line, and all interested with them, will be imprisoned and severely punished; and the goods seized, as well as all other personal property within this department belonging to all implicated, will be confiscated.

IV. Persons residing within the cities of Norfolk and Portsmouth, and Princess Anne County, will not be permitted to pass into Norfolk, Currituck, and Camden Counties, and those living within Norfolk, Currituck, and Camden Counties will not be permitted to pass north of North Landing River and Southern Branch of Elizabeth River and the canal between them, unless in pursuit of their necessary business, with passes of the provost-marshal, and no pass will be given for a longer period than fifteen days.

V. No boat will be permitted to enter the Western Branch of Elizabeth River, Deep Creek, or the Pasquotank River; nor will be permitted to approach the left bank of Elizabeth River below the Western Branch of the same; nor will be permitted to approach the shore between Craney Island and Pig Point, under a penalty of an immediate destruction of the boat, and imprisonment and severe punishment of those taken and interested in the venture.

VI. On or before the 15th day of August, all steamboats, vessels, or boats of any description, must be numbered and registered by the provost-marshal, who will require that they shall be kept at night at such places and in such manner as he may direct. An especial list will be kept for the registry of all permits granted to fishermen and fishing boats. .

VII. Licenses hereafter will be granted only to residents of the counties within the above limits; and all sutlers will be confined strictly to the privileges granted to them, and will not be permitted to trade after the 15th of August, unless the sales of their wares shall be regulated by a scale of prices determined before that time by a council of administration, as provided under the General Orders of the War Department, No. 27, of 1862.

VIII. Merchants will be required to procure stencil plates, with the number of the license in figures, of at least 2 inches in length, cut thereon, and with which they will be required to mark every package sold by them. A penalty of $500 is hereby imposed upon any firm who shall fail to comply with the above. It is, however, not intended that this restriction shall apply to small paper bundles made up for local use.

IX. Merchandise will not be permitted to be carried through any of the canals, nor upon any of the water courses, after it has been received at Norfolk or Portsmouth.

X. All wagons going south with merchandise, or coming north with produce, will be required to pass through Great Bridge, where they will be examined.

XI. Merchants when submitting their invoices for permits for merchandise will be limited to that required for their usual business for three months. Consumers in purchasing from the above will be limited to the quantity required by their families for the same time. The above restrictions being necessary to prevent an accumulation of goods for contraband purposes.

XII. Weapons of all kinds, powder, and all items of a contraband character are prohibited, and will be seized wherever found. All persons attempting to introduce, sell, or conceal any of the above will be imprisoned and severely punished, and their personal property will be confiscated.

XIII. The only currency permitted will be that established by the Government of the United States.

XIV. All passes and privileges at variance with the above order are hereby revoked.

By command of Brig. Gen. Henry M. Naglee:

GEORGE H. JOHNSTON,
Captain, and Assistant Adjutant-General.

HEADQUARTERS ARMY OF THE POTOMAC,
August 17, 1863.

Major-General WARREN,
Commanding Second Corps:

It is reported here that distant firing was heard about daylight in a direction east of south. Did you hear or learn anything of it; if so, in what direction was it; how far distant?

A. A. HUMPHREYS,
Major-General, Chief of Staff.

HEADQUARTERS,
August 17, 1863—9.30 a. m.

Major-General SLOCUM,
Commanding Twelfth Corps:

Did you hear firing about daylight this morning; and, if so, in what direction, and at what distance?

A. A. HUMPHREYS,
Major-General, Chief of Staff.

RAPPAHANNOCK STATION, *August 17, 1863.*
(Received 10.45 a. m.)

Major-General HUMPHREYS:

The following rebel signal message has just been intercepted by our officers:

General LEE:

I am satisfied there is a movement of the enemy of position from front to flank and rear.

STUART.

Also fragments of another message:

As seen from here, none on this side of river. Large trains of wagons appear to be moving up the river on the other side. Quite hazy this a. m.

BARNES.

JOHN NEWTON,
Major-General, Commanding.

HDQRS. ARMY OF THE POTOMAC, *August 17, 1863.*
(Received 11.30 a. m.)

Major-General HALLECK,
General-in-Chief:

On my return, on the 15th, information derived from scouts led to the belief the enemy contemplated a movement by the United States Ford, on my left flank.

The report derived from the soldiers' talk was that the whole army was to be thrown across at that place and an effort made to get in my rear. The scouts reported seeing some 500 negroes cutting logs, supposed for a bridge. Believing it not improbable a raid might be attempted to interrupt my communications, the disposition of the cavalry has been changed so as to place the main body in my rear and toward my left. The pickets toward Falmouth have been strengthened, and every preparation made, should a raid be attempted, to check it as soon as possible.

The cavalry on my right flank, on the 14th, attacked a guerrilla camp at Thoroughfare Gap, capturing 2 men, 10 mules, 27 horses, and a quantity of sutlers' goods. On the evening of the same day an officer of Ewell's staff was captured.

All reports would indicate Lee's army stretched from Madison Court-House to Fredericksburg, with the cavalry at Culpeper. Everything is quiet along the lines this morning.

GEO. G. MEADE,
Major-General, Commanding.

HEADQUARTERS ARMY OF THE POTOMAC,
August 17, 1863—1.30 p. m.

Major-General SCHURZ,
Commanding Eleventh Corps:

The major-general commanding directs that you call in your detachments at Brentsville and on Cedar Run, and that one division of your corps be posted at Manassas Junction and be charged with the protection of the railroad from that vicinity to Warrenton Junction; that the other division of your corps be posted in the near vicinity of Warrenton Junction and be charged with the protection of the road from Warrenton Junction to Bealeton Station; that the number and disposition of the detachments and guards placed upon the road be such as effectually to watch and protect it. The exterior patrols being withdrawn, every possible precaution should be adopted on the line of the road to insure its strict surveillance.

Very respectfully, your obedient servant,
A. A. HUMPHREYS,
Major-General, Chief of Staff.

HEADQUARTERS THIRD DIVISION, CAVALRY CORPS,
August 17, 1863.

Capt. A. J. COHEN,
Assistant Adjutant-General, Cavalry Corps:

CAPTAIN: General Custer reports that some of his people on picket saw upward of 2,000 cavalry passing down the right bank of the Rappahannock this morning. They had eight or ten wagons. He has sent a party down the river to watch them. Nothing has transpired of importance since my last report. I send two letters and a paper captured from a rebel mail carrier this morning. Six rebel soldiers were captured this morning. They will be forwarded as soon as possible.

Very respectfully,
J. KILPATRICK,
Brigadier-General of Volunteers.

AUGUST 17, 1863—2.15 p. m.

Major-General WARREN,
Commanding Second Corps:

The major-general commanding directs me to say that the extended line of picket and patrol assigned to the corps had for its object the prevention of the near approach to our troops of the enemy's scouts, spies, and informers. Recent information renders some change necessary. The river is picketed by infantry to Ellis' Ford, and from that point to United States Ford by cavalry, whence they extend across to the Potomac. Some concentration being desirable, the major-general commanding directs that you concentrate the division stationed at Elkton, calling in the brigade at Bristersburg, and the detachments furnishing the patrols heretofore connecting with Slocum and Schurz, at Ellis' Ford, and near Cedar Run. This line of patrol need not be continued, but a patrol should be kept up between Elkton and Warrenton Junction.

Very respectfully, your obedient servant,

A. A. HUMPHREYS,
Major-General, Chief of Staff.

HEADQUARTERS ARMY OF THE POTOMAC,
August 17, 1863—6.30 p. m.

Major-General SCHURZ,
Commanding Eleventh Corps:

The major-general commanding directs me to say that the disposition you have made of your troops is approved. The regiment at Greenwich may be withdrawn to Bristoe. Be prepared to concentrate at any point that the enemy may threaten to attack in force.

A. A. HUMPHREYS,
Major-General, Chief of Staff.

RAPPAHANNOCK STATION, *August 17, 1863.*
(Received 8 p. m.)

General HUMPHREYS:

The following dispatches have been intercepted by the signal officer of this corps:

Captain M.:

There are but two camps visible between this and Kelly's Ford. A large camp is seen some 3 miles to the left of Warrenton. No troops seen to-day.

B.

Colonel CORLEY:

My command is suffering from want of clothing. What is the difficulty about getting it?

STUART,
General.

General LEE:

Some more troops have been moving to the left of the railroad bridge and are passing yet.

B., *Lieutenant.*

The enemy's signal station is on Pony Mountain.

JOHN NEWTON,
Major-General.

HEADQUARTERS ARMY OF THE POTOMAC,
August 17, 1863.

Commanding Officer Cavalry Corps :

In reference to the report of Brigadier-General Custer of the 13th instant, I am directed by the major-general commanding to request that you will transmit to these headquarters a copy of the instructions sent to that officer, and to say that it is the manifest duty of every officer engaged in the duty General Custer is intrusted with to arrest every one who disregards a parole or pledge ; that paroles or accepted pledges from these headquarters to residents can form no proper excuse for not arresting those paroled or pledged, when they commit any act whatever of disloyalty ; that the instructions from these headquarters do not render him, or any other officer, powerless to act whenever any good reason exists for arrest, but on the contrary, gives ample power when there is reason to suspect any act directly or indirectly disloyal. Authority could not be wider than this, unless it extended beyond the limits possessed even by the commander of this army. But if the power existed, the loose statements upon this subject contained in the letter of General Custer do not impress the major-general commanding with the suitableness of intrusting to that officer the discretion he suggests, of dealing with those within the limits of his command as he might choose.

Very respectfully,

A. A. HUMPHREYS,
Major-General, and Chief of Staff.

WASHINGTON, D. C.,
August 17, 1863—2 p. m.

Brigadier-General LOCKWOOD,
Harper's Ferry, W. Va.:

You will send five companies of your command to report to General W. W. Morris, at Baltimore, for guard duty at Fort Delaware.

H. W. HALLECK,
General-in-Chief.

WASHINGTON, D. C.,
August 17, 1863—2.25 p. m.

Bvt. Brig. Gen. W. W. MORRIS,
Baltimore, Md. :

General Lockwood has been directed to send you five companies from Harper's Ferry for guard duty at Fort Delaware.

H. W. HALLECK,
General-in-Chief.

HEADQUARTERS EIGHTEENTH ARMY CORPS,
New Berne, N. C., August 17, 1863.

Maj. Gen. J. G. FOSTER,
Comdg. Dept. of Va. and N. C., Fort Monroe:

On the 15th, I received a communication from Admiral Lee, U. S. Navy, to the effect that the iron-clad on the Roanoke at Edwards Ferry was nearly completed.

On the 16th, I reached Plymouth and had an interview with General Wessells and Captain Flusser. Some deserters had just arrived, and from them the following information was elicited in respect to Rainbow Bluff, &c. :

Three guns in embrasure to command the approach by river from below, one a rifled 32-pounder, others 24-pounders. One 24-pounder on field carriage in an angle of the fort sweeps the land approaches. There are also two brass 12-pounders and three 6-pounders playing over the breastworks. Rifle-pits on bank below fort 200 yards long. Five pieces field artillery in Hamilton, Graham's battery. Three companies, Pool's battalion, garrison the fort.

At Butler's Bridge, 2 miles from fort, are intrenchments and a place for one gun. Camp of Seventeenth Regiment [North Carolina Infantry], 1,100 strong, near the fort, and the camp of the Fifty-sixth Regiment [North Carolina Infantry] about 1 mile from Hamilton, from fort, and from Butler's Bridge. At Whitney's Bridge (River road), bridge is destroyed, road barricaded, and breastwork 100 yards above. Five thousand men at Garrysburgh. Five hundred men at Edwards Ferry guarding the iron-clad, and iron-clad in course of construction.

These recent dispositions have resulted from your late raids, and will make it a matter of some difficulty to destroy the iron-clad at Edwards Ferry. For this enterprise from 800 to 1,000 good cavalry will be requisite. My plan would be to land the cavalry 6 or 8 miles above Plymouth, and move by Windsor, on an intermediate road, Roxobel, &c., since this route has been less used by our troops than the one via Winton. A demonstration from Norfolk, via Winton, upon Weldon at the same time, would materially enhance the chances of success.

I respectfully submit the above information and suggestions for your consideration.

Very respectfully, your obedient servant,

JOHN J. PECK,
Major-General.

[Indorsement.]

AUGUST 27, 1863.

Letter to be written stating that our force will not permit the proposed movement at present. Letter to be filed.

J. G. FOSTER.

CIRCULAR.]   HDQRS. U. S. TROOPS IN CITY AND HARBOR,
[New York], August 17, 1863.

The duties of the United States troops in the city and harbor of New York are limited to the defense of the forts and the protection of public property, and of the officers of the General Government in the performance of their legal duties. The duty of maintaining order and protecting the properties and rights of private individuals devolves upon the municipal and State authorities, but the troops of the United States will be held in readiness to render any assistance that may be called for by proper authority, or be rendered necessary by the inability of the civil authorities to accomplish these ends.

The commanders of troops, both in the harbor and in the city, will make themselves fully acquainted with the duties they may be called on to perform, and the means under their control for offensive or defensive purposes. The batteries in the harbor will be put in the most perfect state of preparation. The details for service will be arranged and systematized, and the officers and men instructed as rapidly as possible in everything that pertains to their new positions and duties, and especially in the service of heavy guns.

The approaches to any post, by land or water, will be studied; the range, field of fire, and effectiveness of every gun ascertained, and everything kept in constant readiness for the prompt and efficient use of the batteries. Particular care will be taken to guard against the danger to be apprehended from attempts to spike the guns or otherwise destroy the efficiency of batteries in the out-works or dependencies of any of the forts.

If posted in the city, commanders will keep themselves constantly advised of the position of troops in their neighborhood, the communications with them or with other important points, and the means of reaching in the shortest time any point in their neighborhood which may be assailed or threatened.

If officers of the General Government, and, by comity, of the State and municipal governments, in the performance of their legitimate functions, are assailed by lawless violence, it will be the duty of the troops to protect them. If they are charged with the protection of public property, public buildings, or other important interests, it will be their duty to defend them to the last extremity.

If called upon by the civil authorities to aid in the maintenance of order or the enforcement of the laws, the aid will be rendered promptly, cheerfully, and efficiently. The execution of the last duty involves grave responsibilities, and must be executed with the greatest discretion and firmness. It is not to be assumed independently, but will be exercised in connection with and in subordination to the civil authorities.

The troops employed on this duty will be kept well in hand, and will be cautioned to keep cool and steady; to pay no attention to harsh words or other insults that may be offered them; to avoid everything that may provoke unnecessary collision, but to be prepared to act always promptly, efficiently, or decisively. It is made the duty of commanders to see that their troops are fully armed, fully supplied, and prepared in every respect to give the greatest effect to the arms they use.

Troops that are posted in the city will be kept well together and in a state of the most exact discipline. The ordinary course of instruction will be kept up, and no straggling, drunkenness, or other disorderly conduct allowed. Guards and pickets established in streets or other thoroughfares will be carefully instructed to treat all citizens with courtesy and respect, and to perform their duties with as little annoyance or obstruction as is possible. The destruction or injury of public or private property, either wantonly or through neglect, must be prevented.

If posted in parks or improved grounds, the utmost care will be taken that the trees and shrubbery are not injured. Tents will be furnished for officers and men, and temporary stabling for the horses. Sinks and wash-houses will be provided and screened from observation by wooden blinds. The police of the grounds in and about the camps and quarters will be made as perfect as possible, and all accumulations of garbage immediately removed.

The troops that have been brought to this city, and who may be called upon to aid in the maintenance of order and the enforcement of the laws, must themselves set the example of orderly and soldierly conduct, and the attention of all officers and men is specially directed to this point.

The movement of troops to distant parts of the city, or to points in its neighborhood, will be made as far as practicable by water, and for this purpose the quartermaster's department will keep a sufficient number of steamers in constant readiness to move to any point. These steamers, if not armed, will be convoyed by armed steamers, and when moving by night will be distinguished from other vessels by a special signal.

Movements through the streets of the city will be made quietly, and with as little display as possible. Special care must be taken in these movements that the flanks and rear of the cavalry are well guarded, and, if made in connection with artillery, that the supports are stronger than usual. For the troops in the city the police alarm will be the signal for preparation, and will be communicated to the forts and vessels in the harbor in the manner denoted by Special Orders, No. 23, of August 12, 1863. To avoid unnecessary alarm or disturbance in the city, commanders will take the necessary measures for assembling their troops without beating or sounding the usual alarm.

The police authorities have authorized the captains of precincts to put themselves in communication with the commanders of troops posted in their neighborhood, for the purpose of communicating information and rendering such other assistance as may be necessary. They have also authorized the use of the public telegraph for the purpose of making reports and communicating information when the troops are acting in connection with the police for the preservation of order, and police officers will be attached to the several headquarters for the purpose of communicating more directly with the police, and acting as guides when troops are removed to different parts of the city. Commanders of troops in the city will be kept constantly advised of the location of troops in their neighborhood, and when any changes are made by them the new location and the reasons for the change will immediately be made to these headquarters.

The publication or furnishing for publication by persons connected with this command of any information in relation to the numbers, position, movements, or operations of the troops, the strength and condition of the public works, or of any other military information that might be used for improper purposes, is strictly prohibited.

ED. R. S. CANBY,
Brigadier-General, Commanding.

HDQRS. CAVALRY CORPS, ARMY OF THE POTOMAC,
August 18, 1863—8.45 a. m.
(Received 9.15 a. m.)

Major-General HUMPHREYS,
            Chief of Staff:

GENERAL: General Kilpatrick reports that some of his pickets saw upward of 2,000 cavalry passing down the right bank of the Rappahannock yesterday at daylight. Had 8 or 10 wagons with them. He has sent a party down the river to watch them. He also sends two letters and a Richmond paper, which are inclosed, that were captured yesterday from a rebel mail carrier. Six rebel soldiers were also captured.

The brigade of General Gregg at Warrenton has 100 men on Watery Mountain, who picket well toward Salem; another force of 100 men at New Baltimore, who picket and patrol toward White Plains; a regiment which pickets and patrols to Waterloo, Orleans, and the mill beyond on Thumb Run. The pickets report but few of the enemy to be seen and in small parties. Two regiments have also gone direct to Salem, Markham, and Manassas Gap, to return by way of Barbee's Cross-Roads and Orleans.

General Merritt reports that a rebel patrol had been at Union Mills, in the direction of Dumfries, just before his scouting party arrived there yesterday. All else quiet.

Very respectfully,

A. PLEASONTON,
Major-General, Commanding.

HDQRS. THIRD DIVISION, CAVALRY CORPS,
August 18, 1863.

Capt. A. J. COHEN,
Assistant Adjutant-General, Cavalry Corps:

I have the honor to report that my picket line remains undisturbed up to the present. Yesterday afternoon while a party of our men were passing through Falmouth they were fired upon by squads of rebel infantry and cavalry across the river near the old bridge. Our men did not return the fire. Yesterday evening a party of guerrillas stopped a wagon about 6 miles from here on the Warrenton road, carried off the horses and driver, leaving the wagon in the road. I sent a squadron of cavalry in pursuit. They have not yet returned.

A detail has been ordered to put up my end of the telegraph line, as requested. I am going out this morning to inspect my picket line in person.

Very respectfully,

J. KILPATRICK,
Brigadier-General of Volunteers, Comdg. Third Division.

AUGUST 18, 1863—2.30 p. m.

Major-General SYKES,
Commanding Fifth Corps:

The major-general commanding directs me to say that, as it is not contemplated at present to throw a large force across the river to meet or anticipate an attack upon Newton's front or your own, the necessity for the bridge in the vicinity of Beverly Ford no longer exists, and the small force you have on the opposite bank to protect the head of the bridge may be withdrawn to this side, and the bridge be taken up.

General Newton keeps a bridge-head force on the other side, so as to give him time to perfect the arrangement for the defense of the railroad bridge and ford.

Very respectfully, your obedient servant,

A. A. HUMPHREYS,
Major-General, Chief of Staff.

WARRENTON JUNCTION,
August 18, 1863.

General HUMPHREYS,
Chief of Staff:

Two deserters just came in. They left Culpeper Court-House the 8th instant. Longstreet's and Ewell's forces were reported that time at or near Fredericksburg; Hill's corps, between the Rapidan and Orange Court-House; Stuart's cavalry, at Culpeper and Brandy Station.

They met Mosby's force yesterday at Upperville, ready for a raid. Hearing at 12 o'clock of the approach of our cavalry, they were ordered to meet to-day at Rector's Cross-Roads. The deserters cannot tell when Mosby intends to make the attack. The deserters will be sent to general headquarters.

C. SCHURZ,
Major-General.

[Note on original:] General King informed.

HARTWOOD, VA.,
August 18, 1863.

CAPTAIN: I have the honor to report that I went yesterday to Falmouth for the purpose to observe the rebel position on the old battle-ground at Fredericksburg. I could not see any large force of rebels there, except one regiment of cavalry, one battery of light artillery, and an equal force of infantry. The infantry is scattered on the opposite bank of the Rappahannock and fire at every Union soldier they see on this side. Previous to my coming, they fired at our cavalry, and then they fired at me.

They have brought two pieces of artillery nearer the river where our cavalry approached the town, and I noticed that they were moving off loaded wagons from Fredericksburg, as if in anticipation of our crossing.

The inhabitants of Falmouth seem to be—and I think that they really are—totally ignorant of the rebels' position and doings, and they say that only small scouting parties of the rebels are allowed to come over on this side of the river. Our cavalry did not occupy Falmouth the day before yesterday. The rebels have infantry force at Banks' Ford.

I am, sir, very respectfully, your obedient servant,

J. GLOSKOSKI,
Captain, and Acting Signal Officer.

[P. S.]—I submitted a similar report to General Kilpatrick immediately after my return.

ARLINGTON, VA.,
August 18, 1863.

Lieut. Col. THOS. ALLCOCK,
Commanding Fort Ethan Allen:

The following telegram has just been received, and is respectfully forwarded for your information:

WASHINGTON,
August 18, 1863.

General G. A. DE RUSSY:

Colonel Lowell, Second Massachusetts Cavalry, has moved with his entire available force toward Leesburg, where White is reported to be with the main body of his people.

J. H. TAYLOR,
Chief of Staff, and Assistant Adjutant-General.

Respectfully,

G. A. DE RUSSY.

CENTREVILLE, VA., *August* 18, 1863—4 p. m.
(Received 4.20 p. m.)

Col. J. H. TAYLOR,
Chief of Staff:

The following dispatch has just been received from Manassas. Not knowing whether the information has been communicated to headquarters in Washington, I send it to you. I have directed a small party of cavalry to proceed at once to Gainesville and Hay Market, to ascertain, if possible, what truth there is in the report:

MANASSAS JUNCTION, VA.,
August 18, 1863.

Brigadier-General KING:

General Williams telegraphed me last evening that 4,000 cavalry had come down from the Shenandoah Valley, and were making their way around our rear through Hopewell and Hay Market. They were said to be at Salem yesterday morning. My regiment has been under arms since then, and a whole division of the Eleventh Corps has just come down here, and just above, a battery of artillery. My idea is they will endeavor to get around you and go to Fairfax Station, or try to cut the railroad. Can you spare me any cavalry? I have not a single hoof. Our pickets extend out 2¼ miles on the road to Centreville, and half as far on the railroad toward Union Mills. Will be happy to co-operate with you.

ALFRED GIBBS,
Colonel, Commanding 130th New York Volunteers.

RUFUS KING,
Brigadier-General.

CLARKSBURG, W. VA., *August* 18, 1863.
(Received 11.20 p. m.)

Brigadier-General CULLUM:

I came up from Harper's Ferry and New Creek last night. All quiet along line of railroad. General Averell is at Petersburg, in Hardy County, and will move to-morrow on his expedition into Pendleton, Highland, Pocahontas, Bath, and Greenbrier Counties. Will destroy the saltpeter and powder works in Pendleton as he goes through. General Scammon reports all quiet in the Kanawha Valley. Some of the counties in West Virginia are infested with horse-thieves and robbers, and a few men recruiting for Jackson and Imboden. Our scouts killed 2 of the latter in Wirt County yesterday.

B. F. KELLEY,
Brigadier-General.

HETZEL, NEW BERNE, N. C.,
August 18, 1863.

Maj. Gen. J. G. FOSTER,
Comdg. 18*th A. C., Dept. of Va. and N. C., Fort Monroe:*

GENERAL : When you assumed command at Fort Monroe, it was understood that we should together make a reconnaissance of James River, the Sounds, and the mouths of Cape Fear River. There was no definite understanding as to the time or order of doing this. My departure from the Roads was unexpectedly delayed, as was your return there. I hoped then to have found you here, and to have gone over the Sounds and off Wilmington with you before returning to the Roads. In the meantime, you have been up the James, which I did not anticipate would have been done in my absence.

I heartily congratulate you on your escape from the torpedoes, the exposure to which might perhaps have been avoided by dragging in boats in advance of the vessels, and by an examination of the banks under cover of our guns, in suitable force. My recent demonstration up that river would naturally induce the enemy to put down his cheap, destructive, and treacherous defense, and should have suggested a careful approach.

By the end of this week I shall have returned to the blockade off Wilmington, and expect to be there until about the end of the following week; then to return to Hampton Roads. Either now or then, I am ready to make this part of the reconnaissance with you, but I must earnestly say that I regard the destruction of the iron-clads on the Roanoke, if the statement I send you to-day is true, of the first necessity.

I have the honor to be, general, respectfully yours,
S. PHILLIPS LEE,
Acting Rear-Admiral, Comdg. N. A. Bkg. Squadron.

NEW BERNE, N. C.,
August 18, 1863.

Maj. Gen. J. G. FOSTER,
Comdg. Dept. of Virginia and North Carolina:

GENERAL: I inclose a copy of my letter to General Peck, of the 14th instant, and a statement by Michael Cohen, respecting the iron-clads on the Roanoke, near Halifax. If Cohen's statement is correct, the destruction of these iron-clads should not be delayed. I am sure that you will do all you can to effect so desirable an object. Our iron-clads drawing over 12 feet cannot reach or neutralize those of the rebels owing to the shoal waters on the bulkhead at Hatteras Inlet and in Croatan Sound, &c.

I have the honor to be, very respectfully, yours,
S. PHILLIPS LEE,
Acting Rear-Admiral, Comdg. N. A. Bkg. Squadron.

[Inclosure No. 1.]

NEW BERNE, N. C.,
August 14, 1863.

Maj. Gen. JOHN J. PECK:

GENERAL: I hear that the iron-clad in the Roanoke, at Edwards Ferry, above Rainbow Bluff, is nearly completed. If not destroyed she may attack your fortified town on the water side. We have only .wooden vessels to oppose her. I respectfully suggest to you the propriety of an expedition to destroy her at once.

Owing to the fortifications at Rainbow Bluff and the low stage of water on the Roanoke, the expedition must be mainly military. Lieutenant-Commander Flusser, at Plymouth, will give you all the aid in his power.

Respectfully, yours,

S. PHILLIPS LEE,
Acting Rear-Admiral.

[Inclosure No. 2.]

STATEMENT OF MICHAEL COHEN.

NEW BERNE, N. C.,
August 18, 1863.

I am a naturalized citizen of Irish birth. Have lived twenty-one years in the United States and six years in North Carolina. When the war broke out I was carrying on a distillery at Tarborough. This business not being allowed, I turned my distillery into a grist mill. As a miller I was exempt from the conscription. When, on July 20, 1863, General Potter destroyed the vessels at Tarborough, my mill and property, worth $11,000, was burned by mistake by United States troops. Now I became liable to the conscription, and followed the United States troops here, where I am now employed in the quartermaster's department at the request of General Potter.

The work on the gunboat at Tarborough was begun in September last, continued one month, then stopped (in order to work on the iron-clads at Wilmington and afterward on the Roanoke), and was renewed only two weeks before General Potter destroyed it (July 20); at which time, about 20 feet of its amid-ships section had been put up in six parts of the frame of bottom, four parts making sides and angles and tops. More of the frame, in sections, was ready to be put up. General Potter destroyed this, and two unarmed river steamboats. One (of iron, stern-wheel, drawing 20 inches, fast, and in good order) called Governor Morehead, owned by Myers, who took the lights from the house at Hatteras Inlet when the war broke out. The other, called General Hill (old, slow, and stern-wheel, drawing 6 feet), and owned by Willard. There was then a high flood in the river.

There were then no troops guarding the iron-clad building at Smith's, on the Roanoke, in Halifax County, 6 miles below Halifax town, and 40 by land from Tarborough. The iron-clads on the Roanoke are a ram gunboat like the Merrimac, and a floating battery, 40 feet square, with a Merrimac roof. This gunboat was launched about the 1st of July, 1863. Putting on her plating was begun a day or two before General Potter destroyed the boats at Tarborough. The plating is 2 inches through, and was brought from Wilmington;

it is being put on in two layers, one horizontal, the other vertical. The holes are punched with a small engine brought from Richmond.

When the ram is plated, the floating battery will be plated; no guns in either. The ram is to have the Brooke rifle. The boilers (he is not sure about the machinery) were in the ram. The floating battery is to be stationed at Rainbow Bluff, just below Hamilton, a fortified point. This information was got from men taken from my service to work on this gunboat, and is not later than July 20, 1863.

There were, before the war, and are now, three small steamers on the Roanoke, light draught, side-wheel boats. The engine of one of the iron-clads at Wilmington was taken from a steamer, the other was built at Richmond, Va.

Statement made to me August 17 and 18, 1863.

S. PHILLIPS LEE,
Acting Rear-Admiral.

WASHINGTON, D. C.,
August 18, 1863—12.45 p. m.

Major-General GRANT, *Vicksburg, Miss.:*

Brig. Gen. George Crook will repair to the Department of West Virginia, and report for duty to Brigadier-General Kelley.

H. W. HALLECK,
General-in-Chief.

HEADQUARTERS FIRST CORPS,
August 19, 1863—12 m.

Major-General HUMPHREYS,
Chief of Staff, Army of the Potomac:

The following rebel signal message has just been intercepted by our signal officers:

General LEE:

I have moved my headquarters to Culpeper, on account of forage.

STUART,
General.

JOHN NEWTON,
Major-General, Commanding.

GENERAL ORDERS,)   HDQRS. EIGHTEENTH ARMY CORPS,
No. 4. }   *New Berne, N. C., August* 19, 1863.

The limits of the Districts of Beaufort, Albemarle, and Pamlico will, until otherwise ordered, remain as indicated in General Orders, No. 64, from headquarters Department of North Carolina.

The forces and defenses of New Berne will be under the immediate command of Brig. Gen. Innis N. Palmer, with powers and responsibilities analogous to those of district commanders. Necessary stores and supplies will be issued, upon his order, to the troops in his command; and so much of General Orders, No. 111, from these headquarters as is inconsistent herewith is revoked.

By command of Major-General Peck:

BENJ. B. FOSTER,
Assistant Adjutant-General.

WASHINGTON, D. C.,
August 19, 1863—9.55 a. m.

Brigadier-General KELLEY,
        Clarksburg:

When most convenient please come to Washington, as I wish an interview in regard to your department.

H. W. HALLECK,
        General-in-Chief.

CLARKSBURG,
August 19, 1863.

Colonel MOOR,
        Beverly:

General Averell left Petersburg this morning on an expedition into Pocahontas and Greenbrier Counties. He will probably arrive at Huntersville on or about the 25th instant. You will order the Tenth [West] Virginia Infantry and the Second [West] Virginia Mounted Infantry and one section of Keeper's battery to proceed without delay and form a junction with General Averell at Huntersville, and report to him for orders.

The troops will move without camp equipage, taking with them ten days' rations of hard bread, sugar, coffee, and salt, and will depend on the country through which they march for forage and beef. Would suggest you order the infantry and artillery to get off one day in advance of the cavalry.

B. F. KELLEY,
        Brigadier-General.

HEADQUARTERS OF THE ARMY,
        Washington, D. C., August 20, 1863—1.25 p. m.

Major-General MEADE,
        Army of the Potomac:

You will detail a general officer to superintend the detail of guards and the removal of drafted men from Alexandria to the Army of the Potomac. Report.

H. W. HALLECK,
        General-in-Chief.

HDQRS. ARMY OF THE POTOMAC, *August 20, 1863.*
        (Received 1.30 p. m.)

Maj. Gen. H. W. HALLECK,
        General-in-Chief:

In compliance with your instructions contained in dispatch of 12 m., I have directed Brig. Gen. H. S. Briggs to proceed to Alexandria, and superintend the detail of guards and the removal of drafted men from that place to this army. General Briggs will report to you for further orders.

GEO. G. MEADE,
        Major-General.

HDQRS. CAVALRY CORPS, ARMY OF THE POTOMAC,
August 20, 1863—9 a. m. (Received 9.40 a. m.)

Major-General HUMPHREYS,
Chief of Staff:

GENERAL: General Kilpatrick reports there is every indication that the enemy is in large force in and above Fredericksburg. The smoke of their camp fires can be seen along the line of the railroad. Their pickets and stragglers in Fredericksburg, opposite Falmouth, number upward of a thousand men. One of our scouting parties surprised a camp of guerrillas in the night. We recaptured 1 man, 2 negroes, and 3 horses. The party made their escape, but are being pursued by a squadron.

Four Richmond papers are herewith forwarded. It will be seen by an advertisement in the paper of the 17th instant that A. P. Hill's headquarters are near Orange Court-House.

The telegraph to Kilpatrick is completed, and only needs an operator. Can you send him one?

General Gregg reports that his scouting party sent to Hopewell Gap yesterday morning found nothing, and all was quiet beyond.

The two regiments that went to Salem and Manassas have returned, and report that they found nothing but scattered parties of the enemy. They brought in 6 prisoners, supposed to be scouts of the enemy.

General Merritt reports all quiet toward Dumfries and Stafford Court-House. No signs of the enemy.

Very respectfully,

A. PLEASONTON,
Major-General, Commanding.

MORRISVILLE,
August 20, 1863.

Major-General PLEASONTON,
Commanding Cavalry:

The following is just received from General Kilpatrick:

I have reliable information that the enemy is in large force opposite United States Ford; that it is believed our army is retiring on Centreville and Washington. Fitzhugh Lee, with 2,000 men and six pieces of artillery, moved yesterday from Fredericksburg to the vicinity of United States Ford. I am of the opinion that he contemplates crossing at Blind Ford, just above United States Ford. His object will be to gain information. I am ready to meet him.

G. K. WARREN,
Major-General.

[Indorsements.]

Respectfully referred to Major-General Humphreys, chief of staff.

Please return.

A. PLEASONTON,
Major-General, Commanding.

Transmit to Major-General Slocum for his information.

A. A. HUMPHREYS,
Chief of Staff.

HEADQUARTERS THIRD DIVISION, CAVALRY CORPS,
August 20, 1863.

Brig. Gen. G. A. CUSTER, *Commanding Second Brigade:*

GENERAL: You will send your entire train (every wagon) to Hart-wood Church at once. You will hold your command in readiness to move at a moment's notice. Observe the greatest vigilance, leaving your picket line and reserves as they now are. Word has just come in from the right of our line confirming your report of this morning. I believe the rebel army is about to advance.

Very respectfully,

J. KILPATRICK,
Brigadier-General of Volunteers.

———

HEADQUARTERS CAVALRY CORPS, *August 20, 1863.*

Brigadier-General GREGG, *Comdg. Second Cavalry Division:*

GENERAL : The major-general commanding directs me to inform you that there is a rumor that Stuart, with all his cavalry except Lee's brigade, is in the valley. The general desires that you will direct your cavalry to keep a close lookout in the direction of the gaps.

Very respectfully, your obedient servant,

C. ROSS SMITH,
Lieutenant-Colonel, Chief of Staff.

———

HAEDQUARTERS THIRD DIVISION, CAVALRY CORPS,
Hartwood Church, Va., August 20, 1863.

Capt. A. J. COHEN,
Assistant Adjutant-General, Cavalry Corps:

CAPTAIN : I have the honor to report the following, received from my picket line up to 2 p. m. :

Opposite Falmouth the enemy's picket line has been much weak-ened during the night, but few encampments can be seen in that vicinity, and everything indicates a movement of the enemy in some direction—I think to my right. General Custer reports a long col-umn of dust, some 4 miles in length, moving in the rear of Frede-ricksburg, and a complete silence is kept by their men on picket. Near United States Ford the enemy have a few pieces of artillery in position, and a large body of cavalry were reported near this ford this morning. From the latest I can gather, this cavalry force is moving to my right. It is believed by the enemy that our army is retiring upon Centreville and Alexandria. All the fords along my river front are well guarded.

Very respectfully,

J. KILPATRICK.

[Indorsement.]

HEADQUARTERS CAVALRY CORPS,
August 20, [1863]—9 p. m.

Respectfully forwarded to Major-General Humphreys, chief of staff.

This report confirms those of this morning, that the rebel army is on the move. It looks toward Richmond.

A. PLEASONTON,
Major-General, Commanding.

MANASSAS, *August 20, 1863.*

General KING:

Information has been received here that a force of cavalry crossed United States Ford this a. m., between 10 and 11 a. m. Heavy musketry firing was heard in the direction of Elkton. General Slocum has sent this word to headquarters. Cavalry can approach us both by way of Dumfries either to Bristoe, here, or Union Mills, Fairfax, or toward Alexandria. I think they would go pretty low down. No cavalry here.

ALFRED GIBBS,
Colonel.

MORRISVILLE, *August 20,1863.*

Major-General HUMPHREYS:

A report from Elk Run confirms the statement of heavy skirmishing, with no artillery, about 10 a. m. for about one hour, about 5 miles east of Elk Run. General Kilpatrick's communication has no hour mentioned to show when it was written. I do not see how an enemy could have passed between him and me, but the skirmish firing is unexplained. It would be well to warn the guards between you and Alexandria.

G. K. WARREN,
Major-General.

AUGUST 20, 1863—6 p. m.

Brig. Gen. RUFUS KING,
Commanding Division, Centreville:

I am instructed by the major-general commanding to inform you that recent information derived from scouts and spies indicates the probability of a strong raid, or some similar movement, on the part of the enemy from the vicinity of the United States Ford.

Very respectfully, your obedient servant,
A. A. HUMPHREYS,
Major-General, and Chief of Staff.

HEADQUARTERS TWELFTH ARMY CORPS,
August 20, 1863.

Major-General HUMPHREYS:

It is reported by Lieutenant-Colonel Johnstone, Fifth New York Cavalry, said to be at Ballard's Dam, that a large body of the enemy's cavalry crossed below him and passed northward. This reaches me through General Greene, who is at Ellis' Ford.

H. W. SLOCUM,
Major-General.

HEADQUARTERS ARMY OF THE POTOMAC,
August 20, 1863.

Major-General SCHURZ, *Commanding Eleventh Corps:*

General Kilpatrick telegraphs that Lieutenant-Colonel Johnstone denies the report that any cavalry has crossed the river; that the report is not true. The mysterious firing reported as having been heard was probably the cavalry at the mouth of Elk Run discharging their pieces.

A. A. HUMPHREYS,
Major-General, and Chief of Staff.

HDQRS. SECOND DIVISION, TWELFTH ARMY CORPS,
Near Ellis' Ford, Va., August 20, 1863.

Lieut. Col. H. C. RODGERS,
Asst. Adjt. Gen., Twelfth Army Corps:

COLONEL: I have the honor to inform the general commanding corps that the general line of pickets perpendicular to the river has been disturbed by the Second Corps pickets having been withdrawn, leaving a space of about 4 miles open between my left and the right of the Second Corps, through which a body of men could pass between here and Morrisville and toward your headquarters without encountering a picket line.

My command is now drafted upon to its utmost capacity in maintaining 7 miles of pickets on the river, and from thence to Crittenden's Mill, 2 miles farther. From the latter place our line was before connected with that of the Second Corps, but owing to the change the long, broken line leaves unguarded the left flank of the army. I deem it my duty to inform you of this change, feeling cognizant of the precarious condition our flank is placed in by leaving unguarded the line perpendicular to the river northeast of Crittenden's Mill.

I have the honor to be, colonel, very respectfully, your obedient servant,

JNO. W. GEARY,
Brigadier-General, Commanding.

HDQRS. SECOND DIVISION, TWELFTH ARMY CORPS,
Near Ellis' Ford, Va., August 20, 1863.

Lieut. Col. H. C. RODGERS,
Asst. Adjt. Gen., Twelfth Army Corps:

COLONEL: I have this day received information from Aldie (through a source which has always proved reliable and which has served me upon many occasions during the war), that I deem sufficiently important to communicate to the general commanding corps.

My informant states that the rebel citizens in and about Aldie have become exceedingly jubilant within a few days past over a prospect of Lee's army advancing, which is looked for by them daily. They state they have been informed by relatives in the rebel army that Lee, greatly strengthened, intends making a diversion in our front, and under its cover of advancing in two columns, one on our right and one on the left of our lines, one of which will be as a decoy. They suppose the feint will be made on our right flank, while the advance will be made by way of Dumfries toward Washington.

I would hesitate to lay such information before the general if it were not from the tested authority from which it is gleaned.

Very respectfully, your obedient servant,

JNO. W. GEARY,
Brigadier-General, Commanding.

HDQRS. FIRST CAV. DIV., *August 20*, 1863—11.30 p. m.
(Received 9.50 a. m., 21st.)

Col. C. ROSS SMITH,
Chief of Staff:

The report to-day received from pickets in front of Rappahannock Station indicates no change in enemy's line. I have sent for information to be sent to you as well as myself immediately.

W. MERRITT,
Brigadier-General of Volunteers.

GENERAL ORDERS, }   HDQRS. ARMY OF THE POTOMAC,
No. 78.   }   *August 20*, 1863.

The following regulations respecting passes and the transportation of supplies other than public stores have been approved by the Secretary of War, and are published for the information and guidance of all concerned:

1. Passes to leave this army, to be given by the provost-marshal-general, or by his authority. Said passes will authorize the return of the parties, but will not include transportation for property beyond necessary personal baggage.

2. All orders for transportation of property must be given by the quartermaster's department.

3. Supplies for officers may be procured by sending an agent, with a list of the articles to be obtained, signed by a general officer, and approved by the provost-marshal-general, or by his authority.

4. Sutlers and their property to be entirely excluded from transportation by rail for the present.

5. News boys will not be permitted to travel on trains, but packages of papers may be sent to local agents, under charge of a baggage-master, for sale or distribution.

6. No passes to civilians, to visit the Army of the Potomac, shall be given, except by the Adjutant-General of the Army and the general in command of the Army of the Potomac.

7. The principal depot quartermasters at Washington, Alexandria, and at other depots upon the line of the road can pass officers and agents of their departments, and also officers and agents of other departments, traveling on necessary public business, who can procure orders for transportation from them.

8. All orders for cars must be sent to the superintendent of the military railroad, through the proper officers of the quartermaster's department in charge of depots.

9. No officers other than those herein specified will be permitted to give passes beyond the limits of their commands.

10. All boxes or packages sent to, or marked with the name of, any officer shall be accompanied with an accurate list of contents, and shall be placed in custody of the provost-marshal at the place of

destination, to be delivered to the consignee upon satisfactory evidence that the packages contain necessary supplies for his individual use, and contain nothing else.

11. All persons seeking transportation on any railroad from Alexandria shall present their passes for examination at the office of the superintendent in that city.

12. Provost guards at Washington, Alexandria, and other stations will see that the foregoing orders are executed.

13. Train guards, for the protection of each train and to preserve order and keep off stragglers, will be furnished by commanders of troops nearest the points of departure on requisition of superintendent of road.

By command of Major-General Meade:

S. WILLIAMS,
Assistant Adjutant-General.

GENERAL ORDERS, }   HDQRS. ARMY OF THE POTOMAC,
No. 79.   }   *August 20, 1863.*

The following rules, approved by the Secretary of War, will govern the introduction of sutlers' goods into this army:

1. A regiment of cavalry will leave Warrenton Junction on Thursday of each week, at 9 a. m., for Washington or its vicinity, to return on the following Monday at the same hour, for the purpose of protecting such sutlers' goods as may be rightfully brought to this army.

2. Any sutler desiring to avail himself of the privileges herein afforded will furnish the provost-marshal-general with an invoice of the goods he wishes to procure and the number of wagons necessary to transport them. Said invoice, if in accordance with regulations, and if approved by said officer, shall, when presented to the commanding officer of said escort, be sufficient authority for said sutler to join the train with the number of wagons specified. On arriving at the point of destination, the same invoice shall be submitted to the Quartermaster-General of the Army, for permission to load and remove the goods entered therein, from the city, and, with such permission, shall entitle the owner to the protection of the escort on his return.

3. Sutlers' agents will be permitted to represent their employers on presenting their certificates of office, accompanied by written evidence of agency. No certificate will hereafter be issued except the sutler elected under the law be a citizen of the United States.

4. On and after the publication of this order, should any sutler attempt to transport property to Washington, or goods from Washington to this army, in any other mode than is herein prescribed, said property and goods shall be seized and held subject to confiscation.

5. Due notice will be given of any change in the time or place of departure of the escort, both of which must depend upon the movements of the army.

6. The commander of the Cavalry Corps will from time to time furnish the cavalry escort herein provided for.

By command of Major-General Meade :

S. WILLIAMS,
Assistant Adjutant-General.

HARPER'S FERRY, W. VA.,
August 20, 1863—1.25 p. m.

Major-General MEADE,
Headquarters Army of the Potomac:

A gentleman of the highest respectability and reliability has ridden into town to report information just received from Fredericksburg by two men from that place, one a Unionist, the other a secessionist. These men agree in reporting Lee's army very much disorganized; has received no re-enforcements; has lost largely by desertion, and that he will not make a stand this side of Richmond, and is even now preparing to retreat. This is his object in maneuvering to his right, &c.

Very respectfully,

HENRY H. LOCKWOOD,
Brigadier-General.

GENERAL ORDERS, }   HDQRS. DEPT. OF THE SUSQUEHANNA,
No. 11.   }   *August 20, 1863.*

The district of country including the counties of Berks, Schuylkill, Lehigh, Northampton, Carbon, Monroe, Luzerne, and Columbia is placed under the command of Maj. Gen. F. Sigel; headquarters at Reading.

By command of Maj. Gen. D. N. Couch:

JNO. S. SCHULTZE,
Major, and Assistant Adjutant-General.

HEADQUARTERS DEPARTMENT OF VIRGINIA,
Norfolk, Va., August 20, 1863.

Capt. F. A. ROWE,
Ninety-ninth New York Volunteers:

You will continue in command of the army gunboat West End, and your especial duties will be to carry out special orders of August 1, inclosed.* You will destroy or seize all boats upon the Western Branch, prevent any and all persons from passing the same. Any refugees or deserters or contrabands that may come to you, you will bring to headquarters, advising the first named that under no circumstances will they be permitted to recross the line, and that they will be sent to Baltimore or farther north.

Report in person once a week at these headquarters and as much oftener as you may deem necessary to convey information. A gunboat will co-operate with you, and prevent all boats from approaching or leaving the shore from the mouth of Western Branch to Pig Point. Allow no person to pass the creek. Any pass granted by me will be required to report on board your vessel. So dispose of your vessel and boats as to effectually prevent the entrance or crossing of the Western Branch either by day or night.

HENRY M. NAGLEE,
Brigadier-General, Commanding.

---

*See p. 58.

HEADQUARTERS EIGHTEENTH ARMY CORPS,
New Berne, N. C., August 20, 1863.

Maj. Gen. J. G. FOSTER,
    Comdg. Dept. of Virginia and North Carolina:

GENERAL: Your private communication touching the flag of truce and the attack upon the Gaston House, has just reached me. These affairs occurred prior to my arrival, and I presumed that General Palmer had brought them to the notice of the naval authorities. Admiral Lee is here, but has not called upon me, as is his duty, which probably results from a short but plain correspondence I had with him while at Suffolk, upon official matters. Your letter will be presented to him at once, as it embodies all that is necessary, and in better language, &c., than I could present the subject for his consideration. General Palmer will be called upon for a report, with the correspondence, &c.

No mail matter has been received since I left Old Point. If the quartermaster would send to the Norfolk and Old Point postmasters for mail, when about to send a boat to New Berne, many would be obliged.

I am, very respectfully, your obedient servant,
                                        JOHN J. PECK,
                                             Major-General.

————

HEADQUARTERS EIGHTEENTH ARMY CORPS,
New Berne, N. C., August 20, 1863.

Maj. Gen. J. G. FOSTER,
    Comdg. Dept. of Virginia and North Carolina:

GENERAL: Agreeably to your instructions of the 12th instant, I assumed command on the 14th instant of the Eighteenth Army Corps, serving in North Carolina. On the 15th instant, in company with General Palmer, I commenced an inspection of this important command, more especially with respect to the general system of defenses.

Pamlico District.—At Washington I examined the old and new lines, both of which are well arranged. The second or interior line has many advantages over the exterior, especially in its command and the requiring of a lesser force for its defense. Some guns should be added, and some slashing done for the better protection of the artillerists against riflemen.

In this connection I will observe, that on the 14th the cavalry outpost, 1 corporal and 4 men, were surprised. The corporal, 2 men, 4 horses, and the equipments were captured.

The cavalry company at Washington is small and inefficient. It seems proper to make a change. Really, another company ought to be sent there; a good field officer to take charge of both.

General Palmer, General Heckman, and others, urge Colonel Amory, or some new commander, for that place. But in view of your observations on this point, I shall defer any change until I see you. Colonel Amory has been relieved by General Heckman.

Albemarle District.—The line of works at Plymouth is what is demanded for that place. The area of open land is so small that the health and comfort of the troops will be much promoted by a general felling of timber in front of the intrenchments.

On learning that you had given directions for colored troops to occupy Elizabeth City, Jonesburg, Canal Bridge, and South Mills, I at once gave the proper orders for the transportation, and sent Lieutenant King, engineer officer to General Wessells, for the purpose of constructing any light works that might be deemed necessary. In case you place the counties north of the sound under command of General Naglee, as I suggested, the troops of General Wessells can be withdrawn.

My stay at Hatteras Inlet was short, but I was well repaid by the excellent state of things under Captain Allen. The general health of the command is very gratifying.

Defenses of New Berne.—The system comprised under this head is extensive, very complete, and admirably arranged. Any serious operations against New Berne would involve the attempt to seize the works on south side of Trent River. The forests along the Trent must be cut away before the ranges and power of the works can be fully developed. When the timber is cleared there will be a heavy interchange of fire, between the works divided by the Trent.

I am, very respectfully,

JOHN J. PECK,
Major-General.

———

HEADQUARTERS ARMY OF THE POTOMAC,
August 21, 1863—9 a. m.

Commanding Officer Cavalry Corps:

The major-general commanding deems it not advisable to transfer the brigade of Gregg to Gainesville, but in view of the information received last night indicating an abandonment of the design on the part of the enemy of a forward movement on our left flank, and of some movement on his part toward his center, the major-general commanding desires that you dispose of your cavalry now on the right flank (Gregg's division) so as to obtain the earliest intelligence of any change in the position of the enemy's troops or movement to turn our right flank by a route between us and the mountains, or by the way of the Valley of the Shenandoah, or to make a raid by either of these general routes.

The dispositions on our left flank render that as secure as it is possible to make it.

Very respectfully,

A. A. HUMPHREYS,
Major-General, and Chief of Staff.

———

AUGUST 21, 1863—10 a. m.
(Received 12.15 p. m.)

Major-General HALLECK:

The movements of the enemy in the vicinity of Fredericksburg and United States Ford seem to have changed yesterday. My cavalry reported the enemy's pickets opposite Falmouth as being materially reduced in numbers and the men very quiet, refusing to talk. At the same time clouds of dust of considerable length were noticed on the roads leading south from Fredericksburg. A large force of cavalry, which had been near United States Ford, were believed to have moved up the river. Whether these different movements are due to an abandonment of the proposed or suspected movements on my left flank, or whether this movement on the part of the enemy was in reality only a demonstration to draw me down to Falmouth, or whether they ascertained that I was apprised of it and prepared, are all questions the future only can solve.

From scouts and other sources it is reported that a body of cavalry have gone into the valley with a view to turning my right flank. My own idea is that Lee is puzzled to account for my inaction. The Richmond journals of the 19th positively assert I am falling back, object unknown. Deserters say they believe I am about transferring my army to the Peninsula, but our own journals, I regret to see, state that I am falling back. Under this conviction it is not unlikely that Lee may make some demonstration to ascertain whether I am or am not falling back, and if he believes I have been materially weakened (and he only has to read our journals to come to that conclusion), he may attempt to compel me to retire by turning one of my flanks.

I shall endeavor, by the disposition of my cavalry, to be apprised at the earliest moment of any such movement. The necessity of employing my cavalry on both flanks and watching my rear, at such distances from depots and supplies, causes the service to be as hard upon this branch of the army as when in active operations. I have therefore to hope that every effort will be continued, as I know heretofore has been exerted, to keep my cavalry up to the maximum standard.

I attach no importance to the report, by Harper's Ferry, that Lee is concentrating at Fredericksburg preparatory to falling back on Richmond. I do not believe he will fall back until I advance, unless he really believes I am transferring to the Peninsula, when, of course, he will endeavor to get there in advance, and this may be the cause of the movement reported yesterday as being south of Fredericksburg. I shall await events in my present position unless otherwise ordered.

GEO. G. MEADE,
Major-General, Commanding.

HDQRS. ARMY OF THE POTOMAC, *August* 21, 1863.
(Received 3.10 p. m.)

Maj. Gen. H. W. HALLECK,
General-in-Chief:

Can you not let me have the brigade of the Pennsylvania Reserves left at Alexandria? It seems a pity to break up an organization which has gained so much prestige, and they are very anxious to be reunited.

GEO. G. MEADE,
Major-General.

HDQRS. THIRD DIVISION, CAVALRY CORPS,
August 21, 1863.

Capt. A. J. COHEN,
Assistant Adjutant-General, Cavalry Corps:

There is every indication that the enemy is in large force in and above Fredericksburg. The smoke of their camp fires can be seen along the line of the railroad. The telegraph line is completed to these headquarters and awaits an operator. A scouting party from my command surprised a camp of guerrillas last night, numbering about 12 men. In the darkness they succeeded in escaping. We recaptured 1 man, 2 negroes, and 3 horses.

These guerrillas number about 50 men, including scouts, citizens, and soldiers. They have furnished accurate information of our movements to the enemy. One hundred men of my command are now in pursuit and must capture them. I shall arrest all citizens who assist these men or know of their whereabouts. I am compelled to do this to secure my telegraph line and communication. All is quiet along my line. The enemy's pickets and stragglers at Fredericksburg number upward of 1,000 men.

I forward four Richmond papers, of different dates, received from my pickets.

Very respectfully,

J. KILPATRICK,
Brig. Gen. of Vols., Commanding Third Division.

AUGUST 21, 1863—1 p. m.

Major-General WARREN,
Commanding Second Corps:

A scout who was captured by a guerrilla party on the road to Hartwood Church from Warrenton, and has just escaped, reports that there is a Lieutenant Embrey, whose mother lives near Morrisville, whose house is frequented by the officers of our army; that their conversations he overhears, and that he gets newspapers there that are left with his mother by our officers, and that a colonel, particularly, leaves newspapers there daily.

A. A. HUMPHREYS,
Major-General, Chief of Staff.

HARTWOOD CHURCH, *August* 21, 1863.
(Received 10 p. m.)

Lieut. Col. C. ROSS SMITH,
Chief of Staff:

General Custer reports that a large body of troops have been moving since 3 p. m. in a southeasterly direction opposite Falmouth, and large trains are moving along the line of railroad south of Fredericksburg. A signal flag was seen 3 miles south of Fredericksburg at 5 p. m. to-day.

J. KILPATRICK,
Brigadier-General, Commanding Division.

GENERAL ORDERS, }   HDQRS. ARMY OF THE POTOMAC,
    No. 82.   }   *August* 21, 1863.

The duties of the chief of artillery of this army are both administrative and executive; he is responsible for the condition of all the artillery, wherever serving, respecting which he will keep the commanding general fully informed.

Through him the commanding general of the army will take the proper steps to insure the efficiency of the artillery for movement and action, and its proper employment in battle.

All artillery not attached to other troops will be commanded by the chief of artillery. He will, both personally and through his staff, maintain a constant supervision and inspection over the *personnel* and *matériel* of the artillery of the army, and give the orders necessary to insure the instruction of the former and the completeness of the latter, as well as the discipline of the artillery not attached to other troops.

In battle, he will, under the instructions of the major-general commanding, distribute and place in position the reserve artillery, and, when so directed, select positions for the batteries attached to troops, conveying to the commander of the troops the directions of the commanding general.

He will give such directions as are necessary to secure the proper supply of ammunition, and to furnish it promptly to the batteries when in action.

He will give no orders that would interfere with the military control exercised by the commander of a corps or division over the batteries attached to their troops, nor will he withdraw batteries from a corps or transfer them from one corps to another, unless directed to do so by the general commanding the army.

Commandants of the artillery attached to troops will be responsible to the chief of artillery for the condition and efficiency of their batteries, so far as relates to equipments, supplies, and instruction, and will be governed with respect to orders received from him by Paragraph 489, Revised Army Regulations of 1861.

By command of Major-General Meade:

S. WILLIAMS,
Assistant Adjutant-General.

GENERAL ORDERS, }　　　HDQRS. ARMY OF THE POTOMAC,
　　No. 83.　　　}　　　　　　　　　　*August 21, 1863.*

In order that the amount of transportation in this army shall not in any instance exceed the maximum allowance prescribed in General Orders, No. 274, of August 7, 1863, from the War Department, and to further modify and reduce baggage and supply trains, heretofore authorized, the following allowances are established and will be strictly conformed to, viz:

1. The following is the maximum amount of transportation to be allowed to this army in the field:

To the headquarters of an army corps, 2 wagons or 8 pack mules.

To the headquarters of a division or brigade, 1 wagon or 5 pack mules.

To every 3 company officers, when detached or serving without wagons, 1 pack mule.

To every 12 company officers, when detached, 1 wagon or 4 pack mules.

To every 2 staff officers not attached to any headquarters, 1 pack mule.

To every 10 staff officers serving similarly, 1 wagon or 4 pack mules.

The above will include transportation for all personal baggage, mess chests, cooking utensils, desks, papers, &c. The weight of officers' baggage in the field, specified in the Army Regulations, will be reduced so as to bring it within the foregoing schedule.   All excess of transportation now with army corps, divisions, brigades, and regiments, or batteries, over the allowances herein prescribed, will be immediately turned in to the quartermaster's department, to be used in the trains.

Commanding officers of corps, divisions, &c., will immediately cause inspections to be made, and will be held responsible for the strict execution of this order.

Commissary stores and forage will be transported by the trains. Where these are not convenient of access, and where troops act in detachments, the quartermaster's department will assign wagons or pack animals for that purpose; but the baggage of officers, or of troops, or camp equipage, will not be permitted to be carried in the wagons or on the pack animals so assigned.

The assignment for transportation for ammunition, hospital stores, subsistence, and forage will be made in proportion to the amount ordered to be carried.   The number of wagons is hereinafter prescribed.

The allowance of spring wagons and saddle horses for contingent wants, and of camp and garrison equipage, will remain as established by circular, dated July 17, 1863.

2. For each full regiment of infantry and cavalry, of 1,000 men, for baggage, camp equipage, &c., 6 wagons.

For each regiment of infantry less than 700 men and more than 500 men, 5 wagons.

For each regiment of infantry less than 500 men and more than 300 men, 4 wagons.

For each regiment of infantry less than 300 men, 3 wagons.

3. For each battery of four and six guns—for personal baggage, mess chests, cooking utensils, desks, papers, &c., 1 and 2 wagons respectively.

For ammunition trains the number of wagons will be determined and assigned upon the following rules :

First. Multiply each 12-pounder gun by 122 and divide by 112.

Second. Multiply each rifle gun by 50 and divide by 140.   ·

Third. For each 20-pounder gun, 1¼ wagons.

Fourth. For each siege gun, 2½ wagons.

Fifth. For the general supply train of reserve ammunition of 20 rounds to each gun in the army, to be kept habitually with the Artillery Reserve, 54 wagons.

For each battery, to carry its proportion of subsistence, forage, &c., 2 wagons.

4. The supply train for forage, subsistence, quartermaster's stores, &c., to each 1,000 men, cavalry and infantry, 7 wagons.

To every 1,000 men, cavalry and infantry, for small-arms ammunition, 5 wagons.

To each 1,500 men, cavalry and infantry, for hospital supplies, 3 wagons.

To each army corps, except the cavalry, for intrenching tools, &c., 6 wagons.

To each corps headquarters for the carrying of subsistence, forage, and other stores not provided for herein, 3 wagons.

To each division headquarters for similar purpose as above, 2 wagons.

To each brigade headquarters for similar purpose as above, 1 wagon.

To each brigade, cavalry and infantry, for commissary stores for sales to officers, 1 wagon.

To each division, cavalry and infantry, for hauling forage for ambulance animals, portable forges, &c., 1 wagon.

To each division, cavalry and infantry, for carrying armorers' tools, parts of muskets, extra arms and accouterments, 1 wagon.

It is expected that each ambulance and each wagon, whether in the baggage, supply, or ammunition train, will carry the necessary forage for its own team.

By command of Major-General Meade:

S. WILLIAMS,
Assistant Adjutant-General.

WAR DEPARTMENT,
Washington, August 21, 1863—3.45 p. m.
Bvt. Brig. Gen. W. W. MORRIS:

Send immediately a report of the numbers and stations of troops in the Middle Department.

H. W. HALLECK,
General-in-Chief.

WAR DEPARTMENT,
Washington, August 21, 1863—3 p. m.
Major-General FOSTER, *Fort Monroe, Va.:*

Reports from General Meade indicate that a part of Lee's force has moved toward Richmond. This may be a mere feint, or he may intend to trouble you. I send this merely to put you on your guard.

H. W. HALLECK,
General-in-Chief.

FORT MONROE, VA., *August* 21, 1863.
(Received 8.30 p. m.)
Major-General HALLECK, *General-in-Chief:*

Your telegram of to-day is received, and the necessary precautions are taken. Deserters that came into Yorktown to-day report very few troops at Richmond, but extensive new breastworks being constructed there. The telegraph wire between Yorktown and Williamsburg was cut in three places yesterday, which is an unusual occurrence.

J. G. FOSTER,
Major-General, Commanding.

FORT MONROE,
August 21, 1863—5 p. m.
Brigadier-General WISTAR, *Yorktown:*

Reports from the Army of the Potomac indicate that a part of Lee's force has moved on Richmond. Look out sharply, lest this force come down on you suddenly to give you a trial of strength. Have you any recent news from beyond your advance at Williamsburg? If not, send out and try to find out something, and put your outposts on their guard.

J. G. FOSTER,
Major-General, Commanding.

———

[AUGUST 21, 1863.]

Brig. Gen. H. M. NAGLEE,
Commanding District of Virginia:

I have just received a dispatch from General Halleck in which he says:

Reports from General Meade indicate that a part of Lee's force has moved toward Richmond. This may be a mere feint, or he may intend to trouble you.

Please to have things put in order in case Lee should make a move in this direction.

· I would suggest the moving of the Mounted Rifles up the Peninsula to Williamsburg, to scout and obtain information, and also the sending of Spear's cavalry out toward or beyond the Blackwater for the same purpose.

J. G. FOSTER,
Major-General, Commanding.

———

GENERAL ORDERS, }   HDQRS. DEPT. OF VA. AND N. C.,
    No. 8.   }   *Fort Monroe, Va., August 21, 1863.*

The Department of Virginia and North Carolina is hereby divided into two districts of North Carolina and Virginia, commanded, respectively, by Maj. Gen. J. J. Peck and by Brig. Gen. H. M. Naglee.

All reports, returns, and papers for the action of the commanding officer Eighteenth Army Corps must be sent through the district commanders, who will forward them, with their indorsement, to these headquarters.

By command of Maj. Gen. J. G. Foster:

SOUTHARD HOFFMAN,
Assistant Adjutant-General.

———

HEADQUARTERS OF THE ARMY,
Washington, D. C., August 22, 1863—2.40 p. m.

Major-General MEADE,
Army of the Potomac:

General Briggs has been placed in charge of the removal of all drafted men from Alexandria to the Army of the Potomac. When possible, General Heintzelman will supply guards. When he cannot supply them, General Briggs will send his requisitions to you. These escorts will serve as guards to the trains.

H. W. HALLECK,
General-in-Chief.

HDQRS. CAVALRY CORPS, ARMY OF THE POTOMAC,
August 22, 1863—8 a. m.

Brigadier-General KILPATRICK,
  Comdg. Third Cavalry Division, Hartwood Church:

I send you a copy of telegraph sent to you at 10.30 p. m. last night, with request to answer. I fear you have not received it:

The major-general commanding Army of the Potomac wishes to know upon what road the troops opposite Falmouth were moving, and upon what road the trains were moving south of Fredericksburg.

Please answer.

C. ROSS SMITH,
Lieutenant-Colonel, and Chief of Staff.

HDQRS. CAVALRY CORPS, ARMY OF THE POTOMAC,
August 22, 1863—8.30 a. m. (Received 9 a. m.)

Major-General HUMPHREYS,
  Chief of Staff:

GENERAL: Nothing from General Kilpatrick this morning as yet. General Gregg reports all quiet and no changes. General Merritt reports that there has been no perceivable change in front of Rappahannock Station—

No movement indicating withdrawal. Their line continues the same and about the same strength as when the entire division was there.

Very respectfully,

A. PLEASONTON,
Major-General, Commanding.

HARTWOOD, *August 22, 1863—9 a. m.*
(Received 10 a. m.)

Col. C. ROSS SMITH,
  Chief of Staff, Cavalry Corps:

The troops appeared to be moving on the Bowling Green road, the wagons on the Bowling Green road and the telegraph road. A column of cavalry was moving on some road farther south but parallel to the Bowling Green road. The signal flag was seen at 5 p. m. 3 miles south of Fredericksburg. Three deserters will reach you by noon with valuable information.

J. KILPATRICK,
Brigadier-General of Volunteers, Comdg. Division.

HDQRS. THIRD DIVISION, CAVALRY CORPS,
August 22, 1863.

Lieut. Col. C. ROSS SMITH,
  Chief of Staff, Cavalry Corps:

COLONEL: I send you one of three deserters, who came across our lines yesterday. He is very intelligent and can give much reliable information.

Pickett's and Hood's divisions of infantry are near Fredericksburg, back on the telegraph road. Fitzhugh Lee's cavalry, consisting of five Virginia regiments and six companies of a Maryland regiment, picket the river up to the junction of the Rapidan and Rappahannock, and Jenkins' cavalry picket from that point up the river. Fitzhugh Lee's headquarters are on the plank road, 2 miles from Fredericksburg. The cars run to Guiney's Station. Maj. Gen. R. E. Lee's headquarters are at Orange Court-House. Fitzhugh Lee pickets the road from Fredericksburg to Orange Court-House, and the river from United States Ford to Port Conway.

Very respectfully,
J. KILPATRICK,
Brigadier-General, Comdg. Third Div., Cav. Corps.

HARTWOOD CHURCH,
August 22, 1863.

Lieutenant-Colonel SMITH,
Chief of Staff:

The troops seen moving yesterday south of Fredericksburg was a force of infantry and cavalry under General Hood. He passed out on the Bowling Green road a few miles, and thence to Port Conway. He had been informed that we intended to cross below Fredericksburg. All quiet at this hour.

J. KILPATRICK,
Brigadier-General.

HDQRS. DEPARTMENT OF WASHINGTON,
Washington, August 22, 1863.

Maj. Gen. H. W. HALLECK,
Commanding, &c., Armies of the United States:

GENERAL: In reply to General Meade's telegram of yesterday, referred to me, I have the honor to state that when the other two brigades of the Pennsylvania Reserves were sent to the front, I very reluctantly retained this, as it is always objectionable to break up an organization which has acquired distinction. The number of troops in this department has been so much reduced that it is impossible for me to spare even a single regiment unless immediately replaced by another. I can exchange this brigade for two full regiments.

I am, general, very respectfully, your obedient servant,
S. P. HEINTZELMAN,
Major-General.

WASHINGTON, D. C.,
August 22, 1863—1.10 p. m.

Brigadier-General LOCKWOOD,
Harper's Ferry, W. Va.:

Three or four good companies will be immediately sent from your command to Camp Parole, Annapolis, to report for duty to Colonel Root, as camp guard.

H. W. HALLECK,
General-in-Chief.

YORKTOWN, VA.,
August 22, 1863.

General NAGLEE,
        Norfolk:

All my cavalry parties have returned. They have scoured the country on this side the Chickahominy for 15 miles from Williamsburg. All the rebel scouts or pickets hitherto permanently kept in our front were withdrawn within two days and sent to Richmond. The last, 12 in number, passed Twelve-Mile Ordinary last evening at sunset, going to Richmond. This statement was uniformly made by all. I shall have reliable information from Richmond within a few days from another source.

                                I. J. WISTAR,
                                Brigadier-General.

NORFOLK, VA.,
August 22, 1863.

General FOSTER:

General Wistar advises me that all the rebel cavalry pickets for 15 miles in his front have been withdrawn to Richmond.

                                NAGLEE,
                                Brigadier-General.

[FORT MONROE, VA.,
August 22, 1863]—10.30 a. m.

General NAGLEE,
        Norfolk:

I leave the matter to your judgment and discretion. The only objection that I can see to that course is that if there is anything serious, there may not be time to get the regiment into position. But of this you have no doubt estimated carefully.

I have received your second telegram, and will ask the navy to send a gunboat. Is the General Jesup at Norfolk? If so, send her up.

                                J. G. FOSTER,
                                Major-General, Commanding.

SPECIAL ORDERS, } WAR DEPT., ADJT. GENERAL'S OFFICE,
    No. 375.   }   *Washington, August* 22, 1863.

*   *   *   *   *   *   *

19. Brig. Gen. E. L. Viele, U.S. Volunteers, will repair at once to Camp Cleveland, Cleveland, Ohio, and relieve Brig. Gen. John S. Mason, U. S. Volunteers, in command of the depot for drafted men at that place. Lieutenants Field and Van Winkle, aides-de-camp to General Viele, will report to him for duty at Camp Cleveland.

*   *   *   *

By order of the Secretary of War:

                                E. D. TOWNSEND,
                                Assistant Adjutant-General.

SPECIAL ORDERS,) HDQRS. ARMY, ADJT. GENERAL'S OFFICE,
    No. 376.   }   *Washington, August 22, 1863.*

*   *   *   *   *   *

3. Brig. Gen. H. S. Briggs, U. S. Volunteers, will take post at Alexandria, Va., as superintendent for the removal of drafted men from that place to the Army of the Potomac. He will ascertain from the Adjutant-General the quota for each regiment, and will make requisitions upon Major-General Meade and Major-General Heintzelman for the necessary guards to accompany the drafted men to their destination.

By command of Major-General Halleck:

E. D. TOWNSEND,
Assistant Adjutant-General.

HDQRS. CAVALRY CORPS, *August 23* [1863]—8.30 a. m.
                                        (Received 9.20 a. m.)

Major-General HUMPHREYS,
            Chief of Staff:

GENERAL: No further reports from General Kilpatrick since those sent you last evening. General Buford reports all quiet. General Gregg reports that no change has taken place in front of his pickets. A scouting party on the road from Hay Market to Aldie encountered a small party of the enemy, fired into them and dispersed them, killing 1 horse.

Very respectfully,

A. PLEASONTON,
Major-General, Commanding.

HDQRS. CAVALRY CORPS, ARMY OF THE POTOMAC,
    August 23, 1863—11.30 a. m.   (Received 1 p. m.)

Major-General HUMPHREYS,
            Chief of Staff:

GENERAL: General Gregg reports that scouting parties from his brigade near Warrenton went yesterday in the direction of Barbee's Cross-Roads and Little Washington.

The party sent to the latter point found the enemy's pickets at Amissville. Driving these in between Amissville and Little Washington, they found a strong reserve of the enemy.

The party which went to Barbee's Cross-Roads on their return was attacked by some 25 or 30 of the enemy in a wood; 1 lieutenant, 1 non-commissioned officer, and 3 of our men are missing. This party returned by way of Salem, and report a large number of young, stout, hearty men working in the fields in that vicinity. Thirteen were counted in one field. These men are either deserters or the enemy's troops gathering the crops. I have directed General Gregg to send out a regiment to find out who these men are, and also to see if the enemy has anything more than a picket line toward Little Washington.

Very respectfully,

A. PLEASONTON,
Major-General, Commanding.

AUGUST 23, 1863—1.30 p. m.

Major-General PLEASONTON,
    Commanding Cavalry Corps:

The major-general commanding directs that Gregg's division of cavalry resume its former position and picket lines on the south side of the Hedgeman River so far as it is practicable to do so. Sufficient force should be left on this side of Hedgeman River to patrol toward Manassas Gap and the region between that gap and Thoroughfare Gap.

It is evident the major-general commanding considers, from your report and from the Richmond newspapers, that enemy's cavalry are north of the Rappahannock (Hedgeman branch). This he considers should not be permitted.

Very respectfully, your obedient servant,
                                    A. A. HUMPHREYS,
                            Major-General, Chief of Staff.

———

HDQRS. DEPT. OF VIRGINIA AND NORTH CAROLINA,
                    Fort Monroe, Va., August 23, 1863.

Rear-Admiral S. P. LEE,
    Comdg. N. A. Bkg. Squadron, Newport News, Va.:

ADMIRAL: Your letter of the 18th I have just received. I regret, Admiral, that your absence from the roads, and my desire to make myself acquainted with the topography of my new command with as little delay as possible, should have induced me to make the reconnaissance of the James River in your absence. I do not think that "dragging" would have avoided an exposure to the dangers of the torpedoes. They were placed on the bottom of the river and exploded by friction tubes from the shore. The clearing the banks of the river of artillery and musketry I had no force adequate to do. Of course, admiral, it would afford me much pleasure to make any reconnaissance with you within my department that may seem to be needed for the information of our respective arms of the service.

With regard to the iron-clads on the Roanoke River, I sincerely regret that the force at my disposal is not adequate to overcome the resistance I would meet by the concentration of troops from Richmond, Petersburg, and North Carolina. Cohen was taken by General Potter on his recent raid, and was examined by him. His information appeared meager, and from all I know I cannot think that, even if the gunboats be meant for offensive movements, they will be able to move till the spring freshets. Any military movement would, I fear, induce the enemy to strengthen their works, and so, perhaps, block future movements intended for farther up.

I am, admiral, very respectfully and truly, yours,
                                    J. G. FOSTER,
                            Major-General, Commanding.

———

HDQRS. DEPT. OF VIRGINIA AND NORTH CAROLINA,
                    Fort Monroe, Va., August 23, 1863.

Maj. JOHN S. STEVENSON,
    Third Pennsylvania Artillery:

MAJOR: You will proceed with the forces under your command on a reconnaissance up the James and Chickahominy Rivers. The following objects and instructions you will bear in mind: it has been reported that the enemy were collecting boats at the mouth of the Chickahominy, the purpose not known. You are to endeavor to find these boats and destroy them. Obtain any information you can as to the movements of the enemy, and obey any orders you receive from General Wistar, who will communicate with you at either Jamestown Island or Barrett's Ferry. You are not to go farther up the Chickahominy than Barrett's Ferry (7 miles), or the first bluff on the right-hand side ascending. You will remain absent three days. As you will be unsupported, you must not jeopardize your boat, or, unnecessarily, the lives of your men. Should you fail to communicate with General Wistar and need further instructions, return to this point and report. These instructions may be modified, should your information render it necessary.

Relying, major, on your judgment, zeal, and intelligence, I have the honor to be, by order of Major-General Foster, very respectfully, yours,

SOUTHARD HOFFMAN,
Assistant Adjutant-General.

[P. S.]—The steamer C. P. Smith, with three guns (one rifle and two howitzers), 3 commissioned officers, and 60 non-commissioned officers and privates, is under your orders.

———

GENERAL ORDERS, } HDQRS. U. S. TROOPS IN CITY AND HARBOR,
No. 12.   }   *New York, August* 23, 1863.

Under the orders of the major-general commanding the Department of the East, constituting the troops of this command a division, they will be temporarily organized into brigades as follows:

First Brigade, Brig. Gen. R. B. Ayres commanding.—Second U. S. Infantry, Third U. S. Infantry, Fourth U. S. Infantry, Sixth U. S. Infantry, Seventh U. S. Infantry, Tenth U. S. Infantry, Eleventh U. S. Infantry, Twelfth U. S. Infantry, Fourteenth U. S. Infantry, Seventeenth U. S. Infantry, One hundred and fifty-second New York, Second Vermont, Third Vermont, Fourth Vermont, Fifth Vermont, Sixth Vermont, Fourteenth New York Cavalry, Eighteenth New York Cavalry, and Seventh Massachusetts Battery.

Second Brigade, Brig. Gen. Thomas H. Ruger commanding.—Fourth Ohio Infantry, Fifth Ohio Infantry, Seventh Ohio Infantry, Eighth Ohio Infantry, Twenty-ninth Ohio Infantry, Sixty-sixth Ohio Infantry, One hundred and tenth Ohio Infantry, One hundred and twenty-second Ohio Infantry, One hundred and twenty-sixth Ohio Infantry, Fourteenth Indiana Infantry, Twenty-seventh Indiana Infantry, Third Michigan Infantry, Fifth Michigan Infantry, Seventh Michigan Infantry, Second Massachusetts, Third Wisconsin, First Minnesota, and Second Connecticut Battery.

The garrison of the forts in the harbor, the guards at Davids Island and Riker's Island, Battery C, Fifth U. S. Artillery, and the First Delaware Battery will not be brigaded, and their commands will report direct to these headquarters.

The original organizations of the troops from the Army of the Potomac will be resumed as soon as the temporary service upon which they are now engaged has terminated.

By order of Brigadier-General Canby:

C. T. CHRISTENSEN,
Assistant Adjutant-General.

YORKTOWN, *August* 24, 1863.

General NAGLEE,
　　Norfolk :

My object in landing infantry at Wilson's Wharf, near Charles City, was to ascertain the condition of Wise's command, which is mainly at Drewry's Bluff, and by diversion to prevent his crossing the lower Chickahominy in Onderdonk's rear. I submit it to your consideration, but will not do it without further orders from you. One-third of Wise's men would surely desert if a chance offered. Two of his regiments are from this vicinity, and already well represented in our lines by deserters.

　　　　　　　　I. J. WISTAR,
　　　　　　　　　　Brigadier-General.

NORFOLK, *August* 24, 1863.

General WISTAR,
　　Yorktown:

We are fully informed of Wise's command. There is no fear of Wise with 800 infantry making any attempt to capture Onderdonk's cavalry.

　　　　　　　　HENRY M. NAGLEE,
　　　　　　　　Brigadier-General, Commanding.

GENERAL ORDERS, ⎱　　HDQRS. ARMY OF THE POTOMAC,
　　No. 85.　　⎰　　　　　　　　*August* 24, 1863.

The following revised regulations for the organization of the ambulance corps and the management of the ambulance trains are published for the government of all concerned, and will be strictly observed:

1. The army corps is the unit of organization for the ambulance corps, and the latter will be organized upon the basis of captain as the commandant of the corps, one first lieutenant for each division, one second lieutenant for each brigade, one sergeant for each regiment.

2. The privates of this corps will consist of two men and one driver to each ambulance and one driver to each medicine wagon.

3. The two-horse ambulances only will be used, and the allowance, until further orders, to each corps will be upon the basis of three to each regiment of infantry, two to each regiment of cavalry, one to each battery of artillery, to which it will be permanently attached, and two to the headquarters of each army corps, and two army wagons to each division. Each ambulance will be provided with two stretchers.

4. The captain is the commander of all the ambulances, medicine and other wagons in the corps, under the immediate direction of the medical director of the army corps to which the ambulance corps belongs. He will pay special attention to the condition of the ambulances, wagons, horses, harness, &c., and see that they are at all times in readiness for service; that the officers and men are properly instructed in their duties, and that these duties are performed, and that the regulations for the corps are strictly adhered to by those under his command. He will institute a drill in his corps, instructing

his men in the most easy and expeditious method of putting men in and taking them out of the ambulances, lifting them from the ground, and placing and carrying them on stretchers, in the latter case observing that the front man steps off with the left foot and the rear man with the right, &c.; that in all cases his men treat the sick and wounded with gentleness and care; that the ambulances and wagons are at all times provided with attendants, drivers, horses, &c.; that the vessels for carrying water are constantly kept clean and filled with fresh water; that the ambulances are not used for any other purpose than that for which they are designed and ordered. Previous to a march, he will receive from the medical director of the army corps his orders for the distribution of the ambulances for gathering up the sick and wounded previous to and in time of action; he will receive orders from the same officer where to send his ambulances, and to what point the wounded are to be carried.

He will give his personal attention to the removal of the sick and wounded from the field in time of action, going from place to place to ascertain what may be wanted; to see that his subordinates (for whose conduct he will be responsible) attend faithfully to their duties in taking care of the wounded, and removing them as quickly as may be found consistent with their safety to the field hospital, and see that the ambulances reach their destination. After every battle he will make a report in detail of the operations of his corps to the medical director of the army corps to which he belongs, who will transmit a copy, with such remarks as he may deem proper, to the medical director of this army. He will give his personal attention to the removal of sick when they are required to be sent to general hospitals, or to such other points as may be ordered.

He will make a personal inspection at least once a month of everything pertaining to the ambulance corps, a report of which will be made to the medical director of the corps, who will transmit a copy to the medical director of this army. This inspection will be minute and made with care, and will not supersede the constant supervision which he must at all times exercise over his corps. He will also make a weekly report, according to the prescribed form, to the same officer, who will forward a copy to the medical director of this army.

5. The first lieutenant assigned to the ambulance corps for a division will have complete control, under the captain of his corps and the medical director of the army corps, of all the ambulances, medicine and other wagons, horses, &c., and men in that portion of the ambulance corps. He will be the acting assistant quartermaster for that portion of the corps, and will receipt for and be responsible for all the property belonging to it, and be held responsible for any deficiency in anything appertaining thereto. He will have a traveling cavalry forge, a blacksmith, and a saddler, who will be under his orders, to enable him to keep his train in order. His supplies will be drawn from the depot quartermaster upon requisitions approved by the captain of his corps and the commander of the army corps to which he is attached. He will exercise a constant supervision over his train in every particular, and keep it at all times ready for service. Especially before a battle will he be careful that everything be in order. The responsible duties devolving upon him in time of action render it necessary that he be active and vigilant and spare no labor in their execution. He will make reports to the captain of the corps, upon the forms prescribed, every Saturday morning.

6. The second lieutenant will have command of the portion of the ambulance corps for a brigade, and will be under the immediate orders of the commander of the ambulances for a division, and the injunctions in regard to care and attention and supervision prescribed for the commander of the division he will exercise in that portion under his command.

7. The sergeant will conduct the drills, inspections, &c., under the orders and supervision of the commander of the ambulances for a brigade, be particular in enforcing all orders he may receive from his superior officer, and that the men are attentive to their duties.

The officers and non-commissioned officers will be mounted. The non-commissioned officers will be armed with revolvers.

8. Two medical officers and two hospital stewards will be detailed daily, by roster, by the surgeon-in-chief of division, to accompany the ambulances for the division when on the march, whose duties will be to attend to the sick and wounded with the ambulances, and see that they are properly cared for. No man will be permitted by any line officer to fall to the rear to ride in the ambulances unless he has written permission from the senior medical officer of his regiment to do so. These passes will be carefully preserved, and at the close of the march be transmitted, by the senior medical officer with the train, with such remarks as he may deem proper, to the surgeon-in-chief of his division. A man who is sick or wounded, who requires to be carried in an ambulance, will not be rejected should he not have the permission required; the surgeon of the regiment who has neglected to give it will be reported at the close of the march, by the senior surgeon with the train, to the surgeon-in-chief of his division.

When on the march, one-half of the privates of the ambulance corps will accompany, on foot, the ambulances to which they belong, to render such assistance as may be required. The remainder will march in the rear of their respective commands, to conduct, under the order of the medical officer, such men as may be unable to proceed to the ambulances, or who may be incapable of taking proper care of themselves until the ambulances come up. When the case is of so serious a nature as to require it, the surgeon of the regiment, or his assistant, will remain and deliver the man to one of the medical officers with the ambulances. At all other times the privates will be with their respective trains. The medicine wagons will, on the march, be in their proper places, in the rear of the ambulances for each brigade. Upon ordinary marches, the ambulances and wagons belonging to the train will follow immediately in the rear of the division to which they are attached. Officers connected with the corps must be with the train when on the march, observing that no one rides in any of the ambulances except by the authority of the medical officers. Every necessary facility for taking care of the sick and wounded upon the march will be afforded the medical officers by the officers of the ambulance corps.

9. When in camp, the ambulances will be parked by divisions. The regular roll-calls, reveille, retreat, and tattoo will be held, at which at least one commissioned officer will be present and receive the reports. Stable duty will be at hours fixed by the captain of the corps, and at this time, while the drivers are in attendance upon their animals, the privates will be employed in keeping the ambulances to which they belong in order, keeping the vessels for carrying water filled with fresh water, and in general police duties. Should

it become necessary for a regimental medical officer to use one or more ambulances for transporting sick and wounded, he will make a requisition upon the commander of the ambulances for a division, who will comply with the requisition. In all cases when ambulances are used, the officers, non-commissioned officers, and men belonging to them will accompany them; should one ambulance only be required, a non-commissioned officer, as well as the men belonging to it, will accompany it. The officers of the ambulance corps will see that ambulances are not used for any other purposes than that for which they are designed, viz, the transportation of sick and wounded, and, in urgent cases only, for medical supplies. All officers are expressly forbidden to use them, or to require them to be used, for any other purpose. When ambulances are required for the transportation of sick or wounded at division or brigade headquarters, they will be obtained as they are needed for this purpose from the division train, but no ambulances belonging to this corps will be retained at such headquarters.

10. Good, serviceable horses will be used for the ambulances and medicine wagons, and will not be taken for any other purpose except by orders of these headquarters.

11. This corps will be designated: For sergeants, by a green band 1¼ inches broad around the cap, and chevrons of the same material, with the point toward the shoulder, on each arm above the elbow. For privates, by a band the same as for sergeants around the cap, and a half chevron of the same material on each arm above the elbow.

12. No person except the proper medical officers, or the officers, non-commissioned officers, and privates of this corps, will be permitted to take or accompany sick or wounded to the rear, either on the march or upon the field of battle.

13. No officer or man will be selected for this service except those who are active and efficient, and they will be detailed and relieved by corps commanders only.

14. Corps commanders will see that the foregoing regulations are carried into effect.

By command of Major-General Meade:

S. WILLIAMS,
Assistant Adjutant-General.

DIVISION HEADQUARTERS,
Centreville, August 25, 1863.

Capt. C. H. POTTER,
  Assistant Adjutant-General, Washington:

The first information I received about the capture of horses from the Thirteenth New York Cavalry was from Lieut. Col. H. H. Wells, provost marshal in Alexandria, at 4 p. m. yesterday. He telegraphed me that Captain Gillingham, Thirteenth New York Cavalry, was attacked 2½ miles beyond Annandale by about 100 Confederates, who captured 100 horses from him about 2 o'clock. I immediately communicated this intelligence to Colonel Lowell, who at once started out in the direction of Aldie, with two or three hundred cavalry, hoping to intercept the marauders. I have not yet heard the result of the expedition.

A sutler, who came into our lines last evening and was present when the attack was made, told me that the enemy was about 200 strong; that they represented themselves to be part of Stuart's cavalry, and that 2 of our men were killed and 5 wounded in the skirmish. The sutler's horses were taken by the rebels, but his wagon and goods were left untouched. I did not report the affair to headquarters, supposing that Colonel Lowell, to whose command the escort and horses belonged, would do so.

RUFUS KING,
Brigadier-General.

FORT MONROE, VA., *August 25, 1863—10 p. m.*
(Received 10.15 p. m.)
Maj. Gen. H. W. HALLECK,
General-in-Chief:

I do not like to ask for troops at this time, when both the Army of the Potomac and Charleston need all the men, but I have received information, which is quite reliable, to the effect that a force is now collecting to attack the line outside of Portsmouth. I can only bring one weak brigade from North Carolina, and even that ought not perhaps to be brought away. Can you not send me the Eighth New York and Thirty-fourth Massachusetts, now at Harper's Ferry? If so, please send them at once. I should be under no apprehension if the lines of intrenchments were completed, which they are not, and therefore feel obliged to be prepared. Please answer if you can give me the two regiments asked for at once.

J. G. FOSTER,
Major-General.

SUFFOLK, VA.,
August 25, 1863—11 a. m.
General GETTY:

The detachment reported as not returned last report, has returned all right.

Left Suffolk on the Providence Church road; thence via Windsor to Zuni; found picket on the opposite bank of the Blackwater; returned by circuitous route.

The cavalry I reported as Claiborne's at Ivor Station turns out to be Baker's.

Total strength on Blackwater: Griffin's cavalry (one regiment), and two regiments of infantry at or near Franklin; Baker's cavalry and one regiment of infantry at or near Ivor. All on this side of the Blackwater agree in this statement (contrabands, females, &c.).

I have just received information, which I believe to be reliable, as it comes from a source that has previously given me information which invariably proved to be correct, that a force is now collecting near Ivor Station, 3 miles beyond Zuni, to march to Bowers' Hill; informant says "large force infantry and artillery." I give it in the exact words I received it a few moments ago.

The Blackwater is very low, but the Nansemond River is lower than usual. Captain Lee, with gunboat Flora Temple, could not get higher up than Sleepy Hole. He left night before last, sent up by General Naglee, with three ladies to go to Wilmington, N. C. I passed them out. They did not know my strength.

I think a gunboat should patrol the Nansemond River, as the enemy knowing my position could cross the river below Suffolk—it being very low—and cut me off or put me to much inconvenience.

Every point is guarded; I have drawn back my main body this side of Jericho Canal. The town is thoroughly patrolled and every avenue well guarded. Couriers are saddled ready to convey any intelligence to your headquarters. My rear is now all I fear between here and Hargrove's half-way house. I have one day's rations and forage after to-day.

I am, general, with high respect, your obedient servant,

S. P. SPEAR,
Colonel, Commanding.

NORFOLK, VA.,
August 25, 1863.

General FOSTER:

Spear reports Griffin's cavalry and two regiments of infantry at Franklin, and Baker's cavalry and one regiment of infantry at Ivor Station. Spear says a force is now collecting 3 miles beyond Zuni to march to Bowers' Hill. Informant says large force of infantry and artillery. I dislike to recommend you to withdraw any force from North Carolina. Could you not get re-enforcements from the North? Ask for the Eighth New York and Thirty-fourth Massachusetts, at Harper's Ferry, both splendid regiments; 1,700 in the two.

NAGLEE,
Brigadier-General.

HDQRS. U. S. FORCES IN NORTH CAROLINA,
New Berne, August 25, 1863.

Maj. Gen. J. G. FOSTER,
Comdg. Dept. of Virginia and North Carolina:

GENERAL: Since my last communication upon the defenses of this place I have had an interview with Commodore Davenport, senior naval officer on this station. From him I learn that the naval force on the sounds is to be reduced materially by Admiral Lee, and that in all probability not more than one or two gunboats will be retained here. This change of policy results from the belief that the works which have been constructed are sufficient.

In view of this proposed change I must again refer to the defenses of New Berne. The system of works is very complete upon the present *status* of naval co-operation. Without this, Fort Spinola would be untenable with a rebel battery on the opposite bank near Duck Creek. In possession of that point and the south side of the Trent, the enemy would make this position very uncomfortable. By completing the water front of Spinola, or constructing an inclosed work on the point already mentioned, the system would be complete. In this connection, I will state, that it is reported that an old road runs down to the river near Duck Creek.

Batchelder's Creek.—On visiting the command at the outpost under Colonel Claassen, I found everything in most excellent order, and the health of the troops far better than in other localities. There is a large amount of sickness in the Ninth New Jersey, and in some of the Massachusetts regiments, which is attributed to the raid or raids made by them. After consultation, I have decided to send the New Jersey regiment down to the sea-shore for a few weeks.

District of the Albemarle.—On the 14th instant, Colonel Cullen, Ninety-sixth New York, and Captain French, of steamer·Whitehead, captured 5 men and a lieutenant, of the Sixty-sixth North Carolina, in Camden County. On the 16th, they secured 38 muskets, 26 cartridge boxes and waist belts, &c. These officers report that large supplies are brought out from Norfolk, and that many women are engaged in this business.

Pamlico District.—I have ordered the North Carolina company of cavalry to Little Washington, in view of the condition of the detachment at that important place. The medical officers report a strong scorbutic tendency among the troops, and also among the contrabands, as the direct result of the scarcity of fresh vegetables, and recommend the removal of the restrictions upon traffic with the inhabitants, to a certain extent. Your instructions on this point are so full and positive that I do not feel at liberty to relax them without communicating on the subject. Fresh vegetables have been ordered from New York.

Very respectfully, your obedient servant,

JOHN J. PECK,
Major-General.

[Indorsement.]

AUGUST 30, 1863.

Colonel Hoffman will send an extract to General Naglee, relating to our contract and trade from Norfolk. Write to General Peck that he can make a small work on the opposite side of the river, if he judges it important. Army gunboats must be built to replace the naval ones. If he judges it absolutely necessary for health, a very few markets may be established at the picket lines.

J. G. FOSTER.

HDQRS. U. S. FORCES IN NORTH CAROLINA,
New Berne, N. C., August 25, 1863.

Maj. Gen. J. G. FOSTER,
Comdg. Dept. of Virginia and North Carolina:

GENERAL: Not finding any suitable boat here for my use as a dispatch boat, I have acted upon your suggestion, and detained the C. W. Thomas. Deeming the news which she bears important, I have dispatched her with our mails, &c., and desire Lieutenant Stirling, aide-de-camp, to return with the boat.

I am, very respectfully, your obedient servant,

JOHN J. PECK,
Major-General.

WAR DEPARTMENT,
Washington, August 26, 1863—2.35 p. m.

Major-General FOSTER,
Fort Monroe, Va.:

I cannot re-enforce you without withdrawing troops from General Meade. This is perilous, but I will do so if you absolutely require it. A week or two hence I can do it without so great inconvenience.

H. W. HALLECK,
General-in-Chief.

YORKTOWN, VA.,
August 26, 1863.

General NAGLEE,
Norfolk, Va.:

Captain Mitchell, of the navy, reports gunboats Currituck [Reliance] and Satellite captured by the rebel coast guard guerrillas, and carried into Urbanna Creek. They were captured by boarding from four boats, 25 men each. Onderdonk was ordered to start at daylight this morning. His defective preparations detain him till noon. Jenkins' cavalry are said to be at White House and Bottom's Bridge. Doubtful.

I. J. WISTAR,
Brigadier-General.

SPECIAL ORDERS, }   HDQRS. DEPT. OF WEST VIRGINIA,
No. 18.   }   *Clarksburg, August 26, 1863.*

I. Brig. Gen. William F. Smith, commanding at Hagerstown, Md., is, at his own request, relieved from duty at that post and ordered to report by letter to the Adjutant-General, U. S. Army, at Washington City for orders.

*   *   * ·   *   *

By command Brigadier-General Kelley:
THAYER MELVIN,
Assistant Adjutant-General.

WAR DEPARTMENT,
Washington, D. C., August 27, 1863—9 a. m.
(Received 10.20 a. m.)

Major-General MEADE,
Warrenton, Va.:

Walter, Rainese, Folancy, Lai, and Kuhn appealed to me for mercy, without giving any ground for it whatever. I understand these are very flagrant cases, and that you deem their punishment as being indispensable to the service. If I am not mistaken in this, please let them know at once that their appeal is denied.

A. LINCOLN.

HEADQUARTERS ARMY OF THE POTOMAC,
August 27, 1863.

His Excellency ABRAHAM LINCOLN,
President of the United States:

Walter, Rionèse, Folancy, Lai, and Kuhn were to have been executed yesterday. Their execution was postponed by my order till Saturday, the 29th, that time might be given to procure the services of a Roman Catholic priest to assist them in preparing for death. They are substitute conscripts who enlisted for the purpose of deserting after receiving the bounty; and being the first of this class whose cases came before me, I believed that humanity, the safety of this army, and the most vital interests of the country required their prompt execution as an example, the publicity given to which might, and, I trust in God, will, deter others from imitating their bad conduct. In view of these circumstances, I shall therefore inform them their appeal to you is denied.

GEO. G. MEADE,
Major-General, Commanding.

HEADQUARTERS ARMY OF THE POTOMAC,
August 27, 1863—1.10 p. m.

Maj. Gen. H. W. HALLECK,
General-in-Chief:

General Briggs advises me that in the two detachments sent for, the Eighty-third and One hundred and fourth New York Volunteers, there were 7 colored men whom he has retained, awaiting my orders. I presume, as both of the regiments above referred to are filled with white men, that the sending of these men has been accidental. The matter is, however, referred to you for decision, before any action on my part.

GEO. G. MEADE,
Major-General.

WASHINGTON, D. C.,
August 27, 1863—3.15 p. m.

Major-General MEADE,
Army of the Potomac:

Colored troops will in no case be assigned to white regiments. General Briggs will be directed to send none to the Army of the Potomac.

H. W. HALLECK,
General-in-Chief.

HDQRS. CAVALRY CORPS, ARMY OF THE POTOMAC,
August 27, 1863—8.30 a. m.

Major-General HUMPHREYS,
Chief of Staff:

GENERAL: Colonel Gregg reports a reconnaissance sent out met the enemy near Little Washington. Had 1 man wounded and 1 missing; captured 8 horses. A few of the enemy were driven from Flint Hill.

General Buford reports no change in his front. Had sent parties out after guerrillas near Stafford Store; slight skirmish; 1 horse wounded; captured a number of old muskets, shot-guns, ammunition, and caps, with old uniforms (rebel and Union). These were destroyed. The citizens are represented as being anxious to give information concerning the guerrillas. They say the gang is not large, and is now under Jim Tolson, son of old deaf Ben. Tolson, who lives near Stafford Store.

No later report from General Kilpatrick.

Very respectfully,

A. PLEASONTON,
Major-General, Commanding.

HEADQUARTERS THIRD DIVISION, CAVALRY CORPS,
August 27, 1863.

Lieut. Col. C. ROSS SMITH,
Chief of Staff, Cavalry Corps:

COLONEL: I have the honor to report that the enemy is still in force this side of the river. He has a strong line of pickets from Lamb's Creek Church to the Potomac. There are three regiments of infantry, one of cavalry, and four pieces of artillery at King George Court-House.

Forage in large quantities is daily taken across the river at Port Conway. The enemy is in force opposite that point. The boats used by the enemy are boats taken from the river near Port Conway. I had them filled with stones last winter and sunk; there are four. Were these destroyed it would be difficult for them to obtain more. If the major-general commanding thinks it advisable, I should like to move down the river, capture this force on this side, and destroy the boats.

Very respectfully, your obedient servant,

J. KILPATRICK,
Brig. Gen. of Vols., Commanding Third Division.

YORKTOWN, VA., *August 27,* 1863.

General NAGLEE, *Norfolk, Va.:*

A great commotion is in Matthews County. Three companies rebel cavalry have come down there after conscripts, and last night there was a general skedaddle. Six have come in here with canoes, taken oath of allegiance, and want to go to Eastern Shore. May they go direct? Otherwise they must lose their boats.

I. J. WISTAR,
Brigadier-General.

NORFOLK,
*August 27, 1863—*8.20 p. m.

Major-General FOSTER:

Spear, at 12 m. to-day, says the following is definite and certain: Two regiments cavalry and four regiments of infantry, and twelve pieces of artillery; of the above one regiment of cavalry, one of infantry are at Franklin, and all the balance between Ivor Station and the Blackwater. At the crossing is a boat large enough for a loaded wagon and four horses attached. The ferry is guarded by three pieces and one regiment of infantry. Says he is informed there are a party of surveyors in Isle of Wight now at work. Will advise further of this.

NAGLEE,
Brigadier-General.

SPECIAL ORDERS, } HDQRS. U. S. TROOPS IN CITY AND HARBOR,
No. 38.   }   *New York, August 27, 1863.*

*   *   *   *   *

VII. Brig. Gen. Thomas H. Ruger, commanding Second Brigade, will order the six regiments of his command now on Governor's

Island to proceed to-morrow morning for temporary duty to Long Island, to be stationed at the following places: One regiment (one of the strongest) at the village of Jamaica; two regiments at Washington Park, city of Brooklyn; one regiment at the corner of Smith and Carroll streets, Brooklyn.

The draft takes place on Monday, the 31st instant, at the following places: First district, village of Jamaica; second district, No. 26 Grand street, Williamsburg; third district, No. 259 Washington street, Brooklyn.

Two companies will report for duty to the provost-marshal at each of the two last-named places, while the balance of the force will be held in readiness at their respective camping grounds for any emergency that may arise.

The regiment destined for Jamaica will be conveyed by steamer from Governor's Island to Hunter's Point, whence they will proceed by railroad, notifying the provost-marshal by telegraph of their time of departure. The other regiments will cross to Brooklyn in ferry-boats and will be escorted to their respective camping grounds by guides furnished by General Duryea, of the Brooklyn militia. Notification will be sent to him at the Brooklyn Arsenal, corner of Cranberry and Henry streets, of the time when the regiments will arrive in Brooklyn. All the regiments will carry their tents with them. The quartermaster's department will furnish the necessary transportation.

VIII. First Lieut. Ira W. Steward, Twenty-eighth Battery New York Volunteer Artillery, detailed to superintend the recruiting service for the battery in this city, by Special Orders, No. 23, Paragraph III, current series, from these headquarters, will, in addition to his present duties, until further orders, superintend the recruiting service for the battery at Middletown, N. Y., which place he will visit for that purpose as often as the interests of the service may require, though not oftener than three or four times a month. If Lieutenant Steward recommends any changes among the enlisted men at these recruiting stations, the commanding officer at Fort Schuyler is authorized to issue the necessary orders if he thinks proper.

By order of Brigadier-General Canby:

C. T. CHRISTENSEN,
Assistant Adjutant-General.

HDQRS. CAVALRY CORPS, ARMY OF THE POTOMAC,
August 28, 1863—8 a. m.   (Received 8.20 a. m.)

Major-General HUMPHREYS,
Chief of Staff:

GENERAL: General Kilpatrick reports 3 deserters from McLaws' division. They crossed last evening, and state their division left Raccoon Ford four days ago, and marched to Wall's Tavern, where it is receiving supplies from Frederick's Hall, on the Virginia Central Railroad. Pickett's division is on the telegraph road near Fredericksburg. Hood's is between Hamilton's Crossing and Port Royal.

A brigade of infantry under General Cooke is at Fredericksburg, not assigned. Wall's Tavern is about 10 miles northeast from Frederick's Hall.

The force on the peninsula between the Potomac and Rappahannock consists of three regiments of infantry and one of cavalry, with
four guns, near King George Court-House. They have a picket
line from Lamb's Creek Church to the Potomac, and are taking
large quantities of forage to the opposite side of the river from Port
Conway.

Colonel Gregg reports all quiet and no change in his front. Jenkins' and Jones' brigades of cavalry are near Sperryville. General
Buford reports no changes in his front.

Very respectfully,

A. PLEASONTON,
Major-General, Commanding.

HEADQUARTERS CAVALRY CORPS,
August 28, 1863.

Col. JOHN I. GREGG,
Comdg. Second Cav. Div., Watery Mountain Station:

It is rumored that Hampton with 5,000 cavalry has started from
Culpeper Court-House to make a raid into Maryland.

The major-general commanding directs that you will send out and
see if they are moving any force in that direction, and in what
strength, and send in all the information you can gain. Send out
scouts through the country to obtain all information; send word
what force there is at Sperryville.

[C. ROSS SMITH],
Lieutenant-Colonel, and Chief of Staff.

HEADQUARTERS CAVALRY CORPS,
August 28, 1863.

Brigadier-General KILPATRICK,
Comdg. Third Cav. Div., Hartwood Church:

The major-general commanding the army directs that no communication whatever be held between your pickets and the enemy's.

The general commanding also understands that there was a rebel
mail captured by some of your command a few days ago and was
never sent in.

He directs hereafter that anything of that kind that is captured
be forwarded at once.

[C. ROSS SMITH,]
Lieutenant-Colonel, and Chief of Staff.

WARRENTON,
August 28, 1863.

Col. C. ROSS SMITH,
Chief of Staff:

My information is that Jenkins' and Jones' brigades are at Sperryville. The enemy have a strong picket at Gaines' Cross-Roads.

J. IRVIN GREGG.

Circular.]   Headquarters Army of the Potomac,
                                        August 28, 1863.

Commanding Officers of all Corps:

It is deemed advisable to hold communication with the enemy by "flag of truce" at one point only of the lines of this army, and the point designated for that purpose is the picket in front of Rappahannock Station.

Commanding officers will give the necessary order to carry this into effect, and the enemy upon exhibiting a "flag of truce" will be informed of the point at which it will be received.

By command of Major-General Meade:

S. WILLIAMS,
Assistant Adjutant-General.

Arlington House,
August 28, 1863—1.20 p. m.

Lieutenant-Colonel Taylor,
Chief of Staff, A. A. G., Hdqrs. Dept. of Washington:

Major Doubleday has informed me that he has reliable information that 300 rebel cavalry, supposed to be White's, passed last night through the woods west of Difficult Creek, and are now supposed to be lying in the Thornton woods near Thornton Mills. I have sent re-enforcements to the guard at the government farms.

Your obedient servant,

THOS. THOMPSON,
Captain, and Assistant Adjutant-General.

Norfolk,
August 28, 1863.

General Foster:

General Getty telegraphs to me that large bodies of troops have been passing south through Weldon recently. He adds it is not reliable.

NAGLEE,
Brigadier-General.

General Orders, }   Hdqrs. Dept. of Va. and N. C.,
No. 9.   }   *Fort Monroe, Va., August* 28, 1863.

The medical organization of this department is announced as follows:

1. A medical director of the department.

2. A medical director for each of the Districts of Virginia and North Carolina.

3. A superintendent of general hospitals; one for each of the above districts.

No medical officers in this department will be allowed to use the title of medical director, other than those above designated.

The senior medical officers on duty with a division, brigade, or a military sub-district, will, after giving his rank, add "surgeon-in-chief."

No acting medical inspector will be recognized unless appointed by the medical director of the department.

By command of Major-General Foster:

SOUTHARD HOFFMAN,
Assistant Adjutant-General.

HEADQUARTERS CAVALRY CORPS,
August 29, [1863]—3.30 p. m.

Major-General HUMPHREYS,
Chief of Staff:

GENERAL: The regiment sent to Chester Gap reports no signs of the enemy.

General Buford reports one of his scouts states that the rebels know of the order for a regiment of cavalry to escort sutlers on Thursday to Washington and back. Says also that 1,500 cavalry under Imboden have been at Leesburg over one week.

Would it not be well for Buford to send one of his brigades up to Leesburg and give those fellows a good clearing out? They can do it in four or five days.

Very respectfully,

A. PLEASONTON,
Major-General, Commanding.

HEADQUARTERS CAVALRY CORPS,
August 29, 1863.

Col. JOHN I. GREGG,
Comdg. Second Cav. Div., Opposite Sulphur Springs:

The major-general commanding directs that you keep the enemy from concentrating any force at Gaines' Cross-Roads. If the force you have sent out is not strong enough, you had better send a stronger force with two pieces of artillery; that is, if you find them very strong there, as it is important to hold the cross-roads. If your own brigade is not strong enough, you had better order up some of McIntosh's brigade. Watch the enemy's movements as closely as possible.

[C. ROSS SMITH,]
Lieutenant-Colonel, and Chief of Staff.

HARTWOOD CHURCH,
August 29, 1863.

Lieut. Col. C. ROSS SMITH,
Chief of Staff:

I am making every effort to clear my lines and capture the party or parties of the enemy in my rear. Firing was heard about 11 a. m. in the direction of Taggert's Mills; supposed to be between a party of my troops and that of the enemy.

J. KILPATRICK,
Brigadier-General.

RAPPAHANNOCK STATION, *August* 29, 1863.
(Received 7.45 a. m.)

General HUMPHREYS,
Chief of Staff:

The following dispatches were received from our signal officers to-day:

We intercepted the two following rebel messages to-day, No. 1 at 11.55 a. m., and No. 2 at 5.40 p. m.

No. 1.

Captain M.:
Trains are moving down the railroad. Have been for two hours. No troops yet.
B., *Lieutenant.*

No. 2.

Sergeant BUSH:
The trains of wagons reported this a. m. are still passing. A very large train is seen moving in the direction of Warrenton. Camps still the same.
B., *Lieutenant.*

The signal officers also report that Stuart's cavalry command is at last fully supplied with clothing.
Very respectfully,

JOHN NEWTON,
Major-General.

RAPPAHANNOCK STATION,
August 29, 1863.

General HUMPHREYS,
Chief of Staff:

Lieut. N. H. Camp, of our signal corps, took the message that Stuart was supplied with clothing.

JOHN NEWTON,
Major-General, Commanding.

FORT ETHAN ALLEN, *August* 29, 1863.
(Received 10.45 a. m.)

Brigadier-General DE RUSSY,
Arlington:

Lieutenant Phillips, Second Massachusetts Cavalry, from Lewinsville, reports that he is informed by parties just in from Leesburg that a large body of rebel cavalry are at that place and vicinity, and crossing over to Maryland. They went along Thornton woods last evening. Force not known.

THOS. ALLCOCK,
Lieutenant-Colonel.

HARPER'S FERRY, W. VA., *August* 29, 1863.
(Received 2.20 p. m.)

Major-General HALLECK,
General-in-Chief:

My guard extends to the Monocacy. Beyond that is out of this department and of my command. Any transfer of troops from my lines to points beyond the Monocacy exposes these lines. My available cavalry force for excursion operations does not exceed 300 men. Cannot a few hundred good men—say of Scott's Nine Hundred—be added to my present force, with which to clear out the guerrillas now infesting Loudoun County?

Respectfully,

HENRY H. LOCKWOOD,
Brigadier-General.

WAR DEPARTMENT,
Washington, August 29, 1863—12.30 p. m.

Brigadier-General LOCKWOOD,
Harper's Ferry, W. Va:

It is reported that rebel cavalry are crossing into Maryland near Leesburg. They should be looked after.

H. W. HALLECK,
General-in-Chief.

HARPER'S FERRY, W. VA., *August 29, 1863.*
(Received 10.20 a. m., 30th.)

Major-General HALLECK,
General-in-Chief:

Scouting parties went both yesterday and to-day from Point of Rocks within 1½ miles of Leesburg, and report no enemy. A citizen at the point, from Leesburg, spoke of a rumor such as you name. I can learn of no crossing or attempt; certainly none this side of the Monocacy.

Respectfully,

HENRY H. LOCKWOOD,
Brigadier-General.

SPECIAL ORDERS,   HDQRS. ARMY OF THE POTOMAC,
No. 232.   *August 29, 1863.*

*   *   *   *   *   *   *

6. The First Brigade Horse Artillery, now serving in the Cavalry Corps, will be at once relieved by the Second Brigade (Tidball's). As soon as relieved, Captain Robertson, with his command, will report to the chief of artillery.

*   *   *   *   *

By command of Major-General Meade:

S. WILLIAMS,
Assistant Adjutant-General.

SPECIAL ORDERS,   HDQRS. U. S. TROOPS IN CITY AND HARBOR,
No. 40.   *New York, August 29, 1863.*

The Fifth Michigan Infantry, and the Fifth, Seventh, Twenty-ninth, and Sixty-sixth Ohio Infantry, now on board the steamer Baltic, expected to arrive in course of the afternoon, will be attached to the Second Brigade, Brig. Gen. Thomas H. Ruger commanding, and will, for the present, be stationed on Governor's Island. Requisitions will be made as soon as practicable for such camp and garrison equipage as these regiments may need.

By order of Brigadier-General Canby:

C. T. CHRISTENSEN,
Assistant Adjutant-General.

SPECIAL ORDERS, }   WAR DEPT., ADJT. GENERAL'S OFFICE,
No. 388.   }   *Washington, August 29, 1863.*

*   *   *   *   *   *

13. Brig. Gen. J. G. Barnard, U. S. Volunteers; Brig. Gen. G. W. Cullum, U. S. Volunteers, and Col. B. S. Alexander, additional aide-de-camp (major of Engineers), will constitute a Board of Engineers to examine and report upon the proper means of defending the works of the Potomac Aqueduct, as connected with the defense of Washington.

*   *   *   *   *   *

16. Brig. Gen. H. G. Wright, U. S. Volunteers, major of Engineers, is hereby relieved from duty in the Army of the Potomac, and will at once repair to West Point and relieve Lieut. Col. Alexander H. Bowman, Corps of Engineers, in the duties of Superintendent of the Military Academy.* On being relieved, Colonel Bowman will report in person for duty to the Chief of Engineers.

*   *   *   *   *

By order of the Secretary of War :

E. D. TOWNSEND,
Assistant Adjutant-General.

WASHINGTON, D. C.,
August 30, 1863—12 noon.

Major-General MEADE,
Army of the Potomac:

An iron-clad and several gunboats will leave the mouth of the Rappahannock to-morrow morning, and will probably reach Port Royal about night. The object is to recapture the two gunboats taken by the enemy and now in that river. It is very possible that these vessels, being small, may run up toward Fredericksburg, into shallow water, where our vessels cannot pursue. It is, therefore, desirable that you send a force of cavalry and artillery down this side of the river, to assist in destroying them. This force will run the risk of being cut off, by the enemy's throwing troops across the river in their rear. Hence the greatest caution must be taken to watch the river and the enemy's movements. The whole operation will be a delicate one, and the most careful officers should be placed in charge.

H. W. HALLECK,
General-in-Chief.

---

* Order revoked by Special Orders, No. 394, Adjutant-General's Office, September 2, 1863, and Wright ordered to join his command in the Army of the Potomac.

AUGUST 30, 1863—8 p. m.
(Received 10.40 p. m.).

Major-General HALLECK:

In accordance with your telegram, I have directed Brigadier-General Kilpatrick, with his division of cavalry, about 2,000 strong, to proceed to Port Conway, opposite Port Royal, and endeavor to destroy the captured gunboats, if practicable.

To protect his rear and afford him support, Brigadier-General Buford, with a brigade of cavalry and a battery, will hold the crossing at Falmouth, and Major-General Warren, with the Second Corps, about 5,000 infantry, will hold the crossing at Banks' and United States F'ords. I have not much expectation of success, however, for it is known the enemy have a division of infantry at Fredericksburg, and a brigade of cavalry; also a division of infantry at Port Royal, with a brigade on this side, at Port Conway.

What I anticipate is, that Kilpatrick will find the gunboats above Port Royal, where they cannot be reached by our naval forces, and in a position where the enemy's artillery, posted on the right bank, will permit his bringing his batteries to bear on their destruction.

The great distance of Port Conway, 25 miles below Falmouth, the extreme point our cavalry now picket, and the necessity for Kilpatrick awaiting the arrival of the infantry, may prevent his reaching his destination before day after to-morrow.

GEO. G. MEADE,
Major-General, Commanding.

AUGUST 30, 1863—7 p. m.

Major-General WARREN,
Commanding Second Corps:

By direction of the major-general commanding, I transmit you herewith a telegram received from the General-in-Chief.* In pursuance thereof, General Pleasonton will send a strong force of cavalry and artillery, and the major-general commanding directs that you move with your corps to-morrow morning at 3 o'clock to United States Ford and Banks' Ford, and hold those crossings. The cavalry pickets along the river will not be withdrawn, but remain on the river during the operation. And your force will be concealed from the enemy until he makes some demonstration to cross. A cavalry force (a brigade), under General Buford, will hold the ford at Falmouth. Kilpatrick's division will move down the river.

Every man of your command, excepting those on picket, and on the necessary guards, should be with the command. It should be provided with three days' rations.

A. A. HUMPHREYS,
Major-General, Chief of Staff.

Upon the return of the cavalry, of which you will be advised by General Kilpatrick, you will resume your former position at Morrisville and Elkton.

A. A. HUMPHREYS,
Major-General, Chief of Staff.

---

*See Halleck to Meade, August 30, p. 111.

It appearing that the cavalry cannot move so soon as was intended, your corps need not move until 6 a. m.

> A. A. HUMPHREYS,
> *Major-General, Chief of Staff.*

Take as few ambulances as possible, and use your own discretion as to ammunition wagons; no other wagons should accompany the command.

> A. A. H. [HUMPHREYS.]

> HEADQUARTERS FIRST CORPS,
> *August* 30, [1863]—9.45 p. m.

Maj. Gen. A. A. HUMPHREYS,
  Chief of Staff, Hdqrs. Army of the Potomac:

GENERAL : My signal officers have to-day intercepted the following rebel message :

General CHILTON :

I have important dispatches to send to General Lee, at Richmond, in reply to his of yesterday, which I did not receive until this morning. I wish to send them as soon as the telegraph office opens this p. m.

> STUART,
> *General.*

Very respectfully,

> JOHN NEWTON,
> *Major-General.*

> CENTREVILLE, VA.,
> *August* 30, 1863.

Col. J. H. TAYLOR,
  Chief of Staff, Washington, D. C.:

The infantry force which I sent out on Friday to co-operate with the cavalry in a search for guerrillas, returned to camp this morning. They scouted the country thoroughly as far as Dranesville, but only saw 5 or 6 guerrillas, who fled immediately.

Colonel McMahon, commanding the infantry, reports that Mosby, who was severely wounded in the affair on Monday last, has been carried beyond the mountains. White is in the neighborhood of Broad Run, enforcing the Confederate conscription, supported, as is said, by a body of infantry near Leesburg.

> RUFUS KING,
> *Brigadier-General.*

> CENTREVILLE, VA., *August* 30, 1863.
> (Received 6.40 p. m.)

Lieut. Col. J. H. TAYLOR,
  Chief of Staff:

Major Thompson, Second Massachusetts Cavalry, left Dranesville and Guilford Station this morning. White was on Broad Run on Thursday, just before attack on Edwards Ferry. Since that time he is believed not to have been south of Goose Creek. He has from 200 to 300 men with him. Does not move by day, but sends parties of 10 or 20 by night to pick up conscripts and absentees. The supporting force of infantry is said to be between Leesburg and Snicker's Gap, under Major Gilmor. No reliable rumor about number. Major Thompson has had out all my available horses since Friday night. They return this p. m. Unless you wish the reconnaissance to Leesburg made immediately, I shall delay twenty-four hours that the horses may rest.

Very respectfully,

C. R. LOWELL, JR.,
Colonel, Commanding Cavalry.

YORKTOWN,
August 30, 1863.

General NAGLEE,
Norfolk:

Rebels had several squadrons of cavalry at Urbanna withdrawn to Richmond in great hurry Friday night in consequence of our demonstration above. They have got at Urbanna Creek the captured gunboats and schooners and some of our wounded from that affair. Onderdonk's horses cannot move before Tuesday. I will before then submit to you my plans. Rebels are trying to move gunboat machinery to Richmond overland.

I. J. WISTAR,
Brigadier-General.

HEADQUARTERS,
Near Suffolk, August 30, 1863.

General GETTY:

I received your dispatch of last evening at 9 p. m. I send my wagons for five days' forage and rations. Also send for proper papers, data, &c., for completing muster-rolls. I returned at 3.30 this morning. Nothing new. Cannot coax Griffin or Baker to cross the Blackwater. Same force as last reported.

I send a deserter named John H. Crawford, Eleventh North Carolina Battalion, and a captive, Richard Rhoades, Company L, Sixty-second Regiment Georgia Cavalry (Colonel Griffin's). I have examined both and obtained nothing definite.

I think the order for remaining here a good one, and should have recommended it this morning had it not been received; as I believe the moment I left the crossing would commence, at least it appears so from the present force now there "for some purpose."

Animals improving. Men in good health and spirits. I start again to-night in direction of B. W. [the Blackwater]. Will keep you well informed of anything new.

I am, general, with high respect, your obedient servant,

S. P. SPEAR,
Colonel, Commanding Expedition.

SPECIAL ORDERS,⎱ HDQRS. U. S. TROOPS IN CITY AND HARBOR,
No. 41.   ⎰   *New York, August 30, 1863.*

*   *   *   *   *   *   *

III. Brig. Gen. Thomas H. Ruger, commanding Second Brigade, will order the Third and Fifth Regiments Michigan Volunteers (the former now at No. 41 Chambers street, the latter on Governor's

Island) and a section of the Second Connecticut Battery at City Hall Park, to proceed this evening to the city of Troy, N. Y., and to report upon arrival there to Capt. Charles Hughes, provost-marshal.

*   *   *   *   :

By order of Brigadier-General Canby:

C. T. CHRISTENSEN,
Assistant Adjutant-General.

YORKTOWN, VA.,
August 31, 1863.

General NAGLEE,
Norfolk, Va.:

The cavalry will arrive here from Williamsburg this afternoon and start to-morrow. There seems a considerable force about Gloucester Court-House, but cannot get particulars. Have you any further instructions? Shall I send the cavalry direct, or land them at Dudley's Ferry and take enemy in rear? It is three hours from here by steamboat. I have 900 effective for the expedition.

I. J. WISTAR,
Brigadier-General.

CIRCULAR.]   HEADQUARTERS ARMY OF THE POTOMAC,
August 31, 1863—10.30 a. m.

The general commanding desires me to advise you that a movement will be made to-day on our left flank, which may result in some corresponding movement of the enemy and eventually involve other portions of the army. He therefore desires you to enjoin particular vigilance on all pickets and outposts, and that you hold your command in readiness for orders at short notice, as has been hitherto required of you.

A. A. HUMPHREYS,
Major-General, Chief of Staff.

(To commanders of the First, Third, Fifth, Sixth, Eleventh, and Twelfth Army Corps, and the Chief of Artillery.)

SPECIAL ORDERS, }   HDQRS. ARMY OF THE POTOMAC,
No. 234.   }   *August* 31, 1863.

*   *   *   *   *

8. The chief of artillery is authorized to exercise the power of a corps commander with respect to leaves of absence to officers on surgeon's certificates, discharges of soldiers on surgeon's certificate of disability, and transfer to the Invalid Corps under the general orders of the War Department governing that subject.

*   *   *   *   *

By command of Major-General Meade:

S. WILLIAMS,
Assistant Adjutant-General,

HARTWOOD,
August 31, 1863.

Col. C. ROSS SMITH,
    Chief of Staff:

The enemy's scouting parties came up the river, on this side, to within 4 miles of Falmouth last evening. They fell back during the night. All quiet this morning.

J. KILPATRICK,
Brigadier-General.

GENERAL ORDERS, } HDQRS. MIDDLE DEPT., 8TH ARMY CORPS,
    No. 44.   }   *Baltimore, Md., August* 31, 1863.

Having returned from my temporary absence, I hereby resume command of the Middle Department, Eighth Army Corps.

ROBT. C. SCHENCK,
Major-General, U. S. Volunteers.

NORFOLK,
August 31, 1863—2.45 p. m.

General WISTAR,
    Yorktown:

You advised me there was none of the enemy on the Peninsula to prevent a movement in the direction toward Urbanna. Now you advise me there is considerable force at Gloucester. My advice comes through you in relation to the above. Onderdonk can go in no other way than to cross directly to Gloucester; to go by Dudley's Ferry, he could not be crossed alone in a week. If there is a large force in Gloucester, we can do nothing in Matthews County, for we could not send Onderdonk there without holding Gloucester with a strong force of infantry and artillery until he could return. We have not the disposable force.

NAGLEE,
Brigadier-General.

YORKTOWN, VA.,
August 31, 1863.

General NAGLEE,
    Norfolk, Va.:

My intelligence is contradictory, of course. I send you the best I can get, changing from time to time. It is certain some force of rebel cavalry left Urbanna Friday night, and that a force, probably the same, crossed at West Point Saturday morning, going toward Richmond. Cannot hear any news of Emerson Miller's three companies excepting they sent off a number of conscripts. Onderdonk will go direct to Matthews Court-House to-morrow at daylight, unless forbidden. The gunboat will co-operate. I have a guide in view. I think he is about three days too late.

I. J. WISTAR,
Brigadier-General.

YORKTOWN,
August 31, 1863.

General NAGLEE,
          Norfolk:

Colonel Onderdonk reports following information derived from contrabands :

Wise is 2 miles below Bottom's Bridge, with 4,000 infantry, 900 cavalry, and 8 guns.
I send the information for what it is worth.

Expedition starts to-morrow from Gloucester.   Our loss was all in Fifth Pennsylvania Cavalry.

                              I. J. WISTAR,
                                   Brigadier-General.

NORFOLK, VA.,
August 31, 1863.

General WISTAR,
          Yorktown:

Colonel Onderdonk will not be permitted to go to Matthews Court-House unless you know there can be no force of the enemy to intercept his return.

If you have reason to believe the cavalry and conscripts can be intercepted east of Gloucester Court-House, you must send with him one or two infantry regiments, with one or two sections of artillery, to remain at Gloucester for his return.

                         HENRY M. NAGLEE,
                              Brigadier-General, Commanding.

YORKTOWN, VA.,
August 31, 1863—7.15 p. m.

General NAGLEE,
          Norfolk, Va.:

I cannot spare of my effective strength more than 300 infantry to go to Gloucester Court-House.   If that will not answer, I must give up the expedition.   Please answer immediately, as Onderdonk is crossing now.

                              I. J. WISTAR,
                                   Brigadier-General.

NORFOLK, VA.,
August 31, 1863.

General WISTAR,
          Yorktown:

If there is any confirmation of the advance of General Wise, you will send Onderdonk to check and observe his advance.

                              NAGLEE,
                                   Brigadier-General.

Abstract from return of the Army of the Potomac, Maj. Gen. George G. Meade, U. S. Army, commanding, for the month of August, 1863.

Command.	Present for duty.		Aggregate present.	Aggregate present and absent.	Pieces of artillery.	
	Officers.	Men.			Heavy.	Field.
General headquarters *a*	133	1,324	1,672	2,177	......	......
Engineer troops	44	1,172	1,494	1,790	......	......
Artillery Reserve	106	2,622	2,984	3,627	14	74
First Army Corps	506	7,854	9,985	18,323	......	24
Second Army Corps	427	7,171	8,554	20,247	......	26
Third Army Corps	595	10,578	13,198	22,289	......	42
Fifth Army Corps *b*	496	7,724	9,461	14,976	......	28
Sixth Army Corps	686	10,955	13,156	21,759	......	42
Eleventh Army Corps *c*	282	4,863	6,509	11,986	......	25
Twelfth Army Corps	306	6,125	7,132	14,812	......	20
Cavalry Corps	616	11,634	14,905	24,984	......	62
Total	4,197	72,022	89,050	156,920	14	343

a Including camp guards, orderlies, provost guards, and signal corps.
b The First and Second Brigades, Second Division, on detached service in New York Harbor.
c The First Division (Gordon's) transferred to Charleston Harbor.

—

Organization of the Army of the Potomac, Maj. Gen. George G. Meade, U. S. Army, commanding, August 31, 1863.

GENERAL HEADQUARTERS.

PROVOST GUARD.

Brig. Gen. MARSENA R. PATRICK.

80th New York, Col. Theodore B. Gates.
93d New York, Lieut. Col. Benjamin C. Butler.
2d Pennsylvania Cavalry, Lieut. Col. Joseph P. Brinton.
6th Pennsylvania Cavalry (two companies), Capt. James Starr.
Cavalry detachments.*

GUARDS AND ORDERLIES.

Oneida (New York) Cavalry, Capt. Daniel P. Mann.

SIGNAL CORPS.

Capt. LEMUEL B. NORTON.

ORDNANCE DETACHMENT.

Lieut. MORRIS SCHAFF.

ENGINEER BRIGADE.

15th New York, Companies A, B, and C, Maj. Walter L. Cassin.
50th New York, Col. William H. Pettes.
U. S. Battalion,† Capt. George H. Mendell.

*From 1st Maine, and 1st, 2d, 5th, and 6th regular regiments.
† Detached from brigade and reporting direct to army headquarters.

FIRST ARMY CORPS.

Maj. Gen. JOHN NEWTON.

HEADQUARTERS.

Cavalry detachments,* Capt. Robert A. Robinson.

FIRST DIVISION.

Brig. Gen. JAMES C. RICE.†

First Brigade.

Col. WILLIAM W. ROBINSON.

19th Indiana, Col. Samuel J. Williams.
24th Michigan, Col. Henry A. Morrow.
1st New York Sharpshooters (battalion), Capt. Joseph S. Arnold.
2d Wisconsin, Capt. George H. Otis.
6th Wisconsin, Col. Edward S. Bragg.
7th Wisconsin, Maj. Mark Finnicum.

Second Brigade.

Col. GEORGE H. BIDDLE.

7th Indiana, Col. Ira G. Grover.
76th New York, Maj. John E. Cook.
84th New York, Maj. Henry T. Head.
95th New York, Maj. Edward Pye.
147th New York, Maj. George Harney.
56th Pennsylvania, Maj. John T. Jack.

SECOND DIVISION.

Brig. Gen. JOHN C. ROBINSON.

First Brigade.

Col. THOMAS F. McCOY.

16th Maine, Lieut. Col. Augustus B. Farnham.
13th Massachusetts, Lieut. Col. N. Walter Batchelder.
39th Massachusetts, Col. Phineas S. Davis.
94th New York, Maj. Samuel A. Moffett.
104th New York, Col. Gilbert G. Prey.
107th Pennsylvania, Capt. Emanuel D. Roath.

Second Brigade.

Brig. Gen. HENRY BAXTER.

12th Massachusetts, Capt. Charles W. Hastings.
83d New York, Capt. Henry V. Williamson.
97th New York, Capt. Rouse S. Eggleston.
11th Pennsylvania, Col. Richard Coulter.
88th Pennsylvania, Capt. Edmund Y. Patterson.
90th Pennsylvania, Lieut. Col. William A. Leech.

THIRD DIVISION.

Brig. Gen. JOHN R. KENLY.

First Brigade.

Col. CHAPMAN BIDDLE.

121st Pennsylvania, Lieut. Thomas M. Hall.
142d Pennsylvania, Lieut. Col. Alfred B. McCalmont.

Second Brigade.

Col. LANGHORNE WISTER.

143d Pennsylvania, Col. Edmund L. Dana.
149th Pennsylvania, Capt. John Irvin.
150th Pennsylvania, Maj. Thomas Chamberlain.

Third Brigade.

Col. NATHAN T. DUSHANE.

1st Maryland, Lieut. Col. John W. Wilson.
4th Maryland, Col. Richard N. Bowerman.
7th Maryland, Col. Edwin H. Webster.
8th Maryland, Col. Andrew W. Denison.

---

* From 4th and 16th Pennsylvania regiments.
† Assumed command August 23, *vice* Brig. Gen. Henry S. Briggs, who had relieved Brig. Gen. Lysander Cutler August 5.

ARTILLERY.

Col. CHARLES S. WAINWRIGHT.

Maine Light, 2d Battery (B), Lieut. Albert F. Thomas.
Maine Light, 5th Battery (E), Capt. Greenleaf T. Stevens.
1st New York Light, Battery L, Lieut. George Breck.
1st Pennsylvania Light, Battery B, Capt. James H. Cooper.
4th United States, Battery B, Lieut. James Stewart.

SECOND ARMY CORPS.

Maj. Gen. GOUVERNEUR K. WARREN.*

FIRST DIVISION.

Brig. Gen. JOHN C. CALDWELL.

Headquarters.

2d Company Minnesota Sharpshooters, Lieut. Mahlon Black.

First Brigade.	*Third Brigade.*
Col. NELSON A. MILES.	Col. PAUL FRANK.
61st New York, Lieut. Col. K. Oscar Broady.	52d New York, Capt. William Scherrer.
81st Pennsylvania, Col. H. Boyd McKeen.	57th New York. Lieut. Col. Alford B. Chapman.
148th Pennsylvania, Col. James A. Beaver.	66th New York, Lieut. Col. John S. Hammell.
	140th Pennsylvania, Col. John Fraser.
Second Brigade.	*Fourth Brigade.*
Col. PATRICK KELLY.	Col. JOHN R. BROOKE.
28th Massachusetts, Capt. Edmund H. Fitzpatrick.	2d Delaware, Lieut. Col. David L. Stricker.
63d New York (two companies), Capt. Thomas Touhy.	64th New York, Maj. Leman W. Bradley.
69th New York (two companies), Capt. Richard Moroney.	53d Pennsylvania, Lieut. Col. Richards McMichael.
88th New York (two companies), Capt. Denis F. Burke.	145th Pennsylvania (seven companies), Maj. John W. Reynolds.
116th Pennsylvania (four companies), Capt. Seneca G. Willauer.	

SECOND DIVISION.

Brig. Gen. ALEXANDER S. WEBB.†

First Brigade.	*Second Brigade.*
Col. DE WITT C. BAXTER.	Lieut. Col. WILLIAM L. CURRY.
19th Maine. Lieut. Col. Henry W. Cunningham.	69th Pennsylvania, Capt. Thomas Kelly.
15th Massachusetts, Capt. Lyman H. Ellingwood.	71st Pennsylvania, Lieut. Col. Charles Kochersperger.
1st Minnesota, Capt. Henry C. Coates.	72d Pennsylvania, Maj. Samuel Roberts.
82d New York, Capt. Thomas Cummings.	106th Pennsylvania, Capt. John R. Breitenback.

* Assumed command August 16, relieving Brig. Gen. William Hays.
† Relieved Brig. Gen. William Harrow August 15.

Third Brigade.

Lieut. Col. Ansel D. Wass.

19th Massachusetts, Capt. Jonathan F. Plympton.
20th Massachusetts, Capt. Henry L. Abbott.
7th Michigan,* Maj. Sylvanus W. Curtis.
42d New York, Capt. Edward C. Cauret.
59th New York, Capt. Horace P. Rugg.
1st Company Massachusetts Sharpshooters, Lieut. Oscar H. Clement.

THIRD DIVISION.

Brig. Gen. Alexander Hays.

First Brigade.	Second Brigade.
Col. Joseph Snider.	Col. Thomas H. Davis.
14th Indiana,* Lieut. Col. Elijah H. C. Cavins.	14th Connecticut, Maj. Theodore G. Ellis.
4th Ohio,* Lieut. Col. Gordon A. Stewart.	1st Delaware, Lieut. Col. Edward P. Harris.
8th Ohio,* Maj. Albert H. Winslow.	12th New Jersey, Col. J. Howard Willets.
7th West Virginia, Lieut. Col. Jonathan H. Lockwood.	10th New York (battalion), Maj. George F. Hopper.
	108th New York, Col. Charles J. Powers.

Third Brigade.

Brig. Gen. Joshua T. Owen.

39th New York (four companies), Maj. Daniel Woodall.
111th New York, Col. Clinton D. MacDougall.
125th New York, Col. Levin Crandell.
126th New York, Lieut. Col. James M. Bull.

ARTILLERY.

Capt. John G. Hazard.

1st New York Light, Battery G, Capt. Nelson Ames.
1st Pennsylvania Light, Batteries F and G, Capt. R. Bruce Ricketts.
1st Rhode Island Light, Battery A, Capt. William A. Arnold.
1st Rhode Island Light, Battery B, Lieut. Walter S. Perrin.
1st United States, Battery I, Lieut. Frank S. French.

THIRD ARMY CORPS.

Maj. Gen. William H. French.

FIRST DIVISION.

Maj. Gen. David B. Birney.

First Brigade.	Second Brigade.
Col. Charles H. T. Collis.	Lieut. Col. Lorenzo D. Carver.
57th Pennsylvania, Col. Peter Sides.	20th Indiana,* Col. William C. L. Taylor.
63d Pennsylvania, Maj. John A. Danks.	3d Maine, Lieut. Col. Edwin Burt.
68th Pennsylvania, Col. Andrew H. Tippin.	4th Maine, Capt. Robert H. Gray.
105th Pennsylvania, Col. Calvin A. Craig.	86th New York, Lieut. Col. Benjamin L. Higgins.
114th Pennsylvania, Capt. Henry M. Eddy.	124th New York, Lieut. Col. Francis M. Cummins.
141st Pennsylvania, Capt. Edwin A. Spaulding.	1st U. S. Sharpshooters, Maj. George G. Hastings.
	2d U. S. Sharpshooters, Lieut. Col. Homer R. Stoughton.

* On duty in New York.

Third Brigade.

Col. P. REGIS DE TROBRIAND.

17th Maine, Lieut. Col. Charles B. Merrill.
3d Michigan,* Col. Byron R. Pierce.
5th Michigan,† Col. John Pulford.
40th New York, Col. Thomas W. Egan.
99th Pennsylvania, Lieut. Col. Edwin R. Biles.
110th Pennsylvania, Maj. Isaac Rogers.

SECOND DIVISION.

Brig. Gen. HENRY PRINCE.

First Brigade.	*Second Brigade.*
Brig. Gen. JOSEPH B. CARR.	Col. WILLIAM R. BREWSTER.
1st Massachusetts,* Col. Napoleon B. McLaughlen.	70th New York, Capt. William H. Hugo.
11th Massachusetts, Lieut. Col. Porter D. Tripp.	71st New York, Maj. Thomas Rafferty.
16th Massachusetts, Lieut. Col. Waldo Merriam.	72d New York, Col. John S. Austin.
	73d New York, Capt. George Le Fort.
11th New Jersey, Lieut. Col. John Schoonover.	74th New York, Maj. Henry M. Alles.
26th Pennsylvania, Maj. Robert L. Bodine.	120th New York, Capt. Abram L. Lockwood.
84th Pennsylvania, Lieut. Col. Milton Opp.	

Third Brigade.

Brig. Gen. GERSHOM MOTT.

5th New Jersey, Maj. Ashbel W. Angel.
6th New Jersey, Col. George C. Burling.
7th New Jersey, Maj. Frederick Cooper.
8th New Jersey, Col. John Ramsey.
115th Pennsylvania, Lieut. James McIntyre.

THIRD DIVISION.

Brig. Gen. WASHINGTON L. ELLIOTT.

Headquarters.

1st Maryland Cavalry (detachment).

First Brigade.	*Second Brigade.*
Brig. Gen. WILLIAM H. MORRIS.	Col. JOHN W. HORN.
14th New Jersey, Maj. Peter Vredenburgh, jr.	6th Maryland, Maj. Joseph C. Hill.
151st New York, Lieut. Col. Erwin A. Bowen.	110th Ohio,* Col. J. Warren Keifer.
	122d Ohio,* Col. William H. Ball.
10th Vermont, Lieut. Col. William W. Henry.	138th Pennsylvania, Col. Matthew R. McClennan.

Third Brigade.

Col. JOHN W. SCHALL.

106th New York, Lieut. Col. Charles Townsend.
126th Ohio,* Lieut. Col. William H. Harlan.
67th Pennsylvania (two companies), Lieut. Col. Horace B. Burnham.
87th Pennsylvania (four companies), Lieut. Col. James A. Stahle.

---

* On duty in New York.
† On duty at Troy, N. Y.

ARTILLERY.

Capt. GEORGE E. RANDOLPH.

Maine Light, 4th Battery (D), Capt. O'Neil W. Robinson, jr.
Massachusetts Light, 10th Battery, Capt. J. Henry Sleeper.
1st New Jersey Light, Battery B, Capt. A. Judson Clark.
1st New York Light, Battery D, Capt. George B. Winslow.
New York Light, 12th Battery, Capt. George F. McKnight.
1st Rhode Island Light, Battery E, Lieut. John K. Bucklyn.
4th United States, Battery K, Lieut. Francis W. Seeley.

FIFTH ARMY CORPS.

Maj. Gen. GEORGE SYKES.

HEADQUARTERS.

12th New York, Companies D and E, Capt. Henry W. Rider.

FIRST DIVISION.

Brig. Gen. CHARLES GRIFFIN.

First Brigade.

Brig. Gen. JAMES BARNES.

18th Massachusetts, Col. Joseph Hayes.
22d Massachusetts, Lieut. Col. Thomas Sherwin, jr.
1st Michigan, Lieut. Col. William A. Throop.
118th Pennsylvania, Maj. Charles P. Herring.

Second Brigade.

Col. JACOB B. SWEITZER.

9th Massachusetts, Col. Patrick R. Guiney.
32d Massachusetts, Capt. James A. Cunningham.
4th Michigan, Lieut. Col. George W. Lumbard.
62d Pennsylvania, Lieut. Col. James C. Hull.

Third Brigade.

Col. JOSHUA L. CHAMBERLAIN.

20th Maine, Lieut. Col. Charles D. Gilmore.
16th Michigan, Maj. Robert T. Elliott.
44th New York, Lieut. Col. Freeman Conner.
83d Pennsylvania, Maj. William H. Lamont.

SECOND DIVISION.

Brig. Gen. ROMEYN B. AYRES.

*First Brigade.**

Maj. GIDEON R. GIDDINGS.

3d United States (six companies), Capt. Andrew Sheridan.
4th United States (four companies), Maj. Frederick T. Dent.
6th United States (five companies), Capt. Montgomery Bryant.
12th United States (eight companies), Maj. Luther B. Bruen.
14th United States (eight companies), Capt. Jonathan B. Hager.

*Second Brigade.**

Col. SIDNEY BURBANK.

2d United States (six companies), Capt. Samuel A. McKee.
7th United States (four companies), Capt. Peter W. L. Plympton.
10th United States (two companies), Capt. William Clinton.
11th United States (six companies), Maj. Jonathan W. Gordon.
17th United States (seven companies), Capt. Walter B. Pease.

* On duty in New York, under command of Brigadier-General Ayres.

Third Brigade.

Brig. Gen. KENNER GARRARD.

140th New York, Col. George Ryan.
146th New York, Col. David T. Jenkins.
91st Pennsylvania, Lieut. Col. Joseph H. Sinex.
155th Pennsylvania, Capt. John Ewing.

THIRD DIVISION.*

Brig. Gen. SAMUEL W. CRAWFORD.

First Brigade.	*Third Brigade.*
Col. WILLIAM McCANDLESS.	Col. JOSEPH W. FISHER.
1st Pennsylvania Reserves, Col. William C. Talley.	5th Pennsylvania Reserves, Lieut. Col. George Dare.
2d Pennsylvania Reserves, Lieut. Col. George A. Woodward.	9th Pennsylvania Reserves, Lieut. Col. James McK. Snodgrass.
6th Pennsylvania Reserves, Col. Wellington H. Ent.	10th Pennsylvania Reserves, Lieut. Col. James B. Knox.
13th Pennsylvania Reserves, Maj. William R. Hartshorne.	11th Pennsylvania Reserves, Col. Samuel M. Jackson.
	12th Pennsylvania Reserves, Lieut. Col. Richard Gustin.

ARTILLERY.

Capt. AUGUSTUS P. MARTIN.

Massachusetts Light, 3d Battery (C), Lieut. Aaron F. Walcott.
Massachusetts Light, 5th Battery (E), Capt. Charles A. Phillips.
1st New York Light, Battery C, Lieut. Ela H. Clark.
1st Ohio Light, Battery L, Capt. Frank C. Gibbs.
5th United States, Battery D, Lieut. Benjamin F. Rittenhouse.

SIXTH ARMY CORPS.

Maj. Gen. JOHN SEDGWICK.

HEADQUARTERS.

1st Vermont Cavalry (detachment), Capt. Andrew J. Grover.

FIRST DIVISION.

Brig. Gen. HORATIO G. WRIGHT.

First Brigade.	*Second Brigade.*
Brig. Gen. ALFRED T. A. TORBERT.	Brig. Gen. JOSEPH J. BARTLETT.
1st New Jersey, Lieut. Col. William Henry, jr.	5th Maine, Col. Clark S. Edwards.
2d New Jersey, Col. Samuel L. Buck.	121st New York, Lieut. Col. Egbert Olcott.
3d New Jersey, Col. Henry W. Brown.	95th Pennsylvania, Lieut. Col. Edward Carroll.
4th New Jersey, Lieut. Col. Charles Ewing.	96th Pennsylvania, Lieut. Col. William H. Lessig.
15th New Jersey, Col. William H. Penrose.	

* The Second Brigade in Department of Washington.

Third Brigade.

Brig. Gen. DAVID A. RUSSELL.

6th Maine, Lieut. Col. Benjamin F. Harris.
49th Pennsylvania (four companies), Lieut. Col. Thomas M. Hulings.
119th Pennsylvania, Col. Peter C. Ellmaker.

SECOND DIVISION.

Brig. Gen. ALBION P. HOWE.

*Second Brigade.**	*Third Brigade.*
Col. LEWIS A. GRANT.	Col. DANIEL D. BIDWELL.
2d Vermont, Col. James H. Walbridge.	7th Maine, Col. Edwin C. Mason.
3d Vermont, Col. Thomas O. Seaver.	43d New York, Col. Benjamin F. Baker.
4th Vermont, Lieut. Col. George P. Foster.	49th New York, Capt. Reuben B. Heacock.
5th Vermont, Lieut. Col. John R. Lewis.	77th New York, Lieut. Col. Winsor B. French.
6th Vermont, Col. Elisha L. Barney.	61st Pennsylvania, Lieut. Col. George F. Smith.

THIRD DIVISION.

Brig. Gen. HENRY D. TERRY.†

First Brigade.	*Second Brigade.*
Brig. Gen. ALEXANDER SHALER.	Brig. Gen. HENRY L. EUSTIS.
65th New York, Col. Joseph E. Hamblin.	7th Massachusetts, Maj. Joseph B. Leonard.
67th New York, Lieut. Col. Henry L. Van Ness.	10th Massachusetts, Lieut. Col. Joseph B. Parsons.
122d New York, Lieut. Col. Augustus W. Dwight.	37th Massachusetts, ‡ Lieut. Col. George L. Montague.
23d Pennsylvania, Lieut. Col. John F. Glenn.	2d Rhode Island, Col. Horatio Rogers, jr.
82d Pennsylvania, Lieut. Col. John M. Wetherill.	

Third Brigade.

Brig. Gen. FRANK WHEATON.

62d New York, Col. David J. Nevin.
93d Pennsylvania, Maj. John I. Nevin.
98th Pennsylvania, Col. John F. Ballier.
102d Pennsylvania, Col. John W. Patterson.
139th Pennsylvania, Col. Frederick H. Collier.

ARTILLERY.

Col. CHARLES H. TOMPKINS.

Massachusetts Light, 1st Battery (A), Capt. William H. McCartney.
New York Light, 1st Battery, Capt. Andrew Cowan.
New York Light, 3d Battery, Capt. William A. Harn.
1st Rhode Island Light, Battery C, Capt. Richard Waterman.
1st Rhode Island Light, Battery G, Capt. George W. Adams.
5th United States, Battery F, Lieut. Leonard Martin.
5th United States, Battery M, Capt. James McKnight.

* On duty in New York.
† In command from August 4.
‡ On duty at Fort Hamilton, N. Y.

ELEVENTH ARMY CORPS.*

Maj. Gen. OLIVER O. HOWARD.

HEADQUARTERS.

1st Indiana Cavalry, Companies A and B, Capt. Abram Sharra.
8th New York (independent company), Capt. Hermann Foerster.

SECOND DIVISION.

Brig. Gen. ADOLPH VON STEINWEHR.

First Brigade.†

Col. ADOLPHUS BUSCHBECK.

134th New York, Lieut. Col. Allan H. Jackson.
154th New York, Maj. Lewis D. Warner.
27th Pennsylvania, Lieut. Col. Lorenz Cantador.
73d Pennsylvania, Col. William Moore.

Second Brigade.

. Col. ORLAND SMITH.

33d Massachusetts, Col. Adin B. Underwood.
136th New York, Col. James Wood, jr.
168th New York, Col. William R. Brown.
55th Ohio, Col. Charles B. Gambee.
73d Ohio, Maj. Samuel H. Hurst.

THIRD DIVISION.

Maj. Gen. CARL SCHURZ.

First Brigade.

Col. GEORGE VON AMSBERG.

82d Illinois, Col. Frederick Hecker.
45th New York, Maj. Charles Koch.
143d New York, Col. Horace Boughton.
61st Ohio, Lieut. Col. William H. H. Bown.
82d Ohio, Lieut. Col. David Thomson.

Second Brigade.

Col. WLADIMIR KRZYZANOWSKI.

58th New York, Capt. Michael Esembaux.
68th New York, Col. Gotthilf Bourry.
119th New York, Col. John T. Lockman.
141st New York, Col. William K. Logie.
75th Pennsylvania, Maj. August Ledig.
26th Wisconsin, Col. William H. Jacobs.

ARTILLERY.

Maj. THOMAS W. OSBORN.

1st New York Light, Battery I, Capt. Michael Wiedrich.
New York Light, 13th Battery, Capt. William Wheeler.
1st Ohio Light, Battery I, Capt. Hubert Dilger.
1st Ohio Light, Battery K, Lieut. Columbus Rodamour.
4th United States, Battery G, Lieut. Eugene A. Bancroft.

---

* The First Division transferred to Department of the South.
† The 173d Pennsylvania mustered out,

TWELFTH ARMY CORPS.

Brig. Gen. ALPHEUS S. WILLIAMS.*

HEADQUARTERS.

10th Maine (4 companies), Capt. John D. Beardsley.

FIRST DIVISION.

Brig. Gen. JOSEPH F. KNIPE.

First and Second Brigades.†	*Third Brigade.*
Col. SAMUEL ROSS.	Col. EZRA A. CARMAN.
5th Connecticut, Col. Warren W. Packer.	27th Indiana,‡ Col. Silas Colgrove.
20th Connecticut, Lieut. Col. William B. Wooster.	2d Massachusetts,‡ Col. William Cogswell.
3d Maryland, Col. Joseph M. Sudsburg.	13th New Jersey, Lieut. Col. John Grimes.
123d New York, Col. Archibald L. McDougall.	107th New York, Col. Nirom M. Crane.
145th New York, Col. Edward L. Price.	150th New York, Col. John H. Ketcham.
46th Pennsylvania, Col. James L. Selfridge.	3d Wisconsin,‡ Col. William Hawley.

SECOND DIVISION.

Brig. Gen. JOHN W. GEARY.

First Brigade.	*Second Brigade.*
Lieut. Col. ARIO PARDEE, jr.	Col. GEORGE A. COBHAM, jr.
5th Ohio,§ Col. John H. Patrick.	29th Pennsylvania, Col. William Rickards, jr.
7th Ohio,§ Col. William R. Creighton.	109th Pennsylvania, Capt. Frederick L. Gimber.
29th Ohio,§ Col. William T. Fitch.	111th Pennsylvania, Maj. John A. Boyle.
66th Ohio,§ Lieut. Col. Eugene Powell.	
28th Pennsylvania, Capt. John Flynn.	
147th Pennsylvania, Maj. John Craig.	

Third Brigade.

Brig. Gen. GEORGE S. GREENE.

60th New York, Capt. Jesse H. Jones.
78th New York, Lieut. Col. Herbert von Hammerstein.
102d New York, Col. James C. Lane.
137th New York, Lieut. Col. Koert S. Van Voorhis.
149th New York, Maj. Winslow M. Thomas.

ARTILLERY.

Maj. JOHN A. REYNOLDS.

1st New York Light, Battery M, Lieut. Charles E. Winegar.
Pennsylvania Light, Battery E, Capt. Charles A. Atwell.
4th United States, Battery F, Lieut. Edward D. Muhlenberg.
5th United States, Battery K, Lieut. David H. Kinzie.

---

* In temporary absence of Maj. Gen. Henry W. Slocum.
† Temporarily consolidated.
‡ On duty in New York.
§ On duty in New York, under command of Col. Charles Candy.

CAVALRY CORPS.*

Maj. Gen. ALFRED PLEASONTON.

HEADQUARTERS.

19th New York (1st Dragoons), Col. Alfred Gibbs.
6th United States, Capt. James S. Brisbin.

FIRST DIVISION.

Brig. Gen. JOHN BUFORD.

First Brigade.	*Second Brigade.*
Col. GEORGE H. CHAPMAN.	Col. THOMAS C. DEVIN.
8th Illinois, Maj. John L. Beveridge. 12th Illinois, Capt. George W. Shears. 3d Indiana, Col. George H. Chapman. 8th New York, Maj. William H. Benjamin.	4th New York, Lieut. Col. Augustus Pruyn. 6th New York, Maj. William E. Beardsley. 9th New York, Col. William Sackett. 17th Pennsylvania, Lieut. Col. Coe Durland. 3d West Virginia (two companies), Capt. Seymour B. Conger.

SECOND DIVISION.

Col. J. IRVIN GREGG.†

First Brigade.	*Second Brigade.*
Col. JOHN B. McINTOSH.	Col. PENNOCK HUEY.
1st Maryland, Lieut. Col. James M. Deems. 1st Massachusetts (eight companies), Col. Horace B. Sargent. 1st New Jersey, Col. Percy Wyndham. 6th Ohio, Lieut. Col. William Stedman. 1st Pennsylvania, Col. John P. Taylor. 3d Pennsylvania, Maj. Oliver O. G. Robinson. 1st Rhode Island, Lieut. Col. John L. Thompson.	District of Columbia (independent company), Capt. William H. Orton. 1st Maine, Col. Charles H. Smith. 10th New York, Lieut. Col. William Irvine. 4th Pennsylvania, Lieut. Col. William E. Doster. 8th Pennsylvania, Maj. Joseph W. Wistar. 13th Pennsylvania, Col. James A. Galligher. 16th Pennsylvania, Lieut. Col. John K. Robison.

THIRD DIVISION.

Brig. Gen. JUDSON KILPATRICK.

Headquarters.

1st Ohio, Companies A and C, Capt. Noah Jones.

First Brigade.	*Second Brigade.*
Col. HENRY E. DAVIES, jr.	Brig. Gen. GEORGE A. CUSTER.
2d New York, Maj. Samuel McIrvin. 5th New York, Maj. John Hammond. 18th Pennsylvania, Maj. William B. Darlington. 1st West Virginia, Col. Nathaniel P. Richmond.	1st Michigan, Col. Charles H. Town. 5th Michigan, Maj. Crawley P. Dake. 6th Michigan, Col. George Gray. 7th Michigan, Col. William D. Mann. 1st Vermont, Col. Edward B. Sawyer.

* See also Horse Artillery.
† Commanding in temporary absence of Brig. Gen. David McM. Gregg.

ARTILLERY.*

Brig. Gen. HENRY J. HUNT.

HORSE ARTILLERY.†

First Brigade.

Capt. JAMES M. ROBERTSON.

New York Light, 6th Battery, Capt. J. W. Martin.
2d United States, Batteries B and L, Lieut. Edward Heaton.
2d United States, Battery D, Lieut. Edward B. Williston.
2d United States, Battery M, Lieut. Alexander C. M. Pennington, jr.
1th United States, Battery A, Lieut. Rufus King, jr.
4th United States, Battery E, Lieut. Samuel S. Elder.

Second Brigade.

Capt. WILLIAM M. GRAHAM.

Michigan Light, 9th Battery, Capt. Jabez J. Daniel.
1st United States, Batteries E and G, Capt. Alanson M. Randol.
1st United States, Battery K, Lieut. Jacob H. Counselman.
2d United States, Battery A, Lieut. Robert Clarke.
2d United States, Battery G, Lieut. John H. Butler.
3d United States, Battery C, Lieut. William D. Fuller.

ARTILLERY RESERVE.

Brig. Gen. ROBERT O. TYLER.

First Regular Brigade.

Lieut. JOHN G. TURNBULL.

1st United States, Battery H, Lieut. Philip D. Mason.
3d United States, Batteries F and K, Lieut. John G. Turnbull.
4th United States, Battery C, Lieut. Charles L. Fitzhugh.

First Volunteer Brigade.

Lieut. Col. FREEMAN McGILVERY.

Maine Light, 6th Battery (F), Lieut. Edwin B. Dow.
Massachusetts Light, 9th Battery, Capt. John Bigelow.
New York Light, 4th Battery, Capt. James E. Smith.
Pennsylvania Light, Batteries C and F, Capt. James Thompson.

Second Volunteer Brigade.

Capt. ELIJAH D. TAFT.

1st Connecticut Heavy, Company B, Capt. Albert F. Brooker.
1st Connecticut Heavy, Company M, Capt. Franklin A. Pratt.
1st New York Light, Battery B, Lieut. Robert E. Rogers.
New York Light, 5th Battery, Capt. Elijah D. Taft.

Third Volunteer Brigade.

Capt. ROBERT H. FITZHUGH.

Maryland Light, Battery A, Lieut. Thomas Binyon.
New Hampshire Light, 1st Battery, Capt. Frederick M. Edgell.
1st New York Light, Battery K. } Capt. Robert H. Fitzhugh.
New York Light, 11th Battery. }

Fourth Volunteer Brigade.

Capt. JAMES F. HUNTINGTON.

1st New Jersey Light. Battery A. Capt. William Hexamer.
New York Light, 15th Battery, Capt. Patrick Hart.
1st Ohio Light, Battery H, Capt. James F. Huntington.
West Virginia Light, Battery C, Capt. Wallace Hill.

Not Brigaded.

6th New York Heavy Artillery, Col. J. Howard Kitching.

---

* See also the artillery attached to the several corps.
† The Second Brigade was ordered August 29 to relieve the First Brigade serving with Cavalry Corps, the latter to report to General Hunt.

Armament of the artillery in the Army of the Potomac August 31, 1863.

[From monthly report of artillery.]

Battery.	Assignment.	Guns.					
		4.5-inch rifled.	20-pounder Parrott.	3-inch rifled.	10-pounder Parrott.	Light 12-pounder smooth-bore.	Total.
1st Connecticut Artillery:							
Battery B	Artillery Reserve	4					4
Battery M	do	4					4
2d Maine Battery	First Army Corps			4			4
4th Maine Battery	Third Army Corps			6			6
5th Maine Battery	First Army Corps					4	4
6th Maine Battery	Artillery Reserve					4	4
Maryland Artillery, Battery A	do			4			4
Massachusetts Artillery:							
Battery A	Sixth Army Corps					6	6
Battery C	Fifth Army Corps					6	6
Battery E	do			6			6
9th Massachusetts Battery	Second Brigade, Horse Artillery.					4	4
10th Massachusetts Battery	Third Army Corps			6			6
9th Michigan Battery	Artillery Reserve			6			6
1st New Hampshire Battery	do			6			6
1st New Jersey Artillery:							
Battery A	do				5		5
Battery B	Third Army Corps				6		6
1st New York Artillery:							
Battery B	Artillery Reserve				4		4
Battery C	Fifth Army Corps			4			4
Battery D	Third Army Corps					6	6
Battery G	Second Army Corps					6	6
Battery K*	Artillery Reserve			6			6
Battery I	Eleventh Army Corps			5			5
Battery L	First Army Corps			6			6
Battery M	Twelfth Army Corps				4		4
1st New York Battery	Sixth Army Corps			6			6
3d New York Battery	do				6		6
4th New York Battery	Artillery Reserve					6	6
5th New York Battery	do	6					6
6th New York Battery	First Brigade, Horse Artillery.			6			6
12th New York Battery	Third Army Corps			6			6
13th New York Battery	Eleventh Army Corps			4			4
15th New York Battery	Artillery Reserve					4	4
1st Ohio Artillery:							
Battery H	Artillery Reserve			6			6
Battery I	Eleventh Army Corps					6	6
Battery K	do					4	4
Battery L	Fifth Army Corps					6	6
1st Pennsylvania Artillery:							
Battery B	First Army Corps			4			4
Batteries F and G	Second Army Corps			6			6
Pennsylvania, Batteries C and F	Artillery Reserve			5			5
Pennsylvania, Battery E	Twelfth Army Corps				6		6
1st Rhode Island Artillery:							
Battery A	Second Army Corps			6			6
Battery B	do					4	4
Battery C	Sixth Army Corps				6		6
Battery E	Third Army Corps					6	6
Battery G	Sixth Army Corps			6			6
1st U. S. Artillery:							
Batteries E and G	Second Brigade, Horse Artillery.			4			4
Battery H	Artillery Reserve					6	6
Battery I	Second Army Corps					4	4
Battery K	Second Brigade, Horse Artillery.			6			6
2d U. S. Artillery:							
Battery A	do			6			6
Batteries B and L	First Brigade, Horse Artillery.			6			6
Battery D	do					4	4
Battery G	Second Brigade, Horse Artillery.					4	4
Battery M	First Brigade, Horse Artillery.			6			6

* The 11th New York Battery attached.

Armament of the artillery in the Army of the Potomac, &c.—Continued.

Battery.	Assignment.	4.5-inch rifled.	20-pounder Parrott.	3-inch rifled.	10-pounder Parrott.	Light 12-pounder smooth-bore.	Total.
3d U. S. Artillery:							
Battery C	Second Brigade, Horse Artillery.			6			6
Batteries F and K	Artillery Reserve.......					4	4
4th U. S. Artillery:							
Battery A	First Brigade, Horse Artillery.					4	4
Battery B	First Army Corps					6	6
Battery C	Artillery Reserve.......					4	4
Battery E	First Brigade, Horse Artillery.				4		4
Battery F	Twelfth Army Corps ..					6	6
Battery G	Eleventh Army Corps..					6	6
Battery K	Third Army Corps......					6	6
5th U. S. Artillery:							
Battery C*.....							
Battery D	Fifth Army Corps......					4	4
Battery F	Sixth Army Corps......				6		6
Battery K	Twelfth Army Corps...				6		6
Battery M	Sixth Army Corps......					6	6
1st West Virginia Artillery, Battery C.	Artillery Reserve.......				4		4
Total	....	8	6	152	53	136	355

* On detached service in New York City.

Abstract from return of the Department of Washington, Maj. Gen. Samuel P. Heintzelman, U. S. Army, commanding, for the month of August, 1863.

Command.	Present for duty.		Aggregate present.	Aggregate present and absent.	Pieces of artillery.	
	Officers.	Men.			Heavy.	Field.
General headquarters....................................	26	115	157	178	......	......
Artillery Camp of Instruction	27	705	840	1,089	......	38
Railway guards...	25	732	937	966	......	......
Provisional brigades	14	475	529	562	......	......
District of Washington................................	114	2,288	3,513	4,222	......	......
Defenses North of the Potomac	179	4,750	6,395	7,605	81	40
Defenses South of the Potomac*	213	4,560	6,080	7,410	317	115
District of Alexandria	63	1,007	1,330	2,633	......	6
Camp Convalescent, &c	94	3,136	6,668	6,970	......	......
King's division..	424	2,197	2,681	3,852	......	6
Cavalry forces..	32	514	978	1,537	......	......
Fort Washington, Md..	6	110	146	149	70	3
Total..	917	20,589	30,254	36,673	468	208

* Report of pieces of artillery is incomplete.

Troops in the Department of Washington, Maj. Gen. Samuel P. Heintzelman, U. S. Army, commanding, August 31, 1863.

HEADQUARTERS.

111th New York, Companies B and C, Capt. Robert C. Perry.

LIGHT ARTILLERY CAMP OF INSTRUCTION.*

Lieut. Col. J. ALBERT MONROE.

Michigan Light, 10th Battery, Capt. John C. Schuetz.
1st New York Light, Battery F, Capt. William R. Wilson.
1st New York Light, Battery H, Capt. Charles E. Mink.
New York Light, 19th Battery, Lieut. Edward W. Rogers.
Ohio Light, 12th Battery, Capt. Aaron C. Johnson.

1st Pennsylvania Light, Battery H, Capt. Andrew Fagan.
5th United States, Batteries I and L, Lieut. Edmund D. Spooner.
1st West Virginia Light, Battery A, Lieut. George Furst.
1st West Virginia Light, Battery. F. Lieut. James C. Means.

RAILWAY GUARD.

109th New York, Col. Benjamin F. Tracy.

PROVISIONAL BRIGADES.

Maj. Gen. SILAS CASEY.

13th New York Cavalry, Company H, Capt. James P. Batterson.
2d U. S. Colored Troops (six companies), Lieut. Col. Stark Fellows.

DISTRICT OF WASHINGTON.

Brig. Gen. JOHN H. MARTINDALE, Military Governor.

2d District of Columbia, Col. Charles M. Alexander.
14th New Hampshire, Col. Robert Wilson.
153d New York, Col. Edwin P. Davis.
178th New York (battalion), Lieut. Col. Charles F. Smith.
27th Pennsylvania, Company F, Capt. John M. Carson.

150th Pennsylvania, Company K, Capt. Thomas Getchell.
157th Pennsylvania (battalion), Maj. Thomas H. Addicks.
11th New York Cavalry, Col. James B. Swain.
U. S. Ordnance Detachment, Lieut. Col. George D. Ramsay.

DEFENSES NORTH OF THE POTOMAC.†

Lieut. Col. JOSEPH A. HASKIN, Aide-de-Camp, in charge.

First Brigade.	*Second Brigade.*
Col. AUGUSTUS A. GIBSON.	Col. LEWIS O. MORRIS.
2d Pennsylvania Heavy Artillery, Col. Augustus A. Gibson. 1st Vermont Heavy Artillery, Col. James M. Warner.	1st Maine Heavy Artillery, Col. Daniel Chaplin. 7th New York Heavy Artillery, Col. Lewis O. Morris. 9th New York Heavy Artillery, Col. Joseph Welling. 9th New York Battery, Capt. Emil Schubert.

---

* Brig. Gen. William F. Barry, chief of artillery, Department of Washington.
† Troops at Advance Battery, Forts Bunker Hill, Reno, Simmons, Slocum, and Sumner, and in Washington City

Third Brigade.

10th New York Heavy Artillery, Col. Alexander Piper.

DEFENSES SOUTH OF THE POTOMAC.*

Brig. Gen. GUSTAVUS A. DE RUSSY.

First Brigade.

Col. JOSEPH N. G. WHISTLER.

1st Massachusetts Heavy Artillery, Lieut. Col. Levi P. Wright.
2d New York Heavy Artillery, Maj. William A. McKay.
5th New York Heavy Artillery (3d Battalion), Maj. Gustavus F. Merriam.

Second Brigade.

Col. LEVERETTE W. WESSELLS.

2d Connecticut Heavy Artillery, Lieut. Col. Elisha S. Kellogg.
15th New York Heavy Artillery, Capt. Leander Schamberger.

Third Brigade.

Col. HENRY L. ABBOT.

1st Connecticut Heavy Artillery, Col. Henry L. Abbot.
1st Rhode Island Light Artillery, Battery H, Lieut. Charles F. Mason.
Wisconsin Heavy Artillery Company, Capt. Charles C. Meservey.

Fourth Brigade.

Lieut. Col. THOMAS ALLCOCK.

2d Massachusetts Cavalry, Companies B, C, D, and K, Capt. George F. Holman.
4th New York Heavy Artillery (eight companies), Lieut. Col. Thomas Allcock.

DISTRICT OF ALEXANDRIA.

Brig. Gen. JOHN P. SLOUGH.

1st District of Columbia (four companies), Lieut. Col. Lemuel Towers.
3d Pennsylvania Reserves,† Maj. William Briner.
4th Pennsylvania Reserves,† Col. Richard H. Woolworth.
7th Pennsylvania Reserves,† Col. Henry C. Bolinger.
8th Pennsylvania Reserves,† Col. Silas M. Baily.
Pennsylvania Light Artillery, Battery H, Capt. William Borrowe.

CONVALESCENT AND DISTRIBUTION CAMPS.

Lieut. Col. SAMUEL McKELVEY.

Camp Convalescent, Lieut. Col. Samuel McKelvey.
Camp Distribution, Capt. John S. Davis.
Camp Paroled Prisoners, Lieut. Col. Guy H. Watkins.

KING'S DIVISION.

Brig. Gen. RUFUS KING.

The Irish Legion.

Brig. Gen. MICHAEL CORCORAN.

155th New York, Col. William McEvily.
164th New York, Col. Jas. P. McMahon.
170th New York, Col. James P. McIvor.
182d New York,‡ Col. Mathew Murphy.

Not Brigaded.

4th Delaware, Col. Arthur H. Grimshaw.
6th New York Cavalry (two companies), Maj. William P. Hall.
17th New York Battery, Capt. George T. Anthony.

---

* Troops at Battery Gareshé, Forts Albany, Barnard, Bennett, Berry, Blenker, Cass, C. F. Smith, Corcoran, Craig, De Kalb, Ellsworth, Ethan Allen, Haggerty, Lyon, Marcy, Richardson, Scott, Tillinghast, Ward, Whipple, Williams, Woodbury, and Worth, and Redoubts A, B, C, and D.

† Constituting the Second Brigade, Pennsylvania Reserve Corps, under command of Col. Horatio G. Sickel; the 3d and 4th Regiments at Convalescent Camp.

‡ Or 69th New York National Guard Artillery.

CAVALRY.

Col. CHARLES R. LOWELL, jr.

2d Massachusetts (eight companies), Maj. Casper Crowninshield.
13th New York (seven companies), Maj. Douglas Frazar.
16th New York (four companies), Maj. Morris Hazard.

FORT WASHINGTON, MD.

Capt. CHARLES R. DEMING.

16th Indiana Battery, Capt. Charles R. Deming.
4th U. S. Artillery, Regimental Headquarters, Col. Charles S. Merchant.*

Abstract from return of the Middle Department (Eighth Army Corps), Maj. Gen. Robert C. Schenck, U. S. Army, commanding, for the month of August, 1863.

Command.	Present for duty.		Aggregate present.	Aggregate present and absent.	Pieces of artillery.	
	Officers.	Men.			Heavy.	Field.
General headquarters	21	....	21	21	......	......
Defenses of Baltimore	32	734	843	1,072	......	22
Second Separate Brigade *a*	46	1,100	1,444	1,688	136	17
Annapolis, Md...................................	16	400	470	589	... .	....
Fort Delaware	36	639	1,025	1,188	......	......
Elysville, Md..	25	211	298	364	......	......
Monocacy Junction, Md	27	457	596	568	......	......
Relay House, Md....	1	29	82	82	......	....
Delaware Department	21	194	285	358	......	....
Total	225	3,764	4,944	5,880	136	39

a Fort McHenry.

Troops in the Middle Department (Eighth Army Corps), Maj. Gen. Robert C. Schenck, U. S. Army, commanding, August 31, 1863.

DEFENSES OF BALTIMORE.

Brig. Gen. ERASTUS B. TYLER.

1st Delaware Cavalry (four companies), Maj. Napoleon B. Knight.
Baltimore (Maryland) Light Artillery, Capt. Frederic W. Alexander.
Purnell (Maryland) Cavalry, Company B, Capt. Thomas H. Watkins.
Maryland Battery A (Junior Artillery), Capt. John M. Bruce.
Maryland Battery B (Eagle Artillery), Capt. Joseph H. Audoun.
5th New York Heavy Artillery, Companies B and C, Maj. Casper Urban.
3d Pennsylvania Artillery, Light Battery H, Capt. William D. Rank.

Second Separate Brigade.

Bvt. Brig. Gen. WILLIAM W. MORRIS.

5th New York Heavy Artillery (six companies), Lieut. Col. Edward Murray.
8th New York Heavy Artillery (ten companies), Col. Peter A. Porter.
2d U. S. Artillery, Battery I, Lieut. James E. Wilson.

* Relinquished command of the post August 30.

ANNAPOLIS, MD.

Col. CARLOS A. WAITE.

1st Maryland (Eastern Shore), Company B, Lieut. William J. Robinson.
2d Maryland (Eastern Shore), Company B, Capt. Charles H. Wicks.
2d Maryland (Eastern Shore), Company D, Capt. W. Wellington Walker.
2d Maryland Cavalry) Companies A, B, C, D, and E, Capt. William F. Bragg.

FORT DELAWARE, DEL.

Brig. Gen. ALBIN SCHOEPF.

Delaware Heavy Artillery (one company), Capt. George W. Ahl.
Purnell (Maryland) Legion, Col. Samuel A. Graham.
Pennsylvania Artillery, Battery A, Capt. Stanislaus Mlotkowski.
Pennsylvania Artillery, Battery G, Capt. John J. Young.

ELYSVILLE, MD.

3d Delaware, Col. Samuel H. Jenkins.

MONOCACY JUNCTION, MD.

3d Maryland (Potomac Home Brigade), Lieut. Col. Charles Gilpin.

RELAY HOUSE, MD.

5th U.S. Artillery (detachment),* Lieut. Edmund D. Spooner.

DELAWARE DEPARTMENT.

Brig. Gen. DANIEL TYLER.

6th Delaware (detachment), Capt. Charles Heydrick.
Delaware Emergency Artillery (detachment), Lieut. Thomas Crossley.
Purnell (Maryland) Cavalry (one company), Capt. Theodore Clayton.

Abstract from tri-monthly return of the Department of the Susquehanna, Maj. Gen. Darius N. Couch, U. S. Army, commanding, for August 31, 1863.

Command.	Present for duty.		Aggregate present.	Aggregate present and absent.	Pieces of field artillery.
	Officers.	Men.			
General headquarters	11	....	11	11	....
Gettysburg (Ferry)................	7	126	139	187	....
Harrisburg (Stahel)	36	557	1,079	1,904	....
Philadelphia (Cadwalader)............... ;...............	72	1,213	1,757	2,844	....
Reading (Sigel)..	174	3,335	3,791	4,010	14
West Chester...	....	12	20	20	....
York	2	83	†1,088	1,095	....
En route from Reading to Chambersburg........	1	70	71	83	....
Total	303	5,396	7,962	10,253	14

* Left for Camp Barry, D. C., August 12.
† Including an aggregate of 1,001 sick in hospital.

Abstract from return of the Department of the Susquehanna, Maj. Gen. Darius N. Couch, U. S. Army, commanding, for the month of August, 1863.

Command.	Present for duty.		Aggregate present.	Aggregate present and absent.	Pieces of field artillery.
	Officers.	Men.			
General headquarters	11	.....	11	11	......
Carlisle Barracks	9	201	287	310	4
Gettysburg (Ferry)	7	127	140	186	.....
Harrisburg (Stahel)	9	94	108	666	.....
Philadelphia (Cadwalader)	61	827	1,202	2,013	.....
Reading (Sigel)	421	8,205	9,191	9,968	.....
York	5	78	a1,059	1,204	......
Total	523	9,532	11,998	14,358	* 4

a Including an aggregate of 983 sick in hospital.

Troops in the Department of the Susquehanna, Maj. Gen. Darius N. Couch, U. S. Army, commanding, August 31, 1863. *

GETTYSBURG, PA.†

Brig. Gen. ORRIS S. FERRY.

1st Pennsylvania Battalion (militia), Company F, Capt. Joseph A. Ege.
21st Pennsylvania Cavalry, Company B, Lieut. James Mickley.
21st Pennsylvania Cavalry, Company D, Capt. Josiah C. Hullinger.

HARRISBURG, PA.

Maj. Gen. JULIUS STAHEL.

1st Pennsylvania Battalion (militia), Lieut. Col. Joseph F. Ramsey.
20th Pennsylvania Cavalry, Companies G and K, Maj. Robert B. Douglass.
21st Pennsylvania Cavalry, Companies I, K, and L.‡
Company Emergency Pennsylvania Militia (independent guard). ‡

PHILADELPHIA, PA.

Maj. Gen. GEORGE CADWALADER.

10th New Jersey, Lieut. Col. Charles H. Tay.
154th Pennsylvania, Company A, Capt. Charles Fair.
154th Pennsylvania, Company B, Capt. Oliver C. Cunningham.
154th Pennsylvania, Company C, Lieut. John K. Brooker.
Provost Guard, Lieut. Col. Henry A. Frink.
27th New York Battery, Capt. John B. Eaton.
20th Pennsylvania Cavalry, Company B, Capt. Michael B. Strickler.
20th Pennsylvania Cavalry, Company L, Capt. Samuel Comfort, jr.
Nevin's (Pennsylvania) Battery (militia), Capt. Robert J. Nevin.
Independent Pennsylvania Battery (militia), Capt. William H. Woodward.

YORK, PA.

Surg. HENRY PALMER.

Independent Company Patapsco (Maryland) Guard, Lieut. Alexander F. McCrone.

*According to the tri-monthly return for that date. Important discrepancies between that and the monthly return of same date noted.
† The "list of regiments," &c., on monthly return reports this command as consisting of the 31st, 51st, and 52d Regiments (militia), and Company B, 21st Pennsylvania Cavalry, but the face of the return accounts for but two companies, one of infantry and one of cavalry.
‡ Commanders not of record.

LEHIGH DISTRICT.*

Maj. Gen. FRANZ SIGEL.

Pottsville, Pa.

Brig. Gen. WILLIAM D. WHIPPLE.

21st Pennsylvania Cavalry, Companies F, I, K, and L, Col. William H. Boyd.
45th Pennsylvania Militia, Col. James T. Clancy.
52d Pennsylvania Militia, Col. William A. Gray.
U. S. Veteran Reserve Corps (four companies).†
Dana (Pennsylvania) Troop (militia), Capt. Richard W. Hammell.
1st New York Light Artillery, Battery A, Lieut. Isaac B. Hall.
Goodwin's (New York) Battery (militia), Capt. William F. Goodwin.

Reading, Pa.

Maj. Gen. FRANZ SIGEL.

20th Pennsylvania Cavalry, Company A, Capt. George W. Baldwin.
42d Pennsylvania Militia, Col. Charles H. Hunter.
47th Pennsylvania Militia, Col. James P. Wickersham.
48th Pennsylvania Militia, Col. John B. Embich.
53d Pennsylvania Militia, Col. Henry Royer.
Ringgold (Pennsylvania) Battery (militia), Capt. George R. Guss.
5th U. S. Artillery, Battery E,‡ Lieut. James W. Piper.
34th Pennsylvania Militia, Col. Charles Albright.
38th Pennsylvania Militia, Col. Melchoir H. Horn.

Scranton, Pa.

Brig. Gen. FITZ HENRY WARREN.

21st Pennsylvania Cavalry, Companies A, C, E, G, L, and M, Lieut. Col. Richard F. Moson.
49th Pennsylvania Militia, Col. Alexander Murphy.

Abstract from return of the Department of the Monongahela, Maj. Gen. William T. H. Brooks, U. S. Army, commanding, August 31, 1863.

Command.	Present for duty.		Aggregate present.	Aggregate present and absent.
	Officers.	Men.		
General headquarters	9		9	9
Barnesville, Ohio	5	167	177	186
Connellsville, Pa	18	440	523	553
Hendrysburg, Ohio	3	92	95	95
New Wilmington, Pa	1	74	75	75
Pittsburgh, Pa	3	80	90	92
Pulaski, Pa	1	48	52	69
Somerton, Ohio	3	85	88	88
West Finley, Pa	3	89	92	92
Wheeling, W. Va	3	73	160	175
Total	49	1,148	1,361	1,434

*According to the monthly return of department and district. The tri-monthly reports Sigel's command as at Reading, and consisting of the 45th, 48th, 49th, and 52d Regiments Pennsylvania Militia (emergency); a detachment of the U. S. Veteran Reserve Corps; Company A, 20th Pennsylvania Cavalry, and the Dana Troop (ninety days); Battery A, 1st New York Light Artillery; Goodwin's (New York) and the Ringgold (Pennsylvania) Batteries, and Company A, Provost Battalion Pennsylvania, and reports nothing for Pottsville and Scranton.

† Commander not of record.

‡ Also, reported as at Chambersburg, Pa.

Troops in the Department of the Monongahela, Maj. Gen. William T. H. Brooks, U. S. Army, commanding, August 31, 1863.

BARNESVILLE, OHIO.

Ohio Company (Departmental Corps), Capt. James L. Deens.
Ohio Company (Departmental Corps), Capt. Hamilton Eaton.

CONNELLSVILLE, PA.

1st Independent Pennsylvania Cavalry Battalion (militia), Lieut. Col. Richard C. Dale.

HENDRYSBURG, OHIO.

Ohio Company (Departmental Corps), Capt. Joseph P. Arrick.

NEW WILMINGTON, PA.

Pennsylvania Company (emergency militia), Capt. Joseph R. Kemp.

PITTSBURGH, PA.

Pennsylvania Company (emergency militia), Capt. Samuel T. Griffith.

PULASKI, PA.

Pennsylvania Company (emergency militia), Lieut. James M. Brown.

SOMERTON, OHIO.

Ohio Company (Departmental Corps), Capt. Samuel Beard.

WEST FINLEY, PA.

Pennsylvania Company (emergency militia), Capt. John Henderson.

WHEELING, W. VA.

Capt. WESLEY C. THORP.

West Virginia Company (exempts), Capt. Robert Hamilton.
West Virginia Company (exempts), Capt. Perry G. West.

Abstract from return of the Department of West Virginia, Brig. Gen. Benjamin F. Kelley, U. S. Army, commanding, for August 31, 1863.

Command.	Present for duty.		Aggregate present.	Aggregate present and absent.	Pieces of artillery.	
	Officers.	Men.			Heavy.	Field.
General headquarters.. . .	6	......	6	6	......	......
Third Division (Scammon)	195	4,694	5,604	6,533	......	14
Maryland Heights Division	199	4,249	5,011	6,095	32	24
Martinsburg .. .	120	2,621	3,106	3,694	......	6
Separate brigades :						
Averell's brigade	175	3,680	4,398	5,363	......	9
Campbell's brigade	67	1,708	1,956	2,288	......	8
Mulligan's brigade	93	1,712	2,070	2,561	......	13
Wilkinson's brigade	98	2,685	2,893	3,177	......	2
Green Spring Run, W. Va	22	587	689	691	......	......
Hagerstown, Md	9	290	372	398	......	......
Romney, W. Va	26	505	694	779	......	.... ..
Sir John's Run, W. Va	27	333	452	1,062	......	......
Total	1,037	23,059	27,251	32,647	32	76

Troops in the Department of West Virginia, Brig. Gen. Benjamin F. Kelley, U. S. Army, commanding, August 31, 1863.

SCAMMON'S DIVISION.*

Brig. Gen. E. PARKER SCAMMON.

First Brigade.	*Second Brigade.*
Col. RUTHERFORD B. HAYES.	Col. CARR B. WHITE.
23d Ohio, Lieut. Col. James M. Comly.	12th Ohio, Lieut. Col. Jonathan D. Hines.
5th West Virginia, Lieut. Col. Abia A. Tomlinson.	91st Ohio, Col. John A. Turley.
13th West Virginia, Col. William R. Brown.	9th West Virginia, Lieut. Col. William C. Starr.
1st West Virginia Cavalry (two companies), Capt. George W. Gilmore.	1st Ohio Battery, Capt. James R. McMullin.
3d West Virginia Cavalry (one company), Capt. John S. Witcher.	
Kentucky Battery, Capt. Seth J. Simmonds.	

Third Brigade.

Col. FREEMAN E. FRANKLIN.

34th Ohio,† Maj. John W. Shaw.
2d West Virginia Cavalry, Maj. John McMahan.

MARYLAND HEIGHTS DIVISION.

Brig. Gen. HENRY H. LOCKWOOD.

First Brigade.	*Second Brigade.*
Col. GEORGE D. WELLS.	Col. WILLIAM P. MAULSBY.
9th Maryland, Col. Benjamin L. Simpson.	1st Maryland (Potomac Home Brigade), Maj. Roger E. Cook.
10th Maryland, Col. William H. Revere, jr.	1st Maryland (Eastern Shore), Col. James Wallace.
34th Massachusetts, Lieut. Col. William S. Lincoln.	2d Maryland (Eastern Shore), Col. Robert S. Rodgers.
1st Connecticut Cavalry, Companies A, B, and E. ⎱ Capt. Erastus Blakeslee.	Maryland Battalion (Potomac Home Brigade) Cavalry, Maj. Henry A. Cole.
6th Michigan Cavalry, Companies H and M. ⎰	Loudoun (Virginia) Rangers, Capt. Samuel C. Means.
2d Maryland (Potomac Home Brigade), Cavalry Company F, Capt. George D. Summers.	Maryland Light Artillery, Battery B, Capt. Alonzo Snow.
17th Indiana Battery, Capt. Milton L. Miner.	32d New York Battery, Capt. Charles Kusserow.
1st Pennsylvania Light Artillery, Battery C, Capt. Jeremiah McCarthy.	

Unattached.

1st Massachusetts Heavy Artillery (four companies), Maj. Frank A. Rolfe.

---

* At Charleston, Coals Mouth, Fayetteville, Gauley Bridge, Camp Piatt, and Camp White.

† Mounted infantry.

MARTINSBURG.

Col. ANDREW T. McREYNOLDS.

Infantry Brigade.

Lieut. Col. THOMAS F. WILDES.

116th Ohio, Capt. William Myers.
122d Ohio (detachment), Capt. Benjamin F. Sells.
123d Ohio, Maj. Horace Kellogg.
87th Pennsylvania (five companies), Maj. Noah G. Ruhl.
12th West Virginia, Maj. William B. Curtis.

Cavalry and Artillery.

Maryland Battalion (Potomac Home Brigade) Cavalry, Company B, Capt. William Firey.
1st New York Cavalry, Maj. Timothy Quinn.
12th Pennsylvania Cavalry, Col. Lewis B. Pierce.
1st and 3d West Virginia Cavalry (detachments), Capt. George W. McVicker.
30th New York Battery, Lieut. Alfred von Kleiser.

SEPARATE BRIGADES.

Averell's Brigade.

Brig. Gen. WILLIAM W. AVERELL.

28th Ohio, Col. Augustus Moor.
2d West Virginia,* Col. George R. Latham.
3d West Virginia,* Lieut. Col. Francis W. Thompson.
8th West Virginia,* Col. John H. Oley.
10th West Virginia, Col. Thomas M. Harris.
16th Illinois Cavalry, Company C, Capt. Julius Jaehne.
3d Independent Company Ohio Cavalry,† Capt. Frank Smith.
14th Pennsylvania Cavalry, Col. James N. Schoonmaker.

1st West Virginia Cavalry, Company A,† Capt. Harrison H. Hagan.
3d West Virginia Cavalry, Company E,† Capt. Timothy F. Roane.
3d West Virginia Cavalry, Company H,† Capt. William H. Flesher.
3d West Virginia Cavalry, Company I,† Capt. George A. Sexton.
1st West Virginia Light Artillery, Battery B, Capt. John V. Keeper.
1st West Virginia Light Artillery, Battery G, Lieut. Howard Morton.

Campbell's Brigade.‡

Col. JACOB M. CAMPBELL.

54th Pennsylvania, Lieut. Col. John P. Linton.
1st West Virginia, Col. Joseph Thoburn.
Lafayette (Pennsylvania) Cavalry, Sergt. Jefferson G. Van Gilder.

Ringgold (Pennsylvania) Cavalry, Capt. Andrew J. Greenfield.
Washington (Pennsylvania) Cavalry, Lieut. John Dabinett.
1st West Virginia Light Artillery, Battery E, Capt. Alexander C. Moore.

Mulligan's Brigade.§

Col. JAMES A. MULLIGAN.

23d Illinois, Lieut. Col. James Quirk.
2d Maryland (Potomac Home Brigade), Col. Robert Bruce.
14th West Virginia, Col. Daniel D. Johnson.

1st Illinois Light Artillery, Battery L, Capt. John Rourke.
Pennsylvania Light Battery (militia), Capt. Horatio K. Tyler.
1st West Virginia Light Artillery, Battery D, Capt. John Carlin.

---

* Mounted infantry.
† These companies apparently under command of Maj. T. Gibson, 14th Pennsylvania Cavalry.
‡ At Moorefield, Petersburg, and Romney.
§ At New Creek, Petersburg, and Romney.

*Wilkinson's Brigade.**

Col. NATHAN WILKINSON.

6th West Virginia, Maj. John H. Showalter.
11th West Virginia, Col. Daniel Frost.
4th West Virginia Cavalry, Lieut. Col. Samuel W. Snider.

MISCELLANEOUS.

Green Spring Run, W. Va.

2d Pennsylvania Battalion (militia), Lieut. Col. John C. Lininger.

Romney, W. Va.

15th West Virginia, Col. Maxwell McCaslin.

Sir John's Run, W. Va.

20th Pennsylvania Cavalry, Col. John E. Wynkoop.

Hagerstown, Md.

Maj. HENRY PEALE.

18th Connecticut, Maj. Henry Peale.
5th U. S. Artillery, Battery B, Lieut. Henry A. Du Pont.

Abstract from return of the Department of Virginia and North Carolina, Maj. Gen. John G. Foster commanding, for the month of August, 1863.

Command.	Present for duty.		Aggregate present.	Aggregate present and absent.	Pieces of artillery.	
	Officers.	Men.			Heavy.	Field.
General headquarters	19	......	19	19	......	......
Fort Monroe	20	558	822	1,168	......	......
District of Virginia:						
Headquarters	9	......	9	9	......	......
Norfolk	27	651	845	1,013	......	6
Portsmouth	205	3,904	5,298	9,371	......	26
Yorktown and vicinity	146	3,122	4,872	6,168	......	30
Total District of Virginia	387	7,677	11,024	16,461	......	62
District of North Carolina:						
Headquarters	25	33	58	62	......	......
Defenses of New Berne	194	4,051	5,502	7,988	59	64
Sub-District of the Albemarle	60	890	1,470	2,253	13	8
Sub-District of Beaufort	58	1,169	1,647	2,048	52	9
Sub-District of the Pamlico	39	1,180	1,725	2,097	......	6
Detachment Eighteenth Army Corps †	......	......	......	......	......	......
Total District of North Carolina	376	7,323	10,402	14,448	124	87
Grand total	802	15,558	22,267	32,096	124	149

* At Clarksburg, Grafton, and Parkersburg.
† Serving in Department of the South and dropped from return.

Troops in the Department of Virginia and North Carolina, Maj. Gen. John G. Foster, U. S. Army, commanding, August 31, 1863.

FORT MONROE, VA.

3d Pennsylvania Heavy Artillery (nine companies), Col. Joseph Roberts.

DISTRICT OF VIRGINIA.

Brig. Gen. HENRY M. NAGLEE.

NORFOLK, VA.

Lieut. Col. GEORGE M. GUION.

148th New York, Lieut. Col. George M. Guion.
7th New York Battery, Capt. Peter C. Regan.

PORTSMOUTH, VA.

Brig. Gen. GEORGE W. GETTY.

GETTY'S DIVISION.*

Second Brigade.	*Third Brigade.*
Brig. Gen. EDWARD HARLAND.	Col. WILLIAM H. P. STEERE.
8th Connecticut, Col. John E. Ward.	10th New Hampshire, Col. Michael T. Donohoe.
11th Connecticut, Capt. William H. Sackett.	13th New Hampshire, Col. Aaron F. Stevens.
15th Connecticut, Col. Charles L. Upham.	4th Rhode Island, Lieut. Col. Martin P. Buffum.
16th Connecticut, Lieut. Col. John H. Burnham.	

Artillery.

1st Pennsylvania Light, Battery A, Capt. John G. Simpson.
5th United States, Battery A, Lieut. James Gilliss.

Provost Guard.

21st Connecticut, Col. Arthur H. Dutton.

UNATTACHED.

Artillery.†

Capt. FREDERICK M. FOLLETT.

3d Pennsylvania Heavy, Company F, Capt. John A. Blake.	4th United States, Battery D, Capt. Frederick M. Follett.
3d Pennsylvania Heavy, Company G, Capt. Joseph W. Sanderson.	4th United States, Battery L, Capt. Robert V. W. Howard.
3d Pennsylvania Heavy. Company M, Capt. Francis H. Reichard.	99th New York Infantry (detachment), Lieut. James A. Flemming.

Cavalry.

Col. SAMUEL P. SPEAR.

1st New York Mounted Rifles,‡ Col. Benjamin F. Onderdonk.
11th Pennsylvania, Col. Samuel P. Spear.

---

* The First Brigade serving in Department of the South.
† In Forts Butler, Griswold, Reno, Rodman, and Tillinghast.
‡ On detached service at Williamsburg.

YORKTOWN AND VICINITY.*

Brig. Gen. Isaac J. Wistar.

Wistar's Brigade.

Brig. Gen. Isaac J. Wistar.

99th New York, Col. David W. Wardrop.
118th New York, Col. Oliver Keese, jr.
9th Vermont, Lieut. Col. Valentine G. Barney.
19th Wisconsin, Col. Horace T. Sanders.

Artillery.

8th New York Battery, Captain Butler Fitch.
16th New York Battery, Capt. Frederick L. Hiller.
1st Pennsylvania (field and staff), Col. Robert M. West.
1st Pennsylvania Light, Battery E, Capt. Thomas G. Orwig.
2d Wisconsin Battery, Lieut. Carl Schulz.
4th Wisconsin Battery, Capt. George B. Easterly.

Cavalry.

5th Pennsylvania, Lieut. Col. William Lewis.

Unattached Infantry.

139th New York, Col. Samuel H. Roberts.

DISTRICT OF NORTH CAROLINA.

Maj. Gen. John J. Peck.†

DEFENSES OF NEW BERNE.

Brig. Gen. Innis N. Palmer.‡

17th Massachusetts, Lieut. Col. John F. Fellows.
23d Massachusetts, Col. Andrew Elwell.
25th Massachusetts (five companies), Maj. Cornelius G. Atwood.
27th Massachusetts, Maj. William A. Walker.
92d New York, Capt. T. Adams Merriman.
132d New York, Col. Peter J. Claassen.
158th New York, Maj. William M. Burnett.

3d New York Cavalry, Col. Simon H. Mix.
12th New York Cavalry (seven companies), Lieut. Col. Philip G. Vought.
Mix's (New York) Cavalry Battalion, Capt. Emory Cummings.
3d New York Light Artillery (nine batteries), Col. Chas. H. Stewart.
1st Rhode Island Light Artillery, Battery F, Lieut. Thomas Simpson.
5th Rhode Island Heavy Artillery, Col. Henry T. Sisson.

SUB-DISTRICT OF THE ALBEMARLE.§

Brig. Gen. Henry W. Wessells.

First Brigade.

Col. Theodore F. Lehmann.

85th New York, Col. Enrico Fardella.
92d New York, Lieut. Col. Hiram Anderson, jr.
96th New York, Col. Edgar M. Cullen.
101st Pennsylvania, Lieut. Col. Alexander W. Taylor.
103d Pennsylvania, Maj. Audley W. Gazzam.

Not Brigaded.

12th New York Cavalry, Company E, Capt. Raymond Ferguson.
24th New York Battery, Capt. A. Lester Cady.

---

* Including Gloucester Point, Newport News, and Williamsburg.
† Assumed command August 14.
‡ Relieved Brigadier-General Heckman, in command August 14.
§ Troops at Plymouth.

SUB-DISTRICT OF BEAUFORT.*

Brig. Gen. CHARLES A. HECKMAN.†

9th New Jersey, Col. Abram Zabriskie.
81st New York, Col. Jacob J. De Forest.
98th New York, Lieut. Col. Frederick F. Wead.
12th New York Cavalry, Company D, Lieut. James M. Sturgeon.
1st U. S. Artillery, Battery C, Lieut. Redmond Tully.

SUB-DISTRICT OF THE PAMLICO.‡

Lieut. Col. OSCAR MOULTON.

25th Massachusetts (five companies), Capt. Charles H. Foss.
1st North Carolina, Lieut. Col. Joseph M. McChesney.
58th Pennsylvania, Lieut. Col. Montgomery Martin.
12th New York Cavalry, Company C, Capt. Ralph H. Olmstead.
23d New York Battery, Capt. Alfred Ransom.

Abstract from return of the Department of the East, Maj. Gen. John A. Dix, U. S. Army, commanding, for the month of August, 1863.

Command.	Present for duty.		Aggregate present.	Aggregate present and absent.	Pieces of artillery.	
	Officers.	Men.			Heavy.	Field.
General headquarters	79	....	90	90	......	......
New York City and Harbor (Canby):						
Staff	7	......	15	15	......	......
City	542	8,716	10,507	16,809	......	(§)
Harbor	162	3,034	4,018	5,708	327	......
Total Canby's command	711	11,750	14,540	22,532	327	......
Fort Niagara, N. Y	......	1	1	1	16	4
Fort Ontario, N. Y	1	23	26	38	17	......
Fort Trumbull, Conn	6	184	360	391	58	......
Fort Adams, R. I	3	92	136	167	200	......
Portsmouth Grove, R. I	3	64	83	86	......	......
Fort Independence, Mass	10	390	498	578	56	......
Fort Warren, Mass	19	369	505	611	92	......
Fort at Clark's Point, Mass	4	80	96	141	19	......
Fort Constitution, N. H	5	138	150	152	20	4
Fort Knox, Me	1	22	23	26	......	......
Fort Preble, Me	4	70	103	116	44	......
Grand total	846	13,183	16,611	24,929	849	8

*Troops at Beaufort, Caroline City, Fort Macon, Morehead City, and Newport Barracks.
†Assumed command August 18.
‡Troops at Washington.
§Not reported.

Troops in the Department of the East, Maj. Gen. John A. Dix, U. S. Army, commanding, August 31, 1863.

CITY AND HARBOR OF NEW YORK.

Brig. Gen. EDWARD R. S. CANBY.

NEW YORK CITY.

First Brigade.

Brig. Gen. ROMEYN B. AYRES.

152d New York, Col. Alonzo Ferguson.
2d United States (six companies), Capt. Samuel A. McKee.
3d United States (six companies), Capt. Andrew Sheridan.
4th United States (four companies), Maj. Frederick T. Dent.
6th United States (five companies), Capt. Montgomery Bryant.
7th United States (four companies), Capt. P. W. L. Plympton.
10th United States (two companies), Capt. William Clinton.
11th United States (six companies), Maj. Jonathan W. Gordon.
12th United States (eight companies), Maj. Luther B. Bruen.
14th United States (eight companies), Maj. Grotius R. Giddings.
17th United States (seven companies), Capt. Walter B. Pease.
2d Vermont, Col. James H. Walbridge.
3d Vermont, Col. Thomas O. Seaver.
4th Vermont, Lieut. Col. George P. Foster.
5th Vermont, Lieut. Col. John R. Lewis.
6th Vermont, Col. Elisha L. Barney.
14th New York Cavalry (detachment), Capt. George Brenning.
18th New York Cavalry (detachment).*
7th Massachusetts Battery, Capt. Phineas A. Davis.

Second Brigade.

Brig. Gen. THOMAS H. RUGER.

14th Indiana, Lieut. Col. Elijah H. C. Cavins.
27th Indiana, Col. Silas Colgrove.
2d Massachusetts, Col. William Cogswell.
3d Michigan, Col. Byron R. Pierce.
7th Michigan, Maj. Sylvanus W. Curtis.
1st Minnesota, Capt. Henry C. Coates.
4th Ohio, Maj. Gordon A. Stewart.
5th Ohio, Col. John H. Patrick.
7th Ohio, Col. William R. Creighton.
8th Ohio, Maj. Albert H. Winslow.
29th Ohio, Col. William T. Fitch.
66th Ohio, Lieut. Col. Eugene Powell.
110th Ohio, Col. J. Warren Keifer.
122d Ohio, Col. William H. Ball.
126th Ohio, Lieut. Col. William H. Harlan.
3d Wisconsin, Col. William Hawley.
2d Connecticut Battery, Capt. John W. Sterling.

Artillery.

Capt. DUNBAR R. RANSOM.

1st Delaware Battery, Capt. Benjamin Nields.
5th United States, Battery C, Lieut. Gulian V. Weir.

NEW YORK HARBOR.

Davids Island.

Lieut. Col. GEORGE W. MEIKEL.

20th Indiana, Companies A, C, E, and H, Lieut. Col. George W. Meikel.
20th New York Battery (detachment).*
28th New York Battery (detachment), Lieut. Robert F. Joyce.
U. S. Veteran Reserve Corps (detachment).*

Fort Hamilton.

Col. HANNIBAL DAY.

37th Massachusetts, Lieut. Col. George L. Montague.
11th New York Heavy Artillery (detachment), Capt. Seward F. Gould.
13th New York Heavy Artillery (detachment), Capt. George A. Bulmer.
12th United States (headquarters and Company F), Capt. Mathew M. Blunt.
5th U. S. Artillery (headquarters). Lieut. Thompson P. McElrath.

---

* Commander not of record.

Fort at Sandy Hook.

Maj. LEMUEL SAVIERS.

26th Michigan, Company A, Lieut. Sewell S. Parker.
26th Michigan, Company H, Capt. Henry V. Steele.
11th New York Heavy Artillery, Company C, Capt. Henry P. Merrill.

Riker's Island.

Brig. Gen. NATHANIEL J. JACKSON.

1st Massachusetts, Col. Napoleon B. McLaughlen.
Detachments.*

Fort Columbus.

Col. GUSTAVUS LOOMIS.

8th United States, Capt. Edwin W. H. Read.
5th Wisconsin, Col. Thomas S. Allen.

Fort La Fayette.

Lieut. Col. MARTIN BURKE.

Detachments, Lieut. Samuel G. Penney.

Fort Richmond.

Col. MARSHALL S. HOWE.

26th Michigan (eight companies), Capt. James A. Lothian.
12th United States, Company H, Capt. Walter S. Franklin.
11th New York Heavy Artillery, Company A, Capt. William Church.

Fort Schuyler.

Bvt. Brig. Gen. HARVEY BROWN.

20th Indiana, Companies B, D, F, and G, Col. William C. L. Taylor.
20th New York Battery, Lieut. Frank A. Davis.
28th New York Battery, Capt. Josiah C. Hannum.

INDEPENDENT POSTS.

Fort Adams, Newport, R. I.

15th U. S. Infantry (headquarters), Col. Oliver L. Shepherd.

Fort Constitution, N. H.

New Hampshire Heavy Artillery, 1st Company, Capt. Charles H. Long.

Fort Knox, near Bucksport, Me.

1st Maine Heavy Artillery (detachment), Lieut. Thomas H. Palmer.

Fort Preble, Portland, Me.

Maj. GEORGE L. ANDREWS.

17th U. S. Infantry, Company C, 2d Battalion, Capt. Nathaniel Prime.

Fort Warren, Boston, Mass.

Col. JUSTIN DIMICK.

1st Massachusetts Heavy Artillery Battalion, Maj. Stephen Cabot.
1st U S. Artillery (headquarters), Col. Justin Dimick.

Fort at Clark's Point, New Bedford, Mass.

Massachusetts Heavy Artillery, 6th Company, Capt. John A. P. Allen.

Fort Independence, Boston, Mass.

Maj. D. L. FLOYD-JONES.

Massachusetts Heavy Artillery, 3d Company, Capt. Lyman B. Whiton.
11th U. S. Infantry (recruits), Capt. Alfred E. Latimer.

Fort Ontario, Oswego, N. Y.

16th U. S. Infantry (recruits), Capt. Charles H. Lewis.

Fort Trumbull, New London, Conn.

Col. WILLIAM GATES.

Connecticut Volunteer Recruits, Capt. Justin H. Chapman.
3d U. S. Artillery, Battery G, Lieut. Lewis Smith.

Portsmouth Grove, R. I.

Hospital Guards, Rhode Island Volunteers, Capt. Christopher Blanding.

Troy, N. Y.

5th Michigan Infantry, Lieut. Col. John Pulford.

---

* Commander not of record.

SEPTEMBER 1, 1863—1 p. m.
(Received 1.35 p. m.)

Major-General HALLECK:

My infantry and cavalry guarding the lower fords of the Rappahannock got into position last evening, and early this morning General Kilpatrick's division of cavalry left Falmouth for Port Conway. At the latest report the enemy does not seem to have perceived any movement.

On Sunday last, hearing there was a considerable force of the enemy's cavalry at Leesburg, I directed a brigade of cavalry to be sent there and to examine the Loudoun Valley. I should have reported this earlier, that our forces in that vicinity may be apprised of the fact.

GEO. G. MEADE,
Major-General, Commanding.

HARTWOOD CHURCH, *September* 1, 1863.
(Received 11 a. m.)

General HUMPHREYS,
Chief of Staff:

The following just received from General Webb, at Banks' Ford, 8.45 a. m. :

This morning all is as usual on the other side. There is no evidence of unusual caution, or of surprise at the removal of the cavalry reserve; no saddling of horses usually left out to graze. I have 25 men concealed near the crossing, and from the calling of rebel pickets across the river, I judge that the men without arms are still believed to be cavalry.

ALEX. S WEBB,
Brigadier-General.

All quiet at this hour, 11 a. m.

G. K. WARREN,
Major-General.

HARTWOOD, *September* 1, 1863—12 p. m.
(Received 9 a. m., 2d.)

General WILLIAMS,
Assistant Adjutant-General:

Have you heard anything about the enemy crossing below Ellis' Ford ? The cavalry picket from there report that he was driven away by a small party crossing, and some other posts were attacked below at the same time.

C. H. MORGAN,
Lieutenant-Colonel, &c.

[Indorsements.]

HEADQUARTERS ARMY OF THE POTOMAC,
September 2, 1863—9. a. m.

Referred to General Williams, commanding Twelfth Corps, at Kelly's Ford.

Have you heard anything of this ?

A. A. HUMPHREYS,
Major-General, Chief of Staff.

SEPTEMBER 2, 1863.
No such report has reached me.   I discredit it.
A. PLEASONTON,
Major-General.

CIRCULAR.]   HEADQUARTERS ARMY OF THE POTOMAC,
September 1, 1863.
The following is an extract from a note which has been received from the chief engineer of the Defenses of Washington. Corps and other independent commanders are desired to furnish, with as little delay as practicable, statements giving the information asked for.*

The rule now about naming forts and batteries around Washington is to give names of distinguished officers killed in battle, or who have died from wounds or sickness after distinguished services. Will you mention such cases since the commencement of the Pennsylvania campaign, including Gettysburg? Give dates, localities, and, in few words, circumstances of death.

By command of Major-General Meade:
S. F. BARSTOW,
Assistant Adjutant-General.

HEADQUARTERS FIFTH ARMY CORPS,
September 1, 1863.
General S. WILLIAMS,
Assistant Adjutant General, Army of the Potomac:
SIR: Pursuant to the provisions of circular from headquarters Army of the Potomac, of this date, I have the honor to submit the names of the following officers whose memory should be perpetuated in the history of their country, both from distinguished services and from having yielded up their lives in its defense.

1. Brig. Gen. Stephen H. Weed, U. S. Volunteers. Distinguished at Gaines' Mill, June 27, 1862; Malvern Hill, June 30 and July 1, 1862; Bull Run No. 2, August 30, 1862; Antietam, September 17, 1862; Fredericksburg, December 13, 1862; Chancellorsville, especially May 1, 2, and 3, 1863, and Gettysburg, July 2, 1863, where he lost his life.

2. Brig. Gen. Strong Vincent, U. S. Volunteers. Distinguished at the battle of Hanover Court-House, May 27, 1862; Fredericksburg, December 13, 1862; Chancellorsville, May 2 and 3, 1863; cavalry fight in front of Aldie the latter part of June, 1863, and especially at Gettysburg, July 2, 1863, where he was mortally wounded.

3. Col. P. H. O'Rorke, captain of Engineers. Prominent at Chancellorsville, on the 1st of May, and distinguished at Gettysburg, July 2, 1863, where he lost his life, bravely leading his regiment.

4. Lieut. Charles E. Hazlett, Fifth U. S. Artillery. Distinguished at Bull Run, Yorktown, Hanover Court-House, Gaines' Mill, Malvern Bull Run No. 2, Antietam, Fredericksburg, Chancellorsville, and Gettysburg. While stooping by the side of General Weed, to receive his last wishes, a bullet struck the lieutenant in the head and

---

* See Sykes to Williams, September 1; Warren to Williams, September 6, and French to Williams, October 3. Replies from other corps commanders not found.

killed him almost instantly (July 2, 1863). This young officer, for his grade, had no superior in the army.

I am, sir, respectfully, your obedient servant,

GEO. SYKES,
Major-General, Commanding.

HEADQUARTERS CHIEF ENGINEER OF DEFENSES,
Washington, September 1, 1863.

Hon. E. M. STANTON,
Secretary of War:

SIR: The works of Rozier's Bluff, and near Jones' Point are nearly ready to receive guns—in fact they could have been mounted some time ago, had the guns and platforms been available. You are well aware that not only are the large seaport towns, like New York, Boston, and Philadelphia making strenuous exertions to increase their armament of improved guns, but even places of a (comparatively) secondary importance, like Portland, &c. If we have war with a maritime power (a possibility which incites all these preparations), the land defenses of Washington will prove unavailing unless also the access by water is prevented.

There is not now a gun mounted for the defense of the Potomac capable of having the slightest effect upon an iron-clad vessel. As it seems to devolve upon me to represent the necessities of Washington, I would recommend that among the guns which actually do become available, a fair proportion should be assigned to Washington.

The Ordnance Department is doing all that can be done to furnish guns. It has no voice, however, in their distribution, and as there are no Governors of States or commissions of citizens to advocate the needs of Washington, I feel called on to make this representation.

I am, very respectfully, your most obedient,

J. G. BARNARD,
Brigadier-General, and Chief Engineer of Defenses.

CLARKSBURG, *September 1, 1863.*

Brigadier-General AVERELL,
Beverly:

I am not prepared to answer your question definitely. I can see no reason, however, why you should not make the exchange proposed. Send medicine, &c. General Jones' report of your affair appears in Baltimore American to-day; he reports his loss at 200 killed and wounded. I will send you the paper.

[B. F. KELLEY],
Brigadier-General.

HEADQUARTERS FOURTH SEPARATE BRIGADE,
Beverly, September [1], 1863.

Brig. Gen. B. F. KELLEY,
Clarksburg:

The exchange could not be effected without further orders from General Jones. The information received is that they had 2,500 in action and a reserve at hand. They think I had 3,000 in action, when there were not quite half that number. They are quarreling about my return, saying the fate of Morgan ought to have been ours. They pursued to Big Spring with advance at Elkwater. I think they will give it up.

WM. W. AVERELL,
Brigadier-General.

HEADQUARTERS FOURTH SEPARATE BRIGADE,
Beverly, September [1], 1863.

Major GIBSON, *Buckhannon:*

From all I can learn, I think you alone are able to handle any force Jackson may send in by the way of Centreville. He certainly can send no artillery by that route. However, I may be mistaken in the intentions of the enemy. Their principal force is yet in my front. As soon as I am convinced that the movement toward Buckhannon is not a feint, you shall be re-enforced.

I desire you to keep me constantly informed. Remember that your men can fight pretty well. Let me know when you receive your ammunition.

WM. W. AVERELL,
Brigadier-General.

HEADQUARTERS FOURTH SEPARATE BRIGADE,
Beverly, September [1], 1863.

Brig. Gen. B. F. KELLEY, *Comdg. Dept.:*

Dispatch received. I have been acting upon the idea which Colonel Campbell's report conveys. Imboden may scatter his forces upon my communications. One of his men, on his way to capture our mail, was taken in Tucker day before yesterday. I have 25 men after 2 officers and 15 men in the same vicinity. Also scouts to Petersburg, Crab Bottom, and in front. Jackson has been reported by several parties as at Marling's Bottom. Four deserters, just in, report the same. Jenkins reported at Crab Bottom. Have sent to inquire about him. I want some Linden and Burnside carbine ammunition. It may be on the way. I regret that the Seneca route is blockaded. A short communication is thus destroyed. I will cut it out if you think proper. I shall be ready to move to the front again as soon as some horses are furnished.

WM. W. AVERELL,
Brigadier-General.

GENERAL ORDERS, }   HDQRS. DEPT. OF VA. AND N. C.,
No. 11.   }   *Fort Monroe, Va., September* 1, 1863.

Maj. J. L. Stackpole, judge-advocate, is hereby appointed provost judge, and will be respected and obeyed accordingly.

Major Stackpole's powers will be the same as those had by Major Bolles, and as stated in General Orders, Nos. 6 and 41, Department of Virginia.

By command of Major-General Foster:

SOUTHARD HOFFMAN,
Assistant Adjutant-General.

HDQRS. ARMY OF THE POTOMAC, *September 2, 1863.*
(Received 10.20 a. m.)

Maj. Gen. H. W. HALLECK,
General-in-Chief:

The following dispatch of General Kilpatrick's, just received through General Pleasonton, is transmitted for your information:

HEADQUARTERS THIRD CAVALRY DIVISION,
September 1, 1863—3 p. m.

General PLEASONTON:

My advance drove in the rebel pickets one-half mile north of King George Court-House. I am advancing on the three roads I have not yet learned the strength of the enemy. The gunboats came up to Port Conway on Saturday.

KILPATRICK,
General.

GEO. G. MEADE,
Major-General.

———

HEADQUARTERS ARMY OF THE POTOMAC,
September 2, 1863.

Maj. Gen. H. W. HALLECK,
General-in-Chief:

The following dispatch from General Kilpatrick, just received through General Pleasonton, is forwarded for your information:

HEADQUARTERS THIRD CAVALRY DIVISION,
September 2, 1863—5.40 a. m.

I drove the enemy across the river last evening. Have my guns in position below and above the gunboats, near Port Conway. Elder is within 700 yards of one boat. The enemy have shown four guns. No news of the iron-clads.

J. KILPATRICK,
Brigadier-General.

GEO. G. MEADE,
Major-General.

———

HEADQUARTERS FIRST CAVALRY DIVISION,
September 2, 1863.

General PLEASONTON:

Everything is quiet. I have no news from Kilpatrick save what I sent last night. I thought I heard guns at 6 a. m. down the river, but am not positive. There is no change of the enemy in my front.

JNO. BUFORD,
Brigadier-General.

———

HDQRS. SECOND DIVISION, TWELFTH ARMY CORPS,
Near Ellis' Ford, Va., September 2, 1863.
(Received 6 p. m.)

Lieut. Col. H. C. RODGERS,
Assistant Adjutant-General:

COLONEL: I have the honor to state, for the information of the general commanding the corps, that General Greene reported to me at 7.30 o'clock last evening that the cavalry pickets stationed at Skinker's Dam, about a mile below Ellis' Ford, were being fired upon. His brigade was put under arms, and Major Thomas, with 100 men of the One hundred and forty-ninth New York, was sent to that point to reconnoiter, discovering that the rebels, to the number of from 10 to 15, crossed on the dam and attacked the pickets, and after killing one and scattering the rest they recrossed. Major Thomas has been ordered to remain there until relieved by an infantry force to be sent from United States Ford by General Warren. He has discovered no enemy, and the lines have been quiet since his arrival.

I have just returned from a visit to the lines, and find from my officers' statements that there are about 300 cavalry in our front, between Ellis' and Kemper's Fords, and by indications I judge there is also a section of artillery. These movements and changes of the enemy are evidently in apprehension of some movement of ours. I do not apprehend any aggressive step on their part at present.

I have the honor to be, very respectfully, your obedient servant,

JNO. W. GEARY,
Brigadier-General, Commanding.

YORKTOWN, VA.,
September 2, 1863.

General NAGLEE,
    Norfolk:

Colonel Onderdonk returned from Gloucester. Found nothing there. Enemy left on Friday. Reports portions of Fifth and Sixth Virginia Cavalry in Middlesex.

I. J. WISTAR,
Brigadier-General.

WASHINGTON, D. C.,
September 2, 1863—10.30 a. m.

Major-General FOSTER,
    Fort Monroe, Va.:

It is reported that Cape Henry light is not sufficiently guarded, and is in danger. Please look to this.

H. W. HALLECK,
General-in-Chief.

SEPTEMBER 3, 1863—12.15 p. m.

Colonel LOWELL,
    Commanding, &c., Centreville:

Colonel Devin, commanding the cavalry brigade sent to Leesburg, has returned. He reached Leesburg Monday [August 31]. White, with about 300 men, had been there a day or two before, but had retired to Upperville. Imboden had not been there, nor any other force than White's. A Richmond paper of the 1st of September states that Mosby received two serious wounds in the fight near Fairfax Court-House, and has been taken to his father's residence at Amherst.

A. A. HUMPHREYS,
Major-General, and Chief of Staff.

*SEPTEMBER 3, 1863—12.30 p. m.

Circular to Corps Commanders:

The major-general commanding directs me to inform you that the expedition sent from the left flank of this army has returned, after having successfully accomplished its object, by destroying the two gunboats recently captured from us off the mouth of the Rappahannock.

I am instructed to say that although the particular contingency under which the troops were recently ordered to be held in readiness to move at short notice is not likely now to occur, yet the necessity for such movements may arise at any moment, and corps commanders are expected to hold their troops prepared to move at brief notice.

A. A. HUMPHREYS,
Major-General, Chief of Staff.

FORT MONROE, VA., *September* 3, 1863—11 p. m.
(Received 11.45 p. m.)

Major-General HALLECK:

I propose to go to New Berne to-morrow upon urgent business connected with the contraband colony. I start in the Spaulding in the evening, unless you do not desire me to go.. I propose to send the Spaulding directly on to Charleston, with some ammunition for the navy that is waiting shipment here, and to have her bring back the latest news. From Mr. Fulton's statement I infer that something interesting will shortly occur in that quarter. Have you a desire to go down there? If so, this will be the fairest opportunity, as the Spaulding is a safe and swift steamer.

J. G. FOSTER,
Major-General.

WASHINGTON, D. C.,
September 4, 1863—1.24 p. m.

Major-General FOSTER,
Fort Monroe, Va.:

You will exercise your own judgment in regard to visiting other parts of your department. Information received here indicates that Lee's army will soon move. It is not possible for me at present to go to Charleston.

H. W. HALLECK,
General-in-Chief.

CLARKSBURG, W. VA.. *September* 4, 1863.
(Received 5.30 p. m.)

Brigadier-General CULLUM,
Chief of Staff:

Nothing new in my department. All quiet, except we are annoyed in some counties with bushwhackers and horse-thieves. I keep scouts constantly after them.

General Averell is at Beverly, resting his command, shoeing horses, and getting up supplies and ammunition. I am now satisfied that Jones and Jackson contemplated a raid into this part of the State, and that Averell's expedition has frustrated their plans. Deserters report Jones' loss in the late action much more than ours. He lost 4 colonels killed and wounded, and quite a number of line officers.

All safe along line of Baltimore and Ohio and Northwestern Railroads.

B. F. KELLEY,
Brigadier-General.

HEADQUARTERS CHIEF ENGINEER OF DEFENSES,
Washington, September 4, 1863.

Col. J. C. KELTON,
Assistant Adjutant-General: .

SIR: I respectfully recommend that the following works and forts, forming part of the Defenses of Washington, may be called after the officers whose names are set opposite, and who have died or been killed in the service of the United States :

Fort at Rozier's Bluff, on east side of the Potomac River, 2 miles below Alexandria, to be called Fort Foote, after Rear-Admiral A. H. Foote, U. S. Navy, who died of disease June 26, 1863, and whose distinguished services in command of the United States naval forces upon the Western rivers are well known.

Water battery at Alexandria to be called Battery Rodgers, after Fleet Capt. G. W. Rodgers, U. S. Navy, killed August 17, 1863, in a naval attack upon Fort Wagner, Charleston Harbor, S. C.

Fort Blenker, south side of Potomac, to be called Fort Reynolds, after Maj. Gen. J. F. Reynolds, killed July 1, 1863, at Gettysburg, Pa.

Redoubt A, near Fort Lyon, to be called Fort Weed, after Stephen H. Weed, captain Fifth Artillery, brigadier-general of volunteers, killed July 2, 1863, at Gettysburg, Pa.

Redoubt B, near Fort Lyon, to be called Fort Farnsworth, after Brig. Gen. Elon J. Farnsworth, killed July 3, 1863, at Gettysburg, Pa.

Redoubt C, near Fort Lyon, to be called Fort O'Rorke, after Patrick H. O'Rorke, first lieutenant of Engineers, U. S. Army (colonel of volunteers), killed July 2, 1863, at Gettysburg, Pa.

Redoubt D, near Fort Lyon, to be called Fort Willard, after George L. Willard, major Nineteenth Infantry (colonel of volunteers), killed July 2, 1863, at Gettysburg, Pa.

I am, very respectfully, your most obedient,

J. G. BARNARD,
Brig. Gen., Chief Engineer Defenses of Washington.

WAR DEPARTMENT,
Washington City, September 4, 1863.

Brig. Gen. M. C. MEIGS,
Quartermaster-General, Washington, D. C.:

GENERAL: Having, under instructions of the 28th ultimo, visited the Army of the Potomac, you will proceed to make the further inspections prescribed by these instructions.

You will visit the principal armies in the field, and the principal depots of supplies in the Middle States, and in the South and Southwest, so far as time will permit, aiming to return to this city in season to prepare the annual report of your department. If possible, it is desired that your tour should extend to the Army of the Cumberland, and to the depots at Memphis and Vicksburg. On the way, the depots on the Susquehanna and Ohio, and that at Saint Louis should be visited.

All commanding officers will, upon presentation of this order, or of an official copy thereof, afford you every facility in their power to inspect the condition of the department of which you have charge, and the condition of the equipment and outfit of the troops in quarters, tents, clothing, baggage, ammunition, and ambulance wagons, animals, and other supplies furnished by the Quartermaster's Department. The troops should be visited in their camps, and portions of them reviewed and inspected on parade.

You will report from time to time the result of your observations, and will give such orders in relation to the Quartermaster's Department as you find necessary for the correction of abuses and errors, and for promoting efficiency and economy in its operations. Your attention is particularly directed to the subject of steamboat navigation on the Ohio and Mississippi.

You will keep this office informed by telegraph of your address.

Very respectfully, your obedient servant,

P. H. WATSON,
Acting Secretary of War.

NEW YORK CITY, *September 5*, 1863.
(Received 11.40 a. m.)

Hon. E. M. STANTON, *Secretary of War:*

Your note of the 3d is just received. Six thousand men will embark so soon as transportation is ready. Others will follow as soon as possible.

ED. R. S. CANBY,
Brigadier-General, Commanding.

NEW YORK,
September 5, 1863—12 m.

Hon. E. M. STANTON, *Secretary of War:*

Your private letter is just received. I can send you back 5,000 men to-day, if you desire it. Shall I send them?

JOHN A. DIX,
Major-General.

NEW YORK CITY,
September 5, 1863—2.30 p. m.

Hon. E. M. STANTON, *Secretary of War:*

Since telegraphing you I have seen General Canby, and orders have been given for 6,000 men to move. Over 4,000 will embark immediately.

JOHN A. DIX,
Major-General.

WASHINGTON, D. C.,
September 5, 1863—10.25 a. m.

Major-General DIX,
        New York:

Send Colonel Mindil's regiment, as soon as it is mustered, to this place, for the Army of the Potomac. Send by water.

H. W. HALLECK,
                General-in-Chief.

GENERAL ORDERS, ⎱ HDQRS. U. S. TROOPS CITY AND HARBOR,
No. 18.   ⎰   *New York, September 5, 1863.*

I. As the immediate necessity no longer exists, the troops now quartered or encamped in the city, with the exception of the guards at the offices of the provost-marshals and depots of public property, will be removed and encamped at convenient points in the neighborhood.

*   *   *   *   *   ..   *

By order of Brigadier-General Canby:
C. T. CHRISTENSEN,
                Assistant Adjutant-General.

SPECIAL ORDERS, ⎱ HDQRS. U. S. TROOPS IN CITY AND HARBOR,
No. 47.   ⎰   *New York, September 5, 1863.*

I. Brig. Gen. R. B. Ayres will order the Second Regiment Vermont Volunteers to proceed this afternoon, or early this evening, to the city of Poughkeepsie, N. Y., where the draft for the Twelfth Congressional District takes place on Monday, the 7th instant. On its arrival there, the commanding officer will report to Capt. Isaac Platt, provost-marshal.

Brigadier-General Ayres will also order the Fifth and Sixth Vermont Volunteers to proceed this afternoon, or early this evening, to the village of Kingston, Ulster County, N. Y., where the draft for the Thirteenth Congressional District takes place on Monday, the 7th instant. On arrival at that place, the commanding officer of these regiments will report to Capt. Joshua Fiero, jr., provost-marshal. Captain Nields, commanding First Delaware Battery, will detach a section to proceed, in company with the Fifth and Sixth Regiments Vermont Volunteers, to Kingston, N. Y., and to be reported in like manner on arrival at that place.

All these troops will take their tents with them and be provided with one day's cooked rations. Maj. Stewart Van Vliet, quartermaster, U. S. Army, will furnish the necessary transportation.

*   *   *   *   *   *   *

III. Brig. Gen. Thomas H. Ruger, commanding Second Brigade, will order one section of the Second Connecticut Battery to proceed this afternoon, or early this evening, to the village of Kingston, Ulster County, N. Y., where the draft of the Thirteenth Congressional District takes place on Monday, the 7th instant. On its arrival at that place, the commanding officer of the section will report to Capt. Joshua Fiero, jr., provost-marshal.

The men will take their tents with them and be supplied with one day's cooked rations. Maj. Stewart Van Vliet will furnish the necessary transportation.

The section must be ready to leave in company with the Fifth and Sixth Vermont Volunteers, who are destined for the same place.

*   *   *   *   *   *   *

V. Col. A. Ferguson, One hundred and fifty-second New York Volunteers, will proceed to Washington Park, Brooklyn, with his regiment and establish his headquarters there. He will detail one company for duty at each of the following provost-marshal's offices: First District, Jamaica, Long Island; Second District, No. 26 Grand street, Williamsburg; Third District, No. 259 Washington street, Brooklyn.

*   *   *   *   *

By order of Brigadier-General Canby:

C. T. CHRISTENSEN,
Assistant Adjutant-General.

ARTILLERY HEADQUARTERS, ARMY OF THE POTOMAC,
September 5, 1863.

General S. WILLIAMS,
Assistant Adjutant-General, Army of the Potomac:

GENERAL : I have the honor to forward herewith an application* from Capt. F. C. Gibbs, commanding Battery L, First Ohio Volunteer Artillery, for the appointment of an officer to recruit for his battery, made upon the supposition that there will be no draft in Ohio.

I have no reliable information that the draft has been suspended, although it is stated that officers sent to Ohio for drafted men have been ordered to open recruiting offices for volunteers. There is also a prevailing belief that recruits are not to be furnished to the artillery until after the cavalry and infantry regiments are filled.

The batteries have large numbers of men from those two arms. They are reported as "temporarily attached," but are in effect permanently so, and to withdraw them would at once break up the batteries. Besides, many of the men volunteered for the service on the understanding that they were to serve out their terms in the artillery. Many inconveniences, both to the regiments and batteries, result from this, and it is very important that the batteries be filled up, at as early a date as practicable, with men enlisted specially for them.

If the men now serving in the batteries be allowed to re-enlist for them, under Paragraphs VII and VIII, General Orders, No. 191, War Department, current series, it will obviate many of the evils now existing and free the regimental rolls of so many detached men. The balance required should be furnished as soon as possible. If not furnished soon, large additional drafts on the cavalry and infantry regiments of men for "temporary service" will be required, to enable the batteries to take the field. They will weaken the regiments and not be properly instructed in their artillery duties. The applications for permission to recruit for batteries are getting to be so numerous that I respectfully request that some general provision be made to supply recruits to all.

HENRY J. HUNT,
Brigadier-General, Chief of Artillery.

---

* Omitted.

GENERAL ORDERS, } HDQRS. DEPT. OF THE SUSQUEHANNA,
No. 13.   }   September 5, 1863.

Capt. Alexander N. Shipley, assistant quartermaster, U. S. Army, having reported to the major-general commanding the department, in accordance with Paragraph 22, Special Orders, War Department, August 27, 1863, is hereby assigned to duty as acting chief quartermaster of this department, *vice* Lieutenant-Colonel Thompson, additional aide-de-camp and assistant quartermaster, resigned. He will be obeyed and respected accordingly.

By command of Maj. Gen. D. N. Couch:

JNO. S. SCHULTZE,
Major, and Assistant Adjutant-General.

WAR DEPARTMENT,
Washington, September 6, 1863—12.30 p. m.

Major-General MEADE, *Army of the Potomac:*

General Rosecrans seems apprehensive that re-enforcements to Bragg have been sent from Lee's army to East Tennessee by Lynchburg. Employ every possible means to ascertain if this be so. If Lee has sent any troops to Tennessee, I must re-enforce Burnside.

H. W. HALLECK,
General-in-Chief.

HDQRS. ARMY OF THE POTOMAC, *September 6, 1863.*
(Received 3 p. m.)

Maj. Gen. H. W. HALLECK, *General-in-Chief:*

No movement of troops from Lee's army has been reported by scouts or deserters, except that yesterday a deserter said, on his recent trip from Richmond, he had met Cooke's brigade at Hanover Junction, marching, it is said, to Richmond. This brigade has always been stationed in the vicinity of Richmond, and was sent to Fredericksburg when Lee first fell back to the Rapidan.

Some days since, scouts reported McLaws' division, of Longstreet's corps, having moved to Walter's Tavern, about 10 miles north of Frederick's Hall Station, on the Gordonsville railroad. The object of this movement was said to be for the convenience of supplies, but it may have been to cover their withdrawal, though this fact has not been reported.

I think if any movement except Cooke's had taken place, I should have been advised, though it is very difficult to obtain reliable information. The movement of Cooke I considered due to General Foster's operations on the Peninsula. I will endeavor to get scouts across the lines.

GEO. G. MEADE,
Major-General.

HEADQUARTERS ARMY OF THE POTOMAC,
September 6, 1863—4 p. m. (Received 5 p. m.)

Maj. Gen. H. W. HALLECK, *General-in-Chief:*

Wesley Norris, a free negro, came into our lines from Culpeper yesterday about sunset. He states he was formerly the property of George Washington Custis, who died at Arlington, Va., about six

years ago. By his will he was made free, after having served five
years for General Lee. He has been hired out of late to Alexander
Dudley, superintendent of the York River Railroad, who discharged
him a few days before he left Richmond.

He states that he left Richmond on Friday last, with a pass from
General Custis Lee, to go through our lines via Culpeper. He took
the Central cars via Gordonsville, and arrived in Gordonsville about
noon and staid there two hours. Saw no troops on the move or
march. Saw some in camp, to the right of Gordonsville, perhaps
4,000 or 5,000, just out of the town; looked as if they had been in the
camp some little time. The Charlottesville cars run into the same
depot.

He states that if any troops had been moving from or toward Charlottesville he would have known it. He talked with several persons
at Gordonsville. They said nothing about the movement of troops
anywhere. He saw many troops in camp at Orange Court-House.
All in camp; none on the march. He had to get off there to get a
pass, when the cars left him and he walked to Culpeper. Got to Culpeper on Saturday. Yesterday morning saw troops in several places
between Orange Court-House and Culpeper. Went all the way on
the railroad, showing his pass only once. Saw no troops at Culpeper,
but some wagons and a few [sic]. Went to the provost-marshal,
who examined his passes and made some objections to his coming
through. Was put on a horse in the afternoon, blindfolded, and sent
to our pickets at Rappahannock Station.

GEO. G. MEADE,
Major-General.

HDQRS. ELEVENTH CORPS, ARMY OF THE POTOMAC,
September 6, 1863.

Major-General HUMPHREYS,
Chief of Staff:

Captain Sharra, commanding detachment of First Indiana Cavalry, just returned from the neighborhood of Aldie, captured 3 of
Mosby's men near Cool Spring Gap, who will be sent to general
headquarters to-morrow. No signs of any raid. Mosby not dead,
but wounded at Culpeper. The men think he will be fit for duty in
six weeks.

O. O. HOWARD,
Major-General.

HEADQUARTERS SECOND ARMY CORPS,
September 6, 1863.

Brig. Gen. S. WILLIAMS,
Asst. Adjt. Gen., Army of the Potomac:

GENERAL: In reply to circular of September 1, 1863, headquarters
Army of the Potomac, I have the honor to submit the following
statements concerning distinguished officers of this corps killed in
battle during the recent campaign:

1. Brigadier-General Zook. This officer was formerly colonel of
the Fifty-seventh New York Volunteers, and was distinguished for
his bravery on many occasions, particularly at Fredericksburg. He
was killed at the head of his brigade early in the action of July 2,
at Gettysburg.

2. Col. E. E. Cross, Fifth New Hampshire Volunteers. This officer has borne a reputation in this corps for the most intrepid bravery on nearly every battle-field on which this army has fought, and was several times severely wounded. His regiment, under his discipline, was excelled by none. He was killed at the head of his brigade at Gettysburg, July 2, 1863.

3. Col. George H. Ward. This officer lost a leg at Ball's Bluff; returned to his command with an artificial leg, and was killed while mounted, some distance in advance of the main line of battle, at Gettysburg. He was in command of a brigade.

4. Colonel Willard, major Eighth Infantry. Killed at the head of his brigade, at Gettysburg, July 2.

5. First Lieut. A. H. Cushing, Fourth U. S. Artillery. Killed while commanding his battery at Gettysburg, July 3. His gallant conduct was a subject of universal remark in this corps. He was slightly wounded an hour before he was killed.

6. First Lieut. G. A. Woodruff, First U. S. Artillery, commanding Ricketts' (afterward Kirby's) battery. This officer was the associate of the late General Kirby in the different actions in which the battery was engaged, and was himself an officer of marked bravery and of great ability. His services at Gettysburg were highly meritorious. Killed July 3, 1863.

I am, general, very respectfully, your obedient servant,

G. K. WARREN,
Major-General of Volunteers.

RAPPAHANNOCK STATION,
September 6, 1863.

Lieutenant PARSONS,
Acting Assistant Adjutant-General:

My pickets report that about midnight they could hear noises like the tearing up of the railroad track, also the sound of heavy wagons or artillery moving in direction of Brandy Station. The enemy's line remains unchanged since last report.

H. D. MANN,
Captain Eighth New York Cavalry, Comdg. Pickets.

HEADQUARTERS ARMY OF THE POTOMAC,
September 8, 1863. (Received 6.50 p. m.)

Maj. Gen. H. W. HALLECK, *General-in-Chief:*

John Wilson, a citizen of Tennessee, who has been for some time living on the James River, came into our lines yesterday, and reports that he came through Lynchburg, Charlottesville, Gordonsville, &c., and that he neither saw nor heard of any movements of troops from Lynchburg south, except that he met numerous cavalrymen leading their horses, who said they were sent home to remount themselves. Scouts from Fredericksburg report no change in the position of the enemy. Cooke's brigade has gone to Hanover Junction, as previously reported. McLaws' division, they could not say had or had not gone from Walter's Tavern, 10 miles north of Frederick's Hall, where it was last reported.

GEO. G. MEADE,
Major-General, Commanding.

HARTWOOD CHURCH,
September 8, 1863.

Col. C. ROSS SMITH,
Chief of Staff:

Nothing new from my picket lines. General Meade's scouts re-crossed the river near Ballard's Dam this morning at 2 o'clock. They report a brigade of rebel cavalry encamped opposite Ballard's Dam, and a large body of infantry a short distance back.

J. KILPATRICK,
Brigadier-General.

WAR DEPARTMENT,
September 8, 1863.

Major-General MEADE,
Army of the Potomac:

General Heintzelman reports that he has no reliable troops for escorts of drafted men from Alexandria.

H. W. HALLECK,
General-in-Chief.

HEADQUARTERS ENGINEER BRIGADE,
Washington, D. C., September 8, 1863.

General S. WILLIAMS,
Asst. Adjt. Gen., Army of the Potomac:

SIR : I have the honor to make the following report for the information of the commanding general :

The canvas pontoon train to the extent of thirty new boats, or for 600 feet, is essentially complete, with its wagons and trucks, for field service. This makes available 1,000 feet of canvas or 500 feet of trestle bridging, the two being combined in this species of train. The canvas for the additional 200 feet directed is also on hand, but although I have successively ordered the proper lumber from New York and from Baltimore, I have not yet been able to obtain it, and shall now probably have to prepare the remaining boat frames from the balks now on hand.

The mechanics of the command have been vigorously occupied upon the large number of trucks and wagons of the trains that have needed repairs, and in repairing the boats of the different trains, and especially in rebuilding the boats which had been destroyed upon the Upper Potomac, a large number of which had been recovered. In many cases these have been almost entirely renewed, and, it is reported to me, from the details of expenses kept, at much less than one-half the original cost of these boats to the Government by contract.

And while the daily infantry drills of the command have been kept up, the pontoon drills have also progressed, and latterly to my extreme satisfaction. I have to report that within the last week or two, by a method I have proposed since I first took charge of the brigade, and which I have now enforced under my personal supervision (against the preconceived notions, not to say prejudices of perhaps all the officers of the brigade), I have succeeded beyond my most sanguine expectations in a rapid construction and dismantling of a bridge suitable and in most cases applicable for use under fire. By this method, with a force of only 450 to 500 men (all I had available), and not more than one-half of what I could have worked to good advantage (thereby, of course, greatly reducing even the short time occupied during the past week), and on our first trial with so large a bridge, with many of the men new to the work, we have prepared the bridge for crossing the Eastern Branch here, 1,300 feet long, dismantling it in five to six minutes, constructing it in eight to eleven minutes, and swinging it into position ready for a column of infantry to cross in eight to ten minutes.

On yesterday this bridge was dismantled completely in three and a half or in four and a half minutes (as different observers reported), it was constructed in ten and in position so that infantry landed and commenced fire from it in eight more, and it was ready for the passage of artillery in less than twenty minutes from the time the order to "construct" was given; while by my plan this bridge will carry, well concealed, an attacking force equal to one man for every foot of its length.

I have special satisfaction in reporting these facts, as showing the ability and importance of the drill here, and the proficiency attainable, which is absolutely impossible to be accomplished at the front or in the face of the enemy.

And this leads me to the subject of the additions that had been hoped for from the drafted men for these regiments. On the 29th of July, I addressed a letter to your headquarters, asking that application should be made to the proper authority that mechanics or other select men should be assigned or permitted to go to these regiments from the newly drafted men, but to this I have as yet no reply, while I find by the reports of my officers sent to Elmira, according to orders, that while not a single man has been permitted to go to these regiments, notwithstanding the large numbers that desire to, these very officers are kept from my poorly officered regiments, and even put into the permanent garrison company at that post, thus still more weakening instead of strengthening my command.

It is desirable to keep up the efficiency of this brigade, now reduced in its effective force for the two regiments to less than one-third of the organization of one regiment of Engineers, and if the order previously asked for cannot be obtained, I would respectfully request authority for an officer to report at such point in the Army of the Potomac as may be deemed best, to select the mechanics and other men suitable for transfer to this brigade and to these headquarters, where they can be properly drilled, as they can nowhere else, my experience showing me that the new men may be months or years with an army at the front, and still be of no more use as pontooniers than only ordinary infantry, while even one month here may suffice to make them effective.

Very respectfully, your obedient servant,

H. W. BENHAM,
Brigadier-General, Commanding.

———

GENERAL ORDERS, }   HDQRS. DISTRICT OF VIRGINIA,
    No. 2.   }   *Norfolk, Va., September 9, 1863.*

I. Hereafter under no circumstances shall a search be made or shall any property be taken from citizens, within the lines of this command, without the express written order of a general officer, and the search or seizure shall be conducted under the direction of a commissioned officer.

II. Under no circumstances shall property be taken from a citizen without the lines, unless by an officer detailed for the express purpose by order of the officer in command of the detachment; the latter to be of not less rank than that of a field officer.

III. In every instance where property shall be taken, a receipt shall be given by a quartermaster or commissary, specifying the date, place, name of owner, his known loyalty or suspected disloyalty, an accurate description of the kind and quantity and the value thereof, and by whose order it was taken, and in every instance the property shall at once be entered upon the returns of the proper officers.

IV. Commanding officers of detachments who shall capture any property, will include an accurate invoice of the same in their report.

V. The following extract is published and will be rigidly enforced, as follows :

GENERAL ORDERS, }   WAR DEPARTMENT,
    No. 88.   }   *Washington, March 31, 1863.*

*   *   *   *   *   *   *

II. It is further ordered that every officer or private, or persons employed in or with the regular or volunteer forces of the United States, who may receive or have under his control any property which shall have been abandoned by the owner or owners, or captured in any district declared to be in insurrection against the United States, including all property seized under military orders, excepting only such as shall be required for military use of the United States forces, shall promptly turn over all such property to the agent appointed by the Secretary of the Treasury to receive the same, who shall give duplicate receipts therefor.

And every such officer or private, or person employed in or with the regular or volunteer forces of the United States, shall also promptly turn over to such agent, in like manner, all receipts, bills of lading, and other papers, documents, and vouchers showing title to such property, or the rights to the possession, control, or direction thereof, and he shall make such order, indorsement, or writing as he has power to make to enable such agent to take possession of such property or the proceeds thereof.

Arms, munitions of war, forage, horses, mules, wagons, beef cattle, and supplies which are necessary in military operations, shall be turned over to the proper officers of the ordnance or of the quartermaster's or of the commissary departments, respectively, for the use of the army. All other property abandoned or captured or seized as aforesaid shall be delivered to the agent appointed by the Secretary of the Treasury.

The officer receiving or turning over such property shall give the usual and necessary invoices, receipts, or vouchers therefor, and shall make regular returns thereof, as prescribed by the Army Regulations. The receipts of the agent of the Treasury Department shall be vouchers for all property delivered to them, and whenever called upon by the agent of the Treasury Department authorized to receive such abandoned or captured or seized property as aforesaid, or the proceeds thereof, all persons employed in the military service will give him full information in regard thereto, and if requested by him so to do, they shall give him duplicates or copies of the reports and returns thereof, and of the receipts, invoices, and vouchers therefor.

VI. All property captured or seized under military orders, excepting only such as shall be required for military use of the United States forces, shall be promptly turned over to Mr. M. H. Morse, assistant special agent of the Treasury Department, in pursuance of the above General Orders, No. 88, of the War Department.

By command of Brigadier-General Naglee :

                    GEORGE H. JOHNSTON,
                        Assistant Adjutant-General.

SPECIAL ORDERS, } HDQRS. U. S. TROOPS CITY AND HARBOR,
    No. 51.   }   *New York, September 9, 1863.*
          *   *   *   *   *   *

I. By authority from department headquarters, the Fifth Regiment Wisconsin Volunteers is ordered to proceed, as soon as transportation can be furnished, to Albany, N. Y., and report, on arrival, to Maj. Frederick Townsend, Eighteenth U. S. Infantry, acting assistant provost-marshal-general, Northern Division of the State of New York.

On the way to Albany, one company will be left at Kingston, Ulster County, N. Y., and another company at Poughkeepsie, N. Y. The men will take their tents with them and be provided with one day's cooked rations.

The Fifth and Sixth Regiments Vermont Volunteers and the section of the Second Connecticut Battery at Kingston, N. Y.; the Second Vermont Regiment Volunteers, at Poughkeepsie, N. Y.; the Third and Fifth Regiments Michigan Volunteers, at Schenectady, N. Y. (or elsewhere), will, upon being relieved by detachments from the Fifth Regiment Wisconsin Volunteers, proceed without delay to this city.

The Second, Fifth, and Sixth Vermont, and the Third and Fifth Michigan Regiments, will be furnished with transportation to ――――, to be ready, if possible, upon their arrival in this city. The section of the Second Connecticut Battery will proceed to East New York, Long Island, where the battery is encamped, and the company of the Twenty-sixth Michigan Infantry to the headquarters of the regiment at Fort Richmond, Staten Island.

          *   *   *   *   *   *

VI. Brig. Gen. Thomas H. Ruger, after superintending the embarkation of the troops of his brigade, will proceed by railroad to Alexandria, Va., in season to meet his troops upon their arrival at that place.

          *   *   *   *   *   *

IX. Brig. Gen. George J. Stannard, U. S. Volunteers, having reported for duty in accordance with orders from the War Department, is hereby assigned to the command of the district on the west side of the Narrows, including the fort at Sandy Hook, New York Harbor, headquarters at Fort Richmond, New York Harbor.

          *   *   *   *   *   *

By order of Brigadier-General Canby:

C. T. CHRISTENSEN,
Assistant Adjutant-General.

――――――

HDQRS. ARMY AND DISTRICT OF NORTH CAROLINA,
                    New Berne, N. C., September 10, 1863.
Maj. Gen. J. G. FOSTER,
    Comdg. Dept. of Virginia and North Carolina:

GENERAL: Soon after my arrival I proceeded to Plymouth and collected from General Wessells and Captain Flusser, U. S. Navy, all the information respecting the iron-clad and battery at Edwards Ferry, which I communicated to your headquarters. Several thousand men were at Garysburg, Jackson, &c., and several regiments at Hamilton, Rainbow, and vicinity. Five hundred were reported guarding the iron-clad. Your reply was to the effect that the forces of the department would not admit of a movement.

General Wessells and Captain Flusser again report increased efforts for the completion of this boat, and apprehensions that she may come down to Plymouth and the Sounds. The general asks for a small iron-clad, not having much faith in the obstructions which he is preparing. If you have an iron-clad to send, she will not venture down the Roanoke. There is no one here skilled in preparing torpedoes, and while I have not great faith in them, I would request that some person be sent to prepare some at Plymouth.*

Under all the circumstances, a raid upon Edwards Ferry should not be made with less than 1,000 cavalry of good quality. The character of the Twelfth New York Cavalry you fully appreciate, and the effective force of the Third is much reduced, as I'learn from Major Jacobs. He estimates it as 450 or 500.†

General Wessells has been instructed to push the obstructions rapidly, to strengthen his system of works generally, especially on the water front, and to scour the country with his cavalry for the enemy and for information.‡

Major Anderson, of your staff, intimated that the colored troops at Elizabeth City would be relieved, or replaced by troops from Virginia. Upon his advice the former were relieved without waiting for the latter. General Wessells advises that no troops are at Elizabeth City.

Is it your wish that General Wessells should again occupy these points?§

Very respectfully, your obedient servant,

JOHN J. PECK,
Major-General.

———

SUTTON,
September 10, 1863—1 p. m.
Capt. EWALD OVER,
Acting Assistant Adjutant-General:

Some 250 rebels of Jackson's army passed between here and Bull-town yesterday in direction of Glenville. I leave with my command of Sixth and Eleventh to follow them. I sent the wagons and provisions back to Weston, to await further orders.

The rebels may be making for the Burning Springs. They say they are to meet 200 more of their men, but this I doubt. Better send troops to Glenville to support us in case of need; also send troops to Burning Springs. You need not be uneasy if you do not hear from me for two or three days.

We had 10 men of the Eleventh captured on 8th. The latest report says there is a regiment of rebels coming through Webster this way. I expect to be at Glenville on the 11th.

C. J. HARRISON,
Captain, Commanding Forces.

---

* Chief Engineer Lay, U. S. Navy, if in the department, is skilled in making torpedoes. No iron-clads, and torpedoes not thought much of; obstructions are better.—Note by General FOSTER.
† This raid would probably not succeed.—Note by General FOSTER.
‡ If necessary another rifle gun be mounted.—Note by General FOSTER.
§ Do not.—Note by General FOSTER.

CLARKSBURG,
September 10, 1863.

Brigadier-General AVERELL,
   Beverly:

Colonel Campbell reports that his cavalry captured 6 of Imboden's men at Moorefield yesterday. From these prisoners he received such information as leads him to the belief that the late attack on Moorefield was only a feint to cover a movement farther west. Keep your scouts well out and on the alert. Do you know if Jackson's forces have returned to Huntersville?

           B. F. KELLEY,
            Brigadier-General.

HDQRS. DEPARTMENT OF THE SUSQUEHANNA,
Chambersburg, September 10, 1863.

Col. J. C. KELTON,
  Assistant Adjutant General, Army Headquarters:

I respectfully state, for the information of the General-in-Chief, that the enemy are apparently making preparations for a movement of some kind into Pennsylvania. Their spies have been through this county within a few days. My impression is that a raid is intended.

The General-in-Chief is aware that my force is small, one company of infantry, one battery, and three companies of horse in this county; two of cavalry and one of infantry at Gettysburg and vicinity.

   I am, sir, very respectfully, your obedient servant,
           D. N. COUCH,
            Major-General.

GENERAL ORDERS, } HDQRS. ARMY AND DISTRICT OF N. C.,
 No. 12.   }   *New Berne, N. C., September* 10, 1863.

In accordance with the views of the major-general commanding the Department of Virginia and North Carolina, Chaplain Horace James, superintendent of blacks for the District of North Carolina, will assume charge of the colonization of Roanoke Island with negroes.

The powers conferred upon Brigadier-General Wild by General Orders, No. 103, headquarters Department of North Carolina, Eighteenth Army Corps, are hereby transferred to Chaplain James. He will take possession of all unoccupied lands on the island, and lay them out and assign them, according to his own discretion, to the families of colored soldiers, to invalids, and other blacks in the employ of the Government, giving them full possession of the same until annulled by the Government or by due process of United States law.

The authority of Chaplain James will be respected in all matters relating to the welfare of the colony.

  By command of Major-General Peck:
         BENJ. B. FOSTER,
         Assistant Adjutant-General.

HEADQUARTERS ARMY OF THE POTOMAC,
September 11, 1863—9.20 p. m.   (Received 10 p. m.)
Maj. Gen. H. W. HALLECK,
General-in-Chief:

General Kilpatrick, picketing the river from Ellis' Ford to below Falmouth, has reported that within the last two days the enemy's pickets that were in many places of infantry have been replaced by cavalry.   Two scouts this evening have returned who crossed the river below Port Conway, crossed the Fredericksburg railroad at Guiney's Station and went to Walter's Tavern.   McLaws' division was not there; was said to have left last Monday.   The people all told them the army was falling back to the Peninsula.   On their return Law's brigade was met marching from Port Conway to Bowling Green.   It is the conviction of these scouts that the Confederate Army is falling back from the Rapidan.   Still, as their route was so far to the rear of the enemy's right flank, it may be merely a movement of this part of their army, and there is no positive evidence of which way the troops that have moved have gone, but only that they have left their former positions.

I have other scouts out who will endeavor to penetrate nearer Orange Court-House, and if I can get any evidence more positive, I will push to Culpeper and beyond a strong reconnaissance of cavalry and infantry.

GEO. G. MEADE,
Major-General, Commanding.

HEADQUARTERS OF THE ARMY,
Washington, D. C., September 11, 1863.
Brigadier-General WILLIAMS,
Assistant Adjutant-General:

GENERAL: General Canby telegraphs that the following regiments are *en route* to the Army of the Potomac: The Fourth, Fifth, Seventh, Eighth, Twenty-ninth, Sixty-sixth, One hundred and tenth, One hundred and twenty-sixth, One hundred and twenty-second Ohio.

The Second Massachusetts, First Minnesota, Third Wisconsin, Fourteenth and Twenty-seventh Indiana, Seventh Michigan, Third and Fourth Vermont, Thirty-third New Jersey, and First Delaware and Seventh Massachusetts Batteries, and the Second, Third, Eleventh, Fourteenth, Seventeenth, and Twelfth U. S. Infantry are waiting transportation.   The Third Michigan, Second, Fifth, and Sixth Vermont, and Fifth Michigan will sail as soon as relieved.   These regiments have been ordered to march from Alexandria.

Very respectfully, your obedient servant,
J. C. KELTON,
Assistant Adjutant-General.

[Indorsement.]

OFFICIAL.]   HEADQUARTERS ARMY OF THE POTOMAC,
—— —, 1863.

Corps commanders will draw from the quartermaster's department the transportation required by existing orders for such of the above-mentioned regiments as belong to their respective commands, and have the same in readiness on the return of the regiments.

HEADQUARTERS ARMY OF THE POTOMAC,
September 11, 1863.

ADJUTANT-GENERAL OF THE ARMY,
Washington, D. C.:

SIR: As it frequently happens that, through favoritism or other cause, officers and soldiers in the volunteer service are nominated for promotion and appointment who are deficient in the qualifications necessary to enable them to discharge efficiently the duties of the positions for which they are recommended, I have thought that the evil might, at any rate, be partially remedied by requiring all such nominations, before being sent forward to the Governors of States, to be submitted to a board, to the end that an examination may be had into the character and qualifications of the individuals nominated, and I have the honor to inclose the *projet* of a general order, which if it meets with the approval of the General-in-Chief, I will publish for the guidance of this army.

I am, very respectfully, your obedient servant,

GEO. G. MEADE,
Major-General, Commanding.

[Inclosure.]

GENERAL ORDERS, }   HDQRS. ARMY OF THE POTOMAC,
No. —. }   *September* 10, 1863.

I. To the end that Governors of States may have reliable information concerning the qualifications of the officers and soldiers from time to time recommended to them for promotion and appointment, it is ordered that in each division or independent brigade a Board, composed of three experienced officers and a recorder, be appointed by the commander thereof, as occasion may require, to examine into and report upon the character and qualifications of all officers and soldiers, within their commands, who may be nominated for promotion or appointment in the regiments and batteries of the volunteer service.

The Boards thus constituted will make written reports in each case, giving their opinion upon the merits of the officers and soldiers examined, and forward the same, through the usual channel of correspondence, to the War Department for reference to the Governor of the State concerned.

Commanders of regiments and batteries will promptly make nominations to supply vacancies in their respective commands that, under General Orders, Nos. 86 and 182, of 1863, from the War Department, are authorized to be filled, and such nominations will be laid before a Board, constituted as above directed, with as little delay as practicable, and will accompany the report of the Board.

II. In cases not provided for in the foregoing paragraph, special Boards will be appointed by corps commanders, the chief of artillery, or at these headquarters.

III. All direct correspondence with the Governors of States, making nominations for appointments in the volunteer service, is strictly prohibited. Such communications, like all others of a military character, will be forwarded through the channel prescribed by the Regulations.

By command of Major-General Meade:

[———— ————,]
Assistant Adjutant-General.

[First indorsement.]

SEPTEMBER 24.

Colonel TOWNSEND:

I think the plan a good one.   .   .

T. M. V.   [VINCENT.]

[Second indorsement.]

SEPTEMBER 26.

Respectfully submitted to the General-in-Chief.

E. D. TOWNSEND,
Assistant Adjutant-General.

[Third indorsement.]

SEPTEMBER 26.

Approved:

H. W. HALLECK,
General-in-Chief.

[Fourth indorsement.]

OCTOBER 31.

Colonel TOWNSEND:

I submitted this to Secretary of War, but it does not meet his approval at present.

He says before action is taken the views of the respective Governors should be obtained.

Respectfully,

T. M. V.   [VINCENT,]
Assistant Adjutant-General.

SEPTEMBER 11, 1863—10.10 p. m.

Commanding Officer Second Corps:

The commanding general directs that you move your entire corps, in the course of to-morrow, to Rappahannock Station, prepared to cross the river Sunday morning, in support of a cavalry reconnaissance.

Your wagons will be parked at Bealeton, in charge of the guard of the First Corps; only the ambulances and ammunition wagons will be taken across the river.

When you have made all the arrangements for the movement to-morrow, the commanding general desires to see you at headquarters.

S. WILLIAMS,
Assistant Adjutant-General.

WAR DEPARTMENT,
September 11, 1863—6.20 p. m.

Maj. Gen. JOHN A. DIX,
Comdg. Dept. of the East, New York City:

General Canby's proposition of the 8th instant, forwarded by you on the 9th, recommending that the Fourth, Sixth, Seventh, and Tenth Regiments of Infantry be assigned to duty in the harbor of New York, relieving the Twelfth, and that the companies of those regiments be consolidated and the supernumerary officers and non-

commissioned officers be detailed on recruiting service, is approved
and will be carried into effect.

By order of the Secretary of War:

JAS. A. HARDIE,
Assistant Adjutant-General.

WHEELING, W. VA., *September* 11, 1863—8 p. m.
(Received 10 p. m.)

Brigadier-General CULLUM,
Chief of Staff:

The following just received from General Scammon. I think the
force of the enemy exaggerated. Nevertheless, if you have any force
to spare me, I would like to send Scammon two regiments.

Brigadier-General KELLEY:

Enemy reported in large force at Princeton; Twenty-second, Thirty-sixth, Sixtieth [Virginia] Infantry; seven regiments under General Lee. Division, with
Fifty-fifth, Fifty-first, and Third [Virginia] Regiments, at Union. Fifteen hundred
cavalry at Lewisburg under Jenkins and Echols. Enemy's outposts 10 miles south
of Weston. Scout there daily. Can you send me more troops at once?

SCAMMON,
Brigadier-General.

B. F. KELLEY,
Brigadier-General.

FORT MONROE, *September* 11, 1863.
(Received 4.10 p. m.)

Maj. Gen. H. W. HALLECK,
General-in-Chief:

I arrived here from North Carolina last evening While there,
deserters from the enemy represented that the enemy apprehended
an attack by us, re-enforced by 40,000 troops from New York, and
that our object was feared to be the capture of Raleigh, to enable
the peace party to revolutionize the State.

All the disposable troops were concentrated in haste at Kinston,
and a large force of negroes set to work night and day on the defenses of Raleigh. The Union feeling is on the increase in the State,
and peace meetings have been held in several counties. The force
of the enemy in the State is small—not, I should judge by reports,
over 10,000 effective.

Now is a good time to make an attack upon the defenses at the
mouth of Cape Fear River, if you have the force to give me for this
purpose and desire it to be done at this time.

The news by the Spaulding has been anticipated. General
Strong [?] gives some interesting facts. He saw the explosion in
Fort Moultrie on Tuesday morning, and has no doubt of its being
the explosion of the magazine. General Gillmore had said that in
one or two days from that time (Monday) he would plant our flag
upon Fort Sumter; that he would probably have a fight to do it,
as the enemy had 100 or 200 men there yet. General Gillmore
expected to be here within one week, *en route* to Washington, regarding his work as mainly completed by the destruction of Fort
Sumter and the capture of Morris Island.

J. G. FOSTER,
Major-General.

HDQRS. ARMY AND DISTRICT OF NORTH CAROLINA,
New Berne, N. C., September 11, 1863.

General H. W. WESSELLS,
Commanding Sub-District of the Albemarle:

GENERAL: Your favor of the 8th is before me, and I hasten to reply. While at Plymouth I gathered from you and the naval authorities all the information possible respecting the iron-clad and battery in course of construction at Edwards Ferry. On my return, I made a report to Major-General Foster, and suggested a movement from your headquarters in conjunction with a demonstration from Suffolk. The reply was that nothing could be spared for such service, as "the forces of the department will not permit of the proposed movement at present."

From the difficulties connected with its location, and the contiguity of forces about Weldon, Garysburg, Hamilton, and Rainbow Bluff, &c., not less than 1,000 cavalry would be required. There are not boats enough in North Carolina to transport such a force without making two or three trips to your place, which would expose the whole plan. Besides, there is not much over one-half that number of effective cavalry in North Carolina.

As to an iron-clad, it seems to be out of the question. There is not one in North Carolina, and I am told not one north of Charleston that can enter the Sound. You will have two good companies of cavalry, and they must scour the country for rebels and information. Your system of obstructions must be pushed with all vigor, day and night; keep every tool busy in strengthening your works. They can be made so that you can stand a long siege. Particular attention should be given to your water front by closing any works open toward the river and dependent on gunboat service. Additional water batteries may be deemed necessary by you; if so, commence them at once.

Additional artillery will be sent you, if you will state what is required, and, on the approach of the enemy, men and *matériel* of war.

Keep me fully advised, as you have already done, sending reports, rumors, &c.

Very respectfully, your obedient servant,

JOHN J. PECK,
Major-General.

GENERAL ORDERS, }   HDQRS. ARMY AND DISTRICT OF N. C.,
No. 14.   }   *New Berne, N. C., September* 11, 1863.

Complaints having reached the general of depredations upon private property by white and colored troops, it is his duty to republish the standing orders of Major-General Halleck, commander-in-chief, to the end that all may know the views entertained by the Government in respect to these demoralizing offenses.

General Orders, No. 107, of the 15th of August, 1862, says:

III. The laws of the United States and the general laws of war authorize, in certain cases, the seizure and conversion of private property for the subsistence, transportation, and other uses of the army. But this must be distinguished from pillage, and the taking of private property for public purposes is very different from its conversion to private uses. All property lawfully taken from the enemy, or from the inhabitants of an enemy's country, instantly becomes public property, and must be used and accounted for as such. The Fifty-second Article of War authorizes the penalty of death for pillage or plundering, and other articles authorize severe punishment for any officer or soldier who shall sell, embezzle, misapply, or waste military stores, or who shall permit the misapplication of any such public property.

IV. All property, public or private, taken from alleged enemies must be inventoried and duly accounted for.

*   *   *   *   *   *   *

VI. No officer or soldier will, without authority, leave his colors or ranks to take private property, or to enter a private house for that purpose. All such acts are punishable by death, and the officer who permits them is equally as guilty as the active pillager.

If there is one portion of the United States where these regulations should be more rigidly enforced than in any other, it is in the Old North State, for the spirit which prompted North Carolina to make the first declaration of independence of Great Britain still lives in thousands of loyal hearts, in spite of the despotism and bayonets of the Confederacy.

Commanders of every grade will be held responsible for the faithful execution of these orders.

By command of Major-General Peck:

BENJ. B. FOSTER,
Assistant Adjutant-General.

September 12, 1863—12 m.

Commanding Officer Eleventh Corps:

Your telegram received. No report has been made to these headquarters of any attack on Gregg's pickets. On the contrary, General Gregg reports a brigade he had sent to the Bull Run Mountains, and to the country between there and the Blue Ridge, had returned without encountering or hearing of any enemy.

Scouts from below indicate a southerly movement of the enemy, and though I do not rely implicitly on this, yet I shall to-morrow push my cavalry to the front to try and find out something. No further specific instructions can be given than have heretofore been given. In the event of a raid becoming certain, your force should be concentrated at the important points; Warrenton Junction first, as it has the depot and public property, and where there is abundance of artillery, then the bridges at Catlett's and Bristoe. At Manassas there is the regiment of Colonel Gibbs, 700 strong, and General King's force at Centreville, within striking distance.

No information at these headquarters would indicate a raid. At the same time, we should always be ready for one.

GEO. G. MEADE,
Major-General, Commanding.

HEADQUARTERS ARMY OF THE POTOMAC,
September 12, 1863.

Commanding Officer First Corps:

I am instructed to inform you that a movement—reconnaissance—will be made to-morrow in the direction of Culpeper Court-House, and the commanding general orders that you hold your command in readiness to move at short notice in case the development of the movement should be required.

Very respectfully, &c.,

S. WILLIAMS,
Assistant Adjutant-General.

MANASSAS,
September 12, 1863.

General KING:

General Howard has just sent word that there is strong probability of an attack from the direction of Greenwich. It appears so strong that he has directed Von Steinwehr's division to hold itself in readiness—with teams harnessed, wagons packed, &c.—to hold out till the last and then fall back on Catlett's. I have more than half my men away for horses, and have an immense amount of new ordnance just arrived. Can you help me any if I am attacked?

ALFRED GIBBS,
Commanding.

HDQRS. ARMY AND DISTRICT OF NORTH CAROLINA,
New Berne, N. C., September 12, 1863.
(Received Hdqrs. Dept. Cumberland, *October* 16, 1863.)

Major-General FOSTER,
Comdg. Dept. of Virginia and North Carolina:

GENERAL: By a flag of truce, I received some papers, which I send you. Governor Vance issued a proclamation on the 7th, calling upon the people to be united and to support the Confederate Government, &c.

A Mr. Clements, of Pennsylvania, has just arrived from Graham, N. C., where he has a son-in-law. He was on a visit at the outbreak, and has been detained until now. He is a man of sixty years, and very good sense. He says that a large body of troops passed from General Lee's army to the west, for General Bragg, estimated at varying from 15,000 to 20,000. Being a railroad man, from what he saw and learned from others, he judges about 13,000. The last of one portion passed through Raleigh on Tuesday of this week (8th). He conversed with some of the troops, and all said they were going to Bragg, and that it would not be known at the North.

A riot occurred in Raleigh; some of the Georgia troops attacked the office of the Standard; bells sounded, people assembled in a very excited state. Governor Vance addressed them, but the other office was attacked.

This information may be of no great importance when it reaches you, but I deem it proper to communicate it at once. Major Jenney, of my staff, leaves this evening for the Guide, at Beaufort, and will sail at daybreak, or as soon as the vessel can cross the bar.

Very respectfully, your obedient servant,

JOHN J. PECK,
Major-General.

[Indorsement.]

Maj. Gen. W. S. ROSECRANS,
Commanding, &c.:

It may be of service to you hereafter to have a copy of a hasty dispatch sent by me for the information of the Department at Washington.

It was made in the night, and taken by rail to Beaufort, where the bearer sailed at dawn for his destination. The telegram was in

Washington early on the 14th, and doubtless was promptly communicated to you.*

Beyond question it was the most reliable information in possession of the Government at that time. The importance of the news was fully appreciated by the undersigned.

Wishing you all success, I am, very respectfully,

JOHN J. PECK,
Major-General.

HEADQUARTERS DISTRICT OF VIRGINIA,
Norfolk, September 12, 1863.

Lieut. Col. WILLIAM LEWIS,
Commanding Fifth Pennsylvania Cavalry:

You will at present locate your command at or near Great Bridge and relieve the officer now there after forty-eight hours, and he will report for duty with his regiment. Execute the special orders of the 1st of August, a copy of which is herein inclosed.† Ascertain who burned the bridges within the past three days, and arrest and send to Norfolk persons who may be justly suspected. Scour the country in every direction and get rid of the few guerrillas that remain in Camden and Currituck Counties or in the vicinity of Great Bridge. You will watch carefully and prevent all persons from passing the Pasquotank River. Allow no person to pass out whatever. I have ordered that no pass shall be given, and if I desire to pass any one it will be by a special order to yourself or the commanding officer at South Mills.

You will relieve the companies of the Eleventh Pennsylvania at South Mills, and order them to report to their regiment as soon as you are familiar with the country and with the orders. You will send one company to the Currituck Canal, and prevent any vessels from passing with any merchandise whatever.

Mrs. Campbell should occupy your especial attention. She will not be permitted to continue to sell goods after she has closed out her present stock of goods. You will communicate with the Quaker settlement, 20 miles west of South Mills. They will give you reliable information. Send me daily reports and communicate all the names of suspicious persons. Advise Mrs. Bell that after ten days her house will be destroyed unless she removes the guerrilla Sanderlin from it. Advise others to the same purpose who permit their houses to be occupied by guerrillas or their families. Report all persons that give aid and comfort to guerrillas. A severe policy must be adopted in regard to them. Leave one squadron of cavalry, who will report to me for further orders.

Contrabands, deserters, and refugees will be brought directly to the provost-marshal at Norfolk. The latter will be advised, that they will be required to take the oath of allegiance.

No person will be allowed to pass in either direction, except as above specified. I shall hold you responsible for the good conduct of your regiment, and I sincerely hope the confidence I have in you shall only increase with more intimate military connection.

HENRY M. NAGLEE,
Brigadier-General, Commanding.

---

* See Halleck to Rosecrans, September 15.
† See Naglee to Rowe, August 20.

HEADQUARTERS ARMY OF THE POTOMAC,
September 13, 1863—8 p. m.   (Received 8.30 p. m.)
Maj. Gen. H. W. HALLECK,
General-in-Chief:

In accordance with the telegram I sent you on the 11th instant, General Pleasonton, in command of the cavalry, advanced this morning against the enemy, supported by the Second Corps, General Warren.   At the last dispatch received, 5 p. m., General Pleasonton had driven the enemy beyond Culpeper Court-House, which was occupied by General Warren.

General Pleasonton had only encountered cavalry and artillery. He reports a slight loss and the capture of 3 guns and 41 prisoners. He further states that all the information he has been able to gather tends to confirm the reported retrograde movement of the Confederate army.

Both Generals Pleasonton and Warren have been cautioned that their movement was to be restricted to a reconnaissance for obtaining information of the enemy's position, and they were not to compromise matters so as to force on a general engagement, but to retire to the line of the Rappahannock, if the superiority of the force brought by the enemy should compel them to do so.   Should the enemy have withdrawn from the Rapidan, or should he permit of its being done without too great a sacrifice, Culpeper Court-House may be retained by the cavalry.

GEO. G. MEADE,
Major-General.

SEPTEMBER 13, 1863—2 p. m.
Commanding Officer Cavalry Corps:

Remember the object of your expedition is a reconnaissance predicated on the report that the enemy has made a retrograde movement.

I do not desire to bring on a general engagement, and the infantry force was sent to enable you to withdraw with safety in case the enemy appears in such force as to compel or require you so to do.

GEO. G. MEADE,
Major-General, Commanding.

(Copy to commanding officer Second Corps.)

HEADQUARTERS ELEVENTH CORPS,
Bristoe, September 13, 1863—10 p. m.
Brigadier-General VON STEINWEHR,
Commanding Second Division:

GENERAL : The scouts from Bull Run Mountains report no news from the enemy.   Culpeper is in our possession.   General Pleasonton captured three guns and a lot of prisoners.   Have you any news from . General King ?

O. O. HOWARD,
Major-General.

HEADQUARTERS ARMY OF THE POTOMAC,
September 13, 1863.

Commanding Officer Eleventh Corps:

Major-General Pleasonton, with the cavalry under his command, has advanced to a position some 3 miles beyond Culpeper Court-House, after considerable skirmishing with the enemy.   During the day General Pleasonton's command has captured three guns and about 40 prisoners.   The Second Corps is at Culpeper.

S. WILLIAMS,
Assistant Adjutant-General.

(Copy to commanding officers Third and Twelfth Corps.)

———

HEADQUARTERS FIRST CORPS,
September 13, 1863.

Brig. Gen. S. WILLIAMS,
Asst. Adjt. Gen., Army of the Potomac:

GENERAL: I regret very much that the present circumstances exact of me anything like this communication.   Yesterday, when your communication came notifying me of the reconnaissance intended for to-day without any further details, I naturally supposed that it was a cavalry reconnaissance, and that the nearest body of infantry, the First Corps, would support such reconnaissance if required.

Subsequently I heard unofficially that the Second Corps had been detailed to accompany the cavalry in this expedition.   I interpreted this fact, however, in this way: That it was intended to give General Pleasonton, in command of the cavalry, the charge of the reconnaissance, and that the Second Corps was detailed to accompany him because its commander was junior to him.

At an early hour this morning I was informed that my supposition was incorrect; that General Warren, being senior to General Pleasonton, would, of course, take command of the entire expedition in case of necessity.   Under such circumstances you must not be surprised to learn that the officers and men of the First Corps are disappointed and mortified at an occurrence from which others will not fail to draw the inference that the Second Corps was selected and brought from some distance to perform an act for which the First Corps was not qualified.

I cannot believe any such imputation was intended by the major-general commanding, but an ordinary regard for the reputation of the corps which I have the honor at present to command enjoins upon me the duty of forwarding this communication.

I have the honor to be, general, very respectfully, your obedient servant,

JOHN NEWTON,
Major-General, Commanding.

———

HEADQUARTERS ELEVENTH CORPS,
September 13, 1863.

Major-General SEDGWICK,
Commanding Sixth Corps:

GENERAL: I send my orderly to you.   Will you have the kindness to notify me if you move anywhere, or if the enemy makes any raid toward New Baltimore? I have had sundry intimations, but do not deem them altogether reliable, that the rebels contemplate a raid on some of our depots. The work of to-day may prevent it.

I sent out several scouting parties yesterday. One near White Plains met some of Mosby's men and had a skirmish. One of our party was severely wounded and left at a house at White Plains.

I still have a regiment at Greenwich, a brigade at Bristoe, and two brigades here. My force is very small. I will leave my orderly with you till to-morrow. Please send him with everything important. When it is not smoky, I communicate directly with Watery Mountain, and, by telegraph, with headquarters.

Very respectfully,

O. O. HOWARD,
Major-General.

WASHINGTON,
September 13, 1863—10.30 a. m.

General RUFUS KING:

The major-general commanding directs that in the event of Colonel Gibbs being attacked, you furnish him any support which may be necessary. If the occasion arises and you are compelled to detach troops from Centreville, you will receive all possible support from the immediate garrison of the defenses. Please keep these headquarters informed of all that occurs of importance.

Lowell will be informed of the substance of your dispatch and directed to act accordingly.

J. H. TAYLOR,
Chief of Staff.

HEADQUARTERS FOURTH SEPARATE BRIGADE,
Beverly, September 13, 1863.

Brig. Gen. B. F. KELLEY,
Wheeling.

All of Patton's forces at Lewisburg. Jackson at Huntersville with pickets at Marling's Bottom. Jenkins and Imboden at Crab Bottom, with about 3,000, grazing horses and drilling. Colonel Oley, with flag of truce, has effected an exchange for Captain Ewing, who will arrive to-morrow. He is doing well; can walk a little. Major McNally had left arm amputated, also wounded in head; doing well and will live. Captain Parker found dead on field. Sent a supply of medicines to our wounded.

WM. W. AVERELL,
Brigadier-General.

HEADQUARTERS ARMY OF THE POTOMAC,
September 14, 1863—10.30 a. m. (Received 11 a. m.)

Maj. Gen. H. W. HALLECK,
General-in-Chief:

Dispatches received from General Pleasonton subsequent to my telegram of 8 p. m. yesterday announce his having driven the enemy's cavalry and artillery to within 2 miles of the Rapidan at Raccoon Ford and Rapidan Station. An examination of the prisoners sent in shows that Ewell's and A. P. Hill's corps are still on the south side of the Rapidan near Orange Court-House and Raccoon Ford; that Lee has returned from Richmond; he having been seen on Saturday at Orange Court-House. It is believed and reported by the prisoners that Longstreet's corps had gone south, designation said to be Tennessee. McLaws' division, they assert positively, has passed through Richmond.

Pleasonton will this morning continue to press the enemy, and I will report any further authentic intelligence he may send in.

GEO. G. MEADE,
Major-General.

HEADQUARTERS ARMY OF THE POTOMAC,
September 14, 1863.

Commanding Officers Twelfth and other Corps:

As it is not yet known what may be the result of the movement now being made in the front, the commanding general directs that you hold your command in readiness to march at short notice.

S. WILLIAMS,
Assistant Adjutant-General.

SEPTEMBER 14, 1863—9 a. m.

General HERMANN HAUPT, *Washington:*

Our troops now occupy Culpeper Court-House, and General Meade will be glad to have the road opened to that place. The road is believed to be in fair order, but it doubtless requires examination. None of the rails have been removed.

S. WILLIAMS,
Assistant Adjutant-General.

SEPTEMBER 14, 1863—2 p. m.

Maj. Gen. GEORGE SYKES, *Commanding Fifth Corps:*

The commanding general directs me to say, in answer to your dispatch of this morning, that it is not now expected that the result of the reconnaissance sent to the front will be to require a general movement of the army. Should, however, such a movement become necessary, its nature cannot at this time be anticipated, and no instructions can be given as to the trains; such instructions must accompany an order for a move.

S. WILLIAMS,
Assistant Adjutant-General.

HDQRS. ARMY OF THE POTOMAC, *September* 14, 1863.
(Received 2.20 p. m.)

Maj. Gen. H. W. HALLECK, *General-in-Chief:*

The following dispatch, just received, is forwarded for your information:

RAPPAHANNOCK STATION.

Major-General HUMPHREYS:

Two intercepted letters, which I am bringing to headquarters, say General Lee has gone to Charleston or Chattanooga. General Longstreet commands the rebel

Army of the Potomac. General Pleasonton, at 9 a. m., was at Raccoon Ford, on the Rapidan. The enemy's cavalry and a battery of artillery held the opposite bank.

F. C. NEWHALL,
Captain, of Pleasonton's Staff.

GEO. G. MEADE,
Major-General.

CIRCULAR.]   HEADQUARTERS ARMY OF THE POTOMAC,
September 14, 1863—9.45 p. m.

Commanding Officer Eleventh Corps:

The commanding general desires me to make known to you the existing condition of affairs. General Pleasonton has driven the enemy's cavalry and artillery across the Rapidan, but was unable, owing to finding infantry and artillery in position, to effect a crossing at Raccoon, Somerville, or Mitchell's Fords (the railroad crossing). He now holds the north bank of the Rapidan, supported by the Second Corps at Culpeper Court-House. The rest of the army is in the positions formerly occupied. General Pleasonton has sent in 3 guns (2 3-inch and 1 12-pounder howitzer) and 120 prisoners. From the latter it is believed Longstreet's corps has gone south, but that Ewell and Hill are still behind the Rapidan prepared to dispute its passage.

The commanding general desires you to keep your command prepared to move at short notice, your trains supplied, and everything in readiness for an advance, which, from present appearances, will be the character of the movement, if any is made. This communication is confidential.

S. WILLIAMS,
Assistant Adjutant-General.

(To commanding officers First, Third, Fifth, Sixth, Eleventh, and Twelfth Corps.)

SEPTEMBER 14, 1863—9 p. m.
(Received 10.30 p. m.)

Major-General HALLECK :

General Pleasonton reports that he has driven the enemy's cavalry and artillery across the Rapidan, and has to-day unsuccessfully attempted to force a passage at three points, Raccoon Ford, Somerville Ford, and Mitchell's Ford (at the railroad crossing), being at each point met by artillery in position, and rifle-pits manned by infantry. General Gregg, at the railroad crossing, reports taking a prisoner of the Forty-eighth Mississippi Regiment, belonging to A. P. Hill's corps, who said the whole of Hill's corps was at or near Orange Court-House. Other prisoners taken yesterday aver that Ewell's corps is also behind the Rapidan.

My judgment, formed on the variety of meager and conflicting testimony, is, that Lee's army has been reduced by Longstreet's corps, and perhaps by some regiments from Ewell and Hill. What the amount of force left with him, it is difficult to conjecture, but I have no doubt it is deemed sufficient by him, with the advantages of position, to check my crossing the Rapidan, at least until he can withdraw, in case he desires to do so. Under these circumstances, I have

directed General Pleasonton to maintain his position on the Rapidan, to cross if practicable, and in the meantime to endeavor to
obtain more definite information. General Warren, with the Second Corps, will remain in position at Culpeper. I should be glad
to have your views as to what had better be done, if anything.

If Lee's army is as much reduced as the intelligence now received
would lead us to believe, when the detached troops from this army
return, I ought to be his superior in numbers, and should be able to
require him to fall back. At the same time, I see no object in advancing, unless it is with ulterior views, and I do not consider this
army is sufficiently large to follow him to Richmond (in case that
should prove practicable), and lay siege to that place, fortified as we
know it to be.

Moreover, the change of base, in case such a movement were
effected, must be determined—whether it shall be to the Fredericksburg railroad or the James River.

I should be glad if you would communicate the views of yourself
and the Government at the earliest possible moment.

GEO. G. MEADE,
Major-General, Commanding.

SEPTEMBER 14, 1863—7.30 p. m.

Commanding Officer Second Corps:

Your dispatch of 6.30 received. The commanding general does not
deem it expedient at this moment to throw an infantry force across the
Rapidan, and he wishes the operations on that river to be confined to
the cavalry, unless you think it best to support General Gregg with,
say, a brigade of infantry. Information, to be received within a day
or two, may lead the commanding general to move the entire army in
the direction of Gordonsville, but for the present your position will
be Culpeper.

S. WILLIAMS,
Assistant Adjutant-General.

SEPTEMBER 14, 1863—8.30 p. m.

Commanding Officer Second Corps:

Please send the following to General Pleasonton by special messenger.

GEO. G. MEADE.

[Inclosure.]

8.30 p. m.

Commanding Officer Cavalry Corps:

In consequence of the information thus far received, leading to
the opinion that you cannot effect a crossing of the Rapidan unless
strongly assisted by infantry, and as I am not prepared at the present moment to make a general movement of the army in that direction, I desire you to hold the line of the Rapidan, picketing well
above and below your position, and obtaining all the information
you can respecting the movements of the enemy.

If, however, you find you can succeed in crossing the river without hazarding the safety of your command, or risking a severe engagement, you will, of course, do so. The telegraph wire is now in working order to Culpeper, and I wish you to communicate with me frequently, and keep me fully advised of all that transpires in your vicinity.

GEO. G. MEADE,
Major-General, Commanding.

HEADQUARTERS ARMY OF THE POTOMAC,
September 14, 1863.

Maj. Gen. JOHN NEWTON,
     Commanding First Corps:

GENERAL: Your communication of the 13th, instant in reference to the detail of the Second Corps to support the cavalry reconnaissance sent in front of the army yesterday, has been laid before the commanding general, who regrets to learn that the detail has occasioned a feeling of disappointment among the officers and men of your corps.

The considerations which led the commanding general to select the Second Corps for this service were chiefly that the First Corps formed part of a line the continuity of which the general did not wish to break, as he could not foresee the consequences which might flow from our advance, and he was by no means certain that the reconnoitering party, together with its support, might not be driven back upon that line, and moreover, he had in view the fact that the First Corps had for some weeks occupied an advanced position, requiring on its part unusual watchfulness, and far more exhausting duties than had been performed by the corps in rear. The commanding general trusts that this explanation will satisfy you that in assigning the Second Corps to the duty above indicated no distrust was entertained of the qualifications of the First Corps to perform the service equally well.

I am directed to add that, while the commanding general has given in this instance his reasons for issuing a particular order, he does not admit the right of any subordinate commander to call in question his acts, and he regrets that you should have thought it proper to do so.

Very respectfully, your obedient servant,

S. WILLIAMS,
Assistant Adjutant-General.

CENTREVILLE, VA.,
September 14, 1863—1 p. m.

Colonel GRIMSHAW,
     Fairfax Station:

Three guerrillas captured two horses between Union Mills and this place, about half past 10 o'clock to-day. We have sent out cavalry and infantry after them. No train has been captured or interfered with.

RUFUS KING,
Brigadier-General of Volunteers.

CLARKSBURG,
September 14, 1863.

Colonel WYNKOOP,
 Sir John's Run:

You will call in your companies at Bloomery Gap and Bath to Sir John's Run, where you can have them under your own eyes. I fear the affair at Bath the other day was the result of negligence on the part of the officers in command. You will hereafter keep the country in your front constantly and thoroughly scouted, and do it in such a way that the enemy shall not be aware of your movements.

If you have more clothing or other quartermaster's stores than you require for immediate use, you will send the surplus to Cumberland, and store it with Captain Harrison, assistant quartermaster, for safety.

         B. F. KELLEY,
          Brigadier-General.

————

CLARKSBURG,
September 14, 1863.

Brigadier-General AVERELL,
 Beverly:

I will send the passes for Mr. Parker and daughter, as you suggested. Major Stephens was attacked at Moorefield Friday morning by Imboden's men, and 160 of his men were captured. I have no particulars yet. Will order the ammunition sent you at once. Was this ammunition included in the former order?

         B. F. KELLEY,
          Brigadier-General.

————

HEADQUARTERS FOURTH SEPARATE BRIGADE,
Beverly, *September* 14, 1863.

Brig. Gen. B. F. KELLEY,
 Commanding Department:

Major Gibson informed me before Major Bowen's return that he did not want re-enforcements. Nothing was accomplished by Bowen's absence. I understand he allowed his men to get drunk. Ten militiamen escaped from rebels, who retired by Hacker's Lick.

Major Gibson is strengthened by the return of Bowen. I notified the militia the day before they were attacked to look out. If they permitted themselves to be captured after that, on their own ground, I do not think they can be any great loss.

         WM. W. AVERELL,
          Brigadier-General.

————

HEADQUARTERS, *Cincinnati,* *September* 14, 1863.
(Received Barboursville, 15th.)

Major-General BURNSIDE,
 Knoxville:

General Scammon, in the Kanawha Valley, reports the enemy strengthening in his front, with a view to driving him out of West Virginia, as he thinks. Their force is stated at thirteen regiments of infantry and cavalry. If this proves true, my own opinion would be that it is a diversion to bring your troops back to Ohio, and that a show of force moving from Tennessee into Southwestern Virginia would stop them.

J. D. COX,
Brigadier-General.

WAR DEPARTMENT,
Washington, September 14, 1863—1 p. m.

Major-General FOSTER,
Fort Monroe, Va.:

Information received here indicates that a part of Lee's force has gone to Petersburg. There are various suppositions for this. Some think it is intended to put down the Union feeling in North Carolina; others to make an attempt to capture Norfolk; and others, again, to threaten Norfolk, so as to compel us to send re-enforcements there from the Army of the Potomac, and then to move rapidly against Meade. Such was the plan last spring, when Longstreet invested Suffolk. It will be well to strengthen Norfolk as much as possible, and to closely watch the enemy's movements. I think he will soon strike a blow somewhere.

H. W. HALLECK,
General-in-Chief.

FORT MONROE, VA., *September* 14, 1863.
(Received 3 p. m.)

Major-General HALLECK:

I think we can take care of Norfolk, as I have pushed the defenses with all the available force, and have got them in a pretty strong state. I would not like to ask for any re-enforcements from the Army of the Potomac, in view of the splendid chance which it now has before it, if the information given by Bell proves to be true.

J. G. FOSTER,
Major-General.

FORT MONROE,
September 14, 1863.

General NAGLEE,
Norfolk:

Recent information from all sides represents that a considerable movement of troops took place last week, apparently to re-enforce General Bragg from Lee's army. It is probable that the running of the trains incessantly for the past few days has something to do with this, either to carry more troops to Bragg or to bring those back that passed down on the first of last week. I desire that you will send out reconnaissances to obtain all the information on this point that you possibly can.

J. G. FOSTER.

FORT MONROE, VA., *September* 14, 1863—10 a. m.
(Received 12.50 p. m.)

Maj. Gen. H. W. HALLECK,
General-in-Chief:

I have just received a letter from General Peck, at New Berne, dated the 12th, stating that a Mr. Clements, of Reading, Pa., had come through from Graham, N. C., arriving at New Berne that day. Clements states that a large body of troops from Lee's army passed through Raleigh, going to join Bragg, last week, the last of one portion passing on Tuesday last. The estimated strength of the force varied from 15,000 to 20,000, but Clements, who is a railroad man, estimates the number at 13,000. He conversed with the troops, and all said they were going to join Bragg, and that the North would not know of the movement. This information, coupled with the known continuous running of the cars for the past few days, may be of value to you, if it coincides with your own information. There is no doubt that a considerable movement of troops was going on last week, and is continued now in all probability.

Clements also confirms the report of the conflict between the citizens and Georgia troops at Raleigh, resulting in the gutting of the Standard and Register offices. Governor Vance issued a proclamation on the 7th, calling upon the people to be united and support the Confederate Government, &c.

J. G. FOSTER,
Major-General.

———

FORT MONROE, VA., *September* 14, 1863.
(Received 3 p. m.)

Maj. Gen. H. W. HALLECK,
General-in-Chief:

General Getty reports at this moment that a deserter named Bell, from the Sixth Virginia, has come in from Richmond, and reports that Hill's corps, from Lee's army, has gone to Tennessee via Lynchburg, and Longstreet's corps is going there at this time via Weldon. Ewell's corps and the cavalry, 5,000 strong, constitute the only force left with Lee. Bell saw two regiments of Longstreet's corps last Friday in Petersburg on their way to Tennessee, and derived his information from them. I have sent for Bell, and, after closely questioning him, will inform you further.

J. G. FOSTER,
Major-General.

———

FORT MONROE, VA.,
September 14, 1863.

General PECK,
Commanding Forces in North Carolina:

GENERAL: I received your letter this morning by the hand of Major Jenney, and have sent the information to General Halleck. The flag-of-truce boat brought us yesterday information confirmatory of yours, viz, that the cars have been constantly running night and day for some days past. Evidently a considerable movement of troops has been and is taking place, perhaps to the amount of 30,000 men. The objective point appears to be either Knoxville or Chattanooga, to crush either Burnside or Rosecrans, undoubtedly the latter, especially if he has advanced to Atlanta.

With respect to the iron-clads on the Neuse and Roanoke, we can do nothing at present that I can see. The most would be a cavalry raid on Edwards Ferry, and this will take preparation and combination, and even then terminate as the last one did. If it fails it will show the rebels where to prepare for us when we come in force. It is far better to wait until we get an infantry force sufficient to do the work with certainty. I shall write to General Halleck about this, but the understanding is that now as ever the Army of the Potomac is getting all the re-enforcements. Therefore we may have to wait some time.

Very respectfully and truly, yours,

J. G. FOSTER,
Major-General, Commanding.

WASHINGTON, D. C.,
September 14, 1863—3 p. m.

Major-General BURNSIDE,
    Knoxville, Tenn.:

There are reasons why you should re-enforce General Rosecrans with all possible dispatch. It is believed that the enemy will concentrate to give him battle. You must be there to help him.*

H. W. HALLECK.

GENERAL ORDERS,   } HDQRS. U. S. TROOPS CITY AND HARBOR,
   No. 20.   }   *New York City, September* 14, 1863.

In relieving from further duty with this command a large portion of the troops sent here from the Army of the Potomac, the commanding general desires to express his gratification that the exemplary conduct of these troops has added another—less brilliant, perhaps, but not less enduring—to the many laurels already won by them on the field and under the fire of the enemy, and to say that he is authorized from many sources to convey to them the assurance that their sojourn in this city, in more than usually intimate contact with their fellow citizens, has excited for them a personal interest above that ordinarily attached to any army, and that this interest will not pass away with the occasion that gave rise to it, but will follow them wherever they may go, and to whatever field they may be called, with the warmest wishes for their success and welfare.

The commanding general desires to add to this the expression of his thanks to the State troops, the metropolitan police force, and to the local authorities with whom he has been incidentally associated, for the kindness and courtesy shown to the officers and men of his command, and for the spirit of co-operation exhibited in everything that had for its object the advancement of our common wishes and labors.

By order of Brigadier-General Canby:

C. T. CHRISTENSEN,
Assistant Adjutant-General.

---

* For Burnside's reply and other correspondence on this subject, see Series I, Vol. XXX.

WASHINGTON,
September 15, 1863—11 a. m.

Major-General MEADE:

I think preparations should be made to at least threaten Lee, and, if possible, cut off a slice of his army. I do not think the exact condition of affairs is sufficiently ascertained to authorize any very considerable advance. I will write more fully to-day.

H. W. HALLECK.

———

HEADQUARTERS ARMY OF THE POTOMAC,
September 15, 1863—4 p. m. (Received 4.30 p. m.)

Maj. Gen. H. W. HALLECK,
General-in-Chief:

The latest intelligence from the front is to 10 a. m., when General Pleasonton reports that the enemy have increased their forces, both infantry and artillery, at the several crossing places threatened by our cavalry. The enemy have likewise a force of infantry and artillery on this side of the Rapidan (at the railroad crossing), evidently to defend and dispute the possession of the bridge at that place. General Warren remains at Culpeper, to which point our trains run, and the telegraph is being opened to Mitchell's Station, the rebels having left their line intact. Two scouts have arrived from below, having been some 5 miles south of Chancellorsville. They confirm the report of the departure of Longstreet's corps, but heard nothing of Ewell's or Hill's corps leaving.

Your telegram of 11 a. m. this day has been received. I have given orders to concentrate and mass the different corps at the several crossing places on the Rappahannock, but shall await your letter before making any further forward movement.

GEO. G. MEADE,
Major-General.

———

WASHINGTON, D. C., *September* 15, 1863.

Major-General MEADE, *Army of the Potomac:*

GENERAL: After preparing my telegram to you this morning, I received a note from the President, of which I send you a copy. I do not understand this note as materially differing from my dispatch. The main objects are to threaten Lee's position, to ascertain more certainly the actual condition of affairs in his army, and, if possible, to cut off some portion of it by a sudden raid, if that be practicable. And especially every effort should be made to ascertain if any considerable forces have gone by the Valley Railroad toward East Tennessee. This is exceedingly important in regard to General Burnside's operations. His forces were ordered some days ago to move toward Chattanooga to co-operate with Rosecrans against Johnston and Bragg. This will leave East Tennessee comparatively open on the Virginia side. Railroad communication, however, has been entirely destroyed to near Abingdon. The greater danger, however, is that Bragg may attempt to turn Rosecrans' right and cut off his communication on the Tennessee River. It was to enable Rosecrans to strengthen his right that Burnside was ordered to move on Chattanooga. Hurlbut and Sherman were also ordered to concentrate all their available forces at Tuscumbia, or in that vicinity, to co-operate with Rosecrans. This exhausts all the available forces we have in the west on the east side of the Mississippi River. Banks and Steele are operating in Louisiana and Arkansas, and no troops can be withdrawn from them without breaking up their expeditions.

You will see from this statement that I have done all in my power to meet the contingency of the probable re-enforcement of Bragg by a part of Lee's army. The enemy probably fear an attack on Atlanta, or seek to crush Rosecrans and recover East Tennessee.

In regard to your own army, you are aware that it will be impossible at present in any contingency to give you any considerable re-enforcements. No rash movements can, therefore, be ventured. Nevertheless, if Lee's force has been very considerably reduced, something may be done to weaken him or force him still farther back. Moreover, all the country this side of the Rapidan can be stripped of supplies, to support our army and to prevent their falling into the hands of the enemy if he should again advance. All provisions and forage not required for the immediate support of non-combatants should be taken.

The enemy probably saw that if you and Rosecrans could hold your present position till Grant and Banks cleaned out the States west of the Mississippi, the fate of the rebellion would be sealed. His policy undoubtedly was to concentrate all his available forces against you or Rosecrans. All the information I could gather until within the last few days indicated that you would be attacked. It would now seem that Rosecrans and Burnside will be made to receive the shock.

I think, for obvious reasons, that this letter should be immediately destroyed. You can at any time obtain a copy from the archives here.

Very respectfully, your obedient servant,

H. W. HALLECK,
General-in-Chief.

[Inclosure.]

EXECUTIVE MANSION,
Washington, September 15, 1863.

Major-General HALLECK:

If I did not misunderstand General Meade's last dispatch, he posts you on facts as well as he can, and desires your views and those of the Government as to what he shall do. My opinion is that he should move upon Lee at once in manner of general attack, leaving to developments whether he will make it a real attack. I think this would develop Lee's real condition and purposes better than the cavalry alone can do. Of course, my opinion is not to control you and General Meade.

Yours, truly,

A. LINCOLN.

HEADQUARTERS ARMY OF THE POTOMAC,
September 15, 1863—12 p. m.

Major-General HALLECK,
General-in-Chief:

GENERAL: Your letter of this date, per Captain Wager, has been received, read, and destroyed. In accordance with the views therein expressed, I have ordered the army to cross the Rappahannock, and shall take up a position to-morrow with my left at Stevensburg and right at Stone-House Mountain.   I will then picket the Rapidan with infantry, and thus relieve the cavalry, and will endeavor, by means of the latter, to obtain more information.

I have no doubt Longstreet's corps has gone south through Richmond.   I have heard of no troops passing through Lynchburg from Gordonsville, but he can take the road from Petersburg.   He has undoubtedly gone to re-enforce Bragg.   I am satisfied Lee has still Ewell and Hill with him; not less than 40,000 or 45,000 infantry and over 5,000 cavalry.   I hardly think he will cross the Rapidan to meet me at Culpeper, unless he is ignorant of my actual force.   If he does not, it will be a difficult problem to attack him or compel him to fall back, as he has such advantages in the line of the Rapidan, enabling him, by means of artillery and rifle-pits, to hold it with much less force than is required to force the passage.   I will not make the attempt unless I can see my way clear, and I do not much expect any greater success than requiring him to fall still farther back.

I am a little concerned about my line of communications, which will be lengthened by this movement some 20 miles, and I would be glad if the cavalry now in Washington belonging to this army could be sent out, and this arm increased by re-enforcements.   I will advise you further by telegraph.

Respectfully, yours,

GEO. G. MEADE,
Major-General.

·HDQRS. CAVALRY CORPS, ARMY OF THE POTOMAC,
September 15, 1863—8.30 a. m.

Brigadier-General GREGG,
Commanding Second Cavalry Division:

GENERAL : General Kilpatrick will connect with you to-day and give you assistance to push the enemy in front of you across the river, if you think it can be done.   You will occupy the line of the Rapidan until further orders, picketing well above and to your flank, and keeping me fully advised of anything that occurs.   Send your train back for supplies, and, if you can spare the men, send to my headquarters for your share of new horses out of the 1,000 just from Washington.   Let the officers see Lieutenant Spangler about them.   He is to be found near my headquarters, north of the Rappahannock.

Very respectfully,

A. PLEASONTON,
Major-General, Commanding.

SEPTEMBER 15, 1863—1.30 p. m.

Commanding Officer Sixth Corps:

The commanding general directs that you concentrate your corps at Sulphur Springs to-day prepared to cross the river.   You will leave a sufficient guard at Warrenton to protect the depot at that place until broken up.   Please acknowledge.

S. WILLIAMS,
Assistant Adjutant-General.

HEADQUARTERS THIRD DIVISION, CAVALRY CORPS,
September 15, 1863.

Lieut. Col. C. ROSS SMITH,
Chief of Staff, Cavalry Corps:

COLONEL: Colonel Gray, commanding pickets at Somerville Ford, reports that the enemy are constantly throwing up intrenchments opposite the ford and have four field batteries in position. Their people from the rifle-pits are firing upon my men by volleys. I shall strengthen my pickets at the ford. He also reports a large number of camp fires in rear of the batteries. I shall also strengthen my pickets at Robertson's Ford. The enemy have planted a battery of six guns at this ford.

Very respectfully,
J. KILPATRICK,
Brig. Gen. of Vols., Commanding Third Division.

SEPTEMBER 15, 1863—9 a. m.

Commanding Officer Second Corps:

I wish you would send word to Pleasonton to examine the banks of the Rapidan with a view to select some one or two points where a passage can be forced by pontoon bridging, and where the enemy are not now prepared to resist. These points should be between the railroad and the mouth, so as to turn the enemy's right flank. Of course this examination must be made so as not to attract their attention. If you could spare Roebling for this purpose I should be obliged to you.

GEO. G. MEADE,
Major-General, Commanding.

SEPTEMBER 15, 1863—1.50 p. m.

Commanding Officer Twelfth Corps:

The commanding general directs that in the course of to-day you concentrate your command at Kelly's Ford prepared to cross the river. You will, however, leave a thin line of pickets as far down as Ellis' Ford.

Please acknowledge.

S. WILLIAMS,
Assistant Adjutant-General.

HDQRS. TWELFTH CORPS, ARMY OF THE POTOMAC,
September 15, 1863.

Brig. Gen. ALPHEUS S. WILLIAMS,
Commanding Division:

GENERAL: The major-general commanding directs that you hold your command in readiness to cross the river at Kelly's Ford to-morrow morning.

Very respectfully, your obedient servant,
H. C. RODGERS,
Assistant Adjutant-General.

SEPTEMBER 15, 1863—1.30 p. m.

Commanding Officer Third Corps:

The commanding general directs that you concentrate your command at or in the vicinity of Fox's Mills to-day prepared to cross the river. Your headquarters can remain where they now are, unless you think it best to change your position, and in that event you will leave an officer with a suitable party at the telegraph station to receive and forward messages.

Please acknowledge.

S. WILLIAMS,
Assistant Adjutant-General.

SEPTEMBER 15, 1863—6.10 p. m.

Commanding Officer Third Corps:

The commanding general authorizes you to mass your command at Freeman's Ford, instead of Fox's Mills as heretofore ordered. The general wishes you, if practicable, to find a road to Culpeper which does not cut the roads from Sulphur Springs and Rappahannock Station to that place.

S. WILLIAMS,
Assistant Adjutant-General.

RAPPAHANNOCK STATION, *September* 15, 1863.

General WILLIAMS:

My command is all within striking distance of Beverly Ford. Before one portion of it could cross the river, the remainder would be closed on the forward.

GEO. SYKES,
Major-General.

RAPPAHANNOCK STATION, *September* 15, 1863—7.50 p. m.

General S. WILLIAMS:

In one place Beverly Ford is nearly 3 feet deep, the bottom very rough, and the entrance and outcome very soft and boggy. It will be very difficult for the artillery and trains to cross. Is it intended to throw a bridge or not? If it is, the spot in front of Hamilton's house is the best place for it.

GEO. SYKES,
Major-General.

HEADQUARTERS CAVALRY CORPS,
September 15, [1863]—7.50 p. m.

Brigadier-General GREGG,
Commanding Second Cavalry Division:

GENERAL: The major-general commanding directs that you have your command well in hand, so that, if it is necessary to fall back, you will have your command ready to work it. Have your train well out of the way.

Very respectfully, your obedient servant,

C. ROSS SMITH,
Lieutenant-Colonel, and Chief of Staff.

HEADQUARTERS CAVALRY CORPS,
September 15, [1863]—11.50 p. m.

Brigadier-General GREGG,
    Commanding Second Cavalry Division:

The major-general commanding directs that you hold your position as long as you possibly can.

C. ROSS SMITH,
Lieutenant-Colonel, Chief of Staff.

HEADQUARTERS CAVALRY CORPS,
September 15, 1863.

Major-General WARREN,
    Commanding Second Army Corps:

GENERAL: Major-General Pleasonton desires me to say to you that General Kilpatrick reports that the enemy have received heavy re-enforcements; that there has been cheering and bands playing to-night. You can hear the rumbling of artillery and trains. You had better have your corps up here by daylight, for they could make a crossing with their infantry in the morning against the force we could bring against them, as we have such a long line to protect and they have the railroad bridge to cross upon.

C. ROSS SMITH,
Lieutenant-Colonel, Chief of Staff.

SEPTEMBER 15, 1863—10 p. m.

Commanding Officer Cavalry Corps:

What reason have you for supposing the enemy will attempt to drive you back with infantry ? I am not yet prepared to move the whole army forward, awaiting instructions from Washington, but if you have reason to believe, or have any evidence that Lee will cross the Rapidan to give me battle between the two rivers, it would prove his having a greater force than we have supposed, and would militate against the retrograde movement.

GEO. G. MEADE,
Major-General, Commanding.

CIRCULAR.]   HEADQUARTERS ARMY OF THE POTOMAC,
September 15, 1863—11.25 p. m.

To all Corps and Independent Commanders:

The following movements of troops are ordered, and will take place to-morrow, the 16th instant, and will commence punctually at 5 a. m. :

Twelfth Corps, to Stevensburg.

First Corps, midway between Stevensburg and Culpeper Court-House.

Second Corps, Culpeper.

Fifth Corps, in rear of Culpeper.

Third Corps, midway between Culpeper and Stone-House Mountain.

Sixth Corps, at Stone-House Mountain.

Eleventh Corps will be distributed to guard the bridges at Rappahannock crossing, Catlett's, and Bristoe.

The depots at Bealeton, Warrenton, and Warrenton Junction will be broken up, and all supplies drawn from Culpeper Court-House, where a depot will be established.

The Artillery Reserve will move forward and take position in the vicinity of Fifth Corps.

The cavalry will picket the front and guard the flanks of the army.

Headquarters will be at Culpeper Court-House or vicinity.

By command of Major-General Meade:

S. WILLIAMS,
Assistant Adjutant-General.

HDQRS. ARMY AND DISTRICT OF NORTH CAROLINA,
New Berne, N. C., September 15, 1863.

Maj. Gen. J. G. FOSTER,
Comdg. Dept. of Virginia and North Carolina:

GENERAL: The United States is divided into two portions by the Alleghany Mountains, which may be called the Atlantic Slope and the Mississippi Valley. By the successful advance of Rosecrans and Burnside to the eastern limits of Tennessee and Kentucky, the Mississippi Valley is virtually closed, and forever, to the Confederate armies. The rebellion is now hemmed in between the mountains and the Atlantic, and its operations are confined to five States.

Probably concentration will leave but two great armies in the field, aside from the forces in and about Charleston, one in the Old Dominion and the other at the south. Assuming that Burnside cuts effectually, as was his chief business, the Virginia and Tennessee Railway, North Carolina becomes of prime military importance, from her relation to the remaining lines of rebel communication, all of which traverse the State.

Under existing circumstances, actual possession of Hicksford, or Weldon and Gaston, would control the Weldon and Wilmington, the Weldon and Raleigh, and the Weldon, Gaston and Roanoke Valley Railroads. An army of 40,000 men there would beyond question compel the evacuation of Virginia, which would have a very depressing and dispiriting influence upon the rebels in the few remaining States of the Confederacy.

It is well to remember that there is an important line of railway leading from Richmond to Danville, which, upon completion, will connect the principal lines of Virginia and North Carolina without passing through Hicksford, Gaston, or Weldon. This connection is from Danville to Hillsborough or Greensborough, some 35 or 40 miles, and it is certain that it is being pushed to completion with all possible dispatch. Indeed, I was advised in June that this connection was complete, but it lacks confirmation.

Wilmington, or rather the mouth of the Cape Fear River, is daily growing in importance to the rebels, in consequence of our successful operations in the harbor of Charleston. If half the reports are true, many vessels succeed in evading the blockade of the river. Doubtless much of the trade that has been carried on with Charleston will seek a port at Wilmington.

Very respectfully, your obedient servant,

JOHN J. PECK,
Major-General.

WASHINGTON, D. C.,
September 15, 1863—4.30 p. m.

Major-General BURNSIDE,
        Knoxville:

From information received here to-day, it is very probable that three divisions of Lee's army have been sent to re-enforce Bragg. It is important that all the troops in your department be brought to the front with all possible dispatch, so as to help General Rosecrans.

H. W. HALLECK,
General-in-Chief.

WASHINGTON, D. C.,
September 15, 1863—4.30 p. m.

Major-General ROSECRANS,
        Chattanooga:

From information received here to-day, it is very probable that three divisions of Lee's army have been sent to re-enforce Bragg. All the troops in the Departments of the Ohio and the Cumberland should be brought to the front to meet the enemy. Sherman and Hurlbut will bring re-enforcements to the Tennessee River as rapidly as possible.*

H. W. HALLECK.

GENERAL ORDERS, }   HDQRS. DISTRICT OF VIRGINIA,
    No. 4. }   *Norfolk, September 15, 1863.*

The following picket stations are hereby established, and the following orders will be observed by all picket and other guard duty upon the front between the Western Branch and the Dismal Swamp:

No. 1. At the bridge at Davids' Mills.

No. 2. At the bridge at Fort Curtis.

No. 3. At the gate on the main Bowers' Hill road at Fort Rodman.

No. 4. At Deep Creek village.

No. 5. At the gate in the Deep Creek road at Fort Reno.

No. 6. At the intersection of the Deep Creek road with the Portsmouth road from the navy-yard at the house of John Berry.

No. 7. On the main Bowers' Hill road near the late camp of the First New York Mounted Rifles.

No. 8. At the intersection of the main Deep Creek and Bowers' Hill roads. Other posts will be established upon the railroads and at less important places.

No. 1. At Davids' Mills Bridge, the plank of which will be habitually removed, the commissioned officer commanding the guard will

---

* See Halleck to Grant or Sherman, September 13; to Hurlbut, September 14 and 15, and to Pope and Schofield, September 15, Series I, Vol. XXX.

permit no citizen whatever, either with or without a pass, to cross beyond the bridge, and no soldiers will be allowed to pass, except officers and soldiers actually on picket and other duty. No persons will be allowed to pass in, excepting contrabands, deserters, and refugees, who will take the oath of allegiance and an oath that they will remain within the lines until the termination of the war, and all of whom will be sent to the provost-marshal at Norfolk under guard. The plank of the bridge at Fort Curtis will be removed at night.

No. 2. The guard will be furnished with an alphabetical list of all citizens, not exceeding one from each family, who reside between the creeks that pass at Nos. 1 and 2. They will be permitted to pass from their respective houses to and from Portsmouth by the nearest road, passing in on Tuesday and Friday and out on Wednesday and Saturday, but they will not be permitted to travel or be absent from their homes after sundown.

The guards at Nos. 3, 4, 5, 6, 7, will be furnished by General Getty with alphabetical lists of all citizens, not exceeding one from each family, who will be permitted to pass, only upon business, from their respective homes to and from Portsmouth by the nearest road on Monday, Wednesday, and Saturday between sunrise and sunset, and at no other time.

The railroad bridges at certain points will be removed by order of General Getty, and no person whatever will be allowed to pass in either direction along the railroad.

The pickets will arrest all persons who shall leave the roads and attempt to avoid any of the picket stations, and all persons who shall attempt to pass to the front in violation of this order.

No. 8. Colonel Dutton will station a guard at the intersection of the main road from Portsmouth with that from Deep Creek. It will be furnished with the proper list and orders to supervise all travel that may pass at this point, allowing no citizens to pass unless upon the list, and no soldiers without proper passes. All officers passing without proper permission will be reported on the morning guard reports, and to these headquarters through the proper channel. All soldiers or contrabands that attempt to pass without proper authority will be imprisoned at Portsmouth until the following morning, where they will be delivered before it is relieved to the old guard at post No. 6 or 7, who will turn them over; the latter to the provost-marshal, and the former to the colonel of the regiment to which they belong, who will order them before a field officer for punishment.

Any non-residents found within the limits of the above stations, elsewhere than on the way from his or her home to or from Portsmouth, will be arrested.

All passes will be taken up, when the purpose for which they were issued has been fulfilled, and returned to the provost-marshal at Norfolk.

General officers may pass any and all pickets and guards, but if they pass beyond the picket line it will be noted on the guard report. General officers will indicate at these headquarters their intention to pass to Fort Monroe.

Field officers will not pass beyond the limits of their division or their brigade, or, where there is not a division organization, without proper authority.

Line officers will not pass beyond the limits of their brigade without permission of their brigade commanders, nor beyond that of the division without the approval of the division commander, nor across Hampton Roads without the permission of the commanding officer of the district.

Soldiers will not be permitted to leave their regiment without permission of their colonel, nor to leave their brigade or division without the approval of the respective commanders thereof.

Soldiers on duty in the quartermaster's and commissary departments required to go continually to Portsmouth will be entered upon the proper alphabetical list.

In the event of an attack all families will be required to go to Portsmouth.

The discipline of any command may be known by the manner in which the guard duty is performed, and the commanding officer regrets to find it his duty to censure the almost universal neglect and carelessness that now prevails in this respect. The attention of all officers is hereby called to the necessity of an immediate and thorough reformation.

Sentinels who rest their muskets upon the ground, and do not walk their posts, and do talk with any one that will listen to them, may be seen in every direction, and in a tour of inspection to the front, where an attack might have been expected at any moment, pickets not only left their horses, but without exception were lying upon their backs fully absorbed in the perusal of light literature.

Soldiers will not do their duty unless their officers require it to be done, and for inefficiency originating with the latter, they will be held responsible. The heavy labor of the trenches is nearly over, and let us one and all unite and gain for the command a reputation for cleanliness, order, and discipline that all will refer to with pride and satisfaction.

By command of Brigadier-General Naglee:

GEORGE H. JOHNSTON,
Assistant Adjutant-General.

HEADQUARTERS ARMY OF THE POTOMAC,
September 16, 1863—8.40 a. m.   (Received 9.20 a. m.)
Maj. Gen. H. W. HALLECK,
General-in-Chief:

As my advance will materially lengthen my line of communication, the guarding of which I have assigned to the Eleventh Corps, I feel justified in asking that the 500 men of that corps recently sent to Alexandria as a guard for drafted men may, if practicable, be relieved by troops from General Heintzelman's department.

GEO. G. MEADE,
Major-General.

HEADQUARTERS ARMY OF THE POTOMAC,
September 16, 1863—9 p. m.   (Received 11.40 p. m.)
Maj. Gen. H. W. HALLECK,
General-in-Chief:

The army is in position around Culpeper Court-House—the right at Stone-House Mountain, the left at Stevensburg. The cavalry picket the river in front. Artillery firing has been kept up by the enemy all day, and occasionally efforts have been made at one or two points to throw over infantry, but they have been repelled. There is no doubt, however, they can cross whenever they bring a sufficient force to bear. Railroad trains were arriving all night and day, and much cheering on their arrival. I think Lee will concentrate all his available force to resist any attempt on my part to cross the river. His position, immediately in my front, is very strong, and the attempt to force a passage very critical. The river might possibly be crossed by a flank movement, but this would expose my communications or involve the danger of detachments.

I am so far from my base that, should Lee not be so much reduced as we suppose, he might, by crossing at Falmouth, interpose between my army and Washington. This renders me very doubtful of the expediency of advancing farther without some very definite and positive information of his position and numbers. I regret the duty of guarding conscripts could not have been assumed by General Heintzelman at Alexandria, as the 500 men taken from the Eleventh Corps are greatly needed for defending the railroad.

> GEO. G. MEADE,
> *Major-General.*

CULPEPER, *September* 16, 1863—12.15 a. m.
(Received 1 a. m.)

General S. WILLIAMS,
  Assistant Adjutant-General:

Dispatch in regard to movements received. General Warren has just left. I have opened as directed. Will forward at once. Please tell General Patrick that I will be ready to turn over the town as soon as he shall arrive. I have one regiment I will lend him.

> ALEX. S. WEBB,
> *Brigadier-General, Commanding.*

FIFTH CORPS, *September* 16, 1863—1 a. m.

General S. WILLIAMS:

I have received the order directing a movement for to-morrow. The dispatch does not state where I shall cross the Rappahannock, nor what troops have precedence, the First or Fifth Corps. I hear nothing of the bridge that was to be thrown over the river for me near Beverly Ford. Therefore conclude I am to cross at Rappahannock Bridge.

> GEO. SYKES,
> *Major-General.*

SEPTEMBER 16, 1863—1 a. m.

Commanding Officer Cavalry Corps:

Your dispatch of 11.30 p. m. received. The commanding general does not think it expedient to throw General Warren forward until the army is within supporting distance of him, as if you were driven back, he, too, would probably be overcome by numbers.

> S. WILLIAMS,
> *Assistant Adjutant-General.*

HDQRS. CAVALRY CORPS, ARMY OF THE POTOMAC,
September 16, 1863—1.30 a. m.

Brigadier-General GREGG,
    Commanding Second Cavalry Division:

GENERAL: The major-general commanding directs that you hold Cedar Mountain as long as possible, and General Warren will support you at Fox Mountain. The Second Corps will occupy from Culpeper Court-House to Fox Mountain. You had better fall back toward Fox Mountain, if you are forced. The Army of the Potomac crosses and takes up position on this side of the Rappahannock this morning. You can have your pickets withdrawn from Carter's Run.

C. ROSS SMITH,
Lieutenant-Colonel, and Chief of Staff.

HEADQUARTERS ARMY OF THE POTOMAC,
September 16, 1863.

Commanding Officer Third Corps:

Information just received leads to the supposition that the enemy is crossing the Rapidan with his infantry. The commanding general therefore directs that you move up as rapidly as practicable to take the position assigned you in the instructions of last night, communicating with General Sedgwick on your right and General Warren on your left.

Very respectfully, &c.,

S. WILLIAMS,
Assistant Adjutant-General.

HEADQUARTERS ARMY OF THE POTOMAC,
September 16, 1863.

Commanding Officer Sixth Corps:

Information just received leads to the supposition that the enemy is crossing the Rapidan with his infantry. The commanding general therefore directs that you move up as rapidly as possible with your command to take the position indicated in your instructions of last night communicating with General French on your left.

Very respectfully, &c.,

S. WILLIAMS,
Assistant Adjutant-General.

HEADQUARTERS ARMY OF THE POTOMAC,
September 16, 1863.

Commandiny Officer Twelfth Corps:

I am instructed by the commanding general to say that you have been ordered with your command down to Raccoon Ford, to relieve the cavalry pickets and to closely watch the movements of the enemy. Although it is not expected that, in case the enemy should attempt to cross the river in your front in greatly superior force, you will be able to prevent the accomplishment of their object, yet the commanding general looks to you to oppose and retard any movement they may make in this direction sufficiently to enable the commanding general to be informed of such movement, and to make his arrangements to meet it. The commanding general desires you to keep him fully informed of any movements the enemy may make in your vicinity.

Very respectfully, &c.,

S. WILLIAMS,
Assistant Adjutant-General.

CIRCULAR.]   HEADQUARTERS ARMY OF THE POTOMAC,
September 16, 1863—8.30 p. m.

The Second Corps will move at early daylight to-morrow and relieve the cavalry pickets from Somerville Ford to Cedar Mountain, including both places. At the same time the Twelfth Corps will move down to Raccoon Ford, and connect with the pickets of the Second Corps at Somerville and picket the river down to Morton's Ford, relieving the cavalry pickets.

The Fifth Corps will take the position now occupied by the Second Corps, on the ridge in front of the village of Culpeper.

The commander of the Cavalry Corps will assign a brigade to connect with the pickets of the Second Corps and cover the right flank of the army. He will also direct two squadrons, each containing not less than 100 men, to report to the commander of the Second and Twelfth Corps.

The commander of the Cavalry Corps will make suitable dispositions to guard the left flank of the army, and will assemble his reserve force at Stevensburg.

The chief of artillery will furnish such additional batteries as the commanders of the Second and Twelfth Corps may call for.

By command of Major-General Meade:

S. WILLIAMS,
Assistant Adjutant-General.

BEVERLY,
September 16, 1863.

Brig. Gen. B. F. KELLEY,
Commanding Department:

Scouts which left Crab Bottom night before last report Jenkins there with 2,000 mounted men, expecting to be joined by Imboden and Jackson, when they intend moving this way. I have some men in his camp to-day, who will return on Friday.

WM. W. AVERELL,
Brigadier-General.

NORFOLK,
September 16, 1863.

General FOSTER:

By the way of South Mills, I learn a considerable force of Lee's army passed Raleigh for Chattanooga. A Georgia regiment destroyed the Standard. The citizens mobbed and destroyed all the secession papers in Raleigh.

NAGLEE,
Brigadier-General.

FORT MONROE, VA., *September* 16, 1863—10 a. m.
(Received 10.10 a. m.)
Maj. Gen. H. W. HALLECK,
General-in-Chief:

Fresh reports continue to come in, establishing the fact that a considerable force of Lee's army has passed to the south and southwest, principally to Chattanooga. In passing through Raleigh a Georgia regiment destroyed the Standard. The citizens then mobbed and destroyed all the secession papers in the city. Such is the report received this morning.

J. G. FOSTER,
Major-General.

HDQRS. ARMY AND DISTRICT OF NORTH CAROLINA,
New Berne, N. C., September 16, 1863.
Maj. Gen. J. G. FOSTER,
Comdg. Dept. of Virginia and North Carolina:

Yours of the 14th was received at the hands of Major Jenney. Your views accord with mine in the matter of raids at the present. Since my dispatch, General Wessells reports a great movement south, with all the trains in the hands of the Government, so that citizens are unable to travel. This confirms the information I sent you, being from a most reliable source.

In all this movement, which is estimated at 30,000, I am very certain that General Hood's division is to remain in North Carolina for the purpose of collecting deserters from Lee's army, of keeping down the Union feeling, and of sustaining the Confederacy. I have an Irishman who has just arrived from Petersburg. He escaped for the third time, and is under sentence of death. He says Hood's troops were arriving at Weldon when he came through. I have some information that some troops from Lee's army passed south via Salisbury, Charlotte, and Columbia, probably to Charleston.

You will receive a communication in respect to the proper disposition to be made of Mr. Alfred Stanley, brother of the Governor, I believe. Is he an officer? If he is, and I was satisfied of the fact, I would at once forward him as a prisoner of war.

General Wessells still nervous about the gunboat near Halifax.

I am, very respectfully, your obedient servant,
JOHN J. PECK,
Major-General.

HEADQUARTERS,
September 16, 1863.
General NAGLEE and General FOSTER:

Mrs. Charles Swartz, just arrived at outpost, states she is a spy in the Government employ. Goes under the name of Mrs. C. Wilson. Has information which she wishes to take to Washington at once. She went from Chattanooga to Atlanta, and thence through the Confederate lines across the Blackwater to our lines. States that the whole rebel army is on its way to Tennessee. Virginia is to be evacuated. She saw in Petersburg General Robert Lee; badly wounded at

Charleston; not expected to live. Charleston was shelled on Friday, Saturday, and Sunday, and entirely destroyed. Heavy fighting there, and great loss to the enemy.

GEO. W. GETTY,
Brigadier-General.

KEMPSVILLE, VA., *September* 16, 1863—3 p. m.
(Received 5 p. m.)

Brigadier-General NAGLEE,
Commanding at Norfolk:

GENERAL: I have the honor to report that I left camp this morning for the purpose of gaining information in regard to the localities mentioned in your instructions. This step was necessary, as I had no guide.

I marched direct to Princess Anne Court-House, and found that the Pongo and West Neck bridges, over which I must pass in order to arrest those men, had both been burned by guerrillas, thereby stopping my progress. I also found that the fight I had, occurred at Ship's Corner, which must be the place where their encampment is said to be located.

After gaining this information, I returned to this place in order that I might safely send a dispatch, and also allow my wagon to return to camp. I shall await orders, or, not receiving any, shall scout again to-morrow.

Very respectfully, your obedient servant,

A. STETSON,
Captain, Commanding Squadron.

HEADQUARTERS ARMY OF THE POTOMAC,
September 17, 1863.

Commanding Officer Twelfth Corps:

I am instructed by the commanding general to add to the letter I had the honor to address to you last evening, that in the event of your being compelled to yield the position you now hold, you will fall slowly back on this place. And to enable you to do this understandingly, the general wishes you to have an examination made of the country between Raccoon Ford and Culpeper Court-House, so that you may be made acquainted with the defensive points, as well as the roads within the region you may, as a last resort, be required to traverse.

Very respectfully, &c.,

S. WILLIAMS,
Assistant Adjutant-General.

HEADQUARTERS ARMY OF THE POTOMAC,
September 17, 1863.

Maj. J. C. DUANE,
Chief Engineer, Army of the Potomac:

SIR: I have the honor to report the following as the result of my examination of the Rapidan, from Raccoon Ford to Germanna Mills.

I first intended to examine Raccoon Ford, but on arriving at General Buford's headquarters, I found it impossible to get near the ford. The general reported the enemy to have eleven guns in position, with rifle-pits covering the ford.

I next went to Morton's Ford, 2 miles below. Here the enemy was said to have had the previous evening two guns near a house on the hill just back of the ford. These must have been taken away before I got there, for I saw nothing of them. The only intrenchment to be seen was a small rifle-pit on the top of the bank, and a little below the ford. The smoke from camp fires in the woods a short distance to the rear indicate the presence of a regiment or more of men. The ground on this side is higher than that on the other, and intervening between the river and the base of the ridge is a flat some 300 yards wide. Just below the ford is a small island, 100 yards long. It is thickly timbered, the ground on the opposite side rising gradually.

Germanna Ford, 8 miles below, was guarded by a small force of cavalry, say 10 men. There were no indications of infantry or artillery. The ridge on this side commands the opposite side, and artillery suitably placed on the left of the plank road will give us complete possession of the ford. The ford is 3½ to 4 feet deep, and sufficiently wide for cavalry to march by fours. I think that a pontoon bridge can be thrown either at this place or at Morton's with great ease.

Very respectfully,

G. L. GILLESPIE,
First Lieutenant of Engineers.

HEADQUARTERS ARMY OF THE POTOMAC,
September 18, 1863—3 p. m. (Received 6.30 p. m.)

Maj. Gen. H. W. HALLECK,
General-in-Chief:

GENERAL: I have reached such a position that I do not feel justified in making a farther advance without some more positive authority than was contained in your last letter inclosing one from the President. If I apprehend rightly the views of the President and yourself, it was to the effect that I might advance on Lee and threaten him with an attack, and not permit him to cross the Rapidan without giving him battle. After accomplishing this, my feint might be converted into a real attack, if the development of the movement and subsequent information justified the same. It is precisely this question which now embarrasses me, and which I desire to be advised upon.

The situation is simply this: Lee, in command of Ewell's and Hill's corps, estimated at not less than 40,000 infantry, occupies the south bank of the Rapidan, with every available point crowned with artillery, and prepared to dispute the passage. The character of the south bank and its command forbid any attempt being made till Morton's Ford is reached, which is some 10 miles below the railroad. At this place the command is on this side, and I think a passage can be forced, but it would, undoubtedly, result in a considerable sacrifice, and would also, most certainly, involve a general engagement immediately on crossing.

Presuming, for the discussion, that the crossing was effected, and the enemy overcome, he would probably fall back on Gordonsville, as I suppose his policy is to check and retard my advance as long and wherever he can. I do not deem it necessary to discuss the contingencies of a failure, as they will, of course, present themselves to your mind. The whole question, however, in my judgment, hangs upon the advantages to be gained and the course to be pursued in the event of success. I am not in condition to follow Lee to Richmond, and will be less so after being weakened by a severe battle. The only thing I could do would be to change my base to the Fredericksburg railroad, and, after taking a position in front of that place, await an increase of force. The men I should have to sacrifice in this operation would be sufficient to secure the longer line of communication I now have. In fine, I can get a battle out of Lee under very disadvantageous circumstances, which may render his inferior force my superior, and which is not likely to result in any very decided advantage, even in case I should be victorious.

In this view I am reluctant to run the risks involved, without the positive sanction of the Government. If any demonstration on the Peninsula were practicable, or a force could threaten an advance on the Fredericksburg road, Lee would, I think, retire from my front, but I take it for granted either of these contingencies is out of the question.

I send this by an aide-de-camp, who will bring your reply.

GEO. G. MEADE,
Major-General, Commanding.

WAR DEPARTMENT,
Washington, September 18, 1863—4 p. m.

Major-General MEADE,
Army of the Potomac:

General Burnside is very apprehensive that a part of Ewell's corps has gone by Lynchburg to East Tennessee. If you get any evidence to that effect, I wish to send it to Burnside, as his movements must very much depend upon the information.

H. W. HALLECK,
General-in-Chief,

SEPTEMBER 18, 1863—9 p. m.
(Received 9.20 p. m.)

Major-General HALLECK:

There is abundant evidence from deserters and scouts, going to show that Ewell's corps is in my front, and nothing to indicate that any portion of it has gone to East Tennessee.

GEO. G. MEADE,
Major-General, Commanding.

HDQRS. THIRD DIVISION, CAVALRY CORPS,
September 18, 1863.

Lieut. Col. C. ROSS SMITH,
Chief of Staff, Cavalry Corps:

COLONEL: One of my scouts has just returned from across the river. He crossed last night 1 mile below Raccoon Ford, passed through their picket of infantry, and a line of infantry one-fourth of a mile back from the river, and passed out in the country over 2 miles. Saw about one division of infantry passing down the river. He says there is great excitement—never so great as now. The enemy sent for re-enforcements yesterday when the Twelfth and Second Corps marched to the river. They expected an attack last night at Ely's Ford. They have all their dismounted cavalry and one brigade of infantry there. The scout is very much exhausted, or I would send him through to you to-night. The above is all the information he has to impart.

Very respectfully, your obedient servant,

J. KILPATRICK,
Brig. Gen. of Vols., Comdg. Third Division.

HDQRS. TWELFTH CORPS, ARMY OF THE POTOMAC,
September 18, 1863.

General S. WILLIAMS,
Asst. Adjt. Gen., Army of the Potomac:

GENERAL: Your communication of yesterday has been received. I have examined the country in the immediate vicinity of Raccoon Ford, and am satisfied that we could not force a passage of the river at this point, nor can we prevent the enemy from crossing. The advantage in position is entirely with the enemy, the ground on the opposite side commanding every position on this side. I shall park my train well in rear on the road leading to Culpeper. I now think it will be advisable, in case I am obliged to fall back, to have one division, with its train, move on the road to Stevensburg, and the other on the direct Culpeper road. I shall make a careful examination of both roads as soon as possible.

The enemy guard the river at this point very carefully. They fire upon our pickets at sight, and will not allow any person to approach the banks of the river.

Very respectfully, your obedient servant,

H. W. SLOCUM,
Major-General of Volunteers, Commanding.

,SEPTEMBER 18, 1863—1.20 p. m.

Commanding Officer Twelfth Corps:

The major-general commanding directs me to acknowledge the receipt of your communication of to-day's date, and requests that you will examine the river below Raccoon Ford, and particularly at Morton's Ford, to ascertain the practicability of effecting a passage. He is informed that a passage can be forced by him at Morton's Ford.

He desires your views upon the subject as soon as you have made the requisite examinations. He wishes you also to take into consideration the nature of the position this army can take after crossing. He further requests me to say that the examination should be concealed from the enemy, so that the passage, should one be made, may not be anticipated by them.

A. A. HUMPHREYS,
Major-General, Chief of Staff.

HEADQUARTERS SECOND CORPS,
September 18, 1863—9.30 p. m.

General MEADE:

I have been along my whole line to-day. About 3.30 p. m. our cavalry on the right drove the enemy across Crooked Creek and were fired upon several times with artillery. The Valley of the Rapidan above the railroad bridge is such that I think the enemy's left flank could be turned. The railroad bridge head is only a weak trench, and I think was occupied by about 100 men, who seemed to be the reserve of the picket line circulating around it. The trench is only a shelter from our artillery. There seems from the smoke to be a considerable force along the railroad—might be 5,000 men or more. At Robertson's Ford, at the base of Piney Mountain, the enemy are also on this side, and fired on us here. We can easily drive them across, but the high mountain on the other side rises from the stream. At Somerville Ford the banks do not give the enemy much advantage over us. This is as far down as I went. The enemy does not seem to be in much force at Somerville Ford, and none to speak of from there up to the railroad. I do not think there is any prospect of the enemy advancing, nor do I see how he can defend so long a line as he would have to hold from Germanna Ford up. When the firing began on our right, many of the enemy's tents were struck.

Our signal officer, Lieutenant Marston, discovered the enemy's new signals. He made out to-day:

Send me twenty wagons to subsist my division.

FITZ. LEE.

Also that the line would not be open to-night, as they were out of turpentine, and it is not open.

Lieutenant Marston is preparing the new code discovered to send up to chief signal officer. I would like to make some demonstrations to-morrow with my artillery and troops, if it will not interfere with other plans.

G. K. WARREN,
Major-General.

SEPTEMBER 18, 1863—10.15 p. m.

Commanding Officer Second Corps:

Your dispatch is received. The major-general commanding considers that under existing circumstances it is not advisable to make any demonstration. Do you refer to the Valley of the Rapidan or Robertson's River in your dispatch when stating that the Valley of the Rapidan above the railroad bridge is such that you think the enemy's left flank can be turned? How much has the Rapidan on your front risen to-day?

A dispatch from General Kilpatrick, received about 6 p. m., states that one of his scouts who crossed the Rapidan yesterday saw one division moving down the river from Raccoon Ford, and learned that there was one brigade of infantry and all the dismounted cavalry at Ely's Ford.

A. A. HUMPHREYS,
Major-General, and Chief of Staff.

MITCHELL'S,
September 18, 1863.

General MEADE:

I do not know how much the Rapidan has risen. In the present condition of occupancy none of us can visit the river. I refer to the Valleys of both the Rapidan and Robertson's Rivers as being free from mountains and large streams as the cause of our being able to turn the enemy's left flank.

G. K. WARREN,
Major-General.

HEADQUARTERS FIRST ARMY CORPS,
September 18, 1863.

Major-General HUMPHREYS,
Chief of Staff, Army of the Potomac:

1. I moved from Rappahannock via Brandy Station. A portion of my command came directly across the country from Brandy Station to near Pony Mountain, the remainder of my column by Stevensburg.

2. There is a road from here to Stevensburg, and from there to Kelly's Ford.

3. Am not acquainted with any roads from the Rappahannock to the Rapidan between Rappahannock Ford and Kelly's Ford. Mountain Creek in front of my present position is impassable since the rain, except at one point, Stevensburg. I have ordered a bridge constructed over it, which will not be completed before to-morrow night, if then, finding it very difficult to get material to construct it with.

Very respectfully, your obedient servant,
JOHN NEWTON,
Major-General, Commanding.

P. S.—Have not heard of the condition of the roads since the rain.

CLARKSBURG,
September 18, 1863.

Brigadier-General AVERELL:

Colonel Mulligan reports again this morning that he has information, which he deems reliable, that an attack on him at Petersburg at an early date is contemplated. It is to be by Jones', Imboden's, Jenkins', and Jackson's forces combined. What is your information? Is Jackson yet in Pocahontas? Do you think Jones' force is yet in Greenbrier?

Captain Hall, of the Sixth [West] Virginia Infantry, who is scouting Tucker County, reports that there are no pickets or scouts on the Seneca road, at Soldier White's, the Burnt House, or Wyant's. You should keep pickets or scouts constantly on that road watching those points.

[B. F. KELLEY,]
Brigadier-General.

HEADQUARTERS FOURTH SEPARATE BRIGADE,
Beverly, September 18, 1863.

Brig. Gen. B. F. KELLEY,
Commanding Department:

My scouts left Crab Bottom the day before yesterday at 4 o'clock p. m. Jenkins was there with about 1,000 mounted and 1,500 infantry and two guns. They saw a Union man who had come through Monterey the day before, and reported having seen no force on the way. If Jones had moved from Greenbrier northward, I think I should have known it. I have sent a report to the rebels that I have gone to Buckhannon with three regiments. I have a picket of an officer and 10 men on the Seneca road 10 miles out; an officer and 15 men near New Interest, and pickets on every road and path leading to this place, and all the roads are constantly patrolled. I beg to assure you that I understand the importance of pickets, and know from personal attention to the subject that the duties are properly performed.

WM. W. AVERELL,
Brigadier-General.

SPECIAL ORDERS, ⎰ HDQRS. ARMY, ADJT. GENERAL'S OFFICE,
No. 420. ⎱ *Washington, September 18, 1863.*

I. Brig. Gen. J. C. Sullivan, U. S. Volunteers, is hereby relieved from duty with Major-General Grant and assigned to duty with Brigadier-General Kelley, commanding Department of West Virginia.

*   *   *   *   *   *   *

By command of Major-General Halleck:

E. D. TOWNSEND,
Assistant Adjutant-General.

WASHINGTON, D. C.,
September 19, 1863.

Major-General MEADE:

GENERAL : Yours of 3 p. m. of yesterday is received.

It is my duty to point out to the generals commanding the several armies in the field the objects which the Government wishes accomplished, and to assist as far as possible in attaining those objects. But unless directed to do so, I never attempt to direct a general when, where, or how to give battle. He must decide such matters for himself. No one else can do it for him. I have no idea of playing the part of an Austrian ruler.

You are left free to exercise your own judgment on this subject. In regard to Richmond, I do not consider it of any very great military importance, nor as the objective point of the Army of the Potomac. Your objective point, in my opinion, is Lee's army, and the object to be attained is to do it as much harm as possible with as little injury as possible to yourself. If Lee holds a position too strong to be attacked, and he cannot be turned by maneuvering, then his outposts and detachments can be attacked, his communications threatened by raids, or the supplies of the adjacent country collected for the support of our army. The accomplishment of any or all of these objects will necessarily depend upon circumstances which may daily and almost hourly change, and can properly be judged of only by the general in the field.

I gave you in my last a general outline of the condition of our affairs in the south and west and what we have to do there. As soon as the re-enforcements sent to Bragg can be spared, they will probably return against you. Whatever you can do should be done while they are absent. If you really think that nothing of importance can be accomplished, then it seems to me that it will be as well to withdraw your army to some point nearer Washington. In regard to lines of operations, I can see no advantage in a change to Aquia Creek. Indeed, I do not think that line as favorable as the one you are moving on.

I had written thus far when I received the inclosed letter from the President. Please keep me advised of your general plans. I fear that General Rosecrans will be hard pushed.

Very respectfully, your obedient servant,

H. W. HALLECK,
General-in-Chief.

[Inclosure.]

EXECUTIVE MANSION,
Washington, September 19, 1863.

Major-General HALLECK :

By General Meade's dispatch to you of yesterday, it appears that he desires your views and those of the Government as to whether he shall advance upon the enemy. I am not prepared to order or even advise an advance in this case, wherein I know so little of the particulars, and wherein he, in the field, thinks the risk is so great and the promise of advantage so small. And yet the case presents matter for very serious consideration in another aspect. These two armies confront each other across a small river, substantially midway between the two capitals, each defending its own capital, and menacing the other. General Meade estimates the enemy's infantry in front of him at not less than 40,000. Suppose we add 50 per cent. to this for cavalry, artillery, and extra-duty men, stretching as far as Richmond, making the whole force of the enemy 60,000. General Meade, as shown by the returns, has with him, and between him and Washington, of the same classes of well men, over 90,000. Neither can bring the whole of his men into a battle, but each can bring as large a percentage in as the other. For a battle, then, General Meade has three men to General Lee's two. Yet, it having been determined that choosing ground and standing on the defensive gives so great advantage that the three cannot safely attack the two, the three are left simply standing on the defensive also. If the enemy's 60,000 are sufficient to keep our 90,000 away from Richmond, why, by the same rule, may not 40,000 of ours keep their 60,000 away from Washington, leaving us 50,000 to put to some other use ? Having practically come to the mere defensive, it seems to be no economy at all to employ twice as many men for that object as are needed. With no object, certainly, to mislead myself, I can perceive no fault in this statement, unless we admit we are not the equal of the enemy, man for man. I hope you will consider it.

To avoid misunderstanding, let me say that to attempt to fight the enemy slowly back into his intrenchments at Richmond, and there to capture him, is an idea I have been trying to repudiate for quite a year. My judgment is so clear against it that I would scarcely allow the attempt to be made, if the general in command should desire to make it. My last attempt upon Richmond was to get McClellan, when he was nearer there than the enemy was, to run in ahead of him. Since then I have constantly desired the Army of the Potomac to make Lee's army, and not Richmond, its objective point. If our army cannot fall upon the enemy and hurt him where he is, it is plain to me it can gain nothing by attempting to follow him over a succession of intrenched lines into a fortified city.

Yours, truly,   .

A. LINCOLN.

_____

SEPTEMBER 19, 1863—6.30 p. m.

Commanding Officer Twelfth Corps:

The major-general commanding directs me to inquire of you if you received my dispatch of 1.20 p. m. yesterday. It was sent by your orderly, and requested you to examine the vicinity of Morton's Ford (particularly with a view to ascertaining the feasibility of effecting a crossing of the army at that place) and give your views to him. The musketry you heard must have been the cavalry at Stevensburg discharging their carbines. No other report upon the subject than yours has reached these headquarters.

A. A. HUMPHREYS,
Major-General, and Chief of Staff.

_____

HDQRS. TWELFTH CORPS, ARMY OF THE POTOMAC,
September 19, 1863.

Maj. Gen. A. A. HUMPHREYS,
Chief of Staff, Army of the Potomac:

GENERAL: In compliance with instructions contained in your letter of yesterday, I have examined the river from Raccoon Ford down to Stringfellow's Ford. I am of the opinion that a crossing cannot be effected at Raccoon Ford without great loss. At Morton's Ford it would be attended with less difficulty, but even at that point we should labor under many disadvantages. The approaches to this ford from both sides of the river are over a low, marshy ground about one-fourth of a mile in width. There are positions for artillery on this side of the river nearly as good as those on the opposite side, but the enemy have already thrown up one work to command this ford, and are, I think, constructing another.

At Stringfellow's Ford the bluffs approach nearer the river than at either of the other points, and I think a crossing could be effected there with less loss than at either of the other fords. I think, however, it would be necessary to throw a bridge across. I should judge from appearances that a better position could be secured there after crossing than at either of the other points. The enemy have thrown up a work to protect this ford, but I do not think the position has been well taken, and unless they further strengthen it, I think we could make a crossing there. If a crossing is contemplated, I would recommend that an engineer officer be sent here to examine the position. Judging from the camp fires and other indications, I think the main body of the enemy opposite to us are in the vicinity of Raccoon Ford, with from four to six regiments at Morton's Ford. At Stringfellow's Ford I think their force at present is very light.

The contrabands at Dr. Morton's state that Longstreet's corps was sent to Tennessee about ten days since, while the contrabands at Thornton Stringfellow's say it has only gone to Louisa County.

Very respectfully, your obedient servant,

H. W. SLOCUM,
Major-General of Volunteers, Commanding.

HEADQUARTERS ELEVENTH CORPS,
September 19, 1863.

Major-General HUMPHREYS,
　　Chief of Staff, Army of the Potomac:

Quite a force of the enemy's cavalry is reported at Warrenton. Cannot ascertain how large.

O. O. HOWARD,
Major-General.

MITCHELL'S STATION, *September 19, 1863.*
(Received 11.20 a. m.)

General MEADE:

The signal officers have just taken the following dispatch from the signal station on Clark's Mountain:

General LEE:

A deserter this morning reports that all the enemy's cavalry, supported by corps, is moving to our left to flank our position. The cavalry has certainly disappeared from this front and is replaced by infantry. The deserter is on his way to head-quarters.

E. [EARLY,]
General

G. K. WARREN,
Major-General.

SIGNAL DEPT., HDQRS. ARMY OF THE POTOMAC,
September 19, 1863.

Maj. Gen. A. A. HUMPHREYS,
　　Chief of Staff:

GENERAL: The following message was received from the officer at Mitchell's Station, having been intercepted from the enemy's signal station on Clark's Mountain:

SIGNAL STATION—12.45 p. m.
General H..

General Early states a deserter reports that the enemy's cavalry, supported by one corps of infantry, moved up to our left to flank our position. The cavalry has disappeared from his front and is relieved by infantry. Be on your guard and ascertain his movements.

LEE,
General.

I am, general, very respectfully, your obedient servant,

WM. S. STRYKER,
First Lieutenant, and Adjutant Signal Corps.

[SEPTEMBER 19, 1863]—1.30 p. m.

Major-General WARREN,
     Commanding Second Corps, Mitchell's Station:

The following dispatch is sent for your information:

SIGNAL DEPARTMENT, HEADQUARTERS ARMY OF THE POTOMAC,
September 19, 1863.

General HUMPHREYS:

The following message is just received from Pony Mountain:

" 12.50 p. m.

" Captain NORTON:

"A column of infantry, consisting of six regiments, has just passed over the northern face of Clark's Mountain, passing close to the signal station, going in a direction northwest by west. No wagons.

"TAYLOR,
" *Captain.*"

I am, general, very respectfully, your obedient servant,
WM. S. STRYKER.
First Lieutenant, and Adjutant Signal Corps.

A. A. HUMPHREYS,
Major-General, Chief of Staff.

———

MITCHELL'S STATION,
September 19, 1863—2.30 p. m.

General HUMPHREYS:

The movement of the rebel infantry toward his left flank is most likely designed to meet what he thinks is our effort to turn his left.

By camp smokes, show of troops, and the occasional sending of train of cars, we can make him think we have the whole army in his front where we are.

G. K. WARREN,
Major-General.

———

SIGNAL DEPT., HDQRS. ARMY OF THE POTOMAC,
September 19, 1863.

Major-General HUMPHREYS,
     Chief of Staff:

GENERAL: The following message has just been received from Pony Mountain Signal Station:

Captain NORTON:

Between 2 and 4 p. m. a column of infantry, 16 pieces of artillery, 5 ambulances, and 20 wagons passed a point about 1 mile beyond Raccoon Ford, moving down the river.

TAYLOR,
Captain.

I am, general, very respectfully, your obedient servant,
WM. S. STRYKER,
First Lieutenant, and Adjutant Signal Corps.

MITCHELL'S STATION, *September* 19, 1863.
(Received 9.20 p. m.)

Captain NORTON:

The following rebel signal message has been intercepted:

SIGNAL STATION on CLARK'S MOUNTAIN.

General LEE:

Rodes can hold his position. I am just from Morton's Ford. His position is a strong one. Everything very quiet to-day. I am sending a written dispatch.

E. [EWELL?],
General.

F. W. MARSTON,
Captain, and Signal Officer.

WAR DEPARTMENT,
Washington, September 19, 1863—3.20 p. m.

Brigadier-General KELLEY,
Clarksburg, W. Va.:

The Secretary of War directs that a report be made of the recent captures by the enemy in your department, in order that the officers who have neglected their duty may be tried or summarily dismissed. Where such captures result from neglect or carelessness, the commanding general of the department should have the officers tried or reported for dismissal. Unless this is done the Secretary of War holds the commanding general responsible.

H. W. HALLECK,
General-in-Chief.

HEADQUARTERS FOURTH SEPARATE BRIGADE,
Beverly, September 19, 1863.

Brig. Gen. B. F. KELLEY,
Commanding Department:

My picket on the Seneca road has been stationed from half a mile to 2 miles of the Burnt House for several days, with orders to change their position twice every twenty-four hours. A patrol from that picket has gone in the direction of Soldier White's daily, and patrols from here visit the pickets on each road daily. From New Interest a patrol goes to Carrick's Ford. All the pickets have orders not to permit themselves to be seen, which will account for the captain of the Sixth failing to observe them. The Burnt House is a dangerous place for a picket, so I keep them near enough to observe without being seen. I have had several sketches made of all that section, and officers have carefully examined all those roads, and their reports are before me.

Scouts from Pocahontas report that Jackson has gone to McDowell. I do not place implicit reliance upon it. I am not sure that Mulligan ought not to be re-enforced. I have strengthened and extended my pickets in the directions you suggest.

My report this morning is in reply to your dispatch; was intended to relieve you of any disquietude, and not as a manifestation of undue sensitiveness. I trust you will regard it so, and believe that I shall be happy to avail myself of your experience and knowledge of this country at all times.

WM. W. AVERELL,
Brigadier-General.

WAR DEPARTMENT,
Washington City, September 19, 1863.

Maj. Gen. J. G. FOSTER,
Comdg. Dept. of Va. and N. C., Fort Monroe, Va.:

GENERAL: I have the honor to inclose herewith a copy of a letter of the 17th instant from the honorable Secretary of the Navy, in relation to an alleged threatened attack on Plymouth, and the contemplated attempt to take possession of the sounds of North Carolina.

The Secretary of War directs that you will take such action in the premises as may in your judgment be best suited to meet the emergency thus presented.

I have the honor to be, general, very respectfully, your obedient servant,

JAS. A. HARDIE.

[Inclosure.]

NAVY DEPARTMENT,
September 17, 1863.

Hon. E. M. STANTON,
Secretary of War:

SIR: I have the honor to present for your consideration a subject of great importance connected with the maintaining possession of the sounds of North Carolina.

Information received from time to time places it beyond a doubt that the rebels are constructing, and have nearly completed, at Edwards Ferry, near Weldon, on the Roanoke River, a ram and an iron-clad floating battery. It is represented that these vessels will be formidable, and will be completed in the course of four or six weeks. It is further represented that an attack by land and water on Plymouth is contemplated.

Our force of wooden vessels in the sounds, necessarily of light draught and lightly armed, will by no means be adequate to contend against the rebel ram and battery, should they succeed in getting down the Roanoke, and in that event our possession of the sounds would be jeopardized. It is impracticable for our vessels to ascend the Roanoke to any great distance in consequence of the shallowness of the water, their exposed situation from the fire of sharpshooters, and the earth-works represented to be located at different points, particularly at Rainbow Bluff.

Were our iron-clads now completed available for service in the sounds they could not be sent there, as they draw too much water to cross the bulkhead at Hatteras. Our lighter draught ones will not be completed for some time to come. In view of all these facts, I deem it proper to suggest the importance of an effort on the part of the army to surprise and destroy the rebel ram and battery referred to, or of obstructing the river by torpedoes and piles, or otherwise, so as to prevent their descent. Permit me to urge some measure of this sort.

This Department will be happy to co-operate, so far as it may be able, in adopting such steps as may seem practicable and adequate to secure us against threatening disaster.

I am, very respectfully,

GIDEON WELLES,
Secretary of the Navy.

HDQRS. TWELFTH CORPS, ARMY OF THE POTOMAC,
September 20, 1863.

Maj. Gen. A. A. HUMPHREYS,
Chief of Staff, Army of the Potomac:

GENERAL: In reply to your communication of the 18th instant I have the honor to inform you that I have carefully examined the ground from Raccoon Ford down to Stringfellow's Ford. I do not think a crossing could be effected at the former place without great loss of life. At Morton's Ford we might possibly be able to cross, though even then we would labor under great disadvantages. The approaches to this ford are over a low, marshy ground, of about one-quarter of a mile in width on both sides of the river. The positions for artillery at this point are nearly as good on this side of the river as on the other, but the enemy have thrown up some works to protect the ford.

At Stringfellow's Ford the bluffs approach nearer the river on both sides, and I think a crossing could be effected here with less loss of life than at either of the other fords, though I am of the opinion that a bridge should be thrown across in the first place. The enemy have thrown up a work to command this ford also, but I do not think their position is well chosen. After crossing, I should think a fair position might be secured at this point. If a crossing is contemplated, I would suggest that an engineer officer be sent here to examine the ground. From the camp fires and other indications, I am of the opinion that the main body of the enemy opposite us are concentrated near Raccoon Ford; with at least from four to six regiments at Morton's. The force at Stringfellow's is at present quite small, and unless the enemy further strengthen that position, I think it the most feasible point to effect a crossing.

A contraband at Dr. Morton's informed me that Longstreet's corps went to Tennessee some ten days ago, while one at Thornton Stringfellow's says it has only gone to Louisa County, Va.

I have the honor to inform you that a communication of similar import to this was sent to you by an orderly yesterday, and the above information was based upon my examination at that time.

I am, general, very respectfully, your obedient servant,

H. W. SLOCUM,
Major-General, Commanding.

SEPTEMBER 20, 1863—11.30 a. m.

Commanding Officer Twelfth Corps:

The orderly from your headquarters brought a communication to these headquarters about dark last evening, but not the report respecting Morton's Ford.

A. A. HUMPHREYS,
Major-General, and Chief of Staff.

SEPTEMBER 20, 1863—1.15 p. m.

Commanding Officer Second Corps:

Will you have the Rapidan above the fork of Robertson's River and Robertson's River examined, so far as they can be from Cedar Mountain, to ascertain to what degree they are more favorable generally for crossing and taking position upon than the Rapidan below the railroad bridge, and also to ascertain what points upon those rivers should be examined carefully with a view to crossing? There are no engineer officers here at present to send you for the purpose.

A. A. HUMPHREYS,
Major-General, and Chief of Staff.

HEADQUARTERS ELEVENTH CORPS,
September 20, 1863.

Major-General HUMPHREYS,
Chief of Staff, Army of the Potomac:

Captain Higgins, Seventy-third Ohio Volunteers, with a patrol, took 2 rebel prisoners near Brentsville. I send them to General Patrick this a. m.

Respectfully,

O. O. HOWARD,
Major-General.

MITCHELL'S STATION, *September 20, 1863.*
(Received 6.15 p. m.)

Capt. L. B. NORTON, *Chief Signal Officer:*

Dispatch received. The following messages read to-day:

11 a. m.

General LEE:

All quiet in this front; no change observed in enemy's camps.

E. [EWELL?],
General.

1.35 p. m.

All quiet. There is a Yankee signal station on Thoroughfare Mountain.

S. [STUART],
General.

4.20 p. m.

Captain F.:

We have seen only one small party of cavalry to-day. Infantry seem to have taken their places on their whole [*sic*].

WILLIAMSON.

5 p. m.

General E.:

No material change in enemy's camps. Small bodies of infantry moved ; apparently picket reliefs. Small trains moving back from your front.

K.

5 p. m.

General Lee:

All quiet in front.

S. [STUART],
General.

5.50 p. m.

Send wagons of Second North Carolina Cavalry to them to-day near Robertson's River.

F.

Captain Castle will communicate with you as desired. Can you send me another flagman? Goldey is sick. We need message blanks and matches. Did you receive the code I sent?

Please answer.

F. W. MARSTON,
Captain, and Signal Officer.

SIGNAL DEPT., HDQRS. ARMY OF THE POTOMAC,
September 20, 1863—7.30 p. m.

Maj. Gen. A. A. HUMPHREYS,
Chief of Staff:

GENERAL: The following reports have just been received, and are respectfully forwarded for the information of the commanding general:

CEDAR MOUNTAIN SIGNAL STATION,
September 20, 1863.

Captain NORTON,
Chief Signal Officer:

The enemy show a large number of camp fires across the Rapidan and between Robertson's and Rapidan Rivers.

They are working in large numbers on earth-works at Rapidan Station and as far down as Raccoon Ford. They have two brass pieces in position at Rapidan Station.

CASTLE,
Signal Officer.

PONY MOUNTAIN SIGNAL STATION,
September 20, 1863—6.15 p. m.

Captain NORTON:

Enemy are intrenching at Morton's and Stringfellow's Fords to-day. No movements seen.

TAYLOR,
Signal Officer.

I have the honor to be, general, very respectfully, your obedient servant,

L. B. NORTON,
Captain, and Chief Signal Officer.

HEADQUARTERS ARMY OF THE POTOMAC,
September 20, 1863—9.30 p. m.

Commanding Officer Cavalry Corps:

The major-general commanding directs that a reconnaissance be made with two divisions of cavalry, those at Stevensburg, between Robertson's River and the Rapidan, extending from Madison Court-House on the former, and from Burtonsville at the mouth of the Ballard River on the latter, down to Robertson's Ford and to Barnett's Ford.

The object of the reconnaissance is to ascertain the position and force of the enemy between those rivers and along the Rapidan, the number and character of the roads leading to the Rapidan along the extent indicated, and of the character of the fords and of the ground on both sides where these roads cross the Rapidan, and the advantages such points afford for effecting a crossing in the face of the enemy. It is particularly desirable to learn the character of the south bank of the Rapidan along the road leading to Orange Court-House from Burtonsville, since it is along that road that the army may march, should Orange Court-House be approached from above. A sufficient force of cavalry should be left to picket the Rapidan from Stringfellow's Ford to Ely's Ford, and from the right of General Warren's pickets near the foot of Cedar Mountain, along the present cavalry picket line.

If you should deem a less force than two divisions sufficient to make the reconnaissance, you are authorized to send a smaller number. The enemy is reported to have a cavalry force between the two rivers, and some artillery in position at Rochelle, on the pike from Madison Court-House to Orange Court-House. Major Duane will be directed to send an engineer officer with the expedition, if one can be made available; if one is not sent by him an officer should be detailed from your command to perform engineer duty on the reconnaissance.

Very respectfully, &c.,

A. A. HUMPHREYS,
Major-General, and Chief of Staff.

HEADQUARTERS DISTRICT OF VIRGINIA,
Norfolk, September 20, 1863.
Capt. GEORGE J. KER,
Fifth Pennsylvania Cavalry:

You will proceed to Princess Anne Court-House, starting this p. m. or to-morrow a. m., and take command of the detachment of the Fifth Pennsylvania Cavalry now in that neighborhood, with which and yours you will proceed to Ship's Corners, and ascertain the number of guerrillas in the vicinity. If prudent so to do, attack and disperse them. If otherwise you will await the arrival of a detachment of 100 selected men from the One hundred and forty-eighth New York, and make a joint and combined attack. Once dispersed, follow them up as long as any two keep together. You will confine yourself rigidly to the restrictions referred to in the inclosed order.

Permit no pillage nor allow any one to enter any house. Arrest only persons that are justly accused, and invariably send a full report of the circumstances and charges against all arrested. Report daily.

By order of Brigadier-General Naglee:
Very respectfully,

[GEORGE H. JOHNSTON,]
Assistant Adjutant-General.

HEADQUARTERS ARMY OF THE POTOMAC,
September 21, 1863—1 p. m.   (Received 2 p. m.)
Maj. Gen. H. W. HALLECK,
General-in-Chief:

The position of affairs is unchanged since my last, except the enemy is apparently increasing in force, and is busily engaged in strengthening his works. Reconnaissances are being made to ascertain the practicability of further movements. Your letter by Captain Mason was duly received.

GEO. G. MEADE,
Major-General.

SEPTEMBER 21, 1863—10.30 a. m.

Commanding Officer First Corps:

The major-general commanding desires you to examine Pony Mountain and vicinity, in view of the contingency that may arise requiring you to take position upon it with your corps. In such event, the Second and Twelfth Corps would be established between your corps and the Fifth Corps, which is now posted on the high ground in advance of Culpeper, and on the right of the railroad.

A. A. HUMPHREYS,
Major-General, and Chief of Staff.

SEPTEMBER 21, 1863—10.15 a. m.

Commanding Officer Third Corps:

The major-general commanding desires you to examine the high ground upon the right of the Fifth Corps, with a view to establishing your corps in position upon it, in continuation of the position now occupied by the Fifth Corps. Major-General Sykes can indicate to you more exactly the high ground referred to.

A. A. HUMPHREYS,
Major-General, and Chief of Staff.

CONFIDENTIAL.] HEADQUARTERS ARMY OF THE POTOMAC,
September 21, 1863.

*Major-General SLOCUM,
Commanding Twelfth Corps:*

The major-general commanding directs me to inform you that a cavalry reconnaissance in force will be made to-morrow between Robertson's and Rapidan Rivers. The command is that which has been posted at Stevensburg.

A. A. HUMPHREYS,
Major-General, and Chief of Staff.

SIGNAL DEPT., HDQRS. ARMY OF THE POTOMAC,
September 21, 1863.

Maj. Gen. A. A. HUMPHREYS,
Chief of Staff:

GENERAL: The following message has just been received, and is respectfully forwarded for the information of the commanding general:

SIGNAL STATION ON CLARK'S MOUNTAIN,
September 21, [1863]—12.40 p. m.

Captain G.:

A body of cavalry, composed of about a brigade, moving from Stevensburg to Culpeper. Large wagon train coming up and parting at Mitchell's Station. Train of cars now at station.

WILLIAMSON.

I have the honor to be, general, very respectfully, your obedient servant,

L. B. NORTON,
Captain, and Chief Signal Officer.

SIGNAL DEPT., HDQRS. ARMY OF THE POTOMAC,
September 21, 1863.

Maj. Gen. A. A. HUMPHREYS, *Chief of Staff:*

GENERAL : The following dispatches were just received, and are respectfully forwarded for the information of the general commanding :

CEDAR MOUNTAIN SIGNAL STATION,
September 21, 1863.

Captain NORTON, *Chief Signal Officer:*

Not as many troops employed on earth-works along the river as yesterday. Works to protect ten guns nearly finished at Rapidan Station. Nearly two brigades of infantry left Rapidan Station at 11.30 a. m. going southwest. Fifteen wagons left park near station at same time. Camp smokes toward and 3 miles this side of Madison Court-House.

CASTLE,
Captain, and Signal Officer.

The following rebel message was read from Clark's Mountain by Captain Castle on Cedar Mountain :

General S. [STUART:]

The enemy picket all the fords as far as Fredericksburg. When must the expedition start?

FITZ. LEE,
General.

Very respectfully, general, your obedient servant,
L. B. NORTON,
Captain, and Chief Signal Officer.

HEADQUARTERS ARMY OF THE POTOMAC,
September 21, 1863.

Maj. Gen. O. O. HOWARD,
Commanding Eleventh Corps:

An intercepted rebel dispatch from Clark's Mountain this afternoon shows that a cavalry raid by Fitz. Lee's brigade will be set on foot, probably to-night, to move round our left. Among its objects is doubtless a blow at the railroad bridges. A part of our cavalry is on the watch for them, but your command should be on its guard.*

HUMPHREYS,
Major-General, Chief of Staff.

SEPTEMBER 21, 1863—10 p. m.

Commanding Officer Twelfth Corps:

The following rebel dispatch from Clark's Mountain was intercepted this afternoon, indicating an intended raid upon our left flank. Measures have been taken to meet it with our cavalry.

General S. [STUART:]

The enemy picket all the fords as far as Fredericksburg. When must the expedition start?

FITZ. LEE,
General.

A. A. HUMPHREYS,
Major-General, and Chief of Staff.

---

*Substance of this dispatch telegraphed by Howard to commanding officers at Bealeton, Manassas Junction, and Rappahannock Station.

CIRCULAR.] HEADQUARTERS ARMY OF THE POTOMAC,
September 21, 1863.

Until further orders, five days' bread and small rations, including salt, will be carried by the troops in their knapsacks, in addition to the subsistence stores they are required under existing orders to take in their haversacks.

Corps and other independent commanders will take immediate measures to prepare their troops to march, supplied as above directed.

By command of Major-General Meade:

S. WILLIAMS,
Assistant Adjutant-General.

WASHINGTON NAVY-YARD, *September* 21, 1863.
(Received 12.15 p. m.)

Hon. GIDEON WELLES,
Secretary of the Navy:

Referring to your telegram of 19th instant, directing me to examine into the supposed movement of the rebels on or near Mathias Point, Acting Master Hill, commanding the Dragon, a reliable officer, reports that he engaged a negro living between Boyd's Hole and Mathias Point to watch the movements of the enemy. He represents that the force consists of a company commanded by a Captain Todd. This was about the 17th. It is thought probable that there may be more troops there now. A good lookout is kept at Mathias and Boyd's Hole, two vessels always being kept near enough to act together in case of any demonstrations by the rebels.

Mr. Hill states that he has not been able to discover any of the enemy, but that the nature of the ground is such that they can erect batteries without being seen from the river. He suggests that if a small body of troops, say from 50 to 100 men, be sent down to him, he could ma e good use of them as a reconnoitering party without much risk. k

Further information may be looked for shortly.

A. A. HARWOOD,
Commandant.

SPECIAL ORDERS, } WAR DEPT., ADJT. GENERAL'S OFFICE,
No. 422. } *Washington, September* 21, 1863.

*   *   *   *   *   *

13. Brigadier-General Naglee, U. S. Volunteers, is hereby relieved from duty in the Department of Virginia and North Carolina, and will report in person without delay to Major-General Meade, U. S. Volunteers, for duty in the Army of the Potomac, as soon as relieved by Brigadier-General Barnes, U. S. Volunteers, who is assigned to duty in his place.

*   *   *   *

By order of the Secretary of War:

E. D. TOWNSEND,
Assistant Adjutant-General.

WASHINGTON, *September* 22, 1863—11 a. m.
(Received 11.30 a. m.)

Major-General MEADE:

If no immediate movement is contemplated, and you can safely be absent, I would like to see you in Washington. The business, however, is not so pressing as to require your immediate presence if you are wanted there.

H. W. HALLECK,
General-in-Chief.

———

HEADQUARTERS ARMY OF THE POTOMAC,
September 22, 1863—12 m.   (Received 1.10 p. m.)

Maj. Gen. H. W. HALLECK,
General-in-Chief :

The following intercepted rebel dispatch has just been received by our signal officer:

Bragg engaged the enemy. Captured 20 pieces of artillery and 2,500 prisoners.

Your telegram has been received. I will try and get up to Washington some time this evening, so as to return by early to-morrow. Will advise you as soon as an hour can be fixed.

GEO. G. MEADE,
Major-General, Commanding.

———

· HEADQUARTERS ARMY OF THE POTOMAC,
September 22, 1863—5 p. m.   (Received 5.20 p. m.)

Maj. Gen. H. W. HALLECK,
General-in-Chief :

I shall leave here at 5.30 p. m. Be due in Washington at 11 p. m. As I desire, to return at the earliest moment, shall have to ask you to meet me at your office at this late hour.

GEO. G. MEADE,
Major-General.

———

· HEADQUARTERS SECOND ARMY CORPS,
September 22, 1863.

General MEADE:

The firing commenced three hours since, at a point 3 miles south of Madison Court-House. It lasted one and a half hours, and then, after a short interruption, opened again some distance to the east of that point and a little nearer to us.

The rebel signals say that our cavalry is driving theirs. They also report that an hour since we crossed forces at Clark's Ford. The rebel battery at Locust Dale was removed this morning, a regiment of cavalry taking its place. The latter half of a rebel dispatch was just intercepted saying—

A complete victory. We are pursuing the flying enemy.

This is supposed to refer to Rosecrans. From the general direction and progress of the firing, I should say that our cavalry is driving theirs on the Madison and Gordonsville pike.

G. K. WARREN,
Major-General.

HEADQUARTERS FIRST VERMONT CAVALRY,
Grove Church, Va., September 22, 1863.

Capt. L. G. ESTES,
Assistant Adjutant-General:

CAPTAIN: Major Wells, with a portion of this and the Eighteenth Pennsylvania Regiment, went several miles below Falmouth yesterday, but discovered no traces of the enemy this side of the river. He thinks the report made by Major Darlington the night before to be groundless. The major was so much frightened as to withdraw all of his pickets from Banks' and United States Fords, and fell back to Hartwood Church. Major Wells saw the pickets all replaced along the river, and reports everything quiet.

There is a family living 3 or 4 miles from here, consisting of the old people and five sons, four of the latter being in the rebel army. The fifth, a stout, able-bodied man, is at home, he being exempt from conscription by reason of being a shoemaker. The father is also a healthy, able-bodied man. One of the four sons belonging to the army is now lurking about home, engaged in bushwhacking and kindred pursuits, as I have good reason to believe.

There are other similar cases in this vicinity, and I would respectfully ask that I may be advised as to what course I shall pursue with cases of this nature.

I have the honor to be, very respectfully, your obedient servant,

J. HALL,
Major, Commanding Picket.

MANASSAS JUNCTION,
September 22, 1863.

General KING:

Two officers and 15 men, in pursuit of a lost horse, came upon what they supposed to be a company of cavalry, which they were informed was a part of Mosby's force, near the house of one H. Mathews, on the road from Centreville to Gainesville. They were informed by a man named Settle that there was a regiment of cavalry encamped on the old Bull Run battle-field. My horses becoming unmanageable when the firing commenced, I lost 5 men with horses and equipments. My horses are too green to be serviceable as cavalry. I send this information that you may take such action as you deem necessary.

ALFRED GIBBS,
Colonel.

WAR DEPARTMENT,
Washington, September 22, 1863—2 p. m.

Brigadier-General KELLEY,
Clarksburg, W. Va.:

General Burnside reports Sam. Jones, with 6,000 men, at Zollicoffer, between Bristol and Jonesborough, East Tennessee. If so, the country between there and Lynchburg must be undefended. Cannot your cavalry make a raid and cut the road? An attempt will, at least, drive Jones out of Tennessee.

H. W. HALLECK.
General-in-Chief.

PRIVATE AND CONFIDENTIAL.]   FORT MONROE, VA.,
                                                September 22, 1863.
Major-General HALLECK,
            General-in-Chief, Washington, D. C.:

GENERAL : I have the honor to acknowledge receipt of a letter of
date September 19, from Assistant Adjutant-General Hardie, inclosing a communication from the honorable Secretary of the Navy to
the honorable Secretary of War, on the subject of two iron-clads
being built on the Roanoke River, and, in that point of view, on the
subject of the defenses of Plymouth and the mouth of the Roanoke
River.

I have the honor to say that I have long been aware of the building of these iron-clads, and of the necessity of preparing for and
guarding against them. The defenses of Plymouth have been made
strong, and piling has been and is being driven in the bed of the
river across the channel.

As you are aware, several raids by the army and navy have been
made up the Roanoke River. It is possible, if not probable, that
these boats are constructed for river defense and to prevent the
success of any future raids, though I believe that they are intended
to be used against our naval forces at Plymouth, and against Plymouth possibly, in connection with the descent of other boats from
White Hall on the Neuse, and perhaps from other points on rivers
emptying into the Sounds. The attempting the destruction of the ·
boats on the Roanoke River by a cavalry raid (as the proposed iron-
clads on the Tar River were destroyed) has been thought of, but has
not been attempted, as I did not deem that the attempt could be successful, the enemy being strongly posted in some force, and protected by earth-works and provided with artillery, heavy guns, and
light batteries. I have not marched against their works, particularly the one at Rainbow Bluff, for the reason that the available
force at my disposal was not sufficient, my troops being only sufficient to garrison and hold important occupied posts.

I would respectfully state, referring to the foregoing, that if I
could be re-enforced to the extent of 10,000 good infantry (men to
be relied on), I would add all that I could gather from my present
force of infantry, artillery, and cavalry, and endeavor to surprise
and capture the enemy's works at Rainbow Bluff.

Succeeding, I would endeavor to reach Edwards Ferry and destroy
these gunboats, and, if successful there, march on Weldon and Gaston for the purpose of destroying the bridges at those points. I do
not think that any or all of the above operations should be tried by
me without the number of reliable soldiers named above being added
to my command. When I returned, either having been successful
or having been defeated, I could begin the siege of the forts at the
mouth of the Cape Fear River, and might soon accomplish the
blockade of the river, if nothing more.

I shall not be misunderstood, I hope, in adding that, if operations
have ceased or the good of the service permits, my preference is to
have the troops I know and who know me, my detachment now
serving in the Department of the South.

Inclosed* I forward copies of the letters referred to by me.

I have the honor to be, very respectfully, your obedient servant,

                                    J. G. FOSTER,
                                    Major-General, Commanding.

*See p. 212.

FORT MONROE, *September 22, 1863—6.30 p. m.*
(Received 8.10 p. m.)

Hon E. M. STANTON,.
Secretary of War:

I have just arrived from Richmond. Two divisions of Long-street's corps, together with two brigades of Pickett's division, have gone to Tennessee. The remainder of that division, consisting of the brigades cut up at Gettysburg, has relieved Wise's legion, and it also has gone. The entire artillery of the corps accompanied it. Eighty-one pieces were counted crossing the railroad bridge in one day. The movement commenced Wednesday week. It was continuing on Wednesday last, when the prisoners belonging to the Second Virginia Regiment passed through Petersburg. The troops moved by the Shore line, fearing that the East Tennessee road had been destroyed.

There are few troops in Richmond, on the Peninsula, or at Drewry's Bluff. The store-houses in Richmond are filled with provisions, and the impression is that the army will fall back on the city if attacked by General Meade. General Wall [?] and other officers say that the decisive battle of the war will be fought in Tennessee. It is even intimated that General Lee will go there himself. The news from Tennessee has produced no satisfaction. The rebel officers say that the accounts from the west are always favorable at first, but cannot bear the test of time.

CHARLES K. GRAHAM,
Brigadier-General.

———

FORT MONROE, VA.,
September 22, 1863—1 p. m.

General HALLECK,
Washington:

I have the honor to request that you will grant me permission to relieve Brigadier-General Naglee from duty in this department, and to order him to report to you for orders.

J. G. FOSTER,
Major-General, Commanding.

———

WAR DEPARTMENT,
Washington, September 22, 1863—2.20 p. m.

Major-General FOSTER,
Fort Monroe, Va.:

The Secretary of War directs that Brig. Gen. H. M. Naglee be relieved from duty in your command, and that he be ordered to proceed without delay to Vicksburg, Miss., and report for duty to Major-General Grant.

Brigadier-General James Barnes has been ordered to report to you in General Naglee's place.

H. W. HALLECK,
General-in-Chief.

SPECIAL ORDERS, } WAR DEPT., ADJT. GENERAL'S OFFICE,
No. 424.   }   *Washington, September 22,* 1863:

*   *   *   *   *   *

8. Leave of absence for ten days, from the 28th instant, is hereby granted Maj. Gen. R. C. Schenck, U. S. Volunteers.

Bvt. Brig. Gen. W. W. Morris, U. S. Army, is hereby assigned to the command of the Middle Department during the absence of Major-General Schenck.

*   *   *   *

By order of the Secretary of War:

E. D. TOWNSEND,
Assistant Adjutant-General.

SEPTEMBER 23, 1863—9.40 a. m.
(Received 10 a. m.)

Major-General MEADE,
Washington:

Nothing new this morning. Signal officer at Cedar Mountain reported last night that Buford had driven enemy's cavalry across the Rapidan.

A dispatch from Buford, dated 3.40 p. m., received late last night, says: "We are driving the enemy toward the river." Will communicate as soon as any dispatch is received. All is quiet.

A. A. HUMPHREYS,
Major-General, and Chief of Staff.

SEPTEMBER 23, 1863—3.15 p. m.
(Received 3.25 p. m.)

Major-General MEADE:

A dispatch from General Buford is just received, dated 8.30 a. m. The reconnaissance was completely successful.

General Buford wrote from vicinity of Barnett's Ford. He is now returning by way of Robertson's Ford, and the engineer officers have just returned.

A. A. HUMPHREYS,
Major-General, and Chief of Staff.

SEPTEMBER 23, 1863—12.40 p. m.

Commanding Officer Second Corps:

The latest report we had last night from Buford was dated 3.45 p. m. He was then driving the enemy's cavalry. The signal officer on Cedar Mountain reported during the evening, between 8 and 9 o'clock, that Buford had driven the enemy's cavalry across the Rapidan. No more will be expected from your command to-day.

A. A. HUMPHREYS,
Major-General, and Chief of Staff.

MITCHELL'S, *September* 23, 1863.
(Received 3 p. m.)

Captain NORTON :   :

The following intercepted :

SIGNAL STATION—2 p. m.

Captain T. :

The enemy can be seen falling back on the Orange and Culpeper road.
EWELL,
General.

SIGNAL STATION—4.45 p. m.

General Stuart reports the enemy's cavalry as returning from our left on a road parallel to the Orange and Culpeper road.
C.,
Colonel.

NEEL,
Lieutenant.

CEDAR MOUNTAIN, *September* 23, 1863—6.45 p. m.
(Received 7.30 p. m.)

Captain NORTON,
Signal Officer:

Stuart's cavalry is retiring on Madison Court-House road, going on road west of Robertson's River toward Rapidan Station. More camp fires southwest of the station than last evening.
CASTLE,
Signal Officer.

FAIRFAX STATION, *September* 23, 1863.

General KING :

The rebels have just been at Brooks', near this, and taken 10 cavalry. They have struck for the Braddock road. I have sent a small escort to Fairfax Station [Court-House] with Major Willard.
A. H. GRIMSHAW,
Colonel.

CLARKSBURG, W. VA., *September* 23, 1863—3.15 p. m.
Received 8 p. m.)

Brig. Gen. G. W. CULLUM,
Chief of Staff:

In order that the General-in-Chief may fully understand the state of matters in the mountains, I send you copies of last telegrams from Generals Scammon and Averell. If the information contained in these telegrams is reliable, it would be very hazardous to send an expedition at present to the Virginia and Tennessee Railroad, as suggested. I will, however, cause Scammon's and Averell's commands to be in readiness to repel attack, or move forward if you deem it best. Highton is in Highland County, on the Staunton and Beverly pike.

BEVERLY, *September* 23, 1863.

Brigadier-General KELLEY :

Scouts just from Crab Bottom report that three regiments joined Jenkins on Monday evening. He had three pieces of artillery, and expected Imboden to join

15 R R—VOL XXIX, PT II

him. A colonel stated that they had marching orders for yesterday. He has now seven regiments and three batteries. It was reported on the Seneca road yesterday by a citizen that 100 of Jenkins' men were preparing to come down on to Cheat River. I have 150 ready to meet them on Shaffer Mountain.

WM. W. AVERELL,
Brigadier-General.

Brigadier-General KELLEY:

Lieutenant Abbott, Twenty-third Ohio Volunteer Infantry, reports Forty-fifth and Twenty-second [Virginia Infantry], and Edgar's battalion near Lewisburg; Eighth Virginia Cavalry, Derrick's [battalion infantry], and Dittrick's [?] cavalry, at Sinking Creek. Cavalry camp seen distinctly. All passes guarded. Union houses watched. Could not get food for his party. Other party not yet heard from.

SCAMMON,
Brigadier-General.

B. F. KELLEY,
Brigadier-General, Commanding.

HEADQUARTERS CHIEF ENGINEER OF DEFENSES,
Washington, September 23, 1863.

Hon. E. M. STANTON,
Secretary of War:

SIR: By letter of the 1st instant, I represented the importance of speedily arming the two works built for the defense of the Potomac approach to Washington. At your request I mentioned the number of improved sea-coast guns which I thought should be immediately supplied, and I mentioned eight, in consideration of the great demand for guns at the different sea-ports.

This was an off-hand statement, and I have since reflected on the matter, and have come to the conclusion that since there is no armament in Fort Washington of any value whatever, and that these two works will constitute, just now, the real defenses of Washington against maritime attack, the full armament of these works (namely, three 15-inch guns and thirteen 200-pounders) should be furnished very speedily. In case of war with a maritime power, allied with the rebellion, the defense of Washington can hardly be considered second in importance to that of New York.

I have, therefore, to request that in your directions to the Ordnance Department it may be directed to furnish the last-mentioned number of guns as speedily as possible.

I am, very respectfully, your most obedient,

J. G. BARNARD,
Brigadier-General, &c.

SPECIAL ORDERS, }   HDQRS. DEPT. OF VA. AND N. C.,
   No. 65.   }   <i>Fort Monroe, Va., September 23, 1863.</i>

I. In obedience to orders from the Secretary of War, Brig. Gen. H. M. Naglee is hereby relieved from duty in this department, and ordered to proceed without delay to Vicksburg, Miss., and report for duty to Major-General Grant.

II. Brig. Gen. G. W. Getty will assume command of the troops between the James River and Albemarle Sound, exclusive of the towns of Norfolk and Portsmouth, which, with the provost guards therein, are placed under the command of Brig. Gen. Edward E. Potter.

III. Brigadier-General Wistar will command the Sub-District of Yorktown.

Sub-districts will report direct to these headquarters.

*   *   *   *   *

By command of Maj. Gen. John G. Foster:

[SOUTHARD HOFFMAN,]
Assistant Adjutant-General.

HEADQUARTERS ARMY OF THE POTOMAC,
September 24, 1863—4 p. m.   (Received 4.30 p. m.)

Maj. Gen. H. W. HALLECK,
General-in-Chief:

The officers principally engaged in raising funds for the testimonial to General McClellan promptly agreed to my request to stop the whole proceeding on my representing to them the view that had been taken of it. They furthermore disclaimed any intention of doing anything offensive to any one or in violation of regulations.*

I trust this solution will be deemed satisfactory.

GEO. G. MEADE,
Major-General.

HEADQUARTERS ARMY OF THE POTOMAC,
September 24, 1863.

Commanding Officer First Corps:

The major-general commanding directs that you move with your corps immediately and relieve the Twelfth Corps,† Major-General Slocum commanding. It is important that this should be done with the utmost dispatch and that the movement and relief of the Twelfth Corps should be effected without the knowledge of the enemy so far as it is practicable to accomplish it. The Twelfth Corps pickets the Rapidan from Somerville Ford to Stringfellow's Ford. The headquarters and main body of the corps are east of Summerduck River, not far from Raccoon Ford. An officer is sent or will be sent to guide your corps to the Twelfth Corps.

Very respectfully, &c.,

A. A. HUMPHREYS,
Major-General, and Chief of Staff.

RACCOON FORD, *September* 24, 1863.

General HUMPHREYS,
Chief of Staff:

The following rebel dispatch just intercepted:

General R. :

No news relative to the force moving to Germanna. A large force moving toward Morton's Ford.

JOHN NEWTON,
Major-General.

---

* See General Orders, No. 94, headquarters Army of the Potomac, October 6.

† Which, with the Eleventh Army Corps, had been ordered to Tennessee. See Part I, p. 146.

CEDAR MOUNTAIN,
September 24, 1863—3.30 p. m.

Captain NORTON :
    Rebel dispatch :

General EWELL :
    Camps on Culpeper and Stevensburg road, to the right of Pony Mountain, have disappeared within the last two hours.   Infantry can be seen moving toward Stevensburg.   A few wagons also moving in that direction.

NEEL,
Lieutenant.

HEADQUARTERS FIRST ARMY CORPS,
September 24, 1863—5.20 p. m.

A. A. HUMPHREYS,
        Chief of Staff:

The First Corps is in position occupying that recently held by the Twelfth Corps.   The ammunition and ambulance trains were brought down with one wagon for each brigade and division headquarters.
    I suppose I am allowed to bring forage and supplies and required to keep up the full supply trains, &c.   The pickets are not yet entirely relieved.

JOHN NEWTON,
Major-General, Commanding.

HDQRS. DEPT. OF VIRGINIA AND NORTH CAROLINA,
Fort Monroe, Va., September 24, 1863.

Capt. F. VON SCHILLING,
        Commanding Expedition:

You will proceed with the forces under your command to Hog Island and take the necessary steps to protect the light-house on the island from an attack by guerrillas.   If deemed prudent, on consultation with Captain Duvall, or commanding officer of the post, you can cross to the mainland and break up and take or kill this party of guerrillas.   You will obtain all information you can as to these guerrillas.   On landing you will leave a sufficient guard at the light-house to protect it.   You will report immediately on your return, and give your views as to the danger and as to the best means of guarding against it.   The C. W. Thomas is under your orders.
    By order of Major-General Foster:
        I am, very respectfully,

SOUTHARD HOFFMAN,
Assistant Adjutant-General.

[P. S.]—I need hardly suggest the necessity of restraining to the utmost every disposition to plunder by the soldiers should you cross on the mainland.   As commanding officer you are responsible for good order.
    For your information I would inform you that there is a report of a rebel steamer (small) being in Sand Shoal Inlet.   Find out anything you can about her.

HDQRS. DEPT. OF VIRGINIA AND NORTH CAROLINA,
Fort Monroe, Va., September 24, 1863.
Lieut. C. D. WILLARD,
Commanding Gunboat General Jesup:

SIR: You will proceed with secrecy and dispatch to West Point, on the York River, and thence up the Pamunkey to such place as you may deem best to accomplish the purpose of your expedition, which is to intercept and capture a small rebel steamer which plies between White House and West Point. A pilot believed to be reliable is sent to you. Failing of succeeding, you will then return and report to these headquarters. You will endeavor to obtain all information as to a force of cavalry said to be stationed at Matthews Court-House. You will observe every needful precaution to keep the object of this expedition secret.

By order Major-General Foster:
I am, very respectfully,
SOUTHARD HOFFMAN,
Assistant Adjutant-General.

CIRCULAR.]   HEADQUARTERS ARMY OF THE POTOMAC,
September 24, 1863—11.20 a. m.

The major-general commanding directs that all the trains be held in readiness to move to the rear at very short notice.

By command of Major-General Meade:
S. WILLIAMS,
Assistant Adjutant-General.

(Copy to all corps and independent commanders.)

HEADQUARTERS FOURTH SEPARATE BRIGADE,
Beverly, September 25, 1863.
Brig. Gen. B. F. KELLEY,
Commanding Department:

From information received to-night, it is possible that the enemy may make an advance upon this point in the next three or four days. The report which has reached me exaggerates, no doubt, the force advancing on Elkwater road. I have given orders to Gibson, at Buckhannon, and am as nearly ready as well can be.

WM. W. AVERELL,
Brigadier-General.

HEADQUARTERS FOURTH SEPARATE BRIGADE,
Beverly, September 25, 1863.
Major GIBSON,
Buckhannon:

It is possible that this point, or some other in this section, may be attacked by the enemy in considerable force in the course of three or four days. You will send a patrol to Huttonsville daily, and should you become aware of an attack upon Beverly, you will throw your command upon the enemy's flank and rear, via the Huttonsville road,

directing the force at Middle Fork to go to Buckhannon and take
care of your transportation and stores. You will also send a party
to communicate with me at this place, should the telegraph lines be
down. Keep three days' rations constantly in the haversacks. I
believe I am able to hold this valley, if you can take care of that flank.
Let your patrols and your command be provided with axes; and regard this telegram as confidential. Answer if you understand me
fully.

WM. W. AVERELL,
Brigadier-General.

YORKTOWN,
September 25, 1863—6.15 p. m.

General FOSTER:

A discharged railroad engineer from Richmond a week ago has
just arrived. Says Longstreet's corps, also Wise's brigade, went to
Bragg two weeks since; also a few troops went south. Pickett's
headquarters with two brigades at Chaffin's Bluff. No other troops
in or near Richmond. Rebels are discharging many railroad hands
because roads worn out. They are conscripted immediately on discharge.

I. J. WISTAR,
Brigadier-General.

WASHINGTON,
September 25, 1863—3.15 p. m.

Major-General FOSTER:

Brigadier-General Barnes has been assigned to your command, in
the place of General Naglee. It is decided that he be assigned to
duty as commander of Norfolk. You know the high reputation he
enjoys as a military man, and are perhaps personally acquainted
with him. I hope he may be acceptable to you, and that cordial
co-operation in the measures of the Government in weakening the
enemy and in strengthening ourselves by enlisting colored troops,
may exist between you. I have given him a short leave to visit
his family before reporting for duty.

EDWIN M. STANTON.

FORT MONROE, VA., *September 25, 1863—5 p. m.*
(Received 5.40 p. m.)

Hon. E. M. STANTON.
Secretary of War:

I have received your telegram of this day. I have already relieved
General Naglee by Brig. Gen. Edward E. Potter, who is a first-class
man for a position of this kind, and a determined friend to the Government. I propose to have the several districts of Virginia, Norfolk, and Portsmouth, Getty's line of defense, and Yorktown report
to me directly. Brigadier-General Barnes to command Getty's line
in place of Brigadier-General Getty, while the latter is absent on
sick-leave, and then to command Yorktown. General Potter to
command the cities of Norfolk and Portsmouth, and Brigadier-

General Wistar to command at Yorktown at present. I make this
. explanation in order that you may have an opportunity to express
your wishes, which will be fully carried out.

The organization of colored troops is progressing well. They are
now hard at work on the fortifications. The white troops being
much broken down by sickness, cannot the Baltimore regiment be
ordered down at once? I actually need it at Yorktown, where the
regiments are very much enfeebled by sickness.

J. G. FOSTER,
Major-General.

WASHINGTON,
September 25, 1863—7.40 p. m.

Major-General FOSTER:

Your telegram has been received. I am reluctant to interfere with
any arrangement of yours, but for several controlling reasons it is
more important to place General Barnes in command at Norfolk and
Portsmouth than any other arrangement. I shall therefore desire
you to assign him to that command when he reports for duty.

The Baltimore colored regiment is under orders to report to you,
and I had supposed it had reached you by this time.

EDWIN M. STANTON,
Secretary of War.

WAR DEPARTMENT,
Washington City, September 25, 1863—3 p. m.

Major-General SCHENCK, <i>Baltimore:</i>

The President directs that when you take your leave of absence
you will turn over your command to Brig. Gen. Erastus B. Tyler,
who is assigned to the command of the Middle Department during
your temporary absence.*

By order of the President:

EDWIN M. STANTON,
Secretary of War.

FORT MONROE, VA., September 25, 1863.

Maj. Gen. H. W. HALLECK,
General-in-Chief, U. S. Army, Washington, D. C.:

GENERAL: I have the honor to inclose.copy of telegram from Capt.
John E. Graham, provost-marshal at Drummondtown, relative to
the action of guerrillas. I have placed a gun on a transport and
sent a company of soldiers to endeavor to capture this band, and to
take the needful steps to protect Hog Island Light. The counties of
Accomac and Northampton not being in my department, I scarcely
feel authorized to place permanent garrisons there, and so only act
in the emergency. If deemed proper to place these counties in my
command, I will endeavor to prevent any future trouble from guerrillas.

I have the honor to be, very respectfully, your obedient servant,

J. G. FOSTER,
Major-General, Commanding.

---

* Brig. Gen. E. B. Tyler assumed command, under this order, September 28.

[Inclosure.]

DRUMMONDTOWN,
September 24, 1863.

Major-General FOSTER:

A band of guerrillas has visited this shore on the seaside, capturing four boats, one of which they ran ashore, two others they carried to sea and set adrift. The last they retained, containing sutlers' stores bound for Port Royal. Prisoners also retained. This schooner's name is Lydia, from Philadelphia, and had not left on Tuesday, and was stretching in and off Hog Island, the particulars of which were received to-day from part es captured. The parties stated they were bound for Richmond.   i

JOHN E. GRAHAM,
Captain, and Provost-Marshal.

RACCOON FORD,
September 26, 1863—6.45 p. m.

Major-General HUMPHREYS,
Chief of Staff :

The following rebel message just intercepted:

General L.:

Colonel P. has a brigade at Germanna Ford.

STUART,
General.

JOHN NEWTON,
Major-General.

ALEXANDRIA, VA., *September* 26, 1863.
(Received 8.40 p. m.)

Col. J. H. TAYLOR,
Chief of Staff ·

The following dispatch is just received from Colonel Grimeshaw :

FAIRFAX STATION, VA.,
September 26, 1863.

Col. H. H. WELLS,
Provost-Marshal :

It is reported from guard at Burke's Station that rebel force is near the road south (artillery and cavalry), and has taken mules 3 miles from station.

A. H. GRIMESHAW,
Colonel, Commanding Post.

Very respectfully,

H. H. WELLS,
Provost-Marshal.

HEADQUARTERS FOURTH SEPARATE BRIGADE,
Beverly, September 26, 1863.

Brig. Gen. B. F. KELLEY,
Commanding Department :

From Crab Bottom one regiment moved Tuesday, one Wednesday, and one yesterday morning (supposed to be going to Jackson's River), leaving two battalions and two guns in Crab Bottom, besides Sixty-second [Virginia] Regiment, which was at Seneca yesterday morning. All quiet at Parsons' Mills. Jenkins' force is either going to Jones, to Elkwater road, via Back Creek, or to Sutton. I think these men on my right belong to Imboden.

WM. W. AVERELL,
Brigadier-General.

HEADQUARTERS DEPARTMENT OF WEST VIRGINIA,
Clarksburg, September 26, 1863.

His Excellency A. I. BOREMAN,
Governor of West Virginia:

GOVERNOR: I have the honor to inform you that from information which I deem reliable, it is evident that Jenkins, Jackson, and Imboden are either contemplating a combined movement into West Virginia in force, or that they intend sending small detachments and guerrilla bands into the different counties at the same time, for the purpose of destroying the railroads, and capturing and destroying the public stores and property, as well as stealing horses, robbing stores, and plundering and murdering the people.

I respectfully suggest that you issue a proclamation to the people to be on the alert, calling on the militia to organize and arm, and be ready to assemble and move to any point threatened at the shortest possible notice. I do not desire to alarm the people by this action. Indeed, there is no necessity for unnecessary alarm. My object is to put the people on their guard and have them ready to repel the invader whenever or wherever he may show himself.

I am, sir, your obedient servant,

B. F. KELLEY,
Brigadier-General.

WAR DEPARTMENT,
Washington, September 26, 1863—2.30 p. m.

Major-General FOSTER,
Fort Monroe, Va.:

No change of department lines can be made now, but the Secretary of War directs that you take all necessary measures to prevent the operations of guerrillas in the counties of Northampton and Accomac. Any garrisons you may temporarily place there will remain under your command. Operate wherever necessary, without regard to arbitrary department lines.

H. W. HALLECK,
General-in-Chief.

HEADQUARTERS ARMY OF THE POTOMAC,
September 27, 1863—7 p. m. (Received 8 p. m.)

Maj. Gen. H. W. HALLECK,
General-in-Chief:

Two deserters came in yesterday, one last evening. When they left A. P. Hill's corps was in position behind the Rapidan. One of the deserters belonged to Mahone's brigade, Anderson's division, Hill's corps. I will apprise you of the earliest intelligence of any further detachment by Lee, and will make every effort to ascertain it at the earliest moment.

GEO. G. MEADE,
Major-General.

HDQRS. FIRST CAV. DIV., ARMY OF THE POTOMAC,
September 27, 1863—3.30 p. m.

Col. C. ROSS SMITH,
Chief of Staff:

Your note has just been handed to me. The regiments sent to relieve General Kilpatrick's were the Sixth and Ninth New York. They have not been heard from since they started yesterday morning. I have not looked for a report from them yet. Major Beveridge pickets from Richards' to Morton's with 500 men from the First Brigade. He reports all quiet on his line; no cavalry, but infantry and artillery. The rebels are still digging.

I am, very respectfully, your obedient servant,

JNO. BUFORD,
Brigadier-General of Volunteers, Commanding.

HEADQUARTERS FOURTH SEPARATE BRIGADE,
Beverly, September 27, 1863.

Brig. Gen. B. F. KELLEY,
Commanding Department:

Thirty-five rebels camped on Middle Ridge, about 3 miles west of here, last night. They are on their way to the pike. I am trying to catch them. Jenkins was on the move yesterday, 11 a. m., from Crab Bottom toward the pike. A rebel scout told his sister at Huttonsville, night before last, that this post would be attacked within four days. I have good scouts on the road. Have captured two of enemy's scouts, one other wounded and captured. If line remains open, you had better send anything important in cipher.

WM. W. AVERELL,
Brigadier-General.

HDQRS. FIRST CAV. DIV., ARMY OF THE POTOMAC,
September 28, 1863.

Col. C. ROSS SMITH,
Chief of Staff:

I have the honor to report all quiet to-day along the whole length of my picket line, extending from Morton's Ford to the Lacy House. At Morton's the rebels have a large infantry picket, and they are digging like beavers at Germanna. They have thrown up nine earth-works and have them connected, and are still intrenching. A few miles below Fredericksburg they cross at will in small boats.

Last night a small party crossed to this side at Germanna and went back.

The Prince William company of cavalry is fully mounted, and when last heard from were at Stafford Court-House.

I send two Richmond papers.

I am, very respectfully, your obedient servant,

JNO. BUFORD,
Brigadier-General of Volunteers, Commanding.

HEADQUARTERS FIRST ARMY CORPS,
September 28, 1863.

Maj. Gen. A. A. HUMPHREYS,
Chief of Staff:

GENERAL: It is proper for me to state in general terms the disposition I propose to make of the troops of this corps for the information of the commanding general.

This would be to place two divisions on the main road from Raccoon Ford to Culpeper Court-House at or near the house marked "Colvin" on the map, where at present all my batteries save one are posted. The remaining division, with one battery, a little west of Pony Mountain, crossing the road from Morton's Ford to Stevensburg. A road leads from the position of this division to Culpeper Court-House, intersecting the main road from Raccoon Ford to Culpeper at the house marked "Inskip," to the northwest of Pony Mountain.

Necessarily the two bodies into which the corps will be divided must act independently until they nearly reach Pony Mountain, because the cross-roads are few and faintly traced, and on account of the dense woods (imperfectly represented on the map) which interpose.

The main road from Raccoon Ford to Culpeper, as well as the other communication spoken of, are liable to the grave objection of being nearly impassable in wet weather of two or three days' continuance, owing to the character of the soil, and this is the gravest consideration in connection with my position which I feel compelled to call to the attention of the commanding general. In such event, if pressed, I should be very solicitous for the artillery and the necessary wagons.

After carefully considering the ground, I have found it inexpedient to place the two detachments of the corps within supporting distance of each other, having a view to guard the roads to Culpeper. It might be asked why not place the detachment on the left in the forest? The objection to this is the dense character of the woods, with much underbrush and few and blind roads, which would be inconvenient when pressed to operate upon.

I have the honor to be, your obedient servant,

JOHN NEWTON,
Major-General, Commanding.

[SEPTEMBER 28, 1863.—For Naglee to Foster, relating to contraband trade, guerrillas, &c., in the Department of Virginia and North Carolina, see Series I, Vol. XXVII, Part III, pp. 845–856.]

SEPTEMBER 29, 1863.

Major-General NEWTON,
        Commanding First Corps:

By direction of the major-general commanding, I transmit herewith a copy of the instructions given to Major-General Slocum upon his taking up the position on the Rapidan with the Twelfth Corps* which you now occupy with the First Corps. These instructions are intended for your government. The position in front of Culpeper Court-House, which it is intended you shall take up in a certain contingency, has been designated on the ground to the staff officer sent by you for that purpose.

In reference to the movement of your artillery to the rear under the circumstances stated by you, the major-general commanding considers that the roads to Culpeper Court-House should be at once prepared by working parties at those points where heavy rains would render them difficult for the passage of artillery.

In the contingency you anticipate, however, the major-general commanding directs me to say that the enemy would find the same difficulty in bringing forward their artillery that you would in withdrawing yours.

Very respectfully, your obedient servant,
            A. A. HUMPHREYS,
            Major-General, Chief of Staff.

HEADQUARTERS CAVALRY CORPS,
            September 29, 1863.

Brigadier-General GREGG:

The commanding general directs that, unless you have already done so, you withdraw your force from Watery Mountain. He also wishes that, if you have sufficient force for the purpose, you send an occasional scout toward Amissville, as it is reported that the rebels have two regiments of North Carolina cavalry near that place.
            C. C. SUYDAM,
            Assistant Adjutant-General.

YORKTOWN,
            September 29, 1863.

Major-General FOSTER:

Have seen Captain Gillis. I have 434 infantry for duty here. Cannot spare any from Williamsburg. I can use about 300 cavalry for a short expedition, if I had the troops. I think a regiment of infantry should take position at Gloucester Court-House, with battery and 200 cavalry at the Isthmus of Matthews County, with gunboat adjacent at head of North River, while 200 cavalry scoured Matthews County, with another gunboat and transport at the court-house to bring them off if retreat by land should be intercepted. Will write fully by mail.

I have not enough available infantry.
            I. J. WISTAR,
            Brigadier-General.

* See page 197.

FORTRESS MONROE,
September 29, 1863.

General WISTAR,
 Yorktown:

If you will communicate a complete plan which you will engage to carry out, I will see that you have all the means in men and boats, but I want a well-digested plan before I will give an order.

J. G. FOSTER.

RAPPAHANNOCK,
September 30, 1863.

Brigadier-General GREGG:

There is no enemy at Amissville, and the inhabitants report that none have been there.

J. IRVIN GREGG,
Colonel, Commanding.

ARTILLERY HDQRS., ARMY OF THE POTOMAC,
Camp near Culpeper, Va., September 30, 1863.

Brig. Gen. R. INGALLS,[*]
 Chief Quartermaster, Army of the Potomac:

GENERAL : In relation to the transportation of ammunition for the army, I have always been of opinion that it should be transported in caissons. These carriages are constructed specially to transport ammunition, and for this reason alone it might safely be assumed that they are well adapted to the service and possess special advantages. My impression on this subject has been confirmed by experience.

The system of transporting ammunition in the ordinary wagons has led to grave inconveniences. The ammunition trains are apt to be mixed up with other supply trains.

Foreseeing this, I took special pains in the organization of the Artillery Reserve ammunition train in the Peninsula. I obtained orders from General McClellan that the wagons should be covered with black water-proof covers, in order that they might be distinguished at a glance. These orders were not complied with by your predecessor, and the result was much confusion. I took special pains to keep a hundred wagon loads of artillery ammunition of the Artillery Reserve always available. At Malvern Hill, the trains of the divisions having become mingled with the other trains, it was generally found impracticable to find them. I ordered my hundred wagons upon the hill, with direction to issue to all who needed. The consequence was that battery after battery of the different corps, whose supplies were exhausted, and which could not find their own trains, had their chests replenished, and were sent to the field again. I believe this circumstance, the careful watchfulness over this train, and bringing it on to the field of battle, was one of the main causes of our success.

----

[*] See Ingalls' report, Series I, Vol. XIX, Part I, p. 105.

I have frequently seen that trains could not be found when most needed when a battle was going on. It is important that this evil should be removed; the substitution of caissons for army wagons would remove it. On the day of battle, trains of caissons could be easily found and would have unquestioned precedence of movement.

There would be numerous other advantages; the ammunition could always be inspected. Boxed up as it is now such inspection is impossible. It would be better protected. Wagons are now often unloaded of their ammunition that they may be used for other purposes, the ammunition being put in the mud or on wet ground, or, left exposed to the weather, rain beats in at the ends of the wagons, and the covers often leak.

In fine, there can be no security for the condition of the ammunition as long as it is carried in wagons. On the field of battle the boxes must be taken from the wagons, unscrewed, and the ammunition transferred to the caisson, a waste of time when time is too precious to waste, and delay may cause disaster. If transported in caissons, a team from a battery can hitch in and gallop off with a new supply, exchanging an empty caisson for a full one.

There is another point. Each wagon carries 325 pounds of ammunition boxes (14 boxes). The boxes are lost, but the great evil is the transportation of so much unnecessary weight, 23 pounds for each 8 shots. All this would be saved by the use of caissons. About one wagon in six now transport boxes. At need, each caisson can be drawn by a team and one driver as in a wagon, for the train caissons do not maneuver.

For the train, the Gribeauval caisson could be used to advantage if the ordinary wagon team should be found unsuited to the caisson of the present system, but I apprehend no difficulty on this subject. Forges are often drawn by such teams with but one driver, and their limbers are the same as those of the caissons.

I believe, also, that for the same reasons and stronger ones, caissons could be used with advantage for the transport of small-arms ammunition. The present caisson can be arranged with trays for the chests, so as to transport from 25,000 to 30,000 musket cartridges. Properly manned, these caissons could be galloped upon the field and take their places behind infantry brigades, replenish the cartridge boxes, with the help of the file closers, and leave again in ten minutes. There would be no further reports of regiments leaving the field for want of ammunition ; the men would not be weighted down with an oversupply and the consequent waste would be prevented. This, however, would require a higher organization than is required for the transport and supply of artillery ammunition, and that companies of foot artillery should be furnished to act as drivers and guards for the trains. I think this could be done with decided advantage, and the whole ammunition train composed of caissons.

I will add that the subject has been several times brought to the notice of higher authorities, but so far without results. Your department is interested in the subject, and I am certain you will find on examination that the transport of ammunition may be more safely, surely, and economically provided for than by the present system.

Respectfully, your obedient servant,

'HENRY J. HUNT,
Brigadier-General, Chief of Artillery.

Abstract from return of the Army of the Potomac, Maj. Gen. George G. Meade, U. S. Army, commanding, for the month of September, 1863.

Command.	Present for duty.		Aggregate present.	Aggregate present and absent.	Pieces of artillery.	
	Officers.	Men.			Heavy.	Field.
General headquarters	149	1,360	1,711	2,205	......	......
Engineer troops	45	1,145	1,361	1,742	......	......
Artillery Reserve	115	3,154	3,585	4,477	8	99
First Army Corps	558	9,451	11,708	19,745	......	24
Second Army Corps	582	9,890	11,495	21,460	......	26
Third Army Corps	745	12,486	16,560	25,850	......	42
Fifth Army Corps	584	10,925	12,677	19,854	......	28
Sixth Army Corps	826	13,502	16,078	22,196	......	42
Cavalry Corps	614	10,816	13,888	34,903	......	30
Total	4,218	73,729	89,058	142,432	8	291

Abstract from return of the Department of Washington, Maj. Gen. Samuel P. Heintzelman, U. S. Army, commanding, for the month of September, 1863.

Command.	Present for duty.		Aggregate present.	Aggregate present and absent.	Pieces of artillery.
	Officers.	Men.			
General headquarters	31	113	162	184	......
Artillery Camp of Instruction	40	1,208	1,477	1,806	54
District of Washington	120	2,385	3,637	4,317	......
Defenses North of the Potomac	180	4,882	6,375	7,300	417
Provisional brigades	28	730	819	846	......
Defenses South of the Potomac	207	4,353	6,008	7,351	433
King's division	91	1,654	2,117	2,682	6
Cavalry forces (Lowell)	35	590	1,107	1,910	......
District of Alexandria	92	1,462	1,901	3,272	6
Camp Convalescent, &c	85	1,832	6,467	6,749	......
Annapolis Junction (Tracy)	21	744	963	1,005	......
Fort Washington (Brooks)	6	89	153	161	73
Total a	936	20,062	31,186	37,583	989

a Incomplete returns given in Defenses North of the Potomac.

Abstract from return of the Middle Department (Eighth Army Corps), Maj. Gen. Robert C. Schenck, U. S. Army, commanding, for the month of September, 1863.

Command.	Present for duty.		Aggregate present.	Aggregate present and absent.	Pieces of artillery.	
	Officers.	Men.			Heavy.	Field.
General headquarters	21	......	21	21	......	......
Defenses of Baltimore (E. B. Tyler)	38	782	885	1,157	......	16
Second Separate Brigade (Morris)	41	992	1,406	1,700	159	15
Annapolis, Md. (Waite)	19	385	538	577	......	......
Eastville, Va.	3	104	117	190	......	......
Ellicott's Mills, Md. (Gilpin)	23	463	528	569	......	......
Fort Delaware (Schoepf)	24	445	795	927	67	6
Relay House, Md. (Jenkins)	23	243	319	364	......	......
Wilmington, Del. (D. Tyler)	7	326	344	352	......	......
Total	199	3,740	4,953	5,857	226	37

Abstract from return of the Department of West Virginia, Brig. Gen. Benjamin F. Kelley, U. S. Army, commanding, for the month of September, 1863.

Command.	Present for duty.		Aggregate present.	Aggregate present and absent.	Pieces of artillery.		Remarks.
	Officers.	Men.			Heavy.	Field.	
General headquarters	6	......	6	6	......	.	
Third Division (Scammon)	200	4,583	5,580	6,555	......	14	Charleston, W. Va.
Lockwood's division..... ...	210	4,240	5,070	6,204	32	24	Harper's Ferry, W. Va.
Averell's brigade	166	3,830	4,649	5,387	......	9	Beverly, W. Va.
Campbell's brigade.	53	1,601	1,827	2,119	......	7	Romney, W. Va.
Mulligan's brigade	68	1,532	1,827	2,354	......	7	Petersburg, W. Va.
Pierce's brigade	94	2,205	2,779	3,444	......	12	Martinsburg, W. Va.
Wilkinson's brigade............	103	2,750	2,967	3,223	......	5	Clarksburg, W. Va.
Detachments :							
Green Spring Run, W. Va ...	22	587	689	691	......	......	
New Creek, W Va...........	8	185	201	201	......	6	
Romney, W. Va...............	23	458	560	780	......	......	
Sir John's Run, W. Va.......	27	333	452	1,062	......	......	
Total	980	22,305	26,607	31,826	32	84	

Abstract from return of the Department of Virginia and North Carolina, Maj. Gen. John G. Foster, U. S. Army, commanding, for the month of September, 1863.

Command.	Present for duty.		Aggregate present.	Aggregate present and absent.	Pieces of artillery.	
	Officers.	Men.			Heavy.	Field.
General headquarters	32	46	92	95	......	......
Fort Monroe, Va	23	590	850	1,183	......	......
Portsmouth, Va. (Getty)	224	5,209	7,061	11,575	......	24
Portsmouth and Norfolk, Va. (Potter).	48	1,063	1,426	1,721	......	6
Sub-District of Yorktown (Wistar)	109	1,807	3,734	5,106	......	30
District of North Carolina (Peck)	408	7,418	10,959	14,719	135	114
Total...	844	16,133	24,122	34,379	135	174

Abstract from return of the Department of the East, Maj. Gen. John A. Dix, U. S. Army, commanding, for the month of September, 1863.

Command.	Present for duty.		Aggregate present.	Aggregate present and absent.	Pieces of artillery.	
	Officers.	Men.			Heavy.	Field.
General headquarters...	78	......	89	89	......	......
City and harbor of New York (E. R. S. Canby)..........	387	4,002	4,706	8,304	327	......
Fort Ontario, N. Y. (Capt. C. H. Lewis)	1	89	96	110	17	......
Fort Niagara, N. Y	......	1	1	1	16	4
Fort Trumbull, Conn. (W. Gates) ... ..,.............	3	96	192	209	58	......
Fort Adams, R. I. (O. L. Shepherd)	3	67	141	176	200	......
Portsmouth Grove, R. I. (Capt. C. Blanding)............	3	66	82	86	......	......
Fort Independence, Mass (D. L. Floyd-Jones) :..........	10	317	461	477	56	......
Fort Warren, Mass. (Justin Dimick)............	17	468	599	756	92	......
Fort at Clark's Point, Mass. (Capt. J. A. P. Allen).......	4	90	110	148	19	......
Fort Constitution, N. H (Capt. C. H. Long)	7	261	285	287	27	......
Fort Knox, Me (Lieut T. H Palmer)......	1	25	52	58	20	4
Fort Preble, Me. (G. L. Andrews)	4	77	117	127	44	......
Total	518	5,554	6,931	10,898	876	8

MITCHELL'S,
October 1, 1863.

Captain NORTON:

Rebel message from rebel signal station :

General STUART:

    Gregg is at Catlett's Station.

FITZ. LEE,
General.

WM. H. R. NEEL,
Lieutenant, Signal Officer.

SPECIAL ORDERS, }   HDQRS. ARMY OF THE POTOMAC,
   No. 264.   }   October 1, 1863.

    *   *   *   *   *   *

    3. Howe's division, Sixth Corps, is assigned to duty on the railroad for the defense of the bridges at Bristoe, Catlett's, and Rappahannock Stations, a brigade at each bridge, with a battery of artillery with each, to be furnished from the Reserve Artillery. General Gregg's cavalry at Rappahannock, Catlett's, and Bristoe Stations will be relieved by General Howe's infantry. General Gregg's headquarters will be near Bealeton Station, with a portion of one of his brigades of cavalry. He will keep up a force at Kettle Run Bridge and small detachments at the small bridges and culverts, and will patrol the railroad. General Howe's headquarters will be at Catlett's. In conjunction with the cavalry, he will protect the railroad. General Gregg will keep him advised of any movement of the enemy, and will co-operate with him. The movement of Howe's division and artillery will be made during the night as far as Rappahannock Station, so as to be concealed from the observation of the enemy. General Howe will have rifle-pits and other defensive works thrown up by each brigade. General Howe's division will be supplied from Alexandria. General Gregg will send a brigade of cavalry to Hartwood, to relieve Buford's brigade in picketing the Rappahannock River.

    By command of Major-General Meade:

S. WILLIAMS,
Assistant Adjutant-General.

ARTILLERY HDQRS., ARMY OF THE POTOMAC,
October 1, 1863.

Circular to Chiefs of Artillery of Corps:

    The allowance of wagons for the artillery brigades is as follows:

    For headquarters of brigade, 1 wagon for baggage, 1 wagon for forage and supplies, 1 wagon for sales to officers, and 1 wagon for hospital stores.

    For each battery of four guns, 4 wagons for baggage, rations, forage, &c., and for each six-gun battery, 5 wagons, being 1 to each battery in addition to the number heretofore authorized.

    You will please have the necessary requisitions made out. This to enable each battery to transport six days' forage in the wagons.

    By command of General Hunt :

JNO. N. CRAIG,
Assistant Adjutant-General.

WAR DEPARTMENT,
Washington, October 2, 1863—1 p. m.

Major-General MEADE,
 Army of the Potomac:

Colonel McCallum recommends that the troops now at Warrenton Junction be encamped in the woods south of the station, so as to protect the water-tank and wood-choppers at the same time.

Please send me, as nearly as you can, the number of enemy's dead left in our hands at the battle of Gettysburg.

H. W. HALLECK,
General-in-Chief.

———

MITCHELL'S,
October 2, 1863.

General WILLIAMS:

The following report is just received from the picket line:

HDQRS. THIRD BRIGADE, THIRD DIVISION, SECOND ARMY CORPS,
October 2, 1863.

GEORGE P. CORTS,
 Captain, and Assistant Adjutant-General:

SIR: I have the honor to report that unusual activity prevailed all of last night in the enemy's camps. Railroad cars were running the night long, indicating either the arrival or departure of troops.

JOSHUA T. OWEN,
Brigadier-General, Commanding.

G. K. WARREN,
Major-General. ·

———

HDQRS. FIRST ARMY CORPS, ARMY OF THE POTOMAC,
October 2, 1863.

Major-General HUMPHREYS,
 Chief of Staff, Army of the Potomac:

GENERAL: The general officers of the day have been reporting for several days that the enemy has been extending his works at Raccoon Ford, Morton's Ford, and above these places. I cannot account for this except that he intends to cover and sustain a movement in some other direction. Some of the officers on picket imagine that they have recognized a diminution of the force opposite us.

Very respectfully, your obedient servant,

JOHN NEWTON, ·
Major-General, Commanding.

———

HEADQUARTERS SECOND CAVALRY DIVISION,
October 2, 1863.

Col. H. B. SARGENT,
 Commanding First Brigade, Second Division:

Upon being relieved at Catlett's Station and Bristoe Station by brigades of Howe's division of infantry, you will proceed with your brigade to Hartwood Church, and establish a line of pickets on the Rappahannock from Falmouth to Kelly's Ford, relieving the pickets of General Buford's division.   One regiment of your brigade will remain at Kettle Run, to protect the bridge at that point and to patrol the railroad to Bristoe Station.   You will establish the headquarters of your brigade at Hartwood Church, and so dispose your regiments as most effectually to guard the several fords on the river.   Division headquarters and the Second Brigade will be at Bealeton, and from that station you will draw supplies for your brigade.   Should any attempt be made to cross a rebel cavalry force at any point on your line, or should you discover that a crossing had been effected below Falmouth for the same purpose, you will at once communicate the fact to me.   The brigades of infantry will probably relieve you to-day.

Very respectfully, your obedient servant,

D. McM. GREGG,
Brigadier-General of Volunteers, Commanding.

WAR DEPARTMENT,
Washington, October 2, 1863—7.10 p. m.

Major-General FOSTER,
Fort Monroe, Va.:

The Secretary of War directs that you relieve the guard of light-boat at Smith's Point from your command, and send the guard now there to its regiment at Harper's Ferry.   This post will hereafter be considered in your department.

H. W. HALLECK,
General-in-Chief.

FORT MONROE,
October 2, 1863—12.45 p. m.

General WISTAR:

Your plan is approved.   To-morrow 450 cavalry will come up on transports, which vessels can also be used to re-embark them when needed.   Three army gunboats will also come under Major Stevenson, who will report to you.   Arrange with Captain Gillis, U. S. Navy, so as also to have the co-operation of the navy gunboats. Everything must be ready to start on Sunday morning.   Secrecy in your preparations must be carefully observed.   I desire that you will, if your health permits, go in command, so that the expedition may be a success.

J. G. FOSTER,
Major-General, Commanding.

HDQRS. ARMY AND DISTRICT OF NORTH CAROLINA,
New Berne, N. C., October 2, 1863.

Col. SOUTHARD HOFFMAN,
Asst. Adjt. Gen., Dept. of Virginia and North Carolina:

COLONEL: I have the honor to report that I returned last evening from a tour of inspection.   The fortifications at Washington and Plymouth have been pushed very rapidly during the last month.

The progress is very satisfactory in view of the limited force and the unfavorable state of health. A number of heavy guns have been mounted at important points, and two companies Rhode Island artillery have been placed at Washington. The river obstructions have been delayed by high water and other causes. General Wessells will press this branch of defense as fast as possible. I attach much importance to it, situated as it is with respect to the water battery, Fort Gray. This mode of blockading rivers is generally adopted by the rebels.

In reply to a communication of mine upon the subject of torpedoes, General Foster suggested an officer of the navy as being experienced in their construction. Commander Davenport, U. S. Navy, reports that he has no one acquainted with the use of torpedoes. In my judgment, they are very unreliable, and would afford but an uncertain defense at the port of Plymouth.

The suggestion in the letter of General Foster, of the 24th of April, for substituting black labor for white in the District of the Albemarle is a good one, and I shall address General Wessells on the subject.

My expectations in respect to the colony were more than realized by my visit to Roanoke Island. No better place could have been selected, and I see no permanent cause for apprehension on the score of health. The superintendent is actively engaged in laying out the streets and lots. My instructions were to make the avenues of ample width, with a view to increase the beauty and healthfulness of the island. Mules, horses, wagons, &c., have been condemned and ordered to be turned over to the colony. The success of the enterprise I regard as certain, and believe that this African colony can be made self-supporting after the first year.

It is with regret that I learn we are not to be re-enforced in North Carolina and Virginia.

I am, very respectfully, your obedient servant,

JOHN J. PECK,
Major-General.

HEADQUARTERS ARMY OF THE POTOMAC,
October 3, 1863—4.30 p. m. (Received 5.20 p. m.)

Major-General HALLECK:

Reliable intelligence from scouts and deserters would indicate that Lee has been considerably re-enforced within the last week. Cooke's brigade has come from Richmond, and the brigade of Pickett's division left at Drewry's Bluff; also a brigade of North Carolina troops are reported arriving at Orange Court-House, but from whence not known. Intercepted messages, and increased forces at various parts of the enemy's line, together with other indications, would seem to point to some movement on their part, whether a mere raid to intercept my communication, or a reconnaissance in force to ascertain my position and numbers, remains to be seen.

Yesterday 2 of our men came across a party of rebel scouts, 4 in number, in the woods within our lines. One man was killed on each side, when the rebels escaped, after wounding our second man.

Lee, advised of the detachment of this army is undoubtedly anxious to ascertain its strength. The army remains in the same position as last reported, principally massed around Culpeper Court-House, with two corps in front on picket on the Rapidan, and a division of cavalry on each flank; a division of cavalry with one of infantry and five batteries hold the railroad from the Rappahannock to Bull Run.

GEO. G. MEADE,
Major-General, Commanding.

FIRST ARMY CORPS,
October 3, 1863.

Major-General HUMPHREYS:

My officers still report that there are indications of the enemy having reduced his force on my right front, based on sentinels reporting that there were not so many drums and bugles heard this morning as usual! This is all the information I have.

JOHN NEWTON.

MITCHELL'S STATION,
October 3, 1863.

Captain NORTON,
Signal Officer:

Rebel message:

SIGNAL STATION—1.45 p. m.

General LEE:

Ewell, Hill, and Early are here. I have expected it would be safe.

L. [LONG?],
General.

WM. H. R. NEEL.
Lieutenant, Signal Officer.

HEADQUARTERS THIRD ARMY CORPS,
October 3, 1863.

Brig. Gen. S. WILLIAMS,
Asst. Adjt. Gen., Army of the Potomac:

GENERAL: In compliance with circular dated headquarters Army of the Potomac, September 1, 1863, I have the honor to make the following report of distinguished officers killed in battle, or who have died of wounds received in action:

ARTILLERY.

First Lieut. Justin E. Dimick, Battery H, First U. S. Artillery, mortally wounded at Chancellorsville, Va., May 3, 1863, died at Potomac Creek Hospital.

FIRST DIVISION.

Report forwarded.

SECOND DIVISION.

Maj. Gen. Hiram G. Berry, U. S. Volunteers; killed at Chancellorsville, Va., Sunday, May 3, 1863.

Capt. William H. Chester, Seventy-fourth New York Volunteers, and aide-de-camp to Brig. Gen. A. A. Humphreys, commanding division; mortally wounded at Gettysburg, Pa., July 3, 1863.

Maj. Philip J. Kearny, Eleventh New Jersey Volunteers; mortally wounded at Gettysburg, Pa., July 3, 1863.

Col. William O. Stevens, Seventy-second New York Volunteers; killed at the battle of Chancellorsville, May 3, 1862.

Capt. Alfred A. Donalds, Seventy-third New York Volunteers; killed at the battle of Bristoe Station, Va., August 27, 1862.

Col. Louis R. Francine, Seventh New Jersey Volunteers; mortally wounded at Gettysburg, Pa., July 3, 1863.

Col. Francis A. Lancaster, One hundred and fifteenth Pennsylvania Volunteers; killed at Chancellorsville, Va., May 3, 1863.

THIRD DIVISION.

This division, having joined the Army of the Potomac since the battle of Gettysburg, cannot furnish the information called for.

I am, general, very respectfully, your obedient servant,
WM. H. FRENCH,
Major-General, Commanding.

WASHINGTON, D. C.,
October 3, 1863—11.30 a. m.

Major-General MEADE,
Army of the Potomac:

Brig. Gen. Washington L. Elliott will be ordered to immediately report to General Rosecrans.

H. W. HALLECK,
General-in-Chief.

GENERAL ORDERS, }   HEADQUARTERS CAVALRY CORPS,
No. 29.   }   *October* 3, 1863.

I. In consequence of changes which have occurred since the publication of General Orders, No. 19, current series, from these headquarters, the following announcement is made of the staff of the major-general commanding the corps:

Lieut. Col. C. Ross Smith, Sixth Pennsylvania Cavalry, chief of staff, and ordnance officer.

Capt. C. C. Suydam, assistant adjutant-general.

INSPECTOR-GENERAL'S DEPARTMENT.

Lieut. Col. W. H. Crocker, Sixth New York Cavalry, assistant inspector-general.

Capt. F. C. Newhall, Sixth Pennsylvania Cavalry, acting assistant inspector-general.

QUARTERMASTER'S DEPARTMENT.

First Lieut. J. W. Spangler, Sixth U. S. Cavalry, acting chief quartermaster.

COMMISSARY DEPARTMENT.

Lieut. Col. A. S. Austin, chief commissary of subsistence.

First Lieut. W. M. Taylor, Eighth Illinois Cavalry, acting assistant commissary of subsistence.

MEDICAL DEPARTMENT.

Surg. George L. Pancoast, U. S. Volunteers, medical director.
Surg. R. W. Pease, Tenth New York Cavalry, medical inspector.
Asst. Surg. G. M. McGill, U. S. Army, assistant medical inspector.
First Lieut. C. B. McLellan, Sixth U. S. Cavalry, provost-marshal.
Capt. V. E. von Koerber, First Maryland, topographical engineer.
First Lieut. Ferd. Theilkuhl, topographical engineer.
Col. G. A. H. Blake, First U. S. Cavalry, commissary of musters.
First Lieut. I. W. Trask, Eighth Illinois Cavalry, chief ambulance officer.

AIDES-DE-CAMP.

First Lieut. C. Thomson, First New York Cavalry.
First Lieut. G. W. Yates, Fourth Michigan Infantry Volunteers.
First Lieut. James F. Wade, Sixth U. S. Cavalry.
First Lieut. George H. Thompson, First Rhode Island Cavalry.
First Lieut. E. B. Parsons, Eighth New York Cavalry.
First Lieut. D. W. Littlefield, Seventh Michigan Cavalry.
First Lieut. James G. Birney, Seventh Michigan Cavalry.
By command of Major-General Pleasonton:

C. C. SUYDAM,
Assistant Adjutant-General.

THOROUGHFARE MOUNTAIN, CULPEPER COUNTY, VA.,
October 3, 1863.

Capt. L. B. NORTON,
Chief Signal Officer, Army of the Potomac:

SIR: In compliance with General Orders, No. 9, Signal Department, headquarters Army of the Potomac, I have the honor to submit the following report of the set under my charge during the month of September, 1863:

September 5, assumed charge of the signal station on Watery Mountain, near Warrenton, Va., relieving Captain Hall. Second Lieut. W. H. Warts, with one flagman, reported to me for duty. At the time of taking charge, the station was in communication with the following points, viz: Near Germantown, with headquarters of the army and headquarters Cavalry Corps at Warrenton; headquarters Sixth Army Corps, at Catlett's Station; headquarters Eleventh Army Corps, near Jefferson; headquarters Second Cavalry Division, and near Warrenton with Colonel McIntosh's brigade, of the Second Cavalry Division. Communication with the last-named point was had by orderlies, a detail having been made by Colonel McIntosh.

September 8, reported to me for duty, Flagman Charles A. Griffin and James H. Smith. From the 5th to the 12th, inclusive, telescopic reconnaissances were made in direction of the enemy from three to six times daily, but without discovering anything of importance. The atmosphere decidedly unfavorable for observations during the entire period.

The movement of our cavalry upon Culpeper commenced on the morning of September 13. The progress made by it from the time of first engaging the enemy at Muddy Run, 5 miles from Culpeper, was noted and reported to General Sedgwick and yourself.

By the movement of General Gregg's division. signal communication with Colonel McIntosh was discontinued. Though constantly on the lookout for the flag of Captain Dinsmore, accompanying General Gregg, the atmosphere continued too thick to see more than smoke from the artillery.

On the 14th and 15th, nothing of information transpired.

On the 16th, broke up station on Watery Mountain and reported with set to you near Germantown, in compliance with orders. At 7.30 p. m. this day, opened signal communication at headquarters of the army Culpeper with Pony Mountain.

On the 17th, relieved Lieutenants Stryker and Clarke, on Pony Mountain. Captain Wilson and their dismounted men were temporarily attached to my set. Found Pony Mountain station in communication with the following points, viz: Culpeper, with headquarters of the army; near Somerville Ford, Kilpatrick's cavalry division; 2 miles east from Culpeper, headquarters First Army Corps. At 7.30 p. m. Lieutenant Warts opened communication with headquarters of General Buford, at Stevensburg. Owing to Lieutenant Jerome not being acquainted with the cipher words, no message of an important character could be transmitted by signal to General Buford. One message, in consequence, was delayed.

On the 18th, made report to you of fortifications and camp of the enemy seen on opposite side of Rapidan River.

On the 19th, 100 men, 48 axemen, and 52 comprising a guard for working party, reported to me for the purpose of cleaning off timber obstructing river, and constructing a solid and substantial lookout, the old lookout being too unsteady for practical use. Opened communication with headquarters of Twelfth Army Corps near Raccoon Ford. Lieutenant Holland, at these headquarters, informed me that the telegraph was in working order, which would dispense with signal communication.

On the 20th, reported to you column of enemy moving down the river, passing point near Raccoon Ford. At 8.45 a. m. opened communication with Captain Dinsmore, on Thoroughfare Mountain. Reported to you enemy intrenching at Morton's and Stringfellow's Fords.

On the 21st, at 12 m., opened communication with Captain Dinsmore, 3 miles east from Thoroughfare Mountain. At 2.15 p. m. received orders from you to get ready immediately to go to Thoroughfare Mountain. Captain Wilson and his dismounted men by same order relieved from duty with my set. At 4.30 p. m. relieved from duty on Pony Mountain by Lieutenants Stryker and Clarke.

On the 22d, owing to the late hour at which I was relieved yesterday, and in order to obtain supplies for the set, did not start for Thoroughfare until this a. m.; 1.45 p. m. reached the top of Thoroughfare Mountain ; at 2.10 opened communication with Pony Mountain, and at 2.45 p. m. had communication with Captain Paine, accompanying cavalry expedition, on the pike from Madison Court-House to Gordonsville, near Beautiful Run. A message from General Buford to General Pleasonton, through Captain Paine, at 3.25 p. m., I was unable to forward until dark, it being impossible for the officers on Pony Mountain to see my flag on account of the hazy state of the atmosphere. Captain Paine moved forward with cavalry soon after, and communication with him was suspended.

September 23, reported to you that our cavalry was coming in. Saw Captain Paine's flag for a moment ; called, but he was on the move, and I could not get attention. At 3.15 p. m. I saw the flag of Captain Gloskoski calling at the ford of Robertson's River, where General Kilpatrick's division was recrossing under fire of the enemy, enemy having pressed General Kilpatrick to the river. Received message from General Kilpatrick to General Pleasonton, but was unable to dispatch it to Pony Mountain until dark for the reason given in regard to delay of message through Captain Paine.

On the 24th, 5 p. m., established communication with Captain Castle on Cedar Mountain, through whom messages from this station to headquarters are sent whenever the state of the atmosphere precludes the possibility of direct communication with Pony Mountain.

On the 27th, communication opened with Captain Gloskoski, General Kilpatrick's headquarters, near Culpeper. On the 29th, communication opened with Captain Gloskoski, General Kilpatrick's headquarters, 4 miles northeast from this mountain, who reported that General Kilpatrick was desirous of being informed by signal from here of any demonstration of the enemy along his picket line.

During my occupation of Thoroughfare Mountain no important movements of the enemy have been discovered. From a ledge of rocks on the east side of the mountain, where my station proper is established, Orange Court-House and Rapidan Station and their vicinities are distinctly visible with ordinary atmosphere. The greater portion of enemy's lines between Rapidan Station and Raccoon Ford is hidden from our view by the intervention of Cedar Mountain. Besides keeping a close watch from the ledge before mentioned on the enemy's camp around Orange Court-House, and his cavalry forces between Rapidan and Robertson's Rivers, two telescopic reconnaissances are made each day, morning and evening, toward Madison Court-House from a cleared space on the west side of the mountain. As yet no forces of the enemy have been discovered in this latter direction.

I would commend Second Lieut. W. H. Warts for strict attention to duty ; though a new and inexperienced officer, he reads signals as well as many of the old officers of the corps.

Herewith I forward copies of messages sent and received by this set in the month of September. Also copies of messages sent and received by me in the month of August.

All of which is respectfully submitted.

I am, captain, very respectfully, your obedient servant,

P. A. TAYLOR.
Captain, and Signal Officer.

FORT MONROE, VA.,
October 3, 1863.

Maj. Gen. H. W. HALLECK,
General-in-Chief, U. S. Army, Washington, D. C.:

GENERAL: Referring to my communication of September 22, I now have the honor to forward for your information an extract of letter from General Peck, showing that Weldon is being strongly fortified, and that the rebels are in strong defensive position in North Carolina.

I also have the honor to inform you that Irwin Johnson, a native of Wilmington, and a deserter from the rebel army, lately stationed at Smith's Island Light-House, says that he had been employed making military roads on Smith's Island where there were two guns; that the enemy were throwing up fortifications there, and that five hundred shovels and some men were sent to the island the day before he left, September 16. This merely shows that the enemy apprehend danger at those two points, and are preparing for it.

Very respectfully, your obedient servant,

J. G. FOSTER,
Major-General, Commanding.

[Inclosure.]

NEWTON, N. C.,
September 27, 1863.

*   *   *   *   *   *   *

General Wessells has a friend who has been to Weldon. He reports General Ransom there with some 2,500 men, who, with over 1,000 contrabands, are engaged in fortifying all the approaches in a very strong manner, on both sides of the river. Troops at Garysburg, Jackson, &c. At Rainbow 1,500 infantry, field battery, and a number of heavy pieces. A regiment of Georgia cavalry has arrived for duty in Bertie County and an improved class of rangers. He reports they have been somewhat strengthened on the Tar River.

In view of these and other considerations, the general says:

On the whole, I think they are in a more effective condition in North Carolina than at any other time, particularly to resist aggression.

U. S. FLAG-SHIP MINNESOTA,
Off Newport News, Va., October 3, 1863.

Maj. Gen. J. G. FOSTER, U. S. Army,
Comdg. Eighteenth Army Corps, Fort Monroe, Va.:

GENERAL: It was not until you were on board this afternoon that I was fully aware of the number of gunboats necessary to co-operate with the movements of the troops from Yorktown into Matthews and Gloucester Counties, to entrap the rebels, who, with several boats (moved on wheels), have twice recently issued from those counties and committed depredations on the Eastern Shore of Virginia. It was then understood between us that the troops would march from Yorktown to-morrow morning, and that the navy gunboats should rendezvous at Yorktown to-morrow, and leave there the next morning, some to go as high up the North and East Rivers as practicable, to co-operate with the troops, and others to prevent the escape of the rebels by the bay side or the Piankatank.

At 10 o'clock to-night I received your notification that the troops and gunboats (yours and those of the navy on that part of the blockade) had left Yorktown. I immediately dispatched two additional light-draught gunboats to the scene of operations, to assist Lieutenant-Commander Gillis.

I respectfully request that in future the plan of joint operations within the limits of our commands shall, when practicable, be fully and timely arranged between you and myself. In the Sounds of North Carolina emergencies may arise requiring immediate action from the senior army and navy officers present.

I have the honor to be, general, respectfully, yours,

S. PHILLIPS LEE,
Acting Rear-Admiral, Comdg. N. A. Bkg. Squadron.

[Indorsement]

Acknowledge receipt. The dispatch that I wrote said: "The troops and boats have left," meaning this point and not Yorktown. The navy gunboats will be of the greatest service in case of need, but at the first conception it was intended to depend on the army gunboats. Hence the delay in notifying the admiral.

J. G. FOSTER.

———

HEADQUARTERS ARMY OF THE POTOMAC,
October 4, 1863—12 m. (Received 12.50 p. m.)

Major-General HALLECK:

In the various rebel accounts of the battle of the Chickamauga, mention is only made of the divisions of Hood and McLaws, of Longstreet's corps. Furthermore, in an account of an affair with Burnside's people, at Carter's Run, reference is made to Corse's brigade, belonging to Pickett's division. It has occurred to me that possibly that portion of Pickett's division withdrawn with Longstreet may have been sent against Burnside in East Tennessee and Southwest Virginia, and that if Burnside has withdrawn from that part of the country, these troops may have returned to Lee's army, via Lynchburg. This would account for the repeated assertions of deserters and the report of scouts that all of Pickett's division has returned to Lee. Have you any information bearing on this point ?

The enemy this morning from their batteries at Somerville Ford shelled one of our wagon trains collecting forage in the front. Otherwise all is quiet along our lines.

GEO. G. MEADE,
Major-General, Commanding.

———

OCTOBER 4, [1863.]

Major-General SEDGWICK,
Commanding Sixth Corps:

The major-general commanding directs that to-morrow you relieve the Second Corps, Major-General Warren commanding, in the position now occupied and duties performed by it on the Rapidan, and that, as preliminary thereto, staff officers be sent to-day to ascertain the positions and picket lines of General Warren's corps and the roads by which your corps should march. General Warren now watches and pickets the front from Somerville Ford, on the Rapidan, or in that vicinity, to near Robertson's Ford, on Robertson's River. General Wheaton pickets on his left and the cavalry, General Kilpatrick, on his right. General Warren will be directed to communicate his instructions to you.

Only such wagons will be taken with the corps to the front as may be necessary to keep up the supplies directed to be on hand. Mitchell's Station, the headquarters of General Warren, is the point at which your supplies can be obtained from the railroad. Your trains will be parked at some secure point in the rear, from which they may be sent to the rear with facility and without interfering with the routes which may be used for similar purposes by the corps in the vicinity of Culpeper Court-House.

Nothing should be taken to the front that cannot be got out of the way with facility and rapidity.

A copy of the instructions furnished General Slocum in the position adjoining General Warren is sent for your general guidance.

Very respectfully, your obedient servant,

A. A. HUMPHREYS,
Major-General, Chief of Staff.

HEADQUARTERS ARMY OF THE POTOMAC,
October 4, 1863.

Commanding Officer Fifth Corps :

The major-general commanding directs me to inform you that Major-General Sedgwick has been directed to relieve the Second Corps with the Sixth Corps.

The Second Corps has been directed to take post on the heights in rear of Culpeper Court-House, extending across the railroad, as soon as it is relieved.

There will be no force of infantry, therefore, in the vicinity of Stone-House Mountain after to-morrow.

Very respectfully, &c.,

A. A. HUMPHREYS,
Major-General, and Chief of Staff.

SIGNAL DEPT., HDQRS. ARMY OF THE POTOMAC,
October 4, 1863.

General HUMPHREYS:

The following dispatches have just been received, and are respectfully forwarded for the information of the commanding general:

CEDAR MOUNTAIN SIGNAL STATION,
October 4, 1863—7.30 p. m.

Captain NORTON:

All quiet at sunset. Enemy's signals report "all quiet." Yesterday enemy planted a color in one of their works near Raccoon Ford. They are strengthening their works every day between Rapidan Station and Morton's Ford. General F. Lee has his headquarters down the river; I think at or near Halstead's house. General Ewell is somewhere in rear of Clark's Mountain. General Stuart's headquarters can be seen from this station. We have Captain Frayser's station (chief signal officer Stuart's cavalry) in view. Also stations which communicate with Ewell, Early, and F. Lee.

I do not think that General R. E. Lee has been here for a week. The fords as far up the Rapidan as I can see are pretty strongly picketed, with at least a regiment of infantry at each. Stuart's cavalry, with exception of Fitz. Lee's division, lies between Rapidan Station and Madison Court-House. The enemy appeared to be quite short of rations, as in answer to the inquiry, "When do you expect the men's rations," a cavalry colonel replied, "God only knows."

I have the honor to be, general, very respectfully, your obedient servant,

L. B. NORTON,
Captain, and Chief Signal Officer.

HEADQUARTERS DEPARTMENT OF WASHINGTON, .
October 4, 1863.

[Col. J. C. KELTON,]
  Asst. Adjt. Gen., Hdqrs. of the Army:

COLONEL: In reply to indorsed communication of Col. D. C. Mc-Callum, Superintendent Military Railroads, with reference to exposed condition of the Orange and Alexandria Railroad and the absence of guards at the bridges, received at these headquarters October 2, I have the honor to state that the length of railroad from Alexandria to Bull Run is 23 miles.

On this line there are 6 stations, 3 water-tanks, and 10 principal bridges, exclusive of that over Bull Run. Eighteen miles of the line are guarded by the command of Brig. Gen. Rufus King, who has an effective force of 1,362 enlisted infantry. The remaining 5 miles are guarded by the command of Brigadier-General Slough, who has an effective force of 867 enlisted infantry.

In addition to guarding the railroad proper, Brigadier-General King is compelled to hold Fairfax Court-House, and furnish the necessary pickets and picket guards for his camp, and until recently has kept a long line of pickets in front of Centreville. Brigadier-General Slough occupies the town of Alexandria, furnishing the necessary city guards and patrols.

Colonel McCallum submits the following statement:

OFFICE MIL. DIRECTOR AND SUPT. OF RAILROADS,
WAR DEPARTMENT,
Washington, October 2, 1863.

Maj. Gen. H. W. HALLECK,
  General-in-Chief:

SIR: I have the honor to submit the following statement:

A bridge was burned by the enemy at Edsall's. 5 miles west of Alexandria, about September 8. Bridge was burned at Pope's Head, No. 1, about September 27. This is 1¼ miles west of Fairfax. Cameron Run Bridge was burned September 30; located 3 miles from Alexandria. Raid near Burke's, September 24, capturing 8 mules. Raid near Burke's, October 1. Raid near Springfield, October 1, capturing 3 track-men.

Our bridges are constantly exposed; so far as my knowledge extends, none of them are guarded.

I would respectfully suggest that the troops now at Warrenton Junction be changed so as to camp in the woods west of the station, and thus protect the water-tanks and wood-choppers at the same time.

I am, general, very respectfully, your obedient servant,
D. C. McCALLUM,
Colonel, and Military Director and Superintendent of Railroads.

The facts are these, taking the attacks in the order named. First:

A bridge was burned by the enemy at Edsall's, 5 miles west of Alexandria, about September 8.

The bridge was fired as the last train was coming over empty, it is supposed by persons from Alexandria, as they evidently did not know the train time. Trackmen discovered the fire and extinguished it before any damage was done.

Second:

Bridge was burned at Pope's Head, No. 1, about September 27. This is 1¼ miles west of Fairfax.

The bridge was fired by 27 of White's men; the fire was discovered by patrol, extinguished, and reported to Colonel Lowell, Second

Massachusetts Cavalry, commanding cavalry at Centreville, who caused the party to be pursued. I visited the bridge in person, and found the damage done trifling and repaired with little loss of time.

Third:

Cameron Run Bridge was burned September 30; located 3 miles from Alexandria.

Certain parties threw coal-oil or some other inflammable fluid on the bridge and fired it. It was discovered and extinguished without damage and without interruption to the trains.

Fourth:

Raid near Burke's Station, September 24, capturing 8 mules.

These 8 mules were turned over, so far as can be learned, to the railroad company by the assistant quartermaster at Alexandria, and, at the time of capture, were being herded near Burke's Station. There was no notification given to these headquarters of the necessity for a guard for these mules, nor was it ever known that they were there.

Fifth:

Raid near Burke's Station, October 1.

A wood party stationed there were attacked. The guerrillas were beaten off by the guard, doing no damage. The same party captured 3 trackmen at Springfield. It is supposed that if these 3 men were doing their duty at the time of capture, they would have been on the railroad, and consequently that the guerrillas were in possession of it. They did no harm to it, and the inference naturally arises that the 3 men were straggling from their posts.

I invite attention to the appended statement, marked A:

Our bridges are constantly exposed; so far as my knowledge extends, none of them are guarded.

With regard to the troops stationed at Warrenton Junction, I have only to state that, not being in my department, I have no control over them.

The different bridges on the railroad will be protected ·by block-houses.

Their erection was ordered at or about the 6th of June. For reasons why they have not been completed, I respectfully refer to the paper appended, marked B.

With reference to the method pursued at these headquarters to protect property when sent beyond the line of defenses proper, I respectfully refer to the paper appended, marked C.

In conclusion, I would state that the Orange and Alexandria Railroad runs through a country in many places either thickly wooded or covered by undergrowth, rendering it an easy task for two or three active and energetic men to keep the entire available command I have on the road on the *qui vive*, and even with the utmost vigilance exercised, rendering it not strange or unnatural that on any night an inhabitant of the country should place an impediment on the track sufficient to throw a train off, to remove a rail, or even to destroy a bridge with a span of only 4 or 5 feet.

To prevent these incursions, I am enabled to keep only 590 to 600 effective cavalry in camp, near Centreville, ready for instant service.

Very respectfully, your obedient servant,

S. P. HEINTZELMAN,
Major-General, Commanding.

[Inclosure A.]

UNITED STATES MILITARY TELEGRAPH,
Centreville, October 3, 1863—2.30 p. m.
(Received 3.40 p. m.)

Capt. C. H. POTTER,
Assistant Adjutant-General:

The following is the disposition of the forces along the Orange and Alexandria Railroad:

The Fourth Delaware Infantry guards the road from Accotink to Sangster's, with headquarters at Fairfax Station, one company at Accotink, one company at Burke's, one on train, camp guards and pickets at Fairfax Station, 6 men at Hunter's Bridge, and small infantry and cavalry patrols on both sides of road. From Sangster's to Bull Run five companies of infantry guard the road, headquarters at Union Mills; one company at Bull Run Bridge, a platoon at Sangster's, pickets on three roads leading to Union Mills, and patrols moving along the railroad as far as Sangster's at irregular hours. The officers in command are active and vigilant.

RUFUS KING,
Brigadier-General.

[Inclosure B.]

HEADQUARTERS DEPARTMENT OF WASHINGTON,
OFFICE OF CHIEF QUARTERMASTER,
Washington, D. C., October 2, 1863.

Lieut. Col. J. H. TAYLOR,
Chief of Staff, and Assistant Adjutant-General:

COLONEL: In reply to your inquiries of this date, I have the honor to report that the first intimation I ever had of the intention of the military authorities to construct block-houses for the defense of railroad bridges was conveyed to me through the general commanding this department and the Quartermaster-General. These orders were to construct a block-house at every bridge on the Loudoun and Hampshire and Orange and Alexandria Railroads within the limits of this department, and were received by me some time between the 1st and 6th days of June last. My understanding of the matter at that time was that the Engineer Department had been some time previously intrusted with the work of placing the bridges in a defensive condition, but that in consequence of the delay in executing this duty, the Quartermaster-General decided to adopt my suggestion of placing the matter in my hands, with orders to do the work at once, according to plans then in possession of the Engineer Department, which plans subsequently reached me through Major-General Heintzelman. After receiving the orders referred to, I provided the necessary timber for the work, but in consequence of the withdrawal of the troops from our front by General Hooker, the railroads were left in a totally unguarded condition, and the trains ceased running, thus rendering it impossible for me to continue my operations. When the Army of the Potomac returned to its former position in Virginia, I made every effort to procure trains to transport my timber lying along the Orange and Alexandria Railroad near Burke's Station to the specific points, but in consequence of the road being worked to its utmost capacity in transporting supplies, &c., to General Meade's forces, the superintendent, Mr. Devereux was obliged to refuse my repeated applications to him for trains to move my timber as required.

A few days since, however, I was assured that proper facilities would be extended to me for the prosecution of the work, by placing a construction train at my disposal, and I have now resumed operations, and expect to have all the block-houses completed in a short time.

I have the honor to be, very respectfully, your obedient servant,

ELIAS M. GREENE,
Lieutenant-Colonel, Chief Q. M., Dept. of Washington.

[Inclosure C.]

HEADQUARTERS DEPARTMENT OF WASHINGTON,
OFFICE OF CHIEF QUARTERMASTER,
Washington, D. C., October 3, 1863.

Lieut. Col. J. H. TAYLOR,
Chief of Staff, and Assistant Adjutant-General:

COLONEL: I have the honor to state, in answer to your inquiries, that in the raids mentioned by you as occurring from September 8 to October 1, inclusive, none of the public property for which I am accountable was captured or destroyed by the enemy. Its safety has been secured, no doubt by proper precautions on my part, as my orders are not to allow a train of wagons to go beyond the defenses proper without applying for a sufficient military guard for the same, which has been always granted to me.

On one of the occasions referred to (September 28), 8 mules which had been transferred to the authorities managing the Orange and Alexandria Railroad, by Captain Ferguson, assistant quartermaster, in charge of depot at Alexandria, were captured while grazing about three-fourths of a mile from Edsall's Hill. This is the only quartermaster's property captured or destroyed in this department during the above-mentioned period, to my knowledge.

I am firmly convinced that no matter how large a force may be detailed to guard the railroads, the farmer guerrillas within our lines will find occasions when they can, with comparative safety to themselves, make a raid to plunder and destroy public property. My employés south of the Potomac are perfectly familiar with these pretended loyal and peaceable farmers, and I most respectfully, but earnestly, recommend that all such be moved to some locality where they can no longer pursue the double occupation of farming by day and plundering by night. If these doubtful characters are removed from within our lines, danger can only come from without, from larger bodies of the enemy's troops, and in such cases their movements would probably be discovered in time to frustrate their designs.

Very respectfully, your obedient servant,

ELIAS M. GREENE,
Lieutenant-Colonel, Chief Q. M., Dept. of Washington.

CLARKSBURG, W. VA., *October 4, 1863.*
(Received 6.25 p. m.)

Brig. Gen. G. W. CULLUM, *Chief of Staff:*

From information which I deem reliable, I am satisfied that a portion of the rebel force recently in Greenbrier and Pocahontas Counties has been withdrawn, and either sent to Lee's army or to Jones on Virginia and Tennessee Railroad.

If you approve, I will send Averell from Beverly, and a portion of Scammon's force from the Kanawha, and drive the rebels from Greenbrier, Pocahontas, and Monroe, with orders, if the information obtained at Lewisburg will warrant such a movement, to push on to Dublin Station or Christiansburg, on the Virginia and Tennessee Railroad, and destroy the bridges in that neighborhood.

I returned this morning from Harper's Ferry. All quiet along line of railroad.

B. F. KELLEY,
Brigadier-General, Commanding.

WASHINGTON, D. C.,
October 5, 1863—9.25 a. m.

Brigadier-General KELLEY,
   Clarksburg, Va.:

 Your plan is approved.

H. W. HALLECK,
General-in-Chief.

MITCHELL'S STATION,
October 5, 1863.

Captain NORTON,
   Chief Signal Officer:

 Rebel messages:

General E. A. R.:

 Large force of enemy advancing this way through Kirk's farm toward Somerville Ford. Head of column at Cedar Run.

HALL,
Major.

General STUART:

 A large force of the enemy on the road from Culpeper Court-House to Raccoon Ford. Regiments forming in their camps. No tents struck.

C.

General EWELL:

 A brigade of infantry at Mitchell's Station, in line at rest. Column of infantry on Raccoon Ford road. A line of artillery, strongly supported by infantry, at rest on the right of Kirk's house. A long line of infantry advancing from Culpeper Court-House toward Kirk's house. A large wagon train at Mitchell's Station, moving off toward Culpeper Court-House.

CALLOWAY,
Lieutenant.

C. D. R.:

 When do you leave for the Potomac?

[No signature.]

 Cross the river to-night on a scout.

HILL.

 The five last messages from Cedar Mountain.

F. W. MARSTON,
Captain, Signal Officer.

FIRST ARMY CORPS,
October 5, 1863.

General HUMPHREYS,
      Chief of Staff:

The following dispatches of the enemy have just been intercepted by the signal officers of this corps :

General LEE :

The column of infantry camped at Mitchell's Station seems to be going toward Culpeper.

CALLOWAY,
Lieutenant.

General LEE :

I am informed from Clark's Mountain that two columns of infantry are marching on telegraph road toward Rapidan Station, and one on county road from Mitchell's Station to same place.

FITZ. LEE.

JOHN NEWTON,
Major-General.

———

HEADQUARTERS FIRST CORPS,
October 5, 1863.

Major-General HUMPHREYS,
      Chief of Staff:

GENERAL : The following dispatches have been intercepted from the rebel signal station on Clark's Mountain, by Wiggins and Camp, signal officers, First Corps :

General LEE :

The camps at Stone-House Mountain have moved to the front ; gone into camp, and built fires. A battery of six guns moved toward under the mountain.

V.,
Major.

General LEE:

The enemy has made a number of movements to-day, which indicate a purpose of either advancing or falling back. It is hard to tell which. A great quantity of infantry and ambulances have moved to the front, while the forage trains remained back.

E. [EWELL?],
General.

Respectfully forwarded.

JOHN NEWTON,
Major-General.

———

HEADQUARTERS FIRST CORPS,
October 5, 1863—12 m.

Major-General HUMPHREYS,
      Chief of Staff:

The following dispatch of the enemy has just been intercepted by the signal officers of this corps :

General LEE :

A column appeared moving along the road between Culpeper and Raccoon Ford. Force on all roads from toward Culpeper to Stone-House Mountain have disappeared. A signal gun was fired early this morning.

S. G. GLEIMPETER [?],
Aide-de-Camp.

The column referred to was the Sixth Corps. The enemy evidently fear an attack.

JOHN NEWTON,
Major-General.

HEADQUARTERS FIRST ARMY CORPS,
October 5, 1863—1.45 p. m.

Major-General HUMPHREYS, *Chief of Staff:*

GENERAL : The following rebel message has been intercepted-from the rebel signal station on Clark's Mountain :

General LEE:

Troops and trains apparently advancing on the Robertson's, Somerville, and Gordonsville roads. One of the columns is near Long's, and is still going in direction of Cedar Mountain. The head near Wharton's farm.

CALLOWAY,
Lieutenant.

By command of Major-General Newton :

J. C. WIGGINS,
Lieutenant, Signal Officer.

MITCHELL'S STATION,
October 5, 1863.

Captain NORTON :

Rebel signal station, 6.15 p. m. :

General S. [STUART:]

I have been on the mountain. Cannot see anything that indicates a general advance.

LEE. [FITZ. LEE ?],
General.

NEEL,
Signal Officer.

HEADQUARTERS FIRST CORPS,
October 5, 1863.

Major-General HUMPHREYS, *Chief of Staff:*

The summary of news of to-day:

The enemy were stampeded this morning by the several moving columns of the Sixth Corps, some of which passed near the river. They fired an alarm gun. Since which time they have noticed that the position of Stone-House Mountain is evacuated, and that the Second Corps has moved to the rear. I think from this they must fully appreciate the movement.

JOHN NEWTON,
Major-General.

HDQRS. FIRST BRIG., THIRD DIV., CAV. CORPS,
Camp near James City, Va., October 5, 1863.

Captain ESTES, *Assistant Adjutant-General:*

CAPTAIN : I have the honor to submit the following report of the result of the expedition sent yesterday evening, pursuant to orders from the general commanding division, to examine the upper road from Culpeper to Madison Court-House.

A squadron of the First [West] Virginia Cavalry, commanded by Captain Boon, went out yesterday at 5 p. m., and have just returned. They found a vedette of the enemy's cavalry about 2 miles this side of the river, who fell back and crossed the river on their approach. A strong picket was observed on the south bank. This road turns to the right from the Culpeper Court-House and James City road, about 1¼ miles this side of James City, and then runs to Robertson's River in a direction nearly west, somewhat winding, but preserving that line throughout. The road is very bad, narrow, stony, and much washed by the late rains. There are no streams of any size to cross, but many small runs. It is thickly wooded on each side for almost its entire length, with occasional cleared fields at long intervals.

The road, in the opinion of the officer commanding the expedition, is impassable for artillery, and in many places cavalry can only get through it marching by file. The distance to the river from the point of intersection with the James City road is 10 miles. The bank of the river on this side is higher than on the other, but is thickly wooded and rocky, and gives no opportunity for placing artillery in position to advantage. The access to, and egress from, the ford is good, and the ford itself is good and easy. The southerly bank of the river is slightly the lower, but there is on the right an excellent position for artillery on cleared land that would enfilade a crossing, and difficult of approach by reason of a run that falls into Robertson's River just at the ford.

I have the report that all is quiet this morning along my pickets.

Respectfully,

H. E. DAVIES, JR.,
Brigadier-General, Commanding.

WAR DEPARTMENT,
Washington, October 5, 1863—9.30 a. m.

Major-General MEADE,
Army of the Potomac:

The only information I have bearing upon your inquiry is, that the rebels have evacuated the counties of Greenbrier and Pocahontas. Supposed to re-enforce Jones, but possibly to re-enforce Lee.

H. W. HALLECK,
General-in-Chief.

WAR DEPARTMENT,
Washington, October 5, 1863—10 a. m.

Brigadier-General KELLEY,
Clarksburg, W. Va.:

General Lockwood will take the First Regiment Eastern Shore Maryland Volunteers, and report for orders to the commanding officer of the Middle Department, at Baltimore.

H. W. HALLECK,
General-in-Chief.

FIRST ARMY CORPS, *October* 6, 1863.

General HUMPHREYS:

GENERAL: The following rebel messages have been intercepted from the rebel signal stations on Clark's Mountain by Lieutenants Wiggins and Camp, signal officers, First Army Corps:

General LEE:

It has been reported to me that the enemy is falling back. A deserter just brought in confirms the report. Particulars by courier.

G.

General LEE:

Trains of wagons and two columns of infantry, estimated at two corps, moved back on the road, passing Cumberland George's house. Camps at Stevensburg being increased.

S. [STUART,]
General.

Respectfully forwarded.

JOHN NEWTON,
Major-General.

———

MITCHELL'S STATION, *October* 6, 1863.

Captain NORTON:

Rebel message:

General LEE:

Scout reports the whole Yankee army falling back. Deserter just brought in confirms the report.

STUART,
General.

[JOHN NEWTON,
Major-General.]

———

CAMP NEAR CULPEPER, VA.,
October 6, 1863.

General HENRY J. HUNT,
Chief of Artillery, Army of the Potomac:

GENERAL: Your letter of the 30th ultimo, on the subject of the transportation of ammunition, has been received and read with much interest. It so clearly sets forth the advantages of using caissons instead of wagons, and my views so fully coincided with yours as to the benefit which would accrue from the change, that I forwarded a copy of it with my report to the Quartermaster-General, requesting his special attention to a matter of so great importance.

I am, general, very respectfully, your obedient servant,

RUFUS INGALLS,
Brigadier-General, Chief Quartermaster.

———

GENERAL ORDERS, } HDQRS. ARMY OF THE POTOMAC,
No. 94. } *October* 6, 1863.

The major-general commanding calls the attention of all under his command to Paragraph 220, of the General Regulations for the Army, it being as follows:

Paragraph 220.—Deliberations or discussions among any class of military men, having the object of conveying praise, or censure, or any mark of approbation

toward their superiors or others in the military service ; and all publications relative to transactions between officers of a private or personal nature, whether newspaper, pamphlet, or handbill, are strictly prohibited.

This regulation has hitherto, to a certain extent, been practically
disregarded in this army, but recent occurrences* make it incumbent
upon the commanding general to insist upon a rigid observance of
its requirements; and that there may be no misunderstanding upon
the subject, it is declared that meetings or combinations among officers or men for the purpose of expressing their regard for their
superiors or others in the military service, in the way of presenta-
tions, or their disapprobation of the acts of their superiors or others
in the military service, by resolutions, will be considered as viola-
tions of the regulation and noticed accordingly.

By command of Major-General Meade:

S. WILLIAMS,
Assistant Adjutant-General.

———

HEADQUARTERS ARMY OF THE POTOMAC,
October 7, 1863—12 m. (Received 12.25 p. m.)

Major-General HALLECK :

Two deserters who came in yesterday from different parts of the
Confederate army, each state that a rumor was prevalent in their
regiments that a part, say, a division, of A. P. Hill's corps has been
sent to the southwest within a week past. About that time unusual
stir with railroad trains was noted by our pickets.

I have sent out scouts, the return of whom I am hourly expecting,
who will give me some positive information, which will be at once
transmitted.

GEO. G. MEADE,
Major-General, Commanding.

———

WAR DEPARTMENT,
Washington, October 7, 1863—3.45 p. m.

Major-General MEADE,
Army of the Potomac:

The Secretary of War directs me to inquire whether, if a part of
A. P. Hill's corps has gone west, a portion of your army cannot be
spared ; and if so, what corps ?

H. W. HALLECK,
General-in-Chief.

———

HEADQUARTERS ARMY OF THE POTOMAC,
October 7, 1863—4.30 p. m. (Received 6.10 p. m.)

Major-General HALLECK:

The reduction of this army is a question dependent entirely on
the duty that is expected of it. If it is expected that the threat-

———

* See Meade to Halleck, September 24, 1863.

ening attitude against Lee is to be maintained, or, in the event of the rumor of Lee having made any considerable detachment being confirmed, it is expected offensive operations shall be resumed—in either event—the reduction would be in opposition to my judgment.

If, however, it is intended to reduce this army to a defensive position merely, it would be as well to withdraw it to the nearest line in front of the defenses of Washington, in which case, should the Secretary of War think proper to ignore any probable advance of the enemy, it might be materially reduced. As to the particular corps to be withdrawn, I have no opinion to give; it should be a question of numbers, and can be solved by an inspection of the tri-monthly return made for the 30th of September. I mean by having no opinion that I have no choice either as to retaining or sending away any particular corps.

> GEO. G. MEADE,
> *Major-General, Commanding.*

> MITCHELL'S STATION,
> *October 7, 1863.*

Captain NORTON,
 Chief Signal Officer:
 Rebel message :

General R. E. LEE:

 Send me some good guides for country between Madison Court-House and Woodville.

> STUART,
> *General.*

> CASTLE,
> *Signal Officer.*

[Indorsement.]

Transmitted for General Kilpatrick's information.

Are there any officers or intelligent enlisted men in the cavalry who were with General Banks last year, and who know the roads to Stanardsville and Gordonsville, from Madison Court-House ?

> A. A. HUMPHREYS,
> *Chief of Staff.*

> MITCHELL'S,
> *October 7, 1863.*

Captain NORTON:
 Rebel message :

General FITZHUGH LEE:

 Unless you have started, do not come up until to-morrow, as the main army remains as before. The scout's report of yesterday was erroneous.

> S. [STUART,]
> *General.*

PIERCE AND ADAMS.

HEADQUARTERS FIRST ARMY CORPS,
October 7, 1863.

Major-General HUMPHREYS,
     Chief of Staff:

The following rebel dispatch just intercepted :

General LEE:
  Since you were here the wagon train near Mitchell's Station has nearly disappeared · gone toward Culpeper.

                                        PITZER,
                                   Major, Aide-de-Camp.

                          JOHN NEWTON,
                                   Major-General.

———

                         OCTOBER 7, 1863—7 p. m.

Major-General FRENCH,
     Commanding Third Corps:

The major-general commanding directs that a division of your
corps, with one battery of Napoleons, move promptly to-morrow
morning at 4 o'clock, to James City, and support the cavalry in the
event of its being attacked. Should the division be forced to retire
by superior numbers, it will resume its present position. Three days'
rations will be taken with the command. The service being temporary, the trains of the division will remain with those of the corps.
  Information received to-day indicates the probability of a reconnaissance in force by the enemy's cavalry on our right flank to-
morrow.

                          A. A. HUMPHREYS,
                          Major-General, Chief of Staff.

———

Major-General FRENCH :

There was no mistake in the name of James City. It is on the
road from Culpeper Court-House to Madison Court-House, and about
8 miles from Culpeper.

                          A. A. HUMPHREYS,
                          Major-General, Chief of Staff.

———

                         CLARKSBURG, *October 7, 1863.*

Colonel MULLIGAN, *Petersburg:*

  Imboden has been re-enforced with some cavalry from Lee's army,
and is preparing for an expedition near Woodstock. Be on the alert
and ready for him if he intends paying his respects to you.
  I have advised Colonel Campbell.

                          B. F. KELLEY,
                                   Brigadier-General.

———

                    SUB-DISTRICT OF THE ALBEMARLE,
                         Plymouth, N. C., October 7, 1863.

Commanding Officer Norfolk, Va.:

  SIR: Refugees from Edenton and vicinity represent the condition
of affairs in that section as follows: Colonel Hinton (of so-called

rangers) is said to have recently returned from Raleigh, with full authority to arrest or call into service all persons not exempt from military service. A medical examiner accompanies him, also a force (strength not stated) from Bertie or Hertford County. They are posted back of Edenton, and the citizens of that town are in consternation, having mostly fled to the woods. I have sent a gunboat there to afford protection to all who desire it, and another to cruise in the Chowan from Dillard's to Winton, and perhaps to Riddick's Ferry.

A considerable force from the Blackwater, Louisiana Zouaves, or Tigers, variously stated at 300 to 800, is in the direction of South Mills, to cover the conscription, and prevent a movement from Norfolk. A portion of this force is now in the neighborhood of Hertford.

I communicate this without passing through the headquarters of General Peck, and recommend that, if practicable, a cavalry reconnaissance be made from your direction, to disturb, if possible, the operations of the enemy, and to enable the citizens to escape.

My only means of transportation is required to take this to Roanoke, but on its return I shall send a force of infantry to Edenton or Dillard's, as circumstances may demand. The detachments will be very small, having but few men fit for service.

Respectfully, your obedient servant,

H. W. WESSELLS,
Brigadier-General of Volunteers, Commanding.

HEADQUARTERS ARMY OF THE POTOMAC,
October 8, 1863—2 p. m.   (Received 2.15 p. m.)

Major-General HALLECK:

Seven deserters from Anderson's division, Ewell's [A. P. Hill's] corps, came in yesterday evening. They disprove the rumor that this division had been sent away, and say that no detachments from Lee's army have been made since the departure of Longstreet's corps.

GEO. G. MEADE,
Major-General, Commanding.

HDQRS. THIRD DIVISION, CAVALRY CORPS,
October 8, 1863.

Lieut. Col. C. ROSS SMITH,
Chief of Staff, Cavalry Corps:

COLONEL: I found this morning an officer and sergeant from the First Vermont Cavalry, who are acquainted with the road from Madison Court-House to Gordonsville and Stanardsville. One of them was taken prisoner and went by way of Gordonsville to Richmond last year.

This morning my picket at Russell's Ford was attacked, but the enemy were immediately driven back. My loss was 1 man killed.

Very respectfully,

J. KILPATRICK,
Brig. Gen. of Vols., Commanding Third Division.

HEADQUARTERS ARMY OF THE POTOMAC,
October 8, 1863—11 a. m.

Major-General SEDGWICK, *Commanding Sixth Corps:*

The major-general commanding directs me to inform you that the
indications you have reported of a movement of the enemy to our
right are confirmed by intercepted rebel dispatches of last evening,
and that measures have been taken to meet the movement by the
cavalry on our right, and by advancing a division of infantry to
James City this morning.

A. A. HUMPHREYS,
Major-General, Chief of Staff.

FIRST CORPS, *October* 8, 1863.

Major-General HUMPHREYS:

The following report has just been received from Brigadier-General
Cutler, commanding First Division:

Lieutenant-Colonel KINGSBURY, *Assistant Adjutant-General:*

SIR: The lookout on my left reports that about 2 o'clock this p. m. the enemy's
camp opposite my left was broken up, and that the troops moved in the direction
of Raccoon Ford.

L. CUTLER,
Brigadier-General, Commanding First Division.

Very respectfully,

JOHN NEWTON,
Major-General, Commanding.

OCTOBER 8, [1863]—5.45 p. m.

Major-General SEDGWICK, *Commanding Sixth Corps:*

The major-general commanding directs me to transmit for your
information the following intercepted dispatch, transmitted to these
headquarters by General Newton, and requests that you will have
inquiry made as to whether any communication has been made to
the enemy's pickets by officers of your corps upon the subject of
the dispatch or any other.

A. A. HUMPHREYS,
Major-General, Chief of Staff.

[Inclosure.]

FIRST CORPS, *October* 8, 1863—3.30 p. m.

Maj. Gen. A. A. HUMPHREYS:

I have the honor to transmit for your information the following
rebel message intercepted from Clark's Mountain by Lieutenants
Wiggins and Camp, signal officers:

Brigadier-General LEE:

The First Corps pickets from the north of Cedar Run down. This has been ascertained from the field officer of the day of the corps, who called for our officer of the
day to make arrangements about picket firing. I think the Sixth Corps has pickets
above the mouth of Cedar Run.

EARLY,
General.

Very respectfully,

JOHN NEWTON,
Major-General of Volunteers.

SIGNAL DEPT., HDQRS. ARMY OF THE POTOMAC,
October 8, 1863.

Maj. Gen. A. A. HUMPHREYS,
Chief of Staff:

Communication is open with General Kilpatrick, via Pony Mountain and Thoroughfare.

The reason why your question was not previously answered was on account of the thickness of the atmosphere between Cedar Mountain and Thoroughfare.

I have the honor to be, &c.,

L. B. NORTON,
Captain, and Chief Signal Officer.

PRIVATE.]   HDQRS. DEPT. OF VA. AND N. C.,
Fort Monroe, Va., October 8, 1863.

Maj. Gen. H. W. HALLECK,
General-in-Chief, U. S. Army, Washington, D. C.:

GENERAL: I feel desirous to do something, and although my force is very small, I hope, by substituting the defense of citadels for that of the long lines, as Williamsburg, Yorktown, Gloucester, and Getty's line, outside of Portsmouth, to obtain a small but effective movable column. The sickness which has prevailed at Williamsburg, Gloucester, Yorktown, and throughout the whole of North Carolina, has very much enfeebled the troops and made them for a time incapable of long marches. They are, however, available for expeditions by water, and what marches I may be forced to make can be borne by the negro troops. This is the case in the expedition now out scouring Matthews County, of which the infantry is wholly composed of negro troops. To come to the point, I propose (now that I am obliged to understand that the troops sent to the Department of the South cannot be replaced so as to give me force enough to go to Weldon or to take Fort Caswell) to undertake little operations in succession, calculated to attract the attention of the enemy and draw off his force, which can be made very safe by means of the aid of the navy and the army gunboats.

The first point is Fort Powhatan, now deserted, which I propose to seize and turn into a small but strong work for us, from which I can commence a system of cavalry raids. Then, as soon as this has attracted the attention of the enemy so as to accumulate force enough to stop the operations of the cavalry, to seize a point on the other shore of the James, higher up, say, at Wilcox's or Swynyard's Wharves, or Harrison's Landing, and pursue the same game. Then, with a small increase of force, City Point may be seized and fortified, and a dash be made toward Petersburg. To make sure of taking it will require quite an increase of force, say, 20,000 men; but this force can be sent, if you judge expedient, at any time. All that I can do now is to annoy the enemy, and from time to time to accumulate a force to meet an apprehended attack. If this meets with your approval, I will at once enter upon the necessary preparations.

I have the honor to be, general, your obedient servant,

J. G. FOSTER,
Major-General.

Fort Monroe, Va., *October 8, 1863—8 p. m.*
(Received 8.15 p. m.)

Maj. Gen. H. W. Halleck,
General-in-Chief:

Major Mulford, in charge of the flag-of-truce boat, who has a good opportunity to gain information while at City Point, has informed me that on his last visit he saw and heard enough to convince him that the enemy are still sending troops to Bragg, with the determination of holding General Rosecrans in check, if not defeating him.

Jeff. Davis left Richmond for the southwest day before yesterday. Everything indicates a determination to endeavor to regain their lost ground in East Tennessee. They despair of being able to take Chattanooga, but expect to harass the rear of General Rosecrans, and to defeat him if he attacks them. They are, or pretend to be, nervous lest General Rosecrans should not attack.

The attack on the Ironsides in Charleston Harbor was connected with some torpedo arrangement, the exact nature of which could not be ascertained. It did not meet with success.

J. G. FOSTER,
Major-General.

———

Headquarters Army of the Potomac,
October 9, 1863—6.30 a. m.

Commanding Officer Cavalry Corps :

The commanding general directs that you order General Gregg to concentrate as rapidly as possible and march day and night until he reaches Culpeper Court-House. He will leave one regiment to aid General Terry in guarding the railroad.

·General Kilpatrick will be directed to watch the Madison Court-House and Woodville road, as well as the roads leading to Culpeper Court-House which he now watches, and if the enemy moves in force on the Woodville road he will attack him and impede his progress to the utmost.

General Buford will, as soon as possible, force a passage at Germanna Ford, pursue the enemy, and endeavor to uncover Morton's Ford, communicating with General Newton, commanding First Corps, who is instructed to force a passage there also. This being effected, he will continue to follow the enemy, reporting his progress.

Very respectfully, your obedient servant,

A. A. HUMPHREYS,
Major-General, and Chief of Staff.

———

Headquarters Army of the Potomac,
October 9, 1863.

Brigadier-General Gregg,
Commanding Second Cavalry Division :

Concentrate your command at Culpeper Court-House as rapidly as possible, marching by night and day. Leave one regiment to aid General Terry, defending the railroad. Bring in your pickets. Acknowledge receipt of this dispatch at once.

By command of Major-General Pleasonton:

C. C. SUYDAM,
Assistant Adjutant-General.

FIRST ARMY CORPS,
October 9, 1863.

Major-General HUMPHREYS,
   Chief of Staff:

The following just received:

HEADQUARTERS FIRST DIVISION, FIRST ARMY CORPS,
October 9, 1863.

Lieutenant-Colonel KINGSBURY,
  Assistant Adjutant-General, First Army Corps:

SIR: Reveille was sounded in the rebel camps in my front at 3.30 o'clock this morning. From the top of Stone-House Mountain no camps can be discovered in my front. The picket line directly in my front is very much weakened. The enemy seem to move southwest. Whether they are falling back or concentrating to our right, or moving for the Shenandoah, of course I have no means of judging. Not only the tents and men, but most of the smokes have disappeared opposite Morton's Ford. I have an officer on the mountain, and will report any further discoveries. Trains as well as men moved southwest.

   Yours, respectfully,

            L. CUTLER,
       Brigadier-General, Commanding Division.

         JOHN NEWTON,
          Major-General.

HEADQUARTERS FIRST ARMY CORPS,
October 9, 1863.

Major-General HUMPHREYS:

The general officer of the day reports the enemy's lines opposite are remarkably quiet. Says no cannon are to be seen in the earth-works. Officer of Second Division reports that no reveille was heard this morning, and that pickets are fewer than ordinary. Have sent staff officers to see. The Second Division is on the right of my line.

         JOHN NEWTON,
          Major-General.

The rebels, except their pickets, have all gone away from our front. Everything is quiet this morning where usually they held forth for two or three hours at a time. One of Company K's corporals went down to the rebel reserve picket last night unperceived and overheard the conversation, which was to the effect that the Yankees would soon find out if many more troops were taken away from here; that three of Ewell's brigades went away to Bragg yesterday, and that it was the determination of Davis to re-enforce Bragg with every man he had.

            D. J. HYNES,
            Captain, &c.

HDQRS. THIRD DIVISION, CAVALRY CORPS,
October 9, 1863.

Brigadier-General DAVIES,
   Commanding Brigade:

GENERAL: The enemy are reported to be moving in heavy force from Madison Court-House. The general directs that you have your whole command under arms and send the same force to Crig- lersville you had before.

   Very respectfully,

          L. G. ESTES,
       Assistant Adjutant-General.

HDQRS. THIRD DIVISION, CAVALRY CORPS,
October 9, 1863.

Brig. Gen. H. E. DAVIES, Jr.,
Commanding First Brigade.

GENERAL: The enemy have halted about 2 miles from Madison
Court-House, toward Orange Court-House, and have gone into camp.
The general commanding division directs me to say that you will go
into camp as usual, observing, however, the greatest caution and
vigilance on the river.

I am, general, very respectfully,
L. G. ESTES,
Assistant Adjutant-General.

———

HDQRS. THIRD DIVISION CAVALRY CORPS,
October 9, 1863.

Brigadier-General CUSTER,
Commanding Second Brigade:

GENERAL: The enemy are reported to be moving in heavy force
from the direction of Madison Court-House.

The general commanding directs that you will use the greatest
vigilance along your picket line on the river, and keep your command supplied with two days' rations and one day's forage, and
hold yourself ready to move at short notice.

I am, general, very respectfully, your obedient servant,
L. G. ESTES,
Assistant Adjutant-General.

———

FIRST ARMY CORPS,
October 9, 1863.

General HUMPHREYS, *Chief of Staff:*

The indications are that the enemy are evacuating from their right
toward their left. No change at Somerville Ford. So far as seen,
two guns are at Somerville Ford.
JOHN NEWTON,
Major-General.

———

FIRST ARMY CORPS,
October 9, 1863.

Major-General HUMPHREYS, *Chief of Staff:*

e following from Lieutenant Carrington, my aide-de-camp, received:

Appearances indicate that Colonel Prey's report is correct. No guns are in sight
opposite the church. The batteries opposite the church have been removed. Not
more than 5 of the enemy are in sight besides the picket. The picket line is about
as usual. I see a regiment at Somerville Ford moving to the rear; at least 150 men.

Part of Colonel Prey's report was telegraphed you as the general officer of the
day. The enemy's batteries in the vicinity of Raccoon Ford, above and below, have
been removed. The enemy's troop have been seen filing back over the hills.

This postscript is from the information of two staff officers whom
I sent down there to investigate after hearing from the picket.
JOHN NEWTON,
Major-General.

SIGNAL DEPT., HDQRS. ARMY OF THE POTOMAC,
October 9, 1863.

Major-General HUMPHREYS,
    Chief of Staff:

The following dispatch was received from signal officer on Cedar Mountain·

OCTOBER 9, 1863—6.30 p. m.

General Anderson and his command have just left.

FERGUSON,
Assistant Adjutant-General.

I have the honor to be, &c.,

L. B. NORTON,
Captain, and Chief Signal Officer.

———

. HEADQUARTERS FIRST ARMY CORPS,
October 9, 1863.

Major-General HUMPHREYS:

GENERAL: I will be in the neighborhood of Morton's Ford to-morrow morning by daylight with the First Corps. Any communications from General Buford or others will find me there.

Very respectfully,

JOHN NEWTON,
Major-General.

[Indorsement.]

Copy sent to General Pleasonton, with instructions to forward to Buford.

———

FIRST CORPS,
October 9, 1863.

Major-General HUMPHREYS:

The picket officer on our left reports that the enemy's pickets have been relieved by cavalry. No news from the center or right.

JOHN NEWTON,
Major-General.

———

HEADQUARTERS FIRST ARMY CORPS,
October 9, 1863—4.35 p. m.

Major-General HUMPHREYS:

I have the honor to forward for your information the following rebel message intercepted from Clark's Mountain by Lieutenants Wiggins and Camp, signal officers:

General LEE:

General Ewell wishes you to have our pickets relieved by cavalry guards as soon as possible. General Gordon with —— of his regiment to join General Early and send another —— as soon as relieved.

PENDLETON,
Lieutenant-Colonel.

Very respectfully,

JOHN NEWTON,
Major-General.

OCTOBER 9, 1863—7 p. m.

Commanding Officer First Corps:

The major-general commanding directs me to inform you that General Buford has been ordered to force a passage at Germanna as soon as possible and follow the enemy, and endeavor to open Morton's Ford in conjunction with your corps. You will, therefore, as soon as you learn that General Buford has crossed at Germanna, endeavor to carry Morton's Ford, and, upon doing so, will await the arrival of General Buford and follow and support him, moving up the river. You will keep the major-general commanding advised of everything important that transpires, and will also advise General Sedgwick of your crossing and of your movements, as he will be directed, in the event of your success, to endeavor to cross at the fords in his front and move in conjunction with your corps.

A. A. HUMPHREYS,

Major-General, and Chief of Staff.

OCTOBER 9, 1863—7.30 p. m.

Commanding Officer First Corps:

The major-general commanding directs that in the event of your crossing the Rapidan sucessfully, and in moving up the river uncover the front of General Sedgwick and put yourself in communication with him. You will take position on the heights opposite the railroad crossing. The cavalry will follow the enemy in the direction of Orange Court-House.

A. A. HUMPHREYS,

Major-General, and Chief of Staff.

HEADQUARTERS ARMY OF THE POTOMAC,

October 9, 1863—7.30 p. m.

Commanding Officer Cavalry Corps:

The major-general commanding directs that General Buford will inform General Newton as soon as he has crossed at Germanna. General Newton will then cross at Morton's Ford and await the arrival of Buford. General Buford will follow the enemy up the river. Newton will follow and support. Sedgwick will in succession cross at the fords of his front and join in the support of the cavalry.

Very respectfully, &c.,

A. A. HUMPHREYS,

Major-General, and Chief of Staff.

OCTOBER 9, 1863—7.45 p. m.

Commanding Officer Sixth Corps:

The major-general commanding directs me to inform you that General Buford has been ordered to cross at Germanna with his division, and to aid General Newton in effecting a passage at Morton's Ford. General Newton is ordered to cross at Morton's Ford, if practicable, as soon as he learns that General Buford has crossed at Germanna, and await the arrival of Buford, who will move up the river, and, with Newton, co-operate with you in the execution of your orders. General Newton will inform you of his passage of the river. You will hold your corps in readiness to move. Concentrate it as soon as you learn that Newton has crossed, and endeavor to cross at such point as you may deem best, Newton with the First Corps and Buford with his cavalry co-operating with you. In the event of your being successful, General Newton has been ordered to take position on the heights opposite the railroad crossing of the Rapidan, while the cavalry follows the enemy toward Orange Court-House. You will take up a position in conjunction with him. You will keep the major-general commanding advised of your movements, and keep in communication with General Newton.

Additional information received shows that the enemy is either falling back or moving to turn our right flank.

A. A. HUMPHREYS,
Major-General, and Chief of Staff.

HEADQUARTERS FIRST ARMY CORPS,
October 9, 1863—8.30 p. m.

Major-General HUMPHREYS, *Chief of Staff:*

I think there has been a mistake in the report that the enemy's pickets have been relieved by cavalry on the left. I have just received the report of the field officer of the day on the left, stating that the enemy's pickets have not been relieved by cavalry. This is to correct the statement of another officer of the pickets.

JOHN NEWTON,
Major-General.

OCTOBER 9, 1863—8.30 p. m.

General BENHAM,
    Comdg. Engineer Brigade, Rappahannock Station:

The major-general commanding directs that you leave Colonel Spaulding with 200 enlisted men at Rappahannock Station in charge of twenty-three of the pontoons and equipage now at that place. You will, with the remainder of your command and the remainder of the pontoons, proceed with all possible dispatch to Washington, and there prepare pontoons and equipage and obtain the animals to transport the same so as to have sufficient number of boats to build two bridges across the Rappahannock at Fredericksburg. You will make these preparations with the utmost dispatch and hold yourself ready to proceed by water to Aquia Creek Landing and cross from there to the vicinity of Falmouth.

A. A. HUMPHREYS,
Major-General, and Chief of Staff.

HEADQUARTERS FIRST ARMY CORPS,
October 9, 1863—9 p. m.

Major-General HUMPHREYS:

The picket officer on the right reports that the enemy's pickets in his front have not been relieved by cavalry.

JOHN NEWTON,
Major-General.

OCTOBER 9, 1863—9.15 p. m.
Commanding Officer First Corps :

In reply to your inquiry, General Buford has been ordered to communicate to you the fact of his having crossed as soon as he is over. Immediately upon your hearing from him that he has crossed, you will at once move to cross. Have your force in position in readiness to cross. Buford will probably be over the river by daylight.

A. A. HUMPHREYS,
Major-General, and Chief of Staff.

———

HEADQUARTERS ARMY OF THE POTOMAC,
October 9, 1863—10.15 p. m.
Commanding Officer Fifth Corps:

The major-general commanding directs that you move your corps to the vicinity of the point where General Newton has his headquarters, and there mass it, screened from the observation of the enemy. The movement should be made promptly immediately upon receipt of this order, not later than 2 a. m. The regiment in Culpeper will be left there. Your ammunition train and ambulances will accompany you, the other trains will be left.

Upon reaching the point designated you will hold your command ready to support General Newton and General Sedgwick, upon being so directed by the major-general commanding. A copy of the instructions to those officers is sent herewith. General Newton's headquarters are in telegraphic communication with these headquarters. They are near the house marked J. M. Colvin on the map.

Very respectfully, &c.,

A. A. HUMPHREYS,
Major-General, and Chief of Staff.

———

OCTOBER 9, 1863—10.45 p. m.
Commanding Officers First and Sixth Corps:

The major-general commanding directs me to inform you that Major-General Sykes has been directed to move the Fifth Corps to the vicinity of General Newton's headquarters by daylight, and there mass it in the woods screened from the observation of the enemy. It will be held ready to support General Newton, should he require it, in crossing the river or subsequently, or to support Generals Sedgwick and Newton, should they require support at any time during the operations assigned to their corps.

A. A. HUMPHREYS,
Major-General, and Chief of Staff.

———

OCTOBER 9, 1863—11 p. m.
Commanding Officer First Corps :

The major-general commanding directs me to say that the movements ordered for to-morrow are based upon the supposition that the enemy is retiring from the Rapidan. This supposition may prove to be erroneous, and the commanding general desires that you will exercise prudence in the operations to be conducted by you, and not make unnecessary sacrifice in attempting to cross the river should the enemy show himself in strong force, or, in the ulterior operations, should he be found in superior force and position. Care will be taken to keep open communication with the rear.

The ammunition trains should not be taken across the river, but arrangements made to take ammunition to the front by pack mules from the fords. Major-General Newton will communicate which of the fords proves to be the most advantageous for Major-General Sykes to cross at, whether Morton's or Raccoon Ford, or any other, according to the circumstances then existing.

A. A. HUMPHREYS,
Major-General, and Chief of Staff.

(Copy to General Sedgwick.) ·

———

OCTOBER 9, 1863—11.15 p. m.

The following dispatch will be sent to General Sykes at daylight at the station where General Newton's headquarters now are.

A. A. H. [HUMPHREYS.]

Major-General SYKES,
 Commanding Fifth Corps :

The major-general commanding directs that when you arrive in the vicinity of General Newton's headquarters, as specified, you be prepared to move across the Rapidan by Morton's Ford or by Raccoon Ford, and make yourself acquainted with the routes by which these fords are best approached. Your ammunition trains will not cross the river, but will be left near the fords, and arrangements will be made to take forward such infantry ammunition as may be required by pack mules from the fords.

A. A. HUMPHREYS,
Major-General, and Chief of Staff.

———

CIRCULAR.] HEADQUARTERS ARMY OF THE POTOMAC,
October 9, 1863.

Corps commanders will at once have their commands in readiness to move at very short notice.

The five days' rations heretofore directed to be carried in knapsacks will be immediately issued and placed in the knapsacks.

By command of Major-General Meade:

S. WILLIAMS,
Assistant Adjutant-General.

(Addressed to commanding officers First Corps, Second Corps, Third Corps, Fifth Corps, and Sixth Corps, and provost-marshal-general.)

———

HEADQUARTERS FIRST ARMY CORPS,
October 9, 1863.

General HUMPHREYS:

GENERAL: I have received two telegrams, one notifying me General Sykes was to be sent down to my present headquarters, another

that I was to exercise caution in crossing. If information is certain,
audacity is prudence, and I would respectfully suggest that with the
First Corps leading, I would like to have the Fifth and Sixth Corps
as a reserve. As to the point of crossing, I know nothing definite
of the depth of water, my pickets not being able to approach near
enough to obtain it. Morton's Ford, militarily, is half-and-half,
according to who attacks, the advantage being on the side of the
defense. Raccoon Ford is impregnable. This in both cases is on
the supposition that the enemy is in force.

If an attack is to be made, I respectfully recommend a strong
column on one point sufficient to compensate for losses. With the
First Corps I can carry, I think, any point on the river, except Raccoon Ford, but I must be supported, unless information at headquarters is positive that the enemy has evacuated.

Finally, I respectfully recommend that the First, Fifth, and Sixth
Corps, in the order mentioned, take the lead and be concentrated on
one point. I can go anywhere with such a column.

Very respectfully,

JOHN NEWTON,
Major-General.

OCTOBER 9, 1863—7 p. m.
(Received 7.45 p. m.)

Major-General HALLECK :

A movement on the part of the enemy has taken place to-day.
His force guarding the Rapidan has been visibly diminished. A
column of cavalry, artillery, and infantry has been seen moving from
Gordonsville to Madison Court-House. What his intentions are is
as yet uncertain. Whether falling back from the Rapidan, or making a flank movement against me by way of Madison Court-House
and Weaverville, I am unable to say. I have directed one division
of cavalry to cross the Rapidan, if practicable, at Germanna, and
follow the enemy if in retreat. Another division of cavalry is posted
to watch and meet any movement from Madison Court-House. The
rest of the army will be held in hand to meet either contingency, to
pursue in case Lee is withdrawing, or meet his flank movement in
the event of such proving to be his intention.

The enemy's pickets were overheard to say last night that the
Yankees would soon find out that more troops had been sent to
Bragg, and it is reported three brigades from Ewell's corps have
been recently sent.

GEO. G. MEADE,
Major-General, Commanding.

SPECIAL ORDERS, }   HDQRS. DEPT. OF VA. AND N. C.,
No. 81.   }   *Fort Monroe, Va., October 9, 1863.*

*   *   *   *   *   *   *

IV. Major-General Peck, commanding District of North Carolina, will order the following-named regiments to be prepared to
come to this point. The regiments will bring their camp and garrison equipage. Ninth Regiment New Jersey Volunteers, Twenty-
third Regiment Massachusetts Volunteers, Twenty-seventh Regi-

ment Massachusetts Volunteers, Eighty-first Regiment New York Volunteers, Ninety-eighth Regiment New York Volunteers.

General Heckman will come in command. Transportation will be sent for the troops.

*　　　*　　　*　　　*　　　*　　　*

VI. The commanding officer of the Ninety-ninth Regiment New York Volunteers will prepare the regiment to be embarked for New Berne, N. C.

*　　　*　　　*　　　*　　　*　　　*

VII. The commanding officer of the Nineteenth Regiment Wisconsin Volunteers will at once prepare his regiment to be embarked for New Berne, N. C., on steamer Convoy.

*　　　*　　　*　　　*　　　*　　　*

By command of Maj. Gen. J. G. Foster:

SOUTHARD HOFFMAN,
Assistant Adjutant-General.

PRIVATE.]　　　　　　HEADQUARTERS OF THE ARMY,
　　　　　　　　　　　Washington, October 10, 1863.
Maj. Gen. J. G. FOSTER,
　　　　Fort Monroe:

GENERAL: Your letter of the 8th, marked "private," is just received.

Your effective force by your last return was over 19,000 men. You hold many important places and have a very long line of defense. Yet, it is desirable, as you say, that something active should be done by your army, at least to annoy the enemy and keep in check a part of his forces, if nothing more.

As Burnside could not be persuaded to go to Rosecrans' assistance (I telegraphed to him fifteen times to do so, and the President three or four times), it became necessary to send him two corps from the Army of the Potomac, thus destroying all our plans here. Had it not been for this *contretemps,* I proposed to re-enforce you, so that you could co-operate with Meade. The only object, or, at least, the main one, of holding Yorktown and Gloucester has been to keep open the road to West Point, from which place the Army of the Potomac must get its supplies, if the enemy falls back to the defenses of Richmond. At present it seems impossible to give you much assistance without breaking up Meade's army.

I am very certain that a large detachment from Lee's army has been sent west, and that Meade is greatly superior to him in numbers. Nevertheless, Meade seems unwilling to attack him without positive orders. To order a general to give battle against his own wishes and judgment is to assume the responsibility of a probable defeat. If a general is unwilling to fight, he is not likely to gain a victory. That army fights well when attacked, but all its generals have been unwilling to attack, even very inferior numbers. It certainly is a very strange phenomenon.

I am not sufficiently acquainted with localities in your department to advise exactly what you had better undertake. It seems to me, however, that an attempt to hold so many points on the James River will so weaken your active forces that you can accomplish nothing of importance. Fort Powhatan would, I think, be of very little advantage to either party. However, I leave that matter to your own discretion.

General Meade telegraphed last night that Lee's army was in motion, but with what object he did not yet know. Possibly an engagement may follow. If I get important information from that quarter it will be telegraphed to you. I wish I had an additional force to send you, for I am confident you would give it some employment.

Very respectfully, your obedient servant,

H. W. HALLECK.

WAR DEPARTMENT,
Washington, October 10, 1863—10.30 a. m.

Major-General MEADE,
Army of the Potomac:

When King Joseph wrote to Napoleon that he could not ascertain the position and strength of the enemy's army the Emperor replied: "Attack him and you will soon find out." Telegrams from the west say that additional troops from Lee's army are arriving there.

H. W. HALLECK,
General-in-Chief.

HEADQUARTERS ARMY OF THE POTOMAC,
October 10, 1863—12 noon.
(Received 12.40 p. m.)

Major-General HALLECK:

Your telegram of 10.30 received. Orders were last night given for a division of cavalry to cross at Germanna Ford and the two infantry corps on the river were ordered to cross as soon as the cavalry had effected the passage on their left. No intelligence has yet been received from the cavalry at Germanna. On my right, the enemy's cavalry, in force, have crossed Robertson's River, from Madison Court-House, and are now engaged with my cavalry. Every indication would lead to the conclusion that the enemy's cavalry attacking me are supported by a large force of infantry, and there are some reasons to believe there is a movement into the Shenandoah Valley. As yet matters are undeveloped, but I am quite positive no troops have left Lee's army for the West, unless so very recently as to have precluded the possibility of their arrival there being announced by telegraph.

GEO. G. MEADE,
Major-General, Commanding.

WASHINGTON,
October 10, 1863—4.55 p. m.

General MEADE:

Am interested with your dispatch of noon. How is it now?

A. LINCOLN.

OCTOBER 10, 1863—5.30 p. m.
(Received 5.50 p. m.)

Major-General HALLECK:

The enemy have succeeded with their cavalry in forcing back my cavalry and infantry support, and seizing Thoroughfare Mountain, on which was posted my signal officer. This has enabled them to cover their flank movement.

From a deserter and prisoners I learn that A. P. Hill's whole corps and part of Ewell's are turning my right flank, moving from Madison Court-House to Sperryville. Long wagon trains and beef cattle accompany the column. I have no news from the cavalry on my left, although firing has been heard in that direction. As it will be impossible for me to maintain my present position with so considerable a force of the enemy threatening my rear and communications, I shall, to-night, withdraw to the north side of the Rappahannock, and endeavor, by means of the cavalry, to find out what the enemy propose. My belief now is that his movements are offensive.

GEO. G. MEADE,
Major-General, Commanding.

OCTOBER 10, 1863—1.45 a. m.

Commanding Officer First Corps:

Dispatch is received. No change is deemed necessary in the instructions.

A. A. HUMPHREYS,
Major-General, and Chief of Staff.

OCTOBER 10, 1863—9 a. m.

Commanding Officer Third Corps:

The major-general commanding directs me to inform you that the enemy are moving toward our right from Madison Court-House, and directs that you place your corps in position to meet an attack from the direction of James City and from the direction of the Sperryville pike. The division of your corps at James City, if obliged to retire by superior numbers, will fall back to the position now indicated for your corps. General Sykes has advanced to where General Newton's headquarters were yesterday, but will be withdrawn to his position in front of Culpeper in the event of its being necessary. The Second Corps will co-operate with you.

A. A. HUMPHREYS,
Major-General, and Chief of Staff.

HEADQUARTERS CAVALRY CORPS,
October 10, [1863]—8 a. m.

Major-General HUMPHREYS,
Chief of Staff:

GENERAL : The inclosed communication was just received.

A. PLEASONTON,
Major-General.

[Inclosure.]

. MITCHELL'S FORD, RAPPAHANNOCK RIVER,
October 10, 1863—6.30 a. m.

SIR : I have the honor to report that I overtook General Buford's command at 5.30 p. m. He was marching in the direction of Morton's Ford, but, owing to the darkness and slight skirmishing, was delayed, and in consequence of those delays I was unable to send word to you last night. The roads to the fords were blockaded, and it would have been dangerous to send an orderly.

I will remain with the general to-day, and will inform you from time to time how he gets along. He captured 65 prisoners.

Respectfully, your obedient servant,
NICHOLAS NOLAN, •
Lieutenant, Sixth U. S. Cavalry.

OCTOBER 10, 1863—9 a. m.
Commanding Officer First Corps:

The major-general commanding directs me to inform you that the enemy is moving from Madison Court-House upon our right. It is not yet ascertained whether this is a movement of their whole army upon our flank. Should it prove to be so, the whole army will be concentrated around Culpeper Court-House. You will, therefore, hold yourself in readiness to move at a moment's notice back to Culpeper. General Newton will, in such event, place himself in the position heretofore indicated for him, on the left of the Fifth Corps.

A. A. HUMPHREYS,
Major-General, and Chief of Staff.

OCTOBER 10, [1863]—9 a. m.
Brigadier-General CALDWELL,
Commanding Second Corps:

The major-general commanding directs that you place the Second Corps in position immediately to meet an advance of the enemy from the direction of Sperryville, and co-operate with General French, who is ordered to meet the advance of the enemy from the direction of James City, and from the Sperryville road.

A. A. HUMPHREYS,
Major-General, Chief of Staff.

OCTOBER 10, 1863—9 a. m.
Major-General FRENCH,
Commanding Third Corps:

The major-general commanding directs me to inform you that the enemy are moving toward our right from Madison Court-House, and directs that you place your corps in position to meet an attack from the direction of James City and from the direction of the Sperryville pike. The division of your corps at James City, if obliged to retire by superior numbers, will fall back to the position now indicated for your corps.

General Sykes has advanced to where General Newton's headquarters were yesterday, but will be withdrawn to his position in front of Culpeper in the event of its being necessary. The Second Corps will co-operate with you.

A. A. HUMPHREYS,
Major-General, Chief of Staff.

OCTOBER 10, 1863—9.15 a. m.
Commanding Officer Fifth Corps:

The major-general commanding directs that you hold yourself in readiness to return to your former position at a moment's notice. The enemy are advancing upon our right from Madison Court-House, but the attack has not yet fully developed itself. Have you heard from General Newton, and where is he?

A. A. HUMPHREYS,
Major-General, and Chief of Staff.

MORTON'S FORD, *October* 10, 1863—9.30 a. m.
Colonel SMITH,
Assistant Adjutant-General, Cavalry Corps:

SIR: The enemy attacked the rear guard, and a very lively skirmish occurred. Our cavalry made a gallant charge. All our troops have crossed the ford.

NICHOLAS NOLAN,
Lieutenant Sixth U. S. Cavalry.

HEADQUARTERS ARMY OF THE POTOMAC,
October 10, 1863—9.30 a. m.
Commanding Officer Second Corps:

The major-general commanding directs that you get your trains well in your rear on the south side of the railroad, so that they may move either to Rappahannock Station by the road on the south side of the railroad or to Kelly's Ford. Ammunition and ambulance trains are not included.

Very respectfully, &c.,

A. A. HUMPHREYS,
Major-General, and Chief of Staff.

OCTOBER 10, 1863.
Major-General HUMPHREYS,
Chief of Staff:

The courier has just brought back a verbal message from General Prince that Stuart is crossing the river to attack him. I supposed that our cavalry was in his front.

WM. H. FRENCH,
Major-General.

HEADQUARTERS ARMY OF THE POTOMAC,
October 10, 1863—10.15 a. m.

Major-General FRENCH,
    Commanding Third Army Corps:

It is intended by the major-general commanding that your line of battle be formed near to, and in part on that selected by you some time since, your left being in connection with the right of the Fifth Corps, which corps will return to its position as soon as the full character of the enemy's movements is developed, if it should prove to be an advance of his army on our right flank.

A. A. HUMPHREYS,
    Major-General, and Chief of Staff.

[P. S.]—The position of your division on the Sperryville pike, referred to in the dispatch, is not well known to the commanding general. You call it the Second Division, which is General Prince's, now near James City.

A. A. HUMPHREYS,
    Major-General, and Chief of Staff.

———

[*October* 10, 1863.]

General HUMPHREYS:

Prince's old camp, his left at Pendleton's, is the position of the Second Division referred to. I have a strong position, but about a mile from Stone-House Mountain, which commands the Sperryville road. That point is too salient for our line. It would not do to occupy it, as it can be turned on either side easily.

WM. H. FRENCH.

[P. S.]—I should like a staff officer from general headquarters to see the disposition.

———

HEADQUARTERS ARMY OF THE POTOMAC,
October 10, 1863—5.50 p. m.

Major-General FRENCH:

The major-general commanding directs that you withdraw General Prince as soon as it is dark, and be prepared with your corps to make a night march.

A. A. HUMPHREYS,
    Major-General, &c.

———

OCTOBER 10 1863—10.20 a. m.

Major-General HUMPHREYS,
    Chief of Staff:

General Prince has just sent in an aide to report that the enemy crossed this morning; that he sent a regiment to support the cavalry (One hundred and twentieth New York); that it was deployed as skirmishers, and charged by the enemy, and nearly all captured. He reports himself in a good position.

WM. H. FRENCH,
    Major-General, Commanding Third Corps.

HEADQUARTERS,
October 10, 1863—10.30 a. m.

Colonel SMITH,
　Asst. Adjt. Gen.; Cavalry Corps:

COLONEL : The enemy crossed the river, about 2 miles above the ford, with artillery and cavalry. Heavy skirmishing took place, our men driving them back. I saw six guns. We are returning slowly.

NICHOLAS NOLAN.

CIRCULAR.]　　HEADQUARTERS ARMY OF THE POTOMAC,
October 10, 1863—10.25 a. m.

As it is not impossible that the enemy may follow in force the movement of the army to-morrow, the commanding general directs that corps commanders will remain at the rear of their commands, so that they may at the earliest moment receive any instructions the commanding general may wish to send to them.

By command of Major-General Meade :

S. WILLIAMS,
Assistant Adjutant-General.

(To commanding officers.)

HDQRS. ARMY OF THE POTOMAC, *October* 10, 1863.
(Copy received at War Department 12.20 p. m.)

Major-General STONEMAN,
　Chief of Cavalry Bureau:

I desire the Reserve Brigade, or such portions of it as are able to move, to join me without the least delay. My cavalry is now engaged with the enemy, and I am in expectation of the most active operations, in which I shall require every mounted man I can raise. Please send them out as soon as possible.

GEO. G. MEADE,
Major-General.

OCTOBER 10, 1863—1 p. m.

Commanding Officer Sixth Corps:

Your dispatch received. The major-general commanding desires to know whether heavy artillery on Piney Mountain would be serviceable to you? If so, it can be sent to you from the reserve.

A. A. HUMPHREYS,
Major-General, and Chief of Staff.

OCTOBER 10, 1863.

Major-General HUMPHREYS,
　Chief of Staff:

Lieutenant Ordway, of General Prince's staff, has just been here and reported that General Prince had assumed command of the whole force, and that he is convinced that the enemy is greatly superior to him, and would probably turn his position there, and that he deemed it prudent to retire, which he is now doing very slowly, skirmishing with the enemy, Kilpatrick's cavalry bringing up the rear.   He also states that about 75 of the 120 have been taken prisoners.

WM. H. FRENCH,
Major-General, Commanding Third Corps.

HEADQUARTERS ARMY OF THE POTOMAC,
October 10, 1863—2.30 p. m.

Major-General FRENCH :

It is reported to the major-general commanding that General Prince is falling back.   You will direct General Prince to support the cavalry, and not to fall back unless pressed by superior numbers.   So long as General Kilpatrick maintains his position, General Prince should not fall back.

A. A. HUMPHREYS,
Major-General Chief of Staff.

[Indorsement.]

Telegraph : General Prince has since reported that he is going to hold on and has only changed his front.   Kilpatrick is still in position.

WM. H. FRENCH.

OCTOBER 10, 1863—3.15 p. m.

Commanding Officer Fifth Corps:

The major-general commanding directs that you return immediately to your former position in front of Culpeper, and place your troops in position there.   You will hold them in readiness to move at a moment's notice.   The trains will be held ready to move to rear at a moment's notice, and probably along the line of the railroad.

A. A. HUMPHREYS,
Major-General and Chief of Staff.

HEADQUARTERS FIFTH ARMY CORPS,
October 10, 1863.

General A. A. HUMPHREYS,
Chief of Staff:

The Fifth Corps has been massed at the point designated since 8 a. m.   I am at Colvin's house.

GEO. SYKES,
Major-General.

OCTOBER 10, 1863—3.30 p. m.

Commanding Officers First and Sixth Corps:

The major-general commanding directs me to inform you that General Sykes has been ordered to return to his former position at once.   The Sixth and Second Corps will be held ready to move at a moment's notice.

A. A. HUMPHREYS,
Major-General, and Chief of Staff.

CIRCULAR.] HEADQUARTERS ARMY OF THE POTOMAC,
October 10, 1863—4 p. m.

Trains, excepting ammunition and ambulance, will at once fall back to beyond Rappahannock Station, along the two roads adjoining the railroad and along the road to Kelly's Ford.

On the north side of the road: First, the Third Corps trains; second, the Fifth Corps trains.

On the road south side of the railroad: First, the Second Corps trains; second, the Sixth Corps trains; third, Reserve Artillery.

By Kelly's Ford, the First Corps trains.

The depot at Culpeper will be broken up and moved back to Bealeton.

By command of Major-General Meade:

S. WILLIAMS,
Assistant Adjutant-General.

OCTOBER 10, 1863—4.15 p. m.

Commanding Officer First Corps:

The major-general commanding directs that you fall back to your former position on the Stevensburg road as soon as it is dark. Report your arrival at former position. Your trains, except ammunition and ambulances, have been directed to move to Kelly's Ford. General Sedgwick has been ordered to move back at the same time you move and occupy the position on the left of Sykes.

A. A. HUMPHREYS,
Major-General, and Chief of Staff.

OCTOBER 10, 1863—4.30 p. m.

Commanding Officer Sixth Corps:

The major-general commanding directs that as soon as it is dark you fall back and take position on the left of the Fifth Corps, on the ground that General Newton was directed to occupy in the event of falling back. It is in front of Culpeper, and extends from the vicinity of General Sykes' old headquarters (Green's house) to the left of the railroad, as far as the ridge runs. General Newton is directed to fall back at the same hour to his former position on the Stevensburg road. Report your arrival. Your trains have been ordered back to beyond Rappahannock Station.

A. A. HUMPHREYS,
Major-General, and Chief of Staff.

OCTOBER 10, 1863—6 p. m.

Commanding Officer First Corps:

The major-general commanding directs me to say, in reply to your dispatch just received, that the position to which you are to fall back is the same as that which you occupied when you moved to relieve General Slocum. You are to withdraw pickets and everything. Your trains are probably already in motion toward Kelly's Ford, to which point you will also probably withdraw to-night.

A. A. HUMPHREYS,
Major-General, and Chief of Staff.

OCTOBER 10, 1863—7.30 p. m.

Commanding Officer Sixth Corps:

The major-general commanding directs that, instead of halting in front of Culpeper Court-House and taking position in connection with the Fifth Corps, you pass to this side of Culpeper Court-House and Mountain Run, and mass on the south side of the railroad, so as to be in position to move to-morrow morning at about 3 o'clock. Orders for the march will be sent you.

A. A. HUMPHREYS,
Major-General, and Chief of Staff.

OCTOBER 10, [1863]—9.35 p. m.

Major-General HUMPHREYS:

GENERAL: In the event of our moving back, would not it be advisable to destroy the railroad bridge across Cedar Run, and even take up some of the rails, destroy the ties, &c.? The pickets report the same picket line opposite.

JOHN SEDGWICK,
Major-General.

HEADQUARTERS CAVALRY CORPS,
October 10, [1863]—9.45 p. m.

Brigadier-General GREGG,
Commanding Second Cavalry Division:

GENERAL: In consequence of information received, you will place the brigade now with you in position on the Sperryville road to watch the enemy and support Kilpatrick against any movement of the enemy's cavalry on his right. Send me early and frequent reports concerning the enemy.

Very respectfully,

A. PLEASONTON,
Major-General.

OCTOBER 10, 1863—10 p. m.

Commanding Officer Sixth Corps:

The major-general commanding directs that upon reaching Rappahannock Station your corps will be massed and held in readiness to move, until the covering corps arrive, so that in the event of its being required in the rear, it will be available.

Very respectfully, &c.,

A. A. HUMPHREYS,
Major-General, and Chief of Staff.

CIRCULAR.]   HEADQUARTERS ARMY OF THE POTOMAC,
October 10, 1863.

The following movements of troops are ordered for to-morrow, October 11, 1863:

1. The Third Corps will move to the ford on the Hazel River on the road it followed in the march to Culpeper Court-House, and from thence to Sulphur Springs, and take position on the Rappahannock in that vicinity, extending toward Freeman's Ford; will take the eight pontoons to use in crossing the rivers, if it should prove necessary.

2. The Second Corps will move along the north side of the railroad to Rappahannock Station, crossing the Rappahannock on the pontoon bridge above the railroad bridge, and move up to Freeman's Ford, and take position there, extending in the direction of Beverly Ford.

3. The Sixth Corps will move on the south side of the railroad crossing at Rappahannock Station, extending toward Kelly's Ford.

4. The Fifth Corps will move on the north side of the railroad crossing the Rappahannock by the pontoon bridge above the railroad bridge, and take position between Rappahannock Station and Beverly Ford.

5. The First Corps will move to Kelly's Ford and cross the river at that place on a bridge to be laid to-night, taking position at that ford, and extending toward the Sixth Corps at Rappahannock Station, the two corps communicating.

5½. The Artillery Reserve will move as soon as the trains have cleared the road on the south side of the railroad. General Tyler will keep himself advised of the movements of trains, and will so arrange his movements as not to embarrass or delay the march of the troops.

6. Corps commanders will take precaution to have their troops march alongside of the roads, so that the roads may be clear for the movement of artillery and trains.

7. The movement will be commenced simultaneously at 3 a. m. by the Second Corps, the Sixth Corps, and the First Corps.

8. The Fifth and Third Corps, in conjunction with the cavalry, will cover the withdrawal of the army, and, with this object, will not move until the other corps have cleared the road. The Third Corps will cover the Sperryville road, and the Fifth Corps the approach from Rapidan Station, and will withdraw simultaneously. General Gregg will move to Sulphur Springs by the Rixeyville road, moving at the same time as the Third Corps. General Kilpatrick will move along the line of railroad in rear of the Fifth Corps.

9. The headquarters will be in the vicinity of Smith's or Bowen's house, near Rappahannock Station.

10. Corps commanders will see that their ammunition wagons and ambulances precede their troops, and hold the latter well in hand, so as to be prepared to meet the advance of the enemy, should he follow the army.

By command of Major-General Meade:

S. WILLIAMS,
Assistant Adjutant-General.

(Copy to all commanders.)

[OCTOBER 10, 1863.—For abstract from tri-monthly return of the Army of the Potomac, see Part I, p. 226.]

HDQRS. ARMY AND DISTRICT OF NORTH CAROLINA,
New Berne, N. C., October 10, 1863.

Maj. Gen. J. G. FOSTER,
    Comdg. Dept. of Virginia and North Carolina:

GENERAL: I have received a communication from General Wessells, of the 7th, the only one since the one of the 4th, in which he mentioned rumors of troops in the direction of South Mills in search of conscripts. He reports that Colonel Hinton, of Pasquotank County, is authorized by Governor Vance to force into service all persons liable to military duty; that he is accompanied by a medical officer and by a force of militia, &c., for enforcing the conscription. The general says he has sent the gunboat Southfield to Edenton, and the Underwriter up the Chowan to cruise from Dillard's farm to Winton, &c. He also sent the Massasoit, with 100 infantry, to Edenton or such other points as may seem proper. He adds that he has reported this action to the commanding general at Norfolk. Hearing nothing from the commanding general at Norfolk, or from your headquarters respecting the matter, I conclude it was one of the reports so common in rebeldom. I will have some cavalry ready to go to Elizabeth City, in case the information may warrant.

In haste, very respectfully, your obedient servant,

JOHN J. PECK,
Major-General.

HDQRS. ARMY AND DISTRICT OF NORTH CAROLINA,
New Berne, N. C., October 10, 1863.

Maj. Gen. J. G. FOSTER,
Comdg. Dept. of Virginia and North Carolina:

GENERAL: Since my letter of this afternoon, I have thought it advisable to send a force to Elizabeth City, with a view to overawe rebel leaders in that vicinity, and to break up any arrangements that Colonel Hinton, or others, may make for enforcing the conscription. Colonel Mix goes in a few hours with 300 cavalry and a section of Belger's battery. He has particular instructions to protect our friends. His unexpected appearance will create much excitement, and I hope for large results.

JOHN J. PECK,
Major-General.

HDQRS. ARMY AND DISTRICT OF NORTH CAROLINA,
New Berne, October 10, 1863.

Colonel MIX:

You will proceed with 300 cavalry of the Third New York and of Mix's new regiment and a section of Belger's battery to Elizabeth City, N. C., to-night by transports, which the chief quartermaster has been ordered to provide. Your command will have not less than seven days' rations, a proper supply of ammunition, and will be accompanied by a suitable number of medical attendants.

It having been reported that Colonel Hinton is raising a regiment of conscripts in Pasquotank and the adjacent counties, and endeavoring by all means in his power to enforce the rebel conscription law, you will endeavor to ascertain the truth of these representations, and, if possible, break up his operations and disperse his camp. A rumor is in circulation that a force of militia has moved from the Blackwater in the direction of South Mills, where we are supposed to have a cavalry force from Norfolk, for the purpose of watching our forces in that vicinity and preventing any interference with Colonel Hinton. General Wessells has sent one or two gunboats to Edenton, on one of which is a body of infantry.

You will probably find one of our gunboats in the Pasquotank, and it should move with you to Elizabeth City to cover your base of operations. On passing Roanoke Island you will be able to ascertain if there is a boat in the Pasquotank. If there is none, you will take the Bombshell with you for the purpose indicated, with the understanding that upon your return the Bombshell shall go back to the station where you find her.

Lieutenant Stirling, aide-de-camp, is sent this evening by the John Farron to Plymouth, to apprise General Wessells of your movement upon Elizabeth City and its objects. General Wessells has been requested to confer with you and to afford such co-operation as may be practicable.

You will send frequent reports marked "important," by way of Roanoke Island, to be dispatched by the earliest opportunity. On your way up make arrangements at Roanoke for forwarding dispatches in such a way that should their importance require it, they may be sent by a special boat. In case you meet with reverse or serious embarrassments, it will be well to let General Wessells know it. In case of extremity you may send to Roanoke Island for one or two companies temporarily. Much is intrusted to your own discretion, by which you will be guided in unforeseen developments. I write by General Peck's direction.

Very respectfully, your obedient servant,

BENJ. B. FOSTER,
Assistant Adjutant-General.

HDQRS. ARMY AND DISTRICT OF NORTH CAROLINA,
New Berne, N. C., October 10, 1863.

Col. SOUTHARD HOFFMAN,
Asst. Adjt. Gen., Dept. of Va. and N. C.:

The rebel War Department has just made two departments of North Carolina. Wilmington and the region of Cape Fear is placed under command of General W. H. C. Whiting, the remainder is assigned to the command of Maj. Gen. George E. Pickett.

I am, very respectfully, your obedient servant,

JOHN J. PECK,
Major-General.

HDQRS. ARMY AND DISTRICT OF NORTH CAROLINA,
New Berne, N. C., October 10, 1863.

Maj. Gen. J. G. FOSTER,
Comdg. Dept. of Virginia and North Carolina:

GENERAL: Mr. James G. Bryan came in under a flag yesterday from Kinston, where he has been since General Branch evacuated New Berne. He says Branch gave orders to burn the town, as 40,000 Yankees were coming and would burn it. Branch refused to let him return. He is sixty years of age, and a fine specimen of the North Carolina gentlemen, and I am told that he ranked second in the law in this State. The pastor of the Baptist Church at Kinston also came in, and he says Mr. Bryan was a Union man, and made speeches against rebellion. I call your attention to Mr. Bryan as you are probably posted about him. If there is any suspicion I will send him to the North, as I wish no doubtful men within my lines.

JOHN J. PECK.

GENERAL ORDERS, }   HDQRS. MIDDLE DEPT., 8TH ARMY CORPS,
No. 48.   }   *Baltimore, Md., October 10, 1863.*

Having returned from my temporary absence, I hereby resume command of the Middle Department and Eighth Army Corps.

ROBT. C. SCHENCK,
Major-General, U. S. Volunteers.

SPECIAL ORDERS, }   WAR DEPT., ADJT. GENERAL'S OFFICE,
No. 454.   }   *Washington, October 10, 1863.*

*   *   *   *   *   *   *

14. Brig. Gen. E. A. Wild, U. S. Volunteers, is hereby relieved from duty in the Department of the South, and will proceed without delay to New Berne, N. C., to complete the organization of the Third Regiment North Carolina Colored Volunteers.

*   *   *   *   *   *   *

By order of the Secretary of War:

E. D. TOWNSEND,
Assistant Adjutant-General.

CLARKSBURG, W. VA., *October 10, 1863.*
(Received 5 p. m.)

Major-General STONEMAN,
    Chief of Cavalry Bureau:

I ordered General Scammon to direct General Duffié to hold himself in readiness for an important movement. The following telegram just received. Will you please issue an order authorizing Captain Gardner or Captain Stealy, assistant quartermasters, to purchase the horses?

General KELLEY:

General Duffié needs 200 horses at once. So many are unserviceable that his command cannot be efficient without this number in addition.

SCAMMON,
Brigadier-General.

B. F. KELLEY,
Brigadier-General.

HEADQUARTERS ARMY OF THE POTOMAC,
October 11, 1863—8.30 a. m. (Received 8.50 a. m.)

His Excellency ABRAHAM LINCOLN,
    President of the United States:

I am falling back to the Rappahannock. The enemy are either moving to my right and rear or moving down on my flank, I can not tell which, as their movements are not developed. I am prepared for either emergency.

GEO. G. MEADE,
Major-General.

HEADQUARTERS SIXTH ARMY CORPS,
October 11, 1863—1.15 p. m.

Major-General HUMPHREYS,
　　Chief of Staff:

GENERAL : Brigadier-General Wright reports he "can plainly see artillery mounted in the works opposite." This looks as though the enemy was returning a part, at least, of his force to the position in our front, and that he designs holding it.

JOHN SEDGWICK,
Major-General.

OCTOBER 11, 1863—7.30 p. m.

Commanding Officer First Corps:

The major-general commanding directs me to inform you that the enemy followed the rear guard in force to-day, and that it is probable an attempt may be made to-morrow to dislodge us from the present position or to turn us. You will hold your corps prepared to move at very short notice to the support of the corps above you, and also be prepared to maintain your own position. General Pleasonton will be directed to send a cavalry force to picket the river below you. Your trains will be parked sufficiently far from the river to be out of the reach of artillery fire.

A. A. HUMPHREYS,
Major-General, and Chief of Staff.

HEADQUARTERS ARMY OF THE POTOMAC,
October 11, 1863—7.45 p. m.

Major-General SEDGWICK,
　　Commanding Sixth Corps:

The major-general commanding directs me to inform you that the enemy followed and attacked the rear guard to-day in force, and that it appears to be probable that he will make a demonstration or attack to-morrow on our front. You will occupy in force the two hills, on the south side of the river, on your front (those occupied by General Newton), and your pickets will connect with those of General Sykes on the right. General Sykes has been directed to occupy strongly the hills in his front, called the Yew Hills, with infantry and artillery. It is his picket from this force that you are to connect with on your right. Cavalry pickets will likewise cover this part of the front to-night, but they will probably be withdrawn to-morrow. On your left your pickets on this side of the river will connect with those of General Newton.

If there is any ground on this side the river where heavy artillery can be placed to advantage, General Hunt has been directed to send such as you may require.

Your command will be held ready to move at short notice. The two pontoon bridges will be retained for the present.

Very respectfully, your obedient servant,

A. A. HUMPHREYS,
Major-General, and Chief of Staff.

[Indorsement.]

OCTOBER 12, 1863—4 a. m.

Brigadier-General Howe will cross immediately with his division and carry out the instructions contained in the order of the commanding general.

By command of Major-General Sedgwick:

M. T. McMAHON,
Assistant Adjutant-General, and Chief of Staff.

HEADQUARTERS ARMY OF THE POTOMAC,
October 11, 1863—8.15 p. m.

Commanding Officer Third Corps:

The major-general commanding directs me to inform you that the enemy followed and attacked the rear guard to-day in force, with infantry, cavalry, and artillery, and that it is probable he will make a demonstration or attack in our front to-morrow. You will place your corps in position in the vicinity of Freeman's Ford to meet this, and will hold it ready to move to the support of the force on your left or to move to your right.

The Second Corps has moved to Bealeton and the Fifth Corps is on your left at Beverly Ford. Your pickets will connect with those of the Fifth Corps on your left. On your right General Gregg will be directed to picket down as far as Freeman's Ford. General Sykes has been directed to post a stong force of infantry and artillery on the Yew Hills, on the south side of the Rappahannock. You will be responsible for the river as far down as Beverly Ford.

A. A. HUMPHREYS,
Major-General, and Chief of Staff.

HEADQUARTERS ARMY OF THE POTOMAC,
October 11, 1863—8.30 p. m.

Commanding Officer Second Corps:

The major-general commanding directs me to inform you that the enemy followed and attacked our rear guard to-day in force, with infantry, cavalry, and artillery, and that he will probably make a demonstration or an attack to-morrow on our front. You will hold your corps ready to move at very short notice, either in support or to advance or to meet a flank movement. All trains are directed to be moved so far from the river as to be out of artillery fire from the south bank.

Very respectfully, your obedient servant,

A. A. HUMPHREYS,
Major-General, and Chief of Staff.

HEADQUARTERS ARMY OF THE POTOMAC,
October 11, 1863—7.45 p. m.

Corps Commanders:

The major-general commanding directs that all trains be parked at such a distance from the river as to be out of the reach of artillery fire from the south bank.

A. A. HUMPHREYS,
Major-General, Chief of Staff.

CIRCULAR.] HEADQUARTERS FIFTH ARMY CORPS,
October 11, 1863.

The Second Division will cross the river at daylight to-morrow by a bridge to be thrown in front of the Hamilton house. Three batteries of artillery will follow it.

The Third Division will follow the artillery.

General Ayres will take possession of the bald hill (Yew Hill), posting the artillery on the most advantageous points, his infantry behind the crest of the hill, extending well to the right.

The Third Division will be posted on General Ayres' left, and will be made to take advantage of any stone walls or ravines that may be there.

The pickets of these two divisions will precede them and will be thrown well to the front of the position assumed.

The First Division and the remaining batteries will be held ready to cross the river at a moment's notice when so directed from these headquarters.

By command of Major-General Sykes:

FRED. T. LOCKE,
Assistant Adjutant-General.

OCTOBER 12, 1863—11.30 a. m.
(Received 12.30 p. m.)

Major-General HALLECK:

This army was yesterday withdrawn to the north side of the Rappahannock. Although the movement was delayed, the enemy offered no opposition till 1 p. m., when the rear guard of cavalry was attacked by cavalry and artillery supported by infantry.

Brigadier-General Buford, who had crossed the Rapidan the evening before and had moved up on the south side as far as Morton's Ford, here met a superior force of cavalry, supported by infantry, who compelled him to recross to the north side and fall back till he effected a junction with the rear guard of the army.

The intentions of the enemy are as yet undeveloped. My cavalry on the right have not as yet reported any movement in that direction, and the strong force in my rear yesterday renders the theory of their intending to get in my rear less probable. In order to ascertain the condition of things in my front, I have ordered Major-General Sedgwick, with two corps and a division of cavalry, to recross the river and advance to Brandy Station, and ascertain if any considerable force is in my front. If Lee will give me battle between the Rappahannock and the Rapidan I will fight him, although in doing so I feel confident I shall have to attack, and from all the information I can get, it is my opinion his forces are nearly, if not quite, equal to mine.

Our losses yesterday will probably amount to 400 killed, wounded, and missing.

GEO. G. MEADE,
Major-General, Commanding.

OCTOBER 12, 1863—8 p. m. (Received 9 p. m.)

Major-General HALLECK:

General Sedgwick has advanced to Brandy Station, and General Buford to the vicinity of Culpeper Court-House. A small force of cavalry and a few pieces of artillery was all the opposition encountered. General Sedgwick reports that people living on the road say Stuart's whole cavalry force, that was in our front last night, passed up the river to our right this morning, and that the soldiers said Lee's army was moving into Manassas Gap. General Gregg's division of cavalry is on my right, and has sent parties up toward the mountains. I having held in view this movement of Lee as probable, I hope during the night to get some information from him to confirm or disprove this report, now derived only from soldiers' talk with citizens. The moment I can ascertain anything definite, I will fall back by forced marches. In the meantime, it is proper you should be advised of this report, because, if true, Lee may get between me and Washington, and you may be annoyed then.

GEO. G. MEADE,
Major-General, Commanding.

OCTOBER 12, 1863—10 p. m.
(Received 10.10 p. m.)

Major-General HALLECK:

Information has just been received from General Gregg that the enemy have forced the passage of the river at Sulphur Springs, having driven him back, and that large columns of infantry and artillery have been seen passing up the river. There is no doubt the whole of Lee's army is crossing on my immediate right. If I am not attacked to-morrow, I shall move toward him and attack him.

GEO. G. MEADE,
Major-General, Commanding.

WASHINGTON,
October 12, 1863—9 a. m.

Major-General MEADE:

What news this morning? A dispatch from Rosecrans, leaving him at 7.30 p. m. yesterday, says:

Rebel rumors that head of Ewell's column reached Dalton yesterday.

I send this for what it is worth.

A. LINCOLN.

HEADQUARTERS ARMY OF THE POTOMAC,
October 12, 1863—12.30 p. m.   (Received 1.10 p. m.)

His Excellency the President:

Your telegram received. I have just sent a dispatch to General Halleck which will answer your inquiry. We took yesterday some 50 prisoners and some deserters. There is no doubt but that up to yesterday the whole of Hill's and Ewell's corps were here, and some say re-enforced by Pickett's division and other troops from Richmond. Lee never would have made the movements he has, leaving a strong position, if he were weakened by the detachment of any portion of Ewell's or Hill's corps.

GEO. G. MEADE,
Major-General.

BEVERLY FORD,
October 12, 1863—9.50 a. m.

General HUMPHREYS,
    Chief of Staff:

No infantry or artillery discernable opposite the ford. Quite a large force of cavalry massed opposite to the right of where they were grazing this morning early, Dr. Green's house. They seem to be concentrating at this point and in rear of it in the woods.

HOLLAND,
Signal Officer.

P. S.—The ridge this side of Brandy Station has some force upon it. That which can be seen appears to be cavalry and a battery.

GEO. SYKES,
Major-General.

HEADQUARTERS ARMY OF THE POTOMAC,
October 12, 1863—10.15 a. m.

Commanding Officer Sixth Corps:

The major-general commanding directs that you hold your command in readiness to move forward immediately, with ammunition and ambulance trains, leaving the other trains where they are now parked. The major-general commanding desires to see you in person immediately.

Very respectfully, your obedient servant,
A. A. HUMPHREYS,
Major-General, and Chief of Staff.

HEADQUARTERS ARMY OF THE POTOMAC,
October 12, 1863—10.20 a. m.

Commanding Officer Fifth Corps:

The major-general commanding directs that you hold your corps ready to move forward immediately with ammunition and ambulance trains. Instructions to march will be sent you as soon as they can be prepared.

Very respectfully, &c.,
A. A. HUMPHREYS,
Major-General, and Chief of Staff.

HEADQUARTERS ARMY OF THE POTOMAC,
October 12, 1863—10.30 a. m.

Commanding Officer Second Corps:

The major-general commanding directs that you move to Rappahannock Station with your ammunition and ambulance trains, leaving a brigade at Bealeton as a protection to the depot. General Sedgwick is ordered to take position on the heights at Brandy Station with his own corps, the Fifth Corps, and Buford's cavalry. Your corps will be held ready at Rappahannock Station to advance to Brandy Station.

Very respectfully, &c.,
A. A. HUMPHREYS,
Major-General, and Chief of Staff.

ORDERS.]   HEADQUARTERS ARMY OF THE POTOMAC,
                              October 12, 1863—10.30 a. m.

Major-General Sedgwick will, in addition to his own corps, take
command of the Fifth Corps and Buford's division of cavalry, and
advance immediately to Brandy Station, and take position on the
heights there, driving in the enemy and holding the position. He
will report his progress to the commanding general, and also the
force, position, and movements of the enemy.

By command of Major-General Meade:

                              S. WILLIAMS,
                           Assistant Adjutant-General.

(Copy to Generals Sedgwick, Sykes, Pleasonton, and Buford.)

                    HEADQUARTERS ARMY OF THE POTOMAC,
                              October 12, 1863—11 a. m.

Commanding Officer First Corps:

The major-general commanding directs me to inform you that
Major-General Sedgwick, in command of his own corps, the Fifth
Corps, and Buford's division of cavalry, will move immediately to
Brandy Station, and take position on the heights there. You will
hold your corps ready to move to that point, with ammunition and
ambulance trains.

In the event of not being able to send you the pontoons with the
order to march, you can send your ammunition and ambulance trains
to cross on the lower pontoon bridge at Rappahannock Station, the
infantry to cross, if practicable, at Kelly's Ford.

Very respectfully, &c.,

                           A. A. HUMPHREYS,
                        Major-General, and Chief of Staff.

                    HEADQUARTERS ARMY OF THE POTOMAC,
                              October 12, 1863—12 m.

Major-General SEDGWICK,
          Commanding Reconnaissance:

The major-general commanding instructs me to say that the movement intrusted to you is a reconnaissance in force to ascertain if the
enemy is in force and position near Brandy Station or in the vicinity
of Culpeper Court-House, and is prepared to give battle. This will
be accomplished by the movement of your command to the heights
near Brandy Station, and the occupation of the heights by it. This
you will do unless those heights are already held by the enemy in
superior force, of which you will immediately inform the commanding general.

If, upon your occupation of the heights, the enemy displays the
intention of giving battle there, the major-general commanding intends to throw forward rapidly the remainder of his army there and
give battle. You will advise him of the nature of the position and
of the points to which the movement of the three other corps should
be directed in coming up, and will maintain your position until the
arrival of re-enforcements.

Should the enemy make no serious opposition to your occupation of the heights, nor make dispositions to dislodge you, you will send forward Buford's cavalry toward Culpeper Court-House, to ascertain if the enemy is in force and position there or in that vicinity.

A telegraph operator will accompany you. He can attach his instrument to any point of the wire which now connects at these headquarters.

You will keep the commanding general fully acquainted with everything that transpires.

A. A. HUMPHREYS,
Major-General, and Chief of Staff.

HEADQUARTERS FIFTH ARMY CORPS,
Barbour's, October 12, 1863.

General GRIFFIN:

Throw out a strong picket well in front and to your right. Sedgwick wants that hill you are now on held. I will send you two batteries. There are two or three roads through the timber between you and Barbour's camp; but I think in two lines of battle would be best.

Keep a bright lookout to your right, and let me know anything you may learn. I am sorry your troops are not so posted as to give you this place for your headquarters. Let your ambulances and ammunition wagons form somewhere near your troops.

Yours,

GEO. SYKES,
Major-General.

HEADQUARTERS ARMY OF THE POTOMAC,
October 12, 1863—12.30 p. m.

Commanding Officer Second Corps:

The major-general commanding directs that as soon as the Sixth Corps have cleared the bridges, that you cross the river at Rappahannock Station, and, massing your troops, be prepared to move. The ammunition and ambulance trains need not cross the river, but be ready to do so as soon as the infantry moves.

Very respectfully, &c.,

A. A. HUMPHREYS,
Major-General, and Chief of Staff.

[Indorsement.]

General Sedgwick informed.

RAPPAHANNOCK STATION,
October 12, [1863]—12.03 p. m.

Brigadier-General TERRY,
Commanding Railroad Guard:

The major-general commanding directs that you hold your troops in readiness to move promptly and rapidly to the front. They will be provided, as the rest of the army are, with three days' rations in haversack, five days' bread and small rations in knapsack, and the trains with the rations required by existing orders.   The brigade at Catlett's will not, in the event of your troops being ordered up to the front, wait for the troops farther to the rear, but march at once.

A. A. HUMPHREYS,
Major-General, Chief of Staff.

HEADQUARTERS ARMY OF THE POTOMAC,
October 12, 1863—10.20 p. m.

Colonel McCALLUM :

Our military movements render it necessary that all the rolling stock on the Orange and Alexandria Railroad at the different points on the road be withdrawn at once to Alexandria, and that no more trains be sent from that point until further orders are received from these headquarters.

RUFUS INGALLS,
Brigadier-General, Chief Quartermaster.

HEADQUARTERS ARMY OF THE POTOMAC,
October 12, 1863—8 p. m.   (Received 8.05 p. m.)

Brig. Gen. D. H. RUCKER,
    Quartermaster:

I am sending in for 200 artillery horses, to be forwarded by rail.   Our losses in skirmishing from day to day will compel me to call for more artillery and cavalry horses soon.   Buford's cavalry occupy the ridge near Culpeper to-night.   We have three corps over the river, but the enemy has disappeared again, except a few cavalry.   We shall find him shortly.   I am keeping our trains as well parked and protected as possible, and the depot is free of property. The army is in fine condition.

RUFUS INGALLS,
Brigadier-General, Chief Quartermaster.

HEADQUARTERS ARMY OF THE POTOMAC,
October 12, 1863—9.15 p. m.

Commanding Officer Second Corps:

The major-general commanding directs that you fall back to Bealeton immediately.   A dispatch is just received from Gregg, saying that he is fighting the enemy at Sulphur Springs, and that their infantry is passing up the west bank of the Rappahannock.

Very respectfully, &c.,

A. A. HUMPHREYS,
Major-General, and Chief of Staff.

OCTOBER 12, 1863—9.15 p. m.

Commanding Officer Sixth Corps:

The major-general commanding directs that you fall back immediately ; your corps to Rappahannock Station ; General Sykes to

Beverly. Order back General Buford also. The enemy are endeavoring to cross at Sulphur Springs in force. General Sykes should bring his whole force this side of the Rappahannock.

A. A. HUMPHREYS,
Major-General, and Chief of Staff.

HEADQUARTERS ARMY OF THE POTOMAC,
October 12, 1863—9.30 p. m.

Commanding Officer Second Corps:

The major-general commanding directs me to inform you that the enemy are crossing in force at Sulphur Springs, and directs that you move immediately, and with the utmost dispatch, to Warrenton Junction, and take position there looking toward Warrenton. Your ammunition and ambulance trains will accompany you. Order the bridge trains to Rappahannock Station at once. You will be advised of any change of headquarters.

Very respectfully, &c.,

A. A. HUMPHREYS,
Major-General, and Chief of Staff.

(Same to commanding officer Third Corps.)

HEADQUARTERS ARMY OF THE POTOMAC,
October 12, 1863—10 p. m.

Commanding Officer Third Corps:

The major-general commanding directs you to put your corps in position looking toward Sulphur Springs and Warrenton. General Warren is ordered to Fayetteville. General Gregg is at the same place. Orders may be sent to you to move at any moment. Have your corps ready for prompt action.

Very respectfully, &c.,

A. A. HUMPHREYS,
Major-General, and Chief of Staff.

HEADQUARTERS ARMY OF THE POTOMAC,
October 12, 1863—10 p. m.

[General FRENCH :]

GENERAL : General Gregg reports that he has been driven away from Sulphur Springs, and that the enemy are crossing there in large force. There is a regiment of cavalry at Lawson's and Freeman's Fords that should connect with your pickets on the right. They may be driven in in the morning, and you may be attacked. If so, I will immediately support you, but I may also send orders requiring you to fall back. Be ready for either contingency.

GEO. G. MEADE,
Major-General.

HEADQUARTERS ARMY OF THE POTOMAC,
October 12, 1863—10.15 p. m.

Commanding Officer Second Corps:

The major-general commanding directs that you move with the utmost promptitude to Fayetteville, and put your corps in position

looking toward Sulphur Springs.   General Gregg is now at Fayette-
ville.   General French continues for the present at Freeman's Ford.
General Newton is ordered to move at once to Warrenton Junction.
General Sedgwick is ordered back to Rappahannock Station, and
Sykes to Beverly.   They will be moved as soon as they come up.
         Very respectfully, &c.,
                              A. A. HUMPHREYS,
                         Major-General, and Chief of Staff.

                              OCTOBER 12, [1863]—10.15 p. m.
Brigadier-General TERRY, *Catlett's Station:*
    The major-general commanding directs that you concentrate your
command with the utmost dispatch at Warrenton Junction.   General Newton has been ordered to that point to-night from Kelly's
Ford.   You will move your command immediately upon receipt of
this dispatch, and receive your orders from General Newton until
otherwise ordered.   The enemy are crossing the Rappahannock in
force at Sulphur Springs and above.
                              A. A. HUMPHREYS,
                         Major-General, Chief of Staff.

                    HEADQUARTERS ARMY OF THE POTOMAC,
                              October 12, 1863—10.45 p. m.
Commanding Officer First Corps:
    The major-general commanding directs that you move to Warren-
ton Junction by such route as will not carry you along the railroad.
The trains are moving along the railroad.
         Very respectfully, &c.,
                              A. A. HUMPHREYS,
                         Major-General, and Chief of Staff.

                    BALTIMORE, MD., *October 12, 1863—11 a. m.*
                              (Received 11.20 a. m.)
Hon. E. M. STANTON:
    I have heard indirectly that General Lockwood and one regiment
of infantry would be sent back to me, but I get nothing official.
Colonel Fry orders his draft, but I cannot safely let it go on in the
counties of the Eastern Shore without more troops.   If I am to have
such help, it should be immediately ordered.
                              ROBT. C. SCHENCK,
                                   Major-General.

                         WAR DEPARTMENT,
                    October 12, 1863—3.05 p. m.
Major-General SCHENCK, *Baltimore:*
    The General-in-Chief informs me that General Lockwood and a
regiment have been ordered to your command some days ago.   The
regulations in respect to colored recruits have been issued and ordered to be sent you.
                              EDWIN M. STANTON,
                                   Secretary of War.

WAR DEPARTMENT,
Washington, October 12, 1863—3.35 p. m.

Major-General SCHENCK,
Baltimore, Md.:

On the 5th, Brigadier-General Kelley was ordered to relieve General Lockwood from command of Harper's Ferry, and to send him, with a Maryland regiment, to report to the commanding general of the Middle Department.

H. W. HALLECK,
General-in-Chief.

HDQRS. ARMY AND DISTRICT OF NORTH CAROLINA,
New Berne, N. C., October 12, 1863—7 p. m.

JOHN G. FOSTER:

MY DEAR GENERAL: Yours of the 9th and 10th have just reached me, and I have been looking over the ground very closely. You need all the regiments named, and more, but the active force is very small in North Carolina from sickness and other causes. The regiments named in the order, Ninth New Jersey, Twenty-third and Twenty-seventh Massachusetts, Eighty-first New York, and Ninety-eighth New York number about 2,700, and with Heckman are the flower of the command. General Palmer is absent, leaving only General Wessells, who, by the way, reports sickness on the increase in his district. The One hundred and fifty-eighth New York, Colonel Jourdan tells me, has a great deal of sickness, and he thinks he cannot get out much over 200 for drills, &c. I have ordered him to relieve General Heckman and take his regiment to Morehead for sea air.

In view of the length of the line and other considerations, I do not think any more regiments should be drawn from North Carolina at this time. The instruction of the Twelfth New York is being pushed as rapidly as possible, but I fear it will be some time before they will render much service. Colonel Mix is at Elizabeth City with 350 men, as I advised, for the purpose of breaking up Col. James W. Hinton's arrangements for raising a regiment, and had I anticipated your operations, I would not have sent him. However, I think he will be back before the regiments all reach you. At all events, I will write the colonel to shorten his time somewhat.

On the 9th, I mounted my horse for the first time since April, when my horse was thrown down upon me with great violence while forming line of battle. The experiment was not as satisfactory as I wish, but I hope in time to recover from the blow near the spine.

I shall be glad to run up to Plymouth with you, meeting at the outlet of the canal, or here, as you also suggest. It seems to me that you can fix the day, time, and place better than I can, and therefore I leave it to you, with the request that you will give me timely notice. I shall be glad to see you here.

I am, very truly,

JOHN J. PECK,
Major-General.

P. S.—The south part of North Carolina has been made into a new department, under General Whiting. More than the ordinary force is reported under his orders, as an attack is looked for in that quarter.

GENERAL ORDERS, }   HDQRS. DEPT. OF WEST VIRGINIA,
No. 12.   }   *Clarksburg, W. Va., October 12, 1863.*

The troops stationed at Harper's Ferry and Martinsburg, W. Va., and, generally, on the line of the Baltimore and Ohio Railroad from the Monocacy River west to Sleepy Creek, will constitute the First Division of this Department.

Brig. Gen. J. C. Sullivan, U. S. Volunteers, is assigned to the command.

By order of Brigadier-General Kelley :
THAYER MELVIN,
Assistant Adjutant-General.

SPECIAL ORDERS, }   HDQRS. DEPT. OF WEST VIRGINIA,
No. 52.   }   *Clarksburg, W. Va., October 12, 1863.*

I. In pursuance of instructions from the General-in-Chief, Brig. Gen. H. H. Lockwood, U. S. Volunteers, is relieved from duty in this department, and will report to the major-general commanding Middle Department, at Baltimore, Md.

*   *   *   *   *

By command of Brigadier-General Kelley :
THAYER MELVIN,
Assistant Adjutant-General.

HEADQUARTERS ARMY OF THE POTOMAC,
October 13, 1863—1 a. m.

Commanding Officer Cavalry Corps:

I inclose herewith a copy of the order for the movements to-day. The major-general commanding directs that such disposition be made of the cavalry as to protect the flank next the enemy and the rear of the army. A sufficient force of cavalry will likewise be held available to guard the trains in their movement from Weaverton.

Very respectfully, &c.,
A. A. HUMPHREYS,
Major-General, and Chief of Staff.

[Inclosure.]

CIRCULAR.]   HEADQUARTERS ARMY OF THE POTOMAC,
October 13, 1863—12.50 a. m.

The following movements are ordered for to-day, the 13th instant:

1. The Third Corps will move to the Three-Mile Station on the Warrenton Branch Railroad (3 miles from Warrenton Junction), and take position there, looking toward Warrenton. It will move at daylight. In crossing the road from Bealeton to Fayetteville, the commanding general of the Third Corps will send an officer to Fayetteville to inform General Warren that the Third Corps is passing. The route to be pursued by the Third Corps is indicated on the map sent by the guide.

2. The Second Corps will follow close on the Third Corps, and take position in connection with it near the Three-Mile Station.

3. The Fifth Corps will move at sunrise to Warrenton Junction,

taking the road past Anderson's (General Crawford's former head-quarters) and Germantown; it will take position in that vicinity with the Sixth Corps, and just south of the Warrenton Branch Railroad, looking toward Warrenton, and be held ready to move.

4. The Sixth Corps will move at sunrise to Warrenton Junction, on the west side of the railroad, and take position there north of the Warrenton Branch line, looking toward Warrenton, and be held ready to move. General Terry will join the Sixth Corps at this point.

5. The Reserve Artillery will move to Warrenton Junction as soon as the trains clear the road, and be held ready to move.

6. As soon as either the Fifth or Sixth Corps reaches Warrenton Junction, the First Corps will move about 5 miles along the railroad in the direction of Bristoe Station, and there be held ready to move.

7. The corps will be accompanied by their ammunition, ambulance trains, intrenching tools, and medical wagons.

8. The utmost vigilance, promptitude, and celerity will be observed in all the movements. The columns will be kept closed, and those corps next the enemy will throw out advance and rear guards and flankers.

9. Headquarters to-morrow at Warrenton Junction.

By command of Major-General Meade:

S. WILLIAMS,
Assistant Adjutant-General.

(Copy to commanding officers of corps.)

HEADQUARTERS FIFTH CORPS,
October 13, 1863—2 a. m.

Major-General HUMPHREYS,
Chief of Staff:

GENERAL: I have the honor to report that my headquarters are at the same place where they were last night. My troops are on the march back, but will not be here before daylight, the roads being very much obstructed by the troops in front.

GEO. SYKES,
Major-General, Commanding.

HEADQUARTERS,
October 13, 1863.

Major-General FRENCH:

DEAR GENERAL: I send you a guide who is recommended to me as trustworthy.

General Meade desires me to say that the enemy may wish to delay you by partial attacks. Pay no attention to them unless forced to do so. The object of both armies now is to gain certain points. They will hardly make a serious attack upon you. Should they do so, come in upon the main line of march.

The cavalry escort sent with your instructions is directed to return direct to these headquarters. That route is reported to be obstructed by guerrillas in some force.

A. A. HUMPHREYS,
Major-General, and Chief of Staff.

HEADQUARTERS,
October 13, 1863—6 a. m.

Major-General FRENCH,
Commanding Third Corps:

Your dispatch is received. If you are attacked, you must defend yourself, and, if practicable, withdraw in accordance with the order of movement. If the enemy is too strong for you, report it and re-enforcements will be sent you. General Warren is at Fayetteville. Headquarters will move from here to Bealeton.

A. A. HUMPHREYS,
Major-General, and Chief of Staff.

OCTOBER 13, 1863—7 a. m.

Brigadier-General TERRY.

Please hand the following dispatch to General Newton immediately on his arrival:

The commanding general directs that, upon the arrival at Warrenton Junction of either the Fifth or Sixth Corps, the First Corps move about 5 miles along the railroad toward Bristoe Station, and there be held ready to move.

By command of Major-General Meade:

S. WILLIAMS,
Assistant Adjutant-General.

CIRCULAR.]   HEADQUARTERS ARMY OF THE POTOMAC,
October 13, 1863.

There is good reason to believe that the enemy is moving on our left flank, Ewell's corps by the Warrenton pike, and Hill's by Salem and Thoroughfare Gap. It is hoped we are sufficiently far ahead to enable the seizure of the Centreville Heights in advance of the enemy, but if the movement is detected our flank and rear may be attacked, to guard against which all precautions must be taken. The supply trains will run by way of Wolf Run Shoals to Fairfax Station, and will be in striking distance if we are successful.

By command of Major-General Meade:

S. WILLIAMS,
Assistant Adjutant-General.

(Copy to all commanders.)

CIRCULAR.]   HEADQUARTERS ARMY OF THE POTOMAC,
October 13, 1863—1 p. m.

1. Major-General Newton will move and camp for the night at Bristoe.

2. Major-General French, Third Corps, will move to Greenwich, and camp for the night.

3. Major-General Warren, Second Corps, will follow the Third Corps to Auburn, and camp for the night at Auburn.

4. Major-General Sedgwick, Sixth Corps, will move to Kettle Run, on the line of the railroad, and camp for the night,

5. Major-General Sykes, Fifth Corps, will move to Walnut Run, near the railroad, and camp for the night.

6. The Reserve Artillery will move to Slater's Run, on the line of the railroad.

7. The trains will move to the vicinity of Brentsville.

8. Kilpatrick's division of cavalry will be at Buckland Mills, on the Warrenton and Centreville pikes.

9. Gregg's division will be between Warrenton and Auburn.

10. Buford's division will be at Warrenton Junction.

11. The regular brigade will be at Bristoe and Manassas.

This cavalry will picket from Bristoe around by Buckland Mills to Warrenton Junction, and to the right of the trains.

12. Corps commanders will call in the guards with supply and baggage trains, and put every man in the ranks that can carry a musket.

Provost guards will be reduced to the smallest possible numbers.

13. Headquarters to-night at Catlett's, near the fork of the roads to Auburn and Greenwich.

By command of Major-General Meade:

S. WILLIAMS,
Assistant Adjutant-General.

(Copy to corps and independent commanders.)

HEADQUARTERS ARMY OF THE POTOMAC,
October 13, 1863—1.30 p. m.
(Received 2.15 p. m.)

Major-General HALLECK:

The information from General Gregg last night was so positive that the enemy—having driven him from Waterloo, Sulphur Springs, and Fox's Ford, all on my right—were crossing in heavy force, that the army was put in motion as soon as the advance at Brandy could be drawn in and is now falling back. I shall occupy to-night a line from Greenwich to Bristoe Station, and continue my retrograde movement, if possible, till I get to the plains of Manassas or across Bull Run. I cannot ascertain what progress the enemy has made, as he covers his movement by a strong cavalry force, supported by infantry and artillery. General Gregg had very severe fighting with him yesterday, and met with serious loss. I will try to advise you as long as the telegraph is working.

GEO. G. MEADE,
Major-General, Commanding.

OCTOBER 13, 1863—10 p. m.
(Received 10.35 p. m.)

Major-General HALLECK:

I have positive information that Lee's army is moving on my right, Ewell by Warrenton pike, and Hill probably by Salem. This is derived from one of Gregg's men, who was dismounted in the fight of yesterday and lay in the woods all night, and from a regiment of Gregg's command that was cut off, and in getting back passed outside of Hill's corps last night on the other side of the Rappahannock.

I shall to-morrow attempt to gain the heights of Centreville by crossing at the lower fords of Bull Run, and, if I succeed, shall face Lee with my trains in my rear and await his further movements. He may, however, to-night, by a forced march, anticipate me and gain the fords in advance, but I think I am sufficiently ahead to render the success of the movement probable.

GEO. G. MEADE,
Major-General, Commanding.

CIRCULAR.]   HEADQUARTERS ARMY OF THE POTOMAC,
October 13, 1863—10.30 p. m.

The army will be massed at Centreville to-morrow, if practicable.

1. General Newton, First Corps, will move from Bristoe through Manassas Junction, keeping on the north side of the railroad, by way of Milford; thence to Centreville, by way of Mitchell's Ford, seizing and holding the heights and redoubts.

2. General Sedgwick, Sixth Corps, will move along the south side of the railroad to Manassas Junction; thence, by way of Blackburn's Ford, to the heights on the right of Centreville, looking toward Warrenton, forming on the right of the First Corps.

3. General French, Third Corps, will move from Greenwich, crossing Broad Run at Milford, a mile above Bristoe; thence to Manassas Junction on, the north side of the railroad; thence to Centreville, by way of Mitchell's Ford, forming on the left of the First Corps.

4. The Reserve Artillery will follow the Sixth Corps as far as Manassas Junction; thence, moving by way of McLean's Ford, to the rear of Centreville, and park near the pike leading from Centreville to Fairfax Court-House. Such additional batteries as may be required for the heights of Centreville will be placed in position.

5. General Sykes, Fifth Corps, will move along the north side of the railroad, crossing Broad Run at Milford, following the Third Corps, if there is not room for both to move together, and from Manassas Junction moving to Blackburn's Ford, and forming on the left of the Third Corps on the heights of Centreville.

6. General Warren, Second Corps, will move to the railroad, passing by Catlett's house, keep on the south side of the railroad, cross Bull Run at Blackburn's Ford, and mass in rear of Centreville, looking toward Warrenton.

7. Strong working parties will precede the head of each main column for the purpose of working on the crossings of the streams.

8. As the heads of columns approach Manassas Junction and Bull Run great caution will be observed, and at the crossings of Bull Run dispositions will be made to meet any attempt on the part of the enemy to attack in flank or dispute the passage.

9. The movement will commence at daylight by each corps and the Reserve Artillery, and the commanding general calls upon all for the utmost promptitude and dispatch.

Corps commanders will keep their flankers well out on the left flank, and picket all roads coming from that direction.

10. The headquarters will be found along the route of the railroad, and between the First and Sixth Corps; headquarters will be in rear of Centreville.

11. General Kilpatrick will move by way of Hay Market to Sud-

ley Springs, if practicable, and unite with Colonel Gibbs and hold that point.

General Gregg will cover the rear and left flank of General Warren. General Buford will protect the trains.

By command of Major-General Meade:

S. WILLIAMS,
Assistant Adjutant-General.

(To corps and independent commanders and commanding officer Reserve Artillery.)

WAR DEPARTMENT,
October 13, 1863—12 p. m.

Brigadier-General CANBY,
New York:

Please report what forces you have in New York, and hold them in readiness for prompt movement immediately.

EDWIN M. STANTON,
Secretary of War.

NEW YORK, N. Y., *October* 13, 1863—11.40 a. m.
(Received 12.40 p. m.)

Hon. E. M. STANTON,
Secretary of War:

The Twentieth Indiana, One hundred and fifty-second New York, First and Thirty-seventh Massachusetts, Twenty-sixth Michigan, and two batteries, about 2,000 men, can be sent at once. The Fifth Wisconsin is in the interior of the State, but can be recalled and sent immediately. About 1,200 men can be sent from Camp Sprague by consolidating incomplete organizations, and there are about 3,000 men in the interior that can be prepared and sent in a few days. I will send 1,000 to-day.

ED. R. S. CANBY,
Brigadier-General, Commanding.

WAR DEPARTMENT,
Washington, October 13, 1863—4.30 p. m.

General E. R. S. CANBY,
New York City:

Send immediately by rail all the troops that can be spared from your department. Consolidate fractional new regiments, and send them forward with dispatch.

H. W. HALLECK,
General-in-Chief.

NEW YORK CITY, *October* 13, 1863—5.30 p. m.
(Received 6.10 p. m.)

Major-General HALLECK:

Your telegram of 4.30 is received. The movement will commence at once.

ED. R. S. CANBY,
Brigadier-General.

WAR DEPARTMENT,
October 13, 1863—6.45 p. m.

S. M. FELTON, Esq.,
  Prest. of Phila., Wil. and Balt. R. R., Philadelphia:

Please be ready for immediate movement of troops from New York to Baltimore and Washington.

EDWIN M. STANTON,
Secretary of War.

(Similar dispatch to Mr. Garrett.)

WAR DEPARTMENT,
Washington, October 13, 1863—4 p. m.

Mr. GARRETT,
  Baltimore and Ohio Railroad, Baltimore, Md.:

Lee is moving north. Look well to your rolling stock. General Kelley has been notified. Expect new cavalry raids.

H. W. HALLECK,
General-in-Chief.

BALTIMORE, MD., *October 13, 1863.*
(Received 7.05 p. m.)

Major-General HALLECK,
  General-in-Chief:

I am greatly obliged by your information, and I act at once. Have ordered that no trains now west of Cumberland shall pass east of that point, and that none shall be sent to points west of Harper's Ferry until further notice. From your advices, can enemy reach us in less than twenty-four hours? If we can safely use this much time, we can work a large amount of equipment east of Harper's Ferry that may prove important in your military movement. Is any danger of raids indicated east of Harper's Ferry?

J. W. GARRETT.

WASHINGTON, D. C., *October 13, 1863—11.20 p. m.*

Mr. GARRETT,
  Baltimore and Ohio Railroad, Baltimore:

I have nothing definitive; only movement north in general terms. Kelley says a cavalry force near Martinsburg.

H. W. HALLECK,
General-in-Chief.

BALTIMORE, MD., *October 13, 1863—11 p. m.*
(Received 12 p. m.)

Hon. E. M. STANTON,
  Secretary of War:

We will be fully prepared for the movement from New York. We expect to get through to Baltimore a large equipment during the night, which we shall hold here to meet any requirements you may make. Thirteen locomotives, with full trains of loaded cars, passed through Martinsburg at 7.15 this p. m., which we hope to get through the endangered district by midnight.

J. W. GARRETT,
President.

WAR DEPARTMENT,
Washington, October 13, 1863—3.30 p. m.
Brigadier-General KELLEY,
Clarksburg, W. Va.:
Lee's army is moving north, and perhaps will go into the Shenandoah Valley. your attention is called to Harper's Ferry and the railroad in that vicinity, as cavalry raids may be made in that direction.

H. W. HALLECK,
General-in-Chief.

HEADQUARTERS FIRST SEPARATE BRIGADE,
Beverly, October 13, 1863.
Major GIBSON,
Buckhannon:
It is reported that the force at Bulltown was attacked this morning by a superior force. The Eighth and Third and a battery are moving to join you at Buckhannon. Have you heard from your patrol sent to Centreville? How much forage and subsistence is there at Buckhannon? Send some scouts to ascertain which direction the enemy takes as quickly as possible.

WM. W. AVERELL,
Brigadier-General.

CLARKSBURG, W. VA., *October* 13, 1863—3.30 p. m.
(Received 5 p. m.)
Brig. Gen. G. W. CULLUM,
Chief of Staff:
Colonel Pierce, at Martinsburg, reports the combined forces of Jones, Jenkins, and Imboden at or near Winchester last night, and that a portion of Lee's army was approaching that place also. If this information is reliable, they evidently intend a raid on the Baltimore and Ohio Railroad, or a movement into Maryland.

B. F. KELLEY,
Brigadier-General.

WAR DEPARTMENT,
October 13, 1863—7 p. m.
Brigadier-General SLOUGH,
Military Governor of Alexandria:
You are directed to give your attention exclusively to the condition of your command during the present movements, and are relieved from any other duty. On account of the sickness of Gen-

eral Heintzelman, Major-General Augur has been placed in command of the department. Your past promptness and diligence give me assurance that you need no fresh admonition.

EDWIN M. STANTON,
Secretary of War.

BALTIMORE, MD., *October* 13, 1863.
(Received 9 p. m.)

Maj. Gen. H. W. HALLECK,
General-in-Chief:

Have instructed Captain Duvall as to guard at Hog Island Light-House. Ordered (Saturday) a cavalry guard from Drummondtown to Assateague Light-House. Have no other troops but three cavalry companies on the Eastern Shore of Maryland and Virginia. Cannot get any information from General Kelley as to General Lockwood or regiments ordered here.

ROBT. C. SCHENCK,
Major-General.

HEADQUARTERS CHIEF ENGINEER OF DEFENSES,
Washington, October 13, 1863.

Hon. E. M. STANTON,
Secretary of War:

SIR: All the officers to whom the Government has committed the defense of harbors, from General Totten, Chief Engineer, down to his lowest subordinate, and all those who represent the interests of cities to be defended or the civil power of these municipalities or States, are unanimous as to the necessity of providing obstructions in channels to be defended, to arrest and detain iron-clad vessels under the fire of the shore batteries.

For the last six months or more the matter has been undergoing investigation in New York, but as yet, no practical result has flowed from it, and in the case of engineer officers, while all lay down the necessity of the thing, none can answer what it shall be. That the problem is one of exceeding difficulty all admit, but if nothing is decided as to plan even, what shall we do when the time for its use arrives?

The collection of materials alone is an immense undertaking; the fabric must be the result of time. I have devoted some thought to the matter, and have had the assistance of very able engineer officers to sketch out a project of obstructions. I believe the only way to solve the problem is to go at it practically.

An efficient barrier in the Potomac at Rozier's is estimated at about $300,000. If we should get into a war with a maritime power while the rebellion is yet powerful, Washington is, next to New York, a probable point for attack through the Potomac. It has now no formidable batteries, as New York and Boston have. The guns which will be mounted in the two new earth-works (sixteen in all) appear to be the only thing likely, for a long time, to oppose an enemy's reaching Washington through the Potomac. Should the emergency occur, therefore, the engineers and the navy would both be called on to make their opposition efficient by providing the only thing that can do so, viz, obstructions.

But Washington has no such command of resources and material as New York, Philadelphia, and Boston have. Its navy-yard would not be able to furnish the immense amount of cables required; the timber or hulks in such kind and quality as required for such an obstruction are not to be had. Hence, the necessity of a provision beforehand. But, independently of the importance of such an obstruction beforehand, it is particularly important that something should be done at once to solve this problem, and there is no better place for the experiment than here. When the thing has once been done we shall know what to do in all such cases. The importance of obstructions has been fully proved at Charleston Harbor, if we may believe that it is they which have paralyzed our fleet of iron-c ads.

In view of the above statements, I suggest that an appropriation be asked of Congress of $300,000 "for providing obstructions to be moored in the Potomac, to render the shore batteries more efficient for the protection of Washington against maritime attack," and I further request that the Secretary of War authorize a sum of $150,000 from the appropriation for "Contingencies of fortifications," or any available source, to be immediately applied to a partial construction of such obstructions, and in order to arrive speedily at some practical conclusions as to what they shall do.

I am, very respectfully, your most obedient servant,

J. G. BARNARD,
Brigadier-General, &c.

WAR DEPARTMENT,
Washington, October 13, 1863—2 p. m.

Major-General FOSTER,
Fort Monroe, Va.:

It is reported that two boats, with some 30 men, have been hovering around Hog Island, probably intending to destroy that light. Can you not send a steamer to cut off these boats, if they are really there? Lee's army has been moving for the last two days, apparently toward the Shenandoah Valley. General Meade is not yet satisfied whether it is a real movement in that direction or only a demonstration against his flank.

H. W. HALLECK,
General-in-Chief.

FORT MONROE, VA., *October* 13, 1863.
(Received 8 p. m.)

Maj. Gen. H. W. HALLECK,
General-in-Chief:

I have had a strong force in the vicinity of Hog Island for the past four days, and have left a small guard at the light-house. I will send over again at once. I wish the counties of Accomac and Northampton were in my department, so that I could arrange a sure protection by means of a few companies of loyal Virginians, with fixed guards and patrols.

J. G. FOSTER,
Major-General.

WAR DEPARTMENT,
Washington, October 13. 1863—4.15 p. m.
Maj. Gen. J. G. FOSTER,
Fort Monroe, Va.:

It is possible that we may have to call on you for re-enforcements. If so, have you transportation, and how many men can you spare for an emergency?

H. W. HALLECK,
General-in-Chief.

___

FORT MONROE, VA., *October* 13, 1863.
(Received 7.35 p. m.)
Major-General HALLECK,
General-in-Chief:

The utmost of infantry that I can send, even in an extreme emergency, is two weak brigades; but I will send to-night to North Carolina for another good brigade, which ought to be here in three days. I will do whatever you desire, and if artillery is wanted will send it also, in case of need. I think we can muster transportation enough by taking up what vessels are here. If we need more I will telegraph at once. I trust you will remember that any depletion of my force will make some positions hardly defensible in case of a strong attack, and that I shall need the troops back again as soon as the emergency is over.

J. G. FOSTER,
Major-General.

___

WAR DEPARTMENT,
October 13, 1863—11.40 a. m.
Brig. Gen. JAMES BARNES, *Norfolk, Va.:*

The attention of the Secretary of War has this evening, for the first time, been directed to your order of the 9th instant, and he is much surprised and grieved that you should have issued such an order without the authority of this Department. You are directed at once to revoke it, and not to send a flag-of-truce boat, and not to suffer any one to pass or come through your lines without the express permission of this Department. The Secretary directs me to say that he is pained that such an excess of authority should have taken place so early in your administration. You will acknowledge the receipt of this dispatch, and transmit here a copy of your order, revoking your order of the 9th.

By order of the Secretary of War.
JAS. A. HARDIE,
Assistant Adjutant-General.

___

WAR DEPARTMENT,
October 13, 1863—1.40 p. m.
Maj. Gen. J. G. FOSTER,
Comdg. Dept. of Virginia and North Carolina:

A circular issued by Brigadier-General Barnes, dated the 9th of October, and giving notice that persons will be sent beyond the lines on the 15th of this month has this evening, for the first time, reached the knowledge of the Secretary of War.   The circular is an excess of authority which no officer in the service has a right to exercise, unless by express instruction from this Department.   The Secretary has directed General Barnes immediately to revoke it.   He directs that you see that that is done, and that you issue an order prohibiting any officer in your command from permitting any one to pass through your lines without express permission from this Department.   Flags of truce and prisoners exchanged are, of course, excepted.

The Secretary is grieved that such an order should so early have marked the administration of General Barnes, and hopes that you will admonish him against the repetition.

By order of the Secretary of War:

JAS. A. HARDIE,
Assistant Adjutant-General.

WAR DEPARTMENT,
Washington, October 14, 1863—10 a. m.

Major-General MEADE,
Army of the Potomac:

Troops from New York will begin to arrive here to-day.   They will be immediately pushed forward.   General Heintzelman is sick and General Augur temporarily in his place.   Use any of his troops in your vicinity, advising him.   Keep me advised of your own and enemy's movements.

H. W. HALLECK,
General-in-Chief.

BRISTOE STATION, *October* 14, 1863.
(Received 1 p. m.)

Major-General HALLECK:

My movement thus far is successful.   Skirmishing between the cavalry and also with our rear guard.   The enemy are advancing from Warrenton, but will hardly be able to arrest my movement.

GEO. G. MEADE,
Major-General, Commanding.

HEADQUARTERS FIFTH ARMY CORPS,
October 14, 1863—5 p. m.

General HUMPHREYS:

Warren is engaged with the enemy.   His right is at Bristoe.   He says they (the enemy) are along his front.   I shall move to Bristoe at once.   There is no communication between French and myself. Sharp musketry firing is being heard.   If their army is there, two corps are little better than one, but I am afraid when darkness comes they may get between Warren and Manassas, if I do not move toward him, and even then they may get between French and myself.

Send me some word whether I shall unite with the army at Centreville to-night or remain at Bristoe.   I have no information as to where their main force is.

GEO. SYKES,
Major-General.

HEADQUARTERS ARMY OF THE POTOMAC,
October 14, 1863—7.30 p. m.

Commanding Officer Second Corps:

The major-general commanding directs that you withdraw to Centreville to-night, if it be practicable. If it is not practicable, the major-general commanding desires to know it at the earliest moment possible.

Very respectfully, &c.,

A. A. HUMPHREYS,
Major-General, and Chief of Staff.

CENTREVILLE, VA., *October* 14, 1863—10 p. m.
(Received 12.30 a. m. 15th.)

Major-General HALLECK :

The enemy attacked my rear guard, the Second Corps, at Bristoe, about 4 p. m. General Warren repulsed them, capturing a battery and over 100 prisoners. General Warren fought them until dark, the Fifth Corps returning to his support about that time. The Fifth Corps is now withdrawing and the Second will be withdrawn to-night. The army will then be here to await the further movements of the enemy.

The army is somewhat exhausted by the recent marches, and unless the enemy compels a movement to-morrow, I shall give them rest.

GEO. G. MEADE,
Major-General, Commanding.

HEADQUARTERS FIFTH ARMY CORPS,
October 14, 1863—10.30 p. m.

General HUMPHREYS :

I have withdrawn from Bristoe and am now within 2 miles of Blackburn's Ford. Warren will follow. He had withdrawn his artillery before I left him. I think Gregg has gone to Brentsville to join Buford and the trains. I think I shall bivouac between Blackburn's Ford and Centreville.

Respectfully,

GEO. SYKES,
Major-General.

CENTREVILLE, VA., *October* 14, 1863,
(Received 12.30 a. m., 15th.)

Major-General AUGUR :

Please advise me of the troops you have in front of Washington, the position and number; also, what troops are being forwarded to Fairfax Station.

GEO. G. MEADE,
Major-General.

HEADQUARTERS CHIEF ENGINEER OF DEFENSES,
Washington, October 14, 1863.

Hon. E. M. STANTON,
Secretary of War :

SIR : A Commission having been ordered by you a year ago, to examine into the system of the defenses of Washington, and that report having received your approval, I feel it proper to make a brief statement of the operations on the works and their condition.

Previous to my resumption of charge of · these works in August, 1862, the system was but a skeleton, so to speak, of a fortified line. In many important parts, indeed, though the works would be valuable as *points-d'appui* to a line of battle, they would be almost useless unless in connection with an army strong enough to be capable of giving battle. Washington required something more than this. Washington required to have all the strength that could be attained from a line of field-works ; a strength which would enable it to be defended with a moderate force against very superior numbers, at the same time furnishing to an inferior or defeated army, forced to take refuge within its lines, an impregnable barrier. In accordance with this idea, I immediately commenced operations, which were approved and confirmed by the commission. I give a brief sketch.

Fort Lyon.—Four out-works, Forts Willard, O'Rorke, Farnsworth, and Weed, have been completed and armed, and auxiliary batteries and rifle-pits connect them. The position now is a very strong one.

Fort Williams.—On Traitor's (Cooper's) Hill, has been built, also rifle-pits and batteries between it and Ellsworth. With a few pieces of field artillery in these batteries and the opposite one near Fort Lyon, and some watchfulness, a cavalry raid into Alexandria would be difficult, while they complete the system of defense against regular attacks.

Battery Garesché, a small fort, has been built near Fort Blenker. It is armed and efficient.

Fort Berry, occupying an important point between Forts Barnard and Richardson, has been built and armed.

Fort Whipple.—This powerful work, one of the finest field-works in the world, was commenced in the spring, and had its batteries ready early in June. It is now essentially complete.

Fort C. F. Smith, commenced last winter, was in readiness early this spring. It is a powerful work, and is essentially complete.

The various works on the line south of the Potomac, from Fort Lyon to Fort C. F. Smith, have, with few exceptions, undergone important modifications and improvements.

In Forts De Kalb, Craig, and Tillinghast, large bomb-proofs have been made (all the new works, except Berry, have extensive bomb-proofs), and in all, new embrasures and platforms have been made, magazines strengthened, &c. The works have been connected by rifle-pits (more properly covered ways for infantry), and at all points where artillery could be advantageously used, batteries for field guns have been constructed.

Forts Ethan Allen and *Marcy* (at Chain Bridge).—These works have been extensively repaired and improved, and large additional bomb-proofs built. They are connected and supported by covered way rifle-pits, and batteries for field guns arranged where necessary.

Fort Sumner.—The three works, Franklin, Ripley, and Alexander, have been combined into one powerful-work of this name.

Forts Mansfield, Simmons, and Bayard have been built between Sumner and Reno.

Fort Reno (formerly Pennsylvania) has been extensively modified, bomb-proofs added, and the powerful battery in advance constructed. Connecting the works mentioned (from Sumner to Reno) are Batteries Benson and Bailey, and several others, and lines of covered way rifle-pits.

Fort Kearny, a powerful work, has been built between Reno and De Russy, as also Batteries Russell, Smead, Terrill and covered way rifle-pits.

Fort De Russy.—Modified and improved. Between it and Fort Stevens, the Batteries Kingsbury and Sill and lines of rifle-pits have been constructed.

Fort Stevens (formerly Massachusetts) has been extensively enlarged and improved. Between it and Fort Slocum three new batteries and lines of rifle-pits have been constructed.

Fort Slocum, originally one of the weakest, has become one of the largest and most powerful works on the line. Between Forts Bunker Hill and Saratoga, Saratoga and Thayer, Thayer and Lincoln, numerous batteries for field guns have been built and constructed and supported by lines of rifle-pits.

Fort Lincoln has had additional bomb-proofs built. The spur or ridge between it and the Eastern Branch has been occupied by the powerful Battery Jameson, and by rifle-pits arranged as covered ways.

Fort Mahan has been strengthened by the construction of bastionets, for flanking.

Fort Meigs has been extensively enlarged. All other works not mentioned have, with scarce an exception, received considerable improvement and modification.

On nine different points having the most extensive command, 100-pounder Parrott guns have been mounted so as to bring every part of the ground in front of our line under their fire. Two new batteries, Parrott and Kemble, were built expressly for such guns, and their special function is, with Battery Cameron, to sweep the heights across the Potomac between the Chain Bridge and Fort C. F. Smith.

For the defense of the Potomac, the two water batteries (Battery Rodgers and Fort Foote) have been constructed. They are essentially finished, and are receiving their armament. The latter is a powerful inclosed work, and the most elaborate in its internal arrangements of all the defenses of Washington.

The work described is either finished or brought to a state of efficiency; still a system of works of this character demands constant watchfulness and expenditure to keep it up, and there are yet some works that require overhauling, and all of them ought to have their scarps either revetted or sloped and sodded. Fort Ward, in particular, a very important work, was built in great haste, and demands almost complete rebuilding.

It is a maxim among railroad men that "when the cars can go over the road it is half done." Turn-outs have to be made, depots, store-houses, offices, &c., have to be built. The track must be ballasted, tunnels, cuts, and embankments enlarged, and, finally, a second track must be laid. It is quite likely that this maxim will apply fully to the works about Washington. They are, essentially, brought to a condition to render the services expected of them, as a railroad over which the trains begin to pass is brought to a condition to do the service expected of it, and, like the railroad, it is likely to turn out that they are really but half finished.

I have just before indicated, in general terms, how much I can foresee that ought to be done, besides which there will, doubtless, arise innumerable demands for repairs and removal of what was hastily and imperfectly built in the first place, as well as for modifications and improvements.

I have no disposition to magnify this work. I am ready to leave it at any moment. I relinquished command and the more exciting duties of the field at a moment when they would have brought me more palpable recompense, to carry out these works, because I felt that the security of Washington demanded their perfection, and that the security of Washington meant the security of the nation's cause, and that I was the man upon whom the duty fell.

With these remarks, I recommend that an appropriation be asked of Congress of $300,000, for completing and rendering more permanent the defenses of Washington.

I am, very respectfully, your most obedient,

J. G. BARNARD,
Brigadier-General, &c.

FAIRFAX COURT-HOUSE,
October 14, 1863—10 p. m.

Maj. Gen. C. C. AUGUR, *Washington:*

Captain Strang telegraphed me about 7 o'clock that his train had been attacked by guerrillas, this afternoon, on the hill this side of Bull Run Ford. He thinks that there were about 100 wagons which had not yet crossed the ford. He asked me for a cavalry force to overtake them. I had none to send, but I am inclined to think most of the train will get through safely. I have an infantry regiment at Union Mills, within half a mile of the ford.

RUFUS KING,
Brigadier-General.

WAR DEPARTMENT,
Washington, October 14, 1863—9.50 a. m.

Major-General COUCH,
Chambersburg, Pa.:

Have you any troops which could re-enforce Harper's Ferry? It is threatened.

H. W. HALLECK,
General-in-Chief.

WASHINGTON,
October 14, 1863—2.50 p. m.

Major-General COUCH,
Chambersburg:

Will the Pennsylvania troops willingly do duty out of the State?

H. W. HALLECK,
General-in-Chief.

CHAMBERSBURG, PA., *October* 14, 1863—4.40 p. m.
(Received 6.30 p. m.)

Maj. Gen. H. W. HALLECK,
    General-in-Chief:

I have eleven companies of six-months' infantry between this place and Philadelphia. I think they would go readily where ordered. Ten companies of six-months' cavalry are on the border. About one-third of the infantry and cavalry are away now. The Tenth New Jersey is ordered to Harrisburg from Pottsville.

                          D. N. COUCH,
                             Major-General.

CLARKSBURG, W. VA., *October* 14, 1863.
(Received 10.35 p. m.)

Brigadier-General CULLUM,
    Chief of Staff:

General Sullivan reports the return of his cavalry scout from Upperville, in Loudoun County. Saw no enemy.

                          B. F. KELLEY,
                            Brigadier-General.

CLARKSBURG, W. VA., *October* 14, 1863—11 a. m.
(Received 4.35 p. m.)

Brig. Gen. G. W. CULLUM,
    Chief of Staff:

I ordered Brigadier-General Sullivan, now in command at Harper's Ferry, to order all extra stores and baggage from Martinsburg to Harper's Ferry. If cars have been ordered to remove stores from Harper's Ferry, I presume it is a mistake. I have ordered General Sullivan not to remove stores from Harper's Ferry. He reports this a. m. no enemy in sight.

                          B. F. KELLEY,
                            Brigadier-General.

NEW YORK, *October* 14, 1863—10.30 a. m.
(Received 11.40 a. m.)

Hon. E. M. STANTON,
    Secretary of War:

Orders were given yesterday morning to prepare transportation by water, but changed last evening upon the receipt of the telegram from the General-in-Chief, and all will now be sent by rail. The changes to the harbor were made last night and yesterday, and I will be able to send about 3,000 more in the course of to-day.

                    ED. R. S. CANBY,
              Brigadier-General, Commanding.

ALBANY, N. Y., *October* 14, 1863.
(Received 12.05 a. m., 15th.)

Major-General HALLECK:

Governor Seymour directs me to inform you that he has ordered all the volunteer troops in this State to New York; thence to Washington as soon as State bounty is paid. If need be, they can go at once to Washington, and the bounty be paid there. Please answer.

                                        J. B. STONEHOUSE,
                                Acting Assistant Adjutant-General.

                                    BALTIMORE, MD., *October* 14, 1863.
                                            (Received 1.45 p. m.)
Maj. Gen. H. W. HALLECK,
            General-in-Chief:
   The following is the reply of Captain Duvall to the dispatch sent him in relation to the inefficiency of the guard at Hog Island:

                                            EASTVILLE, VA.,
                                                October 14, 1863.
Colonel CHESEBROUGH,
        Assistant Adjutant-General:
   I hope the report is untrue. The island is guarded by a squad of 12 men of Captain Smith's company, and he has assured me the officer, though one of the non-commissioned, is a most faithful man. There can be no danger this time, for there is a force from Old Point with a steamer in the Sound, and troops on the adjoining island. I will look to it at once, and make sure there can come no harm. I will report to you to-morrow.

                                            R. E. DUVALL,
                                                Captain.

                            WM. H. CHESEBROUGH,
                                Assistant Adjutant-General.

                                    MARTINSBURG, VA., *October* 14, 1863.
                                            (Received 3.30 p. m.)
Colonel SHARPE,
        Headquarters Army of the Potomac:
   Have just received information from a scout sent out by me that part of Ewell's corps was this side the Shenandoah River, on the Berryville road.

                                    MICHAEL GRAHAM.

                                    BALTIMORE, MD., *October* 14, 1863.
                                            (Received 10 p. m.)
Col. G. H. SHARPE,
        Assistant Provost-Marshal-General:
   Report from our friends:

                                        RICHMOND, *October* 4.
   Lee advancing with 55,000 men. Hill and Longstreet cannot return. Very few soldiers in and about Richmond. Throwing up more works on Mechanicsville road.

                                    J. L. McPHAIL.

                                        CLARKSBURG,
                                    October 14, 1863—8 p. m.
Brigadier-General AVERELL,
                Beverly:
   Jackson has retreated toward Sutton. He may return to Huntersville through Webster County. Can you not cut him off at some

point? I think some of the officers of the Second or Tenth [West Virginia] know that country thoroughly, and could do it. He has probably from 500 to 600 men. Imboden was at Front Royal last night with about 1,000 men. Thirteen rebels killed and about 60 wounded at Bulltown.

B. F. KELLEY,
Brigadier-General.

HEADQUARTERS FIRST SEPARATE BRIGADE,
Beverly, October 14, 1863.

Brig. Gen. B. F. KELLEY:

I have sent strong patrols from Buckhannon to Elkwater via Centreville. The enemy will, I think, go up Elk via the Glades to Cackleytown, and it would be a waste of time and horses to go after him in Webster. The enemy charged upon my pickets night before last without meeting any success, and at 3 p. m. to-day they were found in considerable strength on Cheat Mountain. I would like to know what they propose to do in front before undertaking anything which would diminish my command. All this activity must be to cover a real attack somewhere, or else the movement of Lee's army to the west. We shall know in a day or two. Cackleytown or Lewisburg would be very good points to cut off Jackson.

WM. W. AVERELL,
Brigadier-General.·

FORT MONROE, VA., *October 14, 1863—9.10 a. m.*

Lieut. Col. J. A. HARDIE,
Assistant Adjutant-General:

· Your telegram received. General Barnes is not to blame, as he acted by my orders.

There are in Norfolk, Portsmouth, and vicinity many paupers and old persons, who are now or soon will be a burden upon the Government, but who have means of support beyond our lines. Also many persons inimical to the Government, who now prefer to go beyond the lines, and whose influence is prejudicial to the restoration of industry and trade, and the proper feeling of loyalty. I decided that all such persons should be sent beyond the lines as a military necessity. This is the same course as that pursued in North Carolina, which resulted in ridding the towns held by us of all disloyal people and white paupers, and in creating a spirit of satisfaction among the remaining ones toward their rulers. I did not consider it necessary to obtain the authority of the Secretary of War, because I suppose it to be my duty to attend to all without troubling the Secretary with matters in my department relating to the welfare of the people under military rule, and necessary to the restoration of a feeling of loyalty to the Government.

Please make my regrets to the Secretary of War that this action does not meet his sanction. Also present reasons for the action, and request that he approve of it, so that it may now be carried out. No persons except those described above sent as a military necessity are ever permitted to pass our lines without a special permit from the Secretary of War.

J. G. FOSTER, ·
Major-General.

WAR DEPARTMENT,
October 14, 1863—2.05 p. m.

Maj. Gen. J. G. FOSTER,
  Commanding at Fort Monroe, Va.:

Your dispatch of this morning has been received. By reference to the circular of the 9th instant, you will find that it is not placed upon any military necessity in your department, but upon the request of numerous persons in Norfolk, and extends the privilege to all persons desiring to avail themselves of that opportunity. The Department had no knowledge of the facts inducing the circular or its purposes excepting as expressed upon its face, and no proceeding could be more objectionable than its purport.

The privilege of passing persons beyond our lines into the rebel territory has never been exercised in any department before, to my knowledge, without the express authority of this Department, save only in the case of a military necessity arising so suddenly that a military commander was compelled to act without previous communication with the Department. Were the privilege confined to the persons enumerated in your telegram, to wit, "Paupers and old persons who are now or soon will be a burden upon the Government," there would be no objection raised; but even for such purpose and applied to such persons, the express authority of the Government ought to be obtained, if circumstances would admit of time enough to present the matter to the Government. Restricting the order to the class of persons enumerated in your telegram, namely, "Paupers and old persons in Norfolk and Portsmouth and the vicinity, who are or soon will be a burden upon the Government," you are authorized to place them beyond your lines. No other persons should be allowed to pass excepting upon the express authority of this Department. A large number of applications are now pending, and persons applying for permission to go by flag-of-truce boat from Fort Monroe are, and for months have been, daily refused.

If, in your judgment, military necessity should require the removal of any other obnoxious persons, or persons of any other class than those enumerated, the convenience and facility of telegraphing will enable you to submit the matter to the Department, together with the facts, and obtain instructions. Very great evils have at different times been occasioned by the indiscriminate privilege of passing from Fort Monroe beyond our lines, or of coming within our lines at that place, and hence so much importance is attributed to the matter.

EDWIN M. STANTON,
Secretary of War.

———

WAR DEPARTMENT,
October 14, 1863—2.05 p. m.

Brigadier-General BARNES,
  Commanding at Norfolk, Va.:

A dispatch received this morning from Major-General Foster assumes the responsibility of the circular of the 9th of October, bearing your name, and relieves you from any responsibility in regard to it. While, therefore, the order itself, in the terms in which it is expressed, is not approved, no blame is attributed to you.

EDWIN M. STANTON,
Secretary of War.

MINNESOTA,
October 14, 1863—a. m.

Maj. Gen. J. G. FOSTER, U. S. Army,
    Comdg. Dept. of Virginia and North Carolina:

GENERAL : The Fahkee came in last evening, and I will send her with the inclosed* to Captain Sands, instructing him to make the reconnaissance of Smith's Island, unless you have a good opportunity to send it. This service will be willingly rendered if you have no better means than ours, and are willing to rely on navy scouting. If you make a detail, I will instruct Captain Sands to afford desired facilities.

I have the honor to be, general, respectfully, yours,
S. PHILLIPS LEE,
Acting Rear-Admiral, &c.

———

GENERAL ORDERS, }   HDQRS. NORFOLK AND PORTSMOUTH,
    No. 13.   }   *Norfolk, Va., October 14, 1863.*

The following order is hereby transmitted:

GENERAL ORDERS, }   HDQRS. DEPT. OF VIRGINIA AND NORTH CAROLINA,
    No. 17.   }   *Fort Monroe, Va., October 10, 1863.*

The proceedings of the Military Commission instituted for the trial of David M. Wright, of Norfolk, Va., by Special Orders, Nos. 195, 196, and 197, of 1863, from the headquarters of the Department of Virginia, having, in accordance with section 5 of the act of Congress approved July 17, 1863, been submitted to the President of the United States, and the sentence having been approved, and the execution ordered by the President at such time and place as the major-general commanding the department may appoint, it is therefore ordered that the sentence that the accused, David M. Wright, of Norfolk, be hung by the neck until he be dead, be carried into execution on Friday next, the 16th day of October, at 10 o'clock in the forenoon, at such place in or near Norfolk as Brig. Gen. James Barnes, commanding United States forces at that place, may designate.

By command of Major-General Foster:
SOUTHARD HOFFMAN,
Assistant Adjutant-General.

In accordance with the above order, the execution of Dr. Wright will take place at the Fair Grounds, near this city, at the time specified above.† The Twenty-first Connecticut Volunteers, One hundred and eighteenth New York Volunteers, and Regan's battery (without pieces), will be present, under the command of Colonel Dutton.

The provost-marshal is charged with the execution of this order.

By command of Brig. Gen. J. Barnes:
GEORGE H. JOHNSTON,
Assistant Adjutant-General.

———

SPECIAL ORDERS, }   WAR DEPT., ADJT. GENERAL'S OFFICE,
    No. 460.   }   *Washington, October 14, 1863.*

*   *   *   *   *   *   *

9. Brig. Gen. Thomas A. Rowley, U. S. Volunteers, will repair without delay to Portland, Me., and relieve Maj. Charles J. Whiting, Second U. S. Cavalry, in command of the depot for drafted men at that place.

———

* Not found.
† See Order of October 22,

As soon as relieved, Major Whiting will at once repair to this city and report in person at the War Department.

*   *   *   *   *   *   *

25. By direction of the President of the United States, Maj. Gen. C. C. Augur will temporarily relieve Major-General Heintzelman from the command of the Department of Washington and of the Twenty-second Army Corps.*

*   *   *   *

By order of the Secretary of War:

E. D. TOWNSEND,
Assistant Adjutant-General.

HEADQUARTERS FIFTH ARMY CORPS,
October 15, 1863—12.30 a. m.

General HUMPHREYS:

Your last dispatch was received after I had crossed Bull Run and was 2 miles this side of it. My troops will be bivouacked there. There is no water that I could see. Shall they continue to Centreville in the morning, in pursuance of the order of yesterday?

Respectfully,

GEO. SYKES.

[P. S.]—My headquarters are about a mile in rear of my troops, at a house on the right-hand side of the road going from Centreville to Bull Run. The orderly who carries this dispatch knows where they are. My troops will not all get to their ground before 3 a. m.

WASHINGTON,
October 15, 1863—2 a. m.

Major-General MEADE:

There are no troops in front of Washington south of the Potomac, excepting those in the works, say 7,000, and the guard in and around Alexandria. I do not know what troops, if any, are on their way to Fairfax Station, but will have you informed before morning. General King has about 2,000 men under him at Fairfax Court-House and other points in that vicinity.

C. C. AUGUR,
Major-General.

WASHINGTON,
October 15, 1863—4.30 a. m.

Major-General MEADE:

To your question to General Augur, what troops are being forwarded to Fairfax Station, the reply is that there are six regiments and two batteries (old volunteer troops) on their way from New York to the Army of the Potomac. These regiments number about 3,000.

JAS. A. HARDIE,
Assistant Adjutant-General.

---

* Major-General Augur assumed command same day.

HEADQUARTERS ARMY OF THE POTOMAC,
October 15, 1863—7 a. m.

Commanding Officer First Corps:

I presume you have an advance force on the pike where it crosses Cub Run. A division was ordered to be sent by you to Bull Run Bridge, but subsequently Cub Run Bridge was substituted for it.

Very respectfully, &c.,

A. A. HUMPHREYS,
Major-General, and Chief of Staff.

———

HEADQUARTERS ARMY OF THE POTOMAC,
October 15, 1863—7 a. m.

Commanding Officer Third Corps:

The major-general commanding directs that you move your corps immediately to Union Mills, so as to hold that position and send a division to Fairfax Station to cover and hold that point.

Very respectfully, &c.,

A. A. HUMPHREYS,
Major-General, and Chief of Staff.

———

HEADQUARTERS ARMY OF THE POTOMAC,
October 15, 1863—7 a. m.

Commanding Officer Fifth Corps:

The major-general commanding directs that you move your corps to Fairfax Court-House, and hold the roads leading to that point. The most important point in that locality is marked Germantown on the map, where three or four roads unite. General Sedgwick holds the Little River turnpike near Chantilly. French will be at Union Mills, with a division at Fairfax Station.

Very respectfully, &c.,

A. A. HUMPHREYS,
Major-General, and Chief of Staff.

———

HEADQUARTERS ARMY OF THE POTOMAC,
October 15, 1863—7 a. m.

Commanding Officer Sixth Corps:

The major-general commanding directs that you concentrate your corps on the Little River turnpike, in the vicinity of the cross-roads at Sanders' toll-gate, so as to prevent the approach of the enemy in that direction.

Very respectfully, &c.,

A. A. HUMPHREYS,
Major-General, and Chief of Staff.

———

HEADQUARTERS ARMY OF THE POTOMAC,
October 15, 1863—7.15 a. m.

Commanding Officer Second Corps:

The major-general commanding directs that you place your corps on the left of General Newton's, so as to hold the heights and Mitchell's and Blackburn's Fords. General French is ordered to

Union Mills, and will cover McLean's Ford. General Sedgwick is on the Little River pike near the cross-roads at Sanders' toll-gate. Sykes is ordered to Fairfax Court-House. Your pickets should connect with Newton's and French's.

Very respectfully, &c.,

A. A. HUMPHREYS,
Major-General, and Chief of Staff:

HEADQUARTERS ARMY OF THE POTOMAC,
October 15, 1863—7.45 a. m.

Brigadier-General KING, *Commanding, &c.:*

The commanding general directs me to advise you that his forces now occupy the line of Union Mills, Centreville, and Chantilly. Any forces you may have had in front of this line he presumes have already fallen back within it. For the present, the general desires that you will, as heretofore, guard the railroad toward Alexandria. He has not at this moment any request to make with regard to Colonel Lowell's cavalry, except to ask that he may be promptly furnished with all information respecting the movements of the enemy.

Very respectfully, &c.,

S. WILLIAMS,
Assistant Adjutant-General.

HEADQUARTERS ARMY OF THE POTOMAC,
·October 15, 1863—8.45 a. m.

Commanding Officer First Corps:

The major-general commanding directs me to say that he considers one division sufficient to hold the works on the heights of Centreville. The remainder of your force should be held massed at some point between you and General Sedgwick, ready to take position. General Sedgwick is ordered to concentrate on the Little River pike in the vicinity of the cross-roads at Sanders' toll-gate. You should retain a force at Cub Run Bridge, and your picket line should connect with Sedgwick on the right and Warren on the left. French is ordered to Union Mills. Sykes to Fairfax Court-House. Warren's troops are now on the heights above Blackburn's and Mitchell's Fords. Pickets should be well out.

Very respectfully, &c.,

A. A. HUMPHREYS,
Major-General, and Chief of Staff.

HEADQUARTERS ARMY OF THE POTOMAC,
October 15, 1863—9.15 a. m.

Commanding Officer Third Corps:

The major-general commanding directs me to say that you should hold McLean's Ford. This ford is about a mile below Blackburn's Ford. General Warren will hold Blackburn's Ford on the left. Your pickets should connect with his on the right. General Buford is directed to picket the Occoquan.

A. A. HUMPHREYS,
Major-General, and Chief of Staff.

HEADQUARTERS ARMY OF THE POTOMAC,
October 15, 1863—10.30 a. m.
Commanding Officer Fifth Corps:

The major-general commanding directs me to inform you that
Brig. Gen. Rufus King has been ordered to report to you with his
division at Fairfax Court-House. Such of his troops as are guard-
ing the railroad (with the exception of those at Fairfax Station) will
remain on that duty.
Very respectfully, &c.,
A. A. HUMPHREYS,
Major-General, and Chief of Staff.

HEADQUARTERS ARMY OF THE POTOMAC,
Centreville, October 15, 1863—12 m.
(Received 1.45 p. m.)
Maj. Gen. H. W. HALLECK,
General-in-Chief:

Generals Warren and Sykes were successfully withdrawn last
night, and the army is now at Union Mills, Centreville, Chantilly,
and Fairfax Court-House, awaiting the movements of the enemy.
The cavalry is out on the flank and the front, endeavoring to ascertain the position and movements of the enemy. General Warren engaged yesterday Heth's division, of Hill's corps, inflicting
serious injury on it, taking 5 guns and 450 prisoners. Among the
prisoners are soldiers just from Charleston. The reports of the prisoners are that Hill's and Ewell's corps, re-enforced to a reported
strength of 80,000, are advancing on me, their plan being to secure
the Bull Run field in advance of me. They started five days ago
with seven days' rations with the men and large supply trains.

I am unable to surmise whether Lee will await opening his communication with Gordonsville, or whether he will continue his advance. In the latter case, I suppose he will turn me again, probably
by the right, with his back to the mountain, in which case I shall
either fall on him or retire nearer Washington, according as his
movements indicate the probability of his being able to concentrate
more rapidly than I can. I have ordered General King, with such
of his troops as are at Fairfax Court-House and Station, to report to
Major-General Sykes, Fifth Corps.
GEO. G. MEADE,
Major-General, Commanding.

UNION MILLS,
October 15, 1863.
General HUMPHREYS,
Chief of Staff:

The enemy are reconnoitering the fords with cavalry and artillery,
not in large force. A rapid crossing of our cavalry at Mitchell's
Ford would break it up.
WM. H. FRENCH,
Major-General.

OCTOBER 15, [1863]—12.30 p. m.

General HUMPHREYS:

Colonel Smith has just sent in a man, whom he directed to say—

That he had got out about 2 miles beyond Bull Run, and finds rebel cavalry at Manassas, and a cloud of dust beyond.

It is not made in writing. I have sent Colonel Smith pencil and paper, and directed him to report hourly, and oftener, if anything important occurs.

G. K. WARREN,
Major-General.

MCLEAN'S FORD,
October 15, 1863—3 p. m.

Major NORVELL,
Assistant Adjutant-General, Third Corps:

MAJOR: The enemy have attacked me with cavalry, supported by a full battery of artillery. I cannot reach them with my guns (one section), light twelves.

G. MOTT,
Brigadier-General.

UNION MILLS,
October 15, 1863.

General HUMPHREYS:

The firing is at McLean's Ford. The enemy have a battery of rifled guns, supported by cavalry.

WM. H. FRENCH,
Major-General.

HEADQUARTERS SECOND ARMY CORPS,
October 15, [1863]—3 p. m.

Major-General HUMPHREYS,
Chief of Staff:

The cannonading has been all by the enemy, and I think is a blind to some other movement. All our cavalry are on this side of the river, and my pickets are firing with the rebel dismounted cavalry, which do not amount to anything.

We see about 1,000 rebel infantry moving across the bottom land toward Union Mills in plain open sight. I also see a single horseman on the high bluff opposite that place.

It cannot be possible that the enemy can intend to advance in this direction. I think I could give them a day's work by myself. It is reported that General French's pickets are coming back from across Bull Run, and that General French says he can be driven from his position.

I may open on the enemy if I get a good chance.

G. K. WARREN,
Major-General.

3.15 p. m.

[P. S.]—Since writing the within, the enemy opened on my wagon train containing the supplies I was issuing, and ran us off. We are replying.

HEADQUARTERS ARMY OF THE POTOMAC,
October 15, 1863—4 p. m.
(Received 4.20 p. m.)
Maj. Gen. H. W. HALLECK,
General-in-Chief:

I have an abundance of artillery, perhaps more even than can be used to advantage, but I should be very glad to have all the infantry and cavalry you can send me.

GEO. G. MEADE,
Major-General, Commanding.

HEADQUARTERS SECOND ARMY CORPS,
October 15, 1863—4 p. m.
Major-General HUMPHREYS:

There is considerable cannonading in the direction of Brentsville, going on now. General Kilpatrick sent an officer just now to ask what the firing here meant, and I told him. He said nothing important was passing along the part of the line he was conversant with. I am more and more convinced that all that is going on in my front is mere humbug. It is meant to cover either a retreat or a flank movement. General Buford is probably in a position to settle which it is. No damage done by the cannonading.

G. K. WARREN,
Major-General, Commanding.

WAR DEPARTMENT,
Washington, October 15, 1863—3 p. m.
Major-General MEADE,
Army of the Potomac:

Advices from Rosecrans that Jeff. Davis was with Bragg's army on Saturday, and promised them more re-enforcements. Reports from Richmond make Lee's present force only 55,000. Is he not trying to bully you, while the mass of the rebel armies are concentrating against Rosecrans? I cannot see it in any other light. Instead of retreating, I think you ought to give him battle. From all the information I can get, his force is very much inferior to yours.

H. W. HALLECK,
General-in-Chief.

OCTOBER 15, [1863]—7 p. m.
General MEADE:

The firing of General Buford toward Brentsville (I suppose it was him near that place) seemed very much to disconcert the enemy in my front. They soon after retired without any special demonstration from me. This force consisted of a battery, one gun (a Whitworth), supported by a pretty large force of cavalry (a brigade at least visible), and some footmen, perhaps 1,000 strong. General Buford seemed to drive the enemy all the time.

I think Lee's game is blocked, and that he will retreat when pressed. It may be, though, that he still contemplates an advance around our right. I believe we can whip him in any fair fight, even by attacking.

If you wish, I can push forward again and see what is going on in my front, if you are still in doubt about the enemy's movements. I am very tired, or I would come down to see you.

Respectfully,

G. K. WARREN.

[P. S.]—The officers of the corps are very much delighted with your compliment, and I am more than pleased—am very grateful.

SIGNAL STATION, GENERAL WARREN'S HEADQUARTERS,
October 15, 1863—9.25 p. m.

Major-General HUMPHREYS:

The enemy, I believe, had a thin picket line at dark along Bull Run. We could see a little force at Manassas, but could not say how much. I think there is no considerable force in my front.

G. K. WARREN,
Major-General.

HEADQUARTERS ARMY OF THE POTOMAC,
October 15, 1863. (Received 6.30 a. m., 16th.)

Major-General FRENCH,
Union Mills:

Buford reports he still needs assistance. Send a brigade at early daylight. Wolf Run Ford is on Bull Run, 1½ miles below Union Mills. It is laid down on the McDowell map.

GEO. G. MEADE,
Major-General.

NEW YORK, *October* 15, 1863.
(Received 3.40 p. m.)

Col. J. C. KELTON,
Assistant Adjutant-General:

The Fifth Wisconsin will leave for Washington this afternoon. Shall I arm the new organizations coming in from the interior of the State? It will perhaps save time to send them on direct.

ED. R. S. CANBY,
Brigadier-General, Commanding.

WASHINGTON, D. C.,
October 15, 1863—6.20 p. m.

General CANBY,
New York City:

I think all troops from the interior should be sent on direct.

H. W. HALLECK,
General-in-Chief.

CHAMBERSBURG, PA., *October* 15, 1863.
(Received 11 p. m.)
Maj. Gen. H. W. HALLECK,
General-in-Chief:

I have ordered Colonel Boyd, with eight companies of cavalry, to Sharpsburg. No artillery has been ordered to Harper's Ferry. Three batteries could be sent.

D. N. COUCH,
Major-General.

WAR DEPARTMENT,
Washington, October 15, 1863—3 p. m.
Major-General COUCH,
Chambersburg, Pa.:

Such troops as you can move will be sent to Harper's Ferry.

H. W. HALLECK,
General-in-Chief.

HEADQUARTERS FIRST SEPARATE BRIGADE,
Beverly, October 15, 1863.
Brig. Gen. B. F. KELLEY,
Commanding Department, Clarksburg:

The following dispatch has just been received from Buckhannon :

Camp Canaan is 23 miles from above this, on the Centreville road. A loyal citizen, by name Waugh, from there an hour since, gives the following information : Seven hundred rebels, he says, will camp to-night at Camp Canaan. This is part of Jackson's force. The force that attacked Bulltown and the force to camp at Canaan were to form a junction at this place on to-morrow or Saturday. At the same time there was to be an attack on Beverly, the rebel force at this place to attack your rear at Beverly. Waugh receives his information from a deserter from Jackson. The force here about 100 fighting men.

H. H. HAGANS,
Captain, Commanding Post.

What do you think of it?

WM. W. AVERELL,
Brigadier-General.

HEADQUARTERS FIRST SEPARATE BRIGADE,
Beverly, October 15, 1863.
Brig. Gen. B. F. KELLEY,
Clarksburg.

Have just heard from Cheat Mountain. It is supposed that Hutton's and Marshall's companies are on the summit. The Tenth [West Virginia] will attempt to surprise them at daylight. Lieutenant-Colonel Scott has gone with the Second [West Virginia] toward Addison, via Elkwater, with instructions to blockade the road and defend it, and picket toward Big Spring. The force at Buckhannon has been directed to investigate the truth of Waugh's report.

WM. W. AVERELL,
Brigadier-General.

CLARKSBURG,
October 15, 1863.

Brigadier-General SCAMMON,
Charleston:

Jackson is retreating up Bryant's Fork of the Little Kanawha toward Addison, in Webster County. Cavalry are pursuing him. Jackson lost 13 killed and 60 wounded in his attack on Bulltown. Our loss trifling. Our men were covered by breastworks.

B. F. KELLEY,
Brigadier-General.

FORT MONROE, *October* 15, 1863.
(Received 11.15 a. m.)

Hon. E. M. STANTON,
Secretary of War:

I have the honor to acknowledge your telegrams of October 14. Hereafter all cases of application to go beyond our lines will be submitted to you for approval. In the present case shall I forward descriptive lists of those proposed to be passed and await your approval?

J. G. FOSTER,
Major-General of Volunteers.

GENERAL ORDERS, }   HDQRS. DEPT. OF VA. AND N. C.,
No. 19.   }   *Fort Monroe, Va., October* 15, 1863.

The people of the county of Norfolk and the cities of Norfolk and Portsmouth having duly elected judicial officers, and such officers having duly entered upon their duties, it is hereby ordered that the provost court of this department shall no longer entertain jurisdiction of civil suits in those places, excepting those in which any officer or enlisted man in the United States Army or Navy, or any person in the employ of the United States military or naval forces, shall be a party, or in which any property, real or personal, owned or claimed by the United States, or the United States forces, or any person serving in them, shall be at stake. This order shall not be held to in any way affect suits now pending in the provost court, nor the existence of martial law in this department.

By command of Major-General Foster:

SOUTHARD HOFFMAN,
Assistant Adjutant-General.

MARTINSBURG, VA., *October* 16 [15], 1863.
(Received 2.30 a. m.)

H. W. HALLECK,
General-in-Chief:

SIR: From rebel prisoners captured to-day I honestly believe that two brigades of Johnson's division, Longstreet's corps, crossed yesterday morning, the 14th, at daylight, near Strasburg, in the direction of Clear Spring or Cherry Run; also Imboden's cavalry. I believe this to be reliable.

MARTINSBURG, VA.—1 a. m.

I also have it from reliable sources that Jenkins is advancing, with 4,000 men, cavalry and infantry, and sixteen pieces of artillery, by the way of Strasburg, Berryville, Charlestown, and Shepherdstown.

MICHAEL GRAHAM.

———

WASHINGTON,
October 16, 1863.

Maj. Gen. GEORGE G. MEADE,
    Army of the Potomac:

GENERAL : I send herewith a copy of a communication just received from the President.

It was reported last night that some of Longstreet's corps was moving from Strasburg toward the Potomac, and that Jenkins' and Imboden's cavalry were also operating in the Shenandoah Valley. Dispatches from Chattanooga say that none of Longstreet's corps have left for the east. About 3,000 of Longstreet's forces went to Charleston before he went west. These may have returned to Lee. This would reconcile the two accounts.

Very respectfully,

H. W. HALLECK,
General-in-Chief.

[Inclosure.]

EXECUTIVE MANSION,
Washington, October 16, 1863.

Major-General HALLECK :

I do not believe Lee can have over 60,000 effective men.

Longstreet's corps would not be sent away to bring an equal force back upon the same road ; and there is no other direction for them to have to come from.

Doubtless in making the present movement, Lee gathered in all the available scraps, and added them to Hill's and Ewell's corps, but that is all, and he made the movement in the belief that four corps had left General Meade ; and General Meade's apparently avoiding a collision with him has confirmed him in the belief. If General Meade can now attack him on a field no more than equal for us, and will do so with all the skill and courage which he, his officers, and men possess, the honor will be his if he succeeds, and the blame may be mine if he fails.

Yours, truly,

A. LINCOLN.

———

HDQRS. ARMY OF THE POTOMAC, *October* 16, 1863.
(Received 6 p. m.)

Maj. Gen. H. W. HALLECK,
    General-in-Chief:

I have directed General Briggs to see that no regiments, old or new, destined for this army, are forwarded till supplied with shelter tents, 40 rounds of ammunition, and three days' rations in haversacks, and five days' hard bread and small rations in their knapsacks.

GEO. G. MEADE,
Major-General.

HEADQUARTERS ARMY OF THE POTOMAC,
October 16, 1863.

Major-General HALLECK,
    General-in-Chief:

GENERAL : I have to acknowledge the receipt of your communication of this date, by the hands of Colonel Cutts, aide-de-camp, inclosing one from the President, and have to say in reply, that it has been my intention to attack the enemy, if I can find him on a field no more than equal for us, and that I have only delayed doing so from the difficulty of ascertaining his exact position, and the fear that in endeavoring to do so my communications might be jeopardized.

    Respectfully, yours,

GEO. G. MEADE,
Major-General.

HDQRS. SECOND DIVISION, THIRD CORPS,
October 16, 1863.

Major NORVELL,
    Assistant Adjutant-General, Third Corps:

MAJOR: General Mott advanced his pickets last night beyond where the enemy's batteries were located, and makes no discovery of the enemy. The general's loss is not accurately ascertained, but will amount to 4 killed and 25 wounded. The corporal who was taken prisoner by the enemy escaped from them, and reports their loss about 60, including a colonel killed and buried on the ground.

    Very respectfully, your obedient servant,

HENRY PRINCE,
Brigadier-General of Volunteers, Commanding.

UNION MILLS,
October 16, 1863.

Major-General HUMPHREYS:

My pickets are now where the enemy's batteries were yesterday, in front of McLean's Ford. No sign of any force beyond. Our loss yesterday was 4 killed and 25 wounded. A corporal who was taken prisoner and escaped reports their loss about 60, including a colonel.

- WM. H. FRENCH,
Major-General.

HEADQUARTERS ARMY OF THE POTOMAC,
October 16, 1863.

Major-General FRENCH :

Did you send a brigade to Wolf Run Ford this morning ? Have you heard from them, or anything of the enemy ?

GEO. G. MEADE,
Major-General.

UNION MILLS, *October* 16, 1863.

Major-General HUMPHREYS:

I sent a brigade as directed to the ford a mile and a half below Union Mills. It is not Wolf Ford, as called in your dispatch, but Yates' Ford on the McDowell map.

WM. H. FRENCH,
Major-General.

UNION MILLS,
October 16, 1863—9 a. m.

General HUMPHREYS:

The enemy are now picketing cavalry in front of McLean's Ford, but showing no force.

WM. H. FRENCH,
Major-General.

HEADQUARTERS ARMY OF THE POTOMAC,
October 16, 1863.

Major-General FRENCH:

Your dispatch is received. The major-general commanding directs that your pickets connect with those of General Gregg.

A. A. HUMPHREYS.

UNION MILLS, *October* 16, 1863.

General HUMPHREYS,
Chief of Staff:

My reconnoitering parties across Bull Run report two small infantry camps to the right of this point, about two brigades. I sent four strong regiments to Wolf Run Ford early this morning. I have heard nothing from that quarter as yet. I expect a dispatch and will communicate it as soon as received.

WM. H. FRENCH,
Major-General.

HEADQUARTERS ARMY OF THE POTOMAC,
October 16, 1863.

Major-General FRENCH:

Your dispatch is received. General Buford reported that all the trains having crossed, he had sent back the brigade you had sent. Should they still be absent from your command, you can bring them back, in fact, should bring them back.

A. A. HUMPHREYS,
Major-General.

HEADQUARTERS CAVALRY CORPS,
October 16, 1863.

Brigadier-General BUFORD,
Comdg. First Cavalry Division, Fairfax Station:

The major-general commanding desires you to picket the Occoquan if your command does not do it already.

The general desires me to say that General Gregg was merely ordered to report to you for your support yesterday. He will report direct hereafter.

C. ROSS SMITH,
Lieutenant-Colonel, and Chief of Staff.

[P. S.]—Please answer when you receive this dispatch.

———

HEADQUARTERS ARMY OF THE POTOMAC,
October 16, 1863—12 m.

Commanding Officer Sixth Corps:

The major-general commanding requests that you will have the route examined from the position now occupied by you to the crossing of Bull Run at Sudley Springs. Your corps will probably advance by that route. The nature of the ground at the Sudley Springs crossing and the facilities it affords for effecting a crossing should be ascertained. Kilpatrick's pickets extend from Sudley Springs to New Market. He also pickets toward Aldie.

Very respectfully, &c.,

A. A. HUMPHREYS,
Major-General, and Chief of Staff.

———

HEADQUARTERS ARMY OF THE POTOMAC,
October 16, 1863.

Major-General HUMPHREYS,
Chief of Staff:

The signal officer at Blackburn's Ford reports that he saw an hour ago about one division of the enemy's cavalry at Manassas Junction moving to our right.

L. B. NORTON,
Captain, and Chief Signal Officer.

———

OCTOBER 16, 1863—3.30 p. m.

Commanding Officer Fifth Corps:

The major-general commanding directs that you move up with your corps on the Centreville pike; and camp for the night near these headquarters. You will leave General King in command of his four regiments at Fairfax Court-House. A communication will be sent to General King in the course of the day respecting his command.

A. A. HUMPHREYS,
Major-General, and Chief of Staff.

———

HDQRS. THIRD BRIG., SECOND DIV., THIRD CORPS,
McLean's Ford, Va., October 16, 1863—6.50 p. m.

Maj. CHARLES HAMLIN,
Assistant Adjutant-General:

MAJOR: Our cavalry crossed Bull Run at 5 p. m. at Blackburn's Ford, and drove the enemy's pickets from my front.

G. MOTT,
Brigadier-General.

HEADQUARTERS SECOND DIVISION, THIRD CORPS,
October 16, 1863.

Respectfully referred to headquarters Third Corps, for information of the major-general commanding.

HENRY PRINCE,
Brigadier-General of Volunteers.

HEADQUARTERS ARMY OF THE POTOMAC,
October 16, 1863—8.20 p. m.

Major-General FRENCH:
Commanding Third Corps, Union Mills:

The major-general commanding desires to know whether the bank of Bull Run on this side of Union Mills is such as to command the crossing of the stream, or if the enemy could prevent it by establishing batteries and throwing up rifle-pits.

A. A. HUMPHREYS.

UNION MILLS, *October* 16, 1863.

General HUMPHREYS:

My answer to your dispatch: The railroad cutting is very deep and oblique to the road on the opposite side of Bull Run. It is not commanded on this side and can be commanded on the other. Whoever holds the crossing must have both sides of the river.

WM. H. FRENCH,
Major-General.

HEADQUARTERS DEPARTMENT OF WASHINGTON,
October 16, 1863—8.45 p. m.

General RUFUS KING,
Fairfax Court-House:

While you remain attached to the Army of the Potomac you will, of course, receive no orders from this office, but while you remain in your present vicinity I would like you to report to me every night what has occurred during the day, and as much oftener as events occur which you may think I ought to know.

C. C. AUGUR,
Major-General, Commanding.

WAR DEPARTMENT,
Washington, October 16, 1863—10 a. m.

Major-General COUCH,
Chambersburg, Pa.:

It is reported that the enemy has appeared on the Potomac near Clear Spring or Cherry Run. I think your troops should act in that direction, instead of going to Harper's Ferry at present.

H. W. HALLECK.
General-in-Chief.

CAMDEN STATION, *October* 16, 1863.
(Received 3.15 p. m.)

Hon. E. M. STANTON and
Maj. Gen. H. W. HALLECK:

At 7.15 last evening I received the following telegram from Brigadier-General Sullivan, in response to inquiries:

HARPER'S FERRY,
[*October*] 15—7.15 p. m.

JOHN W. GARRETT, *President:*

I am convinced there are no rebels in my front. Imboden is reported by my scouts to be in Loudoun. I have a cavalry force in Winchester this evening, and one in the Back Creek country. I am satisfied the road is as safe as it can be made. I will keep you advised of any movement I may learn of the enemy toward the road. Now there is no danger.

JER. C. SULLIVAN,
Brigadier-General, Commanding.

At 9.50 this a. m. I received from Mr. Quincy, of our engineer corps, the following telegram:

HARPER'S FERRY,
October 16, 1863—9.53 a. m.

JOHN W. GARRETT, *President:*

The following has been received here from Martinsburg this morning, dated last night:

"Prisoners say two brigades of Longstreet's corps were marching down Back Creek Valley to-day, with the object of surprising this force; that they are camped near the railroad, 12 miles above here, to-night.

"———— ————,
"*Lieutenant, and Aide-de-Camp.*"

A force of 37 men were advancing on Back Creek yesterday. This entire force was captured, and scouts from Back Creek Valley yesterday morning reported no enemy to be seen. General Sullivan tells me he cannot think the report as to Longstreet correct, yet it comes from headquarters at Martinsburg. I send it to you for such action as to trains as you think best.

W. C. QUINCY.

At 10.40 I have the following:

HARPER'S FERRY, [*October*] 16—10.40 a. m.

JOHN W. GARRETT:

Later advices from Martinsburg, obtained from prisoners, state that on their way to Back Creek Bridge they passed infantry stragglers, who informed them that they belonged to Longstreet's corps, two brigades of which had crossed Valley pike at Strasburg. They also passed five ambulances belonging to same. They saw camp fires in Back Creek Valley. They also state that Jenkins is coming toward Charlestown, with 4,000 men and sixteen pieces of artillery. The prisoners are unusually reticent. General Sullivan tells me he does not believe these reports. I send them to you for such action as you deem proper.

W. C. QUINCY.

As General Sullivan continues not to give credence to these statements, we are working a portion of our trains through. Have you any information on this subject? Is it probable the forces alleged can be in the valley? The continuance of our trains upon the route maintains the military communication, and ability to re-enforce threatened points. We, therefore, are anxious not to cease working unless the danger is real. Please advise us.

J. W. GARRETT,
President.

WAR DEPARTMENT,
October 16, 1863—2.50 p. m.

JOHN W. GARRETT, Esq., *Baltimore:*

One division of Longstreet's corps went to Charleston, while the rest went to Chattanooga. It is believed that the Charleston division have been sent back to Lee, so that the report of the two brigades of Longstreet being at Strasburg, and moving across in rear to Back Creek, really may be true. The utmost vigilance should be observed, and no pains spared to ascertain the direction of the movement from Strasburg.

EDWIN M. STANTON.

MARTINSBURG, VA., *October* 16, 1863.
(Received War Department 7.45 p. m.)

Colonel SHARPE,
Headquarters Army of the Potomac:

The prisoners are from Gilmor's cavalry battalion, not in any brigade. They left Newtown, Va., 40 in number, on Wednesday, 14th instant, at 4 p. m., for the purpose of tapping the Baltimore and Ohio Railroad at Back Creek. We captured 23 of them 9 miles west of this point, on Back Creek road, near Hedgesville,' yesterday. Two of the prisoners say they saw several footmen, regularly armed, near Strasburg, who said they were stragglers from a command of infantry marching in the direction of North Mountain, and had come from Front Royal. One prisoner says the stragglers belonged to Johnson's division, Longstreet's corps, but does not know what regiment or brigade. I do not place so much reliance in their stories now as I did last night. Will send you a copy of a letter found on one of the prisoners, which letter foreshadows intended movement of the rebel army in Virginia. No account of the old man. Will report again as soon as scouts are in.

MICHAEL GRAHAM.

NEW YORK, *October* 16, 1863.
(Received 2.30 p. m.)

Maj. Gen. H. W. HALLECK,
General-in-Chief:

Your telegram of the 15th is just received. The infantry at Camp Sprague (1,700) will be ready this evening. They are being armed this morning. As it involves no delay the cavalry will be sent direct. I had already arranged with the adjutant-general of the State to notify me by telegraph, so that I may have transportation in readiness for the troops from the interior at the moment of their arrival here.

ED. R. S. CANBY,
Brigadier-General.

HDQRS. ARMY OF THE POTOMAC, *October* 17, 1863.
(Received 10 p. m.).

Major-General HALLECK:

Reports from scouts and the cavalry would indicate a movement of the enemy into the Loudoun and, probably, the Shenandoah Valleys. Their cavalry have been seen in the direction of Aldie and their trains passing through Thoroughfare and Hopewell Gaps. My cavalry to-night occupy Manassas Junction, having driven out of it a small force of cavalry and infantry. No information of the position of their infantry has yet been received. So soon as I can form any correct idea of his movements, I shall move to meet him. I send this information that you may warn Generals Kelley and Lockwood.

GEO. G. MEADE,
Major-General, Commanding.

HEADQUARTERS ARMY OF THE POTOMAC,
October 17, 1863.

Major-General FRENCH:

How much has Bull Run swollen at Union Mills? Can you ford it this morning?

A. A. HUMPHREYS,
Chief of Staff.

UNION MILLS, *October* 17, 1863.

General HUMPHREYS,
  Chief of Staff:

The Bull Run is very high this a. m.; 6 feet at McLean's Ford and not less at Union Mills.

WM. H. FRENCH,
Major-General.

UNION MILLS, *October* 17, 1863.

DEAR HUMPHREYS: I am very sorry that I mistook two camps of our own for the other side of Bull Run yesterday, but did not know that Bull Run was bent so. This is for want of a map. I have written this morning to Duane for the Whipple map, and hope either you or he will supply me.

The column of cavalry and artillery I saw day before yesterday 2 or 3 miles west of here moving south was, I am quite satisfied, the force that attacked Mott, at McLean's Ford, going away.

I had a fine view this morning from a height. Saw cavalry pickets opposite to ours. Also saw crossing Manassas Plains (among the redoubts) precisely one squadron (no artillery) of rebels moving north. It met right there an army wagon moving south.

No other evidence of rebels anywhere. Seeing very fine.

HENRY PRINCE.

SIGNAL STATION, *October* 17, 1863.

Major-General HUMPHREYS,
  Chief of Staff:

The signal officer at Blackburn's Ford sends the following report:

No troops can be seen at Bristoe, but a line of camp smokes are seen between Bristoe and Gainesville. No artillery at Manassas, but the earth-works are occupied by a heavy cavalry picket reserve that is always mounted.

L. B. NORTON,
Captain, and Chief Signal Officer.

HDQRS. FIRST ARMY CORPS, ARMY OF THE POTOMAC,
October 17, 1863.

C. KINGSBURY, Jr.,
Assistant Adjutant-General, First Army Corps:

COLONEL: I have the honor to report that while at the right of the picket line, to post orderlies, as instructed by you, a sergeant of the Eighteenth Pennsylvania Cavalry came in and reported the following: That he, with a small squad, was posted on the Aldie pike as a post of observation; that about 50 of the enemy's cavalry came through the woods on the right, thus cutting off their retreat by the Aldie pike; that they retreated across the country to the Gum Springs road, to where their pickets were posted, and found a body of the enemy's cavalry had come down the Gum Springs road, and the pickets had retired toward the Stone Bridge in confusion, leaving everything behind them. The sergeant came down the Gum Springs road, and taking the Warrenton pike, returned to his command.

A citizen, residing near where the cavalry pickets were posted on the Gum Springs road, states the enemy's force that came down the Gum Springs road was not over 20, and supposed they were White's men. None of the enemy's forces were seen by the infantry pickets.

I have the honor to be, very respectfully, your obedient servant,

JAMES P. MEAD,
Lieut., and A. C. M., Second Div., First Army Corps.

HDQRS. CAVALRY CORPS, ARMY OF THE POTOMAC,
October 17, 1863—8 p. m.

Brigadier-General BUFORD,
Commanding First Cavalry Division:

Place one of your brigades at Fairfax Court-House and send the other to Chantilly, to look after the enemy toward Frying Pan and on our right flank. Acknowledge receipt.

A. PLEASONTON,
Major-General, Commanding.

HEADQUARTERS ARMY OF THE POTOMAC,
October 17, 1863.

Brigadier-General GREGG:

You will picket below Wolf Run Shoals and back as far as Occoquan, after General Buford withdraws his pickets, which he is directed to do.

A. PLEASONTON,
Major-General.

SIGNAL STATION, *October* 17, 1863.

Maj. Gen. A. A. HUMPHREYS,
Chief of Staff:

The signal officer on Centreville Heights reports that he sees—

No indications of enemy's forces at Manassas. There are no guns in such works as he can see. Can distinctly observe camp smokes in rear of Bristoe. Too smoky to see into Bristoe Station.

L. B. NORTON,
Captain, and Chief Signal Officer.

SIGNAL STATION,
October 17, 1863.

Major-General HUMPHREYS,
    Chief of Staff:

The signal officer at Blackburn's Ford reports, at 8 p. m., that he sees large camp fires in rear of Bristoe Station. Also, that at dark he heard artillery firing south-southwest from his station and a long distance off.

L. B. NORTON,
Captain, and Chief Signal Officer.

HEADQUARTERS FIFTH ARMY CORPS,
October 17, 1863—9 p. m.

[General GRIFFIN:]

GENERAL: The major-general commanding desires that you move with your division at 5 a. m., and take post where you were stationed yesterday, covering the roads coming in to Germantown. Sedgwick is on the Aldie and Fairfax pike. Let your left rest where it did, and throw your pickets well to the front and right. I will direct two batteries to report to you. The enemy has appeared in some force (mounted) on Sedgwick's right, and a slight skirmish had with his pickets, in which the enemy were driven off. Please communicate direct to general headquarters any information you may obtain

Yours, very respectfully,

GEO. SYKES,
Major-General, Commanding.

HEADQUARTERS ARMY OF THE POTOMAC,
October 17, 1863.

Major-General FRENCH:

The commanding general directs that you order the Twenty-sixth Michigan Volunteers, whose arrival you reported by telegram, to report to Major-General Warren, it having been assigned to the Second Corps, which is now stationed on the heights of Centreville. The regiment should be supplied with 40 rounds of ammunition in the boxes, shelter tents and three days' rations in haversacks, and five days' hard bread and small rations in the knapsacks, before joining the corps.

S. WILLIAMS,
Assistant Adjutant-General.

SIGNAL STATION,
October 17, 1863.

Major-General HUMPHREYS,
    Chief of Staff:

In reply to your inquiries, the signal officer at Blackburn's Ford reports that he could distinguish between camp fires at Manassas and those at Bristoe, but that there are no camp fires at Manassas.

L. B. NORTON,
Captain, and Chief Signal Officer.

OCTOBER 17, 1863—10.30 p. m.

Major-General SEDGWICK,
  Commanding Sixth Corps:

The major-general commanding has directed me to send you the accompanying copy of a dispatch* from General Kilpatrick, received since Colonel McMahon left here. This would indicate that the infantry force near you was small. The fact could probably be ascertained by your pushing the enemy in the morning and making him show his hand. Colonel McMahon will inform you of the disposition made by the commanding general.
  Very respectfully, your obedient servant,
                    A. A. HUMPHREYS,
                    Major-General, Chief of Staff.

————

HEADQUARTERS ARMY OF THE POTOMAC,
  October 17, 1863—10.30 p. m.

Commanding Officer Second Corps:

The major-general commanding directs me to inform you that he has directed a bridge to be thrown at either Mitchell's or Blackburn's Ford, in connection with the advance of the regular cavalry brigade to Manassas, to ascertain the whereabouts of the enemy. The bridge will be thrown at the ford which can be most easily and completely covered by you, and Captain Mendell has been directed to receive your instructions thereupon.
  Very respectfully, &c.,
                    A. A. HUMPHREYS,
                    Major-General, and Chief of Staff.

————

HEADQUARTERS ARMY OF THE POTOMAC,
  October 17, 1863—11.20 p. m.

Commanding Officer Fifth Corps:

The major-general commanding directs me to inform you that General Sedgwick reports that the enemy has infantry pickets on the old ox road, opposite Chantilly, and directs that you move your corps to Fairfax Court-House to-morrow morning at the hour fixed for the movement of Griffin's division.
  Very respectfully, &c.,
                    A. A. HUMPHREYS,
                    Major-General, and Chief of Staff.

[Indorsement.]

Countermanded at 11.30 p. m., and directed to hold himself ready to move at daylight and at any moment after. Griffin ordered to move as before directed.
                    A. A. HUMPHREYS,
                    Major-General, and Chief of Staff.

————————————————————————————

* Not identified.

HEADQUARTERS ARMY OF THE POTOMAC,
October 17, 1863—11.30 p.'m.

Commanding Officer First Corps:

The major-general commanding directs me to inform you that General Sedgwick reports that the enemy has a force of cavalry, infantry, and artillery on the old ox road not far from Chantilly, and directs that you be prepared to move to General Sedgwick's support at any moment after daylight.
Very respectfully, &c.,
A. A. HUMPHREYS,
Major-General, and Chief of Staff.

HEADQUARTERS FIRST CORPS,
October 17, 1863.

Major-General HUMPHREYS,
Chief of Staff, Army of the Potomac:

Having received orders to be in readiness to march to General Sedgwick's support in the morning in case of necessity, what disposition shall I make in the meantime of the four regiments I have at Bull Run, and General Robinson's division at Cub Run?
Very respectfully,
JOHN NEWTON,
Major-General, Commanding.

HEADQUARTERS ARMY OF THE POTOMAC,
October 17, 1863—11.40 p. m.

Commanding Officer Second Corps:

The major-general commanding directs that you support Colonel Gibbs with any force that may be requisite, and that you hold yourself ready to move at daylight either to Manassas or to the support of General Sedgwick, who reports the enemy on the old ox road not far from Chantilly, with cavalry, infantry, and artillery.
Very respectfully, &c.,
A. A. HUMPHREYS,
Major-General, and Chief of Staff.

OCTOBER 17, 1863—11.45 p. m.

Commanding Officer Third Corps:

The major-general commanding directs that you hold your corps in readiness to move at daylight. It is probable you may be ordered up to Manassas at that hour, or soon after.
You will direct General Birney to hold himself in readiness at daylight to move at any hour to Fairfax Court-House, when called upon by General King.
A. A. HUMPHREYS,
Major-General, and Chief of Staff.

OCTOBER 17, 1863—7.45 p. m.

Brig. Gen. RUFUS KING:

The major-general commanding directs me to inform you that the
enemy's cavalry made their appearance in force, with artillery, near
General Sedgwick, on the road from Frying Pan to Sanders' toll-
gate. The indications are that they are moving to Fairfax Court-
House. General Sykes will be ordered to move to Fairfax Court-
House early in the morning, and a cavalry brigade to-night.

A. A. HUMPHREYS,
Major-General, and Chief of Staff.

OCTOBER 17, 1863—9 p. m.

Brigadier-General KING:

I am directed by the major-general commanding to inform you
that General Griffin, with his division of the Fifth Corps and two
batteries, will move from this place to Fairfax Court-House at 5
o'clock to-morrow morning. A brigade of cavalry will be sent to
Chantilly and one to Fairfax Court-House. If it should prove to be
necessary to have additional force, please notify the commanding
general.

A. A. HUMPHREYS,
Major-General, and Chief of Staff.

GENERAL ORDERS, }   HEADQUARTERS KING S DIVISION,
No. 40.   }   *Fairfax Court-House, Va., October* 17, 1863.

An order from the State Department assigns the commanding
general to a different duty.* It is with infinite reluctance that he
takes leave of his comrades in arms. He has received at their hands
all that a general could ask or expect: obedience, respect, and affec-
tion. He leaves them with the earnest hope that their efforts in
behalf of the Union may be crowned with glorious success, and that
once more the "flag of the free" may float in triumph over the entire
Republic.

The command of the division devolves upon Brigadier-General
Corcoran, a gallant and experienced officer, most fit for the post
assigned to him, and devoted to the good cause to which we have
all pledged our lives.

RUFUS KING,
Brigadier-General, Commanding.

FAIRFAX COURT-HOUSE, VA.,
October 17, 1863—2.40 p. m.

General MEADE, *Headquarters:*

I sent out the two companies of cavalry at this post, on the different roads to warn me of the approach of any enemy; and just
learn that 15 men were captured about 5 miles from here, on the

---

* General King was appointed minister resident at Rome. His resignation as an
officer of the army was accepted to date from October 20, 1863, by Special Orders,
No. 471, Adjutant-General's Office, October 21, 1863.

Chantilly road, by about 75 cavalry under Mosby. Three have escaped and arrived here. I am sending out four companies of infantry. I have no cavalry. I have sent word to Colonel Lowell.

MICHAEL CORCORAN,
Brigadier-General.

WAR DEPARTMENT,
Washington, October 18, 1863—12 m.

Major-General MEADE,
Army of the Potomac:

Reported from Harper's Ferry that the enemy attacked Charlestown at 7 o'clock this morning.

H. W. HALLECK,
General-in-Chief.

WAR DEPARTMENT,
Washington, October 18, 1863—11 a. m.

Major-General MEADE,
Army of the Potomac:

If Lee has turned his back on you to cross the mountains, he certainly has seriously exposed himself to your blows, unless his army can move 2 miles to your 1. Fight him before he again draws you at such a distance from your base as to expose your communications to his raids. If he moves on Harper's Ferry, you must not give him time to take that place before you go to its aid. Of course, it cannot hold out long if attacked by his main force.

H. W. HALLECK,
General-in-Chief.

OCTOBER 18, 1863—1 p. m.
(Received 1.40 p. m.)

Major-General HALLECK:

The cavalry report the enemy as having withdrawn from Bristoe, supposed toward the Rappahannock. A reconnaissance to Thoroughfare Gap found the gaps strongly picketed by the enemy's cavalry, but could hear of no large force of the enemy passing through the gap. Stuart, with 4,000 cavalry and six pieces of artillery, passed in the direction of Aldie last evening, doubtless with the intention of making a raid on my rear. I have sent all my available cavalry to watch and oppose him. It is impossible to move this army until I know something more definite of position of the enemy. If he is in the valley, any movement in the direction of the Rappahannock would be lost time. So, also, would any movement be toward Harper's Ferry, if he is retiring to the Rappahannock, which, as far as I can judge, is his direction. Have you any information as to the character of the force at Charlestown this a. m. ? Whatever route he has taken, it is too late for me to overtake him in any short time.

GEO. G. MEADE,
Major-General, Commanding.

WAR DEPARTMENT,
Washington, October 18 1863—7 p. m.

Major-General MEADE:
    Army of the Potomac:
    The attack on Charlestown was not in great force. Enemy finally repulsed. General Sullivan has promised details, but none received. Lee is unquestionably bullying you. If you cannot ascertain his movements, I certainly cannot. If you pursue and fight him, I think you will find out where he is. I know of no other way.   •
                                            H. W. HALLECK,
                                                General-in-Chief.

OCTOBER 18, 1863—8.30 p. m. •
(Received 10 p. m.)
Major-General HALLECK:
    Your telegram of 7 p. m. just received. If you have any orders to give me, I am prepared to receive and obey them, but I must insist on being spared the infliction of such truisms in the guise of . opinions as you have recently honored me with, particularly as they were not asked for. I take this occasion to repeat what I have before stated, that if my course, based on my own judgment, does not meet with approval, I ought to be, and I desire to be, relieved from command.
                                            GEO. G. MEADE,
                                                Major-General, Commanding.

HEADQUARTERS FIFTH CORPS,
October 18, 1863—12.40 a. m.
Major-General HUMPHREYS,
    Chief of Staff:
    GENERAL: Is General Griffin's division (which was the only part of this corps ordered to move) to go to Centreville at daylight or not ? Your dispatch reads thus:

The order to move your corps at 5 a. m. is countermanded. Let Griffin go. Hold the rest of the corps ready to move in any direction at daylight.

    Very respectfully, your obedient servant,
                                            GEO. SYKES,
                                                Major-General, Commanding.

SIGNAL STATION,
October 18, 1863.
Major-General HUMPHREYS,
    Chief of Staff:
    The signal officer at Blackburn's Ford reports "enemy's camp fires · still in rear of Bristoe." Two large regiments of cavalry seen at Manassas.
                                            L. B. NORTON,
                                                Captain, and Chief Signal Officer.

HEADQUARTERS FIFTH ARMY CORPS,
October 18, 1863.
[Maj. Gen. A. A. HUMPHREYS,
Chief of Staff, Army of the Potomac:]

GENERAL: Am I to move the balance of the Fifth Corps toward Centreville at once, or await further orders? The last order says, "Hold it ready to move at daylight." It has been held ready, but no further instructions have been received. The order of 11.20 p. m. did not reach me until 3 a. m. of the 18th. That of 1 a. m. came first. This will explain why I sent to you in reference to Griffin's movement.

Respectfully,

GEO. SYKES,
Major-General.

MANASSAS JUNCTION,
October 18, 1863.
Captain SUYDAM,
Assistant Adjutant-General:

CAPTAIN: Since driving in the enemy's pickets last night everything has remained quiet. Our pickets have been thrown forward within 1½ miles of Bristoe. I shall remain where I am until further instructions from you.

General Warren can give me no support in case of attack, and I think the enemy are moving around in the direction of Chantilly, and, perhaps, retreating.

I send you back, in charge of a courier, a deserter, from whom I think you can get important information.

I am entirely out of forage and rations, and if you wish me to remain here longer, please have me supplied at once.

Respectfully,

ALFRED GIBBS,
Colonel, Commanding Cavalry Reserve Brigade.

HEADQUARTERS ARMY OF THE POTOMAC,
October 18, 1863—8.15 a. m.
Commanding Officer Fifth Corps:

The major-general commanding directs that you move with the remainder of your corps to Fairfax Court-House, and send out a division on the old ox road to the vicinity of Hawxhurst's Saw-Mill or Fox's Mill, or some point intermediate between the two that will afford a good position. General Sedgwick informs me that the enemy seems to be establishing a line of infantry pickets opposite to his, which is taken as an indication that he intends to advance from that direction.

Very respectfully, &c.,

A. A. HUMPHREYS,
Major-General, and Chief of Staff.

HEADQUARTERS ARMY OF THE POTOMAC,
October 18, 1863—11 a. m.

Commanding Officer First Corps :

The major-general commanding directs me to inform you that General Sedgwick reports that the enemy in his front have moved off and that it is not necessary for you to hold your corps under arms.

Very respectfully, &c.,

A. A. HUMPHREYS,
Major-General, and Chief of Staff.

HEADQUARTERS ARMY OF THE POTOMAC,
October 18, 1863—11.15 a. m.

Commanding Officer Second Corps :

The major-general commanding directs me to inform you that General Sedgwick reports that the enemy in his front and on his right had moved off, and that apparently it was not a strong force At present, therefore, there is no probability of your being required to move in the direction of Sedgwick.

Very respectfully, &c.,

A. A. HUMPHREYS,
Major-General, and Chief of Staff.

OCTOBER 18, 1863—11.15 a. m.

Commanding Officer Third Corps :

The major-general commanding directs me to inform you that General Sedgwick reports that the enemy in his front and on his right has moved off. If your troops are under arms, they need not be held so longer.

A. A. HUMPHREYS,
Major-General, and Chief of Staff.

HDQRS. CAVALRY CORPS, ARMY OF THE POTOMAC,
October 18, 1863—12.15 p. m.

Brigadier-General GREGG,
Commanding Second Cavalry Division :

Draw in your pickets and move with your command to Vienna, where you will act in concert with Colonel Lowell's command and push after the enemy's cavalry, reported to be making a raid on our right and rear. Acknowledge receipt.

A. PLEASONTON,
Major-General, Commanding.

HEADQUARTERS SECOND CORPS,
October 18, 1863—5 p. m.

Major-General HUMPHREYS,
Chief of Staff, Army of the Potomac :

The pontoon bridge has just been completed at Blackburn's Ford. I have thrown two regiments as skirmishers three-quarters of a mile beyond the run. They have met nothing, and no enemy is within sight for 2 miles. The cavalry will not be all over by 7 o'clock, if then. The run is not so high as it was yesterday, and is fordable without a bridge. One-half of the cavalry is crossing at a ford above Blackburn's Ford.

G. K. WARREN,
Major-General, Commanding Second Corps.

CIRCULAR.]   HEADQUARTERS ARMY OF THE POTOMAC,
October 18, 1863—10 p. m.

The following movements are ordered for to-morrow, the 19th instant:

1. Major-General Newton, First Corps, will move at 6 a. m. from Centreville, on the Warrenton pike, and take position for the night at Hay Market.

2. Major-General Sedgwick, Sixth Corps, will follow the First Corps, entering the Warrenton pike near Cub Run, commencing the march at 7 o'clock, and take position for the night at Gainesville.

3. Major-General French, Third Corps, will move from Union Mills at 6 a. m., keeping on the south side of the railroad, and take position on Broad Run near Bristoe.

4. Major-General Warren, Second Corps, will move at 6 a. m. by Mitchell's and Blackburn's Fords, keeping on the north side of the railroad, and will take position on Broad Run at Milford.

5. The Reserve Artillery will move on the Warrenton pike, following the Sixth Corps, and camp for the night at Groveton. It will clear the road through Centreville as soon as the First Corps leaves it.

6. Major-General Sykes, Fifth Corps, will move at 6 a. m., and, taking the road south of the Centreville pike, will leave that town on the right, cross Bull Run at Island Ford, pass through New Market to Groveton, and take position there for the night. Strong working parties will precede the column to work on the crossing of Bull Run.

7. The trains at Fairfax Court-House and Station will move to the fords of Bull Run and park there, being covered on the flanks by the cavalry of Generals Buford and Gregg.

8. Headquarters will be at Groveton.

By command of Major-General Meade:

S. WILLIAMS,
Assistant Adjutant-General.

HEADQUARTERS CAVALRY CORPS,
Near Centreville, October 18, 1863—11.30 p. m.

Brigadier-General GREGG,
Comdg. Second Cavalry Division, Fairfax Court-House:

The major-general commanding directs that you stop your column to-night. Major Gaston will bring you orders.

C. ROSS SMITH,
Lieutenant-Colonel, Chief of Staff.

[P. S.]—Have your supply trains filled up.

HEADQUARTERS,
Fairfax Court-House, Va., October 18, 1863.

Captain Batterson, Thirteenth New York Cavalry, reports having seen about 30 rebel cavalry about 8 miles from here, while on his way in charge of train from Washington to this post, via Annandale. He reported to Colonel Baker's command. A private of same regiment has been captured last evening about 3 miles from here toward Centreville.

MICHAEL CORCORAN,
Brigadier-General.

FAIRFAX COURT-HOUSE, VA., *October* 18, 1863.
(Received 12.40 p. m.)

Lieutenant-Colonel TAYLOR,
Chief of Staff, and Assistant Adjutant-General:

The following received from Colonel Lowell, at Vienna:

OCTOBER 18.

We have taken one of Mosby's men this morning, who says that Mosby, with 275 men, is prowling around below here to take supply trains. It will be well to delay all wagon trains without heavy escort till something more definite is learned about Mosby's movements. If you could post strong infantry pickets at points between here and Fairfax, Mosby might be ambushed on his way back.

C. R. LOWELL, JR.

I will communicate the above to General Buford, commanding cavalry, and General Griffin, commanding corps, now stationed here. I have just learned that a company of our cavalry has been attacked about 3 miles from here toward Alexandria, and the captain captured.

MICHAEL CORCORAN,
Brigadier-General, Commanding.

WAR DEPARTMENT,
Washington, October 18, 1863—2 p. m.

Major-General COUCH,
Chambersburg, Pa.:

The enemy has appeared in some force at Charlestown. Your troops will move down in supporting distance of Harper's Ferry, so as to re-enforce Maryland Heights, should the enemy cross the river.

H. W. HALLECK,
General-in-Chief.

HARPER'S FERRY, W. VA.,
October 18, 1863—11 a. m.   (Received 1.40 p. m.)

Maj. Gen. H. W. HALLECK,
General-in-Chief:

I will be prepared to defend Harper's Ferry. Imboden this morning surprised Charlestown and dispersed or captured the force stationed there. The field officers all escaped somehow. I have ordered two regiments and my cavalry to ascertain the movements of the enemy, and whether Imboden is attempting a raid on the Baltimore and Ohio Railroad. I can furnish information by 12 o'clock.

JER. C. SULLIVAN,
Brigadier-General.

CAMDEN STATION, *Baltimore, October* 18, 1863.
(Received 2.45 p. m.)

Hon. E. M. STANTON, *Secretary of War,* and
Maj. Gen. H. W. HALLECK, *General-in-Chief:*

At 10.45 a. m. I received telegram from General Sullivan stating:

> Our forces were driven out of Charlestown by Imboden's forces. I will occupy it again to-day. Our loss I cannot tell.

At 11.45 a. m. the following:

> I have driven Imboden out of Charlestown. Major Cole is pursuing. The Ninth Maryland Infantry is captured. The enemy is retreating in the direction of Berry-ville.
>
> JER. C. SULLIVAN,
> *Brigadier-General.*

Deserters from Imboden report at Martinsburg that White and Gilmor are with him, and that the aggregate is 3,500, all cavalry, 100 being dismounted, the force having six pieces of artillery. We have reports of rebel cavalry being seen this morning near Duffield's and also near Bath. Can Harper's Ferry be re-enforced from Baltimore or Washington? Have you any information of movements of Lee's army toward or into Shenandoah Valley?

J. W. GARRETT,
President.

WASHINGTON,
October 18, 1863—2.15 p. m.

JOHN W. GARRETT,
Baltimore:

Any reliable information that I receive that will be useful to you will be communicated.

H. W. HALLECK,
General-in-Chief.

WAR DEPARTMENT,
Washington, October 18, 1863—11 a. m.

Brigadier-General KELLEY, *Clarksburg, W. Va.,* and
General SULLIVAN, *Harper's Ferry, W. Va.:*

It is reported that the enemy's trains are passing through Thoroughfare, Hopewell, and Aldie Gaps. It is supposed that he is aiming at Harper's Ferry or to cross the Potomac. Every effort should be made to reconnoiter these movements and to defend Harper's Ferry.

H. W. HALLECK,
General-in-Chief.

CLARKSBURG, W. VA., *October* 18, 1863—3 p. m.
(Received 5.30 p. m.)

Brig. Gen. G. W. CULLUM,
Chief of Staff:

The telegram of the General-in-Chief received. Have ordered General Sullivan to keep himself fully advised of the movements of the enemy, and if he is satisfied that he is moving into the valley or

on Harper's Ferry in force, to withdraw his troops from Martinsburg and adjacent posts on Baltimore and Ohio Railroad, by way of
Williamsport or Shepherdstown, to Maryland Heights, and to hold
the heights at all hazards. I may be cut off from him, and unable
to communicate or support him. With this view I have directed
him to communicate direct with you, and to keep you fully advised.
My judgment is clear that Maryland Heights should be held if even
approached by Lee's whole army. If you concur, provision should
be made to support Sullivan from the east if he is assailed.
                                          B. F. KELLEY,
                                   Brigadier-General, Commanding.

                                          WAR DEPARTMENT,
                              Washington, October 18, 1863—7 p. m.
Brigadier-General KELLEY,
            Clarksburg, W. Va.:
   Should the whole of Lee's army attack Maryland Heights, the place
must be held until Meade's army comes to the rescue. It can be so
held, and if the officers fail to do so they should be hung.
                                          H. W. HALLECK,
                                          General-in-Chief.

                                          HARPER'S FERRY,
                                          October 18, 1863.
Col. L. B. PIERCE,
            Martinsburg:
   Imboden surrounded and captured most of the force * at Charlestown. Supposed he had about 1,000 or 1,200 infantry and cavalry,
with some artillery. Put your house in order. Notify Kearneys-
ville to be on the alert.
                                          W. B. KELLEY,
                                          Aide-de-Camp.

            HDQRS. ARMY AND DISTRICT OF NORTH CAROLINA,
                              New Berne, N. C., October 18, 1863.
Maj. Gen. J. G. FOSTER,
            Comdg. Dept. of Virginia and North Carolina:
   GENERAL: Although your communications contemplated the transportation of some of the troops by the Spaulding, momentarily expected, I have deemed it best not to delay longer, and have ordered
the Albany and Jersey Blue to take the Ninth New Jersey. As yet
only the Nineteenth Wisconsin has arrived. The other regiments
are looked for hourly.
   I regret to learn the difficulty upon the canal, and the burning of
one or more boats. In a communication of the 17th, I called attention to the propriety of occupying Elizabeth City, and I believe such
a policy would render the canal navigation much more secure.
   Five Virginia regiments have arrived at Kinston. General Mar-

---

* The Ninth Maryland Infantry.

tin and his brigade have gone south to Wilmington or Charleston. A flag of truce has just been announced at the outpost and probably I shall have additional information before the boat leaves.

The Confederate Governors have been in conference together, and it is said that Governor Vance was entirely reconciled toward the Richmond junta. He is certainly exhibiting more activity than heretofore.

I trust your plan may be entirely successful, and that the troops may be benefited by the change.

Very respectfully, your obedient servant,

JOHN J. PECK,
Major-General.

U. S. FLAG-SHIP MINNESOTA,
Off Newport News, Va., October 18, 1863.

Maj. Gen. J. G. FOSTER, U. S. Army,
Comdg. Dept. of Va. and N. C., Fortress Monroe, Va..

GENERAL: In reply to your communication of yesterday, brought to this flag-ship in my absence at the navy-yard by Major Stevenson, I beg leave to refer you to an extract from the Department's letter to me of May 5, furnished Major Stevenson yesterday, informing me that the War Department had expressly requested the Navy Department not to equip vessels in the employ of the army with articles of navy outfit of any kind, especially ordnance.

As, however, the navy guns, carriages, &c., alluded to in your letter were formerly on board the Smith Briggs, and have been returned to the navy, I have directed Lieutenant-Commander Phenix, in the inclosed letter,* to lend them and the necessary ammunition to you on your application. When, in an emergency, you require for military purposes field or other artillery and ammunition, which we have on hand and which are not needed for immediate naval use, it will be my duty and great pleasure to put them at your disposition. It will at all times afford me much pleasure to afford you every facility.

I beg you to understand, however, that under my instructions from the Department above referred to, such transactions cannot be regarded as final transfer of the property to the army.

I have the honor to be, general, very respectfully, yours,

S. PHILLIPS LEE,
Acting Rear-Admiral, Comdg. N. A. Bkg. Squadron.

[Extract.]

The Department is willing and desirous that the naval should extend to the military branch of the service all the co-operation and assistance that it consistently can; but as regards the arming of steamers, and providing them with articles of outfit within the reach of the quartermaster's department, it does not feel called upon to do this; and the War Department has expressly requested that it should not be done, especially as regards ordnance.

---

* Not found.

WAR DEPARTMENT,
Washington, October 19, 1863—12 m.

Major-General MEADE,
Army of the Potomac:

General Sullivan's cavalry pursued Imboden to Berryville. No other force of the enemy was seen in the valley. General Rosecrans continually reports arrival of troops from Lee's army. Regiments of Virginia cavalry have recently joined Bragg. He thinks the enemy's main force is concentrating there. Under these circumstances it is continually urged upon me that you ought to ascertain Lee's force and position, in order that the Government might at least know the actual facts. As you could not ascertain otherwise, I have repeated the suggestion made to me of the necessity of giving battle. If I have repeated truisms it has not been to give offense, but to give to you the wishes of the Government. If, in conveying these wishes, I have used words which were unpleasing, I sincerely regret it.

H. W. HALLECK,
General-in-Chief.

HEADQUARTERS ARMY OF THE POTOMAC,
October 19, 1863—9.30 p. m.
(Received 9.40 a. m., 20th.)

Maj. Gen. H. W. HALLECK,
General-in-Chief:

The army advanced to-day across Bull Run, and now occupies a line from Hay Market to Bristoe Station. Kilpatrick's division of cavalry in the advance pushed back the enemy's cavalry as far as New Baltimore, where the enemy's infantry appeared in his rear and flank, causing him to fall back to Hay Market. The enemy's infantry followed him up, and are now in front of our infantry pickets. All the intelligence I have been able to obtain indicates the concentration of Lee's army within the last two days at Warrenton. Whether he has moved on and I have now only a rear guard in my front, or whether he will give me battle, are questions that will be decided to-morrow.

Your telegram of 12 m. of this date is received. Your explanation of your intentions is accepted, and I thank you for it.

GEO. G. MEADE,
Major-General, Commanding.

HEADQUARTERS SECOND ARMY CORPS,
Bristoe, October 19, [1863]—12 m.

Major-General HUMPHREYS:

From a Union man living here, I learn that the rebel cavalry pickets left here at daylight this morning. We have sent in a deserter from the Stuart artillery, who has been hiding in the woods since they left. He says their infantry was all going back again across the Rapidan, and the cavalry to Culpeper Court-House. He says the infantry left here the day before yesterday. The cannonading toward Greenwich has ceased for an hour, and seemed to be retiring before that time. I got here about 9.30 a. m.

G. K. WARREN,
Major-General of Volunteers.

HEADQUARTERS ARMY OF THE POTOMAC,
October 19, 1863—4.50 p. m.
Commanding Officer Sixth Corps:

The major-general commanding directs that you will send forward such support of infantry to General Kilpatrick as may be necessary to enable him to withdraw. Probably not less than a division, with its proportion of artillery.
Very respectfully, &c.,

A. A. HUMPHREYS,
Major-General, and Chief of Staff.

HDQRS. FIRST ARMY CORPS, ARMY OF THE POTOMAC,
October 19, 1863—8 p. m.
Major-General. HUMPHREYS,
Chief of Staff, Army of the Potomac:

I consider it necessary to contract my position on General Sedgwick before daylight in the morning, for two reasons:

1. That my pickets have all been disarranged by the necessary falling back of General Kilpatrick, and they cannot be re-established because of the enemy's infantry occupying the ground far in advance of where they originally were, and within close range of my camp.

2. The position is intrinsically bad, and cannot be connected sufficiently strong with General Sedgwick to prevent the enemy getting between us.
Very respectfully, &c.,

JOHN NEWTON,
Major-General, Commanding.

HEADQUARTERS ARMY OF THE POTOMAC,
October 19, 1863—8.30 p. m.
Commanding Officer Second Corps:

Since writing you this afternoon, additional information received from the front indicates the probability of our meeting the enemy to-morrow morning in front of Gainesville. The major-general commanding therefore directs that you move to-morrow morning at 4 o'clock to Gainesville, by the route from Bristoe to Gainesville, marked in red on the map sent herewith.

Upon reaching Gainesville or that vicinity, should General Sedgwick be in position at Gainesville, you will take position on his left. General French will be directed to follow you and form on your left. General Sedgwick will be ordered to move forward to Buckland Mills to-morrow morning at 6 o'clock, followed by Sykes. Newton will be held at Hay Market. Headquarters will be near Gainesville, or between that and Buckland Mills. Information sent by General Kilpatrick indicates that Hill's and Ewell's corps were both at Warrenton to-day.
Very respectfully, &c.,

A. A. HUMPHREYS,
Major-General, and Chief of Staff.

·HEADQUARTERS ARMY OF THE POTOMAC,
October 19, 1863—9 p. m.

Commanding Officer Third Corps:

Information just received indicates the probability of our meeting the enemy to-morrow morning in front of Gainesville. The Second Corps is ordered to move at 4 o'clock to-morrow morning to Gainesville, by the road from Bristoe, marked in red on the map sent you herewith. You will follow the Second Corps, beginning the march at 6 o'clock, and be prepared to take position on the left of the Second Corps. Should it find the Sixth Corps in position at Gainesville, form on its left.

General Sedgwick, followed by General Sykes, will be ordered to move to Buckland Mills at 6 o'clock to-morrow morning. Newton will remain at Hay Market. You should keep well closed on the Second Corps, and move in double column of infantry, artillery between.

Headquarters will be at Gainesville, or between that point and Buckland Mills.

Information received from General Kilpatrick indicates that both Hill's and Ewell's corps were at Warrenton to-day.

Very respectfully, &c.,

A. A. HUMPHREYS,
Major-General, and Chief of Staff.

HEADQUARTERS ARMY OF THE POTOMAC,
October 19, 1863—9 p. m.

Commanding Officer Fifth Corps:

The indications to-night being that the enemy are in front of General Newton and General Sedgwick, the major-general commanding considers it to be important that you should be up at Gainesville by daylight, and directs that you move to Gainesville at 3 o'clock to-morrow morning and mass in rear of Sedgwick, and support him or General Newton, or both, should they require it, without further orders from the commanding general. Upon arriving upon the field, the major-general commanding will acquaint you with the fact.

Very respectfully, &c.,

A. A. HUMPHREYS,
Major-General, and Chief of Staff.

HEADQUARTERS ARMY OF THE POTOMAC,
October 19, 1863—9.15 p. m.

Commanding Officer Sixth Corps:

The major-general commanding directs me to inform you that General Sykes has been ordered to move up to-morrow morning at 3 o'clock and support you or General Newton, or both. Generals Warren and French are ordered to move to Gainesville to-morrow morning at 4 o'clock, and form on your left, should you be in position upon their arrival.

Very respectfully, &c.,

A. A. HUMPHREYS,
Major-General, and Chief of Staff.

HEADQUARTERS ARMY OF THE POTOMAC,
October 19, 1863—9.30 p. m.

Commanding Officer First Corps:

The major-general commanding directs me to inform you that General Sykes has been ordered to be up at Gainesville by daylight to-morrow morning, to support you or General Sedgwick, or both, and to fill up any gaps that may exist between you. The commanding general directs me to say that he considers it important that Hay Market should be held, the numerous roads centering there making it an important point.

Very respectfully, &c.,

A. A. HUMPHREYS,
Major-General, and Chief of Staff.

GENERAL ORDERS, } HDQRS. CORCORAN'S DIVISION,
No. 41. } *Fairfax Court-House, Va., October* 19, 1863.

Until further orders, Col. M. Murphy, Sixty-ninth Regiment New York National Guard, will command the following regiments of the Irish Legion, viz: Sixty-ninth, One hundred and fifty-fifth, and One hundred and seventieth Regiments New York Volunteers.

Colonel Grimshaw, Fourth Delaware; Colonel Alexander, Second District of Columbia; Captain Anthony, Seventeenth New York Battery, and Captain Jackson, commanding detachment Thirteenth New York Cavalry, will report, as formerly directed, to these headquarters.

By command of Brigadier-General Corcoran:

[WM. A. LA MOTTE,]
Acting Assistant Adjutant-General.

WAR DEPARTMENT,
Washington, October 19, 1863—3.30 p. m.

Brigadier-General KELLEY,
Clarksburg, W. Va.:

All of General Couch's forces have been ordered to the Potomac River, so as to be in position to re-enforce General Sullivan. They are now on the march.

H. W. HALLECK,
General-in-Chief.

HEADQUARTERS FIRST DIVISION,
Harper's Ferry, W. Va., October 19, 1863.
- (Received 8.50 p. m.)

Major-General HALLECK,
General-in-Chief:

Two deserters have just been brought in, who left Stuart's command in the mountains at Snicker's Gap. They say the cavalry numbers about 8,000, and are planning a raid into Maryland, by way of Williamsport or Berlin. They also place Lee's army at

somewhere near 65,000, this cavalry included. Their information
tallies with that given by prisoners taken some days ago. I will
start to-morrow morning a strong cavalry reconnaissance through
Berryville, to find out, if possible, their designs.

JER. C. SULLIVAN,
Brigadier-General, Commanding.

CHAMBERSBURG, PA., *October* 19, 1863—2.30 p. m.
(Received 3.45 p. m.)

Maj. Gen. H. W. HALLECK:
Commanding officer at Harper's Ferry has notified General Ferry,
in command of my forces in Maryland, that he only wanted cavalry.
This latter has been sent to him. The infantry and artillery will
return to Hagerstown for the present.

D. N. COUCH,
Major-General.

HAGERSTOWN, MD., *October* 19, 1863.
(Received War Department 4 p. m.)

Colonel SHARPE,
Headquarters Army of the Potomac:
I am satisfied that Longstreet's corps has returned from Bragg
and joined General Lee. I am satisfied, also, that they are going to
invade Maryland and Pennsylvania again. The star they are watching and looking after is Washington and Maryland. Our force was
drawn up in a line of battle at 3 o'clock at Martinsburg. The Potomac River is very high, and cannot be forded by our men or the
rebels before Tuesday or Wednesday.

The force in our front is Imboden's command. Five deserters and
Union men say his force amounts to about 2,500 effective men; Gilmor's Independent Battalion, about 150 men; White's and Mosby's
guerrillas numbering from 300 to 400.

A reliable Union man from Charlestown, who is fleeing from the
rebels, states that there are some 7,000 or 8,000 men marching on to
Martinsburg. They are a portion of Ewell's corps. General Kelley
ought to throw re-enforcements toward Hancock to shelter them.

All my scouts who came in and reported to me say that General
Lee has a large army, and if he cannot capture Washington, Baltimore, and redeem Maryland, that he will fortify South Mountain,
and will winter in Washington County, Md., and draw his supplies
from the richest parts of Maryland and Pennsylvania. I am satisfied
that they are coming. They have had the Union force weighed and
counted, and found them wanting. Prepare for the storm.

Yours, respectfully,

MICHAEL GRAHAM.

HEADQUARTERS ARMY OF THE POTOMAC,
October 20, 1863—8 p. m. (Received 9.05 p. m.)

Major-General HALLECK:
The advance of the army reached Warrenton to-day, the enemy
having all retired beyond the Rappahannock. The railroad from
Bristoe Station, as far as examined to Catlett's Station, has been com-

pletely destroyed, and it is understood this work has been carried as far as the Rappahannock, though not so effectually as immediately at Bristoe. This act is significant of a purpose to detach troops to the southwest, based on the presumed delay in my advance. I will immediately have an estimate made of the time it will require to put the road in repair. I can carry fifteen days' subsistence for the men, but cannot carry more than five or six days' forage for the animals. This would necessitate frequent returns to the depot by the trains, until the road is repaired. This would involve wagoning supplies from Bristoe to Gordonsville, if I advanced thus far, a distance of 70 miles over roads that in bad weather are very difficult of passage, and exposed to the enemy's cavalry. I am afraid the time it will take to repair the road and the difficulty of advance without the railroad, will preclude my preventing the sending of troops to the southwest by the enemy.

· I will endeavor to obtain the earliest intelligence of any movement on their part.

> GEO. G. MEADE,
> *Major-General, Commanding.*

OCTOBER 20, [1863]—3 p. m.

Major-General FRENCH:

I saw General Meade this morning myself. He was not certain whether Lee's army had recrossed the Rappahannock or not, and he wished me to push on and try to find out. From what I learned at Mrs. Green's, I feel almost sure General Lee has recrossed the Rappahannock. General Meade told me he wished me to go at least as far as Auburn, and I know he expects you to follow me. If you do, I will cross Cedar Run and camp on the other side. General Meade indicated he wished me to go farther, and I told him I would if he thought it best when the day's operations had supplied him with information. I inferred he did not intend to push us if Lee really had retreated across the Rappahannock.

> G. K. WARREN,
> *Major-General.*

[OCTOBER 20, 1863.—For abstract from tri-monthly return of the Army of the Potomac, see Part I, p. 226.]

> WAR DEPARTMENT,
> *Washington, October 20, 1863—10.30 a. m.*

Major-General SCHENCK and
JOHN W. GARRETT,
> *Baltimore, Md.:*

Deserters report that Stuart is preparing for another raid into Maryland and Pennsylvania. Every possible care should be taken of rolling stock and bridges.

> H. W. HALLECK,
> *General-in-Chief.*

WAR DEPARTMENT,
Washington, October 20, 1863—10. a.m.

Major-General COUCH, *Chambersburg, Pa.:*

Commanding officer at Harper's Ferry cannot countermand my orders. All of your troops were ordered to move down to the Potomac, in a position to re-enforce Harper's Ferry. It is believed that Stuart will make a cavalry raid into Maryland and Pennsylvania, while Lee will attempt to cut off or reduce Harper's Ferry.

H. W. HALLECK,
General-in-Chief.

MARTINSBURG, VA., *October* 20, 1863.
(Received War Department 2.15 p. m.)

Colonel SHARPE, *Headquarters Army of the Potomac:*

Mr. Patrick Cunningham has returned from Richmond. He arrived at Richmond on Sunday, the 11th. He remained in Richmond two nights and one day. He says, "There are no troops in or around Richmond, excepting what they call the 'Local Guard' of militia." He also says that there are no troops passed from Lee to Bragg or Bragg to Lee, or from any other point to re-enforce Lee.

It is reported in Richmond that General Lee has the finest and the largest army he has ever had heretofore. This is the prevailing opinion of civilians and soldiers. There is no talk of Rosecrans or Charleston, but all eyes seem to be turned upon the army of Lee. They say that Lee will drive Meade into the fortifications around Alexandria and Washington, and again invade Maryland at the following points, viz, Leesburg, Point of Rocks, and Berlin. He also states that there is a force under Imboden encamped on the Shenandoah River, in the neighborhood of White Post, and that White's and Mosby's guerrillas are within re-enforcing distance of Imboden; also Gilmor's and McNeill's. In connection with this he states that—

General Jones' command is posted in the gaps of the Blue Ridge to re-enforce either Imboden or Lee—the one that shall need his assistance first. There is a small rebel force under Jenkins and Jackson in the vicinity of Moorefield, watching the Union troops under Averell. There is no rebel force between Richmond and Gordonsville, and none between Gordonsville and Staunton, and none between Staunton and Winchester. I did not see more than forty rebel wagons between Strasburg and Staunton, and they were employed hauling pig-iron to Richmond. There is a large drove of cattle, numbering about one thousand, for the use of the rebel army. They are grazing in the farm known as Steamburgin's, situated between Mount Jackson and New Market. All the refugees who fled from the presence of the Union forces are returning down the valley with the expectation that the rebels will soon have possession of this country. I did not hear of any re-enforcements—that is, regular troops, joining Lee, or from Lee to any other point—that is, within the last three weeks, except conscripts. This is my honest statement, which I am willing to testify to before any magistrate.

PATRICK CUNNINGHAM.
MICHAEL GRAHAM.

HDQRS. THIRD BRIG., THIRD CAV. DIV., DEPT. WEST VA.,
Charleston, October 20, 1863.

Capt. J. L. BOTSFORD,
Asst. Adjt. Gen., Charleston, W. Va.:

SIR: I have the honor to state that I have received information from reliable Union men that there is a force of rebel cavalry, numbering from 300 to 400 men, under command of Colonel Beckley, now in Boone County, near Boone Court-House. They are engaged in conscripting for the rebel army and stealing horses, &c.

I would respectfully request permission to take my command and go to that place for the purpose of dispersing and capturing this band.

I am, sir, very respectfully, your obedient servant,
A. N. DUFFIÉ,
Brigadier-General, Commanding Cavalry.

WAR DEPARTMENT,
Washington, October 20, 1863—9 p. m.
Major-General FOSTER,
Fort Monroe, Va.:

Advices from Richmond are that every available man, except some local militia or home guards, has moved with Lee's army against Meade. Is it not possible, under these circumstances, to move up the York River, destroy the railroad bridges, and threaten Richmond, so as to draw back some of Lee's forces? Please answer.
H. W. HALLECK,
General-in-Chief.

FORT MONROE, VA., *October* 20, 1863—10.30 p. m.
(Received 11 p. m.)
Major-General HALLECK:

Telegram received. I will attempt what you propose, and do it if possible.
J. G. FOSTER,
Major-General.

HEADQUARTERS ARMY OF THE POTOMAC,
Gainesville, Va., October 21, 1863—10.30 a. m.
(Received 11 a. m.)
Maj. Gen. H. W. HALLECK,
General-in-Chief:

I regret to inform you that from the examination made, I have reason to believe that the Orange and Alexandria Railroad has been destroyed from Bristoe Station to Culpeper Court-House. To repair and put in working order the road to the Rappahannock will require the use of a considerable part of this army for guards and working parties. Under these circumstances, I do not see the practicability of an advance on this line to Gordonsville. A transfer to the Fredericksburg road, if successful in crossing the Rappahannock, would require time to put the road in working order from Aquia Creek, and the enemy would doubtless destroy it in advance of the point we held.

It seems to me, therefore, that the campaign is virtually over for the present season, and that it would be better to withdraw the army to some position in front of Washington and detach from it such portions as may be required to operate elsewhere. Although I have no information but the acts of the enemy, I think it is his intention to detach a portion of his forces for operations elsewhere. I should be glad to have the views of the Government at the earliest possible moment.

GEO. G. MEADE,
Major-General, Commanding.

WASHINGTON, *October* 21, 1863—1.30 p. m.
(Received 9.15 p. m.)
Major-General MEADE:

Your telegrams of 8 p. m. last night and 10.30 this morning were received. I cannot reply till I receive the orders of the President and the Secretary of War.

H. W. HALLECK,
General-in-Chief.

WASHINGTON, *October* 21, 1863—3.30 p. m.
(Received 9.15 p. m.)
Major-General MEADE:

If you can conveniently leave your army, the President wishes to see you to-morrow.

H. W. HALLECK,
General-in-Chief.

SIGNAL DEPT., HDQRS. ARMY OF THE POTOMAC,
October 21, 1863.
Maj. Gen. A. A. HUMPHREYS,
Chief of Staff:

GENERAL: The following report has just been received, and is respectfully forwarded for the information of the commanding general:

WATERY MOUNTAIN SIGNAL STATION,
October 21, 1863—5.30 p. m.
Captain NORTON:

Large camp smokes are seen near Stevensburg, Brandy Station, opposite Rappahannock Station, and Freeman's Ford. Smokes in direction of Stevensburg are heaviest. A force (think of cavalry) is massed on south bank of Rappahannock. Quite a number of lights seen below Sulphur Springs.

TAYLOR,
Signal Officer.

Communication open by flag signals from these headquarters via Watery Mountain, with the headquarters of the Fifth and Sixth Corps.

I have the honor to be &c.,

L. B. NORTON,
Captain, and Chief Signal Officer.

CAMDEN STATION, *Baltimore, Md., October* 21, 1863.
(Received 12.30 p. m.)
Maj. Gen. H. W. HALLECK:

Upon receipt of your telegram yesterday, I instructed the greatest vigilance at all points in reference to our rolling stock and bridges.

We are also endeavoring in every practicable form to obtain information regarding any movements that threaten us, so that we may secure any machinery or property that may be endangered. If the forces that can be concentrated near the Baltimore and Ohio line are active and sufficient to endanger Stuart's return, I strongly hope that he will be deterred from attempting a raid into Maryland and Pennsylvania.

J. W. GARRETT,
President.

HEADQUARTERS DIVISION,
October 21, 1863.

Captain POTTER,
Assistant Adjutant-General:

I have the honor to state that the party of cavalry sent out from here in search of rebel cavalry have returned, who report that the number of the enemy supposed to be in the vicinity of Chichester Mills was greatly exaggerated. Colonel Lowell, in conjunction with Colonel Baker, is still scouring the country.

MICHAEL CORCORAN,
Brigadier-General.

HEADQUARTERS FIRST SEPARATE BRIGADE,
Beverly, October 21, 1863.

Brigadier-General AVERELL,
Clarksburg:

Six of our scouts just in from the front. They were 5 miles beyond Big Spring. Report Captain McNeill's cavalry company at Huntersville, parts of Hutton's and Marshall's companies on Elk Mountain, near Edray; about 100 infantry at Greenbrier Bridge. Colonel Arnett commands all these forces. Headquarters at Greenbrier Bridge. No forces at Green Bank or Dunmore. The force in all that country not over 300.

They also report that they were told by one Sharp, a very reliable Union man living beyond Big Spring, that an officer of Jackson's command told him about a week ago that the forces of Jones and Jenkins were *en route* to the Kanawha Valley, and that Jackson would endeavor to capture Bulltown, and then join forces near Charleston. Nothing known of Jackson since his repulse.

L. MARKBREIT,
Acting Assistant Adjutant-General.

EXECUTIVE MANSION,
Washington, October 21, 1863—2.45 p. m.

Major-General SCHENCK,
Baltimore, Md.:

A delegation is here saying that our armed colored troops are at many, if not all, the landings on the Patuxent River, and by their presence with arms in their hands are frightening quiet people, and producing great confusion. Have they been sent there by any order; and if so, for what reason?

A. LINCOLN.

BALTIMORE, *October* 21, 1863.
(Received 6.45 p. m.)

The PRESIDENT OF THE UNITED STATES,
Washington, D. C.:

The delegation from Saint Mary's County have grossly misrepresented matters. Colonel Birney went under my orders to look for a site for a camp of instruction and rendezvous for colored troops. (See his report this day forwarded to the Adjutant-General.) He took with him a recruiting squad, who were stationed, each with one officer, at Millstone, Spencer's, Saint Leonard's, Duke's, Forest Grove, and Benedict Landings, on the Patuxent. They are under special instructions, good discipline, and have harmed no one. The only disorder or violence has been that two secessionists, named Southeron, have killed Second Lieutenant White at Benedict; but we hope to arrest the murderers. The officer was a white man. The only danger of confusion must be from the citizens, not the soldiers, but Colonel Birney himself visited all the landings, talked with the citizens, and the only apprehension they expressed was that their slaves might leave them. It is a neighborhood of rabid secessionists. I beg that the President will not intervene, and thus embolden them.

ROBT. C. SCHENCK,
Major-General.

HEADQUARTERS SAINT MARY'S DISTRICT,
Point Lookout, Md., October 21, 1863.

Lieut. JOHN MIX,
Comdg. Detachment Second and Fifth U. S. Cavalry:

You will, with 1 commissioned officer and 106 men of your command, proceed by way of the Three Notched road to Leonardtown, in the county of Saint Mary's, at which place you will establish your headquarters. You are charged with the duty of suppressing contraband trade and all disloyal practices, arresting deserters and escaped prisoners, and preserving the public peace. The more effectually to accomplish these objects, you will send small detachments of your force to Charlotte Hall, Chaptico, the mouth of the Patuxent River, and such other points as you may deem necessary. All blockade runners you will cause to be arrested, their goods seized and sent to this point.

It is reported that some persons are now engaged near the mouth of the Patuxent and above there in enlisting into the military service slaves and free persons of color without proper authority from the War Department. You will inquire into the matter, and if you find such to be the case you will cause them immediately to desist and to leave this military district forthwith, if they are not residents therein.

You will take with you rations and forage for three days, and afterward supplies will be sent to Leonardtown for your detachment. I desire that you will be particularly careful that no depredations are committed by any of the men under your command upon the property of any person whatever.

You will report by mail as often as every other day.

Very respectfully, your obedient servant,

GILMAN MARSTON,
Brigadier-General, Commanding.

GENERAL ORDERS, ⎱ HDQRS. MIDDLE DEPT., 8TH ARMY CORPS,
No. 51.   ⎰   *Baltimore, Md., October 21, 1863.*

I. Brig. Gen. H. H. Lockwood, U. S. Volunteers, having reported at these headquarters, is assigned to the command of all that district of country consisting of the counties of the Eastern Shore of Maryland as far north as and including Kent County; the counties of Northampton and Accomac, in Virginia; the county of Calvert, in Maryland, and all the Western Shore of Maryland lying between the Potomac and Patuxent Rivers as far up as the Piscataway River and Upper Marlborough, excepting the county of Saint Mary's.

This command will include all forces that now are, or may be hereafter, assigned for service in any part of said district, and will be known as the First Separate Brigade.

II. All the forces belonging to this department or army corps, now in service, or which may hereafter be assigned to duty, stationed in Baltimore City or County, including all the works of defense therein, except Fort McHenry, Fort Marshall, Fort Federal Hill, and Fort Dix, and except the Second Separate Brigade, shall hereafter be known as the Third Separate Brigade, and will be under the command of Brig. Gen. E. B. Tyler, U. S. Volunteers.

By command of Major-General Schenck:

WM. H. CHESEBROUGH,
Lieutenant-Colonel, and Assistant Adjutant-General.

——

GENERAL ORDERS, ⎱ HDQRS. DEPT. OF WEST VIRGINIA,
No. 16.   ⎰   *Clarksburg, W. Va., October 21, 1863.*

I. The troops formerly designated as the Fourth, Fifth, and Sixth Brigades, First Division, Eighth Corps, and generally those stationed on the Baltimore and Ohio and Northwestern Virginia Railroads, from Sleepy Creek west to the Ohio River, will constitute the Second Division of this department.

II. The counties of Ohio, Brooke, and Hancock, W. Va., are, by order of the Secretary of War, included within and made a portion of this department.

By order of Brigadier-General Kelley:

THAYER MELVIN,
Assistant Adjutant-General.

——

FORT MONROE, VA., *October 21, 1863.*
(Received 8.50 a. m.)

Major-General HALLECK,
        General-in-Chief:

The private information that I get, through rebel sources, is to the effect that Lee will not pursue Meade much farther, but will soon retire to his old position south of the Rappahannock.

J. G. FOSTER,
Major-General.

FORT MONROE, VA., *October 21, 1863*—8 a. m.
(Received 9.10 a. m.)

Maj. Gen. H. W. HALLECK,
General-in-Chief:

The force with which I can move at this moment does not exceed
5,000, of all arms. This would only allow me to make a dash at the
railroad bridge and at Richmond with cavalry, holding certain points
with the infantry. I make this representation before inquiring if
you are decidedly in favor of the demonstration up the York River
instead of the James River. The chances for me in this latter direction are, I think, greater for breaking the railroad connection south
and southwest of Petersburg. Please intimate your wishes upon
this point.

J. G. FOSTER,
Major-General.

WAR DEPARTMENT,
Washington, October 21, 1863—10.30 a. m.

Major-General FOSTER,
Fort Monroe, Va.:

The object is to break railroads between Richmond and General
Lee's army. There would be nothing important gained by destroying bridges south of Richmond at the present time. Having driven
Meade across Bull Run, and destroyed the railroad, Lee is now falling back. If you have not the force to attempt the destruction of
the bridges north of Richmond, I do not insist upon it.

H. W. HALLECK,
General-in-Chief.

WAR DEPARTMENT,
Washington, October 21, 1863—2.30 p. m.

Major-General FOSTER,
Fort Monroe, Va.:

Dispatches from General Meade render it advisable that you make
no movement till further orders.

H. W. HALLECK,
General-in-Chief.

FORT MONROE, VA., *October 21, 1863*—4.30 p. m.
(Received 5 p. m.)

Maj. Gen. H. W. HALLECK,
General-in-Chief:

Your telegram received. I intended to start to-morrow, but am
glad of the delay, as it gives time to get some regiments from North
Carolina and parties from the outposts.

J. G. FOSTER,
Major-General, Commanding.

SPECIAL ORDERS, }   HDQRS. DEPT. OF VA. AND N. C.,
No. 93. }   Fort Monroe, Va., October 21, 1863.

*   *   *   *   *   *   *

VI. Maj. Gen. J. J. Peck, commanding District of North Carolina, will order the following troops under his command to proceed at once to this point with all possible dispatch: Twenty-fifth Regiment Massachusetts Volunteers, Third Regiment New York Cavalry, Battery F, First Rhode Island Artillery; Howell's battery, Third New York Artillery, and Riggs' battery, Third New York Artillery.

*   *   *   *   *   *   *

X. Brig. Gen. E. Harland, commanding Getty's division, will at once take the necessary steps to have his command prepared to embark to-morrow morning.

The troops will be in light marching order; will be provided with three days' cooked rations, seven days' in bulk, and 100 rounds of ammunition.

The fortifications in his front will be garrisoned by the batteries of the Thirteenth New York Artillery, under Major Wetmore, who will divide his command accordingly. The reserve or support to the artillery will be taken from the invalids of the different regiments, who will also garrison the different redans on that front. The field guns left in position will be manned by the invalids of different batteries. All the troops, invalids, and company left in camp by General Harland, will be under the command of Brigadier-General Barnes, who will superintend the above-mentioned distribution of forces.

XI. Col. J. J. De Forest, commanding at Newport News, will have his command prepared to embark to-morrow morning at daylight in light marching order, with three days' cooked rations, seven days' in bulk, and 100 rounds of ammunition per man.

XII. Special Orders, No. 93, Paragraphs 10 and 11, from these headquarters, are hereby suspended until further orders.

XIII. All that part of Virginia comprised within what is known as the interior line of the defenses of Norfolk and Portsmouth, including Fort Norfolk and the fortifications on that line, is hereby placed under the command of Brig. Gen. James Barnes.

By command of Maj. Gen. J. G. Foster:

SOUTHARD HOFFMAN,
Assistant. Adjutant-General.

FORT MONROE, VA., *October* 21, 1863.
(Received 3 p. m.)

Hon. GIDEON WELLES, *Secretary of the Navy:*

The Eutaw is needed at Yorktown to-morrow evening to assist General Foster. I have not a gunboat here, and only the Jones and Putnam there fit for service. Can Eutaw or other aid come?

S. PHILLIPS LEE,
Acting Rear-Admiral.

MANASSAS, *October* 22, 1863.
(Received 12 m.)

Maj. Gen. H. W. HALLECK, *General-in-Chief:*

I will be in Washington by 2 p. m.

GEO. G. MEADE,
Major-General.

HEADQUARTERS ARMY OF THE POTOMAC,
October 22, 1863—6.05 p. m. (Received 11.15 p. m.)

Maj. Gen. GEORGE G. MEADE,
Washington:

Colonel Gregg, commanding brigade of cavalry at Fayetteville, reports that the Second Pennsylvania Cavalry met the enemy's pickets at 12 m. to-day at Bealeton Station. After some skirmishing the enemy moved off in the direction of Rappahannock Station. The officer sent by General Pleasonton with a small party to examine the condition of the railroad was unable to reach Rappahannock Station, being met by a considerable force of the enemy's cavalry, which caused his return. He found the road destroyed to Ratcliffe's Run, the point he reached. A prisoner reports three regiments of the enemy's cavalry and some infantry on this side of the Rappahannock. General Gregg reports that the enemy's vedettes are in sight at Sulphur Springs. The signal officer at Watery Mountain reports that it is too smoky to see anything south of the Rappahannock to-day. Guerrillas seen on Carter's Mountain.

S. WILLIAMS,
Assistant Adjutant-General.

HEADQUARTERS SECOND ARMY CORPS,
Auburn, October 22, 1863.

Major-General HUMPHREYS:

If we are to stay any number of days at this place, would it not be well for me to station a brigade at Greenwich, and detachments at other points between here and Gainesville, so as to prevent guerrillas from infesting the road?

I would not trouble you with such an insignificant matter, but that such a scattering of my force might interfere with my prompt execution of any movements you may have in view for us.

Respectfully,

G. K. WARREN,
Major-General of Volunteers.

CIRCULAR.]   HEADQUARTERS ARMY OF THE POTOMAC,
October 23, 1863.

The several corps of the army are posted as follows, at the present time:

First Corps at Georgetown.

Second Corps where the Warrenton Branch Railroad crosses Turkey Run.

Third Corps at Catlett's Station, with one brigade at Bristoe.

Fifth Corps at New Baltimore.

Sixth Corps at Warrenton.

Reserve Artillery near New Baltimore.

By command of Major-General Meade:

S. WILLIAMS,
Assistant Adjutant-General.

EXECUTIVE MANSION,
Washington, October 22, 1863—1.30 p. m.

Major-General SCHENCK,
Baltimore, Md.:

Please come over here. The fact of one of our officers being killed on the Patuxent is a specimen of what I would avoid. It seems to me we could send white men to recruit better than to send negroes, and thus inaugurate homicides on *punctilio.* Please come over.

A. LINCOLN.

MARTINSBURG, W. VA., *October 22, 1863.*
(Received War Department 5.30 p. m.)

Col. G. H. SHARPE,
Headquarters Army of the Potomac:

Statement of William Arndoff, a native of Jefferson County:

I was informed by a farmer by the name of Joseph Crane, who lives near Charles-town, Jefferson County, and is a very reliable man and a strong rebel, and thinks I am the same, that he would be very much disappointed if General Lee did not cross the Potomac at the Point of Rocks within ten days. This man Crane says he never has been disappointed in his opinion in reference to the rebel movements. He further stated that Imboden's command fell back to Front Royal, there to divide their forces into two separate commands. One is to advance by the way of Berry-ville and Charlestown; the other is to keep north of the turnpike and surround and capture the forces stationed at this post. He also said that General Lee has the largest and finest army he has ever had. He further stated that Jenkins was to unite his forces with Imboden.

This gentleman has been heretofore employed as a spy, and is act-ing in that capacity at present. I this day sent the said Arndoff to Front Royal, Luray, and various other places. He is a responsible man. I took his bond for $5,000.

MICHAEL GRAHAM.

HEADQUARTERS,
Fairfax Court-House, Va., October 22, 1863.

Captain POTTER,
Asst. Adjt. Gen., Dept. of Washington:

I have nothing of importance to report. Three of Mosby's men were captured and 1 killed, near Chichester Mills this afternoon, by the men of Colonel Baker's command at Annandale.

MICHAEL CORCORAN,
Brigadier-General.

FORT MONROE, VA., *October 22, 1863.*
(Received 5 p. m.)

Maj. Gen. H. W. HALLECK,
General-in-Chief:

The Richmond papers of the 19th, 20th, and 21st, which I send you by mail, speak of Lee's intention to retire to a position near Richmond, having failed to bring General Meade to battle. They also report heavy freshets on the Rappahannock and Rapidan Rivers, which destroyed, or at least rendered impassable for a time, the bridges over the latter river. They state that all interest is now centered in the operations of the armies at Chattanooga.

J. G. FOSTER,
Major-General.

GENERAL ORDERS, }   HDQRS. NORFOLK AND PORTSMOUTH,
No. 14.   }   *Norfolk, Va., October 22, 1863.*

The time set·for the execution of Dr. David M. Wright by General Orders, No. 17, headquarters Department of Virginia and North Carolina, promulgated in General Orders, No. 12 [13?], from these headquarters, having been by order of the President postponed until Friday, the 23d, the execution will take place to-morrow (Friday) morning, October 23, 1863, at 10 o'clock.

By command of Brig. Gen. James Barnes:

GEORGE H. JOHNSTON,
Assistant Adjutant-General,

FORT MONROE, VA., *October 23, 1863*—11.20 a. m.
(Received 11.30 a. m.)

Maj. Gen. H. W. HALLECK,
  General-in-Chief:

Dr. Wright was executed this morning at Norfolk, according to orders. Everything passed off very orderly.

J. G. FOSTER,
Major-General, Commanding.

HEADQUARTERS ARMY OF THE POTOMAC,
October 23, 1863—6 p. m.

Maj. Gen. H. W. HALLECK,
  General-in-Chief:

The following dispatch, just received from Colonel Sharpe, deputy provost-marshal-general, is sent for your information. Colonel Sharpe has been directed to send other agents immediately.

GEO. G. MEADE,
Major-General.

[Inclosure.]

ALEXANDRIA, VA.,
October 23, [1863.]

General HUMPHREYS,
  Chief of Staff:

Our men returned this morning. The old man says that Ewell's corps went to Tennessee last Monday. He did not have time to go to the army himself, but yesterday he saw a man from Fredericksburg who had gone up to Culpeper on Monday as claimant to get certificates for damages done to his property and that of citizens around Fredericksburg. These certificates were to come from officers in Ewell's corps. The claimant returned to Fredericksburg on Tuesday, and said that he was unable to complete his business, because Ewell's corps had left for Tennessee on Monday. This is the authority, and the old man thinks it straight.

The old man also says that he is quite sure no troops have come to Lee's army; that it is reported that the division at Petersburg has gone to re-enforce Bragg, and that the main body of the enemy lies at Culpeper, with some troops thrown over the Rapidan. The people about Fredericksburg report that Lee's late advance upon Meade's front has turned out disastrous, and that A. P. Hill is in arrest for the failure.

On the other hand, our men brought with them an Irish refugee from Richmond, who says he left there Wednesday morning, at 7 o'clock; that up to that time Ewell's corps had not passed through; that on Saturday evening last, Governor Smith addressed the citizens of Richmond, urging the home companies to go to protect the salt-works. He did not hear where, but very few went; that Mr. Davis returned from Bragg's army on Monday last, and addressed the citizens the same evening, assuring them of success in the west.

I am writing from Colonel Devereux's office, and shall return to headquarters by the 3 o'clock train if I do not hear from you. If you wish the trip made right over again for absolute confirmation, Captain McEntee must send me one or two other men, as the men I have with me have their feet so blistered as to be unable to walk.

GEO. H. SHARPE,
Colonel, &c.

SIGNAL DEPT., HDQRS. ARMY OF THE POTOMAC,
October 23, 1863.

Brig. Gen. S. WILLIAMS, *Assistant Adjutant-General:*

GENERAL: Communication by flag signal is open between these headquarters and the headquarters of the Second, Third, and Fifth Corps.

Very respectfully, &c.,

L. B. NORTON,
Captain, and Chief Signal Officer.

HEADQUARTERS ARMY OF THE POTOMAC,
October 23, 1863—4 p.m.

Major-General FRENCH,
Commanding Third Corps, Catlett's:

The major-general commanding directs me to say that Colonel Gregg, commanding cavalry brigade, reports that the enemy are in some force at Rappahannock Station, and disposed to fight. They may push forward to ascertain what we are doing, and I am directed to advise you to be on the alert.

A. A. HUMPHREYS,
Major-General, and Chief of Staff.

[Indorsement.]

HEADQUARTERS THIRD ARMY CORPS,
October 23, 1863.

Pursuant to the above, division commanders will hold their commands well in hand, prepared for any emergency that may arise.

By command of Major-General French:

O. H. HART,
Assistant Adjutant-General.

HEADQUARTERS ARMY OF THE POTOMAC,
October 23, 1863.

Major-General HUMPHREYS,
Chief of Staff:

The following dispatch has just been received, and is respectfully forwarded:

WATERY MOUNTAIN SIGNAL STATION,
October 23, 1863—5 p. m.

Captain NORTON:

Large camps of the enemy plainly seen this p. m., south of Rappahannock and between Brandy Station and Culpeper. Five regiments of infantry were drilling on field in vicinity of Brandy Station. Strong cavalry pickets along the Rappahannock. See no camps or smokes west of Jefferson.

TAYLOR,
Signal Officer.

I have the honor to be,

L. B. NORTON,
Captain, and Chief Signal Officer.

HEADQUARTERS ARMY OF THE POTOMAC,
October 23, 1863—8 p. m.

Commanding Officer First Corps:

The major-general commanding directs that you move your corps to Bristoe Station, on the Orange and Alexandria Railroad. The brigade of the Third Corps now there will be relieved by you. As soon as the bridge over Kettle Run is finished, you will have it properly guarded, and will guard the road as fast as finished as far as the crossings of Slaty Run.

Very respectfully, your obedient servant,
A. A. HUMPHREYS,
Major-General, and Chief of Staff.

HEADQUARTERS ARMY OF THE POTOMAC,
October 23, 1863—8.15 p. m.

Commanding Officer Third Corps:

The major-general commanding directs me to inform you that the First Corps is ordered to move to Bristoe Station, and will relieve the brigade of your corps now there. The First Corps will guard the railroad when finished as far as the crossings of Slaty Run. The Third Corps will guard the road from Slaty Run to Warrenton Junction and to the Three-Mile Station, on the Warrenton Branch, as fast as finished.

Very respectfully, your obedient servant,
A. A. HUMPHREYS,
Major-General, and Chief of Staff.

CHARLESTON, W. VA., October 23, 1863—5.20 p. m.
(Received 9.45 p. m.)

Maj. Gen. H. W. HALLECK,
General-in-Chief:

Sergeant Hunnicutt, on secret service, from the Army of the Potomac, passed here September 5, to Dublin, Lynchburg, Gordonsville,

Hanover, Richmond, Petersburg, Weldon, Wilmington, Raleigh, Augusta, Atlanta, and-Chattanooga, and returned here this morning, via Dublin and North River. Reports Clingman's brigade at Wilmington; Colquitt dead, his brigade at Kinston; Ransom's brigade at Weldon; Pickett, with Armistead's brigade, Washington Artillery, and part of the Thirteenth Virginia Cavalry, recruiting at Petersburg; Wise's Legion at Charleston, S. C.; part of Elzey's division at Drewry's Bluff, rest gone to Jones, at Bristol; Imboden, if not with Stuart, aiming at railroad at Piedmont; Tredegar Works making a large number of heavy guns; Reverend Hoge landed at Wilmington, October 10, with from ten to fifteen thousand French tenshooters; Army of Northern Virginia, under Ewell, consists of his corps and A. P. Hill's; Lee, with Bragg's army, 125,000 strong. Hunnicutt says he acts under Colonel Sharpe, deputy provost-marshal, Army of the Potomac. Tried to get into our lines at United States Ford on the Rappahannock, but could not. He leaves in the morning for Washington.

E. P. SCAMMON,
Brigadier-General.

HDQRS. DEPT. OF VIRGINIA AND NORTH CAROLINA,
Fort Monroe, Va., October 23, 1863.

Major-General HALLECK,
Commander-in-Chief, U. S. Army:

GENERAL: I have received information from deserters to the effect that the enemy, seeing the advantage that might accrue to us from the possession of Smith's Island, have occupied it and commenced the erection of a work at Bald Head. I have sent Colonel Dutton, Twenty-first Connecticut Volunteers (Engineer Corps, U. S. Army), to examine and report. This is a very important matter in connection with the commencement of operations against the forts at the mouth of the Cape Fear River. From Bald Head, Fort Caswell can be battered and the channel controlled, while a night attack with infantry might secure the work on Zekes Island, and thus enable us to control the east channel. I do not see what I can do. The small movable force that I have collected here acts now as a reserve for any threatened point, and is available for any movement to the front of our present positions. But to take it so far away as Smith's Island may endanger the safety of the points now held. Besides, the force is too small for the work at Smith's Island and Caswell both, and may even now be too small for the taking of Smith's Island alone. I want to do something, and as soon as Colonel Dutton returns will make a fuller report, and ask for your instructions.

Very respectfully and truly, your obedient servant,
J. G. FOSTER,
Major-General, Commanding.

HDQRS. ARMY AND DISTRICT OF NORTH CAROLINA,
New Berne, N. C., October 23, 1863.

Maj. Gen. J. G. FOSTER,
Comdg. Dept. of Virginia and North Carolina:

Your orders for the additional force came to hand this morning, and found me with less facilities than ever before. Our steamers

were on their routes, or needing repairs, and the quartermaster reported some 12 tons as our whole stock of coal. Commodore Davenport kindly gave us all he had, and the wheels are still in motion.

The Twelfth Cavalry had to be sent to relieve the Third, causing
additional travel and consuming time. At the first, I confess I began
to despair, since so much transportation is called for, cavalry and
artillery.

The Spaulding arrived, and I shall send nine companies of the
Twenty-fifth Massachusetts and two of cavalry upon this vessel.
The Vedette arrived this evening. She is being repaired, and will
leave early in the morning with a schooner in tow for Elizabeth City,
with cavalry. The Patuxent is due in a few hours, I believe. The
Pilot Boy will be due to-morrow evening with the Twenty-fifth Massachusetts from Washington. A tug was sent off with orders for all
vessels, and they will be hurried off as rapidly as our facilities will
admit.

Dr. Rice, Twenty-fifth Massachusetts, was captured yesterday, and
his orderly also. Some of our pickets at Little Washington have
been bagged. I have very little confidence in the Twelfth Cavalry,
and hope you will be able to send back the Third Regiment again.

One of the companies of the Twenty-fifth Massachusetts consti-
tutes the garrison of Fort Gaston, and is well instructed in artillery.
Having nothing to replace it with, I have retained it.

Our sick-list is very large, indeed, and does not run down, as I
anticipated, with the advance of the season.

The small-pox has materially reduced our stock of lumber, by producing a scarcity of hands, but orders have been given to press the
mills for your wants at Fort Monroe.

Very respectfully, your obedient servant,

JOHN J. PECK,
Major-General.

HEADQUARTERS,
Fort Magruder, Va., October 23, 1863.

Brig. Gen. I. J. WISTAR,
Commanding Forces:

GENERAL: Upon the occasion of passing Mrs. Lee out of the lines
yesterday, I deemed it expedient to send out a scouting party in
advance, as far as the Nine-Mile Ordinary. This I did, because upon
a former occasion, I sent a small party out, and afterward heard that
if we did the same thing again the expedition would come to grief.
They said of us that we were too cowardly to come out upon any
other occasion than when ladies accompanied us. It was well that I
sent a good strong party, 1 officer and 50 men, for they were set upon
going out by guerrillas, and returning they were drawn into an
ambush by a party, how strong it was not known, at Six-Mile Ordinary. A considerable volley was delivered into the flank of the
column as it was moving along the road. Telegraph wire had been
stretched across the road to trip their horses as they returned. No
one was hurt, which all parties agree in representing as miraculous.

I should like extremely well to make a dash to-morrow morning
up the road with some cavalry and infantry, say about 100 of each,
not to go beyond the Nine-Mile Ordinary, and see if these fellows

cannot be made to pay a little for their audacity. Will you please allow me to do so?

The captain who commanded the party yesterday had orders to go as far as Nine-Mile Ordinary, but not beyond; to gain all the information he could; if he saw a good chance to make a dash to do so, but avoid an ambush, to be very careful on the latter point. He did not disobey any order, but I think he might have done better. He was also ordered to bring back in safety a buggy and cart driven by two negroes, which went out with Mrs. Lee; this he did.

I have the honor to be, general, very respectfully, your obedient servant,

> ROBT. M. WEST,
> *Colonel, Commanding.*

[First indorsement.]

> HEADQUARTERS,
> *Yorktown, October 23, 1863—12 m.*

Respectfully forwarded to the major-general commanding department, for his information.

I have telegraphed to Colonel West to execute his plan boldly, but take care not to take his infantry too far from support.

Respectfully,

> I. J. WISTAR,
> *Brigadier-General.*

P. S.—Mrs. Lee was sent out under permission from department headquarters, granted some time since, with caution "never to return."

[Second indorsement.]

Action approved.

> J. G. FOSTER.

> WAR DEPARTMENT,
> *Washington, October 24, 1863—11.20 a. m.*

Major-General MEADE,
  Army of the Potomac:

The President desires that you will prepare to attack Lee's army, and, at all hazards, make a cavalry raid, to break the railroad at or near Lynchburg, and such other places as may be practicable. The troops making this raid must mainly subsist upon the country. They should be provided with the proper means of destroying railroads, bridges, &c. There are four lines by which to return; first, to your army; second, through the Valley of the Shenandoah; third, to Gloucester; fourth, to Norfolk. I send herewith a copy of the President's letter, just received.

> H. W. HALLECK,
> *General-in-Chief.*

[Inclosure.]

> EXECUTIVE MANSION,
> *Washington, October 24, 1863.*

Major-General HALLECK:

Taking all our information together, I think it probable that Ewell's corps has started for East Tennessee by way of Abingdon,

· marching last Monday, say, from Meade's front directly to the rail-road at Charlottesville.

First, the object of Lee's recent movement against Meade; his destruction of the Orange and Alexandria Railroad, and subsequent withdrawal, without more motive, not otherwise apparent, would be explained by this hypothesis.

Secondly, the direct statement of Sharpe's man that Ewell has gone to Tennessee.

Thirdly, the Irishman's statement that he has not gone through Richmond, and his further statement of an appeal made to the people at Richmond to go and protect their salt, which could only refer to the works near Abingdon.

Fourthly, Graham's statement from Martinsburg that Imboden is in retreat for Harrisonburg. This last matches with the idea that Lee has retained his cavalry, sending Imboden and perhaps other scraps to join Ewell. Upon this probability what is to be done?

If you have a plan matured, I have nothing to say. If you have not, then I suggest that with all possible expedition, the Army of the Potomac get ready to attack Lee, and that in the meantime a raid shall, at all hazards, break the railroad at or near Lynchburg.

Yours, truly,

A. LINCOLN.

————

OCTOBER 24, 1863—2 p. m.
(Received 3.45 p. m.)

Major-General HALLECK:

Your telegram of 11 a. m. is received. The information given in Colonel Sharpe's dispatch is disproved by two deserters just in, who report Ewell's corps in my immediate front on the Rappahannock, with one division (Anderson's) on this side at the railroad crossing.

My cavalry this morning drove in the enemy's cavalry pickets to the railroad crossing, where they fell back on infantry supports that advanced and compelled our cavalry to retire. From all the information I can get, Lee's army is now between the Rappahannock and the Rapidan, principally at Stevensburg, Brandy, and Jefferson. It would seem as if he intended to dispute the passage of the Rappahannock, and some indications that would lead to the belief of an intention to advance, two pontoon bridges being reported at the rail-road crossing, which would not be required if the defensive was only to be assumed.

Before receiving your dispatch, I had intended to repair the rail-road as far as Warrenton Junction, to establish my base at Warrenton and Warrenton Junction, and then to advance against Lee, Colonel McCallum reporting he could have the road repaired to Warrenton Junction by the 30th instant. I informed you when in Washington that my cavalry was much reduced by the recent active operations, and particularly by the appearance within the last few days of the hoof disease, which is now spreading rapidly. I have called for reports as to the present numbers and condition of the cavalry.

The proposed raid, in my judgment, will be more likely to succeed with small than large numbers. Twenty-five hundred men, I should think, would be sufficient.

The withdrawal of Imboden from the lower valley is not, I apprehend, to send him south, but to hold the passes in the upper valley and resist such expeditions as we now propose, or perhaps to operate on my rear, should I advance.

It has been raining very hard since last evening. This will render all roads, excepting the pike to Gainesville, impassable, and will swell all the small streams and branches. I shall make every preparation with the utmost expedition to advance, and in the meantime select a cavalry command, and arrange the details for the raid ordered.

> GEO. G. MEADE,
> *Major-General, Commanding.*

> WASHINGTON,
> *October 24, 1863—6.45 p. m.*

Major-General MEADE:

Yours of 2 p. m. is just received. I shall not be able to see the President before to-morrow to learn his views on your report of the present aspect of affairs.

> H. W. HALLECK,
> *General-in-Chief.*

> OCTOBER 24, 1863.

Lieut. Col. C. ROSS SMITH:

Report from the cavalry advance toward Bealeton Station:

Colonel Devin's brigade, of the First Division, encamped last night at Liberty, pushing one regiment as far as Bealeton Station. This morning Colonel Devin sent two regiments to drive the enemy's pickets toward or across the river at Rappahannock Station, in order to establish his line at that point. Colonel Devin's men succeeded in driving the enemy from the woods a mile on this side of the river, and close on to the works over the burned bridge, where the enemy had their infantry in line, and from whence they immediately pushed forward about 3,000 men with a force of cavalry, the infantry moving on the north and the cavalry on the south side. Colonel Devin fell back, being closely followed by the enemy's infantry, as far as Liberty, when the enemy halted, and in a short time fell back, followed by our forces, toward Bealeton. Colonel Devin did not engage the enemy, merely observing his movements, losing only 1 man killed and a few wounded.

Colonel Devin expects to have his brigade advanced by sunset close to Bealeton, as the last reports from his advance guard say:

The enemy seem to be retiring to their previous position in the works at Rappahannock Bridge.

Colonel Gregg reports to have learned from a prisoner, or deserter, that Ewell's corps occupy the works at the bridge, two divisions being on this side. Both of our cavalry brigade commanders agree in saying that there is at least one division of rebel infantry on this side.

A locomotive was heard to approach the bridge last night from Culpeper.

Respectfully forwarded.

> MYLES W. KEOGH,
> *Captain, and Aide-de-Camp.*

[Indorsement.]

HEADQUARTERS CAVALRY CORPS,
October 24, [1883]—6.30 p. m.

This report of Captain Keogh, aide-de-camp, to General Buford, just received, and is forwarded for the information of the major-general commanding.

A. PLEASONTON,
Major-General.

———

LIBERTY,
[*October* 24, 1863]—9.20 a. m.

[Maj. Gen. A. PLEASONTON:]

GENERAL: At daybreak I drove in the enemy's pickets to their rifle-pits at the station. They soon after advanced at least a brigade of infantry and one of cavalry. They have not yet reached Bealeton.

Respectfully, yours,

THOS. C. DEVIN,
Colonel, Commanding Brigade.

[P. S.]—We can do nothing here without infantry.

[Indorsement.]

OCTOBER 24, [1863]—11.30 a. m.

This report was just received. It would be well to place some infantry at Bealeton to support the cavalry.

A. PLEASONTON,
Major-General, Commanding.

———

HEADQUARTERS SECOND BRIGADE,
October 24, [1863]—10.30 a. m.

General GREGG:

Colonel Devin reports the enemy advancing in heavy force, pushing forward strong infantry columns.

Very respectfully,

J. IRVIN GREGG,
Colonel, Commanding Brigade.

———

HDQRS. SECOND DIVISION, CAVALRY CORPS,
October 24, 1863.

Lieut. Col. C. ROSS SMITH,
Chief of Staff, Cavalry Corps:

COLONEL: A staff officer from Colonel Gregg reports Devin's brigade falling back upon the Warrenton road, and that Colonel Gregg was in readiness to take a new position. I have sent a staff officer down to get more certain information. The pickets of my first brigade extend from Waterloo to Fox's Ford. This line is still preserved. At Fox's Ford the Second Brigade took up the line and extended to Beverly Ford. Below this point, owing to the presence of the enemy, the line was not established. I have instructed Colonel Gregg to maintain the connection of his right with Colonel Taylor, and extend well off to his left and front. How much Colonel Gregg's line is changed by the falling back, I have not yet learned. Upon the return of my staff officer, I will again report. Should the enemy advance beyond Fayetteville, the pickets at Fox's Ford would be compelled to retire, and the position at Sulphur Springs be endangered.

Yours, respectfully,

D. McM. GREGG,
Brigadier-General of Volunteers.

HDQRS. CAV. CORPS, ARMY OF THE POTOMAC,
October 24, 1863—12 m.

Major-General HUMPHREYS:
Chief of Staff, Army of the Potomac:

GENERAL : General Buford has a brigade of cavalry at Fayetteville. It would be well to have a brigade of infantry near that point to support them.

Very respectfully,

A. PLEASONTON,
Major-General, Commanding.

OCTOBER 24, 1863—1.15 p. m.

Commanding Officer Third Corps:

The major-general commanding directs that you send a brigade to Bealeton, to support the cavalry. Colonel Devin commands the cavalry in that vicinity. His headquarters are at Liberty, and he reports that, after driving in the enemy's pickets this morning at Rappahannock Station, they advanced a brigade of cavalry and one of infantry toward Bealeton.

Should you at any time need support, call upon General Newton at Bristoe. You must protect the telegraph at Warrenton Junction.

A. A. HUMPHREYS,
Major-General, and Chief of Staff.

HEADQUARTERS ARMY OF THE POTOMAC,
October 24, 1863—1.15 p. m.

Commanding Officer Fifth Corps:

The major-general commanding directs that you move your corps to Auburn, and be prepared there to move at a moment's notice or to be in position at that place. You will take with you your ammunition and ambulance trains, leaving your supply trains at New Baltimore under guard of a brigade.

Very respectfully, &c.,

A. A. HUMPHREYS,
Major-General, and Chief of Staff.

CIRCULAR.]   HEADQUARTERS ARMY OF THE POTOMAC,
October 24, 1863—1.30 p. m.

Corps commanders will hold their corps in readiness to move at a moment's notice.

By command of Major-General Meade:

S. WILLIAMS,
Assistant Adjutant-General.

BRISTOE, *October 24, 1863—*4 p. m.

Brigadier-General WILLIAMS:

The head of my column has just arrived here (Bristoe), after an extremely bad march. I do not expect the rear of it until long after dark. I started at 7 a. m.

JOHN NEWTON, •
Major-General.

HDQRS. THIRD DIVISION, CAVALRY CORPS,
October 24, 1863.

Lieut. Col. C. ROSS SMITH,
Chief of Staff, Cavalry Corps:

COLONEL: It was reported to me an hour since that some of Mosby's or White's guerrillas were in the vicinity of Thoroughfare Gap. I have directed General Davies to push out the regiment at Hay Market to that place. I will also see that it moves to Georgetown.

Very respectfully, your obedient servant,

J. KILPATRICK,
Brig. Gen. of Vols., Commanding Third Division.

MARTINSBURG, VA.,   •
October 24, 1863.

Colonel SHARPE,
Headquarters Army of the Potomac:

A deserter from the Fourteenth Louisiana, who left Lee's army on the 21st at Thoroughfare Gap, reports that it is rumored and generally believed that Longstreet's and Hill's corps were returning from Bragg, and will join Lee at or near Gordonsville.   •

MICHAEL GRAHAM.

HEADQUARTERS DIVISION,
Fairfax Court-House, Va., October 24, 1863.

Lieutenant-Colonel TAYLOR,
Chief of Staff, Asst. Adjt. Gen., Dept. of Washington:

I have the honor to report that between 2 and 3 o'clock this a. m. the pickets of the regiment stationed at Fairfax Station were fired upon from the woods. The fire was returned by our men, and two companies immediately sent out, who scoured the country, but no trace of the enemy was found. With the above exception, nothing of any importance has occurred in my command to-day.

Respectfully, &c.,

MICHAEL CORCORAN,
Brigadier-General, Commanding Division.

SIGNAL STATION,
October 25, 1863.

Major-General HUMPHREYS,
Chief of Staff :

The signal officer on Watery Mountain reports that he has seen no movements of the enemy this a. m. between Rappahannock Station and Bealeton, but that movements might have been made between the hours of 10 and 1 o'clock without his knowledge, as he could not see at that time on account of the peculiar state of the atmosphere.

L. B. NORTON,
Chief Signal Officer.

CIRCULAR.]   .HEADQUARTERS ARMY OF THE POTOMAC,
October 25, 1863—12.45 p. m.

The following dispatch is respectfully communicated to corps commanders for their information:

SIGNAL STATION,
October 25, 1863.

Major-General HUMPHREYS,
Chief of Staff :

The signal officer on Watery Mountain reports a considerable force of the enemy on north side of railroad near Brandy Station. Heavy camp smokes opposite Kelly's Ford, and extending from there to Stevensburg. Camp smokes extend from Rappahannock Station toward Bealeton. Enemy occupy the forts opposite Rappahannock Station on south side of river. No camp smokes in immediate vicinity of Culpeper Court-House.

L. B. NORTON,
Captain, and Chief Signal Officer.

By command of Major-General Meade:

S. WILLIAMS,
Assistant Adjutant-General.

CIRCULAR.]   HEADQUARTERS ARMY OF THE POTOMAC,
October 25, 1863.

The attention of corps commanders is directed to the distribution and use of the pioneers on the march. They will be distributed to the troops and trains so as habitually to precede the heads of columns of trains, to repair the roads, prepare the crossings of streams, &c. When the trains are separated a suitable distribution of the pioneers will be made.

In the recent operations it is understood that few if any pioneers accompanied the supply and baggage trains, and various delays occurred for the want of slight repairs on the roads and crossings of streams.

Care will be taken to select faithful and energetic officers for pioneer duty.

By command of Major-General Meade:

S. WILLIAMS,
Assistant Adjutant-General.

OCTOBER 25, 1863—3.15 p. m.

Commanding Officer Third Corps:

I am instructed to say that the movement of the enemy to Kelly's Ford, in connection with the disposition of his force at and near Rappahannock Station, may mean an intention on his part to advance by the line of the railroad and by the route from Kelly's Ford through Bristersburg, crossing Cedar Run at Weaverville and about 2 miles farther down near the house marked "Foulk" on the map. The ground from Catlett's house and vicinity to Weaverville, and along Cedar Run to Foulk's, and that vicinity, should be carefully examined to ascertain what advantages it possesses for posting the troops in such event as that indicated. General Sykes is now at Auburn, and his corps and others would, under the circumstances indicated, be directed toward the general position just pointed out.

Very respectfully, your obedient servant,

A. A. HUMPHREYS,
Major-General, and Chief of Staff.

MITCHELL'S,
[*October*] 25, 1863—6.15 p. m.

Captain NORTON:

Rebel message:

General L.:

I have ordered Chambliss' brigade to Germanna. I will be up to see you.

FITZ. LEE.

WM. H. R. NEEL,
Lieutenant, and Signal Officer.

HDQRS. CAVALRY CORPS, ARMY OF THE POTOMAC,
October 25, 1863.

Major-General HUMPHREYS,
Chief of Staff, Army of the Potomac:

GENERAL: I inclose two reports, one from General Buford,* representing the condition of the cavalry horses in the First Division, and one from General Gregg,* on the same subject, in regard to the Second Division of this corps. General Kilpatrick has not yet sent in his report of the Third Division. I have asked for it, and shall forward it as soon as received. From a conversation with General Kilpatrick yesterday, I am enabled to state to you the condition of his command. He can mount about 2,000 men, but his horses are not fit for hard service, and the disease called "rotten hoof" has made its appearance in that division with great virulence. The Reserve Brigade, under General Merritt, is about 1,600 strong. I am informed they have already sent back several hundred horses to Washington as unfit for service. That brigade only joined from depot about a week ago.

In case the major-general commanding requires any very hard service of the cavalry in a short time, I would respectfully suggest

---

* See p. 400.

that selections of the best mounted men from the different commands be made for the purpose. In such service as the troops are called upon to perform in a raid or in covering a retreat, every man who is dismounted by his horse giving out falls into the hands of the enemy and swells the list of our losses. The very best horses should, therefore, be used on this service.

Should a raid be contemplated at this time in the direction of James River or Lynchburg, a strong diversion in its favor should be made by an attack of the enemy in force, or a demonstration to his opposite flank, for he is watching us closely; his cavalry force at this time is considered as large—and by some of the division commanders larger—than ours, and no raid could succeed if attacked and compelled to fight at its outset.

To prepare and start a raiding party after a general action has commenced, and when the enemy's attention is diverted, would be much more favorable for its success.

I am, very respectfully,

A. PLEASONTON,
Major-General, Commanding.

ARTILLERY HDQRS., ARMY OF THE POTOMAC,
October 25, 1863.

General R. O. TYLER:

GENERAL : I have received your report of the means of transportation for the Artillery Reserve, by which it appears that there are on hand a total of 254 wagons. I cannot understand whether the 20 wagons mentioned by Colonel Morford as belonging to the ammunition train, but used by him in the supply train, are included in the 254. They should have been turned over to the ammunition train.

By reference to the chief quartermaster of this army, he reports to me the following as the allowance of wagons for the Reserve Artillery on October 1 :

Seven six-gun batteries, including siege........	14
Ten four-gun batteries	10
Supply train for them, 3 wagons each...............................	51
(This manifestly excludes Huntington's	5)
Headquarters Artillery Reserve and supplies for employés.................	7
Four brigades, including hospital........,...............................	16
Sixth New York Foot Artillery, baggage.................................	6
Hospital...... ....:.................	2
Supplies..	6
Ammunition..	4

Total Artillery Reserve...	121

This is exclusive of artillery ammunition wagons. Ammunition train required for the guns in the reserve, viz, 28 light 12-pounders, 25 rifles, 6 20-pounders, 16 10-pounders, 8 siege guns to complete the prescribed number of rounds.

For 28 light 12-pounders, 122 rounds each..................................	31
For 41 light rifles, 3-inch and 10-pounders, 2,050 – 140 rounds, ...	15
20-pounders......•...	13
Siege guns........; ....,..;..........,..,..,................,..........	20

	79

For general reserve : ·

136 light 12-pounders, 34 10-pounders, 122 3-inch, 292 guns :

2,440 rounds light 12-pounder, 1,440 ÷ 112.............................	22
2,700 rounds 3-inch and 680 rounds 10-pounder, 3,380 ÷ 140....,........	25

General ammunition train..	47
Artillery Reserve ammunition train.................................	79
Fuses, powder, &c.,...	2
Total ammunition train..	128
Forage for six days	18
Messing, &c., of train	6
	152

Say 150 wagons for the ammunition train, which I wish made up as follows :

1. The 119 wagons for the general reserve of 20 rounds, and spare fuses and powder.

2. Seventy-nine wagons for reserve of guns in Artillery Reserve.

Twenty-two, distribute for forage and mess wagons, so that nothing whatever shall be carried in the ammunition wagons but the ammunition. Every wagon-master or teamster violating this order to be punished and reported for discharge. Artillery wagons sent with the guns from the reserve to the corps to be deducted from the above allowance for the Reserve Artillery, not general trains.

	Wagons.
Colonel Morford reports....................................	254
Allowance to reserve.......................................	121
For ammunition train and supplies as above, 150...........................	271
Leaving due reserve	17

If the 20 wagons spoken of by Colonel Morford are not included in the 254, you have your full supply. If they are, the 17 can be drawn. General Ingalls states that the addition of 1 wagon per battery will be extended to the reserve.

HENRY J. HUNT,
Brigadier-General, Chief of Artillery.

WAR DEPARTMENT,
Washington, October 25, 1863—11.30 a. m.

Brigadier-General KELLEY,
Clarksburg, W. Va.:

Has your cavalry ascertained anything in regard to the enemy in the valley toward East Tennessee or the condition of the railroad? It is reported that Ewell is moving in that direction.

H. W. HALLECK,
General-in-Chief.

CLARKSBURG, W. VA., October 25, 1863.
(Received 8 p. m.)

Brigadier-General CULLUM, Chief of Staff:

I have nothing reliable in regard to the movement of the enemy along the line of the Virginia and Tennessee Railroad. I had hoped ere this to have been able to have sent an expedition, via Lewisburg, in Greenbrier County, through Union, in Monroe County, and destroy the railroad bridge across New River. But as General Echols was at Greenbrier and General Jenkins at Union, each with quite a force, I deemed it not advisable to move until I had force sufficient to drive both of them out. I have, unfortunately, been delayed in getting my force in condition to move for want of horses, arms, &c.

My proposed plan is to send General Averell, now at Beverly, with three regiments of cavalry and mounted infantry, one regiment of infantry, and a battery, via Huntersville, and General Duffié, with two regiments of cavalry, two regiments of infantry, and a battery from the mouth of Gauley, on the Kanawha, and form a junction at or near Lewisburg. After disposing of Echols, for the cavalry to proceed on through Union to destination, unless such information is acquired at Lewisburg of the strength of the enemy at Union or the railroad, as would make the expedition too hazardous.

Averell is about ready, and Duffié will be in a very few days. The expedition will move as soon as possible, as proposed, unless you deem it best to order otherwise.

B. F. KELLEY,
Brigadier-General.

HEADQUARTERS FIRST CAVALRY DIVISION,
October 26, 1863—11.30 a. m.

Col. C. ROSS SMITH,
 Chief of Staff.

COLONEL: The general directs me to say that the enemy advanced on our pickets this morning and have driven them up back beyond Bealeton Station. Have not yet ascertained their numbers. They have infantry.

By command of Brigadier-General Buford:

A. P. MORROW,
Lieutenant, and Aide-de-Camp.

HEADQUARTERS FIRST CAVALRY DIVISION,
October 26, 1863.

Major-General PLEASONTON,
 Commanding Cavalry Corps:

I drove the enemy back to near Bealeton, where they came upon me too strong, with infantry and artillery, and I am falling back to Colonel Smith's infantry brigade, which is half way between Bealeton and Germantown.

 Respectfully,

JNO. BUFORD,
Brigadier-General of Volunteers.

BRISTOE,
October 26, 1863.

General S. WILLIAMS:

Artillery firing pretty frequent when I sent my dispatch. It has now ceased. It lasted about an hour and was very distinct, although the wind is not favorable for my hearing. It appeared by map and compass to have come from the direction of the railroad, and I thought it might be at Bealeton or Rappahannock Station. If it is not our troops, it may have been the enemy shelling the woods somewhere.

JOHN NEWTON,
Major-General.

HEADQUARTERS ARMY OF THE POTOMAC,
October 26, 1863.

General FRENCH:

General Newton reports that he heard firing at Bristoe. Do you hear anything of it? If so, in what direction does it seem to be? Answer.

S. WILLIAMS,
Assistant Adjutant-General.

THIRD CORPS,
October 26, 1863.

Major-General HUMPHREYS:

I have heard no firing at this place and have been around the picket line. I cannot imagine where the firing was heard by Newton. Am I expected to advance from this position to Bealeton or to hold it?

WM. .H. FRENCH,
Major-General.

[P. S.]—Brigade is at Bealeton.

THIRD CORPS,
October 26, 1863—11.45 a. m.

Major-General HUMPHREYS:

This dispatch just received :

Major-General FRENCH,
Commanding Third Army Corps :

The enemy is advancing on us in some force. His artillery has opened upon us. General Buford is here in person, but I think has no force with him. We have about 800 cavalry, one battery, and my brigade.

I have the honor, &c.,

B. F. SMITH,
Colonel, Commanding Brigade.

WM. H. FRENCH,
Major-General.

HEADQUARTERS THIRD CORPS,
October 26, 1863.

Brigadier-General WILLIAMS :

Colonel Smith, commanding brigade at or near Bealeton, reports the enemy in some force as advancing upon him. He states there are about 800 cavalry and his brigade to meet them. In the temporary absence of General French, I deem it prudent to report the fact to you. I have sent an aide for him and expect him momentarily.

O. H. HART,
Assistant Adjutant-General.

OCTOBER 26, 1863—1.45 p. m.

Commanding Officer First Corps:

It is reported from General French's headquarters that the firing is from the enemy, who are advancing in some force toward Bealeton. Whether it is merely a reconnaissance or with some other object, such as collecting railroad iron, or an advance, is not yet developed. Hold yourself in readiness to support General French if he should need it.

A. A. HUMPHREYS,
Major-General, and Chief of Staff.

OCTOBER 26, 1863—2.10 p. m.

Commanding Officer Third Corps:

You are not expected to advance, but to maintain your position. The force at Bealeton should fall back upon you if forced to retire. Please note the hour of sending your dispatches.

A. A. HUMPHREYS,
Major-General, and Chief of Staff.

HEADQUARTERS THIRD CORPS,
October 26, 1863.

Major-General HUMPHREYS,
Chief of Staff:

Your dispatch just received. My line of battle is taken on the range of heights facing south, the right near Stevens' house, round Catlett's residence to Foulk's. At this last place, Cedar Run is commanded at Weaverton, and here the railroad crosses. The command is on the south side. I have sent a staff officer to the brigade at Bealeton, who has not yet returned.

WM. H. FRENCH,
Major-General.

BRISTOE,
October 26, 1863.

General WILLIAMS:

Firing has recommenced. It may be in direction of Kelly's Ford, which does not differ much in direction from the line of the railroad from this point.

JOHN NEWTON,
Major-General.

HEADQUARTERS, *October 26, 1863.*

Colonel HART, *Assistant Adjutant-General:*

The firing was heard at Bristoe by General Newton and seen from Watery Mountain by the signal officer, who reported it to be near Bealeton. General Newton now reports that it has recommenced, perhaps in the direction of Kelly's Ford.

A. A. HUMPHREYS,
Major-General, Chief of Staff.

HEADQUARTERS CAVALRY CORPS,
October 26, 1863.

Brigadier-General MERRITT,
Comdg. Reserve Brigade, Manassas Junction:

The commanding general directs that you move your brigade at once up the railroad toward Bealeton Station, to connect with Buford's left and watch the movements of the enemy, keeping him constantly informed of the approach of the enemy from the extreme left. Do not withdraw your guards from the bridge at Bristoe, unless it is relieved by infantry, in which case do it. General Buford's headquarters are at Germantown. Please communicate with him. Please acknowledge receipt of this.

Respectfully,

C. C. SUYDAM,
Assistant Adjutant-General.

HEADQUARTERS SECOND BRIGADE,
October 26, 1863—4.30 p. m.

Brig. Gen. D. McM. GREGG,
Commanding Second Division:

GENERAL: I have just returned from Liberty. General Buford has fallen back to Germantown. The enemy in their advance paid no attention to my vedettes. About 3 p. m. they advanced on the Fayetteville road a short distance, and then moved off to my right, on the Fox's Ford road. I feel alarmed for my vedettes. The enemy drove my picket from Beverly Ford. I have withdrawn my picket reserve to Fayetteville, and will send out vedettes as far as Liberty and to the junction of the road leading from Fayetteville to Fox's Ford road. I have sent word to the picket at Freeman's Ford to protect itself, and retire, if necessary, on Sulphur Springs. I will soon be without a command.

Very respectfully, your obedient servant,

J. IRVIN GREGG,
Colonel, Commanding Brigade.

SIGNAL STATION, *October 26, 1863.*

Maj. Gen. A. A. HUMPHREYS, *Chief of Staff:*

The signal officer on Watery Mountain reports that a large force of the enemy is now moving from Rappahannock Station toward Bealeton.

L. B. NORTON,
Captain, and Chief Signal Officer.

WATERY SIGNAL STATION,
October 26, 1863—5.15 p. m.

Maj. Gen. A. A. HUMPHREYS, *Chief of Staff:*

The signal officer on Watery Mountain reports that the force that moved from Rappahannock toward Bealeton took forty minutes to pass a given point. One regiment of cavalry, or mounted infantry, passed toward Bealeton. Two regiments of infantry passed forts on south side of river, following cavalry, but halted at Rappahannock Station.

L. B. NORTON,
Chief Signal Officer.

———

HEADQUARTERS ARMY OF THE POTOMAC,
October 26, 1863—5.45 p. m.

Major-General FRENCH, *Commanding Third Corps:*

A report from General Buford states that a regiment of Devin's brigade, on picket toward Morrisville, reported a column of infantry advancing from Kelly's Ford, but that he has heard nothing further from him since 11 a. m. He was directed to retire by Elk Run, if forced to retire. The signal officer on Watery Mountain reports, at 4.30 p. m., a large force was moving from Rappahannock Station toward Bealeton which occupied forty minutes to pass a given point. Other troops were moving in the vicinity of Rappahannock Station. You had better get your trains to the rear. Let them keep on the north or west side of railroad, so as not to interfere with Newton, who will probably be brought up to-night.

A. A. HUMPHREYS,
Major-General, Chief of Staff.

———

HEADQUARTERS FIRST CAVALRY DIVISION,
October 26, 1863.

Col. C. ROSS SMITH:

This is the fourth dispatch that I have sent to-day. The rebels drove in my picket line early this morning to Bealeton. After getting enough men together, I drove them back to Bealeton, where I met the "Stonewall" Brigade of Johnson's division, which would not let me advance.

A regiment of Devin's was on picket toward Morrisville, and reports a column of infantry coming from Kelly's. They will retire by Elk Run, if forced in. No information has been received from the regiment since 11 a. m.

I now hold the flanks of Colonel Smith's brigade of infantry. The enemy does not seem to press now. The next position I intend to hold is where the stage road crosses the railroad, a little south of where general headquarters were before we crossed the Rappahannock.

BUFORD.

———

OCTOBER 26, 1863—7.30 p. m.

Commanding Officers Sixth, Fifth, and Second Corps:

I am instructed to inform you that a report from General Buford, dated 3 p. m., states that a regiment of Colonel Devin's brigade, on

picket on the road from Bealeton to Morrisville, reported to him at
11 a. m. that a column of the enemy's infantry was advancing from
Kelly's Ford. General Buford had heard nothing further from the
regiment, which was directed to fall back to Elk Run, if forced to
retire. General Buford was forced back to near Germantown. The
signal officer on Watery Mountain reported, at 5 or 5.30 p. m., that
a column of infantry was moving from Rappahannock Station
toward Bealeton which took forty minutes to pass a given point.
Other troops were moving about Rappahannock Station.

Corps commanders will be on the alert, prepared to meet the movement of the enemy. The trains will be held ready to go to the rear,
and upon an engagement being imminent, will be sent to Gainesville, where Kilpatrick's division of cavalry is stationed. Ammunition and ambulance trains, hospital wagons, and intrenching tools
will accompany the troops.

A. A. HUMPHREYS,
Major-General, and Chief of Staff.

HEADQUARTERS ARMY OF THE POTOMAC,
October 26, 1863.

Colonel HART,
   Assistant Adjutant-General:

The major-general commanding directs me to say that General ·
Sykes is ordered to hold himself in readiness to support General
French. In the event of requiring support, General French will call
upon General Sykes.

A. A. HUMPHREYS,
Major-General.

HEADQUARTERS FIRST CAVALRY DIVISION,
October 26, [1863.]

Lieut. Col. C. ROSS SMITH:

My division and the brigade of Third Corps are in *statu quo*. The
rebels occupy Bealeton, and are cooking with big camp fires. I
cannot drive them away. I have pickets and scouts beyond Elk
Run, who see no enemy. I know of no way to find out the strength
of the enemy this side of the river with my present means: I
will occupy the road that crosses the railroad south of Licking Run
to-night.

I am, very respectfully,

JNO. BUFORD.

OCTOBER 26, 1863—9.15 p. m.

Commanding Officer First Corps:

I am instructed to say that the last reports indicate that there will
be no necessity for your moving to the front to-night. Be prepared
to move forward at an early hour to-morrow morning. The cavalry
at Manassas Junction is ordered up. Please send a regiment to take
the place of the cavalry in guarding that depot.

A. A. HUMPHREYS,
Major-General, and Chief of Staff.

ARTILLERY HDQRS., ARMY OF THE POTOMAC,
. *Camp near Warrenton, October 26, 1863.*
General W. F. BARRY,
 Inspector of Artillery, U. S. Army:

GENERAL: There is much complaint of the inefficiency, at close quarters, of the canister for the light 12-pounder gun, owing to the small number of balls it contains. This effect was made apparent at Gettysburg, and is complained of frequently now that the batteries of these guns in the horse artillery often come in close contact with the enemy's cavalry and infantry. The present canister shot is so large as to be effective at long ranges, so long that it would be better to use shrapnel.

.I respectfully request that canister with a smaller ball, say of 2 to 3 ounces—or if of smaller diameter than that of a 2-ounce iron ball, then one of lead—may be furnished at as early a day as practicable, in sufficient quantities to furnish at least the horse artillery with one-half their canister of the new pattern. These canisters would carry from 60 to 80 shots, and would probably be much more effective within 200 yards than the present 7-ounce ball of 28 to the canister.

        HENRY J. HUNT,
      Brigadier-General, Chief of Artillery.

———

CLARKSBURG, W. VA., *October 26, 1863—2 p. m.*
         (Received 5 p. m.)
Brig. Gen. G. W. CULLUM,
  Chief of Staff:

I leave this afternoon for the Big Kanawha, for the purpose of ·seeing the condition of General Scammon's division, and to get his portion of the proposed expedition in readiness. I herewith send you a telegram, just received from General Scammon. I think a large portion of the force reported in Greenbrier and Monroe has been ordered to General Samuel Jones.

        B. F. KELLEY,
        Brigadier-General.

[Telegram.]

Brig. Gen. B. F. KELLEY,
  Clarksburg, W. Va.:

Colonel White, at Fayetteville, reports that Lieutenant Blazer's scouting party captured 3 of enemy's pickets on Meadow Creek, attacked pickets on Blue Sulphur, and burned two large houses used as quarters and stables. Reports Sixteenth [Virginia Cavalry] 1½ miles from Blue Sulphur, one mounted regiment at White Sulphur, two at Warm Springs, two at Salt Sulphur, three at the Narrows, one at Centreville; Twenty-second Regiment 1½ miles from Lewisburg, on old pike; Derrick's [Battalion], at Jarrett's, on Muddy Creek, 6 miles from Blue Sulphur; Edgar's [Battalion], 5 miles from Lewisburg, on Anderson's Ferry road; enemy's scouts on Little Sewall.

        E. P. SCAMMON,
        Brigadier-General.

WASHINGTON, D. C.,
October 27, 1863—2 p. m.

Major-General MEADE,
    Army of the Potomac:
Please report condition of affairs in your army and front.
                    H. W. HALLECK,
                        General-in-Chief.

———

OCTOBER 27, 1863—8 p. m.,
(Received 9 p. m.)

Major-General HALLECK:
    Yesterday the enemy advanced a force of infantry and cavalry
from the railroad crossing of the Rappahannock, driving in our cavalry pickets and forcing back Buford's cavalry till they reached their
infantry support in the neighborhood of Bealeton. A column was
reported as crossing at Kelly's Ford, and there were other indications of an advance. This morning, however, the enemy retired to
the river and his former os t on, which appears to be between the
railroad crossing and Kelly's Ford, with a force on this side of the
river at the crossing.
    Last night a supply train coming from the depot at Gainesville
was attacked between New Baltimore and Warrenton and some one
hundred animals taken from it. The train had an escort, which was
in front and rear, but was unable to reach the center of the train
before the guerrillas had made off with the animals. The wagons
were left untouched.
    The railroad will be repaired to Catlett's Station, within 1¼ miles
of Warrenton Junction, by to-morrow night.
                    GEO. G. MEADE,
                        Major-General, Commanding.

———

HEADQUARTERS FIRST CAVALRY DIVISION,
                    October 27, [1863]—12 m.

Lieut. Col. C. ROSS SMITH:
    The firing this morning I cannot understand, unless it is a recon-
naissance I sent to Kelly's. I will let you know as soon as I hear. I
am pushing the enemy from the country between Bealeton and the
river. Nothing but cavalry have been seen this morning, and no
force. Ewell and Johnson were over here at Bealeton yesterday,
with two brigades (Steuart's and Walker's) that I know of. I believe
they came after railroad iron, as portions of it below Bealeton have
been removed.
    Where shall I make my picket line if the rebels are on the south
side of the river? Please give my division trains [instructions] what
to do.
            Respectfully,

                    JNO. BUFORD,
                        Brigadier-General of Volunteers.

[P. S.]—Prisoners say Ewell's corps is at Brandy. The command
that came across yesterday left their camp pitched.

HEADQUARTERS FIRST DIVISION,
Bealeton, October 27, 1863—12.40 p. m.

[Lieut. Col. C. ROSS SMITH,
  Chief of Staff, Cavalry Corps:]

COLONEL : General Merritt I have just seen. He connected with General Buford this morning at 4 o'clock. General Buford is at this place, and has sent a reconnaissance toward the river. I will remain here until it returns. The firing this morning is not yet known, but I shall hear from it before I go back, as General Buford has sent out to ascertain. The general sends these two picket reports.

Yours, &c.,

HUTCHINS.

HEADQUARTERS,
Bealeton, October 27, 1863—2 p. m.

[Lieut. Col. C. ROSS SMITH,
  Chief of Staff, Cavalry Corps:]

COLONEL : The reconnaissance which General Buford sent out toward the river has just returned. The enemy have retreated to the river. A portion is on this side. Their left in the rear of Mr. Smith's house and their right by the station. They have taken up every rail between Bealeton and the station and carried them off. General Buford has now advanced his line of pickets up to within sight of theirs, and will keep you advised of their movements.

B. T. HUTCHINS,
Lieutenant, and Acting Aide-de-Camp.

[Indorsement.]

OCTOBER 27, 1863—4 p. m.

Respectfully forwarded.

Lieutenant Hutchins, my aide, has just returned from General Buford, and makes this report.

A. PLEASONTON,
Major-General, Commanding.

HEADQUARTERS ARMY OF THE POTOMAC,
October 27, 1863.

General FRENCH :

I am instructed to inform you that the enemy has withdrawn to his former position at beyond Rappahannock Station and to Kelly's Ford. No immediate necessity exists for sending trains to the rear, and the construction parties at work upon the railroad should have the use of the wagons heretofore furnished them.

A. A. HUMPHREYS,
Major-General, Chief of Staff.

HEADQUARTERS CHIEF ENGINEER OF DEFENSES,
Washington, October 27, 1863.

Col. J. C. KELTON,
  Assistant Adjutant-General, Hdqrs. U. S. Army:

COLONEL : The works which constitute the defenses of Washington have been separately (and sometimes hastily) armed with such ord-

nance as might be available at the moment. Thinking it probable
that the efficiency of the works would be promoted and economy
consulted by a revision, I would suggest that a Board of Officers be
appointed for that purpose.

I would suggest the names of Brig. Gen. G. A. De Russy, Lieut.
Col. J. A. Haskin, Col. A. A. Gibson, Col. L. O. Morris, Col. A. Piper,
Col. T. R. Tannatt, Col. H. L. Abbot, and Col. J. C. Tidball.

Their instructions should be to report—

1. Whether and how the armament can be simplified by an interchange of calibers, having in view the least number of calibers at
each work.

2. Whether any of the works require additions to their permanent
armament, and what.

3. Whether any reduction of permanent armament may be made
without detriment to efficiency in any of the works, having in view
the relations of each to all the others constituting the system.

4. Whether the number of guns on barbette carriages may or
should be further reduced.

5. Any other recommendations the Board think proper to make.

The Chiefs of Artillery and Engineers should be directed to furnish
all information needed to the Board, and their report should be submitted to them for comment or approval.

I am, very respectfully, your most obedient servant,

J. G. BARNARD,
Brigadier-General, &c.

SPECIAL ORDERS, } WAR DEPT., ADJT. GENERAL'S OFFICE,
No. 480.   }   *Washington, October 27, 1863.*
*   *   *   *   *   *

15. By direction of the President, Brig. Gen. Robert Anderson, U.
S. Army, is hereby relieved from the command of Fort Adams, R. I.,
and will report in person without delay to Major-General Dix, U. S.
Volunteers, commanding Department of the East, at New York City.
*   *   *   *   *   *

19. Brig. Gen. William Hays, U. S. Volunteers, is hereby relieved
from duty as a member of the general court-martial convened by
Special Orders, No. 350, August 6, 1863, from this office, and will at
once proceed to New York City, and enter upon the duties of assistant to the provost-marshal-general, superintendent of volunteer recruiting service, and chief mustering and disbursing officer for the
first ten districts of New York (including New York City).
*   *   *   *   *   *

By order of the Secretary of War:

E. D. TOWNSEND,
Assistant. Adjutant-General.

GENERAL ORDERS, } HDQRS. MID. DEPT., 8TH ARMY CORPS,
No. 53.   }   *Baltimore, Md., October 27, 1863.*

It is known that there are many evil-disposed persons, now at large
in the State of Maryland, who have been engaged in rebellion against
the lawful Government, or have given aid and comfort or encouragement to others so engaged, or who do not recognize their allegiance
to the United States, and who may avail themselves of the indul-

gence of the authority which tolerates their presence to embarrass the approaching election, or, through it, to foist enemies of the United States into power. It is therefore ordered:

I. That all provost-marshals and other military officers do arrest all such persons found at or hanging about, or approaching any poll or place of election on the 4th of November, 1863, and report such arrest to these headquarters.*

II. That all provost-marshals and other military officers commanding in Maryland shall support the judges of election on the 4th of November, 1863, in requiring an oath of allegiance to the United States, as the test of citizenship, of any one whose vote may be challenged on the ground that he is not loyal or does not admit his allegiance to the United States, which oath shall be in the following form and terms:

I do solemnly swear that I will support, protect, and defend the Constitution and Government of the United States against all enemies, whether domestic or foreign; that I hereby pledge my allegiance, faith, and loyalty to the same, any ordinance, resolution, or law of any State convention or State Legislature to the contrary notwithstanding; that I will at all times yield a hearty and willing obedience to the said Constitution and Government, and will not, either directly or indirectly, do any act in hostility to the same, either by taking up arms against them or aiding, abetting, or countenancing those in arms against them; that, without permission from the lawful authority, I will have no communication, direct or indirect, with the States in insurrection against the United States, or with either of them, or with any person or persons within said insurrectionary States; and that I will in all things deport myself as a good and loyal citizen of the United States. This I do in good faith, with full determination, pledge, and purpose to keep this my sworn obligation, and without any mental reservation or evasion whatsoever.

III. Provost-marshals and other military officers are directed to report to these headquarters any judge of an election who shall refuse his aid in carrying out this order, or who, on challenge of a vote being made on the ground of disloyalty or hostility to the Government, shall refuse to require the oath of allegiance from such voter.

By order of Major-General Schenck:

WM. H. CHESEBROUGH,
Lieutenant-Colonel, and Assistant Adjutant-General.

OCTOBER 28, 1863—7 p. m.
(Received 7.40 p. m.)

Major-General HALLECK:

No change in the position of the enemy or of this army. Scouts from Fredericksburg, with information from Gordonsville, report no detachment has been made from Lee's army since withdrawing to the Rappahannock.

GEO. G. MEADE,
Major-General, Commanding.

HDQRS. FIRST CAV. DIV., ARMY OF THE POTOMAC,
Near Germantown, October 28, 1863.

Lieut. Col. C. ROSS SMITH,
Chief of Staff:

My command is in camp on each side of the railroad along the road running from Warrenton to Falmouth. My left is near Kelly's

---

* See General Orders, No. 55, November 2.

Ford. My right connects with Colonel Gregg, near Beverly. The enemy still hold Rappahannock Station with foot troops. Their line runs about three-quarters of a mile from the river, between the river and Smith's house.

The object of the troops coming over on the 26th was to take off the railroad iron. All of it from Bealeton to the river was taken across in wagons. Very large camp fires were seen on the opposite side last night, extending from about Stevensburg, Brandy, and up Hazel Run, in front of Beverly.

I am, very respectfully,

JNO. BUFORD,
Brigadier-General of Volunteers, Commanding.

[Indorsement.]

HEADQUARTERS CAVALRY CORPS,
October 28, [1863]—1.25 p. m.

[General ·PLEASONTON :]

GENERAL : I have the honor to forward you a dispatch from General Buford, which was just received.

Where had General Buford better draw his supplies now ?

Very respectfully,

C. ROSS SMITH,
Lieutenant-Colonel, and Chief of Staff.

———

WASHINGTON,
October 28, 1863.

Brig. Gen. B. F. KELLEY,
Clarksburg, W. Va.:

GENERAL : I have received the reports on the capture of Charlestown, Va., forwarded by you on the 25th. They do not solve the question by whose fault this place was surprised and captured. Either the placé was not a proper one for so large an outpost, or the troops were not properly placed for defense, or they permitted themselves to be surprised, or they did not make proper resistance. Some one has been at fault in this disgraceful surrender, and the officer or officers through whose incompetency or neglect of duty this occurred should be reported for prompt dismissal. It is the duty of the commanding general of the department to investigate this affair, and to report the guilty or negligent parties for prompt punishment. Unless you adopt such measures, you cannot expect to maintain the efficiency of your command, and other disgraceful surrenders will follow.

Very respectfully, your obedient servant,

H. W. HALLECK,
General-in-Chief.

———

WASHINGTON,
October 28, 1863.

Maj. H. S. TURNER,
Philadelphia:

MY DEAR MAJOR : I have received yours of the 26th instant, inclosing a copy of a letter from your brother, dated July 17. They will be sent to General Meade for such remedy as he may be able to apply. Such acts as are complained of are deeply regretted, and every effort is made to prevent them. Nevertheless such things always have and probably always will occur in a border war.

Most of these difficulties are caused by the conduct of the pretended non-combatant inhabitants of the country. They pretend to act the part of neutrals, but do not. They give aid, shelter, and concealment to guerrilla and robber bands like that of Mosby, who are continually destroying our ·roads, burning our bridges, and capturing wagon trains. If these men carried on a legitimate warfare no complaint would be made. On the contrary, they fight in citizens' dress and are aided in all their rascalities by the people of the country. As soon as they are likely to be caught, they go home, put out their horses, hide their arms, and pretend to be .quiet and non-combatant farmers. This thing has often been repeated by your brother's neighbors and, it is alleged, by members of his family. It is not surprising that our people get exasperated at such men and shoot them down when they can. Moreover, men who act in this manner in disguise, and within our lines, have, under the laws of civilized war, forfeited their lives.

Very truly, yours,

H. W. HALLECK.

GENERAL ORDERS, } WAR DEPT., ADJT. GENERAL'S OFFICE,
    No. 350.   } . *Washington, October* 28, 1863.

I. By direction of the President of the United States, Maj. Gen. B. F. Butler, U. S. Volunteers, is appointed to the command of the Eighteenth Army Corps and of the Department of Virginia and North Carolina. Maj. Gen. J. G. Foster, on being relieved by General Butler, will report in person for orders to the Adjutant-General of the Army.

*   *   *   *

By order of the Secretary of War:

E. D. TOWNSEND,
Assistant Adjutant-General.

OCTOBER 29, 1863—10 p. m.

Commanding Officer Third Corps:

The major-general commanding directs that to-morrow you take position in front of Warrenton Junction, on the south side of the railroad on the heights of Licking Run, your right resting on or near the railroad. The teams of the corps now with the construction party can be withdrawn for the purpose of this movement. Have a brigade at Catlett's Station to guard the depot and bridge over Cedar Run, and the railroad to the junction.

A. A. HUMPHREYS,
Major-General, and Chief of Staff.

HEADQUARTERS ARMY OF THE POTOMAC,
October 29, 1863.

Major-General FRENCH:

General headquarters will move to-morrow at 10 a. m. to the vicinity of Colonel Murray's, near Three-Mile Station, Warrenton Branch

Railroad ; the Fifth Corps will move to front of Three-Mile Station, and the Third Corps to front of Warrenton Junction, on Licking Run.

By command of Major-General Meade :

S. WILLIAMS,
Assistant Adjutant-General.

SPECIAL ORDERS, } WAR DEPT., ADJT. GENERAL'S OFFICE,
No. 483.   }   *Washington, October* 29, 1863.

*   *   *   *   *   *   *

9. Brig. Gen. James H. Ledlie, U. S. Volunteers, will proceed without delay to Fort Monroe, Va., and report in person to Major-General Foster, U. S. Volunteers, commanding Department of Virginia and North Carolina, for duty.

*   *   *   *

By order of the Secretary of War :

E. D. TOWNSEND,
Assistant Adjutant-General.

OCTOBER 30, 1863—8 p. m.
(Received 9.30 p. m.)

Major-General HALLECK :

No change in the position of the enemy or this army. Reconnoitering party this p. m. drove in the enemy's pickets at the railroad crossing, capturing a captain and 1 private of Ewell's corps. The enemy appear to have withdrawn the greater portion of the force they had on the north side of the river, keeping, however, a strong picket of infantry and cavalry. The pickets on the right flank at Waterloo report hearing drums about Amissville. The railroad is reported completed this evening to Warrenton Junction. I shall transfer immediately my main depots to this point and Warrenton. The army is now massed from Warrenton to Warrenton Junction, with one corps at Bristoe, the cavalry with some infantry picketing the river from Kelly's Ford to Waterloo.

GEO. G. MEADE,
Major-General, Commanding.

OFFICE OF CAVALRY BUREAU,
Washington, D. C., October 30, 1863.

Col. J. C. KELTON,
Assistant Adjutant-General, U. S. Army:

COLONEL: I have the honor to inclose herewith the papers this day referred to me by the General-in-Chief, with the following remarks :

The issues of cavalry horses to the Army of the Potomac, during the past six months, have been as follows :

During the month of—

May	5,073
June	6,927
July	4,716
August	5,499
September	5,827
October	7,036
Total	35,078

Add to this the number captured from the enemy and taken from citizens.

There are now on hand about 17,000 cavalry horses, which have been turned in and picked up, making about 18,078 horses which have been killed in action, been captured, or have died, or been sold at auction.

To the 17,000 unserviceable horses must be added the number unserviceable now on hand in the Army of the Potomac, which it is impossible to get at.

At the commencement of the withdrawal of the Army of the Potomac from Culpeper Court-House, all the stables were full of horses, serviceable and unserviceable.

Of the number then on hand, 800 have been issued to the Third Maryland Regiment; 500 to the Twentieth New York; 550 to General Foster; 560 to General Kelley; 100 to Colonel Lowell, and 4,804 to the Army of the Potomac, besides several smaller issues, leaving on hand about 2,000,fit for issue. There are also on the way here about 1,000 more.

The whole number issued to the Army of the Potomac during October is 7,036.

It would seem from the inclosed papers that the inefficiency of the Cavalry Corps complained of is due to these causes:

1. Disease of the foot and tongue, both of which yield readily to the remedies used in the hospital at the Cavalry Depot. Great care has been taken in sending forward horses to the army, not to allow any horse to leave the depot afflicted with either of these diseases, as each horse is inspected when he leaves the stables and before he is sent off.

2. The severe duties which the horses have to perform. The remedy for this is within the control of the commanding general of the army with which the cavalry is serving.

3. The great want of forage, without which horses cannot be expected to last long, or be able to perform much service of any kind. The remedy for this is either to furnish more forage, or to keep the cavalry force where it can procure forage if it is [not] furnished.

As to the complaint made by General Kilpatrick, in regard to the demoralization of men and officers by sending them into Washington, and the idea that they "neglect their horses and lose their equipments, knowing in either case that they will be sent in to refit," I agree with him, though General Ingalls and some other officers think such is not the case.

I inclose herewith a copy of a letter* upon the subject to General Ingalls, suggesting that the horses be sent by rail, or that a party be organized of experienced men to take them to the army.

There are two hundred and twenty-three regiments of cavalry in the service, and thirty-six of them are in the Army of the Potomac.

At the rate horses are used up in that army it would require 435,000 per year to keep the cavalry in the army up, and then, according to the inclosed papers, it would be inefficient.

I have the honor to be, very respectfully, your obedient servant,

GEORGE STONEMAN,
Major-General of Volunteers, Chief of Cavalry.

* See p. 402.

[Inclosure No. 1.]

HEADQUARTERS ARMY OF THE POTOMAC,
October 26, 1863.
ADJUTANT-GENERAL OF THE ARMY,
Washington, D. C.:

SIR: I have the honor herewith to transmit for the information of the General-in-Chief reports from the three division commanders of the Cavalry Corps, to which I beg leave to invite attention, as showing the worn and reduced condition of the cavalry of this army at the present time.

I concur with the commander of the Cavalry Corps in the opinion that the practice of sending the dismounted men to the camp at Washington to be refitted has a most injurious and demoralizing effect upon the service, and I earnestly request that it be discontinued, and that the horses, arms, and equipments that may from time to time be required for the dismounted men of this army be sent out as they are needed.

It is believed that in many instances the men neglect their horses and lose their arms for the purpose of being sent to the Dismounted Camp.

I am, very respectfully, your obedient servant,
GEO. G. MEADE,
Major-General, Commanding.

[Sub-inclosure No. 1.]

HEADQUARTERS FIRST CAVALRY DIVISION,
October 24, 1863.
Lieut. Col. C. ROSS SMITH:

In obedience to instructions just received, I have the honor to report that I have equipped and available for duty 2,000 men and horses. One-half of these, in my opinion, are not fit for arduous duty, being poor in flesh and leg-weary. It is impossible to ascertain the number of diseased horses, for the disease is on the increase daily, and to feed them here with grain alone is impossible with my present means of transportation.

The Third Brigade, which crossed at Germanna Mills with 1,488 men to-day, can only turn out 850 men mounted. The First Brigade is better off; can show 1,200 men and fair horses.

I am, very respectfully, your obedient servant,
JNO. BUFORD,
Brigadier-General of Volunteers.

[Sub-inclosure No. 2.]

HEADQUARTERS SECOND CAVALRY DIVISION,
October 24, 1863.
Lieut. Col. C. ROSS SMITH,
Chief of Staff, Cavalry Corps:

COLONEL: I have the honor to make the following report concerning the horses of this division since leaving the Rapidan on the 18th of September:

	Horses.
Reported serviceable	3,144
Reported unserviceable (with hoof and other diseases)	458
Lost in action and abandoned since leaving Rapidan	950
Condemned and turned in at Fairfax Court-House and Gainesville	1,433

Brigade commanders report the horses now in service in their brigades in very poor condition, the result of almost constant use and insufficiency of forage. No hay has been received in this division for more than two weeks, and for several days since leaving the Rapidan but a fractional portion of the allowance of that forage could be procured.

If required to accomplish a march of 150 miles in five days, 20 per cent. of the horses now in use in the division would be totally unfit for service.

I am, very respectfully, your obedient servant,

D. McM. GREGG,
Brigadier-General, Commanding Division.

[Sub-inclosure No. 3.]

HDQRS. THIRD DIVISION, CAVALRY CORPS,
October 25, 1863.

Capt. C. C. SUYDAM,
Assistant Adjutant-General, Cavalry Corps:

In reply to communication dated headquarters Cavalry Corps, October 24, asking for a report of the strength and condition of my command, I have the honor to state that I have 2,100 men for duty.

My men are well armed, but the horses, many of them, not in good condition. Within the last three days I have been obliged to send into the Dismounted Camp 265 men and horses. The men had their arms and equipments and were in every way ready for duty, but their horses, having been affected with the hoof disease and swelled tongue, were totally unserviceable. This disease made its appearance for the first time in my command on the morning of the 20th, and I have now over 200 horses rendered unserviceable from its effects.

The division numbered on the 29th day of June last 3,500 men for duty. Since that time no opportunity has been offered to reorganize or refit. Every effort has been made to keep the division effective and correct irregularities, abuses, and to teach officers and men their duty, of which many of them are totally ignorant. I do not say even now that my division, as a division, is unfit for duty, but we do need rest and a short time for reorganization. Since the battle of James City the division has lost about 400 men killed, wounded, and missing.

Many accounted for as missing are known to be stragglers, and are now at the Dismounted Camp. The men of my command have learned to appreciate the easy life offered them at the Dismounted Camp, and take every opportunity to get there. They neglect their horses, lose their equipments, knowing in either case that they will be sent in to refit. These and various other causes have reduced my command to its present standard, but we are ready now as we ever have been for any duty we may be called upon to perform.

Very respectfully,

J. KILPATRICK,
Brig. Gen. of Vols., Commanding Third Division,

[Indorsement.]

HEADQUARTERS CAVALRY CORPS,
October 26, 1863.

Respectfully forwarded to Major-General Humphreys, for the information of the major-general commanding.

I would earnestly request that hereafter all the dismounted men may be retained in their commands and not be allowed to go to the Dismounted Camp at Washington, but that the dismounted men be remounted in the field.

The sending of dismounted men to the Dismounted Camp at Washington has a very demoralizing influence over the men, and also destroys the discipline of the men.

A. PLEASONTON,
Major-General.

[Inclosure No. 2.]

OFFICE OF CAVALRY BUREAU,
Washington, D. C., October 29, 1863.

Brig. Gen. R. INGALLS,
Chief Q. M., Army of the Potomac, Cavalry Bureau:

GENERAL : I have tried sending out horses in charge of such disposable men as I had in depot, and the plan of sending men back from the Army of the Potomac after the horses has been tried, and there have been found objections to both methods. Cannot the horses be forwarded by rail ? If this is not expedient, how will the plan work of organizing a party of experienced men under a competent officer, to lead the horses out, and an escort be either sent from here, if the men be on hand for that purpose, or sent from the Army of the Potomac, to meet the horses on the road and guard them to the army, the party to return by rail, bringing back broken-down horses.

To take out 500 horses will require a party of horse-leaders of 150 men of experience and energy. The strength of the escort must, of course, depend upon circumstances. The horses should not be sent in droves or squads of more than 500.

There are now in charge of General Rucker and myself upward of 16,000 unserviceable cavalry horses, and it is hoped that the requirements of the Army of the Potomac can be supplied during the remainder of this year from those now on hand.

There are now in depot seven new regiments of cavalry, awaiting arms, accouterments, and equipments. We have had the greatest difficulty in procuring laborers, and have sent all over the country for them.

As soon, however, as the depot is completed we shall have plenty, and the party spoken of above can be organized out of them, or you can organize it yourself and keep it under your own control. If the horses are sent by rail, we can deliver them at Alexandria.

Please let me know your views and wishes upon this subject as soon as may be, and also those of General Meade and General Pleasonton.

I am, general, very respectfully, your obedient servant,
GEORGE STONEMAN,
Major-General of Volunteers, Chief of Cavalry.

GETTY'S HEADQUARTERS,
October 30, 1863.

Major-General FOSTER:

I have received following telegram from Major Wetherill, commanding outpost, Suffolk:

Private John Wynton, *alias* Dunn, Irishman, Sixty-second Georgia Cavalry, got permission to cross the river to bring turkeys, and came in with horse, saddle, &c. Crossed South Quay Ferry at sunset yesterday. Colonel Griffin's headquarters at Murfrees Station, 4 miles from South Quay, on the railroad. Griffin's light battery is at Weldon with five or six companies between Garysburg and Weldon. Griffin's picket on Chowan and Blackwater start at Colerain, below Winton, and extend to South Quay. Here the zouaves have a picket of 4 men and officer, at William Lawrence's.

Wynton states that there is to be a grand ball at Vaughn's house, half a mile this side of Murfrees Station, on the 5th of November; officers are circulating tickets about Gatesville.

The major of the guerrillas who captured the boats at South Mills spends most of his time between Gatesville and Reddick's. Rylander's battalion of infantry is at Franklin.

The stations picketed by Griffin's men from South Quay to Colerain are as follows: South Quay, 1 sergeant, 4 infantry; 1 corporal, mounted. Cherry Grove, no pickets. Manning's Ferry, 1 corporal, 6 privates, 2 on post; the reserve station 4 miles back. Bartonville, 6 privates, 2 on post; reserve half mile back; three-quarters of the time no picket there. Flay Island, at fork of Chowan and Meherrin, 6 privates, reserve 3¼ miles back. Winton, 6 privates and sergeant. California, 3¼ miles below Winton, 6 privates and 1 corporal. Colerain, 17 miles below California, 6 privates and 1 corporal.

It will be observed that Waineoake Ferry, between Cherry Grove and Manning's Ferry, is not picketed, and Cherry Grove only occasionally.

The horse belongs to J. Wynton; cost him $900. One pair Colt's army pistols cost $200, his private property. Shall the man be retained here until his horse rests, and then sent to headquarters with guard, and can any arrangement be made that he could receive anything for his horse and arms?

I would send scout out to Gatesville to pick up officers distributing ball tickets, but it might interfere with the ball. Possibly the commanding general might desire some United States cavalry to attend on the night of the 5th of November.

Wynton suggests if our troops are to attend the ball that the force start early in the night, traveling rapidly to South Quay, sending 2 soldiers in citizens' clothes in buggy in advance, who, on arriving at the ferry at Lawrence, would call for the flat. The pickets collect the ferriage, and are anxious to bring passengers over. The flat could thus be secured and picket captured.

GEO. W. GETTY,
Brigadier-General, Commanding.

HEADQUARTERS ARMY OF THE POTOMAC,
October 31, 1863—6.30 p. m.

Major-General FRENCH:

I learn from General Buford that General Merritt has gone to Elk Run (town), and Colonel Devin is on the road from Bealeton to Morrisville. They are both picketing to the front and toward Kelly's Ford and Ellis' Ford.

General Buford will advise you of everything of any importance that transpires. He knows nothing about the report of the advance of a brigade of rebel infantry toward Morrisville or elsewhere.

A. A. HUMPHREYS,
Major-General, Chief of Staff.

CIRCULAR.]   HEADQUARTERS FIFTH ARMY CORPS,
                 Camp near Three-Mile Station, October 31, 1863.

The commanding general is again compelled to call the attention
of division, brigade, and regimental commanders to the frequent complaints made against the troops for depredating upon the inhabitants in the vicinity of the camps. The evil, instead of being put a
stop to, seems to be daily increasing. It appears that the fields, gardens, poultry, and stock of scarcely any one are respected. The fault
rests wholly with the officers, and either shows that they are unequal
to the positions they occupy or that they are utterly unmindful of
the excesses committed by the troops.

Common humanity demands that the little possessed by women,
children, and aged persons throughout the country we occupy should
be secured to them. Reports of armed parties of marauders from
this corps, numbering from 40 to 60, have been sent from headquarters Army of the Potomac, and, from the fact that a number of
these robbers were fired upon by the provost guard of the Second
Division, the reports are shown to be true.

Company officers will hereafter daily inspect the messing of their
companies and any meat, poultry, vegetables, or other property not
a part of the army ration, will be required to be accounted for by
the soldier in whose possession it may be found, and if improperly
acquired, the offender will be brought at once before a field officer's
court for trial. As most of the stragglers accompany or fall in with
the trains all commissaries and quartermasters will make a like inspection daily of their departments for the same purpose, send to
their regiments for trial all soldiers with plunder in their possession,
and stop the pay of civilian employés, &c., guilty of like disgraceful practices.

The commanding general expects and requires strict compliance
with this order. Division commanders and the commanders of artillery will report weekly whether it has been enforced throughout
their commands.

It will be read at the head of every company to-day, and all men
on detached duty, employés, &c., will be made acquainted with its
provisions.

By command of Major-General Sykes:

                              FRED. T. LOCKE,
                         Assistant Adjutant-General.

                    HEADQUARTERS CAVALRY CORPS,
                              October 31, 1863.

Brig. Gen. R. INGALLS,
        Chief Quartermaster, Army of the Potomac:

GENERAL: In accordance with your request, I have the honor to
inclose tabular statement showing the number of horses received
from all sources since April, 1863, the number of horses lost in
action, and the number turned in as unserviceable during the same
period; also the number of recruits furnished the command.

Very respectfully, your obedient servant,

                              A. PLEASONTON,
                                  Major-General.

[Inclosure.]

Command.	Number of horses—			Number of recruits furnished.
	Received.	Lost in action.	Turned in.	
6th U. S. Cavalry	663	440	192	6
First Division	8,228	1,804	4,951	179
Second Division	4,943	2,217	3,554	258
Third Division	4,842	3,409	3,653	242
Total	18,676	7,870	12,350	685

Abstract from return of the Army of the Potomac, Maj. Gen. George G. Meade, U. S. Army, commanding, for the month of October, 1863.a

Command.	Present for duty.		Aggregate present.	Aggregate present and absent.	Pieces of artillery.	
	Officers.	Men.			Heavy.	Field.
General headquarters b	130	1,080	1,364	1,943		
Engineer troops (Benham and Mendell)	46	1,224	1,527	1,875		
Artillery Reserve (Hunt)	89	2,602	2,974	4,301	8	80
First Army Corps (Newton)	623	11,473	13,819	21,787		34
Second Army Corps (Warren)	682	10,720	12,556	22,640		31
Third Army Corps (French)	881	15,668	18,659	28,184		40
Fifth Army Corps (Sykes)	661	11,273	13,135	20,049		32
Sixth Army Corps (Sedgwick)	916	15,063	17,734	23,813		46
Cavalry Corps (Pleasonton)	652	10,538	13,687	27,263		30
Total	4,680	79,641	95,455	151,855	8	299

a For abstracts from the tri-monthly returns of this army for October 10 and 20, see Part I, p. 226.
b Including provost guard, orderlies, and signal corps.

Abstract from return of the Department of Washington, Maj. Gen. Christopher C. Augur, U. S. Army, commanding, for the month of October, 1863.

Command.	Present for duty.		Aggregate present.	Aggregate present and absent.	Pieces of artillery.	
	Officers.	Men.			Heavy.	Field.
General headquarters	28	22	50	51		
Artillery Camp of Instruction (Barry)	49	1,346	1,505	1,745		60
District of Washington (Martindale) a	129	2,221	3,446	4,269		
Defenses North of the Potomac (Haskin)	213	5,676	7,218	7,814		
Provisional brigades (Casey)	38	989	1,103	1,237		
Defenses South of the Potomac (De Russy)	229	4,875	6,435	7,795	326	118
Corcoran's division (formerly King's)	128	2,226	2,734	3,417		6
Cavalry forces (Lowell)	56	804	1,814	1,921		
District of Alexandria (Slough) b	91	1,303	1,908	3,253		6
Camp Convalescent, &c. (McKelvy)	77	1,553	6,020	6,561		
Falls Church, Va. (Tracy)	19	567	680	982		
Glymont Landing, Md. (Sharra)	6	59	127	168		
Government farms (Greene) c	5	77	97	128		
Fort Washington, Md. (Brooks)	7	129	173	177	70	3
Total	1,075	21,797	32,900	39,518	396	193

a Including 1st District of Columbia Cavalry.   c Detachment of 111th New York, before reported
b And 164th New York.   at general headquarters.

Abstract from return of the Middle Department (Eighth Army Corps), Maj. Gen. R. C. Schenck, U. S. Army, commanding, for the month of October, 1863.

Command.	Present for duty.		Aggregate present.	Aggregate present and absent.	Headquarters.
	Officers.	Men.			
General headquarters	15	....	15	15	
First Separate Brigade (Lockwood)............	35	710	827	912	Drummondtown, Va.
Second Separate Brigade (Morris)............	40	1,049	1,521	1,702	Fort McHenry, Md.
Third Separate Brigade (E. B. Tyler).........	42	850	1,045	1,487	Baltimore, Md.
District of Delaware (D. Tyler)...............	13	506	577	668	Wilmington, Del.
Annapolis, Md. (Waite).	19	364	474	520	
Ellicott's Mills, Md. (Gilpin).................	25	474	540	568	
Fort Delaware (Schoepf).....................	15	277	437	451	
Relay House, Md. (Jenkins)..................	22	265	342	378	
Total.................................	226	4,495	5,778	6,701	

Abstract from return of the Department of West Virginia, Brig. Gen. Benjamin F. Kelley, U. S. Army, commanding, for the month of October, 1863.

Command.	Present for duty.		Aggregate present.	Aggregate present and absent.	Pieces of artillery.		Headquarters.
	Officers.	Men.			Heavy.	Field.	
General headquarters a..................	6	....	6	6	......	......	
First Division (Sullivan) a	311	7,120	8,679	10,882	22	46	Harper's Ferry.
Second Division (Mulligan) b...........	325	7,612	8,811	10,110	1	24	New Creek.
Third Division (Scammon)	192	4,753	5,787	6,782	......	16	Charleston.
First Separate Brigade (Averell)	174	3,761	4,545	5,336	......	12	Beverly.
Wheeling, W. Va (Thorp)..............	7	145	264	281	......	......	
Total.......................	1,015	23,391	28,042	33,397	23	98	

a See General Orders, No. 12, p. 302.   b See General Orders, No. 16, p. 365.

Abstract from return of the Department of Virginia and North Carolina, Maj. Gen. J. G. Foster, U. S. Army, commanding, for the month of October, 1863.

Command.	Present for duty.		Aggregate present.	Aggregate present and absent.	Pieces of artillery.	
	Officers.	Men.			Heavy.	Field.
General headquarters a...............................	34	51	92	95	......	......
Fort Monroe, Va..........	20	671	936	1,295	......	......
Newport News, Va. (Heckman)......................	123	2,680	3,580	4,588	......	......
Norfolk and Portsmouth, Va. (Barnes)..................	102	2,096	2,849	3,580	......	6
Portsmouth, Va. (Getty)...............................	211	4,596	6,050	10,444	......	47
Yorktown, Va., and vicinity (Wistar)..................	179	3,850	4,997	5,776	......	24
Defenses of New Berne, N. C. (Peck).................	174	2,886	3,974	5,067	59	66
Sub-District of the Albemarle, N. C. (Wessells)........	63	991	1,596	1,987	15	13
Sub-District of Beaufort, N. C. (Jourdan)......	65	914	1,227	1,904	58	7
Sub-District of the Pamlico, N. C. (Pickett)..............	45	1,138	1,616	1,961	......	6
Total...........................	1,016	19,803	26,847	37,397	132	169

a Including signal corps.

HEADQUARTERS FIRST CAVALRY DIVISION,
November 1, 1863.

Lieut. Col. C. Ross Smith:

My picket line has been advanced to within carbine range of the enemy's. My right is near Beverly Ford and the line extends past Bowen's house, parallel to the river to half way to Kelly's Ford, where it deflects and strikes the road from Bealeton to Morrisville.

General Merritt's last report says his pickets extend 5 miles from Elk Run toward Morrisville, and nothing has been seen or heard of the enemy. I expect to hear from him soon. I have instructed him to examine Kelly's. There is nothing toward Morrisville, save guerrillas. A negro, who left Richmond on the 23d, says:

The enemy is concentrating at Culpeper. Four thousand came to that point in the cars with him.

The enemy does not show so strong as yesterday.

I am, very respectfully, your obedient servant,
JNO. BUFORD,
Brigadier-General of Volunteers, Commanding.

WASHINGTON,
November 1, 1863—9.30 a. m.

General A. A. Humphreys,
Chief of Staff, Hdqrs. Army of the Potomac:

We have 400 feet of canvas train, with balks and chess on wagons; 900 feet more with balks, chess, and wagons complete; in all, 1.300 feet of canvas pontoon train. Six hundred feet of wooden bridge, with balks and chess in the boats, complete in rafts for towing; 400 feet more of wooden bridge, with balks without chess, ready for placing on trucks or on rafts; 1,000 feet in all of wooden bridge train, and the trucks and wagons for all. We have no pontoon train teams on hand, all having been sent to the front on 30th instant by order, and only about fifteen teams available for engineer tools, forage, &c.
H. W. BENHAM,
Brigadier-General.

HEADQUARTERS ARMY OF THE POTOMAC,
November 1, 1863—2.15 p. m.

Brig. Gen. H. W. Benham,
Commanding Engineers, Washington, D. C.:

The major-general commanding directs that you send immediately by railroad twenty wooden pontoons, with bridge material complete, trucks, and all the corresponding equipage.

One good sized company of the Fiftieth New York Volunteers, say not less than 50 men, should accompany the pontoons. They will take precedence of everything on the road, and will halt at Catlett's Station. The animals and harness for them need not be sent.

The following is a memorandum of the chief parts required: Twenty pontoon wagons, loaded; 2 abutment wagons, loaded; 1 long balk wagon, loaded; 9 chess wagons, loaded; 12 army wagons, and a liberal supply of cordage.
A. A. HUMPHREYS,
Major-General, Chief of Staff.

HEADQUARTERS ARMY OF THE POTOMAC,
November 1, 1863.

Brigadier-General BENHAM,
Navy-Yard:

The major-general commanding directs that you have the following lengths of bridge material made complete immediately in every respect—animals, harness, and drivers—with the requisite number of army wagons, teams and drivers, provisions and forage : Four hundred and fifty feet of wooden pontoon bridging and 800 feet of canvas pontoon bridging. These bridge trains, complete in every respect, must be held ready to move at a moment's notice. They will first be moved by water and then by land to the point where they will be required for use. Another preparation must include that of their transportation by water, as well as their subsequent movement by land. This communication is confidential. The bridging now ordered is in addition to that ordered to-day at 2.15 p. m.

A. A. HUMPHREYS,
Chief of Staff.

HEADQUARTERS ARMY OF THE POTOMAC,
November 1, 1863.

Brigadier-General BENHAM,
Navy-Yard:

I learn from Captain Peirce that he has not animals for the 12 army wagons that are to accompany the pontoons, and requests that you will send the animals, harness, and drivers for them.

A. A. HUMPHREYS,
Chief of Staff.

HDQRS. DEPT. OF VIRGINIA AND NORTH CAROLINA
Fort Monroe, Va., November 1, 1863.

Maj. Gen. H. W. HALLECK,
Commander-in-Chief, U. S. Army:

GENERAL: I have gotten ready to start, and propose to move up the James River, on Wednesday morning, as far as Fort Powhatan; to land there and throw up works on both sides of the river; to start the cavalry at first toward Richmond, whipping and pursuing the force at Charles City Court-House as far as they can go ; then to cross them over the river and to make a raid on Petersburg and the railroad between that city and Weldon. I trust this plan will meet with your approval. I can take a force of 4,500 infantry, 2,300 cavalry, and 500 artillery. I am quite sure that we can make a great noise, if nothing more, and draw off some force from General Lee.

I propose to hold and fortify every point on the James as far as we go, that, by being possessed by the enemy, would give him command of the river. From there, as sheltering points, cavalry raids can be easily made, and our supplies be secured by the way of the river. I wish very much that the force of infantry was greater, so that I could make a solid attack. As it is, I cannot venture to stir far from the river with the infantry and artillery. We will, however, do our best to worry the enemy. We can prevent the enemy gathering the crops on the river and in its vicinity, and thus distress them, as supplies of all kinds are, as I am informed by all deserters and refugees, getting very scarce in Richmond.

I shall report the results of the first movement.

I have the honor to be, very respectfully, your obedient servant,

J. G. FOSTER,
Major-General, Commanding.

HEADQUARTERS ARMY OF THE POTOMAC,
November 2, 1863—-noon.
(Received 1 a. m., 3d.)

Major-General HALLECK:

The railroad to Warrenton Junction, though announced as completed on the 30th ultimo, was not in working order till last night. This has caused a delay in the receipt of supplies.

No material change in the position of the enemy has been reported since my last dispatch, excepting that the forces opposite Freeman's Ford are reported as decreased, and the pickets on my extreme right strengthened. A contraband, who came into our lines yesterday, avers leaving Richmond on the 23d ultimo, and that on the train with him to Culpeper Court-House there came 4,000 troops. The fact, if true, that Lee is receiving re-enforcements, together with other indications already reported, such as moving of camps, strengthening of pickets, &c., would induce the supposition that perhaps he may again advance. From the best judgment I can form, his army is massed between the Rappahannock and Culpeper, prepared to dispute the passage of the river, either at the railroad crossing, or on his immediate right flank by Kelly's Ford, or his left by Sulphur Springs, or any of the intermediate crossings.

I therefore do not think I could, with any probability of success, advance against him in either of the above directions. There remains, then, a flank movement by a decided *détour* either to his left, by way of Amissville and Sperryville, threatening his communications by Culpeper or beyond, or a similar movement to his right, attempting to seize in advance the heights of Fredericksburg and opening communication with Aquia Creek. To the movement on his left there is the objection that I must either abandon my own communications or else weaken myself by the necessary force to protect them; also that the country over which I would have to operate is broken and rough, deficient in roads, and those existing of such a character that a storm of rain or snow, likely to occur at this season, would paralyze all movements. After maturely weighing all these considerations, I have determined to attempt the movement by his right, throwing the whole army rapidly and secretly across the Rappahannock at Banks' Ford and Fredericksburg, and taking position on the heights beyond the town.

The success of this movement will depend on its celerity, and its being kept from the enemy. From my latest information, he had no force below the junction of the two rivers. My present position, and repairing the railroad, has doubtless induced him to believe I shall adhere to this line, and if my movement can be started before he is apprised of it, I have every reason to believe it will be successful, so far as effecting a lodgment on the heights in advance of him; and if he follows and gives me battle, my object will be accomplished. I

can hardly think he will advance in this direction, as he·cannot supply himself for any length of time, unless he continues his movement
into Maryland, in which case, of course, 1 should ·have to retrace my
steps.

It is proper you should be advised of my proposed movement, and
should it not meet with your approval, I desire to be informed at the
earliest moment practicable.

GEO. G. MEADE,
Major-General.

P. S.—For prudential considerations, I send this by an aide-de-
camp.

ARTILLERY HDQRS., ARMY OF THE POTOMAC,
November 2, 1863.

Brig. Gen. S. WILLIAMS,
Asst. Adjt. Gen., Army of the Potomac:

GENERAL : I have the honor to transmit herewith a list of recruits
required to fill up the volunteer batteries of this army, as follows :

From Maine	205
From New Hampshire	32
From Rhode Island	208
From Massachusetts	154
From New York	838
From New Jersey	28
From Pennsylvania	346
From Ohio	76
From Maryland	38
From Virginia	20
Total	1,945

I also transmit a list of the number of recruits required by the
regular batteries, in the hope that some means may be found for
filling them up. The discharges which are constantly taking place
are not made good by re-enlistment, the volunteer service affording
greater inducements to recruits than the regular artillery. The
horse artillery of this army (twelve batteries), with the exception
of one battery, belongs to the regular service.

The duties are very arduous. The batteries (in excellent condition otherwise) are deficient in men. Rather than have the number
of guns reduced, the cavalry furnished them with men from time to
time. These details are temporary, and the men return to their
regiments at every change of position of the batteries. The result
is that the cavalry, when called into action, lose the services of the
men, and the batteries are partly manned by incompetent gunners.

It would be better in every respect to have the men permanently
assigned. I·would, therefore, suggest that a sufficient number of
drafted men, after being credited to their States, be transferred to
the regular artillery, to serve out the term for which they are
drafted. No man should be so assigned, except with his own consent. They should be picked men, not under 5 feet 8 inches, and be
sent from the depots direct, and not from the regiments. Transfers
from the latter, although made from the necessities of the service,
create bitter feelings against the artillery on the part of the regi-

ments. I have reason to believe, also, that the system is injurious to discipline, as it offers to all discontented or worthless men in the regiments a refuge from the results of their bad conduct. The number of men so required for the regular artillery of this army is 896.

Respectfully, your obedient servant,

HENRY J. HUNT,
Brigadier-General, Chief of Artillery.

GENERAL ORDERS, ⎰ HDQRS. MIDDLE DEPT., 8TH ARMY CORPS,
No. 55.   ⎱   *Baltimore, Md., November 2, 1863.*

Paragraph I, of General Orders, No. 53,* from these headquarters, is modified so as to read as follows:

I. That all provost marshals and other military officers are to prevent all disturbance and violence at or about the polls, whether offered by such persons as above described, or by any other person or persons whomsoever.

By command of Major-General Schenck:

WM. H. CHESEBROUGH,
Lieutenant-Colonel, and Asst. Adjt. Gen.

PARKERSBURG, W. VA., *November* 2, 1863—9.30 a. m.
(Received 10.20 a. m.)

Brig. Gen. G. W. CULLUM,
Chief of Staff:

Just arrived here on my return from Kanawha. The expedition is moving. The following telegrams from Brigadier-General Sullivan received here:

HARPER'S FERRY, W. VA.,
October 28, 1863.

Captain MELVIN,
Assistant Adjutant-General, Clarksburg:

Colonel Boyd has returned from his scout through Front Royal and Strasburg, bringing in 1 major, 1 captain, 2 lieutenants, and 18 privates ; 1 four-horse Confederate team and wagon, filled with army goods, valued at $10,000. Imboden's camp on the 25th was near Bridgewater, and Colonel Rosser, with a brigade of cavalry, was within 6 miles of Front Royal. The Shenandoah at Front Royal is not fordable for artillery. I need cavalry horses.

JER. C. SULLIVAN,
Brigadier-General.

HARPER'S FERRY, W. VA.,
November 1, 1863—2.30 p. m.

Capt. T. MELVIN,
Assistant Adjutant-General, Clarksburg:

A scout returned from Middletown and White Post, bringing in 8 prisoners and a lieutenant. No force in the valley of any size ; some small squads only.

JER. C. SULLIVAN,
Brigadier-General.

B. F. KELLEY,
Brigadier-General, Commanding.

---

* Of October 27.

WAR DEPARTMENT,
Washington, November 2, 1863—10 a. m.

Major-General FOSTER,
Fort Monroe, Va.:

Your services being required for another command, orders were issued by the War Department several days ago for you to report here on being relieved by Major-General Butler. These orders should have reached you before now, and General Butler should relieve you immediately. Your proposed expedition should be postponed until your successor arrives.

H. W. HALLECK,
General-in-Chief.

———

FORT MONROE, VA., *November 2, 1863.*
(Received 11.50 p. m.)

Maj. Gen. H. W. HALLECK,
General-in-Chief:

I have the honor to acknowledge the receipt of your telegram of this date. I have given the necessary orders to postpone the expedition.

J. G. FOSTER,
Major-General, Commanding.

———

SPECIAL ORDERS, }   HDQRS. DEPT. OF VA. AND N. C.,
No. 105.   }   *Fort Monroe, Va., November 2, 1863.*

*   *   *   *   *   *   *

II. Brigadier-General Wild is hereby ordered to report to Brigadier-General Barnes for command of colored troops, and such other command as General Barnes may designate.

*   *   *   *   *

By command of Major-General Foster :
SOUTHARD HOFFMAN,
Assistant Adjutant-General.

———

WAR DEPARTMENT,
Washington, November 3, 1863—10 a. m.

Major-General MEADE,
Army of the Potomac:

Your dispatch of 12 m. yesterday, received about 1 o'clock this morning, was submitted to the President at the earliest moment practicable. He does not see that the proposed change of base is likely to produce any favorable result, while its disadvantages are manifest. I have fully concurred in the views he has heretofore communicated on this subject. Any tactical movement to turn a flank or threaten a communication is left to your own judgment ; but an entire change of base under existing circumstances, I can neither advise nor approve.

H. W. HALLECK,
General-in-Chief.

HEADQUARTERS ARMY OF THE POTOMAC,
November 3, 1863.

Commanding Officer Cavalry Corps:

Information is just received that a part of Hampton's old brigade, about 600 strong, crossed at Fredericksburg yesterday, a part of whom were sent to destroy the railroad, and the remainder to scour the country. It was reported at Fredericksburg that a brigade of infantry would follow. The major-general commanding directs that Kilpatrick's division be sent to look after this cavalry and drive them back over the river.

Very respectfully,

A. A. HUMPHREYS,
Major-General, and Chief of Staff.

HEADQUARTERS ARMY OF THE POTOMAC,
November 3, 1863—9 p. m.

Col. D. C. McCALLUM,
Military Superintendent of Railroads:

Your railroad to the junction and Warrenton works well. I was aware that General Meade had paid you a most deserving compliment for the extraordinary labor performed under your direct supervision in rebuilding the road from Bristoe to Warrenton Junction. He desires you will keep your construction parties on the road and put it in working order as far as Bealeton.

RUFUS INGALLS,
Chief Quartermaster.

ARTILLERY HDQRS., ARMY OF THE POTOMAC,
November 3, 1863.

Lieut. Col. J. A. MONROE,
Chief of Artillery, Second Corps:

COLONEL: In reply to your note of this date, I am instructed by the chief of artillery to state:

1. There is no prescribed mode of packing the ammunition of 3-inch guns, as chests of different batteries are often issued marked, and not uniformly. When marked the ammunition should be packed accordingly. There is no objection to your prescribing the mode of packing, but when a mode has been adopted, and systematically followed, it would not be good policy during field operations to change it, unless there is a manifest fault in the packing, which produces injury.

2. For rifled guns, 25 shells, 20 shrapnel to 5 canister is a proper proportion, the shell to be increased to 30 at the expense of the shrapnel, if the commander of the battery desires it. There is too much shrapnel used. Fifty rounds is the load to each chest.

3. As both the Hotchkiss and Schenkl ammunition are provided, commanders of batteries can use either system, but in no case must two projectiles of the same kind be used in a battery. That is, no battery must have both Hotchkiss and Schenkl shell or both Hotchkiss and Schenkl shrapnel. They may have Hotchkiss shell and Schenkl shrapnel, or *vice versa*, but he recommends strongly that,

unless they have a marked preference for special roject es, all should be of one system, either Hotchkiss or Schenkl He believes Schenkl to be best and safest in every respect.

4. The object of the latitude given to battery commanders is to make them responsible for the efficiency of their batteries. Ammunition to which men and officers are most accustomed is the best to supply them. There is an evil, however, in using two kinds of the same description in the same battery or in the same army corps, or even in the same army, but with two systems which have such strong supporters as the Schenkl and Hotchkiss, it can hardly be avoided without a worse evil.

5. There has been no authority of a general character given to depart from the book of tactics in the packing of light 12-pounder ammunition. Permission will, however, be given to increase the number of canister at the expense of shrapnel. The full number of solid shot, 12, and of shell, 4, must be carried. The shrapnel may be reduced to 8, and added either to the canister or shell or both. The use of solid shot is too much neglected. It is the most efficient of our projectiles. He would not object if the allowance were increased to 16 rounds. It was intended that a part of the spherical case should be used as solid shot. The proportion laid down in the tactics is, he believes, the best. If any change should be made it should be to increase the number of solid shot. On no account will a less number be allowed than that prescribed, and the chief of artillery desires that you would impress on battery commanders the importance and superior value of solid-shot fire in almost all cases.

Respectfully, your obedient servant,

JNO. N. CRAIG,
Assistant Adjutant-General.

SPECIAL ORDERS, } WAR DEPT., ADJT. GENERAL'S OFFICE,
No. 489.   }   *Washington, November 3, 1863.*

*   *   *   *   *   *   *

18. Brig. Gen. Solomon Meredith, U. S. Volunteers, will at once return to the Army of the Potomac, and report in person to Major-General Meade, U. S. Volunteers, for duty.

*   *   *   *   *   *   *

By order of the Secretary of War:

E. D. TOWNSEND,
Assistant Adjutant-General.

GENERAL ORDERS, } HDQRS. DEPARTMENT OF WEST VIRGINIA,
No. 18.   }   *Clarksburg, W. Va., November 3, 1863.*

The following officers are announced as assigned to staff duty at these headquarters:

Capt. Thayer Melvin, assistant adjutant-general.

Col. D. H. Strother, Third [West] Virginia Cavalry, acting assistant inspector-general.

Lieut. Col. J. B. Frothingham, additional aide-de-camp, U. S. Army, commissary of musters.

Capt. Robert Adams, jr., Twenty-third Illinois Infantry, acting judge-advocate,

Capt. A. V. Barringer, chief quartermaster.
Capt. William H. Hosack, chief commissary of subsistence.
First Lieut. J. R. Meigs, U. S. Army, chief engineer.
Lieut. Col. William H. Mussey, surgeon, medical inspector.
Maj. J. V. Z. Blaney, surgeon, medical director.
Capt. William J. Matthews, Thirteenth [West] Virginia Infantry,
First Lieut. W. B. Kelley, First [West] Virginia Infantry, and
First Lieut. C. A. Freeman, First [West] Virginia Infantry, aides-
de-camp.

By order of Brigadier-General Kelley:
THAYER MELVIN,
Assistant Adjutant-General.

HEADQUARTERS ARMY OF THE POTOMAC,
November 4, 1863—4 p. m.

Brigadier-General BENHAM,
Comdg. Engineers, Navy-Yard, Washington, D. C.:

I am instructed to say that, it not being probable that the contingency will arise in expectation of which you were directed to hold
certain bridge trains ready for transportation by water and land, it
is not necessary to maintain that state of preparation. The animals
may be returned to the quartermaster's department.
A. A. HUMPHREYS,
Major-General, Chief of Staff.

NOVEMBER 4, 1863—8 p. m.
(Received 8.30 p. m.)

Major-General HALLECK:

Your telegram, of 12 m. yesterday, was duly received. Your dis-
approval of the proposed attempt to secure a lodgment on the Fredericksburg heights of course caused an immediate abandonment of
the plan. I have been since anxiously endeavoring to see my way
clear to make some movement, which, by tactical maneuver on the
enemy's flank, would bring my army in contact with his, without
giving him all the advantage of defense and position. As yet I have
not been able to arrive at any satisfactory conclusion, though most
earnestly anxious to bring matters to a termination. No change has
occurred in the position of this army, nor, as far as I can learn, in
the position of the enemy. Having been informed by scouts that
the enemy had crossed a body of cavalry at Falmouth, I sent Kilpatrick's division to ascertain the character of the force and movement. A report from him at 2 p. m. states he was within a few
miles of Falmouth, driving before him a small force of the enemy's
cavalry.
GEO. G. MEADE,
Major-General, Commanding.

CLARKSBURG, *November 4, 1863.*

Brigadier-General SULLIVAN, *Harper's Ferry:*

General Averell and General Duffié are now moving toward
Lewisburg, one from Beverly, the other from Gauley. Will attack

Lewisburg jointly on Saturday, the 7th. If successful, Averell will go on to the Virginia and Tennessee Railroad, if practicable ; if not, he will proceed to the Valley of the South Branch, and thence to New Creek. I anticipate this movement will draw Imboden's force from the Shenandoah Valley west. I suggest to you to get an expedition ready to move up the valley and attack and disperse any force that may be left there by Imboden. Please give me your views on the subject, and all information you have in regard to the force in the valley.

B. F. KELLEY,
Brigadier-General.

HDQRS. ARMY AND DISTRICT OF NORTH CAROLINA,
New Berne, N. C., November 4, 1863.

Maj. Gen. J. G. FOSTER,
Comdg. Dept. of Virginia and North Carolina:

GENERAL : Your communication by Captain Fitzgerald was received at 9 a. m. this day, and I hasten to say that after extraordinary exertions, I have succeeded in procuring coal from the navy and from Beaufort, and shall leave at 5 p. m. for Plymouth and Winton with a wharf boat, the Rucker, Pilot Boy, Pawtuxent, Ella May, General Berry, and a tug in addition to the Farron. The Delaware will go up, and I shall procure further naval aid from Captain Flusser. .

You say nothing of your numbers, and make no allusion to forage or rations, but to guard against all accidents, I shall take five days' forage for 2,500 animals and five days' rations for 3,000 men.

While writing, I learn that General Ransom has assumed command at Kinston ; General Barton has gone to the Blackwater with his brigade. What this means I am as yet unable to state.

·The steamer Robert E. Lee is about leaving Wilmington with mails for General Magruder, and funds to pay the troops in Texas.

The Jersey Blue has no coal for her trip to New York, and I send her with navy coal to Fort Monroe, with this in the hands of Captain Fitzgerald. Large gangs of contrabands have gone by rail to Weldon and Wilmington. Major-General Whiting advertises for a large number for his works.

In great haste, very respectfully, your obedient servant,
JOHN J. PECK,
Major-General.

HDQRS. DEPT. OF VIRGINIA AND NORTH CAROLINA,
Fort Monroe, Va., November 4, 1863.

Maj. Gen. H. W. HALLECK,
General-in-Chief, U. S. Army, Washington, D. C.:

GENERAL : I have the honor to inclose herewith a copy of a communication received this day from Acting Rear-Admiral S. P. Lee, commanding North Atlantic Blockading Squadron.

I am, general, very respectfully, your obedient servant,
J. G. FOSTER,
Major-General, Commanding.

[Inclosure]

U. S..FLAG-SHIP MINNESOTA,
Off Newport News, Va., November 4, 1863.

Maj. Gen. J. G. FOSTER, U. S. Army,
Comdg. Dept. of Va. and N. C., Fort Monroe, Va.:

GENERAL : The Tribune of the 3d, received to-day, contains a dispatch dated the 2d instant from Washington, in which it is said that I am understood to have more than once made propositions to military commanders on the Peninsula calculated to make the blockade more stringent, but have failed to find reasonable co-operation. It is proper that I should state that I have not made any such proposition to you.

Permit me to avail myself of this occasion to make my acknowledgments for the professional co-operation and official and personal courtesy which I have received from you. Please accept my best wishes for your professional success and personal happiness.

I have the honor to be, general, very respectfully and truly, yours,
S. PHILLIPS LEE,
Actg. Rear-Admiral, Comdg. N. A. Bkdg. Squadron.

HEADQUARTERS ARMY OF THE POTOMAC,
November 5, 1863—1 p. m.

Commanding Officer First Corps:

The major-general commanding directs that you move your corps at once to the vicinity of Catlett's, and hold two divisions of it ready for further orders.

You will assign one division to guarding the railroad from Manassas to Warrenton Junction, as follows: One brigade at Bristoe; one brigade at Warrenton Junction, to protect that depot; the other brigade will be distributed to guard the bridges over Cedar Run and Kettle Run. The small bridges and culverts must be guarded by detachments. The road from Manassas to Warrenton must in addition be patrolled, if practicable, with the force assigned to the duty of protecting the road.

A. A. HUMPHREYS,
Major-General, and Chief of Staff.

NOVEMBER 5, 1863—7.15 p. m.

Commanding Officer Third Corps:

The major-general commanding directs me to inform you that General Newton will assign a division of the First Corps to the duty of guarding the railroad from Manassas to and including Warrenton Junction depot. These troops will be at the posts assigned them to-morrow morning. As soon as they reach them the brigade of your corps at Catlett's, and such other detachments from the corps on the railroad, will rejoin their respective commands.

A. A. HUMPHREYS,
Major-General, and Chief of Staff.

HDQRS. CAVALRY CORPS, ARMY OF THE POTOMAC,
November 5, 1863.

Brig. Gen. S. WILLIAMS,
    Asst. Adjt. Gen., Army of the Potomac:

GENERAL : I have the honor to forward for the information of the major-general commanding this army the accompanying reports, which have come to me from my command.*

Attention is respectfully called to the two prominent grounds of complaint mentioned ; the very general unfitness of the horses furnished for cavalry service, and the want of forage for the animals after they get into the field, both of which conspire to keep a very large portion of this corps actually absent from the army, and many others, in addition, dismounted and unserviceable in the ranks.

The poor quality of the horses sent from Dismounted Camp, and the want of care in the manner of forwarding them to the army, prove, satisfactorily to my mind, the absolute failure of that enterprise, and convince me that some other system must be adopted to keep the cavalry properly mounted and equipped.

I would therefore respectfully suggest that the entire business of fitting out the cavalry of this army be placed under the orders and control of the commanding general; that depots be established (within the actual limits of the army where practicable) where men who have lost horses or equipments can be rapidly re-equipped for the field instead of, as at present, lying sometimes for months together in a Dismounted Camp over which he has no control, where it is reputed there is no discipline or order, and which both officers and soldiers have learned to look to as a comfortable escape from the performance of duty in the field. Depots thus established could receive the attention of the corps commander in an equal degree with any other portion of his command, being under his immediate eye and for the advantage solely of his own troops, suitable officers could and would be selected for their charge, and any evils could and would be promptly checked. Under the present system, although horses of a generally poorer quality than ever before received are furnished the command, although a very large number of officers and men are absent at Dismounted Camp, without the limits of this army, who properly belong to it, and whose services could be usefully employed in the field, I have no power to apply the least remedy.

Very respectfully, your obedient servant,

A. PLEASONTON,
Major-General, Commanding Cavalry Corps.

[Indorsements.]

HEADQUARTERS ARMY OF THE POTOMAC,
November 6, 1863.

Respectfully forwarded to the Adjutant-General, for the information of the General-in-Chief.

GEO, G. MEADE,
Major-General, Commanding.

---

* Inclosures omitted, their substance being in this report and following indorsement.

HEADQUARTERS ARMY,
November 10, 1863.

Respectfully referred to Major-General Stoneman, Chief of Cavalry Bureau, for remarks.

By order of Maj. Gen. H. W. Halleck :

J. C. KELTON,
Assistant Adjutant-General.

OFFICE OF CAVALRY BUREAU,
Washington, D. C., November 12, 1863.

A perusal of the inclosed papers indicates the following :

1. The horses of the Cavalry Corps, Army of the Potomac, are in no small degree affected with diseases, and among them that of the feet and mouth. One remedy, and that used at the depot with success, is the chloride of antimony for sore feet, and a decoction of white-oak bark for the mouth ; another is borax and alum, half and half, pulverized and mixed with sweet oil, and applied with a swab to the tongue, and still another is common salt (chloride of sodium) crisped on a hot shovel and applied to the feet and mouth. A good prevention is to give horses as much salt as they will eat.

2. The extraordinary amount of hard work the cavalry is called upon to perform incident either to the necessities of the case or to an improper use of that arm of the service.

3. The great deficiency of forage, part cu ar y hay. In one instance a whole division (the Second, General Gregg's) has been twenty-one days without any hay. No horses, however good and bought at whatever price, can stand this kind of treatment in a region where but little, if any, grass can be procured.

4. A portion of the horses issued to the Army of the Potomac have been illy adapted to the cavalry service, being too young, unbroken, and unsound. Every effort is being made to remedy, and, as far as possible, to do away with this cause for complaint.

5. Horses which have become unserviceable and having been left behind in various movements of the army or having been sent into depot, have been reissued and sent into the field. It was expected that this would cause complaint, but the Government has these horses on hand, and unless they are disposed of, they must be either kept and fed at great expense or must be reissued for further use. A large portion of these broken-down horses have been during the past summer in pasture, and have been recently collected together and put into stables and sheds, all of which are now full of them. They are divided into four classes, the fourth being considered fit for service, and from this class the best are selected and again sent into the field. Each horse before he is turned over to be sent off is inspected to see if he is affected with any disease, such as sore feet, sore tongue, glanders, farcy, distemper, &c., and none are allowed to leave that are so affected. If, after they have been issued and before they are sent off, any horses develop signs of disease, they are returned to the depot and others issued in their places, the object being to send the best there is and to make the most possible out of the 17,000 on hand on the last of October. But few of the horses purchased by the Cavalry Bureau have been sent to the Army of the Potomac, most of them having been sent to other armies and issued to new regiments, and, as far as is known, have given very general satisfaction.

6. It appears to be a question whether the men shall be sent into depot, either by regiments or in herds, to get their remounts and outfits,
or whether the horses, &c., shall be sent to the army in the field and
there distributed. In this the commanding general must be the
judge, and whatever his decisions may be they will meet with a
hearty co-operation of the Cavalry Bureau, and every effort will be
made to carry them out.

General Pleasonton's opinions in regard to the discipline of the
Dismounted Camp, and also in regard to the quality of the horses
issued by the Cavalry Bureau, might possibly have more weight
had they been founded in either case upon personal observation and
inspection. The plan he proposes of having his own depots under
his own supervision and within the actual limits of the army necessarily indicates that he contemplates that in future the Army of the
Potomac shall remain stationary to protect them from Stuart, or
that his depots shall be of a portable character and capable of being
transported and taken with the army in its various and uncertain
movements.

GEORGE STONEMAN,
Major-General of Volunteers, Chief of Cavalry.

GENERAL ORDERS, }   HDQRS. ARMY OF THE POTOMAC,
No. 100. . }   *November 5, 1863.*

I. The following is the maximum allowance of transportation,
camp and garrison equipage allowed this army while in the field engaged in active operations, and will be strictly conformed to, viz :

1. For the headquarters of an army corps, 2 wagons, or 8 pack-
mules, for baggage; 1 two-horse spring wagon for contingent wants;
5 extra saddle horses for contingent wants; 1 wall tent for personal
use and office of commanding general; 1 wall tent for every 2 officers of his staff.

2. For the headquarters of a division, 1 wagon, or 5 pack-mules,
for baggage; 1 two-horse spring wagon for contingent wants; 2 extra
saddle horses for contingent wants; 1 wall tent for personal use and
office of commanding general; 1 wall tent for every 2 officers of his
staff.

3. For the headquarters of a brigade, 1 wagon, or 5 pack-mules,
for baggage; 1 wall tent for personal use and office of commanding
general; 1 wall tent for every 2 officers of his staff.

4. To every 3 company officers, when detached or serving without
wagons, 1 pack-mule; to every 12 company officers, when detached,
1 wagon, or 4 pack-mules; to every 2 staff officers, when not attached
to any headquarters, 1 pack-mule; to every 10 staff officers, serving
similarly, 1 wagon, or 4 pack-mules.

The above wagons and pack-mules will include transportation for
all personal baggage, mess chests, cooking utensils, desks, papers, &c.
The weight of officers' baggage in the field, specified by Army Regulations, will be reduced so as to bring it within the foregoing schedule. All excess of transportation now with army corps, divisions,
brigades, regiments, or batteries over the allowance herein prescribed will be immediately turned in to the quartermaster's department, to be used in the trains.

5. Commissary stores and forage will be transported by the trains.

When these are not convenient of access, and where troops act in detachments, the quartermaster's department will assign wagons or pack animals for that purpose; but the baggage of officers, or of troops, or camp equipage, will not be carried in the wagons or on the pack animals so assigned. The assignment of transportation for ammunition, hospital stores, subsistence, and forage, will be made on the basis of the amount of each ordered to be carried in orders from general headquarters. The number of wagons is hereinafter prescribed, required by existing orders, to wit:

6. For each full regiment of infantry and cavalry of 1,000 men, for baggage, camp equipage, &c., 6 wagons; for each regiment of infantry less than 700 men and more than 500 men, 5 wagons; for each regiment of infantry less than 500 men and more than 300 men, 4 wagons; for each regiment of infantry less than 300 men, 3 wagons; for each regiment of infantry and cavalry, 3 wall tents for field and staff, 1 shelter tent for every other commissioned officer, 1 shelter tent for every 2 non-commissioned officers, soldiers, servants, and camp followers.

7. For each battery of 4 and 6 guns, for personal baggage, mess chests, cooking utensils, desks, papers, &c., 1 and 2 wagons, respectively; for each 6-gun battery, 3 wall tents for officers; for each 4-gun battery, 2 wall tents for officers; shelter tents, same allowance as for infantry and cavalry regiments.

8. For artillery ammunition trains, the number of wagons will be determined and assigned upon the following rules: Multiply the number of 12-pounder guns by 122 and divide by 112; multiply the number of rifled guns by 50 and divide by 140; multiply the number of 20-pounder guns by 2; multiply the number of $4\frac{1}{2}$-inch guns by $2\frac{1}{2}$; multiply the number of rifled guns in horse batteries by 100 and divide by 140. For the general supply train of reserve ammunition of 20 rounds to each gun in the army, to be kept habitually with Artillery Reserve, the following formula will apply: Multiply the number of 12-pounder guns by 20, divide by 112=number of wagons; multiply the number of rifled guns by 20, divide by 140=number of wagons. To every 1,000 men, cavalry and infantry, for small-arm ammunition, 5 wagons; for Artillery Reserve, for carrying fuses, primers, and powder, 2 wagons.

9. The supply trains will be as follows: To each 1,000 men, cavalry and infantry, for forage, quartermaster's stores, subsistence, &c., 7 wagons; to each cavalry division, for carrying forage for cavalry horses, 30 wagons additional; to each battery, for carrying its proportion of subsistence, forage, &c., 3 wagons; to each horse battery, for the same purpose, 4 wagons; to every 25 wagons of the artillery ammunition train there will be allowed 5 wagons additional for carrying forage for animals of ammunition and additional wagons, baggage, camp equipage, and subsistence of wagon-masters and teamters. Nothing but ammunition will be carried in the artillery ammunition train. The baggage of the drivers of the wagon composing it will be carried in the additional wagons allowed for that purpose.

To each 1,500 men, cavalry and infantry, for hospital supplies, 3 wagons; to each brigade of artillery, for hospital supplies, 1 wagon; to each army corps, except the cavalry, for intrenching tools, &c., 6 wagons; to each corps headquarters, for the carrying of subsistence, forage, and other stores not provided for herein, 3 wagons; to each division headquarters, for similar purposes as above, 2 wagons; to each brigade headquarters, for similar purposes as above, 1 wagon; to each brigade of cavalry, artillery, and infantry, for commissary stores for sales to officers, 1 wagon; to each division of cavalry and infantry, for hauling forage for ambulance animals, portable forges, &c., 2 wagons; to each division, cavalry and infantry, for carrying armorer's tools, parts of muskets, extra arms, and accouterments, 1 wagon. It is expected that each ambulance and each wagon, except-ing those of the artillery ammunition train, will carry the necessary forage for its own team.

10. If corps, division, and brigade commanders take their guards or escorts from commands already furnished with the full allowance of transportation, a corresponding amount should be taken with them to headquarters; but if they have not been provided for at all, then a proper number of wagons will be transferred by the depot quarter-master, on the requisition of the chief quartermaster, certified to and approved by the commanding general. As a rule, neither quarter-master nor commissary sergeants will be allowed to ride public horses.

II. It has been decided that there is no advantage to the service, commensurate with the expense, in keeping up regularly organized pack trains with mules independent of the wagons. All pack-saddles now on hand will be carried in the wagons of the ammuni-tion and supply trains, not to exceed 2 to a wagon.

When it becomes necessary to pack officer's baggage, rations, or ammunition for short distances over rough roads and broken country, pack trains can be made up temporarily by taking mules from the wagons, not to exceed 2 to any 1 wagon.

There will be allowed to each corps 50 extra mules, to supply losses on marches and for packing.

The following modification of Paragraph 1121, Revised Army Regulations, approved by the War Department, General-in-Chief, Quartermaster-General, and the general commanding, is hereby estab-lished, as far as relates to this army, and will be observed until other-wise ordered :

The maximum allowance of forage per day will be, for horses, 10 pounds hay and 14 pounds grain; for mules, 10 pounds hay and 11 pounds grain, and when short forage only can be procured, 18 pounds of grain for horses and 15 pounds of grain for mules can be issued as the daily ration.

When the army is on the march, the above order will not apply. The wagons will carry only the marching ration (10 pounds average to each animal per day).

This increased allowance of grain is intended to be fed only when the animals are at rest, after long marches, to recuperate them, and when hay cannot be procured.

III. Private property shall not be taken, except when required for the public service, and then only on the written order of the general commanding the army, a general commanding a corps, or other in-dependent commander.

A copy of the order and receipts for the property taken must be left with the owner thereof, and a report of all property captured from the enemy, or seized for the public service, will be made monthly to the chief of the department, at these headquarters, to which it appertains.

By command of Major-General Meade:

S. WILLIAMS,
Assistant Adjutant-General.

GENERAL ORDERS, }   HEADQUARTERS CAVALRY CORPS,
No. 42:   }   *November 5, 1863.*

The loss in officers and men sustained in this corps at the hands of guerrillas during the past few days demands the careful attention of all to prevent a recurrence in the future. The command is admonished that we are here in the field for military and not social purposes. Visiting in the families of the country in which our operations are conducted, riding for pleasure, either alone or in small parties, or even any unnecessary exposure when in the line of duty, are directly in violation of every recognized military principle. They will, therefore, be abstained from in future. Every house within or without the lines of the army is a nest of treason, and every grove a lurking place for guerrilla bands. They are on that account to be watched and avoided.

Division commanders are expressly directed to give to this matter their earnest attention.

In the transmission of orders or the conduct of the public business, care will be taken that individuals or small parties are not unnecessarily exposed, and every effort will be made to confine all officers and men to such close attention to their duties as will remove all temptation to go beyond the lines of their immediate command.

Any infringement of the spirit of this order will be reported to these headquarters, that the appropriate remedy for such neglect of duty may be promptly applied.

By command of Major-General Pleasonton:

C. C. SUYDAM,
Assistant Adjutant-General.

CLARKSBURG, W. VA., *November 5, 1863—2 p. m.*
(Received 3.45 p. m.)

Brigadier-General CULLUM,
Chief of Staff:

General Sullivan reports that Captain Bailey, of the First New York Cavalry, had just returned from a scout, bringing 1 major and 5 privates, with horses and equipments. Killed 3 and mortally wounded 1. Imboden is again threatening our lines in the valley.

B. F. KELLEY,
Brigadier-General.

NOVEMBER 6, 1863—7 p. m.
(Received 8 p. m.)

Major-General HALLECK:

General Kilpatrick returned from Falmouth last evening, having driven the enemy's cavalry across the river.

A movement of the enemy's infantry down the river was reported yesterday. Supposed to be in consequence of Kilpatrick's operations.

This morning the enemy crossed at Kelly's Ford, and caused my cavalry pickets at that point to retire a short distance. A scout just in reports Lee having reviewed his army day before yesterday, and that the transportation trains had been increased; also a general report prevailing in the rebel army that a movement was soon to be made.

I had intended to-day advancing to the Rappahannock at the railroad crossing and Kelly's Ford, and attempting the passage of the river. Indications last evening of a storm caused a postponement of the movement. It will be made to-morrow, and I think with a favorable result.

GEO. G. MEADE,
Major-General, Commanding.

HEADQUARTERS CAVALRY RESERVE BRIGADE,
November 6, 1863.

General BUFORD:

My pickets yesterday reported the enemy across the river above Kelly's Ford. A staff officer I sent out by Payne's house from here found the enemy's pickets there, but not in force, only a few vedettes.

This morning the enemy crossed above Kelly's Ford (near Wheatley's, I believe) and drove my pickets at Kelly's in. The report I get from my pickets is very indefinite. The number of the enemy is not reported, nor is it stated how far my pickets were driven. Captain Feilner, at Morrisville, with the reserve of the regiment (the First Cavalry) re-enforced Sumner, but whether he regained his former position or not is not stated. The enemy are on this side the river. My pickets on Hartwood Church road report that Kilpatrick returned toward Warrenton Junction yesterday morning. I have nothing further in regard to the enemy's movement down the river. The enemy hold this side of the river all the way from Rappahannock Bridge to below Kelly's Ford now.

I sent all my wagons for supplies this morning to Warrenton Junction. I have sent to front for more definite reports, and will send them in as soon as received.

Very respectfully,

W. MERRITT,
Brigadier-General of Volunteers, Commanding.

[P. S.]—I inclose report* I have from picket.

HEADQUARTERS CAVALRY RESERVE BRIGADE,
November 6, 1863.

[General BUFORD:]

GENERAL: From further information I conclude that the affair at Kelly's Ford did not amount to much. The enemy hold this side of the ford, though. Shall I drive them across? I would do so without orders, provided our entire line could be advanced, and thus some good result from a fight. My picket line at present is very unsatisfactory. Both parties out stand a chance of being driven in, and have to travel so far that such an occurrence would be extremely demoralizing to the men. There is no additional news.

Very respectfully,

W. MERRITT,
Brigadier-General of Volunteers, Commanding.

---

* Not found.

[Indorsement.]

HEADQUARTERS FIRST CAVALRY DIVISION,
November 6, 1863.

Lieutenant-Colonel SMITH:

I have told Merritt not to molest the pickets at Kelly's unless they attack him, but to watch every movement.

Respectfully,

JNO. BUFORD,
Brigadier-General of Volunteers, Commanding.

CIRCULAR.]   HEADQUARTERS ARMY OF THE POTOMAC,
November 6, 1863.

The following movements are ordered for to-morrow, the 7th instant:

1. The Sixth Corps, Major-General Sedgwick commanding, will move at early daylight to-morrow, and take position at Rappahannock Station, the left resting upon the railroad, the right toward Beverly Ford. The corps will move by way of Fayetteville, and so contract its march as not to interfere with the route of the Fifth Corps.

2. The Fifth Corps, General Sykes commanding, will move at early daylight and take position on the left of the Sixth Corps; it will move by way of Germantown and Bealeton, and will leave the route along the Warrenton Branch Railroad clear for the Second Corps.

3. Major-General Sedgwick will command the Sixth and Fifth Corps, which will compose the right column. He will relieve the cavalry pickets on his front. On reaching his position, his pickets will connect with those of the column at Kelly's Ford.

4. The Third Corps, Major-General French commanding, will move at early daylight to Kelly's Ford, by way of Elk Run and Morrisville.

5. The Second Corps, Major-General Warren commanding, will move at early daylight to Kelly's Ford, taking the route along the Warrenton Branch Railroad and the railroad to Bealeton, and thence by the Morrisville road, diverging so as to pass by Bowen's, former headquarters of the Twelfth Corps.

6. The First Corps, Major-General Newton commanding, leaving a division to guard the railroad, as already directed, will move to Morrisville by way of Elk Run, following the Third Corps, and be prepared to proceed to Kelly's Ford.

7. Major-General French will command the Third, Second, and First Corps, which will compose the left column. He will relieve the cavalry pickets on his front, and connect with the picket line of the column at Rappahannock Station.

8. The chief engineer will assign an officer of Engineers to General Sedgwick and General French. He will assign likewise two bridges to the column at Rappahannock Station and two bridges to the column at Kelly's Ford. The remainder of the bridge train will be held at Warrenton Junction and Bealeton.

9. The chief of artillery will assign ten of the siege guns to Major-General Sedgwick's column, and the remaining four to General French's column. The remainder of the Reserve Artillery, with its

train, will be equally distributed at Bealeton and Morrisville, and held ready to be sent to the columns.

10. Each corps will take with it so much of its small-arms ammunition trains as will give 40 rounds to the troops, its intrenching tools, ambulance trains, and hospital wagons. None of these trains, however, will cross the river, excepting ambulance trains, until specially directed to do so. All other wagons will be left in the rear—those of the Fifth and Sixth Corps parked at Bealeton, those of the Third, Second, and First at Morrisville. The pioneers will accompany the troops.

11. Buford's division of cavalry will move on the right flank, cross on the upper fords, and force the passage of Hazel River at Rixeyville. The chief of cavalry will direct General Buford to communicate and co-operate with General Sedgwick, commanding right column.

General Kilpatrick's division of cavalry will operate on the left flank, crossing at Ellis' or Kemper's Ford. He will communicate and co-operate with General French, commanding left column.

General Gregg's division of cavalry will be held in reserve, guarding the trains at Bealeton and Morrisville, and keeping open the roads communicating between the columns at Rappahannock Station and Kelly's Ford, and between Bealeton and Morrisville. General Buford will leave a sufficient force to protect the signal officer on Watery Mountain.

12. Headquarters will be in the vicinity of the toll-gate near Payne's house.

By command of Major-General Meade:

S. WILLIAMS,
Assistant Adjutant-General.

HEADQUARTERS ARMY OF THE POTOMAC,
November 6, 1863.

Major-General FRENCH,
Commanding Left Column:

GENERAL: The order directing the movements for to-morrow, inclosed herewith,* assigns you to the command of the left column, composed of the Third, Second, and First Corps, which is to effect a crossing of the river at Kelly's Ford, a lodgment on the heights overlooking the crossing, and then moving toward Providence Church, assist the operations of the right column, under General Sedgwick, in dislodging the enemy from his position near Rappahannock Station. Should this be effected, the two columns will move forward to Brandy Station. In the event of General Sedgwick not being able to dislodge the enemy from his position at Rappahannock Station, his column will be withdrawn and thrown across the river at Kelly's Ford, to support you in the movement to Brandy Station.

The main force of the enemy is assembled between Brandy Station, Culpeper Court-House, and Stevensburg. He holds Rappahannock Station and Kelly's Ford in force, with infantry (and probably artillery) at Ellis' Ford, Beverly Ford, &c., and has thrown up defensive works at the crossings of the river. It is to be expected, therefore, that he will oppose your crossing. You will attack him vigor-

* See p. 425.

ously, throwing your whole force upon him, should it be necessary, and drive him from his position, and secure your own upon the high ground.

The movement toward Providence Church to co-operate with General Sedgwick must depend upon the progress he has made. You will maintain communication and connection with him, keeping yourself advised of the result of his operations.

Instructions for the further conduct of your operations will be given during the progress of those just indicated.

Upon reaching the vicinity of Kelly's Ford the presence of your column will be concealed as far as practicable from the enemy. Preparations for effecting the crossing of the river will be made during the night. The chief engineer will furnish two bridges for the use of your column and will send an engineer officer for your staff.

The chief of artillery will supply you with four siege guns.

General Kilpatrick's division of cavalry will cross at Ellis' or Kemper's Ford, and co-operate upon the right. He will communicate and co-operate with you.

A copy of General Sedgwick's instructions is sent herewith. He is furnished with a copy of your instructions. A tracing from a map from Rappahannock Station to Kelly's Ford has been already sent you.

Very respectfully, your obedient servant,

S. WILLIAMS,
Assistant Adjutant-General.

[Inclosure.]

HEADQUARTERS ARMY OF THE POTOMAC,
November 6, 1863.

Major-General SEDGWICK,
Commanding Right Column:

The orders directing the movements for to-morrow, inclosed herewith,* assign you the command of the column, composed of your own and the Fifth Corps, which is to be directed against the enemy in the vicinity of Rappahannock Station. The duty devolving upon you is to drive the enemy from his positions there on this and the other side of the river, and to move toward Brandy Station, between which locality, Culpeper Court-House, and Stevensburg the main force of the enemy is now collected, the crossing at Rappahannock Station and Kelly's Ford being held in force by him with infantry, and probably artillery at Ellis' Ford, Beverly Ford, &c.

Reaching Rappahannock Station before sunset, the enemy should, if practicable, be driven from this side of the river at once, and the operations against their position on the opposite bank be commenced. In connection with these operations, ten siege-guns will be sent you from the Reserve Artillery. A lodgment on the opposite bank at Kelly's Ford and an advance from that point toward Brandy Station is the task assigned to the column commanded by General French, between whom and yourself constant communication and connection will be kept up during your operations against the position at Rappahannock Station and his against that at Kelly's Ford, and during the advance of each upon Brandy Station.

* See p. 425.

The nature of the enemy's position at Rappahannock Station will be sufficiently indicated by the statement that he holds a small redoubt on this side, near the railroad bridge, with rifle-pits, the redoubt and rifle-pit on the hill on the opposite bank on the right of the road, and the wooded hill on the left of the railroad, which commands the level ground on this side of the river and on the line of the railroad on the other. This hill extends a considerable distance nearly parallel with the line of railroad. Upon this hill and others on the right of the railroad, it is highly probable that defensive works have been thrown up. There is some high ground upon this side the river, near Norman's Ford, which, it is understood, will admit of several batteries being placed in position against the wooded hill on the opposite bank.

The contingency should be held in view of your being withdrawn from Rappahannock Station and thrown across at Kelly's Ford, in the event of your not being able to dislodge the enemy from his position at Rappahannock Station.

General Buford's cavalry division is directed to operate upon the right flank and force a crossing at Rixeyville. He will be directed to communicate and co-operate with you.

A copy of General French's instructions is inclosed herewith.* He is furnished with a copy of yours.

A rough sketch of the vicinity of Rappahannock Station, made by Captain Mendell, accompanies this. A tracing of the map, including Rappahannock Station and Kelly's Ford, has already been sent you.

Very respectfully, &c.,

S. WILLIAMS,
Assistant Adjutant-General.

CIRCULAR.]   HEADQUARTERS ARMY OF THE POTOMAC,
November 6, 1863—3.15 p. m.

In the movements ordered for to-morrow, November 7, general headquarters will be at Carter's house, on the road to Kelly's Ford that leaves the road from Bealeton to Morrisville about midway between the two places, instead of at Payne's house, as heretofore indicated.

By command of Major-General Meade:

S. WILLIAMS,
Assistant Adjutant-General.

NOVEMBER 7, 1863—12 m.

Major-General SEDGWICK:

Do you think you can hold the fords in the vicinity of Rappahannock Station with two of your divisions and all your artillery? If the column from Kelly's Ford advances and engages in battle, I desire to make it as strong as possible, as it will, undoubtedly, have to meet the main rebel army, and I ought to leave some force at Kelly's Ford. Let me know at once.

GEO. G. MEADE,
Major-General, Commanding.

---

* See p. 426.

NOVEMBER 7, 1863—9 p. m.
(Received 9.30 p. m.)

Major-General HALLECK:

I advanced to-day with the army to the Rappahannock. Major-General Sedgwick, in command of the Fifth and Sixth Corps, advanced to the railroad crossing, where he drove the enemy to the river, assaulted and captured two redoubts with artillery on this side, taking a number of prisoners. Major-General French, commanding the Third, Second, and part of the First Corps, advanced to Kelly's Ford, driving the enemy in small force across the river, secured a lodgment on the other side, and captured several hundred prisoners at the ford. The advance and attack will be continued to-morrow. Prisoners report Ewell's, Hill's, and part of Longstreet's corps at present under command of General Lee.

GEO. G. MEADE,
Major-General, Commanding.

NOVEMBER 7, 1863—10 p. m.
(Received 10.30 p. m.)

Major-General HALLECK:

General Sedgwick reports capturing this p. m. in his operations 4 colonels, 3 lieutenant-colonels, many other officers, and over 800 men, together with 4 battle-flags. General French captured over 400 prisoners, officers and men.

GEO. G. MEADE,
Major-General, Commanding.

HEADQUARTERS THIRD CAVALRY DIVISION,
Grove Church, Va., November 7, 1863—1.30 p. m.

Major-General PLEASONTON:

GENERAL: I have the honor to report my arrival at Grove Church. Two regiments of Hampton's division of cavalry are on this river. We had a skirmish at Grove Church with a portion of this force. We have captured 1 prisoner. He informs me that the most of their infantry, the day before yesterday, were in the vicinity of Stevensburg. I have sent a staff officer to communicate with Major-General French at Morrisville. I have 2,300 effective men ready for any duty you may please to assign them.

Very respectfully,

J. KILPATRICK,
Brigadier-General, Comdg. Third Cavalry Division.

HEADQUARTERS THIRD CORPS,
Mount Holly Church, November 7, 1863—2 p. m.

Brigadier-General Carr will look out for the left and support all the batteries on the left. He will picket at least a mile to the left.

By command of Major-General Birney:

J. C. BRISCOE,
Captain, and Acting Assistant Adjutant-General.

Hdqrs. Left Column, Army of the Potomac,
Mount Holly Church, November 7, 1863—3 p. m.

Major-General HUMPHREYS,
Chief of Staff:

The head of my column is across the river. Captured 300 prisoners. Troops fording. Division across.

Respectfully,

WM. H. FRENCH,
Major-General, Commanding.

Near New Baltimore,
November 7, [1863]—3.30 p. m.

Major-General PLEASONTON:

My command is on General Sedgwick's right. I found a corn-field, and have halted to feed. I sent a party to White Plains. No enemy there. I await further orders.

JNO. BUFORD,
Brigadier-General of Volunteers.

[Indorsement.]

Orders have been sent.

A. PLEASONTON.

NOVEMBER 7, 1863—4 p. m.

Major-General SEDGWICK,
Commanding Right Column:

The major-general commanding directs me to inform you that French has effected a crossing and lodgment at Kelly's Ford—one division already over. The indications are that the battle will be fought within a mile of Kelly's Ford. He desires to know the condition of things in your front; what the force of the enemy is, and how posted. If you are not confident of being able to cross to-night (Norman's Ford he indicates as probably the best point), he desires you to hold your command ready to be transferred to-night to Kelly's Ford, and cross there.

A. A. HUMPHREYS,
Major-General, and Chief of Staff.

HEADQUARTERS THIRD CAVALRY DIVISION,
Stevensburg, November 7, 1863—4.30 p. m.

Lieutenant-Colonel SMITH,
Chief of Staff:

COLONEL: I have the honor to report that General Kilpatrick has driven the enemy out of Stevensburg and he is now retiring in the direction of Culpeper, and now is at the base of Pony Mountain. Large number of infantry of Ewell's and Hill's corps passed through this place last night toward Culpeper. They were moving all night. He will hold this place until further orders, not deeming it prudent to advance farther. We have only encountered cavalry.

Very respectfully, your obedient servant,

GEORGE W. YATES,
Aide-de-Camp.

[Indorsement.]

HEADQUARTERS CAVALRY CORPS,
November 9, [1863]—8.30 a. m.

Respectfully forwarded.
This is a report of General Kilpatrick's movements.

A. PLEASONTON,
Major-General.

HEADQUARTERS THIRD CORPS,
Kelly's Ford, Va., November 7, 1863—4.45 p. m.

General Carr, commanding Third Division, will leave one brigade to support the left near Mount Holly Church and mass the others in rear of the pontoon bridge, preparatory to crossing the river.
By command of Major-General Birney:

J. C. BRISCOE,
Captain, and Acting Assistant Adjutant-General.

HDQRS. LEFT COLUMN, ARMY OF THE POTOMAC,
November 7, 1863—5.10 p. m.

Major-General HUMPHREYS,
Chief of Staff:

This is the state of things now: The Third Corps is crossing the bridge and getting in position; the Second is massed near. One bridge is down and another in progress. The enemy occupy a rifle-pit covering the road to Brandy. I hope to have it before dark.

Should Sedgwick have to come this way, there is room for him. Should there be an advance of the whole army here, it must for a while be a bushwhacking affair until we seize the plains beyond. I will force the fighting as early to-morrow as the troops can see. The pickets are ordered to push out to-night.
Respectfully,

WM. H. FRENCH.

HEADQUARTERS THIRD CORPS,
Kelly's Ford, Va., November 7, 1863—5.45 p. m.

Brigadier-General Carr will order the brigade and batteries left at Mount Holly to join his command. He will leave one regiment to support battery of heavy guns.
By command of Major-General Birney:

J. C. BRISCOE,
Captain, and Acting Assistant Adjutant-General.

NOVEMBER 7, 1863—6.30 p. m.

Major-General SEDGWICK,
Commanding Right Column:

The major-general commanding is anxiously-waiting your reply to the note of 4 p. m. In the event of your considering that you cannot cross, he desires to know what force of infantry you would require, supposing you retain your artillery, to prevent the enemy from crossing to this side.

A. A. HUMPHREYS,
Major-General, and Chief of Staff.

HEADQUARTERS THIRD CAVALRY DIVISION,
Grove Church, Va., November 7, 1863—7.15 p. m.

Lieut. Col. C. ROSS SMITH,
Chief of Staff, Cavalry Corps:

COLONEL : My people are at Ellis' Ford and have only seen a small force of cavalry. I have heard from General French. He has a division of infantry across the river, and was, at 5 p. m., laying the pontoons. He reports the enemy in rifle-pits about a mile from Kelly's Ford. The whole country here is full of bushwhackers, and several of my men have been killed or taken prisoners. Any messenger you may send should have a strong escort. I shall be at Ellis' Ford ready to cross at an early hour.

Very respectfully,

J. KILPATRICK,
Brig. Gen. of Vols., Comdg. Third Cavalry Division.

SULPHUR SPRINGS, *November* 7, [1863].

Colonel SMITH :

It will be dark before all of General Gregg's pickets can be relieved. To-morrow morning early I will cross at Sulphur Springs, and try to force a crossing of Hazel Run, after which I will try to join the right of Sedgwick. My headquarters to-night are 1 mile in rear of Sulphur Springs.

Respectfully,

JNO. BUFORD.

NOVEMBER 7, 1863—8 p. m.

Major-General SEDGWICK,
Commanding Rignt Column:

Rodes' division of Ewell's corps is at Kelly's Ford. French's command is now crossing. He had one bridge down at 5 p. m., and another under way. He captured 300 prisoners. Your three dispatches are received, that announcing the capture of the redoubts since I began this dispatch. The major-general commanding desires to know whether the enemy's bridge is still down, and whether you can throw a bridge across at once at Norman's Ford.

A. A. HUMPHREYS,
Major-General, and Chief of Staff.

HEADQUARTERS ARMY OF THE POTOMAC,
November 7, 1863—8.30 p. m.

Major-General FRENCH,
Commanding Left Column:

I am instructed to inform you that General Sedgwick took the rifle-pits on this side the river this afternoon and carried the two redoubts on this side the river by assault about dusk, capturing 4 pieces of artillery and a number of prisoners. A second dispatch from him says he has captured 4 colonels, 3 lieutenant-colonels among other officers, and more than 800 men; also, 4 battle-flags.

General Kilpatrick is ordered to cross at Kelly's Ford at daylight and report to you. He will cover your left flank and look out for the enemy toward Mountain Run and Stevensburg.

A. A. HUMPHREYS,
Major-General, and Chief of Staff.

NOVEMBER 7, 1863—9.30 p. m.

Major-General SEDGWICK, *Commanding Right Column:*

The major-general commanding is anxiously waiting your reply to the dispatch sent at 8.30 p. m., inquiring whether you can throw a bridge across at once at Norman's Ford. Do the enemy occupy the heights overlooking the point where Newton had his lower bridge? Please answer at once, as time is of the utmost importance.

A. A. HUMPHREYS,
Major-General, and Chief of Staff.

NOVEMBER 7, 1863—10 p. m.

Major-General SEDGWICK, *Commanding Right Column:*

Your dispatch respecting the number and rank of prisoners you have captured is received. The major-general commanding is highly gratified at the brilliant manner in which your operations have been commenced.

A. A. HUMPHREYS,
Major-General, and Chief of Staff.

HEADQUARTERS ARMY OF THE POTOMAC,
November 7, 1863—10.15 p. m.

Major-General FRENCH, *Commanding Left Column:*

The major-general commanding desires to know where General Newton's command is, and at what hour he will probably be over the river. If he is not ordered down to Kelly's Ford, he should be ordered to be down at early daylight. What indication have you of the force and position of the enemy in your front, and how far out on the roads have your reconnaissances or scouts been?

I sent you a dispatch by your orderly, telling you Sedgwick had carried the rifle-pits and redoubts this side the river. Captured 1,000 prisoners, 4 colonels, 3 lieutenant-colonels, 4 guns, 4 battle-flags. Kilpatrick will cross at Kelly's Ford at daylight and cover your left, and look out for the enemy toward Mountain Run and Stevensburg.

Very respectfully, &c.,

A. A. HUMPHREYS,
Major-General, and Chief of Staff.

11.45 p. m.

P. S.—Kilpatrick will cross at Ellis' Ford or Kemper's, instead of Kelly's.

HEADQUARTERS THIRD CORPS,
Kellysville, November 7, 1863—10.30 p. m.

Lieut. Col. O. H. HART,
Assistant Adjutant-General:

COLONEL: It is reported that a column of the enemy's infantry has been seen, passing a fire for half an hour in front of General Prince's line. The fire bears west by south from this [Kelly's] house, and the column passed to the left. The fire has just now burned so low as not to show the figures passing. The negro who lives there says the enemy have large camps to our left front in the woo s.

Very respectfully,

D. B. BIRNEY,
Major-General, Commanding.

NOVEMBER 7, 1863—11.30 p. m.

Major-General SEDGWICK,
Commanding Right Column:

The major-general commanding directs that the Fifth Corps, General Sykes, move at 4 o'clock to-morrow morning to Kelly's Ford, by the road running past Payne's house and the toll-gate, and be held ready to cross the river. You will also direct two brigades of your corps (Sixth) to follow Sykes to Kelly's Ford and protect the bridges and fords there. A brigade will probably be found sufficient to guard Norman's Ford. You will open upon the enemy's works at daylight, and make every demonstration as if you intended to cross in force, and, if you should find it practicable, you will effect a lodgment on the opposite bank. The force that crosses at Kelly's Ford will move in such a manner that a portion of it will be directed against the enemy near Providence Church, in order to open communication with you and allow you to cross. Keep the commanding general constantly advised of the force and position of the enemy as ascertained by you and of his movements.

A. A. HUMPHREYS,
Major-General, and Chief of Staff.

WAR DEPARTMENT,
Washington, November 7 1863—3.45 p. m.

General KELLEY, *Clarksburg, W. Va.*, and
General SULLIVAN, *Harper's Ferry, W. Va.:*

More troops will be sent west by the Baltimore and Ohio Railroad early next week. See that the road is well guarded, and telegraph if you think that there is any serious danger.

H. W. HALLECK,
General-in-Chief.

HARPER'S FERRY, W. VA., *November 7, 1863—5.30 p. m.*
(Received 6.30 p. m.)

Maj. Gen. H. W. HALLECK,
General-in-Chief:

I believe that all bands of guerrillas are below Strasburg. I have a cavalry force up the valley that will go through Front Royal to-night, and, by way of Luray, to Edenburg. I have 300 cavalry at Strasburg, with orders to watch all movements up that way. I will increase infantry guards on all bridges immediately. I do not think there is need to fear any interruption.

JER. C. SULLIVAN,
Brigadier-General.

HARPER'S FERRY, *November* 7, 1863.

General KELLEY :

Major Rust, of General Rodes' staff, Ewell's corps, is here, my prisoner. He says that General Lee has but two corps; that they are being filled up with conscripts, but do not expect a fight this fall or winter, and that they will make a raid through the valley to collect supplies. The two corps with General Lee are Hill's and Ewell's. My scouts are out.

JER. C. SULLIVAN,
Brigadier-General, Commanding.

NEAR RAPPAHANNOCK STATION, VA.,
November 8, 1863—8 p. m.   (Received 10.20 p. m.)

Maj. Gen. H. W. HALLECK,
General-in-Chief:

This morning, on advancing from Kelly's Ford, it was found the enemy had retired during the night. The morning was so smoky and hazy, it was impossible to ascertain at Rappahannock Station the position of the enemy, and it was not till the arrival of the column from Kelly's Ford it was definitely known the position at Rappahannock Station was evacuated. The army was put in motion, and the pursuit continued by the infantry to Brandy Station and by the cavalry beyond. Major-General Sedgwick reports officially the capture of 4 guns, 8 battle-flags, and over 1,500 prisoners. Major-General French took over 400 prisoners. Sedgwick's loss about 300 killed and wounded; French's, about 70. The conduct of both officers and men in each affair was most admirable.

It will be necessary before I make any farther advance to repair the railroad to the Rappahannock, which the engineers say will take five days.

GEO. G. MEADE,
Major-General.

HEADQUARTERS THIRD CORPS,
November 8, 1863—12.06 a. m.   .

General HUMPHREYS,
Chief of Staff:

General Birney, commanding Third Corps, reports a column of the enemy passing to his left for the last half hour by the light of a fire burning west by south from Kelly's house. The fire is so low now as not to show the figures passing. A negro who lives there says the enemy have large camps on my left front, in the woods. Major-General Newton has not yet reported to me, and I do not know, where the First Corps is.

WM. H. FRENCH,
Major-General, Commanding Third Corps.

Circular.]   HEADQUARTERS THIRD CORPS,
                    Kellysville, Va., November 8, 1863—12.50 a. m.
   Brigadier-General Carr, commanding Third Division, will at daylight carry the hill in his front, which commands this position. He
will be supported by General Prince with his entire command on his
immediate right.   General Ward, with the First Division, will advance so as to keep up the connection with the Second Division.
   The chief of artillery will order a battery to report to each division
commander, and will place the remaining batteries in position to
cover this advance.
   The columns of attack will be formed according to the circular of
the 6th instant from these headquarters.
   By command of Major-General Birney:
                              J. C. BRISCOE,
            Captain, and Acting Assistant Adjutant-General.

                    HEADQUARTERS THIRD CORPS,
                        November 8, 1863—7.15 a. m.
   Brigadier-General Ward, commanding First Division, will flank
the batteries attached to his division with a column of infantry on
both sides wherever practicable.   He will also flank the reserve batteries in his rear in same manner.
   By command of Major-General Birney:
                              J. C. BRISCOE,
            Captain, and Acting Assistant Adjutant-General.

                         NOVEMBER 8, 1863—7.40 a. m.
[General HUMPHREYS:]
   If General Sedgwick has crossed, I would like to send the Second
Corps to Stevensburg.
                         WM. H. FRENCH,
                    Major-General of Volunteers.

                    HEADQUARTERS THIRD CORPS,
                        November 8, 1863.
Major-General HUMPHREYS, *Chief of Staff:*
   GENERAL: Major-General Birney reports that the enemy has left
his front. Johnson went to Brandy Station and across Mountain
Run.
                         WM. H. FRENCH,
                         Major-General.

               HEADQUARTERS ARMY OF THE POTOMAC,
                    November 8, 1863—8.30 a. m.
Commanding Officer Fifth Corps:
   Move forward from Paoli Mills, half way to Stevensburg, where a
road to Brandy Station branches. If you can find a road on north
side of Mountain Run, use it in preference.
      Very respectfully, &c.,
                         A. A. HUMPHREYS,
                    Major-General, and Chief of Staff.

NOVEMBER 8, 1863—8.30 a. m.

Commanding Officer Sixth Corps:

What is the condition of affairs in your front now?

Enemy retiring toward Stevensburg and Brandy Station. Birney with Third Corps moving toward Providence Church, to open communication with you.

A. A. HUMPHREYS,
Major-General, and Chief of Staff.

———

NOVEMBER 8, 1863—9.15 a. m.

Commanding Officer Sixth Corps:

Order up your brigade at Norman's Ford, if you require it.

A. A. HUMPHREYS,
Major-General, and Chief of Staff.

———

NOVEMBER 8, 1863—9.45 a. m.

Commanding Officer Sixth Corps:

Is not the column reported by General Shaler, Birney with Third Corps? Does he know Birney is moving to open communication with you?

A. A. HUMPHREYS,
Major-General, and Chief of Staff.

———

NOVEMBER 8, 1863—11 a. m.

Commanding Officer Sixth Corps:

Move forward to Brandy Station, connecting with the Third Corps on your left. Leave Shaler's brigade to guard trains and bridges.

A. A. HUMPHREYS,
Major-General, and Chief of Staff.

———

KELLY'S, *November 8, 1863—1 p. m.*

Commanding Officer Sixth Corps:

The major-general commanding requests that you will send to the front and ascertain the probable force and position of the enemy near Brandy Station. General Warren, at Thorn's Hill, reports that the enemy are probably concentrating at Brandy Station.

A. A. HUMPHREYS,
Major-General, and Chief of Staff.

———

HEADQUARTERS NEAR BRANDY STATION,
November 8, 1863—1.17 p. m.

Major-General HUMPHREYS, *Chief of Staff:*

The head of my column is occupying Brandy Station. I have ordered up the division of Second Corps and First Corps, and will await orders when they are in position.

Respectfully,

WM. H. FRENCH,
Major-General of Volunteers.

NOVEMBER 8, 1863—12.30 p. m.

Commanding Officer Sixth Corps:

Your dispatch of 12 m. just received.   The Third Corps was ordered to move forward to Brandy Station at 11 a. m.

A. A. HUMPHREYS,
Major-General, and Chief of Staff.

HARPER'S FERRY, W. VA.,
November 8, 1863—7.30 p. m.   (Received 8.05 p. m.)

Major-General HALLECK,
General-in-Chief:

Imboden is certainly on Cedar Creek, near Strasburg, with two regiments of infantry and his cavalry force.   I suppose he means to attack between Martinsburg and Cherry Run.   I have 800 cavalry at Newtown, and will re-enforce Martinsburg with two regiments of infantry to-night, increasing my guards at the bridges along the road.   I have the rebel mail, dated November 4, 1863.

JER. C. SULLIVAN,
Brigadier-General, Commanding.

CLARKSBURG,
November 8, 1863—7 p. m.

Governor BOREMAN,
Wheeling:

General Averell attacked Jackson's forces at Mill Point, in Pocahontas County, on the 5th instant, and drove him from his position with trifling loss.   Jackson fell back to the summit of Droop Mountain, where he was re-enforced by General Echols, with Patton's brigade and one regiment from Jenkins' command.   The position was naturally a very strong one, and was strengthened by breastworks commanding the roads.   General Averell turned the enemy's left with his infantry, and attacked him in front with cavalry, dismounted.

The victory was decisive, and the enemy's retreat became a total rout, his forces throwing away their arms and scattering in every direction.   The cavalry pursued until dark, capturing many prisoners and a large quantity of arms and ammunition, &c.   All the enemy's wounded have fallen into our hands.   Our loss in killed and wounded is about 100.

B. F. KELLEY,
Brigadier-General.

HEADQUARTERS ARMY OF THE POTOMAC,
November 9, 1863—8 p. m.   (Received 10.30 p. m.)

Major-General HALLECK:

Buford's division of cavalry that operated on my right flank, crossed the Hazel River at Rixeyville and pursued the enemy yesterday to the vicinity of Culpeper, which place he occupied this morning.   Kilpatrick's division drove the enemy from Stevensburg toward Raccoon Ford. The enemy, with the exception of a small cavalry force, have all recrossed the Rapidan. From the number of huts, the corduroyed roads, and information derived from citizens, it is evident the enemy contemplated wintering between the Rappahannock and Rapidan; and did not expect a resumption of active operations on my part.

> GEO. G. MEADE,
> *Major-General, Commanding.*

HDQRS. LEFT COLUMN, ARMY OF THE POTOMAC,
Mount Holly Church, November 9, 1863—1.15 a. m.

Major-General HUMPHREYS,
    Chief of Staff, Army of the Potomac:

GENERAL: General Newton has just sent to me a staff officer. He has two divisions massed at Morrisville. I ordered a brigade to report at daylight, but will direct his entire command to move.

The enemy are reported moving to the left of my front, probably on the Stevensburg road. They still hold a rifle-pit at the woods, a mile in front of the ford and covering the Brandy Station road. It would have been attacked last evening, but General Prince reported that he was afraid he would bring on a general engagement (?). It will be attacked at daylight, and I presume it is strongly re-enforced. My skirmishers and pickets are in the woods on the right and nearly enfilading the work.

Very respectfully,

> WM. H. FRENCH,
> *Major-General, Commanding.*

[Indorsement.]

NOVEMBER 9, 1863.

General Prince stated to General Meade that he desired to attack, and asked authority for it, but was refused.

> A. A. HUMPHREYS,
> *Major-General, Chief of Staff.*

HEADQUARTERS CAVALRY CORPS,
November 9, 1863—11.30 a. m.

Major-General HUMPHREYS,
    Chief of Staff:

GENERAL: An officer from General Kilpatrick has just reported, and states he is picketing within 3 miles of Raccoon Ford, up to the enemy's cavalry pickets, which extend to Pony Mountain. The enemy still have a force at Culpeper, but General Kilpatrick thinks that, with infantry to support him, he can take Pony Mountain and see what is going on. Some infantry and cavalry were seen going out the Sperryville road this morning. Shall Kilpatrick make the attempt for Pony Mountain?

> A. PLEASONTON,
> *Major-General.*

BRANDY STATION, VA., NEAR CULPEPER,
November 9, 1863.

Major-General HUMPHREYS,
Chief of Staff, Army of the Potomac:

GENERAL : General Kilpatrick reports that a column of rebel infantry was on yesterday evening marching toward Cedar Mountain
and one of cavalry toward Sperryville. Detachments of infantry
and cavalry (not in force) are seen leaving Culpeper on the Sperryville pike. The rebel pickets are in heavy line between Pony
Mountain across the country to the hills on the south of the railroad and in front of Culpeper.

I am, sir, very respectfully, your obedient servant,
WM. H. FRENCH.

[P. S.]—Kilpatrick could take Pony Mountain if supported by
infantry.

NOVEMBER. 9, 1863—12 m.

Commanding Officer Third Corps :

Your dispatch is received. The major-general commanding directs that you send a support of infantry to General Kilpatrick to
enable him to take Pony Mountain. Your dispatch inquiring as to
the position of the Second and Fifth Corps was received last night.
A. A. HUMPHREYS,
Major-General, and Chief of Staff.

CIRCULAR.]   HEADQUARTERS ARMY OF THE POTOMAC,
November 9, 1863—12 m.

The organization of the army into two columns made for the passage of the Rappahannock is hereby broken up and corps commanders
will, as heretofore, report direct to these headquarters.

By command of Major-General Meade:
S. WILLIAMS,
Assistant Adjutant-General.

CIRCULAR.]   HEADQUARTERS ARMY OF THE POTOMAC,
November 9, 1863—12 m.

The following movements of troops are ordered and will take place
at once:

1. The Fifth Corps, Major-General Sykes, will take position on
north side of Mountain Run, at Paoli Mills, sending a division to
Kelly's Ford to guard the bridges. This division will post a brigade midway between Bealeton and Morrisville, at the point where
the road to Kelly's Ford running to Carter's house leaves the Morrisville road. The division will picket so as to cover the supply
trains moving by that route and the working party on the railroad.

2. The Second Corps, Major-General Warren, will take post between Paoli Mills and Brandy Station in such manner as to have
good communication with the corps at those two points.

3. The Third Corps, Major-General French, will remain at Brandy Station.

4. The Sixth Corps, Major-General Sedgwick, will move to Welford's Ford, on Hazel River. The division of this corps at Kelly's Ford and Rappahannock Station will rejoin the corps upon being relieved.

5. The First Corps, Major-General Newton, will be placed as follows: One division at Rappahannock Station, with a brigade at Beverly Ford; the three brigades of another division will be, one at Bealeton, one at Liberty, and one near the railroad at crossing of Licking Run. These two divisions will picket so as to cover the supply trains passing along the route of the railroad and the working parties on the road.

The division of the First Corps now guarding the railroad from Manassas to Warrenton Junction will remain as now posted. The protection of the railroad is assigned to Major-General Newton.

6. The Artillery Reserve will be in the vicinity of Rappahannock Station.

7. One brigade of Gregg's division of cavalry will take post at Morrisville, and will picket toward Hartwood Church and the crossings of the Lower Rappahannock. The other brigade will take post at Fayetteville, and picket toward Waterloo and beyond Warrenton.

Kilpatrick's division of cavalry will take post at Stevensburg and picket toward the crossings of the Rapidan below the railroad crossing.

Buford's division of cavalry will be posted at Culpeper Court-House, and will picket toward the crossings of Robertson's River and toward the right.

8. Headquarters will be in the vicinity of Brandy Station.

By command of Major-General Meade:

S. WILLIAMS,
Assistant Adjutant-General.

HDQRS. THIRD DIVISION, CAVALRY CORPS,
November 9, 1863.

Brigadier-General DAVIES,
Commanding First Brigade:

GENERAL: You will move your command to-morrow morning to Deep Run, between Hartwood and Grove Church, on the Morrisville road.

You will take on your horses 14 pounds of grain and three days' rations. You will see to this personally, on an inspection which you will make of your command, that each man has three days' rations and 14 pounds of grain before you march. You will place every man capable of doing duty, now on special duty (provided he can be spared from that duty), in the ranks, that your command may be as strong and efficient as possible.

All dismounted men and men having unserviceable horses will report at daylight to the division quartermaster.

By command of Brigadier-General Kilpatrick:

L. G. ESTES,
Assistant Adjutant-General.

HEADQUARTERS THIRD ARMY CORPS,
November 9, 1863—2 p. m.

Major-General HUMPHREYS:

I have ordered a division to support Kilpatrick. General Buford has since reported here through Culpeper. The movement may require the advance of the corps, for which I have prepared.

WM. H. FRENCH,
Major-General, Commanding.

GENERAL: The major-general commanding, G. G. Meade, has passed Rappahannock River on his way here, where his headquarters will be to-night. Cannot reach him with this dispatch.

Very respectfully,

W. C. HALL,
Operator.

HEADQUARTERS ARMY OF THE POTOMAC,
November 9, 1863—6.15 p. m.

Commanding Officer Cavalry Corps:

The major-general commanding has directed General French to give General Kilpatrick sufficient infantry support to enable him to secure Pony Mountain. Direct General Kilpatrick to secure it.

Very respectfully, &c.,

A. A. HUMPHREYS,
Major-General, and Chief of Staff.

HEADQUARTERS THIRD ARMY CORPS,
Brandy Station, Va., November 9, 1863—7.20 p. m.

Major-General HUMPHREYS,
Chief of Staff, Hdqrs. Army of the Potomac:

I have communicated with General Kilpatrick. He has possession of Pony Mountain.

I have withdrawn my supporting force and placed them in line at this place.

Respectfully, &c.,

WM. H. FRENCH,
Major-General of Volunteers.

NOVEMBER 9, 1863—7.30 p. m.

Commanding Officer Third Corps:

The major-general commanding directs me to inform you that General Kilpatrick has possession of Pony Mountain, and that it will not be necessary to send forward the division which you were ordered to have sent to support him.

A. A. HUMPHREYS,
Major-General, and Chief of Staff.

HARRISBURG, PA., *November 9, 1863—7.30 p. m.*
(Received 8.10 p. m.)

Major-General HALLECK:

There are threatenings and serious disturbances in the coal region. Can I withdraw infantry from Maryland?

D. N. COUCH,
Major-General.

———

WASHINGTON, *November 9, 1863—7.30 p. m.*

Major-General MEADE:

I have seen your dispatches about operations on the Rappahannock on Saturday, and I wish to say, "Well done." Do the 1,500 prisoners reported by General Sedgwick include the 400 taken by General French, or do the whole amount to 1,900?

A. LINCOLN.

———

WAR DEPARTMENT,
Washington, November 9, 1863—9.50 p. m.

Maj. Gen. D. N. COUCH, *Harrisburg, Pa.:*

Authority to withdraw your infantry from Maryland has already been given through the Adjutant-General of the Army.

H. W. HALLECK,
General-in-Chief.

———

SPECIAL ORDERS, ⎰ WAR DEPT., ADJT. GENERAL'S OFFICE,
No. 497.   ⎱   *Washington, November 9, 1863.*

*   *   *   *   *   *   *

III. A Board of Officers, to consist of Brig. Gen. W. F. Barry, U. S. Volunteers, lieutenant-colonel First U. S. Artillery; Brig. Gen. J. G. Barnard, U. S. Volunteers, lieutenant-colonel U. S. Engineers; Brig. Gen. G. W. Cullum, U. S. Volunteers, lieutenant-colonel U. S. Engineers; Brig. Gen. G. A. De Russy, U. S. Volunteers, captain Fourth U. S. Artillery; and Lieut. Col. B. S. Alexander, additional aide-de-camp, major U. S. Engineers, will meet in this city on the 10th day of November, 1863, or as soon thereafter as practicable, to examine and report upon the armaments of the works constituting the defenses of Washington.

The Board will report upon the points to be presented to them in a letter of instructions, and will make any other recommendations which in their judgment may seem proper.

The Chiefs of Engineers and of Artillery will furnish all information required by the Board, and the report of the Board will be submitted to them for comment or approval.

The junior member will record the proceedings.

*   *   *   *   *   *   *

XIII. Brig. Gen. E. R. S. Canby, U. S. Volunteers, is hereby relieved from command in the city of New York, and will report for duty in the War Department.

*   *   *   *

By order of the Secretary of War:

E. D. TOWNSEND,
Assistant Adjutant-General.

GENERAL ORDERS, } HDQRS. DEPT. OF VA. AND N. C.,
  No. —. }   *Fort Monroe, Va., November 9, 1863.*

In honor of the gallant dead, who fell while serving their country in its hour of peril—who, to save their country's honor, laid down their young lives on its altar, and whose memories should be preserved by us and coming generations as models of fidelity and truth—the several redoubts constructed and now constructing for the defense of Norfolk and Portsmouth are named as follows:

The redoubt on right of line in rear of Portsmouth, Fort Woodruff, in honor of Lieutenant Woodruff, First U. S. Artillery, who fell while in command of his battery at the battle of Gettysburg.

Center redoubt, same line, Fort Hazlett, in honor of Lieutenant Hazlett, Fifth U. S. Artillery, who fell while commanding his battery at Gettysburg.

Left redoubt, same line, Fort Cushing, in honor of Lieutenant Cushing, Fourth U. S. Artillery, who, although twice severely wounded, still retained command of his pieces until he received his death wound.

Redoubt on Ferry Point, Fort O'Rorke, in honor of Lieutenant O'Rorke, U. S. Engineers, colonel commanding One hundred and fortieth New York Volunteers, who fell while gallantly repulsing the enemy at Gettysburg.

By order of Major-General Foster:

SOUTHARD HOFFMAN,
Assistant Adjutant-General.

HEADQUARTERS SIXTH CORPS,
November 10, 1863.

Major-General HUMPHREYS,
 Chief of Staff:

GENERAL: I have the honor to report that the two divisions of this corps took position last night at the point indicated in your circular of yesterday. When the Third Division joins it will be posted on the left, and I think must extend to near General French's right. It was too dark last night to make the connection of pickets, but it will be made this morning. My headquarters are at the Welford house, nearly opposite the ford.

 Very respectfully,

JOHN SEDGWICK,
Major-General.

CIRCULAR.] HEADQUARTERS ARMY OF THE POTOMAC,
         November 10, 1863.

The following telegram is furnished for the information of corps commanders:

• WASHINGTON, *November 9, 1863.*

Major-General MEADE:

I have seen your dispatches about operations of the Rappahannock on Saturday, and I wish to say, "Well done."

A. LINCOLN.

By command of Major-General Meade:

S. WILLIAMS,
Assistant Adjutant-General.

SPÉCIAL ORDERS, }　　HDQRS. DEPT. OF VA. AND N. C.,
　No. 113.　　　{　　　Fort Monroe, Va., November 10, 1863.

*　　　*　　　*　　　*　　　*　　　*　　　*

VII. Col. S. P. Spear, Eleventh Regiment Pennsylvania Cavalry, is hereby placed in command of the cavalry forces at Portsmouth, consisting of the following regiments: Eleventh Regiment Pennsylvania Cavalry, Fifth Regiment Pennsylvania Cavalry, and Twentieth Regiment New York Cavalry.

*　　　*　　　*　　　*　　　*

By command of Major-General Foster:

SOUTHARD HOFFMAN,
Assistant Adjutant-General.

CLARKSBURG, W. VA., *November* 10, 1863.
(Received 4.15 p. m.)

Brig. Gen. G. W. CULLUM,
　　Chief of Staff:

The following telegram just received from General Sullivan:

HARPER'S FERRY, W. VA.,
November 10, 1863—7.30 a. m.

Brig. Gen. B. F. KELLEY:

Colonel Boyd has returned, having gone to Woodstock. He brings in 21 prisoners. White and Gilmor are reported at Edenburg. Imboden has gone farther down the valley. He is afraid to meet my cavalry. It is reported a regiment of infantry is encamped in Little Fort Valley. The cavalry of this division is becoming very effective and strong enough to keep the railroad secure.

JER. C. SULLIVAN,
Brigadier-General.

B. F. KELLEY,
Brigadier-General.

HEADQUARTERS FIRST CAVALRY DIVISION,
November 11, 1863.

Lieut. Col. C. ROSS SMITH:

I sent in a dispatch last night by Lieutenant Mackenzie. He lost it. It contained no information of the enemy. I inclose * Devin's report.

Merritt sent to within half a mile of Slaughter's Mountain and returned last night, leaving pickets as far as he had advanced—the First Brigade pickets toward Rapidan Station. Nothing has been seen of the enemy save a few scouts. Long line of camp smokes are visible on the other side of Rapidan. I am just starting reconnaissances out to find the enemy. A telegraph operator might save horse-flesh. The line seems to be unharmed.

I am, very respectfully, your obedient servant,

JNO. BUFORD,
Brigadier-General of Volunteers, Commanding.

---

* Not found.

[Indorsement.]

HEADQUARTERS CAVALRY CORPS,
November 11, [1863]—11.30 a. m.
Respectfully forwarded.
It is recommended that a telegraph operator be sent to General Buford.

A. PLEASONTON,
Major-General, Commanding.

———

CULPEPER,
November 11, 1863—7 p. m.
Col. C. ROSS SMITH:

The reconnaissance sent out by Devin has just returned. It proceeded through James City to Robertson's River; saw nothing on this side of the river. The Fourth Virginia Cavalry pickets the south side. Two citizens of Loudoun County were arrested *en route* from Richmond, with some letters. I will send them up in the morning.
Respectfully,

JNO. BUFORD.

———

CLARKSBURG, W. VA., *November* 11, 1863—8 p. m.
(Received 12.15 a. m, 12.)
Brigadier-General CULLUM,
Chief of Staff:

My information from Lewisburg is that General Averell's victory was most decisive at Droop Mountain. The enemy's force engaged was over 4,000. They acknowledged a loss of 300 killed and wounded. General Averell took over 100 prisoners, including field officers, 1 stand of colors, 3 pieces of artillery, large number of small-arms, camp equipage, and wagons. A violent snow-storm prevailed at Lewisburg on the 8th. General Duffié's command had returned to Gauley, and Colonel Moor, with General Averell's infantry, is returning to Beverly.

B. F. KELLEY,
Brigadier-General.

———

GENERAL ORDERS, }   HDQRS. DEPT. OF VA. AND N. C.,
No. 28.   }   *Fort Monroe, Va., November* 11, 1863.

Having been relieved from the command of the Department of Virginia and North Carolina by Maj. Gen. B. F. Butler, in obedience to General Orders, No. 350, from the War Department, the undersigned bids farewell to the officers and men serving in this department.
The conduct of all has been such as to merit his warmest commendation, and he will always remember with pleasure the intercourse,

both official and personal, between himself and those serving under his command.

To the troops which formed a part of his old command in North Carolina, the commanding general bids an affectionate farewell.

From his first association with them at Annapolis, through the perils and trying days at Hatteras, up to the present time, his feeling toward them has been one of unalloyed satisfaction and pride.

Called to another field of duty,* he will continue to watch them with unabated interest, feeling confident that in the future they will exhibit the same qualities of zeal, courage, and devotion to duty which have distinguished their past career.

J. G. FOSTER,
Major-General of Volunteers.

———

GENERAL ORDERS, }   HDQRS. DEPT. OF VA. AND N. C.,
   No. 29.   }   *Fort Monroe, Va., November 11, 1863.*

I. By direction of the President, Maj. Gen. Benjamin F. Butler, U. S. Volunteers, hereby assumes command of the Eighteenth Army Corps and Department of Eastern Virginia and North Carolina.

II. Each commander of division, separate brigade, post, district, or detached command, and each chief of a staff department, will forthwith report to these headquarters the exact condition of his command and the supplies of his department, respectively, accompanied with such remarks in relation thereto as he shall see fit.

Each report shall have minuted thereon the date of the reception of this order, and the date of the transmission of such report.

The utmost dispatch, minuteness, and particularity are required in these reports.

III. The following-named officers are announced as upon the staff of the commanding general:

Col. J. Wilson Shaffer, aide-de-camp, chief of staff.
Lieut. Col. J. McLean Taylor, chief commissary.
Lieut. Col. George A. Kensel, inspector-general.
Maj. Robert S. Davis, assistant adjutant-general.
Lieut. Col. J. Burnham Kinsman, aide-de-camp.
Maj. Joseph M. Bell, aide-de-camp.
Maj. Peter Haggerty, aide-de-camp.
Capt. Alfred F. Puffer, aide-de-camp.
Capt. Haswell C. Clarke, aide-de-camp.
First Lieut. Frederick Martin, volunteer aide-de-camp.

IV. All orders heretofore issued in this department will remain in force until otherwise ordered.

By command of Major-General Butler:

R. S. DAVIS,
Major, and Assistant Adjutant-General.

———

[NOVEMBER 11–DECEMBER 4, 1863.—For correspondence and orders relating to reported organization in Canada of a raid into the United States, see Series III.]

---

*The Department of the Ohio.

HDQRS. 2D BRIG., 3D DIV., CAV. CORPS, A. P.,
November 12, 1863.

Captain SUYDAM,
    Assistant Adjutant-General, Cavalry Corps:

I respectfully submit the following statement, hoping the attention of the proper authorities will be called to it:

Yesterday a detachment of men joined my brigade from Dismounted Camp. The detachment numbers about 80 men. The majority of the horses upon which the men were mounted are unserviceable, and are really a more indifferent lot than those sent to Washington as unserviceable. In the detachment that reported to me yesterday there were 23 men belonging to the Seventh Michigan Cavalry. There were 40 men belonging to this regiment in the detachment when it left the Dismounted Camp, but 17 of that number had to return on account of the horses upon which they were mounted being unable to reach the army.

. Numerous complaints reach me from regimental commanders against the inferior quality of horses sent to them with the men from the Dismounted Camp. So far as my experience and observation extend, my command suffers about as much from the influences and effect of the Dismounted Camp as it does from the weapons of the enemy.

It is an actual fact that there are men in my command who have been captured by the enemy, carried to Richmond, and rejoined my command in less time than it frequently requires for men to proceed to the Dismounted Camp and return mounted.

Very respectfully, &c.,
                        G. A. CUSTER,
        Brig. Gen., Comdg. 2d Brig., 3d Div., Cav. Corps.

[Indorsements.]

HEADQUARTERS CAVALRY CORPS,
November 14, 1863.

Respectfully forwarded.

The attention of the major-general commanding this army is respectfully called to the within report, which is one of many received constantly of a similar nature. The facts therein shown are conclusive, in my mind, in proving that there is in the present system of supplying the cavalry of this army with horses and equipments something so radically wrong that the interests of the service imperatively demand an immediate and entire change and the application of some very stringent remedy.

                        A. PLEASONTON, .
                            Major-General.

OFFICE OF CAVALRY BUREAU,
November 23, 1863.

Respectfully returned.

There are very few if any men belonging to General Custer's brigade in the Dismounted Camp. General Kilpatrick assured me the other day that his division, to which Custer's brigade belongs, was completely mounted; if it is not, horses are on hand to mount it.

All requisitions from the Army of the Potomac up to date have been filled with the best the Government has on hand. I have understood that Custer's brigade are great horse-killers, and it is very likely that the 17 horses were used up as stated, though they were considered serviceable when they left the depot. Inclosed please find copy of indorsement upon a previous communication which was referred to this bureau for a report.*

GEORGE STONEMAN,
Major-General, Chief of Cavalry.

GENERAL ORDERS, } HDQRS. DEPT. OF VA. AND N. C.,
No. 31. } *Fort Monroe, Va., November 12, 1863.*

Representations having been made to the commanding general that certain disloyally disposed persons within this department do occasionally by force interfere with, and by opprobrious and threatening language insult and annoy, loyal persons employed in the quiet discharge of their lawful occupations, it is hereby announced that all such conduct and language is hereafter strictly forbidden, and will be punished with military severity.

All officers in this department are directed to order the arrest of, and to bring such persons as are found offending against this order, before the tribunal established for the purpose of punishing offenses within this department.

By command of Major-General Butler:

R. S. DAVIS,
Major, and Assistant Adjutant-General.

NOVEMBER 13, 1863—11 a. m.
(Received 11.45 a. m.)

Major-General HALLECK:

The enemy occupy in force the line of the Rapidan. My cavalry picket to the river in front. The army is in position from Welford's Ford, on the Hazel River; to Stevensburg, The enemy occasionally fire from their batteries on the Rapidan at the cavalry pickets. If you have no objection, I should like to visit Washington to-morrow to confer with yourself and the Secretary of War. The work on the railroad is progressing; it was to be finished to Bealeton yesterday, and work has been commenced on the Rappahannock Bridge.

GEO. G. MEADE,
Major-General, Commanding.

WASHINGTON, D. C.,
November 13, 1863—1.20 p. m.

Major-General MEADE,
Army of the Potomac:

There is no objection to the proposed visit, and the consultation is desirable.

H. W. HALLECK,
General-in-Chief.

GENERAL ORDERS, } HDQRS. MID. DEPT., 8TH ARMY CORPS,
No. 59. } *Baltimore, Md., November 13, 1863.*

It is known that there are many evil-disposed persons now at large in the State of Delaware who have been engaged in rebellion against

---

*See p. 419.

the lawful Government, or who have given aid or comfort or encouragement to others so engaged, or who do not recognize their allegiance to the United States, and who may avail themselves of the indulgence of the authority which tolerates their presence to attempt to take part in or embarrass the approaching special election in that State. It is therefore ordered:

1. That all provost-marshals and other military officers do prevent all disturbance and violence at or about the polls, whether offered by such persons as above described, or by any person or persons whomsoever.

2. That all provost-marshals and other military officers commanding in Delaware shall support the judges of election on the 19th of November, 1863, in requiring an oath of allegiance to the United States as the test of citizenship, of any one whose vote may be challenged on the ground that he is not loyal or does not admit his allegiance to the United States, which oath shall be in the following form and terms:

I do solemnly swear that I will support, protect, and defend the Constitution and Government of the United States against all enemies, whether domestic or foreign; that I hereby pledge my allegiance, faith, and loyalty to the same, any ordinance, resolution, or law of any State Convention or State Legislature to the contrary notwithstanding; that I will at all times yield a hearty and willing obedience to the said Constitution and Government, and will not, directly or indirectly, do any act in hostility to the same, either by taking up arms against them, or aiding, abetting, or countenancing those in arms against them; that without permission from the lawful authority, I will have no communication, direct or indirect, with the States in insurrection against the United States, or either of them, or with any person or persons within said insurrectionary States, and that I will in all things deport myself as a good and loyal citizen of the United States. This I do in good faith, with full determination, pledge, and purpose to keep this my sworn obligation, and without any mental reservation or evasion whatsoever.

3. Provost-marshals and other military officers are directed to report to these headquarters any judge of election who shall refuse his aid in carrying out this order, or who, on challenge of a vote being made on the ground of disloyalty or hostility to the Government, shall refuse to require the oath of allegiance from such voter.

By command of Major-General Schenck:

WM. H. CHESEBROUGH,
Lieutenant-Colonel, and Assistant Adjutant-General.

STATE OF DELAWARE, EXECUTIVE DEPARTMENT,
Dover, November 13, 1863.

All civil officers and good citizens of this State are enjoined to obey the above military order, issued by the commanding general of the Middle Department, and to give all needful aid for the enforcement of the same.

WILLIAM CANNON,
Governor of Delaware.

CHAMBERSBURG, PA., *November 13, 1863.*
(Received 8.40 p. m.)

Maj. Gen. H. W. HALLECK, *General-in-Chief:*

From your telegram of the 9th instant, I ordered all of my troops from the mouth of Antietam Creek, the Tenth New Jersey being now in the coal regions.

D. N. COUCH,
Major-General.

HDQRS. DEPARTMENT OF THE SUSQUEHANNA,
Chambersburg, Pa., November 13, 1863.
Col. E. D. TOWNSEND,
Assistant Adjutant-General, Washington, D. C.:

SIR: I have the honor to inform you, for the information of the War Department, that I have just returned from the disaffected mining region of Hazelton and vicinity, having during the visit met and conversed with several of the coal operators and others interested in the affairs of that region.

Some of the collieries were stopped last week for the avowed purpose of compelling the General Government to relieve the mining regions from the operations of the draft. However, the prompt arrival of troops, ordered by Major-General Sigel, restored matters to their previous status. The mines are in operation, but the loyal people there live in a state of terror, several brutal murders having been committed within a few weeks.

The operators whom I saw proposed this, that if they could be assured of the protection of the General Government until the work was accomplished, they would discharge the bad characters and employ new men, having eventually a body of men that could be controlled. It is supposed that it would take three months to carry out these desired reforms. If commenced, the troops must not be withdrawn until the work is thoroughly done, otherwise two-thirds of the anthracite region would stop sending coal to market.

I respectfully urge upon the Department to consider the propositions, and recommend that I be instructed to give the guaranties asked for by the operators and proceed to the work with the troops under my command.

I am, colonel, very respectfully, your obedient servant,

D. N. COUCH,
Major-General.

PICKET RESERVE, SECOND NEW YORK CAVALRY,
November 13, 1863.
Capt. L. SIEBERT,
Asst. Adjt. Gen., 1st Brig., 3d Div., Cav. Corps:

CAPTAIN: In pursuance to orders, I made as much show of the small force under my command as I thought might be safely done. I divided my reserve into two parts and moved with the first up the river to Morton's Ford, where the enemy continues to show himself in pretty strong force. He hardly noticed our arrival, but fired occasionally a few shots. I returned to the camping ground of last night shortly after 3 p. m. It is the opinion of the officers on that post that the enemy's reserves are not as large as they were yesterday, although their pickets are just as strong and as close together.

Captain Downing went to Mitchell's Ford with his command, and from there to Sisson's Ford. The enemy showed his strength here on Captain Downing's demonstration to cross. They had close to the river about one battalion of cavalry.

Toward night there has been pretty lively firing, but it has almost ceased at this time.

Your order for a field report could not be obeyed, as we had to send to the various posts, the farthest one of which is between 5 and 6 miles distant. We shall get our reports in to-night, and will send one early to-morrow morning.

Very respectfully, yours,

OTTO HARHAUS,
Lieut. Col., Comdg. Second New York Vol. Cav.

[P. S.]—The duty on our men is very hard, as I have not force sufficient to relieve those who went on yesterday.

HDQRS. ARMY AND DISTRICT OF NORTH CAROLINA,
New Berne, N. C., November 13, 1863.

Acting Rear-Admiral S. P. LEE,
Comdg. N. A. Bkdg. Squadron, Newport News:

SIR: I recently visited Plymouth, &c., and found Captain Flusser somewhat disturbed by a report which had reached General Wessells, to the effect that Mr. Lynch had been examining the channel of the Roanoke, with a view of bringing down the ram. At frequent intervals since I assumed command in North Carolina, I have posted Major-General Foster in relation to the boat at Edwards Ferry, and proposed expeditions for the burning of the same, but he never attached great importance to it, and supposed that it was intended only as a defensive agent. He replied that the troops in the department would not warrant the undertaking.

The works at Plymouth have been pushed with all dispatch possible, and I have added materially to the armament. A work is in progress for a 200-pounder Parrott with a center pintle,' which will make everything very secure there. While waiting for the 200-pounder, I have ordered up a 100-pounder Parrott from Hatteras, which is the only available gun of the kind in North Carolina.

In regard to the report of an examination of the channel, I think it is accounted for by a number of deserters from Fort Branch at Rainbow, who state that week before last it was examined, and torpedoes placed at various points below Rainbow Bluff.

The difficulties of getting at the boat are greatly increased by the fact that an earthen battery for four guns has been constructed at Edwards Ferry, and is garrisoned by from 200 to 500 infantry. The Twenty-fourth North Carolina and one six-gun battery are at Hamilton. Fort Branch is an inclosed work of twelve rifled guns, including one 64-pounder and three 24-pounders.

I am, very respectfully, your obedient servant,

JOHN J. PECK,
Major-General.

HDQRS. ARMY AND DISTRICT OF NORTH CAROLINA,
New Berne, N. C., November 13, 1863.

Mr. DIBBLE,
Merchant:

SIR: A schooner, believed to be the Alice Webb, with a miscellaneous cargo, was beached on the 4th instant, at a point inside of Bogue Inlet, and her cargo taken charge of by the Confederate military authorities. Circumstances seem to indicate that she was run ashore intentionally, with the design of evading the blockade, and the Messrs. Bell, of Newport, and yourself are said to be the parties who freighted and cleared her. The matter is now undergoing investigation, and I am directed by the commanding general to call upon you for a statement of the most explicit character of all your interest in, and connection with, the venture.

I am, sir, very respectfully, your obedient servant,

BENJ. B. FOSTER,
Assistant Adjutant-General.

GETTY'S HEADQUARTERS,
November 13, 1863.

Colonel HOFFMAN,
Assistant Adjutant-General:

The following dispatch just received from Major Cornog, commanding outpost at Suffolk. Be pleased to send one or two gunboats up the Nansemond.

GEO. W. GETTY,
Brigadier-General, Commanding.

[Inclosure.]

SUFFOLK,
November 13, 1863.

General GETTY:

There are now in Suffolk from 30 to 50 infantry, and a much larger force on the South Quay road just below town, removing the obstructions placed there by Major Wetherill. I anticipate an attack here to-night. Is there a gunboat on the river ?

GEORGE T. CORNOG,
Commanding Outpost.

HDQRS. FIRST BRIG., THIRD DIV., CAV. CORPS,
November 14, 1863.

Capt. L. G. ESTES,
Assistant Adjutant-General:

CAPTAIN: I have the honor to inform you that I have been inspecting my picket line on the river this morning, and have observed that the enemy's pickets are not as numerous as they were yesterday, and their infantry posts have been relieved by cavalrymen; that they show less animosity at the presence of our pickets, and I am inclined to believe that they have withdrawn their main force from the river. A sergeant of one of the patrols reports that considerable noise was heard on the other side of the river at about 11 o'clock last night, and near Morton's Ford the officer commanding the pickets heard the beating of drums and the sound of the bugles at 3 oclock this morning also the noise of wheels and shouting of men, as on a march.

I remain, captain, very respectfully,

H. E. DAVIES, JR.,
Brigadier-General, Commanding.

[Indorsement.]

HEADQUARTERS CAVALRY CORPS,
November 14, 1863.

Respectfully forwarded.
The reconnaissances have been ordered.

A. PLEASONTON,
Major-General, Commanding Cavalry Corps.

HEADQUARTERS ARMY OF THE POTOMAC,
November 14, 1863—11 p. m.   (Received 1 a. m., 15th.)

Major-General MEADE, *Washington:*

Information received this evening shows that some movement of
the enemy is on foot. Three contrabands reached headquarters this
afternoon who had crossed the Rapidan 2 miles above Germanna Ford
(at Mitchell's Ford). They state that they heard their master say yesterday afternoon that he had been to Mitchell's or Morton's Ford, and
had found no troops there, and that the army was falling back; that
Rodes' division fell back last night, moving toward Orange Court-
House; that they overheard an officer say to their master that if he
wanted to keep his negroes, he had better carry them off at once, as
the army was falling back.

A deserter from the Fifteenth North Carolina, Rodes' division, was
brought to headquarters this evening. He states that he deserted
early last night. His regiment was on picket at Raccoon Ford yesterday, and at night moved off without being relieved. That the
orderly that brought the order to move said that cavalry pickets
would take their place. That the brigade had already marched, and
that the whole division was in motion. He says they moved toward
some court-house, but does not know whether it was Spotsylvania
Court-House or Orange Court-House. Believes the whole army has
fallen back. This deserter came into Kilpatrick's pickets. General
Davies' report, just received, corroborates these statements. He states
the enemy's pickets are not so numerous as they were yesterday, and
their infantry posts have been relieved by cavalry, and he believes
that their main force has been withdrawn from the river.

There was a good deal of noise about midnight on the other side
of the river and at Morton's Ford; reveille was at 3 o'clock this
morning, and the noise of wheels and the shouting of men was
heard. The cavalry on our front is ordered to push reconnaissances
close in on the enemy not later than daylight to-morrow morning.

Gregg is ordered to send a strong scouting party toward Hartwood
Church and United States Ford. The corps are ordered to hold
themselves in readiness to move at very short notice. They have
four days' forage and about twelve days' rations on hand. Of these
rations, from three to four days' are of salt meat.

The atmosphere has been so hazy all day that the signal officer on
Pony Mountain has not been able to see anything. No scouts have
returned; other scouts have been ordered out on both flanks.

If the enemy is falling back, it is not from any military necessity,
but in consequence of a policy adopted at Richmond. If he is making a flank movement, our left as well as our right has been looked
after. Our left offers some inducements to a concealed movement.

A. A. HUMPHREYS,
Major-General, and Chief of Staff.

HDQRS. DEPARTMENT OF THE SUSQUEHANNA,
Chambersburg, Pa., November 14, 1863.

Major-General FRANZ SIGEL,
Commanding Lehigh District:

GENERAL: I telegraphed you this morning that Captain Roach, deputy provost-marshal, should furnish the charges against those men arrested in Hazelton region. I so told him the morning of the day we met at Reading.

He was informed that the United States could not try men for offenses that were exclusively State ones. But if any of the party, or all, had conspired to resist the draft, or harbored deserters, or resisted the military forces in the execution of their lawful duty regarding the draft, undoubtedly they could be tried by military courts.

The subject is one of exceeding delicacy. The State is utterly powerless in the execution of her laws in the mining region, and we must be very cautious about substituting military law for civil. However, the loyal, good people in that region are desirous of having martial law declared, and would bless you if you would hang 100 men a day for a week. One thing is clear, that these men who have been arrested against whom no charges can be preferred, should not at present be set at liberty.

Have you examined the acts of Congress, Articles of War, &c., in reference to your powers as to appointing a military commission? I confess to you that I am not able to decide, nor have been able to get an opinion on the subject. General Cadwalader some time since ordered a general court-martial, but his authority came directly from the War Department. If we meet at Gettysburg. as I think we shall, perhaps more light can be gathered on the subject.

I am, general, very respectfully, your obedient servant,

[D. N. COUCH,]
Major-General.

HDQRS. ARMY AND DISTRICT OF NORTH CAROLINA,
New Berne, N. C., November 14, 1863.

Maj. Gen. BENJAMIN F. BUTLER,
Comdg. Dept. of Virginia and North Carolina:

GENERAL: During a recent visit at Plymouth, I found the senior naval officer somewhat nervous, in consequence of a report having reached General Wessells of an examination of the Roanoke, with a view to bringing down a ram at Edwards Ferry, some 12 or 15 miles below Halifax. All sorts of reports are put afloat, for the purpose of influencing our operations. My latest advices are that she is not yet complete. Since assuming the command in North Carolina, I have kept strict watch over this matter, and frequently advised General Foster respecting the progress of the work on the iron-clad. I suggested the propriety of burning it in August, but the general did not feel very apprehensive, and replied that the troops at our command would not warrant the enterprise.

The fortifications at Plymouth have been pushed with great vigor, and I have added materially to the armaments. A water battery is in progress for a 200-pounder rifle with a center pintle carriage, which will complete the river works. While waiting for the 200-

pounder, I have moved a 100-pounder from Hatteras, which is the only available gun of the kind in North Carolina. I do not feel very apprehensive, unless the ram moves in conjunction with a land force. The reported examination of the channel is explained by deserters from Fort Branch, at Rainbow Bluff, who state that week before last torpedoes were placed in position in the river below. The destruction of the ram now will be attended with great difficulty, as an earthen battery for four guns has been constructed, and a guard of from 200 to 500 infantry is maintained there. The Twenty-fourth North Carolina and a six-gun battery are at Hamilton, while detach-ments are usually on all the approaches. Its proximity to Weldon renders any raid very uncertain, in consequence of the activity of the rebels.

Fort Branch is at Rainbow Bluff, and is an inclosed work of much strength. At present it is armed with twelve rifles, including one 64-pounder and three 24-pounders.

Doubtless General Foster advised you that he had withdrawn all the best and available troops from North Carolina. There is no reserve force here or in any of the sub-districts. In case of an advance upon the lines, the force would be quite too small for a proper defense.

I am, very respectfully, your obedient servant,

JOHN J. PECK,
Major-General.

HDQRS. ARMY AND DISTRICT OF NORTH CAROLINA,
New Berne, N. C., November 14, 1863.

Maj. Gen. BENJAMIN F. BUTLER,
Comdg. Dept. of Virginia and North Carolina:

GENERAL: I have the honor to inclose some Confederate papers. By examining the telegraphic matter, you will find a telegram of the 8th from East Tennessee, claiming the capture of 850 prisoners, 40 pieces of artillery, 2 stand of colors, 60 wagons, and 1,000 arms. If reliable, these are a part of General Burnside's army. The same paper had a telegram of the 8th from Raleigh, announcing my ar-rival at Winton, with gunboats and troops for a move on Weldon; also that a proper force was at hand to meet the command. They express the opinion that 2,000 cavalry and 15 pieces of artillery were also destined for the same point, showing clearly that the rebel author-ities were advised of your intentions before I was. Norfolk is one city of spies, and communication is kept up day and night by land and water with the rebel army.

Very respectfully, your obedient servant,

JOHN J. PECK,
Major-General.

HDQRS. ARMY AND DISTRICT OF NORTH CAROLINA,
New Berne, N. C., November 14, 1863.

Brig. Gen. H. W. WESSELLS,
Comdg. Sub-District of the Albemarle:

GENERAL: I found Captain Flusser quite nervous about the ram on the Roanoke, in consequence of a report made to you of an exam-ination of the river by Mr. Lynch. Since I assumed command in

North Carolina, I have advised General Foster fully and frequently respecting its progress, and made propositions for its destruction. The general did not feel very apprehensive, and replied that the force in the department would not warrant the undertaking.

The works at Plymouth are in a good state, and when the 200-pounder rifle reaches you, I shall have but little apprehension from the ram, unless it moves in conjunction with a land force. On my return I ordered the 100-pounder rifle at Hatteras to be sent at once to Plymouth, in order to give you all the metal possible while waiting the 200-pounder. I should place it in Fort Gray, and you must have sufficient infantry there to prevent an assault of that work. Any trees that prevent the flanking of the fort by your gunboats should be cut down. Crowd your works all you can, and keep me advised of the progress, and of all reports, &c.

I have examined a number of the artillerists in Fort Branch, Rainbow, who all agree that week before last the channel was examined and numerous torpedoes placed in position. The rebels have constructed a battery of earth at Edwards Ferry of four guns or for four guns, and have an infantry guard there. You will notice that roads from Winton, Weldon, &c., cross at the ferry. Fort Branch has twelve guns, including one 64-pounder and three 24-pounders, one 6-pounder, and the balance 12-pounders, and all rifled.

I am greatly obliged to Captain Flusser for his prompt, cheerful, and valuable co-operation on the recent movement to the headwaters of the Chowan. Captains French and Foster are worthy and deserving officers, and I regret that no opportunity offered for the navy to pay their compliments to the rebels. The demonstration was telegraphed to all the Southern press, and troops moved to meet the advance upon Weldon.

Probably General Butler will arrive by the middle of the week; if so, we shall be at Plymouth.

Very respectfully, your obedient servant,

JOHN J. PECK,
Major-General.

WAR DEPARTMENT,
November 14, 1863—10.10 a. m.

Major-General BROOKS, *Erie, Pa. :*

The Department has no further information in relation to the movement from Canada.* All exposed points are now guarded, so as probably to prevent any present attack. You may employ a tug for a guard-boat. General Dix is at Buffalo; General Cox at Sandusky, and you may communicate with them. Any information received here will be transmitted to you.

EDWIN M. STANTON,
Secretary of War.

BUFFALO, N. Y., *November* 14, 1863.

Hon. E. M. STANTON,
Secretary of War :

SIR: In accordance with the suggestion in your dispatch, I came here yesterday. I found no preparation whatever for the protection

---

*See Series III, dispatches November 11–14, 1863.

of the city. The militia regiments are only partially armed. The arsenal (State) with some 3,000 stand of arms and about 20 pieces of field artillery is without a guard, and the artillery without ammunition.

Although the information I have received shows that Johnson's Island is the immediate object of the combinations in Canada, I deem it important, in view of a probable attack on this city, that the Seventy-fourth Regiment of State Militia, numbering about 400 men, should be called into service for thirty days. I have called on Governor Seymour, in accordance with the authority given me in your telegraphic dispatch, to order it out.

I have ordered a tug to be chartered and armed. There is not even a revenue vessel here. The only armed vessel on the lake is the Michigan, at Johnson's Island.

The most effectual remedy for the existing embarrassment is the removal of the prisoners. Johnson's Island on one side is separated from the land by a sheet of water only 5 feet deep. The whole harbor of Sandusky freezes over; and on the side I refer to the ice becomes strong enough to bear in two or three nights. It usually closes early. With this facility for escape, the security of the prisoners will be further diminished, although it must always be precarious, so immediately on the frontier.

JOHN A. DIX,
Major-General.

BUFFALO, N. Y.,
November 14, 1863.

His Excellency HORATIO SEYMOUR,
Albany, N. Y.:

I find this city utterly unprepared for defense, and deem it very important, in view of combinations among refugees and their sympathizers, in regard to which I have reliable information, that the Seventy-fourth Regiment of Militia should be called into service for thirty days. It is also very desirable that ammunition for the 10-pounder Parrotts in the State arsenal should be sent here immediately. I am authorized by the Secretary of War to call on the proper authority for volunteers, if necessary.

I have seen the mayor, J. Randall, and Colonel Fox, of the Seventy-fourth, and if authorized by you, the regiment will turn out at once.

JOHN A. DIX,
Major-General.

GENERAL ORDERS, }   HDQRS. DEPT. OF VA. AND N. C.,
No. 32.   }   *Fort Monroe, Va., November 14, 1863.*

Maj. Joseph M. Bell, aide-de-camp, is hereby appointed provost judge of this department, and will be obeyed and respected accordingly.

Major Stackpole, judge-advocate, is relieved from his duties as provost judge.

By command of Major-General Butler:

R. S. DAVIS,
Major, and Assistant Adjutant-General.

HEADQUARTERS ARMY OF THE POTOMAC,
November 15, 1863—12.45 p. m.

Major-General MEADE,
    Washington:

From 9 to 10 a. m. the cavalry reconnaissances caused some firing at Raccoon Ford and Rapidan Station. Pony Mountain report, just received, states firing is at Raccoon Ford. Intrenchments at Morton's Ford are filled with infantry. Artillery horses harnessed near the redoubts. One brigade of infantry just came down the hill in rear of the woods opposite Raccoon Ford. A party of soldiers on the hill witnessing the firing. Enemy's camps are nearly all concealed. Camp smokes are visible opposite Raccoon Ford, and behind the hills toward Orange Court-House, and in the direction of Freeman's Ford. Small smokes opposite Morton's and Stringfellow's Fords.

Respecting Freeman's Ford, the signal officer was asked for explanation, and his attention again directed explicitly to certain points and lines. Will report the result.

Railroad bridge at Rappahannock Station just reported finished. The track to that point will be laid to-day.

A. A. HUMPHREYS,
    Major-General, and Chief of Staff.

NOVEMBER 15, 1863—2.30 p.m.

Major-General MEADE,
    Washington:

' Signal officer at Pony Mountain explains that in his previous dispatch Freeman's Ford should be Germanna Ford. No smokes in direction of Madison Court-House. None between Madison and Orange Court-House. Other points not reported on yet.

General Custer, Third Cavalry Division, reports the opposite bank at Morton's Ford completely covered with intrenchments, which are filled with infantry. At least a division of infantry at that point, and batteries of artillery. At Raccoon Ford a strong infantry force was displayed, and artillery in position. Artillery in position between the two fords. Strong force of infantry at Mitchell's Ford. Party sent to Germanna Ford has not yet returned. No cavalry was observed on the entire line of the Rapidan picketed by the Third Division. The infantry have been replaced along the whole front of the Third Division.

General Buford reports that one of his parties passed through James City this morning; saw no enemy, but learned that yesterday a brigade of cavalry passed through there. Other parties not heard from yet.

General Gregg reports nothing new on the left. Has not heard from scouting party.

Signal officer on Pony Mountain now reports that he sees no camp smokes in the direction of United States Ford, Hartwood Church, or thence to Morrisville; the atmosphere is not clear, but he believes that if there were large camp smokes he could see them. His next report states that wagons and infantry in double columns have been passing from Raccoon Ford toward our right for an hour, and that the infantry is still passing—2 p. m.

A camp near Raccoon Ford has just been broken up. Our cavalry reconnaissances have evidently disturbed the enemy. He has not withdrawn from the Rapidan.

A. A. HUMPHREYS,
Major-General, and Chief of Staff.

NOVEMBER 15, 1863—4.15 p. m.

Major-General MEADE,
    Washington:

General Buford reports that his reconnoitering parties found infantry at Rapidan Station, this side the river, and infantry holding Somerville Ford.

A. A. HUMPHREYS,
Major-General, and Chief of Staff.

WASHINGTON,
November 15, 1863—6.40 p. m.

Major-General HUMPHREYS:

Your dispatch of 3 p. m. received. It is evident the enemy have not withdrawn from the Rapidan, but I do not like the reported passing through James City of a brigade of cavalry and the reported movements of infantry from Raccoon Ford. This has the appearance of an advance.

I had intended to leave here to-morrow at 9 a. m., which would bring me at headquarters by noon, but if you think, or have any later intelligence leading to the conclusion, that the enemy is advancing, I will come out at once.

Please let me have an answer as soon as you receive this.

GEO. G. MEADE,
Major-General, Commanding.

NOVEMBER 15, 1863—7.45 p. m.

Major-General MEADE:

Your dispatch of 6.40 p. m. just received. All the information received since my last dispatch indicates that the enemy is not advancing. The movement up the river from Raccoon Ford was probably caused by the advance of our cavalry reconnoitering parties to Rapidan Station, and to the crossings of Robertson's River. The brigade of enemy's cavalry at James City yesterday apparently came forward to reconnoiter, and, so far as yet learned, returned across Robertson's River, which is strongly picketed by cavalry, as Buford has just reported.

The report of the Pony Mountain signal officer at 6 p. m. shows that the enemy is encamped chiefly between Raccoon Ford and Orange Court-House. His camp smokes are likewise seen at Morton's Ford and the fords below that. No camp smokes indicating an advance upon either flank were seen. The movement of troops from Raccoon Ford up the river ceased soon after it was reported; it did not much exceed an hour in duration. The infantry this side the river at Rapidan Station is intrenched as it was formerly.   There is no necessity for you to hasten your return.   The bridge over the Rappahannock is finished.

A. A. HUMPHREYS,
Major-General, and Chief of Staff.

CULPEPER,
November 15, 1863—8.25 a. m.

Colonel SMITH:

I received the dispatch ordering a reconnaissance to ascertain if the enemy's infantry and artillery still held the fords of the Rapidan, particularly if there is infantry on this side at the Rapidan railroad bridge.   I answered that the enemy had a small infantry picket on this side, at Rapidan Station, but there is no force of infantry this side of the Rapidan or Robertson's River.

JNO. BUFORD,
Brigadier-General.

[Indorsements.]

HEADQUARTERS CAVALRY CORPS,
November 15, 1863.

Respectfully forwarded.

A. PLEASONTON,
Major-General, Commanding.

[General PLEASONTON:]

Would it not be well to inform General Buford of the reports received last evening regarding the enemy's movements?   He would then know that we wished by the reconnaissance to ascertain the truth.

JOHN SEDGWICK,
Major-General.

HEADQUARTERS CAVALRY CORPS,
November 15, 1863—noon.

Respectfully returned.

General Buford will be informed.   It is understood, however, that he is aware of the reports mentioned.

A. PLEASONTON,
Major-General.

CULPEPER COURT-HOUSE,
November 15, 1863.

Lieutenant-Colonel SMITH:

Another party has returned.   They found enemy—infantry—intrenched on this side of Rapidan Bridge, with infantry and artillery on opposite side.   Along Robertson's River nothing but cavalry, but in strong force.

BUFORD.

HEADQUARTERS THIRD DIVISION, CAVALRY CORPS,
November 15, 1863—12 m. (Received 2.30 p. m.)

Col. C. ROSS SMITH,
        Chief of Staff:

I have just returned from a personal inspection of the river between Morton's and Raccoon Fords. The Second Brigade of this division was divided into two parties, one of which I sent to Raccoon Ford, the other to Morton's Ford. At the latter I succeeded in driving that portion of the enemy's force which held the ford back to the high ground beyond. The recent rains have rendered the river impassable. The enemy opened a brisk cannonade from six guns, mounted behind earth-works and commanding the approaches to the ford (Morton's). At the same time a battery was planted below the ford, but was not opened. The heights on the opposite bank are completely covered with intrenchments, which are filled with infantry.

Soon after my command made its appearance at Morton's Ford, the enemy marched a heavy column of infantry into their intrenchments. I saw at least a division of infantry at this point. At a point midway between Morton's and Raccoon Fords I saw a battery of the enemy's in position, and from which they fired upon my column. At Raccoon Ford a strong infantry force was displayed, and four guns in position. A few shots were fired from the latter. I sent General Davies, with a portion of the First Brigade, to examine Mitchell's and Germanna Fords. The party sent to the latter point have not yet reported. The other party found a strong force of infantry guarding Mitchell's Ford. No cavalry was observed along the entire line. Although the infantry pickets yesterday were relieved by cavalry, the infantry have been replaced along the river on my front.

Very respectfully, &c.,

G. A. CUSTER,
Brigadier-General, Commanding Division.

WASHINGTON, D. C., *November 15, 1863.*

General JOSEPH G. TOTTEN,
        Chief of Engineers:

SIR: As I believe that a method of laying pontoon bridges which has occurred to me, and which I have directed the practice of in this command, may be of general interest, I would respectfully offer you the following report and description of the same; and it may be the more proper to lay this report before the Department, because, simple as the process has appeared to me, and most extraordinarily expeditious as it has been found—such that a pontoon bridge one-fourth of a mile in length, and with about 450 men only, is laid complete for the passage of artillery in the course of twenty minutes, as has been done repeatedly across the Eastern Branch of the Potomac, opposite this camp—yet I cannot learn, either from books or otherwise, that this method, or any other of the like rapidity of execution, has ever been previously followed in our own or any other service. In fact, by the method I found in practice, in this brigade at least, six to eight hours were necessary for the construction of a bridge of any such length.

It may be remarked that the building of these bridges by making rafts, or by "conversion," as referred to in the books, and as practiced by the regular engineer officers while attached to this brigade, as well as by others, was uniformly by successive pontoons, thereby reducing the time of construction but in a limited degree, and never beyond half of that of the usual method by successive pontoons.

The process is simply to have the wagon bridge trains brought into such position, well closed up, as to be unloaded simultaneously along the shore, as in most cases can be done, and as is the most natural and expeditious method, with ample force of men, and then, with small bridge squads previously detailed, to lay the several bays of the bridge along the shore, also simultaneously, while the abutments on the shore are at the same time being constructed by other squads, when the bridge or long raft, to fill the space between the abutments, can be swung with the oars, aided by the current or wing, into the desired position, and made complete in a very few minutes by connecting the ends of this raft with these abutments.

This method of laying pontoon bridges had occurred to me, and I had directed it to be practiced with the canvas pontoon train at Beaufort, S. C., in May, 1862, and again I proposed it to the officers of this brigade in April of this year, soon after receiving this command. But though I continually described and urged it upon the officers, the want of opportunities for trial while in front of the enemy, and the persistent adherence to the old methods by these officers when the bridges were then laid or removed, with my indisposition to force the new methods in such positions, had delayed the successful practice of it until we reached this depot camp in July of this year. And though this plan was then ordered and minutely described to the officers for their practice here—being designedly left to them for the first three or four weeks—the continued disbelief in it, or the quiet opposition which I was afterward assured had existed with about all the officers of the brigade, was so great that no advance or improvement appeared; in fact, I had the written report of the drills here describing the building of bridges of some 300 feet in forty-five to fifty minutes by the old method of successive pontoons, while the new method was reported as requiring one and a quarter hours.

This satisfied me, then, that my instructions had either been misunderstood or had not been zealously carried out, and I at once took the personal direction of the drills, and at the first trial the bridge of 300 feet was completed in twenty minutes; at the next, after due preparation of the necessary material, the bridge to span the Eastern Branch here, fully 1,300 feet long, was laid complete, swung into position, and connected in half an hour, and in the next three or four drills this time was reduced to twenty minutes or less for the complete construction, swinging around, and connecting of the bridge ready for the passage of artillery.

The detail of time (which I think is now reduced to nearly its minimum) for the several parts of the work, I may mention is very nearly, for squads of 6 to 7 men of some experience, about seven to nine minutes for constructing the bridge or raft along the shore, about seven to nine minutes to swing the bridge to, between the abutments, and about two to three minutes to connect and complete the whole, or some eighteen to twenty minutes in all. The time for swinging the bridge will, of course, vary with the width of the river, currents, wind, &c., while the time for the construction of the raft along the shore and its connection to the abutments will be about the same for any length of bridge.

For removing the bridge I would observe that nearly the same time is required to disconnect the raft from the abutments, about the same time to swing the raft, and for dismantling and placing the roadway on the shore about four or five minutes only, or about fifteen minutes all together for this removal. The squads of men, if the force were available, might be increased from 6 to 7 to 10 to 12 for each bay, which would still further reduce the time of construction and dismantling.

I have been thus particular in showing the delays, not to say opposition, that has been experienced, that, simple as the mode really is, and, as may be supposed, one that would be so readily seized upon, it might be seen how strong the prejudice was in favor of the old slow process, or what total ignorance there was of this mode or of its advantages.

Some of these advantages I would now respectfully call attention to, available as I feel assured it will be in whole or in part for the large majority of cases in actual practice. It would have answered perfectly, I know, for the three bridges which were laid at the United States Ford on the Rappahannock in April last, also at the Franklin's and the Reynolds' crossings, 2 and 4 miles, respectively, below Fredericksburg, where our bridges have been laid repeatedly. It would have applied partially at Banks' Ford, where Sedgwick's troops retired on May 5; also partially and to a greater extent when these same troops were crossed at Edwards Ferry on June 29, 1863, when it would have been of great importance, the river being over 1,400 feet wide here. The old method required some six to eight hours (as reported to me) for the construction of each of the two bridges there, and the labor of carrying upon the shoulders of a limited number of men of these roadways in parts for the space of over one-eighth of a mile, while by this method this labor of carrying the material is needed for from 10 to 20 or 50 feet only.

It also enables the material to be used by the largest number of men from the position where it can most speedily be unloaded from a land train, the wagons and trucks of this train being unloaded at once from the positions of the train as wheeled and closed in a line on the river bank. Or if the bank did not permit the easy approach to the wagons the loads can almost as quickly be distributed there by the large number of troops usually unoccupied while waiting to cross. While the old method required the piling of the whole bridge train by the successive loads as they arrived, around a single abutment, as well as the carrying of this material to be laid, by one or at most two squads of men for ordinary bridges, while all the rest of the command were in a forced idleness.

But more than this, it can carry, fully concealed from view of sharpshooters, a storming column of men equal in number to every foot of its length, as every pontoon can cover, under the bridge floor, or concealed a foot below the gunwale, at least 20 armed men besides its crews (of which the one or two oarsmen only need be exposed), so that as the raft (previously made of full length) comes directly across the stream and grounds at either bank, these men rise, an armed storming column debouching at the instant from the bridge, to be followed in a continuous stream by other troops from the pivot shore, and in power to sweep away everything except the heavy masses of infantry or artillery well posted, in the face of which, of course, the construction of any bridge would be next to impracticable. After the opposite bank shall have been cleared of the enemy, the other abutment and connection could be completed for the passage of artillery.

In the swing of the bridge it may be remarked that with every person in the pontoons, even to the officers (who will occasionally rise up to observe and give directions), with all concealed from view except the one or two boatmen in each boat, who by their double motion of rowing and actual rapid passage in space (especially in the exposed parts of the bridge), there is scarcely any opportunity (as appeared evident in the drills) for the effective use of sharp-shooters against the bridge party, or even for ordinary small volleys of musketry. While the long, weary hours of exposure in laying the bridges by successive pontoons at Fredericksburg in December, 1862, or even the supposed improved plan by which they were afterward laid, by previously embarking masses of men in pontoons to cross first to clear the skirmishers of the enemy, by exposing such masses to large loss by volleys from an enemy, it is believed, offer no pretense of safety, speed of passage, or efficiency like the mode proposed.

The details of the execution or the drill for this construction is very simple, being as follows: Where the shore will allow, the train of pontoon trucks is drawn along the edge of the shore, closed and wheeled to distances of about 20 feet, with the sterns of the boats ready to be run at once into the water and the balks slid off opposite to them. The chess wagons (as chess for two bays are carried on each) are brought at the same time in front of the space between each pair of pontoons, and the chess there run off, the space between each odd pontoon and the next higher numbered boat being left for free communication. If the immediate shore or river edge is a high steep bank (the only case where this method may not be available) and unapproachable by wheels, the pontoons can be placed in the water at the most convenient points and floated to their proper positions, and the balks and chess can be very speedily carried and arranged as above proposed, with the large force of troops usually assisting on such occasions, by whom it can in almost all cases be easily passed down to the boats.

The material being thus placed and ready, and the pontoniers arranged in squads of a non-commissioned officer and 6 to 12 men each, according to the number available, and the boats being numbered from the near-shore abutments or pivot flank of the raft, and the squads assigned and in position at the respective sets of balks, at the order for construction they place the balks (the two outer balks first) between each or any two of the boats by the easy movement of the partial rafts in the water. It has been found that even the laying of these in succession is not requisite. The remaining balks are then placed and lashed, and as soon as the lashings are completed over any even-numbered boat, the placing of the chess commences, being laid both ways from the center line of the pontoon over the adjacent bays, the lashing rails being placed on immediately that any bay is completed. The rails over each pair of boats (as between Nos. 1 and 2, Nos. 3 and 4, &c.), should be laid as inner rails, and between the pairs as outer rails to prevent irregularities. Each squad will lash the rafts upon the bay above its boat, or between that and the next higher numbered boat.

As soon as any squad has lashed the side rails, it takes position at once in the boat, concealed below the gunwales, excepting the one or two oarsmen previously designated, who raise the oars ready to let fall at the word to swing, each oarsman having a relief under cover near him ready to seize the oar in case of any casualty. While the balks are being lashed a minimum number of anchor-boats on the outer side are held ready, with good crews, with anchors from say two not adjacent boats, and are kept head outward on the gentlest strain of their cables. At the word to move, the strain of the oars should be strong on the chord of the arc of movement, as the carelessness which permits these boats to come athwart this line very greatly obstructs and delays the swinging of the bridge. In the rapid passage of the moving end of a long bridge, it is best that the outer or farther anchor-boats should be simply towed alongside the end boat of the raft.

While this work is being executed, a special squad can prepare the hither abutment, and, if no opposition is expected, another such squad can cross with two or three pontoons to complete the opposite or farther abutment.

And as soon as the squads on the raft shall have taken their position, and the officers are all in the boats, if opposition is expected, the oarsmen, at the word, should drop and ply their oars together, at the wheeling flank strongly, near the middle gently, and at the pivot very slightly; in these last cases a constant watch must be kept by the officers and men, not to advance their portions too much. With care at these parts the bridge may be carried round and kept very nearly straight, and of course with the least strain or injury to it, though I was surprised to find no damage of consequence resulted from a cramping of the pivot end of the bridge by which it was curved into about a quarter circle of a radius of not more than 150 to 200 feet. To avoid this the pivot end should always move on a small circle, well clear of the abutment.

As the bridge nears its proper position, the up-stream anchors direct from the pontoons of the bridge should be thrown, first from near the pivot end, to aid in judging of the position, for which range poles on the proper line or distance above the intended position of the bridge should be placed upon the shore. And as the bridge comes between the abutments, previously placed, the connection for vehicles is made at once, while the anchor boats with the down-stream or steadying anchors move off to drop them in position. Or if opposition is expected or is offered, the farther abutment of course not being placed, the bridge is held by its upper anchors as a raft, until the storming column of those concealed in the boats, and as many others as shall be required from our shore, shall have passed over it.

I have the pleasure of inclosing you, for the further explanation of the method of laying these bridges, some photographic views taken during the progress of construction.*

No. 1 shows the pontoons ready with the material, and the boat squads ready for the construction (at foot of East Fifteenth street).

No. 2 shows the progress of construction of the raft after four to five minutes' labor.

No. 3 shows the progress of the bridge raft after six to seven minutes' labor.

No. 4 shows the bridge completed, with the bridge squads formed ready to march off. Parts of a trestle and canvas pontoon bridge across a cove along the shore are in view here.

_____
* Omitted.

No. 5 shows, from a nearer point of view, the pontoon bridge ready for service.

No. 6 gives the view down the Eastern Branch with pontoon bridge to beyond Navy-Yard Bridge, and oarsmen having oars raised ready to move the bridge for dismantling. Parts of pontoon balk-head used for laying the bridge raft are shown in foreground as it was placed to save the men from the water, though rather delaying than expediting the work.

Believing that they would also be interesting at the Department, I have also added two other photographic views.

No. 7, showing the old or generally practiced method of laying bridges by successive pontoons.

No. 8, a view of the pontoon bridges laid by the engineer brigade under my command on the morning of April 29, 1863, at Franklin's Crossing, 2½ miles below Fredericksburg. This shows in the distance the ruins of the villa of Mansfield, the site of General Bayard's death.

Very respectfully, your obedient servant,

H. W. BENHAM,
Brigadier-General.

HDQRS. FIRST BRIG., SECOND DIV., CAVALRY CORPS,
Near Fayetteville, Va., November 16, 1863—9.30 a. m.

Capt. H. C. WEIR,
Asst. Adjt. Gen., Second Division:

SIR: I have the honor to report all quiet along my lines this morning. Night before last, shortly after the line of pickets was established, near Warrenton, 4 men and a corporal were found to be missing; no alarm was given. Last night several shots were fired at the vedettes along the whole front of my lines, but no serious attacks were made.

The guerrillas around Warrenton are very troublesome, always attacking my pickets after nightfall. The citizens do all in their power to help and encourage these people, and I fancy that by putting a section of my battery into position, about 1½ miles this side of the town, with orders to open upon this place in case we are disturbed, no guerrilla raids will hereafter be made upon my lines. We are very short of forage. The missing men belong to First Rhode Island Cavalry.

Very respectfully, your obedient servant,

J. P. TAYLOR,
Colonel, Commanding First Brigade.

[Indorsement.]

HEADQUARTERS SECOND CAVALRY DIVISION,
November 17, 1863.

Respectfully forwarded.

To comply with the instructions to "picket beyond Warrenton," it is found necessary to completely envelop that town, so as to bring it within our lines and cut off communication between its disloyal inhabitants and the guerrillas who infest the country about. These two classes of people, not being permitted to have intercourse, are

very angry, and it results from this that the line of pickets is constantly threatened both in front and rear, and its maintenance will
occasion the loss of men, as in this instance.

D. McM. GREGG,
Brig. Gen. of Vols., Commanding Second Division.

WAR DEPARTMENT,
Washington, D. C., November 16, 1863.

Ordered: Messrs. James C. Wetmere, of Ohio; Gardiner Tufts, of
Massachusetts; W. Y. Selleck, of Wisconsin; A. Chester, of Illinois, and J. C. Rafferty, of New Jersey, are hereby constituted a
Board of Inspectors, whose duty it shall be to inspect from time to
time the Government general hospitals and military prisons in the
Department of Washington, under such special instructions as shall
be given by the War Department.

All officers of these hospitals and prisons are enjoined to treat the
inspectors herein named with respect and courtesy.

The Quartermaster's Department will furnish such transportation
as may be necessary for the Board to perform the duty of visiting
the hospitals and prisons.

By order of the Secretary of War:

JAS. A. HARDIE,
Assistant Adjutant-General.

WAR DEPARTMENT,
Washington City, November 16, 1863.

JAMES C. WETMORE, of Ohio; GARDINER TUFTS, of Massachusetts; W. Y. SELLECK, of Wisconsin; A. CHESTER, of Illinois;
J. C. RAFFERTY, of New Jersey:

GENTLEMEN: As a Board of Inspectors for the Government general hospitals and military prisons in the Department of Washington,
I am directed to convey to you the following instructions for your
guidance:

AS HOSPITAL INSPECTORS.

1. The inspectors are required to inspect the hospitals as to their
general order and cleanliness in all their parts and premises.

2. To observe as to the efficiency, faithfulness, and humanity of
the surgeons and other attendants.

3. To inspect particularly the management of the kitchens, the
condition of stores and supplies, both as to food and clothing, the
nature of the cooking, the quantity and quality of the rations, and, in
general, everything pertaining to the sanitary condition of the
patients.

4. To receive complaints of patients as to grievances, and give them
a reasonable hearing and investigation, yet in no way to interfere
with the military discipline of the hospital. If any just ground for
complaint be found, or any reform be needed, they are to apply for
the remedy to the surgeon in charge. If that does not accomplish
the end, they are to report the facts directly to the Secretary of War,
and, generally, they are to report to him whenever in their judg-

ment anything relating to a hospital or its officers cannot be remedied without his attention.

5. Three of the Board shall constitute a sufficient number to conduct an inspection, and every general hospital in the department is to be visited once in thirty days, and as much oftener as, in the judgment of the Board, it may be expedient. These visits will be made with or without previous notice to the surgeons in charge, as the Board may at any time determine.

6. Generally, in the spirit of the above instructions, the inspectors are to regard the good condition of the hospitals as committed to their keeping, and are to have an eye on everything connected with them that concerns the welfare of the patients and the needs of the military service. It is desired, however, that they shall so act that, as far as it is possible consistently with their duties, they shall not be antagonistic to, but co-operative with, the surgeons in charge for the best good of the hospital.

AS PRISON INSPECTORS.

1. The inspectors are required to inspect the military prisons in the Department of Washington, in all their parts and premises, as to their general management, order, and cleanliness.

2. To observe as to the efficiency, fidelity, and humanity of the officers in charge.

3. To see whether the prisoners are as well cared for with regard to rations, beds, clothing, fuel, and other accommodations for comfort and decency as is consistent with the fact of imprisonment and the necessities of proper discipline.

4. To inspect the records of the prisons, and see that against the name of every person admitted there is a clearly written statement of the offense for which he is committed, and if from time to time persons are found imprisoned for a long period without an official hearing, or who appear to have been overlooked by the proper military authorities, or with regard to whom there is evidently some error in the charge, the inspectors are to report such cases, with a clear statement of the same, to the Secretary of War.

5. Each of the military prisons in the Department of Washington is to be visited by at least three of the Board, together, once in thirty days, and as much oftener as may be deemed expedient. Except by way of suggestion and advice to the superintendent, the inspectors are not to interfere with the discipline of the prisons, but will report to the Secretary of War whenever in their judgment the good of the prisons and of the public service requires it.

By order of the Secretary of War:

JAS. A. HARDIE,
Assistant Adjutant-General.

HARPER'S FERRY, W. VA.,
November 16, 1863—4.30 p. m. (Received 10.15 p. m.)
Maj. Gen. H. W. HALLECK,
General-in-Chief:

I am endeavoring by every means in my power to keep my lines closed against all persons desiring to go south. I have ordered that no passes be given, except at my headquarters, and then upon a care-

ful investigation, and the applicant to be indorsed by the headquarters at Washington, Baltimore, or Clarksburg. My principal
trouble is with a lot of persons, calling themselves scouts and de-
tectives, who pass and repass our lines on passes secured from high
authority. I have abolished the whole system.

> JER. C. SULLIVAN,
> *Brigadier-General.*

> WAR DEPARTMENT,
> *November 16, 1863—4 p. m.*

Maj. Gen. R. C. SCHENCK,
  Commanding Middle Department, Baltimore:
  The Fourth Delaware Infantry has been ordered home. I do not
expect to go to Gettysburg. The President, however, will go on
Wednesday, and if you can leave your command at that time, he will
no doubt be glad to be accompanied by you; but the other matter
that comes off on the same day, the 19th, is of so much importance
that it is for you to consider whether you should be there or in Wilmington. When the order to go to Gettysburg was given, I had
forgotten that the Delaware election occurred on that day, and I
have been informed that it is expected some rebel sympathizers will
be taken to Wilmington to overawe loyal voters. You are, therefore, left to act according to your discretion.

> EDWIN M. STANTON,
> *Secretary of War..*

SPECIAL ORDERS, }   HDQRS. DEPT. OF VA. AND N. C.,
  No. 119.   }   *Fort Monroe, Va., November 16, 1863.*
  *   *   *   *   *   *   *

VIII. Brig. Gen. C. A. Heckman, commanding at Newport News,
will order the following troops to report to Brigadier-General Getty,
commanding United States forces at Portsmouth, Va.: Twenty-fifth
Regiment Massachusetts Volunteer Infantry; Ninth Regiment New
Jersey Infantry; one squadron Third New York Cavalry; Howell's
battery, Third New York Artillery.
  The quartermaster's department will furnish transportation.
  By command of Major-General Butler:

> R. S. DAVIS,
> *Assistant Adjutant-General.*

SPECIAL ORDERS, }   WAR DEPT., ADJT. GENERAL'S OFFICE,
  No. 508.   }   *Washington, November 16, 1863.*
  *   *   *   *   *   *   *

26. Brig. Gen. Charles K. Graham, U. S. Volunteers, is hereby
relieved from duty in the Army of the Potomac, and will report in
person at the expiration of his present leave of absence to the commanding general, Department of Virginia and North Carolina, for
assignment to duty.
  *   *   *   *   ..   *   *

By order of the Secretary of War:

> E. D. TOWNSEND,
> *Assistant Adjutant-General.*

GENERAL ORDERS, }   HDQRS. DEPT. OF WEST VIRGINIA,
   No. 19.   }   *Clarksburg, W. Va., November* 16, 1863.

I. The headquarters of this department will, after this date and until further orders, be at Cumberland, Md.

By order of Brigadier-General Kelley:

THAYER MELVIN,
Assistant Adjutant-General.

HEADQUARTERS ARMY OF THE POTOMAC,
November 17, 1863.

Circular to Corps Commanders:

You will be prepared to move with your command at short notice.

By command of Major-General Meade:

S. WILLLIAMS,
Assistant Adjutant-General.

HEADQUARTERS CAVALRY CAMP,
Vienna, Va., November 17, 1863.

Brigadier-General CORCORAN,
   Comdg. Division, Fairfax Court-House:

GENERAL: I have the honor to request that you will send us information with as little delay as possible when parties of your command are sent out, in order to avoid any trouble that might arise from parties meeting at night.

Two parties of 50 men each from this command had been sent out over an hour with special countersign and parole when your message reached us. The guerrillas captured a sergeant and 2 men, and wounded 1 of the Thirteenth New York Cavalry. No other damage was done. Fifty men are now out with instructions to scout as far as Aldie. It is barely possible that they may fall in with a few of the rebels.

A picket about a mile from camp were alarmed at about 1 o'clock last night, but it is by no means certain that the alarm was not groundless.

I have the honor to be, very respectfully, your obedient servant,

C. R. LOWELL, JR.

HDQRS. SECOND BRIG., THIRD DIV., CAV. CORPS,
November 18, 1863.

Brigadier-General DAVIES:

Major Brewer, First Michigan Cavalry, on picket, reports that the enemy have crossed a few infantry skirmishers at different points all along his front, who are annoying him by constant firing. He has been ordered to hold his position and not fall back unless compelled, and to prevent their crossing if possible.

Respectfully, your obedient servant,

CHAS. H. TOWN,
Colonel, Commanding.

HEADQUARTERS ARMY OF THE POTOMAC,
OFFICE OF CHIEF QUARTERMASTER,
Camp near Brandy Station, November 18, 1863.

Brig. Gen. S. WILLIAMS,
Asst. Adjt. Gen., Army of the Potomac:

GENERAL: I have the honor to report, for the information of the commanding general, that I have examined the capacity of our wagon trains as now allowed by existing orders for carrying of supplies, and find, in round numbers, that each corps can carry ten days' short rations of subsistence and forage in the baggage and supply trains, in addition to the most necessary articles of baggage, camp equipage, &c. To do this, less small-arms ammunition should be carried in wagons. I would suggest that only three wagons, instead of five, be allowed each 1,000 men for that purpose.

I inclose a memorandum of what a wagon can carry, also a memorandum of the wagons in Sixth Corps and what they can carry. I am of the opinion that a wagon cannot carry over 1,000 rations of subsistence, and, say, 600 pounds of grain. This will make the load over 2,000 pounds. The general depot can furnish wagons enough to carry two days' hard bread and four of salt for the army. This will give twelve days' in wagons, with an extra allowance of salt.

If the men carry eight days' on their persons there will be twenty days' in all. I would remind the general commanding that experience has shown that there is no military advantage in loading the men heavily. They become quickly fatigued and waste the rations. In case of battle they abandon them. If eight days' are carried, hardly more than five can be calculated upon.

In any military operations based on amount of supplies carried in wagon trains, calculations must be made for a fresh supply from some reliable source at the expiration of, say, fifteen days.

The army can be furnished with all its prescribed supplies on or before Friday evening.

I am, very respectfully, your obedient servant,

RUFUS INGALLS,
Brig. Gen., and Chief Q. M., Army of the Potomac.

[Inclosure.]

Capabilities of supply of the Sixth Corps, excluding the artillery, computing rations for 18,000 men, at 1,500 pounds weight for 1,000 rations (1½ pounds to a ration), and forage for 2,500 animals, at 10 pounds each. This number of animals includes only those attached to the supply trains and 300 others, estimated not to be provided for otherwise.

	Pounds.
18,000 rations weigh	27,000
2,500 animals' forage	25,000
Daily supply	52,000

The number of wagons procurable for supply trains is 226. Estimating their capacity at 2,500 pounds each, makes 565,000 pounds. Divide this by 52,000, gives ten days and a fraction of about four-fifths.

All the wagons included in the supply trains cannot be devoted to rations and forage. Quartermasters are obliged to carry their blacksmiths' and harness-makers' shops, and commissaries their scales, &c. About ten days' would seem, therefore, to be the full capacity of supply. The same number of days' rations can be carried by the artillery supply train, but not more than five days' forage can be carried in wagons.

One wagon will carry 1,200 rations hard bread; 2,000 rations coffee (1 barrel); 1,800 rations sugar (1 barrel); 300 rations (two-eighths pound) pork (1 barrel, 1 box, 25 pounds); 1,200 rations salt (1 box, 45 pounds); 36 rations (9 pounds to ration) oats (3 sacks); gross weight, 2,674 pounds.

Weight of 1,200 rations, two-eighths pounds pork, 2,520 pounds; weight of 1,200 rations, short, 1,800 pounds; weight of ten days' rations, forage, 600 pounds.

GENERAL ORDERS, } HDQRS. DEPT. OF VA. AND N. C.,
No. 34.   }   *Fort Monroe, Va., November* 18, 1863.

Mr. John D. Sanborn is hereby appointed special provost-marshal in this department, and will be obeyed and respected accordingly

By command of Major-General Butler:

R. S. DAVIS,
Major, and Assistant Adjutant-General.

CUMBERLAND, MD., *November* 19, 1863.
(Received 12 p. m.)

Col. E. D. TOWNSEND,
Assistant Adjutant-General:

The recent success of Brigadier-General Averell at Lewisburg has cleared the new State of West Virginia of any organized force of rebels, and my operations for a time will probably be directed against the enemy in the Valleys of South Branch and Shenandoah. In view of this, and of the fact that the greater portion of the troops of my department are east of or in this vicinity, I have deemed it proper and advisable to change my headquarters from Clarksburg to this place.

B. F. KELLEY,
Brigadier-General.

HEADQUARTERS ARMY OF THE POTOMAC,
November 20, 1863—12 noon. (Received 1.10 p. m.)

Maj. Gen. H. W. HALLECK,
General-in-Chief:

All information tends to the conclusion that Lee has not made any movement with any part of his force, but is awaiting an advance on my part. His army seems to be holding in force the fords of the Rapidan, the left of the infantry at Germanna Ford, and the right toward Orange Court-House, with his cavalry on each flank. Day before yesterday he crossed a considerable body of cavalry at Ely's Ford, who drove in our pickets, surprised an outpost, and after capturing some 30 men, a wagon and ambulance, recrossed the river at Ely's and Germanna. The object of this expedition was, undoubtedly, to ascertain whether I was making any movement to his left.

The railroad was completed on last Monday, but is not yet in good working order, the storm of last Saturday seriously injuring it. So soon as the army is fully supplied, I shall move forward, turning either the right or left flank of the enemy. All general considerations are strongly in favor of operating on his right flank, as this movement will require a change of a portion of the army of only 12 miles, will not uncover my rear or communications, and in case of failure enables the withdrawal of the army without difficulty. To move on his left, and threaten Gordonsville and Orange Court-House, involves a march of 60 miles, entire abandonment of my communications, and exposes the army in case of disaster to having its retreat cut off.

Examinations are being made with a view of determining the practicability of turning the right by Germanna and Ely's. They will be finished by the time the army is supplied, which will be by to-morrow or next day, when I shall decide which movement to make, and at once proceed to its execution.

GEO. G. MEADE,
Major-General, Commanding.

WAR DEPARTMENT,
Washington, November 20, 1863—3.20 p. m.

Major-General MEADE,
 Army of the Potomac :

I respectfully advise that you do not telegraph any tactical movements you propose making. To know them here beforehand can serve no object, and they may be disclosed to the enemy.

H. W. HALLECK,
General-in-Chief.

NOVEMBER 20, 1863—1.30 p. m.

Major-General NEWTON,
 Commanding First Corps :

The major-general commanding directs that you hold your corps in readiness for concentration at Rappahannock Station, providing it with the rations and forage required by existing orders. It is intended that one division of your corps—probably that of General Kenly—shall remain to guard the railroad, and the distribution of which will be governed by information that will be furnished you at the time the order for concentration is issued.

A. A. HUMPHREYS,
Major-General, Chief of Staff.

HDQRS. SECOND BRIG., THIRD DIV., CAV. CORPS, A. P.,
November 20, 1863—2 p. m.

Col. C. ROSS SMITH,
 Chief of Staff :

The officer I sent on a reconnaissance above the Rapidan did not return until a late hour. He reports that the enemy have but very few rifle-pits below Germanna Ford, and they show little or no force below that point. The river is fordable for infantry at Ely's Ford, also at two fords located 2 and 3 miles above Ely's. The roads on this side the river leading to it are in excellent condition, and afford every facility for the passage of troops. In addition to this the signal officer reports great activity among the rebels in the vicinity of Morton's Ford. They could be plainly seen throwing up earthworks and placing guns in position.

This I consider reliable, as a portion of it came under my personal observation.

Very respectfully, &c.,

G. A. CUSTER,
Brigadier-General.

HDQRS. SECOND BRIG., THIRD DIV., CAVALRY CORPS,
November 20, 1863—6 p. m.

Col. C. Roŝs SMITH,
Chief of Staff:

From examination made by an excellent officer of my command, and from citizens who have lived many years in the immediate vicinity of the Rapidan, I learn the following facts:

Ely's Ford is one of the best fords on the river, and artillery can be crossed with the utmost facility. Three miles above Ely's Ford there is a ford known as Hall's, which is an excellent ford, over which artillery can be passed. At this point the enemy have thrown up three small rifle-pits, but they are of trifling importance. At a point about one-half mile above Hall's Ford is a private ford, known as Humphreys' Ford, that is a good ford for infantry, but too rocky and narrow for artillery. One mile below Ely's Ford there is a ford called Urquhart's Ford, which will afford a passage for infantry and has been used for wagons, but it is not a good ford. There is a road running almost parallel with the river from Germanna to Ely's Ford, at an average distance of 1½ miles from the river. Hall's Ford can be plainly seen from Ely's Ford.

Very respectfully,

· G. A. CUSTER,
Brig. Gen., Comdg. Second Brig., Third Div., Cav. Corps.

YORKTOWN,
November 20, [1863.]

Major-General BUTLER:

Our scouts just returned from Twelve-Mile Ordinary report that Pickett is coming down to retaliate, which is my earnest wish. I can hold my Williamsburg line against at least 10,000 men with no heavier artillery than we have a right to apprehend. I have small hopes of such a movement by Pickett, but if so, are there sufficient troops and transportation to throw a force in his rear? A very small force would be safe, as I will press him very close in front.

I. J. WISTAR,
Brigadier-General.

WASHINGTON,
November 21, 1863.
Major-General COUCH,
Chambersburg, Pa.:

GENERAL : In reply to your letter of November 13, I am directed
by the Secretary of War to say that you will dispose of a sufficient
number of troops of your command as will furnish the necessary
protection to the disturbed mining districts.

Very respectfully, your obedient servant,
H. W. HALLECK,
General-in-Chief.

HDQRS. THIRD DIVISION, CAVALRY CORPS,
November 21, 1863—7 p. m.
Lieut. Col. C. ROSS SMITH,
Chief of Staff, Cavalry Corps :

COLONEL: Two deserters have just come in, both very intelligent,
who have been in the service three years.

They informed me that Ewell's corps is in position opposite my
line of pickets, the left at Somerville Ford and the right resting on
Mine Run, at Bartlett's Mill, or Burr Hill Post-Office, about 3 miles
from the river, opposite Sevons' [?] Ford. Early's division and
Rodes' division are on the river from Somerville Ford to Mitchell's
Ford. The third division (Johnson's) occupies a line of intrenchments running back from Mitchell's Ford nearly perpendicular to
the river. They represent the position this division occupies as very
formidable. Rodes' and Johnson's divisions moved up to this point
last Sunday, from near Orange Court-House.

Hampton's cavalry picket the river from Mitchell's Ford to Germanna Ford. There is no infantry on the river below Mitchell's
Ford.

I am satisfied, from the information of these men and other reports
lately received, that the enemy have, infantry and artillery, less than
40,000 men. Ewell's corps consists of three divisions—Johnson's,
Rodes', and Early's—each have from four to five brigades. John-
son's division has four brigades—Steuart's, Walker's, Stafford's, and
Jones'. Rodes' division has five brigades — Ramseur's, Battle's,
Daniel's, and Johnston's. Early's division has four brigades—Hoke's,
Hays', Smith's old brigade, and one brigade, general unknown.
Each brigade will number from 1,300 to 1,500 men, giving the corps
18,200 men.

Hill's corps is less than Ewell's, giving Hill's corps 18,000 men.

Major-General Lee has but 36,000 men in his two corps. Add to
this, Pickett's division, numbering less than 5,000 men, gives him
41,000 men; take from this 1,607, Lee's official report of his loss at
Rappahannock Station, and he then has about 39,000 men all told.

Each division has a battalion of artillery, giving each corps from
forty to forty-eight guns. They have, besides, three battalions of
artillery in reserve.

I have given these facts in detail, as the two men are worn out and
cannot be sent in until morning.

Respectfully submitted.
J. KILPATRICK,
Brig. Gen. of Vols., Commanding Third Division.

SPECIAL ORDERS, ⎰ WAR DEPT., ADJT. GENERAL'S OFFICE,
　　No. 518.　　⎱　　　*Washington, November 21, 1863.*
　　*　　.　　*　　　*　　　*　　　*　　　*　　　*

22. Brig. Gen. H. H. Lockwood, U. S. Volunteers, will relieve Major-General Schenck in command of the Middle Department at such time as the general may notify him of his readiness to turn it over.
　　*　　　*　　　*　　　*　　　*

By order of the Secretary of War:

　　　　　　　　　　　E. D. TOWNSEND,
　　　　　　　　　　　　Assistant Adjutant-General.

　　　　　　　　　　NOVEMBER 22, 1863—11.40 a. m.

Commanding Officer First Corps:

The major-general commanding directs me to say that the railroad having been reconstructed, and the depot at Warrenton Junction broken up, a new disposition of your corps will be made.

He accordingly directs that you assign the duty of guarding the railroad to one division of your corps (General Kenly's), to the commanding officer of which a detachment of 500 cavalry will be ordered to report from Gregg's division, to aid in the execution of the duty. A brigade of infantry, with a battery of artillery, will be posted at Rappahannock Station. A force of infantry, if practicable, will be posted at each of the following points on the road, viz, Bealeton, Warrenton Junction, Catlett's, or Cedar Run bridge, Nokesville, Kettle Run bridge, Bristoe, and Manassas Junction. The road will be strongly picketed from Manassas Junction to Bull Run bridge; the small bridges and the culverts will be guarded as usual, and the road patrolled and picketed.

Cavalry may be substituted for infantry at such points where it is found best suited to the object, and will be used for patrolling. The other two divisions of your corps, with the remaining artillery, will be concentrated at Rappahannock Station, and held ready to move with the supplies required by recent circular to be kept on hand.

　　　　　　　　　　A. A. HUMPHREYS,
　　　　　　　　　Major-General, and Chief of Staff.

　　　HEADQUARTERS SECOND CORPS, *November 22, 1863.*

Major-General HUMPHREYS, *Chief of Staff:*

I had the worst of the roads beyond Mountain Run examined. They are drying up and are not bad, excepting in spots. Mountain Run, where the fords are, is belly deep for a horse.

　　　　　　　　　　G. K. WARREN,
　　　　　　　　　　　　Major-General.

CIRCULAR.]　　　HEADQUARTERS ARMY OF THE POTOMAC,
　　　　　　　　　　November 22, 1863—8 p. m.

The commanding general desires to see corps commanders at his headquarters at 1 p. m. to-morrow, the 23d. Please acknowledge.

By command of Major-General Meade:

　　　　　　　　　　S. WILLIAMS,
　　　　　　　　　Assistant Adjutant-General.

Circular.]   Hdqrs. Second Division, Cavalry Corps,
November 22, 1863.

This command will be in readiness to move at 6 a. m., as the wagon train will not accompany the troops.

Brigade commanders will have their commands supplied with three days' rations from to-morrow evening, and two days' forage from the same period. No wagons will accompany the troops save one wagon for the headquarters of each brigade and one for each battery. All other wagons will be parked, and will report to the division quartermaster before the hour specified for the moving of the troops.

By command of Brigadier-General Gregg:

H. C. WEIR,
Assistant Adjutant-General.

Headquarters Army of the Potomac,
November 23, 1863.

Major-General FRENCH,
Commanding Third Corps:

On account of the unfavorable appearance of the morning, the troops will not move from their camps until further orders from these headquarters. They will, however, be prepared to move at very short notice should the weather clear up after daylight.

Please acknowledge.

S. WILLIAMS,
Assistant Adjutant-General.

Headquarters Third Corps,
November 23, 1863.

Brig. Gen. S. WILLIAMS,
Assistant Adjutant-General:

Your dispatch ordering the temporary suspension of the movement of the troops is received.

WM. H. FRENCH,
Major-General.

Headquarters Army of the Potomac,
November 23, 1863.

Major-General FRENCH, *Comdg. Third Corps:*

The following dispatch is sent for your information and guidance.

A. A. HUMPHREYS,
Chief of Staff.

[Inclosure.]

Headquarters Second Corps,

Major-General HUMPHREYS:

My parties on the road between here and Brandy Station I find are too small to do all the work, and the road will still be in bad condition at sunset. If any troops are to move very soon over that road, there should be very heavy working parties on it at once.

G. K. WARREN,
Major-General.

HEADQUARTERS ARMY OF THE POTOMAC,
November 23, 1863.

Major-General FRENCH,
　Commanding Third Corps:

The brigade near Culpeper may be withdrawn at once. General Warren refers to the condition of the roads from Brandy Station to the crossing of Mountain Run as the one requiring heavy working parties.

A. A. HUMPHREYS,
Major-General, and Chief of Staff.

HEADQUARTERS SECOND CORPS,
November 23, 1863.

Major-General HUMPHREYS, *Chief of Staff:*

I have been busy all day directing and examining, and the meeting escaped my memory. My non-attendance was known to you. I cannot think' I could be supposed to have received any instructions in regard to the movement to-morrow.

G. K. WARREN,
Major-General.

[Indorsement.]

DEAR WILLIAMS: What is this in reply to?
A. A. H. [HUMPHREYS.]

HEADQUARTERS SECOND CAVALRY DIVISION,
November 23, [1863]—12.50 p. m.

Col. C. ROSS SMITH,
　Chief of Staff, Cavalry Corps:

COLONEL: The advance of my division had crossed the Rapidan at Ely's Ford before I received the order countermanding a movement for to-day. There were 7 cavalrymen on picket on the other side. Only one regiment of mine was seen by the enemy. I now have one brigade at Richardsville and one near Ellis' Ford. I have sent my wagon train to Brandy Station to load with forage. A party of 30 rebel cavalry was at Richardsville this morning. My headquarters near Ellis' Ford.

Yours, &c.,

D. McM. GREGG,
Brigadier-General of Volunteers.

HEADQUARTERS SECOND CAVALRY DIVISION,
November 23, 1863.

Col. P. HUEY, *Commanding Second Brigade:*

COLONEL: The command will not cross at United States Ford, as before directed, but will cross the Rappahannock at Ellis' Ford, and the Rapidan at Ely's Ford. Your brigade will move in advance, and at the hour specified in your former instructions.

By command of Brigadier-General Gregg:

H. C. WEIR,
Assistant Adjutant-General.

NOVEMBER 23, [1863]—2 p. m.

Major-General HUMPHREYS,
        Chief of Staff:

GENERAL : I have just heard that United States Ford is blocked
up with fallen timber, and it will take half a day to clear it. Shall
I not send General Gregg's command across at Ely's Ford ? He can
move from Morrisville by way of Ellis' Ford. Please give me an
answer as soon as you can. It is important to change Gregg's orders.

                                            A. PLEASONTON,
                                                    Major-General.

CIRCULAR.]   HEADQUARTERS ARMY OF THE POTOMAC,
                                    November 23, 1863.

The following movements of troops are ordered for to-morrow, the
24th instant :

1. The Second Corps, Major-General Warren commanding, will
move at daylight, marching to Germanna Ford, taking the main dirt
road, keeping on the right-hand side of the road, between Madden's
and Brannan's, to admit of the passage at the same time of the Fifth
Corps. Upon reaching Germanna Ford, the passage of the river will
be forced (should the enemy dispute it). After crossing the Rapidan,
the corps will move on the Germanna plank road to the old turnpike to Orange Court-House, and advance to Robertson's Tavern, if
practicable.

2. The Third Corps, Major-General French commanding, will move
at daylight, crossing Mountain Run at Ross' Mills, enter the Germanna plank road at the first cross-road leading to it (past Holley's),
and diverge from it between Mitchell's and Willis', and cross the
Rapidan by the bridge in the vicinity of Jacobs' Mills. Should the
passage of the river be disputed, the Third Corps will co-operate with
the Second Corps in forcing it. Having crossed, the Third Corps
will move on the Jacobs' Ford and Robertson's Tavern road and
take post on the right of the Second Corps, on the road from Raccoon
Ford to Robertson's Tavern, covering the right from approach in the
direction of Bartlett's Mill.

3. The Fifth Corps, Major-General Sykes commanding, will move
at daylight, enter the main ridge road at Madden's (keeping on the
left-hand side), and proceed by way of Richardsville to Culpeper Ford,
where it will cross the Rapidan, and move by the shortest route to
the Orange and Fredericksburg plank road at Parker's Store, and,
if practicable, advance upon that road to the cross-road from Robertson's Tavern.

4. The Sixth Corps, Major-General Sedgwick commanding, will
move at daylight, and follow the route of the Third Corps, crossing
Mountain Run at Ross' Mills. It will leave a division in the vicinity
of Jacobs' Mills, to cover the removal of the bridge at that ford and
to protect the line of communication by Germanna Ford. The Sixth
Corps will take post in rear of the Third Corps on the Jacobs' Ford
road.

5. The First Corps, Major-General Newton commanding, will move
at daylight by way of Paoli Mills, and follow the route of the Fifth
Corps, crossing the Rapidan at Culpeper Ford. If practicable, it
will move to the Orange and Fredericksburg plank road. It will
take post in rear of the Fifth Corps.

6. The Reserve Artillery will follow the First Corps and park in its vicinity.

7. When two corps take the same route, the commanders will keep each other advised of their position and progress, and the commanders of the leading corps on each of the three routes will communicate and co-operate with each other. All corps commanders will keep the commanding general constantly advised of their progress.

8. Detachments of cavalry, each 100 strong, with 3 commissioned officers, will report for duty, respectively, to Major-General French, Major-General Sykes, and Major-General Warren. A bridge train will likewise be sent to each of these officers. Siege guns will be sent from the Reserve Artillery to Major-General Warren.

9. Each corps will take with it the ammunition trains, ambulance trains, including the brigade medicine wagons, and the spring wagons and ambulances authorized for the several headquarters; but these will not cross the river, excepting one-half the infantry ammunition wagons (30 rounds per man). Ambulances in the proportion of those of one brigade for each division and the spring wagons and ambulances authorized for the several headquarters.

10. The trains not already specified will be parked in the vicinity of Richardsville, under the direction of the chief quartermaster.

11. Gregg's division of cavalry will move on the left flank. Kilpatrick's division of cavalry will continue to guard the fords of the Rapidan until further orders, and will be held ready to move. Buford's division of cavalry will be disposed on the right, to cover the movement.

12. The trains will be so moved as under no circumstances to interfere with the movements of the troops.

13. Headquarters will be in the vicinity of Germanna Ford.

By command of Major-General Meade:

S. WILLIAMS,
Assistant Adjutant-General.

HEADQUARTERS ARMY OF THE POTOMAC,
November 24, 1863.

Major-General FRENCH,
    Commanding Third Corps:

In consequence of the rain, it is not expected that a movement of the army will take place before the 26th instant. Commanders will keep their supplies replenished from the depot.

S. WILLIAMS,
Assistant Adjutant-General.

(Same to other corps commanders.)

CAMP PAOLI MILLS, VA.,
November 24, 1863—10 a. m.

General HUMPHREYS,
    Chief of Staff, Army of the Potomac:

SIR: My command marched this morning at 5.30 o'clock. The order suspending the movement found me at the point where the roads divide, going to Germanna and Ely's Ford. My leading division, with the bridges, was in the vicinity of Richardsville. The rivulets are much swollen, and the roads so much soaked that the trains would have had great difficulty in passing over them. This is e·pecially the case off the main road. The wheels of my leading batteries cut through in places half way to the axle; it would have been much worse for those to come after. My troops are now completing their return to camp.

I am, sir, respectfully,

GEO. SYKES,
Major-General.

HEADQUARTERS CAVALRY CORPS,
November 24, 1863—2 p. m.

Major-General HUMPHREYS,
        Chief of Staff:

GENERAL: I sent this morning to halt General Gregg's command. I have not yet heard the result. It is probable my aide-de-camp would meet him between Ellis' and Ely's Fords, with orders to halt there until the infantry began to move over to the Rapidan.

As the movement is postponed until 26th, shall Gregg remain where he is found or return to Morrisville?

A. PLEASONTON,
Major-General.

HEADQUARTERS DEPARTMENT OF THE EAST,
New York City, November 24, 1863.

Maj. Gen. H. W. HALLECK,
        General-in-Chief, U. S. Army:

GENERAL: It is very desirable that I should have in command of the troops in this city and harbor one who has some familiarity with administration. In the removal of General Canby to Washington I have sustained a very great loss. Major-General Peck, who is now in command at New Berne, would fill his place better than any one whom I now think of, and if he can be spared I request that he may be ordered here with as little delay as possible. He is thoroughly acquainted with men and things here, and can be of great service to me in case of any trouble.

I am very desirous of having 200 men ordered from Elmira (where they are just now not needed) to Fort Porter, Buffalo. They are part of a detachment of 500 belonging to the invalid corps. They can still remain under the control of the provost-marshal of that district, and in case of future need, be recalled to Elmira. The frontier from Erie to Champlain is really defenseless, but I am unwilling to ask for troops fit for service in the field.

The territory of Canada cannot, without a violation of British law and of every rule of international duty, be used for fitting out expeditions against us by disloyal citizens, who have sought a refuge there from calamities they have brought on themselves. On application to the British minister, it seems to me that he must feel bound to give such instructions to the Canadian authorities as to secure an interposition of military force to prevent such a violation of their territory. I am not satisfied that there is any very extensive combination of the refugees from the South for an attack on us, but a few hundred men could take possession of our small towns and inflict serious injury on their inhabitants.

I am, very respectfully, your obedient servant,

JOHN A. DIX,
Major-General.

———

NEW YORK,
November 24, 1863.

General E. D. TOWNSEND,
Assistant Adjutant-General:

SIR: In pursuance with General Orders, No. 276, War Department, Adjutant-General's Office, Washington, D. C., August 8, 1863, I have the honor to make the following report:

I was returning on the steamer Fulton from Hilton Head, S. C., with a conscript guard of 6 officers and 25 enlisted men, and being the senior officer on board was put in command of the troops on board the vessel. I immediately put my guard under order and attended to the proper care of the vessel. Everything passed off quietly until about 7.30 a. m., November 20, when the pilot at the masthead reported a vessel in sight which looked to him like a blockade runner. The captain of the Fulton (Watton) immediately ordered chase to be given. Upon arriving nearer we found her to be a side-wheel steamer with two smoke-stacks and burning soft coal. She was endeavoring to get away from us, and steamed up accordingly. At 9 a. m. we were still gaining upon her, and being within range of the rifle gun on board, the captain of the Fulton ordered the gunners to open fire. Our first shot fell short, but the next two told upon her, one striking her forward, and the other just aft. She then rounded to and Captain Watton detailed Lieut. George W. Darling, First Rhode Island Cavalry, and 12 enlisted men, who were of my guard, to board the vessel as prize crew; these with the chief officer, Mr. A. M. Walker, of the Fulton, and 16 seamen, composed the boarding party, and under their command the prize was placed. She proved to be the steamer Banshee, blockade runner, with general cargo, bound to Wilmington, N. C., from Nassau, this being her fifth trip this season. She is about 200 feet long, 20 wide, and 12 deep, and draws when fully laden only 8 feet of water, and is about 700 tons burden.

When the vessel first appeared in sight, 7.30 a. m., she was the only one to be seen. At about 8 a. m. a boat appeared upon our port beam, which proved to be the side-wheel steamer Delaware, from Stone Inlet to Baltimore. We soon left her far astern and following to see the chase. At 8.30 a. m. we descried upon our port beam and steering southward the U. S. gunboat Grand Gulf, Commander G. M. Ransom. She seeing our chase put on a heavy head of steam and commenced firing at it, but her shots fell far short, and she soon proved to be no match for the Fulton and her guns. We soon left both boats far astern, and when (after we had captured the prize and we had our prize crew on board the Banshee) the Grand Gulf came up and offered to board her, the crew of the Grand Gulf were refused admittance on board the prize and politely referred to the commander of the Fulton. The officers of the Grand Gulf then offered a prize crew, which was very respectfully declined by Captain Watton. This is a prize taken by the Fulton, and she alone.

This proves the speed, safety, and superiority of the Fulton as a steamship, also the faithfulness, courage, and patriotism of her officers and men. The crew of the Banshee were transferred to the Fulton and I had them guarded until I arrived in New York; there I transferred them to the provost-marshal.

All the above I have the honor to submit for your approval.

JAMES E. BAILEY,
Major, Third Rhode Island Artillery.

SPECIAL ORDERS, }   WAR DEPT., ADJT. GENERAL'S OFFICE,
No. 522.   }   *Washington, November 24, 1863.*
*   *   *   *   *   *

XXIII. By direction of the President, so much of Special Orders, No. 445, of October 5, 1863, from this office, as accepts the resignation of Brig. Gen. William Harrow, U. S. Volunteers, is hereby revoked. General Harrow will report immediately in person for duty to Major-General Meade, commanding Army of the Potomac.
*   *   *   *   *   *

By order of the Secretary of War:

E. D. TOWNSEND,
Assistant Adjutant-General.

HEADQUARTERS SECOND ARMY CORPS,
November 25, 1863.

Major-General HUMPHREYS, *Chief of Staff:*

The roads south of Mountain Run are now in a fair condition, needing only occasional repairs. My bridges across Mountain Run are finished, and I have a force working on the roads between here and Brandy Station, which is very bad now from being used during the rain. Those who have the advance in any movement now will be able to move much faster than those who follow them when there is no enemy to oppose.

G. K. WARREN,
Major-General.

HEADQUARTERS ARMY OF THE POTOMAC,
November 25, 1863—10.30 a. m.

Major-General FRENCH,
Commanding Third Corps:

The commanding general desires that you will have the roads examined, and report the condition to these headquarters as soon as practicable.

A. A. HUMPHREYS,
Major-General, and Chief of Staff.

HEADQUARTERS ARMY OF THE POTOMAC,
November 25, 1863—8.15 p. m.

Major-General FRENCH,
Commanding Third Corps:

I am instructed by the major-general commanding to say that in the event of the passage of the Rapidan being disputed, you will co-operate with General Warren by first forcing a passage at Jacobs' Mills, and then directing your operations so as to aid in forcing the passage at Germanna Ford.

Very respectfully, your obedient servant,

A. A. HUMPHREYS,
Major-General, and Chief of Staff.

HEADQUARTERS THIRD ARMY CORPS,
November 25, 1863—8.45 p. m.

Major-General HUMPHREYS,
Chief of Staff, Army of the Potomac:

GENERAL: Your note of 8.15 is just received. I will lose no time in crossing at the point assigned to me. My success, if I am first over, will be attributable to advantages of ground on this side of the Rapidan, of which I will make myself aware early to-morrow.

I am, sir, very respectfully, yours,

WM. H. FRENCH,
Major-General of Volunteers.

HEADQUARTERS THIRD ARMY CORPS,
November 25, 1863.

Lieut. Col. O. H. HART,
Asst. Adjt. Gen., Third Army Corps:

COLONEL: I have the honor to report the condition of the roads between Brandy Station and Jacobs' Ford as follows:

Upon arriving within one-half mile of Mountain Run the road is muddy and deep to the run. The ford is good, and about 2 feet deep. After passing the house of J. Turner, about one-eighth mile, the road is very bad through 1 mile of forest. The road from Germanna plank road to Jacobs' Ford, about 1¼ miles, is bad, and needs repair. The remainder of the road is practicable for artillery and trains.

Very respectfully, your obedient servant,

SAMUEL ALEXANDER,
Acting Engineer.

[Indorsement.]

HEADQUARTERS THIRD ARMY CORPS,
November 25, 1863.

Respectfully transmitted.

This report will give a good general idea of the practicability of the road. Alexander is a man to be relied on.

WM. H. FRENCH,
Major-General.

HDQRS. SECOND DIVISION, THIRD ARMY CORPS,
November 25, 1863.

Lieut. Col. O. H. HART,
Assistant Adjutant-General, Third Corps:

COLONEL: I have had the road examined to the plank road which goes to Germanna Ford.

The road from the position of my division to Ross' Mills is entirely different from that direct from Brandy Station. From here it is in passable condition. From Ross' to Turner's, three-fourths of a mile: Good.

Thence to a main road, 1⅓ miles: Two deep holes, easily repaired.

Along that main road to Madden's, 2½ miles: Good.

At Madden's take right hand for 2 miles to forks: Half dozen bad places.

At forks take right hand to plank road, 2 miles: Good.

Follow plank road 400 yards and take right-hand road, which is not good, but which leads to Jacobs' Ford in 1¼ miles.*

The officer sent by me reconnoitered as far as where the track to Jacobs' Ford leaves the plank road.

Very respectfully, your obedient servant,

HENRY PRINCE,
Brigadier-General of Volunteers, Commanding.

P. S.—The officer rode to Jacobs' Mills and talked with the miller, who says that this evening, by a mark which he knows, the water at the ford is half way up a horse's side, and too deep for men to ford. The cavalry pickets of the enemy were on the other side.

[Indorsement.]

HEADQUARTERS THIRD ARMY CORPS,
November 25, 1863—10.10 p. m.

This report is in accordance with instructions received by me from headquarters Army of the Potomac of this date, and is respectfully furnished.

WM. H. FRENCH,
Major-General of Volunteers.

———

HEADQUARTERS ARMY OF THE POTOMAC,
November 25, 1863—9.30 p. m.

Major-General FRENCH,
Commanding Third Corps:

The report of General Prince upon the road received. That is not the route prescribed, and if taken will interfere with the Second Corps.

A. A. HUMPHREYS,
Major-General, Chief of Staff.

———

HEADQUARTERS ARMY OF THE POTOMAC,
November 25, 1863—8.45 p. m.

Commanding Officer *Third Corps:*

The major-general commanding directs that the wagons containing the intrenching tools accompany each corps, and cross the river with them.

A. A. HUMPHREYS,
Major-General, and Chief of Staff.

———

* For sketch, see p. 932.

HEADQUARTERS FIFTH CORPS,
November 25, [1863]—6 p. m.

General HUMPHREYS,
    Chief of Staff:

I received your dispatch to examine the road at 3 p. m. The officers sent on that duty have just returned, and I forward their reports.* The main road is reported good, the side and cross roads not. In any low country I should fear for the condition of the roads.

    Yours, very respectfully,

GEO. SYKES,
Major-General, Commanding.

[Inclosure.]

HDQRS. ARTILLERY BRIGADE, FIFTH ARMY CORPS,
November 25, 1863.

Lieut. Col. FRED. T. LOCKE,
    Assistant Adjutant-General:

COLONEL: I have the honor to report that I have examined the roads, as directed, in the direction of Richardsville, to within about 2 miles of that place. The road from the present camp, which was taken yesterday, is very soft and bad in many places, until we strike the Stevensburg road, after which the road was very good to within about 2 miles of Richardsville, and was reported by the cavalry to be in passable condition to the river. It would be very difficult moving the artillery from our present camp to the main road, which is about 3 miles, in the present condition of the ground.

    Very respectfully, your obedient servant,

A. P. MARTIN,
Captain, Commanding Artillery Brigade.

HDQRS. THIRD DIVISION, CAVALRY CORPS, A. P.,
November 25, 1863—11 a. m.

Col. C. ROSS SMITH, Chief of Staff:

The officer I sent to Germanna Ford at daylight this morning has just returned. He reports that no change has been made in the number or position of the enemy's troops on the opposite bank of the river. The enemy were engaged in throwing up two small rifle-pits near Germanna Ford. They exhibit their usual watchfulness along the river. Their pickets, both infantry and artillery, are relieved regularly at 9 a. m. daily.

    Very respectfully, &c.,

G. A. CUSTER,
Brigadier-General, Comdg. Third Division.

HDQRS. CAVALRY CORPS, ARMY OF THE POTOMAC,
November 25, 1863.

Major-General PLEASONTON,
    Comdg. Cavalry Corps, Army of the Potomac:

GENERAL: I have the honor to report having proceeded from Stevensburg to Ely's Ford, and finding the roads in that vicinity in

---

* Only Martin's report found.

excellent condition considering the unfavorable weather. The mud caused by the rain did not extend but a few inches below the surface, and could not, in my opinion, impede the passage of artillery or wagons over the good, hard bed found underneath.

I have the honor to remain, sir, very respectfully, your obedient servant,

D. J. HYNES,
Captain, Eighth Illinois Cavalry, A. A. D. C.

[Indorsement.]

HEADQUARTERS CAVALRY CORPS,
November 25, 1863—4.45 p. m.

Respectfully forwarded.

Captain Hynes saw the road after the pontoon train had passed over it and considered it still a good road. He returned from General Gregg last night.

A. PLEASONTON,
Major-General, Commanding.

CIRCULAR.]   HEADQUARTERS ARMY OF THE POTOMAC,
November 25, 1863—8 p. m.

Corps and other independent commanders will have their respective commands in readiness to march at 6 a. m. to-morrow. Further orders will be given at 5 a. m. or earlier.

Please acknowledge.

By command of Major-General Meade:

S. WILLIAMS,
Assistant Adjutant-General.

(To corps commanders.)

ARTILLERY HDQRS., ARMY OF THE POTOMAC,
November 25, 1863—9 p. m.

Brigadier-General TYLER,
Chief of Artillery Corps:

In addition to the ammunition in the chests, 100 rounds per gun will be taken with the batteries of Napoleon guns across the river. The remainder of the ammunition in wagons will be parked near the crossing as ordered.

By command of General Meade:

HENRY J. HUNT,
Brigadier-General, Chief of Artillery.

HEADQUARTERS ARMY OF THE POTOMAC,
November 25, 1863.

Major-General WARREN,
Commanding Second Corps:

The following telegram has just been received. The commanding general desires it to be announced to the troops in the morning before they march.

S. WILLIAMS,
Assistant Adjutant-General.

[Inclosure.]

WASHINGTON, D. C.,
November 25, 1863.

Major-General MEADE:

A great battle has been fought to-day at Chattanooga and our troops were victorious. Thomas took Missionary Ridge by a magnificent charge, and Hooker has penetrated to the rear of the rebels at Rossville, thus placing them between two fires. Telegram from Willcox says courier from Burnside reports thirty days' provisions in Knoxville, and army in good spirits and abundantly strong to resist an attack.

P. H. WATSON.

P. S.—Since writing the above the following is received:

[Sub-inclosure.]

CHATTANOOGA,
November 25, 1863.

Although the battle lasted from early dawn until this evening, I believe I am not premature in announcing a complete victory over Bragg. Lookout Mountain top, all the rifle-pits in Chattanooga Valley, and Missionary Ridge all entirely carried and now held by us. I have no idea of finding Bragg to-morrow.

GRANT.

GENERAL ORDERS, }   HDQRS. DEPT. OF VA. AND N. C.,
No. 38.   }   *Fort Monroe, Va., November 25, 1863.*

All permits for the shipment of goods issued prior to the 15th instant, are hereby rescinded.

By command of Major-General Butler:

R. S. DAVIS,
Major, and Assistant Adjutant-General.

CIRCULAR.]   HEADQUARTERS ARMY OF THE POTOMAC,
November 26, 1863—4 a. m.

The commanding general directs that you move with your command at 6 a. m., as directed in the circular from these headquarters, dated the 23d instant, a copy of which has been furnished you.*

Please acknowledge.

By command of Major-General Meade:

S. WILLIAMS,
Assistant Adjutant-General.

(Sent to Generals French, Newton, Sedgwick, Sykes, and Warren.)

* See p. 480.

HEADQUARTERS ARMY OF THE POTOMAC,
November 27 [26], 1863.
Major-General FRENCH, *Commanding Third Corps:*

The commanding general directs that you move with your command as directed in the circular from these headquarters, dated the 23d instant, a copy of which has been furnished you.*

Please acknowledge.

S. WILLIAMS,
Assistant Adjutant-General.

HEADQUARTERS SECOND CORPS,
November 26, 1863.
General WILLIAMS, *Assistant Adjutant-General:*

Your dispatch ordering the corps to move as before directed received. All the preparations have been made.

G. K. WARREN,
Major-General.

HEADQUARTERS FIFTH ARMY CORPS,
November 26, 1863—12 m.
General HUMPHREYS, *Chief of Staff:*

I have a regiment of infantry and a squad of cavalry over the Rapidan. The bridge will be completed in a few moments. About two regiments of rebel horse passed across my front coming from the direction of Ely's Ford. Gregg has crossed at that point. Only a few cavalry pickets were at this ford.

Respectfully,

GEO. SYKES,
Major-General.

[P. S.]—I shall move on as soon as the bridge is finished.

HEADQUARTERS FIFTH ARMY CORPS,
November 26, 1863—12.20 p. m.
General HUMPHREYS, *Chief of Staff:*

Your dispatch (10.30 a. m.) has just reached me. I have already a division over the river. I shall halt, pursuant to your orders, until I hear from you.

Respectfully.

GEO. SYKES,
Major-General, Commanding.

HEADQUARTERS ARMY OF THE POTOMAC,
Germanna Ford, November 26, 1863—1 p. m.
Major-General FRENCH, *Commanding Third Corps:*

The major-general commanding directs me to inform you that General Warren has crossed his cavalry and meets no opposition.

---

*This is dispatch as recorded in Third Army Corps files, and upon it is noted: "Received 26th instant, at 5.25, headquarters time; 5.45 a. m., our time. Copies sent to everybody at 6 a. m., our time."

He directs that you throw your bridge immediately, and cross without delay. I am also directed to say that your delay in reaching the river has retarded the operations of General Warren more than two hours, and that this delay calls for explanation.

A. A. HUMPHREYS,
Major-General, Chief of Staff.

HEADQUARTERS THIRD ARMY CORPS,
November 26, 1863.

Major-General HUMPHREYS :

In reply to your note, besides the fact that General Prince is very slow, the distance to this ford from my camp is 4 miles farther than General Warren's, who, I believe, was up to Mountain Run. I can easily explain the delay on these two grounds. I have been on the ground for over an hour, endeavoring to urge the leading division.
Respectfully,

WM. H. FRENCH,
Major-General, Commanding.

HEADQUARTERS THIRD ARMY CORPS,
November 26, 1863—1 p. m.

Major-General HUMPHREYS,
Chief of Staff:

GENERAL : General Prince has just concluded his arrangements for launching the pontoons.
Respectfully,

WM. H. FRENCH,
Major-General, Commanding.

HEADQUARTERS THIRD ARMY CORPS,
November 26, 1863—2.30 p. m.

Major-General HUMPHREYS,
Chief of Staff:

My infantry is across the river, and driving the enemy's pickets.

WM. H. FRENCH,
Major-General, Commanding.

HEADQUARTERS FIFTH ARMY CORPS,
November 26, 1863—2.15 p. m.

General HUMPHREYS,
Chief of Staff:

GENERAL : I will cross the remainder of my command at once, and move on toward Parker's Store. Captain Cavada tells me that Warren has not yet crossed. I suppose he will have done so by this time. I cannot communicate with him unless he does. Gregg is on my left. My headquarters will probably be near the rear center of my command. I will endeavor to inform you more minutely when I reach there. It will be very late before the rear of my command gets to its bivouac, and I doubt whether Newton will be able to get more than over the river.

Respectfully,

GEO. SYKES,
Major-General.

HEADQUARTERS ARMY OF THE POTOMAC,
Germanna Ford, November 26, 1863—3 p. m.

Major-General FRENCH, *Commanding Third Corps:*

I am instructed to say that General Sedgwick was so much delayed by being obliged to halt at Brandy Station until the Third Corps had cleared the way, and subsequently by the artillery of that corps being stuck at the crossing of Mountain Run, that he will probably not be able to reach Jacobs' Ford before night. You will not move forward from the river farther than to clear the way for him until he comes up and crosses.

A. A. HUMPHREYS,
Major-General, and Chief of Staff.

HEADQUARTERS THIRD ARMY CORPS,
November 26, 1863.

Major-General HUMPHREYS:

There was nothing at the run to stop the batteries. The head of my rear division was within a mile of the ford by 2 p. m.

WM. H. FRENCH,
Major-General.

HEADQUARTERS THIRD ARMY CORPS,
November 26, 1863—2 p. m.

General HUMPHREYS, *Chief of Staff:*

My troops are crossing rapidly. The road on the south side is impracticable for artillery. Captain Turnbull can do nothing for it.

Respectfully,

WM. H. FRENCH,
Major-General.

JACOBS' MILLS,
November 26, [1863]—4 p. m.

Maj. J. C. DUANE, *U. S. Engineers:*

The crossing here is bad, except for infantry. There is a very steep hill on opposite side. Artillery can only get up by doubling teams, and it is difficult then. Road will ·be impassable on this side if it should rain. I have all seven boats and one trestle in the bridge. I have spoken to General French and advised that all artillery should go by Germanna. It is the worst place I have seen for a pontoon bridge. The Third Corps is now crossing.

CHAS. N. TURNBULL,
Captain of Engineers.

HEADQUARTERS,
November 26, 1863—4.30 p. m.

Major-General FRENCH,
　　Commanding Third Corps:

Send your artillery to cross at Germanna. The road is bad here, but the artillery has crossed. Your artillery can join you by a branch road leading from Germanna plank road, about 1½ miles from the ford. General Warren will encamp at Flat Run Church on plank road. Move forward on your route so as to admit of Sedgwick's crossing and halting for the night.

Send strong working party in at once to put the road in order leading from Germanna plank road to you. Mr. McGee, a guide, is sent to you. He professes to know the road from Jacobs' Ford to Robertson's Tavern. Your pickets should connect with Warren's.

　　　　　A. A. HUMPHREYS,
　　　　　Major-General, and Chief of Staff.

HEADQUARTERS ARMY OF THE POTOMAC,
November 26, 1863.

Major-General FRENCH,
　　Commanding Third Corps:

Send an officer in advance of your artillery to examine the road which it will take until it rejoins you.

By order:

　　　　　A. A. HUMPHREYS,
　　　　　Major-General, Chief of Staff.

HEADQUARTERS THIRD ARMY CORPS,
November 26, 1863—6.30 p. m.

Major-General HUMPHREYS,
　　Chief of Staff:

General Prince got on the wrong road and had to retrograde. His head of column came upon the enemy's cavalry pickets, and had a small skirmish. The guide you sent has joined General Prince.

Respectfully,

　　　　　WM. H. FRENCH,
　　　　　Major-General.

HEADQUARTERS FIRST CORPS,
November 26, 1863—7 p. m.

Major-General HUMPHREYS,
　　Chief of Staff, Army of the Potomac:

One-half of my infantry is just across the river; the remainder and the artillery will encamp on the other side (north). I propose moving on at 3 a. m. to-morrow.

　　　　　JOHN NEWTON,
　　　　　Major-General.

HEADQUARTERS THIRD ARMY CORPS,
November 26, 1863—8 p. m.

Major-General HUMPHREYS, *Chief of Staff:*

My left is 2 miles, and I picket a mile beyond. I have sent an aide with a citizen, who will show the artillery the river road from Germanna, on this side.

Respectfully,

WM. H. FRENCH,
Major-General, Commanding.

P. S.—The bridge cannot be taken up to-night, as the Sixth Corps will be passing.

GENERAL ORDERS, } HDQRS. 18TH A. C., DEPT. VA. AND N. C.,
No. 39.   }   *Fort Monroe, Va., November 26, 1863.*

Hereafter no permits for trade within this department will be valid, unless the same shall have been approved at these head-quarters for the District of Virginia, or by the commanding officer of the District of North Carolina for said last-named district.

By command of Major-General Butler:

R. S. DAVIS,
Major, and Assistant Adjutant-General.

GENERAL ORDERS, } HDQRS. 18TH A. C., DEPT. VA. AND N. C.,
No. 40.   }   *Fort Monroe, Va., November 26, 1863.*

Already large expenses are thrown upon the military within this department, by the numerous applications for requests for permits for imports and exports, and for passports and other permits, for the payment of which no appropriate means have been provided ; and whereas there is no good reason existing why such expenses should not be borne by the persons and property benefited thereby, it is ordered : That all persons hereafter applying for a request for a permit to import into or export from this department shall pay at the rate of 1 per cent. upon the invoice value; that for every pass-port issued there shall be paid the sum of $1; that for every permit granted to any vessel to enter or trade in this department there shall be paid the sum of $3; that all the foregoing fees are to be paid to and received by the provost-marshals, to constitute a provost fund, to meet expenses.

By command of Major-General Butler:

R. S. DAVIS,
Major, and Assistant Adjutant-General.

GENERAL ORDERS, } HDQRS. 18TH A. C., DEPT. VA. AND N. C.,
No. 41.   }   *Fort Monroe, Va., November 26, 1863.*

The following is the staff of Maj. Gen. B. F. Butler as com-pleted :

Col. J. Wilson Shaffer, aide-de-camp, chief of staff.

Col. H. C. Lee, Twenty-seventh Massachusetts Volunteers, pro-vost-marshal-general.

Lieut. Col. Herman Biggs, chief quartermaster.

Lieut. Col. J. McL. Taylor, chief commissary.

Lieut. Col. George A. Kensel, assistant inspector-general.

Lieut. Col. R. V. W. Howard, inspector of artillery.
Maj. R. S. Davis, assistant adjutant-general.
Surg. Charles McCormick, medical director.
Lieut. Col. J. B. Kinsman, aide-de-camp.
Maj. J. M. Bell, aide-de-camp.
Maj. Peter Haggerty, aide-de-camp.
Maj. J. L. Stackpole, judge-advocate.
Capt. William Cogswell, commissary of musters.
Capt. F. U. Farquhar, chief engineer.
Capt. A. F. Puffer, aide-de-camp.
Capt. H. C. Clarke, aide-de-camp.
Lieut. Jasper Myers, chief of ordnance.
Lieut. Frederick Martin, volunteer aide-de-camp.
By command of Maj. Gen. B. F. Butler :

R. S. DAVIS,
Major, and Assistant Adjutant-General.

WAR DEPARTMENT,
Washington, November 27, 1863—12 m.

Major-General MEADE, Army of the Potomac:

General Grant's operations to-day will probably cut Longstreet's line of communication with Bragg. If Burnside holds his position at Knoxville a few days longer, Longstreet will be obliged to retire up the line of the Virginia and Tennessee Railroad, to rejoin Lee. If the Army of the Potomac does not act soon, it may find Lee re-enforced by Longstreet's army.

H. W. HALLECK,
General-in-Chief.

CIRCULAR.]   HEADQUARTERS ARMY OF THE POTOMAC,
November 27, 1863—12.15 a. m.

The following movements of troops are ordered for to-day, November 27:

1. Second Corps, Major-General Warren, will move at 7 a. m. along the turnpike to Old Verdierville.

2. Third Corps, Major-General French, will move at 7 a. m. on the Robertson's Tavern road, and close up on the Second Corps.

3. Fifth Corps, Major-General Sykes, will move at 7 a. m. to New Verdierville.

4. First Corps, Major-General Newton, will move not later than 7 a. m. on the route of the Fifth Corps, and close up on the Fifth Corps.

5. Sixth Corps, Major-General Sedgwick, will move as soon as the Third Corps has cleared the road, and, as his artillery, &c., has joined him, close up on the Third Corps. One division of the Sixth Corps will remain near the river until the trains have crossed at Germanna and the bridges are taken up.

6. The ammunition trains, ambulances, &c., directed to remain on the north bank of the river, will cross and join their corps; those of the Second, Third, and Sixth Corps at Germanna; those of the Fifth and First at Culpeper Ford.

7. Reserve Artillery will cross at Germanna, follow the route of the Second Corps, and halt before reaching Robertson's Tavern, so as not to interfere with the march of the Third Corps.

8. The chief of cavalry will direct a force of that arm to move in advance on the roads in front of the army.

9. The trains, under the direction of the chief quartermaster of the army, will cross at Culpeper and Ely's Fords, and be parked in rear of the army. They will be guarded by Merritt's cavalry division.

9½. Commanders of leading corps will keep up communication with each other, and with the corps in their rear; those of the rear corps with the corps in front. The flank next the enemy will be carefully watched, and the usual precautions against approach will be taken. The commanding general will be kept advised of everything that occurs.

10. Headquarters will be at Robertson's Tavern.

By command of Major-General Meade:

S. WILLIAMS,
Assistant Adjutant-General.

WARREN'S HEADQUARTERS,
November 27, 1863.

Major-General HUMPHREYS:

The road I have had prepared will, I think, enable our ammunition trains and Reserve Artillery to pass up the hill opposite Germanna Ford. It turns to the left, crosses a bad little stream on a good bridge, gains the plateau by a side-hill location (on old road, passes near an old house); thence toward the right of the pine woods, enters the woods, and joins the plank road. It is all the way an old road, and needs now only to dig down the rebel breastworks across it, which is but a moment's work. Tell General Tyler to take a look at it. (See sketch.)

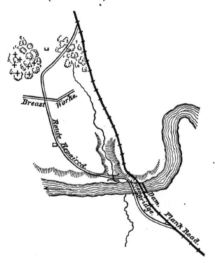

I do not know whether or not to use this route would take Generals French's and Sedgwick's batteries out of the way. I think not, if they moved by daylight, so as not to get lost.

No other news. Lieutenant Matthews brings this and awaits orders.

　　Yours, &c.,
　　　　　　　　　　　G. K. WARREN,
　　　　　　　　　　　　　　Major-General.

　　　　　　　　HEADQUARTERS THIRD ARMY CORPS,
　　　Jacobs' Mills Ford, November 27, 1863—5.45 a. m.

Brigadier-General CARR,
　　　Commanding Third Division:

GENERAL: You will move your division forward as soon as General Prince's division shall have moved; you will keep well closed up on the Second Division. You will look well to your right flank, throwing a strong flanking party well out.

By command of Major-General French:
　　　　　　　　　　　O. H. HART,
　　　Lieutenant-Colonel, and Assistant Adjutant-General.

　　　　　　　　HEADQUARTERS THIRD ARMY CORPS,
　　　　　　　　　November 27, 1863—7 a. m.

Major-General HUMPHREYS:

But one battery has come in; the others are on the road. They have been working twenty-four hours and have had no feed. Captain Randolph reports the horses fagged out. One battery goes with my head of column.

　　Respectfully, .
　　　　　　　　　　　WM. H. FRENCH,
　　　　　　　　　Major-General of Volunteers.

[P. S.]—General Prince reports seeing troops moving over a ridge toward Verdierville during the night. He watched them passing an hour and a half.

　　　　　HDQRS. EN ROUTE FROM JACOBS' MILLS,
　　　　　　　　November 27, 1863—7.05 a. m.

Brigadier-General PRINCE,
　　　Commanding Second Division:

GENERAL: If you require at any time on your advance re-enforcements, you will call upon General Carr for them, who is authorized to supply them, if necessary.

By command of Major-General French:
　　　　　　　　　　　O. H. HART,
　　　Lieut. Col., and Assistant Adjutant-General.

P. S.—Show this to General Carr.

HEADQUARTERS ARMY OF THE POTOMAC,
November 27, 1863—7.30 a. m.   (Received 1 p. m.)

General BENHAM,
        Commanding Engineers:

The major-general commanding directs that you hold your bridge
trains in readiness to move by water and land at a moment's notice.
They should be got in the same stage of readiness ordered in a previous communication about four weeks ago, which order was countermanded.   No further instructions can be sent until the order for
you to move is issued.

                    A. A. HUMPHREYS,
                            Chief of Staff.

HEADQUARTERS THIRD ARMY CORPS,
November 27, 1863—9.20 a. m.

Major-General HUMPHREYS:

The head of my column is near the plank road, and waiting for
General Warren.
        Respectfully, &c.,

                    WM. H. FRENCH,
                    Major-General of Volunteers.

[P. S.]—A few cavalry pickets appeared on my flank, and after
firing a few shots retired.

HEADQUARTERS FIFTH ARMY CORPS,
November 27, 1863—9.30 a. m.

General HUMPHREYS:

My command reached Parker's Store at 9 o'clock.   There Gregg's
cavalry came in.   In order that he may go on toward Orange Court-
House, I have been compelled to halt to give him the road.   He
thinks Hampton's horse has gone back to Spotsylvania Court-
House.   I have seen some few rebel vedettes only, and get no information.   I had to repair a bridge, which delayed me a little.   I have
heard nothing of Warren.   I shall go on to New Verdierville as
soon as the road is open.

                    GEO. SYKES,
                            Major-General.

HEADQUARTERS THIRD ARMY CORPS,
November 27, 1863—10 a. m.

Major-General FRENCH:

GENERAL: General Prince's reconnoitering party has returned,
having communicated with General Warren.   General Warren sent
General Prince word that he understood his position.   General
Prince has withdrawn all his cavalry except 10 men, the enemy
having developed a pretty strong force of cavalry.

                    JNO. M. NORVELL,
                    Assistant Adjutant-General.

HEADQUARTERS THIRD ARMY CORPS,
November 27, 1863—10.30 a. m.

Generals CARR and BIRNEY:

Look out well for your right flank. Guard against the approach of the enemy; we are near them. Throw your flankers well out, and make them strong.

By command of Major-General French:

O. H. HART,
Lieutenant-Colonel, and Assistant Adjutant-General.

HEADQUARTERS SECOND DIVISION,
November 27, 1863.

Col. O. H. HART:

I have ordered the only remaining brigade of my division to occupy the place of the brigade of the Sixth Corps just withdrawn. Our line is very thin. Colonel Brewster reports that the enemy are placing a battery in front.

Very respectfully, your obedient servant,

HENRY PRINCE,
By WILLIAMS.

HEADQUARTERS SECOND CORPS,
November 27, 1863—11 a. m.

[General HUMPHREYS:]

GENERAL: The Fifth Corps is in sight moving up on my left. As soon as I get communication with General French, I intend to move forward and attack. Some musketry and one cannon shot has been heard in front of the Fifth Corps. Slight skirmishing in front of mine. We have possession of a road coming in from General French, besides the forks of a road leading from Raccoon Ford.

G. K. WARREN,
Major-General.

HEADQUARTERS ARMY OF THE POTOMAC,
Near Robertson's Tavern, November 27, 1863—11 a. m.

Major-General FRENCH,
Commanding Third Corps:

General Warren is at Robertson's Tavern, with a considerable force of the enemy in his front. The major-general commanding directs that you move forward as promptly as possible, and send word to General Sedgwick.

A. A. HUMPHREYS,
Major-General, and Chief of Staff.

HEADQUARTERS ARMY OF THE POTOMAC,
November 27, 1863—11.30 a. m.

Major-General FRENCH:

The major-general commanding directs me to inform you that General Warren has met the enemy in strong force—two divisions—

at Robertson's Tavern, and directs that you move forward as rapidly
as oss e to Robertson's Tavern. Communicate this to General
Sedgwick, who is to keep close on you.

A. A. HUMPHREYS,
Major-General, Chief of Staff.

[P. S.]—If you cannot unite with General Warren by the route
you are on, you must move through to him by the left. It is highly
important you should unite with Warren at once.

HEADQUARTERS THIRD ARMY CORPS,
November 27, 1863.

General WARREN:

I am at the junction of the road striking the Raccoon Ford road.
The enemy are moving on my right and toward you. My line of
battle is being made accordingly.
    Communicate to General Meade.
        Respectfully,

WM. H. FRENCH.

HEADQUARTERS THIRD ARMY CORPS,
November 27, 1863.

Major-General SEDGWICK:

General Humphreys desires me to communicate to you that General Warren is engaged with the enemy. I am ordered to go straight
to Robertson's Tavern and communicate with you.

WM. H. FRENCH,
Major-General.

HEADQUARTERS ARMY OF THE POTOMAC,
November 27, 1863—11.30 a. m.

Major-General FRENCH,
    Commanding Third Corps:

Your dispatch of 9.20 is received. What are you waiting for? No
orders have been sent you to wait for General Warren anywhere
upon your route. Robertson's Tavern is the point where he takes
precedence and he is there now engaged with the enemy who are in
strong force. He is waiting for you. The commanding general
directs that you move forward as rapidly as possible to Robertson's
Tavern, where your corps is wanted.

A. A. HUMPHREYS,
Major-General, Chief of Staff.

[P. S.]—Headquarters are on turnpike, 1 mile in rear of Robertson's Tavern. Acknowledge the receipt of this communication as
soon as received.

HEADQUARTERS THIRD ARMY CORPS,
November 27, 1863—11.45 a. m.

Major-General HUMPHREYS,
    Chief of Staff:

General Prince reports from Captain Ford, commanding cavalry, that the enemy are throwing out a large force of infantry upon my right flank on the Raccoon Ford road. I am making dispositions accordingly.

WM. H. FRENCH,
Major-General.

———

HEADQUARTERS FIFTH ARMY CORPS,
November 27, 1863—12.15 p. m.

[Maj. Gen. A. A. HUMPHREYS,
    Chief of Staff:]

GENERAL: The head of my column has not yet reached the point where the Raccoon Ford road intersects the Orange and Fredericksburg plank road. I wrote that the head of the Fifth Corps and the head of Gregg's cavalry met at Parker's Store. Gregg has been skirmishing with the enemy some time, and his progress is slow. I will not move beyond the road running from this one to Robertson's Tavern until I hear from you, as there is no other going to the pike laid down on the map ahead of where I now am.

Gregg, at last accounts, was skirmishing with cavalry. They opened with artillery, also a few shell. Ought he to push beyond Verdierville, if he can get there, and shall I go there, if the road is open to that point?

Respectfully,

GEO. SYKES,
Major-General.

———

HEADQUARTERS ARMY OF THE POTOMAC,
November 27, 1863—1.45 p. m.

Major-General FRENCH,
    Commanding Third Corps:

Your dispatch of 11.45 is received. The major-general commanding directs that you attack the enemy in your front immediately, throwing your left forward so as to connect with General Warren at Robertson's Tavern. The object of the attack is to form a junction with General Warren, which must be effected immediately.

A. A. HUMPHREYS,
Major-General, Chief of Staff.

———

HEADQUARTERS THIRD ARMY CORPS,
November 27, 1863.

Major-General HUMPHREYS:

I had only halted to find the road, and depended upon the reports of the division commanders, assisted as well as my staff could. The map was wrong, and I found it necessary to meet the enemy, who was only 2½ miles from my flank, on the Raccoon Ford road. I have shown Captain Michler the position, and to make the march indi-

cated on your map requires this line to be held strong.   To move on
the only road to the cross-roads to Robertson's Tavern involves an
exposure of flank and rear not anticipated.   Your last order is received, and I will order an advance by the Raccoon Ford road.

WM. H. FRENCH,
Major-General.

NOVEMBER 27, [1863]—2.30 p. m.

General HUMPHREYS :
   I am making an advance with skirmishers, only to better my position and to prevent troops being formed too near it.   The enemy's
thin line falls back along the road to Verdierville.

G. K. WARREN,
Major-General.

HEADQUARTERS THIRD ARMY CORPS,
November 27, 1863—3.15 p. m.

Brigadier-General CARR,
   Commanding Third Division:
   GENERAL : You will move your division up at once, and take
position on the left of General Prince's division.   You will form in
compliance with orders already received from major-general commanding.   Let there be no delay in the movement.

By command of Major-General French :

O. H. HART,
Lieutenant-Colonel, and Assistant Adjutant-General.

HEADQUARTERS THIRD ARMY CORPS,
November 27, 1863—3.30 p. m.

Major-General BIRNEY,
   Commanding First Division:
   GENERAL: You will move your command up at once to the position vacated by General Carr, and hold it in readiness to support
the line.

[By command of Major-General French :

O. H. HART,
Lieut. Col and Assistant Adjutant-General.]

NOVEMBER 27, 1863—3.45 p. m.

[Major-General BIRNEY ?] :
   GENERAL: You will move up on the left to the house occupied by
the major-general commanding for headquarters into the woods, and
form line 300 yards in rear of the line of battle, as supports.

By command of Major-General French:

O. H. HART,
Lieutenant-Colonel, and Assistant Adjutant-General.

NOVEMBER 27, [1863]—3.30 p. m.

General HUMPHREYS:
   I am getting my troops in position, but the country is densely timbered and nothing can be distinguished a hundred yards in front.   I

sent an officer on the road to Robertson's Tavern from this road, and he lost a man and a horse. Said he was fired into by infantry; is positive a small party.

I do not know whether the enemy will try to move on the Catharpin road or not. He seems to be inclining to my left, which extends across the railroad embankment. I am about 3 or 4 miles from Verdierville. The officer of mine who went to Warren reported all quiet there. I do not like the presence of infantry on the road between Warren and me. As I was directed to move cautiously beyond Parker's Store, I shall retain a defensive position until I hear from you.

I know nothing of what is taking place elsewhere. I am on the plank road beyond Parker's Store, at a church. Prisoners taken say they came from Orange Court-House this morning and belong to Heth's division. Let me hear from you by return orderly.

Respectfully,

GEO. SYKES,
Major-General.

HEADQUARTERS ARMY OF THE POTOMAC,
November 27, 1863—6 p. m.

Major-General FRENCH,
Commanding Third Corps:

The major-general commanding desires to know what progress you have made in effecting a junction with General Warren, and whether you are able to take some road leading to Robertson's Tavern instead of passing through the dense wood.

A. A. HUMPHREYS,
Major-General, and Chief of Staff.

[P. S.]—The brigade at Mitchell's should be withdrawn at once.

HEADQUARTERS THIRD ARMY CORPS,
Jacobs' Mills Ford, November 27, 1863—6 p. m.

Major-General BIRNEY,
Commanding First Division:

GENERAL: You will be in readiness to move your division forward as soon as General Carr has stretched out his division. You will keep well closed up on the Third Division, looking well to your right flank, while you will cover with a strong force of flankers thrown well out.

By command of Major-General French:

O. H. HART,
Lieutenant-Colonel, and Assistant Adjutant-General.

HEADQUARTERS THIRD ARMY CORPS,
November 27, 1863—6.15 p. m.

Major-General BIRNEY:

GENERAL: You will send out a strong picket, and direct them to be on the alert for any movement of the enemy. Exercise great caution against the movements of the enemy. Ammunition must be brought up and issued during the night. The mules can be taken from the wagons and parked if necessary.

By command of Major-General French:

O. H. HART,
Lieutenant-Colonel, and Assistant Adjutant-General.

(Same to Brigadier-Generals Prince and Carr.)

HEADQUARTERS FIFTH ARMY CORPS,
November 27, 1863—7 p. m.

General HUMPHREYS:

Your last dispatch has just reached me. My left is at the intersection of the road taken by Gregg from Ely's Ford with the Germanna plank road, at the point where I turn to the right to get on the Orange and Fredericksburg plank road. My whole command is stretched on the Germanna plank road and was before I received your dispatch. I supposed General Warren's left would probably come to where the old turnpike crossed the Germanna road, and therefore I aimed to put my right there. It, however, extends nearly the length of a division to the right in the direction of Germanna Ford.

I am literally in the wilderness; the woods admit of no formation whatever. There must be a considerable interval between my right and Warren's left, and he ought to close it the first thing in the morning. Newton cannot close it, because he would block Warren's road. Newton expects to get on this side of the river and encamp near Vaucluse Mine. Gregg has passed on in the direction of Parker's Store. I requested him to picket down the Orange and Fredericksburg plank road beyond where it meets the Germanna road. My left is 1½ miles from that intersection.

Some citizens said to one of my officers that Hood's division was in Fredericksburg. Mr. Wikoff, whom the general remembers, judges from what the rebel pickets told him that their cavalry is on a line from Hamilton's Crossing to Hanover Junction, and from the latter to Orange Court-House.

I have no position at all, and could get none in the darkness and thick of the woods. I would be glad to receive instructions for to-morrow as early as possible, for I want to get in a better country than I now am. The approaches to the river at Culpeper Ford are tolerable (with some trouble, the artillery can get along pretty well). Woods cover them on the north side—it is open the south side. The banks are of equal height, and have good command, better on the south than north. Newton's pickets cannot possibly connect with mine from his position in rear.

Respectfully,

GEO. SYKES.

HEADQUARTERS THIRD ARMY CORPS,
November 27, 1863—7.30 a. m.

[General HUMPHREYS:]

Your dispatch by Captain Mason is just received. I know of no way to connect with Warren except on an interior road in my rear. General Wright, with an escort of 12 men, has gone by that road, and will give you all the information about affairs to-day. I have lost some 200 killed and wounded, and have that many prisoners. Lee was in my front about dark with Johnson's and Rodes' divisions of Ewell's corps. If I leave this point, it gives the road to Jacobs' Ford to the enemy.

Respectfully,

WM. H. FRENCH,
Major-General.

HEADQUARTERS ARMY OF THE POTOMAC,
November 27, 1863—8.45 p. m.

Major-General FRENCH,
Commanding Third Corps:

I am instructed to say that orders are sent to General Sedgwick to move his corps immediately to Robertson's Tavern, by a route Captain Michler will point out, as the commanding general finds there is great difficulty in your doing so. You will make every effort to carry out the orders heretofore sent you to unite your left with General Warren's right near Robertson's Tavern.

A. A. HUMPHREYS,
Major-General, Chief of Staff.

[P. S.]—General Sedgwick will be posted on General Warren's right so as to aid in effecting a junction with you.

HEADQUARTERS FIRST ARMY CORPS,
November 27, 1863—9.40 [p. m.]

Major-General HUMPHREYS,
Chief of Staff, Army of the Potomac:

GENERAL: I have the honor to report my First Division and artillery in camp on the old turnpike, 1 mile in rear of your headquarters. My Second Division is encamped across the road leading from Parker's Store to Warren's left. I send this in view of any order you may have to communicate to-night.

Very respectfully,

JOHN NEWTON,
Major-General.

HDQRS. THIRD ARMY CORPS,
On the Field, November 28, 1863—2.15 a. m.

Brigadier-General CARR,
Commanding Third Division:

GENERAL: You will withdraw your troops and mass at the corner of the road near where your headquarters were yesterday before the battle. You will not withdraw the pickets until further orders.

By command of Major-General French:

O. H. HART,
Lieutenant-Colonel, and Assistant Adjutant-General.

HDQRS. THIRD ARMY CORPS, *November 28, 1863.*
                               . (Received 3.15 a. m.)
Brigadier-General CARR,
     Commanding Third Division, Third Corps:

GENERAL: You will quietly withdraw your troops from their present position and take up a position back near where your head-quarters were before you advanced yesterday afternoon. On your way down report to the general commanding in person. Commence the movement at once.

By command of Major-General French:

O. H. HART,
     Lieutenant-Colonel, and Assistant Adjutant-General.

HEADQUARTERS THIRD ARMY CORPS,
     November 28, 1863—2.25 a. m.
Major-General BIRNEY,
     Commanding First Division:

GENERAL: You will quietly withdraw your troops from their present position and mass them in the field in rear of this house, leaving your pickets undisturbed until further orders.

By command of Major-General French:

O. H. HART,
     Lieutenant-Colonel, and Assistant Adjutant-General.

HEADQUARTERS THIRD ARMY CORPS,
     November 28, 1863—2.30 a. m.
Brigadier-General PRINCE:

GENERAL: Immediately after the withdrawal of General Birney's troops, you will withdraw from your present position and mass on the road near this house. This withdrawal must be done very quietly. The pickets will remain on their present line until further orders.

By command of Major-General French:

O. H. HART,
     Lieutenant-Colonel, and Assistant Adjutant-General.

HEADQUARTERS THIRD ARMY CORPS,
     November 28, 1863—8 a. m.
Major-General HUMPHREYS:

On the withdrawal of the Sixth Corps I proceeded to take line of battle, the better to secure my line of communications on a new position, but there being no indications of the enemy in my front (he having left his dead and wounded and hospitals behind), I have come up to the rear of Sedgwick, where I am massing.

Respectfully,

WM. H. FRENCH,
     Major-General of Volunteers.

HEADQUARTERS THIRD ARMY CORPS,
Near Robertson's Tavern, November 28, 1863—9 a. m.

General BIRNEY:

You will march your division past General Carr and mass it on the right of the Sixth Corps, leaving room for General Prince between you and General Carr.

General PRINCE:

You will move your division in rear of General Birney and mass between him and General Carr.

By command of Major-General French:

O. H. HART,
Lieutenant-Colonel, and Assistant Adjutant-General.

HEADQUARTERS ARMY OF THE POTOMAC,
November 28, 1863—9.30 a. m.

Major-General FRENCH,
Commanding Third Corps:

GENERAL: Your dispatch is received. General Sedgwick is now moving forward on the old turnpike. As soon as he has cleared the road you will follow him, unless otherwise directed before then.

A. A. HUMPHREYS,
Major-General, Chief of Staff.

CIRCULAR.]   HEADQUARTERS THIRD ARMY CORPS,
November 28, 1863.

As soon as the Sixth Corps moves on so as to clear the road, General Birney (First Division) will move on, keeping closed up to the Sixth Corps trains.

General Prince (Second Division) will follow the First Division, keeping well closed up.

The Third Division will follow General Prince (Second Division), keeping well closed up.

Division commanders will issue their ammunition as soon as possible.

By command of Major-General French:

O. H. HART,
Lieutenant-Colonel, and Assistant Adjutant-General.

HEADQUARTERS ARMY OF THE POTOMAC,
November 28, 1863.

Commanding Officers of Corps:

As soon as you have taken position and examined the position of the enemy in front, you will report to the major-general commanding upon the practicability of carrying their position by assault.

By command of Major-General Meade:

A. A. HUMPHREYS,
Major-General, and Chief of Staff.

HEADQUARTERS FIRST CORPS,
November 28, 1863.

Major-General HUMPHREYS,
      Chief of Staff, Army of the Potomac:

The pickets I ordered advanced on my left report they cannot cross on account of the depth of mud and water. They also report a constant movement of the enemy toward our left.

      Very respectfully,

                              JOHN NEWTON,
                                    Major-General.

HEADQUARTERS THIRD ARMY CORPS,
November 28, 1863—1.20 p. m.

Major-General HUMPHREYS,
      Chief of Staff:

I have been through the dense woods on the left of General Newton. There is no position whatever for artillery, which is lost in the woods. Infantry could not act as well as if massed in rear of the debouch, which they could enter and follow on a dark night or morning, excepting the troops on advance duty.

I have, until informing you, placed my command on a cleared field to the rear of the left of Newton at the opening of the woods. The artillery will be posted there also. My headquarters are under a tree near a pile of rocks on the direct road from your headquarters, about 50 yards from a large barn and outhouses.

      Respectfully,

                              WM. H. FRENCH.

[P. S.]—The hills in front of my position are covered with thick growth.

HEADQUARTERS THIRD ARMY CORPS,
November 28, 1863—1.45 p. m.

Major-General BIRNEY,
      Commanding First Division:

GENERAL: You will send a working party to bridge Mine Run branch. You are also directed to send a reconnoitering party to see the position to be occupied by the corps on the heights beyond the branch at right angles with General Newton's corps.

By command of Major-General French:

                              O. H. HART,
            Lieutenant-Colonel, Assistant Adjutant-General.

HEADQUARTERS THIRD ARMY CORPS,
November 28, 1863—2 p. m.

Major-General HUMPHREYS,
      Chief of Staff:

I am having a reconnaissance made of the ground across Mine Run; also a bridge to be built, and a corduroy in the swamp. As soon as this last is made the artillery can pass.

                              WM. H. FRENCH,
                                    Major-General of Volunteers.

HEADQUARTERS THIRD ARMY CORPS,
November 28, 1863—4 p. m.

General PRINCE,
Commanding Second Division:

GENERAL: You will take up your position on the left of General Carr's division, and on a line with him. You will at once send a staff officer to reconnoiter·the position, so that there may be no delay in movement.

By command of Major-General French:
O. H. HART,
Lieutenant-Colonel, Assistant Adjutant-General.

HEADQUARTERS THIRD ARMY CORPS,
November 28, 1863—4.22 p. m.

Major-General HUMPHREYS:

I have one division in position on the ground across Mine [Run] branch. The remainder of the corps is in motion.

WM. H. FRENCH,
Major-General.

[P. S.]—My headquarters, when changed from here, will be in rear of First Division.

HEADQUARTERS ARMY OF THE POTOMAC,
November 28, 1863.

Major-General FRENCH,
Commanding Third Corps:

GENERAL: The commanding general directs that as the emergency for which the 100 cavalry were assigned to your command has passed, they be ordered to report to Major-General Pleasonton without delay.

I am, general, very respectfully, your obedient servant,
CHAS. E. PEASE,
Assistant Adjutant-General.

HEADQUARTERS ARMY OF THE POTOMAC,
November 28, 1863—12 p. m.

Major-General FRENCH,
Commanding Third Corps:

The major-general commanding directs that you have a division in readiness for a reconnaissance to-morrow morning at daylight, which Major Duane, chief engineer, will conduct.

A. A. HUMPHREYS,
Major-General, Chief of Staff.

HDQRS. FIRST SEPARATE BRIG., 8TH ARMY CORPS,
Drummondtown, Va., November 28, 1863.

Col. SAMUEL A. GRAHAM,
Purnell Legion, Maryland Volunteers:

COLONEL: The brigadier-general commanding directs me to furnish you with the following instructions for the government of

your operations in the country to the command of which you are
assigned:

1. Every precaution must be had to prevent communication between the Maryland and Virginia shores of the Potomac. In order
to effect this, patrols should be sent out along the shores from the
different posts of your command as far as you may deem it safe. All
persons found hovering about the shores of the Potomac should be
arrested and made to give an account of themselves. That part of
your command not at Chapel Point will be so disposed of as to
occupy Liverpool, Chapel, and Lower Cedar, and some point between
Wicomico and Cuckhold Rivers, in such force· as you may deem
sufficient and available. The headquarters of the command will
be established at Chapel Point.

2. You will require all strangers who may be found within your
command to register their names, residence, and their business in
the locality, and to take the oath of allegiance prescribed in Paragraph 2, General Orders, No. 53, headquarters Middle Department,
and then, if you shall be satisfied of the loyalty of the party, you
will issue a pass, and not otherwise. If any one shall refuse to comply with this requirement, you will require him or her to leave the
command immediately, or be detained for further action. In order
to effect this the more certainly, you will issue orders, and have them
posted in the public places within your command, requiring all
strangers and non-residents to report to the nearest office and comply with the regulation above prescribed, and informing all such
persons as refuse to report that they will be arrested as suspicious
characters.

3. You will use all proper efforts to sustain and carry into effect
the policy of the Government in relation to the enlistment of colored
troops. Every protection must be afforded to those engaged in recruiting for this corps, and all persons interfering with these enlistments must be arrested, and the public men made to understand that
the Government will not permit any individual, or band of individuals, to thwart its efforts for the suppression of the rebellion and
the restoration of the national authority.

4. Whenever negroes give you information of any blockade running or other illegal transactions, and it shall appear to you that
by reason of having done so they will be liable to be maltreated or
persecuted, you will in all such cases receive and protect the informers. As a general rule, negroes will not be interfered with in
their embarkation on the Potomac vessels, unless it shall appear to
you that they have been forced by their masters to do so, with a
view of taking them to Virginia, or unless the negroes themselves
shall intend to violate the blockade.

5. All cases of arrests made must be reported to these headquarters, together with the testimony.

6. You will make timely requisition on the proper staff departments for all necessary supplies, which, together with all your
official communications, will be forwarded by mail to Point Lookout, Md.

7. You will keep your men well in hand, and at their posts. No
officer or man will be permitted to be absent from his station without authority from department or these headquarters.

8. Until the arrival of cavalry, which it is expected will shortly
be sent you, you will impress a limited number of horses from the
disloyal inhabitants on which to mount your men when occasion

requires. giving receipts for them which shall entitle them to pay where they make satisfactory exhibition of their loyalty. These receipts will be returned when the horses are delivered up. The number of the horses so seized, and the name of the owner in each case, will be reported to these headquarters.

By command of Brigadier-General Lockwood:

[GEORGE V. MASSEY,]
Captain, and Assistant Adjutant-General.

FORT MONROE, VA., *November 28, 1863.*
(Received 10.25 a. m.)

Capt. G. V. Fox,
Assistant Secretary of the Navy:

We are mounting a 200-pounder Parrott at Plymouth to meet the iron-clad in the Roanoke. Send as early as possible a navy carriage for it. No other will do.

BENJ. F. BUTLER,
Major-General.

HEADQUARTERS ARMY OF THE POTOMAC,
November 29, 1863—8.35 a. m.

Commanding Officer Sixth Corps:

The major-general commanding directs that you send out a strong brigade to picket and hold the Raccoon Ford, about 2 miles out from Robertson's Tavern.

Very respectfully, &c.,

A. A. HUMPHREYS,
Major-General, and Chief of Staff.

HEADQUARTERS SECOND CAVALRY DIVISION,
November 29, 1863—8.35 a. m.

Col. C. Ross Smith,
Chief of Staff, Cavalry Corps:

COLONEL : During the night an advance of cavalry was made on my pickets on the plank road. This morning I find the cavalry in front on the plank road. During the night much noise and cutting of trees to the right of the plank road.

There is a very large swamp off to the right of the plank road. All the approaches to it from the south are covered.

The Second Corps has not yet arrived at the crossing of the plank road and Raccoon Ford road.

Very respectfully,

D. McM. GREGG,
Brigadier-General, Commanding Brigade.

CIRCULAR.] HEADQUARTERS ARMY OF THE POTOMAC,
November 29, 1863—9.30 a. m.

The major-general commanding directs that corps commanders report from time to time the condition of affairs in their front, and whether any changes have taken place in the disposition of the enemy. Each corps commander will also see that a route practicable for wagons as well as troops is open from his rear to Robertson's Tavern, and that a route for communication between the various corps is open in the rear.

·   Very respectfully, &c.,

A. A. HUMPHREYS,
Major-General, and Chief of Staff.

HEADQUARTERS THIRD DIVISION, THIRD CORPS,
November 29, 1863.

Col. O. H. HART,
Assistant Adjutant-General, Third Corps:

COLONEL : I have the honor to report that the party sent to examine the ground in my front have returned, and state that the stream in front is passable at all points.

Very respectfully, your obedient servant,

JOS. B. CARR,
Brigadier-General.

HEADQUARTERS ARMY OF THE POTOMAC,
November 29, 1863—1 p. m.

General HUMPHREYS:

Cline is just in. He went first to Chancellorsville, where he found a detachment of the enemy's cavalry observing the roads leading to Fredericksburg. They belonged to Rosser's brigade. Being pursued, Cline retired, and at the forks of the plank road another party of the enemy's cavalry pursued them. They (Cline's party) then came to Parker's Store and there tried to get through the Wilderness by some of the wood roads, but found them all full of the enemy's cavalry, apparently observing every approach to Fredericksburg and the Catharpin road. Cline tried to reach the Catharpin road, but was unable to do so.

About half way between Robertson's Tavern and New Hope Church, on the plank road, Cline saw a lady who left New Market Cross-Roads day before yesterday morning. Her daughter's husband works in a tobacco factory at Frederick's Hall Station, and she reported that—

Many things were going back on the cars to Richmond and no soldiers were coming up; that from Spotsylvania Court-House toward Chancellorsville the roads were all picketed by cavalry.

She had no idea of the force, and could give nothing more definite. She had seen no infantry.

In the Wilderness, just back of New Hope Church, Cline captured 5 prisoners, whom he turned over to the Fifth Corps. They were from the Fifty-fifth Virginia and Forty-seventh Virginia, of A. P. Hill's corps, and report their division (Heth's) as being the right of the enemy's line. The right of the enemy's line is at New Verdierville, or a little in advance, on the plank road, where they are posted on a ridge, with their encampments in the rear.

Very respectfully,

GEO. H. SHARPE,
Colonel, &c.

HDQRS. SECOND DIVISION, THIRD ARMY CORPS,
November 29, 1863—1.15 p. m.

Colonel HART,
  Assistant Adjutant-General:

COLONEL. I am between Jones' and plank road. Mine Run is in a field in which I am. All open. Jones' house in same opening. Have been to plank road by one path. Am following another nearer to Mine Run. Have driven all pickets to the other side and away back out of the opening into the woods. A rebel soldier from Georgia I have taken says he has seen a battery on the south side of plank road near the west side of Mine Run, but does not think there is any infantry there. Saw perhaps a guard. I shall soon know if it is there.

Yours,

HENRY PRINCE,
Brigadier-General.

———

HEADQUARTERS THIRD ARMY CORPS,
November 29, 1863—3 p. m.

Major-General HUMPHREYS,
  Chief of Staff:

GENERAL: I have received information that General Warren is moving up the plank road. General Prince furnishes it.

WM. H. FRENCH,
Major-General.

———

HDQRS. PA. RES., THIRD DIV., FIFTH ARMY CORPS,
November 29, 1863—3.10 p. m.

Major-General SYKES,
  Commanding Fifth Army Corps:

GENERAL: I have made a careful reconnaissance of the enemy's line in front of the Fifth Corps. It is my opinion that the line of attack for the corps, if it is determined that we should attack simultaneously with Generals French and Newton, should be to the right of the fire of 4½-inch guns in my front. If this view be correct, I should close up the gap toward Bartlett, instead of his closing to the left.

The pine woods in his direct front and where the headquarters of the brigade at present on picket are located, come to a point where the ravines meet directly in our front. An attacking line making use of these woods, and forming upon their edge under cover, would carry the intrenchment in their front over the reduced distance, weakened as their long line must be by the fire from the heavy guns now in position along our front. If the corps attacks over the open space, directly in its front, not only will the artillery in position be unavailable as we descend our own slope and ascend that of the enemy, but the line will be so exposed over the whole space as to offer but a very slight chance of success.

I am, general, very respectfully, your obedient servant,

S. W. CRAWFORD,
Brigadier-General, Commanding Division.

33 R R—VOL XXIX, PT II

HEADQUARTERS FIRST CORPS,
November 29, 1863—3.30 p. m.

Major-General HUMPHREYS,
Chief of Staff:

My signal officers, Lieutenants Wiggins and Camp, have intercepted the following fragment of a rebel message just received from
Clark's Mountain :

We can see a heavy force of the enemy at Somerville.

Very respectfully,

JOHN NEWTON,
Major-General, Commanding First Division.

———

HDQRS. ARMY OF THE POTOMAC, *November 29, 1863.*
(Received 4.20 p. m.)

Major-General FRENCH,
Commanding Third Army Corps:

The major-general commanding desires that General Prince be
instructed to communicate his position to General Warren.

A. A. HUMPHREYS,
Major-General, &c., Army of the Potomac.

———

HDQRS. LINE OF BATTLE ON MINE RUN,
THIRD DIVISION, FIFTH ARMY CORPS,
November 29, 1863—4.35 p. m.

FRED. T. LOCKE,
Lieut. Col., and Assistant Adjutant-General:

COLONEL : The officer sent to make an examination of Mine Run
has returned. He reports that he went in advance of our pickets
until the fire upon him became so strong that he was not able to proceed. He reports that the enemy's pickets are in groups of 5 and 7
men in the pits beyond the creek. He reports a bog or swamp on the
creek making a distance of 150 yards. He reports that he made his
way to the left, and that he saw the picket line of the First Corps
advance, and that they were driven back. I have ordered 3 picked
men to go to-night and make an examination of the ford.

Very respectfully, your obedient servant,

S. W. CRAWFORD,
Brigadier-General, Commanding Division.

———

HEADQUARTERS THIRD ARMY CORPS,
November 29, 1863—7 p. m.

Major-General HUMPHREYS :

Your notes of 5.40 p. m. and 6 p. m. are just received. The
first, in reference to the trains of the Third Corps ordered up, I am
in perfect ignorance. I remember only being informed of the three
days' supply especially directed by the general commanding. I beg
to assure the general commanding that I never will or wish to trans-
cend his orders, and cannot be accessory to others doing so.

I have looked at the ground occupied by the enemy, and cannot see a practicable point or line upon which my command, supported or unsupported, could do anything but carry in such an exhausted state, while they will be in full force to take advantage of it. Should General Warren turn the enemy, a bold movement on the left in conjunction would change the result, but even then there would be no decisive result to compensate.

I am ready, however, to act with all my vigor to carry out such orders as the general commanding, in his knowledge of the whole line, may direct.

Respectfully,

WM. H. FRENCH,
Major-General of Volunteers.

HDQRS. SECOND DIVISION, THIRD CORPS,
November 29, 1863—7.05 p. m.

Lieut. Col. O. H. HART,
Assistant Adjutant-General, Third Corps:

COLONEL: I am encamped on the right of the Second Corps on the continuation of its line. Immediately in rear of my right is Jones' house. I have given orders to have my pickets to connect on the right with General Carr's. A branch of Mine Run is in my rear, but the main body of the run is in my front. The valley of the small branch is between my position and General Carr's. The enemy looks strong in front, and there are crossing places from his position to mine. The space is wide between the Second and Third Divisions.

Very respectfully, your obedient servant,

HENRY PRINCE,
Brigadier-General, Commanding.

HEADQUARTERS ARMY OF THE POTOMAC,
November 29, 1863—7.20 p. m.

Major-General FRENCH,
Commanding Third Corps:

The major-general commanding desires to see you at these headquarters immediately.

A. A. HUMPHREYS,
Chief of Staff.

HEADQUARTERS ARMY OF THE POTOMAC,
November 29, 1863—10.30 p. m.

Major-General FRENCH,
Commanding Third Corps:

The major-general commanding directs that you send two divisions of your corps to report to General Warren on the plank road, the divisions to start at 2 a. m. to-morrow. You will open your batteries to-morrow morning at 8 o'clock punctually. You will hold the remaining division of your corps prepared to resist an attack from the enemy, and also to advance upon him should the result of the attacks at other points be successful, or to move to other points of our front.

A. A. HUMPHREYS,
Major-General, Chief of Staff.

HEADQUARTERS ARMY OF THE POTOMAC,
November 29, 1863—10.45 p. m.

Commanding Officer First Corps:

The major-general commanding directs that you post your corps early to-morrow morning, so as to hold the turnpike. The troops of the Fifth and Sixth Corps left here have been ordered to report to you. With your command you will hold the position on the turnpike, and be prepared to advance and attack the enemy should the results of the other attacks make it desirable, or move to the left or right, according to the dispositions which the enemy may make it necessary to have made. You will open your batteries at 8 o'clock in the morning punctually.

Very respectfully, &c.,

A. A. HUMPHREYS,
Major-General, and Chief of Staff.

———

HEADQUARTERS THIRD ARMY CORPS,
November 29, 1863—11.30 p. m.

Major-General BIRNEY,
Commanding First Division:

GENERAL : In compliance with instructions from headquarters Army of the Potomac, there will be a general assault on the rebel lines at 8 a. m. to-morrow, at which time all the batteries will open fire. At 7 a. m. you will deploy one brigade of your division as skirmishers, the left extending to where the left of our main line now is, and the right to the left of the First Corps. These troops will be placed so as not to expose them to the fire of our own guns.

The other two brigades will be deployed as supports to the batteries, ready to advance as soon as the attack on the enemy's flank proves successful. Every train and encampment must be moved back to Robertson's Tavern, to be out of way of the enemy's shelling.

By command of Major-General French :

JNO. M. NORVELL,
Major, and Assistant Adjutant-General.

———

ORDERS.]   HEADQUARTERS THIRD ARMY CORPS,
November 29, 1863—11.20 p. m.

The divisions of General Prince and General Carr will report to Major-General Warren, on the plank road, starting at 2 a. m. to-morrow, the 30th instant. If practicable, they will draw 20 rounds of ammunition to-night, which the men will carry in their pockets. Take the three days' rations, if you have not already drawn them. Send all teams not required back to Robertson's Tavern. Batteries will open here at 8 a. m.

By command of Major-General French :

JNO. M. NORVELL,
Major, and Assistant Adjutant-General.

WAR DEPARTMENT,
Washington, November 29, 1863—11.30 a. m.

Brigadier-General KELLEY,
　　Clarksburg, W. Va.:

The greater part of Jones' force is now at Knoxville, Tenn., and there can be very little opposition to a movement against the Virginia and Tennessee Railroad.

H. W. HALLECK,
General-in-Chief.

———

CUMBERLAND, MD., *November 29, 1863—9 p. m.*
(Received 10.25 p. m.)

Brigadier-General CULLUM,
　　Chief of Staff:

The General-in-Chief's telegram of this date received. I have been anxiously awaiting the movements of General Meade, hoping that he would be able to drive Lee's army from Gordonsville and Charlottesville, in which event I could move my force up the Valley of the South Branch of the Shenandoah and occupy Staunton, and hold a line west from that point running through Covington, in Alleghany County, and Lewisburg, in Greenbrier County, and thence to the mouth of Gauley, and thereby shorten my present line several hundred miles ; but if you deem your information reliable, and think it best to do so, I can send General Averell, with his whole force, by way of Franklin, Monterey, Covington, and Fincastle, and strike the Virginia and Tennessee Railroad at Salem, in Roanoke, or Bonsack's Station, in Botetourt, or both points. I can also, if you approve, send General Duffié, with his two regiments of cavalry, from Kanawha, via Fayetteville and Raleigh Court-House, and strike the railroad at points between Wytheville and Christiansburg at the same time.

B. F. KELLEY,
Brigadier-General.

———

NOVEMBER 30, 1863—7.45 a. m.

General MEADE :

It is now 7.45 and I have heard no firing from you, from which I fear the enemy has left your front. His position and strength seem so formidable in my present front that I advise against making the attack here. The full light of the sun shows me that I cannot succeed.

G. K. WARREN,
Major-General.

———

HEADQUARTERS ARMY OF THE POTOMAC,
November 30, 1863.

Major-General FRENCH,
　　Commanding Third Corps:

Please advise the commanding general as soon as the division returns to you.

A. A. HUMPHREYS,
Major-General.

[P. S.]—Please acknowledge.

HEADQUARTERS THIRD CORPS,
November 30, 1863.

Major-General HUMPHREYS,
        Chief of Staff:
Your message to General French received at 9.30 a. m., and for-warded immediately to him by orderly.

O. H. HART,
Assistant Adjutant-General.

———

HEADQUARTERS ARMY OF THE POTOMAC,
November 30, 1863—10.15 a. m.

Major-General HUMPHREYS,
        Chief of Staff:
GENERAL : We have but one prisoner so far this a. m., sent in a few minutes ago from the Third Corps. He is from Gordon's bri-gade, Early's division, and was taken by skirmishers of Third Corps to our left of the turnpike. He said his command is between John-son's division and A. P. Hill's corps ; that the enemy is all there ; that three days' rations of flour was issued last night. He stutters, and is very indefinite.

10.30 a. m.
Fourteen prisoners sent in by General Birney from Sixth Louis-iana and Sixty-first Georgia, Early's division, and Forty-eighth Georgia and Fifth Florida, Anderson's division. They were taken by General Birney's skirmishers half a mile to our left of the pike, along the creek. Early's division is the right of Ewell's corps and Anderson's the left of A. P. Hill's corps. They had three days' rations issued last night. One of them had heard a report that Pickett's division had come up, but the more intelligent did not believe it, and nothing had been seen of it.
        Respectfully,

GEO. H. SHARPE,
Colonel.

———

HEADQUARTERS ARMY OF THE POTOMAC,
November 30, 1863—3 p. m.

Commanding Officer Second Corps :
The major-general commanding directs that you order the divis-ion of the Third Corps remaining with you to return to the corps and report to General French. The return movement should be so conducted as to avoid the observation of the enemy. He also desires to know whether any additional information has caused any changes in your views as to the practicability of an attack by our left. General Wright reports that although the enemy have increased the obstacles in the way, yet that he does not deem an attack there im-practicable. He still has hopes of success.
        Very respectfully, &c.,

A. A. HUMPHREYS,
Major-General, and Chief of Staff.

HEADQUARTERS ARMY OF THE POTOMAC,
November 30, 1863.

Major-General FRENCH,
Commanding Third Corps:

Suspend the fire of your batteries and your demonstrations.

A. A. HUMPHREYS,
Major-General, Chief of Staff.

HEADQUARTERS ARMY OF THE POTOMAC,
November 30, 1863.

Major-General FRENCH,
Commanding Third Corps:

Be extremely cautious. The attack on the left will probably not be made.

A. A. HUMPHREYS,
Major-General, and Chief of Staff.

HEADQUARTERS ARMY OF THE POTOMAC,
November 30, 1863.

Commanding Officer Sixth Corps:

The major-general commanding directs me to say that the attack is suspended for to-day, and as soon as it becomes dark you will withdraw the troops to their former position, or in that vicinity. The object of waiting until dark to withdraw is merely to conceal the movement from the observation of the enemy.

Very respectfully, &c.,

A. A. HUMPHREYS,
Major-General, and Chief of Staff.

HEADQUARTERS ARMY OF THE POTOMAC,
November 30, 1863.

Major-General FRENCH,
Commanding Third Corps:

The major-general commanding directs me to inform you that he has gone to the extreme left, and that Major-General Sedgwick will remain here in command until he returns. Suspend your firings and demonstrations. The attack on your left is suspended, as well as that on the left.

A. A. HUMPHREYS,
Major-General, and Chief of Staff.

HEADQUARTERS ARMY OF THE POTOMAC,
November 30, 1863.

Major-General FRENCH,
Commanding Third Corps:

What is the condition of affairs in your front? Have the enemy shown any force or made any movements that you have seen, or changed their dispositions in any way?

A. A. HUMPHREYS,
Major-General, and Chief of Staff.

HEADQUARTERS THIRD CORPS,
November 30, 1863.

General HUMPHREYS, *Chief of Staff:*

Carr's division has joined me. General Carr states that General Warren told him he intended to keep Prince's division.

FRENCH,
General.

ARMY OF THE POTOMAC, *November 30, 1863,*
(Received 7.30 p. m.)

Major-General FRENCH, *Commanding Third Corps:*

The other division of your corps has been ordered to return, and must be on its way, if not near you.

A. A. HUMPHREYS,
Major-General.

HEADQUARTERS ARMY OF THE POTOMAC,
November 30, 1863—8.40 p. m.

GENERAL: The major-general commanding desires to have your opinion upon the practicability of carrying the enemy's intrenchments, so far as they are known to you, within the limits of the front of your command. Please reply immediately.

I am, general, very respectfully, your obedient servant,

S. WILLIAMS,
Assistant Adjutant-General.

(To commanders of First, Third, Fifth, and Sixth Army Corps.)

HEADQUARTERS FIRST ARMY CORPS,
November 30, 1863—9.05 p. m.

Brig. Gen. S. WILLIAMS, *Assistant Adjutant-General:*

In reply to your 8.45, this p. m., I have the honor to report that since dark I have not been able to obtain the information that I desire concerning the topography of the other side of the stream. I will be enabled to answer the note more satisfactorily on receiving from division commanders the information already sent for.

Very respectfully, your obedient servant,

JOHN NEWTON,
Major-General.

HEADQUARTERS FIRST ARMY CORPS,
November 30, 1863—11 p. m.

Brig. Gen. S. WILLIAMS,
Assistant Adjutant-General:

GENERAL: The papers inclosed are the answers of my division commanders* to an inquiry as to the nature of the ground in their respective fronts. I regard any attempt to storm as hopeless, unless the troops can be massed near the point of attack without the knowledge of the enemy, and unless strongly supported on both right and left. The works of the enemy in my immediate front appear to be

---

* Only Cutler's report found.

heavy, and their attention seems to have been drawn to the possibility of an attack here.

Very respectfully, &c.,

JOHN NEWTON,
Major-General.

[Inclosure.]

HEADQUARTERS FIRST DIVISION, FIRST CORPS,
November 30, 1863.

[Lieut. Col. C. KINGSBURY, Jr.,
Assistant Adjutant-General, First Army Corps:]

COLONEL: I think that the works can be carried at or near the first angle of the pike to the left, provided that the enemy is first dislodged from the pines in front of the works by an attack from the left. This is the only practicable way I see, and that at a great sacrifice. If I were to make the assault, I would like to see the officer that is to lead on my left and have daylight to execute it in.

Very respectfully,

L. CUTLER,
Brigadier-General, Commanding Division.

HEADQUARTERS THIRD ARMY CORPS,
November 30, 1863—10.11 p. m.

Major-General HUMPHREYS, *Chief of Staff:*

As to carrying the line in my front, the two divisions being now at my disposal, I say there is no obstacle to success except those incidental to military enterprises.

Very respectfully,

WM. H. FRENCH,
Major-General.

HEADQUARTERS FIFTH ARMY CORPS,
November 30, 1863—9 p. m.

[Brig. Gen. S. WILLIAMS :]

GENERAL: In answer to your question of this evening, I do not think it practicable to successfully carry the intrenchments of the enemy within the front of my command. I mean the front on either side of the old turnpike road, of which I spoke to you yesterday.

I am, sir, respectfully,

GEO. SYKES,
Major-General, Commanding.

HEADQUARTERS FIFTH ARMY CORPS,
November 30, 1863—11 p. m.

[Brig. Gen. S. WILLIAMS :]

GENERAL: In answer to your question, I desire to say that, so far as could be seen, I do not consider it impracticable to carry the front threatened by us to-day, although I regard the chances of success as very much lessened, both because the enemy has prepared to-day to meet the threat there offered, and because I am almost assured that he now knows the nature of the attack it was our design to offer, and has prepared to resist it.

GEO. SYKES,
Major-General.

HEADQUARTERS THIRD ARMY CORPS,
November 30, 1863—9.30 a. m.

Major-General: HUMPHREYS :

The enemy appear the same in my front. Their rifle-pits are full of men. My skirmishers advanced some distance to the front,.but could not draw their fire. We took some 12 prisoners, of Hill's corps.

Very respectfully,

WM. H. FRENCH,
Major-General.

HEADQUARTERS THIRD ARMY CORPS,
November 30, 1863—11.30 a. m.

Major-General HUMPHREYS :

If I could have four 4½-inch guns I could silence the batteries bearing on Warren's right and my front. A staff officer will show a fine road to the position if the guns can be given me. The enemy's fire in my front is in a crochet, thus :

Respectfully,

WM. H. FRENCH,
Major-General.

P. S.—In co-operation I can carry the position as it now stands in my front.

HEADQUARTERS THIRD ARMY CORPS,
November 30, 1863—11.30 p. m.

[General BIRNEY :]

GENERAL : In compliance with instructions from headquarters Army of the Potomac, there will be a general assault along the entire line of the enemy at 8 a. m., at which time all of the batteries will open their fire. At 7 a. m. you will deploy one brigade of your division as skirmishers, the left extending to where the left of our main line now is, and the right to the left of the First Corps. These troops will be placed so as not to expose them to the fire of our own shells or those of the enemy. The other two brigades will be deployed as supports, ready to advance as soon as the attack on the enemy's flank becomes successful. Every train and encampment must be moved back to Robertson's Tavern, or be put out of reach of the enemy's shelling.

By command of Major-General French :

O. H. HART,
Lieutenant-Colonel, and Assistant Adjutant-General.

WAR DEPARTMENT,
Washington, November 30, 1863—9.50 a. m.

Brigadier-General KELLEY,
Cumberland, Md. :

It is not safe to rely upon any movements of General Meade's army. Your operations should be made without regard to him. I can only designate the object. You must determine upon the best way to reach it.

H. W. HALLECK,
General-in-Chief.

GENERAL ORDERS, ⎫ WAR DEPT., ADJT. GENERAL'S OFFICE,
No. 383.   ⎬   *Washington, November 30, 1863.*

I. Commanders of geographical departments are authorized to grant leaves of absence in accordance with the General Regulations of the Army ; but all officers, of whatsoever grade, are prohibited from visiting the city of Washington without the special permission of the War Department.

II. To serve as a check upon the abuse of the authority conferred by the foregoing paragraph, a report of all leaves granted will be made monthly to the Adjutant-General of the Army, stating their length and dates, and the reasons for granting them.

III. No application for extension of leaves of absence will be granted by the War Department unless such extension is recommended by the officer granting the leave.

By order of the Secretary of War :

E. D. TOWNSEND,
Assistant Adjutant-General.

Abstract from return of the Department of Washington, Maj. Gen. Christopher C. Augur, U. S. Army, commanding, for the month of November, 1863.

Command.	Present for duty.		Aggregate present.	Aggregate present and absent.	Pieces of artillery.	
	Officers.	Men.			Heavy.	Field.
General headquarters *a*	26	·22	49	50	......	......
Artillery Camp of Instruction (Barry)	50	1,249	1,477	1,636	......	68
District of Washington (Martindale) *b*	149	2,703	4,259	5,016	......	......
Defenses North of the Potomac (Haskin)	227	5,777	7,336	7,974	......	432
Provisional brigades (Casey)	6	......	6	17	......	......
Defenses South of the Potomac (De Russy)	220	4,798	6,257	7,282	......	444
Corcoran's division *c*	134	2,209	2,748	3,441	......	6
Cavalry forces (Lowell) *d*	39	642	1,124	1,887	......	......
District of Alexandria (Slough) *e*	96	1,410	2,059	2,427	......	6
Camp Convalescent, &c. (Abercrombie)	85	1,618	6,688	7,034	......	......
Glymont Landing (Capt. A. Sharra)	5	73	148	168	......	......
Government farms, Va. (Capt. R. C. Perry)	5	92	106	131	......	......
Mason's Island, D. C. (Tracy)	33	811	946	984	......	......
Fort Washington, Md. (Brooks)	7	128	181	188	70	3
Total	1,082	21,532	33,384	38,235	70	959

a Including band of 17th U. S. Infantry and Brig. Gen. Max Weber and staff. Brigadier-General Abercrombie and staff transferred to Camp Convalescent, &c.
b And 1st District of Columbia Cavalry.
c Fairfax Court-House.
d Centreville, Va.
e Including 4th Delaware.

Abstract from return of the Middle Department (Eighth Army Corps), Maj. Gen. Robert C. Schenck, U. S. Army, commanding, for the month of November, 1863.

Command.	Present for duty.		Aggregate present.	Aggregate present and absent.	Pieces of artillery.		Remarks.
	Officers.	Men.			Heavy.	Field.	
General headquarters............	15	......	15	15	......	......	
First Separate Brigade (Lock-wood).	60	1,027	1,210	1,385	......	......	Drummondtown, Va.
Second Separate Brigade (Morris).	73	1,644	2,054	2,425	159	15	Fort McHenry, Md.
Third Separate Brigade (E. B. Tyler).	41	873	1,103	1,488	......	10	Baltimore, Md.
District of Delaware (D. Tyler)....	10	302	342	392	......	......	Wilmington, Del.
Annapolis, Md. (Waite).......	19	372	448	488	......	......	
Fort Delaware, Del. (Schoepf).....	16	485	665	736	72	6	
Ellicott's Mills, Md. (Gilpin).......	25	469	535	566	......	......	
Relay House, Md. (Jenkins)	22	254	334	379	......	......	
3d Maryland Cavalry (Tevis)	19	482	564	602	......	......	Organizing at Baltimore, Md.
Total	300	5,908	7,270	8,466	231	31	

Abstract from return of the Department of West Virginia, Brig. Gen. Benjamin F. Kelley, U. S. Army, commanding, for the month of November, 1863.

Command.	Present for duty.		Aggregate present.	Aggregate present and absent.	Pieces of artillery.		Remarks.
	Officers.	Men.			Heavy.	Field.	
General headquarters............	8	......	8	8	......	......	
First Division (Sullivan)..........	267	7,089	8,024	10,782	32	40	Harper's Ferry, W. Va.
Second Division (Mulligan)	311	7,775	9,142	10,204	2	29	New Creek, W. Va.
Third Division (Scammon)	187	4,655	5,536	7,001	......	16	Charleston, W. Va.
First Separate Brigade (Averell) ..	165	3,498	4,273	5,384	......	12	New Creek, W. Va.
Wheeling, W. Va. (Thorp).........	7	155	281	301	......	......	
Total	945	23,172	27,864	33,680	34	97	

Abstract from return of the Department of Virginia and North Carolina, Maj. Gen. B. F. Butler, U. S. Army, commanding, for the month of November, 1863.

Command.	Present for duty.		Aggregate present.	Aggregate present and absent.	Pieces of artillery.	
	Officers.	Men.			Heavy.	Field.
General headquarters a...............................	30	61	98	117	......	......
Fort Monroe, Va. (Roberts)..........................	32	804	1,331	1,676	......	......
Norfolk and Portsmouth, Va. (Barnes)	178	3,316	4,297	4,917	......	6
Portsmouth, Va. (Getty)............................	313	6,453	8,145	12,341	16	36
Yorktown and vicinity (Wistar)......................	181	3,740	4,953	5,692	51	50
Newport News, Va. (Heckman)......................	120	2,604	3,388	4,156	......	......
District of North Carolina (Peck):						
Headquarters (New Berne)	22	......	22	22	......	......
Defenses of New Berne (Palmer)	153	3,108	4,153	6,137	59	72
Sub-District of the Albemarle (Wessells)	83	1,207	1,656	2,034	16	13
Sub-District of Beaufort (Jourdan)	75	978	1,335	1,905	55	8
Sub-District of the Pamlico (McChesney)...........	44	1,300	1,691	1,975	......	6
Total..	1,231	23,571	31,064	40,972	197	191

a Including signal corps.

Circular.]   Headquarters Army of the Potomac,
                        December 1, 1863—1.30 a. m.

Corps commanders are directed to place under charge of a competent officer all wagons and ambulances, excepting one-half the infantry and artillery reserve ammunition, and ambulances in the proportion of the ambulances and medicine and hospital wagons of a brigade to each division to be sent to the rear, under the direction of the chief quartermaster of the army.

One-half of the artillery of each corps will accompany the Reserve Artillery, which will be sent to the rear, under the direction of the chief of artillery.

This order will be carried into effect immediately.

The chief quartermaster will designate the roads which the trains will take.

By command of Major-General Meade:

                            S. WILLIAMS,
                            Assistant Adjutant-General.

(To commanding officers First, Second, Third, Fifth, and Sixth Corps, Cavalry Corps, chief of artillery, and chief quartermaster.)

                                        December 1, 1863.

Major-General Humphreys:

All my pickets report the enemy's artillery moving to the left in the night. Infantry is reported moving in the same direction this morning. These reports I do not regard as very positive information. I have ordered a reconnaissance, with infantry, to my left.

General Gregg's cavalry I sent back to him last night. I also withdrew General Terry's division to a position from which it can move free from the observation of the enemy. I am glad the disposition of the artillery, &c., leaves us so free to move.

I would earnestly advise General Meade not to go back till compelled to from lack of provisions. Can we not send infantry to replace our cavalry guarding the trains, and bring it up. I send you a copy of the Army and Navy Journal General Meade gave me, and call your attention to a rebel article on cavalry. Read the part I have marked; it is but a line. We need cavalry for such purposes.

        Respectfully,

                            G. K. WARREN,
                            Major-General of Volunteers.

                                    December 1, [1863]—8.40 a. m.

Maj. J. C. Duane:

The position of the enemy in front of General Warren on the (our) right of the old railroad cut is very strong, there being an almost level plain of nearly 1,000 yards, over which troops must advance to take rifle-pits and batteries on crest, some 30 feet high. On the left of railroad cut the distance to be passed over by troops under fire is about 300 yards. What I could see of this part of the line seemed to be breastworks protected by abatis.

        Very respectfully, your obedient servant,

                            R. S. MACKENZIE,
                            Lieutenant of Engineers.

HDQRS. FIRST CORPS SIGNAL STATION,
December 1, 1863—9 a. m.

Major-General NEWTON:

SIR: The atmosphere is heavy this morning. We can see no change in the position of the enemy from yesterday afternoon. It is too hazy to get any messages from Clark's Mountain.

Very respectfully,

WIGGINS AND CAMP,
Lieutenants, and Signal Officers.

HEADQUARTERS ARMY OF THE POTOMAC,
December 1, 1863—10 a. m.

Major-General HUMPHREYS,
Chief of Staff:

GENERAL: We have just received 6 prisoners of war from the Second Cavalry Division, taken in an affair on Sunday near Parker's Store. They are from the Twelfth Virginia Cavalry, Fifth North Carolina Cavalry, Eleventh Virginia Cavalry, and First North Carolina Cavalry. All from Hampton's division of cavalry. They supposed they were to attack a wagon train. They represent the three brigades of Hampton's division, Gordon's, Rosser's, and Young's, as all being substantially acting together on our right, and having their base (if it may be so called) at Louisa Court-House. One of them, of some intelligence (and who desires to go to his relatives in Ohio), estimates his own brigade, Rosser's, at 1,100 men for duty, and Gordon's and Young's as being a little weaker. Says that the division can turn out about 3,000 for duty.

Respectfully,

GEO. H. SHARPE,
Colonel. &c.

FIRST CORPS SIGNAL STATION,
December 1, 1863—10.15 a. m.

Captain NORTON,
Chief Signal Officer:

A section of 3-inch guns has just moved into the enemy's works, opposite Reynolds' battery, in front of First Corps,

WIGGINS,
Signal Officer.

HEADQUARTERS ARMY OF THE POTOMAC,
December 1, 1863—10.30 a. m.

Major-General FRENCH,
Commanding Third Corps:

The major-general commanding directs that you will hold your command in readiness to move to the support of General Warren in case of additional force being required there.

A. A. HUMPHREYS,
Major-General.

HDQRS. FIRST CORPS SIGNAL STATION,.
December 1, 1863—10.45 a. m.
Major-General NEWTON:

SIR: In the enemy's works exposed to our view we can only count thirty pieces of artillery in position. The enemy is still at work along that portion of their line throwing up intrenchments.

Very respectfully,

WIGGINS AND CAMP,
Lieutenants, and Signal Officers.

HEADQUARTERS ARMY OF THE POTOMAC,
December 1, 1863—11.05 a. m.
Major-General FRENCH,
Commanding Third Corps:

The major-general commanding directs that you send a brigade at once to Parker's Store, on the Orange Court-House plank road, to support the cavalry of General Gregg at that point. This brigade will be held ready to move at any moment. The officer that brings this dispatch knows the road to Parker's Store, and will accompany the commanding officer of the brigade.

You will also send a brigade to the old Wilderness Tavern, at the intersection of the turnpike and Germanna plank road, to support the cavalry at that point. It will be held ready to move at any moment.

The brigades sent should be strong. They will be under the general direction of General Gregg, commanding the cavalry.

A. A. HUMPHREYS,
Major-General, Chief of Staff.

HEADQUARTERS THIRD ARMY CORPS,
December 1, 1863—12 m.
Brigadier-General PRINCE,
Commanding Division:

GENERAL: You will detail a strong brigade, to report to General Gregg at Parker's Store, on the plank road, to support cavalry now at that place. They will proceed immediately, under the guidance of Lieutenant Wade, Sixth U. S. Cavalry. Upon arrival there they will be held in readiness to move at a moment's notice.

By command of Major-General French:

O. H. HART,
Lieutenant-Colonel, and Assistant Adjutant-General.

HEADQUARTERS ARMY OF THE POTOMAC,
December 1, 1863—12.10 p. m.
Brigadier-General CARR,
Commanding Third Division:

GENERAL: You will detail a strong brigade, to report to General Gregg at the old Wilderness Tavern, at the intersection of the turnpike and Germanna plank road.

The commanding officer will be instructed to keep his command in readiness at all times to move at any moment.

An officer of cavalry, Lieutenant Baker, will report to the officer of the brigade, to point out the route.

By command of Major-General French.

O. H. HART,
Lieutenant-Colonel, and Assistant Adjutant-General.

Circular.]   Headquarters Army of the Potomac,
December 1, 1863.

Corps commanders will hold themselves in readiness to move with their trains and artillery at a moment's notice.

Please acknowledge.

By command of Major-General Meade:

S. WILLIAMS,
Assistant Adjutant-General.

Headquarters Army of the Potomac,
December 1, 1863—1 p. m.

Major-General FRENCH,
Commanding Third Corps:

GENERAL: You will be withdrawn to-night by the plank road. Captain Mackenzie's engineers will show you a road by which you can carry your artillery to the plank road. He says it will require a few hours' work on it. Please furnish him with a strong working party under an efficient officer, and have this road ready before dark, so that you will encounter no delay after starting.

Yours,

GEO. G. MEADE.

Headquarters Third Corps,
December 1, 1863—1.25 p. m.

General WILLIAMS,
Asst. Adjt. Gen., Army of the Potomac:

Your dispatch received. Will be in readiness.

WM. H. FRENCH,
Major-General.

Hdqrs. First Corps Signal Station,
December 1, 1863—1.40 p. m.

Major-General NEWTON:

SIR: We can see no change in enemy's position. It has cleared off enough for us to get the following fragment of a rebel message from Clark's Mountain, evidently referring to our trains:

On a road leading from the Wilderness to Germanna.

Very respectfully,

WIGGINS AND CAMP,
Lieutenants, and Signal Officers.

DECEMBER 1, [1863]—2.45 p. m.

Major-General HUMPHREYS:

There is nothing new on our left and front. I send you a sketch* made by Mr. Roebling. Our most advanced cavalryman on the Catharpin road was shot to-day. We have 12 men there now.

The dispatch I received shows some move is contemplated. I was about proposing to go, if nothing else was contemplated, to Tolersville and Frederick's Hall Station. At least, that is the point I should have proposed the day I got here but for the operations yesterday.

Respectfully,

G. K. WARREN,
Major-General.

———

HEADQUARTERS CAVALRY CORPS,
December 1, 1863.

Brigadier-General GREGG,
Commanding Second Cavalry Division:

The major-general commanding Cavalry Corps will dispose of that arm so as to cover the right flank until the infantry corps have crossed the Rapidan and the rear, after crossing, by holding the river. The two brigades of infantry of the Third Corps with General Gregg will remain with the cavalry and take post with them at Culpeper and Ely's Fords until after the passage of all the trains and troops, when they will rejoin their corps at Brandy Station.

Very respectfully, your obedient servant,

C. ROSS SMITH,
Lieutenant-Colonel, and Chief of Staff.

———

HDQRS. CAVALRY CORPS, ARMY OF THE POTOMAC,
December 1, 1863.

Brigadier-General GREGG,
Commanding Second Cavalry Division:

GENERAL: With your division, the brigade from Merritt's division, and the two brigades of infantry of French's corps, at Parker's Store and the Wilderness, you will cover the movement of the army to the other side of the Rapidan River. After performing this duty you will, on crossing that stream, take up positions at Germanna, Culpeper, and Ely's Fords, to prevent the enemy from following.

Place some pickets also on the Rappahannock side, to prevent surprise from that quarter.

All your wagons should be sent over before night, as the movement will take place during the night, and it is expected you will be able to be on the other side of the Rapidan by daybreak.

One of your brigades had best cross at Germanna and protect that road.

The bridges will probably be taken up before you get to the river. Cross your artillery, therefore, at the best ford.

Headquarters to-night at or near Germanna Ford.

Very respectfully,

A. PLEASONTON,
Major-General.

———

* See p. 933.

HEADQUARTERS THIRD CORPS,
December 1, 1863—4.20 p. m. .

General WILLIAMS:

I have nothing new to report. Have you anything to send me before the line is taken up?

WM. H. FRENCH,
Major-General.

———

SIGNAL STATION,
December 1, 1863.

Major-General HUMPHREYS,
Chief of Staff:

The signal officers at the front report the following message as having been sent from Clark's Mountain to General Lee this p. m.:

Enemy's trains moving between Wilderness and Germanna Ford, and also toward Stevensburg on Ely's Ford road.

L. B. NORTON,
Captain, and Chief Signal Officer.

———

HEADQUARTERS THIRD ARMY CORPS,
December 1, 1863.

Brigadier-General CARR,
Comdg. Third Division, Third Army Corps:

GENERAL: Your division will follow the Second Division (Prince). Have staff officers at the heads of your brigades, so that they may follow the route of the troops which are to precede them.

The pickets will remain on until 3 a. m., 2d instant, when they will be assembled on the turnpike with the pickets of the First, Fifth, and Sixth Corps, under the direction of the general officer of the day of the Fifth Corps. After crossing Culpeper Ford, you will mass your corps near the Second Division, picketing on your right and rear. The detached brigade you will direct to remain with the cavalry.

You must keep up your communications with the rear division, and should that halt you will do the same. About this you must be particular.

Very respectfully,

WM. H. FRENCH,
Major-General.

———

CIRCULAR.]   HEADQUARTERS ARMY OF THE POTOMAC,
December 1, 1863.

The following movements of troops are ordered for to-day and to-night:

1. The First Corps, Major-General Newton commanding, will withdraw from its position on Mine Run (part of the Fifth Corps relieving it), concealing the movement from the enemy, and march at 4 p. m. to Germanna Ford, where it will take position and hold the crossing of the river until the Fifth and Sixth Corps cross, when it will follow those two corps as soon as the road on the opposite side is clear. It will then form the rear guard, and use every precaution to insure the safety of the rear. It will take post at the termination

of the plank road, covering the trains on the Stevensburg road and watching the Mitchell's Ford road.

2. The Fifth Corps will withdraw from its position on Mine Run as soon as it is dark (6 o'clock), take the turnpike, and pass to the Germanna plank road by the left, along a wood road which the guide will point out, and move to Germanna Ford and cross the river. After crossing, it will mass on some convenient point near the ford until the Sixth Corps has passed, when it will follow the latter, taking the plank road to its termination, turn into the Stevensburg road at Holley's, and take position at Stevensburg. It will not leave Germanna Ford until the First Corps has crossed so much of its force as not to need its support.

3. The Third Corps will withdraw from its position as soon as it is dark (6 o'clock), and move to the Orange Court-House plank road and proceed to Culpeper Ford, using a cross-road to the Germanna plank road, and turning from the latter by the road to Culpeper Ford. A guide will accompany the corps. The route is that used by the Fifth and First Corps on the recent march. The two brigades of this corps at Parker's Store and Wilderness Tavern will remain with the cavalry, and take post with them at Culpeper and Ely's Fords until after the passage of all the trains and troops, when they will rejoin the Third Corps at Brandy Station. After crossing the river, the Third Corps will mass at some suitable point near the ford until the Second Corps has passed, when it will follow that corps and take the road past Richardsville, moving to Brandy Station, leaving the Stevensburg road at Madden's and crossing Mountain Run at Stony Ford, a mile below Ross' Mills.

4. The Sixth Corps, Major-General Sedgwick commanding, will withdraw as soon as the Fifth Corps has withdrawn and cleared the road; follow the Fifth Corps to Germanna Ford, and, after crossing the river, there precede the Fifth Corps, taking the Germanna plank road; thence past Holley's and through to Stevensburg to the vicinity of Brandy Station, where it will remain until the arrival of the Third Corps, when it will proceed to its former position near Welford's Ford, on Hazel River. The Sixth Corps brings up the rear of the column that crosses at Germanna Ford as far as the Rapidan, and will use every precaution to protect it; it will throw out some force upon the Raccoon Ford road until it has passed Robertson's Tavern.

5. The Second Corps, Major-General Warren commanding, will withdraw after dark in time to follow closely the Third Corps. After that corps has entered the Orange Court-House plank road, it will follow that corps to Culpeper Ford by the route prescribed, and after crossing the river will precede the Third Corps, passing by Richardsville to its former position on Mountain Run, leaving the Stevensburg road at Madden's. The division of the Sixth Corps with it will there rejoin its corps.

The Second Corps will form the rear guard of the column until it crosses the Rapidan, when it will precede the Third Corps. It will use every precaution to insure the safety of the rear.

6. The corps on the same route will maintain constant communication with each other, and keep within close supporting distance. Those that cross at Germanna will look out for their left; those that cross at Culpeper will look out for their right as far as that ford, and every precaution will be used to secure the flanks and rear from surprise.

7. The trains and artillery will precede the head of each corps, excepting such artillery as may be needed for the rear guard of the rear corps.

8. Corps commanders will so conduct the withdrawal of their troops as to avoid the observation of the enemy. In conducting the, march, every effort will be made to prevent any accidental deviation from the route.

9. The major-general commanding the Cavalry Corps will dispose of that arm so as to cover the right flank until the infantry corps have crossed the Rapidan, and the rear, after crossing, by holding the river.

The two brigades of infantry of the Third Corps with General Gregg will remain with the cavalry and take post with them at Culpeper and Ely's Fords until after the passage of all the trains and troops, when they will rejoin their corps at Brandy Station.

10. The pickets will not be withdrawn until 3 o'clock on the morning of the 2d instant. Those of the Sixth, Fifth, Third, and First Corps will be assembled under the command of the officer commanding the pickets of the Fifth Corps, and will be conducted by him on the route of the Fifth Corps. After crossing the Rapidan the pickets will rejoin their corps. The pickets of the Second Corps will follow the route of that corps.

11. Headquarters will take the route of the column that crosses at Germanna, and will be found on the route between the Fifth and Sixth Corps as far as the Rapidan. At Germanna Ford it will be found at the former headquarters there, and afterward on the route to former headquarters near Brandy Station, through Stevensburg. At the close of the march headquarters will be at the former locality, near Brandy Station.

By command of Major-General Meade:

S. WILLIAMS,
Assistant Adjutant-General.

(To commanding officers First, Second, Third, Fifth, and Sixth Corps, Cavalry Corps, chief of artillery, chief commissary of subsistence, chief engineer, and provost-marshal-general.)

CIRCULAR.]   HEADQUARTERS ARMY OF THE POTOMAC,
December 1, 1863.

The commanders of the pickets of the Sixth, First, and Third Corps will arrange with the commanding officer of the pickets of the Fifth Corps as to the time when and order in which they will be withdrawn from their posts and assembled upon the point of assemblage.

By command of Major-General Meade:

S. WILLIAMS,
Assistant Adjutant-General.

BALTIMORE, MD., *December 1, 1863—6 p. m.*
(Received 7 p. m.)

Col. G. H. SHARPE,
Headquarters Army of the Potomac:

Lee has about 40,000 men. There are about 2,500 scattered about and around Richmond. About 2,500 at Hanover Junction and points adjacent. Pickett's division, about 4,000 strong, guards the Petersburg and Weldon Railroad. Bragg has in all 90,000 men.

J. L. McPHAIL,
Provost-Marshal-General of Maryland.

HDQRS. ARMY OF THE POTOMAC, December 1, 1863.
(Received 11.10 p. m.)

General D. H. RUCKER,
Chief of Quartermaster's Department:

I have telegraphed to Ferguson, at Alexandria, to have forage and subsistence loaded on cars and held in readiness to come forward, on my order (probably to-morrow), to Brandy Station. I do not believe we shall want any supplies at Aquia or Bull Run. It looks now as though the campaign must disappoint all our reasonable expectations. I shall deplore it, because the army is in splendid condition, and was handsomely equipped by our department. It is hoped, however, we shall emerge successfully.

If you have caused forage to be put on light-draught vessels, let it remain for the present, though I feel bound to say we shall be back at Brandy to-morrow. From recent indications, the rebels are said by corps commanders to be too strongly intrenched for successful assault by our forces.

RUFUS INGALLS,
Brigadier-General, Chief Quartermaster.

HEADQUARTERS DEPARTMENT OF WEST VIRGINIA,
Cumberland, Md., December 1, 1863.

Brigadier-General SULLIVAN,
Harper's Ferry:

You will order your available cavalry force, with two regiments of infantry and a battery, to move up the Valley of the Shenandoah on Thursday, the 10th instant, with fifteen days' rations of hard bread, sugar, coffee, and salt, and cattle on the hoof; shelter tents, plenty of ammunition, but not extra or unnecessary baggage. Will proceed, by easy marches, to Strasburg, where the force will remain until the 17th instant, when it will move forward, if Imboden retires, to Woodstock, and thence to Mount Jackson, New Market, and Harrisonburg, occupying the latter place on the 20th and 21st, and threatening Staunton with cavalry. On 22d, the force will take up the line of march and return to camp.

B. F. KELLEY,
Brigadier-General.

WAR DEPARTMENT,
Washington City, December 1, 1863—8.10 p. m.

Major-General BUTLER,
Fort Monroe:

Are you willing to take McDowell and spare Peck for General Dix?

EDWIN M. STANTON,
Secretary of War.

GENERAL ORDERS, } HDQRS. 18TH A. C., DEPT. VA. AND N. C.,
No. 44. } *Fort Monroe, Va.; December* 1, 1863.

A Military Commission, of not less than five commissioned officers, of and above the rank of captain, with a recorder and legal adviser, is constituted and appointed for the trial of all high crimes and misdemeanors, which by the laws of any State in the Union or the United States, or the laws martial, are punishable with death, or imprisonment for a long term of years.

The sentences of said Commission will be assimilated to those provided by such laws, due regard being had to the necessity of severity, and for prompt punishment incident to the crimes and disorders arising from a state of war.

The Commission will sit at all convenient hours for the dispatch of business; will be attended by the provost-marshal or his assistants. All its orders will be respected and obeyed, and its summonses complied with.

As the motives of men make so largely the element of the crimes cognizable by this Commission, the rules of evidence of the English common law may be so far relaxed as to allow the accused to be questioned in the presence of the Commission—always leaving it to his free choice to respond or not to the questions proposed.

The accusation will be substantially in the form used in courts-martial, excepting that it should fully set forth a description of the accused, with his residence and business; whether or not he has been a loyal citizen; his antecedents, character, and acts in that regard, so far as known, which portion of the accusation may be put in controversy at the trials, provided the accused be not a soldier of the United States.

All proceedings, findings, and sentences of this Commission are to be subjected to the approval of the commanding general, and will be carried into effect upon his order.

The following-named officers are detailed for and will constitute such Commission:

Col. G. A. Stedman, Eleventh Connecticut Volunteers.
Col. A. G. Draper, Second North Carolina.
Lieut. Col. J. G. Chambers, Twenty-third Massachusetts Volunteers.
Maj. William Grantman, Thirteenth New Hampshire Volunteers.
Capt. W. H. Seip, Eleventh Pennsylvania Cavalry.
Maj. Peter Haggerty, aide-de-camp, recorder and legal adviser.
By command of Maj. Gen. B. F. Butler:

R. S. DAVIS,
Major, and Assistant Adjutant-General.

HEADQUARTERS ARMY OF THE POTOMAC,
December 2, 1863—10 a. m.
Commanding Officer Sixth Corps:

The major-general commanding directs me to say that as your troops are probably very much fatigued, your corps will remain here to-day and move to its former position near Welford's Ford to-morrow. You will send a force down to the ford (Germanna) to relieve the brigade and artillery of General Newton posted there. General Newton will send some force to Mitchell's Ford to hold and watch it until relieved by the cavalry.

Very respectfully,

A. A. HUMPHREYS,
Major-General, and Chief of Staff.

HDQRS. ARMY OF THE POTOMAC, *December 2, 1863.*
Commanding Officer First Corps:

The major-general commanding has directed General Sedgwick's corps to remain here to-day. You will follow the Fifth Corps to Stevensburg. A brigade of the Sixth Corps will relieve your brigade and artillery at Germanna Ford. The brigade you send to Mitchell's Ford will remain there until relieved by the cavalry.

Very respectfully, &c.,

A. A. HUMPHREYS,
Major-General, and Chief of Staff.

———

HEADQUARTERS ARMY OF THE POTOMAC,
December 2,1863—11 a. m.

Major-General WARREN, *Commanding Second Corps:*

The major-general commanding directs me to say that as the Sixth Corps are to remain in the vicinity of Germanna Ford to-day, the division of that corps now with you will remain under your command until to-morrow, when it will rejoin its corps at Welford's Ford.

A. A. HUMPHREYS,
Major-General, Chief of Staff.

———

General HUMPHREYS:

I have already ordered General Terry to his old camp, and all his wagons, tents, &c., have gone there. As I presume there is no military necessity for me to countermand this arrangement, I have assumed the responsibility of letting him go on, as that may be stopped if disapproved.

Respectfully,

G. K. WARREN,
Major-General.

———

HEADQUARTERS ARMY OF THE POTOMAC,
December 2, 1863—11.35 a. m.

Major-General FRENCH, *Commanding Third Corps:*

The major-general commanding directs that the two brigades of the Third Corps detached yesterday to General Gregg will halt at Richardsville, instead of joining their corps, and remain there guarding the trains of the army, and follow in their rear until they have crossed Mountain Run, when the brigades will rejoin their corps.

A. A. HUMPHREYS,
Major-General, and Chief of Staff.

[Indorsement.]

Published to Generals Prince and Carr at once. Detached two regiments from General Birney.

HEADQUARTERS THIRD ARMY CORPS,
December 2, 1863—4.10 p. m.

Major-General HUMPHREYS,
Chief of Staff:

GENERAL: I have one division (Prince's) ahead of the column of
trains. Two brigades are left to cover the rear. The remainder of
the corps I have been enabled to mass about 4 miles from Madden's.
As soon to-night as the trains permit the march will be resumed.
The trains are moving along well in three columns.

Respectfully,

WM. H. FRENCH,
Major-General.

———

HEADQUARTERS ARMY OF THE POTOMAC,
December 2, 1863—11 p. m.

Commanding Officer Fifth Corps:

The major-general commanding directs that you move to Rappahannock Station and assume charge of the protection of the railroad.
Your troops will relieve those of the First Corps under command of
Brigadier-General Kenly, now guarding the road, who will direct
the detachment of cavalry now serving with him to report to you.

The point at which troops are stationed are Rappahannock Station, Bealeton, Warrenton Junction, Cedar Run, or Catlett's, Nokesville, Kettle Run bridge, and Manassas Junction. The force now
stationed at Bristoe, Catlett's, or Cedar Run bridge, and Manassas
Junction is not deemed sufficient, nor is that at Bealeton. The disposition of the First Corps previous to the late movement was as
follows (it will serve as a guide to the views of the major-general
commanding): One brigade at Rappahannock Station; one brigade
at Beverly Ford; one brigade at Bealeton, with a detachment at
Liberty; one brigade at Elk Run bridge and Germantown; one
brigade at Warrenton Junction; one brigade at Bristoe, and one
brigade distributed at the other bridges and stations already enumerated.

The small bridges and culverts were guarded by detachments, and
the road picketed and patrolled. That part between Manassas Junction and Bull Run bridge should be strongly picketed. Pickets
should be established by the brigades and posts.

Some artillery was distributed to the troops at Bristoe and Warrenton Junction; the remainder was at Rappahannock Station, with
some pieces at Beverly.

Very respectfully, &c.,

A. A. HUMPHREYS,
Major-General, and Chief of Staff.

———

HEADQUARTERS ARMY OF THE POTOMAC,
December 2, 1863—11.30 p. m.

Commanding Officer First Corps:

The major-general commanding directs that you move your corps
to Paoli Mills, on Mountain Run, and occupy the position formerly
occupied by the Fifth Corps. You will send a brigade to Kelly's

Ford, which will take post on the north bank. The division of your corps now guarding the railroad will be relieved by the Fifth Corps, when it will report to you.
Very respectfully, &c.,
A. A. HUMPHREYS,
Major-General, and Chief of Staff.

HEADQUARTERS ARMY OF THE POTOMAC,
December 2, 1863—11.45 p. m.
Brigadier-General KENLY,
Commanding Division Guarding Railroad:
I am directed by the major-general commanding to inform you that you will be relieved to-morrow, if practicable, from guarding the railroad by the Fifth Corps.
You will turn over to the commander of that corps, Major-General Sykes, the detachment of cavalry serving with you on that duty.
Upon being relieved you will march your division to Paoli Mills and rejoin your corps.
A. A. HUMPHREYS,
Major-General, and Chief of Staff.

SPECIAL ORDERS, }   HDQRS. DEPT. OF WEST VIRGINIA,
No. 72.   }   *Cumberland, Md., December 2, 1863.*
*   *   *   *   *   *   *

V. It appearing that there are 200 persons residing or remaining at and in the vicinities of Charleston, Fayetteville, and other points in the Kanawha Valley, and belonging to the families of soldiers in the service of the United States; of refugees from sections occupied by rebels in arms, and in some cases of citizens arrested and placed in confinement as dangerous to the Government, who are in a suffering and destitute condition, and that issues of subsistence stores to such persons are absolutely necessary, it is directed, in pursuance of authority given by the honorable Secretary of War, under date of April 22, 1863, that the chief commissary of subsistence of the Third Division of this department make such issues as may be necessary to supply to these destitute persons the needed and proper relief, the issues to be made under the direction of Brig. Gen. E. P. Scammon, commanding Third Division, who will decide as to the amount of issue, and also as to the number of the persons to be benefited by this order, should it hereafter vary from that herein indicated.
*   *   *   *   *   *   *

By order of Brig. Gen. B. F. Kelley:
THAYER MELVIN,
Assistant Adjutant-General.

WASHINGTON CITY,
December 2, 1863—7 p. m.
Major-General BUTLER,
Fort Monroe:
Meade is on the back track again without a fight.
EDWIN M. STANTON.

HEADQUARTERS SECOND CAVALRY DIVISION,
December 3, [1863]—9 a. m.

Col. C. ROSS SMITH,
    Chief of Staff, Cavalry Corps:

COLONEL: Nothing remains at Richardsville.but troops of my division. Ambulances and wagons carrying my wounded are just starting to Brandy Station. I sent an order to Colonel Devin to report at Culpeper. Yesterday, however, Captain Hynes, aide-de-camp, informed me that it was his impression that Devin's brigade had already been ordered away. This morning I sent a force to examine about Morrisville and United States Ford. The lower fords of the Rappahannock cannot be picketed or watched to any purpose, from this position, with my force. Some stragglers must have fallen into the hands of the enemy on the Culpeper Ford road; not many, I think. Some of the enemy's cavalry were seen opposite Ellis' Ford yesterday. I suppose these were guerrilla scouts. The enemy's cavalry were rather late in following. Those that came to Ely's Ford looked rather fagged. I sent away the brigade of infantry this morning.

Yours, respectfully,
                    D. McM. GREGG,
            Brigadier-General of Volunteers.

HEADQUARTERS THIRD ARMY CORPS,
December 3, 1863—10.30 a. m.

Major-General HUMPHREYS, *Chief of Staff:*

GENERAL: One of the brigades which was with Gregg, and which joined at Culpeper Ford, I ordered to remain, according to instructions from the major-general commanding, until all the trains had crossed Mountain Run. The other brigade not reporting before I marched, two regiments were directed to re-enforce the brigade at Richardsville and remain with it. The most of the trains not across Mountain Run were parked at Madden's.

Respectfully,
                    WM. H. FRENCH,
            Major-General of Volunteers.

HEADQUARTERS ARMY OF THE POTOMAC,
December 3, 1863—11.05 p. m. (Received 9.30 a. m., 4th.)

Major-General HUMPHREYS, *Chief of Staff:*

GENERAL: The following dispatch has just been received, and is respectfully forwarded:

PONY MOUNTAIN SIGNAL STATION,
December 3, 1863—6 p. m.

Captain NORTON:

Numerous camp smokes of the enemy appear opposite Raccoon and Morton's Fords and half way between the latter and Germanna. There was firing opposite Morton's Ford about 3 p. m., which lasted for half an hour. Could not communicate with you at 6 p. m., so I sent the above by orderly. Did you get it?
                    PAINE,
                    Signal Officer.

Very respectfully, &c.,
                    L. B. NORTON,
            Captain, and Chief Signal Officer, A. P.

Circular.]   Headquarters Army of the Potomac,
December 3, 1863.—6 p. m.

The major-general commanding directs that you hold your corps in readiness for immediate movement. The enemy are reported by General Custer to be crossing the river at Raccoon Ford and Morton's Ford—cavalry, infantry, and artillery.

By command of Major-General Meade:

S. WILLIAMS,
Assistant Adjutant-General.

(To commanding officers First, Second, Third, Fifth, and Sixth Corps, Cavalry Corps, and chief of artillery.)

December 3, 1863—6.40 p. m.

Commanding Officer Fifth Corps:

The major-general commanding directs that you hold your command in readiness for immediate movement. The enemy are reported by General Custer to be crossing the Rapidan at Raccoon and Morton's Fords in heavy force—cavalry, artillery, and infantry. If you have not yet relieved the division of the First Corps guarding the railroad, the commanding general directs that you delay doing so until further orders.

Please acknowledge, and say whether you have relieved General Kenly's division.

S. WILLIAMS,
Assistant Adjutant-General.

December 3, 1863.

Commanding Officer Fifth Corps:

I am directed by the major-general commanding to say that the order of this evening, requiring you to hold your command in readiness for an immediate movement, may be regarded as recalled, the troops of the enemy that crossed to this side of the Rapidan having been driven back.

S. WILLIAMS,
Assistant Adjutant-General.

Hdqrs. First Army Corps, Army of the Potomac,
December 3, 1863—10 p. m.

Major-General HUMPHREYS,
Chief of Staff:

GENERAL: I have four brigades here. One I have stationed at Kelly's Ford, on the other side of the river; two brigades I will keep in the neighborhood of Paoli Mills, the other I will put on the river road leading from Rappahannock Station to Kelly's Ford, on this side of the river. You will perceive I have not enough troops to make a line of battle from Paoli Mills to the river. May I sug-

·gest to you one thing ? If Sykes continues to relieve my Third Division, you will probably loose the services in this crisis of two divisions instead of one.

Very respectfully, your obedient servant,
JOHN NEWTON,
Major-General, Commanding.

[P. S.]—I have just sent to General Kenly, and ordered him to send me at once all the troops of his that General Sykes has relieved.

CIRCULAR.]   HEADQUARTERS ARMY OF THE POTOMAC,
December 3, 1863.

Corps commanders will have the roads leading from their corps to the depots at Brandy Station and those connecting with the adjoining corps put in good order immediately. The route along the railroad will be put in order by the engineer troops, and the commanders of the Sixth and Third Corps will furnish such details as may be required for that purpose upon the requisition of the engineer officers charged with the works.

The commanding general calls the attention of corps commanders to the fact that serious delays have occurred in the repair of roads, owing to the delay of working parties in repairing to the designated places of work, and to their being imperfectly supplied with tools, and to those they had being in bad order. Proper measures will be taken by corps commanders to insure keeping the intrenching tools in good serviceable condition, and to insure a proper supply of them to working parties.

By command of Major-General Meade:
S. WILLIAMS,
Assistant Adjutant-General.

HEADQUARTERS ARMY OF THE POTOMAC,
December 4, 1863—5 p. m. (Received 5.30 p. m.)
Major-General HALLECK,
General-in-Chief:

I should like to visit Washington to-morrow, if you have no objections.

GEO. G. MEADE,
Major-General, Commanding.

WASHINGTON, D. C.,
December 4, 1863—9.30 p. m.
Major-General MEADE,
Army of the Potomac:

You have my permission to visit Washington whenever you deem proper, reporting to the Adjutant-General at the War Department.

H. W. HALLECK,
General-in-Chief.

HEADQUARTERS SECOND CAVALRY DIVISION,
December 4, 1863—10.15 a. m.

Col. C. ROSS SMITH,
Chief of Staff, Cavalry Corps:

COLONEL: One brigade of the division is now posted at Sheppard's Grove Post-Office, picketing Germanna and Jacobs' Fords, and connecting with the pickets of the Third Division on the right. The other brigade is at Richardsville picketing the lower fords and the Rappahannock. Nothing demonstrative on the part of the enemy. Bushwhackers have begun operations in the rear. I have ordered a force to be crossed at Richards' Ford to go to United States Ford. The force sent yesterday went by Morrisville to Hartwood; hence my report of the distance of 22 miles. The distance to Hartwood from Richardsville is 12 miles by way of Richards' Ford. The road between this point (Sheppard's Grove Post-Office) and Richardsville is very bad. If the enemy's cavalry attempt anything, it will be on the north bank of the Rappahannock. I will send the report of operations as soon as I shall have gotten reports from brigade commanders.

Respectfully, yours,

D. McM. GREGG,
Brig. Gen. of Vols., Commanding Second Division.

HEADQUARTERS ARMY OF THE POTOMAC,
December 4, 1863—3.15 p. m.

Commanding Officer Second Corps:

The major-general commanding directs that you occupy the heights at and in the vicinity of Stevensburg with your corps.

Very respectfully, &c.,

A. A. HUMPHREYS,
Major-General, and Chief of Staff.

HEADQUARTERS SECOND CORPS,
December 4, 1863.

Major-General HUMPHREYS,
Chief of Staff:

Do you wish my corps to move at once or in the morning? It is now half past 3.

G. K. WARREN,
Major-General.

[DECEMBER 4, 1863.]

Major-General WARREN,
Commanding Second Corps:

In the morning will answer.

A. A. HUMPHREYS,
Major-General, Chief of Staff.

HEADQUARTERS ARMY OF THE POTOMAC,
December 4, 1863.

General HUMPHREYS:

The following report has just been received, and is respectfully forwarded·

PONY MOUNTAIN SIGNAL STATION,
December 4, 1863—4.20 p. m.

Captain NORTON:

To-day I see camps in woods back of Morton's house extending nearly a mile to our right and a half mile to our left of that point. The force at Raccoon Ford is not as large as appeared yesterday. I see cavalry camps between Raccoon and Morton's Fords. There is cavalry in the old camp at Somerville Ford. The old camps at Rapidan Station and along the railroad are again occupied. The enemy's cavalry can again be seen at the mouth of Robertson's and along the Locust Dale road. See no force of enemy on this side of Rapidan between Rapidan Station and Morton's Ford. Saw this p. m. a small body of enemy's cavalry, near Cedar Mountain.

CASTLE,
Captain, and Signal Officer.

Very respectfully, &c.,

L. B. NORTON,
Captain, and Chief Signal Officer, A. P.

HEADQUARTERS THIRD CAVALRY DIVISION,
December 4, 1863—p. m.

Col. C. Ross SMITH,
Chief of Staff:

The demonstration made by the enemy yesterday evening on the right of my line was merely to ascertain the strength of my pickets. They were driven back across the river after a brisk skirmish, without loss on either side. I will send you a sketch of my line soon. Everything is quiet along my front to-day.

Very respectfully,

G. A. CUSTER,
Brigadier-General.

HEADQUARTERS COLORED TROOPS,
DISTRICT OF NORFOLK AND PORTSMOUTH,
Norfolk, Va., December 4, 1863.

Brigadier-General GETTY,
Commanding, &c.:

By direction of Major-General Butler, all colored men, women, and children coming into our lines from the enemy's country are to be welcomed by our forces wherever met, and are to be assisted on their way as much as possible. There will be many such coming in soon in consequence of our present expedition. If they are obstructed in any way, it will be very certainly followed by severe punishment to the offenders.

Very respectfully, your obedient servant, ·

EDWARD A. WILD,
Brigadier-General of Volunteers.

[Indorsement.]

HEADQUARTERS UNITED STATES FORCES,
Near Portsmouth, Va., December 6, 1863.

Respectfully transmitted to department headquarters, with a copy of my reply.

The tone of this communication is manifestly improper, and I desire that General Wild may be so notified.

GEO. W. GETTY,
Brigadier-General, Commanding.

[Inclosure.]

HEADQUARTERS UNITED STATES FORCES,
Near Portsmouth, Va., December 6, 1863.

Brigadier-General WILD,
Comdg. U. S. Colored Troops, Norfolk, Va.:

SIR: Your communication of the 4th instant has just been handed to me.

All colored persons coming into the lines occupied by the troops under my command from the enemy's country have at all times and under all circumstances been received and assisted in their way as much as possible. If you possess any knowledge to the contrary, be pleased to inform me. I have no knowledge whatever of the expedition referred to in your communication.

I am, sir, very respectfully, your obedient servant,

GEO. W. GETTY,
Brigadier-General, Commanding.

CIRCULAR.]   HEADQUARTERS ARMY OF THE POTOMAC,
December 5, 1863—11.15 a. m.

Corps commanders will hold their commands in readiness for immediate movement and have the trains ready to move to the rear.

By command of Major-General Meade:

S. WILLIAMS,
Assistant Adjutant-General.

(To commanding officers First, Second, Third, Fifth, and Sixth Corps.)

HEADQUARTERS CAVALRY CORPS,
December 5, 1863.

Brigadier-General GREGG,
Commanding Second Cavalry Division:

GENERAL: The major-general commanding the army directs that you move up one of your brigades here, so that it can be thrown out to the right of the army, if necessary, leaving one brigade to picket the lower fords of the Rapidan, having its headquarters wherever you think best to picket these fords. I think the brigade you move up had better come to near Brandy Station, and then receive orders, if it is necessary, for it to go over to the right. General Merritt reported that some of the enemy crossed at Somerville Ford this morning, and that wagons were heard to move on the Criglersville road last night from left to right.

Have your right connect with General Custer's left at Mitchell's Ford. Custer's officer reports that your officer will not come up as far as Mitchell's Ford.

Very respectfully,

C. ROSS SMITH,
Lieutenant-Colonel, Chief of Staff.

CULPEPER, VA.,
December 5, 1863.

Col. C. ROSS SMITH:

The right of my line of pickets rests to the right of the Rixeyville and Culpeper road, on Muddy Run, this side of Mrs. Major's house. The parties sent out for information in regard to enemy's movements have not yet reported. I will send information as soon as received. The enemy crossed at Somerville Ford to destroy house and hay stack used by our pickets for defense. He has returned to south side of the river.

W. MERRITT,
Brigadier-General.

CULPEPER.
December 5, 1863.

Col. C. ROSS SMITH,
Chief of Staff:

Captain Sweitzer, commanding the picket on Gaines' Mill road, does not know what the wagons heard were. He did not hear them himself, but they were reported by his advanced vedettes this morning. I had sent out a party on the roads toward James City and Madison Court-House before your order reached me. It has orders to find if there is any movement of the enemy.

A staff officer visited Pony Mountain, and reports large camps near Dr. Morton's house, and everything else as far as visible about as it was before the movement. The enemy's camps and position as they were. My picket line connects with General Custer at Somerville Ford, thence runs to the right along Cedar Run a mile and a half beyond Gaines' Mill, southeast of Stone-House Mountain, with right resting on Rixeyville road, near Muddy Run, with Culpeper as a center. It is a curved line, with radius from 4 to 5 miles long. If I throw my line farther to the front, the extent of country is greater than I can cover.

I send parties out daily to reconnoiter well to the front on the principal roads. Captain Clark, just in from a scout, reports the enemy picketing this side the Rapidan, between Morton's and Raccoon Fords; also they are said to be building a bridge between these two fords.

Very respectfully,

W. MERRITT,
Brigadier-General.

HEADQUARTERS FIRST CAVALRY DIVISION,
December 5, 1863.

Col. C. ROSS SMITH,
Chief of Staff:

COLONEL: Captain Sweitzer, commanding First Cavalry, on picket last night, made the report about wagons, &c., that I sent you this morning. As he did not hear the noise himself, I did not attach much importance to the report. The reconnaissance I sent out toward Madison Court-House as soon as I got this report went on very slowly, and the reports sent in are not satisfactory. The squadron went as far as within a mile and a half of James City, but saw nothing save some few scouts on the road. I have ordered out a strong force in that direction which will send reports early to-morrow.

I cannot, with my present force, picket Robertson's River. My line as now posted is 20 miles long. The object desired could be effected by doing as I did when here before—send scouting parties well to the right front on the principal roads. A brigade of cavalry could not insure the safety of a station at Thoroughfare Mountain. It is isolated and the enemy could surround it.

W. MERRITT,
Brigadier-General.

HDQRS. ARMY OF THE POTOMAC, SIGNAL DEPT.,
December 5, 1863.

Major-General HUMPHREYS,
Chief of Staff:

GENERAL: The following report has just been received, and is respectfully forwarded:

PONY MOUNTAIN SIGNAL STATION,
December 5, 1863—4.50 p. m.

Captain NORTON:

It has been too foggy all day to see along the Rapidan. A staff officer of General Merritt's reports the enemy moving cavalry, artillery, and infantry toward Criglersville.

CASTLE,
Captain, and Signal Officer.

Very respectfully, &c.,

L. B. NORTON,
Captain, and Chief Signal Officer, A. P.

HDQRS. THIRD DIVISION, CAVALRY CORPS,
December 5, 1863—5.30 p. m.

Col. C. ROSS SMITH,
Chief of Staff:

The enemy have been skirmishing all the day with my pickets near Raccoon and Somerville Fords. The skirmishing was very slight until this evening, when an attempt was made by the rebels to drive my reserves back; it failed, however, the enemy being driven back by my men in splendid style. I had 6 men wounded. The line is all quiet at this moment.

Very respectfully,

G. A. CUSTER,
Brigadier-General.

HDQRS. ARMY OF THE POTOMAC, SIGNAL DEPT.,
December 5, 1863—8.45 p. m.

Major-General HUMPHREYS,
Chief of Staff:

GENERAL : In answer to your inquiries the signal officer on Pony Mountain states that Lieutenant Myers, of General Merritt's staff, was the officer who reported that a force of the enemy was moving toward Criglersville, and that he informed Captain Castle of it at 12 m., but did not say when the move occurred.

Very respectfully, &c.,

L. B. NORTON,
Captain, and Chief Signal Officer, A. P.

———

HDQRS. THIRD DIVISION, CAVALRY CORPS,
December 5, 1863—11 p. m.

Col. C. Ross SMITH,
Chief of Staff:

I keep myself thoroughly informed of the movements of the enemy on my immediate front. I am positively certain that the enemy have not attempted to throw a bridge across the river at any point of my line. How General Merritt should receive such a report is more than I can imagine. The enemy did cross a regiment of infantry to-day to annoy my pickets, but were driven back.

Two deserters have just come in, belonging to a North Carolina regiment of Ewell's corps, Rodes' division. They report that Ewell's corps occupy the same ground and position they did before the late movement of this army. Hill's corps is near Orange Court-House. The rebels are not supplied with advance rations on hand, but draw each day. They anticipate no movement.

Very respectfully,

G. A. CUSTER,
Brigadier-General, Commanding Division.

———

HEADQUARTERS SECOND CORPS,
December 5, 1863.

General HUMPHREYS,
Chief of Staff :

My troops are in Stevensburg. I remain in my old camp near telegraph office, writing my report. I shall join my command when necessary. I send you the following dispatch, just received:

DECEMBER 5—12 m.

G. K. WARREN,
Major-General:

GENERAL: The cavalry are all in Stevensburg, occupying every piece of woods and available piece of ground. Consequently the divisions have been placed in position in the best places to be found, for the day only, until it is known whether the cavalry is to remain here. Certainly it or our corps should move. Webb is just in the angle between the Raccoon and Germanna Ford roads, say, half a mile out of town. Hays is toward Brandy Station, from Stevensburg, and about 1 mile from Webb. Caldwell is about half a mile between Webb and Hays, and not far from the forks of the Raccoon and Germanna Ford roads.

A report came here just now that the enemy are crossing at Somerville Ford—cavalry. infantry. and artillery. A messenger saw about 100.
Custer's pickets have been driven back to their reserves. I have heard a little random picket firing. I have thought prudent to order the supply and ordnance trains to the other side of Mountain Run.
Headquarters is near General Davies' headquarters.

C. H. MORGAN,
Chief of Staff.

G. K. WARREN,
Major-General.

HEADQUARTERS SECOND ARMY CORPS,
December 5, 1863.

General S. WILLIAMS,
   Adjt. Gen., Army of the Potomac:
   GENERAL : In obedience to circular of the 3d instant, directing the repair of roads, I employed 1,500 men on the road leading from Brandy Station to Stony Ford all of yesterday. To-day I relieved them to move camp, and the road is one we should no longer use in drawing supplies. It will still need a great deal of work to make it passable in all weather.
   I have carefully inspected the approaches to the bridge built by General Webb, just below Ross' Mill, and find them very good for any train taking the road leading to that point, and not likely to be out of order, in the worst of weather. There is no evidence yet of the approach having ever caused any difficulty.
   Very respectfully,

G. K. WARREN,
Major-General of Volunteers.

GENERAL ORDERS, } HDQRS. MID. DEPT., 8TH ARMY CORPS,
   No. 66.   }   *Baltimore, Md., December 5,* 1863.
   Considering it my duty to accept the place in Congress to which I have been elected, I tendered to the President of the United States the resignation of my commission as a major-general of volunteers. My resignation has been accepted, to take effect this day. To-day, therefore, I retire from the military service of my country, and thus relinquish the command of the Middle Department and Eighth Army Corps, which, by authority of the President, I turn over to Brig. Gen. H. H. Lockwood, U. S. Volunteers, the senior officer next in rank within the department.
   In thus passing from military to civil life, I cannot but deeply feel the sundering of associations and relations, which have been so agreeable, with the gallant armies, officers, and soldiers of the Union, with whom I have been connected ever since the beginning of this civil war. It has been my expectation and desire to continue to devote whatever powers and energy I have to the sacred cause of. sustaining our National Government in a more active field of duty ; and I only bring myself to consent to the change in the hope that I may, by earnest endeavor, make myself useful in the new position to which I am called by the voice of fellow-citizens of my native State, whose wishes I am not willing to disregard.
   I especially regret to part with the companions of my present command ; to all the officers and men of which, as well as to the mem-

bers of my staff, who have more immediately worked and sympathized with me, I desire to express my obligation for the zeal and fidelity which they have so generally evinced in the discharge of their part of our joint duty to the Government we serve. That duty and its attendant labors have not been light or inconsiderable. It is now a year since I had the honor to be assigned to this place, and during that space of time the limits of the Middle Department have been, by successive changes, variously expanded and contracted; at one time extending over and embracing the country between the west shore of the Hudson River and the border of Kentucky, and including within those bounds more than 50,000 troops, then constituting the Eighth Army Corps.

But it is within the reduced territory comprising Maryland, Delaware, and the Eastern Shore of Virginia, that the most important responsibility has been incurred. To the loyal people there, of all classes, I return my heartfelt thanks for the cordial support which they have constantly afforded me by their approbation and co-operation. If I have succeeded at all, it has been, I am sure, only owing to the simple fact that I have been unwilling to compromise with treason in any form or expression it might assume. And if, as I am but too conscious may be the case, I have made mistakes, I have a good degree of confidence that in this community I will at least have credit for honesty of purpose in my efforts, at all times, to sustain the just authority of a great and blessed Government, whose existence has been imperiled by devilish and causeless conspiracy and insurrection.

For the effectual putting down of a rebellion, moved and supported by such influences, I believe all good and patriotic men, in every capacity, will strive and pray together until our common efforts are crowned with full success.

ROBT. C. SCHENCK,
Major-General.

GENERAL ORDERS, } HDQRS. MID. DEPT., 8TH ARMY CORPS,
No. 67.   }   Baltimore, Md., December 5, 1863.

In accordance with Special Orders, No. 518, Paragraph 22, dated War Department, Adjutant-General's Office, November 21, 1863, I hereby assume command of the Middle Department and Eighth Army Corps.

It is with a full appreciation of the delicacy and responsibility of the position that I enter upon the discharge of the duties incident thereto, and it is with diffidence that I attempt to exercise the functions of an office which have been discharged with so much ability, sagacity, and justice by the accomplished and respected commander who has just retired to enter upon another sphere of public duty.

I would announce to the citizens resident in this military department that my views as to the government thereof are in consonance with those of its late chief, and that while I earnestly trust there will be no occasion requiring harsh measures, I am, at the same time, determined that any and all disloyal manifestations, declarations, or proceedings shall surely be overtaken by that retributive justice they so properly merit.

HENRY H. LOCKWOOD,
Brigadier-General, Comdg.

HDQRS. ARMY OF THE POTOMAC, SIGNAL DEPT.,
December 6, 1863.

General HUMPHREYS:

The following report has just been received, and is respectfully forwarded:

PONY MOUNTAIN SIGNAL STATION,
December 6, 1863—9 a. m.

Captain NORTON:

Had a fine view of the river at sunrise this morning. Do not see a large force of the enemy on this side of the river at any of the fords. Camp smokes have increased back of Raccoon Ford. See no movements of the enemy on any of the roads leading to the Blue Ridge. No camp smokes at or near Madison Court-House. The enemy appear to occupy their old positions, with a little heavier force opposite the fords than heretofore.

CASTLE,
Captain, and Signal Officer.

Very respectfully, &c.,

L. B. NORTON,
Captain, and Chief Signal Officer, A. P.

HDQRS. ARMY OF THE POTOMAC, SIGNAL DEPT.,
December 6, 1863.

Major-General HUMPHREYS,
Chief of Staff:

GENERAL: The following report has just been received, and is respectfully forwarded:

PONY MOUNTAIN SIGNAL STATION,
December 6, 1863—3.20 p. m.

Captain NORTON:

The enemy's force seems to gradually increase between Morton's and Stringfellow's Fords. Can see large camps there now. All the fords up to Garnett's are well guarded. See quite large camps along the Orange and Alexandria Railroad, from Rapidan Station south. Have seen no demonstration on this side of the river to-day.

CASTLE,
Captain, and Signal Officer.

Very respectfully, &c.,

L. B. NORTON,
Captain, and Chief Signal Officer, A. P.

HEADQUARTERS FIRST CAVALRY DIVISION,
December 6, 1863.

Col. C. ROSS SMITH,
Chief of Staff:

The reconnaissance toward Madison Court-House had got to Thoroughfare Mountain at 11.15 a. m. The officer reports he can see the entire country beyond Madison Court-House to below Clark's Mountain; a signal man with a glass is along. No considerable force of the enemy is this side Robertson's River, above. Camp fires indicate the enemy's position between Rapidan Station and Orange Court-House, as well as along the river below. No movement on our right or in contemplation that can be heard of. The reconnaissance will be pushed forward.

W. MERRITT,
Brigadier-General.

GENERAL ORDERS, } HDQRS. 18TH A. C., DEPT. VA. AND N. C.,
No. 47.   }   *Fort Monroe, Va., December* 6, 1863.

Capt. John Cassels, Eleventh Pennsylvania Cavalry, is announced as aide-de camp to the major-general commanding, and provost-marshal at department headquarters.

He will be obeyed and respected accordingly.

By command of Major-General Butler :

R. S. DAVIS,
Major, and Assistant Adjutant-General.

CUMBERLAND,
December 7, 1863.

Col. AUGUSTUS MOOR :

You will receive orders from General Averell this a. m. You will move at once with all your available force, leaving a force to guard your supplies at Beverly, on the Lewisburg road as far as Droop Mountain, and threaten the enemy. Reach there on Friday if possible.

General Scammon will attack him at Lewisburg on Saturday. When you learn the result of Scammon's movement, you will fall back to Beverly, bringing with you all the wounded able to travel, taking with you two days' rations of hard bread, sugar, coffee, and salt.

B. F. KELLEY,
Brigadier-General.

NEW CREEK,
[*December*] 7, 1863.

Col. AUGUSTUS MOOR :
Beverly, Va.:

March with your command to-morrow morning. Arrive at Marling's Bottom on Friday, the 11th instant. On the 12th and 13th, you will move toward Frankfort, endeavoring to communicate with General Scammon, who is expected to arrive at Lewisburg on the 12th. Remain in the vicinity of Droop Mountain, acting upon any information you may receive and availing yourself of any opportunity to strike the enemy, until the 18th; then return to Beverly, bringing with you the wounded of this command and of the enemy which were left after the battle at Droop Mountain.

By order of General Averell :

WILL. RUMSEY,
Captain, and Aide-de-Camp.

CUMBERLAND,
December 7, 1863—9 a. m.

Brigadier-General SCAMMON,
Charleston:

You will move at once with your cavalry, one battery, and two or three regiments of infantry, on Lewisburg. Time your march so as to arrive at Lewisburg on Saturday, the 12th, when you will attack the enemy vigorously, and capture or drive him out. You will hold the place till the 17th or 18th, threatening the enemy constantly with your cavalry toward Union. The object of this is to engage the attention of the enemy while General Averell is completing his expedition against the Virginia and Tennessee Railroad at Salem and other points. Troops will move to-day from Beverly, and threaten Lewisburg from the north, but will go no farther than Droop Mountain. Take with you fifteen days' rations of hard bread, sugar, coffee, and salt, plenty of ammunition, but no extra or unnecessary baggage.

Having accomplished the object of your expedition, you will return to Charleston, and report by telegraph.

> B. F. KELLEY,
> *Brigadier-General.*

SPECIAL ORDERS, }   HDQRS. ARMY, ADJT. GENERAL'S OFFICE,
No. 543.   }   *Washington, December 7, 1863.*

*   *   *   *   *   *   *

2. The telegraphic order, dated December 5, 1863, from this office, relieving Brigadier-General Garrard, U. S. Volunteers, from duty with the Army of the Potomac, and directing him to report in person without delay to the Adjutant-General of the Army in this city, is hereby confirmed.

*   *   *   *   *   *   *

By command of Major-General Halleck:

> E. D. TOWNSEND,
> *Assistant Adjutant-General.*

HEADQUARTERS FIRST CAVALRY DIVISION,
December 8, 1863.

Col. C. ROSS SMITH,
Chief of Staff, Hdqrs. Cavalry Corps:

All quiet on the lines and in front.

I respectfully call the attention of the proper authorities to the condition of the citizens of Culpeper and its environs. Almost all of them are suffering for the necessaries of life, and some will starve soon if their condition is not bettered by issues from the commissaries. Very few, if any, will take the oath of allegiance to the United States Government ; some refuse from prejudice, others from fear of their neighbors, who, they say, would persecute them for the action. Nor would administering the oath of allegiance to such people do any good, for they would not probably consider themselves bound by it, as they reason that it is forced upon them. I do not allow these people to go out of the town limits, as they steal through the lines, and, being rabid female rebels, give the enemy information. Something must be given them to eat, though.

Very respectfully,

> W. MERRITT,
> *Brigadier-General of Volunteers, Commanding..*

[Indorsement.]

HEADQUARTERS CAVALRY CORPS,
December 8, 1863.

Respectfully forwarded.

What instructions had better be sent to General Merritt ?

> C. ROSS SMITH,
> *Lieutenant-Colonel, and Chief of Staff.*

HDQRS. DEPARTMENT OF WEST VIRGINIA,
Cumberland, Md., December 8, 1863.

Brigadier-General SULLIVAN,
Harper's Ferry:

You will order your available cavalry force, with two regiments of infantry and a battery, to move up the Valley of the Shenandoah on Thursday, the 10th instant, with fifteen days' rations of hard bread, sugar, coffee, and salt, and cattle on the hoof, shelter-tents, plenty of ammunition, but no extra or unnecessary baggage.

Will proceed by easy marches to Strasburg, where the force will remain till the 17th instant, when it will move forward, if Imboden retires, to Woodstock, and thence to Mount Jackson, New Market, and Harrisonburg, occupying the latter place on the 20th and 21st, and threatening Staunton with cavalry. On the 22d, the force will take up the line of march and return to camp.

B. F. KELLEY,
Brigadier-General.

CUMBERLAND, MD., *December* 8, 1863—4 p. m.
(Received 8.45 p. m.)

Brig. Gen. G. W. CULLUM,
Chief of Staff:

Brigadier-General Averell left New Creek this morning with three regiments of cavalry and a battery, for the Virginia and Tennessee Railroad. He will proceed via Petersburg, Franklin, Monterey, Covington, and Fincastle, and strike the railroad in Botetourt and Roanoke Counties. Brigadier-General Scammon will also move from the Kanawha to-day, on Lewisburg and Union, for the purpose of threatening the enemy and the railroad near New River, engaging his attention and making a diversion in Averell's favor. Brigadier-General Sullivan will move a force up the valley via Winchester, Strasburg, Woodstock, &c., threatening Staunton, and engage the attention of Imboden, and prevent him from sending a force against Averell.

Lee may poss b y send a mounted force when he learns of this movement, from his left, for the purpose of cutting Averell off ; but this, if attempted, I hope will be frustrated by corresponding movements of General Meade's cavalry. If my plans and orders are promptly and faithfully executed, I hope to accomplish important results. It will certainly cut off all communication by railroad and telegraph between Lee and Longstreet.

B. F. KELLEY,
Brigadier-General.

WARRENTON,.
December 9, 1863.

H. C. WEIR,
Captain, Assistant Adjutant-General:

CAPTAIN : I sent one squadron to Fayetteville about 11 a. m. to-day, with instructions to scour from Fayetteville to and along Warrenton Railroad. The officer has just returned, and reports no enemy in that locality. Will the 150 men be sent ? All quiet. The two regiments of the Second Brigade have just been relieved. Can the officer in command send one squadron to Foxville on his return to Bealeton ?

Respectfully,

D. GARDNER,
Lieutenant-Colonel, Commanding.

HEADQUARTERS ARMY OF THE POTOMAC,
December 9, 1863—3 p. m. (Received 3.43 p. m.)

Maj. Gen. H. W. HALLECK,
General-in-Chief:

I respectfully request that I may be informed whether it is probable I shall receive instructions which would render it improper for me to grant leaves of absence to officers and furloughs to soldiers in limited numbers and for brief periods. I am confident that the granting of such leaves and furloughs would have a most beneficial effect upon the army, but in ignorance of your views and those of the Government, I now restrict leaves and furloughs to cases of great urgency.

GEO. G. MEADE,
Major-General.

WASHINGTON, D. C.,
December 10, 1863—9.30 a. m.

Major-General MEADE :

General Orders, No. 383, November 30, of War Department, gives the authority which you ask.

H. W. HALLECK,
General-in-Chief.

HDQRS. ARMY OF THE POTOMAC, SIGNAL DEPT.,
December 10, 1863.

Major-General HUMPHREYS,
Chief of Staff:

GENERAL : The following report has just been received and is respectfully forwarded:

PONY MOUNTAIN SIGNAL STATION,
December 10, 1863—6.30 p. m.

Captain NORTON ;

The enemy was busy erecting quarters all day. No working parties seen in the intrenchments. The vicinity of Morton's Ford appears better fortified than ever before. Can see several pieces in position there. At 4 p. m. the enemy's pickets at Morton's and Stringfellow's Fords were relieved by one company each. Observed picket fires to-day from Clark's Ford to a point 5 miles above Humes', on Robertson's River.

HALSTED,
Signal Officer.

Very respectfully, &c.,

L. B. NORTON,
Captain, and Chief Signal Officer, A. P.

HDQRS. CAVALRY CORPS, ARMY OF THE POTOMAC,
December 10, 1863.

Brigadier-General GREGG,
Commanding Second Cavalry Division:

GENERAL: General Custer has been ordered to relieve your pickets on the lower Rapidan. As soon as they are relieved the general commanding directs that you move one of your brigades to Warrenton and one of them to near Bealeton, putting it in camp there, and picketing the country toward Morrisville.

The two batteries that are with your division will be relieved by two batteries from the Second Brigade Horse Artillery. They will report to you before you cross the river.

Very respectfully, your obedient servant,
C. ROSS SMITH,
Lieutenant-Colonel, and Chief of Staff.

HDQRS. CAVALRY CORPS, ARMY OF THE POTOMAC,
December 10, 1863.

Brigadier-General GREGG,
Commanding Second Cavalry Division:

GENERAL: The reports from the reconnoitering party sent to Newby's Cross-Roads indicate that the force sent is not quite strong enough. The general commanding directs that you send 250 men at once to re-enforce them.

I am, very respectfully, your obedient servant,
C. ROSS SMITH,
Lieutenant-Colonel, and Chief of Staff.

FORT MONROE, *December* 10, 1863.
(Received 9.45 p. m.)

The SECRETARY OF WAR:

Richmond Examiner of 8th instant says that Longstreet was at Rutledge, 30 miles northeast of Knoxville, on the Bristol road, on the 6th. They regard him in a position critical, but ultimately safe, and admit that what he has accomplished is nothing.

BENJ. F. BUTLER,
Major-General.

GENERAL ORDERS, } HDQRS. 18TH A. C., DEPT. VA. AND N. C.,
No. 50. } *Fort Monroe, Va., December* 10, 1863.

In accordance with orders received from the President of the United States, any person now under sentence of death is hereby reprieved until further orders from these headquarters.

By command of Major-General Butler:
R. S. DAVIS,
Major, and Assistant Adjutant-General.

HDQRS. CAVALRY CORPS, ARMY OF THE POTOMAC,
December 11, 1863.

Brig. Gen. S. WILLIAMS,
    Asst. Adjt. Gen., Army of the Potomac:

GENERAL: I would respectfully call the attention of the major-general commanding the army to the necessity of keeping up the strength of the Cavalry Corps, to enable it to perform the duties assigned it, more especially in connection with the extensive picket line it is habitually maintaining.

The casualties of the service are very severe upon this arm, and more recently it is being weakened by whole regiments leaving the army for purposes of re-enlistment and re-organization.

In view of this latter fact, I would respectfully suggest that the considerable number of new cavalry regiments now in depot at Washington might properly be drawn on, from time to time, to supply the place of those going away.

I have the honor to be, your obedient servant,
          A. PLEASONTON,
             Major-General.

HDQRS. CAVALRY CORPS, ARMY OF THE POTOMAC,
December 11, 1863.

Major-General HUMPHREYS,
    Chief of Staff, Army of the Potomac:

GENERAL: In consequence of the difficulty of transacting the current business of the Second Division, with one brigade at Warrenton and one east of Bealeton, as well as the necessity of having a sufficient cavalry force on our right flank, I respectfully suggest that the entire Second Division take post at Warrenton, and that the Third Division (Custer's) be posted on the left, between Bealeton and Morrisville. The First Division (Merritt's) has three brigades, one of which could be placed at Stevensburg, to picket on the left, while the other two would be sufficient for the front and right, with some assistance from the infantry, by having the infantry picket lines on the right and left connect with the cavalry, at the same time posting a brigade of infantry in Culpeper, to relieve the cavalry from looking after that place.

Unless some plan of this kind is adopted, the very severe service which the cavalry is now called upon to perform on picket will seriously impair the efficiency of that arm during the coming winter. I may also state that the First Division is nearly as strong as both the Second and Third.

I am, very respectfully, your obedient servant,
          A. PLEASONTON,
            Major-General, Cavalry.

WAR DEPARTMENT,
Washington, December 11, 1863—1.40 p. m.

Brigadier-General KELLEY,
    Cumberland, Md.:

According to the latest advices, Longstreet was at Morristown, East Tennessee, moving up the valley. Troops collected at Abingdon will probably join him. If it is possible to cut the railroad between him and Lee, it would cut off his supplies and retard any junction of their armies. I do not think they will make any serious operations toward the Kanawha Valley at present.

H. W. HALLECK,
General-in-Chief.

CUMBERLAND, MD., *December 11, 1863.*
(Received 11.30 a. m.)

Brig. Gen. G. W. CULLUM,
Chief of Staff:

I transmit the following telegram from Colonel Comly for the information of the General-in-Chief:

CHARLESTON, W. VA.,
December 10, 1863.

Captain MELVIN,
Assistant Adjutant-General:

Captain Witcher, Third [West] Virginia Cavalry, with 50 men, has just returned from a scout through Wayne, Logan, and Boone Counties, bringing as prisoners 1 captain, 2 lieutenants, 1 quartermaster sergeant, and 14 men, and 30 pieces small-arms, having traveled 150 miles in three days, and returning without loss or injury to men. Lost 3 horses and equipments. Captain Witcher reports a considerable force organizing in the region of Abingdon for a raid in Kanawha Valley or Barboursville. He heard of the Lewisburg advance from prisoners captured, who informed him that a large force which had been on the way to join Longstreet was now returning to re-enforce Lewisburg. He reports plenty of grain and large quantities of fat cattle and hogs in Logan; says he could march 10,000 men through. Their roads good. The prisoners captured represent the following commands: Beckley's battalion, Fourteenth [Virginia Cavalry], Twenty-second [Virginia Cavalry], Twenty-sixth [Battalion Virginia Infantry], Thirty-fourth [Battalion Virginia Cavalry], Thirty-sixth [Battalion Virginia Cavalry], and Eighth Virginia Cavalry; Markhead's [?] battalion Kentucky cavalry and First Virginia State Line. General Scammon left Gauley last night.

JAMES M. COMLY,
Lieutenant-Colonel, Commanding.

I have no idea that the force reported to be concentrating at Abingdon contemplates an offensive movement into the Kanawha Valley.

B. F. KELLEY,
Brigadier-General.

HEADQUARTERS ARMY OF THE POTOMAC,
December 12, 1863.

Maj. Gen. H. W. HALLECK,
General-in-Chief:

GENERAL: I desire to call your attention to an important question, requiring immediate action on my part, but which I am undecided what measures to take first without ascertaining more definitely your views in regard to the position and movements of this army. The question I refer to is the re-enlisting of veteran volunteers. General Orders, No. 376, confers upon me the authority to grant a thirty days' furlough to all volunteers re-enlisting as veteran volunteers under General Orders, No. 191, whenever the demand for the same will best permit. It is in deciding the demands of the service that I am in doubt.

I inclose a statement of the number of men in the infantry regiments whose term of service expire by next fall. These amount to over 21,000 officers and men present. It is believed that more than half of them, or over 10,000, will re-enlist provided they can have at once a furlough of thirty days to spend at their homes. It is calculated that over 5,000 of the cavalry will also re-enlist on the same .terms.

Much, however, depends on the furloughs being granted immediately, as it is feared if any system of volition is adopted, only those who at once benefit by the act will re-enlist. I would therefore like, if practicable, to let the whole go, to be absent say the month of January and part of February. The expediency of permitting so large a part this army [to depart], 15,000 men, equal to the largest corps now in it, is a question I do not like to decide in ignorance of your views as to future contingencies. If nothing more is to be done, and I have already reported that in my judgment nothing more can be done this season, the force can be spared provided the enemy remain quiescent. The present position of the army, however, invites an advance from the enemy in case he deems one justifiable.

His position is very different from mine. To move against him I have to make a *détour* of over 50 miles, abandoning my communications and carrying my large wagon trains over impassable roads. If he advances, however, he has only 8 or 10 miles, with his communications intact in his rear, and hence by picking out a favorable moment, when the ground is frozen, he could get his artillery, all he would care to bring, and could make the advance with comparative safety. In this view, I should not like to weaken myself to the extent proposed above ; but would rather propose taking up the line of the Warrenton Railroad, holding in force the covering of the Rappahannock at the railroad bridge.

.Another advantage in occupying this line would be that the troops could be supplied from depots on the railroad, and much of the difficulty of hauling supplies and the labor of making roads now encumbered be avoided. If the army can take up this line, I would send away all willing to re-enlist ; but should it be deemed essential to maintain the present position south of the Rappahannock, I would only permit portions, say one-third, or 5,000, to be absent at a time.

I should be pleased to have your views upon these points at your convenience.

Respectfully, yours,

GEO. G. MEADE,
Major-General.

[Indorsements.]

Case of First [West] Virginia Cavalry referred to Colonel Fry for orders and report.

EDWIN M. STANTON,
Secretary of War.

DECEMBER 5, 1863.

Report : The   ans for securing the re-enlistment of veterans in the field (General Orders, No. 376) requires that they shall have thirty days' leave. I am satisfied that the men will not re-enlist for three years longer without going home. The sooner some of them are permitted to go, the better it will be for the recruiting service. I do not know how necessary this regiment is to military operations in the Army of the Potomac, but if it can possibly be spared I should like to see the system of furlough commenced with it at once. It will show the veterans that the Government is in earnest about the furlough.

JAMES B. FRY,
Provost-Marshal-General.

The provost-marshal-general is directed to communicate with the General-in-Chief and other army commanders on the above-mentioned subject.

EDWIN M. STANTON.

[Inclosure.]

Statement of regiments whose term of service expires previous to September 1, 1864.

MAINE.

Number.	Officers.		Enlisted men.		Aggregate present and absent.	Expiration of term of service.
	Present.	Absent.	Present.	Absent.		
Third	18	9	317	191	535	June 4, 1864.
Fourth	17	4	375	154	540	June 15, 1864.
Fifth	28	5	305	160	498	June 23, 1864.
Sixth	30	6	414	190	640	June 15, 1864.
Seventh					428	August 21, 1864.
Total	93	24	1,411	695	2,641	

VERMONT.

Second					930	June 20, 1864.
Third					700	July 16, 1864.
Total					1,630	

MASSACHUSETTS.

First					613	May 25, 1864.
Seventh	27	6	332	218	583	June 15, 1864.
Tenth	31	4	372	206	613	June 21, 1864.
Eleventh					649	June 13, 1864.
Ninth	27	2	532	208	769	June 11, 1864.
Fifteenth	17	7	285	310	619	July 12, 1864.
Sixteenth					620	July 12, 1864.
Eighteenth	15	12	375	281	683	August 24, 1864.
Nineteenth	12	17	223	222	474	August 28, 1864.
Twentieth	16	5	249	296	566	July 10, 1864.
Twelfth	15	16	261	377	a453	June 26, 1864.
Thirteenth		..9...	186	276	462	July 16, 1864.
Total	160	69	2,815	2,394	7,104	

a 154 conscripts.

RHODE ISLAND.

Second	29	5	518	189	741	June 6, 1864.
Total	29	5	518	189	741	

Statement of regiments whose term of service expires, &c.—Continued.

NEW YORK.

Number.	Officers.		Enlisted men.		Aggregate present and absent.	Expiration of term of service.
	Present.	Absent.	Present.	Absent.		
Fortieth	20	14	554	406	994	June 14, 1864.
Thirty-ninth	6	3	187	149	345	May 1, 1864.
Forty-second	14	9	317	233	573	June 22, 1864.
Sixty-second	17	7	298	116	438	June 30, 1864.
Sixty-fifth	15	10	302	103	430	August 24, 1864.
Sixty-seventh	17	9	385	119	530	June 24, 1864.
Seventieth					487	June 29, 1864.
Seventy-first					433	July 18, 1864.
Seventy-second					572	June 21–October 31, 1864.
Seventy-third					505	August 19, 1864.
Seventy-fourth					412	September 1, 1864.
Eighty-second	12	14	155	278	459	May 21, 1864.
Eighty-third	22	6	98	121	247	
Fourteenth a	26	5	242	248	521	April 18, 1864.
Total	149	77	2,538	1,773	7,036	

a State militia.

NEW JERSEY.

Number.	Present.	Absent.	Present.	Absent.	Aggregate	Expiration.
First	24	7	362	130	523	June 4, 1864.
Second	28	6	402	139	575	May 30, 1864.
Third	23	5	348	110	486	June 4, 1864.
Fourth	24	6	389	84	503	August 17, 1864.
Fifth					444	August 29, 1864.
Sixth					389	August 29, 1864.
Total	99	24	1,501	463	2,920	

PENNSYLVANIA.

Number.	Present.	Absent.	Present.	Absent.	Aggregate	Expiration.
First a	26	6	312	123	467	May 15, 1864.
First b	25	7	355	169	556	July 26, 1864.
Second	17	10	223	123	373	July 31, 1864.
Fifth	24	9	337	146	516	May 15, 1864.
Sixth	23	10	315	177	525	July 27, 1864.
Ninth	21	12	333	137	503	June 28, 1864.
Tenth	25	8	465	92	590	April 15, 1864.
Eleventh	28	3	332	144	507	June 9, 1864.
Twelfth	21	8	309	145	483	May 15, 1864.
Eleventh c	18	9	230	183	440	July 19, 1864.
Sixty-second	28	3	427	142	600	July 22–September 1, 1864.
Sixty-third	30	4	308	155	497	August 1, 1864.
Sixty-ninth	13	7	165	164	349	August 19, 1864.
Seventy-first	15	6	218	219	458	May 28, 1864.
Seventy-second	16	8	268	353	645	August 10, 1864.
Twenty-third	25	12	545	140	731	August 2, 1864.
Forty-ninth	17	12	303	146	478	September —, 1864.
Ninety-eighth	30	5	363	112	510	August 17, 1864.
One hundred and second	31	2	440	156	629	August 6, 1864.
One hundred and sixth	19	12	229	182	442	August 28, 1864.
Eighty-eighth	18	8	214	154	394	
Total	470	151	6,691	3,371	10,693	

a Reserves.　　*b* 1st Rifles or 13th Reserves.　　*c* Coulter's regiment.

MARYLAND.

Number.	Present.	Absent.	Present.	Absent.	Aggregate	
First					661	
Total					661	

Statement of regiments whose term of service expires, &c.—Continued.

[WEST] VIRGINIA.

Number.	Officers.		Enlisted men.		Aggregate present and absent.	Expiration of term of service.
	Present.	Absent.	Present.	Absent.		
Seventh	15	2	254	157	428	July 4, 1864.
Total	15	2	254	157	428	

OHIO.

Fourth	27	6	336	166	535	June 5, 1864.
Eighth	26	9	221	131	387	June 25, 1864.
Total	53	15	557	297	922	

INDIANA.

Fourteenth	23	8	257	119	407	June 7, 1864.
Nineteenth	......	......	......	......	422	July 28, 1864.
Twentieth	20	14	423	135	642	July 22, 1864.
Total	43	22	680	304	1,471	

MICHIGAN.

First	19	9	214	122	364	August 17, 1864.
Third	20	7	275	165	467	June 10, 1864.
Fourth	20	12	243	160	435	June 20, 1864.
Fifth	21	5	210	168	404	August 28, 1864.
Total	80	33	942	615	1,670	

WISCONSIN.

Second	22	7	159	237	425	June 11, 1864.
Fifth	33	2	480	130	645	July 12, 1864.
Sixth	21	10	225	216	472	July 15, 1864.
Seventh	24	12	189	245	470	August 16–September 2, 1864.
Total	100	31	1,053	828	2,012	

MINNESOTA.

First.......................	19	9	220	323	571	April 21, 1864.
Total	19	9	220	323	571	

UNITED STATES SHARPSHOOTERS.

First	4	2	50	15	71	
Total	4	2	50	15	71	

RECAPITULATION a

State.	Officers		Enlisted men		Aggregate.
	Present.	Absent.	Present.	Absent.	
Maine	93	24	1,411	695	2,641
Vermont					1,639
Massachusetts	160	60	2,815	2,394	7,104
Rhode Island	29	5	518	189	741
New York	149	77	2,588	1,773	7,086
New Jersey	99	24	1,501	463	2,920
Pennsylvania	470	161	6,691	3,371	10,693
Maryland					661
[West] Virginia	15	2	254	157	428
Ohio	53	15	557	297	922
Indiana	43	22	680	304	1,471
Mi·higan	80	33	942	615	1,670
Wisconsin	100	31	1,053	828	2,012
Minnesota	19	0	230	333	571
United States Sharpshooters	4	2	50	15	71
Total	1,314	474	19,280	11,424	40,580

a The discrepancy in the recapitulation arises from the fact that in many regiments only the aggregate strength present and absent is given.

NEW BERNE, N. C., *December* 12, 1863.

Maj. Gen. BENJAMIN F. BUTLER,

 Comdg. Dept. of Virginia and North Carolina.

GENERAL: The brilliant affair near Greenville, which I reported on the 28th, produced great commotion throughout North Carolina, and was generally noticed in the Richmond, Raleigh, and Wilmington papers, although I have failed to discover any allusion to it in ours. In consequence of this and other moves, Governor Vance called out the entire State or home guards by proclamation on the 2d. Brigadier-General Ransom, with a portion of a brigade, moved to Tarborough, which is equally distant from Greenville and Rainbow Bluff, and connected by rail with Weldon, &c. A large force, of all arms, is at the railway near Kenansville, where but a single company has usually been kept. All concur in material additions to the command of General Whiting.

The gunboat has not yet been reported in North Carolina, but I look for her daily.

No part of the Third [New York] Cavalry has arrived, as I hoped. In my judgment, it is needed for the public service.

The 200-pounder has arrived, but without a carriage. It will be placed in its proper position so soon as a carriage can be prepared.

Your General Orders, No. 46, on the recruitment of colored troops have been received. Orders have been issued calling the attention of all to the subject-matter and requiring a hearty co-operation. It seems to remove all obstacles, and there is a fair promise of an abundant harvest.

Rev. Mr. James may labor under some difficulty from not being a bonded officer. I nominated him to the War Department for an appointment as superintendent of blacks. Failing to receive that, a commissioner's appointment would remove all embarrassment, and increase his very small compensation.

I am, very respectfully, your obedient servant,

    JOHN J. PECK,

     Major-General.

YORKTOWN,
December 12, 1863.

Major-General BUTLER:

The movement spoken of is in progress. The infantry marched at 7 this morning by a circuitous route to seize the crossings at the forge. Cavalry marched this evening, and will be at same place about 3 o'clock to-night, whence they will make a dash with sabers only—carbines left behind. A colored regiment with ambulances and rations of bread for the returning troops marches from here at 4 a. m. to-morrow, and will meet them to-morrow evening at Twelve-Mile Ordinary, where all will encamp.

I. J. WISTAR,
Brigadier-General.

ELIZABETH CITY,·
Saturday, December 12, 1863.

Brigadier-General BARNES,
Commanding, Norfolk:

SIR: I have the honor to report that we occupy this place, and thus far without accident. Below South Mills we built a solid bridge on the piles previously standing, but partly burned, and marched hither.

Our two steamers, I. D. Coleman and Three Brothers, arrived beforehand, and lay off out of sight, but signals from our cannon soon brought them up. They are now unloaded, and in use for other purposes. A gunboat has made two calls here very recently, having quite a salutary influence in confirming our footing here. But I would be glad to keep one around us as long as we stay. At her last call she carried off a steam mill and machinery, some said for Roanoke, some for Fort Monroe. We keep hearing of considerable bodies of State partisan rangers, *alias* guerrillas, but not strong enough to harm us. All we dread is the sending of a regular force from Suffolk, Winton, or even from Richmond.

I have sent out to-day four expeditions hence, one to Hertford for contrabands, &c.; one in search of guerrillas; one for forage for our cavalry and artillery; one for fire-wood, which we need much—this party takes the lightest steamer up the river. Also, I am just sending the other steamer down to Roanoke Island with a load of contrabands, including horses and carts, on a schooner in tow, to return with a load of coal for both steamers. Thus every man is employed.

I send this via Roanoke Island.

We are greatly favored with weather, but cool.

Very respectfully, your obedient servant,
EDWARD A. WILD,
Brigadier-General of Volunteers.

P. S.—I shall have serious complaints to make against Colonel Ward, of General Getty's command, for his conduct in attempting to defeat the objects of our expedition. He sent out cavalry in advance to warn the inhabitants that "nigger-stealers were coming to plunder them of everything," and he interfered in other ways.

New York City, *December* 12, 1863—2.30 p. m.
(Received 2.40 p. m.)

Hon. P H Watson,
Assistant. Secretary of War:

Information has been sent to the enemy that the United States forces contemplate a land attack on Wilmington, N. C., and preparations therefor going on at New Berne.

JOHN HORNER.

War Department,
Washington, December 13, 1863—3 p. m.

Major-General Butler,
Fort Monroe, Va.:

It has been suggested that Lee, since Meade's failure to attack him, has or may send re-enforcements to Longstreet by rail through to Lynchburg. Please send all information on that point which you may be able to obtain.

H. W. HALLECK,
General-in-Chief.

Fort Monroe, Va., *December* 14, 1863.
(Received 5.20 p. m.)

Secretary of War:

I have much to do with the Eastern Shore, Accomac and Northampton Counties. I am now trying men for murder committed there. I could obtain a large number of recruits for my colored troops from there had I authority. Please either annex these counties to this department or give me leave to send a recruiting party there if judged best for the service.

BENJ. F. BUTLER,
Major-General, Commanding.

War Department,
December 15, 1863—4.20 p. m.

Maj. Gen. Benjamin F. Butler,
Commanding, &c., Fort Monroe:

I am directed by the Secretary of War to say, in reply to your telegram of yesterday in relation to the annexation of the Eastern Shore of Virginia, Accomac and Northampton Counties, to your department, that until the question in respect to the command of the Middle Department is determined, it is not deemed expedient to make any change in the departmental boundaries, and that Colonel Birney is authorized to recruit colored troops in that region, so as to render it unnecessary to send recruiting parties there from your department.

ED. R. S. CANBY,
Brig. Gen., and Assistant Adjutant-General.

CUMBERLAND, MD., *December 15, 1863*—10 a. m.
(Received 2.10 p. m.)

Brig. Gen. G. W. CULLUM, *Chief of Staff:*

The following telegram just received. I have no news yet from Averell. I expect he will reach the Virginia and Tennessee Railroad to-day at or near Salem. Scammon was directed to reach Lewisburg on Saturday, the 12th. I hope to hear from him to-day. It appears from Sullivan's telegram that Imboden is being re-enforced by Lee. May I ask you to direct General Meade's cavalry to keep a close watch upon any movement into the Shenandoah Valley?

DECEMBER.15, 1863—9 a. m.

Brigadier-General KELLEY,
Cumberland:

Full reports from my troops at Strasburg this morning; skirmishing continually. Reports that the enemy have re-enforced Imboden, and intend occupying the valley. I have taken 32 prisoners—some from Ewell's corps. Colonels Wells and Boyd are vigilant.

JER. C. SULLIVAN,
Brigadier-General, Commanding.

B. F. KELLEY,
Brigadier-General, Commanding.

WAR DEPARTMENT,
December 16, 1863—10.45 p. m.

Brig. Gen. B. F. KELLEY, *Cumberland:*

The following is taken from the Richmond Whig, of December 16:

Although there appears to be no doubt of the movement of Averell from Kanawha in the direction of the East Tennessee and Virginia Railroad, the War Department has received no additional information from that quarter. The enemy's movements, so far as known, seem to indicate a raid on the railroad or probably upon the counties of Botetourt, Rockbridge, or Augusta.

By order of the Secretary of War:

THOS. T. ECKERT,
Major, and Asst. Supt. U. S. Military Telegraph.

NORFOLK, *December 16, 1863.*

Col. J. W. SHAFFER, *Chief of Staff:*

The following communication has just been received:

ELIZABETH CITY,
Sunday, December 13, 1863.

Brigadier-General BARNES,
Commanding, Norfolk:

SIR: I have the honor to report that we still hold Elizabeth undisturbed. The forage sent by the gunboat has arrived on another steamer, the gunboat having exploded her cylinder. I am just sending a request to General Graham for another gunboat to be sent in her stead immediately to this place. Our expedition meets with moderate success. No casualties excepting 2 men wounded, and 1 captured by guerrillas. I send this by Roanoke Island.

Very respectfully, &c.,

EDWARD A. WILD,
Brigadier-General of Volunteers.

JAMES BARNES,
Brigadier-General.

GENERAL ORDERS, } HDQRS. 18TH A. C., DEPT. VA. AND N. C.,
No. 56. }   Fort Monroe, Va., December 16, 1863.

The provost-marshal of each district in this department will cause to be made and reported to these headquarters, on or before the 5th day of January, 1864, an enrollment of all able-bodied citizens (distinguishing between white and colored in their reports) between the ages of eighteen and forty-five, in order that the commanding general may know upon what able-bodied force he can rely for the defense of the Union.

By command of Major-General Butler :

R. S. DAVIS,
Major, and Assistant Adjutant-General.

WAR DEPARTMENT,
Washington, December 17, 1863—2.30 p. m.
Maj. Gen. GEORGE G. MEADE,
Army of the Potomac:

The subject-matter of your letter of the 12th instant was laid before the Secretary of War immediately on its receipt, but I have not been able to give you an earlier answer. The policy of furloughing now a part, at least, of those who re-enlist, is approved. Perhaps the number who so re-enlist may not be so great that you cannot spare them all. General Orders, No. 376, leave that to your discretion.

If you deem a position on the line of the Rappahannock more favorable than that you now occupy, no objections are made to the change. I have received no intimation in regard to future enterprises. If any should be made, I will immediately communicate them. General Kelley seems to apprehend a movement from Lee's army into the Shenandoah Valley, and asks that your attention be called to the subject.

H. W. HALLECK,
General-in-Chief.

HEADQUARTERS ARMY OF THE POTOMAC,
December 17, 1863.
Circular to Corps Commanders :

The commanding general directs that you send to these headquarters, in the course of to-morrow, if possible, a statement showing the number of men that will re-enlist in your command, under the provisions of General Orders, Nos. 191, 305, and 376, of the present year, from the War Department, upon the condition that the men so re-enlisting are at once allowed the furlough of at least thirty days provided for in the last-mentioned order. The statement will be arranged by regiments and show the number of men that will re-enlist in each regiment, as well as the number that will not re-enlist or do not come within the provisions of the orders applicable to the subject.

No man can re-enlist at this time who has more than a year to serve.

By command of Major-General Meade :

S. WILLIAMS,
Assistant Adjutant-General.

FAIRFAX-COURT-HOUSE, VA.,
December 17, 1863.

Commanding Officer at Burke's Station:

The rebels have attacked our front at Sangster's Station. The commanding general directs that your troops rest on their arms and that all guards and patrols be on the alert.

WM. A. LA MOTTE,
Assistant Adjutant-General.

HEADQUARTERS DIVISION,
December 17, 1863.

Lieut. Col. J. H. TAYLOR,
Assistant Adjutant-General:

Colonel Flood reports the bridge this side of Sangster's Station on fire, and found it impossible to cross on account of the swollen stream. He sent some men across on the burning string-pieces, who, on their arrival on the other side, were fired at by a volley of 60 or 70 shots. Captain McAnally, with 34 men, are missing. The force of guerrillas is estimated between 200 to 400 men. The company at Sangster's are said to have fought well. Will report from time to time.

MICHAEL CORCORAN,
Brigadier-General, Commanding.

[P. S.]—I gave Colonel Lowell early notice.

YORKTOWN,
December 17, 1863.

Major-General BUTLER:

This afternoon rebel cavalry came down to my lines at Gloucester. Captain Poor, with one squadron, was sent out to reconnoiter, drove in the advance, and found a large force of rebel cavalry 4 miles out in line of battle. Being too many to attack, he returned to a position 1 mile in front of the pickets. I am sending over a detachment of cannoneers to man Fitch's battery, whose men have just gone on furlough, also 300 colored infantry. I am in no condition to-night to make an attempt on their rear with infantry by way of the river. It is raining violently, and the men exhausted, many of them without shelter. Will try it to-morrow if the opportunity continues. They will not attack, I fear.

I. J. WISTAR,
Brigadier-General.

HEADQUARTERS CAVALRY CORPS,
December 18, 1863.

Colonel TAYLOR:

COLONEL: A dispatch from Washington, from General Augur, says General Rosser's brigade left Fredericksburg Wednesday night last. Crossed the Orange and Alexandria Railroad last night at Sangster's Station, attempting to destroy the bridge, but, failing to do so, have gone in the direction of Centreville, with the view probably of operating on our rear. Colonel Lowell, with all the cavalry at command, is after them. Rosser is reported to have about 1,000 men and no artillery. The general directs that you be on the lookout for General Rosser, and if possible intercept him.

Answer.

C. ROSS SMITH,
Lieutenant-Colonel, Chief of Staff.

HEADQUARTERS CAVALRY CORPS,
December 18, 1863.

Col. JOHN P. TAYLOR,
Commanding Second Cavalry Division:

It is reported that Rosser's brigade, Stuart's cavalry, 800 strong, struck the Orange line of railroad at Sangster's last night at 8 o'clock. They cut the wires and set fire to two bridges on Pope's Run. The general commanding directs that you notify your brigade at Warrenton to keep a good lookout toward Salem and New Market, as the enemy are reported to have gone in that direction toward the Blue Ridge, and if they come within reach of your brigade at Warrenton, tell it to "pitch into" them and whip them, as their horses will be tired out. Have your whole command on the lookout, as they may try another point. Please answer when you receive this.

Very respectfully,

C. ROSS SMITH,
Lieutenant-Colonel, Chief of Staff.

BEALETON,
December 18, 1863.

Lieutenant-Colonel SMITH:

Dispatch received. I have ordered two regiments from this brigade to re-enforce brigade at Warrenton, and brigade at that place to send strong reconnaissances to Salem and New Market. All quiet and nothing new.

J. P. TAYLOR,
Commanding Second Division Cavalry.

WARRENTON,
December 18, 1863.

Capt. H. C. WEIR:

I have the honor to inform you that the officer in command of the scouting party sent out this afternoon has returned, and reports having been to New Baltimore, and found no signs of any force of the enemy. I have sent two regiments to Salem as directed.

Respectfully,

D. GARDNER,
Lieutenant-Colonel, Commanding Brigade.

GENERAL ORDERS, } HDQRS. MIDDLE DEPT., 8TH ARMY CORPS,
No. 68.   }   *Baltimore, Md., December 18, 1863.*

I. General Orders, No. 51, from these headquarters, bearing date October 21, 1863, constituting the First and Third Separate Brigades, Eighth Army Corps, is hereby revoked.

II. The following troops of this command will constitute the First Separate Brigade: Third Regiment Delaware Volunteer Infantry, Col. S. H. Jenkins; Third Regiment (Potomac Home Brigade) Maryland Volunteer Infantry, Lieut. Col. Charles Gilpin; Purnell Legion Maryland Volunteer Infantry, Col. Samuel A. Graham, and such other troops as may be assigned to duty in that section of country within this department lying west of the Chesapeake Bay, south of and adjacent to the line of the Baltimore and Ohio Railroad, excepting the command of Col. C. A. Waite, U. S. Army, and the hospitals at Annapolis Junction.

Brig. Gen. E. B. Tyler, U. S. Volunteers, is assigned to the command of the First Separate Brigade, with his headquarters at the Relay House, Baltimore and Ohio Railroad.

III. The following batteries will constitute the Artillery Reserve of this army corps: Baltimore Battery Light Artillery, Capt. F. W. Alexander; Battery H, Third Regiment Pennsylvania Volunteer Artillery, Captain Rank; Battery A (Junior Artillery), Maryland Volunteers, Captain Bruce; Battery B (Eagle Artillery), Maryland Volunteers, Capt. Joseph H. Audoun.

Capt. F. W. Alexander, Baltimore Battery, senior officer of light artillery, will assume command of the Artillery Reserve, receiving orders from, and reporting directly to, these headquarters.

IV. The following regiments and detachments of cavalry will constitute the cavalry reserve of this army corps: Third Regiment Maryland Volunteer Cavalry, Lieut. Col. C. C. Tevis; First Regiment Connecticut Cavalry, Capt. E. W. French, commanding; First Battalion Delaware Volunteer Cavalry, Maj. N. B. Knight.

Lieut. Col. C. C. Tevis, Third Maryland Cavalry, senior officer of cavalry, will assume command of the Cavalry Reserve, receiving his orders from, and reporting directly to, these headquarters.

All orders conflicting with the present organization of the command are hereby revoked.

By command of Brigadier-General Lockwood:

WM. H. CHESEBROUGH,
. *Lieutenant-Colonel, and Assistant Adjutant-General.*

YORKTOWN,
December 18, 1863.

Major-General BUTLER:

Followed the enemy in Gloucester two hours before daylight this morning, with 100 cavalry, artillery, and infantry following in close support. The rebels ran—would not fight at any price. My cavalry chased them 10 miles, and are now returning. The destruction here is terrific. All hands not engaged in pursuing the enemy are busy clearing the wreck. The very surface of the solid earth is altered at the scene of the explosions. Whole loss to the Government which the troops' labor cannot replace will not exceed $40,000, which will be reduced by picking up shell, shot, and bullets. No life lost. Conduct of most of the troops entirely soldierly. No confusion. An attack by the enemy could have been met and repelled while the explosions were taking place and the whole fort filled with flying missiles. A few Sibley tents would do us good.

I. J. WISTAR,
Brigadier-General.

CUMBERLAND, MD., *December* 18, 1863.
(Received 11.30 a. m.)
Brig. Gen. G. W. CULLUM,
Chief of Staff:

General Sullivan reports that a cavalry scout has just returned from Loudoun County, commanded by Captain Keys, of the Twenty-second Pennsylvania. Near Upperville he captured Colonel Carter, of the First Virginia Cavalry, 5 men, and 6 horses. Keys' loss, 1 man killed and 2 captured. Enemy's, 1 man and 2 horses killed.

B. F. KELLEY,
Brigadier-General.

DECEMBER 19, 1863—10 p. m.
(Received 10.30 p. m.)
Major-General HALLECK:

General Gregg reports the return of the command sent to Salem and Manassas Gap after Rosser. They report Rosser's command as having passed through Front Royal yesterday morning, and that they moved toward Luray. One of Rosser's men was captured.

GEO. G. MEADE,
Major-General, Commanding.

(Copy to Major-General Augur.)

DECEMBER 20, 1863—11 p. m.
(Received 12.10 a. m., 21st.)
Major-General HALLECK:

I have directed General Pleasonton to send a brigade of cavalry to Luray, but I hardly think they can overtake Rosser, who will have had time to pass up the valley and rejoin Stuart.

GEO. G. MEADE,
Major-General, Commanding.

HEADQUARTERS UNITED STATES FORCES,
Near Portsmouth, Va., December 20, 1863.
Col. J. W. SHAFFER,
Chief of Staff:

SIR: In compliance with the communication of the 18th, from the major-general commanding, requesting a report as to the feasibility of holding a line to include the six northeastern counties of North Carolina, and of affording protection to the people thereof, I have the honor to state:

A line including these counties should be traced as follows: From Albemarle Sound, ascending the Chowan and Blackwater Rivers some 50 miles, and thence across the country to Suffolk and the Nansemond River, a whole distance of not less than 70 miles. While the Chowan and Blackwater would offer a considerable obstacle to the inroads of the enemy, from the Blackwater to Suffolk, some 30 miles, there are no natural defenses whatever. To hold a line of this character, would require a movable force equal to the force which the enemy can bring against it, besides strong outposts and guards at the passes of the river, with their proper supports. I have to report, therefore, that with the force at my disposal, 6,655 of all arms effective, it is impossible to hold the line in question.

Our present line, which includes the counties of Nansemond, Norfolk, and Princess Anne, Va., beginning on the James River, extends up the Nansemond to Suffolk; thence along Jericho Canal to Lake Drummond, in the Dismal Swamp; thence by the feeder to the Dismal Swamp Canal, and thence by the Little Canal and Northwest River to Currituck Sound. By abandoning the positions at Pongo Bridge and on Northwest River, and throwing the troops now garrisoning them forward to South Mills and the Pasquotank River, a new line can be formed to include the counties of Currituck and Camden, N. C. This line would be identical with the present as far as Lake Drummond, thence following the line of the Pasquotank south to Albemarle Sound, instead of east by the feeders, Little Canal, and Northwest River to Currituck Sound. But all the positions which are or may be occupied to hold these lines, as Suffolk, South Mills, Northwest Landing, Pongo Bridge, &c., are simply outposts, and, although affording present protection to the people inside, would, in the event of the advance of a heavy force of the enemy from the Blackwater, have to be abandoned and the troops drawn in to the fortified lines around Norfolk and Portsmouth.

I am, sir, very respectfully, your obedient servant,

GEO. W. GETTY,
Brigadier-General, Commanding.

CUMBERLAND, MD., *December* 20, 1863—8 p. m.
(Received 10.15 p. m.)

Brig. Gen. G. W. CULLUM,
Chief of Staff:

Brigadier-General Sullivan reports that a citizen has just come in to the ferry, and reports that Colonel Rosser, with a brigade of Stuart's cavalry, is in the Luray Valley, maneuvering to get in the rear of General Sullivan's force, now near Harrisonburg, engaging the attention of Imboden. If General Meade would send a cavalry force to Luray, he could cut off Rosser.

B. F. KELLEY,
Brigadier-General.

WASHINGTON, D. C.,
December 21, 1863—1 p. m.

Brigadier-General KELLEY:

General Meade has sent a brigade to Luray. I hear nothing of Averell.

H. W. HALLECK,
General-in-Chief.

HEADQUARTERS ARMY OF THE POTOMAC,
December 21, 1863—1 p. m. (Received 2 p. m.)

Major-General HALLECK:

Scouts just in, state it was reported at Orange Court-House that Averell had been into Staunton, burning the depot and doing other damage to the railroad, and that he had beaten Imboden and Jenkins.   On receipt of this intelligence, Fitzhugh Lee's and Wickham's brigades of cavalry, with seven batteries of artillery, were sent to Albemarle County; they were traced as far as Stony Point, and are believed to have gone to Staunton.   No other movements of troops reported; rebel soldiers said it was expected Longstreet would return to Lee's army.

GEO. G. MEADE,
Major-General, Commanding.

———

CUMBERLAND, MD., *December 21, 1863—11 p. m.*
(Received 6.50 a. m., 22d.)

Brigadier-General CULLUM,
Chief of Staff:

Brigadier-General Sullivan reports that he has just received information that Fitzhugh Lee's cavalry were crossing at Berry's Ferry, on Saturday, and that two brigades of infantry were crossing at Front Royal.   I think this information is doubtful, but if true General Meade can certainly prevent their safe return east of the Blue Ridge.

B. F. KELLEY,
Brigadier-General.

———

WAR DEPARTMENT,
December 21, 1863—8.50 p. m.

Maj. Gen. BENJAMIN F. BUTLER,
Fort Monroe, Va.:

You have subjoined an order of this Department, placing the county of Saint Mary's, in Maryland, and the counties of Northampton and Accomac, in Virginia, under your command, as a part of the Department of Virginia.   You will please assume command immediately, and direct the commandant of the prisoners' camp at Point Lookout to report to you.   It is deemed expedient that you make an immediate inspection of that post, with the view to ascertain its security against any effort of the prisoners to escape, or of the rebels to aid them in that purpose.   You will communicate a copy of the order to Brigadier-General Marston, commanding at Point Lookout, and acknowledge the receipt of this telegram.

By order of the Secretary of War:

ED. R. S. CANBY,
Brigadier-General, and Assistant Adjutant-General.

[Inclosure.]

WAR DEPARTMENT,
December 21, 1863.

Ordered, that the county of Saint Mary's, in the State of Maryland, and the counties of Northampton and Accomac, in the State of Virginia, be, and they are hereby annexed to the Department of Virginia, under the command of the general commanding that department.

By order of the Secretary of War:

ED. R. S. CANBY,
Brigadier-General, and Assistant Adjutant-General.

———

DECEMBER 21, [1863]—7 a. m.
Col. J. W. SHAFFER,
Chief of Staff, Fort Monroe:

Fugitives from South Mills arrived last night, report a force of the enemy (cavalry and infantry) between Elizabeth City and South Mills, within 8 miles of Pasquotank Bridge, numbers not stated. I will obtain further information in the course of the day.

GEO. W. GETTY,
Brigadier-General, Commanding.

(Same to Colonel Stetzel, Suffolk.)

———

DECEMBER 21, [1863]—9 p. m.
Colonel STETZEL,
Suffolk :

Major Wetherill, who has gone to South Mills, reports, on the authority of Mr. Duke, of Lake Drummond, that there is quite a force of rebel infantry and artillery at Zuni, with the intention of making a move, via Suffolk, with a view of drawing off attention from a force operating in the direction of South Mills. Be on your guard and advise me of all that is going on in your neighborhood.

GEO. W. GETTY,
Brigadier-General, Commanding.

———

DECEMBER 21, 1863.
Major-General BUTLER,
Fort Monroe:

If General Wild is in Currituck County, it would be well to send a steamer to Pongo to be in readiness to transfer the Ninety-eighth New York from that place to Coinjack Bridge or Northwest Landing, as may be most needed. I have sent a squadron of cavalry to South Mills to obtain information and watch the movements of the enemy. Commanders of posts have been instructed to afford all possible assistance to General Wild.

GEO. W. GETTY,
Brigadier-General, Commanding.

———

HEADQUARTERS UNITED STATES FORCES,
Near Portsmouth, Va., December 21, 1863.
General GRAHAM,
Commanding Naval Brigade, Norfolk:

Will you be pleased to send a gunboat to Pongo, to report to General Ledlie or Lieutenant-Colonel Wead, commanding Ninety-eighth

Regiment New York Volunteers. General Ledlie has received full instructions from me. It may be necessary to use the gunboat to transfer the Ninety-eighth New York from Pongo to Coinjack Bridge, Currituck Court-House, or Northwest Landing, as the exigencies of the service may demand.

GEO. W. GETTY,
Brigadier-General, Commanding.

HEADQUARTERS ARMY OF THE POTOMAC,
December 22, 1863.

ADJUTANT-GENERAL OF THE ARMY,
Washington, D. C.:

SIR: I have the honor herewith to transmit a copy of an order issued by me, designed to carry out, in this army, the orders and instructions of the War Department relative to the re-enlistment of veteran volunteers.

It is not in my power, at the present moment, to say what number of men have re-enlisted or agreed to re-enlist prior to this date, but I place the number, approximately, at 10,000 infantry and 2,500 cavalry.

I do not consider that a greater number of men can be spared at present, although it is hoped that a considerable number will yet re-enlist; and, if so, they can be furloughed when the men about to leave return to duty.

Under the discretion left to me in General Orders, No. 376, of the 21st ultimo, from the War Department, I have directed that individual furloughs be given, believing that this would be more acceptable to the men generally than an order to report to the superintendents of the recruiting service, in their respective States, for furloughs and reorganization. When, however, three-fourths of a regiment or company re-enlist, the men will be allowed to go home in a body with their officers, and to take their arms with them.

The period of the furlough has been fixed at thirty-five days, so as to allow the men, as far as practicable, thirty days within the limits of their States.

Very respectfully, your obedient servant,

GEO. G. MEADE,
Major-General, Commanding.

[Inclosure.]

SPECIAL ORDERS, }   HDQRS. ARMY OF THE POTOMAC,
No. 329.   }   *December 21, 1863.*

1. With the exception hereinafter indicated, corps and other independent commanders are now authorized to grant individual furloughs for thirty-five days, which must cover the entire period of the soldier's absence from his company and regiment, to such men of their respective commands as may have, up to this date, re-enlisted, or having, since the issue of the circular from these headquarters dated December 17, 1863, signified their intention to do so, shall at once re-enlist as veteran volunteers, under the provisions of General Orders, Nos. 191, 305, and 376, from the War Department.

2. When three-fourths of the men of a regiment or company re-enlist, such portion of the regiment or company will be allowed

to go home in a body, and take with it its arms and equipments. In all other cases, the arms and equipments of the men granted furloughs will be turned in, before leaving camp, to the division ordnance officer, by whom they will be transferred to the officer in charge of the ordnance depot, to be held subject to his call on the return of the men to duty. Three-fourths of a veteran regiment will be understood to mean three-fourths of the men belonging to it who are within the limits of this army, and not to include those absent as prisoners of war, in general hospitals, &c. When there are men in a veteran organization who do not come within the limits for re-enlistment, all men who have joined the army since July 1, 1863, excepted, and are yet willing to re-enlist, they will be permitted to go on furlough with the regiment, in case it goes in a body, and those only will be left behind who are within the limits and yet refuse to re-enlist, and the aforesaid men who have recently joined. The men willing to re-enlist will, of course, not be discharged and remustered till they come within the limits; that is, have less than one year to serve, but they will be required to affirm, in writing, their intention to re-enlist, and such affirmation must be witnessed by two commissioned officers, and filed with the muster-rolls of the company to which they belong.

3. Furloughs will not be granted in cases where three-fourths of a regiment or a company have agreed to re-enlist under the foregoing provisions until after corps commanders shall have sent to these headquarters, for the orders of the commanding general thereon, a statement showing the strength present with the army of such regiment or company, and the number of men who have re-enlisted or can re-enlist under the orders and instructions of the War Department.

4. When an organization may be broken up for the time being by the departure of the men going on furlough, corps commanders will transfer, temporarily, the officers and men who remain to other regiments and companies from the same State, or organize them into a battalion, as may be thought best.

5. Every furlough granted under this order will have an indorsement showing that the holder, as a veteran volunteer, is entitled to transportation to and from his home, as provided for by Paragraph 4, of General Orders, No. 376, from the War Department. Corps commanders will make requisitions upon the chief quartermaster for transportation for the men of their commands who may be granted furloughs, and the chief quartermaster will make the necessary arrangements with the proper officer of his department at Washington to have all such men promptly forwarded to their homes.

6. The necessities of the service will not admit of the granting of furloughs at present to a larger number of men than are embraced in this order. But the men not herein included, who may be entitled to re-enlist as veterans, will be granted a similar furlough on the return to duty of the men now furloughed.

7. Corps and other independent commanders will report at the earliest moment practicable the number of men who have re-enlisted or may re-enlist in their respective commands, and who may receive furloughs under the provisions of this order.

By command of Major-General Meade :

S. WILLIAMS,
Assistant Adjutant-General.

CIRCULAR.]   HEADQUARTERS ARMY OF THE POTOMAC,
                                        December 22, 1863.

1. The pickets of the Sixth Corps will extend from Freeman's Ford to the Rixeyville road, about 3 miles from Culpeper.

2. The pickets of the Third Corps will extend from the left of those of the Sixth Corps on the Rixeyville road to Mountain Run, opposite Gaines' Mill, where they will connect with the right of the pickets of the First Corps. They will commence again at the left of the pickets of the First Corps at Inship's, foot of Pony Mountain, and extend along the front of Mountain Run, joining those of the Second Corps near the road from Stevensburg to Morton's Ford.

3. The pickets of the First Corps will extend from Mountain Run, near Gaines' Mill on the right, around to Inship's on the left. They will connect on the right and left with the pickets of the Third Corps.

4. The pickets of the Second Corps will extend from the Stevensburg and Morton's Ford road to the Rappahannock River, and up that river above Kelly's Ford.

5. The general line to be occupied by the pickets is indicated on the map sent herewith.

By command of Major-General Meade :

                                        S. WILLIAMS,
                                Assistant Adjutant-General.

(To commanding officers First, Second, Third, Fifth, and Sixth Corps, Cavalry Corps, and chief engineer.)

SPECIAL ORDERS, }   HDQRS. ARMY OF THE POTOMAC,
   No. 331.   }   *December 22,* 1863.

I. The First Corps will move to Culpeper and post one division near the line of railroad, well toward Mitchell's Station, to support the cavalry picketing from Raccoon Ford to the right. With this object in view, the division will throw forward a brigade close up to the cavalry at Mitchell's Station (the infantry will move at the same time as the cavalry). The infantry brigade will picket the open ground in its front, and connect with the cavalry pickets on its right and left. The duty of supporting the cavalry will be performed by the divisions of the First Corps in turn.

A special guard around the town of Culpeper will be maintained by the First Corps.

II. The Second Corps will keep one brigade posted in the vicinity of Sheppard's Grove Post-Office, and one in advance of Stevensburg, on the road to Morton's Ford, to support the cavalry picketing from Morton's Ford to the left.

III. Special directions have been given for posting the cavalry corps.

IV. The infantry picket line will be established in accordance with the instructions and map inclosed herewith.*

V. Daily memoranda, similar to those required at the camp near Falmouth, will be made and transmitted daily to these headquarters,

------
* Not found.

as soon as the necessary blanks are furnished, and they will be sent
to corps commanders and to the chief of staff departments as soon
as practicable.

By command of Major-General Meade:

S. WILLIAMS,
Assistant Adjutant-General.

GETTY'S HEADQUARTERS,
December 22, 1863.

Maj. R. S. DAVIS,
Assistant Adjutant-General:

A dispatch from General Wild addressed to yourself has just been
handed me. I have positive information that none of the enemy are
at or about South Mills. The force that visited that place have
retired, a portion across the Blackwater and the remainder across
the Chowan. They could not possibly be overtaken by a force marching via Suffolk.

GEO. W. GETTY,
Brigadier-General, Commanding.

HEADQUARTERS UNITED STATES FORCES,
Near Portsmouth, Va., December 22, 1863.

Major-General BUTLER,
Fort Monroe:

I submit the following, derived from best information, of the recent
movements and designs of the enemy:

On Wednesday and Thursday of last week, a considerable force
advanced from the Blackwater, passing through Gates County, N.
C., for the purpose of opposing the march of the troops under Gen-
eral Wild, who, it was reported, intended marching from Elizabeth
City upon Hertford, Edenton, &c., and from thence through Gates
County to Suffolk. A portion of this force advanced as far as the
Pasquotank, and after destroying the bridges, ferries, &c., returned.

To draw attention from the force sent against General Wild,
infantry and artillery were concentrated at each of the points,
Franklin and Zuni, for the purpose of making a demonstration in
this direction via Suffolk. The force at Franklin advanced as far as
Carrsville. Of that at Zuni I have no information. No doubt the
movement was suspended in consequence of the withdrawal of General Wild's force to the east side of the Pasquotank. All is quiet at
Suffolk and South Mills to-night.

GEO. W. GETTY,
Brigadier-General.

GENERAL ORDERS, ⎱ HDQRS. 18TH A. C., DEPT. OF VA. AND N. C.,
No. 58.   ⎰   *Fort Monroe, Va., December 22, 1863.*

In compliance with the following general orders from the War
Department, command is assumed of the counties of Saint Mary's,
in Maryland, and Northampton and Accomac, in Virginia, and they
are hereby annexed to this department.

WAR DEPARTMENT,
Washington City, December 21, 1863.

Ordered, that the county of Saint Mary's, in the State of Maryland, and the counties of Northampton and Accomac, in the State of Virginia, be, and they are hereby, annexed to the Department of Virginia, under the command of the general commanding that department.

By order of the Secretary of War:

ED. R. S. CANBY,
Brigadier-General, Assistant Adjutant-General.

GENERAL ORDERS,   HDQRS. 18TH ARMY CORPS, DEPT. OF VA. AND N. C.,
No. 29.   *Fort Monroe, Va., November 11, 1863.*

EXTRACT.

II. Each commander of division, separate brigade, post, district, or detached command, and each chief of a staff department, will forthwith report to these headquarters the exact condition of his command and the supplies of his department, respectively, accompanied with such remarks in relation thereto as he shall see fit. Each report shall have minuted thereon the date of the reception of this order, and the date of the transmission of such report.

The utmost dispatch, minuteness, and particularity are required in these reports.

By command of Major-General Butler:

R. S. DAVIS,
Major, and Assistant Adjutant-General.

All officers in command of troops and posts in those counties will immediately report to these headquarters, in accordance with Paragraph II, General Orders, No. 29, from these headquarters, hereunto annexed.

By command of Maj. Gen. B. F. Butler:

R. S. DAVIS,
Major, and Assistant Adjutant-General.

HEADQUARTERS ARMY OF THE POTOMAC,
December 23, 1863.

Commanding Officer Second Corps:

The following dispatch has just been received from the Adjutant-General's office, and is published to corps commanders for their information and government. It will be seen that it modifies somewhat Paragraph 2, Special Orders, 329.

WASHINGTON, D. C.,
December 23, 1863.

Major-General MEADE:

Under the telegram of the 21st instant, in relation to meaning three-quarters veteran volunteer regiments: No drafted men will be permitted to go on furlough with regiments. To volunteer recruits, or those who have joined since original organization of regiments or company, only those will be permitted to go on furlough with the regiment who are willing to re-enlist, and who, within three months, will come within the limits of re-enlistments.

E. D. TOWNSEND,
Assistant Adjutant-General.

By command of Major-General Meade:

S. WILLIAMS,
Assistant Adjutant-General.

HDQRS. ARMY OF THE POTOMAC, SIGNAL DEPT.,
December 23, 1863—3.55 p. m.

Major-General HUMPHREYS,
        Chief of Staff:

GENERAL: In reply to an inquiry of mine, concerning the last report from Pony Mountain, the signal officer on that station reports that—

The camps at Morton's and Raccoon Fords appear as usual, but those between the two fords have disappeared. Camp smokes appear this morning about a mile to the rear of where the camps were.

Very respectfully, &c.,

L. B. NORTON,
Captain, and Chief Signal Officer, A. P.

HDQRS. EIGHTY-THIRD PA. VOLS., MEDICAL DEPT.,·
                        December 23, 1863.

Dr. [————]:

SIR: I have the honor to report the facts and circumstances as far as I am able relative to the death of Dr. Jared Free, assistant surgeon Eighty-third Pennsylvania Volunteers, who was killed in an encounter with guerrillas on the 10th of December, 1863.

Dr. Jared Free joined the regiment on the 26th of June, 1863, at Frederick City, Md., when the army was on the march to Gettysburg, Pa. He participated in the battle of Gettysburg, and after the battle was retained at the First Division (Fifth Corps), hospital, where he remained until some time in September, when he rejoined the regiment at Beverly Ford, since which time until the time of his death he had been on duty with the regiment.

On the 10th of December, 1863, Dr. Free, accompanied by E. W. Bettis, quartermaster sergeant, went to the country, in charge of 20 guards and three wagons, for lumber. The pass granting them permission did not arrive at these headquarters very early in the morning, and the wagons started in advance, while Dr. Free, E. W. Bettis, quartermaster sergeant, and guard remained behind awaiting permission from brigade headquarters. By the time the pass returned from brigade headquarters, the wagons had proceeded some distance on the road toward Kelly's Ford. Dr. Free, E. W. Bettis, quartermaster sergeant, and guard followed in the direction of Kelly's Ford, whither they supposed the wagons had gone. But on the way they met a wagon and some guards of the Forty-fourth New York Volunteers. The guard informed them that the Eighty-third wagons had gone up to Mount Holly Church. Dr. Free and party proceeded to Mount Holly Church, and were informed by some soldiers of the Forty-fourth New York Volunteers that the Eighty-third wagons had gone in the direction of the old camping ground near Captain Payne's.

Dr. Free and party concluded to take a near cut across the ravine and strike the road at the nearest point. They passed down into the ravine without molestation, but found the opposite side of the hill too difficult of ascent, so they dismounted and followed the path up the ravine until they would come to a place that they could ascend. While following this path they were attacked by a band of guerrillas, who came rushing down the hill, at the same time ordering the quartermaster sergeant to halt and surrender, or they would blow his brains out; but notwithstanding their threats he quickly mounted his steed and escaped, but not without being shot at. The last he saw of Dr. Free, who was in the advance, was in the act of mounting his horse. The quartermaster sergeant distinctly heard two shots fired afterward, but knew nothing of the fate of Dr. Free until the next day, December 11, 1863, when a detachment of men and an officer of the Eighty-third Pennsylvania Volunteers went out in search of the guerrillas, and to gain some information, if possible, in regard to the fate of Dr. Free. When they arrived at the place' where the attack had been seen made the day previous, they saw no guerrillas, of course, but found the body of Dr. Free, pierced by two balls and seven buckshot, lying by the side of a log, some 30 feet from where he had last been seen the day previous by the quarter-master sergeant. He was shot in the right hypochondriac region, and all the bullet holes could be covered by the palm of the hand, showing conclusively that his antagonist could not have been more than 10 or 15 feet from him when he fired.

The body of Dr. Free was brought to camp late in the evening of the 11th of December, and having been properly cleansed, was confined in a rough board coffin and kept until the 18th of December, awaiting permission for some one to accompany the body home. Nothing having been heard from the papers that were sent up on the 11th of December, we concluded that, having kept the body six days, it would be best to forward it to Washington and have it expressed from there to his friends. His body was sent on the 18th of December in charge of Sergeant McKee, and ordered to be confined in a metallic coffin and expressed to his brother, Dr. John L. Free, Shrewsbury, York County, Pa.

Very respectfully, your obedient servant,

J. P. BURCHFIELD,
Surgeon, Eighty-third Pennsylvania Volunteers.

CUMBERLAND, MD., *December 23, 1863*—9 a. m.
(Received 11 a. m.)

Brig. Gen. G. W. CULLUM,
Chief of Staff:

General Sullivan telegraphs that Colonel Wells, commanding column, reached Strasburg last evening, and that Early's division, of Ewell's corps, is certainly following him, and was at Mount Jackson yesterday. It was currently reported at Harrisonburg before Wells left that Averell had destroyed the depot at Salem, locomotives, trains, &c. I have nothing definite from Averell yet.

B. F. KELLEY,
Brigadier-General.

CUMBERLAND, MD., *December 23, 1863.*
(Received 7 p. m.)

Brigadier-General CULLUM,
Chief of Staff:

Just received telegram from General Averell announcing his brilliant success. He informs me he has forwarded a copy direct to the general. Has it been received? If not, I will forward at once.

B. F. KELLEY,
Brigadier-General,

CUMBERLAND, MD., *December 23, 1863*—8 p. m.
(Received 9.40 p. m.)

Brig. Gen. G. W. CULLUM,
 Chief of Staff:

Colonel Mulligan reports that Colonel Thoburn, who accompanied General Averell as far as Monterey with two regiments of infantry and a battery, and who was ordered to threaten Staunton from the west during Averell's absence at Salem, has reached the North Fork of the Potomac, on the Seneca road, in safety on his return, bringing with him General Averell's train. The enemy blockaded the road on him, but he has come through without loss. Will reach Petersburg to-night.

     B. F. KELLEY,
      Brigadier-General.

HEADQUARTERS DEPARTMENT OF WEST VIRGINIA,
December 23, 1863.

Governor BOREMAN,
 Wheeling:

General Averell has succeeded in cutting the Virginia and Tennessee railroad at Salem, in Roanoke County. He reached there on the 16th. Destroyed three depots containing an immense amount of public property, unquestionably collected there for the use of Longstreet's army, which is supposed to be falling back into Virginia.

The following comprises a portion of the property destroyed : 2,000 barrels flour, 10,000 bushels of wheat, 100,000 bushels of shelled corn, 50,000 bushels of oats, 2,000 barrels of meat, 1,000 sacks of salt, several cords of leather, 31 boxes of clothing, 20 bales of cotton, large amount of harness, shoes, saddles, equipments, tools, oil, tar, and various other stores, and 100 wagons ; water stations, bridges, several culverts, and much of track torn up and rails destroyed ; large quantity of bridge timber and repairing materials were also destroyed.

General Averell captured about 200 prisoners, and lost about 60 men in killed, wounded, and missing. He says :

My command has marched, climbed, slid, and swum 355 miles since the 8th instant.

This is undoubtedly one of the most hazardous, important, and successful raids since the commencement of the war. General Averell will reach Beverly to-night.

     [B. F. KELLEY,]
      Brigadier-General.

FORT MONROE, *December 23, 1863.*
(Received 6.20 p. m.)

SECRETARY OF WAR :

Flag-of-truce boat in. No difficulty, I think, at Point Lookout. Have strengthened the post. Telegrams from Lynchburg to Richmond papers say that—

A force of the enemy—3,000 cavalry and mounted infantry—under Averell, reached Salem, on Virginia and Tennessee Railroad, December 16, at 10.30 o'clock. Telegraphic communication has been interrupted. Nothing heard since,

By Richmond papers of the 22d, under date—

BRISTOL, *December* 21.

Officers from the front state that our Confederate forces are moving forward in the direction of Knoxville. Three hundred prisoners captured in the engagement at Bean's Station. Reports from below state that Imboden and Echols have surrounded the Salem raider, Averell, and that the entire party will probably be captured. The enemy have burned their wagons and destroyed their artillery to prevent their falling into our hands.

CHARLESTON, *December* 21.

Little change in the position of affairs. No important movement of the fleet. A calcium light has been displayed for two nights past, reflecting on the city. No other news of importance.

CHARLESTON, *December* 21.

Twenty-nine vessels, including the Ironsides, are inside the bar. The usual number in the stream and off the bar.

BENJ. F. BUTLER,
Major-General, Commanding.

WAR DEPARTMENT,
December 23, 1863—9.40 a. m.

Major-General BUTLER, *Fort Monroe:*

Your extracts from Richmond papers received. Averell has got safely back with loss of 6 men drowned, 4 wounded, and 90 missing. He reports having reached Salem; burned three depots with a large amount of stores; destroyed 15 miles of railroad and 5 bridges. The enemy made vigorous and extensive combinations to surround him, but he got through with the loss stated, having burned some ambulances, a few wagons, and two caissons.

The Adjutant-General informs me that the order assigning Point Lookout and Accomac and Northampton Counties to your command has not been acknowledged.

You will please report if received.

EDWIN M. STANTON,
Secretary of War.

HEADQUARTERS UNITED STATES FORCES,
Near Portsmouth, Va., December 23, 1863.

Major-General BUTLER, *Fort Monroe, Va.:*

Lieutenant-Colonel Stetzel, commanding outpost at Suffolk, reports this morning that there were sixteen companies of rebel cavalry in Suffolk last night from 9 till 11 o'clock, at which time they retired. They came from Elizabeth City to Suffolk, and have gone back to the Blackwater.

GEO. W. GETTY,
Brigadier-General, Commanding.

NORFOLK, *December* 23, 1863.

Major-General BUTLER:

General Wild has just arrived here. His command will be in this evening by 11 o'clock. He has lost 4 men killed, 1 mortally wounded, and 2 taken prisoners; about 12 men wounded. I will send a preliminary report in the morning as soon as it can be made, and a more full report afterward. Your dispatch stopping the publishing of the Old Dominion paper is received.

Respectfully,

JAMES BARNES,
Brigadier-General, Commanding.

HEADQUARTERS SUB-DISTRICT OF BEAUFORT,
Morehead City, N. C., December 23, 1863.

Major-General PECK,
Comdg. Army and District of North Carolina:

GENERAL: In consequence of information received that a schooner had run into Bear Inlet with a cargo of salt, which schooner had been destroyed by one of our war vessels, and that about 400 sacks of salt were lying on the beach, I proceeded on board the steamer Howquah this morning at daylight, by permission of Commander Dove, for the purpose of ascertaining the facts of the case. On my arrival, and after reconnoitering well with my glass, I sent a boat through the inlet to examine the beach and sound, on the return of which the officer in charge reported about 400 sacks of salt and about 500 barrels of turpentine on the beach.

If you deem it advisable to destroy or capture said stores, I can do so by taking a gunboat and launches to land and protect about 100 infantry, keeping a proper force in reserve. The steamer Fasier is here on her way to Port Royal, which only draws 3 feet of water. She could assist materially. I suppose the stores are protected by a company of cavalry, and probably one field piece. I reconnoitered carefully. Dispatch only will secure success. I await instructions.

J. JOURDAN,
Colonel.

SPECIAL ORDERS, } HDQRS. ARMY, ADJT. GENERAL'S OFFICE,
No. 569.   }   *Washington, December 23, 1863.*

*   *   *   *   *   *   *

2. Brig. Gen. R. O. Tyler, U. S. Volunteers, is hereby relieved from duty with the Army of the Potomac, and will repair without delay to this city and report in person to Major-General Augur, U. S. Volunteers, commanding Department of Washington.

By command of Major-General Halleck:

E. D. TOWNSEND,
Assistant Adjutant-General.

DECEMBER 24, 1863—9 p. m.

Major-General HALLECK:

The command sent to Luray has returned. They report that Rosser and his command left Luray for Madison Court-House last Monday. The command captured 9 men and killed 1.

GEO. G. MEADE,
Major-General, Commanding.

(Copy to Major-General Augur.)

HEADQUARTERS CAVALRY CORPS,
December 24, 1863.
Colonel TAYLOR,
Commanding Second Cavalry Division:
The within communication is furnished for your information.
The major-general commanding directs that you have your brigades at Warrenton and Bealeton, keep a sharp lookout, and report at once to these headquarters any information that you may gain.
Very respectfully,
E. B. PARSONS,
Captain, Acting Assistant Adjutant-General.

[Inclosure.]

WASHINGTON, *December 24, 1863.*
Major-General MEADE :
A woman comes in and reports that one of the rebel cavalry engaged in the last raid was at her house, and said that the affair was a failure, but they were preparing for another on a large scale ; that there would be about 5,000 engaged in it. Should this prove true, I have no competent force to prevent it or save the road. She reported that the expedition will start the last of this week.
C. C. AUGUR,
Major-General.

———

HDQRS. ARMY OF THE POTOMAC, *December 24, 1863.*
(Received 2 p. m.)
Maj. Gen. C. C. AUGUR,
Commanding, Washington:
I doubt if the enemy can spare 5,000 cavalry for a raid. I have, however, directed General Crawford to relieve your people at Bull Run bridge and assume the defense of that point. It will be almost impossible to prevent some damage being done by raids in force, but by holding the most important points we can easily repair damage at other places. My cavalry in the rear are directed to be on the alert.
GEO. G. MEADE,
Major-General.

———

WASHINGTON, *December 24, 1863.*
Colonel ALEXANDER :
It is reported here that another raid upon the Alexandria and Orange Railroad is to be made the latter part of this week. You will please have every possible precaution taken to make a successful resistance. Where block-houses are not completed, have such a disposition of the timber made as will afford protection to parties and stores. Have strong barricades on the roads from the Occoquan, and the roads themselves well patrolled. Let every officer on the line of the railroad know of this, so that precaution can be used. The block-house at Bull Run bridge can be used by all for defense now. The one at Devereux Station should also be defensible.
By command of Major-General Augur :
J. H. TAYLOR,
Chief of Staff.

WASHINGTON,
December 24, 1863.

Colonel ALEXANDER :

Major-General Meade has decided to relieve, by a detachment from the Pennsylvania Reserves, the guard from your command now at Bull Run bridge. When the change is made, employ the guard relieved in strengthening the most important posts on the road between Fairfax Station and Bull Run bridge. Investigate and report the rumor that the four vedettes were captured and hung by guerrillas yesterday, near Flint Hill.

J. H. TAYLOR,
Asst. Adjt. Gen., and Chief of Staff.

FORT MONROE, VA., *December* 24, 1863.
(Received 11.40 a. m.)

General THOMAS,
Adjutant-General, U. S. Army:

Secretary of War's dispatch announcing Averell's return received. The dispatch assigning Point Lookout, Accomac, and Northampton to this command was received. General Butler left yesterday for Point Lookout. Will return to-night.

J. W. SHAFFER,
Colonel, and Chief of Staff.

HDQRS. FIRST ARMY CORPS, ARMY OF THE POTOMAC,
December 25, 1863.

Brig. Gen. S. WILLIAMS,
Asst. Adjt. Gen., Army of the Potomac:

GENERAL : I cannot conceal my astonishment that General Merritt should have reported to headquarters that "General Newton tells me he does not know what is expected of him," a sentence calculated to give an entirely wrong interpretation to my views. All the specifications of Special Orders, 331, and circular of December 22, were carried out. The picket line was established, and one division sent to the neighborhood of Mitchell's Station yesterday. The brigade directed to advance close on to Mitchell's Station may not yet have done so, but its commander conferred with the officer commanding cavalry here (as directed), and if it has not, the fault is not with the infantry. The brigade of infantry and the cavalry were by the order to advance at the same time. The cavalry division were by this morning were ordered back.

It will thus be seen that I clearly comprehended the instructions given me, and have acted on them to the utmost of my power. The only sense in which I am ignorant of the object of my being sent here is this, that I am uncertain whether our coming here is a premonitory sign of an advance against the enemy, or whether it is intended as a precaution against his advance. I think General Merritt has been led into his mistake by the expression of some such views as the above on my part.

Very respectfully, your obedient servant,

JOHN NEWTON,
Major-General, Commanding.

HEADQUARTERS ARMY OF THE POTOMAC,
December 25, 1863.
Colonel TAYLOR,
    Commanding Second Division Cavalry:
    Dispatch just received states that Mosby has made great prepa-
ration to have a frolic, with his principal officers, at the house of Dr.
Bispham and Mrs. Murray, in Salem, to-night. Dr. Bispham's is the
second house as you go in the village from Warrenton, and Mrs.
Murray lives about the middle of the street, in a large white house.
The major-general commanding directs that you send a party from
the brigade which is at Warrenton, under the command of a smart
and competent officer, to capture them.
                                        E. B. PARSONS,
                        Captain, Acting Assistant Adjutant-General.

HEADQUARTERS CHIEF ENGINEER OF DEFENSES,
Washington, December 26, 1863.
Brig. Gen. JOSEPH G. TOTTEN,
    Chief Engineer, &c., Washington, D. C.:
    SIR : By letter of the Secretary of War to you, of the 2d instant,
you are instructed to detail me—

> To make an examination of the shore of Lake Erie, and designate at what
> points defensive works can be advantageously erected to guard the States of New
> York, Pennsylvania, and Ohio against hostile raids from Canada.

    In compliance with the tenor of the above, I have, after first visit-
ing and consulting the Governor of Ohio, at Columbus, visited the
following points on the shore of Lake Erie, viz, Sandusky, Toledo,
Cleveland, Erie, Dunkirk, and Buffalo.
    I understood my instructions to refer solely to the actual condition
of things, and not to refer to another state of things in which war
shall exist betwixt Canada itself (and the Government to which she
belongs) and the United States. I have of course made it a point,
so far as I was able in a brief time and at such a season, to form in
my mind some idea of the positions and character of works required
for the latter supposition, but report only in reference to the former.
    There seems to me to be two objects, and only two, for which
"hostile raids" might be made by parties of the numerous secessionists in Canada. One of these objects would be the rescue of the prisoners on Johnson's Island; the other, to destroy shipping, railroad
depots, grain elevators, machine shops, &c., which are situated con-
tiguous to the harbors of the places I have mentioned. Plunder
might perhaps be considered an object, but the risks would be great
of penetrating into the interior of such places as Buffalo, Cleveland,
&c., where alone there is anything to be carried off, and the means
of guarding against it are identical with those to be used against
destruction.
    First, in reference to the rescue of prisoners. There are now 2,800
of them, all officers, confined on Johnson's Island. This island is
almost a mile long and one-half mile broad (at its broadest part).
Its nearest distance to the mainland is over a half mile. The permanent guard is a battalion of four companies of Ohio Volunteers
(to be, as I understood, speedily increased to a regiment) and a
company of heavy artillery. Besides this, there was stationed on

the island a part of a regiment of dismounted cavalry. There are three (I think) 20-pounder Parrotts, one 30-pounder, and a battery of 3½-inch ordnance rifled guns, in charge of the artillery company. It seems to me that the above gives all reasonable security against an aquatic raid. How can a gang of raiders get together in a friendly country vessels to carry men enough to overcome the guard, to encounter the artillery now on the island, or if successful in these things, how could they get their prisoners away?

With the permanent guard raised to a full regiment (as it should be) and the artillery force on the island, I think we have reasonable security, and that the light battery may be sent elsewhere.

During the recent alarm, the light battery was placed on Cedar Point, behind a rude sand epaulement, and a detachment of the artillery company had charge of it. This point is unquestionably the key-point to the harbor defense, but with my ideas of the chance of maritime attack, it does not seem to me necessary. If a battery is kept up there hereafter (it is now withdrawn for the winter), it is proper it should be made secure. Surprise will be the main feature of the attack, and a body of men strong enough to overcome the Johnson's Island guard will, a fortiori, be more than strong enough to overpower and capture a fraction of a company of artillery (a landing being made on some point on the shore to the eastward). It will be a difficult and expensive matter to make the battery or epaulement itself an impassable obstacle, and unless that is done there is no use in closing its gorge. Short of these expensive measures, a strong block-house between the epaulement and the light-house would be required.

In the winter of 1837, during the "patriot war," a party of American sympathizers or Canadian refugees crossed from near the west shore of Sandusky Bay on the ice to Point Pelee Island. They were there met by a body of British troops coming from the Canadian shore (also on the ice), and a skirmish occurred. This suggests a species of raid upon Johnson's Island within the bounds of probability, and makes more important the intended increase of the permanent guard, especially during the winter months.

As to raids having the object of destruction of property, I will mention, to illustrate my opinions as to defensive works, what seems to me one of the most feasible. From the pier and harbor of Buffalo to the Canadian shore the distance is not more than 2 miles. Two hundred bold men might conspire to meet on this Canadian shore, have three or four boats ready to embark in the night, land in the harbor, and, proceeding from one end to the other, set fire to all the elevators, shipping, &c. Against such a proceeding defensive works would be useless, or nearly so; for if we suppose batteries on the pier and shore, and a watch so perfect that the hostile approach could not be made unobserved (a thing really impossible), it would only increase somewhat the risks to the raiders by causing a landing at a more remote point. The end of the lake near Buffalo is frequently bridged by ice, suggesting another way of operating a raid of this character.

At Cleveland, Erie, Dunkirk, Toledo, and Sandusky, the most obvious methods of raiding would not differ much in general character, though perhaps each place would suggest somewhat different means of operating. Toledo, Sandusky, and Dunkirk may be approached by ice in winter. Cleveland and Erie probably cannot. While defensive works would not be a protection, all that they could do would be accomplished by rifled field artillery. At every point mentioned there are exceedingly favorable locations for a field battery to act upon vessels attempting to enter the harbors, and such a battery, instead of being fixed, could ply to any point where a landing might be threatened.

In conclusion, I consider the way to "guard the States of New York, Pennsylvania, and Ohio against hostile raids from Canada" is by home guards and not defensive works. Artillery companies should be organized, supplied with field artillery (if not already done), at the following places, viz: Buffalo, Erie, Cleveland, and Toledo, and battalions or regiments of State militia should be organized at all the places I have named, and kept in a complete state of drill and efficiency; the Governors of the several States and the mayors of the several towns mentioned should be informed that upon their own vigilance mainly must repose the security of their property. In conjunction with these measures by the State authorities, it would be advisable to employ a few intelligent men of the right sort to spend their time mainly in Canada and the provinces, keeping themselves informed of what is going on along the lake and river shores, and so far as practicable of what is taking place among the secessionists themselves and their Canadian or provincial sympathizers.

I have to acknowledge much useful information and assistance in making my examinations from Colonel Bliss, of Governor Tod's staff, whom the Governor kindly directed to accompany me.

I am, very respectfully, your most obedient,

J. G. BARNARD,
Brigadier-General, &c.

BEVERLY,
December 26, 1863.

Brig. Gen. B. F. KELLEY,
Commanding, Cumberland:

I will move toward the railroad to-morrow. From the fact that Early and Fitzhugh Lee are in the department, I think it highly important that my mounted force should be taken into the valley as soon as possible. Will you order cars for my transportation to be at Webster on Tuesday, 29th instant? I will endeavor to reach Cumberland to-morrow night myself.

WM. W. AVERELL,
Brigadier-General.

HEADQUARTERS FIRST CORPS,
December 28, 1863.

Major-General HUMPHREYS,
Chief of Staff, Army of the Potomac:

In my orders of 22d instant from your headquarters, I am directed to "throw forward a brigade close up to the cavalry at Mitchell's Station." In accordance with these orders, a brigade was posted there. I now find that the cavalry which I supposed to be at that point are about 1½ miles to the rear, though with their pickets in front. General Merritt gives as a reason for not posting his cavalry there that "the ground is low, clayey, and wet—the animals would be over ears in mud and water in a very short time."

This report is confirmed by the commanding officer of my troops there, and I now desire to ask, if possible, that they be allowed to fall back to the high ground in rear of the station, near where the cavalry are encamped.

The pickets can remain to the front, as they now are.

Very respectfully, your obedient servant,

JOHN NEWTON,
Major-General, Commanding.

HEADQUARTERS CAVALRY CORPS,
December 28, 1863—2.30 p. m.

Col. JOHN P. TAYLOR,
Commanding Second Cavalry Division:

COLONEL: Mosby's whole command was ordered to rendezvous this morning at Rector's Cross-Roads for an attack to-night on Colonel Baker's command. The commanding general directs that you send at once a party to attack him, and report as soon as they return.

I am, colonel, very respectfully, your obedient servant,

E. B. PARSONS,
Acting Assistant Adjutant-General.

WARRENTON,
December 28, 1863.

Captain WEIR:

Your message of 4.55 received at 7 p. m. ; your dispatch by orderly at 7.30 p. m. Colonel Kester, with 500 men, is ordered to carry out your instructions. This number comprises nearly all my available force.

D. GARDNER,
Lieutenant-Colonel, Commanding.

HEADQUARTERS DIVISION,
Fairfax Court-House, Va., December 28, 1863.

Col. J. P. McMAHON,
Commanding Brigade:

COLONEL: The colonel commanding division, in consequence of having received intimation that Mosby is about making an attack on the camp of Colonel Baker's cavalry this night, directs that you send two companies of infantry on the road between here and Flint Hill, in order to intercept him. Your men will patrol the road in strong force, and be on the alert in case of the approach of the enemy.

Let them be careful not to fire into our own men.

Yours, respectfully,

WM. A. LA MOTTE,
Captain, and Assistant Adjutant-General.

FORT MONROE, VA.,
December 28, 1863.

Hon. E. M. STANTON,
Secretary of War:

I have twelve brigadier-generals in this department, and about seventeen or eighteen thousand effective troops. Another one has just been sent me this morning without application. I should like permission to relieve such as I do not need.

BENJ. F. BUTLER,
Major-General, Commanding.

———

WASHINGTON, D. C.,
December 29, 1863—12.30 p. m.

Major-General MEADE,
Commanding Army of the Potomac:

My attention has been called by the War Department to the difficulty and expense of foraging so large a number of animals in the Army of the Potomac, and it is suggested whether a part of the cavalry cannot be subsisted in the Shenandoah Valley on the enemy, or some portion of the animals be sent where food can be supplied at less expense. I submit the matter for your consideration.

H. W. HALLECK,
General-in-Chief.

———

DECEMBER 29, 1863—8.45 p. m.

Brigadier-General MERRITT:

General French reports that his picket officer reports the enemy's pickets on the Sperryville road, and that a reconnoitering party of the enemy was also observed. Is one of your brigades on that road? Have you pickets and patrols on it? The major-general commanding directs that you send out immediately and ascertain what force of the enemy are there.

A. A. HUMPHREYS,
Major-General, and Chief of Staff.

———

WARRENTON,
December 29, 1863—4 p. m.

H. C. WEIR,
Assistant Adjutant-General, Cavalry Corps:

Colonel Kester, First New Jersey Cavalry, has just returned from his scout, agreeably with your instructions of the 28th. He reports having captured at Rectortown 100 suits clothing and 8 horses. The enemy in two charges on the rear guard were repulsed, and owing to the fleetness of their horses escaped. I will send his report to-morrow.

D. GARDNER,
Lieutenant-Colonel, Commanding First Brigade,

CUMBERLAND, MD., *December 30, 1863*—7 p. m.
(Received 8.30 p. m.)

Brig. Gen. G. W. CULLUM,
    Chief of Staff:

The following telegram just received. I have ordered Averell's command to move by railroad to Martinsburg. We will be in readiness for Early:

HARPER'S FERRY, W. VA.,
December 30, 1863.

Brig. Gen. B. F. KELLEY:

Nine deserters from the valley, just in, report General Early, with 9,000 men, between New Market and Mount Jackson. Rosser has 700 men; Imboden 1,500 men. Great dissatisfaction among the rebels. These deserters heard the President's proclamation and required oath with great surprise, and declared if it was printed and circulated thousands would come into our lines.

JER. C. SULLIVAN,
Brigadier-General.

B. F. KELLEY,
Brigadier-General.

MARTINSBURG, VA.,
December 30, 1863.

Capt. WILLIAM M. BOONE,
    A. A. G., 1st Div., Dept. W. Va., Harper's Ferry, Va.:

My scout from Shanghai came in yesterday at 4 p. m. The scout to Winchester was ordered to remain at Bunker Hill last night. I received intelligence from Back Creek yesterday evening, which seemed to be creditable, that a party of the enemy, 30 in number, under command of Captain Ross, of Gilmor's command, were in the neighborhood of Tomahawk at sunset yesterday. I accordingly sent Major Morris, One hundred and sixteenth Ohio, to throw forward strong parties from Back Creek and North Mountain before daylight this morning, and sent Captain McDonald, Twelfth Pennsylvania Cavalry, with 40 men, to Captain Henry at Bunker Hill, and to proceed immediately down the Green Spring road, via Shanghai, to Tomahawk, scouring the Back Creek Valley; and I am in hopes they will make some captures.

Six deserters, from White's and Gilmor's commands, were sent in last night from Winchester, by Captain Henry. They are intelligent men, and represent these commands to be very much dissatisfied, and anxious to desert, but are afraid to do so, as they believe if they do they will be put into our service. Frequent parties to Winchester may succeed in dispelling them of this idea. They (Gilmor and White) are represented to be in camp near Mount Jackson.

Very respectfully, your obedient servant,

R. S. RODGERS,
Colonel. Commanding.

CUMBERLAND, MD., *December, 31, 1863*—noon.
(Received 3 p. m.)

Brig. Gen. G. W. CULLUM,
    Chief of Staff:

The following received from General Sullivan. I am pushing Averell's command to Martinsburg as rapidly as possible. My infantry is so scattered in the western portion of my department that I cannot concentrate any considerable force at once. May I, therefore, suggest that two or three regiments of infantry be held in readiness to be sent from Washington or Baltimore to Sullivan, if necessary:

HARPER'S FERRY, W. VA.,
December 31, 1863—2.10 a. m.

Brigadier-General KELLEY:

Information from deserters and my own scouting party teaches me to think that General Early will make an attack on some point near us within twenty-four hours. He was at Strasburg, and expected to·reach Winchester to-night. Can Averell's forces be hurried here? Early is reported to be about 6,000 strong.

JER. C. SULLIVAN,
Brigadier-General.

B. F. KELLEY,
Brigadier-General.

CAMDEN STATION,
Baltimore, Md., December 31, 1863.

Maj. Gen. H. W. HALLECK, *General-in-Chief*, and
Hon. E. M. STANTON, *Secretary of War:*

General Sullivan has information that the enemy is at Winchester, under command of Early, and General Averell advises us to keep our rolling stock in hand to move if necessary. I trust the forces that can be concentrated will be sufficient to prevent the enemy destroying our communications. I know your interest in doing all that is possible for the protection of this important line.

J. W. GARRETT,
President Baltimore and Ohio Railroad.

WAR DEPARTMENT,
December 31, 1863—3.45 p. m.

JOHN W. GARRETT, Esq.,
Baltimore:

Please have your trains, &c., in readiness for rapid movement of troops from Washington and Baltimore west, if necessity should require. Suspend everything that may interfere with this object within the next twelve hours.

EDWIN M. STANTON,
Secretary of War.

WASHINGTON CITY,
December 31, 1863—4 p. m.

Major-General HUMPHREYS,
Headquarters Army of the Potomac:

Has any intelligence of Early's movements been received since I left? General Kelley reports him advancing on Winchester with 6,000 men. Arrangements must be made and the necessary orders issued to have a division of cavalry and two divisions of the Sixth Corps ready to move at a moment's notice. Notify General Ingalls and Mr. Devereux to be ready to transport troops by rail from camp to Alexandria.

GEO. G. MEADE.

WAR DEPARTMENT,
Washington City, December 31, 1863—4 p. m.

Major-General HUMPHREYS,
            Chief of Staff:

Direct a strong brigade from the Sixth Corps to be immediately sent here by rail; the commander to report to Major-General Augur by telegraph for orders.

Direct General Pleasonton to immediately send a division of cavalry into the Shenandoah Valley to cut off, if practicable, the retreat of Early's command reported at Winchester to-day. The division now in rear, Gregg's, will probably be the one most available. A portion of Merritt's, say one brigade, should be sent to hold the principal points now held by Gregg.

                        GEO. G. MEADE,
                            Major-General.

───────

DECEMBER 31, 1863—5.30 p. m.

Commanding Officer Sixth Corps:

A dispatch from Major-General Meade just received. He orders that a strong brigade from the Sixth Corps be sent immediately by rail to Washington; it is wanted for immediate service in connection with the enemy, who, under General Early, are in Winchester to-day. The commander of the brigade will report immediately by telegraph to General Augur at Washington for orders. Hold two divisions ready to move at a moment's notice, by rail or otherwise.

                        A. A. HUMPHREYS,
                    Major-General, and Chief of Staff.

───────

DECEMBER 31, 1863—5.45 p. m.
(Received 9.20 p. m.)

Major-General MEADE,
            Washington:

Your two dispatches were received together half an hour ago; the orders have been all issued and the brigade will leave to-night. The two divisions of infantry (excepting one brigade) will be held ready to move at a moment's notice, and the arrangements for their transport made. No intelligence respecting General Early has been received since you left.

                        A. A. HUMPHREYS,
                    Major-General, and Chief of Staff.

───────

DECEMBER 31, 1863—8.30 p. m.
(Received 9.30 p. m.)

Major-General MEADE,
            Washington:

The brigade, 2,000 strong, General Wheaton commanding, is on its way to Brandy Station, and will leave there immediately upon arriving. The two divisions of infantry (less this brigade) are ready to move at a moment's notice, with a due proportion of artillery, and such parts of their trains as may be required, or without any trains. As the dispatches did not mention whether they would move by rail or into the Upper Valley of the Shenandoah from here, I gave directions that would meet both cases.

Please let me know in regard to it, lest preparations for moving so many men by railroad might interfere with the transport of the brigade. It should not do so, but might.

General Merritt reports that 4 deserters (conscripts) from the Fifty-fourth North Carolina, Hoke's brigade, Early's division, came in to-day. They say they heard that part of Ewell's corps had gone to the Shenandoah Valley to winter, confirming the composition of Early's present command.

A. A. HUMPHREYS,
Major-General, and Chief of Staff.

WASHINGTON,
December 31, 1863—11 p. m.

Major-General HUMPHREYS,
Chief of Staff, Hdqrs. Army of the Potomac:

Your two telegrams received. Later intelligence from General Kelley would show that Early had not advanced beyond Woodstock. I do not think the divisions of infantry will be required. The movements of the cavalry should be predicated on the information now sent; that is, ascertain whether Early contemplates or is making a raid on the Baltimore and Ohio Railway, or whether he is stationary between New Market and Woodstock. I shall leave for headquarters at 9 a. m. to-morrow; have my ambulance at the depot.
GEO. G. MEADE,
Major-General.

HEADQUARTERS FIRST ARMY CORPS,
December 31, 1863.

Major-General HUMPHREYS,
Chief of Staff:

GENERAL: The movement ordered by you yesterday, viz, the concentration of Robinson's division at Cedar Mountain, is unavoidably postponed until a change of weather. In the meantime, permit me to request that the cavalry should so picket and scout the roads leading from Madison Court-House and running to the north of Cedar Mountain, and likewise the roads from Raccoon Ford, by which Cedar Mountain could be turned, as to give timely notice to commanding officer at the mountain of a movement of the enemy in force. General Pleasonton's instructions to his cavalry, based upon a previous disposition of the First Corps, might now require a slight modification, though an important one, of his pickets. All I desire is that the commanding officer at Cedar Mountain may get timely notice, as the lookout on Cedar Mountain is useless in hazy weather.
Very respectfully,

JOHN NEWTON,
Major-General, Commanding.

CIRCULAR.]   HEADQUARTERS ARMY OF THE POTOMAC,
        OFFICE OF THE PROVOST-MARSHAL-GENERAL,
                        December 31, 1863.

In compliance with instructions from headquarters Army of the Potomac, all newspaper correspondents connected with this army are prohibited from publishing, or causing to be published, the number or designation of regiments re-enlisting in the army, or leaving the same, the number of re-enlistments, or the number of men being furloughed.

Corps provost-marshals are directed to see that the newspaper correspondents in their respective corps are notified of the above order.

Assistant adjutant-generals of independent commands are requested to see that a copy of this circular is furnished to any correspondent connected with their respective departments.

                        M. R. PATRICK,
                        Provost-Marshal-General.

                        WAR DEPARTMENT,
        Washington, December 31, 1863—2.30 p. m.
Brigadier-General SULLIVAN,
        Harper's Ferry, W. Va.:

Have you any positive information in regard to the rebel force at Winchester? Is it cavalry?

                        H. W. HALLECK,
                        General-in-Chief.

                        HARPER'S FERRY, W. VA.,
        December 31, 1863—4 p. m.   (Received 5 p. m.)
Major-General HALLECK,
        General-in-Chief:

The information of last night is not correct. My cavalry are to-day in Winchester, and sent to Strasburg, with orders to bring back reliable news. The rebel force is said, by deserters, to be two brigades of infantry and about 2,500 cavalry, under Imboden, Rosser, White, and others, all commanded by Early. I do not apprehend the least danger of an attack. The Shenandoah is so high that they will not venture lower down than New Market. I will, under permission from General Kelley, keep you advised of any movements that seem important.

                        JER. C. SULLIVAN,
                        Brigadier-General.

                        WAR DEPARTMENT,
        December 31, 1863—8 p. m.
JOHN W. GARRETT, Esq., *Baltimore:*

It was designed to forward troops to Harper's Ferry. The latest information from General Sullivan reports no enemy at Winchester, or any nearer than Woodstock. It will be well, however, to guard the valley with a larger force, and transportation for 1,500 men from here to Harper's Ferry should be ready here by to-morrow noon.

                        EDWIN M. STANTON,

HEADQUARTERS OF THE ARMY,
Washington, December 31, 1863.

Major-General AUGUR,
  Commanding, &c.:

GENERAL: It is possible that General Kelley may ask 'for two or three regiments and some batteries to be sent to Harper's Ferry via railroad. General Meade will send up a brigade from his army to report to you for this purpose, and General Barry will have the batteries in readiness. If the demand should be pressing from General Kelley, I hope you may be able to send him some infantry in advance of the arrival of the brigade from General Meade. No troops will be sent forward unless further demands are made from General Kelley or Harper's Ferry.

  Yours, truly,

  H. W. HALLECK,
  General-in-Chief.

———

CUMBERLAND,
December 31, 1863—10 a. m.

Major-General COUCH,
  Chambersburg:

Your telegram of yesterday received, and this morning received the order from the War Department. General Sullivan reports that General Early is moving down the Shenandoah Valley with a large force, and was last night between Strasburg and Winchester. I will therefore be compelled to detain Colonel Boyd's command until further developments, but will send it the earliest moment I can safely spare it. I presume the best route for him to take will be by Hagerstown, as he is now near Harper's Ferry.

  B. F. KELLEY,
  Brigadier-General.

———

GENERAL ORDERS, }   HDQRS. DEPT. OF WEST VIRGINIA,
  No. 24.   }   *Cumberland, Md., December 31, 1863.*

I. The troops of the First Separate Brigade will hereafter constitute the Fourth Division of this department.

Brig. Gen. W. W. Averell, U. S. Volunteers, will command the Fourth Division.

II. Capt. Horace Turner, commissary of subsistence, volunteers, is announced as inspecting commissary of this department.

  By order of Brigadier-General Kelley:

  THAYER MELVIN,
  Assistant Adjutant-General.

———

HDQRS. 18TH ARMY CORPS, DEPT. OF VA. AND N. C.,
Fortress Monroe, December 31, 1863.

Hon. E. M. STANTON,
  Secretary of War:

SIR: I have the honor to report that General Wild was dispatched by my order upon an expedition with two regiments of colored troops into the northeastern counties of North Carolina. Our navigation on the Dismal Swamp Canal had been interrupted, and the Union inhabitants plundered by the guerrillas.

General Wild took the most stringent measures, burning the property of some of the officers of guerrilla parties, and seizing the wives and families of others as hostages for some of his negroes that were captured, and appears to have done his work with great thoroughness, but perhaps with too much stringency. The effect has been, however, that the people of Pasquotank, Currituck, Camden, Perquimans, and Chowan Counties have assembled, and all passed resolutions similar to those which I inclose, which were passed by the inhabitants of Pasquotank County, and three of the counties have sent committees to me with their resolutions. These resolutions are signed by 523 of the inhabitants of the county, an average vote being 800, and every prominent man, I am informed by the committee who presented them, that had not signed them had left and gone across the lines.

The guerrillas have also been withdrawn from these counties, to the relief of the inhabitants.

I have promised the committees of the several counties that so long as they remain quiet, keep out the guerrillas, and stop blockade running, that they shall be afforded all possible protection by us, and be allowed to bring their products into Norfolk and receive goods in exchange.

Until I can get sufficient force organized to make it safe to throw my lines around them, I have further informed them I shall not require the oath of allegiance.

I think we are much indebted to General Wild and his negro troops for what they have done, and it is but fair to record that while some complaints are made of the action authorized by General Wild against the inhabitants and their property, yet all the committees agree that the negro soldiers made no unauthorized interferences with property or persons, and conducted themselves with propriety.

I find between some of the officers in this department in command of white soldiers, a considerable degree of prejudice against the colored troops, and in some cases impediments have been thrown in the way of their recruiting, and they interfered with on their expeditions. This I am investigating, and shall punish with the most stringent measures, trusting and believing my action will be sustained by the Department. I also find some incompetent officers in the negro regiments. The Board of Examination cannot always develop the character of the officer, although it may make some possible guess at his requirements.

I shall take leave, therefore, to report for dismissal those who in my judgment, upon investigation, are not fit for the service. The negro troops, to have a fair chance, ought to have first-class officers, for from their habits of obedience and discipline, they are more apt to depend upon their officers than are white soldiers.

I beg leave to inclose * a copy of General Wild's report, and also the original proceedings of the citizens of Pasquotank.

I have the honor to be, very respectfully, yours,
                                        BENJ. F. BUTLER,
                                    Major-General, Commanding.

_____

* See Part I, p. 911.

[Inclosure.]

PETITION OF 523 CITIZENS OF PASQUOTANK.

At a meeting of the citizens of Pasquotank County, N. C., held at the court-house in Elizabeth City, December 19, 1863,. Dr. William G. Pool being called to the chair and Isaiah Fearing selected secretary, a committee consisting of George W. Brooks, John C. Ehringhause, R. F. Overman, William H. Clark, and (by motion) William G. Pool were appointed to present suitable matter for the action of this meeting.

Being called upon, George W. Brooks, chairman, submitted the following preamble and resolutions, which were unanimously and enthusiastically adopted:

Whereas the county of Pasquotank has suffered immensely since the fall of Roanoke Island, without aid or protection from any source; and whereas we have been lately visited, by order of General Benjamin F. Butler, by such force and under such circumstances as to cause universal panic and distress; and whereas we have been assured by General E. A. Wild, in command of this force, that he will continue to operate here, even to the destruction, if necessary, of every species of property for the purpose of "ridding this county of partisan rangers;" and whereas we believe that these rangers cannot be of any service to us, but that their further presence here will bring upon us speedy and inevitable ruin; and whereas we are promised to be "let alone" if these rangers be removed or disbanded and return quietly home, and, further, if that species of business known as "blockade running" be desisted from: Therefore, in view of these facts and of this condition of things,

Resolved, That we earnestly petition the Governor and Legislature of North Carolina, satisfied that you cannot protect us with any force at your command, to remove or disband these few rangers; on motion,

Resolved, That we denounce that species of business carried on here by private citizens for private gain known as "blockade running," and that we will hereafter use our best efforts to suppress such trade.

On motion, Barney Berry, Dr. J. J. Shannonhouse, John D. Markham, Thomas I. Murden, B. F. Whitehurst, Timothy Hunter, Frank Vaughan, and D. D. Raper, being one from each captain's district in the county, were appointed to obtain the signature of every male citizen in the county above the age of eighteen years to this application to the Governor and Legislature of North Carolina and to General B. F. Butler.

On motion, Jerry Wilcox and C. L. Cobb were appointed to furnish to the above committee, from the census returns and other sources, the names of all white males in this county above the ages of eighteen years.

On motion, William H. Clark, Dr. J. J. Shannonhouse, and Richard B. Creecy were appointed a committee to bear these proceedings to the Governor and Legislature of North Carolina, and to ask their immediate attention to the same.

On motion, a committee consisting of George W. Brooks, George D. Pool, and John J. Grandy was appointed to bear the proceedings to General B. F. Butler, at Fort Monroe, and to learn of him whether the removal of partisan rangers from this county, and the ceasing of all persons in this county to run the blockade, will secure us, through him, from raids by United States forces through this county and the further destruction of our property.

On motion, George W. F. Dashiel and Reuben F. Overman were appointed a committee to raise funds to defray the expenses of the committee to Raleigh and Fort Monroe.

On motion, the following persons were appointed to bear the proceedings of this meeting to the following counties, viz: Charles C. Pool, to Chowan; Andrew J. Perry, to Gates; John H. Perry, to Perquimans; J. B. Shaw, to Camden; and C. L. Cobb, to Currituck.

On motion, the meeting adjourned, to be called together by the chairman whenever he might deem it advisable.

(Signed by W. G. Pool, chairman; Isaiah Fearing, secretary; Benoni Cartright, John W. Graves, Jesse M. Rhodes, Charles Meeds, Marmaduke Rhodes, James Gannon, Barney Perry, *et al.*)

ELIZABETH CITY, *December 26, 1863.*

I certify on honor that the above list of names is a true copy, as handed to me by each committee from each district.

ISAIAH FEARING,
Secretary.

Abstract from return of the Army of the Potomac, Maj. Gen. John Sedgwick, U. S. Army, commanding, for the month of December, 1863.

Command.	Present for duty.		Aggregate present.	Aggregate present and absent.	Pieces of artillery.	
	Officers.	Men.			Heavy.	Field.
General headquarters *a*	71	743	947	1,970		
Engineer troops	37	1,041	1,858	1,848		
Artillery Reserve	85	2,649	3,015	3,501	8	78
First Army Corps	516	11,081	13,443	21,161		28
Second Army Corps	587	10,505	12,382	22,340		31
Third Army Corps	655	14,638	17,474	26,294		46
Fifth Army Corps	582	11,096	12,914	19,618		32
Sixth Army Corps	676	13,429	16,530	23,558		46
Cavalry Corps	494	12,889	16,068	25,923		30
Total	3,703	78,011	94,151	146,208	8	291

a Includes staff, provost-guard, and signal corps.

Organization of the Army of the Potomac, Maj. Gen. John Sedgwick, U. S. Army, [*] *commanding, December 31, 1863.*

GENERAL HEADQUARTERS.

PROVOST GUARD.

Brig. Gen. MARSENA R. PATRICK.

1st Maryland Cavalry, Capt. Joseph H. Cook.
80th New York (20th Militia), Col. Theodore B. Gates.
93d New York, Maj. Samuel McConihe.
1st U. S. Cavalry (squadron), Capt. Isaac R. Dunkelberger.
2d, 5th, and 6th United States and 1st Maine Cavalry (detachments from).

ENGINEER BRIGADE.

Brig. Gen. HENRY W. BENHAM.

15th New York (battalion), Maj. William A. Ketchum.
50th New York, Col. William H. Pettes.

BATTALION U. S. ENGINEERS.

Capt. CHARLES N. TURNBULL.

---

[*] Maj. Gen. George G. Meade temporarily absent.

ORDNANCE DETACHMENT.

Lieut. MORRIS SCHAFF.

GUARDS AND ORDERLIES.

Oneida (New York) Cavalry, Capt. Daniel P. Mann.

SIGNAL CORPS.

Capt. LEMUEL B. NORTON.

FIRST ARMY CORPS.

Maj. Gen. JOHN NEWTON.

ESCORT.

4th and 16th Pennsylvania Cavalry (detachments), Capt. Robert A. Robinson.

FIRST DIVISION.

Brig. Gen. LYSANDER CUTLER.

First Brigade.	*Second Brigade.*
Col. WILLIAM W. ROBINSON.	Brig. Gen. JAMES C. RICE.
19th Indiana, Maj. John M. Lindley. 24th Michigan, Col. Henry A. Morrow. 1st New York Sharpshooters (battalion), Capt. Joseph S. Arnold. 2d Wisconsin, Lieut. Col. John Mansfield. 6th Wisconsin, Col. Edward S. Bragg. 7th Wisconsin, Maj. Mark Finnicum.	7th Indiana, Col. Ira G. Grover. 76th New York, Lieut. Col. John E. Cook. 84th New York (14th Militia), Col. Edward B. Fowler. 95th New York, Maj. Edward Pye. 147th New York, Col. Francis C. Miller. 56th Pennsylvania, Col. J. William Hofmann.

SECOND DIVISION.

Brig. Gen. JOHN C. ROBINSON.

First Brigade.	*Second Brigade.*
Col. THOMAS F. McCOY.	Brig. Gen. HENRY BAXTER.
16th Maine, Maj. Archibald D. Leavitt. 13th Massachusetts, Lieut. Col. N. Walter Batchelder. 39th Massachusetts, Lieut. Col. Charles L. Peirson. 94th New York, Maj. Samuel A. Moffett. 104th New York, Lieut. Col. John R. Strang. 107th Pennsylvania, Maj. Henry J. Sheafer.	12th Massachusetts, Capt. Charles W. Hastings. 83d New York (9th Militia), Col. Joseph A. Moesch. 97th New York, Col. Charles Wheelock. 11th Pennsylvania, Maj. John B. Keenan. 88th Pennsylvania, Capt. John S. Steeple. 90th Pennsylvania, Lieut. Col. William A. Leech.

THIRD DIVISION.

Col. NATHAN T. DUSHANE.*

First Brigade.	*Second Brigade.*
Col. LANGHORNE WISTER.	Lieut. Col. CHARLES E. PHELPS.
121st Pennsylvania, Lieut. Col. Alexander Biddle. 142d Pennsylvania, Lieut. Col. Alfred B. McCalmont. 143d Pennsylvania, Lieut. Col. John D. Musser. 149th Pennsylvania, Lieut. Col. Walton Dwight. 150th Pennsylvania, Lieut. Col. Henry S. Huidekoper.	1st Maryland, Capt. Robert W. Reynolds. 4th Maryland, Capt. J. Bailey Orem. 7th Maryland, Capt. Edward M. Mobley. 8th Maryland, Capt. Charles T. Dixon.

---

*Brig. Gen. John R. Kenly temporarily absent.

ARTILLERY BRIGADE.

Col. CHARLES S. WAINWRIGHT.

Maine Light, 5th Battery (E), Capt. Greenleaf T. Stevens.
Maryland Light, Battery A, Capt. James H. Rigby.
1st New York Light. Battery H, Capt. Charles E. Mink.
1st New York Light, Batteries E and L, Capt. Gilbert H. Reynolds.
1st Pennsylvania Light, Battery B, Capt. James H. Cooper.
4th United States, Battery B, Lieut. James Stewart.

SECOND ARMY CORPS.

Maj. Gen. WINFIELD S. HANCOCK.

ESCORT.

10th New York Cavalry, Company M, } Lieut. Robert Brown.
13th Pennsylvania Cavalry, Company G, }

FIRST DIVISION.

Brig. Gen. JOHN C. CALDWELL.

First Brigade.

Col. H. BOYD MCKEEN.

26th Michigan, Col. Judson S. Farrar.
61st New York, Capt. Thomas G. Morrison.
81st Pennsylvania, Maj. Thomas C. Harkness.
140th Pennsylvania, Col. John Fraser.

Third Brigade.

Col. PAUL FRANK.

52d New York,* Maj. Henry M. Karples.
57th New York, Lieut. Col. Alford B. Chapman.
66th New York, Lieut. Col. John S. Hammell.
148th Pennsylvania, Lieut. Col. George A. Fairlamb.

Second Brigade.

Col. PATRICK KELLY.

28th Massachusetts, Col. Richard Byrnes.
63d New York, Capt. Peter T. Boyle.
69th New York (detachment).
88th New York, Capt. Patrick Ryder.
116th Pennsylvania (battalion), Capt. Garrett Nowlen.

Fourth Brigade.

Col. WILLIAM P. BAILY.

2d Delaware, Lieut. Col. David L. Stricker.
64th New York, Maj. Leman W. Bradley.
53d Pennsylvania (seven companies), Capt. Archibald F. Jones.
145th Pennsylvania, Lieut. Col. David B. McCreary.

SECOND DIVISION.

Brig. Gen. ALEXANDER S. WEBB.

First Brigade.

Col. HENRY W. HUDSON.

19th Maine, Lieut. Col. Henry W. Cunningham.
15th Massachusetts, Capt. Charles H. Eager.
1st Minnesota, Lieut. Col. Charles P. Adams.
82d New York (2d Militia), Maj. Thomas W. Baird.
152d New York, Lieut. Col. George W. Thompson.

Second Brigade.

Col. ARTHUR F. DEVEREUX.

69th Pennsylvania, Capt. Patrick S. Tinen.
71st Pennsylvania, Col. R. Penn Smith.
72d Pennsylvania, Lieut. Alexander McCuen.
106th Pennsylvania, Lieut. Col. William L. Curry.

* Detachment 7th New York attached.

Third Brigade.

Col. TURNER G. MOREHEAD.

19th Massachusetts, Maj. Edmund Rice.
20th Massachusetts, Lieut. Col. George N. Macy.
7th Michigan, Col. Norman J. Hall.
42d New York, Lieut. Col. William A. Lynch.
59th New York (battalion), Lieut. Col. Horace P. Rugg.
1st Company (Andrew) Massachusetts Sharpshooters, Lieut. Samuel G. Gilbreth.
2d Company Minnesota Sharpshooters, Lieut. William Harmon.

THIRD DIVISION.

Brig. Gen. ALEXANDER HAYS.

First Brigade.	*Second Brigade.*
Col. SAMUEL S. CARROLL.	Col. CHARLES J. POWERS.
14th Indiana, Col. John Coons.	14th Connecticut, Col. Theodore G. Ellis.
4th Ohio, Maj. Peter Grubb.	1st Delaware, Col. Thomas A. Smyth.
8th Ohio, Lieut. Col. Franklin Sawyer.	12th New Jersey, Col. J. Howard Willets.
7th West Virginia (battalion), Capt. Isaac B. Fisher.	10th New York (battalion), Maj. George F. Hopper.
	108th New York, Lieut. Col. Francis E. Pierce.

Third Brigade.

Col. LEVIN CRANDELL.

39th New York, Capt. Bernard Bear.
111th New York, Lieut. Col. Isaac M. Lusk.
125th New York, Capt. Edward P. Jones.
126th New York, Lieut. Col. William H. Baird.

ARTILLERY BRIGADE.

Lieut. Col. J. ALBERT MONROE.

1st New York Light, Battery G, Lieut. Samuel A. McClellan.
Pennsylvania Light, Battery C, Capt. James Thompson.
Pennsylvania Light, Battery F, Capt. Nathaniel Irish.
1st Pennsylvania Light, Batteries F and G, Lieut. Charles B. Brockway.
1st Rhode Island Light, Battery A, Capt. William A. Arnold.
1st Rhode Island Light; Battery B, Capt. John G. Hazard.
5th United States, Battery C, Lieut. Richard Metcalf.

THIRD ARMY CORPS.

Maj. Gen. WILLIAM H. FRENCH.

FIRST DIVISION.

Maj. Gen. DAVID B. BIRNEY.

First Brigade.	*Second Brigade.*
Col. CHARLES H. T. COLLIS.	Col. ELIJAH WALKER.
57th Pennsylvania, Col. Peter Sides.	3d Maine, Maj. William C. Morgan.
63d Pennsylvania, Lieut. Col. John A. Danks.	4th Maine, Capt. Edwin Libby.
105th Pennsylvania, Col. Calvin A. Craig.	20th Indiana, Col. William C. L. Taylor.
110th Pennsylvania (battalion), Maj. Levi B. Duff.	86th New York, Lieut Col. Jacob H. Lansing.
114th Pennsylvania, Maj. Edward R. Bowen.	124th New York, Lieut. Col. Francis M. Cummins.
141st Pennsylvania, Col. Henry J. Madill.	99th Pennsylvania, Col. Asher S. Leidy.
	2d U. S. Sharpshooters, Lieut. Col. Homer R. Stoughton.

Third Brigade.

Col. BYRON R. PIERCE.

17th Maine, Col. George W. West.
3d Michigan,* Maj. Moses B. Houghton.
68th Pennsylvania, Lieut. Col. Jacob W. Greenawalt.
1st U. S. Sharpshooters, Capt. Frank E. Marble.

SECOND DIVISION.

Brig. Gen. HENRY PRINCE.

First Brigade.	*Second Brigade.*
Col. WILLIAM BLAISDELL.	Col. WILLIAM R. BREWSTER.
1st Massachusetts, Lieut. Col. Clark B. Baldwin.	70th New York, Col. J. Egbert Farnum.
11th Massachusetts, Lieut. Col. Porter D. Tripp.	71st New York, Col. Henry L. Potter.
16th Massachusetts, Lieut. Col. Waldo Merriam.	72d New York, Lieut. Col. John Leonard.
11th New Jersey, Col. Robert McAllister.	73d New York, Lieut. Col. Michael W. Burns.
26th Pennsylvania, Lieut. Col. Robert L. Bodine.	74th New York, Maj. Henry M. Alles.
84th Pennsylvania, Lieut. Col. Milton Opp.	120th New York, Maj. John R. Tappen.

Third Brigade.

Brig. Gen. GERSHOM MOTT.

5th New Jersey, Maj. Ashbel W. Angel.
6th New Jersey, Lieut. Col. Stephen R. Gilkyson.
7th New Jersey, Capt. James McKiernan.
8th New Jersey, Maj. Virgil M. Healey.
115th Pennsylvania, Lieut. Col. John P. Dunne.

THIRD DIVISION.

Brig. Gen. JOSEPH B. CARR.

First Brigade.	*Second Brigade.*
Brig. Gen. WILLIAM H. MORRIS.	Col. J. WARREN KEIFER.
14th New Jersey, Col. William S. Truex.	6th Maryland, Maj. Joseph C. Hill.
151st New York, Lieut. Col. Erwin A. Bowen.	110th Ohio, Capt. William S. McElwain.
10th Vermont, Maj. Charles G. Chandler.	122d Ohio, Col. William H. Ball.
	138th Pennsylvania, Capt. George W. Guss.

Third Brigade.

Col. BENJAMIN F. SMITH.

106th New York, Lieut. Col. Charles Townsend.
126th Ohio, Capt. George W. Voorhes.
67th Pennsylvania, Col. John F. Staunton.
87th Pennsylvania, Lieut. Col. James A. Stahle.

---

* Detachment 5th Michigan and 40th New York attached.

ARTILLERY BRIGADE.

Capt. O'NEIL W. ROBINSON, jr.

Maine Light, 4th Battery (D), Capt. O'Neil W. Robinson, jr.
Massachusetts Light,.10th Battery, Capt. J. Henry Sleeper.
New Hampshire Light, 1st Battery, Capt. Frederick M. Edgell.
1st New Jersey Light, Battery B, Capt. A. Judson Clark.
1st New York Light, Battery D, Capt. George B. Winslow.
New York Light, 12th Battery, Capt. George F. McKnight.
1st Rhode Island Light, Battery E, Lieut. John K. Bucklyn.
4th United States, Battery K, Lieut. John W. Roder.

FIFTH ARMY CORPS.

Maj. Gen. GEORGE SYKES.

PROVOST GUARD.

12th New York, Companies D and E, Lieut. Joseph Hilton.

FIRST DIVISION.

Col. JACOB B. SWEITZER.

First Brigade.	*Second Brigade.*
Col. JAMES GWYN.	Lieut. Col. JAMES C. HULL.
18th Massachusetts, Maj. Thomas Weston.	9th Massachusetts, Lieut. Col. Patrick T. Hanley.
22d Massachusetts, Maj. Mason W. Burt.	32d Massachusetts, Lieut. Col. Luther Stephenson, jr.
1st Michigan, Maj. George C. Hopper.	4th Michigan, Lieut. Col. George W. Lumbard.
118th Pennsylvania, Maj. Henry O'Neill.	62d Pennsylvania, Capt. Samuel Conner.

Third Brigade.

Col. JOSEPH HAYES.

20th Maine, Maj. Ellis Spear.
16th Michigan, Lieut. Col. Norval E. Welch.
44th New York, Lieut. Col. Freeman Conner.
83d Pennsylvania, Maj. William H. Lamont.

SECOND DIVISION.

Brig. Gen. ROMEYN B. AYRES.

First Brigade.	*Second Brigade.*
Col. SIDNEY BURBANK.	Col. EDGAR M. GREGORY.
2d United States (six companies), Capt. James W. Long.	140th New York. Col. George Ryan.
3d United States (six companies), Capt. Richard G. Lay.	146th New York, Col. David T. Jenkins.
11th United States (six companies), Maj. Jonathan W. Gordon.	91st Pennsylvania, Lieut. Col. Joseph H. Sinex.
12th United States, Maj. Luther B. Bruen.	155th Pennsylvania, Lieut. Col. Alfred L. Pearson.
14th United States (eight companies), Capt. Edward McK. Hudson.	
17th United States (seven companies), Capt. Walter B. Pease.	

THIRD DIVISION.

Brig. Gen. SAMUEL W. CRAWFORD.

First Brigade.

Col. WILLIAM McCANDLESS.

1st Pennsylvania Reserves, Col. William C. Talley.
2d Pennsylvania Reserves, Lieut. Col. Patrick McDonough.
6th Pennsylvania Reserves, Col. Wellington H. Ent.
11th Pennsylvania Reserves, Col. Samuel M. Jackson.
13th Pennsylvania Reserves (1st Rifles), Maj. William R. Hartshorne.

Third Brigade.

Col. JOSEPH W. FISHER.

5th Pennsylvania Reserves, Lieut. Col. George Dare.
9th Pennsylvania Reserves, Maj. Charles Barnes.
10th Pennsylvania Reserves, Capt. C. Miller Over.
12th Pennsylvania Reserves, Lieut. Col. Richard Gustin.

ARTILLERY BRIGADE.

Capt. ALMONT BARNES.

Massachusetts Light, 3d Battery (C), Lieut. Aaron F. Walcott.
Massachusetts Light, 5th Battery (E), Capt. Charles A. Phillips.
1st New York Light, Battery C, Lieut. Ela H. Clark.
1st Ohio Light, Battery L, Capt. Frank C. Gibbs.
3d United States, Batteries F and K, Lieut. George F. Barstow.
5th United States, Battery D, Lieut. Benjamin F. Rittenhouse.

SIXTH ARMY CORPS.

Maj. Gen. JOHN SEDGWICK.

ESCORT.

1st Vermont Cavalry (detachment), Capt. Andrew J. Grover.

FIRST DIVISION.

Brig. Gen. DAVID A. RUSSELL.

First Brigade.

Brig. Gen. ALFRED T. A. TORBERT.

1st New Jersey, Lieut. Col. William Henry, jr.
2d New Jersey, Lieut. Col. Charles Wiebecke.
3d New Jersey, Maj. William E. Bryan.
4th New Jersey, Lieut. Col. Charles Ewing.
15th New Jersey, Col. William H. Penrose.

Second Brigade.

Col. EMORY UPTON.

5th Maine, Maj. Aaron S. Daggett.
121st New York, Lieut. Col. E. Olcott.
95th Pennsylvania, Lieut. Col. Edward Carroll.
96th Pennsylvania, Lieut. Col. William H. Lessig.

Third Brigade.

Lieut. Col. GIDEON CLARK.

6th Maine, Maj. George Fuller.
49th Pennsylvania, Lieut. Col. Thomas M. Hulings.
119th Pennsylvania, Maj. Henry P. Truefitt, jr.
5th Wisconsin, Lieut. Col. Theodore B. Catlin.

SECOND DIVISION.

Brig. Gen. ALBION P. HOWE.

Second Brigade.	*Third Brigade.*
Col. THOMAS O. SEAVER.	Brig. Gen. THOMAS H. NEILL.
2d Vermont, Col. James H. Walbridge. 3d Vermont, Lieut. Col. Samuel E. Pingree. 4th Vermont, Lieut. Col. George P. Foster. 5th Vermont (battalion), Capt. Leonard D. Tice. 6th Vermont, Lieut. Col. Oscar A. Hale.	7th Maine (six companies), Col. Edwin C. Mason. 43d New York, Lieut. Col. John Wilson. 49th New York, Lieut. Col. George W. Johnson. 77th New York, Lieut. Col. Winsor B. French. 61st Pennsylvania, Lieut. Col. George F. Smith.

THIRD DIVISION.

Brig. Gen. HENRY D. TERRY.

First Brigade.	*Second Brigade.*
Col. JOSEPH E. HAMBLIN.*	Brig. Gen. HENRY L. EUSTIS.
65th New York, Capt. David I. Miln. 67th New York, Col. Nelson Cross. 122d New York, Lieut. Col. Augustus W. Dwight. 23d Pennsylvania, Lieut. Col. John F. Glenn. 82d Pennsylvania, Lieut. Col. John M. Wetherill.	7th Massachusetts, Col. Thomas D. Johns. 10th Massachusetts, Lieut. Col. Joseph B. Parsons. 37th Massachusetts, Col. Oliver Edwards. 2d Rhode Island, Col. Horatio Rogers, jr.

Third Brigade.

Brig. Gen. FRANK WHEATON.

62d New York, Lieut. Col. Theodore B. Hamilton.
93d Pennsylvania, Lieut. Col. John S. Long.
98th Pennsylvania, Col. John F. Ballier.
102d Pennsylvania, Col. John W. Patterson.
139th Pennsylvania, Lieut. Col. William H. Moody.

ARTILLERY BRIGADE.

Maj. JOHN A. TOMPKINS.

Massachusetts Light, 1st Battery (A), Capt. William H. McCartney.
New York Light, 1st Battery, Capt. Andrew Cowan.
New York Light, 3d Battery, Capt. William A. Harn.
1st Rhode Island Light, Battery C, Capt. Richard Waterman.
1st Rhode Island Light, Battery G, Capt. George W. Adams.
4th United States, Battery C, Lieut. Charles L. Fitzhugh.
5th United States, Battery F, Lieut. Alexander J. McDonald.
5th United States, Battery M, Capt. James McKnight.

---

*Brig. Gen. Alexander Shaler temporarily absent.

CAVALRY CORPS.

Maj. Gen. ALFRED PLEASONTON.

HEADQUARTERS GUARD.

6th United States, Capt. Andrew W. Evans.

FIRST DIVISION.

Brig. Gen. WESLEY MERRITT.

First Brigade.	*Second Brigade.*
Col. WILLIAM GAMBLE.	Lieut. Col. GEORGE S. NICHOLS.
8th Illinois, Lieut. Col. David R. Clendenin.	4th New York, Maj. William R. Parnell.
3d Indiana (six companies), Maj. William Patton.	6th New York, Maj. William P. Hall.
8th New York, Lieut. Col. William L. Markell.	9th New York, Capt. Wilber G. Bently.
	17th Pennsylvania, Maj. Coe Durland.
	3d West Virginia, Companies A and C, Maj. Seymour B. Conger.

Reserve Brigade.

Col. ALFRED GIBBS.

19th New York (1st Dragoons), Maj. Howard M. Smith.
6th Pennsylvania, Capt. Benoni Lockwood.
1st United States, Capt. Napoleon B. Sweitzer.
2d United States, Capt. George A. Gordon.
5th United States, Capt. Abraham K. Arnold.

SECOND DIVISION.

Col. JOHN P. TAYLOR.*

First Brigade.	*Second Brigade.*
Lieut. Col. DAVID GARDNER.	Col. CHARLES H. SMITH.
1st Massachusetts, Capt. Benjamin W. Crowninshield.	1st Maine, Lieut. Col. Stephen Boothby.
1st New Jersey, Lieut. Col. John W. Kester.	10th New York, Lieut. Col. William Irvine.
6th Ohio, Lieut. Col. William Stedman.	2d Pennsylvania, Maj. Joseph Steele.
1st Pennsylvania, Capt. Alex. Davidson.	4th Pennsylvania, Maj. George H. Covode.
3d Pennsylvania, Maj. James W. Walsh.	8th Pennsylvania, Maj. Joseph W. Wistar.
1st Rhode Island, Lieut. Col. John L. Thompson.	13th Pennsylvania, Maj. George F. McCabe.
	16th Pennsylvania, Lieut. Col. John K. Robison.

THIRD DIVISION.

Brig. Gen. JUDSON KILPATRICK.

Headquarters Guard.

1st Ohio Cavalry, Companies A and C, Capt. Samuel N. Stanford.

First Brigade.	*Second Brigade.*
Brig. Gen. HENRY E. DAVIES, jr.	Brig. Gen. GEORGE A. CUSTER.
2d New York, Lieut. Col. Otto Harhaus.	1st Michigan, Col. Charles H. Town.
5th New York, Maj. Amos H. White.	5th Michigan, Maj. Stephen P. Purdy.
18th Pennsylvania, Col. Timothy M. Bryan, jr.	6th Michigan, Lieut. Col. Henry E. Thompson.
	7th Michigan, Lieut. Col. Allyne C. Litchfield.
	1st Vermont, Lieut. Col. Addison W. Preston.

* Brig. Gen. D. McM. Gregg temporarily absent.

ARTILLERY.*

Brig. Gen. HENRY J. HUNT.

ARTILLERY RESERVE.

Lieut. Col. JAMES BRADY.

First Volunteer Brigade.	*Second Volunteer Brigade.*
Capt. WALLACE HILL.	Capt. ELIJAH D. TAFT.
Massachusetts Light, 9th Battery, Capt. John Bigelow.	1st Connecticut Heavy, Battery B, Capt. Albert F. Brooker.
1st New York Light, Battery B, Capt. Albert S. Sheldon.	1st Connecticut Heavy, Battery M, Capt. Franklin A. Pratt.
1st Ohio Light, Battery H, Lieut. George W. Norton.	New York Light, 5th Battery, Capt. Elijah D. Taft.
1st West Virginia Light, Battery C, Lieut. John G. Theis.	

Third Volunteer Brigade.

Maj. ROBERT H. FITZHUGH.

Maine Light, 6th Battery (F),† Capt. Edwin B. Dow.
1st New Jersey Light, Battery A, Capt. William Hexamer.
1st New York Light, Battery K, Capt. J. E. Burton (11th N. Y. Battery attached).
New York Light, 15th Battery, Capt. Patrick Hart.
1st United States, Battery H, Lieut. John D. Wilson.

HORSE ARTILLERY.

First Brigade.

Capt. JAMES M. ROBERTSON.

New York Light, 6th Battery, Capt. Joseph W. Martin.
2d United States, Batteries B and L, Lieut. Samuel B. McIntire.
2d United States, Battery D, Lieut. James A. Sayles.
2d United States, Battery M, Lieut. Carle A. Woodruff.
4th United States, Battery A, Lieut. Frederick A. Fuger.
4th United States, Battery E, Lieut. Terrence Reily.

Second Brigade.

Capt. DUNBAR R. RANSOM.

1st United States, Battery E, Lieut. Frank S. French.
1st United States, Battery I, Capt. Alanson M. Randol.
1st United States, Battery K, Lieut. John Egan.‡
2d United States, Battery A, Lieut. John H. Calef.§
2d United States, Battery G, Lieut. William N. Dennison.§
3d United States, Battery C, Capt. Dunbar R. Ransom.

Unattached.

6th New York Heavy Artillery, Maj. Absalom Crookston.

---

* All organizations of artillery except the reserve will be found in the rosters of the commands with which they served.
† Temporarily attached to the First Army Corps.
‡ Serving with Second Cavalry Division.
§ Serving with First Cavalry Division.

Abstract from return of the Department of Washington, Maj. Gen. Christopher C. Augur, U. S. Army, commanding, for the month of December, 1863.

Command.	Present for duty.		Aggregate present.	Aggregate present and absent.	Pieces of artillery.
	Officers.	Men.			
General headquarters a	26	22	48	50	......
Artillery Camp of Instruction	48	1,215	1,479	1,681	70
District of Washington b	143	2,977	4,379	5,297	......
Defenses North of the Potomac	236	6,697	8,182	8,907	432
Provisional brigades	5	11	16	16	......
Defenses South of the Potomac	220	5,178	6,548	7,664	445
Tyler's division	183	3,349	4,566	5,918	6
District of Alexandria	93	1,308	2,002	2,443	6
Camp Convalescent, &c	83	1,115	5,209	5,608	......
Fort Washington, Md	8	136	199	208	78
Glymont Landing, Md	6	72	144	169	......
Government farms, Va	5	90	106	130	......
Mason's Island, D. C	37	785	987	983	......
Total	1,089	23,040	33,905	39,069	1,082

a Includes Brigadier-Generals Abercrombie and Weber, and staffs, and band of the 17th U. S. Infantry.
b And 1st District of Columbia Cavalry.

Troops in the Department of Washington (Twenty-second Army Corps), Maj. Gen. Christopher C. Augur, U. S. Army, commanding, December 31, 1863.

HEADQUARTERS.

Brig. Gen. John J. Abercrombie and staff.
Brig. Gen. Max Weber and staff.

LIGHT ARTILLERY CAMP OF INSTRUCTION.*
Lieut. Col. JAMES A. HALL.

Connecticut Light, 2d Battery, Lieut. Walter S. Hotchkiss.

Delaware Light, Nields Battery, Lieut. Charles G. Rumford.

Maine Light, 2d Battery (B), Lieut. Benjamin F. Carr.

Massachusetts Light, 7th Battery (G), Lieut. Wilbur G. McCurdy.

New Jersey Light, 3d Battery, Capt. Christian Woerner.

New Jersey Light, 4th Battery, Capt. George T. Woodbury.

New Jersey Light, 5th Battery, Capt. Zenas C. Warren.

1st New York Light, Battery F, Capt. William R. Wilson.

New York Light, 19th Battery, Capt. Edward W. Rogers.

New York Light, 33d Battery, Lieut. J. De Witt Wood.

1st Pennsylvania Light, Battery H, Capt. Andrew Fagan.

1st Rhode Island Light, Battery H, Lieut. Walter M. Knight.

5th United States, Battery I, Lieut. W. Butler Beck.

5th United States, Battery D, Lieut. Samuel Peeples.

DISTRICT OF WASHINGTON.

Brig. Gen. JOHN H. MARTINDALE, Military Governor.

14th New Hampshire, Col. Robert Wilson.

153d New York, Col. Edwin P. Davis.

27th Pennsylvania, Company F, Capt. John M. Carson.

150th Pennsylvania, Company K, Capt. Thomas Getchell.

9th U. S. Veteran Reserve Corps, Col. George W. Gile.

U. S. Veteran Reserve Corps (fifteen companies), Lieut. Col. Fabian Brydolf.

U. S. Ordnance Department, Maj. James G. Benton.

1st District Columbia Cavalry, Maj. Everton J. Conger.

11th New York Cavalry, Col. James B. Swain.

---

*Camps Barry and Marshall. Brig. Gen. William F. Barry was chief of artillery, defenses of Washington.

DEFENSES NORTH OF THE POTOMAC.*

Lieut. Col. JOSEPH A. HASKIN.

First Brigade.	Second Brigade.
Col. AUGUSTUS A. GIBSON.	Col. LEWIS O. MORRIS.
2d Pennsylvania Heavy Artillery, Col. Augustus A. Gibson. 1st Vermont Heavy Artillery, Col. James M. Warner.	1st Maine Heavy Artillery, Col. Daniel Chaplin. 7th New York Heavy Artillery, Col. Lewis O. Morris. 9th New York Heavy Artillery, Col. Joseph Welling. 9th New York Battery, Capt. Emil Schubert.

Third Brigade.

Col. ALEXANDER PIPER.

9th New York Heavy Artillery, 2d Battalion,† Maj. Edward P. Taft.
10th New York Heavy Artillery, Col. Alexander Piper.

Provisional Brigades.

Maj. Gen. SILAS CASEY.

[No troops.]

DEFENSES SOUTH OF THE POTOMAC. ‡

Brig. Gen. GUSTAVUS A. DE RUSSY.

First Brigade.	Third Brigade.
Col. THOMAS R. TANNATT.	Col. JOHN C. TIDBALL.
1st Massachusetts Heavy Artillery, Col. Thomas R. Tannatt. 2d New York Heavy Artillery, Col. Joseph N. G. Whistler.	4th New York Heavy Artillery, Col. John C. Tidball. 16th New York Cavalry, Company D, Capt. Λ. Livingston Washburne.
Second Brigade.	Fourth Brigade.
Col. HENRY L. ABBOT.	Col. LOUIS SCHIRMER.
1st Connecticut Heavy Artillery, Col. Henry L. Abbot. 2d Connecticut Heavy Artillery, Lieut-Col. Elisha S. Kellogg.	15th New York Heavy Artillery, Col. Louis Schirmer. Wisconsin Heavy Artillery, Company A, Maj. Charles C. Meservey.

*Troops at Advance Battery and Forts Baker, Bunker Hill, Reno, Simmons, Slocum, and Sumner.
† At Fort Foote.
‡ Headquarters at Arlington; troops at Batteries Garesché and Rodgers, and at Forts Albany, Barnard, Bennett, Berry, Cass, Corcoran, Craig, Ellsworth, Ethan Allen, Farnsworth, Haggerty, Lyon, Marcy, O'Rorke, Reynolds, Richardson, Runyon, C. F. Smith, Strong, Tillinghast, Ward, Weed, Whipple, Willard, Williams, Woodbury, and Worth.

TYLER'S DIVISION.*

Col. CHARLES M. ALEXANDER.

Irish Legion.

Col. JAMES P. McIVOR.

182d New York (69th New York National Guard Artillery), Lieut. Col. Thomas M. Reid.
155th New York. Col. Hugh C. Flood.
164th New York, Col. James P. McMahon.
170th New York, Lieut. Col. Michael C. Murphy.

Cavalry Brigade.

Col. CHARLES R. LOWELL, jr.

2d Massachusetts, Maj. Casper Crowninshield.
13th New York, Lieut. Col. Henry S. Gansevoort.
16th New York, Col. Henry M. Lazelle.

Not Brigaded.

2d District of Columbia, Maj. William F. Garrett.
157th Pennsylvania, Companies A, B, C, and D, Maj. Thomas H. Addicks.
17th New York Battery, Capt. George T. Anthony.

DISTRICT OF ALEXANDRIA.

Brig. Gen. JOHN P. SLOUGH, Military Governor.

Second Brigade (Pennsylvania Reserve Corps).

Col. HORATIO G. SICKEL.

3d Pennsylvania Reserves,† Maj. William Briner.
4th Pennsylvania Reserves,† Lieut. Col. Thomas F. B. Tapper.
7th Pennsylvania Reserves, Col. Henry C. Bolinger.
8th Pennsylvania Reserves, Lieut. Col. William Lemon.

Not Brigaded.

4th Delaware,‡ Col. Arthur H. Grimshaw.
1st District of Columbia, Lieut. Col. Lemuel Towers.
5th New York (veteran), Lieut. Col. Cleveland Winslow.
1st Michigan Cavalry, Company D,§ Capt. Thurlow W. Lusk.
Pennsylvania Light Artillery, Battery H, Capt. William Borrowe.

CAMP CONVALESCENT, ETC.

Lieut. Col. SAMUEL McKELVEY.

Camp Convalescent, Lieut. Col. Samuel McKelvey.
Camp of Deserters, Maj. Charles G. Freudenberg.
Camp of Distribution, Lieut. Frank T. Stewart.

FORT WASHINGTON, MD.

Col. HORACE BROOKS.

16th Indiana Battery, Capt. Charles R. Deming.

DETACHMENTS.

Glymont Landing, Md.

1st Indiana Cavalry, Companies I and K, Capt. Abram Sharra.

Government Farms, Va.

111th New York, Companies B and C, Capt. Robert C. Perry.

MASON'S ISLAND, D. C.

109th New York, Col. Benjamin F. Tracy.

---

* Constituted December 30, 1863, and Brig. Gen. Robert O. Tyler assigned to the command.
† On duty at Camp Convalescent.
‡ On special duty, under Brig. Gen. Henry S. Briggs, at Alexandria, Va.
§ Under command of Lieut. Col. Henry H. Wells, provost-marshal, at Alexandria, Va.

Abstract from return of the Middle Department (Eighth Army Corps), Brig. Gen. Henry H. Lockwood, U. S. Army, commanding, for the month of December, 1863.

Command.	Present for duty.		Aggregate present.	Aggregate present and absent.	Remarks.
	Officers.	Men.			
General headquarters	15	....	15	15	
First Separate Brigade (Tyler)	86	1,137	1,382	1,514	Relay House, Md.
Second Separate Brigade (Morris)......	79	1,791	2,399	2,844	Fort McHenry, Md.
District of Delaware (D. Tyler)	14	392	432	760	Headquarters Wilmington.
Annapolis, Md. (Waite)	13	192	244	311	
Baltimore, Md	42	976	1,248	1,630	
Benedict, Md. (Birney)..............	59	1,498	2,067	2,389	
Drummondtown, Va. (Comegys).......	29	646	716	751	
Eastville, Va. (Duvall)	1	69	78	92	
Fort Delaware, Del. (Schoepf)	14	274	404	443	
Total	352	6,975	8,985	10,749	

Troops in the Middle Department (Eighth Army Corps), Brig. Gen. Henry H. Lockwood, U. S. Army, commanding, December 31, 1863.

FIRST SEPARATE BRIGADE.

Brig. Gen. ERASTUS B. TYLER.

3d Delaware, Col. Samuel H. Jenkins.
3d Maryland (Potomac Home Brigade), Lieut. Col. Charles Gilpin.
Purnell (Maryland) Legion, Col. Samuel A. Graham.
Purnell (Maryland) Cavalry, Company B, Capt. Thomas H. Watkins.

SECOND SEPARATE BRIGADE.

Bvt. Brig. Gen. WILLIAM W. MORRIS.

10th Maryland, Col. William H. Revere, jr.
5th New York Heavy Artillery, Maj. Casper Urban.
8th New York Heavy Artillery (ten companies), Lieut. Col. Willard W. Bates.
2d U. S. Artillery, Battery I, Capt. Thomas Grey.

DISTRICT OF DELAWARE.

Brig. Gen. DANIEL TYLER.

5th Maryland, Capt. Samuel Ford.
1st Delaware Cavalry, Company A, Capt. William P. Lord.
1st Delaware Cavalry, Company D, Lieut. Solomon Townsend.
Purnell (Maryland) Cavalry, Company C, Capt. Theodore Clayton.

BALTIMORE, MD.

Artillery Reserve.

Capt. FREDERIC W. ALEXANDER.

Maryland Light, Battery A (Junior Artillery), Capt. John M. Bruce.
Maryland Light, Battery B (Eagle Artillery), Capt. Joseph H. Audoun.
Baltimore Light Artillery, Capt. Frederic W. Alexander.
3d Pennsylvania, Battery H, Capt. William D. Rank.

Cavalry Reserve.

Col. C. CARROLL TEVIS.

1st Connecticut, Capt. William E. Morris.
1st Delaware, Maj. Napoleon B. Knight.
3d Maryland, 2d Battalion, Maj. William Kelsey.

BENEDICT, MD.

Brig. Gen. WILLIAM BIRNEY.

7th U. S. Colored Troops, Col. James Shaw, jr.
9th U. S. Colored Troops, Col. Thomas Bayley.
19th U. S. Colored Troops, Maj. Theodore H. Rockwood.

ANNAPOLIS, MD.

Col. CARLOS A. WAITE.

2d Maryland Cavalry, Companies A, B, C, D, and E. Capt. William F. Bragg.
3d Delaware   } (detachments), Capt. Wilson W. Walker.
2d Maryland (Eastern Shore) }

FORT DELAWARE, DEL.

Brig. Gen. ALBIN SCHOEPF.

Delaware Heavy Artillery Company, Capt. George W. Ahl.
Pennsylvania Artillery, Battery A, Capt. Stanislaus Mlotkowski.
Pennsylvania Artillery, Battery G, Capt. John J. Young.

EASTVILLE, VA.

Purnell (Maryland) Cavalry, Company A, Capt. Robert E. Duvall.

DRUMMONDTOWN, VA.

Lieut. Col. WILLIAM H. COMEGYS.

1st Maryland (Eastern Shore) Infantry, Lieut. Col. William H. Comegys.
Smith's Independent Company (Maryland) Cavalry, Lieut. Joseph T. Fearing.

Abstract from return of the Department of the Susquehanna, Maj. Gen. Darius N. Couch commanding, for the month of December 1863.

Command.	Present for duty.		Aggregate present.	Aggregate present and absent.	Pieces of artillery.
	Officers.	Men.			
Department staff..	9	....	9	9	....
Philadelphia (Maj. Gen. George Cadwalader):					
Staff..	2	....	2	2	......
Infantry.......................................	18	173	468	505	......
Cavalry..	2	123	148	157	......
Artillery.......................................	2	70	90	96	4
Total......................................	24	366	708	760	4
Reading, Pa. (Maj. Gen. Franz Sigel):					
Staff..	2	....	2	2	......
Infantry.......................................	24	437	589	670	......
Cavalry..					
Artillery.......................................	2	77	89	99	4
Total......................................	28	514	680	771	4

Abstract from return of the Department of the Susquehanna, &c.—Continued.

Command.	Present for duty.		Aggregate present.	Aggregate present and absent.	Pieces of artillery.
	Officers.	Men.			
Harrisburg, Pa. (Maj. Gen. Julius Stahel):					
Staff..	4	....	4	4	.....
Infantry...	6	123	150	151	.....
Cavalry..	78	1,635	1,881	2,051	.....
Artillery...	5	76	105	106	.....
Total..	93	1,834	2,140	2,312	.....
Chambersburg (Brig. Gen. Orris S. Ferry), staff...............	2	....	2	2	.....
Gettysburg (Capt. Thomas S. McGowan), infantry..............					
Harrisburg (Lieut. Col. James V. Bomford), infantry	4	....	4	4	....
York, Pa., infantry	3	77	85	88	.....
Chambersburg (Lieut. James W. Piper), Battery E, 5th U. S. Artillery	3	88	95	100	4
Assistant quartermasters and chief quartermaster (Capt. Alex. N. Shipley).......	8	......	8	8	.....
Company F, First Battalion, Pennsylvania Volunteers (Capt. J. A. Ege)...................................	3	78	84	88	.....
Harrisburg (Capt. Jeremiah H. Gilman), commissaries of subsistence, U. S. Army, and chief commissary of subsistence.	8	....	8	8	.....
Total.................................	31	243	286	298	4
Grand total, Department of the Susquehanna.. ...	185	2,957	3,823	4,150	12

Troops in the Department of the Susquehanna, commanded by Maj. Gen. Darius N. Couch, December 31, 1863.

CHAMBERSBURG, PA.

Brig. Gen. ORRIS S. FERRY.

1st Battalion Pennsylvania Infantry, Company F, Capt. Joseph A. Ege.
5th U. S. Artillery, Battery E, Lieut. James W. Piper.

HARRISBURG, PA.

Maj. Gen. JULIUS STAHEL.

20th Pennsylvania Cavalry, (seven companies), Col. John E. Wynkoop.
21st Pennsylvania, (seven companies).*
Nevin's (Pennsylvania) Light Artillery, Battery I, Capt. Robert J. Nevin.

PHILADELPHIA, PA.

Maj. Gen. GEORGE CADWALADER.

27th New York Battery, Capt. John B. Eaton.
20th Pennsylvania Cavalry, Company B, Capt. Michael B. Strickler.
20th Pennsylvania Cavalry, Company L, Capt. Samuel Comfort, jr.
1st Battalion Pennsylvania Infantry (three companies), Lieut. Col. Joseph F. Ramsey.
2d Battalion Pennsylvania Infantry (five companies), Lieut. CoL T. Elwood Zell.
147th Pennsylvania Infantry, Company I, Capt. Charles Fair.

READING, PA.

Maj. Gen. FRANZ SIGEL.

10th New Jersey, Lieut. Col. Charles H. Tay.
1st New York Light Artillery, Battery A, Capt. Thomas H. Bates.
20th Pennsylvania Cavalry, Company G, Capt. Hugh A. Kelley.
Ten companies U. S. Veteran Corps.*

* Commander not of record.

CAMP WILLIAM PENN, PA.

Lieut. Col. LOUIS WAGNER.

8th U. S. Colored Troops, Col. Charles W. Fribley.
22d U. S. Colored Troops (seven companies), Lieut. James E. Griffin.

YORK, PA.

Surg. HENRY PALMER.

Patapsco (Maryland) Guards, Capt. Thomas S. McGowan.
50th Company, 2d Battalion, U. S. Veteran Reserve Corps, Capt. Robert T. Knox.

Abstract from return of the troops in the Department of West Virginia, Brig. Gen. Benjamin F. Kelley commanding, for the month of December, 1863.

Command.	Present for duty.		Aggregate present.	Aggregate present and absent.	Pieces of artillery.		Headquarters.
	Officers.	Men.			Heavy.	Field.	
Commanding general and staff	9	....	9	9	......	......	
First Division (Brig. Gen. Jeremiah C. Sullivan):							
Staff................................	3	....	3	3	......	......	Harper's Ferry.
First Brigade (Col. George D. Wells)	58	1,084	2,101	2,287	......	16	Do.
Second Brigade (Col. William P. Maulsby).	46	1,149	1,308	1,704	......	13	Do.
Third Brigade (Col. Robert S. Rodgers).	66	2,184	2,007	3,101	......	6	Do.
Cavalry forces at Charlestown... .	56	1,380	1,764	2,705	......	......	Do.
Heavy artillery	20	553	722	798	32	......	Do.
Cavalry..............................	3	56	62	72	......	...	Point of Rocks, Md.
Total	252	7,015	8,567	10,725	32	40	
Second Division (Col. James A. Mulligan):							
Staff	2	....	2	2	......	......	New Creek, W. Va.
First Brigade (Col. James M. Campbell).	80	2,230	2,463	2,640	... .	12	Do
Second Brigade (Col. Joseph Thoburn).	77	2,340	2,862	3,458	....	13	Do.
Third Brigade (Col. N. Wilkinson)	108	2,984	3,313	3,514	2	9	Do.
Total	267	7,563	8,640	9,623	2	34	
Third Division (Brig. Gen. E. P. Scammon):							
Staff........	5	... .	5	5	......	......	Charleston, W. Va.
First Brigade (Col. Rutherford B Hayes).	56	1,438	1,695	2,446	.. .	.....	Do.
Second Brigade (Col. Carr B. White)	58	1,462	1,721	2,306	....	.....	Do.
Third Brigade (Brig. Gen. Alfred N. Duffié).	10	378	480	702	.....	.....	Do.
Division cavalry	40	965	1,096	1,290	... .	.	Do.
Division artillery	7	196	227	313	... .	16	Do.
Total	176	4,430	5,230	7,122	...	16	
First Separate Brigade, Fourth Division (Brig. Gen. William W. Averell):							
Staff	9	......	9	10	......	......	New Creek, W. Va.
Infantry	44	1,067	1,231	1,578	... .	.....	Do.
Mounted infantry.	55	1,192	1,427	2,081	... .	.....	Do
Cavalry...........	32	732	932	1,437	... .	... .	Do.
Artillery...........	5	162	174	221	......	12	Do.
Detachment of signal corps	3	14	17	20	... .	.....	Do.
Total	148	3,167	3,790	5,347	...	12	
Virginia Exempts (Capt. W. C. Thorp)	4	74	170	187	......	... .	Wheeling, W. Va.
Grand total.	856	22,258	26,406	33,013	34	102	

Troops in the Department of West Virginia, Brig. Gen. Benjamin
F. Kelley, U. S. Army, commanding, December 31, 1863.

FIRST DIVISION.

Brig. Gen. JEREMIAH C. SULLIVAN.

First Brigade.

Col. GEORGE D. WELLS.

9th Maryland, Col. Benjamin L. Simpson.
34th Massachusetts, Lieut. Col. William S. Lincoln.
12th West Virginia, Maj. William B. Curtis.
17th Indiana Battery, Capt. Milton L. Miner.
1st Pennsylvania Light Artillery, Battery D, Lieut. Andrew Rosney.
1st West Virginia Light Artillery, Battery A, Capt. George Furst.

Second Brigade.

Col. WILLIAM P. MAULSBY.

1st Maryland (Potomac Home Brigade), Lieut. Col. Roger E. Cook.
2d Maryland (Eastern Shore), Capt. Seth W. Herrick.
Maryland Light Artillery, Battery B, Capt. Alonzo Snow.
30th New York Battery, Lieut. Alfred von Kleiser.
32d New York Battery, Capt. Charles Kusserow.

Third Brigade.

Col. ROBERT S. RODGERS.

18th Connecticut, Maj. Henry Peale.
116th Ohio, Col. James Washburn.
123d Ohio, Maj. Horace Kellogg.
12th Pennsylvania Cavalry, Col. Lewis B. Pierce.
1st West Virginia Cavalry, Company K, Lieut. Anderson Dawson.
5th U. S. Artillery, Battery B, Lieut. Henry A. Du Pont.

Cavalry Brigade.

Col. WILLIAM H. BOYD.

1st Connecticut (detachment), Maj. Erastus Blakeslee.
Maryland (Potomac Home Brigade) Battalion, Maj. Henry A. Cole.
2d Maryland (Potomac Home Brigade), Company F, Capt. Norval McKinley.
6th Michigan, Company M, Capt Harvey H. Vinton.
1st New York, Maj. Timothy Quinn.
21st Pennsylvania (five companies), Maj. Charles F. Gillies.
22d Pennsylvania, 1st Battalion, Maj. B. Mortimer Morrow.

Heavy Artillery.

Maj. GUSTAVUS F. MERRIAM.

5th New York Heavy Artillery, 3d Battalion.
Tyler's (Pennsylvania) Battery,* Capt. Horatio K. Tyler.
1st West Virginia Light Artillery, Battery H, Capt. James H. Holmes.

Unattached.

Engineer Company (Pennsylvania), Capt. William Penn Gaskell.
Loudoun (Virginia) Rangers, Capt. Samuel C. Means.

---

* On one of the returns this is designated as the " Park (Pennsylvania) Battery."

SECOND DIVISION.

Col. JAMES A. MULLIGAN.

First Brigade.

Col. JACOB M. CAMPBELL.

2d Pennsylvania Battalion, Lieut. Col. John C. Lininger.
54th Pennsylvania, Lieut. Col. John P. Linton.
15th West Virginia, Col. Maxwell McCaslin.
1st West Virginia Light Artillery, Battery E, Lieut. Francis M. Lowry.

Second Brigade.

Col. JOSEPH THOBURN.

23d Illinois, Lieut. Col. James Quirk.
2d Maryland (Potomac Home Brigade), Maj. John H. Huntley,
1st West Virginia, Lieut. Col. Jacob Weddle.
14th West Virginia. Capt. Jacob Smith.
Lafayette (Pennsylvania) Company Cavalry, Sergt. Jefferson G. Van Gilder.
Ringgold (Pennsylvania) Cavalry (five companies), Capt. James Y. Chesrow.
Washington (Pennsylvania) Company Cavalry, Lieut. John Dabinett.
1st Illinois Light Artillery, Battery L, Capt. John Rourke.
1st West Virginia Light Artillery, Battery D, Capt. John Carlin.

Third Brigade.

Col. NATHAN WILKINSON.

6th West Virginia, Lieut. Col. John F. Hoy.
11th West Virginia, Lieut. Col. Van H. Bukey.
4th West Virginia Cavalry, Col. Joseph Snider.
1st West Virginia Light Artillery, Battery F, Lieut. George W. Graham.

THIRD DIVISION.

Brig. Gen. E. PARKER SCAMMON.

First Brigade.

Col. RUTHERFORD B. HAYES.

23d Ohio, Maj. James P. McIlrath.
5th West Virginia, Col. Abia A. Tomlinson.
13th West Virginia, Col. William R. Brown.
1st West Virginia Cavalry, Company A. Lieut. James Abraham.
1st West Virginia Cavalry (one company), Capt. George W. Gilmore.
3d West Virginia Cavalry, Company G, Capt. John S. Witcher.

Second Brigade.

Col. CARR B. WHITE.

12th Ohio, Lieut. Col. Jonathan D. Hines.
91st Ohio, Col. John A. Turley.
9th West Virginia, Col. Isaac H. Duval.
1st Ohio Battery, Capt. James R. McMullin.

Third Brigade.

Brig. Gen. ALFRED N. DUFFIÉ.

34th Ohio,* Capt. Luther Furney.
2d West Virginia Cavalry, Lieut. Col. David Dove.
3d West Virginia Cavalry (three companies), Capt. George W. McVicker.
Simmonds' (Kentucky) Battery, Lieut. Daniel W. Glassie.

----

* Mounted.

FOURTH DIVISION.*

Brig. Gen. WILLIAM W. AVERELL.

28th Ohio, Col. Augustus Moor.
2d West Virginia,† Lieut. Col. Alexander Scott.
3d West Virginia.† Lieut. Col. Francis W. Thompson.
8th West Virginia,† Col. John H. Oley.
10th West Virginia, Col. Thomas M. Harris.
16th Illinois Cavalry, Company C, Capt. Julius Jaehne.

3d Independent Company Ohio Cavalry, Capt. Frank Smith.
14th Pennsylvania Cavalry, Col. James N. Schoonmaker.
1st West Virginia Cavalry, Company A, Capt. Harrison H. Hagan.
3d West Virginia Cavalry, Companies E, F, and H, Capt. Lot Bowen.
1st West Virginia Light Artillery, Battery B, Capt. John V. Keeper.
1st West Virginia Light Artillery, Battery G, Capt. Chatham T. Ewing.

WHEELING, W. VA.

.Capt. WESLEY C. THORP.

West Virginia Exempts (one company), Capt. Robert Hamilton.
West Virginia Exempts (one company), Capt. Perry G. West.

Abstract from return of the Department of the Monongahela, Maj. Gen. William T. H. Brooks, U. S. Army, commanding, for the month of December, 1863.

Command.	Present for duty.		Aggregate present.	Aggregate present and absent.
	Officers.	Men.		
General headquarters..	9	.....	9	10
Barnesville, Ohio...	6	143	149	186
Hendrysburg, Ohio..	2	66	68	89
New Wilmington, Pa..	3	63	66	86
Pittsburgh, Pa..	3	85	89	100
Pulaski, Pa...	1	45	46	71
Somerton, Ohio...	3	79	82	90
West Alexander, Pa...	1	34	35	43
West Finley, Pa..	3	82	89	96
Total...	.31	597	633	771

Troops in the Department of the Monongahela, Maj. Gen. William T. H. Brooks, U. S. Army, commanding, December 31, 1863.

BARNESVILLE, OHIO.

Departmental Corps (Ohio Emergency Militia), Capt. James L. Deens.
Departmental Corps (Ohio Emergency Militia), Capt. Hamilton Eaton.

HENDRYSBURG, OHIO.

Departmental Corps (Ohio Emergency Militia), Capt. Joseph P. Arrick.

NEW WILMINGTON, PA.

Departmental Corps (Pennsylvania Emergency Militia), Capt. Joseph R. Kemp.

---

* Reported on the return as the "First Separate Brigade;" organization changed by department general orders of December 31 (see p. 595).
† Mounted infantry.

PITTSBURGH, PA.

Pennsylvania Emergency Militia (one company), Capt. Samuel T. Griffith.

PULASKI, PA.

Departmental Corps (Pennsylvania Emergency Militia), Lieut. James M. Brown.

SOMERTON, OHIO.

Departmental Corps (Ohio Emergency Militia), Capt. Samuel Beard.

WEST ALEXANDER, PA.

Departmental Corps (Pennsylvania Emergency Militia), Lieut. John C. Porter.

WEST FINLEY, PA.

Departmental Corps (Pennsylvania Emergency Militia), Capt. John Henderson.

Abstract from return of the Department of Virginia and North Carolina, Maj. Gen. Benjamin F. Butler, U. S. Army, commanding, for the month of December, 1863.

Command.	Present for duty.		Aggregate present.	Aggregate present and absent.	Pieces of artillery.	
	Officers	Men.			Heavy.	Field.
General headquarters a	26	71	100	125	.....	.....
Fort Monroe, Va	68	1,734	2,069	2,416	.....	2
Norfolk and Portsmouth, Va. (Barnes)	175	3,611	4,147	4,686	.....	6
Portsmouth, Va. (Getty)	303	6,574	8,312	12,450	57	34
Newport News, Va. (Heckman)	141	2,877	3,837	4,956	.....	18
Yorktown, Va., and vicinity (West)	183	3,932	5,106	5,956	51	51
District of Saint Mary's (Marston)	71	1,968	2,483	3,077	.....	9
District of North Carolina (Peck):						
Headquarters	21	.....	21	23	.....	..
Defenses of New Berne (Palmer)	148	3,114	4,060	6,060	61	49
Sub-District of the Albemarle (Wessells)	82	1,224	1,700	2,058	17	13
Sub-District of Beaufort (Jourdan)	65	1,219	1,594	2,115	55	9
Sub-District of the Pamlico (McChesney)	47	1,316	1,648	1,926	.....	7
Total	1,330	27,640	35,092	45,878	241	198

a Including signal corps.

Troops in the Department of Virginia and North Carolina, Maj. Gen. Benjamin F. Butler, U. S. Army, commanding, December 31, 1863.

FORT MONROE.

3d Pennsylvania Heavy Artillery, Col. Joseph Roberts.
U. S. Veteran Reserve Corps, 2d Battalion, Maj. James W. H. Stickney.
1st U. S. Colored Cavalry, Col. Jeptha Garrard.
Army gunboats, Brig. Gen. Charles K. Graham.
Signal Corps, Capt. Henry R. Clum.

NORFOLK AND PORTSMOUTH, VA.

Brig. Gen. JAMES BARNES.

African Brigade,.

Brig. Gen. EDWARD S. WILD.

55th Massachusetts Colored (detachment). }
1st North Carolina Colored (detachment). } Capt. Charles A. Jones.
2d North Carolina Colored, Col. Alonzo G. Draper.
3d North Carolina Colored, Lieut. Col. Abial G. Chamberlain.
1st U. S. Colored Troops, Col. John H. Holman.
5th U. S. Colored Troops, Col. James W. Conine.
10th U. S. Colored Troops, Col. John A. Nelson.

Not brigaded.

27th Massachusetts, Col. Horace C. Lee.
148th New York, Company A, Lieut. Col. John B. Murray.
11th Pennsylvania Cavalry, Company A, Capt. George S. Ringland.
2d Massachusetts Heavy Artillery, Companies G and H, Capt. Ira B. Sampson.
7th New York Battery, Capt. Peter C. Regan.

PORTSMOUTH, VA.

Brig. Gen. GEORGE W. GETTY.

*GETTY'S DIVISION, EIGHTEENTH ARMY CORPS.**

Second (Harland's) Brigade.

Col. FRANCIS BEACH.

8th Connecticut, Capt. Henry M. Hoyt.
15th Connecticut, Lieut. Col. Samuel Tolles.
16th Connecticut, Lieut. Col. John H. Burnham.

Third Brigade.

Col. WILLIAM H. P. STEERE.

10th New Hampshire, Lieut. Col. John Coughlin.
13th New Hampshire, Lieut. Col. William Grantman.
4th Rhode Island, Maj. James T. P. Bucklin.

Cavalry Brigade.

Col. SAMUEL P. SPEAR.

20th New York, Col. Newton B. Lord.
5th Pennsylvania, Lieut. Col. William Lewis.
11th Pennsylvania, Lieut. Col. George Stetzel.

Artillery Brigade.

Capt. FREDERICK M. FOLLETT.

3d New York Light, Battery M, Capt. John H. Howell.
13th New York Heavy, Companies A, B, C, and D, Maj. Oliver Wetmore, jr.
1st Pennsylvania Light, Battery A, Capt. John G. Simpson.
4th United States, Battery D, Capt. Frederick M. Follett.
5th United States, Battery A, Lieut. James Gilliss.
4th Wisconsin Battery, Capt. George B. Easterly.

---

*The First Brigade serving in the Department of the South.

DISTRICT OF CURRITUCK, N. C.

Brig. Gen. JAMES H. LEDLIE.

81st New York, Col. Jacob J. De Forest.
96th New York, Col. Edgar M. Cullen.
98th New York, Lieut. Col. Frederick F. Wead.
3d New York Cavalry, Company B. Capt. John Ebbs.
3d New York Cavalry, Company C, Lieut. John Mayes.
5th Pennsylvania Cavalry (squadron), Lieut. J. Frank Cummings.

NEWPORT NEWS, VA.

Brig. Gen. CHARLES A. HECKMAN.

21st Connecticut, Col. Arthur H. Dutton.
23d Massachusetts, Col. Andrew Elwell.
25th Massachusetts, Lieut. Col. Orson Moulton.
9th New Jersey, Col. Abram Zabriskie.
118th New York, Col. Oliver Keese, jr.
3d New York Cavalry, Col. Simon H. Mix.
3d New York Light Artillery, Battery H, Capt. William J. Riggs.
16th New York Battery, Capt. Frederick L. Hiller.

YORKTOWN, VA., AND VICINITY.

Col. ROBERT M. WEST.*

Infantry.

11th Connecticut, Maj. Joseph H. Converse.
139th New York, Col. Samuel H. Roberts.
148th New York, Col. George M. Guion.
4th U. S. Colored Troops, Col. Samuel A. Duncan.
6th U. S. Colored Troops, Col. John W. Ames.

Artillery.

8th New York Battery, Capt. Butler Fitch.
16th New York Heavy Artillery (five companies), Capt. James H. McLaughlin.
1st Pennsylvania Light Artillery, Battery E, Capt. Thomas G. Orwig.
4th U. S. Artillery, Battery L, Lieut. John S. Hunt.
2d Wisconsin Battery, Lieut. Carl Schulz.

Cavalry.

1st New York Mounted Rifles, Col. Benjamin F. Onderdonk.

DISTRICT OF SAINT MARY'S.

Brig. Gen. GILMAN MARSTON.

2d New Hampshire, Col. Edward L. Bailey.
5th New Hampshire, Col. Charles E. Hapgood.
12th New Hampshire, Capt. John F. Langley.
U. S. Cavalry (detachment), Lieut. John Mix.
1st Rhode Island Light Artillery, Battery F, Lieut. Thomas Simpson.

* Commanding in temporary absence on duty of Brigadier-General Wistar.

DISTRICT OF NORTH CAROLINA.

Maj. Gen. JOHN J. PECK.

Defenses of New Berne, N. C.

Brig. Gen. INNIS N. PALMER.

17th Massachusetts, Lieut. Col. John F. Fellows.
12th New York Cavalry, Col. James W. Savage.
3d New York Light Artillery, Col. Charles H. Stewart.
92d New York, Lieut. Col. Hiram Anderson, jr.

99th New York, Lieut. |Col. Richard Nixon.
132d New York, Col. Peter J. Claassen.
5th Rhode Island Heavy Artillery,* Col. Henry T. Sisson.
19th Wisconsin, Maj. Rollin M. Strong.

Sub-District of Beaufort, N. C.

Col. JAMES JOURDAN.

2d Massachusetts Heavy Artillery, Company C. Capt. Charles B. Newton.
2d Massachusetts Heavy Artillery, Company D, and detachment Company A, Capt. Russell H. Cornwell.
2d Massachusetts Heavy Artillery, Companies A and B. } Capt. Nehemiah P. Fuller.
1st U. S. Artillery, Battery C.
Mix's New York (Battalion) Cavalry, Capt. Emory Cummings.

158th New York (seven companies), Lieut. Col. William H. McNary.
158th New York, Companies B, D, and E. } Capt. Peter B. Steele.
2d North Carolina, Company A.
5th Rhode Island Heavy Artillery, Company A, Lieut. Dutee Johnson.
9th Vermont, Col. Edward H. Ripley.
19th Wisconsin, Company F, Capt. Martin Scherff.

Sub-District of the Albemarle, N. C.

Brig. Gen. HENRY W. WESSELLS.

12th New York Cavalry (detachment), Capt. John S. Ellison.
24th New York Battery, Capt. A. Lester Cady.
85th New York, Col. Enrico Fardella.
96th New York (detachment), Lieut. Col. Stephen Moffitt.

2d North Carolina (recruits), Lieut. Isaiah Conley.
101st Pennsylvania, Lieut. Col. Alexander W. Taylor.
103d Pennsylvania, Col. Theodore F. Lehmann.

Sub-District of the Pamlico, N. C.

Col. JOSEPH M. McCHESNEY.

12th New York Cavalry (two companies), Capt. Rowland R. West.
23d New York Battery, Lieut. Thomas Low.
1st North Carolina, Maj. Charles C. Graves.
58th Pennsylvania, Lieut. Col. Montgomery Martin.

5th Rhode Island Heavy Artillery, Company C, Lieut. George H. Pierce.
5th Rhode Island Heavy Artillery, Company E, Capt. George G. Hopkins.

---

* Detachment 2d Massachusetts Heavy Artillery attached.

Abstract from return of the Department of the East, Maj. Gen. John A. Dix, U. S. Army, commanding, for the month of December, 1863.

Command.	Present for duty.		Aggregate present.	Aggregate present and absent.	Pieces of artillery.	
	Officers.	Men.			Heavy.	Field.
General headquarters	85	10	95	95	....	......
City and harbor of New York	86	2,013	2,946	4,284	548	......
Riker's Island, New York Harbor.	51	1,788	2,084	2,137	....	......
Madison Barracks, N. Y..............................	.	1	1	1	1	......
Fort Ontario, N. Y..................................	1	120	138	173	17	4
Fort Niagara, N. Y	.	1	1	1	16	......
Fort Trumbull, Conn..................................	6	376	500	523	62	......
Fort Adams, R. I....................................	1	83	124	100	200	......
Portsmouth Grove, R. I................................	3	60	74	81	....	......
Fort Independence, Mass...........	10	209	366	385	56	......
Fort Warren, Mass	24	631	773	789	101	......
Fort at Clark's Point, Mass..........................	4	84	104	147	19	......
Fort at Eastern Point, Mass	5	138	151	151	....	......
Winter Island, Mass................................	5	132	152	152	....	......
Fort Constitution, N. H.............................	4	131	142	150	27	......
Forts Preble and Scammel, Me	4	143	219	233	44	......
Fort Knox, Me	1	41	45	50	20	4
Fort McClary, Me...........	5	134	149	151	4	......
Total	295	6,090	8,014	9,673	1,114	8

Troops in the Department of the East, Maj. Gen. John A. Dix, U. S. Army, commanding, December 31, 1863.

CITY AND HARBOR OF NEW YORK.

Brig. Gen. GEORGE J. STANNARD.

Davids Island.

U. S. Veteran Reserve Corps (detachment), Capt. Isaac H. Baker.

Fort Hamilton.

Col. HANNIBAL DAY.

6th United States, Maj. George W. Wallace.
12th United States, Maj. Dickinson Woodruff.
14th New York Heavy Artillery, Companies E and F, Capt. Oliver B. Flagg.
5th U. S. Artillery (regimental headquarters), Lieut. Thompson P. McElrath.

Fort Schuyler.

Bvt. Brig. Gen. HARVEY BROWN.

7th United States (seven companies), Capt. Gurden Chapin.
20th New York Battery, Lieut. Arthur Wiecker.
28th New York Battery, Lieut. Ira W. Steward.

Fort at Sandy Hook.

Lieut. Col. ENOCH STEEN.

14th New York Heavy Artillery. Company C, Capt. George S. Green, and Company D, Capt. Lorenzo J. Jones.

Fort Columbus.

Col. GUSTAVUS LOOMIS.

8th United States (six companies), Capt. Milton Cogswell.

Fort Richmond.

Lieut. Col. CLARENCE H. CORNING.

14th New York Heavy Artillery (six companies), Lieut. Col. Clarence H. Corning.
4th United States, Capt. Charles H. Brightly.

Fort La Fayette.

Lieut. Col. MARTIN BURKE.

10th United States, Capt. William Clinton.

Fort Wood.

Col. CHARLES S. MERCHANT.

48th Company Veteran Reserve Corps, Capt. Charles W. Gibbs.
49th Company Veteran Reserve Corps, Capt. Michael Walsh.

INDEPENDENT POSTS.

Fort Adams, Newport, R. I.

Col. OLIVER L. SHEPHERD.

15th United States, Company A, 3d Battalion.

Fort Constitution, N. H.

New Hampshire Heavy Artillery (one company), Capt. Charles H. Long.

Fort Independence, Boston, Mass.

Lieut. Col. D. L. FLOYD-JONES.

Massachusetts Heavy Artillery, 3d Company, Lieut. Benjamin A. Ball.
11th United States (detachment), Capt. Alfred E. Latimer.

Fort McClary, Kittery Point, Me.

New Hampshire Heavy Artillery, 2d Company, Capt. Ira McL. Barton.

Forts Preble and Scammel, Portland, Me.

Maj. GEORGE L. ANDREWS.

17th United States, 2d Battalion, Company B, Capt. John P. Wales.
17th United States, 2d Battalion, Company C, Capt. Edward J. Conner.

Fort Warren, Boston, Mass.

Massachusetts Heavy Artillery, 1st Battalion and 7th Company (unattached), Maj. Stephen Cabot.

Riker's Island, N. Y.

Brig. Gen. NATHANIEL J. JACKSON.

8th United States, Company E, Lieut. Hanson E. Weaver.
8th United States, Company G, Lieut. Samuel J. Franks.
20th U. S. Colored Troops, Col. Nelson B. Bartram.

Fort at Clark's Point, New Bedford, Mass.

Massachusetts Heavy Artillery, 6th Company, Capt. John A. P. Allen.

Fort at Eastern Point, Gloucester, Mass.

Massachusetts Heavy Artillery, Capt. Thomas Herbert.

Fort Knox, near Bucksport Me.

1st Maine Heavy Artillery (detachment), Lieut. Thomas H. Palmer.

Fort Ontario, Oswego, N. Y.

16th United States (detachment), Capt. Charles H. Lewis.

Fort Trumbull, New London, Conn.

Col. WILLIAM GATES.

Connecticut Volunteer Recruits, Lieut. Joseph Talcott.
3d U. S. Artillery, Battery G, Lieut. Lewis Smith.
14th United States (detachment), Capt. John D. O'Connell.

Portsmouth Grove, R. I.

Hospital Guards, Rhode Island Volunteers, Company A, Capt. Christopher Blanding.

Winter Island, Salem, Mass.

Massachusetts Heavy Artillery, 12th Company, Capt. James M. Richardson.

Report of the number of deserters returned to the Army of the Potomac from July 1 to December 31, 1863, the number tried, the number found guilty, the number sentenced to be shot, and the number shot.

Command.	Returned.	Found guilty.	Sentenced to be shot.	Shot.	Tried.
First Corps...........		80	10	3	146
Second Corps.................................		84	20	9	160
Third Corps.......................................		64	11	3	171
Fifth Corps...		39	15	8	114
Sixth Corps...	2,465	106	35	2	199
Cavalry...		22	1	......	30
Artillery Reserve...		......	2	......	8
Engineer Brigade...		......	......	... ..	7
Engineer Battalion		3	....	... ..	4
Provost Marshal's Department...............		2	......	......	3
Total .....:...	2,465	402	94	25	842

HEADQUARTERS ARMY OF THE POTOMAC, *January* 1, 1864.

CONFEDERATE CORRESPONDENCE, ETC.

HEADQUARTERS ARMY OF NORTHERN VIRGINIA,
August 4, 1863.

General S. COOPER,
Adjutant and Inspector General, Richmond:

GENERAL: The movements of the enemy north of the Rappahannock, rendering it difficult for me to ascertain whether he intended to advance through Culpeper or fall down the river to Fredericksburg, determined me to unite the army south of the Rapidan. General Ewell's corps, which after crossing the Blue Ridge had been posted in Madison, had been previously ordered to Orange Court-House.

Longstreet's and Hill's corps were yesterday ordered to the Rapidan. I could find no field in Culpeper offering advantages for battle, and any taken could be so easily avoided should the enemy wish to reach the south bank of the Rapidan, that I thought it advisable at once to retire to that bank. Should he advance by this route, I shall endeavor to resist him; and if he falls down to Fredericksburg, will oppose him on that line.

I am, very respectfully, your obedient servant,
R. E. LEE,
General.

WELDON, *August 4, 1863.*

General S. COOPER:

Following dispatch received:

My scouts from Nansemond report that General Getty's brigade is preparing to move, some say to Charleston, some to Petersburg, others to Meade; but my scouts think he will join Colonel Spear, who is preparing for another raid. Colonel Spear is going to move his headquarters to between Norfolk and Edenton. Five thousand infantry and 2,000 cavalry in force at Norfolk and Portsmouth—so estimated.
J. F. MILLIGAN,
Major, and Signal Officer.

M. W. RANSOM,
Brigadier-General.

HEADQUARTERS ARMY OF NORTHERN VIRGINIA,
August 5, 1863.

Col. L. B. NORTHROP,
Commissary-General, C. S. Army:

COLONEL: Your letter of the 23d ultimo, and a subsequent one without date, have been received. If it becomes necessary to reduce the soldiers' rations, I shall regret it from the effect I fear it will have upon the army, as I do not think the present allowance more than sufficient to keep the men well and satisfied. If the reduction is made, I think it ought to extend to all the armies, and not to this alone, as was the case last spring.

When ordered, I shall, of course, conform to it, and do all in my power to render it satisfactory to the troops. In all the operations of this army, I have endeavored to economize the supplies as much as possible, and to obtain as great an amount from the country occupied as could be collected.

As regards your latter communication, I agree with you that every effort should be made to accumulate subsistence in Richmond. The necessities of this army and the uncertainty of depending upon our railroads render this apparent. Every assistance that I can give with the army transportation in collecting the grain and transporting it to the depots will be afforded, and immediately on the reception of your letter, Colonel Corley was directed to furnish to the commissary agents you have named the number of wagons you require, or as many in proportion as could be spared for that purpose. He reports that he cannot find Thomas J. Foster, but that he can place at his disposal thirty four-horse wagons under one of his own quartermasters. He has directed Major Bell, at Staunton, to use all his surplus transportation in that district as Mr. Nelson may desire. Major Bell answered that Mr. Nelson is unable to say at present how many teams he may need or can use, but that he (Major Bell) can furnish him fifty teams, probably one hundred, on condition that he procure teamsters. To collect supplies in the Rappahannock Valley, he can furnish twenty teams. These teams will all be placed in charge of quartermasters, and will be set to work as soon as informed that the grain is ready for transportation. As they form a part of the army transportation, and may be needed for its use at any time, there is an objection to turning them over to the commissary agents, but I desire they shall be used in the way you propose.

The arrangement you propose for the railroads I think ought to be made, but I have no means of controlling their operations.

I am, very respectfully, your obedient servant,

R. E. LEE,
General.

———

PETERSBURG,
August 5, 1863.

Major-General ELZEY,
Richmond:

Colonel Baker reports no enemy this side of Bowers' Hill. Force at Portsmouth, &c., some 5,000. All new troops. Old troops sent to Charleston. General Ransom reports no enemy this side of Chowan.

M. JENKINS,
Brigadier-General.

BRIGADE HEADQUARTERS, CHAFFIN'S FARM,
August 5, 1863.

Maj. T. O. CHESTNEY,
Assistant Adjutant-General: .

MAJOR : I beg respectfully to report that, having been informed through the signal corps that one iron-clad and three gunboats have passed Varina, I have sent a company to Cox's Landing to protect Captain Davidson's submarine batteries from interference by landing. I have ordered Major Stark, with four pieces of artillery, to Deep Bottom, to fire on them returning. I have also sent eight companies of the Twenty-sixth [Virginia] Regiment to support the artillery and to act as sharpshooters. I hope this disposition will meet your approval.

Please let me know if you expect to see me at 10 in the morning, under the existing state of affairs.

Very respectfully, your obedient servant,
P. R. PAGE,
Colonel, Commanding Brigade.

ENGINEER BUREAU,
August 5, 1863.

Col. W. H. STEVENS,
C. S. Army:

COLONEL : The honorable Secretary of War directs that a competent engineer officer be sent to examine the works for defense of the bridges over the South Anna and North Anna Rivers. If they are not in good condition, or require modification to make them susceptible of defense by a few companies, you will have the necessary work done, calling on the troops guarding the bridges for the necessary labor. For the defense of each bridge there should be a closed work of sufficient strength of profile to resist cavalry and light artillery.

Your obedient servant,
J. F. GILMER,
Colonel of Engineers, and Chief of Bureau.

RICHMOND,
August 6, 1863.

General SAMUEL JONES,
Dublin, Va.:

GENERAL : I am directed by the Adjutant and Inspector General to inform you that reports of stragglers in Southwestern Virginia, from the Army of Northern Virginia, have been received at this office.

It is believed if a few companies of reliable men, under the command of a vigilant, active, and energetic officer, were sent to Goshen, and the adjacent counties, with orders to arrest such absentees and send them under guard to their commands, much good would be effected. It would not only increase the strength of the army, but deter others, who have the disposition, from leaving the ranks. The offense has become so frequent that the utmost effort should be made to arrest and return all who cannot show some sufficient authority for their absence. In this connection, it may be noted that there are said to be many stragglers from the command of Col. W. L. Jackson, and that even some of the officers of his regiment have been permitted to remain absent several months at a time. To what extent this may have existed is not alleged, and it is hoped there may, in fact, be but little foundation for the assertion.

Your attention is also requested to the report that many able-bodied men are employed in the quartermaster's and commissary departments within the limits of your command. General Orders, No. 105, current series, direct the disposition to be made of such persons; and, as the army greatly needs re-enforcements, it is expected the requirements of the orders will be rigidly enforced.

Very respectfully, &c.,

H. L. CLAY,
Assistant Adjutant-General.

ENGINEER BUREAU,
August 6, 1863.

Col. W. H. STEVENS, C. S. Army,
Richmond, Va..

COLONEL: It is the desire of the honorable Secretary of War that immediate steps be taken to construct a suitable work for the defense of the bridge of the Petersburg and Weldon Railroad over the Meherrin River, and I have to request that you will take measures at once, in concert with the commanders of the forces at Weldon and Petersburg, to construct the proposed work. The bridge is one of considerable length, and if destroyed would break the southern connection for a considerable time.

An officer of Engineers must be assigned at once to the duty of locating and building a closed work in proper relations for defending the approaches to the bridge, and of such strength of profile as to resist cavalry and light artillery, and suitable for a garrison of two or three companies. It is understood that negro labor will be furnished to some extent by the citizens in the neighborhood, and the commanders of troops should be urged to furnish fatigue labor. Can you assign Lieutenant Bender, or some officer now in North Carolina or Petersburg, to the duty, with proper instructions from yourself? The bridge over the Nottoway River should be guarded also, and possibly a small work built for its protection. I repeat, the Secretary of War desires that prompt measures be taken to build a defensive work at the bridge over the Meherrin. Home guards, in an emergency, it is believed, could be obtained to defend the bridge when the work shall have been built.

The Secretary of War has decided that the agricultural interests will not admit of a call on the slaves for labor on the fortifications sooner than the 10th of September. He has urged upon General Elzey that details of troops be made from his command for fatigue service, say 500 men daily. These to be employed on the connection between Randolph and Chaffin's Bluff. Please see General Elzey, and urge prompt action.

Your obedient servant,

J. F. GILMER,
Colonel of Engineers, and Chief of Bureau.

HEADQUARTERS ARMY OF NORTHERN VIRGINIA,
August 7, 1863.

Hon. JAMES A. SEDDON,
Secretary of War, Richmond:

SIR: I have the honor to inform you that there are 1,700 unarmed men in this army, and the commanding officer of the Richmond Arsenal has informed Lieutenant-Colonel Baldwin, chief of ordnance, that he could only furnish a portion of the needed arms. In addition to the present deficiency, we will need about 5,000 stand of arms in a fortnight, and probably 10,000 within a month. In order to supply these deficiencies, I would respectfully recommend that the reserved arms of this army, which I hear have been distributed among the local troops and the second-class militia, be again collected and forwarded to us, while this class of troops wait for the gradual supply from the arsenals. I need not urge upon you the importance of keeping this army thoroughly equipped.

I am, very respectfully, your obedient servant,
R. E. LEE,
General.

HEADQUARTERS ARMY OF NORTHERN VIRGINIA,
August 7, 1863.

Hon. JAMES A. SEDDON,
Secretary of War, Richmond:

SIR: In a late letter from Colonel Northrop he alluded to the difficulties of railroad transportation from the south, and suggests that when the freight trains cannot bring the usual supplies or sufficient supplies, that the passenger trains should be temporarily stopped, and the whole force of the road devoted to supplying the army. I think the suggestion an important one. Besides the important deficiencies in the commissary department due to these difficulties, I regret to say that we receive now only 1,000 bushels of grain *per diem* for all the animals of this army. On this it would be impossible to bring up our cavalry and artillery horses, even if we gave it all to them. I hope that something can be done to procure a greater proportion of the transportation of our railroads for army purposes than we ever have had at our disposal.

I am, very respectfully, your obedient servant,
R. E. LEE,
General.

RICHMOND,
August 7, 1863.

Maj. Gen. W. H. C. WHITING,
Wilmington, N. C.:

The President directs that the regiments of Colquitt's brigade be sent to Charleston, as indicated to you yesterday.
S. COOPER,
Adjutant and Inspector General.

WRIGHTSVILLE,
August 7, 1863.

General S. COOPER:

The order of the President is obeyed, and the movement commenced. The enemy will attack the railroad in force this week, according to my information. Please to let me know who will command General Ransom's troops, and what force he has. Please to move Ransom's troops at once, as indicated in your dispatch of yesterday.

W. H. C. WHITING,
Major-General.

HEADQUARTERS DEPARTMENT OF NORTH CAROLINA,
Wilmington, August 7, 1863.

Brig. Gen. J. G. MARTIN,
Commanding, &c., Kinston, N. C.:

MY DEAR GENERAL: Your notes received. I have modified the orders about Saunders as you desired. About that raid, I am uncertain whether they mean to fortify the line of White Oak or come upon the line of railroad bridge at, say, Warsaw, when they have seen the country, and then fortify either against you or against me. The first thing for both to do would be to try to meet or intercept them; at any rate, to attack them before they could fortify. On the receipt of news there, you should send out at once. I shall put a regiment with Jackson to hold the Gaklun(?) passes and the Cape Fear at Hallsville. They might move, however, to South Washington. I wish you would spare at once to Jackson a section of artillery. I have so few batteries, and horses have been dying so, that I cannot do it. I shall be compelled to put a guard at South Washington.

Very respectfully,

W. H. C. WHITING,
Major-General.

HEADQUARTERS DISTRICT OF CAPE FEAR,
Wilmington, August 7, 1863.

Major JACKSON,
Kenansville:

MY DEAR MAJOR: I regret I did not see you. I send you a letter* from General Martin which will put you on your guard. I will endeavor to-night to send up one of Colquitt's regiments, commanded by Major Ballenger, to report to you, and have told Martin to send you at once another section of artillery.

You had better send down and ascertain the chance of the enemy taking the left-hand road down the Cape Fear, near Hallsville, and, crossing at South Washington, attacking the Rockfish Creek bridge. If there is a bridge at South Washington, it ought to be strongly watched, and, if obliged, burned. Ascertain if there are fords. I will endeavor, though I am greatly pressed, to keep the Holly Shelter road. Keep your communications well open with Harris.

Yours, truly,

W. H. C. WHITING,
Major-General.

* Not found.

KINSTON, *August 7*, 1863.

General COOPER, *Richmond:*

Captain Brown, quartermaster at Tarborough, reports he has information, he thinks reliable, that enemy is advancing from Washington upon some point of the Wilmington and Weldon Railroad.

J. G. MARTIN,
Brigadier-General.

RICHMOND,
August 7, 1863.

Maj. Gen. ᵛARNOLD ELZEY:

GENERAL: I have just received a letter from Gilmer, informing me that the Secretary of War cannot allow the slaves to be impressed until the 10th of September, and that he said he would urge you to give me details from your troops. If you can comply with his request, please give the necessary orders, and be kind enough to let me have a copy of them.

Very respectfully, yours,

W. H. STEVENS,
Colonel.

[RICHMOND,]
August 8, 1863.

General ELZEY:

GENERAL: I inclose you a dispatch just received from General Whiting, with the rough of my answer sent to him. Please be governed by it, and advise General Ransom accordingly. Please return the telegram here for file.

Yours,

S. COOPER,
Adjutant and Inspector General.

[Inclosures.]

WRIGHTSVILLE,
[*August*] 8, 1863.

General COOPER:

Please let me know what troops General Ransom has, and whether he will report to me. I have directed General Martin, as the former moves down and occupies his position, to concentrate his own forces near Kinston, leaving the garrison of Fort Branch.

W. H. C. WHITING,
Major-General.

[RICHMOND,]
August 8, 1863.

[General WHITING:]

General Ransom has with him his entire brigade of five regiments, besides two batteries of artillery. He is in direct correspondence with General Elzey, to whose command he belongs. He will keep you advised by reports of all matters touching his movements, &c.

S. C. [COOPER.]

RICHMOND, VA.,
August 8, 1863.

General RANSOM:
Keep General Whiting advised of your own movements and of everything that may be of interest to him.
Respectfully,

A. E. [ELZEY.]

RICHMOND, VA.,
August 8, 1863.

Brigadier-General RANSOM,
Weldon:

In reply to your telegram, just received, I have to say that your brigade is under my command. You will be governed by the instructions you have received from me and General Cooper, and advise General Whiting of the movements you have made.
Very respectfully, your obedient servant.

ARNOLD ELZEY,
Major-General, Commanding.

WAR DEPARTMENT, C. S.,
Richmond, Va., August 9, 1863.

General R. E. LEE,
Commanding, &c.:

GENERAL: I am pleased to be able to relieve you from the anxiety manifested in your letter of the 7th instant, in relation to the due supply of arms for your army. I am informed by the Chief of Ordnance that there are at Staunton already, subject to your order, 3,000 arms; that he can command here, subject to your requisition, from 5,000 to 7,000 more, and that he does not apprehend any difficulty in meeting the larger number (10,000) which you expect to require within a month.

I am using all means at the command of the Department to increase both the manufacture and import of arms, and I am always pleased to receive announcements of anticipated deficiencies, that they may be used to stimulate efforts on the part of officers and agents, and assist me in providing for the coming need.
Very truly, yours,

J. A. SEDDON,
Secretary of War.

HEADQUARTERS ARMY OF NORTHERN VIRGINIA,
August 9, 1863.

Brig. Gen. J. D. IMBODEN,
Comdg. Northwestern Virginia Brigade:

GENERAL: Your letter of August 7 has been received.

I hope ere this the people from the lower valley have been able to move up within our lines, with much of their cattle and other property. You will, I hope, give them all the protection you can.

The government wagons, hauling grain and other supplies, must be protected. If the cattle and horses belonging to the Government are in danger in lower Rockingham, they should be moved higher up.

Instruct the officers sent to the passes on your flank to be very watchful, and take every precaution against any attempt of Averell to get into your rear, or to make a raid upon our resources in Rockingham. After the removal of everything of value about Strasburg, you must take position so as to protect the valley, whether the attack comes from the direction of Winchester, the eastern gaps, or from the South Branch Valley.

I hope that McNeill's expedition has proved successful, and that he may return without loss.

Spare no efforts to recruit your command. Arrest all deserters from this army whom you may find in the valley, and send them to Staunton,

Did you give McNeill notice of the attempt of Averell to cut him off? If you have not, you must make a movement to divert attack from him.

I am, very respectfully, your obedient servant,

R. E. LEE,
General.

WILMINGTON, N. C.,
August 9, 1863.

Brigadier-General MARTIN :

The general instructs me to send you the following dispatch from Lieutenant Fairly last night at Swansborough:

News from the lines indicate a raid on Kinston. No re-enforcements have passed up to New Berne since last report. Reports appoint next Wednesday or Thursday as the day of departure from New Berne.

S. J. FAIRLY.

T. B. VENABLE,
Major, and Assistant Adjutant-General.

HEADQUARTERS ARMY OF NORTHERN VIRGINIA,
August 10, 1863.

General S. COOPER,
Adjutant and Inspector General, Richmond, Va.:

GENERAL: General Imboden reports that on the 5th instant, General Kelley left Bunker Hill, in the vicinity of which he had been encamped, with his infantry force, for Romney. On the same evening about 9 p. m., General Averell, with his cavalry, started for Moorefield. This movement is believed to have been occasioned by a demonstration of Captain McNeill, on the Baltimore and Ohio Railroad west of Cumberland, to which point he had been directed to go about the 1st of August, with this view. No report has been received from Captain McNeill, but citizens from Hampshire informed General Imboden that Captain McNeill had had a fight near New Creek, in which he had been successful, with a loss of 4 men on our side. The route taken by General Averell may force Captain McNeill to retire, by the Dry Fork of Cheat, into Pendleton

County, and thus some time must elapse before he can be heard from. General Imboden believes that the enemy has evacuated the valley south of Bunker Hill.

I have the honor to be, very respectfully, your obedient servant,

R. E. LEE, ·
General.

HEADQUARTERS ARMY OF NORTHERN VIRGINIA,
August 10, 1863.

Brig. Gen. J. D. IMBODEN,
Comdg. Northwestern Virginia Brigade:

GENERAL: In your letter of 7th instant, you state that the enemy removed from Winchester to Harper's Ferry tents, damaged ordnance, and other stores, while in a previous letter it was stated that Colonel Imboden had destroyed what he could not remove. I had hoped that this was the case, and that nothing had been left on which the enemy could make a boast of recapture. Please state the facts more fully.

I am, very respectfully, your obedient servant,

R. E. LEE,
General.

HEADQUARTERS DEPARTMENT OF WESTERN VIRGINIA,
Dublin, August 10, 1863.

Maj. Gen. SAMUEL JONES,
Mouth of Indian Creek, via Narrows:

The following telegram just received:

ORANGE COURT-HOUSE,
August 10, 1863.

Maj. Gen. SAMUEL JONES:

General Imboden reports Kelley concentrating his force at Moorefield; anticipated attack on Staunton by Franklin and McDowell. Have you any troops so disposed as to move by Huntersville, and aid or make diversion in his favor?

R. E. LEE.

CHAS. S. STRINGFELLOW,
Assistant Adjutant-General.

HEADQUARTERS DEPARTMENT OF WESTERN VIRGINIA,
August 10, 1863.

General R. E. LEE,
Orange Court-House:

Dispatch received and forwarded to General Jones, who is on his way to Lewisburg, where there is a regiment and a battalion of infantry and four companies of cavalry. Col. William L. Jackson is near Huntersville, with the Nineteenth Virginia Cavalry, and ten companies to be organized next week. General Jones will receive your dispatch to-night.

Respectfully,

CHAS. S. STRINGFELLOW,
Assistant Adjutant-General.

HEADQUARTERS DEPARTMENT OF WESTERN VIRGINIA,
Dublin, August 10, 1863.

Col. GEORGE S. PATTON,
Lewisburg, via Union:

The enemy reported concentrating heavily at Moorefield to attack Staunton, via Franklin and McDowell. Send courier to Colonel Jackson and put him on the lookout. Tell him to be ready to move at shortest notice to co-operate with General Imboden, or make a diversion in his favor.

By order:

CHAS. S. STRINGFELLOW,
Assistant Adjutant-General.

CAMP NEAR MOUTH OF INDIAN CREEK,   •
Monroe County, Va., August 10, 1863.

General S. COOPER,
Adjt. and Insp. Gen., C. S. Army, Richmond, Va. :

GENERAL: I have received a letter from Lieutenant-Colonel Clay, assistant adjutant-general, written by your direction, informing me that there were many deserters from the Army of Northern Virginia in Southwestern Virginia, and suggesting that a few reliable companies might be well employed at "Goshen and the adjoining counties" in arresting these deserters.

The greater part of Southwestern Virginia is not in my department. It was attached to the Department of East Tennessee in January last, and I do not feel at liberty to send troops on such duty into another department than my own, nor do I suppose you desire me to do so, as Brigadier-General Preston's troops, being already in that section of country, can more readily perform the duty.

I know of no place in my department called Goshen. There is a railroad depot of that name on the Central road, but I believe it is in Rockbridge County, and, if so, is not in my department. I really cannot tell from Colonel Clay's letter where you wish me to send companies to arrest deserters. Will you please inform me definitely?

I am also informed by Colonel Clay that it is reported there are many stragglers from Col. W. L. Jackson's command, and that some of the officers of his regiment have been permitted to remain absent several months at a time. I am on my way now to Colonel Jackson's command, and if any such abuses exist, will endeavor to correct them. It is but just to Colonel Jackson, however, to say that his command is new, and is now only in formation and organization, and it is probable that those who are represented as stragglers and absentees have been employed recruiting and collecting men from within the enemy's lines.

Colonel Clay also calls my attention to the report that many able-bodied men are employed in the quartermaster's and commissary departments within my command. There are a number of able-bodied men employed in my command in the quartermaster's and commissary departments. They are employed as blacksmiths, teamsters, boatmen, &c., duties which cannot be performed by disabled men. I have directed the provisions of General Orders, 105, current series, to be rigidly enforced, and will see that the order is obeyed.

I respectfully ask that you will inform me how the reports of these irregularities and abuses in my command reached you, and from whom you obtained the information, that I may trace up and correct all such irregularities and abuses.

Very respectfully, your obedient servant,

SAM. JONES,
Major-General.

[Indorsement.]

As General Jones appears to be indisposed to send out the companies referred to for the important object contemplated, it is scarcely necessary to pursue the subject further in respect to his command.

FORT BOYKIN,
August 10, 1863.

[Maj. JAS. F. MILLIGAN:]

Our scout from Norfolk could not get any reliable information about the Yankees' intention to evacuate Norfolk.

They have one regiment at Deep Creek, and that place is well fortified. One regiment of infantry and one of cavalry (Eleventh Penusylvania) at Oak Grove, 1 mile from Portsmouth. One regiment at Norfolk. The whole amount of forces at and around the cities is estimated at 4,000.

He saw the steamer that was fired into by our forces up the James River the other day. She was badly crippled—four shots into her, besides many bullets also.

A torpedo exploded while one of the gunboats was very near it, and the concussion of the water threw 14 men overboard, 3 of whom were drowned. One of the gunboats came to her assistance, and the captain of the first gunboat, thinking his boat was sinking, and in the attempt to jump on the steamer coming to his assistance, was struck by a cannon ball from the shore and cut in two. This is Yankee news.

A regiment of 1,300 negroes left Fort Monroe for Charleston, August 8. Small-pox is said to be bad among the negroes at Norfolk. One English man-of-war and one Yankee are all the shipping at Fort Monroe. They are trying to raise the Cumberland.

Yours, respectfully, &c.,

JOS. R. WOODLEY,
Lieutenant, Commanding.

ENGINEER BUREAU,
August 10, 1863.

His Excellency ZEBULON B. VANCE,
Governor of North Carolina, Raleigh, N. C.:

SIR: For completing the defenses of Wilmington at an early day, slave labor is required, and Major-General Whiting, commanding in the eastern part of your State, urges that immediate steps be taken to procure it. The works ought to be pressed forward without delay, and to this end I am instructed by the honorable Secretary of War to appeal to your excellency for aid, and to ask you as Governor of North Carolina to call on the patriotic citizens in the neighboring counties, and elsewhere, to send a portion of their hands, say one-fifth of the negroes (male), to the city of Wilmington, to be employed under the command of General Whiting, on the fortifications. What we do for the safety of your principal sea-port should be done quickly, and if possible before our bitter foes meet with further successes at Charleston or elsewhere. Should any military organization be required for the collection of the requisite number of negroes, at least 1,000, General Whiting can furnish the force. He will be directed to confer with you on this point.

I have the honor to be, very respectfully, your obedient servant,

J. F. GILMER,
Colonel of Engineers, and Chief of Bureau.

Abstract from field return of the Army of Northern Virginia, General Robert E. Lee, C. S. Army, commanding, for August 10, 1863; headquarters Orange Court-House.

Command.	Present for duty.		Aggregate present.	Aggregate present and absent.	Aggregate present last field return.
	Officers.	Men.			
General staff	16	....	16	16	17
First Army Corps (Longstreet):					
Headquarters	10	....	10	12	10
McLaws' division	487	4,861	6,298	12,201	5,999
Pickett's division	355	3,611	4,839	11,373	4,591
Hood's division	509	5,087	6,612	11,758	6,386
Total First Army Corps	1,361	13,559	17,759	35,344	16,986
Second Army Corps (Ewell):					
Headquarters	18	....	18	20	18
Rodes' division	495	5,420	6,990	15,159	6,207
Early's division	501	5,006	6,367	12,899	5,477
Johnson's division	482	3,996	5,253	12,297	4,650
Total Second Army Corps	1,496	14,422	18,628	40,375	16,352
Third Army Corps (A. P. Hill):					
Headquarters	17	....	17	17	16
Anderson's division	495	4,999	6,543	12,962	6,159
Heth's division	276	3,378	4,206	8,234	3,957
Pender's division	431	4,021	4,978	11,690	4,592
Total Third Army Corps	1,219	12,398	15,744	32,903	14,724
Cavalry (Stuart)a	634	8,404	10,210	19,354	....
Artillery (Pendleton):					
First Army Corps	90	1,760	2,025	2,886	1,996
Second Army Corps	94	1,440	1,733	2,675	1,704
Third Army Corps	84	1,680	1,989	2,764	1,832
Total artillery b	277	4,880	5,747	8,325	5,532
Grand total	5,003	53,663	68,104	136,317	53,611

a Aggregate present last field return not reported on original return. A note on above return states that some of the enlisted men reported present for duty are dismounted, but the number is not given.

b Guns not reported on original, but see statement following.

Artillery in the Army of Northern Virginia after Gettysburg.a

Battalions.	20-pounder Parrotts.	10-pounder Parrotts.	3-inch rifles.	Whitworths.	Napoleons.	24-pounder howitzers.	12-pounder howitzers.	Battery wagons.	Caissons.	Forges.	Rounds of ammunition, average per gun.	Serviceable horses.	Total.
FIRST CORPS.													
Colonel Cabell: b													
Has		4	4		3	1	3	1	15	2	118	213	....
Lost			1						1		..	..	
Major Henry: c													
Has		6	1		11		..	1	All.	4	156		
Lost			1				1						
Major Dearing has d.	2	3	1		12				All.	3	140	258	....
Colonel Alexander: e													
Has	2	1	7		6	4	2	1	All.	3	147		
Lost							2						
Major Eshleman: f													
Has			1		8		1	1	All.	2	138		
Lost					1		1						
The corps has	4	14	14		40	5	6	4	81	14			83
SECOND CORPS.													
Lieutenant-Colonel Andrews: g													
Has	2	5	3		6			1	11	2	124	223	....
Lost									1				
Lieutenant-Colonel Carter has. h		4	6		6				16	2	132	200	....
Lieutenant-Colonel Jones: i													
Has		2	6		8				All.	2	120	221	....
Lost					1								
Colonel Brown: j													
Has	4	4	10		2				19	1	100	282	....
Lost								1	1	4			
Lieutenant-Colonel Nelson: k													
Has		1	4		8				13	1	131	210	....
Lost										3			
The corps has.	6	16	29		30			1	78	8			81

a From a statement in General William N. Pendleton's handwriting, but undated. The artillery of Cavalry Corps not accounted for.

b Transportation good and sufficient; men enough in Manly's and Carlton's companies; not in McCarthy's and Fraser's. Lost 1 3-inch rifle, turned into ordnance train, and 1 caisson, disabled at Gettysburg.

c Horses for most part in good condition Transportation good and sufficient. Men enough in Reilly's and Latham's companies; greatly deficient in Bachman's and Garden's. Lost 1 6-pounder, said to be turned in, and 1 12-pounder howitzer, abandoned; 1 3-inch rifle burst. Took of captured 3 10-pounder Parrotts. Needs a number of men for Bachman and Garden and 26 horses.

d Men enough. Transportation good and sufficient.

e Transportation sufficient. Lost 1 12-pounder howitzer, injured and abandoned, and caisson; 1 12-pounder howitzer sent to rear. Needs men for Fickling's South Carolina battery and Parker's.

f Transportation reported indifferent. Lost 1 Napoleon and 1 12-pounder howitzer, disabled in action; 1 limber blown up, caissons.(?) Needs guns and horses to fill up battalion.

g Transportation sufficient. Two forges assigned to Colonel Carter. Lost 1 caisson, blown up at Gettysburg (other ?). Needs men for Brown's and Dement's Maryland companies and 32 horses.

h Transportation insufficient. Two forges borrowed from Lieutenant-Colonel Andrews. Lost forges and wagons by enemy on road. Needs men in case of emergency.

i Transportation in part sent to the rear. Lost 1 Napoleon, disabled, Gettysburg. (Where is it?) Captured. Needs men in Garber's and Green's companies and 14 horses.

j Horses—many lame, though serviceable. Transportation insufficient. Lost 1 caisson, blown up at Gettysburg, 4 forges, 1 battery wagon, and a number of wagons captured on road. Needs men in all companies excepting Hupp's, wagons and clothing.

k Transportation insufficient. Lost 3 forges and a number of wagons on road, captured. Needs forges and transportation; also clothing.

Artillery in the Army of Northern Virginia after Gettysburg—Continued.

Battalions.	20-pounder Parrotts.	10-pounder Parrotts.	3-inch rifles.	Whitworths.	Napoleons.	24-pounder howitzers.	12-pounder howitzers.	Battery wagons.	Caissons.	Forges.	Rounds of ammunition, average per gun.	Serviceable horses.	Total.
THIRD CORPS.													
Major McIntosh has *a*			7	2	6			1	14	4	100	206	....
Major Poague: *b*													
Has . . .		1	2		7		6		14	2	100	187	....
Lost . .									1				
Major Pegram: *c*													
Has		3	4		9		2	1	14	3	66	184	....
Lost		1			1				7				....
Lieutenant-Colonel Garnett: *d*													
Has		2	4		3		2	1	11	1	165	159	....
Lost									6	3			....
Lieutenant-Colonel Cutts: *e*													
Has	2	3	4		3		5		16	2		205	....
Lost									1	1			....
In all	2	9	21	2	28		15	3	69	10			77
Grand total *f*	12	39	64	2	98	5	21	8	228	32			241

a Transportation sufficient when rear wagons return. Two of the forges loaned in battalion. Lost 1 gun disabled and turned in and 1 rear part of caisson. Needs men in Lusk's and Hurt's companies.

b Transportation insufficient. Forges borrowed from other battalion. Lost 1 caisson on march to Falling Waters. Needs men for Wyatt's and Brooke's companies and 25 horses.

c Transportation sufficient. Lost 1 10-pounder Parrott, disabled in action and sent to rear; 1 Napoleon, disabled and captured on road with General Imboden; 1 caisson, turned in; 1 caisson and 8 horses captured; 1 caisson disabled and left on the field; 3 caissons blown up by the enemy, and 1 abandoned on march to Falling Waters. Needs detailed men to be returned to companies and some conscripts for each.

d Transportation insufficient. Lost 2 guns, captured near Falling Waters; 2 guns turned over by Major Richardson to Captain Hart to save them; 6 caissons and 3 forges captured under General Imboden; 70 horses and 40 sets of harness captured or abandoned, besides ordnance stores. Needs no men, but general refitting.

e Caissons full. Transportation sufficient. The forge captured under General Imboden. Three of the 3-inch guns are navy Parrotts.

f The grand total is not given on original statement.

Abstract from return of the Department of Richmond, Maj. Gen. Arnold Elzey, C. S. Army, commanding, for August 10, 1863.

Command.	Present for duty.		Effective total present.	Aggregate present.	Aggregate present and absent.	Pieces of field artillery.
	Officers.	Men.				
General headquarters	11			11	11	
Ransom's division *a*	369	5,920	6,202	6,989	9,784	40
Wise's command	141	2,276	2,423	2,869	3,750	8
Chaffin's Bluff	24	339	304	475	501	
Drewry's Bluff	18	263	380	432	467	
Richmond defenses	80	1,432	1,569	1,830	2,181	16
40th Virginia Cavalry Battalion	12	204	228	263	547	
Total	655	10,443	11,286	12,869	17,241	64

a Cooke's brigade transferred to the Army of Northern Virginia.

Abstract from return of the Department of North Carolina, Maj. Gen. W. H. C. Whiting, C. S. Army, commanding, for August 10, 1863.

Command.	Present for duty.		Effective total.	Aggregate present.	Aggregate present and absent.	Pieces of artillery.
	Officers.	Men.				
General headquarters	9	3	3	12	14	.....
District of the Cape Fear	252	3,857	4,406	5,163	6,206	119
District of North Carolina	216	3,919	4,197	4,764	6,104	33
Total	477	7,779	8,606	9,939	12,324	152

RICHMOND, VA.,
August 11, 1863.

General R. E. LEE,
Commanding Army of Northern Virginia:

Yours of 8th instant has been received. I am glad that you concur so entirely with me as to the want of our country in this trying hour, and am happy to add that after the first depression consequent upon our disaster in the west, indications have appeared that our people will exhibit that fortitude which we agree in believing is alone needful to secure ultimate success.

It well became Sidney Johnston, when overwhelmed by a senseless clamor, to admit the rule that success is the test of merit;* and yet there has been nothing which I have found to require a greater effort of patience than to bear the criticisms of the ignorant, who pronounce everything a failure which does not equal their expectations or desires, and can see no good result which is not in the line of their own imaginings. I admit the propriety of your conclusions, that an officer who loses the confidence of his troops should have his position changed, whatever may be his ability, but when I read the sentence I was not at all prepared for the application you were about to make. Expressions of discontent in the public journals furnish but little evidence of the sentiment of an army. I wish it were otherwise, even though all the abuse of myself should be accepted as the results of honest observation. I say I wish I could feel that the public journals were not generally partisan nor venal.

Were you capable of stooping to it, you could easily surround yourself with those who would fill the press with your laudations, and seek to exalt you for what you had not done, rather than detract from the achievements which will make you and your army the subject of history and object of the world's admiration for generations to come.

I am truly sorry to know that you still feel the effects of the illness you suffered last spring, and can readily understand the embarrassments you experience in using the eyes of others, having been so much accustomed to make your own reconnaissances. Practice will, however, do much to relieve that embarrassment, and the minute knowledge of the country which you have acquired will render you less dependent for topographical information.

---

* See Series I, Vol. VII, p. 261.

But suppose, my dear friend, that I were to admit, with all their implications, the points which you present, where am I to find that new commander who is to possess the greater ability which you believe to be required? I do not doubt the readiness with which you would give way to one who could accomplish all that you have wished, and you will do me the justice to believe that if Providence should kindly offer such a person for our use, I would not hesitate to avail of his services.

My sight is not sufficiently penetrating to discover such hidden merit, if it exists, and I have but used to you the language of sober earnestness when I have impressed upon you the propriety of avoiding all unnecessary exposure to danger, because I felt our country could not bear to lose you. To ask me to substitute you by some one in my judgment more fit to command, or who would possess more of the confidence of the army, or of the reflecting men of the country, is to demand an impossibility.

It only remains for me to hope that you will take all possible care of yourself, that your health and strength may be entirely restored, and that the Lord will preserve you for the important duties devolved upon you in the struggle of our suffering country for the independence which we have engaged in war to maintain.

As ever, very respectfully and truly, yours,
                                    JEFFERSON DAVIS.

HEADQUARTERS DEPARTMENT OF WESTERN VIRGINIA,
        Camp near Red Sulphur Springs, August 11, 1863.

General R. E. LEE,
        Orange Court-House, Va.:

Your telegram of yesterday received. One regiment of infantry has just started from here, and another will start from Lewisburg to move via Huntersville, for the purpose you mention. Where is General Imboden? Has he any idea of the strength of Kelley's force? Reply by telegraph via Dublin. It will reach me at Union or Lewisburg.

                                    SAM. JONES,
                                        Major-General.

HEADQUARTERS DEPARTMENT OF WESTERN VIRGINIA,
        Dublin, August 11, 1863.

Maj. Gen. SAMUEL JONES:

The following telegram just received from General Lee:

                    ORANGE COURT-HOUSE,
                            August 11, 1863.

Maj. Gen. SAMUEL JONES:

I am not certain General Imboden is correct in his supposition. Telegraph to him at Staunton to keep you advised. He represents Kelley's strength—infantry, artillery, and cavalry—at 4,000. If you two could unite upon him, you could demolish him.

                                    R. E. LEE.

I have telegraphed Imboden as suggested.
                        CHAS. S. STRINGFELLOW.

HEADQUARTERS RICHMOND DEFENSES,
August 11, 1863.

Maj. T. O. CHESTNEY,
 Assistant Adjutant-General:

SIR: I desire to make the following statements and suggestions for the consideration of the general commanding:

About a week ago I mentioned to him that the batteries of the inner line were by no means in the condition I should like to have them, and urged upon him the necessity of making an effort to obtain negro labor. He expressed some surprise, but he will see that there really was no room for it. During the absence of the commander at Gordonsville, some representations were made as to the unpreparedness of these works, which I think were not justified by the facts. I said then and I say now that the works were in fighting condition, with the exception of one, whose ammunition was near at hand, if the officer sent there had only known it, and then, as now, every gun which was mounted could have been fought.

However, so great a stir was made that I determined to overhaul all the works, and received orders from you so to do. The work was commenced at once, and has been steadily going on. From twelve to fifteen barbettes for light guns have been designated for each battery, and many of them are completed; but in making these changes it was found that in most of the work, portions of the plank revetment was rotting, so that the work to be done was quite extensive, and after two months' labor I find that much remains unfinished.

Moreover, upon consultation with Col. W. H. Stevens, Engineers, it was concluded that the gorges of all these batteries should be closed with rifle-pits, and that a military road should be made conveniently connecting the parts of the whole line. This involves a good deal of labor, and can only be accomplished by the employment of negroes. This I respectfully urge upon the general commanding. Last winter Colonel Stevens employed constantly some 3,000 or 4,000 negroes, but not an hour's work was done on these batteries by them. Indeed, they were sent back to their masters before the intermediate line was completed, and at present all the labor Colonel Stevens can possibly get is very properly at once put on that line as the most important.

At Nos. 1, 2, 3, 4, 8, 9, and 10, the work is in good progress, and No. 5 will in a week show a great improvement, but Nos. 6 and 7 are very backward, due especially to the fact that they are large works, and the companies which occupy them are weak. At present these companies are absent, and I would take occasion respectfully to ask that they be returned to their post as soon as possible.

General Hood's division I learn has been moved to Fredericksburg, thus I presume relieving Cooke's brigade, which in its turn I trust may relieve the Eighteenth and Twentieth Battalions, now at the bridges on the South Anna.

 Very respectfully, your obedient servant,
       T. S. RHETT,
   Colonel, Commanding Richmond Defenses.

GENERAL ORDERS, } ADJT. AND INSP. GENERAL'S OFFICE,
 No. 109.   }   *Richmond, August 11, 1863.*

I. A general pardon is given to all officers and men within the Confederacy, now absent without leave from the army, who shall, within twenty days from the publication of the address of the President in the State in which the absentees may then· be, return to their posts of duty.

II. All men who have been accused or convicted, and undergoing sentence for absence without leave or desertion, excepting only those who have been twice convicted of desertion, will be returned to their respective commands for duty.

By order:

S. COOPER,
Adjutant and Inspector General.

SPECIAL ORDERS, }   ADJT. AND INSP. GENERAL'S OFFICE,
   No. 190.   }   *Richmond, Va., August 11,* 1863.
    *   *   *   *   *   *   *

XV. Lieut. Col. James W. Watts, Second Virginia Cavalry, is assigned to duty as commandant of the post at Liberty, Va., and will report accordingly.

    *   *   *   *   *   *   *

XVII. Brig. Gen. Francis T. Nicholls, Provisional Army, C. S., will relieve Lieut. Col. M. S. Langhorne as commandant of the post at Lynchburg, Va., and its environs.

    *   *   *   *   *   *

By command of the Secretary of War:

JNO. WITHERS,
Assistant Adjutant-General.

UNION, MONROE COUNTY, *August* 12, 1863.

General R. E. LEE,
    Commanding, &c., Orange Court-House:

GENERAL: I received yesterday, in camp near Red Sulphur Springs, your telegram of the day before, and immediately started a regiment of infantry to Lewisburg, and telegraphed you that I would send it and another from Lewisburg, by Huntersville, to aid or make diversion in General Imboden's favor, as you desired.

I supposed at the time that General Imboden had with him the troops you mentioned when you last wrote me, but this morning I hear, unofficially, that the troops I sent to the valley under Colonel Wharton are now with you, and I have not heard if their places are supplied in the valley.

If I am to give aid, it is very desirable that I should know what force I am aiding; but your telegram gives me no information on the subject. The telegraph line is down at some point between here and Dublin, cutting me off from communication with Imboden by that means.

Will you please inform me, as soon as you can, what forces there are in the valley, and where they are? I will communicate with Imboden as soon as practicable.

With great respect, your obedient servant,

. SAM. JONES,
Major-General.

P. S.,—I have just received information that about 500 of the enemy are engaged removing obstructions from one of the roads

(Coal Knob) leading to Lewisburg, indicating a move on that place. It is probably a demonstration to prevent me from detaching any of my troops to interfere with General Kelley.

I am on my way to Lewisburg now.

HDQRS. ARTILLERY, ARMY OF NORTHERN VIRGINIA,
August 13, 1863.

General R. E. LEE,
Commanding Army of Northern Virginia:

GENERAL: On day before yesterday, when visiting the artillery battalion of the Second Corps, near Liberty Mills, I met with an intelligent citizen of Albemarle County, a near connection of Mr. William C. Rives, who stated some facts respecting horses which it seems to me to be proper to submit to yourself:

First, he related several instances that had fallen under his own immediate observation, of worn and reduced army horses injuriously neglected through the carelessness or incompetency of the agents or officials having them in charge. One case he particularly dwelt upon in which 50 feeble horses were temporarily pastured on his farm, and in a few days 10 of the number perished. Had the same number of horses belonged to a careful and sensible farmer, he believed that not one would have died. The difficulty was want of salt and proper care of, and supplying each animal with the food, water, &c., needed, within reach.

Another case he described was where diseased horses were permitted freely to circulate among a large collection, with the certainty of spreading contagion, suffering, and loss. He declined mentioning the names of parties, believing the evils rather attributable to the system pursued with our decrepid horses than to the special culpableness of particular individuals.

Some plan which should bring into requisition the strong and ceaseless motive of interest toward restoring these horses seems at once suggested by these facts.

Instead of waiting to collect large numbers of broken-down horses at certain points, turning them over to certain officers who have inadequate means of watering, feeding, &c., and who depend on employés without special knowledge of or interest on the subject—a plan under which so many horses die—might not farmers in suitable districts, not too far off, be induced to take such horses in small numbers as they fail, use them as they become strong, and return them or keep them, as the case may be, for suitable payments at the proper time.

This gentleman assured me that not less than 300 good artillery horses might be very soon gotten in Albemarle County alone without any serious detriment to the farming interests, if the right course was pursued. Such course he believed would not be the sending out of quartermasters, or their agents, unacquainted with the people or country, and with no deep interest in the great object, but the employment of an esteemed, judicious, and reliable citizen, with authority to secure the right kind of horses, either by paying suitable prices or exchanging worn and feeble horses for fresh ones, with proper boot. The prices would range near $600, he thought, and if parties would not sell, impressment as granted by law might be used. The name of a suitable citizen was mentioned, but one has occurred to myself, Mr. Littleton Macon, now sheriff of Albemarle. He served in my battery the first year of the war, and is as true a man as lives, full of energy, zeal for our cause, and of good qualities that commend him to general confidence.

If this plan cannot be tried, I would beg that something be attempted in another way, viz, that the artillery officers themselves be authorized to exercise their energies toward finding and securing good horses. Bonded officers alone need have or dispense the funds, but, unless those who have the deepest interest in having good horses are allowed to act in the matter, the evil of poor horses may be expected to continue without at all disparaging the quartermaster's department; and satisfied that many of the officers in that department are very faithful, I am also satisfied that they must be superior to human nature in general if they can do as well for the artillery in this respect as the artillery officers themselves. They do not know the need as well. They do not begin to feel the same interest in success. They are not actuated by the motives that command success in the case. If under existing regulations nothing of this kind can be done, I respectfully suggest that in a question of so much importance suitable provisions be asked of the Department in Richmond.

I have the honor to be, general, respectfully, your obedient servant,

W. N. PENDLETON,
Brigadier-General, &c.

CAMP NEAR LEWISBURG, VA.,
August 13, 1863.

Hon. JAMES A. SEDDON,
Secretary of War:

SIR: I have reason to believe that some persons, citizens, within the limits of the Department of Western Virginia, are endeavoring to have me removed from the command of the department, and Brigadier-General Echols, or some other general officer, assigned to the command. To effect this object, I am informed that a petition has been circulated for signature, addressed to you or the President, asking that I be removed. What reason they may assign why this should be done, I cannot imagine unless it be that I have undertaken no expedition of any magnitude against the enemy.

This military department has had the reputation of being cursed with intrigue and political plotters ever since the war commenced. No commander, not even General Lee, has, I believe, given satisfaction while in command here, and I doubt exceedingly if any gentleman who looks to the interests of the Confederacy generally, can command here and give satisfaction to all. I was not ignorant of the condition of the department in that respect when I was assigned to the command, and it is known to you, I believe, that I was very far from desiring the command.

I was ordered, however, to command the department, and have administered the trust confided to me with a view single to what I regarded as the interest of the country. I am sure that if either you or the President had disapproved of my course, I should have been informed of it, and I am quite as sure that neither of you will act upon representations prejudicial to me, made by interested parties, without giving me an opportunity of explaining anything that may be represented as objectionable in my course.

I believe I know something of the interests and requirements of the department, and the various conflicting and disturbing elements in it, and I respectfully suggest that if it is in contemplation to relieve me from the command of it, the interest of the service may be promoted by deferring the selection of my successor until I have communicated further with you on the subject. I am now on a tour of inspection, will go on to Pocahontas County day after to-morrow, and when I have completed the inspection, I will, if I can with propriety do so, go to Richmond and have a personal interview with you, if you can give it me.

With great respect, sir, your obedient servant,

SAM. JONES,
Major-General, Comdg. Dept. of Western Virginia.

[Indorsement.]

AUGUST 18, 1863.

Read. Lay aside for future answer on his return from his trip of inspection.

J. A. S. [SEDDON],
Secretary.

RICHMOND,
August 13, 1863.

Maj. Gen. WILLIAM SMITH:

GENERAL: In forwarding the inclosed commission as major-general, Provisional Army, C. S., the Secretary of War directs me to say that you will be assigned at once to the special duty of visiting the people of Virginia and the adjacent States.

It is desired that you will on this mission employ every effort to reanimate our people, inspire them with hope and renewed zeal for the cause, and especially induce those liable to service to come forward to their places promptly, and without awaiting the regular process of conscription.

In many parts of the country are to be found large numbers of men absent beyond, or without leave. Many of these are thus absent without criminal intent, and by the mere inadvertence of not appreciating the importance of one individual to the service. It is believed that a stirring appeal to them, but especially to the influence of patriotic women of the country, will be sufficient to cause the return of these laggards to the ranks.

In some localities, however, the stragglers and deserters have manifested a disposition to resist the efforts toward their return to duty. In such cases it will devolve upon you to devise means for enforcing their obedience, and to this end you are authorized to employ and direct the services of any local companies already existing, or which may be formed, and invoke and encourage the co-operation of the militia officers and local authorities.

In view of impending raids by the enemy, it is important that in every neighborhood companies be formed for local defense and special service, under the act approved August 21, 1861, of non-conscripts to be mustered into Confederate service, armed and equipped. It is desirable that such companies should, in the terms prescribed in their muster-rolls, hold themselves ready for service anywhere in the State. But while such limits are preferred, it is not probable that in any instance a company of this kind would be called upon to go beyond its own locality; and companies for more restricted service will be accepted.

It is expected that an earnest presentation of the subject to the people will induce them to perfect such organizations promptly.

By personal conference with the leading men of each section, and your well-directed appeal to the masses, we may confidently expect that you will succeed in diffusing a new spirit, and imparting to our cause a more certain, rapid, and enduring progress.

I am, general, very respectfully, your obedient servant,

S. COOPER,
Adjutant and Inspector General.

ENGINEER BUREAU, ·
August 13, 1863.

Col. W. H. STEVENS,
Corps of Engineers:

COLONEL: The honorable Secretary of War has considered your letter of the 7th instant, representing that labor is imperatively needed at this time for the construction of fortifications in Virginia, and has indorsed as follows:

This is as favorable a season as can be found for the withdrawal, temporarily, of agricultural labor. Calls may be made for slave labor till the 5th of October, and from the grain-growing districts especially.

J. A. S. [SEDDON,]
· *Secretary.*

In conversation with me the Secretary expressed the opinion that labor could be better spared from the grain-growing districts than from the tobacco fields at this time. On this point it will be difficult to discriminate, but you will please to arrange your call, or rather the date of the call, as equitably as possible, regard being had in all cases to the number of slaves in each county, the extent of former service, and burdens resulting from depredations of the enemy. You will please to prepare your call without delay, and forward it to this Bureau, when the President will be requested to make application to the Governor of Virginia for the force you may name.

Very respectfully,

J. F. GILMER,
Colonel of Engineers, and Chief of Bureau.

HEADQUARTERS DEPARTMENT OF WESTERN VIRGINIA,
Lewisburg, Va., August 14, 1863.

General R. E. LEE:

I have heard nothing from Imboden of the movements of the enemy, nor do I know anything of the strength of his force. I will not move my two regiments until I hear further from him or you.

· Col. W. L. Jackson reports all quiet in his front, and no indication of a movement by the enemy.

SAM. JONES,
Major-General.

HEADQUARTERS DEPARTMENT OF WESTERN VIRGINIA,
Lewisburg, via Union, August 14, 1863.

Brigadier-General IMBODEN:

I expect to be at Huntersville day after to-morrow, and will remain there two or three days. I Would like very much to meet you somewhere, but as I do not know where you are, I cannot designate place of meeting. Communicate with me if you can before I leave Huntersville.

SAM. JONES,
Major-General.

HEADQUARTERS ARMY OF NORTHERN VIRGINIA,
Orange Court-House, August 15, 1863.

General S. COOPER:
Adjutant and Inspector General, Richmond, Va.:

GENERAL: Lists of absentees without leave from this army, arranged separately, according to the county or congressional district in which the men are supposed to be, have been called for, and are being forwarded to the Bureau of Conscription, with the request that the commandants of conscripts in the several States be instructed to cause efforts to be made to arrest these men, and return them to their commands.* I deem it expedient to make every exertion to increase the effective strength of this army, and respectfully request that the Department will call the attention of the Superintendent of the Bureau of Conscription to the importance of the earnest co-operation of the enrolling officers in causing to return to duty the number of soldiers wandering at large through the country, who should be with their commands in the field.

I am, most respectfully, your obedient servant,

R. E. LEE,
General.

HEADQUARTERS ARMY OF NORTHERN VIRGINIA,
August 15, 1863.

General S. COOPER,
Adjutant and Inspector General, Richmond:

GENERAL: I am satisfied, from the habits of our soldiers, that the stragglers, the disaffected, and the sick who wander away from the army leave a great many arms and accouterments along the different lines of travel in the country. I would, therefore, respectfully suggest that the enrolling officers be instructed to cause vigorous search to be made in their respective districts to collect these arms, and forward them to the Ordnance Department at Richmond. From what I can learn, I think a considerable number of arms may be obtained in this way.

I am, with great respect, your obedient servant,

R. E. LEE,
General.

---

* See Preston to Cooper, August 20.

HEADQUARTERS ARMY OF NORTHERN VIRGINIA,
August 15, 1863.

Maj. Gen. J. E. B. STUART,
    Commanding Cavalry Division:

GENERAL: In reply to your different communications on the subject of the deficiency of good arms in the cavalry, I have to say that I have sent Colonel Baldwin to Richmond to see what can be done there. I have also issued an order that the infantry arms be thoroughly inspected, so as to obtain all the arms from among them which are better adapted for the cavalry service. There are many difficulties, however, in the way of arming the cavalry thoroughly, and keeping it in that condition. Few cavalry arms are imported, and those manufactured in the Confederacy are generally rejected. I fear there is great carelessness, too, in the preservation of arms in the whole army. Company and regimental officers do not hold their men to sufficient responsibility. Men who leave the camp on furlough should be compelled to turn in their arms and accouterments to the ordnance sergeant or brigade ordnance officer. Where infantry arms have been issued to the cavalry, it is stated that they have either been turned in or thrown away in nine cases out of ten. Before the army went into Maryland, 2,000 Austrian rifles were sent to Culpeper Court-House. Of these, very few were issued to the men, and after the fight at Brandy Station, nearly all that had been issued were returned or thrown away. Recently 600 Enfield rifles and Mississippi rifles were sent to Culpeper for the cavalry division. The brigade ordnance officer declined to receive them, saying the men would not take them.

From the nature of the cavalry service, it is almost impossible for the ordnance officers to enforce the rules of the Department. Regimental and company commanders should be held to rigid account, and be required to make frequent returns. Where an arm or accouterment is missing and not properly accounted for, the soldier should not only be charged with it, but military punishment should be inflicted.

Colonel Baldwin has ordered blank forms for cavalry armament returns to be prepared, which will be issued to every company commander in the division. To-day he reports having forwarded 220 Enfield rifles, and between 400 and 500 Sharp's carbines, with some accouterments, ammunition, &c.; this on yesterday.

I think your dismounted men should be speedily organized, and thoroughly drilled as infantry, and armed to be used as infantry, until they can be mounted.

Your letter of August 14, with inclosed dispatches, was received. I thank you for the information of the enemy's position which it contains.

Respectfully, &c.,

R. E. LEE,
General.

HEADQUARTERS ARMY OF NORTHERN VIRGINIA,
August 15, 1863.

Col. J. GORGAS,
    Chief of Ordnance, C. S. Army:

COLONEL: I send Lieutenant-Colonel Baldwin down this morning to consult with you on the subject of arms for this army. We are in especial need of good arms for the cavalry division, and, as you will see from his report, there is a considerable deficiency of arms in the infantry, which deficiency will become greater as the number of returning convalescents increases. I have heard from several sources that there are arms in Charleston, S. C., held in reserve for troops, which are still to be reserved. If this is so, I think that they should be distributed to troops in the field. In fact, I should think, in the present condition of things, that no ordnance, arms, or other supplies should be kept in Charleston, excepting such as are necessary for the troops engaged in its defense. I hope you will be able to make some arrangements by which the deficiencies in this army may be speedily supplied.

I am, very respectfully, your obedient servant,

R. E. LEE,
General.

RICHMOND, *August* 15, 1863.

Brig. Gen. M. JENKINS, *Petersburg, Va.:*

The militia referred to by you are neither Confederate nor State troops, but are simply militia in the service of the Confederacy for the period of thirty days.

You are authorized to permit the militia called out at Petersburg to remain at their homes, instead of going into camp, upon condition of drilling once or twice a day, and being within call at a moment's notice.

S. COOPER,
Adjutant and Inspector General.

SIGNAL OFFICE,
Richmond, August 15, 1863.

Hon. JAMES A. SEDDON, *Secretary of War:*

SIR: I have the honor to report the following items received to-day by a scout who left Washington August 8:

Ten thousand men (New York troops) have recently been discharged from Meade's army, their time having expired. A large force, stated by some to be at least 30,000 men, has also recently been withdrawn from the same army and sent to Charleston. To pay off this latter force, six paymasters have been sent down, which item our informant in Washington furnishes as a fact by which the strength of the force may be estimated.

Very respectfully,

WM. NORRIS,
Major, and Chief of Signal Corps.

HEADQUARTERS ARMY OF NORTHERN VIRGINIA,
August 17, 1863.

His Excellency JEFFERSON DAVIS,
President of the Confederate States:

Mr. PRESIDENT: The number of desertions from this army is so great, and still continues to such an extent, that unless some cessation of them can be caused, I fear success in the field will be endangered. Immediately on the publication of the amnesty, which I thought would be beneficial in its effects, many presumed on it, and absented themselves from their commands, choosing to place on it a wrong interpretation. In one corps, the desertions of North Carolinians, and, to some extent, of Virginians, has grown to be a very serious matter. The Virginians go off in many cases to join the various partisan corps in the State. General Imboden writes that there are great numbers of deserters in the valley, who conceal themselves successfully from the small squads sent to arrest them. Many cross the James River near Balcony Falls, *en route* for .the south, along the mountain ridges. Night before last, 30 went from one regiment and 18 from another. Great dissatisfaction is reported among the good men of the army at the apparent impunity of deserters.

In order to remove all palliation from the offense of desertion, and as a reward to merit, I have instituted in the army a system of furloughs, which are to be granted, in the most meritorious and urgent cases, at the rate of one for every 100 men present for duty.

I would now respectfully submit to your excellency the opinion that all has been done which forbearance and mercy call for, and that nothing will remedy this great evil which so much endangers our cause excepting the rigid enforcement of the death penalty in future in cases of conviction.

I have the honor to be, with great respect, Your Excellency's obedient servant,

R. E. LEE,
General.

HEADQUARTERS ARMY OF NORTHERN VIRGINIA,
August 17, 1863.

Brig. Gen. J. D. IMBODEN,
Commanding Valley District:

GENERAL: Your letter of the 14th instant has been received.

So long as you are undetermined as to the movements of the enemy, the position you have taken may be well, but I desire you to dispose your troops to cover the valley, and to repress any expedition above Winchester, if possible. The best way of effecting this is to keep the enemy constantly apprehensive for the safety of the Baltimore and Ohio Railroad, and to strike at it whenever you can. He will then be obliged to distribute himself, and cannot mass his troops for attack. This will require your cavalry to be active, which can serve at the same time to collect cattle, &c., from the exposed districts, for your own support and for the rest of the army.

I desire you to keep yourself informed of the position of Col. William L. Jackson, and the infantry about Lewisburg and Huntersville of Gen. Samuel Jones' command, that you may inform them of any movements affecting the country in which they operate. Co-operate with them if advantageous, which they could reciprocate under similar circumstances. I am glad to hear that the prospect of raising local troops in Rockingham and Augusta is so favorable. This will enable you, by leaving guards of your feeble men at certain points, to be strengthened by the local troops, to use the mass of your force in offensive operations.

It will be necessary to keep bold scouts constantly in front of the enemy to apprise you of his movements and positions, so that you may regulate yours. All the iron, cloth. leather, subsistence, &c., should be collected in the valley and in Northwest Virginia that is possible, and I hope you will give unremitting attention to this subject and all the aid you can afford. It is very important, too, that you should collect, and send back to the army all stragglers and deserters, and summary means must be resorted to for this purpose, if necessary. You will, therefore, try to ascertain their lurking places, send parties for their capture, and disperse them. There is much desertion, I regret to say, from this army, principally from the North Carolina troops, but it also occurs among others, and, I am pained to add, among the Virginians. The punishment you recommend has been resorted to, but I begin to fear nothing but the death penalty, uniformly, inexorably administered, will stop it.

I am, very respectfully, your obedient servant,

R. E. LEE,
General.

HEADQUARTERS DEPARTMENT OF NORTH CAROLINA,
Wilmington, N. C., August 17, 1863.

Hon. JAMES A. SEDDON,
Secretary of War, Richmond:

SIR: The time has come in which I am obliged to have for the public service at this place a steamer in the river. Heretofore I relied upon the Lizzie or Mariner coming back, which boat, you will remember, I strongly urged should be taken. But she has been captured by the enemy. In the meantime, the business of the Government and the importance of this place has increased in a most extraordinary degree. Independent of the government work on blockading steamers, of the defense of the city, the quartermaster's department, the commissary department, for transportation, I have just received notice that the private blockaders heretofore running to Mobile from Havana are to be consigned here, and that the business of the Government is to be very largely increased by the charter of many steamers. Already I have not the means of proper communication between the city and the forts, from 21 to 26 miles distant, for the military service simply. I have but two small and defective river steamers. The navy is in a worse plight. I have constant and necessary demands for transportation of guns, ammunition, coal, provisions, and all that belongs to an important *entrepôt* like this, as well as a place largely and extensively fortified.

To-day, for instance, I am called upon to lighten the steamer Advance, belonging to the State of North Carolina, aground on the rips. More important still, the steamer Gibraltar (formerly the Sumter), having on board two 700-pounder Blakely guns, besides arms and ammunition, is still outside the bar, but under the guns of Fort Fisher, and so far safe. She requires to be lightened to come in. I have put troops, &c., on board of her. The necessity of additional steam transportation is evident.

There are now twelve steamers in this port. I recommend that we purchase at once. If that is not practicable, impress the steamer Flora, a small double propeller just arrived. She grounded on the rips, but by the assistance of the garrison of Fort Fisher, and the loss of entire cargo, thrown overboard, has been saved and brought in. She is just what I want, and I understand she is owned in the

Confederate States. Nothing, but the most imperious necessity would induce me to recommend this course, but I think we must have a good steamer here, that it is essential, and that you will entirely agree with me.

I beg leave to present this matter for your immediate and prompt consideration.

Very respectfully,

W. H. C. WHITING,
Major-General.

HEADQUARTERS,
Orange, August 18, 1863.

General STUART,
Commanding, &c.:

GENERAL: The report of Major Mosby, of 4th instant, relative to his expeditions toward Fairfax Court-House and below, has been forwarded to the War Department. I greatly commend his boldness and good management, which is the cause of his success. I have heard that he has now with him a large number of men, yet his expeditions are undertaken with very few, and his attention seems more directed to the capture of sutlers' wagons, &c., than to the injury of the enemy's communications and outposts. The capture and destruction of wagon trains is advantageous, but the supply of the Federal Army is carried on by the railroad. If that should be injured, it would cause him to detach largely for its security, and thus weaken his main army. His threat of punishing citizens on the line for such attacks must be met by meting similar treatment to his soldiers when captured.

I do not know the cause for undertaking his expeditions with so few men, whether it is from policy or the difficulty of collecting them. I have heard of his men, among them officers, being in rear of this army selling captured goods, sutlers' stores, &c. This had better be attended to by others. It has also been reported to me that many deserters from this army have joined him. Among them have been seen members of the Eighth Virginia Regiment. If this is true, I am sure it must be without the knowledge of Major Mosby; but I desire you to call his attention to this matter, to prevent his being imposed on.

I am, very respectfully, your obedient servant,

R. E. LEE,
General.

HEADQUARTERS ARMY OF NORTHERN VIRGINIA,
August 18, 1863.

Maj. Gen. SAMUEL JONES,
Commanding Southwestern Department:

GENERAL: Your letter of August 12 has been received.

I thank you for your prompt arrangements to lend aid to Imboden in the valley. He has only his own infantry and cavalry operating with him. Colonel Wharton is near here with his brigade. General Imboden has taken position at Bridgewater, in order to protect the upper valley, and cover the gaps from Brock's Gap to the pass via McDowell. My proposition to you was to threaten the enemy's flank, in making any movement through these passes, by a demonstration toward Huntersville, especially any approach via Monterey.   I hope you will be successful in beating back any attempt he may make on your lines in the direction of Lewisburg.

I am, very respectfully, your obedient servant,

R. E. LEE,
General.

———

WAR DEPARTMENT, C. S.,
Richmond, Va., August 18, 1863.

Capt. W. B. MALLORY,
Commanding Post, Charlottesville, Va.:

SIR: In the Examiner of to-day it is stated that—

At a sale of Yankee plunder taken by Mosby and his men, held at Charlottesville last week, thirty odd thousand dollars were realized to be divided among the gallant band.

You are requested to inquire whether such sale was made, and to report the facts to the Department.

Respectfully,

J. A. SEDDON,
Secretary of War.

———

HEADQUARTERS CAVALRY DIVISION,
August 19, 1863.

Hon. JAMES A. SEDDON,
Secretary of War:

SIR: In a conversation with Major Mosby, the partisan leader, I suggested to him the use of Rains' percussion torpedoes on the Orange and Alexandria Railroad.   He cordially approved of the suggestion, and requested me to write to you for a supply of the explosives in question.   If, therefore, you concur with us in thinking that much damage may be done to the enemy by means of these bombs placed beneath the rails of that particular road, which is used exclusively for the transportation of troops and army supplies, you will confer a favor upon Major Mosby by ordering him to be supplied with them immediately.

While writing, I take occasion to ask another favor of the Department, which is, to revoke the commission to raise a company, which, on my application, was granted some three months ago to Edward P. Castleman, of Clarke County.   I do this also at Mosby's request, as I find from him that Castleman's conduct is not what I thought it would be when I recommended him to you for a command.   He has not succeeded in raising a company, has only some 20 men under him, has failed to report to Mosby as he promised to do, and in the exercise of his own independent will has been committing depredations and taking horses from our own citizens.   If Castleman's commission, as I resume it is a contingent one, be revoked, those with him can be added to our own army as conscripts.

No news here.   All quiet along the lines in front.

I have the honor to be, most respectfully, your obedient servant,

A. R. BOTELER.

P. S.—General Stuart suggests that some one acquainted with the use of the torpedoes be sent up with them, as they are dangerous things in unskillful hands,

[Endorsements.]

AUGUST 26, 1863.
ADJUTANT-GENERAL:
If Castleman has not mustered and sent in rolls of a company,
revoke his authority.

J. A. S.   [SEDDON,]
Secretary.

[P. S.]—Then Ordnance Bureau, for consideration and report.

AUGUST 31, 1863.
No rolls of Castleman's company on file in this office. The authority should be revoked in orders.

E. A. PALFREY,
Lieutenant-Colonel, and Assistant Adjutant-General.

ADJUTANT AND INSPECTOR GENERAL'S OFFICE,
September 2, 1863.
Respectfully referred to Chief of Ordnance.
By command of Secretary of War:

H. L. CLAY,
Assistant Adjutant-General.

SEPTEMBER 3, 1863.
Unless these torpedoes can be continually replaced as exploded, I
doubt the policy of using them at all. To use them once only is to
irritate, not intimidate. If, therefore, we have no sufficient command
of the vicinity to continue the use of these impediments, it seems to
me impolitic to begin their use. They can be furnished here whenever called for.

J. GORGAS.

SEPTEMBER 3, 1863.
ORDNANCE BUREAU:
Have you an officer or employé you can send to use them?

J. A. S.   [SEDDON],
Secretary.

A man can be sent.

J. GORGAS.

SEPTEMBER 9, 1863.
ADJUTANT-GENERAL:
Revoke Castleman's authority.

J. A. S.   [SEDDON],
Secretary.

———

BUREAU OF CONSCRIPTION,
Richmond, August 20, 1863.
General S. COOPER,
Adjutant and Inspector General:
GENERAL: I respectfully return the inclosed letter from General
R. E. Lee,* and use the occasion to urge that all officers who may

———
* Of August 15,

be sent out by the general commanding be ordered to report to the commandants of conscripts in the respective States, and furnish them with the list of absentees, and to co-operate generally with enrolling officers in the discharge of the duties to which they are assigned. Instructions have been issued to all officers under the control of this bureau to increase their vigilance and energy in carrying out the purposes indicated by General Lee. The list of absentees furnished to this bureau are in progress of distribution, and every possible agency will be employed to arrest and send back the absentees.

I regard it as important to success that the officers sent from the army should by order be required to report to the commandants. I venture to suggest that it might facilitate the execution of this matter if all officers commanding were specially required forthwith and regularly to send to this bureau a roll of the absentees arranged according to the county and congressional district in which they are supposed to be. Also a roll of substitutes, giving the name and post-office of the principal.

Very respectfully, your obedient servant,
JOHN S. PRESTON,
Colonel, and Superintendent.

OFFICE INSP. GEN. OF FIELD TRANSPORTATION,
Richmond, August 20, 1863.

General LAWTON,
Quartermaster-General:

SIR: In obedience to the Secretary of War's indorsement concerning the discrepancy between the indorsement of General Elzey and that of my own on the application of the Commissary Department for wagons and teams to haul wheat into Richmond, I have the honor to make the following report:

Captain Tucker, assistant quartermaster at Danville, the only officer there charged with transportation, has under his charge 32 four-horse wagons and teams; 8 two-horse wagons and teams; 19 serviceable and 15 unserviceable animals not used in the teams habitually, and 37 surplus serviceable and unserviceable wagons, without teams.

This transportation is in daily use, as follows: Nine four-horse wagons and teams hauling iron, &c., for Ordnance Department, at Leaksville; 11 four-horse wagons and teams hauling and accumulating wood for the hospitals at post; 7 four-horse wagons and teams and 1 two-horse wagon and team hauling forage for the Government and support of teams; 5 four-horse and 1 two-horse wagons and teams hauling lumber from mills for hospitals building in neighborhood; 4 two-horse wagons and teams employed at the different hospitals; 1 two-horse wagon and team employed by the Commissary Department; 1 two-horse wagon and team employed at stables at the posts.

The 19 serviceable animals are used, about 10 for saddle purposes by wagon-masters, forage agents, &c., and 9 kept as relay animals to supply the places in the teams of such as become, from any cause, unserviceable. The 15 unserviceable animals are at pasture recruiting. I have endeavored in this report to show explicitly the number and description of wagons and teams available at Danville, and how they are daily employed, and from which, I think, the honorable Secretary cannot fail to conclude that the correctness of my indorse-

ment is fully sustained. In that indorsement I stated that "the number of wagons and teams at Danville, being only about half the
number named by General Elzey," meaning only four-horse wagons
and teams, such only being suitable for hauling grain over long
lines.

General Elzey's indorsement says, "There are 70 wagons at Danville,
30 of which ought to be used for transportation purposes elsewhere."
The general was mainly correct as to the number of wagons, but evidently he either lost sight of or was uninformed as to the number of
animals at Danville, wherein the discrepancy alone arises between
his indorsement and mine.

I have the honor to be, very respectfully, your obedient servant,

A. H. COLE,
Major, and Inspector-General of Transportation.

[Inclosure No. 1.]

BUREAU OF SUBSISTENCE,
Richmond, August 3, 1863.

Col. L. B. NORTHROP,
Commissary-General of Subsistence:

COLONEL: The incessant rains of the past month have not only
damaged the wheat crop to a considerable extent, but materially delayed the planters in their farming operations, very few being now
engaged in thrashing, and nearly all will be prevented from sending
their crops to market in consequence of the want of transportation.

With the limited stock of flour now in this market, and the very
small quantity in the State under control of this Department (rendered so entirely by want of transportation and not scarcity), I would
suggest that it is of the utmost importance that all the available
transportation in this city, and attached to the various commands
defending it, should be immediately offered to the farmers, as the
prospect of obtaining facilities to send their crops to market will no
doubt induce them to commence and prosecute their thrashing operations with energy and vigor.

It would doubtless be well to call the attention of the Secretary of
War to the existing state of affairs, and impress upon him the
necessity and importance of immediate action. The wagons could
be recalled at any time when necessary for the movement of troops.

Col. A. H. Cole, chief of field transportation, has offered to loan 25
wagons for the purpose mentioned, and states that he could, with
the sanction of the Secretary of War, increase the number to 150
from the commands in the vicinity of Richmond.

I am, very respectfully, your obedient servant,

S. BASSETT FRENCH,
Major, and Commissary of Subsistence.

[First indorsement.]

OFFICE COMMISSARY-GENERAL OF SUBSISTENCE,
August 3, 1863.

Respectfully referred to the Secretary of War, asking the order to
Major-General Elzey, directing that all the arrangements suggested
by Colonel Cole may be carried out.

L. B. NORTHROP,
Commissary-General of Subsistence,

AUGUST 3, 1863.

Colonel Cole is authorized to furnish such transportation as can be spared from the commands around Richmond, to aid the bringing of supplies to the Subsistence Bureau.

J. A. S. [SEDDON],
Secretary.

[Third indorsement.]

OFFICE INSPECTOR-GENERAL OF TRANSPORTATION,
August 12, 1863.

Respectfully submitted to General Elzey.

The Commissary Department has called for 50 wagons and teams to be furnished by 9 a. m. to-morrow. I will be able to furnish by that time 30 of the number, leaving 20 to be provided from the commands around Richmond. That number might be made up from the following troops, and still leave sufficient for the necessary daily service of each command: From Forty-sixth Virginia, 5 wagons and teams; from Twenty-sixth Virginia, 4 wagons and teams; from Fourth Virginia [Heavy Artillery], 5 wagons and teams; from Fifty-ninth Virginia, 3 wagons and teams; from Major Stark's artillery battalion, 2 wagons and teams, and from General Wise's staff teams, 1 wagon and team, making the 20 required to fill the requisition.

If General Elzey approves, I request that these teams be ordered to report immediately.

A. H. COLE,
Major, and Inspector-General.

[Fourth indorsement.]

HEADQUARTERS DEPARTMENT OF RICHMOND,
August 12, 1863.

The transportation of General Wise's brigade is constantly employed in supplying that brigade, and cannot be spared without destroying its efficiency. I therefore earnestly but respectfully protest against its being taken from it. There are 70 wagons at Danville, 30 of which ought to be used for transportation purposes elsewhere.

Very respectfully,

ARNOLD ELZEY,
Major-General, Commanding.

[Fifth indorsement.]

OFFICE INSPECTOR-GENERAL OF TRANSPORTATION,
August 13, 1863.

Respectfully forwarded through the Quartermaster-General.

The transportation referred to by General Elzey, at Danville, has been and is now employed in hauling supplies, the number of wagons and teams belonging to that depot being only about half the number named by General Elzey.

A. H. COLE,
Major, and Inspector-General.

[Sixth indorsement.]

QUARTERMASTER-GENERAL'S OFFICE,
August 17, 1863.
Major Cole's position and information are such that his indorsement
is adopted, and respectfully forwarded to the Secretary of War.
A. R. LAWTON,
Quartermaster-General.

[Seventh indorsement.]

AUGUST 17, 1863.
The transportation of supplies is so important that the requisition
of the Quartermaster-General is approved.
J. A. SEDDON,
Secretary of War.

[Eighth indorsement.]

OFFICE INSPECTOR-GENERAL OF TRANSPORTATION,
August 17, 1863.
Respectfully forwarded to General Elzey.
A. H. COLE,
Major, and Inspector-General.

[Ninth indorsement.]

AUGUST 18, 1863.
In lieu of the indorsement last made by me, General Wise having
undertaken to send all the wagons his brigade can possibly spare,
but desiring that they should be under the charge of his wagon-
master while hauling supplies, let him be ordered to send, under
charge of his wagon-master, such wagons as he can spare, to be employed in hauling supplies, as indicated by the Commissary-General
or the Quartermaster-General.
J. A. SEDDON,
Secretary of War.

[Tenth indorsement.]

AUGUST 18, 1863.
QUARTERMASTER-GENERAL:
There appears a discrepancy between General Elzey's indorsement
and that of Major Cole in regard to the number of wagons, &c., at
Danville. General Elzey's statement was made, he informs me, on
the authority of recent inspection. Cause inquiry and report as to
the number, so that the number at command may be undoubtedly
ascertained.
J. A. S. [SEDDON],
Secretary.

[Eleventh indorsement.]

HEADQUARTERS DEPARTMENT OF RICHMOND,
August 18, 1863.
General Wise has been ordered to furnish all the transportation
he can spare, under his own wagon-master, to report to Major Cole
for the purpose of hauling wheat in the neighborhood of Richmond.
Very respectfully,
ARNOLD ELZEY,
Major-General, Commanding.

[Inclosure No. 2.]

QUARTERMASTER'S OFFICE, WISE'S BRIGADE,
August 18, 1863.

Capt. J. H. PEARCE, *Assistant Adjutant-General:*

I beg leave most respectfully to submit that the transportation of this brigade has been so reduced by a recent order that nearly the whole of it is required for foraging, excepting at intervals of short duration, when we might furnish 12 or 15 wagons; but ordinarily, unless a move is contemplated, we can furnish 8 or 10 wagons.

Very respectfully, your obedient servant,

H. CARRINGTON WATKINS,
Major, and Brigade Quartermaster.

SPECIAL ORDERS, }   ADJT. AND INSP. GENERAL'S OFFICE,
No. 198.   }   *Richmond, August 20, 1863.*

*   *   *   *   *   *   *

XIV. Brig. Gen. G. J. Rains will procee without delay to Charleston, S. C., and report to General G. T. Beauregard, commanding, &c., for assignment to duty.

*   *   *   *   *   *   *

XXIII. Brig. Gen. John Pegram, Provisional Army, C. S., will report to General R. E. Lee, commanding Army of Northern Virginia, for assignment to duty.

By command of the Secretary of War:

JNO. WITHERS,
Assistant Adjutant-General.

Abstract from field return of the Army of Northern Virginia, General Robert E. Lee, C. S. Army, commanding, for August 20, 1863; headquarters Orange Court-House.

Command.	Present for duty.		Aggregate present.	Aggregate present and absent.
	Officers.	Men.		
General headquarters...................................	14	....	14	14
First Army Corps a (Longstreet)	1,326	13,323	17,749	33,951
Second Army Corps (Ewell)......................................	1,491	14,900	19,206	40,022
Third Army Corps (A. P. Hill)......................................	1,189	13,059	16,555	32,500
Cavalry (Stuart)......................................	658	8,004	10,101	19,338
Artillery (Pendleton)......................................	300	4,906	5,857	8,317
Total..	4,978	54,282	69,542	134,142

a Note on original states that two regiments of Hood's division (aggregate present, 580) are not reported.

WAR DEPARTMENT, C. S., *Richmond, August 21, 1863.*

General WHITING, *Wilmington, N. C.:*

Your letter about Flora not received. Have you got out the Blakely guns, and can you send them by railroad to Charleston? They are so urgent that both had better go at once.

J A. SEDDON,
Secretary of War.

PETERSBURG, *August 21, 1863.*

Maj. Gen. ARNOLD ELZEY:

Captain Bird, of Florida, returned prisoner, late from Fort Norfolk, says in the last two weeks 20,000 men, including Eleventh Army Corps, have passed to Charleston.

M. JENKINS,
Brigadier-General.

CONSCRIPT OFFICE, CAMP VANCE,
August 21, 1863.

Col. P. MALLETT,
Commanding Conscripts, North Carolina:

COLONEL: Several peace meetings have been held in the Ninth and Tenth Districts, at which I understand, not officially, that the most treasonable language was uttered, and Union flags raised. Can I have authority to break up any such assemblages, and arrest the ringleaders who are not of conscript age?

I feel it my duty to complain against the publication of the Standard newspaper, which is issued in Raleigh, and extensively circulated throughout this section. From common report, which can be made official intelligence if necessary, I am constrained to believe that most of the trouble in North Carolina, as well as of the desertions from the army, are the direct consequence of the circulation of this incendiary publication.

I am, colonel, your obedient servant,

J. C. McRAE,
Captain, &c., Commanding.

[Indorsement.]

CONSCRIPT OFFICE, NORTH CAROLINA,
August 27, 1863.

Respectfully referred to the Bureau of Conscripts.

The state of things described by Captain McRae to a great extent exists in other parts of the State. The attention of the Department is earnestly recommended to this matter.

PETER MALLETT,
Colonel, Commanding Conscripts, North Carolina.

CAMP NEAR ORANGE COURT-HOUSE,
August 22, 1863.

His Excellency JEFFERSON DAVIS,
President Confederate States, Richmond, Va.:

Mr. PRESIDENT: Your note by General Davis has been received. General Fitz. Lee has sent from his brigade, now near Fredericksburg, Colonel Rosser's regiment of cavalry, to the counties of Middlesex and Gloucester, to be in readiness to afford protection if needed to the expedition you mentioned. Colonel Rosser will take a convenient position between Urbanna and Gloucester, and keep out vedettes for observation.

The scouts on the Potomac, placed by me since my return from Maryland, have reported no increased activity on the river since the passage of General King's division from Suffolk, Norfolk, &c. No troops have been reported going up till Thursday, 13th instant, when a large steamer, with probably a regiment aboard, ascended the river. About a fortnight since, twenty-four steamers were reported passing down, apparently loaded. It was about the time troops were said to have been landed at Old Point for Charleston. As I have not been able to hear of them further, this was probably the case. The Eleventh Army Corps, General Howard, was sent back about the 1st instant, and reported to have been disbanded and distributed. It was very much reduced, and General Stuart thinks did not exceed 1,000 men for duty. A scout, recently from Washington, reports that the order for its disbandment was rescinded on the 7th instant by General Halleck, and that it was ordered to Charleston. Major Mosby, recently from Alexandria, says that up to the time he left there none had embarked at that place.

Colonel White, from Loudoun, reports 10,000 Federal troops passing Fredericktown toward Washington from the west. I can learn of no troops joining General Meade since General King's division, which is posted at Centreville, excepting conscripts. General Meade was in Washington on the 15th instant. His army is posted along the Orange and Alexandria Railroad, in Fauquier and Prince William. His cavalry is guarding each flank and picketing the Rappahannock from Waterloo to Falmouth; none have yet gone below the latter place. Up to the 17th, no operations had been commenced at Aquia, nor had any force been in that vicinity either by land or water. A large amount of timber, said to have been shipped to Aquia, had not arrived, nor can I hear of a large quantity of stone shipped to a point unknown. Supply transports are passing up and down the Potomac, but not in unusual numbers. The enemy's attention seems to be now devoted to the capture of Charleston, which I trust he will never get. As soon as I can get the vacancies in the army filled, and the horses and men recruited a little, if General Meade does not move, I wish to attack him.

I have received another application from General Jenkins to join me with his brigade. I should like much to have him if he can be spared, and would replace it by General Davis', which he thinks would enable him to refill this regiment [brigade ?], if you approve it.

I am, with great respect, your obedient servant,

R. E. LEE.

RICHMOND, *August 22, 1863.*

General R. E. LEE,
 Orange Court-House, Va.:

The following received through the signal office here, from agent in Maryland, dated August 20 :

I learned from a gentleman, on Tuesday, direct from Washington, and in position to know how things are moving, that it was generally believed there that the Army of the Potomac will be reduced 50,000 to enforce the draft in New York. It looks very much like it, from the great numbers of troops already gone down the Potomac, and there are evidences of more to come. There are large steamers now up the river, and will return to-morrow.

The signal officer on the Potomac states that from certain indications the troops could not have gone farther than Fort Monroe.

S. COOPER,
Adjutant and Inspector General.

RICHMOND, *August 22, 1863.*

Maj. Gen. SAMUEL JONES,
    Dublin Station, Va.:

The following dispatch just received from General Buckner, viz:

Burnside is advancing on East Tennessee. Force heavy, but numbers not known; chiefly mounted infantry with heavy trains. Points not developed; probably by Big Creek Gap and Wartburg. Will you ask General Jones to re-enforce me, if possible? Preston covers the salt-works now.

You will do what you can, consistent with the safety of your department, to re-enforce General Buckner.

S. COOPER,
Adjutant and Inspector General.

UNION, *August 22, 1863.*

General S. COOPER,
    Adjutant and Inspector General:

Your telegram of this date received. I cannot re-enforce General Buckner without moving the troops from Saltville, and I do not think it prudent to do that.

SAM. JONES,
Major-General.

HEADQUARTERS DEPARTMENT OF WESTERN VIRGINIA,
    Union, August 22, 1863.

Maj. Gen. S. B. BUCKNER,
    Knoxville, Tenn.:

I cannot give you any aid without moving my troops from Saltville, and I cannot move them without an order to do so.

SAM. JONES,
Major-General.

HEADQUARTERS DEPARTMENT OF WESTERN VIRGINIA,
    Dublin, August 22, 1863.

Maj. Gen. SAMUEL JONES, *Union:*

I telegraphed you yesterday that I declined, in your absence, to send any troops to Knoxville. Telegram just received from General Buckner, who proposes to give you, at Saltville, equal number of dismounted cavalry for the Sixty-third [Virginia] Regiment, and begs you to send it. Under General Cooper's telegram, ought it not to be done? I have ordered McMahon to hold himself in readiness. Please let me hear from you immediately.

CHAS. S. STRINGFELLOW,
Major, and Assistant Adjutant-General.

RICHMOND, *August 23, 1863.*

General BUCKNER, *Knoxville, Tenn.:*

General S. Jones, to whom your dispatch for aid was sent, reports he cannot re-enforce you without moving troops from Saltville, which he does not think it would be prudent to do.

S. COOPER.

SALT SULPHUR SPRINGS, *August 23, 1863.*
Col. W. H. BROWNE,
    Little Levels, Pocahontas County, Va.:

COLONEL: I have just received a dispatch from Colonel Jackson, dated yesterday. He was at Gatewood's house, on Back Creek, 12 or 15 miles from Huntersville, on the road to Warm Springs. He left two companies at his old camp, 3 miles from Huntersville, on same road. He thinks this move of the enemy was designed to surround and capture him, and not to make a raid on Staunton. Colonel Jackson has a strong position on Back Creek, and expresses entire confidence in his ability to hold it, if attacked. He was skirmishing all day Friday, the 21st, with the enemy on Knapp's Creek.

If the enemy attempts to move on Colonel Jackson by the road from Huntersville to Warm Springs (he thinks they are moving both by the Knapp's Creek and Back Creek roads), I think you can get in their rear, and you and Jackson together, perhaps, capture them.

It is impossible at this distance, and without full knowledge of the enemy's movements and strength, to give minute instructions. I trust with confidence to your own judgment to profit by any opportunity that offers to punish the enemy.

I do not think that Averell had more than 1,200 or 1,300 cavalry. If he has divided that force and is moving by the two routes, as Colonel Jackson says, you will be fully able to manage the column nearest you.

Communicate fully with Colonel Jackson, and co-operate with him. I believe you rank him, but unless the two commands actually come together, there need be no question of rank raised. Colonel Jackson has served long in that section of country and knows it well.

I trust that you two will so manage as to punish the enemy severely before they extricate themselves from the mountainous country into which they have penetrated.

Communicate with me freely by way of Lewisburg.

Very respectfully, &c.,
                                    SAM. JONES,
            Major-General, Comdg. Dept. of Western Virginia.

SALT SULPHUR SPRINGS, *August 23, 1863.*
Lieutenant-Colonel DERRICK,
                    Commanding, &c.:

COLONEL: The major-general commanding directs that you move without delay, with your whole command, transportation, &c., to Greenbrier Bridge, and there await further orders.

I am, colonel, very respectfully, &c.,
                                    WM. B. MYERS,
                        Assistant Adjutant-General.

SALT SULPHUR SPRINGS, *August 23, 1863.*
Col. W. L. JACKSON,
        Back Creek, Bath County:

COLONEL: I received this morning, between 8 and 9 o'clock, your dispatch of yesterday.

Colonel Browne, of the Forty-fifth Virginia, left Lewisburg early yesterday with his own regiment and two companies of cavalry (two other companies of cavalry had preceded him) for Little Levels and Marling's Bottom, with orders to scout the roads toward Beverly and Monterey. I have sent a dispatch to him communicating the substance of your dispatch of yesterday.

If the enemy is advancing on you by both the Back Creek and Knapp's Creek roads, Colonel Browne ought to be able to get in the rear of the column that goes by the road from Huntersville toward the Warm Springs, and between you that column will be in a fair way of being cut off or captured.

I have directed Colonel Browne to communicate and co-operate with you. I shall look anxiously for news from you.

Very respectfully, &c.,

SAM. JONES,
Major-General.

SALT SULPHUR SPRINGS, *August 23, 1863.*

Col. GEORGE S. PATTON, *Lewisburg:*

COLONEL : Both of your dispatches to-day were received within about half or three-quarters of an hour of each other.

Move without delay, as you suggest, with your infantry and artillery, up Antony's Creek, toward the Huntersville and Warm Springs roads, and co-operate with Colonel Jackson. Take with you one company of cavalry, leaving the remainder on the Frankfort and Pocahontas roads, to watch the enemy from that direction. I can give you no more minute directions at present. Keep me informed of your own movements and those of the enemy as fully as you can. Colonel Derrick will be ordered to or near Lewisburg.

In haste, yours, &c.,

SAM. JONES,
Major-General.

[AUGUST 23, 1863.—For Jones to Cooper, in reference to Averell's operations, see Part I, p. 42.]

HEADQUARTERS,
Orange Court-House, August 24, 1863.

His Excellency JEFFERSON DAVIS,
President Confederate States, Richmond:

Mr. PRESIDENT : The information from the signal officer in Maryland, telegraphed me by General Cooper, is confirmed by the scouts on the Potomac. They report that on the 17th three steamers passed down the river loaded with troops; on the 18th, one; on the 19th, two; on the 20th, a very large steamer, with two smoke-stacks, crowded; and on the 21st, one large steamer filled with troops. These troops may belong to the Eleventh Army Corps on their way to Charleston, mentioned in my previous letter, or those said to have passed through Maryland from the west on their way to Washington.

A scout from north of the Rappahannock states, on Sunday, 16th instant, the Twelfth Army Corps went back to Alexandria. Whether he confounded the Eleventh with the Twelfth, or that an additional corps has gone back, I do not know yet. The enemy's lines are so closely watched and our scouts have to make so wide a circuit, that their information is frequently late reaching me.

I can discover no change of importance in the enemy's position on the Rappahannock. Nothing prevents my advancing now but the fear of killing our artillery horses. They are much reduced, and the hot weather and scarce forage keeps them so. The cavalry also suffer, and I fear to set them at work. Some days we get a pound of corn per horse and some days more; some none. Our limit is 5 pounds per day per horse. You can judge of our prospects. General Fitz. Lee is getting from north of the Rappahannock, below Fredericksburg, about 1,000 pounds per day, which is a considerable relief on that wing. Everything is being done by me that can be to recruit the horses. I have been obliged to diminish the number of guns in the artillery, and fear I shall have to lose more.

I am, with great respect, your obedient servant,

R. E. LEE,
General.

ORANGE COURT-HOUSE,
August 24, 1863.

General S. COOPER:

On application of General Sam. Jones, I have directed Jenkins' and Wharton's brigades to report to him.

R. E. LEE.

HEADQUARTERS ARMY OF NORTHERN VIRGINIA,
August 24, 1863.

Maj. Gen. J. E. B. STUART,
Commanding, &c.:

GENERAL: General Sam. Jones telegraphs, under date of to-day,* that the enemy has driven Colonel Jackson out of Pocahontas, and is pressing him back toward the Warm Springs, and that another column is moving down through Beverly toward Lewisburg. He desires to have the troops belonging to his command now with this army returned as soon as possible. I have telegraphed to you to order Jenkins' brigade to rejoin him, and desire that they be sent without delay. They will proceed, by the best route, by way of Staunton and the Warm Springs.

Very respectfully, your obedient servant,

R. E. LEE,
General.

HEADQUARTERS ARMY OF NORTHERN VIRGINIA,
August 24, 1863.

General G. C. WHARTON,
Commanding Brigade:

GENERAL: General Sam. Jones reports by telegraph that the enemy has driven Colonel Jackson out of Pocahontas, and is press-

* See Part I, p. 42.

ing him back toward Warm Springs. Another column is moving down from Beverly toward Lewisburg. He represents himself in great need of all the troops sent to this army.

I have, therefore, to request that you will make arrangements at once to report to him, proceeding via Staunton and Warm Springs, with your brigade and three field batteries. Jenkins' brigade is also ordered.

I have directed Colonel Corley to use the railroad to the extent of its ability, without stopping supplies, to transport the sick and feeble, &c., of your command to Staunton. You had better send him the number you wish forwarded by rail.

You can take the road through Charlottesville or Stanardsville, as you may deem best.

Very respectfully, your obedient servant,

R. E. LEE,
General.

HEADQUARTERS DEPARTMENT OF WESTERN VIRGINIA,
Dublin, August 24, 1863.

Brigadier-General IMBODEN,
Commanding, &c., Harrisonburg:

The enemy, 3,000 strong, are pressing Colonel Jackson back toward Warm Springs and may advance on Staunton.

By order of Maj. Gen. Sam. Jones:

GILES B. COOKE,
Assistant Adjutant and Inspector General.

HEADQUARTERS DEPARTMENT OF WESTERN VIRGINIA,
Dublin, August 24, 1863.

Major KENT, *Comdg. Home Guard, Wytheville:*

MAJOR: When the enemy were last heard from, which was yesterday, they were pressing Colonel Jackson back to Warm Springs. Their whole force reported 3,000 strong. It is thought that their cavalry, numbering 1,200, will make a raid on some point of the railroad—most probably New River Bridge.

There is no telling when Wytheville will be threatened from Prestonsburg or from some other point on your front. This information is given that you may be ready for any move they may make.

Very respectfully, your obedient servant,

GILES B. COOKE,
Assistant Adjutant and Inspector General.

HEADQUARTERS DEPARTMENT OF WESTERN VIRGINIA,
Dublin, August 24, 1863.

Major KENT, *Wytheville:*

Have your guns and ammunition issued to your company immediately. The enemy's cavalry, 1,200 strong, are reported advancing on New River Bridge. Hold your command in readiness to move at a moment's warning.

By order of Maj. Gen. Sam. Jones:

GILES B. COOKE,
Assistant Adjutant and Inspector General.

HEADQUARTERS DEPARTMENT OF WESTERN VIRGINIA,
Dublin, August 24, 1863.

Colonel McCAUSLAND,
Commanding, &c., Princeton :

Telegrams, dated Union, August 23 and 24, inform me that the enemy, reported 3,000 strong, have pressed Colonel Jackson back toward Warm Springs, and that a body of cavalry numbering 1,200 may make a raid on the railroad near New River Bridge; that another heavy column is moving on Lewisburg.

In view of the above, General Lee has ordered Wharton's and Jenkins' brigades to report to General Jones, via Staunton and Warm Springs.

GILES B. COOKE,
Assistant Adjutant and Inspector General.

WAR DEPARTMENT, C. S.,
Richmond, August 24, 1863.

Brig. Gen. F. T. NICHOLLS,
Lynchburg, Va. :

Send such force as you can command, including the local militia, who will go as they did to Wytheville, to defend the bridge over New River, on the line of the railroad. There are guns at the ordnance depot. Call on Captain Getty, at Lynchburg, for the number you need, as also for munitions.

J. A. SEDDON,
Secretary of War.

HEADQUARTERS DEPARTMENT OF WESTERN VIRGINIA,
Dublin, August 24, 1863.

Brigadier-General NICHOLLS,
Lynchburg :

The enemy, 3,000 strong, are pressing Colonel Jackson back toward Warm Springs. It is thought the cavalry, 1,200 strong, will advance on the railroad, probably at New River Bridge. I would suggest that you hold all of your available force in readiness to proceed at a moment's warning to the support of the threatened point.

GILES B. COOKE,
Assistant Adjutant and Inspector General.

HEADQUARTERS DEPARTMENT OF WESTERN VIRGINIA,
Dublin, August 24, 1863.

Col. ROBERT T. PRESTON,
Christiansburg :

The enemy are reported 1,200 strong, moving on New River Bridge. Hold your command in readiness to move at a moment's warning, and await further orders.

By order, &c. :

GILES B. COOKE,
Assistant Adjutant and Inspector General.

HEADQUARTERS DEPARTMENT OF WESTERN VIRGINIA,
Dublin, August 24, 1863.

Colonel TERRILL,
Commanding Home Guard, Salem:

COLONEL : I have notified you by telegram that I have sent you by this evening's train 50 guns and ammunition. These are all I can furnish at present. I will try and collect more at New River Bridge, whence you may be able to get more if you meet them.

A telegram dated 23d instant, from the general, who is at Union, says the enemy, 3,000 strong, are pressing Colonel Jackson back toward Warm Springs.

I am apprehensive that the cavalry, reported 1,200 strong, will start on a raid to the railroad. Let me know if you want the "howitzers" I promised you.

I am, colonel, respectfully, yours, &c.,
GILES B. COOKE,
Assistant Adjutant and Inspector General.

(Same to Col. R. L. Preston.)

HEADQUARTERS DEPARTMENT OF WESTERN VIRGINIA,
Dublin, August 24, 1863.

Colonel TERRILL,
Salem:

The enemy's cavalry are reported 1,200 strong, moving on New River Bridge. Hold your command in readiness to move at a moment's warning, and await further orders. Notify Captain Tayloe, at Big Lick, to do the same.

By command of Maj. Gen. Sam. Jones :
GILES B. COOKE,
Assistant Adjutant and Inspector General.

HEADQUARTERS DEPARTMENT OF WESTERN VIRGINIA,
Dublin, August 24, 1863.

General JOHN S. WILLIAMS :

I received a telegram from General Jones this morning, stating that 3,000 of the enemy are pressing Colonel Jackson back toward Warm Springs, and that he was apprehensive of a raid on some point of the railroad by their cavalry, numbering 1,200. Steps have been taken to give them a warm reception if they should come this way. I have notified Major Kent, commanding home guard company, to hold himself in readiness to repel any demonstration on Wytheville from Prestonsburg, or from any point in his front.

I received a telegram from General Buckner, just now, asking General Jones to place you in command of General Preston's district in his absence. You have been authorized by telegraph to assume command of said district. You will please telegraph me the number of effective men—now that the Sixty-third Virginia is gone and has been replaced by an equal number of cavalry—under your command that may be used for the defense of the salt-works, including the troops that General Preston left, and all of the home guards you may be able to call into service. It is important that couriers should be kept at the telegraph office at Glade Spring, so that communication between us may be had with as much dispatch as possible.

I am, general, very respectfully, &c., your obedient servant,

GILES B. COOKE,
Assistant Adjutant and Inspector General.

HEADQUARTERS DEPARTMENT OF WESTERN VIRGINIA,
Dublin, August 24, 1863.

Brigadier-General WILLIAMS,
Commanding, Saltville:

In the absence of General Preston, you will take command of the district. The substitute for the Sixty-third [Virginia] Regiment will be mounted instead of dismounted cavalry.

By order of Maj. Gen. Sam. Jones:

GILES B. COOKE,
Assistant Adjutant and Inspector General.

RICHMOND, VA.,
August 24, 1863.

Brig. Gen. M. JENKINS,
Commanding at Petersburg, Va.:

By the demonstration on the Blackwater, the enemy may design to draw you away from Petersburg so as to enable him to throw a force up the river in transports, land at Bermuda Hundred, and turn Drewry's Bluff. Keep this in view.

ARNOLD ELZEY,
Major-General, Commanding.

CHAFFIN'S FARM,
August 24, 1863—7 p. m.

Maj. J. R. ROBERTSON:

MAJOR: Information has this moment been received from the major-general commanding of the ascent of the Chickahominy River by the gunboat.

I am directed by General Wise to order you to concentrate your cavalry at the Chickahominy River, dismount your men, and give the best fight you can. This order you will obey immediately upon its receipt. If the boat remains up the Chickahominy or comes up the James, you will report promptly to the general. Establish a courier line from any point you may move your command to to these headquarters, and probably you had better add an extra courier to each post, to make the trips easier. General Elzey's orders are to destroy the boat, if possible. It is probable she will not remain up the Chickahominy all night; so you will see the necessity of moving promptly and quietly, avoiding all unnecessary noise that might alarm her. A dispatch from Lieutenant Harkey has just been received, conveying the intelligence above named.

Very respectfully, your obedient servant,

JAMES H. PEARCE,
Assistant Adjutant-General.

HEADQUARTERS,
Wilmington, August 24, 1863.

Hon. James A. Seddon,
    Secretary of War, Richmond:

SIR: I have for some time been greatly concerned on account of the exposed and dangerous situation of this place, and this district, due to want of force. I hope to call your earnest attention to it, and through you that of the President. As the siege of Charleston continues, so the importance of this port grows every day. I do not know now that there is another place, excepting perhaps Richmond, we should not sooner see lost than this. But as to a place so vulnerable, by reason of the very large field in which points of attack may be selected, the entire confidence had in the fortifications, and the reliance evidently had on either the want of enterprise of the enemy or the supposition that he has his hands full elsewhere, seem to me like tempting Providence.

I have but one regiment in this district, to constitute a movable force. It is called upon to operate sometimes at Topsail (22 miles from town), sometimes at Fisher (21 miles in the opposite direction), sometimes at points intermediate on the coast. In addition, I have but three or four of probably the poorest and worst appointed field batteries in the service, batteries formed at a late date with refuse guns, and which have never seen a battle. The duties of the garrison of the city and the forts are unusually heavy and exhausting, while the season is very sickly. This regiment has also to help them. The enormous increase of the government trade, the increasing activity of the enemy in trying to prevent it, gives the garrison of the forts constant employment and almost ceaseless battle. The duty devolving on the city garrison is overwhelming in the guarding and transportation of stores, enforcement of the quarantine, guarding vessels to carry out the regulations for detection of spies, &c. But the sense of security which is felt, either in the supineness of the enemy or the safety and strength of the place, sometimes receives a rude shock.

Yesterday the enemy took a fancy to destroy what remained of the wreck of the Hebe, a Crenshaw steamer run ashore some days ago, and from which a company of the garrison of Fort Fisher were engaged in saving property. The steam frigate Minnesota and five other gunboats approached the beach, and, under a terrific fire, attempted to land, but were gallantly repulsed by Captain Munn, with a Whitworth and two small rifle guns of short range. The site was about 9 miles from Fisher, on the narrow and low beach between the Sounds and the ocean, and completely under the fire of the enormous batteries of the enemy. A portion of the squadron, steaming farther up the beach, effected a landing some 2 miles off in largely superior force, and came down upon Captain Munn, still gallantly fighting his little guns against the Minnesota, they being moved by hand, and, having fired his last round, the Whitworths disabled, 1 gunner killed, lieutenant and 4 men wounded, Captain Munn, with his small party, was compelled to fall back, under a heavy enfilade fire, toward Fort Fisher, with the loss of his guns.

This took place 9 miles from Fort Fisher and about the same distance from the city. The narrow beach, separated from the mainland by the Sounds, gives every facility to the enemy, and secures them from us who are without boats or means of getting at them. The

Fiftieth [North Carolina] Regiment—the only one I have—was off at a distance, called by a landing made by the enemy at Topsail, in which they burned, the night before, a schooner, a salt-work, and took 2 artillerymen prisoners.

These little affairs, however, are only mentioned in illustration. This is the first time they have landed; but what they have done once they can do again, and doubtless will. There is no day scarcely until the winter gales set in but what they could put 5,000 men on the beach; they can get them from New Berne and Beaufort before I could know·it. I only say if they do, they can get either Fort Fisher or the town as they elect, if they set about it at once.

Few persons are aware of the extreme difficulty of this position, the necessity of an army here, and the trouble and uncertainty in providing by the disposition of a supporting force to anticipate the movements of the enemy. But at all times, and especially now, I assure you, sir, and it is my duty to warn you, that at least a strong brigade ought always to cover this important and vital point. I cannot draw them from other points of the department. It is extensive, and our line of communication very vulnerable and much exposed. Nor have I control of all troops in it.

You no doubt remember that 10,000 of the best troops from this section were sent west to endeavor to save Vicksburg. Vicksburg has fallen and Charleston hard pressed, yet no doubt those troops are still necessary, until Pemberton's are exchanged, where they are. A brigade is far from the force which would be absolutely necessary here when this place is attacked in force, but it might be disposed so as to secure it from a *coup de main.* I most urgently urge it. I beg you will say to the President that in my judgment nothing here, of all other places, should be left to chance or good fortune. I am pushing my works; the Governor is supplying me now with labor. Do not let this be thrown away or rendered useless. A single brigade from anywhere, stationed here, made familiar with the position, would be worth 10,000 men who should arrive after a *coup de main* of the enemy, or when they should have succeeded in making lodgment, when they would be too late.

It is not necessary for me to repeat to you, who are so well acquainted with the subject, our dependence on the safety of this place for future and now needed supplies. I know you appreciate the matter. I only say most earnestly, looking as I do from a point of view best enabling one to judge, that I regard the state of affairs and the position as dangerous. I need also cavalry, not only against raids, but even here more than anywhere else. The efforts of the enemy to stop our steamers are increasing. Their force is largely increased. I have met with a serious and heavy loss in that Whitworth, a gun that in the hands of the indefatigable Lamb has saved dozens of vessels and millions of money to the Confederate States. I beg that a couple of the Whitworth guns originally saved by him from the Modern Queen may be sent here at once. Their long range makes them most suitable for a sea-board position. Could I get them with horses, we could save many a vessel that will now be lost to us. But chiefly in this letter I beg of you, if you concur in my views, to lay the matter of the necessity of increasing the force here before the President.

Very respectfully,

W. H. C. WHITING,
Major-General.

[Indorsements.]

August 26, 1863.

Respectfully submitted for the consideration of the President, whose attention is specially invoked to the apprehensions expressed, as I fear with so much reason, by General Whiting.

J. A. SEDDON,
Secretary of War.

If the local-defense men promised from North Carolina are in position to guard the road, there can no longer be any difficulty about sending General Martin's brigade to Wilmington.

JEFFERSON DAVIS.

———

HEADQUARTERS DEPARTMENT OF NORTH CAROLINA,
Wilmington, August 24, 1863.

Hon. JAMES A. SEDDON,
Secretary of War, Richmond:

SIR: I wrote you this morning relative to the urgent and increasing necessity for troops in this district. The state of affairs at Charleston now, though I by no means despair of the place whether Sumter falls or not, is very critical.

I wish to point out one thing of importance which the present condition of Charleston perfectly illustrates, and which I have often called attention to. With the immense navy and force of the enemy, to make on our part a successful resistance, it is absolutely necessary to prevent them getting a foothold on the approaches. They must be attacked on their landing. It will not do to let them quietly establish themselves on the islands and approaches, and wait for our re-enforcements, to go through exhausting process of the engineering of siege attack.

You are already aware that though I am strengthening Fisher, it is a work more designed to repel sea attack than land, an extensive line of sea-coast batteries connected by covered ways. Its garrison is sufficient to man its guns. The plan of defense here has always been predicated on the support of a movable army, and indeed no other, in my judgment, could be adopted with effect,

I say now that, as far as my opinion in the matter is of value, it is time to commence assembling troops for the defense of Wilmington, whether the enemy fail or succeed at Charleston. The fleet here is being increased. It is strong enough now to land a formidable force for a *coup de main.*

I have not the means to meet it without leaving to the enemy the whole line of communication in North Carolina. I could answer for Fort Caswell for a short time, but not for Fort Fisher unless I have troops; of these there ought to be enough to enable me to make a formidable resistance at the very beginning.

I must repeat, it will not do to wait for the attack. Pardon my urgency, but this matter is indeed very urgent.

Very respectfully,

W. H. C. WHITING,
Major-General.

HEADQUARTERS DEPARTMENT OF NORTH CAROLINA,
Wilmington, August 24, 1863.

Governor ZEBULON B. VANCE,
Raleigh:

SIR: I have written pressing letter to the Secretary of War, urging that the time has arrived to commence assembling troops for the defense of Wilmington. It will not do to wait until we are attacked, and then depend on assembling re-enforcements. We must be prepared. The whole plan of defense of this now vital and most important point, not only to the Confederacy, but to your State, is predicated on the presence of an army to support the works and to crush the first effort of the enemy either to advance or to land. The present condition of Charleston shows that we should never let the enemy possess himself, with his immense means, of the approaches. I do not despair of Charleston, but whether it falls or not, I say, as one in the position to judge, that it is time to look out for Wilmington.

I hope that a response will be made, and that from some of the armies of the Republic I may receive some troops. I fear a *coup de main.* This district is stripped. I cannot take from other parts of the department without laying Raleigh, Fayetteville, Goldsborough, and Weldon open, and the entire communication liable to be destroyed, thus preventing my ever getting troops. Please to urge this matter yourself, not that I expect other than a perfect comprehension and appreciation of the wants of the district, but to add the weight of your influence. In the meantime, I would suggest, if you have the power, that you would order into the field four or five regiments of militia infantry. If they could be put on foot at once, I think we could arm them and get them, by means of an excellent staff, into good discipline and drill. Think of this.

If permitte, I will send you a copy of my letter to the Secretary of War. I assure you the matter is urgent.

Very respectfully,

W. H. C. WHITING,
Major-General.

———

HEADQUARTERS DEPARTMENT OF NORTH CAROLINA,
Wilmington, August 25, 1863.

Hon. JAMES A. SEDDON,
Secretary of War, Richmond:

SIR: Should the enemy design attacking this place from the southward, as is likely, whether they succeed or fail at Charleston, there is a feasible line of attack which they might well adopt, now that the extraordinary range of their siege guns is shown, and with disastrous consequences to us here.

It is to land at either Shallotte or Little River, or both, and move directly on the city, plant their batteries, and destroy it. This move on their part, unless promptly defeated, would result in the turning and capture of Smithville, the Saint Philip lines, the isolation of Fort Caswell, and eventually the loss of the harbor.

As in all other cases heretofore demonstrated, this is a line of attack which must be met by a supporting army. The works are not sufficient.

With the force now at my command, I do not hesitate to say that the large fleet now off here have men enough to land and effect this object. I regard this district as very much exposed. The enemy have commenced boat raiding to destroy salt-works. I cannot prevent it. I hope you will be able to let me have infantry, cavalry, and artillery. I need every man that can be had.

I do not want to permit the enemy to acquire any knowledge of the approaches. At present he can learn what he pleases, but, independent of this, the port of Wilmington and its harbors, uncovered of support, are not now safe.

Very respectfully,

W. H. C. WHITING,
Major-General.

COMMANDANT'S OFFICE,
Drewry's Bluff, Va., August 25, 1863.

Maj. Gen. ARNOLD ELZEY,
Commanding Defenses, Richmond, Va.:

GENERAL: I inclose you the only telegram that has been sent me to-day. I sent you one to General Wise last evening. I think it would be well to keep some force near these creeks, so that when the Yankees enter they will meet with a sufficient force to capture them, or at least to break up their plundering. I think from there being one vessel and 150 men, it is for the purpose of firing the crops and getting in the negroes.

It would be well if we could put a stop to the boats entering our rivers, &c., for they come to destroy all the crops and break up the farmers.

I am, very respectfully, your obedient servant,

. S. S. LEE,
Commandant.

[Inclosure.]

AUGUST 25, 1863—11.05 a. m.

Captain LEE:

The gunboat is in Chickahominy River. She lay at Lambert's Wharf last night. Has bales of hay aboard for protection. About 150 troops on board. No gunboat above Hog Island.

HARKEY,
Lieutenant.

11.10 a. m.

The fleet off Newport News consists of three schooners and one brig. One gunboat off Hagan's Creek.

·WOODLEY,
Lieutenant.

SALT SULPHUR SPRINGS, *August 25, 1863.*

Major CLAIBORNE, *Commanding Dunn's Battalion:*

MAJOR: The major-general commanding directs that you hold yourself in readiness to move at a moment's notice.

Very respectfully, your obedient servant,

WM. B. MYERS,
Assistant Adjutant-General.

P. S.—The general also directs that you send four men, well mounted, to report to him at Union for temporary duty as couriers.

LYNCHBURG,
August 26, 1863.

General S. COOPER:

Enemy, reported from 4,000 to 6,000 strong, are advancing on New River Bridge. I am so advised by Major-General Jones.

FRANCIS T. NICHOLLS,
Brigadier-General, Commanding Post.

LYNCHBURG,
August 26, 1863.

General S. COOPER,
Adjutant and Inspector General:

Pursuant to orders, all my available force was sent this evening to New River Bridge. Should General Jones be mistaken and the enemy strike for Bonsack's or Salem, as is my own impression, every thing east of those points would be utterly without defense. I would wish to have troops indicated upon whom I could call for assistance, if necessary. If transportation were ready and the troops in readiness, I could get them down in time from Gordonsville.

I received a dispatch from Mr. Anderson, chairman of committee of safety of Botetourt County, saying the enemy are reported to be in Covington this morning.

FRANCIS T. NICHOLLS,
Brigadier-General, Commanding Post.

HEADQUARTERS DEPARTMENT OF WESTERN VIRGINIA,
Dublin, August 26, 1863.

Col. G. C. WHARTON:

Telegram received. Proceed to Warm Springs at once, via Staunton, and there await orders. Let me know when you reach Warm Springs. Enemy pressing Jackson near Warm Springs. Strength, between 5,000 and 6,000 mounted infantry.

By order, &c.:

GILES B. COOKE,
Assistant Adjutant and Inspector General.

HEADQUARTERS DEPARTMENT OF NORTH CAROLINA,
Wilmington, N. C., August 26, 1863.

General MARTIN,
Kinston:

MY DEAR GENERAL: I have your two notes by the hand of Colonel Moore, and first I must say that I am quite ignorant of the arrangements for defense about Kinston. It is, however, so important at least that the enemy should not have it, that in my opinion we must hold on as long as we can. If the deserter and Whitford news is correct, Peck has not the force to drive you from the position, especially if Ransom assists you. It seems to me that to give up Kinston would be to give up Goldsborough and all our picket line now so important in giving information.

I directed, for your immediate needs, one of Ransom's regiments to Goldsborough. I learn to-day that it has arrived there. It had better probably remain there for a while. The pressing calls I have made on the President, and the representations I have made of the dangerous condition of this department will, I think, meet with a response, and I shall have some more force. I want to come to Kinston very much, but just now, in view of the state of affairs at Charleston, and my being my own engineer, hurrying up important work, makes me loth to leave at this juncture. If a large force is gathered at Kinston I shall come on; but the probability is that at no distant time both friends and enemies will be gathered round this place, now become the most important point in the Confederacy. It will require an army to attack it and one to defend it.

As to the gunboat, I care very little. I never expect it to be finished, or if finished to do anything. So far the gunboats have caused more trouble, interfered more with government business and transportation, been bound up more and accomplished less than any other part of the service. Here I do not permit them to interfere any longer. They must give place to more useful business.

I am glad to learn that Peck has no greater force. Neither he nor Potter are much.

I consider Kenansville a very important point. You may add the remaining section to the one now there. I wish that they would push Claiborne's case and get rid of him.

Very truly, yours,

W. H. C. WHITING,
Major-General.

EXECUTIVE DEPARTMENT, NORTH CAROLINA,
Raleigh, August 26, 1863.

Hon. JAMES A. SEDDON,
Secretary of War, Richmond, Va.:

DEAR SIR: The vast numbers of deserters in the western counties of this State have so accumulated lately as to set the local militia at defiance and exert a very injurious effect upon the community in many respects. My home guards are poorly armed, inefficient, and rendered timid by fear of secret vengeance from the deserters. If General Lee would send one of our diminished brigades or a good strong regiment to North Carolina, with orders to report to me, I could make it increase his ranks far more than the temporary loss of his brigade, in a very short time. Something of this kind must be done.

Very respectfully,

Z. B. VANCE.

[Indorsements.]

Referred to General Lee by Secretary of War, August 29, 1863.

HEADQUARTERS,
September 8, 1863.

General Hoke, with two regiments and a squadron of cavalry, has been sent to Governor Vance.

R. E. LEE,
General,

BOTTOM'S BRIDGE, *August* 27, 1863.

Major-General ELZEY, *Richmond, Va.:*

A courier has just arrived with intelligence that the enemy is coming up in force, both infantry and cavalry. The advance guard was at Barhamsville this morning. Six flags seen in the infantry.

J. G. McKISSICK,
Captain, Commanding Cavalry, Holcombe Legion.

Mr. Kendrick will send the above dispatch to General Elzey forthwith, and oblige, very respectfully,

J. G. McKISSICK,
Captain, Commanding, &c.

WHITE SULPHUR SPRINGS, *August* 27, 1863.

Brigadier-General IMBODEN, *Commanding, &c.:*

We fought the enemy near here all yesterday and to-day again. About midday they retreated toward Warm Springs. They suffered severely here, and are much exhausted, both men and horses, and I believe they are short of ammunition. I have ordered Wharton's and Jackson's brigades to hurry to Warm Springs and attack them. Look out for them and damage them as much as possible.

SAM. JONES,
Major-General.

WHITE SULPHUR SPRINGS,
August 27, 1863.

Commanding Officer Jenkins' Brigade:

Press forward as rapidly as possible to Warm Springs, and attack the enemy. He was whipped and punished severely here yesterday, and to-day retreated toward Warm Springs about midday, men and horses much exhausted; cavalry and infantry pursuing them. Colonels Wharton and Jackson are ordered to Warm Springs on same duty I now order you.

SAM. JONES,
Major-General.

WHITE SULPHUR SPRINGS,
August 27, 1863.

Col. W. L. JACKSON, *Commanding, &c.:*

Fought the enemy near here all day yesterday, and again to-day, until about midday, when he abandoned his position, and retreated toward Warm Springs, pursued by cavalry and artillery. They have about 3,000 men and six field pieces, under General Averell. They left one regiment at Warm Springs. I hope you and Jenkins' brigade will intercept the retreating enemy at Warm Springs, and follow and cut them up. They suffered severely here. One of their surgeons, whom we have, estimates their loss at 500. We have taken about 150 prisoners. They are much exhausted, both men and horses, and I believe they are short of ammunition. Push them to the utmost, and help destroy them, if possible.

SAM. JONES,
Major-General.

WHITE SULPHUR SPRINGS, *August* 27, 1863.

Col. G. C. WHARTON,
Commanding, &c.:

We fought the enemy near here all yesterday and again to-day. About midday he abandoned his position, and retreated toward Warm Springs, followed by cavalry and artillery. He suffered severely. A surgeon estimates their loss at 500. They are much exhausted, both men and horses, and I believe they are short of ammunition. They were about 3,000 strong, and had six pieces of artillery, General Averell commanding. They left a regiment at Warm Springs, and may attempt to make a stand there. Push forward as rapidly as possible, and do your utmost to cut them up. I have telegraphed to Colonel Jackson and the commanding officer of Jenkins' brigade. You will be the senior officer until I get up, and will, of course, command.

SAM. JONES,
Major-General.

CALLAGHAN'S, *August* 28, 1863.

Brig. Gen. A. E. JACKSON:

Our troops are all occupied; fought the enemy on the 26th. It is impossible at present to send you any re-enforcements. General Williams has been telegraphed at Saltville to be on the alert.

By command Maj. Gen. Sam. Jones:

WM. B. MYERS,
Assistant Adjutant-General.

PETERSBURG, *August* 28, 1863.

Major-General ELZEY:.

Your dispatch received. I send four regiments without delay. Will this be sufficient? Two regiments will leave the depot at 7 o'clock, the other two as soon as transportation can be furnished. Shall I send for any portion of Ransom's brigade? I expect to come over, unless you think differently.

M. JENKINS,
Brigadier-General.

HEADQUARTERS, WILMINGTON,
August 28, 1863.

Hon. JAMES A. SEDDON,
Secretary of War, Richmond:

SIR: While the foreign business of the Government at this place is daily increasing and its importance to the country growing in still greater ratio, the enemy are enlarging their force and redoubling their efforts to stop the trade, to break off our communications, and to attack the last port which remains to us. In the meantime, I am powerless for want of troops. I hope you will pardon me for my running to this subject, but it is one of so great importance that I can leave no effort unmade either to illustrate the state of affairs or to ask for relief.

The necessity here for a very strong movable force, the stronger the better, is daily more apparent, and it should be of all arms. It is hard to say which I need most, infantry, artillery, or cavalry, all are so necessary and so important. Two batteries of 10-pounder Parrott guns, so long since applied for, might have saved the Hebe with her large and valuable cargo of government stores. I have lost my little Whitworth, which has so often driven off the enemy and saved our steamers, in an unequal contest with a frigate and six steamers. But it is not to save steamers that I want force. It is to make this vital point secure, to leave nothing to chance or good fortune, or the supineness or the imbecility of the enemy, secure against sudden attack; above all, independent of the raids which every day threaten our line of communication, and may result in leaving this place defenseless and not to be relieved at the most critical time. It must be recollected that, almost entirely without cavalry, with, besides this district, the whole department to look after, stripped almost of troops, it may be in the enemy's power to establish himself in force immediately on the railroad. Even now such a design is being prepared by Peck, who has succeeded to the command in New Berne.

In this district, of such paramount importance, I have but one regiment of infantry and three small companies of cavalry. It is out of my power to place more here. Really it seems to me like tempting Providence. Please try to send me troops.

Very respectfully,

W. H. C. WHITING,
Major-General.

[Indorsement.]

SEPTEMBER 1, 1863.

Respectfully submitted to the President.

Another urgent appeal from General Whiting for re-enforcements, which I am at a loss to provide.

J. A. SEDDON.

WARM SPRINGS,
August 30, 1863.

General R. E. LEE,
Commanding, &c., Orange Court-House:

The enemy that fought us on the 26th and 27th retreated very rapidly by Huntersville, and passed Greenbrier Bridge at Marling's Bottom early yesterday morning. My cavalry pursued them to that point, and a small force still following them. A part of Colonel Wharton's brigade arrived here yesterday. Jenkins' cavalry was about 3 miles west of Staunton last evening, coming on to this place. From what I hear of Imboden, he was probably at Monterey last night, with the intention of moving on to Huntersville. I fear he cannot reach there in time to intercept the retreating enemy. They have been severely punished, and when they reach Beverly will not, I think, be fit for service for several weeks. A captain of artillery whom I have prisoner says they started from Moorefield with between 4,000 and 5,000, General Averell commanding. Is that the force referred to by you in your dispatch of the 26th instant ?

SAM. JONES,
Major-General.

(Similar dispatch, same date, to Adjutant and Inspector General.)

WARM SPRINGS,
August 30, 1863.

Colonel FERGUSON,
    Commanding Jenkins' Cavalry:

COLONEL: The major-general commanding directs that you proceed to this place and thence to Pocahontas County and establish your command at or near Marling's Bottom, wherever in that immediate vicinity you can find forage for your horses.

In case you have turned on to the Staunton and Parkersburg turnpike in the direction of Monterey, you will continue to that place; otherwise you will proceed according to the instructions contained above.

In either event, the major-general commanding directs that your command be established near Marling's Bottom until further orders, as soon as your present movement is completed.

Very respectfully, your obedient servant,
WM. B. MYERS,
Assistant Adjutant-General.

WARM SPRINGS,
August 30, 1863.

Colonel FERGUSON,
    Commanding, &c.:

COLONEL: The major-general commanding directs that instead of coming to this place, as instructed in the dispatch sent you this morning, that you proceed by the shortest route to McDowell and occupy the country in that vicinity, scouting the road as far as Hightown. If pressed by the enemy, you will fall back to Shenandoah Mountain, and hold that pass as long as possible.

The general is not only desirous of guarding the approaches from that direction, but it being a good grass country, he wishes your horses recuperated, and that you get them in efficient condition with the least possible delay. You will also scout the Franklin road. Draw your supplies from the nearest depot, and send up reports and communications for headquarters to the general commanding at Dublin depot, via Staunton.

Very respectfully, your obedient servant,
WM. B. MYERS,
Assistant Adjutant-General.

HEADQUARTERS DEPARTMENT OF WESTERN VIRGINIA,
Dublin, August 30, 1863.

Brigadier-General WILLIAMS,
    Saltville:

General A. E. Jackson, at Jonesborough, telegraphs for re-enforcements, and says:

The enemy, in large force, are advancing on Knoxville. On their return, I apprehend they will come this way.

In view of the above, the major-general commanding directs that you will be on the alert.

GILES B. COOKE,
Assistant Adjutant and Inspector General.

RICHMOND,
August 31, 1863.

General SAMUEL JONES,
 Union Springs, Va.:

I hear, yet unofficially, that the enemy are advancing on and probably have taken Knoxville. Can you not aid to defend Southwestern Virginia and East Tennessee bordering thereon ?
J. A. SEDDON,
Secretary of War.

Abstract from return of the Army of Northern Virginia, General Robert E. Lee, C. S. Army, commanding, for the month of August, 1863; headquarters Orange Court-House.

Command.	Present for duty.		Effective total present.	Aggregate present.	Aggregate present and absent.	Pieces of artillery.
	Officers.	Men.				
General headquarters.............................	15	....	....	15	15	.....
First Army Corps (Longstreet):						
Staff..	11	....	5,277	11	11	......
McLaws' division..............................	530	5,277	5,277	6,789	12,107	......
Pickett's division.............................	356	4,009	4,009	5,316	11,344	......
Hood's division	527	5,382	5,382	7,041	11,700	......
Total.................................	1,424	14,668	14,068	19,157	35,162	....
Second Army Corps (Ewell):						
Staff..	18	....	....	18	21	......
Rodes' division...............................	485	5,640	5,640	7,401	14,984	..:....
Early's division...............................	488	5,279	5,279	6,802	12,757	......
Johnson's division	460	4,509	4,509	5,746	12,056	......
Total.................................	1,451	15,428	15,428	19,967	39,818	......
Third Army Corps (A. P. Hill):						
Staff...	15	....	....	15	17	......
Anderson's division...........................	470	5,499	5,499	6,937	12,775	......
Heth's division...............................	264	3,686	3,685	4,646	8,307	......
Wilcox's division	396	4,416	4,416	5,736	11,234	......
Total.................................	1,145	13,601	13,600	17,334	32,333	......
Cavalry (Stuart):						
Headquarters.................................	11	....	....	11	16	......
Hampton's brigade	1 9	1,332	1,332	1,725	3,878	......
Fitz. Lee's brigade	152	2,295	2,295	2,730	4,814	......
W. H. F. Lee's brigade.........................	99	1,305	1,305	1,773	3,631	......
Jones' brigade	110	1,754	1,754	2,103	3,288	......
Robertson's brigade	44	623	623	787	1,486	......
Beckham's artillery battalion	18	392	392	451	568	14
Total.................................	573	7,701	*a*7,701	9,580	17,681	14
Artillery (Pendleton):						
First Army Corps.............................	99	1,807	1,807	2,099	2,889	87
Second Army Corps............................	86	1,470	1,470	1,782	2,569	79
Third Army Corps.............................	82	1,652	1,652	2,020	2,787	66
Total.................................	267	4,929	4,929	5,901	8,245	232
Grand total	4,875	56,327	56,326	71,954	133,254	246

a Of the 7,701 men reported as "Effective total," cavalry division, 1,333 are dismounted.

Organization of the Army of Northern Virginia, General R. E. Lee, C. S. Army, commanding, August 31, 1863.

FIRST ARMY CORPS.

Lieut. Gen. JAMES LONGSTREET.

M'LAWS' DIVISION.

Maj. Gen. L. McLAWS.

Kershaw's Brigade.

Col. JOHN W. HENAGAN.

2d South Carolina, Col. John D. Kennedy.
3d South Carolina, Col. James D. Nance.
7th South Carolina, Col. D. Wyatt Aiken.
8th South Carolina, Col. John W. Henagan.
15th South Carolina, Lieut. Col. Joseph F. Gist.
3d South Carolina Battalion, Lieut. Col. W. G. Rice.

Wofford's Brigade.

Brig. Gen. W. T. WOFFORD.

16th Georgia, Col. Goode Bryan.
18th Georgia, Lieut. Col. S. Z. Ruff.
24th Georgia, Col. Robert McMillan.
Cobb's (Georgia) Legion, Lieut. Col. Luther J. Glenn.
Phillips (Georgia) Legion, Lieut. Col. E. S. Barclay.
3d Georgia Battalion Sharpshooters, Maj. P. E. Davant.

*Humphreys' Brigade.**

Brig. Gen. B. G. HUMPHREYS.

13th Mississippi, Col. John W. Carter.
17th Mississippi, Col. W. D. Holder.
18th Mississippi, Col. Thomas M. Griffin.
22st Mississippi, Lieut. Col. W. L. Brandon.

Semmes' (late) Brigade.

Col. GOODE BRYAN.

10th Georgia, Col. John B. Weems.
50th Georgia, Col. W. R. Manning.
51st Georgia, Col. E. Ball.
53d Georgia, Col. James P. Simms.

PICKETT'S DIVISION.

Maj. Gen. GEORGE E. PICKETT.

Corse's Brigade.

Brig. Gen. M. D. CORSE.

15th Virginia, Col. T. P. August.
17th Virginia, Col. Morton Marye.
29th Virginia, Col. James Giles.
30th Virginia, Col. A. T. Harrison.

Hunton's Brigade. †

Brig. Gen. EPPA HUNTON.

8th Virginia, Lieut. Col. N. Berkeley.
18th Virginia, Col. R. E. Withers.
19th Virginia, Col. Henry Gantt.
28th Virginia, Col. William Watts.
56th Virginia, Lieut. Col. P. P. Slaughter.

Armistead's Brigade.

Col. W. R. AYLETT.

9th Virginia, Col. J. J. Phillips.
14th Virginia, Col. William White.
38th Virginia, Col. E. C. Edmonds.
53d Virginia, Col. W. R. Aylett.
57th Virginia, Col. C. R. Fontaine.

Kemper's Brigade.

Col. JOSEPH MAYO, jr.

1st Virginia, Col. Frederick G. Skinner.
3d Virginia, Col. Joseph Mayo, jr.
7th Virginia, Lieut. Col. C. C. Flowerree.
11th Virginia, Col. David Funsten.
24th Virginia, Col. William R. Terry.

*Assigned, August 17, by General Lee.
†Assigned, August 15, by General Lee.

HOOD'S DIVISION.

Brig. Gen. E. M. LAW.

Law's Brigade.

Col. JAMES L. SHEFFIELD.

4th Alabama, Col. P. D. Bowles.
15th Alabama, Maj. A. A. Lowther.
44th Alabama, Col. William F. Perry.
47th Alabama, Lieut. Col. M. J. Bulger.
48th Alabama, Col. James L. Sheffield.

Anderson's Brigade.

Col. W. W. WHITE.

7th Georgia, Col. W. W. White.
8th Georgia, Col. John R. Towers.
9th Georgia, Col. Benjamin Beck.
11th Georgia, Col. F. H. Little.
59th Georgia, Col. Jack Brown.

Robertson's Brigade.

Brig. Gen. J. B. ROBERTSON.

3d Arkansas, Col. Van H. Manning.
1st Texas, Lieut. Col. P. A. Work.
4th Texas, Col. J. C. G. Key.
5th Texas, Col. R. M. Powell.

Benning's Brigade.

Brig. Gen. H. L. BENNING.

2d Georgia, Col. Edgar M. Butt.
15th Georgia, Col. D. M. Du Bose.
17th Georgia, Col. Wesley C. Hodges.
20th Georgia, Col. J. D. Waddell.

SECOND ARMY CORPS.

Lieut. Gen. R. S. EWELL.

RODES' DIVISION.

Maj. Gen. R. E. RODES.

Daniel's Brigade.

Brig. Gen. JUNIUS DANIEL.

32d North Carolina, Col. E. C. Brabble.
43d North Carolina, Col. Thomas S. Kenan.
45th North Carolina, Lieut. Col. Samuel H. Boyd.
53d North Carolina, Col. W. A. Owens.
2d North Carolina Battalion, Maj. John M. Hancock.

Ramseur's Brigade.

Brig. Gen. S. D. RAMSEUR.

2d North Carolina, Col. W. R. Cox.
4th North Carolina, Col. Bryan Grimes.
14th North Carolina, Col. R. Tyler Bennett.
30th North Carolina, Col. Francis M. Parker.

Doles' Brigade.

Brig. Gen. GEORGE DOLES.

4th Georgia, Col. Philip Cook.
12th Georgia, Col. Edward Willis.
21st Georgia, Col. John T. Mercer.
44th Georgia, Col. Samuel P. Lumpkin.

Battle's Brigade.

Brig. Gen. C. A. BATTLE.

3d Alabama, Lieut. Col. Charles Forsyth.
5th Alabama, Col. J. M. Hall.
6th Alabama, Col. James N. Lightfoot.
12th Alabama, Col. Samuel B. Pickens.
26th Alabama, Col. E. A. O'Neal.

Iverson's (late) Brigade.

5th North Carolina, Col. Thomas M. Garrett.
12th North Carolina, Col. Henry Eaton Coleman.
20th North Carolina, Col. Thomas F. Toon.
23d North Carolina, Lieut. Col. Robert D. Johnston.

EARLY'S DIVISION.

Maj. Gen. JUBAL A. EARLY.

Hays' Brigade.

Brig. Gen. HARRY T. HAYS.

5th Louisiana, Col. Henry Forno.
6th Louisiana, Col. W. Monaghan.
7th Louisiana, Col. David B. Penn.
8th Louisiana, Lieut. Col. Alcibiades De Blanc.
9th Louisiana, Col. Leroy A. Stafford.

Hoke's Brigade.

Brig. Gen. R. F. HOKE.

6th North Carolina, Col. Robert F. Webb.
21st North Carolina, Col. W. W. Kirkland.
54th North Carolina, Col. Kenneth M. Murchison.
57th North Carolina, Col. Archibald C. Godwin.
1st North Carolina Battalion Sharpshooters, Maj. R. W. Wharton.

Gordon's Brigade.

Brig. Gen. J. B. GORDON.

13th Georgia, Col. James M. Smith.
26th Georgia, Col. E. N. Atkinson.
31st Georgia, Col. Clement A. Evans.
38th Georgia, Col. J. D. Mathews.
60th Georgia, Col. W. H. Stiles.
61st Georgia, Col. John H. Lamar.

Smith's (late) Brigade.

Col. JOHN S. HOFFMAN.

13th Virginia, Lieut. Col. James B. Terrill.
31st Virginia, Col. John S. Hoffman.
49th Virginia, Lieut. Col. J. Catlett Gibson.
52d Virginia, Lieut. Col. James H. Skinner.
58th Virginia, Col. F. H. Board.

JOHNSON'S DIVISION.*

Maj. Gen. EDWARD JOHNSON.

"Stonewall" Brigade.

Brig. Gen. JAMES A. WALKER.

2d Virginia, Col. J. Q. A. Nadenbousch.
4th Virginia, Col. Charles A. Ronald.
5th Virginia, Col. J. H. S. Funk.
27th Virginia, Col. James K. Edmondson.
33d Virginia, Col. F. W. M. Holliday.

Steuart's Brigade.

Brig. Gen. G. H. STEUART.

1st Maryland Battalion, Lieut. Col. J. R. Herbert.
1st North Carolina, Col. John A. McDowell.
3d North Carolina, Col. William L. De Rosset.
10th Virginia, Col. E. T. H. Warren.
23d Virginia, Col. A. G. Taliaferro.
37th Virginia, Col. T. V. Williams.

Jones' Brigade.

Brig. Gen. J. M. JONES.

21st Virginia, Col. W. A. Witcher.
25th Virginia, Col. John C. Higginbotham.
42d Virginia, Lieut. Col. R. W. Withers.
44th Virginia, Col. Norvell Cobb.
48th Virginia, Lieut. Col. R. H. Dungan.
50th Virginia, Col. A. S. Vandeventer.

Iverson's Brigade.

Brig. Gen. ALFRED IVERSON.

1st Louisiana, Col. W. R. Shivers.
2d Louisiana, Col. J. M. Williams.
10th Louisiana, Col. Eugene Waggaman.
14th Louisiana, Col. Z. York.
15th Louisiana, Col. Edmund Pendleton.

*On face of the returns, only three brigadier-generals are reported present for duty.

THIRD ARMY CORPS.

Lieut. Gen. A. P. HILL.

ANDERSON'S DIVISION.*

Maj. Gen. R. H. ANDERSON.

Wilcox's (late) Brigade.

Col. J. C. C. SANDERS.

8th Alabama, Col. Y. L. Royston.
9th Alabama, Col. J. H. King.
10th Alabama, Col. W. H. Forney.
11th Alabama, Col. J. C. C. Sanders.
14th Alabama, Col. L. Pinckard.

Wright's Brigade.

Brig. Gen. A. R. WRIGHT.

3d Georgia, Col. Edward J. Walker.
22d Georgia, Col. Joseph Wasden.
48th Georgia, Col. William Gibson.
2d Georgia Battalion, Maj. George W. Ross.

Mahone's Brigade.

Brig. Gen. WILLIAM MAHONE.

6th Virginia, Col. George T. Rogers.
12th Virginia, Col. D. A. Weisiger.
16th Virginia, Col. Joseph H. Ham.
41st Virginia, Col. William A. Parham.
61st Virginia, Col. V. D. Groner.

Perry's Brigade.

Brig. Gen. E. A. PERRY.

2d Florida, Lieut. Col. L. G. Pyles.
5th Florida, Lieut. Col. T. B. Lamar.
8th Florida, Col. David Lang.

Posey's Brigade.

Brig. Gen. C. POSEY.

12th Mississippi, Col. W. H. Taylor.
16th Mississippi, Col. Samuel E. Baker.
19th Mississippi, Col. N. H. Harris.
48th Mississippi, Col. Joseph M. Jayne.

HETH'S DIVISION.

Maj. Gen. HENRY HETH.

Pettigrew's (late) Brigade.

Col. T. C. SINGELTARY.

11th North Carolina, Col. Collett Leventhorpe.
26th North Carolina, Lieut. Col. John R. Lane.
44th North Carolina, Col. Thomas C. Singeltary.
47th North Carolina, Col. George H. Faribault.
52d North Carolina, Col. J. K. Marshall.

Walker's Brigade.

Brig. Gen. H. H. WALKER.

40th Virginia, Col. J. M. Brockenbrough.
47th Virginia, Col. R. M. Mayo.
55th Virginia, Col. W. S. Christian.
22d Virginia Battalion, Lieut. Col. E. P. Tayloe.

Archer's Brigade.

Brig. Gen. H. H. WALKER.

5th Alabama Battalion, Maj. A. S. Van de Graaff.†
13th Alabama, Col. B. D. Fry.
1st Tennessee (Provisional Army), Col. Peter Turney.
7th Tennessee, Col. John A. Fite.
14th Tennessee, Col. William McComb.

Davis' Brigade.

Brig. Gen. J. R. DAVIS.

2d Mississippi, Col. J. M. Stone.
11th Mississippi, Col. F. M. Green.
42d Mississippi, Lieut. Col. Hillery Moseley.
55th North Carolina, Col. John K. Connally.

---

*Only two of the brigadier-generals reported present for duty.
†Detached.

WILCOX'S DIVISION.*

Maj. Gen. C. M. WILCOX.

Lane's Brigade.

Brig. Gen. J. H. LANE.

7th North Carolina, Col. Edward G. Haywood.
18th North Carolina, Col. John D. Barry.
28th North Carolina, Col. Samuel D. Lowe.
33d North Carolina, Col. Clark M. Avery.
37th North Carolina, Col. William M. Barbour.

Thomas' Brigade.

Brig. Gen. E. L. THOMAS.

14th Georgia, Col. Robert W. Folsom.
35th Georgia, Col. Bolling H. Holt.
45th Georgia, Col. Thomas J. Simmons.
49th Georgia, Col. S. T. Player.

McGowan's Brigade.

Brig. Gen. S. McGOWAN.

1st South Carolina (Provisional Army), Col. D. H. Hamilton.
1st (Orr's) South Carolina Rifles, Col. F. E. Harrison.
12th South Carolina, Col. John L. Miller.
13th South Carolina, Col. B. T. Brockman.
14th South Carolina, Col. Abner Perrin.

Scales' Brigade.

Brig. Gen. A. M. SCALES.

13th North Carolina, Col. Joseph H. Hyman.
16th North Carolina, Col. John S. McElroy.
22d North Carolina, Lieut. Col. W. L. Mitchell.
34th North Carolina, Col. W. L. J. Lowrance.
38th North Carolina, Col. William J. Hoke.

CAVALRY CORPS.†

Maj. Gen. J. E. B. STUART.

Hampton's Brigade.

Brig. Gen. WADE HAMPTON.

Cobb's (Georgia) Cavalry, Col. P. M. B. Young.
Phillips (Georgia) Cavalry, Lieut. Col. W. W. Rich.
Jeff. Davis (Mississippi) Legion, Lieut. Col. J. F. Waring.
1st North Carolina Cavalry, Col. J. B. Gordon.
1st South Carolina Cavalry, Col. John L. Black.
2d South Carolina Cavalry, Col. M. C. Butler.

Robertson's (late) Brigade.

Col. D. D. FEREBEE.

4th North Carolina Cavalry (59th North Carolina Troops), Col. D. D. Ferebee.
5th North Carolina Cavalry (63d North Carolina Troops), Lieut. Col. S. B. Evans.

W. H. F. Lee's Brigade.

Col. JOHN R. CHAMBLISS, jr.

2d North Carolina Cavalry, Col. W. G. Robinson.
9th Virginia Cavalry, Col. R. L. T. Beale.
10th Virginia Cavalry, Col. J. Lucius Davis.
13th Virginia Cavalry, Col. John R. Chambliss, jr.
15th Virginia Cavalry, Col. William B. Ball.

Fitzhugh Lee's Brigade.

Brig. Gen. FITZHUGH LEE.

1st Battalion Maryland Cavalry, Lieut. Col. R. Brown.
1st Virginia Cavalry, Col. R. W. Carter.
2d Virginia Cavalry, Col. Thomas T. Munford.
3d Virginia Cavalry, Col. Thomas H. Owen.
4th Virginia Cavalry, Col. Williams C. Wickham.
5th Virginia Cavalry, Col. Thomas L. Rosser.

---

* Only three of the brigadier-generals reported present for duty. Major-General Wilcox assigned by General Lee, August 15.
† Only two brigadier-generals (Fitzhugh Lee and Jones) reported present for duty.

Jones' Brigade.

Brig. Gen. W. E. JONES.

6th Virginia Cavalry, Lieut. Col. John Shac Green.
7th Virginia Cavalry, Col. R. H. Dulany.
11th Virginia Cavalry, Lieut. Col. O. R. Funsten.
12th Virginia Cavalry, Col. A. W. Harman.
35th Battalion Virginia Cavalry, Lieut. Col. E. V. White.

Horse Artillery.

Maj. R. F. BECKHAM.

Breathed's (Virginia) Battery, Capt. James Breathed.
Chew's (Virginia) Battery, Capt. R. P. Chew.
McGregor's (Virginia) Battery, Capt. W. M. McGregor.
Moorman's (Virginia) Battery, Capt. M. N. Moorman.

ARTILLERY.

Brig. Gen. WILLIAM N. PENDLETON.

FIRST ARMY CORPS.

Col. J. B. WALTON.

Cabell's Battalion.	*Dearing's Battalion.*
Col. H. C. CABELL.	Lieut. Col. JAMES DEARING.
Manly's (North Carolina) Battery, Capt. B. C. Manly.	Blount's (Virginia) Battery, Capt. J. G. Blount.
Pulaski (Georgia) Artillery, Capt. J. C. Fraser.	Fauquier (Virginia) Artillery, Capt. R. M. Stribling.
1st Richmond (Virginia) Howitzers, Capt. E. S. McCarthy.	Hampden (Virginia) Artillery, Capt. W. H. Caskie.
Troup (Georgia) Artillery, Capt. H. H. Carlton.	Richmond Fayette (Virginia) Artillery, Capt. M. C. Macon.
Henry's Battalion.	*Alexander's Battalion.*
Maj. M. W. HENRY.	Col. E. P. ALEXANDER.
Branch (North Carolina) Artillery, Capt. A. C. Latham.	Bedford (Virginia) Artillery, Capt. Tyler C. Jordan.
German (South Carolina) Artillery, Capt. W. K. Bachman.	Brooks (South Carolina) Artillery, Capt. W. W. Fickling.
Palmetto (South Carolina) Light Artillery, Capt. Hugh R. Garden.	Madison (Louisiana) Light Artillery, Capt. G. V. Moody.
Rowan (North Carolina) Artillery, Capt. James Reilly.	Parker's (Virginia) Battery, Capt. William W. Parker.
	Taylor's (Virginia) Battery, Capt. Osmond B. Taylor.
	Woolfolk (Virginia) Battery, Capt. Pichegru Woolfolk, jr.

Washington (Louisiana) Artillery.

Maj. B. F. ESHLEMAN.

1st Company, Capt. C. W. Squires.
2d Company, Capt. J. B. Richardson.
3d Company, Capt. M. B. Miller.
4th Company, Capt. J. Norcom.

SECOND ARMY CORPS.

Col. S. CRUTCHFIELD.

Andrews' Battalion.

Lieut. Col. R. S. ANDREWS.

Alleghany (Virginia) Artillery, Capt. J. C. Carpenter.
Chesapeake (Maryland) Artillery, Lieut. John E. Plater.
Lee (Virginia) Battery, Capt. Charles I. Raine.
1st Maryland Battery, Capt. W. F. Dement.

Carter's Battalion.

Lieut. Col. T. H. CARTER.

Jeff. Davis (Alabama) Artillery, Capt. William J. Reese.
King William (Virginia) Artillery, Capt. W. P. Carter.
Morris (Virginia) Artillery, Capt. R. C. M. Page.
Orange (Virginia) Artillery, Capt. C. W. Fry.

Jones' Battalion.

Lieut. Col. H. P. JONES.

Charlottesville (Virginia) Artillery, Capt. James McD. Carrington.
Courtney (Virginia) Artillery, Capt. William A. Tanner.
Louisiana Guard Artillery, Capt. C. A. Green.
Staunton (Virginia) Artillery, Capt. A. W. Garber.

Brown's Battalion.

Col. J. T. BROWN.

Powhatan (Virginia) Artillery, Capt. W. J. Dance.
Rockbridge (Virginia) Artillery, Capt. A. Graham.
Salem (Virginia) Artillery, Capt. A. Hupp.
2d Richmond (Virginia) Howitzers, Capt. David Watson.
3d Richmond (Virginia) Howitzers, Capt. Benjamin H. Smith, jr.

Nelson's Battalion.

Lieut. Col. WILLIAM NELSON.

Amherst (Virginia) Artillery, Capt. Thomas J. Kirkpatrick.
Fluvanna (Virginia) Artillery, Capt. John L. Massie.
Milledge (Georgia) Artillery, Capt. John Milledge, jr.

THIRD ARMY CORPS.

Col. R. L. WALKER.

Poague's Battalion.

Maj. W. T. POAGUE.

Brooke's (Virginia) Battery, Capt. James V. Brooke.
Graham's (North Carolina) Battery, Capt. Joseph Graham.
Madison (Mississippi) Light Artillery, Capt. George Ward.
Wyatt's (Virginia) Battery, Capt. J. W. Wyatt.

McIntosh's Battalion.

Maj. D. G. McINTOSH.

Hardaway (Alabama) Battery, Capt. W. B. Hurt.
Johnson's (Virginia) Battery, Capt. Marmaduke Johnson.
Lusk's (Virginia) Battery, Capt. William K. Donald.
Rice's (Virginia) Battery, Capt. R. Sidney Rice.

Garnett's Battalion.

Lieut. Col. J. J. GARNETT.

Grandy's (Virginia) Battery, Capt. C. R. Grandy.
Lewis' (Virginia) Battery, Capt. John W. Lewis.
Donaldsonville (Louisiana) Artillery, Capt. V. Maurin.
Moore's (Virginia) Battery, Capt. J. D. Moore.

Pegram's Battalion.

Maj. W. J. PEGRAM.

Crenshaw's (Virginia) Battery, Lieut. A. B. Johnston.
Fredericksburg (Virginia) Artillery, Capt. E. A. Marye.
Letcher (Virginia) Artillery, Capt. T. A. Brander.
Pee Dee (South Carolina) Artillery, Capt. E. B. Brunson.
Purcell (Virginia) Artillery, Capt. Joseph McGraw.

Cutts' Georgia Battalion.

Lieut. Col. A. S. CUTTS.

Ross' (Georgia) Battery, Capt. H. M. Ross.
Patterson's (Georgia) Battery, Capt. George M. Patterson.
Irwin (Georgia) Artillery, Capt. John T. Wingfield.

Abstract from the return of the Department of Richmond, Maj. Gen. Arnold Elzey, C. S Army, commanding, August 31, 1863.

Command.	Present for duty.		Effective total present.	Aggregate present.	Aggregate present and absent.	Pieces of field artillery.
	Officers.	Men.				
General headquarters	11	......	......	11	11	......
Ransom's division	444	7,132	7,539	8,525	11,017	40
Wise's command a	165	2,533	2,689	3,256	4,456	10
Chaffin's Bluff	21	271	329	466	503	18
Drewry's Bluff	18	248	358	445	491	......
Richmond defenses	73	1,448	1,586	1,851	2,121	14
Total	732	11,632	12,501	14,554	19,199	82

a And the 40th Virginia Cavalry Battalion.

Troops in the Department of Richmond, Maj. Gen. Arnold Elzey, C. S. Army, commanding, August 31, 1863.

RANSOM'S DIVISION.[*]

Ransom's Brigade.

Brig. Gen. M. W. RANSOM.

24th North Carolina, Col. William J. Clarke.
25th North Carolina, Col. H. M. Rutledge.
35th North Carolina, Col. John G. Jones.
49th North Carolina, Col. Lee M. McAfee.
56th North Carolina, Col. Paul F. Faison.

Artillery Battalion.

Maj. FRANCIS J. BOGGS.

Martin's (Virginia) Battery.
Sturdivant's (Virginia) Battery.
Webb's (North Carolina) Battery.

Jenkins' Brigade.

Brig. Gen. M. JENKINS.

1st South Carolina (Volunteers), Col. F. W. Kilpatrick.
2d South Carolina Rifles, Col. Thomas Thomson.
5th South Carolina, Col. A. Coward,
6th South Carolina, Col. John Bratton.
Hampton's (South Carolina) Legion, Col. M. W. Gary.
Palmetto (South Carolina) Sharpshooters, Col. Joseph Walker.

Artillery Battalion.

Maj. JAMES R. BRANCH.

Bradford's (Mississippi) Battery.
Coit's (South Carolina) Battery.
Pegram's (Virginia) Battery.
Wright's (Virginia) Battery.

---

[*] Jenkins probably in command.

Artillery Battalion.

Maj. E F. MOSELEY.

Dabney's (Virginia) Battery.
Talley's (Virginia) Battery.
Young's (Virginia) Battery.

Unattached.

10th Georgia Battalion.
32d Virginia.
C. S. Zouaves (Louisiana Battalion.)
3d North Carolina Cavalry, Col. John A. Baker.
Moore's (North Carolina) Battery.
Slaten's (Georgia) Battery.

WISE'S COMMAND.

Brig. Gen. HENRY A. WISE.

Wise's Brigade.	*Cavalry.*
Brig. Gen. HENRY A. WISE.	Holcombe (South Carolina) Legion.
	10th Virginia, Company D.
4th Virginia Heavy Artillery, Col. J.	15th Virginia, Company C.
Thomas Goode.	32d Virginia Battalion.
26th Virginia, Col. P. R. Page.	40th Virginia Battalion, Lieut. Col. W.
46th Virginia. Col. R. T. W. Duke.	T. Robins.
59th Virginia, Col. William B. Tabb.	

Artillery Battalion.

Maj. A. W. STARK.

McComas (Virginia) Light Artillery, Capt. D. A. French.
Matthews (Virginia) Light Artillery, Capt. A. D. Armistead.

CHAFFIN'S BLUFF.

Lieut. Col. J. M. MAURY.

Gloucester (Virginia) Artillery, Capt. T. B. Montague.
King and Queen (Virginia) Artillery, Capt. A. F. Bagby.
Lunenburg (Virginia) Artillery, Capt. C. T. Allen.
Pamunkey (Virginia) Artillery, Capt. A. J. Jones.

DREWRY'S BLUFF.

Maj. F. W. SMITH.

Johnston (Virginia) Artillery, Capt. B. J. Epes.
Neblett (Virginia) Artillery. Capt. W. G. Coleman.
Southside (Virginia) Artillery, Capt. J. W. Drewry.
United (Virginia) Artillery, Capt. Thomas Kevill.

RICHMOND DEFENSES.

Col. T. S. RHETT.

First Division.	*Second Division.*
Lieut. Col. J. W. ATKINSON.	Lieut. Col. JAMES HOWARD.
10th Virginia Heavy Artillery Battalion,	18th Virginia Heavy Artillery Battalion,
Maj. James O. Hensley.	Maj. M. B. Hardin.
19th Virginia Heavy Artillery Battalion,	20th Virginia Heavy Artillery Battalion,
Maj. N. R. Cary.	Maj. James E. Robertson,

Light Artillery.

Lieut. Col. C. E. LIGHTFOOT.

Alexandria (Virginia) Light Artillery, Capt. D. L. Smoot.
Caroline (Virginia) Artillery, Capt. Thomas R. Thornton.
Nelson (Virginia) Artillery, Capt. J. Henry Rives.
Surry (Virginia) Artillery, Capt. J. De Witt Hankins.

Abstract from return of the Department of North Carolina, Maj. Gen. W. H. C. Whiting, C. S. Army, commanding, August 31, 1863.

Command.	Present for duty.		Effective total present.	Aggregate present.	Aggregate present and absent.	Pieces of artillery.	
	Officers.	Men.				Heavy.	Field.
General headquarters *a*	8	40	40	49	61		
District of the Cape Fear:							
General staff	10			10	11		
City and river defenses	34	752	835	1,053	1,431		22
Forts Anderson and Branch	20	291	386	458	504	21	
Fort Caswell	22	525	636	784	913	28	
Fort Fisher	25	518	688	817	1,074	47	
Kenansville	30	531	566	663	830		2
50th North Carolina *b*	34	582	595	728	823		
Total	175	3,199	3,706	4,513	5,586	96	24
District of North Carolina:							
General staff	5			5	5		
Goldsborough	22	253	276	321	391		
Kinston and vicinity	104	1,757	1,936	2,281	3,525		12
Salsbury prison guard	6	95	98	111	202		
Between the Roanoke and the Tar	53	1,158	1,215	1,461	1,878		
Detachments *b*	9	108	113	129	243		
Total	199	3,371	3,638	4,308	6,244		12
Grand total	382	6,610	7,384	8,870	11,801	96	36

a Including signal corps.
b Stations not reported in original.

Troops in the Department of North Carolina, Maj. Gen. W. H. C. Whiting, C. S. Army, commanding, August 31, 1863.

DISTRICT OF THE CAPE FEAR.

42d North Carolina* (two companies).
50th North Carolina, Col. J. A. Washington.
61st North Carolina* (three companies).
7th Confederate Cavalry* (three companies).
5th North Carolina Cavalry,* Company E.
5th South Carolina Cavalry* (two companies).
1st North Carolina Artillery, Company I (section).
1st North Carolina Heavy Artillery Battalion, Company A.
2d North Carolina Artillery, Col. William Lamb.

3d North Carolina Artillery, Maj. John J. Hedrick.
3d North Carolina Artillery Battalion, Maj. John W. Moore.
10th North Carolina Heavy Artillery Battalion.
13th North Carolina Artillery Battalion, Company D, Capt. Z. T. Adams.
Staunton Hill (Virginia) Artillery, Capt. A. B. Paris.
Forts Anderson and Branch, Maj. John J. Hedrick.
Fort Caswell, Col. T. M. Jones.
Fort Fisher, Col. William Lamb.
Wilmington, Maj. W. H. Gibbes.

---

*Mounted force, under command of Maj. George Jackson, at Kenansville.

DISTRICT OF NORTH CAROLINA.

62d Georgia (three companies).
8th North Carolina Infantry Battalion,
    Maj. John H. Nethercutt.
12th North Carolina Cavalry Battalion,
    Maj. Samuel J. Wheeler, jr.
13th North Carolina Infantry Battalion.
17th North Carolina, Col. William F.
    Martin.
42d North Carolina, Col. George C.
    Gibbs.
North Carolina Infantry Battalion, Maj.
    John N. Whitford.
Croom's (North Carolina) Company.
Foy's (North Carolina) Partisan Company.

7th Confederate Cavalry, Col. W. C.
    Claiborne.
1st North Carolina Artillery (three companies).
Saunders' Artillery Battalion,[*]
Cogdell's (North Carolina) Battery.
Ells' (Georgia) Battery (detachment).
Graham's (Virginia) Battery.
Starr's (North Carolina) Battery.
Southerland's (North Carolina) Battery (detachment).
Tillery's (North Carolina) Heavy Artillery Company

RICHMOND, VA., *September* 1, 1863.

Lieut. Gen. JAMES LONGSTREET,
    Commanding, Orange Court-House:

GENERAL : I inclose you herewith a letter from Lieutenant Peden, referred by the Governor of North Carolina to the honorable Secretary of War, relative to the organization of deserters in Wilkes County, in that State,[†] and the means by which it is proposed to remedy this formidable and growing evil. I desire to send on this mission a regiment of North Carolina troops from Brigadier-General Ransom's command, and a squadron of cavalry from the troops under Jenkins, and a regiment of North Carolina troops from the Army of Northern Virginia, the whole to be under the command of a good officer. I wish you therefore to select either Brigadier-General Hoke or Brigadier-General Ramseur as the officer to be intrusted with the general charge of the matter in question, and to send him with one of his regiments, by way of this place, to North Carolina, where he will be joined by the other troops above mentioned, and where he will receive more explicit instructions from Governor Vance, who has been requested to make the necessary arrangements for provisioning the troops, &c.

I wish a small regiment sent from the brigade of Hoke or Ramseur, as I think a good opportunity will be presented of filling its ranks to the legal standard, and I desire whichever of these officers General Ewell thinks the best and most suitable for the duty to be selected. Please send him at once, and caution him not to speak of the character of his duty, as it is desired it shall be kept quiet.

Very respectfully, your obedient servant,

R. E. LEE,
General.

RED SWEET SPRINGS,
September 1, 1863.

Col. W. L. JACKSON, *Commanding, &c.:*

COLONEL : The major-general commanding directs that you communicate with him at your earliest convenience, giving him full information of the movements of the enemy in your front.

---

[*] Consisting of Andrews' (Alabama), Cumming's (North Carolina), and Dickson's (North Carolina) Batteries, at Kinston.
[†] See Vance to Seddon, August 26,

He wishes you to do all in your power to collect together your command, which he learns has a large amount of stragglers from your old camp. as far as Millborough. Communicate with the general at Dublin Depot.

Very respectfully,

WM. B. MYERS,
Assistant Adjutant-General.

UNION,
September 1, 1863.

Col. JOHN MCCAUSLAND,
Commanding, &c.:

COLONEL: The major-general commanding desires you to advise yourself fully of the movements of the enemy in the Kanawha Valley; any change in their force, their numbers, stations, &c. He wishes this done through scouts, and any information which you acquire please forward to the major-general commanding, at the Narrows, by letter.

He also desires to know where your cavalry now is.

Very respectfully,

WM. B. MYERS,
Assistant Adjutant-General.

RED SWEET SPRINGS,
September 1, 1863.

Col. GEORGE S. PATTON,
Commanding, &c.:

COLONEL: The major-general desires that you communicate with him at Dublin by way of Union until further instructions. He wishes you to scout to Gauley, and send some reliable men to the Kanawha Valley, as he is anxious to learn, as soon as possible, any information of the forces, &c., in that locality.

Will you please send a courier up the Antony's Creek road to a Mr. Hall's, 5 miles above Dolan's, and direct him to bring a wagon left there by our teamster on the march. The horse had best be turned over to the quartermaster at Lewisburg.

Respectfully,

WM. B. MYERS,
Assistant Adjutant-General.

HEADQUARTERS,
September 2, 1863.

General R. E. LEE,
Commanding, &c.:

GENERAL: Your letter of the 31st is received. I have expressed to Generals Ewell and Hill your wishes, and am doing all that can be done to be well prepared with my own command. Our greatest difficulty will be in preparing our animals. I do not know that we can reasonably hope to accomplish much here by offensive operations, unless you are strong enough to cross the Potomac. If we advance to meet the enemy on this side, he will, in all probability, go into one of his many fortified positions; these we cannot afford to attack.

ı know but little of-the condition of our affairs in the west, but am inclined to the opinion that our best opportunity for great results' is in Tennessee. If we could hold the defensive here with two corps, and send the other to operate in Tennessee with that army, I think that we could accomplish more than by an advance from here.

The enemy seems to have settled down upon the plan of holding certain points by fortifying and defending, while he concentrates upon others. It seems to me that this must succeed, unless we can concentrate ourselves, and, at the same time, make occasional show of active operations at all points. I know of no other means of acting upon that principle at present, excepting to depend upon our fortifications in Virginia, and concentrate with one corps of this army, and such as may be drawn from others, in Tennessee, and destroy Rosecrans' army. I feel assured that this is practicable, and that greater advantage will be gained than by any operations from here.

I remain, general, very respectfully, your most obedient servant,

JAMES LONGSTREET,
Lieutenant-General.

HEADQUARTERS,
Petersburg, Va., September 2, 1863.

General S. COOPER,
Adjutant and Inspector General, C. S. Army:

GENERAL : I respectfully request that a question of vital importance to the success of our cause be settled, if it can be done.

I spoke to you in an interview of the difficulties to be apprehended next April, when the term of enlistment of our three-years' men expires. I do not wish to encumber your office with useless papers, but I speak knowingly when I say that serious trouble may be apprehended unless the question of reorganization is settled now before parties for office and change of arms of service are organized, and while the men are doubtful of their right to reorganize. Such a right, if allowed them, will be ruinous, and as the conscript law does not allow new organizations to be formed till the old are filled to the maximum, I think the law will cover reorganizations, which of course will be new organizations.

An official announcement that the old organizations will not be disturbed and the soldiers not allowed to change their arm of service, made at this time, would prevent most injurious discussion and demoralization.

I am, general, most respectfully, your obedient servant,

M. JENKINS,
Brigadier-General.

[Indorsements.]

OCTOBER 2, 1863.

Respectfully submitted to Secretary of War.

There would seem to be a necessity for an early decision in cases of this kind in order to settle the question in doubtful minds. My view is that soldiers who engage for three years or the war are liable to serve for the war or three years according to the determination of the Government.

S. COOPER,
Adjutant and Inspector General.

Respectfully submitted to Secretary of War.

The language of the conscription acts of April and September is that the persons in service whose term shall expire, and those called out and placed in service, "shall serve for three years, unless the war shall have been sooner ended." The inquiry is one of the utmost gravity, and the policy of the Government cannot be determined too early in reference to the probabilities of the future.

J. A. CAMPBELL,

HEADQUARTERS,
Wilmington, September 2, 1863.

Hon. JAMES A. SEDDON,
Secretary of War:

SIR: I send by Colonel Tansill, assistant inspector-general of this department, and a member of my staff, a distingushed and able officer, a special letter to you, relative to the condition of this department, especially as regards the Cape Fear District, and the necessity for some immediate action to supply a force to meet emergencies.

Colonel Tansill is acquainted with my views and plans, and thoroughly knows the country.

If you will refer to the maps accompanying my memoir to the President, he can illustrate and point out the features of the country, with the weak points and strong ones of the plan.

I request you will give him an audience, and, if you think proper, that you will introduce him to the President. He has some other letters of mine to you—copies of them, rather—intrusted to him as a member of my staff to aid as memoranda.

I have said that an army was necessary here, and that in my judgment it is time to commence assembling it.

I beg you implicitly to believe that if my opinion in this matter is deemed by the President to be correct, and that an army will be sent here, I hope and wish that as far as I am concerned there will be no difficulty as to command. All I want is to secure the safety of this most important place, and to do that I desire to use all my personal endeavors either as engineer or as commanding a division. Any one of the generals of the army or the corps commanders to take the command of such a body of men as I deem necessary to secure this, will be all that can be desired by me at any rate.

With great respect, your obedient servant,

W. H. C. WHITING,
Major-General.

[Indorsement.]

SEPTEMBER 4, 1863.

Respectfully submitted to the President.

General Whiting has sent these papers* by a trusted officer, to whom he refers for more special information, and seems to desire he should have the opportunity of presenting his views to the President. If it be your pleasure to see him, I will call with him at any hour to-morrow you may prefer.

---

*See also Whiting's letters of August 24 and 25, copies of which were inclosed with that of August 31.

I have written to Governor Vance begging the employment of his State troops and militia for the defense of the railroad line, so as to leave at least General Martin's brigade free to re-enforce Wilmington,

J. A. SEDDON,
Secretary of War,

[Inclosure.]

HEADQUARTERS DEPARTMENT OF NORTH CAROLINA,
Wilmington, August 31, 1863.

Hon. JAMES A. SEDDON,
Secretary of War, Richmond :

SIR : Suppose the map of North Carolina before you, and allow me to illustrate briefly only a single phase in the condition of Wilmington, and its probable attack or defense.

Suppose me without an army, or at most with but a single brigade, a force much larger than I really have at my command. The enemy, after due preparation, of which we may or may not have received notice, lands a strong force at Shalotte, 18 miles from Fort Caswell and 36 from Wilmington, a point much more suitable for his operations and more convenient than Light-House Inlet at Charleston.

Once landed, as I have not the force at hand to fight at once, three courses are open to him, any of which will be demonstrably fatal. He can advance on Fort Caswell as he is doing on Sumter, slowly but securely, strengthening always his position and the tenacity of his grip on the land, or, which a bolder foe would do at once, march upon Smithville, take its batteries in reverse, cut off Fort Caswell and shortly destroy it, or march directly upon the city and in its front, secure from attack by the obstacles of Brunswick River and the Cape Fear, plant his long-range guns and at the easy distance of 2 miles destroy the city, close the river, and turn all the formidable batteries against naval attack, on which so much labor has been expended. All this is not only possible but highly probable. There are besides other lines of attack equally feasible.

I use the description of this in particular only to illustrate what I wish to impress, that the whole system of the plan of defense adopted here, the only plan, indeed, which can be successful, depends on the presence, I might almost say the constant presence, of an army. On that, and that alone, depends the safety of the flanks, and not only that, but on the rapidity and success of the attack of that army rests the safety of Caswell and Fisher, of this the last harbor left to us, and of the city, an important point however considered.

To have this army assemble, but assemble too late, would, it seems to me, only increase the disaster. I hope that nothing here will be left to chance. The assembling a force, and such a force as would undoubtedly be required, will take, in the present condition of our transportation .and resources, a long time—time that we cannot afford to lose.

While the railroads are constantly deteriorating, they are liable also to be cut off daily. I have intimated that a large force is required here.

Let me illustrate by again referring to the map, and suppose the enemy attempting the southerly line of attack. With but a small force at my command, I throw my troops to the west of the Cape Fear to oppose him, for I cannot in this case sit down and wait the progress of events, and the enemy, landing a few thousand men at Masonborough before the movement can be arrested, cuts off the peninsula between the ocean and the Cape Fear River, and the fate of Fort Fisher and the harbor is sealed. I know no place now in the Confederacy where the presence of a large body of veteran troops is more necessary or more important than this. It is necessary now to prevent possible and by no means improbable disaster and to be ready. In the event of an attack this presence will be indispensable.

I beg that you will not consider me importunate in this matter. It oppresses me. It is not at all for me to make a comparison with the importance of this as compared with any other part or movement of the war. It is only for me to call attention to the case and to point out the necessities and indicate the means of defense.

I hope you will please to lay the subject before the President for his consideration.

When Vicksburg was threatened, if I am correctly informed, 20,000 troops were not thought insufficient. At that time Vicksburg was a point first in importance. It has fallen. I think now that this place is quite as important as Vicksburg was then. When it is attacked in the changed circumstances which now may be observed, the fewer objects of attack for the enemy, the greater power of concentrating his forces on a single point, and the increased need on our part to hold this with certainty, I must say that less than 20,000 men will hardly succeed.

Very respectfully,

W. H. C. WHITING,
Major-General.

HEADQUARTERS ARTILLERY CORPS,
September 3, 1863.

Major COLE,
Supt. of Transportation, &c., Richmond, Va.:

MY DEAR MAJOR: The question of our artillery horses of course occupies much of my attention, not only as to the difficult problem of having fidelity exercised in preserving those we have, but as to the scarcely less difficult achievement of filling the gaps occasioned by losses from hard service, deficient food, and inadequate care.

Respecting both the preservation and the supply, I wish to submit to you, and through you to the Department, a few considerations. I do this because General Lee has informed me that all final arrangements on these subjects were made in Richmond, and not by the authority of any commanding general in the field.

1. The preservation of our horses, after all we can do in battling against the intrinsic difficulties of our situation and the common negligence of officers and men, leaves many things yet to be desired. Multitudes of those left too long in the field because of inadequate provisions for relieving them, and too far gone for restoration before they are relieved, are, when relieved, committed to unskilled or unfaithful agents, and either perish on the way to the point where they are to be permanently provided for, or die after reaching those points through lack of the care, food, &c., essential for their resuscitation.

Toward remedying these evils and others connected with them, I some time since submitted a paper furnished me by Major Paxton, quartermaster to Jenkins' cavalry brigade, for General Lee's information, Major Paxton having had considerable experience with horses, and being extensively acquainted with the resources of those portions of Virginia where worn-down horses can be best recruited. There are three main ideas in the plan proposed, viz:

First. The establishment of a sort of general horse district in the counties of Halifax, Pittsylvania, Henry, Patrick, Franklin, Campbell, and Bedford, with depots, stables, &c., under the care of a responsible superintendent, who should select his own agents, and have the care of all horses for this army to be resuscitated, &c.

Second. The procurement from time to time, by this same officer or others in connection with his charge, of a number of fresh horses, to be taken to the depots in said district and kept with those renovated, for transfer when needed to the field.

Third. The establishment of suitable places of accommodation for horses removed to and from this district and the army, so as to insure their being suitably provided for in transit.

Out of this plan good can be made, I am persuaded. Major Paxton would himself be a good superintendent, and I could wish you might have him called for a brief season to Richmond, that you might have with him a full exchange of views. The district of country is full of forage, away from railroads, &c., so that it can hardly be otherwise available. Slave labor is there cheap, for attending to all the menial work. There is abundance of material for sheds, &c., and the region is eminently safe from the risk of raids, &c. Pray revolve it, consult the Quartermaster-General and any others requisite, and see if something valuable cannot be wrought out.

2. As to a supply of serviceable horses now, much exhaustion has been experienced, I am aware, but careful inquiry satisfies me that there are still horses enough for the army and for agriculture, &c., if the requisite means were adopted for getting them. Two things are necessary: First, prices proportioned to the cost of useful articles among us generally, and, second, agents interested in the cause and reliable. As to prices, much as I abominate the extortion of the times, and earnestly as I insist our State and Confederate legislatures ought to adopt measures for enforcing a scale of prices gradually descending to the ante-war standard, I am satisfied it is now wise to supply ourselves at high rates, at an average of $600. I am informed some 300 horses, good for artillery, might probably be gotten in the county of Albemarle alone, but to get them, the county must be explored and purchases made by other than those ordinary agents, who either know little of the necessities of the case or care little for meeting the emergency.

This matter of purchasing agents is, I well know, one of peculiar difficulty, and in avoiding one evil nothing is more likely than to run into another. Still it seems to me clear that in a case so important as this, the most influential motives governing men ought to be brought into requisition. Within a few weeks we ought to have some 300 additional and fresh horses for the artillery of this army. If the officers commanding battalions be authorized to have purchased, at rates averaging about $600, the number they severally need, they superintending the operation, and their quartermasters making the payments, I think the best security will be gotten that the want will be supplied, and the operation will be fairly and effectually performed. Pray consider and submit this matter also, and let us have the best results you can reach for our need.

I am, major, respectfully, your obedient servant,
W. N. PENDLETON,
Brigadier-General, and Chief of Artillery.

HEADQUARTERS,
September 5, 1863.

General R. E. LEE,
Commanding, &c.:

GENERAL: Your letter of the 4th is received. Colonel Walton expressed the desire to have a command at Mobile some time ago. He is getting almost too old for our active and severe winter service in this climate.

I do not know enough of our facilities for transporting troops, &c., west, to say what time would be consumed in moving my corps to Tennessee and back.

Your information will enable you to determine this much better than I. I believe, though, that the enemy intends to confine his great operations to the west, and that it is time that we were shaping our movements to meet him.

If this army is ready to assume offensive operations, I think that it would be better for us to remain on the defensive here, and to re-enforce the west, and take the offensive there. We can hold here with a smaller force than we would require for offensive operations; and if it should become necessary to retire as far as Richmond temporarily, I think that we could better afford to do so than we can to give up any more of our western country. I will say more; I think that it is time that we had begun to do something in the west, and I fear if it is put off any longer we shall be too late.

If my corps cannot go west, I think that we might accomplish something by giving me Jenkins', Wise's, and Cooke's brigades, and putting me in General Bragg's place, and giving him my corps. A good artillery battalion should go with these brigades. We would surely make no great risk in such a change and we might gain a great deal.

I feel that I am influenced by no personal motive in this suggestion, and will most cheerfully give up, when we have a fair prospect of holding our western country.

I doubt if General Bragg has confidence in his troops or himself either. He is not likely to do a great deal for us.

Mr. Hyden will give the ladies quarters. I believe that he has a very pleasant place.

I remain, most respectfully, your obedient servant,
JAMES LONGSTREET,
Lieutenant-General.

HEADQUARTERS DEPARTMENT OF WESTERN VIRGINIA,
Dublin, September 5, 1863.

Col. GEORGE S. PATTON,
Commanding, &c.:

COLONEL: The major-general commanding directs me to say that the threatening aspect of affairs in front of Saltville makes it necessary to move Wharton's brigade and the Forty-fifth [Virginia] Regiment, at least temporarily, in that direction.

In view of this, the major-general commanding enjoins extra vigilance on the part of the commanding officers defending the line of Lewisburg and Princeton.

Please communicate anything of importance promptly to these headquarters.

I am, colonel, respectfully, &c.,

WM. B. MYERS,
Assistant Adjutant-General.

(Similar letter to Major Claiborne, commanding Dunn's battalion, and to Colonel McCausland.)

WAR DEPARTMENT, C. S.,
Richmond, Va., September 5, 1863.

His Excellency ZEBULON B. VANCE,
Governor of North Carolina, Raleigh, N. C.:

SIR: General Whiting, in several late communications, expresses grave apprehension for the safety of Wilmington, and urges earnestly the necessity of having more troops at that point. He is, as you are aware, in command of the Department of North Carolina, and might summon the aid of the forces within it to that city ; but he is unwilling to remove any of them from the long line of defense over which they are scattered without some arrangement made to substitute them. I regret to confess that, with the formidable columns of the enemy threatening at so many vital points, the resources of the Department do not allow the withdrawal from our armies or the command from other quarters of the force that will be necessary to meet General Whiting's requirements.

Under these circumstances, remembering the confident expectation entertained by you when I had the privilege of seeing you here, that you would be enabled speedily to command from 10,000 to 20,000 troops, either militia or for State defense, I venture to inquire if it would not be in your power with them to undertake the defense of the railroad line from Weldon to Wilmington, or at least so much of it as is protected by the forces under General Martin, so as to allow them to be thrown at once to Wilmington.

I may add that this inquiry is at the suggestion of the President himself, and if it be in your power to afford such protection to the railroad line, I unite in urging that application of your State forces.

Very truly, yours,

J. A. SEDDON,
Secretary of War.

RICHMOND, VA.,
September 6, 1863.

His Excellency the PRESIDENT OF THE CONFEDERATE STATES:

Mr. PRESIDENT : I have arranged with the Quartermaster-General for the transportation of Longstreet's Corps, and have given the necessary orders for the movement of the troops and their subsistence on the road. I go to the Army of Northern Virginia to-morrow

morning to assist in carrying out what has been directed, and to
make whatever other arrangements may be necessary. As regards
myself, should you think that the service will be benefited by my
repairing to the Army of Tennessee, I will of course submit to your
judgment. From your knowledge of all the circumstances attending the operations of both armies, you can come to a more correct
conclusion than I can from my point of view. In my conversation
with you on this subject when the question was proposed, I did
not intend to decline the service, if desired that I should undertake
it, but merely to express the opinion that the duty could be better
performed by the officers already in that department.

I am, with great esteem, your obedient servant,

R. E. LEE,
General.

———

GENERAL ORDERS, ⎱ HDQRS. DEPT. OF WESTERN VIRGINIA,
No. 23.   ⎰   *Abingdon, September 6, 1863.*

In compliance with orders from the Secretary of War, the undersigned assumes temporarily command of that portion of Southwestern Virginia which belonged to the Department of East Tennessee,
and all the forces east of Knoxville that belong to that department.

SAM. JONES,
Major-General.

———

GENERAL ORDERS, ⎱ HDQRS. DEPT. OF WESTERN VIRGINIA,
No. 24.   ⎰   *Abingdon, September 6, 1863.*

Brig. Gen. J. S. Williams is hereby temporarily assigned to the
command of that portion of Southwestern Virginia which belonged
to the Department of East Tennessee, and all forces east of Knoxville that belong to that department.

By order of Maj. Gen. Sam. Jones:

J. G. MARTIN,
Assistant Adjutant-General.

———

DUBLIN,
September 7, 1863.

Lieut. Col. J. FLOYD KING,
Chief of Artillery, Union:

Bring your command direct to this place, via the Narrows. Use
all efforts to get it here as soon as possible.

WM. B. MYERS,
Assistant Adjutant-General.

———

SPECIAL ORDERS, ⎱ HDQRS. ARMY OF NORTHERN VIRGINIA,
No. 224.   ⎰   *September 7, 1863.*

* * * * * * *

VII. Brig. Gen. W. W. Kirkland, Provisional Army, C. S., will
report to Lieut. Gen. A. P. Hill, commanding Third Corps, for
assignment to the command of the brigade formerly commanded by
General Pettigrew.

VIII. Brig. Gen. Goode Bryan, Provisional Army, C. S., will report to Lieut. Gen. J. Longstreet, commanding First Corps, for assignment to the command of the brigade formerly commanded by General Semmes.

By command of General R. E. Lee:

R. H. CHILTON,
Assistant Adjutant and Inspector General.

RICHMOND,
September 8, [1863].

General R. E. LEE:

Have considered your letter. Believe your presence in the western army would be worth more than the addition of a corps, but fear the effect of your absence from Virginia. Did not doubt your willingness to do whatever was best for the country, and suggest your aid to determine that question. Have sent you all additional information, to aid your further consideration of problems discussed with you here.

JEFFERSON DAVIS.

ABINGDON,
September 8, 1863.

Hon. JAMES A. SEDDON,
Secretary of War, Richmond:

Labor is needed to construct defensive works at Saltville. Governor Letcher says he can give me no authority to impress slaves, because you have called out all available slave labor for public defense. May the slaves called out in this and adjoining counties be employed on works at Saltville?

SAM. JONES,
Major-General.

HEADQUARTERS,
Wilmington, N. C., September 8, 1863.

Hon. JAMES A. SEDDON,
Richmond, Va.:

I have reason to believe the enemy designs an attempt to occupy Bald Head and Smith's Island. It is all important that we should anticipate him. Can you send me troops? I have none.

W. H. C. WHITING,
Major-General.

WAR DEPARTMENT, C. S.,
Richmond, Va., September 8, 1863.

Maj. Gen. W. H. C. WHITING,
Commanding, &c., Wilmington, N. C.:

GENERAL: I have received your several communications relative to the condition of the defense at Wilmington, and the necessity for more troops, with much interest, and have likewise had the advantage of a personal conference with the intelligent officer sent by you to press your views on the Department. The subject has been presented on several different occasions to the President, and has received his anxious consideration, aided, too, by the counsels of General Lee, who has been with him for some days. With the limited resources of the Department, and the urgent pressure of the enemy's forces at other (for the present) even more vital points, the conclusion has been that no troops beyond those already in North Carolina can be spared for the re-enforcement of Wilmington. Governor Vance has been urged to use the local troops and State militia which he has been organizing for the defense of the line of railroad from Weldon, which would liberate the troops now stationed there and enable you to concentrate them at Wilmington. I hope he will be enabled to effect this in a short time, for I do not see any other means of supplying additional troops to your department. You will, of course, remember that you are commanding general within that department, and must appreciate and judge of the relative necessities of different points.

To weaken the extended line of defense against incursions in the State would certainly be very objectionable, unless the withdrawal of troops be, in your judgment, demanded by the necessity of defending the more important point of Wilmington. During the progress of the siege of Charleston, I incline to think the attention and resources of the enemy will be too much employed to render an attack on Wilmington probable; still, it will undoubtedly be wiser if in our power to guard against contingency, and your anxiety to point out and guard against danger is both natural and laudable. The formidable modes of hostile approach have certainly been indicated by you with force; but I cannot doubt your skill and prescience are even more exercised in devising and arranging the modes of successful resistance.

With high regard, your obedient servant,

J. A. SEDDON,
Secretary of War.

HEADQUARTERS,
Wilmington, September 8, 1863.

Hon. JAMES A. SEDDON,
Secretary of War, Richmond:

SIR: The city of Charleston may not be taken, but as a Confederate port it has well nigh ceased to belong to us. The news of to-day settles that question. In this crisis the importance of this place grows hourly. At this moment there is absolutely nothing to prevent, say, 3,000 of the enemy from landing at Lockwood's Folly, 23 miles from Wilmington, and turning all our positions.

In any such event the harbor and the ports must go. We shall have a repetition of the Morris Island business, perhaps worse. The danger here is not from naval attack, I believe, as against monitors and fleets; if that is the enemy's line, I am able to maintain my position and beat them. It is against land forces. As Charleston is closed in the danger increases. If the Department considers this position as worth anything, I beg that troops may be gathered here. At no time in the history of this war has it been so entirely stripped, or in so great danger.

It is my earnest conviction and opinion that from this moment to the close of the war there should be an army always here. All-important as Vicksburg was to us, the presence of an army was always deemed necessary to its defense. The importance of Vicksburg then is not greater than that of this place now, the last outlet to the Confederacy. I repeat, however, that at no time has this place been so unprotected by supporting forces.

The artillery garrison is not adequate to man the works. The infantry force is nothing. I am endeavoring to occupy Smith's Island. I have neither the troops nor the labor.

I beg that you will lay all my letters before the President; as he has intrusted me with this defense he will consider my opinions for what they are worth.

I am not an alarmist, but I see danger not far off, and my only desire is to provide against it.

Very respectfully,

W. H. C. WHITING,
Major-General.

P. S.—Unless some great disaster occurs to the enemy, Charleston, as a Confederate port, is closed. The enemy have it in their power to hold their position and transfer in any two nights their operations here. It will not do to trust to work to be done and force to be gathered afterward.

[Indorsement.]

SECRETARY OF WAR:

General Clingman's brigade cannot now be withdrawn from Charleston. Martin's brigade, if full and well instructed, would afford a garrison, or, if it be better suited to an interior position, the brigade of General Ransom would be entirely reliable for protection of approaches to Wilmington. Pickett's brigades when filled up will be able to extend farther on the railroad, and the local-defense men of North Carolina, it is hoped, will soon be in the field.

The importance of Wilmington is evident, and it is desirable to have troops in position to cover the country and its proper defenses.

JEEFERSON DAVIS.

———

HEADQUARTERS,
Wilmington, September 8, 1863.

Hon. JAMES A. SEDDON,
Secretary of War, Richmond:

SIR : In connection with my late letters to you urging my immediate need of troops, I inclose to-day a letter from Col. T. M. Jones, commanding at Fort Caswell.

The occupation of Bald Head on our part is a matter of necessity, daily growing greater. It should be held by a large force. My artillery garrison is now far too small to man the batteries and works already constructed, without considering those in process of erection. Of infantry support I have but one regiment, occupied entirely in picket duty over a large extent of country, and unable from its distribution even to meet and repulse the landings of the enemy. This matter of Bald Head is one of very great importance. I beg of you so to consider it and no longer to allow this district to remain in its present exposed, dangerous, and defenseless position.

Very respectfully,

W. H. C. WHITING,
Major-General.

[Inclosure.]

HEADQUARTERS FORT CASWELL,
September 7, 1863.

ASSISTANT ADJUTANT-GENERAL,
Headquarters:

SIR: I have the honor to state that yesterday one of the enemy's gunboats went off within one-half or three-quarters of a mile of the Cape of Bald Head, and sent two boat-loads of men ashore. I sent men over to discover what they were doing, but they had gone back before my men reached the point. I am disposed to think that the enemy is planning to occupy the island before we do, and therefore request permission to keep one of my companies over on Bald Head, or at least a detachment of men and a piece of artillery, until the battery is erected over there.

The inspection ordered by the general to be made by Major Hedrick, Captain Sweetman, and myself, was made the day after the receipt of his order, and a suitable place for a battery was found near the point of Bald Head Island, and also a suitable place for a wharf was selected.

I am, sir, very respectfully, your obedient servant,

THOS. M. JONES,
Colonel, Provisional Army, C. S.

HEADQUARTERS DEPARTMENT OF NORTH CAROLINA,
Wilmington, September 8, 1863.

MEMORANDUM FOR LIEUTENANT-COLONEL FROBEL.

Proceed immediately to occupy Bald Head. Rankin's company is ordered there, and force will be increased if necessary. The Whitworth gun should be sent there from Caswell. The engineer department will proceed to construct wharves; one near proposed fort, one for the rip near light-house.

Intrenchments and the works of the fort should be at once commenced, and should receive your constant and vigilant supervision. In this I desire that Major Hedrick should assist you. Timber must be immediately secured for bomb-proofs, and no time must be lost in the construction. *Têtes-de-pont* should be built to cover the wharves.

Recollect this work is of the utmost importance and will require all your energy.

Very respectfully,

W. H. C. WHITING,
Major-General.

SPECIAL ORDERS, ⎱ HDQRS. ARMY OF NORTHERN VIRGINIA,
  No. 225.   ⎰   September 8, 1863.
    *   *   *   *   *   *   *

V. Brig. Gen. Robert D. Johnston, Provisional Army, C. S., will report to Lieut. Gen. R. S. Ewell, commanding Second Corps, Army of Northern Virginia, for assignment to the command of the North Carolina brigade, of Rodes' division, formerly commanded by Brigadier-General Iverson.
    *   *   *   *   ..   ..

By command of General R. E. Lee:

R. H. CHILTON,
Assistant Adjutant and Inspector General.

CAMP AT ORANGE COURT-HOUSE, *September 9, 1863.*

His Excellency JEFFERSON DAVIS,
  President Confederate States, Richmond, Va.:

Mr. PRESIDENT: I have placed the troops on march toward Richmond. Two divisions will reach Hanover Junction this morning. The third will reach or pass beyond Louisa Court-House to-day. General Longstreet proposes that Pickett's division take the place of Wise's and Jenkins' brigades about Richmond, and that they accompany him. Pickett's division wants many officers, owing to the number wounded and captured, who cannot now be replaced. He also thinks it might increase its ranks in that locality. Wise's and Jenkins' brigades will probably exceed Pickett's division in numbers, though they will not give the Virginia troops you desire for the south. I know no other objection. General Longstreet has selected two Georgia brigades for Charleston, one from McLaws' and one from Hood's division. He does not want to take them into Georgia, for fear of desertion. If he takes Wise's and Jenkins', instead of Pickett's, he will assign them to McLaws and Hood, respectively, in their stead. The division of Pickett, according to the arrangement of the Quartermaster-General, will be moved last. It is on march to Richmond; you can therefore decide. The two Georgia brigades are also directed to march to Richmond, and can be sent to Charleston whenever transportation is furnished.

Your dispatch of yesterday is not very clear in reference to Burnside's movement, but I understand it to mean that it is approaching Rosecrans. I think Rosecrans is maneuvering to cause the evacuation of Chattanooga, and for Burnside to form a junction with him. He ought to be attacked as soon as possible. I think it probable that Gillmore will now seize upon Sullivan's Island, to cause the evacuation of Fort Moultrie, and thus close the entrance to Charleston.

With great respect, your obedient servant,

R. E. LEE,
General.

ORANGE COURT-HOUSE, *September 9, 1863.*

The PRESIDENT:

Anderson's brigade, of Hood's division, is designated as one of the brigades for Charleston. Please direct accordingly. It will march to Richmond.

R. E. LEE.

WAR DEPARTMENT, C. S.,
Richmond, September 9, 1863.

C. S. STRINGFELLOW,
Assistant Adjutant-General, Dublin, Va.:

The salt-works the more important to be defended.   If satisfied of the impending danger, order the Sixtieth [Virginia] Regiment as you propose; instruct Colonel McCausland to be on his guard, and fall back if necessary.   Inform General Jones, as soon as you can, of this movement.

J. A. SEDDON,
Secretary of War.

HEADQUARTERS DEPARTMENT OF WESTERN VIRGINIA,
Dublin, September 9, 1863.

Maj. Gen. SAMUEL JONES,
Commanding, &c., Abingdon:

Wharton's brigade leaves here to-day at 9 a. m. ; reach Saltville this afternoon.   Forty-fifth [Virginia Infantry] and artillery will reach here the 10th at 12 m.; and will be sent on at once.

WM. B. MYERS,
Assistant Adjutant-General.

Reorganization of the Cavalry Corps of the Army of Northern Virginia, Maj. Gen. J. E. B. Stuart, C. S. Army, commanding, September 9, 1863. *

FIRST DIVISION.

Maj. Gen. WADE HAMPTON.

Jones' Brigade.

Brig. Gen. W. E. JONES.

6th Virginia, Lieut. Col. John Shac Green.
7th Virginia, Col. R. H. Dulany.
12th Virginia, Col. A. W. Harman.
35th Virginia Battalion, Lieut. Col. E. V. White.

Baker's Brigade.

Brig. Gen. L. S. BAKER.

1st North Carolina, Col. J. B. Gordon.
2d North Carolina, Lieut. Col. W. G. Robinson.
4th North Carolina, Col. Dennis D. Ferebee.
5th North Carolina, Col. Stephen B. Evans.

Butler's Brigade.

Brig. Gen. M. C. BUTLER.

Cobb's (Georgia) Legion, Col. P. M. B. Young.
Jeff. Davis (Mississippi) Legion, Lieut. Col. J. F. Waring.
Phillips (Georgia) Legion, Lieut. Col. W. W. Rich.
2d South Carolina, Lieut. Col. T. J. Lipscomb.

---

* Under Special Orders, No. 226, headquarters Army of Northern Virginia, of that date.

SECOND DIVISION.

Maj. Gen. Fitzhugh Lee.

Lee's Brigade.

Brig. Gen. W. H. F. Lee.

1st South Carolina, Col. John L. Black.
9th Virginia, Col. R. L. T. Beale.
10th Virginia, Col. J. Lucius Davis.
13th Virginia, Col. John R. Chambliss, jr.

Lomax's Brigade.

Brig. Gen. L. L. Lomax.

1st Maryland Battalion, Lieut. Col. Ridgely Brown.
5th Virginia, Col. Thomas L. Rosser.
11th Virginia, Col. O. R. Funsten.
15th Virginia, Col. William B. Ball.

Wickham's Brigade.

Brig. Gen. Williams C. Wickham.

1st Virginia, Col. R. W. Carter.
2d Virginia, Col. Thomas T. Munford.
3d Virginia, Col. Thomas H. Owen.
4th Virginia, Lieut. Col. William H. Payne.

RICHMOND,
September 10, 1863.

General R. E. Lee,
Orange Court-House, Va.:

Your dispatch and letter received. It will involve delay to send the brigade of General Wise. Cannot a brigade of Pickett's division be advantageously substituted. Jenkins will go.

JEFFERSON DAVIS.

ORANGE COURT-HOUSE,
September 10, 1863.

His Excellency JEFFERSON DAVIS:

Anderson's brigade, Hood's division, and Bryan's brigade, Mc-Laws' division, are selected by General Longstreet to go to Charleston. If preferred, Wise and Jenkins could go in their place and Pickett's division remain in vicinity of Richmond. Three battalions of artillery are ordered to Richmond. Their horses cannot accompany the guns farther, and their guns should not be forwarded unless horses can be obtained at the scene of operations.

R. E. LEE.

[Indorsement.]

This seems to me better, unless there be reason to fear straggling from the brigades named, or unless the orders given will obstruct execution.

If you prefer this, give orders at once.

J. D. [DAVIS.]

HEADQUARTERS ARMY OF NORTHERN VIRGINIA,
September 10, 1863.

Brig. Gen. J. D. IMBODEN,
Commanding, Valley District:

GENERAL: Your letters of August 25, 27, and 31 have been received.

I regret exceedingly that the enemy escaped with so little damage to himself. I am sorry you could not go on to Huntersville to see General Jones when he sent for you in order to form some combined plan of operations before the attack.

It seems to me the command of Averell should have been more seriously punished. Unless we are active in inflicting all the loss we can upon the parties sent on these expeditions, and in using every opportunity of cutting them off, they will continue to be sent out, will desolate the country, and bring great distress upon the people. I hope you will be more successful in future.

The success of Captain Hill's expedition into Barbour County is gratifying and his boldness commendable. It shows what can be accomplished in the mountains by energy and skill. I desire you to seize every favorable occasion for inflicting damage upon the enemy.

Prominent citizens of the valley have made serious complaints of the conduct of Captain Shearer's company, of Gilmor's battalion. I wish you would see to it. If they cannot be brought under proper discipline, and continue to harass our own citizens by their bad conduct, they had much better be disbanded. Hon. R. Y. Conrad, of Winchester, is one of the citizens preferring the complaint.

There is a company of Missourians here, and three other companies in Richmond, exchanged prisoners, who appear to be bold, brave men, who have been in the cavalry service. I telegraphed you to know whether you can mount them within a reasonable time. If you can, they will prove a valuable addition to your brigade.

Very respectfully, your obedient servant,

R. E. LEE,
General.

Abstract from return of the Army of Northern Virginia, General Robert E. Lee, C. S. Army, commanding, September 10, 1863; headquarters Orange Court-House.

Command.	Present for duty.		Aggregate present.	Aggregate present and absent.
	Officers.	Men.		
General headquarters	14	....	14	15
Second Army Corps (Ewell)	1,387	15,804	20,196	30,131
Third Army Corps (A. P. Hill)	1,135	14,087	17,828	31,973
Cooke's brigade	143	2,100	2,601	3,270
Cavalry Corps a	594	7,547	9,530	18,011
Artillery	147	3,226	3,840	5,376
Total b	3,420	42,764	54,009	97,776

a Of the enlisted men present for duty, 1,361 are reported as dismounted.
b The First Army Corps detached.

HEADQUARTERS DEPARTMENT OF WESTERN VIRGINIA,
Dublin, September 10, 1863.
Brig. Gen. JOHN S. WILLIAMS,
Bristol.

The Forty-fifth [Virginia Infantry] left at 6 o'clock this morning—marched all night and were started without delay.

WM. B. MYERS,
Assistant Adjutant-General.

RALEIGH, *September* 10, 1863.
President DAVIS, *Richmond:*

A Georgia regiment (of Benning's brigade) entered this city last night at 10 o'clock and destroyed the office of the Standard newspaper. This morning a mob of citizens destroyed the office of the State Journal in retaliation. Please order immediately that troops passing through here shall not enter the city. If this is not done, the most frightful consequences may ensue.

Respectfully,

Z. B. VANCE.

RICHMOND, VA., *September* 10, 1863.
Governor VANCE, *Raleigh, N. C.:*

Your dispatches of this date received. I deeply regret the occurrence you announce, and have sent by telegraph the following order:

Maj. W. W. PEIRCE,
Quartermaster, Raleigh, N. C.:

You will not allow the troops in transit to be detained at Raleigh, and will communicate to the commanding officer of each detachment passing there that he is instructed not to permit his men to enter the city ; but if transportation is not furnished to enable the detachment to proceed immediately by railroad, will march it before halting to an encampment at safe distance from Raleigh.

JEFFERSON DAVIS.

KINSTON, N. C., *September* 10, 1863.
General S. COOPER, *Richmond:*

Scouts report General Foster was in New Berne one night last week and left the next morning, taking with him some troops, number not known. Some horse artillery or cavalry left New Berne the same time on the cars, number unknown. Day before yesterday Foster reached Washington, N. C., with some troops, number not known.

J. G. MARTIN,
Brigadier-General.

ORANGE COURT-HOUSE,
September 11, 1863.
His Excellency JEFFERSON DAVIS :

Pickett's brigades are small. If his division is retained, it had better be kept entire. It will require some days for it to march to Richmond.

R. E. LEE.

HEADQUARTERS ARMY OF NORTHERN VIRGINIA,
September 11, 1863.

His Excellency JEFFERSON DAVIS,
President Confederate States:

Mr. PRESIDENT : Your letter of September 9, with.the accompanying extract of a letter from Governor Brown, of· Georgia, has been received. General Wofford is now with his brigade on the march to Tennessee, and will be much needed in his brigade at the present juncture. I regard him as one of the best brigadiers in the division in which he is serving, and I do not see well how his services can be spared. I think everything should be done to check the progress of the evil of which Governor Brown speaks. General A. R. Wright, of Georgia, whose brigade is with that portion of the army which remains here, might be spared for this duty, I hear ˙that he is a gentleman of some political influence in his State. If Governor Brown should desire his services and make application for him, I think he might be assigned. He is a gallant and efficient officer. I hope all good citizens will aid the Governor in inculcating a spirit of harmony and in suppressing these treasonable demonstrations.

I am, with great respect, your obedient servant,
R. E. LEE,
General.

CAMP NEAR ORANGE COURT-HOUSE,
September 11, 1863.

His Excellency JEFFERSON DAVIS,
President Confederate States, Richmond, Va.:

Mr. PRESIDENT : I replied by telegraph to your dispatch of the 10th instant.* I think if Pickett's division is retained it had better be kept entire. Its brigades are small. Should, if possible, be recruited, and it will be more efficient united. It will require some days for it to march to Richmond, and in the meantime Wise can be made ready. Longstreet should .have reached Richmond last evening, and can make all necessary arrangements.

The defenses around Richmond should now be completed as soon as possible. I did not see any connection or communication between the redoubts for the defense of Drewry's Bluff from a land attack, and the defensive line around Manchester. This is important, and also that there should be obstructions in the river connecting this intermediate line (as it was termed) on both sides of the river. Should the enemy's land forces drive us from Drewry's Bluff, they would remove the obstructions at that point, and although we might be able to hold the intermediate line, his gunboats could ascend the river and destroy Richmond. I think, too, Colonel Gorgas should commence at once to enlarge his manufacturing arsenals, &c., in the interior, so that if Richmond should fall we would not be destitute. These are only recommended as prudential measures, and such as, should the necessity for them ever arise, we will then wish had been taken.

Scouts on the Potomac report 4 large schooners crowded with troops, passing up the river on the 8th instant. I think they must have come from south of James River. Scouts should be sent to Suffolk and elsewhere to ascertain what points have been evacuated.

* See p. 710.

If I was a little stronger, I think I could drive Meade's army under cover of the fortifications of Washington before he gathers more re-enforcements. When he gets all his re-enforcements I may be forced back to Richmond. The blow at Rosecrans should be made promptly, and Longstreet returned.

I am, with great respect, your obedient servant, .

R. E. LEE,
General.

HEADQUARTERS DEPARTMENT OF WESTERN VIRGINIA,
Dublin, September 11, 1863.

Maj. Gen. SAMUEL JONES,
Abingdon:

There is a report that the enemy, 800 strong, cavalry and infantry, breakfasted at Mr. Taylor's, this side of Tazewell Court-House, this morning. I do not know that the authority is good. Please instruct me if you wish the home guards called out, &c.

WM. B. MYERS,
Assistant Adjutant-General.

HEADQUARTERS DEPARTMENT OF WESTERN VIRGINIA,
Dublin, September 11, 1863.

Maj. Gen. SAMUEL JONES,
Abingdon:

Your dispatch regarding the enemy just received. Have telegraphed to the commanding officers at Salem, Big Lick, and Christiansburg; also to Dodamead, to furnish transportation to New River Bridge.

Am sending down rations. Scouts are watching the Walker's Creek road and all the other approaches. Lieutenant-Colonel Gardner and Colonel Gray, of Newbern, are stationing the scouts.

I have telegraphed Major Kent, at Wytheville, to keep me advised of any approach in that direction. Riders are out collecting the home guards. Every one seems inclined to respond promptly to the call.

WM. B. MYERS,
Assistant Adjutant-General.

HEADQUARTERS DEPARTMENT OF WESTERN VIRGINIA,
Dublin, September 11, 1863.

Colonel TERRILL,
Salem:

The following dispatch has just been received from General Jones, at Abingdon:

Four hundred Yankees reported in Tazewell. Call out the home guards of Pulaski, Montgomery, and Roanoke, to protect Dublin and New River Bridge. You will collect your force at once and be ready to come to New River Bridge. You will be informed when transportation will be ready.

WM. B. MYERS,
Assistant Adjutant-General.

HEADQUARTERS DEPARTMENT OF WESTERN VIRGINIA,
Dublin, September 11, 1863.

Capt. J. M. WADE,
   Christiansburg:

Report of raid by the enemy in direction of Wytheville via Tazewell. Collect your force and hold them in readiness to come to New River Bridge. You will be informed when transportation will be ready.

By order:

WM. B. MYERS,
Assistant Adjutant-General.

SPECIAL ORDERS, }   ADJT. AND INSP. GENERAL'S OFFICE,
No. 216.   *Richmond, September 11, 1863.*

*   *   *   *   *   *   *

XXVII. The brigade of Brig. Gen. M. Jenkins is assigned to Hood's division, Longstreet's army corps, and will proceed with that division to its destination under existing orders.

XXVIII. The brigade of Brigadier-General Wise will proceed without delay to Charleston, S. C., and report for duty to General Beauregard.

By command of the Secretary of War:

JNO. WITHERS,
Assistant Adjutant-General.

EXTRACT OF LETTER FROM GENERAL LONGSTREET.

HEADQUARTERS,
Richmond, September 12, 1863.

General R. E. LEE,
   Commanding:

GENERAL: Henry's artillery has come down here, to my surprise. I have ordered * * *. Anderson's brigade was so far on its way toward Charleston when your telegram got here that it could not be diverted, and fearing that if I sent Jenkins on to take his place that General Béauregard would keep both, I concluded that the wisest and safest plan would be to put Jenkins' brigade in Anderson's place in Hood's division. It has been so arranged. I intended to have suggested before leaving you, that our defenses around Richmond be so arranged that we might (in the event we should be forced to give up Richmond) hold Drewry's and Chaffin's Bluffs, with a garrison of 15,000 or 20,000 men, until we could collect army enough here to retake Richmond. I suppose that we might hold our vessels here, under the protection of these fortifications, until we could recover the city. But if we should give up the river to the enemy, there would be but little prospect of our getting back the capital during the war. As I have never seen the positions of these bluffs, I do not know whether this arrangement is a practicable one.

I hope to start west on Monday morning. If I can do anything there, it shall be done promptly. If I cannot, I shall advise you to recall me. If I did not think our move a necessary one, my regrets

at leaving you would be distressing to me, as it seems to be with the
officers and men of my command. Believing it to be necessary, I
hope to accept it and my other personal inconveniences cheerfully
and hopefully. All that we have to be proud of has been accomplished under your eye and under your orders. Our affections for
you are stronger, if it is possible for them to be stronger, than our
admiration for you.

I remain, general, most respectfully and affectionately, your obedient servant,

JAMES LONGSTREET,
Lieutenant-General.

HEADQUARTERS ARMY OF NORTHERN VIRGINIA,
September 12, 1863.

General S. COOPER,
Adjutant and Inspector General:

GENERAL: In reply to the question whether he can furnish horses
for the dismounted Missouri cavalry, which it was proposed to assign
to him, General Imboden writes that he cannot do it. He proposes
to aid them, by guides and otherwise, to capture horses from the
enemy on the border. This plan I do not approve, as the parties
sent out are too liable to take horses from friends as well as foes.
General Imboden states that he has 200 government horses under
charge of his quartermaster, on grass, and thinks it would be well to
sell them out to individuals at an appraisement, and thinks they
would recuperate more rapidly in this way. This is a matter, however, for the consideration of the Quartermaster-General, as he may
be more in need of those horses for other branches of the service,
and the horses well taken care of ought to improve rapidly as they
are.

I am, very respectfully, your obedient servant,
R. E. LEE,
General.

[Indorsements.]

·SEPTEMBER 17, 1863.

Respectfully referred to the Quartermaster-General, for his views
as to the proposed sale of horses by General Imboden, and return of
this communication requested.

By order:

C. H. LEE,
Assistant Adjutant-General.

QUARTERMASTER-GENERAL'S OFFICE,
September 18, 1863.

Respectfully referred to Maj. A. H. Cole, Inspector-General, for
consideration and report to this office.

By order:

J. B. HOGE,
Major.

OFFICE INSPECTOR-GENERAL OF TRANSPORTATION,
September 21, 1863.

Respectfully returned to the Quartermaster-General.

Provision has been made for the recruiting by the Government of all public animals, with the view of returning them to service, where they are much needed for artillery and transportation, as rapidly as possible. I cannot therefore recommend the adoption of General Imboden's suggestion.

A. H. COLE,
Major, and Inspector-General.

QUARTERMASTER-GENERAL'S OFFICE,
September 21, 1863.

Respectfully returned to the Adjutant-General.

Major Cole's indorsement is approved.

By order of Quartermaster-General:

J. B. HOGE.

———

WILMINGTON, N. C.,
September 12, 1863.

Hon. JAMES A. SEDDON,
Richmond, Va.:

Is it likely that my troops will be sent to me in accordance with my many requests? Must have some.

W. H. C. WHITING,
Major-General.

———

HEADQUARTERS,
Wilmington, September 12, 1863.

Hon. JAMES A. SEDDON,
Secretary of War, Richmond:

SIR : I have to-day received your letters of the 8th and 9th instant. While I regret exceedingly our want of means, I cannot but recognize the pressure upon the Department as very great. We must accordingly do the best we can with what we have.

I am informed by Colonel Hinton that he has been very successful in raising and equipping a respectable force of State troops in the northeastern part of the State, and that Governor Vance will place them under my control. In this case, I can move, no doubt, the greater part of Ransom's brigade here.

I regret exceedingly to have to report the existence of armed and hostile bands of North Carolinians in the western counties. It is believed, however, that the measures already taken will shortly break them up.

Your impression is correct as to No. 4 of the regulations in regard to steamers to which you refer. No authority to issue passports is claimed. It was simply deemed necessary that we should know who is permitted to leave the country. Passports from the War Department are therefore only *visé* in this office.

With regard to Colonel Duncan, although I have as yet seen no reason to be otherwise than satisfied with his efficient performance of business, I must regard your suggestion. He is not a commissioned officer. I have accordingly transferred the business in question to Major Gibbes, of South Carolina, who has lately been ordered to report to me as an officer of artillery. He will perform it faithfully. In fact, as you may well understand, I prefer all of this business to be transacted by officers not belonging to my military family. I have so constantly and persistently opposed the blockade running (government business excepted) as to make it a matter of principle that none of us should be at all connected with it, or even exposed to the imputation of so being.

If I had any embarrassment in the case of Colonel Duncan, who volunteered, as an old friend, to serve me as an aide, he has properly and gracefully relieved me of it. I communicated to him only the fact that the Department preferred that the business in question should be transacted by an officer bearing a commission. I was aware imperfectly that Colonel Duncan had some official dispute with one of the Departments of the Government, but presumed it to be entirely in the nature of a civil or legal transaction. I am sure he is actuated by patriotic motives in his desire to serve his country. I am not aware of his private business circumstances, but I think it is due to him to express the conviction I have that he has never allowed it to interfere with his public duties in his connection with me.

Very respectfully,

W. H. C. WHITING,
Major-General.

Special Orders, } Hdqrs. Artillery Corps, A. N. Va.,
No. —. }   *September* 13, 1863.

The officers commanding Cabell's and Henry's artillery battalions will march them by reasonable stages, so as not to worry their horses, to the neighborhood of Gordonsville; there select satisfactory camping ground, and report without delay to these headquarters. On the march, which had best be by way of Louisa Court-House, they will be careful to forage their animals as well as practicable, and if they have to resort to the purchase of standing corn, they will see that it is used with proper caution and with such rations of drier food as can be procured.

W. N. PENDLETON,
Brig. Gen., and Chief of Arty., Army of Northern Va.

WYTHEVILLE,
September 13, 1863.

Hon. JAMES A. SEDDON,
Secretary of War:

SIR: It is reported that a Federal force of mounted men and infantry, 4,000, advancing through Tazewell County on the road and bridge. Sixteen of the advance were captured last night. No troops, except two or three companies of home guards, here. Wires down between Wytheville and Abingdon. These facts are deemed correct. Can any assistance be furnished? The Otey Battery is here.

LANDON C. HAYNES,
C. S. Senator.

CHRISTIANSBURG,
September 13, 1863.

SECRETARY OF WAR:

We are threatened with a heavy and formidable raid upon the railroad. Force estimated from 5,000 to 7,000. Can you send us any assistance? We beg that you will send us re-enforcements immediately.

WALLER R. STAPLES.
ROBERT T. PRESTON.

SEPTEMBER 13, 1863.

SECRETARY OF WAR:

After considering the telegrams and note sent to me, though I am left to hope that the "locals" ordered by you may suffice, there is reason to apprehend that, with due allowance for exaggeration, it will be otherwise. It seems to me well that a brigade of Pickett's division should be sent up for temporary service. Communication opened with General Jones may give more reliable information. Should it prove to be a false alarm the brigade can be ordered back from any point on the road, if it should have started before an answer can be received.

Wharton's and Jenkins' brigades may be in position to afford the earliest assistance. The raiders should, if possible, whether in large or small numbers, be not only checked but punished.

Yours,

JEFFERSON DAVIS.

HEADQUARTERS DEPARTMENT OF WESTERN VIRGINIA,
Dublin, September 13, 1863.

Capt. W. T. HART,
New River Bridge:

The following dispatch just received from Captain Walker, Otey Battery, at Wytheville:

A party of raiders are supposed to be working their way to New River Bridge. I have information of 800 cavalry in Tazewell. What direction they will take not known.

D. N. WALKER.

WM. B. MYERS,
Assistant Adjutant-General.

HEADQUARTERS DEPARTMENT OF WESTERN VIRGINIA,
Dublin, September 13, 1863.

Brigadier-General NICHOLLS,
Commanding, Lynchburg:

There is a force of 700 of the enemy reported advancing through Tazewell County in this direction or on Saltville. Prisoners report it as the advance guard of a heavy force from 4,000 to 7,000. Please keep your command in readiness to move in this direction. I will keep you fully advised of any information I receive.

WM. B. MYERS,
Assistant Adjutant-General.

HEADQUARTERS DEPARTMENT OF WESTERN VIRGINIA,
Dublin, September 13, 1863.
Capt. D. N. WALKER,
Otey Battery, Wytheville:

I have about 200 home guards here, will have about 250 at New River Bridge this morning, and have telegraphed to Brigadier-General Nicholls, commanding at Lynchburg, to be prepared to assist if needed. Keep me informed of anything you can learn.

WM. B. MYERS,
Assistant Adjutant-General.

HEADQUARTERS DEPARTMENT OF WESTERN VIRGINIA,
Dublin, September 13, 1863.
Col. G. C. WHARTON, *Commanding, Glade Spring:*

A large force of the enemy reported in Abb's Valley. Seven hundred supposed to be advancing either on Saltville or some point east of that place on the railroad. This is rumored to be an advance guard of a force of from 4,000 to 7,000. Please keep me informed of anything you may learn.

WM. B. MYERS,
Assistant Adjutant-General.

HEADQUARTERS DEPARTMENT OF WESTERN VIRGINIA,
Dublin, September 13, 1863.
Maj. Gen. SAMUEL JONES, *Abingdon:*

I have telegraphed General Nicholls, at Lynchburg, to keep his command in readiness to start if necessary. About 600 men (home guards) reported to me at New River Bridge. I have 200, with one piece of artillery, stationed at Cloyd's Mountain. The force at Wytheville has not been reported to me. I suppose about 300. Is it worth while to bring the Lynchburg Home Guards to Central Depot, or shall I only keep them on the alert?

WM. B. MYERS,
Assistant Adjutant-General.

HEADQUARTERS DEPARTMENT OF WESTERN VIRGINIA,
Dublin, September 13, 1863.
Col. G. C. WHARTON, *Commanding, Glade Spring:*

The enemy, reported 800 strong, are supposed to be advancing through Tazewell, either on Wytheville or in this direction. The home guards of Pulaski are stationed on Cloyd's Mountain with one piece of artillery. They number 200. I have about 600 more from Roanoke reported at New River Bridge. I do not know the force at Wytheville. If anything occurs in your front please let me know. The raid may be on the salt-works. Some prisoners taken yesterday near Marion reported it as the advance of a large force. It may be so. The salt-works would in that case probably be their destination.

WM. B. MYERS,
Assistant Adjutant-General.

WAR DEPARTMENT,
September 13, 1863.
Brigadier-General NICHOLLS,
Lynchburg:
The enemy are reported as making a serious raid toward Wytheville. Send thither whatever local force you can command at once.·
J. A. SEDDON,
Secretary of War.

HDQRS. DEPT. SOUTH CAROLINA, GEORGIA, AND FLORIDA,
Charleston, S. C., September 13, 1863.
Col. W. H. STEVENS,
Engineer in Charge, Richmond, Va.:
COLONEL: I will ask you to give special study to the question of a second obstruction in James River. If one could be located even as high as Warwick Bar, just below the pontoon bridge, we would have a river defense but slightly salient from our best line, the intermediate around the city. The bottom at Warwick Bar is good for driving piles—depth of water only 13 feet and the work partially done. Possibly a pile structure may be planned that would be formidable, when commanded by three or four 10-inch columbiads, mounted in good chambers on the point where preparations were commenced some time ago. Four good columbiad chambers and platforms might be constructed, with the hope of getting the guns after some time. The length of infantry line from the intermediate line of defense to embrace this battery will be much shorter, of course, than the one stretching on Chaffin's Bluff.

With your increase of negro force you may find it judicious to build the batteries referred to and establish a good pile obstruction. Cribs filled with stone, I fear, will take too long to construct as well as too much labor. Please give the subject your earliest and most careful study.

Your obedient servant,
J. F. GILMER,
Major-General, and Chief of Engineer Bureau.

HEADQUARTERS ARMY OF NORTHERN VIRGINIA,
September 14, 1863.
His Excellency JEFFERSON DAVIS,
President Confederate States:
MR. PRESIDENT: The guns of three battalions of artillery have been called for, to go with General Longstreet, and have been forwarded to Richmond with that object. I think before they go it should be fully ascertained whether they can obtain horses for them in that region. If this cannot be done it would be worse than useless to carry them, as they would not only undergo the wear and tear and damage of transportation, but we might possibly lose them.*

＊   ＊   ＊   ＊   ＊   ＊   ＊

I have been informed that the New York Herald, of the 9th instant, contained the movement of Longstreet's corps in the order in

---

* For portion here omitted, see Part I, p. 134.

which his divisions moved, and even contained the announcement that two of his brigades would probably stop in Richmond and Wise's and Jenkins' take their places. I only communicated the movement to the Quartermaster-General on the night of the 6th instant, and it must have reached New York on the 7th or 8th in order to be in the Herald of the 9th. I fear that there has been great imprudence in talking on the part of our people, or that there may be improper persons among the officers or railroad clerks.

I am, with great respect, your obedient servant,

R. E. LEE,
General.

HEADQUARTERS ARMY OF NORTHERN VIRGINIA,
September 14, 1863.

His Excellency JEFFERSON DAVIS,
    President Confederate States, Richmond:

MR. PRESIDENT: My letter of this morning will have informed you of the crossing of the Rappahannock by the cavalry of General Meade's army, and of the retirement of ours to the Rapidan. The enemy's cavalry so greatly outnumbers ours, and is generally accompanied by so large a force of infantry in its operations, that it must always force ours back. I advanced last night to the Rapidan a portion of Early's and Anderson's divisions, and arrested the farther progress of the enemy.

I have just returned from an examination of the enemy's cavalry on the Rapidan. It seems to consist of their entire force, three divisions, with horse artillery, and, as far as I can judge, is the advance of General Meade's army. All the cavalry have been withdrawn from the lower Rappahannock, excepting some reduced pickets from Richards' Ford to Fredericksburg. Our scouts report that their whole army is under marching orders, and that two corps have already crossed the Rappahannock. The Eleventh Corps, which has been guarding the line of the railroad, marched through Manassas on the 12th instant, for the Rappahannock. Three steamers heavily loaded with troops reached Alexandria on the 9th, and the troops were forwarded in trains, on the 10th, to the same destination.

Everything looks like a concentration of their forces, and it is stated by our scouts that they have learned of the large reduction of this army. I begin to fear that we have lost the use of troops here, where they are much needed, and that they have gone where they will do no good. I learn by the papers of to-day that General Rosecrans' army entered Chattanooga on the 9th, and that General Bragg has retired still farther into the interior. It also appears that General Burnside did not move to make a junction with Rosecrans, but marched upon Knoxville. General Bragg must, therefore, either have been misinformed of his movements, or he subsequently changed them. Had I been aware that Knoxville was the destination of General Burnside, I should have recommended that General Longstreet be sent to oppose him, instead of to Atlanta.

If General Bragg is unable to bring General Rosecrans to battle, I think it would be better to return General Longstreet to this army, to enable me to oppose the advance of General Meade with a greater prospect of success. And it is a matter worthy of consideration whether General Longstreet's corps will reach General Bragg in time and condition to be of any advantage to him.

If the report sent to me by General Cooper since my return from Richmond is correct, General Bragg had, on the 20th of August last, 51,101 effective men; General Buckner, 16,118. He was to receive from General Johnston 9,000. His total force will therefore be 76,219, as large a number as I presume he can operate with. This is independent of the local troops, which you may recollect he reported as exceeding his expectations.

Should General Longstreet reach General Bragg in time to aid him in winning a victory. and return to this army, it will be well, but should he be detained there without being able to do any good, it will result in evil. I hope you will have the means of judging of this matter and of deciding correctly. There seems to be no prospect now of General Burnside effecting a junction with General Rosecrans, but it is to be apprehended that he will force General Jones back and thus aid the advance of General Meade.

I am, with great respect, your obedient servant,

R. E. LEE,
General.

GENERAL ORDERS, } HDQRS. CAVALRY CORPS, A. N. VA.,
No. 2.   }   *September* 14, 1863.

In accordance with Special Orders, No. 229, Paragraph IV, headquarters Department of Northern Virginia, Lieut. Col. George St. Leger Grenfel, Provisional Army, C. S., is hereby assigned to duty as assistant inspector-general, Cavalry Corps, Army of Northern Virginia.

By command of Maj. Gen. J. E. B. Stuart:

H. B. McCLELLAN,
Major, and Assistant Adjutant-General.

BRISTOL, TENN., *September* 14, 1863.

Maj. WILLIAM B. MYERS,
Assistant Adjutant-General, Dublin:

Keep the home guards together, or ready to turn out in short notice, until you receive information from Colonel McCausland that there is no immediate danger from the direction of Tazewell and Mercer. Ascertain to what extent I can rely on the home guards to protect the salt-works. It would help me very much to be able to take Wharton's troops away from that service.

SAM. JONES,
Major-General.

JONESBOROUGH, TENN., *September* 14, 1863.

Capt. J. G. MARTIN,
Assistant Adjutant-General, Abingdon:

The enemy reported advancing from Cumberland Gap to Saltville. How true I cannot say. Instruct Majors Chivworth [Chenoweth] and Prentice to send scouts and ascertain the truth of the rumor.

SAM. JONES,
Major-General.

JONESBOROUGH,
September 14, 1863.

Brig. Gen. G. C. WHARTON,
Glade Spring:

Order down to Saltville the whole of the Otey Battery immediately. I have ordered Stamps' battery to report to you. The enemy is reported moving from Cumberland Gap toward Saltville. The report not authentic, but be on the alert.

SAM. JONES,
Major-General.

———

HEADQUARTERS DEPARTMENT OF WESTERN VIRGINIA,
Dublin, September 14, 1863.

Col. W. L. JACKSON,
Commanding, &c.:

COLONEL: The major-general commanding directs that you communicate with and co-operate with Colonels Ferguson and Patton in resisting and obtaining early information of any advance of the enemy in your direction.

The major-general commanding desires me to say that he is so far removed necessarily at present from your command that he is unable to give you any minute instructions. He relies with confidence on your good judgment and ability to do all that can be done to keep back the enemy in your front while the other troops of this command are engaged elsewhere.

I have the honor to remain very respectfully, your obedient servant,

WM. B. MYERS,
Assistant Adjutant-General.

(Same to Col. George S. Patton and Colonel Ferguson.)

———

HEADQUARTERS DEPARTMENT OF WESTERN VIRGINIA,
Dublin, September 14, 1863.

Col. JOHN MCCAUSLAND,
Commanding, &c.:

COLONEL: The major-general commanding is informed that there are 600 or 700 Yankees in Wyoming, and it is supposed they intend making a raid through Tazewell to the railroad. The party (he thinks) sent a day or two since may have only been a reconnoitering party. He directs you to be watchful and vigilant.

Please keep me informed at these headquarters. I have only the local home guards to defend this portion of the railroad.

Very respectfully, your obedient servant,

WM. B. MYERS,
Assistant Adjutant-General.

———

GENERAL ORDERS, }   HDQRS. DEPT. OF WESTERN VIRGINIA,
No. 38.   }   *Dublin, September* 14, 1863.

By order of the major-general commanding, the home guards of the counties lately threatened are hereby relieved from duty, and will return to their homes.

The major-general commanding returns thanks to the home guards of Wythe, Pulaski, Roanoke, and Montgomery for the promptitude with which they met the third call for their assistance in repelling a threatened raid.

While he feels confidence in their ability and determination to repel any attack when their services are needed, he at the same time takes this opportunity of cautioning them to feel no disappointment when they are disbanded without a conflict with the enemy, for the track of the invader, no matter how small his encroachment on our boundaries, is marked with waste and devastation.

Let us, on the contrary, return thanks to God that we have been once more protected from the destruction of our homes and property.

By command of Maj. Gen. Sam. Jones:

CHAS. S. STRINGFELLOW,
Assistant Adjutant-General.

WAR DEPARTMENT, C. S.,
Richmond, Va., September 14, 1863.

His Excellency ZEBULON B. VANCE,
  Governor of North Carolina, Raleigh, N. C.:

SIR: Your excellency's letter of the 20th ultimo, with regard to the causes of dissatisfaction among the North Carolina troops in the Army of Northern Virginia, was referred to General Lee, and I now have the honor to inclose a copy of his reply.

Very respectfully, your obedient servant,

J. A. SEDDON,
Secretary of War.

[Inclosure.]

HEADQUARTERS ARMY OF NORTHERN VIRGINIA,
September 9, 1863.

Hon. JAMES A. SEDDON,
  Secretary of War, Richmond, Va.:

SIR: The letter of Governor Vance, of North Carolina, of August 20, with regard to the causes of dissatisfaction among the North Carolina troops in this army, with your indorsement, has been received.

I regret exceedingly the jealousies, heart-burnings, and other evil consequences resulting from the crude misstatements of newspaper correspondents, who have, necessarily, a very limited acquaintance with the facts about which they write, and who magnify the deeds of troops from their own States at the expense of others. But I can see no remedy for this. Men seem to prefer sowing discord to inculcating harmony.

In the reports of the officers, justice is done the brave soldiers of North Carolina, whose heroism and devotion have illustrated the name of their State on every battle-field in which the Army of Northern Virginia has been engaged, but the publication of these reports during the progress of the war would give the enemy information which it is desirable to withhold. With regard to a correspondent of the press from North Carolina, the way is open to him as to those from other States. I cannot, however, in my judgment,

consistently with the good of the public service, detail a soldier from
the army for this purpose. *I believe it would be much better to
have no correspondents of the press with the army.

In the appointment of officers I do not think there is any ground
for complaint. The attempt has been as far as possible to have all
the regiments from the same State brigaded together under officers
from their own States, or old army officers. The cavalry regiments
from North Carolina have been placed in a brigade to be commanded
by General Baker. In a mixed brigade of Virginia and North Carolina regiments I some time ago removed a Virginia brigadier, on
the representations of Governor Vance, and placed over the brigade
an old army officer from Maryland. Shortly after the battle of Chancellorsville two brigadiers from North Carolina were promoted major-
generals in this army, their former positions being filled at once by
promotions from that State. Of one of these, the noble Pender, the
casualties of battle, alas, deprived us; and the other, General Ransom, has been called to take charge of an important military department, succeeding another distinguished North Carolinian, General
Hill, of the Army of Northern Virginia, promoted and sent to the
Department of the West. Another, the lamented Pettigrew, whose
brigade, under his skillful leadership, emulated the deeds of veterans
in the battles of Gettysburg, fell on the banks of the Potomac. He
has been succeeded by the promotion of an officer from the same
State. General Iverson, of Georgia, has been transferred from the
North Carolina brigade which he commanded to a Louisiana brigade,
and his place filled by the promotion of a North Carolinian. You will
perceive from this statement how far I have succeeded in arranging
the brigades from North Carolina in conformity to the rule spoken
of above, and though the accidents of war and the wants of the
service in other departments have deprived this army of the services
of many accomplished North Carolinians, they have been replaced
almost entirely by promotions from that State.

I need not say that I will with pleasure aid Governor Vance in removing every reasonable cause of complaint on the part of men who
have fought so gallantly and done so much for the cause of our
country. And I hope that he will do all in his power to cultivate a
spirit of harmony, and to bring to punishment the disaffected who
use these causes of discontent to further their treasonable designs.

I am, with great respect, your obedient servant,

R. E. LEE,
General.

HEADQUARTERS,
Orange, September 15, 1863.

Brig. Gen. WILLIAM N. PENDLETON :

GENERAL : Your letter of the 8th instant, inclosing one from Major
Page, reached me at a time when I was pressed by business that had
accumulated during my absence. I cannot now give the matter
much attention, and have only been able to read partially Major
Page's letter. I think the report of my dissatisfaction at your conduct is given upon small grounds, the statement apparently of your
courier, upon whom I turned my back. I must acknowledge I have
no recollection of the circumstances, or of anything upon which it
could have been based. The guns were withdrawn from the heights

of Fredericksburg under general instructions given by me. It is difficult now to say, with the after knowledge of events, whether these instructions could, at the time, have been better executed, or whether if all the guns had remained in position, as you state there was not enough infantry supports for those retained, more might not have been captured.

I am, very respectfully, your obedient servant,

R. E. LEE,
General.

P. S.—I return Major Page's letter* and the copy of your report.*

HEADQUARTERS DEPARTMENT OF WESTERN VIRGINIA,
Dublin, September 15, 1863.

Brig. Gen. F. T. NICHOLLS,
Lynchburg:

Send both companies, as soon as you can, to report to Colonel Wharton at Glade Spring.

CHAS. S. STRINGFELLOW,
Assistant Adjutant-General.

HEADQUARTERS DEPARTMENT OF WESTERN VIRGINIA,
Dublin, September 15, 1863.

Maj. Gen. SAMUEL JONES,
Jonesborough:

Will send Stamps immediately. There are 1,500 regular troops at Lynchburg and *en route* to that place. Do not know commander— Dodamead desires to know where to send them. Telegraph him direct, as I am not informed of your wishes or plans, and cannot order him under Warwick's telegram. Major Myers sent the home guards away. Sorry I cannot be with you, but cheerfully remain as you desire. Will send Myers to-morrow.

CHAS. S. STRINGFELLOW,
Assistant Adjutant-General.

RICHMOND, VA., *September 16, 1863.*

General R. E. LEE,
Comdg. Army of Northern Virginia, Orange C. H.:

GENERAL: Your two letters of the 14th have been received. In relation to the guns of General Longstreet's corps, I had taken the same view which you present, and upon inquiry have learned that a supply of artillery horses were to be obtained at Atlanta. On account of the necessity for rapid operations and the delays consequent upon insufficient transportation, I suggested to General Longstreet the propriety of supplying himself with guns, if practicable, from those in depot at Atlanta and at Augusta. At the latter place a battery of Napoleons were being prepared to be shipped to General Whiting at Wilmington. I proposed to Colonel Gorgas to exchange them for similar guns here belonging to General Longstreet's corps.

---

* Not found.

I have been disappointed, by the retreat of General Bragg from Chattanooga, which I saw defeated the purpose for which Longstreet's corps had been sent by way of Atlanta. Could this have been foreseen, it would no doubt have been better to have carried out the original design, and sent him by way of Bristol, to attack Burnside from the east. The information communicated by General Jones is confirmatory of the inexplicable surrender of Cumberland Gap. This opens to the enemy approaches into Southwest Virginia and gives them the command of that portion of East Tennessee which otherwise General Jones would have been able to defend against such force as the enemy could under existing circumstances detach. The disaffected population in East Tennessee and Northwest North Carolina will materially aid the enemy and embarrass our future operations.

General Bragg, after leaving Chattanooga, moved toward the mountains in a southwest direction, and reports that he was unable to bring the enemy to battle. I had previously telegraphed to him that from his reports I inferred the plan of Rosecrans to be to cause him to evacuate Chattanooga, and then to make a junction with Burnside, and urged upon him, as had been previously done, the importance of prompt action and the advantage of attacking the enemy while his columns were separated. I conversed freely with General Longstreet, and he seemed to concur with me in the propriety of the most active operations, both by attack upon the enemy and expeditions against his lines of communication. It is most unfortunate that Burnside should have been permitted to get possession of that portion of Tennessee which alone could have enabled him to continue his operations independently of the base on which he had relied for supplies. I can but hope, however, that with the large army which General Bragg commands he will recover by force the country out of which he seems to have been maneuvered by the enemy, and this reasonable hope is sustained by the dispatch which has just come in from Lafayette, bearing date 15th instant:

The enemy has retired before us at all points. We shall now turn on him in the direction of Chattanooga.

Thus, you see, is to be fulfilled my apprehension as communicated to him that, if Rosecrans could induce him to evacuate Chattanooga, by demonstrations upon his line of communication, he would then reverse his movement to make a junction with Burnside at Chattanooga, and there we shall probably have to fight the whole force of the enemy in an intrenched position, unless it may be possible so to confine him as to compel him to march out for the want of subsistence. The numerical superiority of the enemy, and their vast means of transportation, offer serious objections to any attempt on our part to besiege him. The opportunity has been lost which was presented in the earlier stages of the campaign, and the question now is, what is the best which it remains for us to do? On this point, if you should have the necessary leisure, I would be glad to have your views.

The demonstrations of the enemy in your front have very probably resulted from the knowledge that Longstreet's corps had been detached. I cannot imagine how the information was acquired at so early a date as that which you mention. I have despaired in the present condition of Richmond of being able to keep secret any movement which is to be made from or through this place. When

Colonel Wood made his boat expedition to the Chesapeake, his purpose and destination were not known to the other members of my staff, nor to the Secretary of the Navy, yet he found the vessels he boarded had been put on their guard against his coming.

I called Mr. Seddon's attention to your remarks on the subject of the information given in relation to the movement of General Longstreet's corps and other troops. He could suggest nothing as to the way in which the fact had transpired.

The War Department assures me that no effort shall be spared to fill up the ranks of your army, and as soon as circumstances permit, the divisions which you have sent to the southwest will be directed to hasten back to you. Should the Legislature of Virginia make provision for forcing all men able to bear arms into service as militia, it will probably benefit the enrollment of recruits for the army.

Very respectfully and truly, yours,

JEFFERSON DAVIS.

HEADQUARTERS ARMY OF NORTHERN VIRGINIA,
September 16, 1863.
His Excellency JEFFERSON DAVIS,
President Confederate States, Richmond, Va.:

Mr. PRESIDENT: No attempt has been made by the enemy to cross the Rapidan since the 14th. He seems to be collecting forces in the vicinity of Culpeper Court-House. Whether it is with a view of its occupancy or of a farther advance, is not yet apparent. A few days will probably disclose.

Col. Bradley T. Johnson, who was commissioned for a command in the Maryland Line, is now without one. He has commanded General John M. Jones' brigade since the battle of Gettysburg, But General Jones, having recovered from his wounds, has returned to duty. The Maryland Line has been divided; the cavalry assigned to Fitz. Lee's brigade and the infantry to George H. Steuart's.

There are eight companies of infantry, seven of cavalry, and a battalion of light artillery. It is desired to keep the Maryland Line united, as I believe was contemplated by the act of Congress organizing it. I could place the whole under Colonel Johnson, assign it to duty at Hanover Junction, and bring Cooke's brigade to this army. The troops of the Maryland Line were temporarily separated on the expedition to Pennsylvania, as they could not do duty together with advantage. The infantry ought to be sufficient to guard the bridges over the Annas and the cavalry to guard the roads of approach in that direction. Cooke's brigade would give some strength to this army.

I am, very respectfully, your obedient servant,

R. E. LEE,
General.

HDQRS. DEPT. OF W. VA. AND EAST TENN.,
Zollicoffer, September 16, 1863.
His Excellency President DAVIS,
Richmond:

The indications in front of Jonesborough yesterday were such that I did not think it necessary to withdraw to the line of the Watauga and Holston, being reluctant to yield any more ground. I have tolerably reliable information that the main body of the enemy's force left Cumberland Gap on the 12th. Do not know where they went. There are indications that it is coming by Rogersville toward Blountsville. If so, I must return from Jonesborough. From two to four regiments of infantry reported occupying Cumberland Gap.

General Corse telegraphed me from Bonsack's this morning that his orders from General Pickett were to go to Wytheville, and if the reports of the enemy's advance were false, to return without further orders to Petersburg. Was that your intention? I had ordered him here. If he can be spared, it is important to retain him. I cannot withdraw any more troops from Lewisburg or Princeton without exposing too much of the Virginia and Tennessee Railroad. I left Jenkins' cavalry brigade on the Staunton and Parkersburg turnpike, near Monterey. Can I withdraw it with safety to Staunton?

SAM. JONES,
Major-General.

———

HEADQUARTERS,
Wilmington. September 16, 1863.

Hon. JAMES A. SEDDON,
Secretary of War, Richmond:

SIR: I send you a letter from the Governor of North Carolina on a matter of great importance. I am not able to give him an engineer of the ability he desires, but have asked the Engineer Department to furnish one. I have suggested to him to employ the services of either Col. Robert H. Cowan, late of the Eighteenth North Corolina, or Colonel De Rosset, late of the Third North Carolina, both excellent soldiers and now out of service.

In the meantime, if you will allow General Pickett to extend one of his brigades to the vicinity of Weldon, it will enable me to make use of Ransom and his command. This thing ought to be crushed at once.

Very respectfully, your obedient servant,
W. H. C. WHITING,
Major-General.

[Indorsements.]

ENGINEER BUREAU, September 26, 1863.

Respectfully referred to Col. W. H. Stevens, for his consideration and action.

It is suggested that Lieut. W. G. Bender could perform the within duties satisfactorily, and that Lieut. J. B. Tapscott could be ordered probably to take Lieutenant Bender's present position. Please return these papers, with an indorsement informing the bureau of your action.

ALFRED L. RIVES,
Lieutenant-Colonel, and Acting Chief of Bureau.

SEPTEMBER 27, 1863.

Respectfully returned to Engineer Bureau.
I have ordered Lieutenants Bender and Tapscott as suggested.

W. H. STEVENS,
Colonel, Engineers.

ENGINEER BUREAU, *October* 1, 1863.

Respectfully returned to honorable Secretary of War.

An officer of Engineers of good reputation has been ordered to Western North Carolina, as desired by General Whiting and Governor Vance.

ALFRED L. RIVES,
Lieutenant-Colonel, and Acting Chief of Bureau.

OCTOBER 1, 1863.

ADJUTANT-GENERAL:

If Corse's brigade be returned, it might be expedient for General Pickett to extend command to Weldon and leave General Ransom's brigade in part free. Suppose you consult General Pickett on this point.

J. A. S. [SEDDON.]

OCTOBER 3, 1863.

SECRETARY OF WAR,:

I have seen and conversed with General Pickett, and we both think I would be unwise to send any part of Brigadier-General Ransom's brigade to Western North Carolina, General Hoke having been sent some time since by General Lee with sufficient force, including a regiment of Ransom's, besides cavalry, for this purpose.

S. COOPER,
Adjutant and Inspector General.

[Inclosure.]

STATE OF NORTH CAROLINA, EXECUTIVE DEPARTMENT,
Raleigh, September 14, 1863.

General WHITING:

MY DEAR SIR: By the occupation of East Tennessee by the enemy, the mountain region of North Carolina has become exposed to destructive raids and incursions of the Federals and tories.

Large numbers of deserters are also crowding in there.

The mountains have a strong force of warlike militia, used to the rifle, who are calling upon me to organize them for a fight. I desire to send them an engineer to show them how to fortify the passes, &c., and a brigadier to organize them and command. Can you send me the engineer—an active, intelligent man, who could comprehend the topography and probable operation of a large extent of country? Let me know immediately.

Very respectfully, your obedient servant,

Z. B. VANCE.

GENERAL ORDERS, }   HDQRS. CAVALRY CORPS, A. N. VA.,
No. 3.   }   *September* 17, 1863.

Officers immediately in command on the battle-field will be held to strict accountability for the safety of artillery operating with their commands. They will see that a sufficient support of cavalry sharpshooters is in every case specially charged with its support and protection at all hazards.

By command of Maj. Gen. J. E. B. Stuart:

H. B. McCLELLAN,
Major, and Assistant Adjutant-General.

HEADQUARTERS DEPARTMENT OF WESTERN VIRGINIA,
Dublin, September 17, 1863.

Maj. Gen. SAMUEL JONES, *Zollicoffer:*

General Lee can send you no troops. Will send his letter to-morrow. Expects a fight.

CHAS. S. STRINGFELLOW,
Assistant Adjutant-General.

DUBLIN, *September* 17, 1863. (Received 19th.)

Hon. JAMES A. SEDDON,
Secretary of War, Richmond, Va.:

Captain Martin, assistant adjutant-general, reports from Abingdon
that enemy are advancing slowly on that place. He says Colonel
Carter, First Tennessee [Cavalry] Regiment, engaged enemy 7 miles
this side of Bristol this morning, and fell back to Abingdon. Enemy
have seven regiments and six or more pieces of artillery. I have
heard nothing from General Jones to-day, and therefore presume the
above to be true. He was at Zollicoffer yesterday.

CHAS. S. STRINGFELLOW,
Assistant Adjutant-General.

HEADQUARTERS DEPARTMENT OF WESTERN VIRGINIA,
Dublin, September 17, 1863.

Lieut. Col. E. A. PALFREY, *Assistant Adjutant-General:*

In the absence of the commanding general in East Tennessee, I
have the honor to report, in reply to your letter of the 15th instant,
that Col. G. C. Wharton was ordered to the valley with his brigade
on the 8th of July, 1863.

Very respectfully, your obedient servant,

CHAS. S. STRINGFELLOW,
Assistant Adjutant-General.

HEADQUARTERS ARMY OF NOTHERN VIRGINIA,
September 18, 1863.

His Excellency JEFFERSON DAVIS,
President Confederate States:

MR. PRESIDENT: I have had the honor to receive your letter of
the 16th instant. Should Generals Rosecrans and Burnside unite at
Chattanooga, as now seems to be probable, and there fortify themselves, they will have, as you say, such vast means at their disposal
as to render an attack upon that position by us extremely hazardous.
I can see no other way, at this distance, of causing them to abandon
that strong position than that which you suggest of attacking their
line of communication. For this purpose their position will be
favorable, for, although from Stevenson two routes are open to the
enemy, one to Memphis, and the other to Nashville, from Stevenson
to Chattanooga there is but a single route. General Bragg, by concentrating his cavalry, and sending it to cut the lines of communication beyond Stevenson, will cause General Rosecrans to detach
largely for its maintenance. Then, by moving with his whole force
upon a vulnerable point, according to the nature of the ground, he
will in all human probability break up his position.

From the report of our scouts General Meade's whole army is this side of the Rappahannock, and it is stated that he is preparing to march against us. The route he will take is not certain, though a deserter who came in last night reported that he was to force a passage across the Rapidan at Morton's Ford to-day. The heavy rains of this morning may interfere with his plans. It has also been reported by our scouts that on the 10th instant two very large steamers passed up the Potomac loaded with troops. On the 12th, a very large ocean steamer passed up heavily laden, and on the 14th, another steamer passed up, also loaded with troops. They have been forwarding troops on the Orange and [Alexandria] Railroad for the last few days, which I think are those I have mentioned as having ascended the Potomac. I think it also probable that these troops are conscripts, as the deserter referred to stated that the party he. came with was shipped at Philadelphia to prevent their desertion. I also see it stated in the Northern papers that General Meade has been promised that his army shall be filled up to its full organization by conscripts as fast as obtained. The only re-enforcements for this army that I can now obtain is Cooke's brigade, stationed at Hanover Junction. If a portion of Pickett's division could be sent there for the occasion, I should like to draw it to me.

Very respectfully, your obedient servant,

R. E. LEE,
General.

HEADQUARTERS ARMY OF NORTHERN VIRGINIA,
September 18, 1863.

His Excellency JEFFERSON DAVIS,
President Confederate States:

MR. PRESIDENT: Since my letter of this morning I have received reports from various scouts, all concurring in the statement that General Meade's whole army is between the Rappahannock and the Rapidan. All the corps forming his army have been mentioned and all seem to be present. The Eleventh Corps alone is still north of the Rappahannock guarding the line of the railroad. The reports that have been circulated of some of the corps having been sent to Charleston would appear to have been erroneous, unless they have been recently returned. Their force is apparently so much greater than our own that it is probable we may be forced back, and I am sending off all surplus articles from Orange and Gordonsville.

If it can be ascertained that the enemy has withdrawn his troops from the coast of Virginia and North Carolina, all of ours that are available had better be placed in marching condition for service with this army. I inclose a report* just sent me by General Fitz. Lee, which corroborates others that I have received. Lieutenant-Colonel White, who is operating in Loudoun and Fauquier, says it is reported on the upper Potomac that General Heintzelman has taken command at Harper's Ferry and that re-enforcements are being sent there. I have written to General Imboden to ascertain if this is true and what is its object.

I have the honor to be, with great respect, your obedient servant,

R. E. LEE,
General.

---

* Not found.

SPECIAL ORDERS, }   HDQRS. ARMY OF NORTHERN VIRGINIA,
No. 235.   }   September 18, 1863.

I. Col. D. H. Hamilton is, at his own request, relieved from the command of McGowan's brigade and his own regiment (First South Carolina Regiment), and will report to the Adjutant and Inspector General, C. S. Army, Richmond, Va., with the request that he be ordered to Charleston, S. C., for duty.

*   *   *   *

By command of General R. E. Lee:

R. H. CHILTON,
Assistant Adjutant and Inspector General.

HEADQUARTERS DEPARTMENT OF WESTERN VIRGINIA,
Dublin, September 18, 1863.

Col. M. J. FERGUSON,
Comanding Jenkins' Brigade, via Staunton
(Care of commanding officer at that point):

Order one regiment of your brigade to Little Levels, in Pocahontas County, station one regiment near Lewisburg, and order one to report to Colonel McCausland; send Witcher's battalion to Zollicoffer, East Tennessee, near Bristol.

Report execution of this order, the number of the regiment sent to each place, and use all possible dispatch. Notify General Imboden and Col. W. L. Jackson of the move.

By order of Maj. Gen. Sam. Jones:

CHAS. S. STRINGFELLOW,
Assistant Adjutant-General.

Officer Commanding at Staunton:

Please forward the accompanying dispatch to Colonel Ferguson, commanding General Jenkins' brigade, on Staunton and Parkersburg turnpike, near Monterey, with all possible haste, as also the one to General Imboden. They are of greatest importance,

CHAS. S. STRINGFELLOW.

P. S.—Deliver copy of dispatch for Colonel Ferguson to commander of post, to be sent to General Imboden.

HEADQUARTERS DEPARTMENT OF WESTERN VIRGINIA,
Dublin, September 18, 1863.

Col. J. GORGAS,
Chief of Ordnance, Richmond:

From report of Major Bowyer, the ammunition in the department is fearfully short. Exposed troops have only 23 rounds. Unless ammunition is hurried here immediately, the consequences will be most disastrous. Am satisfied Major Bowyer could not have made reports required. If necessary, that can be inquired into hereafter. Ammunition is needed now.

In absence of the general commanding:

CHAS. S. STRINGFELLOW,
Assistant Adjutant-General.

HEADQUARTERS DEPARTMENT OF WESTERN VIRGINIA,
Dublin, September 18, 1863.

Col. GEORGE S. PATTON,
Commanding First Brigade:

Order the Eighth Virginia Cavalry to report to Colonel McCausland immediately. Jenkins' brigade has just been ordered from its present position. One regiment ordered to Little Levels, Pocahontas, one to Colonel McCausland, one to Lewisburg, and Witcher's battalion to Zollicoffer, East Tennessee.

You must employ the Greenbrier cavalry and such portions of Dunn's battalion as you think proper to scout in your front until the regiment of Jenkins' brigade gets up. Send a copy of this to Col. William L. Jackson immediately. He will notify General Imboden of this move.

CHAS. S. STRINGFELLOW,
Assistant Adjutant-General.

HEADQUARTERS DEPARTMENT OF WESTERN VIRGINIA,
Dublin, September 19, 1863.

Hon. JAMES A. SEDDON,
Secretary of War, Richmond:

Am satisfied, from information sent you in my telegram, that the salt-works are in imminent danger. The Sixtieth Virginia Regiment is at Narrows of New River. I think it can be spared, though Colonel McCausland will then be left at Princeton with less than two regiments. In any event he can retreat safely to the Narrows. Shall I order the Sixtieth to Saltville, and take the risk in front?

I cannot hear from General Jones. The enemy is between us, if reports are true, and I therefore ask that you will reply to-night. Wharton cannot resist the force opposed to him if as reported, and they move on him instead of against General Jones.

If Scammon and Kelley make a simultaneous move in front, the withdrawal of the Sixtieth may lead to serious consequences here and on the Staunton line.

Please instruct me immediately.

CHAS. S. STRINGFELLOW,
Assistant Adjutant-General.

HEADQUARTERS DEPARTMENT OF WESTERN VIRGINIA,
Dublin, September 19, 1863.

Maj. JOSEPH F. KENT,
Wytheville:

Collect every man you can and go at once to Glade Spring. The defense of Wytheville will be best made there. Enemy 7 miles this side of Bristol this morning, and steadily advancing on Abingdon and Saltville.

Reply.

CHAS. S. STRINGFELLOW,
Assistant Adjutant-General.

HEADQUARTERS DEPARTMENT OF WESTERN VIRGINIA,
Dublin, September 19, 1863.
Col. W. L. JACKSON,
Commanding, &c.:

COLONEL: By direction of the major-general commanding, I inform you that orders have been given for the disposition of General Jenkins' brigade as follows, viz: One regiment at Little Levels, Pocahontas, one near Lewisburg, and one to report to Colonel McCausland. Witcher's battalion reports to the general at Zollicoffer, East Tennessee.

Very respectfully, colonel, your obedient servant,
CHAS. S. STRINGFELLOW,
Assistant Adjutant-General.

HEADQUARTERS DEPARTMENT OF WESTERN VIRGINIA,
Dublin, September 19, 1863.
Col. B. H. JONES,
Comdg. Sixtieth Regiment Va. Vols., Narrows:

Report at Dublin with your regiment, with the least possible delay. Be ready to take the cars for Saltville. When can you get here? Reply at once, that transportation may be ordered. Lose no time. Send the accompanying dispatch to Colonel McCausland by special courier.

By order, &c.:
CHAS. S. STRINGFELLOW,
Assistant Adjutant-General.

HEADQUARTERS DEPARTMENT OF WESTERN VIRGINIA,
Dublin, September 19, 1863.
Colonel McCAUSLAND,
Commanding Brigade:

The enemy are so vigorously pressing General Jones and with such superior force, while they threaten Saltville also, that the Sixtieth Regiment has been ordered to Saltville immediately.

You must do the best you can with your remaining force, and the Eighth Virginia Cavalry; another regiment of General Jenkins' brigade, is on its way to you. Be on your guard and fall back if necessary to the Narrows and Rocky Gap, or either of those places, as may be best under the circumstances.

Will order a company of First Brigade to Narrows as a guard. The emergency is pressing. Promptness and watchfulness were never more needed.

By order of Maj. Gen. Sam. Jones:
CHAS. S. STRINGFELLOW,
Assistant Adjutant-General.

HEADQUARTERS DEPARTMENT OF WESTERN VIRGINIA,
Dublin, September 19, 1863.
Col. GEORGE S. PATTON, Union:

Order the Eighth [Virginia Cavalry] to McCausland at Princeton. Forgetting you had a company of the Fourteenth [Virginia Cavalry], I merely ordered a regiment to you. It is on the move but

I do not know yet which you will have. The enemy vigorously pressing General Jones, and threatening Wharton. I shall immediately order the Sixtieth [Virginia Infantry] to Glade Spring to aid Wharton. Keep, therefore, the closest lookout in your front. Report fully anything that occurs. Send the Eighth immediately. By order of Maj. Gen. Sam. Jones:

CHAS. S. STRINGFELLOW,
Assistant Adjutant-General.

HEADQUARTERS DEPARTMENT OF WESTERN VIRGINIA,
Dublin, September 19, 1863.

Col. GEORGE P. TERRILL,
Salem:

If you can carry any of your men to Glade Spring, report there at once to Brigadier-General Wharton. The enemy this side of Bristol and steadily advancing. Call on all your men to stand by you and rally to Wharton's support.

CHAS. S. STRINGFELLOW,
Assistant Adjutant-General.

(Similar dispatches to the above were sent to the following addresses: Col. H. M. Bowyer, Bonsack's; Brigadier-General Nicholls, Lynchburg; Maj. James M. Wade, Christiansburg.)

HEADQUARTERS DEPARTMENT OF WESTERN VIRGINIA,
Dublin, September 19, 1863.

Brig. Gen. G. C. WHARTON;
Glade Spring:

Have called on the home guards of Montgomery, Roanoke, Botetourt, Bedford, Wythe, Smyth, and Pulaski to aid you. Am afraid to order Sixtieth [Virginia Infantry] away. Communicate with the general by special courier if possible and ask the order from him.

CHAS. S. STRINGFELLOW,
Assistant Adjutant-General.

HEADQUARTERS DEPARTMENT OF WESTERN VIRGINIA,
Dublin, September 19, 1863.

Brig. Gen. G. C. WHARTON,
Glade Spring:

Have ordered the Sixtieth [V rg n a] Regiment to your aid, and will send you quite a large body of home guards. Will order transportation as soon as I can, when they will be ready. Promptness, energy, and skill will yet bring us all right. I rely on you confidently, but use your forces to best advantage to aid General Jones, and defend the salt-works. Communicate with the general at all hazards, but in such a way as to guard against capture of dispatches. Will aid you by every means in my power. Inform General Jones of this move as soon as you can.

By order of Maj. Gen. Sam. Jones:

CHAS S. STRINGFELLOW,
Assistant Adjutant-General.

HEADQUARTERS DEPARTMENT OF WESTERN VIRGINIA,
Dublin, September 19, 1863.

Brig. Gen. G. C. WHARTON,
Glade Spring:

Keep me fully informed of affairs in your front. I hear Bristol is in the hands of the enemy. Do you know anything about this?

CHAS. S. STRINGFELLOW,
Assistant Adjutant-General.

HEADQUARTERS DEPARTMENT OF WESTERN VIRGINIA,
Dublin, September 19, 1863.

G. A. WINGFIELD, *Liberty:*

Call on every man who will rally to the support of General Wharton to go with you at once to Glade Spring. Enemy 7 miles this side of Bristol this morning, and steadily advancing. Reply.

CHAS. S. STRINGFELLOW,
Assistant Adjutant-General.

HEADQUARTERS ARMY OF NORTHERN VIRGINIA,
September 20, 1863.

His Excellency JEFFERSON DAVIS,
President Confederate States:

MR. PRESIDENT: I have had the honor to receive your letter of yesterday, giving the statements of gentlemen from Norfolk with regard to negro troops and cavalry which the enemy are collecting in that quarter for an attack on Weldon. I do not apprehend that these negro regiments will prove a very formidable body, though unopposed they might do us great damage. But as the enemy are now in possession of the East Tennessee road, and the progress on the line from Danville to Greensborough has been so small in the past year, Weldon becomes to us a point of much importance, and I think it would be well to send Colonel Stevens, of the Engineers, to have some works erected for its defense, as well as for the defense of other vulnerable points on the railway. These could be so arranged as to be held by a small force until re-enforcements could be sent.

If the navigation of the Roanoke has not been yet obstructed, there may be danger from light-draught steamers on that river, which is navigable very high up. It can be readily obstructed, no doubt, and may be a good stream for the use of torpedoes.

It is of the greatest importance to us now that the line from Danville to the North-Carolina Railway should be speedily finished.

I am, very respectfully, your obedient servant,

R. E. LEE,
General.

RICHMOND,
September 20, 1863.

General SAMUEL JONES,
Watauga Bridge, via Bristol:

If you can with safety spare Corse's brigade, send it here.

S. COOPER,
Adjutant and Inspector General.

HEADQUARTERS DEPARTMENT OF WESTERN VIRGINIA,
Dublin, September 20, 1863.

Col. JOHN McCAUSLAND, *Commanding, &c.*:

COLONEL : I telegraphed you last night that the situation of affairs in East Tennessee and near Saltville renders it absolutely necessary to order to the latter place the Sixtieth Virginia Regiment. The enemy are between Generals Jones and Wharton, and the utmost promptness can alone save us. This exposes you, but I hope you can maintain yourself with the Eighth Virginia Cavalry until another regiment of General Jenkins' brigade, now on its way to you, gets up. Of course, you must fall back, if necessary, and try to hold the Narrows and Rocky Gap. A company from the First Brigade has been ordered to the Narrows as a guard.

If Scammon learns the state of things at Zollicoffer and Bristol, an advance will doubtless be made. Be prepared, therefore, for any move, and keep a sharp lookout in your front and in the direction the raiders last came. Nothing but the most urgent necessity would have caused this move.

Very respectfully, colonel, your obedient servant,

CHAS. S. STRINGFELLOW,
Assistant Adjutant-General.

Abstract from field return of the Army of Northern Virginia, General Robert E. Lee, C. S. Army, commanding, September 20, 1863; headquarters Orange Court-House.

Command.	Present for duty.		Aggregate present.	Aggregate present and absent.
	Officers.	Men.		
General headquarters..	14	....	14	15
Second Army Corps (Ewell).......................................	1,507	16,235	20,084	38,264
Third Army Corps (A. P. Hill)	1,175	14,207	17,975	31,667
Cooke's brigade...	145	2,045	2,534	3,367
Cavalry Corps a (Stuart)..	594	7,547	9,530	18,011
Artillery (Pendleton)...	184	3,337	3,931	5,406
Total..	3,619	43,461	54 068	96,630

a From return for September 10 of the enlisted men present for duty, 1,361 are reported as dismounted.

Abstract from return of the Department of North Carolina, Maj. Gen. W. H. C. Whiting, C. S. Army, commanding, September 20, 1863.

Command.	Present for duty.		Effective total.	Aggregate present.	Aggregate present and absent.	Pieces of field artillery.
	Officers.	Men.				
General headquarters..............................	9	3	3	13	14	......
District of the Cape Fear	180	3,179	3,646	4,459	5,631	22
District of North Carolina........................	170	2,807	3,242	3,968	6,223	31
Total...	359	5,989	6,891	8,440	11,868	53

RICHMOND, VA., *September* 21, 1863.

General R. E. LEE,
    Commanding Army of Northern Virginia:

GENERAL : Yours of the 20th has been received. I concur with you in your estimate of the movement from Norfolk, but even thus regarded, it seems difficult to make the needful provision against it. The division sent here was numerically not equal to the two brigades taken away, and the necessities of General S. Jones caused the brigade of General Corse to be sent to him. I directed the Adjutant-General, in furtherance of your wish, to send another of Pickett's brigades to relieve General Cooke's, so that you might draw that to you.

Since I commenced writing, a dispatch from General Bragg has arrived from Chickamauga River, September 21. He says :

After two days' hard fighting we have driven the enemy, after a desperate resistance, from several positions, and now hold the field, but he still confronts us. The losses are heavy on both sides, especially so in our officers. We have taken over 20 pieces of artillery and some 2,500 prisoners.

Have this moment received the following dispatch from the adjutant-general of General S. Jones, from Dublin, September 21 :

Courier from General Jones arrived at Bristol yesterday. He was at Zollicoffer. Enemy moved on that point yesterday at 8 o'clock. Skirmished with our forces. Moved off in the direction of Blountsville and Jonesborough. Colonel Carter started after them with cavalry and artillery last night.

These dispatches indicate that the attention of the enemy will be concentrated on General Bragg, and that General Jones will thereby be relieved for the present. I have been, since you left, anxious to go to the Army of Tennessee, but have been delayed by causes which you readily understand. Unless we receive more decisive intelligence than that herein communicated, it is still my purpose to go as soon as other duties will permit. If we can obtain a complete victory in that quarter, and drive the enemy, broken and discouraged, from the present field of operations, the forces you sent can most readily return to you through East Tennessee and Southwestern Virginia, and I trust it may be practicable then to bring them to you before the enemy shall render their presence with you a necessity. In the meantime, I have urged that the greatest efforts should be made to procure and send recruits to you, and I hope the Legislature, now in session here, will adopt such action as will bring out the arms-bearing population who are not subject to enrollment for the Confederate Army, and thus afford to you an auxiliary force, which will relieve you from the necessity of detaching troops to guard localities and lines of communication.

I have not been able to avoid vain regrets at the detachment of troops by the southern route, which, if the course of General Bragg could have been foreseen, would have been more valuable in East Tennessee, whence they could have been more readily withdrawn to support you in time of need. If, however, General Bragg's operations should be successful, and rapidly followed up, it may prove that the course adopted was, after all, the best.

Only one battalion of artillery (Alexander's) has gone beyond Petersburg, and I have directed that no horses should be sent. The supply at Atlanta, if correctly reported, will suffice for that battalion, but no more, and you will no doubt require all the artillery horses which General Longstreet had,

Colonel Ives, who some time since gave his attention to the obstruction of rivers in North Carolina, informs me that torpedoes are in the course of construction, and it is intended, as soon as any are ready, to place them in the Roanoke River. He says, however, a difficulty has been encountered in the want of a proper officer to take charge of laying them. He will inquire what has been done, and is doing, in relation to works of defense at Weldon and other vulnerable points on the railroad. The works some time since commenced at Weldon were too extensive for a small force, and we could not expect to keep a large garrison there.

The progress of the Danville and Greensborough Railroad, if recent promises are fulfilled, should be more rapid hereafter than heretofore.

No recent intelligence from Charleston of importance, and no indication of any withdrawal of troops by the enemy. I received private information that 30,000 troops were about to be shipped from the North to go southward. Those you mention as coming up to General Meade may be from New York, and if so are new levies mainly. I deeply regret your want of an adequate force to avail yourself of the opportunity afforded by the present condition of the enemy, but hope before he is prepared to attack that you will be re-enforced. Like the people generally, I feel secure in the confidence you and your army inspire ; that, in the meantime, nothing worse can befall us than a temporary withdrawal to a more interior line.

Very respectfully and truly, yours,

JEFFERSON DAVIS.

HEADQUARTERS ARMY OF NORTHERN VIRGINIA,
September 21, 1863.

Gen. J. D. IMBODEN,
Commanding, &c.:

GENERAL : General Lee directs me to acknowledge the receipt of your letter of the 16th instant, and say that he is gratified to learn that injustice has been done to Major Gilmor and his command. He says that he considers it necessary that every means should be used to capture or destroy the lawless men who have brought discredit upon the army. The interests of the cause and the character of our troops, particularly that of Major Gilmor's command, require that these deserters be arrested or destroyed, and a stop put to their marauding. The general desires that you will instruct your officers and men to take them whenever they can, dead or alive. They must be exterminated, and every one who comes across them must take or shoot them.

Very respectfully, your obedient servant,

CHARLES MARSHALL,
Major, and Aide-de-Camp.

SPECIAL ORDERS, } HDQRS. ARMY OF NORTHERN VIRGINIA,
No. 237. { *September 21, 1863.*

I. Brig. Gen. A. Perrin, Provisional Army, C. S., will report to Lieut. Gen. A. P. Hill, commanding Third Corps, Army of North-

ern Virginia, for assignment to the temporary command of McGowan's brigade, Wilcox's division.

*   *   *   *   *   ..   ..

By command of General R. E. Lee.

R. H. CHILTON,
Assistant Adjutant and Inspector General.

STATE OF NORTH CAROLINA, EXECUTIVE DEPT.,
Raleigh, September 21, 1863.

Hon. JAMES A. SEDDON,
Secretary of War:

MY DEAR SIR: The occupation of East Tennessee by the enemy,
and the great assemblage of tories and deserters in the mountains of
the border, renders Western North Carolina, with all its supplies of
beef and pork, open to the incursions of the Federals and tories.   It
is inhabited, however, by quite a warlike militia who are calling
upon me to arm and organize them for a fight.   I am doing so to the
utmost of my ability, but shall not be able to accomplish much
without your assistance.   I have the honor, therefore, to request that
you will constitute that mountain country a district and assign a
competent brigadier to the command.   With a battery or so, and a very
few regular troops, the various passes could be easily held with the
help of some 2,000 home guards whom I can order to his support.
If you have no suitable officer to be spared for such a purpose, I would
recommend that Col. C. M. Avery, of the Thirty-third North Carolina Infantry, or Col. Stephen Lee, late of the Sixteenth North
Carolina Infantry, be made a brigadier and assigned to that duty.
They are both residents of that section, acquainted with the country
and people.   The first named would, in my opinion, be the best appointment, being younger, more active, and better adapted to the
management of militia and the people generally.

I cannot furnish arms to them without leaving unarmed the home
guards on the eastern border of the State, and so I beg you, if possible, to spare me 1,000 or 1,500 muskets.

Please let me know if these suggestions meet your view immediately; there is no time to be lost.

Very respectfully, yours,

Z. B. VANCE.

[Indorsements.]

SEPTEMBER 23, 1863.

I will send 600 muskets to Captain Brenizer, Salisbury, and 200
or more rifles may be obtained at Asheville Armory, N. C.

J. GORGAS,
Colonel.

SEPTEMBER 23, 1863.

Respectfully submitted to the President.
Governor Vance requests early action.

J. A. SEDDON,
Secretary of War.

Every assistance should be given which is practicable.   I do not
know the present position of Colonel Avery and therefore cannot

judge of the feasibility of the proposition to assign him to duty as proposed. It will be observed that a request is made for the appointment of a brigadier-general, but it does not appear that there is a brigade to justify such appointment. If there should be a brigade of local-defense men, a brigadier may be appointed or assigned as may be found best.

J. D. [DAVIS.]

SEPTEMBER 26, 1863.

ADJUTANT-GENERAL:

What is the present position of Colonel Avery? Is he not with General Lee in command of a regiment?

J. A. S. [SEDDON],
Secretary.

ADJUTANT AND INSPECTOR GENERAL'S OFFICE,
September 29, 1863.

Respectfully returned to the Secretary of War.

Colonel Avery commands the Thirty-third North Carolina Regiment, Lieut. Gen. A. P. Hill's corps, General Lee's army.

By order of the Adjutant and Inspector General:

E. A. PALFREY,
Lieutenant-Colonel, and Assistant Adjutant-General.

Abstract from field return of Pickett's division, Maj. Gen. George E. Pickett, C. S. Army, commanding, September 21, 1863.

Command.	Present for duty.		Aggregate present.	Aggregate present and absent.	Average last field report.	Remarks.
	Officers.	Men.				
Division headquarters	8	....	8	9	7	Petersburg, Va.
Armistead's brigade	69	1,033	1,354	3,109	1,272	Do.
Corse's brigade	....	....	....	....	....	Detached.
Hunton's brigade	71	781	1,050	2,669	1,048	Chaffin's Farm, Va.
Kemper's brigade	92	1,000	1,349	3,130	1,319	Do.
Total	240	2,814	3,761	8,917	3,646	

HEADQUARTERS,
Wilmington, September 22, 1863.

Hon. JAMES A. SEDDON,
Secretary of War, Richmond:

SIR: The demands for transportation here have now become so great, and my means so small and so rapidly deteriorating, that I am compelled to ask for one or two steamers at once, either to be purchased or impressed, for service in the river.

For the engineer service, river obstructions, commissariat, quartermaster's department, transportation of ordnance, assistance to government steamers pursuing the blockade, and for the coal supply from Fayetteville (this most important), I have but two small iron steamers of very limited capacity, and almost entirely unserviceable from wearing out.

Please give me authority either to purchase or impress. The matter of coal alone is one of the greatest importance. If I can get serviceable steamers for the lower river, I shall be able to put one of those now attending to general business in the coal trade.

Very respectfully,

W. H. C. WHITING,
Major-General.

HEADQUARTERS ARMY OF NORTHERN VIRGINIA,
Camp at Orange Court-House, September 23, 1863.

His Excellency JEFFERSON DAVIS,
President Confederate States, Richmond, Va.:

Mr. PRESIDENT: I have had the honor to receive your letter of the 21st instant. I was rejoiced yesterday to learn by a dispatch from the War Department of the complete victory gained by General Bragg. I hope he will be able to follow it up, to concentrate his troops and operate on the enemy's rear. I infer, from the accounts I have seen, that Buckner has not joined him. Unless he is occupying a superior force to his own, he ought at once to unite with Bragg, that he may push the advantage gained. If that can be done, Longstreet can successfully move to East Tennessee, open that country, where Sam. Jones can unite with him, and thence rejoin me. No time ought now to be lost or wasted. Everything should be done that can be done at once, so that the troops may be speedily returned to this department. As far as I can judge, they will not get here too soon. The enemy is aware of Longstreet's departure. They report in their papers the day he passed through Augusta, and give the position of Ewell's and Hill's corps. General Meade is strengthening himself daily. Our last scouts report the return of the troops sent north to enforce the draft. Nine trains loaded with troops reached Culpeper Thursday night. Three trains arrived on Monday, and three on Tuesday last, in addition to between 4,000 and 5,000 by marching.

It was apparently expected by the enemy that we would abandon the line of the Rapidan on his approach. His advance seems to be delayed by doubts as to our strength from the maintenance of our position. His reconnoitering parties and cavalry are brisk in observation. During Monday and Tuesday he quietly massed his cavalry on his right, and moved through Madison to turn our left. Gregg came down the road to Orange Court-House by Burnett's Ford, Kilpatrick the road by Liberty Mills, and Buford the road by Barboursville leading to Gordonsville. General Stuart, with one division of cavalry guarding our left flank, opposed so obstinately the progress of these three divisions of the enemy that he brought them to a halt last night at the Rapidan. By that time, General Fitz. Lee had hastened from the right and joined him. During the night the enemy commenced to retire. General Stuart is now pursuing him on his route back to Culpeper. I presume his next attempt will be on our right, unless he determines to move his whole army around our army to Gordonsville. General Stuart showed his usual energy, promptness, and boldness in his operations yesterday; keeping with the front line of his troops, his horse was shot under him. Citizens report the enemy's loss heavy. I hope ours is not large. I have only heard the death of Colonel Rogers, of North Carolina, Scales' brigade, who was killed by a shell at Barnett's Ford, and of Lieutenant-Colonel Delony, of the cavalry, wounded.

I am, with great respect, your obedient servant,

R. E. LEE,
General.

P. S.—From the details brought by the train to-day of the battle of Chickamauga, I see that Buckner had united with Bragg. I am grieved to learn the death of General Hood. I fear also, from the accounts, that General Wofford is dead ; he was one of Georgia's best soldiers. I am gradually losing my best men—Jackson, Pender, Hood. There was no braver soldier in the Confederacy than Deshler. I see he is numbered among the dead.

HEADQUARTERS ARMY OF NORTHERN VIRGINIA,
September 23, 1863—2 p. m.

General STUART,
Commanding, &c.:

GENERAL : I have just received your note of to-day, reporting the retirement of the enemy's cavalry. I hope you may be able to deal him a damaging blow before he gets out of your reach. I congratulate you on defeating his plans and arresting his advance. The energy and promptness of yourself and command elicits my high admiration. With inferior numbers you concentrated your troops, and successfully opposed his progress, and obliged him to relinquish his purpose. His next attempt will be on our right. We must either be prepared for him there or prostrate him by a movement on his rear.

I hope your loss has been small, and that your troops are in good condition. Cherish and refresh them all you can.

Very respectfully, your obedient servant,

R. E. LEE,
General.

HEADQUARTERS DEPARTMENT OF WESTERN VIRGINIA,
Dublin, September 23, 1863.

General S. COOPER,
Richmond, Va.:

Captain Reid just reached Glade Spring from fight at Blountsville, Tenn., yesterday. Reports enemy, infantry and artillery and cavalry, 6,000 strong, attacked Colonel Carter and drove him toward Zollicoffer. Believes their intention to attack Saltville. Prisoner informed him Burnside in command. General Wharton reports he has sent Fifty-first Virginia Regiment toward Bristol. Has Otey Battery and Clarke's battalion on trains ready to start. Asks for the Sixtieth Regiment at once. Says he has no late intelligence from General Jones. The Sixtieth goes to him as soon as transportation is procured. It was delayed here after communications with General Jones were opened.

McCausland ordered to hold Rocky Gap and approaches to the railroad through Tazewell and Wyoming.

Have directed General Echols to be ready to garrison the Narrows in event of advance by Scammon. This would expose Greenbrier and Monroe temporarily, but the railroad seems of greater importance.

CHAS. S. STRINGFELLOW,
Assistant Adjutant-General.

HEADQUARTERS DEPARTMENT OF WESTERN VIRGINIA,
Dublin, September 23, 1863.

Brig. Gen. JOHN ECHOLS,
Lewisburg, via Union:

We cannot possibly afford to have the railroad cut now. Be prepared to garrison the Narrows at a moment's notice in event of advance by Scammon. McCausland will protect Rocky Gap and the line west of that point. Keep the closest lookout and inform me promptly of enemy's movements. Send couriers to hurry up movements of Jenkins' brigade. Colonel Patton will inform you of this. Reply at once. This exposes you for a few days, but cannot be avoided. To-day's papers confirm Bragg's great victory. Enemy's loss immense. All his killed and wounded in our hands. He retreated to Chattanooga.

By order of Maj. Gen. Sam. Jones:

CHAS. S. STRINGFELLOW,
Assistant Adjutant-General.

DUBLIN, *September 23, 1863.*

Col. JOHN McCAUSLAND, *Princeton:*

Orders have been given General Echols to be prepared to send a garrison as suggested, on a moment's notice. Carry out your plan, but give me and General Echols the earliest information.

CHAS. S. STRINGFELLOW,
Assistant Adjutant-General.

Operator will see that this is put in the courier mail when it reaches the Narrows. If courier has passed, send by special messenger.

C. S. [STRINGFELLOW.]

HEADQUARTERS DEPARTMENT OF WESTERN VIRGINIA,
Dublin, September 23, 1863.

Col. H. M. BOWYER,
Bonsack's:

Following just received from Glade Spring:

Major STRINGFELLOW ·

Order the home guards of Botetourt to be in readiness for any emergency.

ROBERT T. PRESTON.

Your men may be needed at any moment.

CHAS. S. STRINGFELLOW,
Assistant Adjutant-General.

SPECIAL ORDERS, } HDQRS. ARMY OF NORTHERN VIRGINIA,
   No. 239.   }   September 23, 1863.

*   *   *   *   *   *   *

X. Brig. Gen. A. L. Long, Provisional Army, C. S., will report to Lieut. Gen. R. S. Ewell, commanding Second Corps, for assignment to duty as chief of the artillery of his corps.

By command of General R. E. Lee:

R. H. CHILTON,
Assistant Adjutant and Inspector General.

NAVY DEPARTMENT, C. S.,
Richmond, September 23, 1863.

Hon. JAMES A. SEDDON,
   Secretary of War:

SIR: I have the honor to inclose herewith, for your information, an extract from a letter of Flag-Officer W. F. Lynch, C. S. Navy, commanding naval defenses of North Carolina.

I am, very respectfully, your obedient servant,

S. R. MALLORY,
Secretary of the Navy.

[Inclosure.]

HALIFAX, N. C.,
September 12, 1863.

* * * After a careful examination of a chart of the coasts of North and South Carolina, I am persuaded that you will concur with me in thinking an attack upon the forts defending the entrances to the Cape Fear River by iron-clads impracticable for months to come.

Within a week, in all probability, we shall have the equinoctial gale, after which the weather becomes unsettled, and is frequently tempestuous.

From Baldhead Light at the southwest and principal entrance* of the Cape Fear, to Bull Bay, in South Carolina—the first harbor in a southerly direction, for any but vessels of a light draught—is a distance of 60 miles, and from New Inlet entrance to Beaufort, N. C., the nearest in that direction of sufficient draught of water, is 80 miles.

The Ironsides may ride out the gales which spring up so suddenly and with such force in the vicinity of Frying-Pan Shoals, but the monitors cannot, and therefore would scarce venture an attack during the forthcoming season.

If the south end of Smith's Island be as much neglected as was the south end of Morris Island, the enemy may transport guns to and erect batteries upon it, but I think that General Whiting has not overlooked the importance of that position.

[Indorsement.]

SEPTEMBER 28, 1863.

Returned, with acknowledgments, to honorable Secretary of the Navy.

---

* Heretofore most important, but now with less water on its inner bar or rip than at New Inlet.—Note on original.

General Whiting concurs in reference to naval attack, but dreads effort to assail by land.   ⋅ ♦

J. A. S. [SEDDON,]
Secretary.

SPECIAL ORDERS, ⎱   ADJT. AND INSP. GENERAL'S OFFICE,
  No. 226.   ⎰   *Richmond, September 23, 1863.*

*   *   *   *   *   *

XXIII. Maj. Gen. George E. Pickett, Provisional Army, C. S., is assigned to the command of the Department of North Carolina, headquarters at Petersburg, Va.

*   *   *   *   *

By command of the Secretary of War:

JNO. WITHERS,
Assistant Adjutant-General.

GENERAL ORDERS, ⎱   HDQRS. ARMY OF NORTHERN VIRGINIA,
  No. 89.   ⎰   *September 24, 1863.*

The commanding general announces to the army, with profound gratitude to Almighty God, the victory achieved at Chickamauga by the army of General Braxton Bragg.

After a fierce and sanguinary conflict of two days, the Federal forces under General Rosecrans were driven, with heavy loss, from their strong positions, and, leaving their dead and wounded on the field, retreated under cover of night on Chattanooga, pursued by our cavalry.

Rendering to the Great Giver of Victory, as is most justly due, our praise and thanksgiving for this signal manifestation of His favor, let us extend to the army that has so nobly upheld the honor of our country the tribute of our admiration for its valor, and sympathy for its suffering and loss.

Invoking the continuous assistance of Heaven upon our efforts, let us resolve to emulate the heroic example of our brethren in the south, until the enemy shall be expelled from our borders and peace and independence be secured to our country.

[R. E. LEE,]
General.

DUBLIN,
September 24, 1863.

Maj. Gen. SAMUEL JONES:

I have heard nothing from you since the 18th. In reply to Colonel Wharton's request I sent the Sixtieth [Virginia Infantry] to him last night. As I delayed it on his statement that such was your order, I presume you had also instructed him when to call for it.

Nothing yet heard from Colonel Ferguson. I have directed General Echols to be ready to garrison the Narrows in the event of an advance by Scammon. McCausland is ordered to cover Rocky Gap and the approaches through Tazewell and Wyoming to protect the railroad. I shall use the home guards of the county as circumstances seem to require. The arrival of Ferguson's regiments is anxiously looked for, as I am well persuaded that as soon as Scammon learns the situation, he must advance. I will do all in my power in this contingency. I repeat that I am in absolute ignorance of everything connected with affairs at Zollicoffer—have no idea of even the number of your troops. Under such circumstances you will see I have to wait direct orders from you on almost every subject, or in the exercise of my own judgment, on the reports and information received here, be liable to mistakes when mistakes may possibly be fatal. You omitted in your order of the 18th to dispose of Sweeney's battalion. Where do you desire it posted?

Very respectfully, yours, &c.,

CHAS. S. STRINGFELLOW,
Assistant Adjutant-General.

HEADQUARTERS DEPARTMENT OF WESTERN VIRGINIA,
Dublin, September 24, 1863.

Col. JOHN McCAUSLAND,
Commanding Fourth Brigade:

COLONEL : I telegraphed you last night that I have given General Echols orders to garrison the Narrows in event of Scammon's advance, and that you could look mainly to the defense of the line west of that point.

I am trying to hurry up the cavalry regiments, but cannot hear from them yet. When the regiment ordered to you arrives, could you not hold the line you had previous to the withdrawal of the Sixtieth [Virginia Infantry] ?

I am uneasy in regard to the very large force which General Kelley has at Beverly; to weaken General Echols, exposes not only Greenbrier and Monroe, but the line to Staunton also. General Lee, in all probability, has his hands full to attend to the enemy in his front.

Very respectfully,

CHAS. S. STRINGFELLOW,
Assistant Adjutant-General.

HEADQUARTERS ARMY OF NORTHERN VIRGINIA,
September 25, 1863.

General COOPER :
Adjt. and Insp. Gen., C. S. Army, Richmond, Va.:

GENERAL : The reports of the operations of this army have been forwarded from time to time, as the receipt of those of subordinate officers enable me to prepare my own. It was my purpose to have them all arranged in chronological order so as to form a continuous narrative ; those of 1862, extending from the battles at Richmond to the first battle at Fredericksburg, December 15, 1862, being placed together. Owing to the manner in which they were transmitted, all of them with the exception of the reports of the battles of Sharpsburg, Boonsborough, and Harper's Ferry were addressed to you in the form of a letter, and some changes will therefore be necessary before they can be arranged in the form I desire.

During my last visit to Richmond, I caused the necessary alterations to be made in some of them, but one being missing—that of Cedar Mountain—I was unable to have them put in the form I wished. I now beg leave to call your attention to the subject, and ask that the reports may be arranged, as I request, before being submitted to Congress. To do so I respectfully request that you will direct all my reports of 1862, from Mechanicsville to the first battle of Fredericksburg, inclusive, be put together as a continuous report. The address to you of the first report will serve for the address of the whole, and the signature to the last will also serve for the signature to the whole. All the intermediate reports will then have the address to you stricken out, and over each will be written a caption showing to what part of the campaign it relates. The words "respectfully submitted" and my signature will also be erased from all the reports excepting the last.

The series will then be made to form a continuous narrative addressed to yourself, in the following order:

First. Report of operations around Richmond, including the battles of Mechanicsville, Gaines' Mills, or battle of the Chickahominy, Savage Station, Frazier's [Frayser's] Farm, and Malvern Hill.

Second. Battle of Cedar Mountain.

Third. Report of operations of the army from August 13 to September 2, embracing the battles of Manassas and Ox Hill.

Fourth. Maryland Campaign, embracing the battles of Boonsborough, Sharpsburg, capture of Harper's Ferry, and the return of the army to the line of the Rappahannock.

Fifth. Battle of Fredericksburg, December 13, 1862.

The first only will be addressed, the last only will have my signature. Some of these alterations have been made, as before stated. Should there be any difficulty in making the others, if my reports could be sent to me, I will have the necessary changes made.

Very respectfully, your obedient servant,

R. E. LEE,
General.

HEADQUARTERS ARMY OF NORTHERN VIRGINIA,
September 25, 1863.

General ARNOLD ELZEY,
Commanding, &c., Richmond, Va.:

GENERAL: I judge by the enemy's movements in front and the reports of my scouts in his rear that he is preparing to move against me with all the strength he can gather. The troops sent to New York have returned and pontoon trains are being brought up. I wish every man who can possibly be sent to re-enforce me, and, therefore, would be glad for you to make your arrangements so as to send me all you can spare at the proper moment. Please let me know whether Pickett has yet gone to Hanover Junction, so that I can draw Cooke up at once.

Very respectfully, your obedient servant,

R. E. LEE,
General.

P. S.—I have delayed sending the Maryland troops down until after the battle.

HEADQUARTERS,
Orange, September 25, 1863.

Lieut. Gen. JAMES LONGSTREET:

GENERAL: If it gives you as much pleasure to receive my warmest congratulations as it does me to convey them, this letter will not have been written in vain. My whole heart and soul have been with you and your brave corps in your late battle. It was natural to hear of Longstreet and Hill charging side by side, and pleasing to find the armies of the east and west vying with each other in valor and devotion to their country. A complete and glorious victory must ensue under such circumstances. I hope the result will equal the beginning and General Bragg will be able to reoccupy Tennessee. I grieve for the gallant dead and mourn for our brave Hood. The names of others have reached me, but I hope the report of their fall may not prove true. Finish the work before you, my dear general, and return to me. I want you badly and you cannot get back too soon. Your departure was known to the enemy as soon as it occurred. General Meade has been actively engaged collecting his forces and is now up to the Rapidan. All his troops that were sent north have returned and re-enforcements are daily arriving. His cavalry and engineers are constantly reconnoitering, and a vigorous effort was made Monday and Tuesday to turn our left. We are endeavoring to maintain a bold front, and shall endeavor to delay them all we can till you return.

Present my sincere compliments and admiration to the officers around you, and accept for yourself and command my ardent wishes for the welfare and happiness of all.

Very truly, yours,

R. E. LEE,
General.

HEADQUARTERS DEPARTMENT OF WESTERN VIRGINIA,
Dublin, September 25, 1863.

Maj. Gen. SAMUEL JONES,
Zollicoffer:

Colonel Ferguson reports all orders being executed as directed in your telegram of 18th excepting in regard to the regiment to go to Little Levels. Does not mention that my telegram must have been incorrectly received at Staunton. Ferguson remains at Crab Bottom Highland, with the Fourteenth [Virginia Cavalry] and Sweeney's battalion. Shall I repeat the order as to Little Levels? If so, do what with Sweeney?

CHAS. S. STRINGFELLOW,
Assistant Adjutant-General.

HDQRS. DEPT. SOUTH CAROLINA, GEORGIA, AND FLORIDA,
Charleston, September 25, 1863.

Col. W. H. STEVENS,
Corps of Engineers, Richmond, Va.:

COLONEL: In reply to your letter of the 21st instant, in which you give me an extract from a confidential letter written by General Lee, in reference to a connection between the "intermediate" line around Manchester and the defenses landward at Drewry's Bluff and a second

line of river obstructions connected with the same line ("the intermediate"), I would say that my judgment is still in favor of making
the obstruction at Warwick Bar just below the pontoon bridge,
because the work is partially done now and can be completed sooner
than any other, and because two or three guns mounted on the favorable point on the left bank of the James, just above the line of the
obstructions, would afford a strong protection for the same. A much
shorter connection would suffice to place these second obstructions
in relation with the intermediate line around Manchester than is
required to connect it with Drewry's Bluff. At Richmond Bar the
banks of the river do not, I fear, offer good positions for guns bearing on the channel, while Warwick Bar can be swept by cannon, and
at the same time by sharpshooters, in rifle-pits. All along the frown-
ing bluff, formerly the left bank, a pocket shape would have to be
given to the intermediate line on the right bank to make it embrace
the Warwick obstructions, but the length would be much less than
that required to embrace Drewry's Bluff. I would advise that whatever is done toward connecting the Manchester (intermediate) line
with Drewry's Bluff be done first at the end next to this line, with a
view to turn it in when opposite Warwick. If this be found to be
the best position for a second river obstruction, as I think it will be,
two of our bridges will then be within our best line of defense.

Please give the subject your most careful study and decide as
promptly as possible. I hope you will soon have a full force of
negroes.

Your obedient servant,

J. F. GILMER,
Major-General.

HEADQUARTERS ARMY OF NORTHERN VIRGINIA,
September 26, 1863.
Maj. Gen. SAMUEL JONES,
Comdg. Southwestern Virginia Department:

GENERAL: So far as I am able to judge, the enemy is preparing to
move against me at this point with all the strength he can gather.
I need every man that I can possibly get to re-enforce me.

The enemy in Tennessee will, no doubt, draw all their forces from
the region of Knoxville and the northern portion of the State, to re-
enforce the defeated army of General Rosecrans. I hope, therefore,
unless you are able to strike them a blow very speedily, you will
make arrangements to spare all the troops you can, and at least send
Corse's brigade back to me.

If you find by using all your force you can damage the enemy and
drive him out of the country, it is a positive advantage not to be
neglected. But if you cannot do this, this brigade will be comparatively idle there while its services are much needed here.

I am, very respectfully, your obedient servant,

R. E. LEE,
General.

DUBLIN, [*September*] 26, 1863.
Brig. Gen. JOHN ECHOLS:

GENERAL: Your letter of the 24th has just been received. Colonel
Ferguson has received my order of the 18th instant, issued by di-

rection of the major-general commanding. The Seventeenth Virginia Cavalry, Col. W. H. French commanding, is on its way to report to you at Lewisburg, and will very probably be there before this reaches you. Orders have been given to have supplies hurried on to the Narrows, as soon as the exigencies of the service will permit. The Sixteenth Virginia Cavalry, Lieut. Col. W. L. Graham, is on its way to Princeton. I wrote you yesterday in regard to this regiment.

Very respectfully, general, your obedient servant,
CHAS. S. STRINGFELLOW,
Assistant Adjutant-General.

HEADQUARTERS DEPARTMENT OF WESTERN VIRGINIA,
Dublin, September 26, 1863.
Brig. Gen. JOHN ECHOLS,
Commanding Brigade:

GENERAL: Colonel McCausland informs me he cannot possibly forage another cavalry regiment. The Sixteenth Regiment, Lieutenant-Colonel Graham, has been ordered to report to him. It is necessary, therefore, to change this disposition somewhat, and I inclose you an order for the Sixteenth to report to you temporarily.

Please station one of your battalions at such point as you may deem best, with a view to its being thrown either to the Narrows or Lewisburg, as occasion may require, and report in regard to this matter.

Kelley is so far off he can only move on you with cavalry. The mounted force in Colonel McCausland's front has been considerably increased. Brigadier-General Duffié has reached Charleston, to take command of their cavalry.

Very respectfully, your obedient servant,
CHAS. S. STRINGFELLOW,
Assistant Adjutant-General.

HEADQUARTERS DEPARTMENT OF WESTERN VIRGINIA,
Dublin, September 26, 1863.
Maj. Gen. SAMUEL JONES,
Zollicoffer:

McCausland says it is impossible for him to forage more cavalry. Have therefore ordered the Sixteenth Virginia Regiment to report to Echols also, and directed him to place a battalion so that it can easily reach the Narrows if required. Brigadier-General Duffié arrived at Charleston to take command of all the Yankee cavalry, and has 1,800 men.

CHAS. S. STRINGFELLOW,
Assistant Adjutant-General.

WAR DEPARTMENT, C. S.,
Richmond, Va., September 26, 1863.
Maj. Gen. W. H. C. WHITING,
Wilmington, N. C.:

GENERAL: I have received your letter asking authority either to purchase or impress one or two steamers.

You will endeavor to purchase such steamers at a fair price, and, failing to do so, you will proceed to impress, observing carefully the requirements of the law.

Your obedient servant,

J. A. SEDDON,
Secretary of War.

SPECIAL ORDERS, }   ADJT. AND INSP. GENERAL'S OFFICE,
No. 229.   }   *Richmond, Va., September 26, 1863.*

*   *   *   *   *   *   *

VII. Major-General Whiting is assigned to the separate command of the Cape Fear District, and is charged with the defense of Wilmington, N. C. He will make his reports directly to this office.

*   *   *   *   *   *   *

By command of the Secretary of War:

JNO. WITHERS,
Assistant Adjutant-General.

RICHMOND,
September 26, 1863.

General W. H. C. WHITING,
Wilmington, N. C.:

You will have the separate command of the Cape Fear District for the defense of Wilmington, and will make your reports directly to this office, as heretofore. Major-General Ransom is on duty in Southwestern Virginia and cannot be spared.

S. COOPER,
Adjutant and Inspector General.

RICHMOND,
September 26, 1863.

Major-General PICKETT,
Petersburg, Va.:

Major-General Whiting has been assigned to the separate command of the Cape Fear District, and will make his reports directly to this office. In case of emergency, you will afford him such aid of troops as the circumstances of your command will permit.

S. COOPER,
Adjutant and Inspector General.

CAMP AT ORANGE COURT-HOUSE,
September 27, 1863.

His Excellency JEFFERSON DAVIS,
President Confederate States, Richmond, Va.:

Mr. PRESIDENT: The enemy has made no serious advance yet. All his preparations indicate that intention. The troops in his rear have been closed up on the Rapidan. General King's division, which has been stationed for some time at Centreville watching the passes through the Bull Run Mountains, has been brought forward to Culpeper. Our scouts also report that the troops from about Washington, under General Heintzelman, have joined General Meade. The report that the former officer had taken command at Harper's Ferry I find is not correct. He visited that post, and inspected the troops along the line of the Baltimore and Ohio Railroad, probably with a view to withdrawing all that could be spared, which gave rise to the report. The pontoon trains have again been brought up from Centreville, and a Confederate soldier that escaped from Point Lookout and crossed the Potomac on the 9th instant, brings the report that some of the troops lately landed at Alexandria came from Washington, [N. C.,] and Charleston.

Every effort seems to be making to collect a large army under General Meade, and I fear, as usual, he will come in overwhelming numbers. I have brought Cooke's brigade to Gordonsville, to have him as near as possible, while retaining him on the line of the railroad. The North Carolina companies of Pettigrew's and Daniel's brigades left last spring in Richmond, which I have several times requested might be returned to their regiments, have not yet been sent to me. I know of no other troops that I could get, unless Corse's brigade could be withdrawn from General Sam. Jones. The enemy will now send from East Tennessee to General Rosecrans all the regular troops in that quarter, and if General Sam. Jones could re-occupy Knoxville he could materially assist General Bragg. If he cannot, the troops with him will be in a measure idle. I am much obliged to your excellency for the information contained in your dispatch of last evening in reference to Generals Hood and Wofford. It has given me great relief.

I am, with great respect, your obedient servant,

R. E. LEE,
General.

HEADQUARTERS DEPARTMENT OF WESTERN VIRGINIA,
Dublin, September 27, 1863.

Maj. Gen. SAMUEL JONES,
Zollicoffer:

Have sent orders to Pegram as directed. General Lee writes he expects enemy to move on him immediately, with all the force he can get. Needs all his troops.

If you can strike the enemy a damaging blow, do so immediately. If his troops be kept idle he needs them badly.

Send him all you can. Refers especially to Corse's brigade. Headquarters not given. On the 24th, Bragg reports he has 7,000 prisoners, 36 cannon, and 15,000 small-arms. I think the enemy still at Chattanooga. Bragg in their immediate front.

CHAS. S. STRINGFELLOW,
Assistant Adjutant-General.

CAMP AT ORANGE COURT-HOUSE,
September 28, 1863.

His Excellency JEFFERSON DAVIS,
President Confederate States, Richmond, Va.:

MR. PRESIDENT: A report was sent to me yesterday from Shenandoah Valley which, if true, furnishes additional reason for prompt action on the part of General Bragg. It is stated that Generals Slocum and Howard's corps, under General Hooker, are to re-enforce General Rosecrans. They were to move over the Baltimore and Ohio Railroad, and to commence on the night of the 25th.

I see by the Washington Chronicle of the 25th, that on the 24th the Twelfth Corps, which is the one commanded by General Slocum, was reviewed by Sir Henry Holland and Assistant Adjutant-General Townsend. A review of a corps was noticed on that day by our lookouts, and the disappearance of a large encampment east of Culpeper Court-House and some changes in those west of that place were reported. The Eleventh Corps, Howard's, has been stationed along the Orange and Alexandria Railroad, and I have not heard of its withdrawal, though it may have been replaced by other troops from the rear. By last accounts, the railroad was still closely guarded.

If the report from the valley is true, it will no doubt be corroborated to-day or to-morrow. I sent yesterday to General Imboden and Major Gilmor, in the valley, to endeavor to break the Baltimore and Ohio Railroad. But it has occurred to me, if the withdrawal of these two corps under General Hooker is true, that they may be intended to operate on the Peninsula as a diversion to Meade's advance. I therefore request that reliable scouts be sent to the Peninsula to ascertain if any troops are arriving there.

A person from Washington City reports that there are no troops now in that place or Alexandria, and that 22,000 men have recently been brought over the Washington and Baltimore Railroad for Meade's army.

I am, with great respect, your obedient servant,

R. E. LEE,
General.

HEADQUARTERS,
Orange Court-House, September 28, 1863.

General ARNOLD ELZEY,
Commanding at Richmond, Va.:

GENERAL : It has been reported to me that Slocum's and Howard's Corps, Twelfth and Eleventh, under General Hooker, are to re-enforce General Rosecrans, and that the movement of those corps was to have commenced on the evening of the 25th. The disappearance of a large encampment east of Culpeper Court-House and some change of camps west of that place were reported to me on the 25th, which would give some corroboration to the report. But if true, I shall no doubt ascertain in a day or two. It was said that these troops were to have been moved on the Baltimore and Ohio Railroad, but it has occurred to me, coupling the report with what has been previously stated in the Washington papers in reference to General Hooker, that these corps may be intended for operations on the Peninsula or south of the James River, as a diversion for General Meade's advance. I therefore request that you will send bold and reliable scouts to ascertain if any troops are arriving in those quarters.

I have the honor to be, your obedient servant,

R. E. LEE,
General,

HEADQUARTERS ARMY OF NORTHERN VIRGINIA,
September 28, 1863.

J. M. McCUE, Esq., *House of Delegates, Richmond, Va.:*

DEAR SIR : Your letter of the 25th instant is received.

I do not think that it would be advantageous to the service to increase the number of partisan corps or augment those already in existence. Much inconvenience has already been experienced from these organizations, and I am satisfied that they do not accomplish as much as the same number of men in the regular service. For this reason, I cannot advise the increase of Captain McNeill's company, although I consider him a brave and efficient officer, and his company has done as good service as any other of the same kind. I would be very glad if Captain McNeill could increase his command to a battalion or a regiment for regular service, and in that event would recommend his being detached from the regiment to which he now belongs. But I do not think that in any case it would be practicable or judicious to give him the independent command of which you speak. It would be necessary for him to act under the orders of the officer commanding the department in which he serves, in order to secure that prompt and ready co-operation of all the troops which is indispensable to success. To do otherwise would be to place two officers in command in the same district and divide the forces required for its defense.

The policy which our necessities and the experience of the war have taught is the reverse of this, and nothing should be done which may interfere with the concentration of our forces.

I inclose the petition* to the President contained in your letter.

Very respectfully, your obedient servant,

R. E. LEE.

HEADQUARTERS DISTRICT OF CAPE FEAR,
Wilmington, September 28, 1863.

Hon. JAMES A. SEDDON, *Secretary of War, Richmond:*

SIR: I wish you would cause, if possible, one regiment at least to be sent here. I have, as you know, but one in the whole district of infantry, and have not now the power to transfer at a moment's warning as heretofore. I had intended previous to the change of command to make the transfer. This is an important matter and I beg your attention to it.

The defense of Wilmington is now a separate command, including the District of Cape Fear, this much reducing the responsibility of the department commander, and I should think, the defense of Weldon being very properly conducted from Petersburg, so much nearer than Wilmington, that one regiment at least could be sent to me. I have not troops enough for garrison duty.

W. H. C. WHITING.

HEADQUARTERS DISTRICT OF CAPE FEAR,
Wilmington, September 28, 1863.

His Excellency Governor VANCE, *Raleigh, N. C.:*

SIR : I have to inform you that, in consideration of the increasing importance of this place, and that the attention of the officer in com-

---

* Not found.

mand is constantly required here, the War Department has constituted the defense of Wilmington and the District of the Cape Fear
a separate command assigned to me. Maj. Gen. George E. Pickett,
headquarters at Petersburg, is assigned to the command of the remainder of North Carolina.

I write you this for your information.

Very respectfully,

W. H. C. WHITING,
Major-General.

CAMP AT ORANGE COURT-HOUSE,
September 29, 1863.

His Excellency JEFFERSON DAVIS,
President Confederate States, Richmond, Va.:

Mr. PRESIDENT: I have not yet ascertained, with certainty, the
correctness of the report that re-enforcements were being sent from
General Meade's army to General Rosecrans. The report has been
repeated from the valley without giving the circumstances on which
it was based. On the other hand, scouts north of the Rappahannock
state re-enforcements as coming to General Meade. Those on the
Potomac report a large steamer laden with troops as having passed
up the river on the 21st, one on the 22d, one on the 23d, and two on
the 25th. These may have been conscripts. If it is true that re-enforcements are being sent from General Meade to General Rosecrans,
it shows that the enemy is not as strong as he asserts. General Sam.
Jones reports that Burnside has carried nearly all his troops to
re-enforce Rosecrans, leaving only a brigade or two of mounted men
between him and Knoxville. It would seem probable, from statements of their prisoners, that Grant was also re-enforcing Rosecrans.
If this latter is true, General Johnston should be moving either to
Bragg or to General Rosecrans' lines.

I have informed General Sam. Jones that if he can advance and
operate advantageously, to retain Corse; if not, to return him.

General Imboden reports that 400 of his cavalry returned yesterday from an expedition north of Winchester. They report the railroad too strongly guarded to attack. He reports every bridge in
Hampshire with a stronger guard than he can attack successfully.
I have repeated my orders to endeavor to break it at some vulnerable
point.

I am, with great respect, your obedient servant,

R. E. LEE,
General.

HEADQUARTERS DEPARTMENT OF WESTERN VIRGINIA,
Dublin, September 29, 1863.

Brig. Gen. JOHN ECHOLS, *Commanding, &c.:*

GENERAL: Your letter of the 27th has just been received. I am
aware of the difficulties attaching to your position and fully appreciate them. But though you are badly off in some respects, others
are in a yet worse strait. At Saltville there are only a few detachments of volunteers. The rest of the garrison is composed mainly
of local troops, with the Sixtieth [Virginia] Regiment at Glade
Spring in supporting distance,

Colonel McCausland has therefore to guard the advances through Tazewell and Rocky Gap. It will certainly take the regiment of cavalry and the regiment of infantry with him to do that, for he has no other troops.

To resist an advance upon Lewisburg, you could concentrate all of Colonel Jackson's command, Colonel Ferguson's three regiments, Dunn's battalion, the Twenty-second Regiment, and certainly one infantry battalion. Indeed, you would in no event be weakened by the major-general's order of the 26th instant, for, by placing the battalion as directed on that day, if your cavalry is vigilant the battalion could reach you before you were attacked by the enemy in force.

I do not think the enemy is likely to move from the Kanawha on you, when he can strike Colonel McCausland, who would have to meet him with only about 1,000 men, with about as much ease.

The cavalry force at Beverly seems to me to be the one against which you have to guard most carefully, and against that force you could concentrate the troops of Jackson and Ferguson, and I think the battalion of infantry in question. I do not, therefore, feel that I could change the disposition of this battalion, approved by the commanding general, without his order. Please, therefore, station it as requested in my letter of the 26th, and let me know where it is stationed with as little delay as possible, that I may inform Colonel McCausland on the subject.

I have this morning sent both of your letters to the commanding general, requesting his particular attention to them. I will communicate with you immediately if he makes any change. I asked his special attention to the difficulty in regard to forage, &c.

So soon as Major-General Ransom reports for duty, I think he will be put in command in East Tennessee, when General Jones will return to this end of his line, at least for a few days. I expect, therefore, that he will very shortly be with you.

I presume the major-general commanding was not aware that Davidson's battery was attached to Jenkins' brigade. I had forgotten it myself, the battery having joined General Jenkins after he left this department. As the rest of his brigade has been ordered away, I presume Colonel Ferguson will bring that battery with him. So soon as he reports I will issue an order to that effect, if he has not anticipated it.

Very respectfully, general, your obedient servant,

CHAS. S. STRINGFELLOW,
Assistant Adjutant-General.

P. S.—My attention has been called to the fact that a report was received from Colonel Ferguson during my absence in which Captain Davidson's battery is mentioned. I see he has only two guns in the field, the rest being without horses.

CAMP AT ORANGE COURT-HOUSE,
September 30, 1863.

His Excellency JEFFERSON DAVIS,
President Confederate States, Richmond, Va.:

MR. PRESIDENT: Reports are coming in corroborating the statement that two corps, Eleventh and Twelfth, of General Meade's army, will proceed to General Rosecrans. A scout, in whom I have not entire confidence, sends me information to that effect from Washington City, under date of 26th of September, and adds that General Meade's army will be transferred to the Peninsula. The latter I do not believe. Another scout in Prince William County, under date of 27th, states that it is currently reported "that one division of the Eleventh Corps, and First and Third of the Twelfth Corps, have passed through Alexandria to re-enforce Rosecrans." None of the scouts have yet seen the troops in motion, nor can any material change be observed in their camps in our front. If sent, their most probable route would be down the Ohio and up the Tennessee to Clarksburg, and thence by rail to Stevenson. It would be well to advise General Bragg that his cavalry, if possible, might break the line.

No indications this morning of a movement on the part of General Meade. His army occupies the ridge north of Culpeper Court-House, extending some miles east and west. His cavalry massed in front of his right and our left. His position answers as well for defense as attack. General Jones writes that he does not believe there is any enemy between him and Knoxville. I presume he does not intend to advance, as he says he has ordered back Corse's brigade.

With great respect, your obedient servant,

R. E. LEE,
General.

HEADQUARTERS ARMY OF NORTHERN VIRGINIA,
September 30, 1863.

General S. COOPER,
Adjutant and Inspector General, C. S. Army:

GENERAL: I send by courier to-day thirty-two packages and letters sent over by flag of truce, inclosing effects found on persons of deceased Confederate soldiers. I have advised company and regimental commanders, requesting them to send in the addresses of representatives of the deceased in order that their effects may be forwarded to them. So soon as received they will be forwarded. As the amount of money inclosed is considerable, I have considered it best to send it where it can be properly cared for until known to whom it may be sent.

I am, general, respectfully, yours,

R. H. CHILTON,
Assistant Adjutant and Inspector General.

SIGNAL OFFICE,
Richmond, September 30, 1863.

Hon. JAMES A. SEDDON,
Secretary of War:

SIR: I have the honor to inclose copy of dispatch just received at this office, from Washington, from a source which may be considered reliable.

Very respectfully,

WM. NORRIS,
Major, and Chief of Signal Corps.

SEPTEMBER 25, 1863.

The Eleventh Army Corps, 30,000 strong, is at Alexandria; is to be forwarded at once to the relief of Rosecrans. General Meade, if circumstances demand it, will fall back on Washington.

The President has telegraphed railroad presidents to meet here, and it is said they are already here. The troops are to be hurried through on shortest time. There is immense trepidation here with the "powers that be," in regard to Rosecrans. General Meade is already, it is said, at Warrenton. (Evening.)

Recent information shows that two of Meade's army corps are on the move; large numbers of troops are at the cars, now loaded with cannon.

There is no doubt as to the destination of these troops—part for Rosecrans, and perhaps for Burnside. Eleventh Army Corps commanded by General Howard (the Dutch corps).

A. HOWELL.

SEPTEMBER 27.

It is reported that Joe Hooker is in command of these troops, and their destination is the White House.

The troops are at the Relay House this evening.

HEADQUARTERS EARLY'S DIVISION,
September 30, 1863.

Col. R. H. CHILTON,
Asst. Adjt. Gen., Army of Northern Virginia:

COLONEL: I must call the attention of the commanding general to the embarrassments under which regimental officers, especially company officers, labor in regard to their subsistence in the present state of things. No funds for the payment of the troops have been furnished for several months, notwithstanding the fact that the regular estimates have been sent in, and the consequence is that officers cannot be paid, and as the regulations of the Commissary Department require sales to officers to be made for cash, officers who are dependent on their pay, as is the case with a vast majority of them, are without the means of subsistence. They cannot buy from citizens or the commissaries without money, and the only resource they have left is to share the rations of the men.

I would respectfully suggest that commissaries be authorized to sell to officers provisions without requiring cash payments, tickets being given to show the amount of purchases, which could be turned over to the regimental quartermaster, to be deducted from the pay of the officer giving them. A system of this sort, properly regulated, would be a convenience to all parties, and would serve to diminish the volume of the currency to the extent of purchases made by officers, as money would not be required for that purpose. Fraud upon the Government could be prevented by rendering any payment to an officer, except by his proper quartermaster, invalid, which would also curtail the cases of absence without leave.

These suggestions, if deemed of any value, can be submitted to the War Department, but the present necessities of the officers must be relieved in some way, or they must starve, or live entirely upon the rations furnished for the men, which is not calculated to enhance their authority or respectability. A vast number of my officers are in this condition, and I must urge immediate attention to the matter.

Respectfully, your obedient servant,

J. A. EARLY,
Major-General, Commanding Division.

[Indorsements.]

HEADQUARTERS SECOND ARMY CORPS,
October 1, 1863.

Respectfully forwarded.

I recommend that brigade commissaries of subsistence be authorized to receive officers' pay accounts in payment for subsistence stores, to be passed through the hands of the quartermaster, so as to prevent fraud, and to be returned by the Commissary of Subsistence to the Quartermaster's Department for payment, when it has funds. This plan has this advantage over that proposed by General Early, that it can go into operation at once. Either this should be done or the Commissary of Subsistence should be directed to sell on credit or to issue rations to the officers, who are in some cases (not in Early's division) reduced to living on the rations issued to their men. I would also approve the recommendation of General Early, that officers should only be paid by the quartermasters of their own commands, with this addition, that whenever an officer absent from his command applies for payment, he be required to append to his pay account a copy of the order authorizing such absence.

R. S. EWELL,
Lieutenant-General.

HEADQUARTERS ARMY OF NORTHERN VIRGINIA,
October 4, 1863.

Respectfully forwarded, and the suggestions of General Ewell recommended.

R. E. LEE,
General.

OCTOBER 7, 1863.

Respectfully referred to the Commissary-General.

S. COOPER,
Adjutant and Inspector General.

OFFICE COMMISSARY-GENERAL OF SUBSISTENCE,
Richmond, Va., October 9, 1863.

Respectfully returned to Adjutant and Inspector General.

The difficulties within alleged were long since anticipated, and, it is believed, are fully provided for by the provisions of the inclosed circular.

L. B. NORTHROP,
Commissary-General.

[Inclosure.]

CIRCULAR.]   SUBSISTENCE DEPARTMENT, C. S. A.,
Richmond, Va., October 17, 1862.

No subsistence stores will be sold to officers' families. When an officer has his family with him, where he is stationed on duty, he may draw a limited amount of such stores on his certificate on honor that the stores are exclusively for himself and his family. He must pay cash, or deposit a pay account with the commissary, on which he may draw. Under no other circumstances whatever will commissaries be permitted to issue stores to officers, and then only such articles as are a part of the ration regularly issued to soldiers at the time.

L. B. NORTHROP,
Commissary-General.

Approved:

G. W. RANDOLPH,
Secretary of War.

HEADQUARTERS,
Wilmington, September 30, 1863.

Hon. JAMES A. SEDDON,
Secretary of War, Richmond:

SIR : I inclose you a letter which I have just received from General Clingman, in Charleston. I beg you will read it to the President. It tends to confirm anticipations I have long had. Troops are absolutely necessary here ; I have but 600 men that I can move. It is time that some were being collected.

The whole plan of defense here depends upon the presence of force, as often demonstrated, and I fear, unless that is supplied, a great and irremediable disaster.

Very respectfully,

W. H. C. WHITING,
Major-General.

[Inclosure.]

SULLIVAN'S ISLAND,
September 28, 1863.

Maj. Gen. W. H. C. WHITING :

GENERAL : I have learned that General Ripley, on examination yesterday from Fort Sumter of the enemy's works (I have not myself been in Sumter for some weeks), has become satisfied from the position of the enemy's guns, being protected by high traverses against the fire of this island, and being directed toward the inner harbor chiefly, that they will not attack us on Sullivan's Island at all. He also says that the guns in Wagner are chiefly directed seaward, as if to guard against an attack from the sea. It is his impression also that, when their batteries are completed, they will probably send off their monitors and retain only the Ironsides and some wooden vessels.

I think it probable, from the news of this morning from the North, that they will mostly direct the fire of their guns on the city to destroy it. I should not be surprised, therefore, if the monitors should go up to give you some trouble at Wilmington, The number of vessels that are running the blockade there, and other things, will make them very anxious to interfere there. If they do not design an immediate attack here, they may also send a part of their land forces up to endeavor to close that harbor. I make these suggestions because I know your force is small.

I see from the indorsement of the Secretary of War on Radcliffe's application for his companies, that he thinks it was dangerous for you to send my brigade here. As far as I am personally concerned, I am well situated here, being in command of this sub-division, as I have been for some weeks, on the most exposed point, and with twelve infantry regiments under my command, besides the large artillery force in the heavy batteries, as well as light artillery and cavalry. As this island is considered a very dangerous place I do not think any of the other generals here covet it, and I can probably remain here indefinitely.

If, however, I cannot be actively engaged here, if the enemy attack Wilmington I should be willing to go there, and think my observations of affairs here has been of service to me and that I could do better now than before I went into a fight of batteries against iron-clads.

In haste, yours, truly, &c.,

T. L. CLINGMAN,
Brigadier-General.

[Indorsements.]

Returned to Secretary of War.

In addition to arrangements made to concentrate General Martin's brigade at Wilmington, it will be well to give contingent instructions so that if required, Clingman's brigade might be promptly returned to Wilmington.

JEFFERSON DAVIS.

[General BEAUREGARD:]

From information received by General Whiting, as well as from general inference of what may be the policy of the enemy, that vigilant commander is apprehensive that a portion of the forces now assailing Charleston may be suddenly diverted and thrown in attack on Wilmington. He dreads an attack even by the iron-clads from sea, much less than a descent in force on some exposed point on the coast, and an attack in reverse.

These apprehensions, it is hoped, may prove unfounded; but as the enemy may well despair of triumphing in a land attack on your strong defenses, it may be that he will seek to cover his failure by an attempt at a *coup de main* elsewhere. It behooves, therefore, the Department that such arrangements as circumstances allow should be adopted to guard against the contingency of an attack on Wilmington. General Whiting has, therefore, been provided with Martin's brigade, and in addition has been instructed, in the event of certain intelligence being received of any contemplated land attack on him, to call on you for the prompt return of Clingman's brigade to him. I have to request that, as far as may be practicable without disturbing your plans of defense, you hold Clingman's brigade so prepared that on such call it may be thrown rapidly to Wilmington, and that, in the event of General Whiting making the requisition, it may be sent to his re-enforcement without delay. He will be cautioned not to make the demand unless satisfied that the enemy's land forces are being withdrawn from before Charleston for attack on him.

Very truly, yours,

J. A. S. [SEDDON.]

Write, informing General Whiting of the above instructions to General Beauregard, and authorize him, on certain intelligence that

₍the enemy are preparing to attack him by land with forces drawn in whole or in part from Charleston, to make requisition for the return of Clingman's brigade.

                                        J. A. S. [SEDDON.]

———

                                        HEADQUARTERS,
                                Wilmington, September 30, 1863.

Colonel GORGAS,
    Chief of Ordnance, Richmond:

COLONEL: Captain Porter, of the Phantom, goes on to Richmond this evening to make his report to you. I beg that you will not consider the loss of the ship as his fault. From all I can learn, the accident has been unavoidable, and due to no mismanagement.

Captain Porter has, with great gallantry and much personal exposure, directed successfully the troops and his crew in saving the cargo, under a daily and heavy fire, and in this he deserves in every way the consideration and commendation of the Department.

The loss of the vessel is what may happen to any commander. The course he has pursued since belongs to himself, and I hope that he will be continued in service for the good of our cause.

Backed by our brave soldiers, I think that the saving of the cargo of the Phantom is due to the personal skill and gallantry of Captain Porter.

    Very respectfully,

                                        W. H. C. WHITING,
                                            Major-General.

[Inclosure.]

                            AGENCY OF WAR DEPARTMENT,
                                Wilmington, September 30, 1863.

Col. J. GORGAS,
    Chief of Ordnance, Richmond:

COLONEL: I have refrained from alluding, excepting briefly, to the loss of the Phantom, as Captain Porter could make his own report, and I did not desire to anticipate any statements which would appear from him. But Captain Porter's attention to duty, his earnestness in its discharge, his acknowledged capacity, and the coolness and gallantry he has exhibited in saving the cargo of the Phantom, entitle him to every consideration, and I trust he will be continued in a service for which he has sacrificed great inducements and for which he is peculiarly fitted.

    I am, very respectfully, your obedient servant,

                                        J. M. SEIXAS,
                                    Agent of War Department.

[Indorsement.]

                                        OCTOBER 5, 1863.

Respectfully referred to the Secretary of War for notice and return.

I am satisfied that Captain Porter is an efficient and brave officer, and I shall be glad to recommend him for the command of any new steamer purchased.

In the meantime, he is still retained in service, securing stores and machinery of steamer Phantom.

J. GORGAS,
Chief of Ordnance.

HDQRS. DEPT. OF WESTERN VA. AND EAST TENN.,
Carter's Depot, Tenn., September 30, 1863.

His Excellency President DAVIS, *Richmond:*

I have ordered General Ransom forward with a sufficient force, I think, to drive the enemy's rear guard beyond Greenville, and if practicable beyond Bull's Gap. I shall return to Dublin, as accounts I have from the Kanawha I think make it desirable. I have heard nothing from General Bragg.

SAM. JONES,
Major-General.

Abstract from return of the Army of Northern Virginia, Maj. Gen. Robert E. Lee, C. S. Army, commanding, for the month of September, 1863.

Command.	Present for duty.		Effective total.	Aggregate present.	Aggregate present and absent.	Pieces of artillery.
	Officers.	Men.				
General headquarters	12	....	....	12	13	......
Second Army Corps (Ewell)	1,599	16,688	16,688	20,974	39,190	......
Third Army Corps (A. P. Hill)	1,224	15,073	15,068	18,814	31,926	......
Cooke's brigade	150	2,150	2,150	2,605	3,260	4
Cavalry Corps (Stuart)a	490	6,744	6,744	8,376	14,797	16
Artillery (Pendleton)b	225	3,762	3,762	4,440	5,978	154
Total	3,700	44,367	44,362	55,221	95,164	174

a Baker's brigade of Hampton's division not reported. Of the effective total, 904 men are reported as dismounted.
b Haskell's battalion not reported.

Abstract from return of the Department of Richmond, Maj. Gen. Arnold Elzey, C. S. Army, commanding, September 30, 1863.

Command.	Present for duty.		Effective total present.	Aggregate present.	Aggregate present and absent.	Pieces of field artillery.
	Officers.	Men.				
General headquarters	11	....	....	11	11	......
Hunton's command a	110	1,288	1,288	1,719	3,256	10
Terry's command b	88	1,080	1,074	1,402	3,224	......
40th Virginia Cavalry Battalion	11	259	284	331	574	......
Chaffin's Bluff	20	262	327	405	505	18
Drewry's Bluff	17	250	375	453	498	12
Richmond defenses	78	1,493	1,630	1,879	2,179	......
Total	335	4,582	4,928	6,200	10,247	40

a Hunton's brigade and attached cavalry and artillery, at Chaffin's Farm. See p. 765.
b Kemper's brigade and attached artillery, at Hanover Junction. Pieces of artillery not reported. See p. 765.

Abstract from return of Pickett's division, Maj. Gen. George E. Pickett, C. S. Army, commanding, for the month of September, 1863; headquarters Petersburg, Va.

Command.	Present for duty.		Effective total present.	Aggregate present.	Aggregate present and absent.
	Officers.	Men.			
Field and staff	9			9	9
Armistead's brigade	67	1,116	1,116	1,484	3,123
Kemper's brigade a	86	999	999	1,319	3,114
Corse's brigade	120	1,342	1,342	1,596	2,334
Hunton's brigade b	87	962	962	1,268	2,882
Dearing's artillery battalion c	19	345	345	306	527
Total	388	4,764	4,764	6,022	11,989

a Detached at Hanover Junction. See Terry's command, Department of Richmond, p. 764.
b Detached at Chaffin's Farm. See Department of Richmond, p. 764.
c Three batteries, 18 guns.

Abstract from return of the Defenses of Wilmington, N. C., Maj. Gen. W. H. C. Whiting, C. S. Army, commanding, September 30, 1863.

Command.	Present for duty.		Effective total present.	Aggregate present.	Aggregate present and absent.	Pieces of field artillery.
	Officers.	Men.				
General staff a	9	34	34	51	58	
Infantry	62	770	798	964	1,140	
Cavalry	17	311	345	413	544	
Light artillery	19	399	413	458	617	23
Heavy artillery	82	1,795	2,281	2,741	3,549	
Total	189	3,309	3,866	4,627	5,908	23

a Including the signal corps.

Troops in the Defenses of Wilmington, N. C., September 30, 1863.

Infantry.

42d North Carolina (two companies).
50th North Carolina, Col. James A. Washington.
61st North Carolina (three companies).

Light Artillery.

3d North Carolina Battalion, Maj. John W. Moore.
13th North Carolina Battalion, Battery D, Capt. Z. T. Adams.
Staunton Hill (Virginia) Artillery, Capt. A. B. Paris.

Cavalry.

7th Confederate (three companies).
5th North Carolina (one company).
5th South Carolina (three companies).

Heavy Artillery.*

Fort Anderson, Maj. John J. Hedrick.
Fort Caswell, Col. T. M. Jones.
Fort Fisher, Col. William Lamb.
Fort Pender, Maj. John J. Hedrick.
Wilmington, Col. George A. Cunningham.

* Troops not indicated on original.

CAMP AT ORANGE COURT-HOUSE,
October 1, 1863.

His Excellency JEFFERSON DAVIS,
President Confederate States, Richmond, Va. :

Mr. PRESIDENT : From the additional evidence received since my letter of yesterday, I consider it certain that two corps have been withdrawn from General Meade's army to re-enforce General Rosecrans. One of the scouts saw General Howard take the cars at Catlett's Station, where his headquarters had been established, and saw other troops marching toward Manassas, which he believes to have been the Twelfth Corps. Transportation on the railroad was interrupted all last Saturday, which may have been owing to the operations of Mosby or White, to whom I had sent instructions to that effect.

Everything that can be done to strengthen Bragg ought now to be done, and if he cannot draw Rosecrans out in any other way, it might be accomplished by operating against his re-enforcements on their line of travel. If he found they could not reach him, he would be obliged to go to them.

I send this morning Major Clarke, of the Engineers, to General Longstreet, to whom I think he may be useful. I part with him with reluctance.

I am, with great respect, your obedient servant,

R. E. LEE,
General.

———

HEADQUARTERS,
Wilmington, October 1, 1863.

His Excellency President DAVIS,
Richmond :

SIR : I think it is quite time to collect troops for this place. I am convinced that very shortly a large part of the force now engaged against Charleston will be diverted here. The character of their operations leads me to this opinion, especially their works on Morris Island.

While they have long-range guns, these are mounted against the city alone, and not against Sullivan's Island.

The defenses of Fort Wagner are chiefly in the channel, which indicates the probable absence of their own iron-clads and apprehension from ours. By rendering Morris Island very strong they seal up Charleston Harbor, and can hold their position with comparatively small force, while the rest can attempt the same thing here. If they make a lodgment they will do it. If successful in closing these two ports they inflict a heavier blow than the capture of either, and they are at liberty to pursue their operations at will, to the final reduction of both. When it is considered that I have but 500 men to prevent their occupation of any place they see fit to take, I hope that every effort will be made to forward a force at once; otherwise I am greatly apprehensive of disaster without remedy. I cannot answer for the safety of this place in its present condition.

Very respectfully,

W. H. C. WHITING,
Major-General.

[Indorsement.]

SECRETARY OF WAR:

As the division of General Pickett is reunited and filled up, so will the power increase ,to extend on the line of railroad, and by moving General Ransom's brigade to the south, the brigade of General Martin may be concentrated at Wilmington.

J. D. [DAVIS.]

RICHMOND, VA.,
October 2, 1863.

His Excellency JEFFERSON DAVIS:

SIR: The undersigned, senators and delegates in the General Assembly of Virginia, from Central, Western, and Southwestern Virginia, deeply impressed with the great importance (not only to our immediate section, but to the entire Confederacy) of having in command in that district one who combines all the elements essential to success, do most respectfully and earnestly request the removal of Maj. Gen. Sam. Jones, now in command, and that your excellency assign to that command some one of the numerous gallant and efficient generals who, in our judgment, are far better adapted to the pressing wants of that all-important military field.

We make this appeal in no spirit of captious opposition to the Government. On the contrary, we have an abiding confidence in its wisdom, as well as its ability to attain final triumph. Nor do we feel inclined to do any injustice to General Jones; but our opportunities have been ample for observing the numerous manifest errors and defects in his command, errors which have been mortifying to the gallant army under his command, and have resulted in great loss to the producing interests of that section, from raids which have been repeatedly made and feebly resisted, when, in our judgment, as well as in the judgment of the army and country, these raids might have been prevented, or the enemy destroyed in his efforts to return from his visits of destruction upon our people.

In conclusion, sir, we feel assured that, aside from the promptness with which our section has responded to all calls to arms emanating from proper sources, the great lead, iron, copper, salt, and other interests (a proper defense of which is so materially essential to the welfare of our entire Confederacy) cannot fail to secure your earnest and, we trust, favorable consideration.

We have the honor to be, sir, with sentiments of great esteem, your obedient servants:

[Signed by R. Crockett, House of Delegates, Wythe County; R. A. Richardson, House of Delegates, Mercer County; Geo. W. Duval, House of Delegates, Roane County; Wilson Lively, House of Delegates, Monroe County; A. J. Deyerle, House of Delegates, Roanoke County; Abraham Fry, House of Delegates, Giles County; James B. Johnson, House of Delegates, Carroll County; S. M. Dickey, House of Delegates, Grayson County; Jno. M. Rowan, House of Delegates, Monroe County; J. W. M. Witten, Fortieth Senatorial District of Virginia; R. M. Bales, Forty-second Senatorial District of Virginia; Jas. C. Taylor, Thirty-ninth Senatorial District of Virginia; J. A. Alderson, Forty-fourth Senatorial District of Virginia; Wm. E. Herndon, House of Delegates, Putnam; Jas. A.

Nighbert, House of Delegates, Logan, Boone, and Wyoming Counties; J. H. Thompson, House of Delegates, Smyth County; R. T. Bowen, House of Delegates, Tazewell County; Wm. J. Kendrick, House of Delegates, Russell County; John S. Draper, House. of Delegates, Pulaski County.]

[Indorsement.]

Secretary of War for attention and reply.

J. D. [DAVIS.]

HEADQUARTERS DEPARTMENT OF WESTERN VIRGINIA,
Dublin, October 2, 1863.

Capt. J. G. MARTIN,
  Commanding, &c. :

CAPTAIN : The general commanding directs me to reply to your letter of the 1st instant. He desires you to remain in your present position for the time being. He expresses himself entirely satisfied with the action you have hitherto taken, and wishes you to continue to follow the instructions given you by Brigadier-General Preston and himself.

You will order Captain Fields to proceed forthwith with his company to Pound Gap and remain at that place. Lieutenant-Colonel Prentice will, after he has wiped out the enemy at Guest's Station, scout the country between that place and Pound Gap. Direct Mr. Page to return to Jonesville and report to the major-general commanding any information from that place. The general thinks it probable that a commandant will be sent to the district which you now command.

He is perfectly satisfied with your course, and desires you to remain until relieved by such commandant.

I have the honor to remain, very respectfully,
WM. B. MYERS,
Assistant Adjutant-General.

WAR DEPARTMENT, C. S.,
Richmond, Va., October 2, 1863.

Brig. Gen. ROBERT F. HOKE :

GENERAL : Mr. Jones, who is largely interested in iron contracts with the Government, has been sent to me by Governor Vance, with the representation of dangerous combinations and violent proceedings of deserters and tories in and about Watauga County, N. C., in which the works of Mr. Jones are situated. The accounts induce me to believe that a visit with your command, or a portion of it, to that district would be eminently serviceable.

I do not know the precise nature of the instructions you have received from General Lee, nor do I mean to contravene them ; but if, without a departure from them, you can appropriately visit and repress disorders in the county named, and in one or two adjoining, liable, as I am informed, to similar outrages, it would be gratifying to the Department.

Mr. Jones, who will hand you this, is commended to a favorable audience, and will inform you more in detail both of the nature of the outrages and of the readiest avenues of approach to the infected district. He is particularly urgent that the disloyal men who may be arrested, if conscribed, should be totally removed from the State and sent to our more distant armies. I would suggest that if there be any troops from North Carolina serving with General Johnston, that army, being most remote, would probably offer fewest opportunities of escape; next to that being the army of General Lee, and to one or the other I think they had better be assigned.

Very respectfully,

J. A. SEDDON,
Secretary of War.

CAMP AT ORANGE COURT-HOUSE,
October 3, 1863.

His Excellency JEFFERSON DAVIS,
President Confederate States, Richmond, Va. :

Mr. PRESIDENT : A dispatch from Major Gilmor, in the valley, last night states that the re-enforcements for Rosecrans have all passed over the Baltimore and Ohio Railroad. The force, composed of Slocum's and Howard's corps, under General Hooker, was estimated at between 20,000 and 25,000 men. He states he made several attempts to break the railroad, but could accomplish nothing. I do not expect that Imboden has been more successful in his efforts farther west. Unless more than two corps have been forwarded to General Rosecrans' army, the estimate of their strength is, in my opinion, too great, and they will probably not exceed 12,000. They are considered two of the smallest and most indifferent corps.

A small detachment of General R. D. Johnston's North Carolina brigade crossed the Rapidan on the night of the 1st and attacked a cavalry picket of the enemy. Lieut. P. Durham, commanding the detachment, returned with 1 prisoner, 8 horses, 9 saddles and bridles, 4 sabers, and 4 pistols. He left 1 of the enemy killed, 1 wounded, and 2 horses killed.

The army has not been paid for some months, and it is reported that the company officers find difficulty in subsisting themselves. All the estimates, excepting for the cavalry, forwarded some weeks since. If it is possible, I should like to have the men paid regularly.

I am, with great respect, your obedient servant,

R. E. LEE,
General.

DUBLIN,
October 4, 1863.

Brig. Gen. G. C. WHARTON,
Glade Spring:

Place your brigade in the vicinity of the depot, so that you can move readily to Saltville, on the railroad, as desired.

By order of Maj. Gen. S. Jones:

CHAS. S. STRINGFELLOW,
Assistant Adjutant-General.

HEADQUARTERS, *Wilmington, October* 4, 1863.

General S. COOPER,
    Adjutant and Inspector General, Richmond:

GENERAL: I must continue to call attention to the serious exposure of this important place, its danger, and our great need of troops.

Never since the commencement of the war has this danger been so imminent, and never in the way of troops, at least (and they are all important), has there been so few to meet it. As I have many times demonstrated, the only plan of successful defense to be adopted here depends on a supporting force or movable column. All the works which have been put up for the protection of the harbor and the city are based upon this, and without this are of but little avail.

Even those works, though pushed with all the means at my command, are not yet complete.

Instead of a supporting force, estimated at from 10,000 to 20,000 men, necessary, according to the magnitude of the enemy's preparation for even a show of defense, I have but one regiment of infantry and a few batteries of very inferior artillery, none of which have ever been in action.

My heavy artillery force is not sufficient to man the guns which have been mounted. It is, moreover, compelled to labor constantly, owing to the backwardness of the people in furnishing negroes to work upon the fortifications, which impairs its efficiency. I have not, literally, troops enough at my disposal to perform the required guard duty over the public property, now very great, at this important sea-port, and daily increasing.

In the meantime, the operations of the enemy indicate the permanent occupation, by powerful defensive works, of Morris Island. That should be his plan, as it seals up the port of Charleston, still enables him to go on to destroy the city at long range without exposure to himself, and releases his fleet and army for the attack on the last remaining port on this coast. He may endeavor to do the same here ; that is, seal up the port, and that he will surely and inevitably do unless an army is present. I do not think it will do to wait until after he has landed. It has never done yet. An army of 27,000 men was gathered to support Vicksburg. I do not pretend to decide on the relative importance of the two places at that time, but surely this place is as important now as Vicksburg was then. I assure you now, positively, as this place is now situated, 2,000 men can land and either take the city in twenty-four hours, or else render fruitless all the labor that has been expended. I am not very apprehensive of the naval attack. The fortifications that have been erected against that are of the best character, but they depend on security by land, and there can be no security, no system of defense in this peculiar locality without the presence of a large body of troops. It seems to me time to collect them.

It is needless to call attention to the vast importance this port has assumed of late. All are aware of that. It will be easy for the enemy to close it unless I can crush him on his landing ; but I have nothing. You are, perhaps, not aware that the defenses here, though vastly increased and totally different in design from the original batteries projected before the monitors were called in play, have not had the increase of a man to garrison them since General French was in command.

At that time there were no advance works at Fort Caswell, none at Fisher, none at the important point of Smithville, none at all on Smith's Island, and but few on the river. At all these points powerful works have been erected, absolutely essential to the defense, but I have had no increase of force. But this, the garrisoning of the forts, is but a trifle compared to the vital necessity of the army of support. I have many times shown this in reports, plans, and memoirs. The responsibility is great. I must leave the subject with you, only assuring you that as matters stand here now I cannot answer for the safety of this place for any forty-eight hours.

Very respectfully,

W. H. C. WHITING,
Major-General.

P. S.—My previous letters on this subject, which are very numerous, have been addressed to the Secretary of War, in continuation of a direct correspondence commenced with Mr. Randolph. Having received your telegram, in future I will be careful to address you.

[Indorsement.]

OCTOBER 6, 1863.

Respectfully submitted to the Secretary of War.

A brigade of Pickett's division has been sent to Kinston to relieve Martin's brigade, which is ordered to Wilmington.

General Beauregard should be instructed to watch the movement of the enemy from Charleston and the coast in the direction of Wilmington, and promptly send re-enforcements to General Whiting, should such movements be made.

S. COOPER,
Adjutant and Inspector General.

CAMP AT ORANGE COURT-HOUSE,
October 5, 1863.

His Excellency JEFFERSON DAVIS,
President Confederate States, Richmond, Va.:

MR. PRESIDENT: I have had the honor to receive your letter of the 1st. I hope there was a mistake as to the strength of Bragg's army. His effective strength, given me by General Cooper before the battle, and before the addition of Longstreet's corps, was 76,219; Bragg's 51,101 and Buckner's 16,118, plus 9,000 from Johnston's army. I think if Your Excellency could make it convenient to visit that country, you would be able to reconcile many difficulties and unite the scattered troops.

I wrote to you that I could spare General Iverson for the cavalry in Georgia. He is the only man I can think of for the situation. I would also recommend that General W. E. Jones be assigned to the command of the cavalry lately under Deshler, unless there is with that army a better man for the place. I consider General Jones a brave and intelligent officer, but his feelings have become so opposed to General Stuart that I have lost all hope of his being useful in the cavalry here. He tendered his resignation before the expedition to Pennsylvania, which I withheld. He has been subsequently tried by court-martial for disrespect and the proceedings are now in Richmond. I understand he says he will no longer serve under Stuart, and I do not think it would be advantageous for him to do so, but I wish to make him useful. I can replace him by Colonel Rosser, Fifth Virginia Cavalry, an excellent officer in the field, who is prompt, cool, and fearless, and has been twice wounded in this war. He resigned his position as cadet at the U. S. Military Academy, just before the period of his graduation. When the war commenced, served first in the artillery, with some distinction, and subsequently was transferred to the cavalry. As soon as the proceedings of the court are published, I shall be obliged to relieve Jones from the command of his brigade, which, in fact, has been without its commander ever since the army crossed the Potomac.

I am, with great respect, your obedient servant,

R. E. LEE,
General.

ORANGE COURT-HOUSE, *
October 5, 1863.

General S. COOPER,
Adjutant and Inspector General:

Please send the North Carolina cavalry regiment at once.

R. E. LEE,
General.

SPECIAL ORDERS, } HDQRS. ARTILLERY CORPS, A. N. VA.,
No. —. } *October 5, 1863.*

Captain Lamkin, commanding Nelson Artillery, having reported for assignment under orders from general headquarters, is hereby assigned to the battalion now commanded by Major Haskell. He will proceed as soon as practicable to the camp of said battalion, a short distance beyond Gordonsville on the Charlottesville road, and report for duty to Major Haskell.

W. N. PENDLETON,
Brigadier-General, and Chief of Artillery.

HEADQUARTERS DEPARTMENT OF NORTH CAROLINA,
Petersburg, October 5, 1863.

General S. COOPER,
Adjt. and Insp. Gen., C. S. Army, Richmond, Va.:

GENERAL: General Whiting telegraphed me this morning that he wanted the Forty-seventh North Carolina Regiment. I immediately sent word to General Martin to order it to report to Whiting; he replies there is no such regiment there, but the Forty-second is, and the only one at that point. Just at the same time I received a dispatch from Captain Leitch, who tells me you wish a brigade gotten in readiness to relieve Martin at Kinston. I have ordered Barton's brigade to be ready to move to-morrow and the quartermaster to furnish transportation by rail. The wagons had better be sent by road, I suppose, and at once; or will they take the transportation which Martin will leave behind? In consequence of the intended movement of Martin's brigade, I did not repeat the order for a regiment to go to Whiting. Have you any further instructions relative to this case? I inclose telegram from Weldon just received from my aide-de-camp whom I sent to General Ransom this morning.

I am, general, very respectfully, your obedient servant,
GEO. E. PICKETT,
Major-General, Commanding.

[Inclosure.]

WELDON,
October 5, 1863.

Major-General PICKETT:

General Ransom had received the information some time before Colonel Hinton, who received it merely through him. He considers it by no means reliable and certainly not at all probable that they will make that their main attack. It will be on Weldon, which he would leave uncovered by moving; therefore he will not go. I will return on the night train and give you the particulars. If you wish anything further, telegraph at once. Telegraph anyway.

E. R. BAIRD,
Aide-de-Camp.

HEADQUARTERS DEPARTMENT OF NORTH CAROLINA,
October 5, 1863.

General S. COOPER:

GENERAL: Major Morfit, transportation agent at this place, informs me that 4 o'clock to-morrow evening is the earliest moment at which he can furnish transportation for the brigade. They can all go at that time.

I am, general, very respectfully, your obedient servant,
G. E. P. [PICKETT.]

HEADQUARTERS DEPARTMENT OF NORTH CAROLINA,
Petersburg, October 5, 1863.

General S. COOPER,
Adjutant and Inspector General, C. S. Army:

GENERAL: I have just learned from General Barton that a telegram arrived last night from General Longstreet, calling for my division. It is proper that I should state to you before any movement is made the condition of the command. There have been some few conscripts assigned to us since our arrival in this neighborhood, say, 100. At this time there are 2 officers, 1 non-commissioned officer, and 3 privates absent on recruiting service from each regiment, making 40 officers and 80 privates. The plan of reorganizing this shattered division is in fact but just commenced. The steps I have taken to gather up the numbers of men on detailed service in and about Richmond are in progress, but should we move now it will be with ranks not recruited, and in fact in no better condition than upon our arrival. The object for which we were left here has not been carried out. In time I will be able to get the division together and in fighting trim it most emphatically is not so now. And until the ranks are filled up and some more officers come back to us by exchange, and opportunity is given to those promoted to learn some little of their duties, it will not be the crack division it was, and I decidedly would not like to go into action with it. If more troops are needed in the southwest and we go, it is plain other troops must be sent here to replace us. Why not let this division remain till it is fit for service? I think, general, the final benefit to the service would be increased by this arrangement. It was the intention when we were put in our present position, and the circumstances are not altered. I am informed by the Conscript Bureau that I will have some two hundred and odd men assigned to me within a month. These men are to be returned from Jones and Imboden.

By last field return I have 329 officers and 4,007 rank and file effective in the division. Aggregate present and absent, 11,344.

I send this over to you by a staff officer, Captain Leitch, and will come over this evening by train in case you might wish to see me.

I am, general, in haste, your obedient servant,

GEO. E. PICKETT,
Major-General.

WAR DEPARTMENT, C. S.,
Richmond, Va., October 5, 1863.

Maj. Gen. W. H. C. WHITING,
Commanding, &c., Wilmington, N. C.:

GENERAL: The President has directed that obstructions be placed in the Roanoke River, and Lieut. F. L. Hoge, C. S. Navy, has been detailed by the Secretary of the Navy for that service. You are requested to furnish such assistance and protection as may be needed and can be spared, and, also, such material and transportation as can be conveniently supplied from your department. Lieutenant Hoge will receive all the aid that can be given by the Engineer and other Bureaus here.

Very respectfully, yours,

J. A. SEDDON,
Secretary of War.

RICHMOND,
October 6, 1863.

Maj. Gen. GEORGE E. PICKETT,
Petersburg, Va.:

Order Barton's brigade to Kinston to relieve Martin's, and direct General Martin to proceed with his brigade to Wilmington and report to General Whiting. Both brigades now being in your department, your orders will be sufficient.

S. COOPER,
Adjutant and Inspector General.

RICHMOND, *October 6, 1863.*

General PICKETT, *Petersburg, Va.:*

Order Seventh Confederate Cavalry Regiment, late Claiborne's, to repair to Orange Court-House, Va., and report to General Lee.

S. COOPER.

SPECIAL ORDERS, }   ADJT. AND INSP. GENERAL'S OFFICE,
No. 237.   }   *Richmond, Va., October* 6, 1863.

* * * * * * *

XXI. Brigadier-General Iverson is relieved from duty with the army in the Department of Northern Virginia. He will repair to Atlanta, Ga., and report to Major-General Cobb.

XXII. Brig. Gen. W. M. Gardner is relieved from assignment in Special Orders, No. 223, Paragraph XXVI, and will proceed to Quincy, Fla., and assume command of Department of West Florida, lately held by Major-General Cobb.

By command of the Secretary of War:

JNO. WITHERS,
Assistant Adjutant-General.

HEADQUARTERS DEPARTMENT OF WESTERN VIRGINIA,
Dublin, October 6, 1863.

Brig. Gen. JOHN ECHOLS,
Commanding, &c.:

GENERAL: The major-general commanding directs me to say, in reply to your letter of yesterday, that he desires Colonel Ferguson to co-operate with you, but to report direct to these headquarters.

I am, general, very respectfully, your obedient servant,

WM. B. MYERS,
Assistant Adjutant-General.

HEADQUARTERS DEPARTMENT OF WESTERN VIRGINIA,
Dublin, October 6, 1863.

Brig. Gen. JOHN ECHOLS,
Commanding First Brigade:

GENERAL: The Sixtieth [Virginia] Regiment has been ordered back to the Narrows. So soon as you learn that it has arrived at that point, the major-general commanding directs that you can order the infantry battalion back to Lewisburg, and also recall the company of Dunn's battalion, now at the Narrows.

Very respectfully, your obedient servant,

CHAS. S. STRINGFELLOW,
Assistant Adjutant-General.

WAR DEPARTMENT, C. S.,
Richmond, Va., October 7, 1863.

Maj. Gen. W. H. C. WHITING,
Commanding, Wilmington, N. C.:

GENERAL: I have received your letter inclosing a communication from General Clingman, suggesting the probability of a force being sent from Charleston to attack Wilmington, and have written to General Beauregard requesting that, as far as may be practicable, without disturbing his plans of defense, he hold Clingman's brigade so prepared that on a call from you it may be thrown rapidly to Wilmington, and that, in the event of your making the requisition, it may be sent to your re-enforcement without delay.

You are, therefore, authorized, on the receipt of certain intelligence that the enemy are preparing to attack you by land with forces drawn in whole or in part from Charleston, to make requisition for the return of Clingman's brigade.

Very truly, yours,

J. A. SEDDON,
Secretary of War.

P. S.—Orders have likewise been given to General Pickett, by which General Martin's brigade will be at once placed in Wilmington or its vicinity as a present re-enforcement.

HEADQUARTERS DEPARTMENT OF NORTH CAROLINA,
Petersburg, Va., October 8, 1863.

General S. COOPER,
Adjt. and Insp. Gen., C. S. Army, Richmond, Va.:

GENERAL: I have the honor to state I have ordered 200 cavalry from Colonel Griffin's regiment, headquarters Franklin, to North Carolina, as far as possible to relieve Claiborne's regiment. You will have perceived that General Whiting declines sending the three companies of Claiborne's cavalry which are in his district. I have sent a courier to Lieutenant-Colonel Waddell, commanding Baker's cavalry, to close in to the right and cover the ground formerly occupied by the 200 cavalry withdrawn and sent to North Carolina. I sent down by railroad to-day, to Ivor, the Seventeenth Virginia, Lieutenant-Colonel Herbert commanding. The Ninth Virginia, the regiment first ordered to that point, I, of course, sent off with its brigade (Barton's). Colonel Herbert is a most efficient officer, and I shall feel more confidence in the conduct of affairs on the Blackwater after his arrival. I also thought of sending down a battery in a day or two. I think an expedition might possibly be made with effect toward Suffolk; I shall not make one, however, till I find out something more. The Seventeenth can occupy the points left vacant by Baker's cavalry.

I inclose you telegrams received from General Barton and my reply.

Lieut. Hawes E. Marshall is here under arrest. I was directed by telegram that his case would be brought before the military court in Richmond. Do you wish him sent over at once, with the witnesses, or will the court notify me when they wish him brought before them?

I shall be happy to receive any instructions or suggestions, and to know whether the distribution of troops made by me meets with your approbation.

Do you think more cavalry ought to be taken from the Blackwater and sent to North Carolina?

I am, general, with much respect, your obedient servant,

GEO. E. PICKETT,
Major-General, Commanding.

[Inclosure No. 1.]

OCTOBER 8, 1863.

Maj. C. PICKETT:

It will be impracticable for me to picket the line as at present established with the force I have. That part from Hamilton to Greenville, inclusive, will require 800 men. Now that the cavalry has been ordered away, it will take every man I have to do the duty from Greenville south. Cannot General Ransom furnish a regiment to each of the points, Hamilton and Greenville? I will not relieve Martin's troops there till I hear from you. •

> S. M. BARTON,
> *Brigadier-General.*

[Sub-Inclosure.]

> KINSTON,
> *October 7, 1863.*

General PICKETT:

If the Seventh Confederate Cavalry leaves this place there will not be more than 200 effective cavalry from the Roanoke to Wilmington.

> J. G. MARTIN,
> *Brigadier-General.*

[Inclosure No. 2.]

> HEADQUARTERS DEPARTMENT OF NORTH CAROLINA,
> *October 8, 1863.*

Brig. Gen. S. M. BARTON,
   Commanding, Kinston, N. C.:

Relieve General Martin as far as you can. Two hundred cavalry of Griffin's command have been ordered to relieve the Seventh Confederate Cavalry, which is that you speak of as being ordered away.

> C. PICKETT,
> *Assistant Adjutant-General.*

> RICHMOND,
> *October 8, 1863.*

General GEORGE E. PICKETT,
   Petersburg, Va:

Revoke the order requiring the Seventh Confederate Cavalry to report to General Lee. Under existing circumstances it must be retained where it is in North Carolina.

> S. COOPER,
> *Adjutant and Inspector General.*

> RICHMOND,
> *October 8, 1863.*

General R. E. LEE,
   Orange Court-House:

I have been compelled to suspend the movement of the cavalry regiment from North Carolina on account of present state of things there. Colonel Stafford has just been appointed brigadier-general, to report to you.

> S. COOPER,
> *Adjutant and Inspector General.*

HEADQUARTERS DEPARTMENT OF WESTERN VIRGINIA,
Dublin, October 8, 1863.

Brig. Gen. JOHN ECHOLS,
  Commanding First Brigade:

GENERAL: The major-general commanding directs me to say that if the enemy is at Bowyer's Ferry in no larger force than represented in your letter of the 6th instant, he can see no reason to prevent your organizing a force to drive them off without [delay.] They should be allowed neither to construct boats nor clear out the roads. You will immediately prepare to attack this force, unless you have very urgent reasons against this course.

Very respectfully, your obedient servant,
  CHAS. S. STRINGFELLOW,
    Assistant Adjutant-General.

SPECIAL ORDERS, } ADJT. AND INSP. GENERAL'S OFFICE,
  No. 239.   } *Richmond, October 8,* 1863.

* * * * * * *

XXIV. The Eighth and Fourteenth Regiments Virginia Cavalry, now serving in the Department of Southwestern Virginia, will proceed without delay to Orange Court-House, Va., and report to General R. E. Lee, commanding Department of Northern Virginia, for assignment to duty with the cavalry divisions of his army.

* * * * * * *

By command of the Secretary of War:
  JNO. WITHERS,
    Assistant Adjutant-General.

ORANGE COURT-HOUSE,
  October 9, 1863.

General S. COOPER,
  Adjutant and Inspector General:

Your dispatch received. Report indicates the enemy will attempt a raid north of James River. Troops should be withdrawn from south side to meet it.

R. E. LEE.

RICHMOND, VA.,
  October 9, 1863.

General PICKETT,
  Petersburg, Va.:

Information received excites suspicion that a raid in force is contemplated by enemy either toward Weldon or on the north side toward Hanover Junction. Movements are not yet sufficiently decided to enable us to decide which is the design. It may be contemporaneous on both points. Under the circumstances, it is recommended, while retaining force on watch at Weldon, you concentrate such other as you can command at or near Petersburg ready to be thrown either way.

S. C. [COOPER.]

RICHMOND,
October 9, 1863.

General R. E. LEE,
Orange Court-House:

GENERAL: The proceedings, findings, and sentence in the case of Brig. Gen. W. E. Jones have been received and duly approved. The usual general order in such cases will be forwarded you as soon as it can be prepared, and in the meantime special orders will be sent directing that officer to report for duty to Maj. Gen. Samuel Jones. The President approves your suggestion with respect to Colonel Rosser.

Very respectfully, &c.,

S. COOPER,
Adjutant and Inspector General.

P. S.—Colonel Rosser will be immediately appointed brigadier-general for cavalry service in your command.

SPECIAL ORDERS, }   ADJT. AND INSP. GENERAL'S OFFICE,
No. 240.   }   *Richmond, October* 9, 1863.

*   *   *   *   *   *   *

XXIV. Brig. Gen. W. E. Jones will proceed to Dublin Depot,Va., and report for duty to Maj. Gen. Sam. Jones for assignment to the cavalry in his command.

By command of the Secretary of War:

JNO. WITHERS,
Assistant Adjutant-General.

HEADQUARTERS ARMY OF NORTHERN VIRGINIA,
October 9, 1863.

Maj. Gen. ARNOLD ELZEY,
Commanding, &c., Richmond, Va.:

GENERAL: I presume from the fact that Colonel Spear is transferring his cavalry to the Peninsula that he designs making a raid in that quarter. I think you had better draw your troops from the south side to meet them. As far as I can judge, there is no force of consequence south of James River; you have better means of information, however.

My scouts on the Potomac report that on the 2d two small steamers with troops passed up the river, and on the 5th, four, one a large one, also laden with troops. This shows that the enemy is still re-enforcing General Meade, and the troops referred to doubtless came from the direction of Fort Monroe.

I do not therefore attach any importance to the report of troops in large force at Norfolk or Portsmouth. Unless your information is positive on the subject, a small force might be left to guard our lines south of James River, and the rest moved to meet the anticipated raid. It is impossible for me to spare any cavalry from this army at present.

Troops could better be spared from General Sam. Jones at this time than from this army.

.Very respectfully, your obedient servant,

R. E. LEE,
General.

HEADQUARTERS ARMY OF NORTHERN VIRGINIA,
October 9, 1863.

Brig. Gen. J. D. IMBODEN,
Commanding, &c.:

GENERAL: It is a matter of great importance, in my judgment, that our troops should advance upon the enemy in all quarters, for the purpose of preventing him from re-enforcing points more seriously threatened, if nothing better can be accomplished. I desire you to move some part of your force to Strasburg and scout over toward Manassas and Thornton's Gaps, to prevent anything from coming in rear of those of our troops which will now be operating in the direction of Woodville and Sperryville. Should you find no opposition, or such as you can overcome, you may continue your advance farther down the valley, taking care to observe closely the points above indicated.

Very respectfully, your obedient servant,

R. E. LEE,
General.

HEADQUARTERS ARMY OF NORTHERN VIRGINIA,
October 9, 1863.

Maj. Gen. SAMUEL JONES,
Commanding, &c.:

GENERAL: I think it very important that our troops everywhere should advance upon the enemy, even if nothing else can be accomplished excepting preventing him from re-enforcing points now threatened. Of course, if opportunity offers to do more, it should be made use of. I hope you will be able at least to make some demonstration which will detain such force as the enemy may now have in your department, and thus co-operate with the movement going on in other quarters.

Very respectfully, your obedient servant,

R. E. LEE,
General.

ORDERS, }
No. — }   HEADQUARTERS ARTILLERY CORPS,
                   October 9, 1863.

Colonel Cabell will with his artillery battalion take position near Gordonsville, for the purpose of guarding that point against incursions of the enemy while the army is in motion. He will have the roads picketed, especially those north and east of Gordonsville. He will keep his battalion ready for moving forward at very short notice should occasion therefor occur. Captain Lamkin's company, now with Major Haskell's battalion, and without equipments, will report to Colonel Cabell, and be subject to his command until further orders.

Major Haskell will with his battalion move forward toward Liberty Mills, and act under verbal orders which he will receive.

W. N. PENDLETON,
Brigadier-General, and Chief of Artillery.

HDQRS. DEPT. OF WESTERN VA. AND EAST TENN.,
Dublin, October 9, 1863.

General R. E. LEE,
Commanding Army of Northern Virginia:

GENERAL: I received to-day your letter of the 7th instant. There is no such body of men as Dunn's battalion at or near the salt-works. Lieut. Col. D. C. Dunn, of the Sixty-third Virginia Regiment, attempted to raise a battalion under authority which he said was given him by Brigadier-General Williams. I have stopped him and ordered him to his regiment, and ordered all the men and officers purporting to belong to that unauthorized battalion to be arrested and turned over to the conscript officers.

The Captain Pasley whom you mention belongs to Colonel Peters' regiment. That organization has given me and others great trouble, and I have no doubt whatever that there are many deserters in it. Lieutenant-Colonel Murray, of your staff, visited my camp a few weeks since, by your order, to reclaim deserters who were supposed to be in that regiment, and I gave him all the aid he asked to enable him to carry out his instructions. I cannot tell now, nor do I think Colonel Peters can, what men in his regiment are and what are not deserters. I will, however, if you desire it, order the regiment to report to you. In your army perhaps the deserters may be recognized and reclaimed.

Please let me know your wishes on my suggestions.

With great respect, your obedient servant,

SAM. JONES,
Major-General.

ORANGE COURT-HOUSE,
October 9, 1863.

Maj. Gen. SAMUEL JONES,
Dublin Depot:

GENERAL: I arrived here yesterday; Hill's corps was moving and passed, going to the front and left of this place.

This morning early, Ewell's corps passed, or at least two divisions. General Lee moves to-day. General Early's division will, I think, bring up the rear. I think I shall be able to get my troops here. Cooke's brigade has already arrived.

It is supposed the enemy has fallen back to Culpeper Court-House, and perhaps beyond that place. A deserter reported yesterday that only a small body was in that town. I am sorry to find General Lee quite unwell from an attack of rheumatism. He expressed great interest in getting supplies from Tennessee and Kentucky. Any horses you can have sent to him will be more than acceptable.

I shall go down to-day. If a fight comes off I can hardly be in it.

Everything indicates rapidity of motion, and if the enemy is going to his intrenchments about Washington, there is no time to lose. Every one says the army is in fine condition. What I have seen appears to be. They are mobile and prompt.

When I reach Richmond I will write again. Regards to your staff.

Very truly,

R. RANSOM, Jr.

———

DUBLIN, *October 9,* [1863.]

Col. B. H. JONES,
    Sixtieth Virginia Regiment:

COLONEL: The major-general commanding directs that you move your regiment to the Narrows at once; permit as little delay as is practicable at this point.

Very respectfully, colonel, your obedient servant,

CHAS. S. STRINGFELLOW, •
Assistant Adjutant-General.

———

HEADQUARTERS ARMY OF NORTHERN VIRGINIA,
October 10. 1863.

Hon. JAMES A. SEDDON,
    Secretary of War:

SIR: The report of a scout received on 10th instant (to-day) states that General Gillmore has been ordered to take Charleston at all hazards, and failing in this, to make a flank movement and endeavor to seize upon Branchville. The latter does not look like a probable movement, but I send you the statement, as it may indicate some movement against Charleston by the enemy. General Stuart attacked a body of the enemy near James City and drove them back, capturing 125 prisoners.

I am, very respectfully, your obedient servant,

R. E. LEE,
General.

———

HDQRS. DEPT. OF WESTERN VA. AND EAST TENN.,
Dublin, October 10, 1863.

Brig. Gen. A. R. LAWTON,
    Quartermaster-General, Richmond, Va.:

GENERAL: The troops under my command are so greatly in need of clothing that I have directed Major Brown, post quartermaster at this place, to go to Richmond himself to procure as full a supply as he can.

I know from personal inspection that the clothing is necessary, chiefly pants and shoes. I have seen large numbers of men in the ranks and marching to meet the enemy without shoes, and many others have been excused from certain duty because they were, as I was assured, so destitute of clothing that they could not with decency appear on duty.

Very respectfully, your obedient servant,

SAM. JONES,
Major-General.

Troops in the Department of Richmond, Maj. Gen. Arnold Elzey, C. S. Army, commanding, October 10, 1863.

Hunton's Brigade.

Brig. Gen. E. HUNTON.

8th Virginia, Capt. Henry C. Bowie.
18th Virginia, Capt. Henry T. Owen.
19th Virginia, Capt. J. G. Woodson.
28th Virginia, Capt. W. L. Wingfield.
56th Virginia, Capt. John Richardson.
Holcombe (South Carolina) Legion, Col. W. P. Shingler.
32d Virginia Cavalry Battalion, Maj. J. R. Robertson.

Artillery Battalion.*

Maj. A. W. STARK.

Alexandria (Virginia) Artillery, Capt. D. L. Smoot.
McComas (Virginia) Artillery, Capt. D. A. French.
Matthews (Virginia) Artillery, Capt. A. D. Armistead.

Detached Cavalry.

42d Virginia Cavalry Battalion, Lieut. Col. W. T. Robins.

Chaffin's Bluff.

Lieut. Col. J. M. MAURY.

19th Virginia, Companies B and G.
Goochland (Virginia) Artillery, Capt. J. Talley.
Lunenburg (Virginia) Artillery, Capt. C. T. Allen.
Pamunkey (Virginia) Artillery, Capt. A. J. Jones.
Howitzer (Virginia) Battery, Capt. E. R. Young.

Kemper's Brigade.

Col. W. R. TERRY.

1st Virginia, Lieut. Col. F. H. Langley.
3d Virginia, Maj. W. H. Pryor.
7th Virginia, Col. C. C. Flowerree.
11th Virginia, Capt. R. W. Douthat.
24th Virginia, Lieut. Col. R. L. Maury.
Claytor's (Virginia) Battery, Capt. R. B. Claytor.

Richmond Defenses.

Col. T. S. RHETT.

10th Virginia Heavy Artillery Battalion,† Maj. J. O. Hensley.
18th Virginia Heavy Artillery Battalion,‡ Maj. M. B. Hardin.
19th Virginia Heavy Artillery Battalion,† Maj. N. R. Cary.
20th Virginia Heavy Artillery Battalion,‡ Maj. J. E. Robertson.
Caroline (Virginia) Artillery, Capt. T. R. Thornton.
2d Nelson (Virginia) Artillery, Capt. J. H. Rives.
Surry (Virginia) Artillery, Capt. J. D. Hankins.

Drewry's Bluff.

Maj. F. W. SMITH.

Johnston (Virginia) Artillery, Capt. B. J. Epes.
Neblett (Virginia) Artillery, Capt. W. G. Coleman.
Southside (Virginia) Artillery, Capt. J. W. Drewry.
United (Virginia) Artillery, Capt. Thomas Kevill.

SPECIAL ORDERS, }   HDQRS. DEPT. OF NORTHERN VIRGINIA,
No. 255.   }   *October* 11, 1863.

Brig. Gen. John Pegram, Provisional Army, C. S., will report to Lieut. Gen. R. S. Ewell, commanding Second Army Corps, for assignment to the command of the brigade formerly commanded by Brigadier-General Smith.

By command of General Lee:

W. H. TAYLOR,
Assistant Adjutant-General.

---

*Attached to Hunton's command at Chaffin's Farm.
† First Division, Inner Line, Lieut. Col. J. W. Atkinson commanding.
‡ Second Division, Inner Line, Lieut. Col. James Howard commanding.

DUBLIN,
October 11, 1863.

Brig. Gen. G. C. WHARTON,
    Commanding, &c., Glade Spring:

GENERAL : The major-general commanding directs you to assume command of all the troops between Saltville and the Tennessee line and be prepared for the defense of the salt-works. Capt. J. G. Martin, at Abingdon, can give you the necessary information in regard to the detached companies, &c. It is reported that the enemy is interposed between General Williams and yourself.

Should you and he be compelled to unite your forces, he will, of course, be in command as the ranking officer. If communication between this point and Glade Spring should be interrupted, you must of course act promptly on your own judgment.

Have your troops well in hand and secure the earliest and most reliable information.

I am, general, your obedient servant,
CHAS. S. STRINGFELLOW. .
Assistant Adjutant-General.

RICHMOND,
October 12, 1863.

General R. E. LEE,
    Comdg. Army of Northern Va., Orange C. H., Va.:

GENERAL : I am in the receipt of your recent letter in which, after stating that your army is much in want of shoes for men and horses, and blankets for the former, you request that all that can be furnished may be placed at the disposal of your chief quartermaster, and also that you may be informed what provision can be made to meet your wants.

It was not my fortune to see Lieutenant-Colonel Corley while he was here. You have no doubt heard from him of the limited supplies on hand at this point. Such as were here were placed at his disposal, and I immediately telegraphed to distant points to secure the number of shoes—some 8,000—required by Colonel Corley's report, to provide for the barefooted men of your command. Some 2,000 pairs of shoes have been forwarded by Lieutenant-Colonel Cone, direct from his depot here ; 1,229 pairs, also, received from Wilmington, and 3,500 are daily expected that were ordered from Columbus, Ga. I regretted very much to learn on Saturday that Maj. C. D. Hill, established at this point by Colonel Corley himself, had on hand, at the date of that officer's visit and call for supplies, over 3,000 pairs of shoes which were entirely overlooked. I have directed that these too be sent up immediately. In this way nearly 10,000 pairs will be supplied, which is a little in excess of the very pressing demand ; and others will be added so soon as they can be provided through our home resources or from foreign arrivals. There are some 15,000 overcoats on hand here, and a fair supply of clothing at this and other depots ; but blankets are extremely scarce. About 4,000 have been issued to your troops within the past month, leaving in the depot here only 1,500, which, with 12,000 at Atlanta, . Ga., for which the commands in that section of the country are clamorous, constitute the entire supply ; and unfortunately our domestic resources in this particular are very limited. All the horse-shoes here and some that have been drawn from other points are on their way to you.

I have postponed some days my reply that I might learn the contents of a cargo just arrived at Wilmington. I am glad to say that some 10,500 pairs shoes and 6,500 blankets, besides a quantity of leather, are reported as received. These will relieve, I hope, your present necessities to a great extent, and the requisitions of Colonel Corley shall be filled as promptly as possible. In view of the exhausted condition of our resources here, I am using every effort to draw a winter's supply from abroad, and while the difficulties and uncertainties are such as to forbid my stating results in advance, I still hope to be able to provide, with economy, for the pressing wants of our armies in the field.

A. R. LAWTON,
Quartermaster-General.

———

HEADQUARTERS DEPARTMENT OF WESTERN VIRGINIA,
Dublin, October 12, 1863.

Brig. Gen. JOHN ECHOLS:

The major-general commanding directs me to say, in reply to your letter of the 10th instant, that he approves of your course and the suggestions contained in your letter of that date. He has been requested by General Lee to keep the enemy in his front occupied by an apparent if not a real move, that they may not send re-enforcements to any of the points against which our forces are now moving in the general plan adopted by the Government. He therefore directs you to advance your brigade in the direction of Gauley.

Should you have any opportunity of striking the enemy an effective blow, remove the blockade, push on, and attack him with vigor. If, however, you are satisfied from the information you obtain that no blow can be struck at the enemy with advantage at Bowyer's Ferry or elsewhere, you will simply make such a demonstration as will occupy his attention and prevent his sending troops elsewhere. A regiment of cavalry may be sent to scout in the direction of Summerville.

Colonel Ferguson will be directed to co-operate with you, and be under your orders, for the purposes herein indicated.

I am, general, very respectfully,
CHAS. S. STRINGFELLOW,
Assistant Adjutant-General.

———

HEADQUARTERS DEPARTMENT OF WESTERN VIRGINIA,
Dublin, October 12, 1863.

Col. M. J. FERGUSON,
Commanding Cavalry Brigade:

COLONEL: Directions have been given General Echols in regard to the purposes and objects of a contemplated move in the direction of Gauley. As the general commanding desires you to co-operate with General Echols, he directs you to report to him at once, and act under his orders, for the object of the movement above referred to.

Very respectfully, your obedient servant,
CHAS. S. STRINGFELLOW.

HEADQUARTERS,
Wilmington, October 13, 1863.

General COOPER,
Adjutant and Inspector General, Richmond:

GENERAL: The President informed me in a personal interview in passing through here that he thought I might have some marines and artillerists spared from the forts on James River, and directed me to apply to you in the matter. On account of the increased extent of the works here since General French had charge, and the fact that the artillery (heavy) force had not since been increased, I need very much a re-enforcement of experienced artillerists. If, therefore, in accordance with the President's suggestion, I can get from Mr. Mallory some marines, and from the army some artillerists, will you please to make the necessary application in the first case and the order in the second.

Very respectfully,

W. H. C. WHITING,
Major-General.

HEADQUARTERS DEPARTMENT OF WESTERN VIRGINIA,
Dublin, October 13, 1863.

Col. JOHN McCAUSLAND:

Brigadier General Echols reports that persons who have just come from the Kanawha inform him that nearly all the cavalry force of the enemy in that section have gone below Charleston. Our troops in East Tennessee have been pressed very hard, and forced to retire to Zollicoffer.

It is supposed that the cavalry of the enemy have been sent from the Kanawha to East Tennessee, or else so disposed as to make an advance by way of the Sandy. The commanding general, therefore, desires you to send forward reliable scouts without delay, and obtain such information as you can, and report at once to these headquarters.

Very respectfully, your obedient servant,

CHAS. S. STRINGFELLOW,
Assistant Adjutant-General.

HEADQUARTERS DEPARTMENT OF WESTERN VIRGINIA,
Dublin, October 14, 1863.

Col. JOHN McCAUSLAND,
Commanding, &c., Princeton:

COLONEL: I am directed to inform you that Brig. Gen. John Echols has been ordered forward to make a demonstration against the enemy in his front, for the purpose of distracting their attention and preventing the detaching of troops to re-enforce their armies at other points against which we are moving. Should he have the opportunity, he will convert this feint into a real blow. The enemy are reported at Bowyer's Ferry, constructing boats, &c. If General Echols can do so, he will probably attack this force.

Very respectfully, your obedient servant,

CHAS. S. STRINGFELLOW,
Assistant Adjutant-General.

DUBLIN, *October* 14, 1863.

Col. M. J. FERGUSON,
    Commanding Cavalry Brigade, Lewisburg:

Order the Seventeenth Virginia [Cavalry] Regiment to report immediately to Colonel McCausland at Princeton, to replace the Eighth [Virginia Cavalry], ordered to Bristol. Order Dunn's battalion to report immediately to Brig. Gen. W. E. Jones at Bristol. Inform General Echols of these moves. The enemy is pressing.

By order of Maj. Gen. Sam. Jones:
                CHAS. S. STRINGFELLOW,
                    Assistant Adjutant-General.

DUBLIN, *October* 14, 1863.

Col. JOSEPH F. KENT, *Wytheville:*

Call out the home guards of Wythe County to go to Glade Spring. Lose no time; the necessity is urgent.

By order:
                CHAS. S. STRINGFELLOW,
                    Assistant Adjutant-General.

DUBLIN, *October* 14, 1863.

Capt. J. M. SHEFFEY, *Marion:*

Call out the home guards of Smyth, to go immediately to Glade Spring. Give full notice and lose no time; the enemy is pressing.

By order:
                CHAS. S. STRINGFELLOW,
                    Assistant Adjutant-General.

DUBLIN, *October* 14, 1863.

Captain SPILLER, *Wytheville:*

Collect your men from Grayson and other places, and report with them at once to Colonel Kent, at Glade Spring.

By order of Maj. Gen. S. Jones:
                CHAS. S. STRINGFELLOW,
                    Assistant Adjutant-General.

PETERSBURG, VA.,
October 14, 1863.

Maj. Gen. ARNOLD ELZEY,
    Commanding Department of Richmond:

GENERAL: I sent dispatch from Ivor to-day in regard to the report of the scouts from the Peninsula; upon my arrival here I sent another, for fear that the first would not reach you. Yorktown being some distance from my base of operations, I can get opportunities very seldom to send there.

The papers sent you will give you all reliable information as to the bearing of affairs in Yankeeland. I am watching for the Yankee papers with some degree of interest with regard to the Ohio and

Pennsylvania elections. I will forward as soon as received. I keep General Pickett fully posted.

It is evident to me that Foster designs making some move on North Carolina, perhaps to try his same old route of November last. The raids will certainly take place, and their object is to cut off our southern communications by tapping the Wilmington and Weldon Railroad. The force left about Norfolk and Portsmouth is very insignificant, mostly negroes.

Your obedient servant,

J. F. MILLIGAN,
Major, Comdg. Independent Signal Corps.

SPECIAL ORDERS, } HDQRS. ARMY OF NORTHERN VIRGINIA,
No. 256.   }   *October* 15, 1863.

I. Brig. Gen. Thomas L. Rosser, Provisional Army, C. S., will report to Maj. Gen. J. E. B. Stuart, commanding cavalry, for assignment to the command of the brigade formerly commanded by Brig. Gen. W. E. Jones.

II. Brig. Gen. P. M. B. Young, Provisional Army, C. S., will report to Maj. Gen. J. E. B. Stuart, commanding cavalry, for assignment to the command of Butler's brigade.

*   *   *.   *   *   *

By command of General R. E. Lee :

W. H. TAYLOR,
Assistant Adjutant-General.

RICHMOND, *October* 15, 1863.

Maj. Gen. GEORGE E. PICKETT,
    Petersburg, Va.:

Send a brigade of infantry of your immediate command forthwith to Dublin, Va., to report to Maj. Gen. Samuel Jones. It is required there with the least possible delay.

S. COOPER,
Adjutant and Inspector-General.

PETERSBURG,
October 15, 1863.

General S. COOPER:

Your dispatch in reference to sending brigade of infantry to Dublin is received. I have ordered General Corse, with three regiments, numbering 1,200 men, all that I have. The following dispatch was received last night from Ivor:

My scouts returned from the Peninsula last night report as follows: All the troops have left the Peninsula except a small force at Yorktown; the general impression is that Foster has gone with his expedition to New Berne, N. C. The troops that left Norfolk and Portsmouth on Saturday did not stop at Old Point, but went to New Berne; this accounts for Foster's light-draught fleet, and his intention no doubt is to make a raid up some of the shallow streams running into the Sound.

MILLIGAN,
Major.

GEO. E. PICKETT,
Major-General.

HEADQUARTERS DEPARTMENT OF NORTH CAROLINA,
Petersburg, Va., October 15, 1863.

General S. COOPER,
Adjutant and Inspector General :

GENERAL : Your telegram in reference to sending a brigade of infantry to report to General Sam. Jones at Dublin has been received. I have accordingly ordered off General Corse with three regiments, all the infantry I have here, about 1,200 aggregate. I have directed Corse to take only his cooking utensils and three day's rations, as your object seems to be celerity of action.

I have the honor, general, to call your attention to the reported movements of Foster to New Berne, N. C. This threatening attitude, if not already developed, we have good reason to believe may be in a day or two.

Under the existing circumstances, I respectfully request that General Corse may be sent back to me as soon as possible, as, should an emergency occur, I have not a man to re-enforce with.

I am, general, very respectfully, your obedient servant,

GEO. E. PICKETT,
Major-General.

[P. S.]—The troops will take the train at 4 p. m. this evening. A dispatch received late last night from Blackwater says two batteries and some infantry recently arrived at Suffolk. An extra published in Norfolk says a flag of truce, with 350, mostly women and children, will be in Suffolk to-day. What these poor destitute creatures are to do for food or transportation I do not know. The proximity of the enemy forbids any assistance being sent them, even were it in the country. Is our Government aware of the fact ?

PETERSBURG,
October 15, 1863.

General S. COOPER:

The following telegram just received from General Barton. at Kinston:

It seems probable that a movement will be made against this point soon, the gun-boat being the attraction. The expedition I learn is waiting for re-enforcements.

GEO. E. PICKETT,
Major-General.

DUBLIN,
October 15, 1863.

Brig. Gen. JOHN ECHOLS,
Lewisburg, via Union :

Recall your infantry to Lewisburg without delay. The enemy is pressing us on the west, in very heavy force. Was at Bristol last night. Keep your scouts well out, and your men ready for any move.

C. S. S. [STRINGFELLOW.]

HEADQUARTERS DEPARTMENT OF WESTERN VIRGINIA,
Dublin, October 15, 1863.

Col. JOHN McCAUSLAND,
 Commanding Fourth Brigade:

COLONEL: The major-general commanding directs me to urge upon you the importance of obtaining the earliest information in regard to the force of the enemy in your front. If possible, learn whether any of Scammon's forces have been sent to the Sandy.

The enemy is pressing us hard at and near Bristol, with a very heavy force.

Very respectfully,
    CHAS. S. STRINGFELLOW,
     Assistant Adjutant-General.

RICHMOND,
October 16, 1863.

President DAVIS,
 Meridian, Miss.:

No decisive events in Virginia since you left. General Lee has moved, crossing the river and turning Meade's right flank. There have been several sharp cavalry fights with success to our arms, and the capture of about 700 prisoners. More prisoners are being sent in daily. General Lee, however, fears Meade will elude him by a retreat to his strongholds in and near Washington. Heavy rains now prevailing will probably impede General Lee's movements. In East Tennessee the enemy are reported advancing, with superior force, from Bristol toward Abingdon, to which place General Williams has retired. General Jones is collecting his forces to concentrate at that point. On his call, I have returned Corse's brigade to him. Reports, probable but not wholly reliable, indicate concentration of the enemy under Foster for a raid somewhere in eastern part of North Carolina. Plans of enemy yet undeveloped. Force in Peninsula reported very small. Nothing of special interest in this city.

    J. A. SEDDON,
     Secretary of War.

PETERSBURG,
October 16, 1863.

General S. COOPER,
 Adjutant and Inspector General:

Following telegram just received from General Ransom:

My scouts report the enemy in heavy force at Elizabeth City and in Perquimans County. The scouts' estimate is 10,000, but this must be excessive. The same reports say they have 12 gunboats and 10 transports. General Barton informs me that he expects an advance on Kinston. The enemy, if he intends anything, must design a feint here and advance on Kinston, or *vice versa.* I will let you know in time.

I suppose General Whiting is instructed to assist me in case of necessity.

    GEO. E. PICKETT,
     Major-General.

RICHMOND, *October* 16, 1863.

Maj. Gen. GEORGE E. PICKETT,
    Petersburg, Va. :

Proceed immediately to Goldsborough, N. C., and assume command of forces within your department, leaving at Petersburg a competent staff officer to attend to affairs of your habitual headquarters. You will use your best efforts below to repel advance of the enemy. General Whiting is telegraphed to re-enforce you, on your requisition to him, to the extent of his means.

        S. COOPER,
        Adjutant and Inspector General.

RICHMOND, *October* 16, 1863.

Major-General WHITING,
    Wilmington, N. C. :

General Pickett is ordered to Goldsborough to repel advances of the enemy, threatening Weldon and Kinston in force. Furnish him such aid in troops on his requisition as extent of your means will permit.

        S. COOPER,
        Adjutant and Inspector General.

OCTOBER 16, 1863.

General BEAUREGARD,
    Charleston, S. C. :

Following dispatch received :

Following dispatch just received from General Ransom : " My scouts report the enemy in heavy force at Elizabeth City and in Perquimans County. The scouts' estimate is 10,000, but this must be excessive. The same report says they have 12 gunboats and 10 transports. General Barton informs me that he expects an advance on Kinston. The enemy, if he intends anything, must design a feint here and advance on Kinston, or *vice versa.* I will let you know in time."

        GEO. E. PICKETT,
        Major-General.

This may be concerted plan with Gillmore. Please give me earliest possible information of any change in enemy's disposition against you. Foster is in command of enemy's force. Pickett ordered to Goldsborough to protect Kinston and Weldon. I am directed to aid if possible.

        W. H. C. WHITING,
        Major-General.

HEADQUARTERS DEPARTMENT OF WESTERN VIRGINIA,
    Dublin, October 16, 1863.

Brig. Gen. JOHN ECHOLS,
    Commanding, &c. :

GENERAL: The major-general commanding directed me yesterday to telegraph you to draw your infantry back to Lewisburg without delay. This order, I presume, was duly received.

The Sixtieth [Virginia] Regiment will leave for Abingdon this evening. The Eighth Virginia Cavalry and Thirty-seventh [Virginia] Battalion should be already on the march.

You will see the necessity for keeping your men well in hand, and prepared for any move, as it can hardly be presumed that the enemy in your front will again be so inactive as on the former advance of General Burnside.

General Williams has been forced back to Abingdon. The force óf the enemy is variously estimated at from eight to seventeen regiments, and a battle is deemed imminent. The major-general commanding and staff left here on a special train this morning. Let me have the earliest information of affairs in your front, that I may communicate it to him.

Very respectfully, your obedient servant,

CHAS. S. STRINGFELLOW,
Assistant Adjutant-General.

HEADQUARTERS DEPARTMENT OF WESTERN VIRGINIA,
Dublin, October 16, 1863.

Col. JOHN McCAUSLAND,
Commanding, &c.:

COLONEL : The advance of the enemy on Abingdon has again required that' the Sixtieth [Virginia] Regiment should be hurried to that point. The enemy was last night about 3 miles this side of Bristol, and a fight is daily expected. General Williams has been driven back by a very largely superior force.

The major-general commanding desires you to hold your troops ready for any move, and to forward the earliest information of affairs in your front. It can hardly be expected that General Scammon will again remain inactive, but the certainty of active operations near Saltville requires the immediate concentration of our forces at and near that point, though you are thereby exposed.

Very respectfully, your obedient servant,

CHAS. S. STRINGFELLOW,
Assistant Adjutant-General.

DUBLIN, *October 17, 1863.*

Maj. Gen. SAMUEL JONES,
Abingdon:

The Thirty-sixth [Virginia] Battalion will be here this evening, in accordance with your order. What disposition shall I make of them ? McCausland says he does not need the cavalry. Do you want them ?

CHAS. S. STRINGFELLOW,
Assistant Adjutant-General.

HEADQUARTERS DEPARTMENT OF WESTERN VIRGINIA,
October 17, 1863.

Col. JOHN McCAUSLAND,
Commanding, &c.:

COLONEL : I have received your telegram of this morning, but not your letter alluded to in it. Have sent your telegram to the major-general commanding, who left here for Abingdon in a special train yesterday morning, and will forward you his answer without delay. Burnside in command at Bristol, but information very meager. General Williams has been skirmishing every day since the 8th instant, but steadily driven back.

Very respectfully, your obedient servant,

CHAS. S. STRINGFELLOW.

HEADQUARTERS DEPARTMENT OF WESTERN VIRGINIA,
Dublin, October 18, 1863.

Maj. Gen. SAMUEL JONES,
Abingdon:

Colonel McCausland's scouts report enemy's cavalry in Kanawha gone to Tennessee. One regiment from Fayetteville gone below Charleston. Twelfth and Ninety-first Ohio at Fayette Court-House. Fifth [West] Virginia Infantry from Gauley, and Twenty-third Ohio from Charleston, gone to Tennessee, and report is they are destined for Chattanooga. Scammon has gone to Washington, and Duffié is in command. McCausland thinks Scammon has gone to Rosecrans, with his cavalry, two regiments of infantry, and one battery, leaving Duffié with two regiments at Fayetteville, one at Charleston, and one scattered, with one battery. I think if you were here a good move on Gauley and Charleston could be made. May not the enemy have pushed forces to Rosecrans and made this move on Williams to cover them ?

CHAS. S. STRINGFELLOW,
Assistant Adjutant-General.

KINSTON,
October 18, 1863.

General S. COOPER,
Richmond:

New Berne was re-enforced by from 1,000 to 2,000 men, 13th. Steamers left New Berne on the 13th with re-enforcements, excepting one regiment, and with a part of the original garrison; the avowed destination Fort Monroe, the citizens thought for Weldon. Five more regiments were under marching orders for Fort Monroe, to leave on the 15th. General Ransom reported all quiet this morning.

GEO. E. PICKETT,
Major-General.

GOLDSBOROUGH,
October 18, 1863.

General S. COOPER :

Reliable information just received by General Barton's scouts as follows : The enemy were re-enforced at New Berne on the evening of the 11th, by one regiment of infantry and seven companies of cavalry, the latter supposed to be conscripts. On the 11th, Heckman's brigade, consisting of four regiments, left the vicinity of New Berne, by steamer from Beaufort ; destination said to be Portsmouth or Fort Monroe. Do not apprehend any movement toward Kinston.

GEO. E. PICKETT,
Major-General.

HEADQUARTERS ARMY OF NORTHERN VIRGINIA,
October 19, 1863.

Brig. Gen. J. D. IMBODEN,
    Commanding, &c., Staunton, Va..

GENERAL : Your letter of the 14th instant is received. After my letter of the 9th, the army moved against General Meade, who retreated rapidly and was forced to retire into Fairfax County. We then returned to the Rappahannock. The cavalry is still in Fauquier County, and until its withdrawal I wish you to continue to scout toward the gaps of the mountains, to secure it from any advance in that direction. Your plan of keeping the enemy at the lower end of the valley is approved, and I hope you may be able to break up the railroad.

Very respectfully, your obedient servant,

R. E. LEE,
General.

HEADQUARTERS ARMY OF NORTHERN VIRGINIA,
October 19, 1863.

Brig. Gen. A. R. LAWTON,
    Quartermaster-General, Richmond, Va.:

GENERAL : I have received your letter of the 12th instant,.and am very glad to find that your exertions to supply the army have been so successful. The want of the supplies of shoes, clothing, overcoats, and blankets is very great. Nothing but my unwillingness to expose the men to the hardships that would have resulted from moving them into Loudoun in their present condition induced me to return to the Rappahannock. But I was averse to marching them over the rough roads of that region, at a season, too, when frosts are certain and snows probable, unless they were better provided to encounter them without suffering. I should otherwise have endeavored to detain General Meade near the Potomac, if I could not throw him to the north side.

The supplies you now have at your disposal for this army will be most welcome, and I trust that your exertions to increase them will meet with full success.

Very respectfully, your obedient servant,

R. E. LEE,
General.

HEADQUARTERS ARMY OF NORTHERN VIRGINIA,
October 19, 1863.

Maj. Gen. J. E. B. STUART,
    Commanding Cavalry Corps:

GENERAL : Your note announcing your victory over General Kilpatrick, by your combined divisions, has been received. I congratulate you and your officers and men on this handsome success. The plan was well conceived and skillfully executed. It is not my design for you to advance or to cross the Potomac, but to withdraw on the line formerly designated, when you think it advantageous to do so. I have ordered the iron from the railroad for some miles north of the Rappahannock to be hauled across the river. I desire you, while this operation continues, to have a brigade near the railroad, with pickets at Catlett's, in order to give the working parties and wagons notice of any advance of the enemy's cavalry, and to cover their movements as much as possible. Be sure, also, to send back, at once, any stragglers from the infantry whom you may find in the country north of the Rappahannock.

I am, very respectfully, your obedient servant,

R. E. LEE,
General.

DUBLIN,
October 19, 1863.

Maj. Gen. SAMUEL JONES,
Abingdon:

Colonel Jackson dispatches General Echols that Averell is about to move in connection with Scammon. Says Averell has 4,000 men. One regiment already moving to Cheat Pass; Staunton or Lewisburg his destination. As Scammon co-operates, I think it must be the latter place. Send me your orders immediately.

CHAS. S. STRINGFELLOW,
Assistant Adjutant-General.

NOTE.—Send above to Colonel McCausland, excepting the last sentence. Substitute, "Be on the alert to guard against surprise, and try to guard the Narrows." Send the earliest information.

DUBLIN,
October 19, 1863.

General S. COOPER:

Dispatch just received from General Echols. He says that Col. W. L. Jackson reports that General Averell about to move from Beverly, with 5,000 men; one regiment already moving to Cheat Pass. He co-operates, it is supposed, with Scammon; their destination is Staunton or Lewisburg. Have forwarded this to General Jones at Abingdon, but deem it right to inform you immediately.

CHAS. S. STRINGFELLOW,
Assistant Adjutant-General.

HEADQUARTERS DEPARTMENT OF WESTERN VIRGINIA,
Dublin, October 19, 1863.

Brig. Gen. JOHN ECHOLS,
Lewisburg, via Union:

Have sent your dispatch to General Jones. If the enemy advances on you, make the best defense you can. Have forwarded copy of your telegram to Colonel McCausland. Communicate with him fully. Will try to get re-enforcements for you, but if compelled to fall back, protect this line of railroad. If cut, the effect will be disastrous to our troops at Abingdon.

Respectfully, &c.,

CHAS. S. STRINGFELLOW,
Assistant Adjutant-General.

HDQRS. DEPT. OF WESTERN VA. AND EAST TENN.,
Abingdon, Va., October 20, 1863.

Maj. C. S. STRINGFELLOW,
Assistant Adjutant-General, Dublin:

Direct General Echols to disregard Scammon ; unite his command
with Col. W. L. Jackson, and devote his entire attention to General
Averell. If they can concentrate at Jackson's old camp near Huntersville, it will be the best position. It is probably too late for that.
Callaghan's is the next best place to concentrate. It is impossible
to give minute directions for meeting the raid when it is not known
at what point it aims. Echols and Jackson combined ought to whip
Averell.

If the force in the Kanawha Valley is as small as McCausland represents, we have not much to fear from that quarter. Direct Mc-
Causland to be on the alert, and employ the Seventeenth Cavalry to
watch the enemy on this side of New River. They may make a demonstration on Monroe by way of Pack's Ferry. If so, McCausland
can, I think, move by Shanklin's Ferry in time to stop them.

Warn commanders of home guards of Averell's move, that they
may be ready, but not turn out until called. Keep me fully advised.
If Averell aims at the railroad, I will send part of the force from
here.

Colonel Witcher had a spirited skirmish yesterday 2 miles south
of Zollicoffer, with enemy's rear guard. Captured 43, and left 18
killed and wounded on the field. Lieutenant-Colonel Bottles the
only one on our side killed.

SAM. JONES,
Major-General.

————

HEADQUARTERS DEPARTMENT OF WESTERN VIRGINIA,
Dublin, October 20, 1863.

Brig. Gen. JOHN ECHOLS, *Lewisburg:*

Nothing from you since last night. The major-general commanding directs that if Averell advances, Colonel Jackson shall join his
forces with yours. He thinks the best point to concentrate is at
Colonel Jackson's old camp, near Huntersville. If too late for that,
unite at Callaghan's. Colonel McCausland is directed to watch
Scammon. You and Colonel Jackson and Ferguson must turn
your attention entirely to General Averell. I have the home guards
notified of this move, and will call them out if necessary.

CHAS. S. STRINGFELLOW,
Assistant Adjutant-General.

————

HEADQUARTERS DEPARTMENT OF WESTERN VIRGINIA,
Dublin, October 20, 1863.

Col. JOHN McCAUSLAND, *Princeton:*

The general commanding desires you to hold your command ready
to move as circumstances may require, at shortest notice. Do not
let the Seventeenth [Virginia] Cavalry go any farther west. Have
you any information corroborating General Echols' dispatch ?

By order :

CHAS. S. STRINGFELLOW,
Assistant Adjutant-General.

HEADQUARTERS DEPARTMENT OF WESTERN VIRGINIA,
Dublin, October 20, 1863.

Col. JOHN MCCAUSLAND,
Princeton:

Scout this side of New River with the Seventeenth [Virginia] Cavalry. General Echols must look entirely to Averell. Keep in communication with General Echols and guard against a demonstration or movement by Pack's Ferry. In that event could you not move by Shanklin's Ferry? Communicate any move of Scammon's.

CHAS. S. STRINGFELLOW,
Assistant Adjutant-General.

———

HEADQUARTERS DEPARTMENT OF WESTERN VIRGINIA,
Dublin, October 20, 1863.

Col. J. M. WADE,
Christiansburg:

Notify your men to be ready to turn out on short notice. General Averell is reported advancing on Lewisburg with 5,000 men. It is believed that Scammon will co-operate with him.

CHAS. S. STRINGFELLOW.

NOTE.—Send similar messages to Col. George P. Terrill, Salem; Capt. G. A. Wingfield, Liberty; Maj. Joseph F. Kent, Wytheville, and James McDowell, at Fincastle. Bonsack's is, I think, the place for the latter.

———

ABINGDON, *October 21, 1863.*

Brig. Gen. A. R. LAWTON,
Quartermaster-General, Richmond:

I am detained here now for want of shoes. May I ask that you will hurry them forward? When may I expect them?

SAM. JONES,
Major-General.

———

PETERSBURG, *October 21, 1863.*

General S. COOPER,
Richmond:

The following has just been received from Lieutenant-Colonel Herbert, commanding at Ivor Station:

The flag-of-truce boat has arrived at Suffolk with 500 persons. Part of them will be here to-day.

GEO. E. PICKETT,
Major-General, Commanding.

———

PETERSBURG, *October 21, 1863.*

General S. COOPER:

The following dispatch just received from Colonel Herbert:

Would like to send down a flag of truce for the purpose of sending wagon train to bring up refugees.

A. HERBERT,
Commanding.

I have telegraphed Herbert to send flag. The refugees are mostly women and children.

Just received from General Barton:

Scouts from within enemy's lines report that Foster's expedition has gone to Mobile.

From Colonel Griffin:

Enemy carried off from Perquimans and Chowan Counties during the late raid between 400 and 500 negroes, mostly women and children. They have returned to New Berne. All quiet to-day.

GEO. E. PICKETT,
Major-General.

HEADQUARTERS PICKETT'S DIVISION,
October 21, 1863.

General S. COOPER:
Adjt. and Insp. Gen., C. S. Army, Richmond, Va.:

GENERAL: I have the honor to inclose return of division for the month of September.* Numbers of applications for the return of detailed men on work in Navy Department, &c., have been sent back disapproved. I have received every encouragement in believing that many of, if not all, these men should be sent back. The division has not increased as rapidly as it would have done had the exchanges been accomplished and detailed men returned to their regiments.

I am, general, very respectfully, your obedient servant,
GEO. E. PICKETT,
Major-General, Commanding.

[Indorsements.]

OCTOBER 23, 1863.

Respectfully submitted to Secretary of War.

By last return, September 30, the strength of this division is as follows:

Effective total	4,764
Total present	5,610
Aggregate present	6,022
Present and absent, total	11,192
Present and absent, aggregate	11,989

When filled according to organization, the strength of the division should be about 24,000—more than twice its present strength. I recommend that all detailed men now absent from the command be returned to it.

S. COOPER,
Adjutant and Inspector General.

OCTOBER 24, 1863.

ADJUTANT-GENERAL:

I am endeavoring to return detailed men as far as the interests of the general service will possibly allow.
J. A. S. [SEDDON,]
Secretary.

* See p. 765.

WAR DEPARTMENT, C. S.,
Richmond, Va., October 22, 1863.

ADJUTANT-GENERAL :

Information has been received that a large number of women and children have been landed at Suffolk, by the Federal commander of that department, who are without transportation. Give an order to Major-General Pickett to afford all proper assistance to them to come into our lines, and for transportation to a reasonable distance. Lieutenant Foster may bear the order.

By order:

J. A. CAMPBELL,
Assistant Secretary of War.

ABINGDON, *October 22, 1863.*

General BRAXTON BRAGG.
Missionary Ridge, via Chickamauga :

Your telegram received. I will move on the enemy as soon as practicable, which will be in two or three days. Will inform you when I move.

SAM. JONES,
Major-General.

ABINGDON, *October 22, 1863.*

Hon. JAMES A. SEDDON,
Secretary of War:

I understand that General Meade has fallen back to his intrenched camp, and General Lee this side of the Rappahannock. If so, might not a few thousand of General Lee's infantry be sent here to aid in the effort to drive Burnside from East Tennessee? They are greatly needed.

SAM. JONES,
Major-General.

HEADQUARTERS DEPARTMENT OF WESTERN VIRGINIA,
October 22, 1863.

Brig. Gen. JOHN ECHOLS, *Commanding, &c.:*

GENERAL: The views expressed in your letter of yesterday are in strict accordance with the wishes of the major-general commanding. The directions given to Colonel McCausland were based upon the representation made in regard to the withdrawal of troops from the Kanawha, in consequence of which it was supposed he would be able to check such a move on the part of General Scammon as you suggest. The general commanding did not intend to designate the two points indicated for concentration in the way of an order, as he is too far off to know exactly the situation of affairs. Of course he expects you to exercise your best judgment and dispose your forces so as to best protect this line of railroad. Huntersville and Callaghan's were designated as the points which in his opinion were best for concentration.

Very respectfully, your obedient servant,

CHAS. S. STRINGFELLOW,
Assistant Adjutant-General.

HEADQUARTERS ARMY OF NORTHERN VIRGINIA,
October 23, 1863.

Hon. JAMES A. SEDDON, *Secretary of War, Richmond:*

SIR : I have had the honor to receive your letter of the 20th instant. As soon as your dispatch with reference to Averell's movement reached me, I directed General Imboden, whom I had ordered to the lower valley of the Shenandoah when this army crossed the Rapidan, to return toward Staunton, ascertain, if possible, the truth of the report, and be prepared to meet Averell's advance. I think there are enough troops in Western Virginia, if properly managed, not only to resist all attacks of the enemy, but to drive them farther from our present positions. The retreating before every advance of the enemy upon the Tennessee Railroad, I fear will entail upon us heavy loss, and the assaults of such troops as they have in that region, home guards and cavalry, could, by proper dispositions, be easily repulsed. I hope you will cause to be investigated the truth of the report which you mention of a force of the enemy being in York River, as another attack upon our railroad from that quarter may be in contemplation.

I have not been able to ascertain the future movements of General Meade's army. Our scouts report that bridge timber and cross-ties have been brought forward to Broad Run, and that a portion of the enemy's infantry had advanced as far as Catlett's Station on the railway. It is also stated that his cavalry is in Warrenton, and a portion of his infantry on the turnpike leading from that place to Centreville. It may be his intention to advance to Warrenton and bring his supplies to that point by the turnpike until the railroad is reconstructed. Our scouts on the Potomac still report transports with troops ascending that river. A steamer passed up on the 13th instant laden with troops, estimated at 600, and on the 17th, two large ocean steamers passed up, estimated to contain 1,200. I see it stated in the Northern papers that all the volunteers in the State of New York have been ordered to Washington. They are, therefore, strengthening themselves on that front.

I hope you will endeavor to provide the army with shoes, clothing, and blankets, for the season is approaching when the want of these articles will entail great suffering and sickness on the troops, and incapacitate them for military movements.

I am, very respectfully, your obedient servant,

R. E. LEE,
General.

————

HDQRS. CAV. CORPS, ARMY OF NORTHERN VIRGINIA,
October 23, 1863.

General S. COOPER,
Adjutant and Inspector General, C. S. Army:

GENERAL : I have the honor to request that the Eighth and Fourteenth Regiments Virginia Cavalry, lately ordered to this command, which order was temporarily suspended, be now ordered to proceed to join in compliance with the original order. My cavalry force has been always inadequate in number to the work to be performed, and none can be better spared to augment it than the regiments designated.

I have the honor to be, most respectfully, your obedient servant,

J. E. B. STUART,
Major-General.

[Indorsement.]

HEADQUARTERS ARMY OF NORTHERN VIRGINIA,
October 23, 1863.

Respectfully forwarded and recommended; but I fear that as soon as the order is issued it will give rise to a report of an advance by the enemy, and the operation of the order be again suspended.

R. E. LEE,
General.

———

HDQRS. DEPT. OF WESTERN VA. AND EAST TENN.,
Dublin, October 25, 1863.

Maj. Gen. R. RANSOM, Jr.,
Abingdon:

Send the Sixtieth Regiment Virginia Infantry to Wytheville without delay. I would like it to start at night so as to attract as little attention as possible. A force of cavalry with three pieces of artillery is moving from below Charleston on the Kanawha toward Logan Court-House; will probably strike at the railroad or salt-works.

SAM. JONES,
Major-General.

———

HEADQUARTERS DEPARTMENT OF WESTERN VIRGINIA,
Dublin, October 25, 1863.

Col. W. H. BROWNE,
Commanding, &c.:

A large body of the enemy's cavalry are reported passing up Coa. River toward Wyoming Court-House, with three pieces of artilleryl It is supposed they are moving to Logan Court-House after Colonel Beckley, and thence into Tazewell, or else to the rear of Colonel Mc-Causland. The commanding-general directs you to have your forces ready for any movement that circumstances may require, and to forward the inclosed dispatch * to Colonel Bowen without delay.

Very respectfully, your obedient servant,

CHAS. S. STRINGFELLOW,
Assistant Adjutant-General.

(Copy of above sent to Major-General Ransom and Col. H. S. Bowen.)

———

DUBLIN, *October 25, 1863.*

Col. W. H. FRENCH,
Commanding, &c.:

COLONEL: The major-general commanding directs you to proceed with your command to Abb's Valley without delay, to repel a reported advance of the enemy. You will go by the shortest route, and report your move to Colonel McCausland immediately. He further instructs me to say that he has received information of many depredations having been committed by your men between Crab

———

* Not found.

Orchard and Greenbrier. He does not know the truth of these charges, but directs that you will take such steps as will prevent a repetition of them.

Very respectfully, &c.,

CHAS. S. STRINGFELLOW,
Assistant Adjutant-General.

HEADQUARTERS ARMY OF NORTHERN VIRGINIA,
October 26, 1863.

Hon. JAMES A. SEDDON,
Secretary of War, Richmond, Va.:

SIR: I have to acknowledge the receipt of your letter of the 22d instant.

Our pickets are now below the Orange and Alexandria Railroad, and the enemy is altogether west of it, so far as I can learn.

I can arrange to give notice to the working parties engaged in removing the iron from the Aquia Creek road, but have no doubt that as soon as the enemy learn that it is being done they will send a larger force to prevent it than I can spare to meet them. Under these circumstances, timely notice of the approach of the enemy will serve as good a purpose as the small force I could now spare to protect the work. I think it should be undertaken at once, and with energy and secrecy. By taking a few railroad trucks across the river and beginning the work at the remote end of the line, the rails might be transported to the river opposite Fredericksburg, without risking our wagons. If a pontoon bridge could be thrown across the river to remove the iron as fast as it is brought down, it would greatly facilitate the work.

I desire to be notified as soon as the operations begin, in order that I may put our pickets and scouts on the watch, to notify those engaged of any danger that may threaten.

Very respectfully, your obedient servant,

R. E. LEE,
General.

[Indorsement.]

ENGINEER BUREAU,
October 31, 1863.

Contents carefully noted and attended to.

Respectfully returned to the honorable Secretary of War.

ALFRED L. RIVES,
Lieutenant-Colonel, Acting Chief of Bureau.

HDQRS. CAV. CORPS, ARMY OF NORTHERN VIRGINIA,
October 26, 1863.

Col. O. R. FUNSTEN,
Eleventh Virginia Cavalry:

COLONEL: In relieving you from command of the brigade to which Brigadier-General Rosser has been assigned, I feel it but just that I should give expression to my high appreciation of your good conduct, and the highly satisfactory manner in which you discharged the duty of brigade commander. The brigade never rendered more efficient service, or performed such prodigies of valor under any former commander, and at the same time exhibited the true characteristics of good patriots and true soldiers, a cheerful endurance of hardship, hunger, and fatigue.

I beg you to consider Capt. W. K. Martin, assistant adjutant-general, as included in my commendation.

I have the honor to be, colonel, most respectfully, your obedient servant,

J. E. B. STUART,
Major-General.

HDQRS. DEPT. OF WESTERN VA. AND EAST TENN.,
Dublin, October 26, 1863.

Maj. Gen. R. RANSOM, Jr.,
Commanding, &c., Abingdon :

The shoes are on the way ; will be hurried forward as fast as possible. Press forward with the cavalry and two batteries, or more if you think proper, but press with the cavalry. If Williams asks for leave of absence give it to him, and give Brig. Gen. W. E. Jones charge of all the cavalry.

SAM. JONES,
Major-General.

HDQRS. DEPT. OF WESTERN VA. AND EAST TENN.,
Dublin, October 26, 1863.

Hon. JAMES A. SEDDON,
Secretary of War :

SIR : Brig. Gen. John S. Williams desires to be transferred from this to some other department. He thinks, and under the circumstances I concur with him, that he can serve with more pleasure and satisfaction to himself and benefit to the cause in some other department than this. At the request of General Williams, I respectfully recommend and ask that when he makes his application to be transferred you will grant it.

With great respect, your obedient servant,

SAM. JONES,
Major-General.

HDQRS. DEPT. OF WESTERN VA. AND EAST TENN.,
Dublin, October 26, 1863.

Hon. JAMES A. SEDDON,
Secretary of War :

SIR : I telegraphed you a few days since suggesting that if, as reported, General Lee had driven General Meade to his intrenched camp at or near Centreville, and had fallen back himself behind the Rappahannock, a part of his infantry might be employed greatly to the interest of the service in East Tennessee at this time.

The cavalry I have will not, I am afraid, accomplish much unless well supported by infantry. I need not bring to your notice the importance of driving the enemy from East Tennessee. You know as well as I do not only the importance to us of that country from its geographical position, but from the supplies of subsistence it can furnish the Government.

While I do not pretend to know what number of troops General Lee can spare, or if he can with safety spare any for this service, I think it proper to bring the matter again to your notice, that you may take such action on it as you may think proper.

With great respect, your obedient servant,

SAM. JONES,
Major-General.

[Indorsement.]

Submitted to General Lee November 9, 1863.*

HEADQUARTERS DEPARTMENT OF WESTERN VIRGINIA,
Dublin, October 26, 1863.

Col. B. H. JONES,
Commanding Sixtieth [Virginia] Regiment:

COLONEL: Your regiment has been ordered to Wytheville, to protect that place against the reported advance of a large body of the enemy's cavalry by way of Coal River and thence through Tazewell. The major-general commanding thinks you had best post your command at or near Walker's Mountain. The enemy may attempt to pass in the rear of Colonel McCausland. Be on your guard against this move.

Very respectfully, your obedient servant,

CHAS. S. STRINGFELLOW,
Assistant Adjutant-General.

PETERSBURG, *October 27, 1863.*

General S. COOPER,
Adjutant and Inspector General:

Following dispatch just received from General Barton, at Kinston, dated October 26:

Three steamers, each with a schooner in tow, and carrying troops supposed to be Third New York Cavalry, passed down Neuse River yesterday; destination given out to be Portsmouth, Va.

No report from signal corps as to their arrival at Portsmouth.

GEO. E. PICKETT.

RICHMOND, *October 27, 1863.*

Governor ZEBULON B. VANCE,
Raleigh, N. C.:

The Ordnance Bureau places at your disposal 600 arms at Salisbury, all that can be at once conveniently commanded in that direction. General Hoke is acting under General Lee's orders, but he will be instructed, if not inconsistent with such orders, to co-operate with you.

J. A. SEDDON,
Secretary of War.

---

* See Lee to Secretary of War, November 11.

WAR DEPARTMENT, C. S.,
Richmond, October 27, 1863.

Maj. Gen. W. H. C. WHITING,
Commanding, &c., Wilmington, N. C.:

GENERAL: Information has been received by me that the loss of both the Hebe and the Venus might have been prevented by the possession at Fort Fisher, or on the beach near, of one or two more guns of long range. I would be pleased to learn if this be so, and the character and number of guns required, and whether, in your judgment, their possession would add materially to the security of vessels running the blockade.

Respectfully,

J. A. SEDDON,
Secretary of War.

———

RICHMOND, *October 28, 1863.*

Maj. Gen. SAMUEL JONES:

General Lee has again urged sending him the Eighth and Fourteenth Virginia Cavalry. Can they be spared from your command? If so, send them.

S. COOPER,
Adjutant and Inspector General.

———

HDQRS. DEPT. OF WESTERN VA. AND EAST TENN.,
Dublin, October 28, 1863.

General S. COOPER,
Adjutant and Inspector General, Richmond, Va.:

I cannot spare either the Eighth or Fourteenth Regiment of Cavalry, or any other troops. The Eighth is on the border of Virginia and Tennessee and the Fourteenth in front of Lewisburg, and are greatly needed where they are. If I must send General Lee a portion of my cavalry, I beg that I may be allowed to retain these two regiments, which are my best and largest.

SAM. JONES,
Major-General.

———

WAR DEPARTMENT, C. S.,
Richmond, Va., October 28, 1863.

Brig. Gen. ROBERT F. HOKE:

GENERAL: Governor Vance telegraphs me that the enemy are advancing from Tennessee into Western North Carolina in such force that he fears General Vance, with the home guards, will be unable to resist them, and asks that one of your regiments be sent to his assistance. I would be pleased, if the instructions given you by General Lee will allow, and if more pressing claims upon your attention do not exist, to have your co-operation with the Governor in repressing such disorders by moving a force toward the point indicated.

Respectfully,

J. A. SEDDON,
Secretary of War.

SPECIAL ORDERS, } ADJT. AND INSP. GENERAL'S OFFICE,
No. 257. {   *Richmond, October* 29, 1863.

 * * * * * * *

III. Col. Walter H. Stevens, Engineers, will assume command of artillery defenses of Richmond, in addition to his duties of chief engineer of fortifications of Department of Richmond.

 * * * * * * *

By command of the Secretary of War:

JNO. WITHERS,
Assistant Adjutant-General.

SPECIAL ORDERS, } HDQRS. ARTILLERY CORPS, A. N. VA.,
No. —. {   *October* 29, 1863.

Maj. James Reilly, having reported for duty with Major Haskell's battalion artillery, under commission dated September 25, 1863, is hereby assigned to that battalion. He will report accordingly, and be obeyed and respected as a field officer of the battalion.

W. N. PENDLETON,
Brigadier-General, and Chief of Artillery.

DUBLIN, *October* 29, 1863.

Col. J. GORGAS, *Chief of Ordnance, Richmond:*

COLONEL: I have the honor to inclose a requisition* for ordnance and ordnance stores. The army is now on the move to East Tennessee, and the limited supply of these stores has already been exhausted, and was not sufficient to satisfy the wants of the army before the march was begun, and as they are daily calling for more, I earnestly beg that the requisition may be filled entire, that no lack of ordnance stores can be urged as cause of failure of the campaign.

Respectfully, colonel, your obedient servant,

T. M. BOWYER,
Major, Chief Ord. Officer, Dept. W. Va. and E. Tenn.

HDQRS. ARMY OF NORTHERN VA., *October* 30, 1863.

Hon. JAMES A. SEDDON, *Secretary of War, Richmond:*

SIR: Your telegram, directing a respite in the cases of Privates Newton and Scroggin, Forty-first Virginia Infantry, is received, and the order has been issued accordingly. At the same time I beg leave to express my serious apprehension of the consequences of a relapse into that lenient policy which our past experience has shown to be so ruinous to the army, and in the end so much more cruel to the men. Early in the war, it was found that stringent measures alone would keep the army together. After a few executions a number of men were pardoned, and the consequence was a recurrence of desertion to a most alarming extent. A return to a sterner discipline was found to be absolutely necessary, and by the executions that have taken place since the proclamation of the President, and by them only, has a stop been put to a spirit that was rapidly growing, that seized eagerly upon the slightest hope of escape from the consequences of crime, and that seriously threatened the existence of the army.

---

* Not found.

A return to the lenient system that formerly prevailed will assuredly be productive of like results in the future, and render still harsher measures necessary hereafter, if the army is to continue to exist. I fear that pardons, unless for the best of reasons, will not only make all the blood that has been shed for the maintenance of discipline useless, but will result in the painful necessity of shedding a great deal more. I hope I feel as acutely as any one the pain and sorrow that such events occasion, and I am sure that no one would more willingly dispense with them if they could be avoided, but I am convinced that the only way to prevent them is to visit the offense, when committed, with the sternest punishment, and leave the offender without hope of escape, by making the penalty inevitable. It must be remembered that the punishment of death for desertion is inflicted almost exclusively for the warning of others, and no one without experience can conceive how readily the slightest prospect of escape is embraced.

I have felt it my duty to bring this subject strongly to your attention, as I am satisfied that in it, more than in any other, is involved the strength and efficiency of the army and its ability to cope with the enemy. And I am further convinced that in a strict adherence to a stern discipline will be found the only means of avoiding the recurrence of these sad occasions.

Very respectfully, your obedient servant,

R. E. LEE.

ABINGDON, *October* 30, 1863.

General BRAXTON BRAGG, *Chickamauga:*

Your telegram of yesterday received. My cavalry is on the Watauga and Holston, from Carter's Station to Kingsport. Infantry moving to the same line. I cannot move my infantry beyond the Holston. Will use cavalry to make raids and, if practicable, collect cattle and hogs. It is important that there should be additional force on this end of the line. I have asked for it repeatedly. I believe there is no enemy this side of Jonesborough.

SAM. JONES,
Major-General.

HDQRS. DEPT. OF WESTERN VA. AND EAST TENN.,
Abingdon, October 30, 1863.

General S. COOPER,
Adjt. and Insp. Gen., C. S. Army, Richmond, Va.:

GENERAL : I received day before yesterday, at Dublin, a telegram from you, informing me that General Lee was again calling for the Eighth and Fourteenth Regiments Virginia Cavalry, and directing me to send them to him if I could spare them. I immediately replied by telegraph that I could not spare these regiments, or any other troops.

Since the withdrawal of Major-General Buckner's troops from Southwestern Virginia and East Tennessee, and the evacuation of Cumberland Gap, my line has been greatly extended, and this part of it, in particular, much more exposed than it has been at any time since the war began. While the enemy holds Cumberland Gap and East Tennessee this section of country is open to invasion, and the salt-works and lead mines alone, which are so essential to us, offer to the enemy the strongest inducement to attempt the invasion in large force. Of course, it is for the War Department to designate the points at which troops are needed, and to order them there. But I deem it my duty to state strongly to the Department my conviction that no troops can be withdrawn from this department without running great risk of losing for a time this section of country, including the salt-works and lead mines.

So far from being able to spare any part of my command, I think an additional force should be sent here, and have so stated to the Secretary of War and General Lee. I hope they will concur with me and send the force. General Bragg has pressed the enemy from Loudon back upon Knoxville. If an additional force were placed upon this end of the line, he might be so pressed as to draw him out of East Tennessee, either by force or by so stripping the country of supplies as to render it impracticable to winter his troops in that country.

The Eighth Virginia Cavalry is now in East Tennessee, and the Fourteenth in front of Lewisburg. To reach General Lee's army, the Eighth Regiment would have to march 300 miles or more. It probably would not be fit for service for a week or two after so long a march, and thus its services would be lost during all the month of November. This I think an additional reason why it should not be moved from here at this time.

I am somewhat surprised that Major-General Stuart should have designated the two best cavalry regiments in my command, and ask that those particular regiments be taken from me and given to him. If he needed a part of my cavalry, it would, I think, have been more in accordance with military usage and courtesy to have specified the number and left me to designate the troops.

I sent the greater part of my cavalry to General Stuart last spring. It has been recently returned to me reduced far beyond what might have been expected from the casualties of a campaign, and the greater part of that returned to me was in wretched condition, and much of it is not yet fit for service. I do not wish the Eighth and Fourteenth Regiments to share the same fate, and must, therefore, most respectfully urge that the order assigning them to General Stuart be revoked.

With very great respect, your obedient servant,
SAM. JONES,
Major-General.

[Indorsement.]

NOVEMBER 2, 1863.

Respectfully referred to General Lee.

The Secretary of War is of opinion that if it becomes absolutely necessary to withdraw any cavalry from Major-General Jones' command, it would be better to take any than the regiments already called for by General Stuart.

S. COOPER,
Adjutant and Inspector General.

RICHMOND, *October 30, 1863.*

Maj. Gen. W. H. C. WHITING, *Wilmington, N. C.:*

There is no cavalry force here to send you, and I know not where it is to be had from any quarter.

S. COOPER,
Adjutant and Inspector General.

HEADQUARTERS ARMY OF NORTHERN VIRGINIA,
October 31, 1863.
Maj. Gen. ARNOLD ELZEY,
    Commanding, &c., Richmond, Va..

GENERAL : Your telegram is received. I wish to put you on your guard against the mischief that may result from sending dispatches containing information as to the number and position of our troops, unless they be put in cipher. Whenever such matters cannot be made the subject of a letter, which is always preferable when possible, they should be sent by telegraph in cipher, as facts have before this found their way to the public, and of course to the enemy, under such circumstances as to induce me to abstain from sending open telegrams about things that ought not to be known. I advise you to pursue this course. You can order the troops from Hanover Junction to you, as soon as you see proper, giving me notice when you do.

If it be true that all of General Foster's troops are being withdrawn from the coast of North Carolina, the forces that have been opposing them can also be withdrawn, and if you ascertain the fact satisfactorily, you can apply to the Secretary of War to order up the disposable troops from North Carolina, including such as can be spared from Wilmington, who will no longer be of service there after the enemy has withdrawn, excepting a sufficient guard to prevent raids by small parties.

Very respectfully, your obedient servant,
R. E. LEE,
General.

_____

HEADQUARTERS ARMY OF NORTHERN VIRGINIA,
October 31, 1863.
Maj. Gen. J. E. B. STUART, *Commanding, &c.:*

GENERAL : Colonel Willis has been ordered to proceed with two regiments of infantry to scour the counties of Rappahannock, Page, Madison, and Greene for deserters. I desire you to send a squadron of cavalry to report to him at Rixeyville, where he will probably arrive Monday evening. I also wish you to send him guides acquainted with the counties named, if you have them, selecting those who are acquainted with the country, and who can aid him in finding the haunts of deserters or put him in communication with those who can. Please direct General Rosser, or whoever commands the cavalry near the scene of his operations, to notify Colonel Willis of any danger, and should he call for any cavalry besides the squadron, to furnish it.

Very respectfully, your obedient servant,
R. E. LEE,
General.

_____

HDQRS. DEPT. OF WESTERN VA. AND EAST TENN.,
Abingdon, October 31, 1863.
Hon. JAMES A. SEDDON, *Secretary of War:*

SIR : Brig. Gen. W. E. Jones was at Jonesborough, Tenn., yesterday with a part of my cavalry. He thinks the enemy has fallen back to Bull's Gap. General Bragg informs me by telegraph, dated day before yesterday, that the enemy had been driven from Loudon back to Knoxville. My cavalry is now beyond the Holston. My infantry will occupy the line of the Holston from Zollicoffer toward Kingsport to-morrow. I cannot move the small force of infantry I now have so far into East Tennessee as to uncover this section of country and the salt-works and lead mines. The enemy's force in my front is chiefly cavalry or mounted infantry. They have guides who know the country well, and if the enemy is enterprising and active, they may do us much damage while my force occupies the line it will occupy to-morrow. The damage done in my rear while I was at Zollicoffer warns me of what may be done while I occupy the position I have taken.

With a few thousand additional infantry, I think I could do much toward driving the enemy from East Tennessee; but while my force is so small as it is at present, I cannot thrust it far into East Tennessee without exposing this section of country, which it seems to me of the utmost importance that we should hold. So far from receiving any of the re-enforcements I have asked for, I received a telegram from General Cooper, day before yesterday, informing me that General Lee had again called for my two best regiments of cavalry, and directing me to send them if I could spare them. I have not sent them, and shall not without a more positive order, and I trust that the order in regard to the transfer of those two regiments (the Eighth and Fourteenth Virginia Cavalry) to General Lee's army may be revoked.

With great respect, your obedient servant,

SAM. JONES,
Major-General.

HDQRS. DEPT. OF WESTERN VA. AND EAST TENN.,
Abingdon, October 31, 1863.

Maj. Gen. R. RANSOM, Jr.,
Commanding, &c. :

GENERAL: Your note this morning is very satisfactory. You wrote apparently in haste, and I could not decipher all of it, but enough to show that the enemy is falling back. If I could get a few thousand additional infantry now, I think we could press General Burnside out of East Tennessee. With our present force, however, we may do much. Push the cavalry well to the front and right. Do not allow the infantry to go beyond the Holston. Keep a strong cavalry picket at or near Kingsport to prevent a cavalry raid by our right without our knowing it. I have directed Brigadier-General Williams to be relieved. Place all the cavalry under Brig. Gen. W. E. Jones. Williams has had time enough to make up his mind to stand a trial or not, as he thinks best. Let me know where you will encamp to-morrow night. If I can get through with a mass of paper business here, I will try to go to your headquarters. Nothing new to-day that I have heard.

Very respectfully and truly,

SAM. JONES,
Major-General.

P. S.—Get from General W. E. Jones all the information you can as to the extent of damage done the railroad, if any, south of Carter's Station.

Abstract from return of the Army of Northern Virginia, General Robert E. Lee, C. S. Army, commanding, for the month of October, 1863; headquarters Brandy Station, Va.

Command.	Present for duty.		Effective total present.	Aggregate present.	Aggregate present and absent.	Pieces of artillery.
	Officers.	Men.				
General headquarters................................	13	....	....	13	13	.....
Second Army Corps (Ewell):						
Staff..	19	....	....	19	23	.....
Early's division....................................	486	5,445	5,445	6,909	11,702	.....
Johnson's division.................................	530	4,850	4,850	6,248	11,485	.....
Rodes' division....................................	600	6,802	6,802	8,555	14,839	.....
Total..	1,635	17,097	17,097	21,782	38,069	.....
Third Army Corps (A. P. Hill):						
Staff..	17	....	....	17	18	.....
Anderson's division...............................	513	5,896	5,896	7,421	12,616	.....
Heth's division	425	5,044	5,044	6,305	10,807	.....
Wilcox's division..........	506	5,593	5,593	6,993	11,268	.....
Total..	1,461	16,533	16,533	20,826	34,799	.....
Cavalry Corps (Stuart):						
Staff	13	....	....	13	15	....
Hampton's division................................	261	3,731	3,731	4,622	8,789	6
Fitz. Lee's division................................	304	4,108	4,108	5,042	8,847	5
Artillery division..................................	4	78	78	90	135	3
Total..	582	7,917	7,917	9,767	17,786	14
Artillery (Pendleton):						
Second Army Corps	81	1,566	1,566	1,898	2,634	79
Third Army Corps..................................	93	2,048	2,048	2,449	3,217	80
Reserve...........	23	453	453	516	674	15
Total..	197	4,067	4,067	4,863	6,525	174
Grand total	3,888	45,614	45,614	57,251	97,192	.....

Abstract from return of the Department of Richmond, Maj. Gen. Arnold Elzey, C. S. Army, commanding, October 31, 1863.

Command.	Present for duty.		Effective total.	Aggregate present.	Aggregate present and absent.	Pieces of field artillery.
	Officers.	Men.				
General headquarters...........................	10	....	....	10	11	.....
Hunton's brigade	90	958	948	1,307	2,559	.....
Kemper's brigade (Terry)...........................	80	1,198	1,179	1,831	3,241	.....
Cavalry...........................	36	513	539	778	1,149	.....
Chaffin's Farm a...................................	11	226	222	276	315	10
Chaffin's Bluff	20	310	388	443	562	18
Drewry's Bluff.....................................	21	272	372	459	502	....
Richmond defenses b	85	1,464	1,706	1,948	2,206	14
Total...	353	4,936	5,354	7,052	10,545	42

a Art'llery serving with Hunton's brigade
b Col. Walter H. Stevens, C. S. Engineers, assigned to command October 29.

Abstract from return of the Army of Western Virginia and East Tennessee, Maj. Gen. Samuel Jones, C. S. Army, commanding, October 31, 1863; headquarters Dublin Depot, Va.

Command.	Present for duty.		Effective total.	Aggregate present.	Aggregate present and absent.	Aggregate last return.	Pieces of field artillery.	Remarks.
	Officers.	Men.						
General staff	20	....	....	20	21	20	......	Dublin, Va.
Ransom's division:								
Staff...................	7	....	....	7	7	7	....	
Corse's brigade, infantry.	84	1,092	1,092	1,299	1,817	1,844	....	
Wharton's brigade, infantry.	56	904	904	1,071	1,438	1,438	......	
Jackson's brigade, infantry.	52	309	309	398	1,049	1,049	......	
Jones' brigade, cavalry.	103	1,480	1,480	1,699	2,644	....	......	
Williams' brigade, cavalry.	139	1,253	1,253	1,528	2,510	....	......	
King's battalion, artillery.	20	386	386	441	566	....	20	
Total	461	5,424	5,424	6,443	10,031	4,838	20	
Unattached:								
Echols' brigade, infantry.	92	1,306	1,306	1,558	2,225	2,158	......	
McCausland's brigade, infantry.	37	692	692	814	931	916	......	63d Virginia not included in abstract.
Jenkins' brigade, cavalry.	22	293	293	348	1,756	....	......	
60th Virginia Infantry.	......	....	....	....	755	755	......	Detached from their respective brigades.
45th Virginia Infantry.	......	....	....	....	897	897	......	
Three companies of artillery.	11	206	206	230	378	380	15	
Company of engineer troops.	4	54	54	58	73	64	......	
Total	166	2,551	2,551	3,008	7,015	5,170	15	
Grand total a	647	7,975	7,975	9,471	17,067	9,528	35	

a See also Jones to Cooper, November 6.

Organization of the Army of Western Virginia and East Tennessee, Maj. Gen. Samuel Jones, C. S. Army, commanding, October 31, 1863.

RANSOM'S DIVISION.

Maj. Gen. R. RANSOM, jr.

Corse's Brigade.

Brig. Gen. M. D. CORSE.

15th Virginia, Lieut. Col. E. M. Morrison.
29th Virginia, Col. James Giles.
30th Virginia, Col. A. T. Harrison.

Jackson's Brigade.

Brig. Gen. A. E. JACKSON.

Thomas' (North Carolina) Regiment, Lieut. Col. J. R. Love.
Walker's (North Carolina) Battalion, Maj. J. A. McKamy.

Wharton's Brigade.

Brig. Gen. G. C. WHARTON.

30th Virginia Battalion Sharpshooters, Lieut. Col. J. Lyle Clarke.
45th Virginia,* Col. William H. Browne.
51st Virginia, Col. Aug. Forsberg.

Jones' Cavalry Brigade.	*Williams' Cavalry Brigade.*
Brig. Gen. W. E. JONES.	Brig. Gen. JOHN S. WILLIAMS.

8th Virginia, Col. J. M. Corns.
21st Virginia, Col. W. E. Peters.
27th Virginia Battalion, Lieut. Col. H. A. Edmundson.
34th Virginia Battalion, Lieut. Col. V. A. Witcher.
36th Virginia Battalion, Capt. C. T. Smith.
37th Virginia Battalion, Maj. J. R. Claiborne.

16th Georgia Battalion, Maj. E. Y. Clarke.
4th Kentucky, Col. H. L. Giltner.
10th Kentucky Battalion, Maj. J. T. Chenoweth.
May's (Kentucky) Regiment, Lieut. Col. E. Trimble.
1st Tennessee, Col. J. E. Carter.
64th Virginia, Col. C. Slemp.

Jenkins' Cavalry Brigade.

Brig. Gen. A. G. JENKINS.

14th Virginia, Col. James Cochran.
16th Virginia, Col. M. J. Ferguson.
17th Virginia, Col. William H. French.

Artillery Battalion.

Lieut. Col. J. F. KING.

Otey (Virginia) Battery, Capt. D. N. Walker.
Ringgold (Virginia) Battery, Capt. C. Dickenson.
Virginia Battery, Capt. G. S. Davidson.
Virginia Battery, Capt. W. M. Lowry.

INDEPENDENT BRIGADES.

Echols' Brigade.	*McCausland's Brigade.*
Brig. Gen. JOHN ECHOLS.	Brig. Gen. JOHN MCCAUSLAND.

22d Virginia, Col. George S. Patton.
23d Virginia Battalion, Lieut. Col. C. Derrick.
26th Virginia Battalion, Lieut. Col. George M. Edgar.

36th Virginia, Lieut. Col. B. R. Linkons.
60th Virginia,* Col. B. H. Jones.
63d Virginia, Col. J. J. McMahon.†

UNATTACHED.

3d C. S. Engineers, Company E, Capt. William T. Hart.
Botetourt (Virginia) Artillery,† Capt. Henry C. Douthat.
Levi (Virginia) Battery, Capt. John T. Levi.‡
McClung's (Tennessee) Battery, Capt. H. L. W. McClung.‡

Rhett (Tennessee) Artillery, Capt. William H. Burroughs.
Virginia Battery, Capt. Thomas A. Bryan.
Virginia Battery, Capt. G. B. Chapman.
Virginia Battery, Capt. Thomas E. Jackson.

---

* Detached.
† Serving under General Buckner since August last.
‡ Reported on return as having no guns.

Abstract from return of the District of Cape Fear and Defenses of Wilmington, Maj. Gen. W. H. C. Whiting, C. S. Army, commanding, October 31, 1863; headquarters Wilmington, N. C.

Command.	Present for duty.		Effective total present.	Aggregate present.	Aggregate present and absent.	Pieces of artillery.	
	Officers.	Men.				Heavy.	Field.
General staff	9	30	31	48	68		
Martin's brigade	100	1,729	1,830	2,143	2,852		
61st North Carolina (two companies).	6	104	99	119	151		
2d C. S. Engineers, Company A	3	78	80	94	101		
Cavalry	18	336	376	431	552		
Heavy artillery	98	1,829	2,321	2,839	3,616	132	
Light artillery	21	500	524	577	740		30
Total	255	4,606	5,261	6,251	8,074	132	30

Organization of troops in the District of Cape Fear and Defenses of Wilmington, Maj. Gen. W. H. C. Whiting, C. S. Army, commanding, October 31, 1863.

Martin's Brigade.

Brig. Gen. J. G. MARTIN.

42d North Carolina, Col. G. C. Gibbs.
50th North Carolina, Col. J. A. Washington.
61st North Carolina (two companies).
66th North Carolina, Col. A. D. Moore.

Cavalry.

Col. GEORGE JACKSON.

5th North Carolina (one company).
5th South Carolina (two companies).
7th South Carolina (three companies).

Light Artillery.

3d North Carolina Battalion, Maj. John W. Moore.
Adams' (North Carolina) Battery, Capt. Z. T. Adams.
Paris' (Virginia) Battery, Capt. A. B. Paris.
Southerland's (North Carolina) Battery, Capt. T. J. Southerland.

Heavy Artillery.*

Fort Caswell, Col. T. M. Jones.
Fort Fisher, Col. William Lamb.
Fort Pender. ⎫
Fort Anderson. ⎬ Col. J. J. Hedrick.
Fort Holmes. ⎭
Wilmington, Col. G. A. Cunningham.

HEADQUARTERS ARMY OF NORTHERN VIRGINIA,
November 2, 1863.

Brig. Gen. J. D. IMBODEN,
Commanding, &c.:

GENERAL: I have received your letter of the 31st ultimo, by Capt. George W. Stump.

I think it very important, in the quiescent state of affairs in your department, to endeavor to drive the enemy from Hardy and Hampshire Counties, and break up his position at Romney and Petersburg; but I am unable, at this time, to detach any portion of this army to your assistance. The enemy is reported to be again advancing toward the Rappahannock, and, until I can discover his intentions, I do not think it prudent to diminish my present force.

---

* Troops not indicated on original.

But should an opportunity offer of re-enforcing you, I should be glad to do so. In the meantime, I hope you will take advantage of every occasion to annoy and harass the enemy, even if you cannot drive him north of the Potomac.

I would not recommend an attack on Romney or Petersburg, if they are so strongly fortified as you suppose, but suggest that you endeavor to draw the enemy out, by either attacking his line of communication, or some point on the railroad which will necessitate his moving against you. A thousand bold men, which you say you can mount, can accomplish a great deal by the promptness of their movements.

I will write to General Sam. Jones to see if the operations in his department will enable him to re-enforce you; or, at any rate, to make a demonstration upon the enemy to prevent his concentrating upon you.

Your late exploit at Charlestown gives me great reason to hope that you will be able, before the approach of winter, to deal another serious blow upon the enemy at some point of his line. I hope, at any rate, you will be able to get out all the cattle, hogs, and horses that can be made available for our use.

It will be very advantageous to get out the flour you propose from Frederick, and the wheat from Clarke, if possible; but at this time I can do nothing to aid you.

In a conversation with Captain Stump, he thinks great damage can be done to the transportation on the Baltimore and Ohio Railroad by the operations of a party of picked men constantly hovering along its line and watching their opportunity.

I agrée with him in thinking that much could be done in this way, but am aware of the difficulty of raising such a force. If you think it feasible, detachments might be made temporarily from your companies, under Captain Stump, and the practicability of the plan tested.

Very respectfully, your obedient servant,

R. E. LEE,
General.

———

HEADQUARTERS ARMY OF NORTHERN VIRGINIA,
November 2, 1863.
Maj. Gen. SAMUEL JONES,
Commanding, &c.:

GENERAL: I have received your letter of the 22d ultimo,* and regret that I cannot at this time spare any troops from this army to re-enforce you. General Meade is again advancing on this line, repairing the railroad as he moves forward.

I had desired to take advantage of any lull in his operations and the good weather of this fall to drive General Kelley's forces out of Hardy and Hampshire, and make another attempt to interrupt transportation on the Baltimore and Ohio Railroad, but in the present condition of affairs, I am unable to re-enforce General Imboden, who thinks himself too weak to accomplish it.

Your movement upon East Tennessee may attract the attention of the enemy in Northwestern Virginia, so as to prevent a combination of his forces upon General Imboden. I hope you will be able

---

*See Jones to Seddon, October 22.

to occupy Knoxville. It is the best manner of securing the line of the Virginia and Tennessee Railroad, and preventing the constant and annoying demonstrations against you, and I suggest that you unite your whole force, leaving out only detachments to observe the enemy and keep up appearances, while you strike rapid and strong blows upon the force in Tennessee. Should you not be able to do this, a movement upon Northwestern Virginia, combined with a movement of Imboden upon the railroad, might enable both detachments to injure the enemy.

As far as I can learn, I believe there is little probability of the threatened movement of Averell from Beverly, of which you advise me, nor have I any reason to believe that an advance will be made by him in that direction this fall.

It behooves us to be active, to give the enemy no rest, and to prevent his re-enforcing his army about Chattanooga, which now seems to be the important point of his operations.

Very respectfully, your obedient servant,

R. E. LEE,
General.

HEADQUARTERS ARMY OF NORTHERN VIRGINIA,
November 2, 1863.

Maj. Gen. J. E. B. STUART,
Commanding, &c. .

GENERAL : Your letter of the 31st ultimo, with reference to the inspection report of the batteries in your command, is received.

I am aware of the difficulties under which those batteries labor, and am disposed to make proper allowances for them. The matters which I mentioned in my letter, however, are such as require only a due degree of attention on the part of the officers. As far as grease for the harness is concerned, all that is used in the artillery is made in the same way as that you refer to, and as it is impossible in our condition to have all the facilities and means that we would desire, it is necessary to exert increased effort to supply the deficiencies, and render available such as we have. We are compelled to depend upon the resources of our officers and men in making the most of what we have, and not to wait until we get what we would prefer. The subject of greasing the harness was not mentioned in the report. I only referred to its being dirty and suffered to lie on the ground for want of proper racks. This can be easily remedied.

In the case of Chew's battery, the report does not mean that it has not changed camp in eight days, but only that it has not been on the march or in action during that time, so that it has had opportunity to wash and clean the guns and equipments.

The report of General Chilton was a simple statement of facts, and as I have extracted all that require your attention, I see no good that would result from departing from usages in such matters by sending you a copy. I know that you and the officers of your artillery will do all in your power to correct these evils, and it was only with that view that they were brought to your attention.

. Very respectfully, your obedient servant,

R. E. LEE,
General.

WAR DEPARTMENT, C. S.,
Richmond, Va., November 2, 1863.

General SAMUEL JONES,
Abingdon, Va.:

There are indications of enemy threatening a raid upon the Peninsula in formidable force. Do your plans allow the return of Corse's brigade? If so, hold it ready to move on order.

J. A. SEDDON,
Secretary of War.

ABINGDON,
November 2, 1863.

Hon. JAMES A. SEDDON,
Secretary of War, Richmond:

Your telegram received. I shall not move Corse's brigade or any other infantry beyond the Holston, unless I receive re-enforcements. It can be sent to you whenever you order it, but not without serious danger to this section of country.

SAM. JONES,
Major-General.

SPECIAL ORDERS,)   ADJT. AND INSP. GENERAL'S OFFICE,
No. 261.   )   *Richmond, November 3, 1863.*

*   .   *   .   *   .   *   .   *

XXI. Maj. Gen. Wade Hampton, Provisional Army, C. S., having reported for duty, will proceed via Charlottesville to the headquarters Army of Northern Virginia, and report to General Robert E. Lee, commanding.

*   *   *   *   *   ..   ..

By command of the Secretary of War:

JNO. WITHERS,
Assistant Adjutant-General.

HEADQUARTERS DEPARTMENT OF WESTERN VIRGINIA,
Dublin, November 3, 1863.

Maj. Gen. SAMUEL JONES,
Abingdon:

Following dispatch just received:

Enemy reported to be moving toward Lewisburg, by way of Huntersville. General Imboden has been directed to follow them, communicating with you, and in concert to strike them. Forces said to be from 5,000 to 7,000—cavalry, artillery, and infantry.

R. E. LEE,
General.

[Indorsement.]

I have sent General Echols' dispatch to Colonel McCausland, and directed both of them to keep communications open. Have notified the home guards to be in readiness.

C. S. S. [STRINGFELLOW.]

PETERSBURG,
November 3, 1863.

General S. COOPER :

The following dispatch just received :

Maj. E. Burroughs, of guerrillas, reports enemy crossing the Sound to Elizabeth City in force—infantry, artillery, and cavalry ; marching from thence to Float Bridge and crossing into Camden County, on supposed route to Norfolk. Float Bridge is on the Pasquotank River. All quiet in my front. Enemy's cavalry 4 miles below Suffolk, about 200 strong. Some armed negroes 1 mile below them.

The above is from Franklin, and signed "Joel R. Griffin, colonel, commanding."

GEO. E. PICKETT,
Major-General.

HEADQUARTERS,
Wilmington, November 3,.1863.

Hon. JAMES A. SEDDON,
Secretary of War, Richmond :

SIR : Captain McKinney, the chief commissary here, has received an order from the Commissary-General to issue only one-third of a pound of meat to negro laborers. The labor here is very severe and exhausting, the more so that I am but scantily supplied with negroes. It is, however, absolutely necessary to us and very pressing. It is with great difficulty I can procure sufficient force or retain it at all unless I can feed them. I beg you will cause this order to be rescinded, to allow one-half pound.

Very respectfully,

W. H. C. WHITING,
Major-General.

WAR DEPARTMENT,
Richmond, Va. November 3, 1863.

His Excellency ZEBULON B. VANCE,
Governor of North Carolina :

I owe you an apology for having allowed your letter of the 26th ultimo, handed me some days since, respecting the effort made to enlist troops east of the Chowan River, amid the press of other matters, to escape my attention. I understand the embarrassments presented by the condition of the people in the counties east of the Chowan, for similar ones have been experienced in various districts of this State, which, without being in the actual occupancy of the enemy, are at all times open to their control. It is an embarrassing question in such cases to determine whether to exercise any authority over those districts, and by exacting from the people manifestations of the loyalty which fully possesses the very great majority, expose them and their property to the insolence and ravages of the enemy, or to have them in apparent subjection to await the events of the war.

I am inclined to think your judgment suggests the best practicable course, which is to draw forth, as far as possible, the younger and more disconnected men for service, and such means and productions as can be conveniently obtained, but to leave heads of families undisturbed, and such supplies as are necessary for the comfortable maintenance of the weak and dependent. The course, therefore, adopted by you has the concurrence of my opinion, and while, of course, I can release no obligation the law has imposed, nor relinquish the right, should more favorable circumstances be secured by the ascendency of our arms, of exacting both the service and contributions the law demands, you may expect such sanction as my authority warrants.

Very truly, yours,

J. A. SEDDON,
Secretary of War.

HEADQUARTERS ARMY OF NORTHERN VIRGINIA,
November 4, 1863.

General S. COOPER,
Adjutant and Inspector General:

GENERAL: The application of Colonel Hamilton, of South Carolina, for the transfer of the First Regiment South Carolina Volunteers, formerly commanded by him, to that State for duty, has been received. If the regiment could really be recruited in South Carolina, it might be well to transfer it thither, provided, meantime, a good regiment from that department could be sent to this army to take its place, and thus preserve the integrity of McGowan's brigade, to which it belongs. As to the transfer of troops from the Army of Northern Virginia to the Department of South Carolina at this period, I will make a statement of the facts as I conceive them, and leave it to the Department to decide the question. Meade is in our front, gradually advancing and repairing the railroad, having already reached Warrenton Junction. His army, consisting of five corps of infantry and three divisions of cavalry, has been re-enforced to some extent since its late retreat on Washington, and is variously estimated at from 60,000 to 80,000 effective men. To oppose this the Army of Northern Virginia presents an effective total not greatly exceeding that of General Beauregard's army, which has opposed to it, so far as I can learn, one corps of the enemy which will hardly number more than 20,000 men, exclusive of the naval forces engaged in the attack on Charleston.

I believe the troops of this army have been called upon in winter, spring, and summer to do almost as active service as those of any other department, and I do not see that the good of the service will be promoted by scattering its brigades and regiments along all the threatened points of the Confederacy. It is only by the concentration of our troops that we can hope to win any decisive advantage.

I am, very respectfully, your obedient servant,

R. E. LEE,
General.

HEADQUARTERS ARMY OF NORTHERN VIRGINIA,
November 4, 1863.

General S. COOPER,
Adjutant and Inspector General, C. S. Army:

GENERAL: I have had the honor to receive your letter of October 30, inclosing a telegram from Maj. Gen. S. Jones, with regard to the Eighth and Fourteenth Virginia Cavalry. Upon reference to General Stuart to know why these two regiments were especially desired, he states that it is because he believes that these are the only two regiments in that command which were not raised under some implied promise to serve in a certain locality.   In addition to the great want of cavalry in this army to oppose the greatly superior numbers of the enemy in that arm of the service, I will urge, from my own experience and observation in the mountain country of Virginia, that it is a very poor region for the operations of cavalry, and that it was very difficult to forage there.

I do not know whether this is the case in Southwest Virginia, but I still think that General Jones has more cavalry than is needed or can be used in his department advantageously. The Department, however, is the best judge in the matter, but if it is left to the decision of each general whether he will spare any troops when they are needed elsewhere, our armies will be scattered instead of concentrated, and we will be at the mercy of the enemy at all points.

I am, very respectfully, your obedient servant,

R. E. LEE,
General.

HEADQUARTERS ARMY OF NORTHERN VIRGINIA,
November 4, 1863.

Hon. SECRETARY OF WAR,
Richmond:

SIR : I have the honor to acknowledge the receipt of your letter of the 2d instant, with reference to punishment and deserters.

I think the course you have pursued with regard to the latter is the best; no terms should be made with them while they remain deserters.   It would encourge others with hopes of a like immunity, but in fact the courts-martial invariably take into account in their decisions the voluntary return of a prisoner, and I have never known one who had so returned to be sentenced to death.   I think this is the best way to extend indulgence to them.

Very respectfully, your obedient servant,

R. E. LEE,
General.

HEADQUARTERS ARMY OF NORTHERN VIRGINIA,
November 4, 1863.

Maj. Gen. J. E. B. STUART,
Commanding, &c.:

GENERAL : By inspection report of Hart's battery, it appears that there will be wanted, to mount the men now present for duty and for four guns and caissons, 62 horses.   The wagons and forge must be supplied with mules, of which there are 19 with the battery, 1 having been condemned, and including 2 riding mules.   As this company had no record of property, and no morning reports, it was impossible to ascertain how many horses it had, or what had become of them.   All that could be learned was what the orderly sergeant remembered.   I suppose some of the horses must have been sent back to the horse infirmary, and desire to know how many you can procure from there to supply the deficiency in this battery, as the quartermaster's department will not be able to furnish them all.

The condition of this battery is reported to be bad. I call your attention particularly to the necessity of having morning reports and a proper record, without which it is impossible to have proper responsibility in the command. The horses are said to be in worse condition, and to show more evidences of want of attention than those of the other batteries. The guns have not been washed off recently, nor the harness greased, and a chain is substituted for a pole yoke in one of the guns. The grounds about the guns and caissons are badly policed.

It is due to Captain Hart to say that he has but recently returned to the battery.

Very respectfully, your obedient servant,

R. E. LEE,
General.

SPECIAL ORDERS, }   HDQRS. ARMY OF NORTHERN VIRGINIA,
No. 273.   }   *November 4, 1863.*

I. Col. J. C. C. Sanders, commanding brigade, is relieved from duty as a member of the general court-martial convened by Paragraph II, Special Orders, No. 195, current series, from these headquarters, and Col. D. A. Weisiger, Twelfth Virginia Regiment, is detailed in his stead.

II. Brig. Gen. A. Iverson having been relieved from duty with this army, Brig. Gen. L. A. Stafford is detailed in his stead as a member of the Board of Examiners convened by Paragraph XVIII, Special Orders, No. 222, current series, from these headquarters.

*   *   *   *   *   *   *

By command of General Lee:

W. H. TAYLOR,
Assistant Adjutant-General.

HEADQUARTERS DEPARTMENT OF WESTERN VIRGINIA,
Dublin, November 4, 1863.

Maj. Gen. SAMUEL JONES,
Abingdon:

Colonel Jackson sent dispatch to General Echols that 1,000 of the enemy were yesterday evening at Green Bank, in Pocahontas. Jackson will fall back on Lewisburg, if pressed too hard.

CHAS. S. STRINGFELLOW,
Assistant Adjutant-General.

BRANDY,
November 5, 1863—10.30 [a. m.]

Hon. JAMES A. SEDDON:

Advance of enemy to Falmouth was to break up party removing iron. I wish a telegraphic operator placed at Hamilton's Crossing to communicate with me.

R. E. LEE.

HEADQUARTERS DEPARTMENT OF WESTERN VIRGINIA,
Dublin, November 5, 1863.

Maj. Gen. SAMUEL JONES,
           Abingdon:

Dispatch just received from General Echols. At 7 p. m. yesterday, enemy, not less than 2,000 strong, were pressing Colonel Jackson, and within 3 miles of him, advancing by the Beaver Creek route. Suppose they came from Huntersville. General Echols is in motion to relieve Colonel Jackson. No more from the Kanawha yet. May not some of your troops be needed?

CHAS. S. STRINGFELLOW,
Assistant Adjutant-General.

HEADQUARTERS DEPARTMENT OF WESTERN VIRGINIA,
Dublin, November 5, 1863.

Colonel McCAUSLAND,
           Princeton:

At 7 o'clock last night the enemy not less than 2,000 strong were within 3 miles of Colonel Jackson, and pressing upon him. They were advancing by the Beaver Creek route. Keep in communication with General Echols, and watch for any advance on your lines.

By order, &c.:

CHAS. S. STRINGFELLOW,
Assistant Adjutant-General.

HEADQUARTERS DEPARTMENT OF WESTERN VIRGINIA,
Dublin, November 5, 1863.

Brig. Gen. JOHN ECHOLS,
           Lewisburg:

Telegram received and communicated to Colonel McCausland. If the number of the enemy is estimated correctly, you can readily manage them. Have directed Colonel McCausland to keep open communication with you and advise you of any move on his front. Will forward your dispatch immediately, and ask the general commanding to assist you, if necessary.

CHAS. S. STRINGFELLOW,
Assistant Adjutant-General.

HEADQUARTERS DEPARTMENT OF WESTERN VIRGINIA,
Dublin, November 5, 1863.

JAMES McDOWELL,
           Fincastle:

Enemy reported advancing in heavy force on Lewisburg. Please notify your men to be in readiness for any move.

CHAS. S. STRINGFELLOW,
Assistant Adjutant-General.

(Similar dispatches to Col. James M. Wade, Christiansburg; Col. George P. Terrill, Salem; Capt. G. A. Wingfield, Liberty; Col. J. F. Kent, Wytheville, and Henry M. Bowyer, Bonsack's.)

SPECIAL ORDERS, }   HDQRS. DEPT. OF NORTHERN VIRGINIA,
No. 274.   }   *November 5, 1863.*

*   *   *   *   *   *

II. In accordance with the act of Congress (No. 26, approved 13th of October, 1862), as published in General Orders, No. 93, Adjutant and Inspector General's Office, of 22d of November, 1862, a Board of Examiners, to consist of Col. E. J. Walker, Third Georgia Regiment; Lieut. Col. E. M. Feild, Twelfth Virginia Regiment, and Maj. John P. Emrich, Eighth Alabama Regiment, will meet at the camp of Anderson's division on the 9th day of November, 1863, or as soon thereafter as practicable—

To examine into the cases of such officers of the division as may be brought to their attention, for the purpose of determining their qualifications for the discharge of the duties properly appertaining to their several positions, whether they are careless or inattentive in the discharge of the same, and their fitness for promotion to any existing vacancies in their respective commands.

The Board will be sworn, will have power to summon witnesses, will keep a record of its proceedings, will give an opinion in each case, and will be careful to conform to the requirements of General Orders, No. 50, of 29th of March, 1863, from these headquarters.

By command of General Lee:

W. H. TAYLOR,
Assistant Adjutant-General.

HEADQUARTERS ARMY OF NORTHERN VIRGINIA,
November 6, 1863.

JOHN S. BARBOUR, Esq.,
Pres. Orange and Alexandria Railroad, Lynchburg, Va.:

SIR : The enemy were in possession of the Orange and Alexandria Railroad as far as the Rapidan River, and by certain movements of this army, beginning on the 8th of October, they were driven beyond Bull Run. In their retreat, they destroyed the bridge over the Rappahannock and rendered the road useless to our army north of the river. For reasons of a military nature, I ordered the destruction of the road from Cub Run beyond Broad to the Rappahannock, which was accordingly done. The enemy advanced when we retired, and I learn have repaired the road to Warrenton Junction, and are continuing to repair it in the direction of Rappahannock.

Very respectfully, your obedient servant,

. R. E. LEE,
General.

HEADQUARTERS ARMY OF NORTHERN VIRGINIA,
November 6, 1863.

His Excellency JOHN LETCHER,
Governor of Virginia:

GOVERNOR : At its late called session the legislature made an appropriation for the relief of the families of soldiers. I find that there is great suffering among the people in this region for want of the necessaries of life. The farms and gardens have been robbed, stock and hogs killed, and these outrages committed, I am sorry to say, by our own army to some extent, as well as by the Federals. I hear of like destitution in Stafford, where the Federal Army alone has been.

Would it not be well to forward such supplies of flour and meat as can be obtained to Culpeper Court-House and Fredericksburg, with agents for its distribution to those soldiers' families in distress, so as to relieve their wants during the coming winter?

Very respectfully, your obedient servant,

R. E. LEE,
General.

HEADQUARTERS DEPARTMENT OF WESTERN VIRGINIA;
Dublin, November 6, 1863.

General S. COOPER,
Richmond:

Your telegram received. Questions cannot be answered with entire accuracy just now, owing to movements of the troops.

Major-General Ransom's field return for October 31, including troops at Saltville, showed: Present for duty, 506 officers and 6,096 enlisted men; sick and inefficient, 33 officers and 822 enlisted men; total, 539 officers and 6,918 enlisted men; aggregate, 7,457.

Brigadier-General Echols and Colonel McCausland's brigades show: Present for duty, 148 officers and 2,552 enlisted men; absent, 55 officers and 993 enlisted men; aggregate present and absent, 227 officers and 3,885 enlisted men.

Col. W. L. Jackson's return not in, but he has not more than 1,000 men for duty.

Colonel Ferguson has two regiments of Jenkins' brigade in front of Lewisburg, with 72 officers and 810 enlisted men present for duty; aggregate present and absent, 1,629. Complete returns will arrive in a few days.

Fifteenth, Twenty-second, Twenty-ninth, Thirtieth, Thirty-sixth, Forty-fifth, Fifty-first, and Sixtieth [Virginia Infantry] Regiments, and Twenty-third, Twenty-sixth, and Thirtieth Virginia Infantry [Battalions]; Eighth, Fourteenth, Sixteenth, Seventeenth, Nineteenth, Twentieth, and Twenty-first Regiments [Virginia Cavalry], and Thirty-fourth, Thirty-sixth, and Thirty-seventh Battalions Virginia Cavalry; First Tennessee and Fourth Kentucky Regiments Cavalry; Sixteenth Georgia Battalion of Cavalry; fragments of Thomas' Legion, aggregating 399, under Brig. Gen. A. E. Jackson.

Reports are made on every variety of blanks, and it will be impossible to fill out the form sent for the Department until the brigades are supplied with blanks of the same kind.

I send the above message in cipher as directed.

SAM. JONES,
Major-General.

DUBLIN, *November* 6, 1863.

Col. JOHN MCCAUSLAND, *Princeton:*

The Sixtieth [Virginia] Regiment will be at the Narrows in ample time to assist you in case of necessity.

By order:

WM. B. MYERS,
Assistant Adjutant-General.

WAR DEPARTMENT, C. S.,
Richmond, November 7, 1863.

General R. E. LEE,
Culpeper Court-House, Va..

GENERAL: A telegram just received from General Jones says:

General Echols has been defeated with heavy loss, and is endeavoring to retreat by Salt Pond Mountain. Enemy advancing, about 7,000 strong.

General Jones asks aid, if it can be given. I have no force to send, as General Pickett, under information of raid toward Weldon, has just moved thither with his disposable force. Can you render aid?

J. A. SEDDON,
Secretary of War.

BRANDY STATION,
November 7, 1863.

Hon. JAMES A. SEDDON,
Secretary of War:

Your telegraph received. Imboden's command was to have reached Millborough by noon yesterday. He said he would push on. I hope he has formed junction with other forces in that quarter. Enemy commenced a demonstration in our front about noon to-day. Cannot detach any force from here now.

R. E. LEE,
General.

HEADQUARTERS DEPARTMENT OF WESTERN VIRGINIA,
Dublin, November 7, 1863.

Maj. Gen. R. RANSOM, Jr.,
Commanding, &c.:

GENERAL: In consequence of the movements of the enemy on Greenbrier, I shall not be able to send to you at present the additional infantry mentioned in the note from my aide (Lieutenant Warwick) to you night before last.

Make, therefore, no change whatever in your plans for the move on Rogersville. I hope that move has not been interfered with by the rain of yesterday and last night. It was slight here. The enemy under Brigadier-General Averell, variously estimated at from 3,000 to 7,000 strong, is moving toward Lewisburg, skirmishing all yesterday in the lower end of Pocahontas. I will go up there.

SAM. JONES,
Major-General.

HDQRS. DEPT. OF WESTERN VA. AND EAST TENN.,
Dublin, November 7, 1863.

General R. E. LEE,   •
Brandy Station:

General Echols was badly defeated, with heavy loss, at Droop Mountain yesterday; is pursued by forces estimated at 7,000, mostly mounted. Echols will retreat by Salt Pond Mountain if he can, but I fear he cannot escape, and will be cut up and destroyed. If you

can send aid, please do it. If sent by rail to Millborough and
thence by the Warm Springs toward the White Sulphur, it may
deter the enemy from pressing on.

SAM. JONES,
Major-General.

HDQRS. DEPT. OF WESTERN VA. AND EAST TENN.,
Dublin, November 7, 1863.

Brig. Gen. JOHN D. IMBODEN,
 Via Millborough:
 General Echols was badly defeated, with heavy loss, at Droop
Mountain. Is closely pursue by enemy, estimated at 7,000. Echols
will retreat over Salt Pond Mountain if he can. If possible strike
the enemy's flank or rear.

SAM. JONES,
Major-General.

[Indorsement.]

Agent at Millborough will forward with all possible speed.

DUBLIN, *November 7, 1863.*

Col. B. H. JONES
 (Care of Captain Gibboney, Asst. Q. M., Wytheville):
 Proceed with your regiment overland to the Narrows. Carry
transportation, &c., and lose no time on the road. The enemy is
pressing heavily.
 By order of, &c.:

CHAS. S. STRINGFELLOW,
Assistant Adjutant-General.

[Indorsement.]

Captain Gibboney will immediately forward this by special courier.

DUBLIN, *November 7, 1863.*

Col. JOSEPH F. KENT, *Wytheville:*
 Assemble all your men at Wytheville. General Echols is retreating before vastly superior forces.

CHAS. S. STRINGFELLOW.
Assistant Adjutant-General.

(Same to Capt. J. M. Sheffey, Marion.)

DUBLIN, *November 7, 1863.*

JAMES McDOWELL,
 Fincastle:
 Call out every man you can and go at once to Salem. General
Echols is retreating before vastly superior forces. Lose no time.

CHAS. S. STRINGFELLOW,
Assistant Adjutant-General.

DUBLIN, *November 7, 1863.*

Brigadier-General NICHOLLS,
    Lynchburg.

General Echols is retreating before a superior force, heavily
pressed. Call out every man you can to go to Salem.

CHAS. S. STRINGFELLOW,
    Assistant Adjutant-General.

DUBLIN, *November 7,* 1863.

Col. GEORGE P TERRILL,
    Salem:

Assemble all your men at Salem. General Echols heavily pressed
by vastly superior forces. He is retreating rapidly.

CHAS. S. STRINGFELLOW,
    Assistant Adjutant-General.

(Same to Capt. G. A. Wingfield, at Liberty.)

DUBLIN, *November 7,* 1863.

Col. J. M. WADE,
    Christiansburg:

Call out every man you can. Enemy pressing heavily on General
Echols. Go at once to New River Bridge.

CHAS. S. STRINGFELLOW,
    Assistant Adjutant-General.

PETERSBURG,
    November 7, 1863.

General S. COOPER,
    Adjutant and Inspector General:

The following dispatches just received:

Col. J. W. Hinton just dispatches me, received at 3 p. m.:
"I am pressed by enemy in considerable force, coming from Winton—artillery,
infantry, and cavalry. Send me re-enforcements immediately to Murfreesborough."
I go, by General Ransom's order, with my two cavalry companies and one piece
of artillery, leaving my infantry to guard Blackwater. Detachments of enemy's
cavalry came within 8 miles of Franklin yesterday evening, but fell back at night.

JOEL R. GRIFFIN,
    Colonel, Commanding Forces at Franklin.

Enemy 10,000 strong at Winton—artillery, infantry, and cavalry. My force is
1,200. The re-enforcements ought to be sent.

M. W. RANSOM,
    Brigadier-General, Commanding, Weldon, N. C.

I do not know whether the enemy can be in such force as represented. I think not. General Whiting should be ordered to re-enforce, if necessary. If this movement is a feint toward Weldon,
Petersburg is left entirely uncovered when Barton's brigade leaves
here.

GEO. E. PICKETT,
    Major-General.

PETERSBURG,
November 7, 1863.

General S. COOPER,
Adjutant and Inspector General:

Following dispatch just received from General Ransom:

WELDON, *November 7, [1863.]*

The enemy, from 10 gunboats and transports, are landing at Winton, on their way to Weldon. If there are no demonstrations elsewhere, send out what forces you can spare. I have two regiments.

M. W. RANSOM,
Brigadier-General.

I have ordered Barton's brigade to get ready to move. Do you know of any demonstrations to prevent this re-enforcement being sent to Weldon? I shall go myself if report is verified.

GEO. E. PICKETT,
Major-General.

WILMINGTON,
November 7, 1863.

General CUSTIS LEE,
President's Staff, Goldsborough:

Following dispatch received from Weldon:

Last night between 11 and 12 m. received information of the enemy landing at Winton; forces, 10 boats and transports; destination supposed to be Weldon. Two cavalry regiments reported 20 miles below Winton.

W. H. C. WHITING,
Major-General.

WAR DEPARTMENT, C. S.,
Richmond, November 7, 1863.

Maj. Gen. W. H. C. WHITING,
Commanding, Wilmington, N. C.:

GENERAL: Colonel Gorgas, Chief of Ordnance, informs me that you can be supplied in a few days, from the Tredegar Works, with some 10 and 20 pounder Parrott guns, and that as soon as a rifling machine is put in working order some 30-pounder Parrotts can be furnished.

Very respectfully,

J. A. SEDDON,
Secretary of War.

SPECIAL ORDERS,   }   HDQRS. ARMY OF NORTHERN VIRGINIA,
No. 277.   }   *November 8, 1863.*

Maj. Gen. Wade Hampton, having reported for duty, will assume command of the division of the Cavalry Corps assigned to him in Paragraph XIV, Special Orders, No. 226, current series, from these headquarters. He will report to Maj. Gen. J. E. B. Stuart for further orders.

By command of General R. E. Lee:

W. H. TAYLOR,
Assistant Adjutant-General.

HEADQUARTERS DEPARTMENT OF WESTERN VIRGINIA,
Dublin, November 8, 1863.

Col. J. M. WADE, *Christiansburg:*

Take your entire force to Salt Pond Mountain immediately, to meet General Echols at this place.

By order of, &c.:

WM. B. MYERS,
Assistant Adjutant-General.

LYNCHBURG, *November 8, 1863.*

General S. COOPER:

The militia have turned out so badly—only 40—that I have organized, under convalescent Confederate officers, 300 convalescent soldiers who would not be returned to duty within a week, and, if not otherwise ordered, will send them to-night to the aid of General Sam. Jones. The emergency seems to be very great.

FRANCIS T. NICHOLLS,
Major-General.

WELDON, *November 8, 1863.*

General S. COOPER:

Following dispatch just received from Murfreesborough:
Are there any demonstrations being made elsewhere?

I arrived here this morning at 3 o'clock; enemy are landing troops and lumber from three transports at Winton; four gunboats went up river this morning. The gunboats at Reddick's Ferry yesterday have gone back. It is supposed the enemy are building pontoons at Winton; they have pontoon boats. Captain Duval, of my regiment, drove enemy's pickets into Winton yesterday; thinks they have small force, yet I do not think they will move across Potecasi Creek as before, but think they will take the plain road toward Weldon. The style of their preparations would indicate, I think, a raid or series of raids of some magnitude. I will keep you informed of movements. Enemy's landing at Winton may be for the purpose of establishing a permanent post for the purpose of cutting off from us large supplies of provisions, &c. The situation of Winton rather inclines me to this opinion. This would complete chain of posts on river and coast of North Carolina.

Respectfully,

JOEL R. GRIFFIN,
Colonel,
Per W. A. HOPSON,
Adjutant.

GEO. E. PICKETT,
Major-General.

HEADQUARTERS DEPARTMENT OF NORTH CAROLINA,
Weldon, November 9, 1863.

General S. COOPER,
Adjutant and Inspector General, Richmond:

GENERAL: I have the honor to state I forwarded by telegram last night the latest intelligence which has been received from Winton. I also asked whether there was anything in the way of a demonstration elsewhere. Not getting any reply, and conceiving it advisable to dislodge the enemy at once, I have sent off General Ransom this morning, with two regiments (1,200 strong in all) and a battery of artillery, which will make his force in addition to his infantry, six companies of cavalry and nine pieces of artillery, among them four Napoleons.

The first report from Colonel Hinton was that there were 10,000 men. The next was in the same spirit, calling for re-enforcements; now it appears that he does not think it so formidable. The infantry under his command—State troops—it seems were scattered over the country upon the appearance of the enemy, and were not collected; fact is, they are not to be depended on, and I will send some competent officers there.

In meantime I keep Barton's brigade at this point, ready to re-enforce if necessary, or to be brought back to Petersburg, should this only be a feint.

The expedition under General Ransom will return within a week, and if successful in driving off the gunboats, I very much desire that torpedoes may be furnished at once, so as to obstruct the river below Winton. Otherwise, should they make it a base of operations, it will lose us a very valuable country for supplies, and will compel us to keep constantly a strong force at this point. We cannot occupy it with our present limited numbers. It will be necessary, of course, to keep some good cavalry and artillery in that neighborhood.

I return to Petersburg to-day if no more important developments are made.

I sent down to Ivor, to Colonel Herbert, before coming here, to move a body of cavalry, infantry, and battery of artillery toward Suffolk, to-night or as soon as possible. I could not uncover the line of the Blackwater by sending troops to the right, and I deemed it best to make a small demonstration myself to the front in that direction.

I forward this letter by Captain Baird, assistant quartermaster.

I am, general, very respectfully, your obedint servant,

GEO. E. PICKETT,
Major-General, Commanding.

HEADQUARTERS ARMY OF NORTHERN VIRGINIA,
November 10, 1863.

Hon. JAMES A. SEDDON,
Secretary of War, Richmond, Va.:

SIR: I beg leave to urge upon your attention the fact that many of our men in this army are still barefooted, and the weather has become very cold. The shoes received a short time since relieved much hardship and added much to the efficiency of the army, but it is a matter of great importance to the comfort and health of the men that they should all be well shod and clothed in such weather as we may expect now for some months. Another subject gives me great anxiety also. Corn for our animals comes in very slowly, and I fear that unless the amount can be very much increased, we shall lose many horses and mules this winter. I would beg you, therefore, to urge on the officers who have charge of this matter to use great diligence and activity in bringing forward the corn from the south and elsewhere.

I am, very respectfully, your obedient servant,

R. E. LEE.
General.

WAR DEPARTMENT,
Richmond, Va., November 10, 1863.

Maj. Gen. W. H. C. WHITING,
Commanding, Wilmington, N. C.:

GENERAL: I have received your letter asking me to rescind the order of the Commissary-General reducing the quantity of meat allowed negro laborers to one-third of a pound per day. I should most cheerfully comply with your request if the amount of supplies at the command of the Department would allow, but the necessity of the case constrains me to sanction the order reducing the ration.

Respectfully,

J. A. SEDDON,
Secretary of War.

EXECUTIVE DEPARTMENT, NORTH CAROLINA,
Raleigh, November 10, 1863.

Hon. JAMES A. SEDDON,
Richmond, Va.:

DEAR SIR: Lest it may not be known to you, I desire to say that the position in which the enemy have established themselves at Winton, on the Chowan River, in this State, will effectually cut us off from four or five million pounds of pork, which we expected to get from the counties east of that stream. It would be a terrible loss to the army and the State. If possible for General Pickett to drive them off and prevent their fortifying (which I learn they are doing), it ought by all means to be done. It will be positively ruinous for our troops to stand at Weldon and surrender all the rich country below. I beg your attention to this matter.

Very respectfully, your obedient servant,

Z. B. VANCE.

HEADQUARTERS ARMY OF NORTHERN VIRGINIA,
November 11, 1863.

Hon. SECRETARY OF WAR,
Richmond, Va.:

SIR: I have the honor to acknowledge the receipt of the letter of General Sam. Jones referred to me by you, and at the same time a copy of a letter of Senator Henry.* I am very desirous to meet the views expressed in both these letters, and if I had the troops to spare would willingly send them to East Tennessee. At the present time, however, I cannot detach any from this army. Whether the troops could penetrate Tennessee in the manner indicated by Mr. Henry, I am unable to decide, but at present the withdrawal of any part, and especially so large a part of this army as he speaks of, is impracticable.

Very respectfully, your obedient servant,

R. E. LEE,
General.

---

* See Jones to Seddon, October 26.

DUBLIN, *November 11, 1863.*

Brig. Gen. J. D. IMBODEN, *Millborough:*

That part of the enemy's force that did not go with General Averell left Lewisburg yesterday. The cavalry left went with Averell. The infantry returned through Pocahontas. The force from Kanawha went toward Kanawha. I am anxious to know something more of Averell's movements. Can you enlighten me?

SAM. JONES, ·
Major-General.

HEADQUARTERS ARMY OF NORTHERN VIRGINIA,
November 12, 1863.

His Excellency JEFFERSON DAVIS,
President Confederate States, Richmond:

Mr. PRESIDENT: Our scouts report the Orange and Alexandria Railroad finished as far as Bealeton. They report, moreover, that the road from Union Mills to that point is almost entirely stripped of troops, nearly all the road guards having been sent forward. Trains have lately passed up bringing artillery. Cavalry has passed up with led horses. The route from Bealeton to Kelly's Ford is almost as short as that from Brandy Station to the same point, and the above movements indicate, I think, an advance on the part of General Meade. There are indications also that this advance will take place on our right by the lower fords, Germanna and Ely's, as if with the intention of striking for the Richmond and Fredericksburg. Railroad. Should he move in that direction, I will endeavor to follow him and bring him to battle, but I do not see how I can do it without the greatest difficulty. The country through which he will have to pass is barren. We have no forage on hand and very little prospect of·getting any from Richmond. I fear our horses will die in great numbers, and, in fact, I do not know how they will survive two or three days' march without food. I hope every effort will be made to send some up, and I think it would be well to stop the transportation of everything on the railroad excepting army supplies.

One of the scouts brings an extravagant report coming from an official in Washington, that the United States Government is collecting a large number of horses—40,000—to mount a body of infantry for the purpose of making a raid on Richmond, with a view to the release of their prisoners. The rescue of these prisoners has been for some time a theme with the Northern papers. I think they should, for many reasons, be removed from that city as soon as practicable.

I am, with great respect, your obedient servant,

R. E. LEE,
General.

HEADQUARTERS ARMY OF NORTHERN VIRGINIA,
November 12, 1863.

Hon. JAMES A. SEDDON,
Secretary of War, Richmond, Va.:

SIR: The condition of the Virginia Central Railroad, on which we depend almost entirely for our supplies, seems to become worse every day. Colonel Corley reports the frequent accidents of cars running off the track, and that the track, in many places, is very bad. I beg you to consult with the president and superintendent of the road as to what measures can be taken for its repair before the winter fairly sets in.   To make details from this army for the purpose, in the present reduced condition of our regiments, is next to impossible. I hope, however, something may be done to put it in good repair, so that it may be relied on for the regular transportation of our supplies. If this cannot be done, the only alternative will be to fall back nearer to Richmond.

This would leave not only the railroad, but the richest portion of the State of Virginia at the mercy of the enemy. If the Engineer Department can do the work and the railroad company cannot, I think they might set a portion of the force employed on the defenses of Richmond at work at once and charge the work done to the company, to be deducted from the tolls on supplies transported to the army.

It is of great importance that the work should be done while the good weather lasts.

Very respectfully, your obedient servant,

R. E. LEE,
General.

HEADQUARTERS ARMY OF NORTHERN VIRGINIA,
November 12, 1863.
Brig. Gen. ROBERT F. HOKE,
Commanding, &c.:

GENERAL: I hope you have nearly finished the work for which you were detached, and will soon be able to rejoin the army.

I regret to inform you that in the recent advance of the army at Rappahannock Bridge, that part of your brigade which is here sustained a loss of 3 killed, 19 wounded, and 906 missing, most of whom were taken prisoners. As the number reported captured by the enemy is smaller than the number of missing, I suppose some of the men may have availed themselves of the opportunity for concealment presente by the capture of so large a part of the command, and returned home.

While you are in the State it would be well for you to give the matter your attention, and arrest any stragglers you can find.

This unfortunate affair greatly reduces your brigade, leaving only 29 officers and 257 men present for duty, and a total present of 30 officers and 321 men. I hope you will endeavor to procure some additional regiments from the Governor to fill up your brigade, as it could not be spared from the army, and I shall be glad to see you back aga n as soon as possible, with your command at least as strong as beforei

Very respectfully, your obedient servant,

R. E. LEE,
General.

HEADQUARTERS DEPARTMENT OF NORTH CAROLINA,
Petersburg, Va., November 12, 1863.
General S. COOPER,
Adjutant and Inspector General, Richmond:

GENERAL : I have the honor to report that the enemy had some seventeen steamers at Winton. They left without committing any

depredation, and made no advance excepting a very short distance
into the country, when they were immediately driven back by Colonel Griffin's cavalry, Captain Bower's company. General Ransom,
whom I had sent down with two regiments, has returned to Weldon,
the enemy having left before he arrived. About the same time, I
had ordered Colonel Herbert from the Blackwater to the front, intending to make a diversion had the enemy intended anything in
North Carolina. I inclose his report.* He captured some 7 prisoners, 1 wagon, and 8 horses.

Barton's brigade is now at this point, having been sent back from
Weldon upon the receipt of instructions from Richmond.

The prisoners captured report 6,000 infantry in Portsmouth; this
I consider doubtful.

I am, general, very respectfully, your obedient servant,

GEO. E. PICKETT,
Major-General, Commanding.

[Indorsement.]

NOVEMBER 14, 1863.

ADJUTANT-GENERAL:

Answer that he will do well, unless some move in North Carolina
requires otherwise, to return a brigade to Petersburg. I see in
Northern papers indications of a sudden dash on Richmond to release the prisoners, &c. It is well to be fully on guard about this,
especially just now when we are removing them, and I wish that
your scouts should be urged to special vigilance for early notice
of any contemplated movement on the Peninsula, Lower James, or
Blackwater.

J. A. S. [SEDDON,]
Secretary.

DUBLIN,
November 13, 1863.

Brig. Gen. JOHN ECHOLS,
Commanding, &c.:

GENERAL: I am instructed by the general commanding to say that
he has received information that the enemy have entirely abandoned
Greenbrier and gone back to Beverly and Kanawha. He will not
therefore for the present order the movement of Colonel McCausland, as contemplated when he saw you last.

Very respectfully,

CHAS. S. STRINGFELLOW,
Assistant Adjutant-General.

HDQRS. DEPT. OF WESTERN VA. AND EAST TENN.,
Dublin, November 13, 1863.

Col. JOHN McCAUSLAND,
Commanding, &c.:

The enemy is reported as moving in the direction of Kanawha,
from Lewisburg, and said to be in great confusion. The major-gen-

---

*See raid on Suffolk, Va., Part I, p. 638.

eral commanding directs you to send out reliable scouts, and obtain as accurate information as you can in regard to their movements and present disposition.

Very respectfully, your obedient servant,

CHAS. S. STRINGFELLOW,
Assistant Adjutant-General.

WAR DEPARTMENT, C. S.,
Richmond, Va., November 14, 1863.

General R. E. LEE,
Commanding, &c.:

GENERAL: I owe you an apology for not sooner acknowledging the receipt of your letter calling my attention to the deficiency of the supplies, both of shoes for the soldiers and of forage for the animals of your command. I had been apprised only the day before its receipt of the falling off in the quantity of corn received by railroad transportation from the south, and had immediately sent an active officer of the Quartermaster's Department on the southern line to discover the causes of delay, and, if possible, remove them at once. I likewise instructed the Quartermaster-General to send forward whatever small supplies he could command from this city, or any other convenient depots in the State.

I trust relief will be afforded by these measures, and supplies in future will be more regular and abundant. The time is near at hand when we shall be less dependent than for months past we have been on the transportation of corn from such distant points as South Carolina and Georgia. The attention of the Quartermaster-General had been before, and was again on the receipt of your letter, called specially to the necessity of supplying your troops with shoes. He assures me every effort will be made, and mentions in excuse that some of the supplies sent by the railroad had not been forwarded as promptly as he expected. Directions have been given that such delays be not again allowed.

I have directed that if our supplies are too limited to allow due provision for all the armies, those serving in Northern Virginia and the mountainous districts should be preferred. Deficiency, if existing at all, is due to the unfortunate loss of two or three steamers, which were laden mainly with quartermaster's stores.

This has compelled us to rely almost exclusively on internal manufacture.

Yours, with esteem,

J. A. SEDDON,
Secretary of War.

GENERAL ORDERS, } HDQRS. ARMY OF NORTHERN VIRGINIA,
No. —.   }   *November 14, 1863.*

I. It is absolutely necessary that the forage in this department which is near enough to the railroad and canal for convenient transportation should be reserved for the use of this army. Officers in charge of animals sent back to be recruited or held in reserve, and those herding cattle for the use of this army, are forbidden to use this forage. They must avail themselves, as far as possible, of fodder and cornstalks, and must confine their stock to regions remote from the railroads and canal, and from which this army does not draw its supplies.

II. In the inspection of troops of this army, the inspector will be accompanied by the ordnance officer of the command inspected. In all inspections of transportation, he will be accompanied by the quartermaster in charge of the same.

By command of General Lee:

R. H. CHILTON,
Assistant Adjutant and Inspector General.

WAR DEPARTMENT, C. S.,
Richmond, Va., November 16, 1863.

Maj. Gen. GEORGE E. PICKETT,
Commanding, Petersburg, Va.:

GENERAL: Your report of the 12th instant has been received. You will do well, I think, unless some movement of the enemy in North Carolina requires other disposition of your forces, to retain a brigade in Petersburg. I see in the Northern papers indications of a sudden dash on Richmond to release the prisoners confined here. It is well to be fully on guard about this, especially just now, when we are removing them to the interior; and I wish that your scouts should be urged to special vigilance, so as to give early notice of any contemplated movement on the Peninsula, the Lower James, or the Blackwater.

Respectfully,

J. A. SEDDON,
Secretary of War.

EXECUTIVE DEPARTMENT, NORTH CAROLINA,
Raleigh, November 18, 1863.

Hon. JAMES A. SEDDON,
Secretary of War:

DEAR SIR: I beg to inclose you my brother's letter, which will explain his situation better than I can. With about 300 troops and some militia, he is succeeding well in getting out pork from East Tennessee, and I would most respectfully urge the increase of his command if possible. A vast amount of provisions could thus be saved to the Government, which, I fear, will otherwise be lost.

Most respectfully, yours,

Z. B. VANCE.

[Inclosure.]

HEADQUARTERS,
Paint Rock, November 12, 1863.

His Excellency ZEBULON B. VANCE,
Raleigh, N. C.:

DEAR BROTHER: I have raided Cocke County and a part of Greene, pretty thoroughly, and brought out safely 800 hogs and some horses and cattle.

On yesterday I started to Greeneville, but was overtaken by a courier stating that 300 Yankees had attacked Lieutenant Richie and took 100 hogs from him. I immediately tacked about with 60 men and made after them. We met them, 200 strong, 5 miles of Newport, and had a brisk fight, driving the enemy back several hundred yards. We had 2 men wounded, 1 of whom is at Hawk's house, the other here. The enemy's loss, 1 captain killed and 2 men wounded. My men fought well. The wounded are of Captain Boykin's company, South Carolina cavalry.

My hogs (800) are all above the springs. Colonel Mallett has ordered Captain McRae back, and I will not let him go; it is impossible to do without him, and I wish you to lay the facts before the War Department. I am not only saving property for the Government, but threatening the enemy on his lines, and keeping him uneasy, and drawing some of his force away to watch me. Please haste to lay this matter before the authorities. The enemy went to mouth of Chucky last night. No other news excepting that heavy cannonading was heard toward Rogersville yesterday.

Your brother,

ROBT. B. VANCE,
Brigadier-General.

P. S.—I had to let Captain Boykin go home this morning; this shears me of a good portion of my strength. Why can I not get some of General Hoke's men, or him and his whole command? The field is so inviting and I am so anxious to do something. There is also Colonel Williams' regiment at Greenville, S. C. Let it be understood at Richmond that I ask for men not to defend North Carolina simply, but to work for the Government in East Tennessee.

[Indorsement.]

NOVEMBER 23, 1863.

I hope General Lee will be able to spare Hoke's remaining men to this service. The recommendation of General Vance to that effect has been commended to his favorable consideration.

J. A. SEDDON.

HEADQUARTERS ARMY OF NORTHERN VIRGINIA,
November 19, 1863.

Hon. JAMES A. SEDDON,
Secretary of War, Richmond, Va.:

SIR: I inclose you the copy* of a letter received yesterday from Colonel Northrop on the subject of impressment of supplies for this army. If the imperative necessity has arisen which Major Noland mentions in the paper prepared by him for Colonel Northrop, it will doubtless continue, and from Colonel Northrop's indorsement I judge the same prevails for all the armies of the Confederacy. It is not, then, a case of mere temporary exigency, like that alluded to in Paragraph II, General Orders, No. 31, repeated in General Orders, No. 144, current series, where the general commanding an army is authorized to impress. I do not think, therefore, that I am the proper authority to command the agents of the Bureau of Subsistence to impress supplies in the manner desired.

---

* Not found.

Again, if the operations of the impressment law, in its full extent, are to be limited to those portions of the Confederacy where armies are situated, it would bear very unequally on the States and the people. Nor will the employment of the impressing power in all its stringency in the regions already harassed and stripped by large armies serve to obtain adequate supplies. I would therefore suggest, if this necessity exists with regard to the supply of our different armies, and if it is impossible to subsist them longer by purchase from the citizens, that it will be better for the Department to give the requisite authority to the agents of the Subsistence Bureau in all the States than for the commander of a particular army to increase the burdens of a country already much exhausted by the continued presence of that army.

I think every effort should be made to render equal the action of the impressment law, and so to fix the proportion of the produce to be taken from each farmer as to make its operations gentle and regular, and not dependent upon the will or caprice of the impressing agent.

If the Department, however, wishes me to issue the order requested by Colonel Northrop, I will do so.

Very respectfully, your obedient servant,

R. E. LEE,
General.

WAR DEPARTMENT, C. S.,
Richmond, Va., November 20, 1863.

General R. E. LEE, *Commanding:*

GENERAL: I am not prepared to command the resort to military impressment recommended to your consideration by the Commissary-General; first, because I do not consider myself warranted in controlling the discretion which is imposed by law on commanders in the field, under circumstances of exigency which can only be fully known to themselves, of relieving their army by the summary process of unlimited impressment; and, secondly, because, while not free from serious anxiety about our future prospects of subsistence, I do not accord with the Commissary-General in the extent or immediate pressure of the dearth of provisions. Colonel Northrop does not seem to have fully explained to you why he made the application in the manner he did, direct to you. The impressment law, as you may have observed, gives the power of impressment to the Department for the purpose of accumulating supplies for the army, but limits it merely to the surplus of production, requiring that a sufficiency for the reasonable support of the holder, his family, or employés should be exempted.

The construction of the Department, in conformity with the spirit if not the letter of this restriction, exempts supplies which may have been purchased, as well as those raised for private consumption, and likewise, to secure provisions for consumers in the cities who are not able to make such permanent provision, allows exemption of products for subsistence *in transitu* to market. This restriction, thus interpreted, in the apprehension of the Commissary-General, with the scant supplies, as he supposes, really existing in the country, renders it impracticable for him to accumulate supplies sufficient for the support of the army.

In casting around for the means of avoiding the effect of this restriction. he finds another clause of the impressment law reposes in commanders in the field the discretion of unlimited impressment when necessity requires, and believing, as he insists, that such necessity is actually existing, 'he wishes what was intended as a power for casual exercise should be brought into general and immediate operation.   Considering that the discretion was reposed by law in the generals commanding to be determined on their convictions of the necessity existing, I have not felt at liberty to prohibit the Commissary General from presenting his view of such necessity and suggesting the exercise of the discretionary power referred to.

At the same time I have declined myself to command, or even recommend to the generals in the field, the general use of the unlimited power of impressment given them by the law.   I do not wonder at the reluctance which is felt by you to the employment of such summary means, and I certainly think they should be foreborne unless upon information possessed by yourself or communicated by officers of the commissariat, who have ampler means of judgment than I can possess, your conviction of the necessity should make it imperative.

Impressment as a mode of supply for the army, even with the restrictions imposed upon the Department, is unequal and odious, and I shall earnestly urge at the approaching session of Congress the expediency of adopting other modes of supply, or of so tempering and regulating this as to make it less harsh and more equal in its operation.

Yours, with esteem,

J. A. SEDDON,
Secretary of War.

HDQRS. ARTY. CORPS, ARMY OF NORTHERN VIRGINIA,
November 20, 1863.

General R. E. LEE,
Commanding, &c.:

GENERAL: In obedience to your instructions I have carefully reconsidered all the recommendations for promotion in the artillery service with this army, availing myself of the matured counsels of General Long, chief of artillery, Second Corps, and Colonel Walker, chief of artillery, Third Corps, and of General Stuart for the batteries serving with the cavalry.   The result I have now the honor to report.

The legitimate armament of batteries actually in the field with the army, including those attached to the First Corps and those with the cavalry, amounts to 276 guns.   At present there is a deficiency of guns in some of the batteries, owing to the fact that Napoleons have not been supplied in sufficient numbers to replace all the 6-pounders and howitzers turned in to be recast, and the additional fact that casualties in action and the wear and tear of service have deprived us at this juncture of some pieces and teams, for the replacing of which arrangements are in progress.   The existing incomplete number thus produced is 244.

As all the elements of our organization, companies, battalions, and corps groups, are based upon the legitimate number expected to be restored as soon as practicable, it is believed to be the proper standard by which to adjust our legal proportion of field officers.   This num-

ber entitles us, under the law, to 3 brigadier-generals, 7 colonels, 11
lieutenant-colonels, and 17 majors. We now have on our rolls 2
brigadier-generals, 6 colonels, 6 lieutenant-colonels, and 17 majors,
viz: W. N. Pendleton and A. L. Long, brigadier-generals; S. Crutch-
field, J. B. Walton, J. T. Brown, H. C. Cabell, R. L. Walker, and
E. P. Alexander, colonels; A. S. Cutts, R. S. Andrews, Thomas H.
Carter, H. P. Jones, W. Nelson, and John J. Garnett, lieutenant-
colonels; Charles Richardson, B. F. Eshleman, S. P. Hamilton, R.
F. Beckham, James Dearing, T. J. Page, jr., W. J. Pegram, D. G.
McIntosh, W. T. Poague, C. M. Braxton, R. A. Hardaway, J. B.
Brockenbrough, John Lane, F. Huger, John C. Haskell, J. P. W.
Read, James Reilly, majors.

Of the colonels, Crutchfield is understood to be so far disabled for
active field service, by the effects of a severe wound received at
Chancellorsville, that it is due equally to the service and to himself
that he be assigned to some position better adapted to his physical
condition. His eminent merit and services deserve reward. General
Jackson desired him to be made brigadier-general of artillery and
to continue in his post of chief of artillery for the Second Corps.
This, by General Jackson's death and his own protracted disability,
seems to be now precluded, but it is hoped a congenial and useful
position may be assigned him in connection with the defense of
Richmond, or with some other department of home defense.

Colonel Walton is also a meritorious officer for whom some other
sphere of duty seems required, in justice to the service and to himself. His junior colonel, Alexander, is believed to be better adapted
to promote the efficiency of the artillery with the First Corps as its
chief, and he must therefore be recommended for promotion to that
position. In this event, however, it is understood Colonel Walton
prefers duty elsewhere, Mobile being mentioned as the locality most
agreeable to him. It is hoped the interests of the service may admit
of his being thus accommodated.

Colonel Cabell is another estimable officer whom it is best to transfer to another position. His worth as a gentleman, his patriotism
as a citizen, and his gallantry as a soldier deserve honorable mention,
but it is believed he could render better service in a command requiring less prompt activity than that he now holds. It is therefore
respectfully recommended that he be transferred, by exchange with
Lieutenant-Colonel Lightfoot, to command the battalion of field artillery at Richmond, now under charge of Lieutenant-Colonel Lightfoot, and that the latter be assigned to the command of the battalion
with this army of which Colonel Cabell has had charge.

Of the lieutenant-colonels, Andrews, a most gallant and distinguished officer, ought, in duty to the cause and to himself, to be relieved from field exposure and employed in less trying service, that
he may recover from the threatening consequences of a dangerous
wound received at Cedar Run, nearly eighteen months ago. He is
admirably adapted to usefulness in the Ordnance Department, and it
is hoped a position therein may be assigned him with an additional
grade. Were it really proper for him to remain in the field, senior-
ity and merit would together place him first on our list of lieutenant-colonels for promotion.

Lieutenant-Colonel Garnett may with advantage to the service be
relieved of his command and assigned to other duty. He has proved
less efficient in the field than was expected of so well trained and
capable a soldier. It is believed he can be more useful on conscript

service than in his present position. Such change for him is therefore respectfully recommended.

Of the majors, Brockenbrough, entitled to praise for extended and good service, is disabled, and will probably long so continue, by the lingering effects of a wound received at Fredericksburg last December. He ought to be relieved of responsible connection with this army and assigned some post of comparatively light duty.

To fill the vacancies thus occurring and others now existing, I respectfully recommend, on the testimonials of other commanders, as well as on my own judgment, the following promotions, viz: Col. E. P. Alexander, to be brigadier-general and chief of artillery, First Corps; Lieutenant-Colonels Carter, Jones, and Cutts, to be colonels; Majors Dearing, Eshleman, Huger, Braxton, Pegram, McIntosh, Poague, Beckham, Hardaway, and Richardson, to be lieutenant-colonels, and Captains Cutshaw, Jordan, Miller, Stribling, Raine, R. C. M. Page, Watson, McGraw, M. Johnson, Ward, Maurin, Moorman, Chew, and Breathed, to be majors.

Our list of assignments will then stand:

FIRST CORPS.

E. P. ALEXANDER, Brigadier-General, and Chief of Artillery.

Lieut. Col. F. Huger, South Carolina.
Major Jordan, Virginia...... } Huger's Battalion.

Lieutenant-Colonel Beckham, Virginia.
Major Read, Georgia......... } Beckham's Battalion.

Lieutenant-Colonel Eshleman, Louisiana.
Major Miller, Louisiana...... } Eshleman's Battalion.

Lieutenant-Colonel Lightfoot, North Carolina.
Major Hamilton, Georgia..... } Lightfoot's Battalion

Major Haskell, South Carolina
Major Reilly, North Carolina. } Haskell's Battalion.

} Col. Jones.

SECOND CORPS.

A. L. LONG, Brigadier-General.

Maj. R. C. M. Page, Virginia.
Major Moorman, Virginia.... } Page's Battalion....

Major Cutshaw, Virginia.....
Major Stribling, Virginia..... } Cutshaw's Battalion.

Lieutenant-Colonel Braxton, Virginia.
Major Raine, Virginia........ } Braxton's Battalion.

} Col. Carter, Virginia.

Lieutenant-Colonel Hardaway, Alabama.
Major Watson, Virginia...... } Hardaway's Battalion.

Lieutenant-Colonel Nelson, Virginia.
Maj. T. J. Page, jr., Virginia. } Nelson's Battalion..

} Col. Brown, Virginia.

THIRD CORPS.

R. L. WALKER, Colonel, and Chief of Artillery.

Lieutenant-Colonel Pegram,
  Virginia. } Pegram's Battalion.
Major McGraw, Maryland....

Lieutenant-Colonel McIntosh,
  South Carolina. } McIntosh's Battalion.
Major Johnson, Virginia.....

Lieutenant-Colonel Poague,
  Maryland. } Poague's Battalion.
Major Ward, Mississippi.....

Lieutenant-Colonel Richardson, Louisiana. } Richardson's Battalion. } Col. Cutts,
Major Maurin, Louisiana....   Georgia.
Colonel Cutts, Georgia....... } Cutts' Battalion.....
Major Lane, Georgia.........

Lieutenant-Colonel Dearing,
  Virginia. } With the cavalry.
Major Chew, Virginia........
Major Breathed, Virginia....

In this schedule will be noticed 2 colonels less and 1 lieutenant-colonel and 3 majors more than the literal legal ratio, an exchange deemed allowable, as 2 colonels are on the numerical scale of the law more than equivalent to a lieutenant-colonel and 3 majors, and these are needed, as the schedule shows, for the best organization.

General Long wishes his battalion grouped as above under Colonels Carter and Brown.

I concur with him in deeming it a good arrangement, and have provided similarly for the two reserve battalions, First Corps, on this line, under Colonel Jones.

The best men are believed to be herein presented in each case; at the same time the fairest distribution practicable is made of promotions in the corps, respectively, and among the several States. From the First Corps, including a brigadier-general, there are 7 promotions; from the Second, 8; from the Third, 9, and from the Horse Artillery, 4.

These promotions are much needed and it is believed they will greatly benefit the artillery service; encouragement to this arm has not been, as it should be, commensurate with that in the others.

Even with the recommendations now submitted, the number of artillery field officers will be only about three-fourths of those belonging to three brigades of cavalry, or infantry having anything like the number of men, companies, &c., constituting the artillery.

I have the honor to be, general, respectfully, your obedient servant,

W. N. PENDLETON,
Brigadier-General, and Chief of Artillery.

ORDNANCE OFFICE,
Dublin Depot, November 21, 1863.

Lieut. Col. W. LE ROY BROWN,
Commanding Arsenal:

COLONEL: In compliance with circular of March 31 and July 8, 1863, from Ordnance Bureau, I have the honor to report the number of troops in this department, as follows :

Infantry.. 8,635
Artillery 908
Cavalry 6,467
                                                                              ———
    Total... 16,010

This is a statement of enlisted men alone.

Respectfully, your obedient servant,
T. M. BOWYER,
Major, Chief Ord. Officer, Dept. W. Va. and East Tenn.

BUREAU OF SUBSISTENCE, C. S. A.,
Richmond, November 22, 1863.

General R. E. LEE, *Commanding:*

GENERAL : Your letter of the 19th instant to the Secretary of War has by him been placed in my hands. Your general views that the application of the impressment laws should be equal, and proportionate to the amount of each man's production and necessities, should be gentle and regular, and not dependent on the caprice or will of the impressing agent, must commend themselves to the mind of every just and reasonable man. Nothing to the contrary was implied in my late communication to you.

You have not appreciated my presentation of the existing state of things, because you have connected its consideration with the principle of Orders Nos. 31 [March 19, 1863] and 144 [November 6, 1863], so far as pertaining to these things, which imply that there is enough in the country for full supply both for the people and army.

As that basis does not exist, no inferential reasoning from these orders are of moment.

There are two classes of impressment, one to meet exigencies of armies in the field, of such character as to make impressments absolutely necessary for its subsistence ; second, when the Secretary of War shall be of opinion, &c. See section 4 of General Orders, No. 37 [April 6, 1863].

The first section overrides all exemptions, and secures the property. The second class is so crippled as to leave the army only the surplus, after everybody has secured one year's supply. This process has been elaborated in Major Noland's letter, and has frequently been set forth to the War Department. There being no surplus, but actual deficiency, and there being no penalty attached to a refusal to hold impressed property, or against selling to another for higher prices, impressments under section No. 4 can accomplish but little. I consider that the exigency contemplated in section No. 1 is really in every army on this side of the Mississippi.

Your proposition that the Secretary of War should issue appropriate directions to the generals commanding is beyond his power, and he has no resource in case of non-acquiescence on the part of the people. Section 1 gives legality to the physical power in the hands of the generals commanding. The troops will be in want before the tithe meat comes in sufficient (if it ever will be) to meet that want.

There exists an urgent difficulty. Last winter I stated to you that this was impending, and the generals in the field alone have the legal and actual power to combat it, and using the organization of this bureau in their respective departments enables them to shift the burden from their immediate proximity and expand it over the whole of their departments respectively.

Furthermore, such action will rouse the nation to a sense of its real condition, brought on or allowed by the timidity of the political leaders in Congress and the Legislatures. The first class appreciated the emergency, but failed to sanction the law by adequate penalties; the second class failed to sustain the principle of the joint appraisement by not fixing maximum prices near those of the joint appraisers; therefore, no holder would exchange his commodities for an inflating, depreciating currency so long as he is not obliged to sell. Permit me to suggest that you re-examine General Orders, No. 37, with the law, and reconsider my proposition, which is of importance.

Very respectfully, your obedient servant,

L. B. NORTHROP,
Commissary-General of Subsistence.

HEADQUARTERS ARMY OF NORTHERN VIRGINIA,
November 23, 1863.

Col. L. B. NORTHROP,
Commissary-General, Richmond, Va..

COLONEL: Your letter of the 17th instant is received. I understand the power of impressment conferred upon commanding generals, to which you refer, to be designed to provide against emergencies and exigencies in the service, such as the case of an army cut off from its base of supplies, and the like. I do not think Congress intended it as a means for accumulating stores for the use of the army, as other provisions were made for that purpose by law.

I am also of opinion that if I possess the power you suppose, its exercise would be attended with evil consequences. It would, of necessity, be partial in its application, and therefore unjust and oppressive. I think that the system of impressment, if we must resort to it, should be by some uniform regulation, applicable not only to all the States, but to every part of each State. I prefer this arrangement to the one proposed by you, conceding that your views as to the meaning of the law are correct.

Very respectfully, your obedient servant,

R. E. LEE,
General.

HEADQUARTERS ARMY OF NORTHERN VIRGINIA,
November 24, 1863.

Brig. Gen. J. D. IMBODEN, *Commanding, &c.:*

GENERAL: Inclosed please find lists,* Nos. 1 and 3, of deserters from this army, serving with your command, furnished by Lieut. Col. Edward Murray, one of the inspectors of this army. Those of

---

* Not found.

list No. 1, you claim as having been enlisted within the enemy's lines, upon the authority considered by you as having been granted in letters, one of May 7, from Hon. George W. Randolph, then Secretary of War, another of December 23, 1862, from General S. Cooper, Adjutant and Inspector General, and Special Orders, No. 251, of October 27, 1862.

The War Department, in extending amnesty to deserters received into other commands, would do so in the shape of an order, both to inform their proper officers of their pardon and its conditions, and to relieve the deserters and officers receiving them from the penalties ordered under the twenty-second Article of War. No such order is on record among files from the Adjutant and Inspector General's Office, nor can it be discovered upon perusal that the letters give authority to enlist deserters. They do authorize you to "recruit all the men you can from counties within the enemy's lines, and also from non-conscripts;" the latter privilege extending to those within and out of our lines; the former to those of conscript age outside of our lines, thus removing the prohibition against such enlistments contained in General Orders, No. 53, Adjutant and Inspector General's Office, of July 31, 1862. As General Orders, No. 43, Adjutant and Inspector General's Office, of June 13, 1862, prohibits the transfer of men from the line to partisan corps, partisan officers knowingly violating the order forfeit authority to raise troops, and deserters belonging to the line come as fully under this prohibition as others, as their connection cannot be severed from original commands excepting by transfer or discharge by proper authority.

In addition to these considerations, policy requires the return of these men. If discovered that desertion into the enemy's lines instead of punishment secures the reception of the offenders into commands serving near their homes, all anxious to serve in such vicinities have but to desert, thus destroying all military organization and discipline.

In view of these facts, the commanding general directs that you cause these men to be turned over, with their descriptive and clothing lists, to the nearest provost-marshal, to be forwarded to their proper companies.

List No. 3 contains names of those claimed by you as having been illegally transferred by General Jackson from the militia. It is presumed these transfers were made under consultation with the Governor and the laws of the State. They were acquiesced in by all but the small number who deserted as either legal or necessary under pressure of the occasion, and were recognized by the Confederate authorities as legal, as General Orders, No. 36, Adjutant and Inspector General's Office, last series, provides for the discharge of all so drafted who were over thirty-five years of age, without embracing those of conscript age. Waiving the question of law, the transfer having been made by an officer high in rank and in the confidence of the State and Confederate Governments, it is not for individual opinion to determine it; but in order that the question may be definitely settled by a proper tribunal, and to prevent the withdrawal from this army of the large number of drafted men who under your claim, if admitted in behalf of these men, would be justified in leaving to join other commands, the commanding general directs that they also be forwarded, in the same manner as those of list No. 1, for trial.

I am, general, very respectfully, your obedient servant,

R. H. CHILTON.

HEADQUARTERS,
November 25, 1863.

His Excellency JEFFERSON DAVIS,
   President Confederate States, Richmond:

Mr. PRESIDENT: I have the honor to send herewith * a letter committed to my care from the office of the Adjutant and Inspector General, received last evening. A scout from Culpeper reported last night that the First Army Corps of General Meade's army, encamped near the court-house, had been provided with eight days' rations and received marching orders, their destination unknown, but their own men reported they were to move forward. A scout from Stafford also reported last night that Gregg's division of cavalry moved from Morrisville yesterday, with two batteries of artillery and a train of wagons, to Ellis' Ford, on the Rappahannock, where they were crossing when he left. They had eight days' rations and inquired the distance to Ely's Ford, on the Rapidan, from which it was presumed that point was their destination. He also heard that the infantry along the railroad was in motion. From these reports and the indications in the Washington papers, I infer that General Meade intends to advance. Pickett's division should be held in readiness and advanced to Hanover Junction if nothing prevents. As far as I can judge, the Federal army greatly exceeds this in numbers, and every precaution should be taken to prevent disaster. I hear of no forces of the enemy south of James River or on the Peninsula. General Butler may project a movement up the Rappahannock to Fredericksburg.

I am, with great respect, your obedient servant,

R. E. LEE,
General.

HEADQUARTERS ARMY OF NORTHERN VIRGINIA,
November 25, 1863.

General J. D. IMBODEN,
   Commanding Valley District, Staunton, Va.:

GENERAL: I have been much gratified by the result of your recent operations, Major White's and Captain McNeill's.

The reports have been forwarded to the War Department, and I beg to tender to you and to the officers and men of each command my high appreciation of their services. Similar success will always attend like efforts. It is only by constant watchfulness and labor that the invasion of the enemy can be prevented.

It is important that you impress upon your scouts the necessity of giving you correct information. I think the strength of the enemy's column is always greatly exaggerated. I need only refer to the number of Averell's troops and the expedition said to have advanced up the Kanawha in this last expedition. Proper dispositions cannot be made to repel these attacks unless the number of the enemy be correctly stated.

From the reports of scouts, I think it probable that the army of General Meade is about to advance from the Rappahannock. Whether it will attempt to cross the Rapidan, there is nothing now to indicate. In the event of its advance, I have thought you might

----

* Not found.

give material aid by sending a force east of the Blue Ridge to aid Major Mosby to break up the railroad north of the Rappahannock and interrupt its communications. Major Gilmor's battalion could at least operate advantageously in that way. I will telegraph you if an advance of General Meade is made.

Very respectfully, your obedient servant,

R. E. LEE,
General.

PETERSBURG, VA., *November 25, 1863—10.*30 p. m.
(Received 26th.)

General S. COOPER,
Adjutant and Inspector General, C. S. Army:

One brigade of my division, Kemper's, at Hanover Junction. Hunton's brigade is at Chaffin's Bluff. Barton's brigade is here. Corse's, in East Tennessee. The only brigade under my immediate command, Barton's, I will hold in readiness to move.

GEO. E. PICKETT,
Major-General.

[Indorsement.]

NOVEMBER 26, 1863.

ADJUTANT-GENERAL:

I had not seen this telegram when I conversed with you just now. One brigade (Barton's) should proceed to Hanover Junction; another should be drawn back from North Carolina to Petersburg.

J. A. S.   [SEDDON,]
Secretary.

NOVEMBER 26, 1863.

General route of wagon train of Second Corps:

Turn off the plank road at Verdierville and go to Antioch Church; thence, via Jacobs' Mills, Richards', Briscoe's, and Parker's, to the Catharpin road. Follow the Catharpin road to Shady Grove Church, then turn to the right and go, via Buchanan's, Pool's, and Waite's, to the new court-house.

The above is the route to be pursued by the baggage trains (all wagons not necessary in an engagement) and the reserve artillery. The trains will move as the progress of the army requires, and when halted will be located at such point as will enable them readily to take roads leading directly to the Fredericksburg plank road or to the Virginia Central Railroad, so that they can at once leave the above routes and move up to the army, or move to the south of the roads above indicated, thereby clearing them.

The brigade ordnance wagons will keep with the troops; the corps reserve ordnance trains will keep with the general reserve ordnance train, under orders of Lieutenant-Colonel Baldwin, chief of ordnance. Chief ordnance officers of the corps will report to him for further instructions.

By command of General Lee:

W. H. TAYLOR,
Assistant Adjutant-General.

* WAR DEPARTMENT, C. S.,
Richmond, Va., November 26, 1863.

Maj. Gen. GEORGE E. PICKETT,
Commanding at Petersburg:

I find your force less than I had supposed. It will not do wholly to uncover Petersburg. Can you not draw some forces from North Carolina to take their place, yet leaving Weldon protected? I suggest your sending such portion of Barton's brigade at Petersburg as you can spare to Hanover Junction at once, retaining the balance until you draw some force from North Carolina. Take care not to interfere with the movements of corn.

J. A. SEDDON,
Secretary of War.

HEADQUARTERS DEPARTMENT OF NORTH CAROLINA,
Petersburg, November 26, 1863.

Hon. JAMES A. SEDDON,
Secretary of War, Richmond, Va.:

SIR: I have the honor to acknowledge the receipt of your telegram of this morning in reference to the sending of a portion of Barton's brigade to Hanover Junction and not leaving Petersburg uncovered. Barton's brigade numbers about 1,200 muskets; therefore it would not do to divide it. Petersburg is not covered by any means against an attack. I have so reported before. All that I could do would be to hold the enemy in check, should they advance in force, till I could get re-enforcements.

The only infantry I have in the department, besides Barton's brigade, is Ransom's brigade, one regiment of which is in Western North Carolina. Please inform me what the emergency is. If I am to take my division into the field, I wish to take the whole division, and not a portion of it, as I did at Gettysburg, and I beg of you not to split it up when going into action. If I am to keep command of this department, do not entirely denude it. I refer you to many of my communications on the subject. If the enemy make an advance on General Lee, the probability is they will make a simultaneous advance on this point and up the river.

Rest assured I will use my utmost endeavors to comply with whatever order I may receive with my whole ability.

I am, general, very respectfully, your obedient servant,

GEO. E. PICKETT,
Major-General, Commanding.

PETERSBURG,
November 26, 1863.

General S. COOPER:

The following dispatch just received:

The French steamer has anchored off Berkley. Colonel Herbert reports enemy re-enforced at Suffolk by two regiments of infantry and three companies of cavalry from Newport News. Pickets do think it is impossible to obtain news of enemy's movements,

GEO. E. PICKETT,
Major-General,

NOVEMBER 27, 1863.

General ELZEY:

Can you not manage to get intelligence through your pickets or scouts?

J. A. SEDDON,
Secretary.

HEADQUARTERS DEPARTMENT OF RICHMOND,
November 28, 1863.

My pickets and scouts on this side are unable to pass through the enemy's lines to obtain information of what is going on in their interior.

Respectfully,

ARNOLD ELZEY,
Major-General.

NOVEMBER 30, 1863.

Noted.   They should make every effort and be on the alert.

J. A. SEDDON,
Secretary.

FORT BOYKIN,
Isle of Wight County, Va., November 26, 1863.

Hon. JAMES A. SEDDON,
Secretary of War, Richmond, Va.:

HONORABLE SIR: I herewith send you a file of Heralds, from the 12th to the 20th instant. They contain much news of interest as to the general bearing of affairs at the North which may be of interest to you. I send the papers as received regularly to General Elzey, and all other news of interest, &c.

You will perceive that the Herald of the 17th instant contains an editorial upon a project freely discussed by the officers about Old Point, viz, advancing by the south side from a point above City Point. Bermuda Hundred, opposite Shirley, is spoken of as the place they purpose landing in order to flank Drewry's Bluff and cut off Petersburg. We have the means of knowing their conversation, and it is faithfully and regularly reported to us.

The enemy on Saturday last sent two regiments of infantry and three companies of cavalry from Newport News by transport up the Nansemond River, to re-enforce their troops in the vicinity of Suffolk. I would respectfully state that this line of communication of theirs could be easily stopped, and effectively, by a few torpedoes judiciously distributed by those competent to set them. They should be so arranged as to go off by concussion; none other would do on account of the width of the river at the place where they should be set to prove effective. General Pickett approves of this plan, and has applied for the means to accomplish his purpose.

Butler is enrolling everything in shape of men, black and white. I would respectfully ask to be officially informed if it is General

Butler's purpose to put to death our scouts caught within his lines, uniformed as soldiers of the Confederacy. My scouts are everywhere in this locality, often visiting Norfolk, Old Point, and Yorktown. Such a threat I deem against the laws of Christian warfare, and not sustained by the laws of war or nations. Would it be intruding too much upon your kindness to have the inquiries made through the proper official channel, that I may govern myself accordingly?

It is more than probable from their own talk that they will advance by the peninsula to a point opposite their intended landing on the south side in order that they be mutually supported by their gunboats.

Their talk gives evidence of a deeply laid plan by Foster to capture Richmond, or at least Petersburg, and these officers do not hesitate to say had Foster remained, he would at least have attempted it.

It has become particularly hazardous to land on the north side of the James within their lines, owing to the fact of deserters and other evil-disposed persons giving them information of our line of communication. My scouts are active and vigilant, and I most truly hope, with proper prudence, to be able to keep this communication open.

Respectfully, your obedient servant,
J. F. MILLIGAN,
Major, &c.

RICHMOND,
November 27, 1863.

Major-General PICKETT,
Petersburg:

Send Barton's brigade to Hanover Junction, as first directed to-day, and bring forward Ransom's brigade, as also instructed this morning. Arrangements will be made to replace.
S. COOPER,
Assistant and Inspector General.

PETERSBURG,
November 27, 1863.

General S. COOPER:

Barton's brigade leaves here at 5 a. m. to-morrow for Richmond; transportation should be ready there to take it to Hanover Junction. I have ordered Ransom to concentrate at Weldon, leaving two companies at Kinston and two at Hamilton. Should General Whiting be ordered to send some of his forces to Goldsborough or some other point on the railroad, then I could bring Ransom or a portion of his brigade to Petersburg, which is now entirely uncovered. Please send an order to the regiment of Ransom, in Western North Carolina, to return, or let Whiting relieve it. I have ordered Seventeenth Virginia to be ready to move up from Blackwater.
GEO. E. PICKETT,
Major-General, Commanding.

Abstract from field return of the troops commanded by Maj. Gen. George E. Pickett, C. S. Army, November 27, 1863.

Command.	Present for duty.		Aggregate present.	Aggregate present and absent.	Remarks.
	Officers.	Men.			
General headquarters *a*	17	166	198	217	
Barton's brigade	76	1,280	1,549	3,115	Near Petersburg.
Ransom's brigade	132	2,324	2,603	3,392	Goldsborough and Weldon.
Confederate Zouaves	19	43	62	9	Franklin Station.
10th Georgia Battalion	15	278	343	466	Do.
Whitford's North Carolina battalion.	30	600	688	812	
17th Virginia	29	214	274	477	Ivor Station.
18th Virginia	11	223	278	573	Petersburg.
Provost guard at Kinston	4	54	65	98	
Total infantry	309	5,016	5,862	9,022	
7th Confederate Cavalry	18	197	309	638	Ivor Station.
62d Georgia Cavalry	35	498	621	835	Franklin Depot.
3d North Carolina Cavalry	32	589	733	971	Near Weldon.
Total cavalry	85	1,284	1,663	2,444	
Branch's artillery command	48	387	1,164	1,451	Near Petersburg. *b*
Dearing's battalion	14	266	313	404	Do.
Washington (La.) Artillery	17	310	359	480	Do.
1st North Carolina Artillery (three companies).	12	211	275	373	Near Goldsborough.
3d North Carolina Artillery, Company F.	4	70	85	98	
Andrews' battery	2	59	72	92	
Cumming's battery	3	69	83	95	
Dickson's battery	1	102	126	137	
Starr's battery	4	126	137	156	
Total artillery	100	2,200	2,614	3,286	
Grand total	511	8,666	10,337	14,969	

a Including "Independent Signal Corps."   *b* Two batteries at Weldon.

HDQRS. DEPT. OF WESTERN VA. AND EAST TENN.,
Dublin, November 28, 1863.

Hon. A. T. CAPERTON:

SIR: I received yesterday your letter of the 26th. I am fully aware of the importance of having additional troops in my department, and especially of having an adequate force to prevent the enemy from penetrating into Botetourt and Rockbridge. I have repeatedly asked for re-enforcements, and shall do so again whenever I think that there is the slightest possibility that they can be procured. At present I regret to say that I can get none.

For reasons not necessary now to mention, I cannot send any more of my own troops to Greenbrier. At this late season of the year I do not think the enemy will move into Greenbrier for the purpose of occupying the county, and I hope and believe that we can prevent any raiding party from penetrating into Rockbridge and Botetourt.

I shall be glad if you will ascertain and inform me what cavalry committed the depredations you mention on your own property and that at the Red Sweet Springs, that I may have reparation made and the officers commanding punished.

SAM. JONES,
Major-General.

HDQRS. DEPT. OF WESTERN VA. AND EAST TENN.,
Dublin, November 28, 1863.

Brig. Gen. JOHN ECHOLS:

Your note of the 26th instant has been received. It is impossible to send you re-enforcements at present. Colonels Ferguson and Jackson have been directed to receive and obey orders from you, and to report through you to these headquarters.

If the offensive move you contemplate should be made from the Kanawha, you must not make a stand at Lewisburg, but fall back with your infantry and artillery and take position south of Greenbrier River at or near the burned bridge, leaving your cavalry to skirmish with the enemy in front of Lewisburg, and, if too heavily pressed, to fall back and join you at the bridge. Meanwhile use every exertion to effectually blockade the road by Alderson's Ferry and any other road by which the enemy can turn your left and penetrate into Monroe. For their own protection the people of Monroe should furnish you the labor needed for this work. If they will do this (and your influence will accomplish it if it can be accomplished at all), the roads can be so obstructed as to delay the enemy a day or so, should he attempt to come in on your left. At this late season I do not think the enemy will enter Greenbrier for the purpose of permanent occupation. They cannot subsist their troops in that country, and before they can draw supplies from the Kanawha the roads will probably be too bad for them to rely on the chances of subsistence from that direction.

Should the enemy move on you now, it will be for the purpose of cutting up and dispersing your command.

Their late raid shows how reluctantly they venture far into the country. By keeping your troops well in hand in a strong position near the burned bridge, and obstructing the roads already mentioned, should the enemy move with the purpose of penetrating farther than Lewisburg, he will have to fight you in a strong position where, unless my information is at fault, you can resist any force they can send from the Kanawha. Should they attempt to turn your left, the obstructions should delay them long enough to enable you to take a new position, if necessary.

Should they attempt to move by Covington, they would have to make a *détour* by way of Frankford and come down the Antony's Creek road (for they would hardly pass directly by your front, exposing both flanks and rear). If they attempt such a thing, you can move by a much shorter line and stop them between Dry Creek and Callaghan's.

SAM. JONES,
Major-General.

NOVEMBER 28, 1863.

Col. GEORGE JACKSON, *Commanding at Magnolia, Kenansville:*

You will proceed immediately to Kinston, N. C., and assume command. The Fiftieth North Carolina Infantry has gone on this morning, with orders to report to you at Kinston. Turn over your command at Kenansville to the next in rank. Instructions will be sent you by mail.

By command of Major-General Whiting:

T. B. VENABLE,
Major, and Assistant Adjutant-General.

SPECIAL ORDERS, }   ADJT. AND INSP. GENERAL'S OFFICE,
No. 283.   }   *Richmond, November* 28, 1863.

*   *   *   *   *   *   *

XIII. Brigadier-General Clingman will proceed with his brigade without delay to North Carolina and replace Brigadier-General Ransom's brigade at Goldsborough and Weldon. The latter brigade, on being relieved, will proceed to Petersburg, Va., and report to Major-General Pickett.

Brigadier-General Barton will forthwith proceed with his brigade to Hanover Junction, and hold himself subject to the orders of General Lee.

*   *   *   *   *

By command of the Secretary of War:

JNO. WITHERS,
Assistant Adjutant-General.

HEADQUARTERS ARMY OF NORTHERN VIRGINIA,
November 29, 1863.

His Excellency JEFFERSON DAVIS,
President Confederate States, Richmond, Va.:

MR. PRESIDENT: I have the honor to acknowledge the receipt of your letter of the 25th instant, inclosing one from General Bragg.

The enemy is in force in my front and I shall necessarily be brief, but will give you the substance of the views which have suggested themselves to me, after much previous reflection, on the subjects referred to by General Bragg.

1. I think it a matter of the first importance that our armies now in the field shall be retained in service and recruited by wise and effectual legislation. This cannot be done too soon. The law should not be open to the charge of partiality, and I do not know how this can be accomplished without embracing the whole population capable of bearing arms, with the most limited exemptions, avoiding anything that would look like a distinction of classes. The exemptions of persons of particular and necessary avocations had better be made as far as possible by authority of the Department rather than by special enactment.

I think the general exemption of such persons by law is open to much abuse, and many escape service under color of them who are only nominally within the provisions of the law, and who can be taken into service without prejudice to the necessary productions of the country.

I also am of opinion that the skeleton regiments should be consolidated under the authority of the Department when necessary, and the provision should extend to all arms of the service. If possible, some prospective bounty should be provided for the men who have been and will be again retained in service. As to the imperative necessity for retaining them, and adding sufficiently to their numbers to enable them to cope with the enemy, there can be no doubt, and all the constitutional power of Congress should be fully exerted for this purpose.

2. With reference to mounting the cavalry on government horses, I should be glad if it could be accomplished, but do not see how the

horses could be procured. It is difficult now to meet the wants of our artillery and transportation. But I think the law should invest the Government with complete authority for the time being over every horse mustered into the service, and authorize the use of them in such manner as will most promote the public interests, providing at the same time proper compensation for the owners should it be found necessary to deprive them of the use of their horses. A cavalry soldier cannot perform the terms of his enlistment without a horse, and the Government should be able to control the horse on this ground and to this extent at least.

I fully concur in what General Bragg says with reference to depredations, whether committed by cavalry or any other part of the army. Any legislation that can repress this evil would be most beneficial.

3. I am not in favor of increasing the pay of any officer, but think it would be well to allow rations and clothing to company officers and their servants (such as they may lawfully have), and to other officers of like rank and pay with company officers. I see no necessity to extend the law to officers of a higher rank.

4. I think that the evil of officers and men absenting themselves without leave should be provided against as far as practicable by legislation. The ordinary mode of punishing by court-martial does not effectually check it, and I do not think General Bragg exaggerates the extent of the practice. In the case of officers, I think the law should vacate their commissions by its own operation and subject them to conscription.

5. In this connection, I would call your attention to the evils that flow from the absence of officers permanently disabled. Regiments are frequently commanded by captains, from this cause, companies by sergeants, and sometimes brigades by majors and lieutenant-colonels. Many officers are borne on the rolls who are unfit for service. It would be hard to drop them, and yet they prevent the promotion of other officers and interfere with the efficiency of their commands.

I would suggest the establishment of an invalid corps, to which such officers might be transferred, retaining their rank and pay. This corps might be made useful in many ways and relieve troops fit for field service.

6. I concur in the remarks of General Bragg in reference to the rank of the chief staff officer of our armies and those of the personal staff of commanding generals. The number and rank of the latter should correspond with their duties. These officers have no opportunity of promotion, and their importance is not overestimated by General Bragg.

7. If any change in our hospital system can diminish the vice of absence without leave, I think it should be made. I do not know the particular features of the system to which General Bragg refers.

I herewith return General Bragg's letter,* as you request.

I think it very important in providing for the personal staff, which should be adequate to the wants of the officer with whom they serve, that he should be strictly confined to the staff allowed by law.

Very respectfully, your obedient servant,

R. E. LEE,
General.

---

* Not found.

HDQRS. DEPT. OF WESTERN VA. AND EAST TENN.,
Dublin, November 29, 1863.

Col. M. J. FERGUSON,
 Commanding, &c.
 (Care Brigadier-General Echols, Lewisburg):

Receive and obey all orders from Brigadier-General Echols.
By order, &c.:

    CHAS. S. STRINGFELLOW,
     Assistant Adjutant-General.

OPERATOR:

Send the same message, same direction, to Col. William L. Jackson.

DUBLIN,
November 29, 1863.

Col. B. H. JONES,
 Commanding Fourth Brigade:

Put your command in readiness to move without delay. Enemy advancing on General Echols again.
By order, &c.:

    CHAS. S. STRINGFELLOW,
     Assistant Adjutant-General.

HDQRS. DEPT. OF WESTERN VA. AND EAST TENN.,
Dublin, November 29, 1863.

Col. JOHN MCCAUSLAND,
 Commanding, &c.:

COLONEL: The enemy reported to be again advancing on General Echols.

I am directed by the major-general commanding to say that you must proceed to your command, without delaying on the road. It will be in readiness to move as soon as possible. Orders will be sent by telegram.
 Very respectfully,

    CHAS. S. STRINGFELLOW,
     Assistant Adjutant-General.

HDQRS. DEPT. OF WESTERN VA. AND EAST TENN.,
Dublin, November 29, 1863.

Col. JOHN MCCAUSLAND,
 Commanding, &c., Narrows:

Leave a guard at the Narrows, and proceed with the rest of your command to Lewisburg, without delay, to re-enforce General Echols.
By order, &c.:

    CHAS. S. STRINGFELLOW,
     Assistant Adjutant-General.

HDQRS. DEPT. OF WESTERN VA. AND EAST TENN.,
Dublin, November 29, 1863.

Brigadier-General ECHOLS, *Lewisburg:*

Col. John McCausland has been ordered to re-enforce you immediately with his command. If the enemy advance in force, fall back to the burned bridge. Do not attempt to hold Lewisburg. Colonels Jackson and Ferguson have been placed under your command. I send telegrams for them to your care. Sent you written directions yesterday by mail. Orders to Colonels Jackson and Ferguson similar to telegrams of to-day.

By order, &c. :

CHAS. S. STRINGFELLOW,
Assistant Adjutant-General.

PETERSBURG, *November 29, 1863.*

General S. COOPER,
Adjutant and Inspector General:

Following dispatch just received :

Colonel Herring [?] reports that, on the 26th, 200 Yankee cavalry surprised and captured 20 men of Whitford's battalion, State forces, at Huddock's Cross-roads, below Greenville. Yankee deserters report Butler at New Berne. On Friday, our cavalry drove the Yankees back to Washington. Thirty-fifth North Carolina will leave for Petersburg to-day at 12 m. If there is no need for them at Petersburg, I suggest the propriety of keeping the Twenty-fourth North Carolina at Tarborough until Clingman's brigade relieves it. There might be a dash on that point of the line. There is railroad to Tarborough, and the regiment can be carried from there directly to you. The presence of Butler at New Berne and the affair with Whitford's pickets make me apprehend it.

M. W. RANSOM,
Brigadier-General.

I have ordered the Twenty-fourth North Carolina to remain until Clingman arrives.

GEO. E. PICKETT,
Major-General, Commanding.

Abstract from return of the Department of Richmond, Maj. Gen. Arnold Elzey, C. S. Army, commanding, November 30, 1863.

Command.	Present for duty.		Effective total.	Aggregate present.	Aggregate present and absent.	Pieces of field artillery.
	Officers.	Men.				
Department headquarters	10	......	......	10	11	......
Hunton's brigade (Chaffin's Farm)	92	1,118	1,105	1,417	2,581	......
1st Maryland (Col. B. T. Johnson)	23	253	253	319	511	......
Cavalry *a*	49	803	825	1,232	1,787	......
Chaffin's Farm (Stark)	12	220	216	277	310	10
Chaffin's Bluff (Maury)	10	322	414	475	576	18
Drewry's Bluff (Smith)	18	331	302	447	502	12
Baltimore Artillery (Griffin)	4	58	58	73	100	3
Richmond defenses (Stevens)	89	1,619	1,795	2,073	2,220	14
Total	316	4,784	5,058	6,323	8,598	57

a The 1st Maryland Battalion, Holcombe Legion, and 42d Virginia Battalion.

Abstract from return of the District of Cape Fear and Defenses of Wilmington, Maj. Gen. W. H. C. Whiting, C. S. Army, commanding, November 30, 1863; headquarters Wilmington, N. C.

Command.	Present for duty.		Effective total.	Aggregate present.	Aggregate present and absent.	Pieces of artillery.	
	Officers.	Men.				Heavy.	Field.
General headquarters	14	3	3	17	21		
Engineer troops	2	82	84	92	99		
Signal corps	2	33	33	39	55		
Martin's brigade	102	1,931	2,035	2,338	3,968		
61st North Carolina (two companies)	8	108	112	124	150		
Cavalry	18	358	390	427	546		
Light artillery	26	591	61ɔ	672	744		29
Heavy artillery	106	1,952	2,558	2,960	3,678	139	
Total	278	5,053	5,830	6,669	9,261	139	29

Abstract from return of the Army of Western Virginia and East Tennessee, Maj. Gen. Samuel Jones, C. S. Army, commanding, November 30, 1863; headquarters Dublin Depot, Va.

Command.	Present for duty.		Effective total.	Aggregate present.	Aggregate present and absent.	Aggregate last return.	Pieces of field artillery.
	Officers.	Men.					
General staff a	21			21	21	21	
Ransom's division:							
Staff	6			6	7	7	
Corse's brigade, infantry	83	1,062	1,062	1,291	1,824	1,817	
Wharton's brigade, infantry	58	900	900	1,055	1,383	1,438	
Jackson's brigade, infantry	51	312	312	421	1,012	1,049	
Jones' brigade, cavalry b	133	1,913	1,913	2,253	3,474	2,644	
Williams' brigade, cavalry	125	1,197	1,197	1,496	2,575	2,610	
King's battalion, artillery c	25	459	459	527	693	566	24
Total	481	5,873	5,873	7,049	10,968	10,131	24
Echols' brigade:							
Infantry	109	1,395	1,395	1,675	2,313	2,416	
Chapman's battery	5	100	100	114	152	151	
Jackson's horse artillery	4	45	45	51	67	68	
McCausland's brigade:							
Infantry d	77	1,294	1,294	1,420	1,682	1,686	
17th Virginia Cavalry	(e)	(e)	295	380	565	511	
Bryan's battery	3	117	117	131	158	169	6
Troops at Saltville, infantry f	43	623	623	709	893	897	
Jenkins' brigade, cavalry g							
W. L. Jackson's brigade, cavalry	92	777	777	938	1,611	1,598	
Lurty's battery	5	43	43	48	77	77	
Company of engineer troops	2	54	54	56	73	70	
Total	340	4,378	4,673	5,522	7,591	7,633	6
Grand total	842	10,251	10,546	12,592	18,580	17,785	30

a Dublin, Va.
b 21st Virginia Cavalry, aggregating 794, not on return of October 31.
c McClung's battery, aggregating 53, and Burroughs' battery, aggregating 78, not on last return.
d 60th Regiment included in this brigade.
e Not given.
f 45th Virginia detached at Saltville.   Two partisan companies, aggregating 191, not on last return.
g No reports received from 14th and 16th Regiments for November.

DUBLIN,
December 1, 1863.

Brig. Gen. JOHN S. WILLIAMS:
     Abingdon:
General Jones is in front. I do not know whether he will be here
on Thursday.

CHAS. S. STRINGFELLOW,
Assistant Adjutant-General.

ORANGE COURT-HOUSE,
December 2, 1863.

General S. COOPER,
     Adjutant and Inspector General:
Barton with two brigades has been ordered to Louisa Court-
House.

R. E. LEE.

ORANGE COURT-HOUSE,
December 2, 1863.

General S. COOPER,
     Adjutant and Inspector General:
The order for movement of two brigades from Hanover Junction
has been countermanded.

R. E. LEE,
General.

HEADQUARTERS ARMY,
Parker's Store, December 2, 1863—12 m.

General EARLY:
GENERAL : General Lee directs me to say that the head of Anderson's column has reached this point, and has been halted. General
Stuart writes from the intersection of the Brock and plank roads
that the enemy turned off at that point, taking the Brock road to
the left toward Ely's Ford. When you are satisfied that the enemy
have crossed the river and are too far in advance for you to overtake them, you will halt and send word back to Johnson to go on to
Morton's Ford.
     Respectfully,

W. H. TAYLOR,
Assistant Adjutant-General.

HEADQUARTERS ARMY OF NORTHERN VIRGINIA,
December 3, 1863.

His Excellency JEFFERSON DAVIS,
     President Confederate States, Richmond:
MR. PRESIDENT : I have considered with some anxiety the condition of affairs in Georgia and Tennessee. My knowledge of events
has been principally derived from the public papers, and the impres-

sions I have received may be erroneous, but there appears to me to be grounds to apprehend that the enemy may penetrate Georgia and get possession of our depots of provisions and important manufactories. I see it stated that General Bragg has been relieved from command, and that General Hardee has been relieved from command, and that General Hardee is only acting until another commander shall be assigned to that army. I know the difficulties that surround this subject, but if General Beauregard is considered suitable for the position, I think he can be replaced at Charleston by General Gilmer. More force, in my opinion, is required in Georgia, and it can only be had, so far as I know, from Mississippi, Mobile, and the Department of South Carolina, Georgia, and Florida. The occupation of Cleveland by the enemy cuts off General Longstreet from his base, and unless he succeeds quickly in defeating General Burnside, he will have to retire either into Virginia or North Carolina. I see no reason why General Sam. Jones should not be ordered to advance to his support, or at least to divert the attention of the column that is said to be moving on Charleston, Tenn.

I have ventured to trouble Your Excellency with these suggestions, as I know how much your attention is occupied with the general affairs of the country, especially as the session of Congress approaches. I think that every effort should be made to concentrate as large a force as possible, under the best commander, to insure the discomfiture of Grant's army. To do this and gain the great advantage that would accrue from it, the safety of points practically less important than those endangered by his army must be hazarded. Upon the defense of the country threatened by General Grant depends the safety of the points now held by us on the Atlantic, and they are in as great danger from his successful advance as by the attacks to which they are at present directly subjected.

Very respectfully, your obedient servant,

R. E. LEE,
General.

ORANGE COURT-HOUSE,
December 4, 1863.

General S. COOPER,
  Adjutant and Inspector General:

Pickett's brigades can return to their former positions when required.

R. E. LEE.

HEADQUARTERS SECOND ARMY CORPS,
December 4, 1863.

In turning over the command of the corps to its proper commander, Major-General Early takes occasion to express to the officers and men of the entire corps his high appreciation of their good conduct during the recent operations. The cheerful spirit with which the men have endured unusual hardships, and the zeal with which they have met all demands upon them for work and vigilance, are deserving of the highest praise.

To Major-General Johnson and his division great credit is due for the spirited manner in which they met and repulsed the column of the enemy which was endeavoring to get in their rear, on the afternoon of the 27th ultimo.

The spirit manifested by all would have insured a signal victory to our arms had not the exceeding caution of the enemy caused him to withdraw from the contest which he at one time appeared to court.

J. A. EARLY,
Major-General.

PETERSBURG,
December 4, 1863.

General S. COOPER,
Adjutant and Inspector General:

The following dispatch received from General Ransom:

The raiders, who doubtless were a small party, I think have gone back to New Berne. Nothing new.

GEO. E. PICKETT,
Major-General, Commanding.

PETERSBURG,
December 4, 1863.

General S. COOPER,
Adjutant and Inspector General:

The enemy was reported yesterday as making a raid with 1,000 and upward of cavalry toward Tarborough. I ordered Ransom, with a regiment, to Rocky Mount, and to stop some of Clingman's troops so as to cover the railroad. The following is the latest dispatch:

ROCKY MOUNT, *December* 3.

I am here. Met Clingman at Enfield *en route* to Weldon. Shall stop some of his forces here until all danger is over. So far have heard of no damage. I do not think the enemy has advanced above Greenville.

M. W. RANSOM,
Brigadier-General.

GEO. E. PICKETT,
Major-General, Commanding.

SPECIAL ORDERS,	HDQRS. DEPARTMENT OF TENNESSEE,
No. 62.	*Dalton, Ga., December* 4, 1863.

I. Brig. Gen. R. B. Vance is assigned to the command of the Western District of North Carolina. His headquarters will be at Asheville, N. C.

II. Col. J. B. Palmer, Fifty-eighth North Carolina Regiment, is relieved from the command of the Western District of North Carolina and will report to Brigadier-General Vance for instructions.

*   *   *   *   *   *   *

By command of Lieutenant-General Hardee:

GEORGE WM. BRENT,
Assistant Adjutant-General.

RICHMOND,
December 5, 1863.

General R. E. LEE,
Orange Court-House:

Could you consistently go to Dalton, as heretofore explained?
JEFFERSON DAVIS.

RICHMOND,
December 5, 1863.

General R. E. LEE,
Orange Court-House:

The following dispatch has just been sent to commanding officer at Hanover Junction:

Send Hunton's brigade immediately to relieve the local troops at Chaffin's Farm.

S. COOPER,
Adjutant and Inspector General.

SPECIAL ORDERS, }   ADJT. AND INSP. GENERAL'S OFFICE,
No. 289.   }   *Richmond, Va., December 5, 1863.*

*   .   *   *   *   *   *   *

VI. Brig. Gen. R. B. Vance will proceed with his command to Knoxville, Tenn., and report to Lieut. Gen. J. Longstreet, commanding, &c., for duty.

*   *   *   *   *   *   *

By command of the Secretary of War:

JNO. WITHERS,
Assistant Adjutant-General.

HEADQUARTERS ARMY OF NORTHERN VIRGINIA,
Rapidan, December 7, 1863.

His Excellency JEFFERSON DAVIS,
President Confederate States, Richmond:

MR. PRESIDENT: I have had the honor to receive your dispatch, inquiring whether I could go to Dalton. I can if desired, but of the expediency of the measure you can judge better than I can. Unless it is intended that I should take permanent command, I can see no good that will result, even if in that event any could be accomplished. I also fear that I would not receive cordial co-operation, and I think it necessary if I am withdrawn from here that a commander for this army be sent to it. General Ewell's condition, I fear, is too feeble to undergo the fatigue and labor incident to the position. I hope Your Excellency will not suppose that I am offering any obstacles to any measure you may think necessary. I only seek to give you the opportunity to form your opinion after a full consideration of the subject. I have not that confidence either in my strength or ability as would lead me of my own option to undertake the command in question.

I am, with great respect, your obedient servant,

R. E. LEE,
General.

HEADQUARTERS ARMY OF NORTHERN VIRGINIA,
December 7, 1863.

Col. L. B. NORTHROP,
Commissary-General, C. S. Army, Richmond, Va.:

COLONEL: I have considered your letter of the 22d ultimo, and am unable to take the view entertained by you of my powers under the impressment act. I have not time to state the reasons that govern me more fully than was done in my former letter. The power that you desire rests, in my opinion, with the War Department; was intended by Congress to be exercised by the Department excepting in casual emergencies provided for, and can be more uniformly and judiciously exerted than by the commanders of the armies.

I regret to learn that the necessity for impressment by commanders of armies has, in your opinion, arrived. I shall endeavor to collect all the supplies for this army that I can legitimately do, and keep it in the best condition I can. But unless it is supplied with food, it will be impossible for me to keep it together.

I am, with great respect, your obedient servant,
R. E. LEE,
General.

[Indorsements.]

OFFICE COMMISSARY-GENERAL OF SUBSISTENCE,
December 9, 1863.

Respectfully referred to the Secretary of War.

The power of meeting the present crisis, as far as is possible, rests somewhere, because that necessity is absolute which has no law to limit it.

L. B. NORTHOP,
Commissary-General.

I know, as an officer, no greater necessity than to obey the law.
J. A. S.   [SEDDON,]
Secretary.

HEADQUARTERS HAMPTON'S DIVISION,
December 7, 1863.

General R. E. LEE,
Commanding, &c.:

GENERAL: I have the honor to submit the following suggestions, which are prompted by an earnest desire to place my command in the best condition before the opening of the spring campaign:

Two of the brigades of my division are composed of troops from the two Carolinas, Georgia, Alabama, and Mississippi. Owing to the great distance they are from home, the men in these brigades find great difficulty in keeping themselves well mounted, and horses have reached such prices that I greatly fear many of my best men will be forced to go into the infantry. If these two brigades can be spared this winter, I advise that they be sent to the Roanoke River, near Weldon, where forage is abundant, and where they will have an opportunity not only of procuring fresh horses, but of doing good service by protecting a very valuable portion of our country. The North Carolina brigade could be largely augmented if it was allowed to winter in its own State, and I feel sure that the other brigades would also be increased in numbers. I recommend that

Rosser's brigade be sent to the valley, where they can be of eminent service, and where they can take good care of their horses.

In Butler's brigade there are two battalions—the Jeff. Davis and the Phillips Legions—each consisting of six companies. I advise that Millen's battalion of four companies from Georgia be added to the former, and that four additional companies from the same State be ordered on to join the latter, so that both can be increased to regiments. Anderson's regiment from Georgia desires to come on, and if it was ordered here a brigade could be formed for General Young. Two regiments from South Carolina could well be spared to add to Butler's brigade. There are four full regiments, numbering each from 1,000 to 1,350 men, I am told, in South Carolina, besides several independent companies and battalions. Men could be detached from these plethoric regiments to fill up the depleted companies in the First and Second South Carolina now here.

Five new companies have just been raised in my State, and they are to be disbanded, I am informed. If this is the case they might be ordered on, and the men comprising them assigned to the regiments just named. By these means, Butler's, Young's, and Gordon's could each have a full brigade ready for the spring campaign. But if the horses are kept here this winter on short forage, these brigades will not be in condition for active service, nor will they ever be able to fill up their ranks.

If my division is disposed of for the winter as I have suggested, I respectfully ask to be transferred for the time during which my command is recruiting to Mississippi. General Johnston has done me the honor to ask that I might be sent there, and it would give me great pleasure to join him. I hope that my acquaintance with that country would enable me to be of service there, and I could thus be on active duty while my command was recruiting.

I am, very respectfully, yours,

WADE HAMPTON,
Major-General.

SPECIAL ORDERS, }   HDQRS. ARTILLERY CORPS, A. N. VA.,
No. —.   }   *December 7, 1863.*

Maj. John Page and Lieuts. George W. Peterkin and E. P. Dandridge are hereby detailed on special duty of examining into and reporting upon the forage facilities in the district of country between the Virginia Central Railroad and James River, for a short distance west of Charlottesville to a line not far east of Beaver Dam Depot; Major Page to examine the district east of a line joining Louisa Court-House and Goochland Court-House, and to extend his inquiries into a corresponding district north of the Virginia Central Railroad; Lieutenant Dandridge to explore the region between the line bounding Major Page's district and a line joining Lindsay's Turnout and Columbia, and Major Wolffe to examine the country indicated west of Lieutenant Dandridge's line, the object of this examination being to provide support for our army animals during the winter.

The officers thus detailed will include in their inquiries all questions pertaining to that object. the supply of straw as well as corn, oats, hay, and fodder, and the number and kind of mills for grinding grain to be used as chop feed; also good camping ground. It is supposed that, by availing themselves of information to be derived .

from intelligent citizens, these officers may accomplish the duty assigned and have in their reports at the end of four days; that is, by
Thursday evening, 10th instant.

W. N. PENDLETON,
Brigadier-General, and Chief of Artillery.

HDQRS. ENGINEER DEPT., DEPT. OF NORTHERN VA.,
Richmond, December 8, 1863.

Lieut. Col. S. G. WILLIAMS,
  Commissary-General's Office:

COLONEL : There is an engineer regiment near this city, commanded by Colonel Talcott, numbering some 250. The regiment is
under the directions of the Engineer Bureau, and as by regulations
road repairing is a part of their duties, I respectfully recommend
that you see the Chief of the Engineer Bureau, who, no doubt, will
order that the regiment repair the Mechanicsville road at once.

Very respectfully, your obedient servant,

W. H. STEVENS,
Colonel of Engineers.

[First indorsement.]

RICHMOND, VA.,
December 9, 1863.

Respectfully referred to Chief of Engineer Bureau, with the request that the work may be done as soon as possible.

Inclosed herewith is a copy of an indorsement on the letter of
Captain Wilson with regard to this matter.

L. B. NORTHROP,
Commissary-General of Subsistence.

[Inclosure.]

OFFICE COMMISSARY-GENERAL OF SUBSISTENCE,
December 5, 1863.

Respectfully referred to honorable Secretary of War, with the request that he will order Colonel Stevens, commanding Richmond
defenses and engineers, to at once use a portion of the forces (negro
laborers) under his control to repair this road, particularly that
portion between Mechanicsville and the outer line of fortifications.
The Quartermaster-General has been consulted, and, as he also receives large amounts of corn over this road, he cordially unites in
the above request.

L. B. NORTHROP,
Commissary-General of Subsistence.

[Second indorsement.]

ENGINEER BUREAU,
December 11, 1863.

Respectfully returned to the Commissary-General.

After consultation with the honorable Secretary of War, the recommendation of Colonel Stevens is not approved, for the following
reasons : The engineer troops, now numbering but little if any over
150 effective men, are in camp being drilled and organized. If they
are taken from their camp to be employed on road repairs in the
vicinity of this city, they will become mere "navvies," not engineer
troops, without pride or drill to make them efficient in difficult and

trying circumstances. Moreover, their officers would strongly object to such duty being assigned them. It is only in the field and on the march that such duties fall to them in the judgment of this bureau.

ALFRED L. RIVES,
Lieutenant-Colonel, and Acting Chief of Bureau.

[Third indorsement.]

Troops should hold all useful service honorable, but further leave for drill and organization is desirable.

J. A. S. [SEDDON.]

[Fourth indorsement.]

OFFICE COMMISSARY-GENERAL OF SUBSISTENCE,
Richmond, Va., December 12, 1863.

Respectfully returned to Secretary of War, with the renewal of the request that Colonel Stevens be directed to use a portion of the negro force under his control for the purpose of repairing the road in question. The importance of the work is daily enhanced as the season advances.

It is expected that large supplies of subsistence and quartermaster's supplies will have to be hauled over that road, and serious inconvenience will be felt not only by the army, but by the people of this city, if the work is not done promptly.

L. B. NORTHROP,
Commissary-General of Subsistence.

HEADQUARTERS ARMY OF NORTHERN VIRGINIA,
December 8, 1863.

Brig. Gen. J. D. IMBODEN, *Commanding Valley District:*

GENERAL: I have received a petition addressed to the Secretary of War and signed by the Hon. Moses Walton, Jacob Olt, Laurence Keller, and numerous other citizens of the lower valley, setting forth their exposed condition, and the losses sustained by invasions of the enemy, &c., and suggesting that Major Myers, with the Seventh Virginia Cavalry, be ordered to that region, or, if that could not be done, that Major Myers be assigned to the command of the battalions under Majors White and Gilmor, for the protection of the lower valley. I know the advantages of having a larger force in the valley, and wish the Seventh Virginia Cavalry could be spared for that purpose, but at this time it is impossible; nor can I now detach any regiment from this army.

My object is to know whether you can make any arrangements to give greater protection to the inhabitants down the valley, and have a force near Strasburg, so as at least to close the valley above that point against the incursions of the enemy, and what officer of your command had better be charged with this special duty. If you could so dispose your command as to guard the approaches from the lower valley, as well as those from the west, and be ready to re-enforce either party, or unite your whole force on either, as occasion may require, you might be able so to punish invading parties of the enemy as to deter them from making the attempt.

I am, very respectfully, your obedient servant,

R. E. LEE,
General.

SPECIAL ORDERS, }   ADJT. AND INSP. GENERAL'S OFFICE,
    No. 291.   }   *Richmond, Va., December 8*, 1863.

*   *   *   *   *   *

XVI. Brig. Gen. S. M. Barton will proceed with his brigade to Petersburg, Va., and report to Maj. Gen. G. E. Pickett, commanding.

*   *   *   *   *

By command of the Secretary of War:

JNO. WITHERS,
Assistant Adjutant-General.

CAMP, *December 9*, 1863.

General STUART:

GENERAL: I am called to Richmond this morning by the President. I presume the rest will follow.* My heart and thoughts will always be with this army. Please look out for positions for the cavalry, where they can be foraged, and be not too far away from the field of operations. I have set Colonel Corley to work. I expect to be back.

Very truly,

R. E. LEE.

Abstract from field return of the Army of Northern Virginia, General Robert E. Lee, C. S. Army, commanding, December 10, 1863.

Command.	Present for duty.		Aggregate present.	Aggregate present and absent.	Aggregate present last field report.
	Officers.	Men.			
General headquarters a	40	325	633	790	166
Second Army Corps (Ewell)	1,551	15,447	19,969	37,018	20,011
Third Army Corps (A. P. Hill)	1,535	17,872	22,202	35,061	21,756
Cavalry Corps (Stuart)	614	7,481	9,381	17,239	8,915
Artillery Corps (Pendleton)	244	4,371	5,233	6,925	5,240
Total	3,984	45,596	57,418	97,033	56,088

a Including provost guard, scouts, guides, and couriers.

EXECUTIVE DEPARTMENT, NORTH CAROLINA,
Raleigh, December 11, 1863.

Hon. JAMES A. SEDDON,
Secretary of War:

DEAR SIR: Referring to your letter of the 29th of October in relation to the petition of the First and Third Regiments North Carolina Infantry to be put into a North Carolina brigade, in which you

---

*See Lee to Davis, December 3; Davis to Lee, December 5, and Lee's reply, December 7.

say that it cannot be done because all the North Carolina brigades are full, I have the honor to ask now that the First, Third, and Fifty-fifth North Carolina Regiments, which belong to brigades from other States, and the Thirty-third, belonging to Lane's brigade, which has five regiments, be constituted a brigade. I have no disposition to interfere unduly with the arrangements of the generals in the field, but so great is the desire of these brave men for this arrangement that I am induced to urge it, if it can be done without injury to the service. They have petitioned me to assist them in getting it accomplished.

Respectfully, yours,

Z. B. VANCE.

[First indorsement.]

DECEMBER 15, 1863.

ADJUTANT-GENERAL:

Let this be referred to the generals under whose commands these regiments are serving, with an expression of my desire that, when the interests of the service will permit, troops from the same State may be brigaded together.

J. A. SEDDON,
Secretary of War.

[Second indorsement.]

ADJUTANT AND INSPECTOR GENERAL'S OFFICE,
December 18, 1863.

Respectfully referred to General R. E. Lee, commanding.
Please see indorsement of the Secretary of War.
By command of Secretary of War:

H. L. CLAY,
Assistant Adjutant-General.

[Third indorsement.]

HEADQUARTERS,
January 7, 1864.

Respectfully returned.

On several occasions when this subject has been referred to me, I have stated that the First and Third Regiments North Carolina troops were brigaded with three Virginia regiments, the whole under General George H. Steuart, an officer of experience of the old army, from the State of Maryland. This, at the time, was rendered necessary from the fact that I had no North Carolina regiments to brigade with them, all the other North Carolina brigades having been filled. These troops have been serving together for some time. Their commander cannot be disposed to treat them unfairly, and is very attentive to their comfort and interests. I cannot withdraw them without breaking up this brigade.

The Fifty-fifth North Carolina Regiment was brigaded with three Mississippi regiments before it joined this army, and while serving in the vicinity of Richmond or south of James River. To take it away now would break up that brigade (Davis'). General Lane's brigade by the last return numbered 2,398, aggregate. To take from it the Thirty-third North Carolina, one of the largest in the brigade, would reduce it to about 1,900 men. This brigade is composed entirely of North Carolina regiments, is one of the oldest in service, and I think it would be disadvantageous to reduce it, unless I had more North Carolina regiments. The only change that could be made, if there is any advantage in so doing, would be to join the Fifty-fifth to Steuart's brigade. There would then be three North Carolina and three Virginia regiments together; but that would break up Davis' brigade.

I see no public benefit that would result from the changes within proposed; therefore cannot recommend them. The men, I believe, would be satisfied if let alone. In connection with this subject I inclose a letter received from General Lane which I did not previously understand.

R. E. LEE,
General.

[Fourth indorsement.]

JANUARY 7, 1864.

Respectfully returned to Secretary of War, with General Lee's indorsement.

S. COOPER,
Adjutant and Inspector General.

[Inclosure.]

HEADQUARTERS LANE'S BRIGADE,
November 12, 1863.

Col. R. H. CHILTON,
Asst. Adjt. and Insp. Gen., and Chief of Staff:

COLONEL: Some of the friends of Col. C. M. Avery, Thirty-third North Carolina Troops, are anxious to have him promoted and assigned to the command of a new North Carolina brigade, to be carved out of Davis', Steuart's, and my own. To accomplish their object, I am told they are endeavoring to persuade the officers of the First, Third, Thirty-third, and Fifty-fifth North Carolina Regiments to petition for the formation of this new brigade, with the view of forwarding their petition to Governor Vance, of North Carolina, who will be urged to use his influence in Colonel Avery's behalf. I believe the Thirty-third Regiment, if let alone, would be very well satisfied to remain where it is, and I am opposed to having my command reduced to gratify the aspirations of any of my subordinate officers.

As the President will, of course, consult General Lee before making such a change in this army, I most earnestly and respectfully ask the commanding general, through you, to use his influence to prevent the Thirty-third or any other regiment being taken from this, the oldest North Carolina brigade in the Confederate States Army, for the purpose of making a brigade for any one.

Most truly, your obedient servant,

J. H. LANE,
Brigadier-General.

[Indorsements.]

HEADQUARTERS WILCOX'S LIGHT DIVISION,
November 13, 1863.

Respectfully forwarded.

I have no knowledge of any effort being made to create a new brigade for some colonel who expects or hopes to be promoted; but if there should be such a scheme in contemplation, I beg that the brigade of General Lane may not be mutilated for any such purpose, and that the Thirty-third North Carolina Regiment may be permitted to stay where it is. I believe five regiments to be a better brigade organization than four.

C. M. WILCOX,
Major-General, Commanding.

HEADQUARTERS THIRD ARMY CORPS,
November 14, 1863.

Respectfully forwarded.
I have no knowledge of any such movement.

A. P. HILL,
Lieutenant-General.

HEADQUARTERS,
January 4, 1864.

Respectfully forwarded in connection with the letter from Governor Vance of December 11, 1863, this day returned to War Department.

R. E. LEE,
General.

———

HEADQUARTERS TEXAS BRIGADE,
December 12, 1863.

To the Texas Delegation in C. S. Congress:

GENTLEMEN : The casualties of the service have reduced my brigade to so small a number that, without some plan is adopted to fill up its ranks with recruits, it must ere long lose its identity and be merged into other commands. Of the services rendered by the Texas brigade I may not be the proper one to speak, but, as they are a part of the history of our struggle, I will be excused for asking in the name of the surviving officers and men that the regiments shall not be consolidated. The memory of our common toils and sufferings and that of our fallen comrades alike forbid a course that would destroy our organization. The next question that arises is, how can the brigade be recruited ? The number present for duty this morning is 677 men and 87 officers, and this includes the Third Arkansas Regiment. I have four regiments in the brigade. The strength of the three Texas regiments is 516 men and 66 officers.

It is evident from these figures that we must either have our ranks filled up or soon cease to be an organization. We have tried the plan of sending recruiting officers to Texas and it failed. There is one other plan that offers to my mind a fair, if not certain, chance of success. It is to furlough the whole command as soon as the present campaign closes, and let it return home, making each officer and man a recruiting officer. Let them, by the conditions of the furlough, be required to rejoin their commands at such point west of the Mississippi as shall be ordered by Generals Smith or Magruder, or by the Secretary of War, on, say, the 1st day of April. I feel very confident that they would not only return promptly, but each officer and man would bring with him more or less recruits. An order from the Secretary of War allowing individual transfers from commands in Texas to the regiments of the brigade would render it certain. By this course we would have a brigade but little, if any, inferior in numbers or ability to what it was at the start.

The officers and men of the brigade have served for two years and a half faithfully, neglecting home, business, and everything personal to themselves. They have seen fall around them from the casualties of the service more than two-thirds of their original number, and believing that the approaching winter will offer an opportunity for them to enjoy the rest they require and attend to their necessary business at home without detriment to the service, they appeal with confidence to the governmental authorities for this indulgence. We make the application jointly with the officers and men of the Third Arkansas Regiment. The same reasoning will apply to them.

I have written to General Hood on the subject, with the hope of getting his concurrence and assistance, and hope you will confer with him. If you and he can agree, I hope you will act in concert. I address the delegation, and earnestly hope that you will all give us your aid in this matter. I shall visit Richmond as soon as I can get off. I am joined in this effort by all the officers of the command.

I am, gentlemen, very respectfully, your obedient servant,
                            J. B. ROBERTSON,
                            Brigadier-General, Commanding.

[Indorsements.]

The undersigned members of Congress from Texas beg leave most respectfully to refer the foregoing communication to His Excellency the President of the Confederate States, and to add their most earnest request that some arrangement consistent with the public service may be made for the transfer of First, Fourth, and Fifth Texas Regiments to the State of Texas in order to be recruited. We think that the extraordinary services rendered and hardships endured by these regiments eminently commend them to the special favor of the Government.

[Signed by F. B. Sexton, M. D. Graham, W. B. Wright, John A. Wilcox, W. S. Oldham, L. T. Wigfall, and P. W. Gray.]

                            RICHMOND,
                            December 29, 1863.

I will never consent to the consolidation of this brigade. I approve the plan proposed within.

                            J. B. HOOD,
                            Major-General.

HDQRS. DEPT. OF WESTERN VA. AND EAST TENN.,
                            Dublin, December 12, 1863.

Brig. Gen. JOHN ECHOLS,
                            Union:

Fall back slowly unless you are heavily pressed. Do not engage the enemy until you are joined by McCausland. If this rain continues, I do not think the enemy will cross the Greenbrier River. Where is Colonel Jackson and in what direction is he moving? Do you need anything to prepare your troops for action?

                            SAM. JONES,
                            Major-General.

HDQRS. DEPT. OF WESTERN VA. AND EAST TENN.,
Dublin, December 12, 1863.
Col. JOHN MCCAUSLAND,
Narrows:
Brigadier-General Echols has fallen back this side of Greenbrier River on the road to Union. Move up your command to his support, leaving only a sufficient guard for the public property. Move in the morning.
SAM. JONES,
Major-General.

HDQRS. DEPT. OF WESTERN VA. AND EAST TENN.,
Dublin, December 12, 1863.
Col. JOHN MCCAUSLAND,
Narrows, Va.:
Brigadier-General Echols reports the enemy encamped at Meadow Bluff last night and advancing on Lewisburg. Hold your command in readiness to move to his support at the shortest notice. Send if you can a courier to Major Smith, of the Seventeenth Cavalry, informing him of the enemy's move. It will give him more freedom of action, and he can avail himself of their absence to accomplish much.
SAM. JONES,
Major-General.

HEADQUARTERS,
Chaffin's Farm, December 13, 1863—9.15 p. m.
Maj. T. O. CHESTNEY,
Assistant Adjutant-General:
MAJOR: Your dispatch is received and its directions shall be complied with. The last information I have received of the strength and movements of the enemy is in a dispatch from signal corps. It states that the enemy crossed Forge Bridge about daylight, and attacked the cavalry at Charles City Court-House, about an hour by sun, capturing nearly the whole command. Major Robertson escaped. The enemy's force is estimated at 400. I presume Forge Bridge was picketed; my orders were positive to that effect. The dispatch from signal corps informs me that the enemy retired about 10 a. m. to-day toward Forge Bridge.

As soon as I heard of the capture of Major Robertson's command, I sent out Lieutenant-Colonel Berkeley, with about 150 men, to picket in my front. He is at New Market, with a picket on the river road and one on the Long Bridge road where it is crossed by the Central or Darbytown road. This guards all the approaches, I think, to Richmond and this point, excepting the Charles City and Williamsburg roads, which Colonel Shingler is directed to watch and hold. I also ordered Colonel Shingler to watch, as far as the capacities of his command would allow, the defiles of the Chickahominy until a cavalry force could be procured to take the place of that captured. I hope General Elzey will be able to furnish me with this cavalry.

I feel exceedingly indignant at what I suppose to be a complete surprise, and somebody should suffer for it. I have directed Major

Robertson to report all the facts of the case to me, and they shall be forwarded to you.

I have just learned from the signal corps that two brigades of Yankees landed on Friday at Newport News.

I am, major, yours, respectfully,

EPPA HUNTON,
Brigadier-General.

P. S.—Colonel Shingler sent out a scout to ascertain the whereabouts and strength of the enemy to-day, and I am expecting to hear from him.

HEADQUARTERS DEPARTMENT OF NORTH CAROLINA,
Petersburg, Va., December 15, 1863.

General S. COOPER,
Adjt. and Insp. Gen., C. S. Army, Richmond, Va.:

GENERAL: I have the honor to inclose a dispatch just received from Colonel Griffin. It is impossible with my force to prevent these raids. The section of country that the enemy is now operating in is too far from our line to do more than watch their operations.

It is evident from the statement in Mr. Lincoln's message concerning the numbers of negro troops in the Federal service and their boasted efficiency, that their policy will be to increase that description of material as much as possible, as it strengthens their numbers and weakens our labor force. General Butler is evidently pursuing a steady course to effect this object wherever it is in his power, and in a short time all the country that he can overrun will be entirely denuded of slaves.

Would it not be advisable to cause all the slaves in the country so exposed to be brought back within our lines? We could send a cavalry expedition of our own down in such neighborhoods to collect and bring in the negroes. Whatever is determined on should be carried out at once, as every day loses so much valuable property to the Confederacy. In many cases, doubtless, objections may be made by the owners; but I think the case one of emergency. I inclose copy of Colonel Griffin's telegram.

Respectfully asking a reply, I am, general, your obedient servant,

GEO. E. PICKETT,
Major-General, Commanding.

[Inclosure.]

FRANKLIN,
December 15, 1863.

Major-General PICKETT:

Enemy, 1,500 strong, negroes and whites, reported yesterday 12 miles of Gatesville, committing all kinds of excesses; insulting our ladies in the most tantalizing manner. People are fleeing their wrath. They are shipping all meat, grain, &c., in carts; taking clothing from men and women's backs, and destroying or carrying it off.

Yankee cavalry were in Suffolk on Friday and Saturday last in small detachments. Gunboats came up Nansemond River at night, and detachments came out and patrolled town; cavalry dismounted at Ivor and attacked them from northeast side of river with great success, with one or two rifled cannon.   Force at Bernard's Mill small.   A battalion of cavalry (Yankees) with one piece of artillery landed at Colerain, on Chowan, Saturday and Sunday, from gunboats.   Some 50 marines were gathering up negroes and carrying them off.   They had arrested several citizens there.   Two companies of infantry should be located near this point, or placed at Winton, and cavalry sent there.

. Beast Butler it is reported issued orders everything people had would be destroyed if they did not take the oath in his lines.   Some have already made a sacrifice.   Something might be done to keep them out of Gates County, by use of cavalry and regiment of infantry.

JOEL R. GRIFFIN,
Colonel, Commanding.

HEADQUARTERS DEPARTMENT OF NORTH CAROLINA,
Petersburg, Va., December 15. 1863.

[General S. COOPER:]

GENERAL: I have the honor to inclose a second telegram received from Colonel Griffin.   I have ordered him to send all the cavalry force he has down into Gates County.   The report I look upon probably as a little exaggerated; but doubtless these fiends, backed, or rather instigated, by such a beast as Butler is, will be set on to commit any outrage.   I inclose copy of my telegram to Colonel Griffin.

I will not stand upon terms with these fellows any longer.   If our cavalry force was sufficient, we could, in a measure, prevent these inroads.   The only other alternative is to evacuate the country. Butler's plan, evidently, is to let loose his swarm of blacks upon our ladies and defenseless families, plunder and devastate the country. Against such a warfare there is but one resource—to hang at once every one captured belonging to the expedition, and afterward any one caught who belongs to Butler's department.

Let us come to a definite understanding with these heathens at once.   Butler cannot be allowed to rule here as he did in New Orleans.   His course must be stopped.

I am, general, respectfully, your obedient servant,

G. E. P. [PICKETT.]

[Inclosure No. 1.]

PETERSBURG,
December 15, 1863.

General COOPER:

Following dispatch received:

Two thousand of enemy's infantry, mostly negroes, and 50 cavalry are at Elizabeth City conscripting negroes and plundering generally.

JOEL R. GRIFFIN,
Colonel, Commanding at Franklin.

I wrote concerning the above by courier.

GEO. E. PICKETT,
Major-General, Commanding.

[Inclosure No. 2.]

HEADQUARTERS DEPARTMENT OF NORTH CAROLINA,
December 15, 1863.

Col. J. R. GRIFFIN,
Commanding, &c., Franklin Depot:

Send all the cavalry force you have at once down to the scene of devastation. If they cannot drive off the enemy, they can at least hold them in check. Send orders to Colonel Hinton. Any one caught in the act (negroes or white men) of burning houses or mal-treating women, must be hung on the spot, by my order.

GEO. E. PICKETT,
Major-General, Commanding.

UNION, MONROE COUNTY, VA.,
December 15, 1863

Maj. WILLIAM B. MYERS,
Assistant Adjutant-General, &c.:

There seems to be no doubt that the enemy have passed Sweet Springs, taking the Fincastle road. On the first intimation that they are coming toward Dublin, have the entire bottom of the turnpike bridge over New River taken up and carried to the Newbern side. If General Ransom has arrived at Bristol with his command, order Corse's brigade with the least possible delay to New River Bridge. If General Ransom has not reached Bristol, order Forty-fifth [Virginia] Regiment to New River Bridge immediately. Give all orders necessary to impress all railroad trains, whether carrying salt or anything else, to get the troops to New River Bridge. Hurry up the home guards. Concentrate them at New River Bridge, and under no circumstances allow Averell to get on the left bank of New River.

SAM. JONES,
Major-General.

DUBLIN, *December 15, 1863.*

Col. W. H. BROWNE, *Saltville:*

The enemy is advancing on the railroads, probably toward Salem. Move your regiment to New River Bridge at once. Impress any trains you require at Saltville, whether loaded with salt or not. The utmost dispatch required.

WM. B. MYERS,
Assistant Adjutant-General.

DUBLIN, *December 15, 1863.*

Maj. Gen. R. RANSOM, Jr., *Bristol:*

The enemy, under Averell, are moving on the railroad; have passed Sweet Springs to-day *en route* to Fincastle and Bonsack's; will reach the latter place to-morrow evening. Send Corse and Wharton at once to New River Bridge. Telegraph McMahon when transportation will be needed. The utmost rapidity is necessary. The enemy has passed Echols, and there is nothing between him and the railroad.

By order, &c.:

WM. B. MYERS,
Assistant Adjutant-General.

Quartermaster at Bristol forward this dispatch with all haste to General Ransom.

WM. B. MYERS,
Assistant Adjutant-General.

DUBLIN,
December 15, 1863.

Maj. Gen. R. RANSOM, Jr.,
Bristol:

When can Corse's brigade reach New River Bridge? If it cannot get there to-morrow morning early, I will order the Forty-fifth [Virginia] Regiment from Saltville.

By order, &c.:

WM. B. MYERS,
Assistant Adjutant-General.

DUBLIN,
December 15, 1863.

Col. GEORGE P. TERRILL,
Commanding Home Guards, Salem, Va.:

Averell, with force reported 3,000 strong, is advancing on railroad from Sweet Springs. You will immediately move your command to Salem.

By order, &c.:

WM. B. MYERS,
Assistant Adjutant-General.

HDQRS. DEPT. OF WESTERN VA. AND EAST TENN.,
Dublin, December 15, 1863.

Maj. J. M. WADE,
Christiansburg:

General Averell reported moving toward Sweet Springs. Collect your command at the rendezvous and hold it in readiness to move at a moment's warning. Report to these headquarters.

By order of Maj. Gen. Sam. Jones:

WM. B. MYERS,
Assistant Adjutant-General.

(Copy of same sent to Col. George P. Terrill, Salem; Maj. H. M. Bowyer, Bonsack's, Botetourt; Maj. G. A. Wingfield, Liberty, Bedford; Maj. Joseph F. Kent, Wytheville; Maj. James M. Sheffey, Marion; Maj. Joseph Graves, Newbern, Pulaski; General Nicholls, Lynchburg, Va.)

DUBLIN, *December* 15, 1863.

Maj. J. M. WADE, *Christiansburg:*

The enemy, 3,000 strong, is advancing from Sweet Springs, on the railroad. Assemble your command and telegraph at once the amount of transportation required to move them to New River Bridge.

By order:

WM. B. MYERS,
Assistant Adjutant-General.

(Copy of same sent to Maj. Joseph F. Kent, Wytheville.)

DUBLIN, *December* 15, 1863.

Col. G. A. WINGFIELD,
Commanding Home Guards, Liberty:

Move your command to Salem at once. Averell is advancing on railroad from Sweet Springs.

By order, &c.:

WM. B. MYERS,
Assistant Adjutant-General.

SPECIAL ORDERS, } HDQRS. ARMY OF NORTHERN VIRGINIA,
No. 308.   }   *December* 15, 1863.

*   *   *   *   *   *   *

XIV. Maj. Gen. J. A. Early, Provisional Army, C. S., will proceed to Staunton, Va., and assume command of the troops there and in the Valley of Virginia, and make the best disposition of the same to resist the advance of the enemy.

*   *   *   *   *   *   *

By command of General R. E. Lee:

W. H. TAYLOR,
Assistant Adjutant-General.

HDQRS. DEPT. OF NORTH CAROLINA, *December* —, 1863.
(Received 17th.)

General S. COOPER,
Adjutant and Inspector General:

GENERAL: I have ordered all the cavalry from the Blackwater, Colonels Griffin's and Taliaferro's regiments, numbering some 600 effective men, to the scene of operations in Pasquotank. I have directed General Ransom to relieve the cavalry at and near Franklin, by infantry from Weldon, and send down 400 men by special train to Ivor to-night, to relieve the cavalry between Ivor and Franklin. I have also ordered General Ransom to mount, if possible, 200 men to proceed to same destination as Colonel Griffin. Major Dearing, with 200 mounted men from his battalion, I have ordered to be ready to leave here to-morrow for same place. This will be all the mounted force I can send. It would not be prudent to risk an infantry force so far, with both flanks assailable, and the rear open and liable to be cut off by a force operating from Suffolk.

I inclose a communication from Colonel Hinton, received to-day.

Should the enemy be dislodged, they have it in their power to return at any time and carry out their plundering designs, unless we have a strong cavalry force (such as we have not in this department) to continually harass them.

I am, general, very respectfully, your obedient servant,

GEO. E. PICKETT,
Major-General, Commanding.

[Inclosure.]

HEADQUARTERS NORTH CAROLINA STATE FORCES,
Murfreesborough, December 14, 1863.

General GEORGE E. PICKETT,
Comdg. Department of North Carolina, Petersburg:

GENERAL: Two regiments of armed negroes and one of Yankees (all infantry), and one regiment of cavalry, are quartered in Elizabeth City. They are committing all manner of depredations upon the unarmed and defenseless citizens of the surrounding country. They express a determination to remain in Elizabeth City until they shall have completed the destruction of property in that section. My little force—about 500 strong—are doing all they can to hold them in check, but cannot operate successfully against so large a force. Can you not, general, send a brigade to the relief of that community? They can be easily captured, or driven off. Their position would be exceedingly precarious if opposed by an equal force. If they are not speedily dislodged, the Confederacy need not expect to get any more provisions from that section of country, but if they are driven off, the quantity of pork and bacon that will come to the Confederacy from the east side of the Chowan will be truly incredible. Please let me hear from you.

I am, general, very respectfully, your obedient servant,

J. W. HINTON,
Colonel, Commanding Cavalry.

———

DUBLIN, *December 16, 1863.*

Capt. W. R. PRESTON, *Christiansburg:*

The telegraph operator left Salem about three hours ago. Said the enemy was near there. Nothing new. Please let me hear if they move in this direction. I hope to prevent their crossing New River.

WM. B. MYERS,
Assistant Adjutant-General.

———

DUBLIN, *December 16, 1863.*

Major-General RANSOM, Jr., *Bristol:*

Hurry Corse's brigade down to New River Bridge. The enemy in possession of Salem.

By order, &c.:

WM. B. MYERS,
Assistant Adjutant-General.

———

LYNCHBURG, *December 16, 1863.*

General S. COOPER,
Adjutant and Inspector General:

Captain Otey's company, sent to General Jones' assistance, were obliged to come back to Bonsack's. The enemy in strong force are at Salem and have burned the depot. Otey's company alone is at Bonsack's; the militia declined going up.

FRANCIS T. NICHOLLS,
Brigadier-General, Commanding.

LYNCHBURG, *December 17, 1863.*

ADJUTANT AND INSPECTOR GENERAL:

By a dispatch from Captain Otey, at Liberty, the enemy are reported advancing toward Bonsack's from Salem. I have no force here but about 100 infantry (militia) and one or two pieces of artillery.

FRANCIS T. NICHOLLS,
Brigadier-General, Commanding Post.

LYNCHBURG, *December 17, 1863.*

General S. COOPER,
Adjutant and Inspector General:

GENERAL: Information which I deem reliable represents Averell to have retreated by the Sweet Springs or New Castle road. They are about 2,500 strong, with artillery. I have communicated from the beginning with Staunton.

FRANCIS T. NICHOLLS,
Brigadier-General, Commanding.

LYNCHBURG, *December 17, 1863.*

General S. COOPER,
Adjutant and Inspector General:

A later dispatch states that the main body of the enemy left Salem last night and encamped, about 4 miles from there, at Mason's Cove. Supposed to be from 2,000 to 3,000 strong.

FRANCIS T. NICHOLLS,
Brigadier-General, Commanding Post.

DUBLIN, *December 17, 1863.*

Col. W. H. BROWNE,
New River Bridge, via Central Depot:

Do you wish the home guards of Pulaski to remain at the bridge? If they are of no use they may be disbanded. What do you think?

WM. B. MYERS,
Assistant Adjutant-General.

DUBLIN, *December 17, 1863.*

Capt. W. R. PRESTON,
Christiansburg:

The wires down between here and Union. Have sent a courier off. No news yet from Echols. Do not know where he is.

WM. B. MYERS,
Assistant Adjutant-General.

HEADQUARTERS ARMY OF NORTHERN VIRGINIA,
December 17, 1863.

General Orders, No. 107, refers to the men actually carrying muskets—the effective strength. The same principle will be applied to the detailed or extra-duty men of a division or brigade, two to every hundred such for duty, provided their services can be temporarily dispensed with without detriment.

'y order of General Lee:

W. H. TAYLOR,
Assistant Adjutant-General.

DUBLIN, *December 18, 1863.*
Col. W. H. BROWNE,
Commanding:

When you arrive there you had best get a good guide, and I understand there is a strong pass, which can be easily held, between Salem and Red Sulphur, about half way. If McCausland then advances, the enemy will have but one way of escape, in direction of Echols' force. You can decide on the position to take when you reach Salem better than I can designate it. Answer.

WM. B. MYERS,
Assistant Adjutant-General.

DUBLIN, *December 18, 1863.*
Col. W. H. BROWNE,
New River:

The enemy has returned to Salem. Under these circumstances you had best remain in your present position until further orders.

WM. B. MYERS,
Assistant Adjutant-General.

DUBLIN, *December 18, 1863.*
Col. W. H. BROWNE,
Commanding &c.:

Telegrams from Preston last night and this morning report enemy at Roanoke, Red Sulphur, about 12 miles from Salem. If McCausland can come to Blacksburg, and you hold their rear, the enemy will be forced to go toward Sweet Springs, and Echols can meet them. Do you want rations? Can you communicate with McCausland from Christiansburg? He is at Newport.

WM. B. MYERS,
Assistant Adjutant-General.

DUBLIN, *December 18, 1863.*
Col. W. H. BROWNE,
Commanding, &c.:

It is important to find out if he is advancing. It would be well to send a courier from Salem to Bonsack's, to communicate with Rich-

mond or Lynchburg.   I telegraphed General Cooper two days ago
to send up some troops.   They may be between Bonsack's and Lynchburg.   If so, they should march to Fincastle from Bonsack's, to stop
the retreat in that direction.   I think that would fix the thing.   You
had best hold the home guards from Christiansburg to Salem.   I will
send rations.

WM. B. MYERS,
Assistant Adjutant-General.

HEADQUARTERS,
Lynchburg, December 18, 1863.

General S. COOPER,
    Adjutant and Inspector General:
    I send you the following dispatch just received:

Our superintendent, J. M. Crowley, who is 1 mile this side of Salem with a mag-
net, reports Yankees returning back to Salem.   I judge they have found their
retreat cut off.

LE FAUCHEUR,
Manager.

I have no information other than the above.

FRANCIS T. NICHOLLS,
Brigadier-General, Commanding Post.

LYNCHBURG,
December 18, 1863.

General S. COOPER,
    Adjutant and Inspector General:
    The following dispatch has just been received by me from D. C.
Booth, commanding Roanoke Home Guards, dated Bonsack's:

Scouts report that the enemy have been intercepted on their retreat, and are coming in this way again.

Salem, I presume, on the Botetourt Springs road.   I communicate
just such information as I get myself.

FRANCIS T. NICHOLLS.

LYNCHBURG,
December 19, 1863.

General S. COOPER,
    Adjutant and Inspector General:
    I forward the following dispatch just received by me:

BONSACK'S,
December 19, 1863.

A scout has just arrived from Fincastle, reports that the enemy were seen up
to dark last night on this side of Craig's Creek, which was too high to ford.

D. C. BOOTH.

FRANCIS T. NICHOLLS,
Brigadier-General.

HDQRS. DEPT. OF WESTERN VA. AND EAST TENN.,
Dublin, December 20, 1863.

Col. W. H. BROWNE,
Commanding, &c., Central Depot:

Night before last enemy divided at Cray's [Craig's] Creek, part going toward Newport, part toward Sweet Springs. If repulsed at either point, they may attempt to return by Salem and New River Bridge. I will relieve you as soon as possible.

WM. B. MYERS,
Assistant Adjutant-General.

HEADQUARTERS, *Wilmington, December 20, 1863.*

Col. W. M. BROWNE,
Aide-de-Camp to the President, Richmond, Va.:

COLONEL: I have received your confidential note and its important information. I beg you will call the attention of the President to my numerous letters to the War Department, demonstrating that the safety and whole plan of defense for this place depends on the presence of a strong army to oppose a movement by land. If there is danger, it must be assembled at once and be prepared to meet it. It will not do to wait until after the enemy have landed and are advancing. At present I have but a single brigade which has never yet been in battle, and a few light batteries which have never been engaged. I earnestly entreat that I may at once receive such an addition to my force as may at least enable me to guard the approaches and do something toward retarding the enemy long enough to have a little chance to receive re-enforcements. Undoubtedly, if this place is attacked, the enemy will make strenuous efforts to cut the communication. If they succeed, they will get me with my present means.

Please ask General Custis Lee to examine some of my letters to the Secretary of War on the defense of this place and the necessity of a supporting army.

Very respectfully,

W. H. C. WHITING,
Major-General.

HEADQUARTERS DEPARTMENT OF NORTH CAROLINA,
December 20, 1863.

General S. COOPER:

GENERAL: I have the honor to report that the enemy have been committing the most brutal outrages upon our loyal citizens in the vicinity of Elizabeth City. Immediately upon hearing of their appearance at that place, which is 50 miles from Franklin, our nearest post, I gave orders to collect all the cavalry from the Blackwater, relieving them with infantry, and sending also 130 mounted artillery from Dearing's battalion. The enemy being also reported as fortifying opposite Harrellsville, which is in Bertie County, and just below Winton, I ordered General Ransom with three regiments of infantry, via Franklin, to the scene of devastation, and to move down with infantry, cavalry, and artillery against them. You will see by telegram inclosed that the enemy decamped upon hearing of the approach of our forces. You will perceive that they have with their negro troops hung one of our soldiers and manacled ladies, and have taken them off in irons. They have run riot over all the country east of the Perquimans River, behind which they fell, burning the bridges upon the first approach of a squadron of our cavalry. My orders were to spare no one. But unfortunately our foe is too wary. They, like the Indians, only war on the defenseless. You will see likewise that they are going to play the same game in Suffolk that they did in Norfolk—make all take the oath of allegiance to the Federal Government or confiscate their property. I really do not know what advice to give in answer to the question they ask me. With my force it is impossible to protect such distant points. Still it makes my blood boil to think of these enormities being practiced, and we have no way of arresting them.

Eight thousand men are reported as at Washington. This I doubt. Probably they intend making a similar trip from Washington in the adjoining county to the Elizabeth City one.

I inclose also report of General Barton about the capture of some of our cavalry. A few days before, the enemy attacked our pickets near Free Bridge and were repulsed, leaving 5 killed on the field and 2 horses.

I will give orders to the cavalry now at or near Franklin to make an expedition to Suffolk and the vicinity. We of course cannot hold the place, but might possibly do the enemy some damage.

What answer had I better give the Suffolk people? I understand that the citizens of Norfolk have mostly taken the oath asked for by Butler. I communicated with General Butler in reference to Major Borroughs, but have as yet received no reply.

I have the honor to be, general, very respectfully, your obedient servant,

GEO. E. PICKETT,
Major-General, Commanding.

[Indorsement.]

It is impossible for the Department to answer the question propounded by General Pickett in respect to the deputation of ladies from Suffolk further than to state that taking the compulsory oath exacted of them by an infuriated [foe], for their safety, &c., should not, under the pressing necessities of the case represented by them, be considered as an indication of their want of fidelity to the Southern cause. General Pickett, in all other respects, appears to have taken the necessary measures, to the extent of his means, to check the outrages complained of.

S. C. [COOPER.]

[Inclosure No. 1.]

HEADQUARTERS OUTPOST,
Greenville, N. C., December 17, 1863.

Capt. J. D. DARDEN,
Assistant Adjutant-General:

CAPTAIN: It is my painful duty to announce the capture of about 35 men of Capt. J. W. Moore's company (H), of my command. A battalion of Yankee infantry crossed a foot ford which had been blockaded, avoiding my pickets, and making their way to and surrounding Captain Moore's encampment, about 6 miles below here, on this side of the river, and capturing, with the exception of 4 men and 2 horses, that portion of the command which was there. As soon as I received information of their approach, I immediately moved after them, but, on arriving at Cheod Creek bridge, found that they had captured my pickets there from the same company, and had forded the stream at that point, leaving a wagon which they had captured with the command. One Yankee was killed there by the picket. I am at a loss to account for the surprise, as I had only last evening, through my adjutant, cautioned Captain Moore to increased vigilance, from rumors that I had heard of a body of 35 armed deserters making their way through the county toward Washington. My scouts around Washington and citizens coming from below all report that no passing is now allowed by the Yankees, and that they are very busy making preparations for a raid from Plymouth and Washington, to concentrate at some point in the interior. A lady direct from Washington reports an increased force there; that they have 300 negro cavalry constantly drilling, and that they are very busy preparing for something, and, from what she could learn, were very nearly ready. I have applied, captain, to General Ransom, Colonel McKethan, and through Colonel Waddell for some infantry at this point. I again most respectfully urge it. One of my companies picket 16 miles below here, on the other side of the river, one to 12 miles below on this side, and I have only one small company as a reserve here and as a support to the battery, and none to act independently. My men are very poorly equipped.

I inclose my returns.* Would have sent them sooner, but moved at daylight this morning, and have just returned. Hoping that I will be re-enforced, and most respectfully urging it,

I am, very respectfully, your obedient servant,

ROGER MOORE,
Major, Commanding.

[Inclosure No. 2.]

WHITE MILLS, ON DISMAL SWAMP,
[*December*] 19, [1863.]

Major-General PICKETT :

Enemy have escaped me by river bridge, Pasquotank River. They were warned of my first advance to Gatesville. Their cavalry have gone to Norfolk, through Currituck County, N. C., the negroes, by Dismal Swamp Canal, to Portsmouth. They are on forced march. Last left South Mills this morning. My men are near the place. Nothing now to be done but collect all hogs and drive them out, which is a considerable item here; also bring out Colonel Hinton's guerrillas, which he requests. Enemy had at Elizabeth City 2,900 negroes and 500 cavalry. They hung Private Daniel Bright, of Company L, of my Sixty-second Georgia Regiment; hung him to a beam in a house; body remained suspended forty hours. Lieutenant Mundin's wife, with other ladies, were arrested, tied, and placed in jail at Elizabeth City, and carried in irons to Norfolk; even their feet tied. Negroes killed a child in Camden County, committing all other kinds of excesses.

JOEL R. GRIFFIN,
Colonel, Commanding.

_____

* Not found.

[Inclosure No. 3.]

WELDON,
December 20, 1863.

Major-General PICKETT:

No news from Hamilton; no danger there yet. Can we do any. thing for the people of Suffolk? I fear not. If possible, I will go there and fight Butler over, anyhow. I shall withdraw troops to-morrow from Franklin, unless you think we could catch them below Suffolk. I will move down, and, if the enemy are certainly gone, recall Griffin. Excuse me for troubling you so much.

M. W. RANSOM,
Brigadier-General.

[Inclosure No. 4.]

WELDON,
[*December*] 20, [1863.]

General GEORGE E. PICKETT:

The following dispatch received from Franklin, dated 20th, to General Ransom:

A deputation of 2 ladies from Suffolk came last night. General Butler has noti-fied the citizens of Suffolk that they must take the oath of allegiance to the Federal Government or leave immediately. They are loyal to the South, and wish your advice on the subject. Those left in Suffolk, if they should leave it, would lose their all, and not be able to support themselves in our Confederacy. Tuesday is the day fixed. He is to send a provost-marshal and troops there on that day to administer the oath. All quiet here.

DE BORDENAVE,
Major, Commanding Forces, Blackwater.

Abstract from return of the Army of Northern Virginia, General Robert E. Lee, C. S. Army, commanding, December 20, 1863.

Command.	Present for duty.		Aggregate present.	Aggregate present and absent.
	Officers.	Men.		
General headquarters *a*	19	106	151	209
Second Army Corps (Ewell)	1,543	15,785	20,327	37,095
Third Army Corps (A. P. Hill) *b*	1,291	15,543	19,303	29,928
Cavalry Corps (Stuart)	609	7,53)	9,487	17,227
Artillery Corps (Pendleton)	244	4,371	5,283	6,925
Total	3,706	43,285	54,451	91,384

a Including scouts, guides, &c. The provost guard dropped and not accounted for.
b Thomas' and Walker's brigades detached.

DECEMBER —, 1863.

The honorable delegation in Congress from State of Florida:

GENTLEMEN: The undersigned, a committee appointed by a meet-ing composed of the officers of Perry's brigade, to communicate with you upon a subject of vital importance to our existence as a military organization, beg leave to represent that in view of the reduced condition of this brigade, the commandants of the regiments composing the same have united in an application to the Secretary of War asking that the brigade be temporarily transferred to Florida, with the view of recruiting our decimated ranks during the winter months, and returning to the field, upon the resumption of active hostilities in the spring, in an effective condition.

In the application, the strength and condition of the regiments are fully set forth, as well as the reasons upon which the same is based, and the committee deem their duty discharged when they invite your attention to the above-named application and ask your co-operation in securing its success. The committee, however, cannot let the occasion pass without urging upon you the importance of taking such steps as will preserve our organizations; they feel that you share with them the reputation earned by our brigade upon the battlefields of Virginia and will unite with them in perpetuating its existence.

[Signed by W. K. Partridge, captain, Fifth Florida, and chairman; F. Worth, captain, Eighth Florida; B. Frank Whitner, captain, Eighth Florida; H. C. Simmons, captain, Eighth Florida; J. T. Bernard, captain and assistant quartermaster, Eighth Florida; B. F. Simmons, adjutant, Eighth Florida; J. L. Taylor, captain, Company K, Fifth Florida; C. A. Bryan, captain, Company C, Fifth Florida; N. B. Walker, second lieutenant, Second Florida; D. F. Bradley, lieutenant, Company A, Second Florida.]

[First indorsement.]

DECEMBER 23, 1863.

ADJUTANT-GENERAL:

Has any application of this kind come up through military channels? If not, refer to commanding general for his views.

J. A. S. [SEDDON.]

[Second indorsement.]

ADJUTANT AND INSPECTOR GENERAL'S OFFICE,
. *December* 30, 1863.

Respectfully referred to General Lee for his views.
By order of Adjutant and Inspector General:

JOHN W. RIELY,
Captain, and Assistant·Adjutant-General.

[Third indorsement.]

HEADQUARTERS,
January 4, 1864.

Respectfully returned.

This subject has been one of consideration and correspondence for a year, and has come up in every shape. The officers think that recruits can only be obtained by sending the brigade to Florida. I have no doubt if it went back with the assurance of remaining that it would receive its share of conscripts, but if it was known that the brigade was to return to the field, I cannot see the advantage that would be gained. If men are to be obtained for it in Florida, by the aid of the recruiting officers, it seems they can as well be sent to the brigade as the brigade to the men.

In answer to His Excellency the Governor of Florida, who recommended the return of the brigade to the State, I stated it could be done in my opinion if a full regiment was sent to take its place until its ranks could be filled. If this cannot be done, I recommend that the brigade be consolidated into a regiment. I should much regret for the brigade to lose its identity. It has served long and faithfully; but I have tried every way to recruit its ranks without success. If this brigade was sent to Florida, others equally deserving could not be denied a similar indulgence, and the army would be broken up.

R. E. LEE,
General.

[Fourth indorsement.]

ADJUTANT AND INSPECTOR GENERAL'S OFFICE.
January 22, 1864.

Respectfully returned to the Secretary of War.

A former application of Messrs. Maxwell and Hilton, requesting that this command be returned to Florida, was referred to General Beauregard January 7, 1864, and has not yet been returned to this office.

H. L. CLAY,
Assistant Adjutant-General.

[Fifth indorsement.]

Inform these Representatives of the action taken, if the paper has to be sent by Adjutant-General.

J. A. S. [SEDDON.]

HDQRS. DEPT. OF WESTERN VA. AND EAST TENN.,
Dublin, December 21, 1863.

Maj. Gen. SAMUEL JONES,
Sweet Springs:

Following dispatch just received from operator at Salem, dated to-day:

A courier just arrived says the enemy was in New Castle about dark this evening.

WM. B. MYERS,
Assistant Adjutant-General.

(Copy of same sent to General Nicholls, commanding at Lynchburg.)

DECEMBER 21, [1863.]

President DAVIS:

Information from Colonel Browne received yesterday. Please communicate to General Pickett and War Department. Pickett reports enemy re-enforced at Washington. May be to cut railroad. Only one brigade here, and I can do no more than I am doing.

W. H. C. WHITING,
Major-General.

HEADQUARTERS,
Wilmington, December 21, 1863.

His Excellency President DAVIS,
Richmond:

SIR: Since receiving a note from your aide, Colonel Browne, conveying me confidential information of the enemy's designs, I have been shown a letter from a gentleman in New York to an officer of the staff of General Martin—from his father, in fact—dated near the latter part of November, which tends to confirm your information. He states the intention to attack here; that the new gunboats, sharp at both ends, are (at that date) about completed. They are armed with heavy guns, not ironed, intended to attack here. He states further that Dahlgren and Gillmore are used up.

Your aide tells me the information was sent for my guidance. Without a larger force, I can do nothing but what I am doing. All of my plans depend on a supporting army. Information from Major-General Pickett is received to-day that the enemy are heavily re-enforcing at Washington. He ask me to be ready to re-enforce him. If this be so, it is, doubtless; to cut communication prior to or simultaneous with attack here. I need much more force than I have, and it ought to be here now. In my opinion, the permanent force to support should always be three brigades, in order to insure the chance of re-enforcement before the enemy may acquire fatal advantages, as I am entirely too weak, especially when it is considered that the enemy can take his choice of points and position, may come from above or below, or both, and can move faster than I can, to oppose him. The position is very difficult, and yet it is so important to us that nothing should be left to chance that can be done.

The city is much more vulnerable than Charleston. There, the city does not fall though the harbor is closed. Here, the city is open to attack first. Without troops, it must go and with it the harbor.

Before an attempt is made on our communication, I most earnestly entreat for re-enforcements, or consequences may be serious.

Very respectfully,

W. H. C. WHITING,
Major-General.

———

HEADQUARTERS,
Wilmington, December 21, 1863.

General S. COOPER,
Adjutant and Inspector General, Richmond:

GENERAL: The event of an attack on Wilmington is now regarded as imminent. Information to this effect has been received from the Executive Department, and I have further tending to same from New York via Nassau. It is considered in New York that Gillmore and Dahlgren have utterly failed at Charleston, and that the enemy's attack will be transferred here. General Pickett reports that the enemy is being heavily re-enforced at Washington, said to be 8,000. He calls on me for help. I want it too much myself to afford him any aid. If they are placing troops there, it is very probable it is for the purpose of cutting off communication with Richmond on the railroad, either prior to or simultaneous with a demonstration on this place. Either would have the effect of delaying, if not of preventing, aid to me. Such aid will be indispensable to the safety of this place, and should be here or gathering here now. This point has been frequently demonstrated, and on it depends all my plans to save this important position. A timely assembly of force may have the effect of diverting attack.

If my opinion of the enemy's intentions is correct, it will be necessary to have a strong force between Weldon and this place. In all probability, I shall have to move the small force at Kenansville (a very important position) to operate on the Holly Shelter road, or to re-enforce here. This will require to be replaced. A brigade, at the least, with batteries of light artillery, ought to come here at once, and I think Pickett's command should move into North Carolina, and forces be drawn from the Army of Virginia, where, probably, no very formidable movement of the enemy from Meade's army may be anticipated in the winter months. If General Beauregard is relieved from apprehension at Charleston, he may be able to assist me, but it is all important that I should have the means in hand to prevent the enemy gaining a fatal advantage before re-enforcements can reach me.

It must be recollected that the enemy have the choice of approaching the coast by sea either above or below me, or by both routes at once, and, in the event of his landing undisturbed, the city itself is in great danger. If he can advance upon it, all goes—harbor, forts, and all.

I am doing all I can, and have been so doing, outside the want of force.

I send this by special messenger, the son of Dr. Wright, who was executed in Norfolk, a very gallant and trustworthy lad. Please answer receipt by telegraph, and send him back.

Very respectfully,

W. H. C. WHITING,
Major-General.

HEADQUARTERS,
Wilmington, December 21, 1863.

Flag-Officer LYNCH,
Comdg. C. S. Naval Forces of North Carolina, Wilmington:

FLAG-OFFICER: I have received information from the President to the effect that the enemy, despairing of taking Charleston, propose to attack this place very shortly. At the same time, I learn from New York, via Nassau, that such is the object, and that Gillmore and Dahlgren are regarded as having failed at Charleston; also that gunboats of a peculiar construction, said to be sharp at both ends and of light draught of water, and completed at New York, are destined for here. General Pickett telegraphs me to-day that he learns from Washington, N. C., that the enemy are re-enforcing there (said to be 8,000). No doubt, if true, they intend to try to cut off communication by railroad, to prevent or delay re-enforcements either prior to or simultaneous with a demonstration here.

Any attack on this place, to be successful, must be accompanied by a strong land force, and it is not known whether they will prefer to come from above or below, or both. I do not anticipate a successful attack on the forts by gunboats, but some might succeed in getting by them, to attempt to cut off communication in the river, if built of light draught and great speed. I would, therefore, in conveying to you this information, suggest that you have your available force in readiness for action, and posted, say, near the Drum Shoals, being above the New Inlet rip, to protect that point. You would then be in readiness to observe which bar would be attacked, and certainly in the best position to render service in the defense. That rip is most exposed, owing to its distance from any guns.

I would also suggest that, in the limited and defective character of my river transportation and the heavy draft upon it, if possible, you would aid the engineer department and quartermaster, with your steamers, should they be compelled to call upon you.

Very respectfully,

W. H. C. WHITING,
Major-General.

SPECIAL ORDERS, } HDQRS. ART., ARMY NORTHERN VIRGINIA,
No. —.   }   *December 21, 1863.*

Maj. John Page, chief quartermaster, artillery, will supervise the operations of his department with the artillery in winter quarters, so as to have irregularities corrected and all requisite supplies appropriately furnished.

He will ordinarily be the medium of communication between the chief quartermaster of the artillery of each corps, the reserve, and the chief quartermaster of the army.

Maj. B. L. Wolffe, chief commissary, artillery, will occupy a like position and discharge like duties in reference to supplies in his department.

W. N. PENDLETON,
Brigadier-General, and Chief of Artillery.

HEADQUARTERS ARMY OF NORTHERN VIRGINIA,
December 22, 1863.

Maj. Gen. JUBAL A. EARLY,
Commanding, &c. :

GENERAL : I telegraphed you to-day with reference to obtaining supplies for the army while the troops are in the valley, and now write to explain my views more fully. I wish you to avail yourself of the present opportunity to collect and bring away everything that can be made useful to the army from those regions that are open to the enemy, using for this purpose both the cavalry and infantry under your command. I hear that in the lower valley, and particularly in the country on the South Branch of the Potomac, there are a good many cattle, sheep, horses, and hogs. Besides these, there is said to be a quantity of bacon, cloth, and leather, and all these supplies are accessible to and can be used by the enemy. I desire to secure all of them that it is in our power to get, and you will use your command for the purpose of keeping back the enemy while the work is being done. You will buy from all who are willing to sell, and where you cannot buy, you must impress and give certificates to the owners. Of course you will not take what is necessary for the subsistence of the people, but leave enough for that, and secure all the rest of the articles named, and any others—such as shoes, horse-shoes, and horse-shoe nails—that you can get. While so engaged, I wish you to subsist the troops on those supplies that are most difficult of transportation, such as bacon, potatoes and other vegetables, which I hear can be had, sending back those that are easy to transport, such as cattle, particularly sheep and hogs. If you cannot get enough bacon and vegetables, you might use some of the sheep and hogs.

You will understand that these instructions have no application to those parts of the country that are accessible to our ordinary agents engaged in procuring supplies. You will make requisition on Major Bell for such transportation as he can furnish, and also try to get additional facilities from the people. The cloth, leather, and other quartermaster's stores should be collected as fully as possible, leaving, of course, enough for the wants of our people. Horses and cattle can be driven back at once. I write to Major Bell by this mail to assist you as far as he is able.

Very respectfully, your obedient servant,

R. E. LEE,
General.

P. S.—You will give out that your movement is intended as a military one against the enemy, and, of course, will do them all the harm you can. You will use all the troops, including those of Imboden and Gilmor, that you may require.

HEADQUARTERS ARMY OF NORTHERN VIRGINIA,
December 22, 1863.

Maj. H. M. BELL,
Quartermaster of the Post, Staunton, Va..

MAJOR : I have written to General Early to endeavor, while the troops are in the valley, to get all the supplies of cattle, horses, hogs, sheep, cloth, leather, and other quartermaster's stores from those parts of the country that are easily accessible to the enemy. I have directed him to call upon you for transportation, and desire you to furnish all you can, and aid him in getting any more he may require from the people. I wish you to render all the assistance in your power in this work ; send your agents with the army, and wherever you can buy supplies belonging to your department—particularly horses, horse-shoes, cloth, and leather—do so, but where they cannot be bought they must be taken, giving certificates to the owners. The horses should be driven back as fast as they are procured. In taking any of the articles referred to, you will instruct your agents that while nothing must be left that can be made use of by the enemy, a sufficient supply for the necessities of the people must of course remain in their hands.

Very respectfully, your obedient servant,

R. E. LEE,
General.

P. S.—These instructions only apply to those portions of the country not accessible to our ordinary agents engaged in procuring supplies.

SALT SULPHUR SPRINGS,
December 22, 1863.

Brig. Gen. JOHN ECHOLS,
          Commanding, &c.:

GENERAL: The following has just been received from Major Myers:

Major-General JONES:

Following dispatch just received from operator at Salem, dated to-day:

"A courier just arrived says enemy was at New Castle about dark this evening."
                                        WM. B. MYERS,
                                Assistant Adjutant-General.

In view of the above you will not move your command from near Sweet Springs until you can find out positively as to whether the report is correct or not, or if your command has moved, send back a sufficient force to prevent the enemy, if he be at New Castle, from making his escape over Sweet Springs Mountain. It is suggested that the force referred to is a part or the whole of the Fourteenth Pennsylvania Cavalry.

Respectfully, &c.,

SAM. JONES,
Major-General.

———

HDQRS. DEPT. OF WESTERN VA. AND EAST TENN.,
          Dublin, December 23, 1863.

Brig. Gen. JOHN ECHOLS,
          Commanding, &c., Monroe, via Union:

It is unnecessary to move your command to Sweet Springs. Give us the latest information of the enemy's movements, where Averell went to after leaving White Sulphur.

By order, &c.:

. WM. B. MYERS,
Assistant Adjutant-General.

———

DUBLIN, *December 23, 1863.*

Col. W. H. BROWNE, *New River Bridge:*

The general directs that you impress a train, and move your command at once to Salem. A body of the enemy is reported approaching from New Castle to Heavenly Gap, near Salem. Return your train to be enabled to move either way, as necessity demands.

By order, &c.:

WM. B. MYERS,
Assistant Adjutant-General.

———

HDQRS. DEPT. OF WESTERN VA. AND EAST TENN.,
          December 24, 1863.

Col. W. H. BROWNE.
          Comdg. Forty-fifth Virginia Regiment, Salem, Va.:

The general directs that you call on the home guards and mounted men, to assist you in hunting the enemy. Report progress to these headquarters.

JAMES L. FRASER,
· *Aide-de-Camp.*

HDQRS. DEPT. OF WESTERN VA. AND EAST TENN.,
Dublin, December 24, 1863.
Brig. Gen. W. PRESTON,
Richmond, Va.:

Your letter of 22d received to-day. Please return to Abingdon and resume command of District of Southwestern Virginia.

SAM. JONES,
Major-General.

DECEMBER 27, 1863.
General J. E. B. STUART:

GENERAL: I send you the report from Clark's Mountain received this morning:

The enemy's camps of about two corps are in sight, as before reported, near Mitch-ell's Station and along the railroad between Mitchell's Station and Culpeper Court-House. No movements in their camp this morning. It is too smoky to see plainly about Brandy and vicinity, but the rising of columns of smoke indicates increased camps about Stone-House Mountain and Culpeper Court-House.

I wish if to-morrow is favorable you would ride to Clark's Mount-ain and observe the position of the enemy, and let me know your conclusion. The report from the mountain does not coincide with Lomax's of 11.15 to-day, just received.

Very respectfully,

R. E. LEE.

WILMINGTON,
December 28, 1863.
General COOPER:

My scouts bring me information, considered trustworthy, that heavy re-enforcements are daily arriving at New Berne. It is re-ported that Kinston will be attacked in a few days, that Butler designs extending his lines to Kinston and New River. Kinston should be re-enforced at once.

W. H. C. WHITING,
Major-General.

WILMINGTON, N. C.,
December 28, 1863.
General S. COOPER,
Adjutant and Inspector General, Richmond:

GENERAL: Kinston is a strategic point which should never be allowed to fall into the enemy's hands. It is undoubtedly of the very greatest importance to the defense of Wilmington. While we hold it, we may consider our communication secure, and we seriously threaten any advance on this place from toward New Berne. I am sure that an attack is meditated on that point, and imminent. The enemy are preparing for an active campaign in North Carolina, the ultimate object of which is doubtless to close the only remaining port we possess.

You are in possession of my plans of defense, and are aware of what is indispensable to success. I think I am not premature, nor ill advised, in saying that it is full time to throw a strong force into

North Carolina and here, that we may be ready. I trust that nothing in a matter of such importance will be left either to chance or to the supineness of the enemy.

I consider Barton's position as critical now, and if he is driven back mine will be very greatly endangered.

Very respectfully,

W. H. C. WHITING,
Major-General.

[Indorsements.]

ADJUTANT-GENERAL:

It would be well, under the circumstances, as shown in this and other communications, to order General Clingman's brigade to Goldsborough; and, if needed, other troops may be sent to Petersburg.

JEFFERSON DAVIS.

This has been verbally communicated to General Pickett, commanding the Department of North Carolina, who contemplates a movement into Suffolk, where the enemy are understood to be making preparations for a movement, and not in the direction which these letters intimate.

S. C. [COOPER.]

———

HEADQUARTERS,
Wilmington, December 28, 1863.

General S. COOPER,
Adjutant and Inspector General, Richmond:

GENERAL: I have received information, which I consider entirely trustworthy, that large re-enforcements are daily arriving at New Berne and Beaufort. Positive numbers not yet ascertained, but there is no doubt that the enemy is concentrated for an attack. Kinston is supposed to be the point. Butler is reported as intending to extend his lines to New River and Kinston; and this would undoubtedly be his design as preliminary to attack here, for it would place our communications in his power, and advance his front much nearer to me. Kinston ought certainly to be strengthened at once, and a heavy force thrown into North Carolina, to be ready to repel Butler's advance at first, and to re-enforce me. I telegraphed this information to you and to General Pickett to-day. Please call the President's attention to it.

Very respectfully,

W. H. C. WHITING,
Major-General.

———

DECEMBER 28, 1863.

Colonel JACKSON,
Kenansville:

The general says keep a strict lookout along your entire front. The enemy, it is believed, intends trying to extend their lines to New River.

J. H. HILL,
Major, and Assistant Adjutant-General.

HDQRS. DEPT. OF WESTERN VA. AND EAST TENN.,
Dublin, December 29, 1863.

General S. COOPER,
Adjt. and Insp. Gen., C. S. Army, Richmond, Va.:

GENERAL: The recent raid on Salem shows, I think, very clearly the importance of having on this line of railroad a force adequate to its protection. I have been satisfied ever since I assumed command in this department of the importance of keeping a regular force directly on this road, and placed such a force on it last spring, but in July last, under orders from the War Department, I was obliged to send that force away, and have not been able since then to replace it.

Under the conviction that it is important to keep some regular force on this road, I respectfully and earnestly recommend that the Fifty-fourth and Sixty-third Virginia Regiments, now serving with the army lately commanded by General Bragg, be ordered to report to me for duty, that I may employ them to protect this important line. Both of those regiments were under my command a year ago. The Fifty-fourth was sent last spring, under orders from the War Department, to East Tennessee. About the 1st of September last, under an urgent call from Major-General Buckner, which you desired me to comply with, I sent the Sixty-third Regiment to East Tennessee, for temporary duty, as I supposed. They both, I think, belong properly to my command. The exigencies of the service have caused them to be temporarily detached; they have rendered valuable and distinguished service under General Bragg, and are now greatly reduced in numbers.

I think the interests of the service will be promoted by bringing them back to this department, where they were raised and organized. The senior officer of the two regiments, Col. R. C. Trigg, of the Fifty-fourth, is an officer of great merit, who distinguished himself at Chickamauga by his gallantry and general good conduct, and is held in high esteem by the officers under whom he has served, is thoroughly acquainted with this section of country, and, I think, could aid materially in its defense. If those two regiments are brought here I am sure they can render most valuable aid in protecting this section of country. I believe that under the laws which it is understood will be passed by the present Congress, they can be filled up nearly, if not quite, to the maximum, by the opening of spring. It is probable they will diminish rather than increase in strength where they are.

I earnestly commend my suggestion to the favorable consideration of the War Department.

Very respectfully, your obedient servant,

SAM. JONES,
Major-General.

———

HDQRS. DEPT. OF WESTERN VA. AND EAST TENN.,
Dublin, December 29, 1863.

General S. COOPER,
Adjutant and Inspector General, Richmond:

GENERAL: In consequence of information received from Brig. Gen. W. E. Jones, I desire to withdraw my indorsement of the 24th instant on a letter from Major-General Ransom regarding the Twenty-first Virginia Cavalry, better known as Colonel Peters' regiment. The regiment has been for some time in W. E. Jones' brigade, and I have confidence in his judgment as to the best course to pursue with regard to it. It is at least due to Colonel Peters that no action be taken in the matter until he has made the representation in regard to it which he proposes to do in two or three days.

Very respectfully, your obedient servant,

SAM. JONES,
Major-General.

WELDON, N. C.,
December 30, 1863.

Maj. C. PICKETT,
Assistant Adjutant-General, &c.:

MAJOR: I beg leave to represent to the major-general commanding this department the propriety of forming a new regiment of cavalry and artillery, to be composed of the following troops, viz:

1. The Twelfth North Carolina Battalion, now at Kinston, consisting of three companies (mounted). This organization was formerly known as Wheeler's.

2. Company L, Sixty-second Georgia Regiment, commanded by Captain Barham, numbering 136 men. This company makes the eleventh company belonging to the Sixty-second Georgia, and Captain Barham, under authority from the Secretary of War to raise a battalion, has increased his company to its present numbers. This company of 136 men would make two very respectable companies, sufficiently large for efficient action. This company may very well be detached from the Sixty-second Georgia.

3. There are in the Seventh Confederate Cavalry, Colonel Taliaferro, now at Ivor, twelve companies. The two extra companies might very well be taken from this regiment and made part of the new organization.

4. To these seven companies of cavalry I propose to attach one or two batteries of field artillery, and suggest the Macon Light Artillery, Captain Slaten, now stationed here, and one other battery to be selected from Lieut. Col. J. R. Branch's command.

These troops, organized into a regiment under an enterprising and vigorous soldier, would render valuable services to this department. At present at least one-half of this force is entirely inefficient for want of proper organization and management.

Our present lines of defense run at a distance of about 100 miles from the ocean, leaving a large area of country unoccupied by the enemy, but still unable for permanent occupation by our small force. This cavalry and artillery force, under a daring and skillful chief, would do much to secure to us this intermediate section. I need not say how important such an organization would be in meeting the raids of the enemy and harassing their outposts and transports. Over this command a good cavalry and artillery officer ought to be placed. As a valuable adjunct to this force might be added two companies of cavalry, under Lieutenant-Colonel Wynn. These companies now belong to the State forces and could not be combined with regular Confederate troops, but might be made of great service if attached to this new command. At present two companies of cavalry not acting in concert with the main Confederate force can be but of little effect. I understand the Governor of North Carolina has directed Colonel Hinton, commanding these forces, to report to Major-General Pickett.

I trust the major-general will pardon these suggestions, but I regard the matter as important.

I am, sir, very respectfully,

M. W. RANSOM,
Brigadier-General.

[Indorsement.]

HEADQUARTERS DEPARTMENT OF NORTH CAROLINA,
Petersburg, January 12, 1864.

I respectfully forward this communication, and recommend Maj. James Dearing as an officer well known to me. He has served with me for two years under my immediate command. I know of no one more justly entitled to promotion than Major Dearing. The service needs an efficient officer in the section of country to which he will go.

GEO. E. PICKETT,
Major-General.

HEADQUARTERS,
Wilmington, December 30, 1863.

Colonel LAMB,
Commanding Fort Fisher:

COLONEL: I have been giving the subject of the defense of your post much consideration. As you know, its weak point has always been the land approach. Topsail will be rendered secure, as I am now throwing up exterior lines on Virginia Creek just beyond Topsail and controlling that point. If the enemy design a land attack on this side the river and the fort, I think a work somewhat similar to Fort Campbell, though not so extensive, can be put up just below Gatlin, inclosed from the Sound to the beach, together with a battery at A to flank the approaches ; the direction of the faces armed with cannon to be varied to suit the ground, and that toward the enemy and seaward to be provided with ample traverses. In connection with this, the troops might throw up a line from Burns and the river over toward the battery which you have between Gatlin and Fisher, and occupy the hill near Fisher.

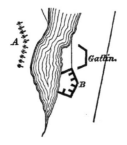

I want to know what force you will be able to spare from other works now going on at the fort and which may be postponed in favor of this. Also, how soon you might get one or even two guns in position and covered.

As to guns, you would want four or five, and they might be taken from Fisher, to be supplied hereafter. The 10-inch on your left flank could very well go there, and perhaps an 8-inch.

An advanced work like that proposed would, I think, secure the fort. It is likely the enemy would interrupt you by firing. Gatlin and another Whitworth, with the one you have, might keep them off. After getting the new work well advanced you might leave Gatlin.

Let me hear from you on the points suggested.

Every effort is being made to procure more labor.

Very respectfully,

W. H. C. WHITING,
Major-General.

———

HEADQUARTERS DEPARTMENT OF NORTH CAROLINA,
Petersburg, Va., December 31, 1863.

General S. COOPER,
Adjt. and Insp. Gen., C. S. Army, Richmond, Va.:

GENERAL: I have the honor to report that there is every probability of a raid in a few days from the direction of Suffolk. I think there will probably be a combined movement—Spear with cavalry from direction of Suffolk, and a negro expedition up the James, landing on the south side. I will try and make preparations to receive them.

Some pontoons are indispensable, as I must cross the Blackwater and get in their rear, if possible. The river (Blackwater) is very high, and not fordable. There are no pontoons in the department. There were a few which were taken from the Appomattox and sent to Richmond.

Will you please be kind enough to give Capt. Raymond Fairfax, chief of my pioneer corps, who will deliver this, an order for eight? I understand they have them to spare in Richmond. I wish to have them put in the river near Ivor as soon as possible, say Sunday at latest.

I shall report in person at your office on Saturday, and get some advice and assistance about the North Carolina affairs.

Whiting is much alarmed, as you doubtless have seen by his letters to the Department, though Barton reports all quiet.

I am, general, very respectfully, your obedient servant,

GEO. E. PICKETT,
Major-General.

P. S.—The enemy advanced on Greenville yesterday, but were ambuscaded and repulsed; so says telegram just received. Enemy 2,000 strong.

[Indorsements.]

JANUARY 1, 1864.

ENGINEER BUREAU:
Have you the pontoons at command? If so, they should be sent
without delay, as requested.

J. A. SEDDON.

ENGINEER BUREAU,
January 5, 1864.

Pontoons promptly sent.
This letter respectfully returned to honorable Secretary of War.

ALFRED L. RIVES,
Lieutenant-Colonel, and Acting Chief of Bureau.

---

*Abstract from return of the Army of Northern Virginia. General Robert E. Lee,
C. S. Army, commanding, for the month of December, 1863.*

Command.	Present for duty.		Effective total.	Aggregate present.	Aggregate present and absent.	Pieces of artillery.
	Officers.	Men.				
General headquarters *a*	32	270	270	409	644	......
Second Army Corps:						
Headquarters	10	......	......	10	21	......
Early's division	450	4,675	4,675	6,225	10,768	......
Johnson's division	421	4,553	4,553	5,651	10,646	......
Rodes' division	546	6,312	6,312	8,201	14,102	......
Total	1,427	15,540	15,540	20,087	35,537	......
Third Army Corps:						
Headquarters	11	......	......	11	18	......
Anderson's division	497	6,180	6,180	7,592	12,409	......
Heth's division *b*	326	4,331	4,331	5,332	8,271	......
Wilcox's division *c*	429	4,998	4,998	6,241	9,156	......
Total	1,263	15,468	15,468	19,176	29,854	......
Cavalry Corps:						
Headquarters	13	......	......	13	17	......
Hampton's division	306	3,927	3,927	4,953	9,354	......
Fitz. Lee's division	272	3,623	3,623	4,461	7,881	......
Total	591	7,550	7,550	9,427	17,252	......
Artillery Corps:						
First Army Corps	18	382	382	439	563	13
Second Army Corps *d*	65	1,294	1,294	1,559	2,268	62
Third Army Corps	117	2,096	2,096	2,483	3,352	78
Cavalry Corps	17	366	366	415	585	19
Total	217	4,138	4,138	4,896	6,768	172
Maryland Line *e*	39	592	592	720	1,198	3
Grand total *f*	3,569	43,558	43,558	54,715	91,253	175

a Including provost guard, scouts, guides, and couriers.
b Walker's brigade detached.
c Thomas' brigade detached.
d Nelson's battalion not reported.
e Also reported in Department of Richmond.
f The Valley District not reported.

Organization of the Army of Northern Virginia, General R. E. Lee, C. S. Army, commanding, December 31, 1863.

GENERAL HEADQUARTERS.

1st Virginia Infantry Battalion, Maj. D. B. Bridgford.
39th Virginia Cavalry Battalion, Maj. J. H. Richardson.

SECOND ARMY CORPS.

Lieut. Gen. R. S. EWELL.*

EARLY'S DIVISION.

Brig. Gen. HARRY T. HAYS.†

Hays' Brigade.

Brig. Gen. HARRY T. HAYS.

5th Louisiana, Col. Henry Forno.
6th Louisiana, Col. William Monaghan.
7th Louisiana, Col. David B. Penn.
8th Louisiana, Maj. G. A. Lester.
9th Louisiana, Col. W. R. Peck.

Gordon's Brigade.

Brig. Gen. J. B. GORDON.

13th Georgia, Col. J. H. Baker.
26th Georgia, Col. E. N. Atkinson.
31st Georgia, Col. Clement A. Evans.
38th Georgia, Col. J. D. Mathews.
60th Georgia, Col. W. H. Stiles.
61st Georgia, Col. John H. Lamar.

Pegram's Brigade.

Brig. Gen. JOHN PEGRAM.

13th Virginia, Col. James B. Terrill.
31st Virginia, Col. John S. Hoffman.
49th Virginia, Col. J. Catlett Gibson.
52d Virginia, Col. James H. Skinner.
58th Virginia, Col. F. H. Board.

Hoke's Brigade.

Brig. Gen. R. F. HOKE.

6th North Carolina, Col. R. F. Webb.
21st North Carolina, Lieut. Col. W. S. Rankin.
54th North Carolina, Col. Kenneth M. Murchison.
57th North Carolina, Col. A. C. Godwin.
1st North Carolina Battalion Sharpshooters, Capt. John A. Cooper.

JOHNSON'S DIVISION.‡

Maj. Gen. EDWARD JOHNSON.

"Stonewall" Brigade.

Brig. Gen. J. A. WALKER.

2d Virginia, Col. J. Q. A. Nadenbousch.
4th Virginia, Lieut. Col. R. D. Gardner.
5th Virginia, Col. J. H. S. Funk.
27th Virginia, Lieut. Col. C. L. Haynes.
33d Virginia, Col. F. W. M. Holliday.

Steuart's Brigade.

Brig. Gen. GEORGE H. STEUART.

1st North Carolina), Col. H. A. Brown.
3d North Carolina, Col. S. D. Thruston.
10th Virginia, Col. E. T. H. Warren.
23d Virginia, Col. A. G. Taliaferro.
37th Virginia, Col. T. V. Williams.

Jones' Brigade.

Brig. Gen. J. M. JONES.

21st Virginia, Col. W. A. Witcher.
25th Virginia, Col. J. C. Higginbotham.
42d Virginia, Col. R. W. Withers.
44th Virginia, Col. Norvell Cobb.
48th Virginia, Col. R. H. Dungan.
50th Virginia, Col. A. S. Vandeventer.

Stafford's Brigade.

Brig. Gen. L. A. STAFFORD.

1st Louisiana, Col. W. R. Shivers.
2d Louisiana, Col. J. M. Williams.
10th Louisiana, Col. E. Waggaman.
14th Louisiana, Col. Z. York.
15th Louisiana, Col. Edmund Pendleton.

---

* Resumed command of the corps on or about December 4, relieving Major-General Early.

† Commanding *vice* Early, assigned to command in the Valley District December 15. On the face of the return but two brigadier-generals are reported as present for duty in the division.

‡ Only two brigadier-generals reported present for duty.

RODES' DIVISION.*

Maj. Gen. R. E. RODES.

Daniel's Brigade.

Brig. Gen. JUNIUS DANIEL.

32d North Carolina, Col. E. C. Brabble.
43d North Carolina, Col. T. S. Kenan.
45th North Carolina, Col. S. H. Boyd.
53d North Carolina, Col. W. A. Owens.
2d North Carolina Battalion, Maj. J. J. Iredell.

Ramseur's Brigade.

Brig. Gen. S. D. RAMSEUR.

2d North Carolina, Col. W. R. Cox.
4th North Carolina, Col. Bryan Grimes.
14th North Carolina, Col. R. T. Bennett.
30th North Carolina, Col. F. M. Parker.

Doles' Brigade.

Brig. Gen. GEORGE DOLES.

4th Georgia, Col. Philip Cook.
12th Georgia, Col. Edward Willis.
21st Georgia, Col. John T. Mercer.
44th Georgia, Col. S. P. Lumpkin.

Battle's Brigade.

Brig. Gen. C. A. BATTLE.

3d Alabama, Col. C. Forsyth.
5th Alabama, Col. J. M. Hall.
6th Alabama, Col. J. N. Lightfoot.
12th Alabama, Col. S. B. Pickens.
26th Alabama, Col. E. A. O'Neal.

Johnston's Brigade.

Brig. Gen. R. D. JOHNSTON.

5th North Carolina, Col. T. M. Garrett.
12th North Carolina, Col. H. E. Coleman.
20th North Carolina, Col. T. F. Toon.
23d North Carolina, C. C. Blacknall.

THIRD ARMY CORPS.

Lieut. Gen. A. P. HILL.

ANDERSON'S DIVISION.†

Maj. Gen. R. H. ANDERSON.

Mahone's Brigade.

Brig. Gen. WILLIAM MAHONE.

6th Virginia, Col. G. T. Rogers.
12th Virginia, Col. D. A. Weisiger.
16th Virginia, Col. J. H. Ham.
41st Virginia, Col. W. A. Parham.
61st Virginia, Col. V. D. Groner.

Posey's Brigade.

Col. N. H. HARRIS.

12th Mississippi, Col. W. H. Taylor.
16th Mississippi, Col. Samuel E. Baker.
19th Mississippi, Col. N. H. Harris.
48th Mississippi, Col. J. M. Jayne.

Wilcox's Brigade.

Col. J. C. C. SANDERS.

8th Alabama, Col. Y. L. Royston.
9th Alabama, Col. J. H. King.
10th Alabama, Col. W. H. Forney.
11th Alabama, Col. J. C. C. Sanders.
14th Alabama, Col. L. Pinckard.

Wright's Brigade.

Brig. Gen. A. R. WRIGHT.

3d Georgia, Col. E. J. Walker.
22d Georgia, Capt. George W. Rush.
48th Georgia, Col. William Gibson.
2d Georgia Battalion, Maj. C. J. Moffett.

Perry's Brigade.

Brig. Gen. E. A. PERRY.

2d Florida, Col. L. G. Pyles.
5th Florida, Lieut. Col. T. B. Lamar.
8th Florida, Col. David Lang.

---

* Only three brigadier-generals reported present for duty.
† Only two general officers (brigadier-generals) reported present for duty.

HETH'S DIVISION.*

Maj. Gen. HENRY HETH.

Davis' Brigade.

Brig. Gen. J. R. DAVIS.

2d Mississippi, Col. J. M. Stone.
11th Mississippi, Col. F. M. Green.
42d Mississippi, Col. Hillery Moseley.
55th North Carolina, Col. J. K. Connally.

Kirkland's Brigade.

Brig. Gen. W. W. KIRKLAND.

11th North Carolina, Col. C. Leventhorpe.
26th North Carolina, Col. J. R. Lane.
44th North Carolina, Col. T. C. Singeltary.
47th North Carolina, Col. G. H. Faribault.
52d North Carolina, Col. J. K. Marshall.

Cooke's Brigade.

Brig. Gen. J. R. COOKE.

15th North Carolina, Col. William MacRae.
27th North Carolina, Col. J. A. Gilmer, jr.
46th North Carolina, Col. E. D. Hall.
48th North Carolina, Lieut. Col. Samuel H. Walkup.

Walker's Brigade.†

Brig. Gen. H. H. WALKER.

40th Virginia, Col. J. M. Brockenbrough.
47th Virginia, Col. R. M. Mayo.
55th Virginia, Col. W. S. Christian.
22d Virginia Battalion, Lieut. Col. E. P. Tayloe.

Archer's Brigade.‡

13th Alabama, Col. B. D. Fry.
1st Tennessee (Provisional Army), Col. Peter Turney.
7th Tennessee, Col. John A. Fite.
14th Tennessee, Col. William McComb.

WILCOX'S DIVISION.

Maj. Gen. CADMUS M. WILCOX.

Lane's Brigade.

Brig. Gen. J. H. LANE.

7th North Carolina, Col. E. G. Haywood.
18th North Carolina, Col. J. D. Barry.
28th North Carolina, Col. S. D. Lowe.
33d North Carolina, Col. C. M. Avery.
37th North Carolina, Col. William M. Barbour.

Perrin's Brigade.

Brig. Gen. ABNER PERRIN.

1st South Carolina (Provisional Army), Col. D. H. Hamilton.
1st South Carolina Rifles, Col. F. E. Harrison.
12th South Carolina, Col. J. L. Miller.
13th South Carolina, Col. B. T. Brockman.
14th South Carolina, Col. J. N. Brown.

Scales' Brigade.

Brig. Gen. A. M. SCALES.

13th North Carolina, Col. J. H. Hyman.
16th North Carolina, Lieut. Col. William A. Stowe.
22d North Carolina, Col. Thomas S. Gallaway.
34th North Carolina, Col. W. L. J. Lowrance.
38th North Carolina, Col. W. J. Hoke.

Thomas' Brigade.§

Brig. Gen. E. L. THOMAS.

14th Georgia, Col. Robert W. Folsom.
35th Georgia, Col. B. H. Holt.
45th Georgia, Col. Thomas J. Simmons.
49th Georgia, Col. S. T. Player.

---

* Only one brigadier-general reported present for duty.
† Detached; probably in the Valley District, where it is reported January 31, 1864.
‡ Not accounted for on original. Probably yet consolidated with Walker's brigade.
§ Detached; probably in Valley District, where it is reported January 31, 1864.

MARYLAND LINE.*

Col. BRADLEY T. JOHNSON.

1st Maryland Battalion, Lieut. Col. J. R. Herbert.
1st Maryland Cavalry Battalion, Lieut. Col. Ridgely Brown.
Baltimore (Maryland) Light Artillery, Capt. W. H. Griffin.

CAVALRY CORPS.

Maj. Gen. J. E. B. STUART.

HAMPTON'S DIVISION.

Gordon's Brigade.	*Young's Brigade.*
Brig. Gen. JAMES B. GORDON.	Brig. Gen. P. M. B. YOUNG.
1st North Carolina, Col. W. H. Cheek.	1st South Carolina, Col. J. L. Black.
2d North Carolina, Col. W. G. Robinson.	2d South Carolina, Col. T. J. Lipscomb.
4th North Carolina, Col. D. D. Ferebee.	Cobb's (Georgia) Legion, Col. G. J.
5th North Carolina, Lieut. Col. S. B.	Wright.
Evans.	Jeff. Davis (Mississippi) Legion, Lieut.
	Col. J. F. Waring.
	Phillips (Georgia) Legion, Lieut. Col. W.
	W. Rich.

Rosser's Brigade.

Brig. Gen. T. L. ROSSER.

7th Virginia, Col. R. H. Dulany.
11th Virginia, Col. O. R. Funsten.
12th Virginia, Col. A. W. Harman.
35th Virginia Battalion, Lieut. Col. E. V. White.

FITZHUGH LEE'S DIVISION.

Maj. Gen. FITZHUGH LEE.

W. H. F. Lee's Brigade.	*Lomax's Brigade.*
Col. J. R. CHAMBLISS, jr.	Brig. Gen. L. L. LOMAX.
9th Virginia, Col. R. L. T. Beale.	5th Virginia, Lieut. Col. H. Clay Pate.
10th Virginia, Col. J. Lucius Davis.	6th Virginia, Col. Julian Harrison.
13th Virginia, Col. J. R. Chambliss, jr.	15th Virginia, Col. William B. Ball.

Wickham's Brigade.

Brig. Gen. W. C. WICKHAM.

1st Virginia, Col. R. W. Carter.
2d Virginia, Col. T. T. Munford.
3d Virginia, Col T. H. Owen.
4th Virginia, Lieut. Col. W. H. Payne.

ARTILLERY.

Brig. Gen. W. N. PENDLETON.

SECOND ARMY CORPS.

Brig. Gen. A. L. LONG.

Andrews' Battalion.	*Carter's Battalion.*
Lieut. Col. R. S. ANDREWS.	Lieut. Col. T. H. CARTER.
Alleghany (Virginia) Artillery, Capt. J. C. Carpenter.	Jeff. Davis (Alabama) Artillery, Capt. W. J. Reese.
Chesapeake (Maryland) Artillery, Lieut. W. S. Chew.	King William (Virginia) Artillery, Capt. W. P. Carter.
1st Maryland Battery, Capt. W. F. Dement.	Morris (Virginia) Artillery, Capt. R. C. M. Page.
Lee (Virginia) Battery, Lieut. C. W. Statham.	Orange (Virginia) Artillery, Capt. C. W. Fry.

* Also reported as in the Department of Richmond.

ARTILLERY—Continued.

Jones' Battalion.

Lieut. Col. H. P. JONES.

Charlottesville (Virginia) Artillery, Capt. J. McD. Carrington.
Courtney (Virginia) Artillery, Capt. W. A. Tanner.
Louisiana Guard Artillery, Capt. C. A. Green.
Staunton (Virginia) Artillery, Capt. A. W. Garber.

Nelson's Battalion.

Lieut. Col. WILLIAM NELSON.

Amherst (Virginia) Artillery, Capt. T. J. Kirkpatrick.
Fluvanna (Virginia) Artillery, Capt. John L. Massie.
Milledge (Georgia) Artillery, Capt. John Milledge, jr.

First Virginia Regiment.

Col. J. THOMPSON BROWN.

Powhatan Artillery, Capt. W. J. Dance.
2d Richmond (Virginia) Howitzers, Capt. David Watson.
3d Richmond (Virginia) Howitzers, Capt. B. H. Smith, jr.
Rockbridge (Virginia) Artillery, Capt. Archibald Graham.
Salem (Virginia) Flying Artillery, Capt. C. B. Griffin.

THIRD ARMY CORPS.

Col. R. L. WALKER.

Cutts' Battalion.

Lieut. Col. A. S. CUTTS.

Georgia Battery, Capt. G. M. Patterson.
Georgia Battery, Capt. H. M. Ross.
Irwin (Georgia) Artillery, Capt. J. T. Wingfield.

Pegram's Battalion.

Maj. W. J. PEGRAM.

Crenshaw (Virginia) Battery, Capt. Thomas Ellett.
Fredericksburg (Virginia) Artillery, Capt. E. A. Marye.
Letcher (Virginia) Artillery, Capt. T. A. Brander.
Pee Dee (South Carolina) Artillery, Capt. E. B. Brunson.
Purcell (Virginia) Artillery, Capt. J. McGraw.

Garnett's Battalion.

Lieut. Col. J. J. GARNETT.

Donaldsonville (Louisiana) Artillery, Capt. V. Maurin.
Huger (Virginia) Artillery, Capt. J. D. Moore.
Lewis (Virginia) Artillery, Capt. N. Penick.
Norfolk (Virginia) Light Artillery Blues, Capt. C. R. Grandy.

Poague's Battalion.

Maj. WILLIAM T. POAGUE.

North Carolina Battery, Capt. J. Graham.
Albemarle (Virginia) Artillery, Capt. J. W. Wyatt.
Brooke (Virginia) Battery, Capt. A. W. Utterback.
Madison (Mississippi) Artillery, Capt. George Ward.

McIntosh's Battalion.

Maj. D. G. McINTOSH.

Danville (Virginia) Artillery, Capt. R. S. Rice.
Hardaway (Alabama) Artillery, Capt. W. B. Hurt.
2d Rockbridge (Virginia) Artillery, Capt. W. K. Donald.
Virginia Battery, Capt. M. Johnson.

Haskell's Battalion.

Maj. J. C. HASKELL.

Branch (North Carolina) Artillery, Capt. John R. Potts.
Nelson (Virginia) Artillery, Capt. J. N. Lamkin.
Palmetto (South Carolina) Battery, Capt. H. R. Garden.
Rowan (North Carolina) Artillery, Capt. John A. Ramsay.

CAVALRY CORPS.

Maj. R. F. BECKHAM.

Virginia Battery, Capt. J. Breathed.
South Carolina Battery, Capt. J. F. Hart.
Virginia Battery, Capt. R. P. Chew.
Virginia Battery, Capt. W. M. McGregor.
Virginia Battery, Capt. M. N. Moorman.

ARTILLERY RESERVE.

Col. H. C. CABELL.

North Carolina Battery, Capt. B. C. Manly.
1st Richmond (Virginia) Howitzers, Capt. E. S. McCarthy.
Pulaski (Georgia) Artillery. Lieut. M. Callaway.
Troup (Georgia) Artillery, Capt. H. H. Carlton.

VALLEY DISTRICT.

Maj. Gen. JUBAL A. EARLY.*

Imboden's Command.

Brig. Gen. J. D. IMBODEN.

62d Virginia, Col. George H. Smith.
2d Maryland Cavalry Battalion, Maj. H. W. Gilmor.
18th Virginia Cavalry, Col. G. W. Imboden.
41st Virginia Cavalry Battalion, Maj. Robert White.
Virginia Battery, Capt. J. H. McClanahan.

Abstract from return of the Department of Richmond, Maj. Gen. Arnold Elzey, C. S. Army, commanding, December 31, 1863.

Command.	Present for duty.		Effective total.	Aggregate present.	Aggregate present and absent.	Pieces of field artillery.
	Officers.	Men.				
General headquarters	10	......	......	10	11	......
Hunton's brigade	76	1,093	1,085	1,345	2,565	......
Kemper's brigade	96	1,256	1,256	1,682	3,212	4
Maryland Line†	39	592	592	720	1,198	3
Cavalry	32	424	419	562	1,101	......
Richmond defenses	81	1,621	1,787	2,082	2,290	14
Chaffin's Farm artillery	12	239	235	291	312	10
Chaffin's Bluff	24	323	412	465	524	18
Drewry's Bluff	15	352	420	452	508	12
Total	397	5,900	6,206	7,559	11,716	61

* The original return reports Imboden as commanding the district, but see Early's assignment of December 15.
†Also accounted for in return of the Army of Northern Virginia for this date.

Organization of troops in the Department of Richmond, Maj. Gen. Arnold Elzey, C. S. Army, commanding, December 31, 1863.

Hunton's Brigade.

' Brig. Gen. E. HUNTON.

8th Virginia, Capt. Henry C. Bowie.
18th Virginia, Capt. Henry T. Owen.
19th Virginia, Capt. J. G. Woodson.
28th Virginia, Capt. W. L. Wingfield.
56th Virginia, Capt. John Richardson.

Kemper's Brigade.

Col. W. R. TERRY.

1st Virginia, Lieut. Col. F. H. Langley.
3d Virginia, Maj. W. H. Pryor.
7th Virginia, Col. C. C. Flowerree.
11th Virginia, Capt. R. W. Douthat.
24th Virginia, Lieut. Col. R. L. Maury.
Cooper's (Virginia) Battery, Capt. R. L. Cooper.

Maryland Line.

Col. BRADLEY T. JOHNSON.

1st Battalion Infantry, Col. B. T. Johnson.
1st Battalion Cavalry, Lieut. Col. R. Brown.
2d Maryland Battery, Capt. W. H. Griffin.

Cavalry.

Holcombe (South Carolina) Legion, Col. W. P. Shingler.
42d Virginia Battalion. Lieut. Col. W. T. Robins.

RICHMOND DEFENSES.

Col. W. H. STEVENS.

First Division, Inner Line.

Lieut. Col. J. W. ATKINSON.

10th Battalion Virginia Heavy Artillery, Maj. J. O. Hensley.
19th Battalion Virginia Heavy Artillery, Maj. N. R. Cary.

Second Division, Inner Line.

Lieut. Col. JAMES HOWARD.

18th Battalion Virginia Heavy Artillery, Maj. M B. Hardin.
20th Battalion Virginia Heavy Artillery, Maj. J. E. Robertson.

Light Artillery.

Lieut. Col. C. E. LIGHTFOOT.

Caroline (Virginia) Light Artillery, Capt. T. R. Thornton.
2d Nelson (Virginia) Light Artillery, Capt. J. H. Rives.
Surry (Virginia) Light Artillery, Capt. J. D. Hankins.

CHAFFIN'S BLUFF.

Lieut. Col. J. M. MAURY.

Richmond Fayette (Virginia) Artillery, Capt. M. C. Macon.
Goochland (Virginia) Artillery, Capt. J. Talley.
Howitzer (Virginia) Battery, Capt. E. R. Young.
Lunenburg (Virginia) Artillery, Capt. C. T. Allen.
Pamunkey (Virginia) Artillery, Capt. A. J. Jones.

DREWRY'S BLUFF.

Maj. F. W. SMITH.

Johnston (Virginia) Artillery, Capt. B. J. Epes.
Neblett (Virginia) Artillery, Capt, W. G. Coleman.
Southside (Virginia) Artillery, Capt. J. W. Drewry.
United (Virginia) Artillery, Capt. T. Kevill.

CHAFFIN'S FARM.

Alexandria (Virginia) Artillery, Capt. D. L. Smoot.
Matthews (Virginia) Artillery, Capt. A. D. Armistead.
McComas (Virginia) Artillery, Capt. D. A. French.

Abstract from return of the Department of North Carolina, Maj. Gen. George E. Pickett, C. S. Army, commanding, December 31, 1863; headquarters Petersburg, Va.

Command.	Present for duty.		Effective total present.	Aggregate present.	Aggregate present and absent.	Pieces of field artillery	Stations as reported December 20.
	Officers.	Men.					
General headquarters a	16	173	173	200	229	....	
Barton's brigade	84	1,300	1,300	1,647	3,156	.	Kinston and vicinity.
Clingman's brigade	145	1,930	1,930	2,447	3,159	......	Petersburg, Va.
Ransom's brigade	152	2,589	2,589	2,869	3,510	......	Weldon, N. C.
C S. Zouaves (Lieut. Col. A. Coppens).	19	43	43	62	91	......	Franklin Depot, Va.
10th Georgia Battalion (Maj. J. E Rylander).	21	304	304	365	457	......	Do.
North Carolina Battalion (Lieut. Col John N. Whitford).	26	512	512	627	847	......	Near Kinston, N. C.
17th Virginia (Col. Morton Marye).	23	247	247	322	533	......	Ivor Station.
18th Virginia (Col. R E Withers).	13	244	244	989	687	......	Petersburg, Va.
44th Virginia Battalion (Maj. Peter V. Batte).	8	128	128	167	244	......	Do.
Provost guard	5	32	32	39	75	......	Kinston, N. C.
Total infantry	406	7,329	7,329	8,834	12,759	......	
7th Confederate Cavalry (Col. V. H Taliaferro)	24	409	409	528	666	3	Ivor Station.
62d Georgia Cavalry (Col. J. R. Griffin).	32	376	376	510	866	6	On the Blackwater, &c,.
3d North Carolina Cavalry (Col. John A. Baker).	34	554	554	684	971	......	Near Kinston.
Total cavalry	90	1,339	1,339	1,722	2,500	9	
Artillery command b (Walton's).	33	614	614	717	1,024	30	Petersburg, Va.
Artillery command c (Branch's).	35	684	684	895	1,025	35	Do.
1st North Carolina Artillery, Battery E	3	91	91	100	160	8	Weldon, N. C.
1st North Carolina Artillery, (headquarters and two batteries).	13	123	123	148	266	......	Fort Branch, N. C.
Andrews' (Alabama) battery	2	51	51	67	86	4	Near Kinston.
Cumming's (North Carolina) battery)	3	70	70	84	98	4	Do.
Dickson's (North Carolina) battery.	1	102	102	125	135	4	Do.
Graham's (Virginia) battery	4	73	73	86	91	4	Weldon, N. C.
Macon (Georgia) Light Artillery.	3	91	91	108	138	4	Do.
Robertson's (North Carolina) heavy battery.	4	66	66	83	99	2	Near Kinston.
Starr's (North Carolina) battery.	3	125	125	140	153	5	Do.
Total artillery	104	2,090	2,090	2,483	3,275	100	
Grand total	700	10,931	10,931	13,239	18,763	109	

a Including the Independent Signal Corps.
b Embracing Dearing's and the Washington (Louisiana) battalions.
c Embracing Boggs', Coit's, and Moseley's battalions.

Composition of the infantry brigades in the Department of North Carolina, December 31, 1863.

Barton's Brigade.

Brig. Gen. SETH M. BARTON.

9th Virginia, Col. J. J. Phillips.
14th Virginia, Col. William White.
38th Virginia, Lieut. Col. J. R. Cabell.
53d Virginia, Col. William R. Aylett.
57th Virginia, Col. C. R. Fontaine.

Clingman's Brigade.

Brig. Gen. T. L. CLINGMAN.

8th North Carolina, Col. H. M. Shaw.
31st North Carolina, Col. J. V. Jordan.
51st North Carolina, Col. Hector McKethan.
61st North Carolina, Col. J. D. Radcliffe.

Ransom's Brigade.

Brig. Gen. M. W. RANSOM.

24th North Carolina, Col. William J. Clarke.
25th North Carolina, Col. H. M. Rutledge.
35th North Carolina, Col. J. G. Jones.
49th North Carolina, Col. Lee M. McAfee.
56th North Carolina, Col. P. F. Faison.

Abstract from return of the troops in the Defenses of Wilmington, N. C., Maj. Gen. W. H. C. Whiting, C. S. Army, commanding, December 31, 1863.

Command.	Present for duty.		Effective total.	Aggregate present.	Aggregate present and absent.	Pieces of artillery.	
	Officers.	Men.				Heavy.	Field.
General headquarters a	19	38	38	59	77	......	......
Engineer troops..............................	1	73	75	85	99	......	......
Martin's brigade	130	2,502	2,637	2,965	3,971	......	......
Cavalry......................................	26	363	00	455	579	......	......
Light artillery...................	26	623	647	683	761	......	28
Heavy artillery................................	104	2,159	2,688	3,052	3,728	150	.....
Total	306	5,758	6,485	7,299	9,215	150	28

a Including signal corps.

Troops in the Defenses of Wilmington, N. C., Maj. Gen. W. H. C. Whiting, C. S. Army, commanding, December 31, 1863.

Martin's Brigade.

Brig. Gen. J. G. MARTIN.

17th North Carolina, Col. W. F. Martin.
42d North Carolina, Col. G. C. Gibbs.
50th North Carolina, Maj. J. C. Van Hook.
66th North Carolina, Col. A. D. Moore.

Cavalry.

Col. GEORGE JACKSON.

7th Confederate (three companies).
5th North Carolina (one company).
5th South Carolina (two companies).

Light Artillery.

1st North Carolina, Battery I, Capt. T. J. Southerland.
3d North Carolina Battalion, Maj. John W. Moore.
13th North Carolina Battalion, Battery D, Capt. Z. T. Adams.
Staunton Hill (Virginia) Artillery, Capt. A. B. Paris.

Heavy Artillery.

Fort Caswell,* Col. T. M. Jones.
Fort Fisher,* Col. William Lamb.
Fort Holmes.* } Col. John J. Hedrick.
Fort Pender.* }
Wilmington, Col. G. A. Cunningham.

*These forts under command of Brig. Gen. Louis Hébert.

Abstract from return of the Army of Western Virginia and East Tennessee, Maj. Gen. Samuel Jones, C. S. Army, commanding, December 31, 1863; head-quarters Dublin Depot, Va.a

Command.	Present for duty.		Effective total.	Aggregate present.	Aggregate present and absent.	Aggregate last return.	Pieces of field artillery.
	Officers.	Men.					
General staff	9	....	......	9	21	21	......
Ransom's division : b							
Staff...........................	7	....	....	7	7	7	......
Corse's brigade, infantry..	95	1,093	1,093	1,324	1,833	1,834	......
Wharton's brigade, infantry	69	915	915	1,066	1,388	1,383	......
A. E. Jackson's brigade, infantry	43	313	313	402	961	1,012	......
Troops at Saltville (45th Virginia)..........	35	617	617	702	918	803	......
Jones' brigade, cavalry	111	1,193	1,193	1,477	3,490	3,474	......
Williams' brigade, cavalry	98	786	786	1,088	2,228	2,575	......
King's battalion, artillery	26	453	453	516	689	693	24
Total	484	5,370	5,370	6,582	11,514	11,861	24
Echols' brigade :							
Infantry..	98	1,310	1,310	1,564	2,282	2,313	......
Chapman's (Virginia) battery	4	107	107	128	154	152	......
Jackson's (Virginia) horse artillery	3	45	45	53	60	67	......
McCausland's brigade :							
Infantry	65	1,122	1,122	1,325	1,676	1,683	......
Bryan's (Virginia) battery..................	4	119	119	133	155	154	6
Jenkins' brigade, cavalry :							
14th Virginia Cavalry c	16	172	172	220	452	466	......
17th Virginia Cavalry d............	29	295	295	345	578	565	......
W. L. Jackson's brigade, cavalry e	74	604	604	736	1,607	1,611	......
Lurty's (Virginia) battery	5	43	43	55	79	77	3
22d Virginia Cavalry, unattached	44	488	488	539	788	....	......
Botetourt (Virginia) Artillery, unattached	4	85	85	97	168	....	8
Hart's company of engineer troops.	3	43	43	50	65	73	......
Total	349	4,433	4,433	5,245	8,064	7,161	17
Grand total...........................	842	9,803	9,803	11,836	19,599	19,043	41

a Stations of troops not indicated on return.
b Serving with Longstreet in East Tennessee.
c On detached service with Echols' brigade.
d On detached service with McCausland's brigade ; 1 lieutenant and 36 men prisoners of war.
e Three officers and 90 men prisoners of war.

Troops in the Department of Western Virginia and East Tennessee, Maj. Gen. Samuel Jones, C. S. Army, commanding, December 31, 1863.

RANSOM'S DIVISION.

Maj. Gen. ROBERT RANSOM, jr.

Corse's Brigade.

Brig. Gen. M. D. CORSE.

15th Virginia, Lieut. Col. E. M. Morrison.
29th Virginia, Col. James Giles.
30th Virginia, Lieut. Col. R. S. Chew.

Wharton's Brigade.

Brig. Gen. G. C. WHARTON.

45th Virginia,* Col. W. H. Browne.
51st Virginia, Lieut. Col. John P. Wolfe.
30th Virginia Battalion Sharpshooters, Lieut. Col. J. Lyle Clarke.

* On detached service at Saltville.

A. E. Jackson's Brigade.

Lieut. Col. J. R. LOVE.

Thomas' (North Carolina) Regiment, Maj. W. W. Stringfield.
Walker's (North Carolina) Battalion, Maj. J. A. McKamy.

Jones' Cavalry Brigade.	*Williams' Cavalry Brigade.*
Brig. Gen. W. E. JONES.	**Col. J. E. CARTER.**
8th Virginia, Lieut. Col. A. F. Cook.	16th Georgia Battalion, Lieut. Col. S. J. Winn.
21st Virginia, Capt. W. H. Balthis.	
27th Virginia Battalion, Capt. J. B. Thompson.	4th Kentucky, Maj. N. Parker.
34th Virginia Battalion, Lieut. Col. V. A. Witcher.	May's (Kentucky) Regiment, Lieut. Col. E. Trimble.
36th Virginia Battalion, Capt. C. T. Smith.	1st Tennessee, Lieut. Col. Onslow Bean.
37th Virginia Battalion, Maj. J. R. Claiborne.	64th Virginia, Col. C. Slemp.

Artillery Battalion.

Lieut. Col. J. FLOYD KING.

Otey (Virginia) Battery, Capt. D. N. Walker.
Rhett (Tennessee) Battery,* Capt. W. H. Burroughs.
Ringgold (Virginia) Battery, Capt. Crispin Dickenson.
Tennessee Battery,* Capt. H. L. W. McClung.
Virginia Battery, Capt. George S. Davidson.
Virginia Battery, Capt. W. M. Lowry.

Independent Brigade.

Echols' Brigade.	*McCausland's Brigade.*
Brig. Gen. JOHN ECHOLS.	**Col. JOHN McCAUSLAND.**
22d Virginia, Col. George S. Patton.	36th Virginia, Maj. T. Smith.
23d Virginia Battalion, Lieut. Col. C. Derrick.	60th Virginia, Col. B. H. Jones.
26th Virginia Battalion, Lieut. Col. George M. Edgar.	Virginia Battery, Capt. Thomas A. Bryan.
Partisan Rangers, Capt. W. D. Thurmond.	
Partisan Rangers, P. J. Thurmond.	
Virginia Battery, Capt. G. B. Chapman.	
Virginia Battery, Capt. T. E. Jackson.	

Jenkins' Cavalry Brigade.†	*Jackson's Cavalry Brigade.*
14th Virginia, Col. J. A. Gibson.	**Col. W. L. JACKSON.**
16th Virginia, Col. M. J. Ferguson.	
17th Virginia, Maj. F. F. Smith.	19th Virginia, Lieut. Col. W. P. Thompson.
	20th Virginia, Col. W. W. Arnett.
	Detachment (six companies).
	Virginia Battery, Capt. Warren S. Lurty.

Unattached.

3d Confederate Engineers, Company E, Capt. William T. Hart.
22d Virginia Cavalry, Col. H. S. Bowen.
Botetourt (Virginia) Artillery,‡ Capt. Henry C. Douthat.

---

*On detached service at Saltville.
†Regiments dispersed on detached service.
‡At New River Bridge.

JANUARY 11, 1864.

INDORSEMENT ON MAJOR-GENERAL WHITING'S LETTER.[*]

Returned to the honorable Secretary of War.

I am unable to judge at this distance of the danger threatening Wilmington. I cannot see that the enemy is collecting any force against it, and when he does he must withdraw it from some other point, whence our forces must also move to meet it. This is the only way I know of resisting an attack upon it. If the defenses of Wilmington require "the constant presence of an army," I do not see where it is to come from. I see no danger in using the garrisons of the forts to resist a landing or approach at other points to gain time for concentration of troops. I think Martin's brigade and two light batteries sufficient to watch the threatened point.

The custom of the enemy when he wishes to attack one point is to threaten a distant one. The troops are rushed to the threatened points and the real point is exposed. I could at this time send some troops from here, but when should I get them back? Then, it would be seen that it was impossible to withdraw them. Three divisions of this army, and they of the best, are now scattered over the country, and I see no prospect of recovering them. The troops want some rest, some time for reorganization and recruiting their ranks. The enemy is making great efforts to reorganize their army in my immediate front. Large bounties are given to those who re-enlist; many are re-enlisting by means of their people at home, so as to prevent the draft. Conscripts to their ranks are also daily arriving. According to our scouts on the Potomac over 2,000 have come up to Alexandria since the beginning of this year. I see nothing doing on our part, and I fear the spring will open upon us and find us without an army.

R. E. LEE.

GENERAL ORDERS, }   ADJT. AND INSP. GENERAL'S OFFICE,
No. 5.   }   *Richmond, January 13, 1864.*

I. The President having approved the following joint resolution of Congress, directs its announcement in General Orders, expressive of his gratification at the tribute awarded the patriotic officers and soldiers to whom it is addressed.

For the military laggard, or him who, in the pursuits of selfish and inglorious ease, forgets his country's need, no note of approbation is sounded. His infamy is his only security from oblivion. But the heroic devotion of those who, in defense of liberty and honor, have periled all, while it confers, in an approving conscience, the best and highest reward, will also be cherished in perpetual remembrance by a grateful nation. Let this assurance stimulate the armies of the Confederacy everywhere to greater exertion and more resolute endurance, till, under the guidance of Heaven, the blessings of peace and freedom shall finally crown their efforts. Let all press forward in the road to independence, and for the security of the rights sealed to us in the blood of the first revolution. Honor and glory await our success. Slavery and shame will attend our defeat!

---

[*] Probably on his letter of December 20, p. 881. This indorsement is found in General Lee's indorsement book.

II.—JOINT RESOLUTIONS of thanks to General Robert E. Lee, and to the officers and soldiers under his command.

Whereas the campaigns of the brave and gallant armies covering the capital of the Confederate States during the two successive years of 1862 and 1863, under the leadership and command of General Robert E. Lee, have been crowned with glorious results, defeating greatly superior forces massed by the enemy for the conquest of these States, repelling the invaders with immense losses, and twice transferring the battle-fields from our own country to that of the enemy ; and whereas the masterly and glorious achievements, rendering forever memorable the field of the "Seven days of great battles," which raised the siege of Richmond, as well as those of Cedar Run, Second Manassas, Harper's Ferry, Boonsborough, Sharpsburg, Shepherdstown, Fredericksburg, Winchester, Gettysburg, and Chancellorsville, command the admiration and gratitude of our country; and whereas these and other illustrious services rendered by this able commander since the commencement of our war of independence have especially endeared him to the hearts of his countrymen, and have imposed on Congress the grateful duty of giving expression to their feelings : Therefore,

Resolved by the Congress of the Confederate States of America, That the thanks of Congress are due and are tendered to General Robert E. Lee, and to the officers and soldiers of the Confederate armies under his command, for the great and signal victories they have won over the vast hosts of the enemy, and for the inestimable service they have rendered in defense of the liberty and independence of our country ;

Resolved, That the President be requested to communicate these resolutions to General Robert E. Lee, and to the officers and soldiers herein designated.

Approved January 8, 1864.

By order :

S. COOPER,
Adjutant and Inspector General.

———

HOUSE OF REPRESENTATIVES,
Clerk's Office, January 15, 1864.

Hon. JAMES A. SEDDON, *Secretary of War :*

SIR : I have the honor to inform you that the following resolution was this day adopted by the House of Representatives, viz :

Resolved, That the Secretary of War be requested to inform this House by what authority Generals Sam. Jones and Imboden have prohibited the transportation of food from the military district in which they are located to the city of Richmond for private use and consumption.

A. R. LAMAR,
Clerk.

[First indorsement.]

JANUARY 16, 1864.

Referred to the Adjutant-General, for inquiry of the generals as to the facts and the reasons for such orders.

J. A. SEDDON,
Secretary of War.

[Second indorsement.]

ADJUTANT AND INSPECTOR GENERAL'S OFFICE,
January 20, 1864.

Respectfully referred to the Commissary-General, C. S. Army, who will please give whatever information he may be possessed of in regard to the orders alluded to in this resolution, and as to the causes which induced their issuance.

By command of Secretary of War :

JNO. WITHERS,
Assistant Adjutant-General.

OFFICE COMMISSARY-GENERAL OF SUBSISTENCE,
January 23, 1864.

As the orders referred to were issued by generals in the field, it is not practicable for this bureau to report the motives which actually prompted them respectively. I learned from General Sam. Jones that he had issued his orders. I wrote to General Imboden in consequence of an application from his commissary on the commissary at Lynchburg for flour, which was referred to this bureau. My suggestion was, that under the necessities of his command he had better impress for supply. He had either anticipated the letter by his order, or preferred to have recourse to another procedure.

I inclose a copy of my letter to General Jones, of November 11, and of General Imboden's published orders of November 28. I refer to my report of November 15 for my views of the necessities of the situation. I fully concur in the action of both, so far as my judgment extends.

L. B. NORTHROP,
Commissary-General of Subsistence

FEBRUARY 4, 1864.

Respectfully submitted to the Secretary of War in answer to the within resolution.

S. COOPER,
Adjutant and Inspector General.

SUBSISTENCE DEPARTMENT,
Richmond, November 11, 1863.

Maj. Gen. SAMUEL JONES,
Commanding, &c.:

GENERAL: A telegram from Major Galt, of the 9th instant, states that Major King, chief commissary of your command, has called on him for flour. The chief commissary of that district has been addressed on the subject.

I now write to say that it is quite impossible for purchases to be made by officers of this bureau, and that impressments by them are constantly met by declarations of having no surplus over that needed for the consumption of their families, or for companies, railroads, corporations, &c. In fact, the people are individually and collectively arrayed against the army, the former being considered by the War Department as at liberty to collect and hold a year's supply, or up to the next crop. They have no restriction in prices, and are anxious to convert their money into substantials, while we are limited to schedule prices.

Yours is now precisely the case provided for, when the exigencies of troops in the field require impressments under orders of the general commanding. Against this class there are no exemptions in the law. I recommend, therefore, as you are straitened, that you direct Major King to gather subsistence under the first class of impressments, which override all other demands.

Very respectfully, your obedient servant,

L. B. NORTHROP,
Commissary-General of Subsistence.

[Inclosure No. 2.]

SPECIAL ORDERS, } · HEADQUARTERS VALLEY DISTRICT,
     No. 78.   }   *Linville Creek, November 28, 1863.*

It having been reported to the general commanding that the officers and agents of the subsistence department of this district are
unable to procure the supplies imperatively required for the army
by purchase, because speculators are in the market paying higher
prices than those fixed by the government commissioners, and sending such supplies out of the district to be sold again, it is ordered
that the commissaries of subsistence at New Market, Harrisonburg,
Staunton, and Lexington, and those on duty with the command in
the field, do impress, for the use of the army, all the necessaries of
subsistence found in the hands of speculators, or which have been
sold to speculators, though not delivered, to be sent out of the district, and by the term "speculator" is meant any one who buys to sell
again; and any one in this military district making alleged purchases
for private consumption, or for the use of the poor, or soldiers'
families in other districts, for the use of railroad employés or government contractors, will not be permitted to remove supplies from
this district, excepting by special orders from these headquarters, or
from the War Department, and the commissary officers and agents
named in this order will see that no purchases are carried into effect
by the contracting parties. This order is not intended to apply to
necessaries in the hands of producers *in transitu* to market, which
have not been sold, or engaged to be sold, before or on their arrival
at market.

By order of Brig. Gen. J. D. Imboden, commanding:

                    G. W. McPHAIL,
                Lieutenant, and Aide-de-Camp.

HDQRS. DEPT. OF WESTERN VA. AND EAST TENN.,
                Dublin, January 15, 1864.

General S. COOPER,
     Adjutant and Inspector General, C. S. Army:

GENERAL: I forward herewith the returns of my command for
November and September.

I have received several copies of a circular of June last, issued
from your office, requiring tri-monthly returns. Shortly after receipt
of the first copy, I forwarded my department return, which was
inaccurate in one or two trifling particulars, and for this was
returned. I have since tried to insure entire accuracy, and consequently have in almost every case had to send back the reports of
subordinate officers for correction. This has heretofore and must
hereafter cause great delay in department returns, when it is considered that my troops are scattered over a line extending from beyond
Huntersville, Va., to Rogersville, in Tennessee.

These troops are in places accessible only by couriers, some of
whom necessarily require several days to go and return. In illustration of this, I will add that I have only been enabled to get this
morning the connected reports from two commands for making up
the returns forwarded herewith.

General Ransom's report was incorrect.   He was so far in Tennessee, and the means of communication so uncertain, that I feared to return it for correction, lest it might fall into the hands of the enemy, and it was therefore retained until General Ransom returned nearer to Bristol. My report of course detained in consequence.

Very respectfully, your obedient servant,

SAM. JONES,
Major-General.

APPENDIX.

HEADQUARTERS FIRST BRIGADE,
Harper's Ferry, Va., August 20, 1863.

Colonel SIMPSON,
Commanding Ninth Maryland Infantry:

COLONEL: The general is very anxious that you should be in Charlestown to-night, and fearing that my first messenger has not reached you I send another. You will get to Charlestown as soon as possible. When there you will communicate with Captain Summers. The remainder of your regiment, with subsistence stores, is now on its way from this place to join you there.

I am, very respectfully, your obedient servant,
GEO. D. WELLS,
Colonel, Commanding First Brigade.

HEADQUARTERS FIRST BRIGADE,
Harper's Ferry, Va., September 12, 1863.

Lieutenant-Colonel CLOWDSLEY,
Commanding Ninth Maryland Infantry:

COLONEL: The colonel commanding desires that your report of the demonstration to-day which caused the alarm be accompanied by a full and detailed report by Captain Summers of the events of the day, and the force and operations of the enemy in your vicinity. He also desires to remind you of the instructions he has often given you verbally—that the holding of Charlestown is no object. If there is any force of the enemy within your reach that you can whip, then whip them. If advanced upon by a superior force retire.

So far as Charlestown itself is concerned there is no more object in holding that than if you were encamped in an open plain.

I am, very respectfully, your obedient servant,
SAM'L F. WOODS,
Acting Assistant Adjutant-General.

HEADQUARTERS FIRST BRIGADE,
Harper's Ferry, Va., September 28, 1863.

Colonel SIMPSON,
Ninth Maryland Infantry:

COLONEL: I am instructed by the colonel commanding to state that information has been received here that a force of cavalry and infantry are between your place and Winchester. You will direct

(915)

Captain Summers to ascertain and report as soon as possible upon this, and will bear in mind the written instructions you have received in reference to your action if advanced upon by a superior force.

I am, very respectfully, your obedient servant,

SAM'L F. WOODS,
Acting Assistant Adjutant-General.

HEADQUARTERS FIRST BRIGADE,
Harper's Ferry, Va., September 29, 1863.

Capt. WILLIAM M. BOONE,
Assistant Adjutant-General:

CAPTAIN: I have the honor to state that by my order Captain Summers scouted yesterday p. m., and reported late last night that there was probably a force of less than 500 cavalry, composed in part of the Twelfth Virginia and Gilmor's battalion, somewhere in the neighborhood of Winchester. No infantry or artillery. He added that with 250 men he could find and whip them.

I ordered all the cavalry under my command to report to Captain Summers at daybreak this morning, and was about to venture to awake the brigadier-general commanding and ask him for the Cole's cavalry, when I learned that they had already been sent in that direction.

I am, very respectfully, your obedient servant,

GEO. D. WELLS,
Colonel, Commanding Brigade.

MITCHELL'S STATION, *October 7, 1863.*

Captain NORTON,
Chief Signal Officer:

The enemy intend some movement. Stuart sent to Lee for guides; Lee sent him 5 from Wickham's brigade. Stuart has given orders about supplying regiments at or near Madison Court-House with horses. James City, Madison Court-House, and Woodville have been mentioned in their dispatches this a. m.

Have strengthened the infantry force at Barnett's Ford, also moved a battery near that ford; placed a section of artillery at Clark's Ford, on Robertson's River, this a. m. Most of the rebel generals have met at either R. E. Lee's headquarters this p. m., or at Hill's. No troops moving that I can see.

D. E. CASTLE,
Captain and Signal Officer.

HEADQUARTERS FIRST BRIGADE,
Harper's Ferry, Va., October 7, 1863.

Col. BENJAMIN L. SIMPSON,
Ninth Maryland Infantry:

COLONEL: The colonel commanding desires me to say that information from Martinsburg states that Imboden intends a raid on the railroad between this and Martinsburg the latter part of this week or first of the coming one. He has directed the cavalry detachment under his command to report to you, and you will employ them and Captain Summers in ascertaining where Imboden is, and if any such movement is contemplated.

I am, very respectfully, your obedient servant,

SAM'L F. WOODS,
Acting Assistant Adjutant-General.

HEADQUARTERS SIXTH ARMY CORPS,
October 9, 1863—4.20 p. m.

Major-General HUMPHREYS,
Chief of Staff:

Is it not possible that the enemy have discovered our camp at James City, and their move is to counteract that? A message from F. Lee to Stuart would indicate that.

JOHN SEDGWICK,
Major-General, Commanding.

SPECIAL ORDERS, }   HEADQUARTERS FIRST BRIGADE,
No. 33.   }   *Harper's Ferry, Va., October* 11, 1863.

Col. Benjamin L. Simpson, commanding at Charlestown, Va., will immediately direct all the available cavalry at that post (picket excepted) to proceed at once to re-enforce Major Cole, who is now or will be this p. m. in the vicinity of Berryville, and receive their orders from him. Captain Means' company has been ordered to Charlestown and placed under the command of Colonel Simpson.

By command of Col. George D. Wells, commanding First Brigade:

SAM'L F. WOODS,
Acting Assistant Adjutant-General.

BRANDY STATION, *October* 12, 1863.

Major-General HUMPHREYS,
Chief of Staff:

The following is from General Griffin. Its contents were told Colonel Chamberlain, who, General Griffin says, is a clear-headed and reliable officer:

General SYKES:

At a house near Beverly Ford, just to my right, the occupants say that the enemy's cavalry this morning said that their infantry was at Manassas Gap; that they had no infantry here. The occupants report that the cavalrymen made the subject common talk, stating that their infantry was certainly at Manassas Gap.

CHARLES GRIFFIN.

Further reports confirm this. Citizens say Stuart left with his cavalry this morning in the direction of our right.

JOHN SEDGWICK,
Major-General, Commanding.

♦Brandy Station, *October* 12, 1863.

Major-General Humphreys,
            Chief of Staff:

Another citizen fully confirms the information contained in General Griffin's note. He seems to be reliable and thinks all their cavalry and about two regiments of infantry were here yesterday. He says General Stuart with the cavalry, all but one regiment, and the infantry moved this morning toward our right, but the soldiers said A. P. Hill was at Waterloo, and that the impression seemed to be that we were falling back to Bull Run, where there would be another fight.

                    JOHN SEDGWICK,
                    Major-General, Commanding.

                    Headquarters Third Corps,*
                        October 13, 1863.

Major-General Humphreys,
            Chief of Staff:

An officer from General Gregg's cavalry who has been picketing at Fox's Ford reports being driven in, and the enemy crossing their infantry and artillery.

I have my right strongly picketed, and the road to Bealeton also, opposite F——'s Ford.

It will be necessary for me to change my front, and I must move my trains to-night.

                    WM. H. FRENCH,
                    Major-General, Commanding.

                    Headquarters Third Army Corps,
                        October 13, 1863—10 p. m.

Major-General Humphreys,
            Chief of Staff:

Arrived here after a hard day's march. Had a skirmish with the enemy at Auburn, driving him before me. He had cavalry and artillery.

                    WM. H. FRENCH,
                    Major-General, Commanding.

                    Headquarters Second Army Corps,
                        October 13, 1863—7.30 p. m.

Major-General Humphreys,
            Chief of Staff:

By lapping by General French I have nearly reached Auburn with the head of my column. General French had a slight skirmish here with the cavalry, but they soon cleared out. He has probably reached Greenwich by this time. His trains, however, are not past Auburn by 2 miles. My men are bivouacking along the road. They are tired and sleepy, but have marched splendidly and are in fine spirits.

Kilpatrick is moving along parallel to me and French, and with much difficulty, having to make his own road. The position at Auburn is one of great strength.

G. K. WARREN,
Major-General, Commanding.

SPECIAL ORDERS, }   HEADQUARTERS FIRST BRIGADE,
      No. 35.   }   *Harper's Ferry, Va., October* 13, 1863.
*   *   *   *   *   .   *   *

II. By order of the brigadier-general commanding, Colonel Simpson will direct Captain Means to send a scout of 10 men, under a reliable non-commissioned officer, to follow the summit of the Blue Ridge as far down as Front Royal, with orders to observe diligently on both sides and send back all information as to the enemy, who is reported to be advancing in large force toward the Potomac. The scout will reach the mountains by daylight to-morrow, and will carry four days' rations and short forage.

III. Colonel Simpson will at once send out a scout to go as far as Berryville and bring in all intelligence that can be gathered. The lieutenant handing you this will report to you with 16 men. Two relays of horsemen are stationed between here and Charlestown to bring through information with the least possible delay. Do you hear anything of any advance? Get all the information possible from every quarter, and send at once any of importance.

By order of Col. George D. Wells, commanding First Brigade ·
SAM'L F. WOODS,
Acting Assistant Adjutant-General.

HEADQUARTERS SECOND ARMY CORPS,
October 14, 1863. (Received 5 p. m.)
General SYKES:

I have whipped Heth's division, captured a battery and some hundreds of prisoners. I cannot retire under the fire. Support my right; they still threaten me heavily.

G. K. WARREN,
Major-General, Commanding.

SPECIAL ORDERS, }   HEADQUARTERS FIRST BRIGADE,
      No. 36.   }   *Harper's Ferry, Va., October* 14, 1863.
*   *   *   *   *   *   *

III. Colonel Simpson will immediately send an infantry scout with three days' rations up the crest of the mountains as far as Chester Gap, if possible. There is a practicable road up the mountain as far as Snicker's Gap. You will instruct them to be cautious, but move as rapidly as possible.
*   *   *   *   *   *   *

By order of Col. George D. Wells, commanding First Brigade:
SAM'L F. WOODS,
Acting Assistant Adjutant-General.

HEADQUARTERS FIRST BRIGADE,
Harper's Ferry, Va., October 14, 1863.

Lieut. S. B. McCULLOCH,
Acting Assistant Adjutant-General:

LIEUTENANT : I have the honor to report that Colonel Simpson, commanding forces at Charlestown, informs me that all his available cavalry force is out with orders to proceed to Berryville. He has pickets well out on the Smithfield and Summit Point roads. Will send immediately any information he may receive. He reports everything quiet and no news.

While writing the above, I received another dispatch from Colonel Simpson, which states that he learns from a reliable source 6 miles beyond Berryville that there is no force in the valley advancing, and there is no rumor there to that effect. Sunday last some of our cavalry passed through bound up the valley, supposed to be Cole's.

In Winchester it is rumored that the citizens were expecting a force there last night.

I am, very respectfully, your obedient servant,

GEO. D. WELLS,
Colonel, Commanding Brigade.

HEADQUARTERS FIRST BRIGADE,
Harper's Ferry, Va., October 14, 1863.

Lieut. S. B. McCULLOCH,
Acting Assistant Adjutant-General :

LIEUTENANT : I have the honor to report that I am informed by Colonel Simpson that the scout sent out by my orders have returned to Charlestown. They proceeded to within sight of Berryville, and drove in the enemy's pickets, supposed to be White's battalion. Some 80 or 90 of the enemy came out and attempted to flank them, and our scout fell back, their number being too small for attack. They could learn of no force approaching down the valley. The scout of 2 men sent to the Blue Ridge returned, being unable to proceed by that route. . Colonel Simpson asks if it is desired that they should attempt any other.

I am, very respectfully, your obedient servant,

GEO. D. WELLS,
Colonel, Commanding Brigade.

HEADQUARTERS FIRST BRIGADE,
Harper's Ferry, Va., October 14, 1863.

Colonel SIMPSON,
Ninth Maryland Infantry:

COLONEL : The colonel commanding directs me to inquire of you the reason why the cavalry scout were unable to proceed along the Blue Ridge. He instructs me to direct that you will continue to scour the country in front of you with small parties of cavalry, and send in any information which may be obtained.

I am, very respectfully, your obedient servant,

SAM'L F. WOODS,
Acting Assistant Adjutant-General.

HEADQUARTERS FIRST BRIGADE,
Harper's Ferry, Va., October 14, 1863.
Lieut. S. B. McCULLOCH,
Acting Assistant Adjutant-General:

LIEUTENANT: I have the honor to acknowledge receipt of your communication of this date, and in reply would say I am unable to give any reason, other than in the words of Colonel Simpson, as to why the scout (which was a cavalry scout) did not succeed: "They were unable to proceed along the crest of the mountain." An infantry scout sent out sometime since by General Lockwood in the same direction returned and reported the road impassable.

I am, very respectfully, your obedient servant,
GEO. D. WELLS,
Colonel, Commanding Brigade.

HEADQUARTERS FIRST BRIGADE,
Harper's Ferry, Va., October 14, 1863.
Lieut. S. B. McCULLOCH,
Acting Assistant Adjutant-General:

LIEUTENANT: I have the honor to report that I am informed by Colonel Simpson of the return of the scout of two men sent to the Blue Ridge, they having proceeded as far as Berryville, when they met part of Gilmor's battalion. He now has scouts out to go as far as Keys' and Meyers' Fords, with orders to report any information they may gain. He reports a small number of rebels at Smithfield, but can learn of no force in the valley.

I am, very respectfully, your obedient servant,
GEO. D. WELLS,
Colonel, Commanding Brigade.

HEADQUARTERS SECOND ARMY CORPS,
October 15, 1863.
Major-General HUMPHREYS,
Chief of Staff:

I gave what information I had to the colonel of the First Maine Cavalry, and have orderlies from him to communicate any information I receive. He has been off for an hour. My cavalry provost guard were out to within 2 miles of the battle-field this morning, and have returned about half an hour ago. Two of our tired men on the battle-field were fired on this morning by the enemy, and they escaped. The provost guard brought in all stragglers. Tell General Pleasonton I have kept his two batteries till the artillery-reserve batteries General Hunt was to send me arrive; they will then go in, all my batteries having gone back to replenish. My infantry is unsupplied with ammunition, and provisions are coming up. Men are somewhat tired and sore, but in good fighting condition. We have seen a column, apparently our own, about 2 miles east of Blackburn's Ford on a road, moving northward. We suppose it was our troops moving toward Centreville from Blackburn's Ford.

G. K. WARREN,
Major-General, Commanding.

Headquarters First Brigade,
Harper's Ferry, Va., October 15, 1863.

Colonel Simpson,
 Ninth Maryland Infantry:

Colonel : A man is in town to-day who reports that last evening Imboden was at Berryville with something of a force, and that he was sending a force around between Charlestown and the river to cut off your train on the Charlestown road. Will you look into the matter ? Colonel Clowdsley was saying the other day that there was some rascality about the house near which Summers was attacked. Will you investigate this and report ? General Halleck's alarm seems to have been without foundation so far as we are concerned. You can resume the even tenor of your way at Charlestown the same as before.

Very respectfully,
 GEO. D. WELLS,
 Colonel, Commanding Brigade.

P. S.—You will keep Captain Means for the present.

Headquarters First Brigade,
Harper's Ferry, Va., October 15, 1863.

Colonel Simpson,
 Ninth Maryland Infantry:

Colonel : The colonel commanding is informed that a force of cavalry is on the road from Martinsburg to Winchester and Berryville with orders to send to Charlestown both going and coming any information which they may procure. You will immediately forward to these headquarters any report which may reach you from this scout.

I am, very respectfully, your obedient servant,
 SAM'L F. WOODS,
 Acting Assistant Adjutant-General.

Headquarters First Brigade,
Harper's Ferry, Va., October 16, 1863.

Lieut. S. B. McCulloch,
 Acting Assistant Adjutant-General:

Lieutenant : I have the honor to report that I am just informed by Colonel Simpson, commanding at Charlestown, that the cavalry scouts sent out in pursuance to orders from these headquarters yesterday p. m., by the Summit Point and river roads, to meet at Ripon, have returned. They report that they neither saw nor heard anything of the enemy except that a portion of Gilmor's battalion, supposed to be about 100, were at Berryville. The infantry scout has returned, being unable to cross the river, having attempted several of the fords and finding them impassable on account of the depth of water. They returned via Kabletown, and could gain no information of the presence of the enemy in that vicinity.

I am, very respectfully, your obedient servant,
 GEO. D. WELLS,
 Colonel, Commanding Brigade.

HEADQUARTERS FIRST BRIGADE,
Harper's Ferry, Va., October 17, 1863.

Lieut. S. B. McCulloch :

LIEUTENANT : A dispatch from Colonel Simpson, just received, informs me that one of White's battalion, caught by our picket about daylight this a. m., reports that White's battalion, being 150 cavalry and 80 dismounted, have been at Berryville for the last few days. They reconnoitered our position yesterday, but found that " it was little more than he would like to attack."

The person says White left Berryville for White Post at 8.30 o'clock last night, and Imboden with 800 men is 8 miles above Winchester.

The cavalry scout from Martinsburg arrived there last night, reporting that they were unable to reach Berryville on account of White. No other forces are reported in the valley.

I am, very respectfully, your obedient servant,

GEO. D. WELLS,
Colonel, Commanding Brigade.

MARTINSBURG, *October* 18, 1863.

Brigadier-General SULLIVAN :

Captain Jones has just returned. He reports having visited Winchester and Berryville this forenoon, returning down the Opequon. His force was too small and jaded to risk any demonstration in Imboden's rear. There is no other force in the valley but that with Imboden, which deserters say numbers about 3,000.

L. B. PIERCE,
Colonel, Commanding.

HEADQUARTERS FIFTH ARMY CORPS,
October 20, 1863—5.15 p. m.

Major-General HUMPHREYS,
Chief of Staff:

My command is encamped at New Baltimore. The Sixth Corps is just moving on Warrenton. Before it is stretched out it will be dark. For this reason, and because my men have been up since 1 a. m. this morning, I have decided to remain here for the night.

GEO. SYKES,
Major-General, Commanding.

HEADQUARTERS FIFTH ARMY CORPS,
Auburn, October 25, 1863—9.30 a. m.

Major-General HUMPHREYS,
Chief of Staff:

My command reached here last night. One brigade and my supply trains are at New Baltimore. I have heard nothing from headquarters since 2.30 p. m. yesterday. I would be glad to know the disposition of the other corps and receive any other information that may be useful or proper.

GEO. SYKES,
Major-General, Commanding.

HEADQUARTERS SIXTH ARMY CORPS,
November 7, 1863.

Major-General HUMPHREYS.
Chief of Staff:

Your dispatch received. I have taken the rifle-pits in front of the redoubts and our pickets are on the river above and below the works, which we have not succeeded in taking. Prisoners report Ewell's corps at Brandy Station, with one division here. Hill's corps near Culpeper and Stevensburg, with one division at Kelly's Ford. I don't think I can cross to-night.

JOHN SEDGWICK,
Major-General, Commanding.

HEADQUARTERS SIXTH ARMY CORPS,
November 7, 1863.

Major-General HUMPHREYS,
Chief of Staff:

The assault on the redoubts is successful; both are carried. I have taken four guns and a number of prisoners. I cannot tell yet how many. Three guns are reported taken, but of this I am not certain. We can drive them, I think, from the works on the other side in the morning.

JOHN SEDGWICK,
Major-General, Commanding.

HEADQUARTERS SIXTH ARMY CORPS,
November 7, 1863—7.40 p. m.

Major-General HUMPHREYS,
Chief of Staff:

Your dispatch of 6.30 just received. I sent you two messengers. I have taken the redoubt on this side by assault, and I think I can knock them out of the works on the other side in the morning. I think two strong divisions [sufficient] to hold this place [and] guard both fords.

JOHN SEDGWICK,
Major-General, Commanding.

HEADQUARTERS SIXTH ARMY CORPS,
November 7, 1863—9 p. m.

Major-General HUMPHREYS,
Chief of Staff:

We have taken prisoners 4 colonels, 3 lieutenant-colonels, and many other officers, 800 men, and more coming in. We have also taken 4 battle-flags. All works on this side of the river are in our possession. We hold the bridge.

JOHN SEDGWICK,
Major-General, Commanding.

HEADQUARTERS SIXTH ARMY CORPS,
November 7, 1863—9.45 p. m.

Major-General HUMPHREYS,
    Chief of Staff:

My loss is estimated at 75 killed and 200 wounded; chiefly in Wright's division. All are not yet collected, as the assault continued until after dark. Prisoners are still coming in; they will probably exceed a thousand.

JOHN SEDGWICK,
Major-General, Commanding.

HEADQUARTERS SIXTH ARMY CORPS,
November 7, 1863—10 p. m.

Major-General HUMPHREYS,
    Chief of Staff:

The enemy's bridge is still down and under our control. I have sent for Colonel Spaulding, commanding the bridge train. I think we can throw a bridge across at Norman's Ford. We have 1,100 prisoners. Had not the escort better be increased? Dispatch of 9.30 received. Yes, the enemy occupy those heights in force, so General Sykes reports.

JOHN SEDGWICK,
Major-General, Commanding.

HEADQUARTERS THIRD ARMY CORPS,
November 8, 1863—7.35 a. m.

Major-General HUMPHREYS,
    Chief of Staff:

I have just received the following information through a deserter: General Lee is not with his command, but gone south. Has been gone a week. Early's division moved to Fredericksburg. Rodes' upon Brandy Station.

WM. H. FRENCH,
Major-General, Commanding.

P. S.—If General Sedgwick has crossed I should like to send the Second Corps to Stevensburg.

WM. H. FRENCH.

HEADQUARTERS SIXTH ARMY CORPS,
November 8, 1863—7.40 a. m.

Major-General HUMPHREYS,
    Chief of Staff:

The enemy attempted to burn the bridge this morning. I think they will leave. Pickets are forming across the river. Wright is watching to open on them. In the event of getting the works on the other side I shall throw another bridge over. Shall I order up my brigade from Norman's Ford?

JOHN SEDGWICK,
Major-General, Commanding.

HEADQUARTERS SIXTH ARMY CORPS,
November 8, 1863—8.35 a. m.

Major-General HUMPHREYS,
 Chief of Staff:

I have just sent to Bealeton 9 officers and 100 men prisoners, in addition to those already forwarded.

I am collecting and burying the dead. I am afraid my loss is larger than I reported, but I hope not.

JOHN SEDGWICK,
Major-General, Commanding.

HEADQUARTERS SIXTH ARMY CORPS,
November 8, 1863—9.05 a. m.

Major-General HUMPHREYS,
 Chief of Staff:

The enemy are retiring in our front. We are taking possession of the works on the other side. I have ordered a bridge laid. Their bridge was partly burned. Skirmishers are going forward.

JOHN SEDGWICK,
Major-General, Commanding.

HEADQUARTERS SIXTH ARMY CORPS,
November 8, 1863—10.55 a. m.

Major-General HUMPHREYS,
 Chief of Staff:

The Third Corps is halted in front of this position in line of battle, about a mile from the river, with skirmishers on the wooded crest in its front. The bridges here are about completed. I am ready to cross and await orders. Wright is on the other side. We captured 8 battle-flags yesterday.

JOHN SEDGWICK,
Major-General, Commanding.

CULPEPER, VA.,
November 11, 1863—6.30 p. m.

Col. C. ROSS SMITH,
 Chief of Staff, Cavalry Corps:

The Eighth Illinois has just returned from a reconnaissance down the railroad to Rapidan Bridge. They could not see the bridge without exposing themselves too much. Nothing was found on this side save a few scouts. The river was visited at several points. Strong pickets were discovered on the other side at each point. Rodes' division crossed at Raccoon; no troops crossed below. The civilians all say that the rebel army was much frightened, and never saw it in so much confusion. The First U. S. Cavalry started out this morning on a reconnaissance to Robertson's River and beyond, if practicable. It has not returned. When last heard from it was near Robertson's River. A regiment of Devin's went toward Madison Court-House. No report from it yet. My impression is that Lee's army has gone farther south than the line of the Rapidan.

JNO. BUFORD,
Brigadier-General, Commanding.

HEADQU'ARTERS CAVALRY CORPS,
November 15, 1863—7.30 p. m.

Major-General HUMPHREYS,
Chief of Staff:

I have just received a letter from Mr. Smith, stating he has seen an acquaintance who left Richmond on the 3d and Fredericksburg on the 6th instant. At that date there were no troops in Richmond except the home guard, consisting of boys and old men; that De Courcey's [?] brigade left Richmond on the 1st of November for Tennessee, and that Garrett's [?] brigade was at Taylorsville, on the Richmond and Fredericksburg Railroad, on the 3d instant, with marching orders to go, so report said, to Tennessee; that at that time there was no guard at the railroad bridge across the South Anna River, and that the heavy guns had been removed from the fortifications around Richmond, but did not know where they had taken them; that, on the 4th, Cobb's Legion, comprising about 300 men, were at Fredericksburg; these were all the troops he saw between Richmond and Fredericksburg; that there is no force in Lynchburg; that he had been as far south as Wilmington, N. C., and that there was no force there; that three vessels arrived there while he was there, and a very large amount of Government stores were received thereabout daily.

He also says that it is reported and freely talked about in Richmond of abandoning Virginia, and they are now moving things quietly from the different parts of the State, and that the troops will all be drawn off; that is one reason of a show to hold Culpeper to better enable them to carry out their plans. I send this information in the words it has been conveyed to me, and from its source I deem it of sufficient importance to suggest it be telegraphed to General Meade before he leaves Washington, as it may be useful to him there.

A. PLEASONTON,
Major-General, Commanding.

HEADQUARTERS SIXTH CORPS,
November 27, 1863.

[Major-General HUMPHREYS,
Chief of Staff:]

SIR: My troops have been in line since 7 o'clock this morning, waiting for the Third Corps, all closed up. I have understood General French was retarded by the enemy. One of French's brigades was left on the other side of the river, at Mitchell's Ford. I supposed it on the other side, and was about to retire; discovered it was on the other side and the bridge taken up. To relieve it now a brigade would have to go down to Germanna Ford, a distance of 5 miles, and up, making 10. Did the general expect it to be left there?

JOHN SEDGWICK,
Major-General, Commanding.

HEADQUARTERS SIXTH CORPS,
November 29, 1863.

[Major-General HUMPHREYS,
Chief of Staff:]

My right brigade rested very near the Raccoon road. I have moved it a short distance to the right, and it now covers the road.

JOHN SEDGWICK,
Major-General, Commanding.

HEADQUARTERS SIXTH CORPS,
November 29, 1863.

[Major-General HUMPHREYS,
Chief of Staff :]

I think I am not mistaken in the Raccoon road. The one Mr. Barlow mentioned is the road that runs into the Raccoon. My staff officers have not yet returned, and Mr. Barlow has gone to meet them.

JOHN SEDGWICK,
Major-General, Commanding.

HEADQUARTERS SIXTH CORPS,
November 29, 1863.

[Major-General HUMPHREYS,
Chief of Staff:]

SIR : I should like to have the general commanding or yourself to take a look at the enemy's position from this point. It cannot be more than three-quarters of a mile.

JOHN SEDGWICK,
Major-General, Commanding.

HEADQUARTERS SIXTH ARMY CORPS,
November 29, 1863.

[Major-General HUMPHREYS,
Chief of Staff :]

There is no material change in my front. The enemy were at work last night slashing timber and working on their rifle-pits. I believe it to be impossible to take wagons to the rear except by the main road. My artillery could have come in near general headquarters.

General Wright has officers out examining further.

JOHN SEDGWICK,
Major-General, Commanding.

HEADQUARTERS CAVALRY CORPS,
November 29, 1863—2 p. m.

[Major-General HUMPHREYS,
Chief of Staff:]

SIR : There is no truth in the report about our wagon train 2 miles from here having been attacked. I have just heard from Old Wilderness. The enemy's cavalry appear to be making for Ely's Ford. Our troops there have been notified.

A. PLEASONTON,
Major-General, Commanding.

HEADQUARTERS FIRST CAVALRY DIVISION,
November 29, 1863.

[Capt. C. C. SUYDAM,
 Assistant Adjutant-General:]

SIR: There is nothing new to report. I will move my headquarters to-day to near Ely's Ford, and will throw one brigade over the river to scout the country there.

W. MERRITT,
Brigadier-General, Commanding.

———

HEADQUARTERS SECOND CAVALRY DIVISION,
November 29, 1863—3.20 p. m.

[Col. C. ROSS SMITH,
 Chief of Staff, Cavalry Corps:]

SIR: A strong attack of about one brigade of cavalry, and possibly infantry, is being made on the brigade near New Hope Meeting-House. The First Brigade, at the Wilderness, has also been attacked and communication cut between the two. These points are very important, and so assailable that considerable force will be required to hold either. The road from this point back to Robertson's Tavern is blocked with wagons, which do not move beyond this point. With my division here I could hold this point. The brigade here has been hard pressed, but I think we will hold. I have communicated with General Warren in front.

D. McM. GREGG,
Brigadier-General, Commanding.

I think it probable General Warren will send some infantry here.

———

HEADQUARTERS SIXTH ARMY CORPS,
November 30, 1863.

[Major-General HUMPHREYS,
 Chief of Staff:]

I do not think our position has been discovered. They evidently know of some movement near here by their random firing over the troops. Your P. S. is noted.

JOHN SEDGWICK,
Major-General, Commanding.

———

HEADQUARTERS SIXTH CORPS,
November 30, 1863.

[Brig. Gen. S. WILLIAMS:]

In answer to your dispatch just received, I respectfully report that I do not believe the enemy's works can be carried in my front by an assault without numerous sacrifices. I regard the chances as three to one against the success of such an attack.

JOHN SEDGWICK,
Major-General, Commanding.

HEADQUARTERS SIXTH CORPS,
November 30, 1863—11.30 p. m.

[Brig. Gen. S. WILLIAMS:]

I respectfully report that I think the changes made by the enemy to-day on his left, in strengthening his lines and increasing the number of troops, render it doubtful whether the position could now be carried. I think it could have been carried this morning without great loss.

JOHN SEDGWICK,
Major-General, Commanding.

HEADQUARTERS FIRST DIVISION, SIXTH CORPS,
November 30, 1863.

[General SEDGWICK:]

I believe the chances of success materially diminished by the delay, owing to changes by the enemy in the position of batteries, strengthening of his lines, and additional troops, and a strong suspicion, if not certainty, of the position of our forces. If the attack is made it is vital that it be made at once.

H. G. WRIGHT,
Brigadier-General, Commanding.

HEADQUARTERS THIRD CAVALRY DIVISION,
Morton's Ford, November 30, 1863—2 p. m.

[Col. C. ROSS SMITH,
Chief of Staff, Cavalry Corps:]

Two contrabands, who crossed the river near Rapidan Station last night, report that the enemy is moving all his trains toward Gordonsville. One contraband stated that he had counted over 500 wagons moving from Orange Court-House to Gordonsville. There was scarcely any guards with the train. A man belonging to my command who was taken prisoner two weeks ago at Raccoon Ford, made his escape from the enemy and has just come in. He reports that he has been at Orange Court-House for one week; that now there are but very few troops at that point, all having been marched toward Fredericksburg. He confirms the report which states that the trains of the enemy are moving to Gordonsville. He was dressed in the rebel uniform, and associated freely with the rebel soldiers after making his escape.

They are all aware of Bragg's disaster and expect that Lee's army will be forced back. The enemy have withdrawn all infantry from the fords above this point, and do not show as large a force of cavalry as usual. I can cross Morton's Ford at my pleasure. A few minutes ago I received through General Merritt's headquarters a dispatch from you, stating that our batteries would open at 8 a. m. The dispatch was dated 7 a. m.

G. A. CUSTER,
Brigadier-General, Commanding.

[Indorsement.]

This dispatch just received.   Shall I send orders for Custer to cross in the morning and pitch in, in case an attack is made?   The rebels are evidently preparing to leave in case we succeed.   They evidently are not sanguine of the result.

A. PLEASONTON,
Major-General, Commanding Cavalry Corps.

HEADQUARTERS FIRST DIVISION, SIXTH CORPS,
December 1, 1863—3.30 p. m.

[General SEDGWICK :]

I have neither seen nor heard of anything to induce me to alter the opinion I expressed last night, but I should say that I have made no examination to-day of any importance.   I was much fatigued and have remained most of the day in camp.   One of my officers thinks the works on the enemy's right have been strengthened, and his view from the point where we were yesterday corresponds with what we see from here.

H. G. WRIGHT,
Brigadier-General, Commanding.

CONFEDERATE CORRESPONDENCE, ETC.

FAUQUIER COUNTY, VA.,
October 12, 1863.

Major-General STUART,
Commanding Cavalry Corps:

GENERAL : I have just returned from a reconnaissance into Fairfax.   I destroyed 3 wagons and captured 16 horses and equipments and 9 prisoners.

I was accompanied by only 8 men.   Captain Smith was to have followed me with my command on the next day, but a heavy force of cavalry appearing near Middleburg rendered it impracticable

Respectfully,

JNO. S. MOSBY,
Major &c.

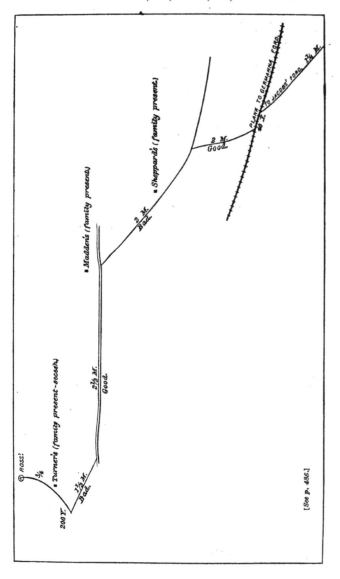

[See p. 486.]

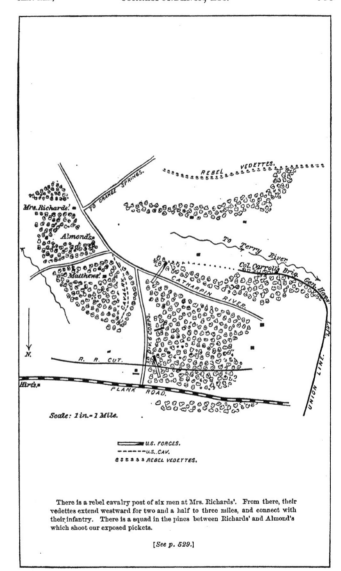

Scale: 1 in.= 1 Mile.

▭▭▭ U.S. FORCES.
------- U.S. CAV.
≈≈≈≈≈ REBEL VEDETTES.

There is a rebel cavalry post of six men at Mrs. Richards'. From there, their vedettes extend westward for two and a half to three miles, and connect with their infantry. There is a squad in the pines between Richards' and Almond's which shoot our exposed pickets.

[See p. 529.]

Abbot's (Henry L.) **Heavy Artillery.** See *Connecticut Troops, 1st Regiment.*
Abbott's (Henry L.) **Infantry.** See *Massachusetts Troops, 20th Regiment.*
Abraham's (James) **Cavalry.** See *West Virginia Troops, 1st Regiment.*
Adams' (Charles P.) **Infantry.** See *Minnesota Troops, 1st Regiment.*
Adams' (George W.) **Artillery.** See *Rhode Island Troops, 1st Regiment, Battery G.*
Adams' (Zachariah T.) **Artillery.** See *North Carolina Troops, Confederate,* 13th Battalion, Battery D.
Addicks' (Thomas H.) **Infantry.** See *Pennsylvania Troops, 157th Regiment.*
Ahl's (George W.) **Heavy Artillery.** See *Delaware Troops.*
Aiken's (D. Wyatt) **Infantry.** See *South Carolina Troops, 7th Regiment.*
Albemarle **Artillery.** See *Virginia Troops, Confederate.*
Albright's (Charles) **Infantry.** See *Pennsylvania Troops,* 34th Regiment Militia.
Alexander's (Charles M.) **Infantry.** See *District of Columbia Troops, 2d Regiment.*
Alexander's (Frederic W.) **Artillery.** See *Baltimore Artillery, Union, post.*
Alexandria **Artillery.** See *Virginia Troops, Confederate.*
Allcock's (Thomas) **Heavy Artillery.** See *New York Troops, 4th Regiment.*
Alleghany **Artillery.** See *Virginia Troops, Confederate.*
Allen's (C. Tacitus) **Heavy Artillery.** See *Lunenburg Heavy Artillery, post.*
Allen's (John A. P.) **Heavy Artillery.** See *Massachusetts Troops, 6th Unattached Company.*
Allen's (Thomas S.) **Infantry.** See *Wisconsin Troops, 5th Regiment.*
Alles' (Henry M.) **Infantry.** See *New York Troops, 74th Regiment.*
Ames' (John W.) **Infantry.** See *Union Troops (Colored), 6th Regiment.*
Ames' (Nelson) **Artillery.** See *New York Troops, 1st Regiment, Battery G.*
Amherst **Artillery.** See *Virginia Troops, Confederate.*
Anderson's (Hiram, jr.) **Infantry.** See *New York Troops, 92d Regiment.*
Anderson's (Robert H.) **Cavalry.** See *Georgia Troops, 5th Regiment.*
Andrew **Sharpshooters.** See *Massachusetts Troops, 1st Company.*
Andrews' (William G.) **Artillery.** See *Montgomery True Blues, Artillery, post.*
Angel's (Ashbel W.) **Infantry.** See *New Jersey Troops, 5th Regiment.*
Anthony's (George T.) **Artillery.** See *New York Troops, 17th Battery.*
Armistead's (A. D.) **Artillery.** See *Matthews Artillery, post.*
Arnett's (William Wiley) **Cavalry.** See *Virginia Troops, Confederate, 20th Regiment.*
Arnold's (Abraham K.) **Cavalry.** See *Union Troops, Regulars, 5th Regiment.*
Arnold's (Joseph S.) **Sharpshooters.** See *New York Troops, 1st Battalion.*
Arnold's (William A.) **Artillery.** See *Rhode Island Troops, 1st Regiment, Battery A.*
Arrick's (Joseph P.) **Infantry.** See *Ohio Troops.*
Ashland **Artillery.** See *Virginia Troops, Confederate.*
Atkinson's (E. N.) **Infantry.** See *Georgia Troops, 26th Regiment.*

---

* References, unless otherwise indicated, are to index following.

Atwell's (Charles A.) Artillery. See *Pennsylvania Troops, Battery E.*
Atwood's (Cornelius G.) Infantry. See *Massachusetts Troops, 25th Regiment.*
Audoun's (Joseph H.) Artillery. See *Maryland Troops, Union, Battery B (six months).*
August's (T. P.) Infantry. See *Virginia Troops, Confederate, 15th Regiment.*
Austin's (John S.) Infantry. See *New York Troops, 72d Regiment.*
Avery's (Clark M.) Infantry. See *North Carolina Troops, Confederate, 33d Regiment.*
Aylett's (W. R.) Infantry. See *Virginia Troops, Confederate, 53d Regiment.*
Bachman's (William K.) Artillery. See *German Artillery, post.*
Bagby's (Alexander F.) Heavy Artillery. See *Virginia Troops, Confederate, 4th Regiment, Battery K.*
Bailey's (Edward L.) Infantry. See *New Hampshire Troops, 2d Regiment.*
Baily's (Silas M.) Infantry. See *Pennsylvania Troops, 8th Reserves.*
Baird's (Thomas W.) Infantry. See *New York Troops, 82d Regiment.*
Baird's (William H.) Infantry. See *New York Troops, 126th Regiment.*
Baker's (Benjamin F.) Infantry. See *New York Troops, 43d Regiment.*
Baker's (J. H.) Infantry. See *Georgia Troops, 13th Regiment.*   •
Baker's (John A.) Cavalry. See *North Carolina Troops, Confederate, 3d Regiment.*
Baker's (Samuel E.) Infantry. See *Mississippi Troops, 16th Regiment.*
Baldwin's (Clark B.) Infantry. See *Massachusetts Troops, 1st Regiment.*
Baldwin's (George W.) Cavalry. See *Pennsylvania Troops, 20th Regiment.*
Ball's (Benjamin A.) Heavy Artillery. See *Massachusetts Troops, 3d Unattached Company.*
Ball's (E.) Infantry. See *Georgia Troops, 51st Regiment.*
Ball's (William B.) Cavalry. See *Virginia Troops, Confederate, 15th Regiment.*
Ball's (William H.) Infantry. See *Ohio Troops, 122d Regiment.*
Ballier's (John F.) Infantry. See *Pennsylvania Troops, 98th Regiment.*
Balthis' (W. H.) Cavalry. See *Virginia Troops, Confederate, 21st Regiment.*
Baltimore Artillery. See *Maryland Troops, Confederate.*
Baltimore Artillery. See *Maryland Troops, Union.*
Baltimore (Colored) Infantry. See *Union Troops (Colored), 4th Regiment.*
Bancroft's (Eugene A.) Artillery. See *Union Troops, Regulars, 4th Regiment, Battery G.*
Barbour's (William M.) Infantry. See *North Carolina Troops, Confederate, 37th Regiment.*
Barclay's (E. S.) Infantry. See *Phillips Legion, post.*
Barnes' (Charles) Infantry. See *Pennsylvania Troops, 9th Reserves.*
Barney's (Elisha L.) Infantry. See *Vermont Troops, 6th Regiment.*
Barney's (Valentine G.) Infantry. See *Vermont Troops, 9th Regiment.*
Barry's (John D.) Infantry. See *North Carolina Troops, Confederate, 18th Regiment.*
Barstow's (George F.) Artillery. See *Union Troops (Regulars), 3d Regiment, Batteries F and K.*
Barton's (Ira McL.) Heavy Artillery. See *New Hampshire Troops, 2d Battery.*
Bartram's (Nelson B.) Infantry. See *Union Troops (Colored), 20th Regiment.*
Batchelder's (N. Walter) Infantry. See *Massachusetts Troops, 13th Regiment.*
Bates' (Thomas H.) Artillery. See *New York Troops, 1st Regiment, Battery A.*
Bates' (Willard W.) Heavy Artillery. See *New York Troops, 8th Regiment.*
Batte's (Peter V.) Infantry. See *Virginia Troops, Confederate, 44th Battalion.*
Batterson's (James P.) Cavalry. See *New York Troops, 13th Regiment.*
Bayley's (Thomas) Infantry. See *Union Troops (Colored), 9th Regiment.*
Beale's (R. L. T.) Cavalry. See *Virginia Troops, Confederate, 9th Regiment.*
Bean's (Onslow) Cavalry. See *James E. Carter's Cavalry, post.*
Bear's (Bernard) Infantry. See *New York Troops, 39th Regiment.*
Beard's (Samuel) Infantry. See *Ohio Troops.*
Beardsley's (John D.) Infantry. See *Maine Troops, 10th Regiment.*

Beardsley's (William E.) **Cavalry.** See *New York Troops, 6th Regiment.*
Beaver's (James A.) **Infantry.** See *Pennsylvania Troops, 148th Regiment.*
Beck's (Benjamin) **Infantry.** See *Georgia Troops, 9th Regiment.*
Beck's (W. Butler) **Artillery.** See *Union Troops, Regulars, 5th Regiment, Battery I.*
Beckley's (H. M.) **Infantry.** See *Virginia Troops, Confederate, 45th Battalion.*
Bedford Artillery. See *Virginia Troops, Confederate.*
Belger's (James) **Artillery.** See *Rhode Island Troops, 1st Regiment, Battery F.*
Benjamin's (William H.) **Cavalry.** See *New York Troops, 8th Regiment.*
Bennett's (R. Tyler) **Infantry.** See *North Carolina Troops, Confederate, 14th Regiment.*
Bently's (Wilber G.) **Cavalry.** See *New York Troops, 9th Regiment.*
Berkeley's (N.) **Infantry.** See *Virginia Troops, Confederate, 8th Regiment.*
Beveridge's (John L.) **Cavalry.** See *Illinois Troops, 8th Regiment.*
Biddle's (Alexander) **Infantry.** See *Pennsylvania Troops, 121st Regiment.*
Bigelow's (John) **Artillery.** See *Massachusetts Troops, 9th Battery.*
Biles' (Edwin R.) **Infantry.** See *Pennsylvania Troops, 99th Regiment.*
Binyon's (Thomas) **Artillery.** See *Maryland Troops, Union, Battery A.*
Black's (John L.) **Cavalry.** See *South Carolina Troops, 1st Regiment.*
Black's (Mahlon) **Sharpshooters.** See *Minnesota Troops, 2d Company.*
Blacknall's (C. C.) **Infantry.** See *North Carolina Troops, Confederate, 23d Regiment.*
Blake's (John A.) **Heavy Artillery.** See *Pennsylvania Troops, 3d Regiment, Battery F.*
Blakeslee's (Erastus) **Cavalry.** See *Connecticut Troops, 1st Regiment; also Michigan Troops, 6th Regiment.**
Blanding's (Christopher) **Infantry.** See *Hospital Guards, post.*
Blount's (Joseph G.) **Artillery.** See *Virginia Troops, Confederate.*
Blunt's (Mathew M.) **Infantry.** See *Union Troops, Regulars, 12th Regiment.*
Board's (F. H.) **Infantry.** See *Virginia Troops, Confederate, 58th Regiment.*
Bodine's (Robert L.) **Infantry.** See *Pennsylvania Troops, 26th Regiment.*
Bolinger's (Henry C.) **Infantry.** See *Pennsylvania Troops, 7th Reserves.*
Boothby's (Stephen) **Cavalry.** See *Maine Troops, 1st Regiment.*
Borrowe's (William) **Artillery.** See *Pennsylvania Troops, Battery H.*
Botetourt Artillery. See *Virginia Troops, Confederate.*
Botetourt Home Guards. See *Virginia Troops, Confederate.*
Boughton's (Horace) **Infantry.** See *New York Troops, 143d Regiment.*
Bourry's (Gotthilf) **Infantry.** See *New York Troops, 68th Regiment.*
Bowen's (Edward R.) **Infantry.** See *Pennsylvania Troops, 114th Regiment.*
Bowen's (Erwin A.) **Infantry.** See *New York Troops, 151st Regiment.*
Bowen's (H. S.) **Cavalry.** See *Virginia Troops, Confederate, 22d Regiment.*
Bowen's (Lot) **Cavalry.** See *West Virginia Troops, 3d Regiment.*
Bowerman's (Richard N.) **Infantry.** See *Maryland Troops, Union, 4th Regiment.*
Bowie's (Henry C.) **Infantry.** See *Virginia Troops, Confederate, 8th Regiment.*
Bowles' (P. D.) **Infantry.** See *Alabama Troops, 4th Regiment.*
Bown's (William H. H.) **Infantry.** See *Ohio Troops, 61st Regiment.*
Boyd's (Samuel H.) **Infantry.** See *North Carolina Troops, Confederate, 45th Regiment.*
Boyd's (William H.) **Cavalry.** See *Pennsylvania Troops, 21st Regiment.*
Boyle's (John A.) **Infantry.** See *Pennsylvania Troops, 111th Regiment.*
Boyle's (Peter T.) **Infantry.** See *New York Troops, 63d Regiment.*
Brabble's (Edmund C.) **Infantry.** See *North Carolina Troops, Confederate, 32d Regiment.*
Bradford's (William D.) **Artillery.** See *Confederate Guards, Artillery, post.*
Bradley's (Leman W.) **Infantry.** See *New York Troops, 64th Regiment.*
Bragg's (Edward S.) **Infantry.** See *Wisconsin Troops, 6th Regiment.*
Bragg's (William F.) **Cavalry.** See *Maryland Troops, Union, 2d Regiment.*
Branch Artillery. See *North Carolina Troops, Confederate.*

---

* Temporarily commanding.

Brander's (Thomas A.) **Artillery.** See *Letcher Artillery, post.*
Brandon's (W. L.) **Infantry.** See *Mississippi Troops, 22d Regiment.*
Bratton's (John) **Infantry.** See *South Carolina Troops, 6th Regiment.*
Breathed's (James) **Artillery.** See *Virginia Troops, Confederate.*
Breck's (George) **Artillery.** See *New York Troops, 1st Regiment, Battery L̇.*
Breitenback's (John R.) **Infantry.** See *Pennsylvania Troops, 106th Regiment.*
Brenning's (George) **Cavalry.** See *New York Troops, 14th Regiment.*
Bridgford's (D. B.) **Infantry.** See *Virginia Troops, Confederate, 1st Battalion.*
Brightley's (Charles H.) **Infantry.** See *Union Troops, Regulars, 4th Regiment.*
Briner's (William) **Infantry.** See *Pennsylvania Troops, 3d Reserves.*
Brinton's (Joseph P.) **Cavalry.** See *Pennsylvania Troops, 2d Regiment.*
Brisbin's (James S.) **Cavalry.** See *Union Troops, Regulars, 6th Regiment.*
Broady's (K. Oscar) **Infantry.** See *New York Troops, 61st Regiment.*
Brockenbrough's (J. M.) **Infantry.** See *Virginia Troops, Confederate, 40th Regiment.*
Brockman's (B. T.) **Infantry.** See *South Carolina Troops, 13th Regiment.*
Brockway's (Charles B.) **Artillery.** See *Pennsylvania Troops, 1st Regiment, Batteries F and G.*
Brooke's (James V.) **Artillery.** See *Virginia Troops, Confederate.*
Brooker's (Albert F.) **Heavy Artillery.** See *Connecticut Troops, 1st Regiment, Battery B.*
Brooker's (John K.) **Infantry.** See *Pennsylvania Troops, 154th Regiment.*
Brooks **Artillery.** See *South Carolina Troops.*
Brown's (H. A.) **Infantry.** See *North Carolina Troops, Confederate, 1st Regiment.*
Brown's (Henry W.) **Infantry.** See *New Jersey Troops, 3d Regiment.*
Brown's (Jack) **Infantry.** See *Georgia Troops, 59th Regiment.*
Brown's (James M.) **Infantry.** See *Pennsylvania Troops.*
Brown's (J. N.) **Infantry.** See *South Carolina Troops, 14th Regiment.*
Brown's (Ridgely) **Cavalry.** See *Maryland Troops, Confederate, 1st Battalion.*
Brown's (Robert) **Cavalry.** See *Pennsylvania Troops, 13th Regiment; also New York Troops, 10th Regiment.*
Brown's (William D.) **Artillery.** See *Chesapeake Artillery, post.*
Brown's (William R.) **Infantry.** See *New York Troops, 168th Regiment.*
Brown's (William R.) **Infantry.** See *West Virginia Troops, 13th Regiment.*
Browne's (William H.) **Infantry.** See *Virginia Troops, Confederate, 45th Regiment.*
Bruce's (John M.) **Artillery.** See *Maryland Troops, Union, Battery A (six months).*
Bruce's (Robert) **Infantry.** See *Maryland Troops, Union, 2d Regiment, P. H. B.*
Bruen's (Luther B.) **Infantry.** See *Union Troops, Regulars, 12th Regiment.*
Brunson's (Ervin B.) **Artillery.** See *Pee Dee Artillery, post.*
Bryan's (Goode) **Infantry.** See *Georgia Troops, 16th Regiment.*
Bryan's (Thomas A.) **Artillery.** See *Virginia Troops, Confederate.*
Bryan's (Timothy M., jr.) **Cavalry.** See *Pennsylvania Troops, 18th Regiment.*
Bryan's (William E.) **Infantry.** See *New Jersey Troops, 3d Regiment.*
Bryant's (Montgomery) **Infantry.** See *Union Troops, Regulars, 6th Regiment.*
Buck's (Samuel L.) **Infantry.** See *New Jersey Troops, 2d Regiment.*
Bucklin's (James T. P.) **Infantry.** See *Rhode Island Troops, 4th Regiment.*
Bucklyn's (John K.) **Artillery.** See *Rhode Island Troops, 1st Regiment, Battery E.*
Buffum's (Martin P.) **Infantry.** See *Rhode Island Troops, 4th Regiment.*
Bukey's (Van H.) **Infantry.** See *West Virginia Troops, 11th Regiment.*
Bulger's (M. J.) **Infantry.** See *Alabama Troops, 47th Regiment.*
Bull's (James M.) **Infantry.** See *New York Troops, 126th Regiment.*
Bulmer's (George A.) **Heavy Artillery.** See *New York Troops, 13th Regiment.*
Burke's (Denis F.) **Infantry.** See *New York Troops, 88th Regiment.*
Burling's (George C.) **Infantry.** See *New Jersey Troops, 6th Regiment.*
Burnett's (William M.) **Infantry.** See *New York Troops, 158th Regiment.*

Temporarily commanding.

Burnham's (Horace B.) Infantry. See *Pennsylvania Troops, 67th Regiment.*
Burnham's (John H.) Infantry. See *Connecticut Troops, 16th Regiment.*
Burns' (Michael W.) Infantry. See *New York Troops, 73d Regiment.*
Burrough's (William H.) Artillery. See *Rhett Artillery, post.*
Burt's (Edwin) Infantry. See *Maine Troops, 3d Regiment.*
Burt's (Mason W.) Infantry. See *Massachusetts Troops, 22d Regiment.*
Burton's (John E.) Artillery. See *New York Troops, 11th Battery;* also *New York Troops, 1st Regiment, Battery K.* *
Butler's (Benjamin C.) Infantry. See *New York Troops, 93d Regiment.*
Butler's (John H.) Artillery. See *Union Troops, Regulars, 2d Regiment, Battery G.*
Butler's (M. C.) Cavalry. See *South Carolina Troops, 2d Regiment.*
Butt's (Edgar M.) Infantry. See *Georgia Troops, 2d Regiment.*
Byrnes' (Richard) Infantry. See *Massachusetts Troops, 28th Regiment.*
Cabell's (J. R.) Infantry. See *Virginia Troops, Confederate, 38th Regiment.*
Cabot's (Stephen) Heavy Artillery. See *Massachusetts Troops, 1st Battalion.*
Cady's (A. Lester) Artillery. See *New York Troops, 24th Battery.*
Calef's (John H.) Artillery. See *Union Troops, Regulars, 2d Regiment, Battery A.*
Callaway's (Morgan) Artillery. See *Pulaski Artillery, post.*
Cantador's (Lorenz) Infantry. See *Pennsylvania Troops, 27th Regiment.*
Cape Fear Artillery. See *North Carolina Troops, Confederate.*
Carlin's (John) Artillery. See *West Virginia Troops, Battery D.*
Carlton's (Henry H.) Artillery. See *Troup Artillery, post.*
Caroline Artillery. See *Virginia Troops, Confederate.*
Carpenter's (John C.) Artillery. See *Alleghany Artillery, ante.*
Carr's (Benjamin F.) Artillery. See *Maine Troops, 2d Battery.*
Carrington's (James McD.) Artillery. See *Charlottesville Artillery, post.*
Carroll's (Edward) Infantry. See *Pennsylvania Troops, 95th Regiment.*
Carson's (John M.) Infantry. See *Pennsylvania Troops, 27th Regiment.*
Carter's (James E.) Cavalry. See *Tennessee Troops.*
Carter's (John W.) Infantry. See *Mississippi Troops, 13th Regiment.*
Carter's (R. W.) Cavalry. See *Virginia Troops, Confederate, 1st Regiment.*
Carter's (William P.) Artillery. See *King William Artillery, post.*
Cary's (N. R.) Heavy Artillery. See *Virginia Troops, Confederate, 19th Battalion.*
Caskie's (William H.) Artillery. See *Hampden Artillery, post.*
Cassin's (Walter L.) Engineers. See *New York Troops, 15th Regiment.*
Catlin's (Theodore B.) Infantry. See *Wisconsin Troops, 5th Regiment.*
Cauret's (Edward C.) Infantry. See *New York Troops, 42d Regiment.*
Cavin's (Elijah H. C.) Infantry. See *Indiana Troops, 14th Regiment.*
Chamberlain's (Abial G.) Infantry. See *North Carolina Troops, Union, 3d Regiment (Colored).*
Chamberlain's (Thomas) Infantry. See *Pennsylvania Troops, 150th Regiment.*
Chambliss' (John R., jr.) Cavalry. See *Virginia Troops, Confederate, 13th Regiment.*
Chandler's (Charles G.) Infantry. See *Vermont Troops, 10th Regiment.*
Chapin's (Gurden) Infantry. See *Union Troops, Regulars, 7th Regiment.*
Chaplin's (Daniel) Heavy Artillery. See *Maine Troops, 1st Regiment.*
Chapman's (Alford B.) Infantry. See *New York Troops, 57th Regiment.*
Chapman's (George B.) Artillery. See *Monroe Artillery, post.*
Chapman's (George H.) Cavalry. See *Indiana Troops, 3d Regiment.*
Charlottesville Artillery. See *Virginia Troops, Confederate.*
Cheek's (W. H.) Cavalry. See *North Carolina Troops, Confederate, 1st Regiment.*
Chenoweth's (J. T.) Infantry. See *Kentucky Troops, Confederate, 11th Regiment.*
Chesapeake Artillery. See *Maryland Troops, Confederate.*
Chesrow's (James Y.) Cavalry. See *Ringgold Cavalry, post.*
Chesterfield Artillery. See *South Carolina Troops.*

---

* Temporarily commanding.

Chew's (R. Preston) **Artillery.** See *Virginia Troops, Confederate.*
Chew's (R. S.) **Infantry.** See *Virginia Troops, Confederate,* 30th *Regiment.*
Chew's (Walter S.) **Artillery.** See *Chesapeake Artillery, ante.*
Christian's (W. S.) **Infantry.** See *Virginia Troops, Confederate,* 55th *Regiment.*
Church's (William) **Heavy Artillery.** See *New York Troops,* 11th *Regiment.*
Claassen's (Peter J.) **Infantry.** See *New York Troops,* 132d *Regiment.*
Claiborne's (James R.) **Cavalry.** See *Virginia Troops, Confederate,* 37th *Battalion.*
Claiborne's (William C.) **Cavalry.** See *Confederate Troops, Regulars,* 7th *Regiment.*
Clancy's (James T.) **Infantry.** See *Pennsylvania Troops,* 45th *Regiment Militia.*
Clark's (A. Judson) **Artillery.** See *New Jersey Troops,* 2d *Battery.*
Clark's (Ela H.) **Artillery.** See *New York Troops,* 1st *Regiment, Battery C.*
Clarke's (E. Y.) **Cavalry.** See *Georgia Troops,* 16th *Battalion.*
Clarke's (J. Lyle) **Infantry.** See *Virginia Troops, Confederate,* 30th *Battalion.*
Clarke's (Robert) **Artillery.** See *Union Troops, Regulars,* 2d *Regiment, Battery A.*
Clarke's (William J.) **Infantry.** See *North Carolina Troops, Confederate,* 24th *Regiment.*
Clayton's (Theodore) **Cavalry.** See *Purnell Legion, Cavalry, post.*
Claytor's (Robert B.) **Heavy Artillery.** See *Virginia Troops, Confederate,* 10th *Battalion, Battery B.*
Clement's (Oscar H.) **Sharpshooters.** See *Massachusetts Troops,* 1st *Company.*
Clendenin's (David R.) **Cavalry.** See *Illinois Troops,* 8th *Regiment.*
Clinton's (William) **Infantry.** See *Union Troops, Regulars,* 10th *Regiment.*
Coate's (Henry C.) **Infantry.** See *Minnesota Troops,* 1st *Regiment.*
Cobb's (Norvell) **Infantry.** See *Virginia Troops, Confederate,* 44th *Regiment.*
Cobb's Legion. See *Georgia Troops.*
Cochran's (James) **Cavalry.** See *Virginia Troops, Confederate,* 14th *Regiment.*
Cogdell's (Daniel) **Artillery.** See *North Carolina Troops, Confederate,* 1st *Regiment, Battery B.*
Cogswell's (Milton) **Infantry.** See *Union Troops, Regulars,* 8th *Regiment.*
Cogswell's (William) **Infantry.** See *Massachusetts Troops,* 2d *Regiment.*
Coit's (James C.) **Artillery.** See *Chesterfield Artillery, ante.*
Cole's (Henry A.) **Cavalry.** See *Maryland Troops, Union.*
Coleman's (Henry Eaton) **Infantry.** See *North Carolina Troops, Confederate,* 12th *Regiment.*
Coleman's (Wiley G.) **Heavy Artillery.** See *Neblett Artillery, post.*
Colgrove's (Silas) **Infantry.** See *Indiana Troops,* 27th *Regiment.*
Collier's (Frederick H.) **Infantry.** See *Pennsylvania Troops,* 139th *Regiment.*
Comegys' (William H.) **Infantry.** See *Maryland Troops, Union,* 1st *Regiment, E. S.*
Comfort's (Samuel, jr.) **Cavalry.** See *Pennsylvania Troops,* 20th *Regiment.*
Comly's (James M.) **Infantry.** See *Ohio Troops,* 23d *Regiment.*
Confederate Guards, **Artillery.** See *Mississippi Troops.*
Confederate Zouaves, **Infantry.** See *A. Coppens' Infantry, post.*
Conger's (Everton J.) **Cavalry.** See *District of Columbia Troops,* 1st *Regiment.*
Conger's (Seymour B.) **Cavalry.** See *West Virginia Troops,* 3d *Regiment.*
Conine's (James W.) **Infantry.** See *Union Troops (Colored),* 5th *Regiment.*
Conley's (Isaiah) **Infantry.** See *North Carolina Troops, Union,* 2d *Regiment.*
Connally's (John K.) **Infantry.** See *North Carolina Troops, Confederate,* 55th *Regiment.*
Conner's (Edward J.) **Infantry.** See *Union Troops, Regulars,* 17th *Regiment.*
Conner's (Freeman) **Infantry.** See *New York Troops,* 44th *Regiment.*
Conner's (Samuel) **Infantry.** See *Pennsylvania Troops,* 62d *Regiment.*
Converse's (Joseph H.) **Infantry.** See *Connecticut Troops,* 11th *Regiment.*
Cook's (A. F.) **Cavalry.** See *Virginia Troops, Confederate,* 8th *Regiment.*
Cook's (John E.) **Infantry.** See *New York Troops,* 76th *Regiment.*
Cook's (Joseph H.) **Cavalry.** See *Maryland Troops, Union,* 1st *Regiment.*
Cook's (Philip) **Infantry.** See *Georgia Troops,* 4th *Regiment.*

Cook's (Roger E.) **Infantry.** See *Maryland Troops, Union, 1st Regiment, P. H. B.*
Coons' (John) **Infantry.** See *Indiana Troops, 14th Regiment.*
Cooper's (Frederick) **Infantry.** See *New Jersey Troops, 7th Regiment.*
Cooper's (James H.) **Artillery.** See *Pennsylvania Troops, 1st Regiment, Battery B.*
Cooper's (John A.) **Infantry.** See *North Carolina Troops, Confederate, 1st Battalion.*
Cooper's (Raleigh L.) **Artillery.** See *Stafford Artillery, post.*
Coppens' (A.) **Infantry.** See *Louisiana Troops.*
Corning's (Clarence H.) **Heavy Artillery.** See *New York Troops, 14th Regiment.*
Corns' (James M.) **Cavalry.** See *Virginia Troops, Confederate, 8th Regiment.*
Cornwell's (Russell H.) **Heavy Artillery.** See *Massachusetts Troops, 2d Regiment.*
Coughlin's (John) **Infantry.** See *New Hampshire Troops, 10th Regiment.*
Coulter's (Richard) **Infantry.** See *Pennsylvania Troops, 11th Regiment.*
Counselman's (Jacob H.) **Artillery.** See *Union Troops, Regulars, 1st Regiment, Battery K.*
Courtney Artillery. See *Virginia Troops, Confederate.*
Covode's (George H.) **Cavalry.** See *Pennsylvania Troops, 4th Regiment.*
Cowan's (Andrew) **Artillery.** See *New York Troops, 1st Battery.*
Coward's (A.) **Infantry.** See *South Carolina Troops, 5th Regiment.*
Cox's (William R.) **Infantry.** See *North Carolina Troops, Confederate, 2d Regiment.*
Craig's (Calvin A.) **Infantry.** See *Pennsylvania Troops, 105th Regiment.*
Craig's (John) **Infantry.** See *Pennsylvania Troops, 147th Regiment.*
Crandell's (Levin) **Infantry.** See *New York Troops, 125th Regiment.*
Crane's (Nirom M.) **Infantry.** See *New York Troops, 107th Regiment.*
Creighton's (William R.) **Infantry.** See *Ohio Troops, 7th Regiment.*
Crenshaw's (William G.) **Artillery.** See *Virginia Troops, Confederate.*
Crookston's (Absalom) **Heavy Artillery.** See *New York Troops, 6th Regiment.*
Croom's (Allen) **Infantry.** See *North Carolina Troops, Confederate.*
Cross' (Edward E.) **Infantry.** See *New Hampshire Troops, 5th Regiment.*
Cross' (Nelson) **Infantry.** See *New York Troops, 67th Regiment.*
Crossley's (Thomas) **Artillery.** See *Delaware Troops.*
Crowninshield's (Benjamin W.) **Cavalry.** See *Massachusetts Troops, 1st Regiment.*
Crowninshield's (Casper) **Cavalry.** See *Massachusetts Troops, 2d Regiment.*
Cullen's (Edgar M.) **Infantry.** See *New York Troops, 96th Regiment.*
Cumming's (James D.) **Artillery.** See *Cape Fear Artillery, ante.*
Cummings' (Emory) **Cavalry.** See *New York Troops, 23d Battalion.*
Cummings' (J. Frank) **Cavalry.** See *Pennsylvania Troops, 5th Regiment.*
Cummings' (Thomas) **Infantry.** See *New York Troops, 82d Regiment.*
Cummins' (Francis M.) **Infantry.** See *New York Troops, 124th Regiment.*
Cunningham's (Henry W.) **Infantry.** See *Maine Troops, 19th Regiment.*
Cunningham's (James A.) **Infantry.** See *Massachusetts Troops, 32d Regiment.*
Cunningham's (Oliver C.) **Infantry.** See *Pennsylvania Troops, 154th Regiment.*
Curry's (William L.) **Infantry.** See *Pennsylvania Troops, 106th Regiment.*
Curtis' (Sylvanus W.) **Infantry.** See *Michigan Troops, 7th Regiment.*
Curtis' (William B.) **Infantry.** See *West Virginia Troops, 12th Regiment.*
Dabinett's (John) **Cavalry.** See *Washington Cavalry, post.*
Dabney's (William J.) **Artillery.** See *Virginia Troops, Confederate.*
Daggett's (Aaron S.) **Infantry.** See *Maine Troops, 5th Regiment.*
Dake's (Crawley P.) **Cavalry.** See *Michigan Troops, 5th Regiment.*
Dale's (Richard C.) **Cavalry.** See *Pennsylvania Troops, 1st Battalion.*
Dana's (Edmund L.) **Infantry.** See *Pennsylvania Troops, 143d Regiment.*
Dana Troop, Cavalry. See *Pennsylvania Troops.*
Dance's (Willis J.) **Artillery.** See *Powhatan Artillery, post.*
Daniel's (Jabez J.) **Artillery.** See *Michigan Troops, 9th Battery.*
Danks' (John A.) **Infantry.** See *Pennsylvania Troops, 63d Regiment.*
Danville Artillery. See *Virginia Troops, Confederate.*

Dare's (George) Infantry. See *Pennsylvania Troops, 5th Reserves.*
Darlington's (William B.) Cavalry. See *Pennsylvania Troops, 18th Regiment.*
Davant's (P. E.) Sharpshooters. See *Georgia Troops, 3d Battalion.*
Davidson's (Alexander) Cavalry. See *Pennsylvania Troops, 1st Regiment.*
Davidson's (George S.) Artillery. See *Virginia Troops, Confederate.*
Davis' (Edwin P.) Infantry.   See *New York Troops, 153d Regiment.*
Davis' (Frank A.) Artillery. See *New York Troops, 20th Battery.*
Davis' (J. Lucius) Cavalry. See *Virginia Troops, Confederate, 10th Regiment.*
Davis' (Phineas A.) Artillery. See *Massachusetts Troops, 7th Battery.*
Davis' (Phineas S.) Infantry. See *Massachusetts Troops, 39th Regiment.*
Dawson's (Anderson) Cavalry. See *West Virginia Troops, 1st Regiment.*
De Blanc's (Alcibiades) Infantry. See *Louisiana Troops, 8th Regiment.*
Deems' (James M.) Cavalry. See *Maryland Troops, Union, 1st Regiment.*
Deens' (James L.) Infantry. See *Ohio Troops.*
De Forest's (Jacob J.) Infantry. See *New York Troops, 81st Regiment.*
Dement's (William F.) Artillery. See *Maryland Troops, Confederate.*
Deming's (Charles R.) Artillery. See *Indiana Troops, 16th Battery.*
Denison's (Andrew W.) Infantry. See *Maryland Troops, Union, 8th Regiment.*
Dennison's (William N.) Artillery. See *Union Troops, Regulars, 2d Regiment, Battery G.*
Dent's (Frederick T.) Infantry. See *Union Troops, Regulars, 4th Regiment.*
De Rosset's (William L.) Infantry. See *North Carolina Troops, Confederate, 3d Regiment.*
Derrick's (Clarence) Infantry. See *Virginia Troops, Confederate, 23d Battalion.*
Dickenson's (Crispin) Artillery. See *Ringgold Artillery, post.*
Dickson's (Henry) Artillery. See *North Carolina Troops, Confederate, 13th Battalion, Battery E.*
Dilger's (Hubert) Artillery. See *Ohio Troops, 1st Regiment, Battery I.*
Dimick's (Justin) Artillery. See *Union Troops, Regulars, 1st Regiment.*
Dittrick's [?] Cavalry. Official designation not of record. See —— *Dittrick.*
Dixon's (Charles T.) Infantry. See *Maryland Troops, Union, 8th Regiment.*
Donald's (William K.) Artillery. See *Rockbridge Artillery, No. 2, post.*
Donaldsonville Artillery. See *Louisiana Troops.*
Donohoe's (Michael T.) Infantry. See *New Hampshire Troops, 10th Regiment.*
Doster's (William E.) Cavalry. See *Pennsylvania Troops, 4th Regiment.*
Douglass' (Robert B.) Cavalry. See *Pennsylvania Troops, 20th Regiment.*
Douthat's (Henry C.) Artillery. See *Botetourt Artillery, ante.*
Douthat's (R. W.) Infantry. See *Virginia Troops, Confederate, 11th Regiment.*
Dove's (David) Cavalry. See *West Virginia Troops, 2d Regiment.*
Dow's (Edwin B.) Artillery. See *Maine Troops, 6th Battery.*
Draper's (Alonzo G.) Infantry. See *North Carolina Troops, Union, 2d Regiment (Colored).*
Drewry's (John W.) Artillery. See *Southside Artillery, post.*
Du Bose's (D. M.) Infantry. See *Georgia Troops, 15th Regiment.*
Duff's (Levi B.) Infantry. See *Pennsylvania Troops, 110th Regiment.*
Duke's (R. T. W.) Infantry. See *Virginia Troops, Confederate, 46th Regiment.*
Dulany's (R. H.) Cavalry. See *Virginia Troops, Confederate, 7th Regiment.*
Duncan's (Samuel A.) Infantry. See *Union Troops (Colored), 4th Regiment.*
Dungan's (Robert H.) Infantry. See *Virginia Troops, Confederate, 48th Regiment.*
Dunkelberger's (Isaac R.) Cavalry. See *Union Troops, Regulars, 1st Regiment.*
Dunn's (A. C.) Cavalry. See *Virginia Troops, Confederate, 37th Battalion.*
Dunne's (John P.) Infantry. See *Pennsylvania Troops, 115th Regiment.*
Du Pont's (Henry A.) Artillery. See *Union Troops, Regulars, 5th Regiment, Battery B.*
Durland's (Coe) Cavalry. See *Pennsylvania Troops, 17th Regiment.*
Dutton's (Arthur H.) Infantry. See *Connecticut Troops, 21st Regiment.*

Duval's (Isaac H.) **Infantry.** See *West Virginia Troops, 9th Regiment.*
Duvall's (Robert E.) **Cavalry.** See *Purnell Legion, Cavalry, post.*
Dwight's (Augustus W.) **Infantry.** See *New York Troops, 122d Regiment.*
Dwight's (Walton) **Infantry.** See *Pennsylvania Troops, 149th Regiment.*
Eager's (Charles H.) **Infantry.** See *Massachusetts Troops, 15th Regiment.*
Eagle Artillery. See *Maryland Troops, Union, Battery B (six months).*
Easterly's (George B.) **Artillery.** See *Wisconsin Troops, 4th Battery.*
Eaton's (Hamilton) **Infantry.** See *Ohio Troops.*
Eaton's (John B.) **Artillery.** See *New York Troops, 27th Battery.*
Ebbs' (John) **Cavalry.** See *New York Troops, 3d Regiment.*
Eddy's (Henry M.) **Infantry.** See *Pennsylvania Troops, 114th Regiment.*
Edgar's (George M.) **Infantry.** See *Virginia Troops, Confederate, 26th Battalion.*
Edgell's (Frederick M.) **Artillery.** See *New Hampshire Troops, 1st Battery.*
Edmonds' (E. C.) **Infantry.** See *Virginia Troops, Confederate, 38th Regiment.*
Edmondson's (James K.) **Infantry.** See *Virginia Troops, Confederate, 27th Regiment.*
Edmundson's (H. A.) **Cavalry.** See *Virginia Troops, Confederate, 27th Battalion.*
Edwards' (Clark S.) **Infantry.** See *Maine Troops, 5th Regiment.*
Edwards' (Oliver) **Infantry.** See *Massachusetts Troops, 37th Regiment.*
Egan's (John) **Artillery.** See *Union Troops, Regulars, 1st Regiment, Battery K.*
Egan's (Thomas W.) **Infantry.** See *New York Troops, 40th Regiment.*
Ege's (Joseph A.) **Infantry.** See *Pennsylvania Troops, 1st Battalion.*
Eggleston's (Rouse S.) **Infantry.** See *New York Troops, 97th Regiment.*
Elder's (Samuel S.) **Artillery.** See *Union Troops, Regulars, 4th Regiment, Battery E.*
Ellett's (Thomas) **Artillery.** See *William G. Crenshaw's Artillery, ante.*
Ellingwood's (Lyman H.) **Infantry.** See *Massachusetts Troops, 15th Regiment.*
Elliott's (Robert T.) **Infantry.** See *Michigan Troops, 16th Regiment.*
Ellis' (Theodore G.) **Infantry.** See *Connecticut Troops, 14th Regiment.*
Ellison's (John S.) **Cavalry.** See *New York Troops, 12th Regiment.*
Ellmaker's (Peter C.) **Infantry.** See *Pennsylvania Troops, 119th Regiment.*
Ells' (H. N.) **Artillery.** See *Macon Artillery, post.*
Elwell's (Andrew) **Infantry.** See *Massachusetts Troops, 23d Regiment.*
Embich's (John B.) **Infantry.** See *Pennsylvania Troops, 48th Regiment Militia.*
Ent's (Wellington H.) **Infantry.** See *Pennsylvania Troops, 6th Reserves.*
Epes' (Branch J.) **Artillery.** See *Johnston Artillery, post.*
Esembaux's (Michael) **Infantry.** See *New York Troops, 58th Regiment.*
Evans' (Andrew W.) **Cavalry.** See *Union Troops, Regulars, 6th Regiment.*
Evans' (Clement A.) **Infantry.** See *Georgia Troops, 31st Regiment.*
Evans' (Stephen B.) **Cavalry.** See *North Carolina Troops, Confederate, 5th Regiment.*
Ewing's (Charles) **Infantry.** See *New Jersey Troops, 4th Regiment.*
Ewing's (Chatham T.) **Artillery.** See *West Virginia Troops, Battery G.*
Ewing's (John) **Infantry.** See *Pennsylvania Troops, 155th Regiment.*
Exempts' Battalion, Infantry. See *West Virginia Troops.*
Fagan's (Andrew) **Artillery.** See *Pennsylvania Troops, 1st Regiment, Battery H.*
Fair's (Charles) **Infantry.** See *Pennsylvania Troops, 154th Regiment; also Pennsylvania Troops, 147th Regiment.*
Fairlamb's (George A.) **Infantry.** See *Pennsylvania Troops, 148th Regiment.*
Faison's (Paul F.) **Infantry.** See *North Carolina Troops, Confederate, 56th Regiment.*
Fardella's (Enrico) **Infantry.** See *New York Troops, 85th Regiment.*
Faribault's (George H.) **Infantry.** See *North Carolina Troops, Confederate, 47th Regiment.*
Farnham's (Augustus B.) **Infantry.** See *Maine Troops, 16th Regiment.*
Farnum's (J. Egbert) **Infantry.** See *New York Troops, 70th Regiment.*
Farrar's (Judson S.) **Infantry.** See *Michigan Troops, 26th Regiment.*
Fauquier Artillery. See *Virginia Troops, Confederate.*
Fearing's (Joseph T.) **Cavalry.** See *George W. P. Smith's Cavalry, post.*

Fellows' (John F.) **Infantry.** See *Massachusetts Troops*, 17th *Regiment*.
Fellows' (Stark) **Infantry.** See *Union Troops (Colored)*, 2d *Regiment*.
Ferebee's (Dennis D.) **Cavalry.** See *North Carolina Troops, Confederate*, 4th *Regiment*.
Ferguson's (Alonzo) **Infantry.** See *New York Troops*, 152d *Regiment*.
Ferguson's (M. J.) **Cavalry.** See *Virginia Troops, Confederate*, 16th *Regiment*.
Ferguson's (Raymond) **Cavalry.** See *New York Troops*, 12th *Regiment*.
Fickling's (William W.) **Artillery.** See *Brooks Artillery, ante*.
Fields' (William J.) **Cavalry.** See *Kentucky Troops, Confederate*.
Finnicum's (Mark) **Infantry.** See *Wisconsin Troops*, 7th *Regiment*.
Firey's (William) **Cavalry.** See *Henry A. Cole's Cavalry, ante*.
Fisher's (Isaac B.) **Infantry.** See *West Virginia Troops*, 7th *Regiment*.
Fitch's (Butler) **Artillery.** See *New York Troops*, 8th *Battery*.
Fitch's (William T.) **Infantry.** See *Ohio Troops*, 29th *Regiment*.
Fite's (John A.) **Infantry.** See *Tennessee Troops*, 7th *Regiment*.
Fitzhugh's (Charles L.) **Artillery.** See *Union Troops, Regulars*, 4th *Regiment, Battery C*.
Fitzhugh's (Robert H.) **Artillery.** See *New York Troops*, 1st *Regiment, Battery K;* also 11th *Battery*.*
Fitzpatrick's (Edmund H.) **Infantry.** See *Massachusetts Troops*, 28th *Regiment*.
Flagg's (Oliver B.) **Heavy Artillery.** See *New York Troops*, 14th *Regiment, Batteries E and F*.
Flemming's (James A.) **Infantry.** See *New York Troops*, 99th *Regiment*.
Flesher's (William H.) **Cavalry.** See *West Virginia Troops*, 3d *Regiment*.
Flood's (Hugh C.) **Infantry.** See *New York Troops*, 155th *Regiment*.
Flowerree's (C. C.) **Infantry.** See *Virginia Troops, Confederate*, 7th *Regiment*.
Fluvanna Artillery. See *Virginia Troops, Confederate*.
Flynn's (John) **Infantry.** See *Pennsylvania Troops*, 28th *Regiment*.
Foerster's (Hermann) **Infantry.** See *New York Troops*, 8th *Regiment*.
Follett's (Frederick M.) **Artillery.** See *Union Troops, Regulars*, 4th *Regiment, Battery D*.
Folsom's (Robert W.) **Infantry.** See *Georgia Troops*, 14th *Regiment*.
Fontaine's (C. R.) **Infantry.** See *Virginia Troops, Confederate*, 57th *Regiment*.
Ford's (Samuel) **Infantry.** See *Maryland Troops, Union*, 5th *Regiment*.
Forney's (William H.) **Infantry.** See *Alabama Troops*, 10th *Regiment*.
Forno's (Henry) **Infantry.** See *Louisiana Troops*, 5th *Regiment*.
Forsberg's (August) **Infantry.** See *Virginia Troops, Confederate*, 51st *Regiment*.
Forsyth's (Charles) **Infantry.** See *Alabama Troops*, 3d *Regiment*.
Foss' (Charles H.) **Infantry.** See *Massachusetts Troops*, 25th *Regiment*.
Foster's (George P.) **Infantry.** See *Vermont Troops*, 4th *Regiment*.
Fowler's (Edward B.) **Infantry.** See *New York Troops*, 84th *Regiment*.
Foy's (Christopher D.) **Infantry.** See *North Carolina Troops, Confederate*.
Franklin's (Walter S.) **Infantry.** See *Union Troops, Regulars*, 12th *Regiment*.
Franks' (Samuel J.) **Infantry.** See *Union Troops, Regulars*, 8th *Regiment*.
Fraser's (John) **Infantry.** See *Pennsylvania Troops*, 140th *Regiment*.
Fraser's (John C.) **Artillery.** See *Pulaski Artillery, post*.
Frazar's (Douglas) **Cavalry.** See *New York Troops*, 13th *Regiment*.
Fredericksburg Artillery. See *Virginia Troops, Confederate*.
French's (David A.) **Artillery.** See *McComas Artillery, post*.
French's (E. W.) **Cavalry.** See *Connecticut Troops*, 1st *Regiment*.
French's (Frank S.) **Artillery.** See *Union Troops, Regulars*, 1st *Regiment, Batteries E and I*.
French's (William H.) **Cavalry.** See *Virginia Troops, Confederate*, 17th *Regiment*.
French's (Winsor B.) **Infantry.** See *New York Troops*, 77th *Regiment*.

---

* Temporarily commanding.

Fribley's (Charles W.) Infantry. See *Union Troops (Colored), 8th Regiment.*
Frost's (Daniel) Infantry. See *West Virginia Troops, 11th Regiment.*
Fry's (B. D.) Infantry. See *Alabama Troops, 13th Regiment.*
Fry's (C. W.) Artillery. See *Orange Artillery, post.*
Fuger's (Frederick A.) Artillery. See *Union Troops, Regulars, 4th Regiment, Battery A.*
Fuller's (George) Infantry. See *Maine Troops, 6th Regiment.*
Fuller's (Nehemiah P.) Heavy Artillery. See *Massachusetts Troops, 2d Regiment.*
Fuller's (William D.) Artillery. See *Union Troops, Regulars, 3d Regiment, Battery C.*
Funk's (John H. S.) Infantry. See *Virginia Troops, Confederate, 5th Regiment.*
Funsten's (David) Infantry. See *Virginia Troops, Confederate, 11th Regiment.*
Funsten's (Oliver R.) Cavalry. See *Virginia Troops, Confederate, 11th Regiment.*
Furney's (Luther) Infantry. See *Ohio Troops, 34th Regiment.*
Furst's (George) Artillery. See *West Virginia Troops, Battery A.*
Gallaway's (Thomas S.) Infantry. See *North Carolina Troops, Confederate, 22d Regiment.*
Galligher's (James A.) Cavalry. See *Pennsylvania Troops, 13th Regiment.*
Gambee's (Charles B.) Infantry. See *Ohio Troops, 55th Regiment.*
Gansevoort's (Henry S.) Cavalry. See *New York Troops, 13th Regiment.*
Gantt's (Henry) Infantry. See *Virginia Troops, Confederate, 19th Regiment.*
Garber's (Asher W.) Artillery. See *Staunton Artillery, post.*
Garden's (Hugh R.) Artillery. See *Palmetto Artillery, post.*
Gardner's (Robert D.) Infantry. See *Virginia Troops, Confederate, 4th Regiment.*
Garrard's (Jeptha) Cavalry. See *Union Troops (Colored), 1st Regiment.*
Garrett's (Thomas M.) Infantry. See *North Carolina Troops, Confederate, 5th Regiment.*
Garrett's (William F.) Infantry. See *District of Columbia Troops, 2d Regiment.*
Gary's (M. W.) Infantry. See *Hampton Legion, post.*
Gaskell's (William Penn) Engineers. See *Pennsylvania Troops.*
Gates' (Theodore B.) Infantry. See *New York Troops, 80th Regiment.*
Gazzam's (Audley W.) Infantry. See *Pennsylvania Troops, 103d Regiment.*
German Artillery. See *South Carolina Troops.*
Getchell's (Thomas) Infantry. See *Pennsylvania Troops, 150th Regiment.*
Gibbs' (Alfred) Cavalry. See *New York Troops, 19th Regiment.*
Gibbs' (Charles W.) Infantry. See *Union Troops, Veteran Reserve Corps, 1st Battalion, 48th Company.*
Gibbs' (Frank C.) Artillery. See *Ohio Troops, 1st Regiment, Battery L.*
Gibbs' (George C.) Infantry. See *North Carolina Troops, Confederate, 42d Regiment.*
Gibson's (Augustus A.) Heavy Artillery. See *Pennsylvania Troops, 2d Regiment.*
Gibson's (J. A.) Cavalry. See *Virginia Troops, Confederate, 14th Regiment.*
Gibson's (J. Catlett) Infantry. See *Virginia Troops, Confederate, 49th Regiment.*
Gibson's (William) Infantry. See *Georgia Troops, 48th Regiment.*
Giddings' (Grotius R.) Infantry. See *Union Troops, Regulars, 14th Regiment.*
Gilbreth's (Samuel G.) Sharpshooters. See *Massachusetts Troops, 1st Company.*
Giles' (James) Infantry. See *Virginia Troops, Confederate, 29th Regiment.*
Gilkyson's (Stephen R.) Infantry. See *New Jersey Troops, 6th Regiment.*
Gillies' (Charles F.) Cavalry. See *Pennsylvania Troops, 21st Regiment.*
Gilliss' (James) Artillery. See *Union Troops, Regulars, 5th Regiment, Battery A.*
Gilmer's (John A., jr.) Infantry. See *North Carolina Troops, Confederate, 27th Regiment.*
Gilmor's (Harry W.) Cavalry. See *Maryland Troops, Confederate, 2d Battalion.*
Gilmore's (Charles D.) Infantry. See *Maine Troops, 20th Regiment.*
Gilmore's (George W.) Cavalry. See *West Virginia Troops.*
Gilpin's (Charles) Infantry. See *Maryland Troops, Union, 3d Regiment, P. H. B.*
Giltner's (H. L.) Cavalry. See *Kentucky Troops, Confederate, 4th Regiment.*
Gimber's (Frederick L.) Infantry. See *Pennsylvania Troops, 109th Regiment.*

Gist's (Joseph F.) **Infantry.** See *South Carolina Troops, 15th Regiment.*
Glassie's (Daniel W.) **Artillery.** See *Seth J. Simmonds' Artillery, post.*
Glenn's (John F.) **Infantry.** See *Pennsylvania Troops, 23d Regiment.*
Glenn's (Luther J.) **Infantry.** See *Cobb's Legion, ante.*
Gloucester Heavy Artillery. See *Virginia Troops, Confederate, 4th Regiment, Battery A.*
Godwin's (Archibald C.) **Infantry.** See *North Carolina Troops, Confederate, 57th Regiment.*
Goochland Artillery. See *Virginia Troops, Confederate.*
Goode's (J. Thomas) **Heavy Artillery.** See *Virginia Troops, Confederate, 4th Regiment.*
Goodwin's (William F.) **Artillery.** See *New York Troops.*
Gordon's (George A.) **Cavalry.** See *Union Troops, Regulars, 2d Regiment.*
Gordon's (James B.) **Cavalry.** See *North Carolina Troops, Confederate, 1st Regiment.*
Gordon's (Jonathan W.) **Infantry.** See *Union Troops, Regulars, 11th Regiment.*
Gould's (Seward F.) **Heavy Artillery.** See *New York Troops, 11th Regiment.*
Graham's (Archibald) **Artillery.** See *Rockbridge Artillery, post.*
Graham's (Edward) **Artillery.** See *Petersburg Artillery, post.*
Graham's (George W.) **Artillery.** See *West Virginia Troops, Battery F.*
Graham's (Joseph) **Artillery.** See *North Carolina Troops, Confederate, 1st Regiment, Battery C.*
Graham's (Samuel A.) **Infantry.** See *Purnell Legion, Infantry, post.*
Graham's (William L.) **Cavalry.** See *Virginia Troops, Confederate, 16th Regiment.*
Graham's (William M.) **Artillery.** See *Union Troops, Regulars, 1st Regiment, Battery K.*
Grandy's (Charles R.) **Artillery.** See *Norfolk Blues, Artillery, post.*
Grantman's (William) **Infantry.** See *New Hampshire Troops, 13th Regiment.*
Graves' (Charles C.) **Infantry.** See *North Carolina Troops, Union, 1st Regiment.*
Gray's (George) **Cavalry.** See *Michigan Troops, 6th Regiment.*
Gray's (Robert H.) **Infantry.** See *Maine Troops, 4th Regiment.*
Gray's (William A.) **Infantry.** See *Pennsylvania Troops, 52d Regiment Militia.*
Green's (Charles A.) **Artillery.** See *Louisiana Guard, Artillery, post.*
Green's (F. M.) **Infantry.** See *Mississippi Troops, 11th Regiment.*
Green's (George S.) **Heavy Artillery.** See *New York Troops, 14th Regiment, Battery C.*
Green's (John Shac) **Cavalry.** See *Virginia Troops, Confederate, 6th Regiment.*
Greenawalt's (Jacob W.) **Infantry.** See *Pennsylvania Troops, 68th Regiment.*
Greenfield's (Andrew J.) **Cavalry.** See *Ringgold Cavalry, post.*
Grey's (Thomas) **Artillery.** See *Union Troops, Regulars, 2d Regiment, Battery I.*
Griffin's (Charles B.) **Artillery.** See *Salem Artillery, post.*
Griffin's (James E.) **Infantry.** See *Union Troops (Colored), 22d Regiment.*
Griffin's (Joel R.) **Cavalry.** See *Georgia Troops, 62d Regiment.*
Griffin's (Thomas M.) **Infantry.** See *Mississippi Troops, 18th Regiment.*
Griffin's (William H.) **Artillery.** See *Baltimore Artillery, Confederate, ante.*
Griffith's (Samuel T.) **Infantry.** See *Pennsylvania Troops.*
Grimes' (Bryan) **Infantry.** See *North Carolina Troops, Confederate, 4th Regiment.*
Grimes' (John) **Infantry.** See *New Jersey Troops, 13th Regiment.*
Grimshaw's (Arthur H.) **Infantry.** See *Delaware Troops, 4th Regiment.*
Groner's (V. D.) **Infantry.** See *Virginia Troops, Confederate, 61st Regiment.*
Grover's (Andrew J.) **Cavalry.** See *Vermont Troops, 1st Regiment.*
Grover's (Ira G.) **Infantry.** See *Indiana Troops, 7th Regiment.*
Grubb's (Peter) **Infantry.** See *Ohio Troops, 4th Regiment.*
Guiney's (Patrick R.) **Infantry.** See *Massachusetts Troops, 9th Regiment.*
Guion's (George M.) **Infantry.** See *New York Troops, 148th Regiment.*
Guss' (George R.) **Artillery.** See *Pennsylvania Troops.*

Guss' (George W.) Infantry. See *Pennsylvania Troops*, 138th *Regiment.*
Gustin's (Richard) Infantry. See *Pennsylvania Troops*, 12th *Reserves.*
Hagans' (Harrison H.) Cavalry. See *West Virginia Troops*, 1st *Regiment.*
Hagers' (Jonathan B.) Infantry. See *Union Troops, Regulars,* 14th *Regiment.*
Hale's (Oscar A.) Infantry. See *Vermont Troops*, 6th *Regiment.*
Hall's (Edward D.) Infantry. See *North Carolina Troops, Confederate,* 46th *Regiment.*
Hall's (Isaac B.) Artillery. See *New York Troops,* 1st *Regiment, Battery A.*
Hall's (J. M.) Infantry. See *Alabama Troops,* 5th *Regiment.*
Hall's (Norman J.) Infantry. See *Michigan Troops,* 7th *Regiment.*
Hall's (Thomas M.) Infantry. See *Pennsylvania Troops,* 121st *Regiment.*
Hall's (William P.) Cavalry. See *New York Troops,* 6th *Regiment.*
Ham's (Joseph H.) Infantry. See *Virginia Troops, Confederate,* 16th *Regiment.*
Hamblin's (Joseph E.) Infantry. See *New York Troops,* 65th *Regiment.*
Hamilton's (D. H.) Infantry. See *South Carolina Troops,* 1st *Regiment, P. A.*
Hamilton's (Robert) Infantry. See *Exempts' Battalion, ante.*
Hamilton's (Theodore B.) Infantry. See *New York Troops,* 62d *Regiment.*
Hammell's (John S.) Infantry. See *New York Troops,* 66th *Regiment.*
Hammell's (Richard W.) Cavalry. See *Dana Troop, ante.*
Hammerstein's (Herbert von) Infantry. See *New York Troops,* 78th *Regiment.*
Hammond's (John) Cavalry. See *New York Troops,* 5th *Regiment.*
Hampden Artillery. See *Virginia Troops, Confederate.*
Hampton Legion. See *South Carolina Troops.*
Hancock's (John M.) Infantry. See *North Carolina Troops, Confederate,* 2d *Battalion.*
Hankins' (J. De Witt) Artillery. See *Surry Artillery, post.*
Hanley's (Patrick T.) Infantry. See *Massachusetts Troops,* 9th *Regiment.*
Hannum's (Josiah C.) Artillery. See *New York Troops,* 28th *Battery.*
Hapgood's (Charles E.) Infantry. See *New Hampshire Troops,* 5th *Regiment.*
Hardaway Artillery. See *William B. Hurt's Artillery, post.*
Hardin's (Mark B.) Heavy Artillery. See *Virginia Troops, Confederate,* 18th *Battalion.*
Harhaus' (Otto) Cavalry. See *New York Troops,* 2d *Regiment.*
Harkness' (Thomas C.) Infantry. See *Pennsylvania Troops,* 81st *Regiment.*
Harlan's (William H.) Infantry. See *Ohio Troops,* 126th *Regiment.*
Harman's (A. W.) Cavalry. See *Virginia Troops, Confederate,* 12th *Regiment.*
Harmon's (William) Sharpshooters. See *Minnesota Troops,* 2d *Company.*
Harn's (William A.) Artillery. See *New York Troops,* 3d *Battery.*
Harney's (George) Infantry. See *New York Troops,* 147th *Regiment.*
Harris' (Benjamin F.) Infantry. See *Maine Troops,* 6th *Regiment.*
Harris' (Edward P.) Infantry. See *Delaware Troops,* 1st *Regiment.*
Harris' (N. H.) Infantry. See *Mississippi Troops,* 19th *Regiment.*
Harris' (Thomas M.) Infantry. See *West Virginia Troops,* 10th *Regiment.*
Harrison's (A. T.) Infantry. See *Virginia Troops, Confederate,* 30th *Regiment.*
Harrison's (F. E.) Infantry. See *South Carolina Troops,* 1st *Regiment Rifles.*
Harrison's (Julian) Cavalry. See *Virginia Troops, Confederate,* 6th *Regiment.*
Hart's (James F.) Artillery. See *Washington (S. C.) Artillery, post*
Hart's (Patrick) Artillery. See *New York Troops,* 15th *Battery.*
Hart's (William T.) Engineers. See *Confederate Troops, Regulars,* 3d *Regiment.*
Hartshorne's (William R.) Infantry. See *Pennsylvania Troops,* 13th *Reserves.*
Hastings' (Charles W.) Infantry. See *Massachusetts Troops,* 12th *Regiment.*
Hastings' (George G.) Sharpshooters. See *Union Troops, Volunteers,* 1st *Regiment.*
Hawley's (William) Infantry. See *Wisconsin Troops,* 3d *Regiment.*
Hayes' (Joseph) Infantry. See *Massachusetts Troops,* 18th *Regiment.*
Haynes' (C. L.) Infantry. See *Virginia Troops, Confederate,* 27th *Regiment.*
Haywood's (Edward G.) Infantry. See *North Carolina Troops, Confederate,* 7th *Regiment.*

Hazard's (John G.) **Artillery.** See *Rhode Island Troops, 1st Regiment, Battery B.*
Hazard's (Morris) **Cavalry.** See *New York Troops, 16th Regiment.*
Heacock's (Reuben B.) **Infantry.** See *New York Troops, 49th Regiment.*
Head's (Henry T.) **Infantry.** See *New York Troops, 84th Regiment.*
Healey's (Virgil M.) **Infantry.** See *New Jersey Troops, 8th Regiment.*
Heaton's (Edward) **Artillery.** See *Union Troops, Regulars, 2d Regiment, Batteries B and L.*
Hecker's (Frederick) **Infantry.** See *Illinois Troops, 82d Regiment.*
Hedrick's (John J.) **Heavy Artillery.** See *North Carolina Troops, Confederate, 3d Regiment.*
Henagan's (John W.) **Infantry.** See *South Carolina Troops, 8th Regiment.*
Henderson's (John) **Infantry.** See *Pennsylvania Troops.*
Henry's (William, jr.) **Infantry.** See *New Jersey Troops, 1st Regiment.*
Henry's (William W.) **Infantry.** See *Vermont Troops, 10th Regiment.*
Hensley's (James O.) **Heavy Artillery.** See *Virginia Troops, Confederate, 10th Battalion.*
Herbert's (Arthur) **Infantry.** See *Virginia Troops, Confederate, 17th Regiment.*
Herbert's (James R.) **Infantry.** See *Maryland Troops, Confederate, 1st Battalion.*
Herbert's (Thomas) **Heavy Artillery.** See *Massachusetts Troops, 11th Unattached Company.*
Herrick's (Seth W.) **Infantry.** See *Maryland Troops, Union, 2d Regiment, E. S*
Herring's (Charles P.) **Infantry.** See *Pennsylvania Troops, 118th Regiment.*
Hexamer's (William) **Artillery.** See *New Jersey Troops, 1st Battery.*
Heydrick's (Charles) **Infantry.** See *Delaware Troops, 6th Regiment.*
Higginbotham's (John C.) **Infantry.** See *Virginia Troops, Confederate, 25th Regiment.*
Higgins' (Benjamin L.) **Infantry.** See *New York Troops, 86th Regiment.*
Hill's (Joseph C.) **Infantry.** See *Maryland Troops, Union, 6th Regiment.*
Hill's (Wallace) **Artillery.** See *West Virginia Troops, Battery C.*
Hiller's (Frederick L.) **Artillery.** See *New York Troops, 16th Battery.*
Hilton's (Joseph) **Infantry.** See *New York Troops, 12th Regiment.*
Hine's (Jonathan D.) **Infantry.** See *Ohio Troops, 12th Regiment.*
Hodges' (Wesley C.) **Infantry.** See *Georgia Troops, 17th Regiment.*
Hoffman's Battalion, Infantry. See *Ohio Troops.*
Hoffman's (John S.) **Infantry.** See *Virginia Troops, Confederate, 31st Regiment.*
Hofmann's (John William) **Infantry.** See *Pennsylvania Troops, 56th Regiment.*
Hoke's (William J.) **Infantry.** See *North Carolina Troops, Confederate, 38th Regiment.*
Holcombe Legion. . See *South Carolina Troops.*
Holder's (W. D.) **Infantry.** See *Mississippi Troops, 17th Regiment.*
Holliday's (F. W. M.) **Infantry.** See *Virginia Troops, Confederate, 33d Regiment.*
Holman's (George F.) **Cavalry.** See *Massachusetts Troops, 2d Regiment.*
Holman's (John H.) **Infantry.** See *Union Troops (Colored), 1st Regiment.*
Holmes' (James H.) **Artillery.** See *West Virginia Troops, Battery H.*
Holt's (Bolling H.) **Infantry.** See *Georgia Troops, 35th Regiment.*
Hopkins' (George G.) **Heavy Artillery.** See *Rhode Island Troops, 5th Regiment, Battery E.*
Hopper's (George C.) **Infantry.** See *Michigan Troops, 1st Regiment.*
Hopper's (George F.) **Infantry.** See *New York Troops, 10th Regiment.*
Horn's (Melchoir H.) **Infantry.** See *Pennsylvania Troops, 38th Regiment Militia.*
Hospital Guards, Infantry. See *Rhode Island Troops.*
Hotchkiss' (Walter S.) **Artillery.** See *Connecticut Troops, 2d Battery.*
Houghton's (Moses B.) **Infantry.** See *Michigan Troops, 3d Regiment.*
Howard's (Robert V. W.) **Artillery.** See *Union Troops, Regulars, 4th Regiment, Battery L.*

Howell's (John H.) **Artillery.** See *New York Troops, 3d Regiment, Battery M.*
Hoy's (John F.) **Infantry.** See *West Virginia Troops, 6th Regiment.*
Hoyt's (Henry M.) **Infantry.** See *Connecticut Troops, 8th Regiment.*
Hudson's (Edward McK.) **Infantry.** See *Union Troops, Regulars, 14th Regiment.*
Huger **Artillery.** See *Joseph D. Moore's Artillery, post.*
Hugo's (William H.) **Infantry.** See *New York Troops, 70th Regiment.*
Huidekoper's (Henry S.) **Infantry.** See *Pennsylvania Troops, 150th Regiment.*
Huling's (Thomas M.) **Infantry.** See *Pennsylvania Troops, 49th Regiment.*
Hull's (James C.) **Infantry.** See *Pennsylvania Troops, 62d Regiment.*
Hullinger's (Josiah C.) **Cavalry.** See *Pennsylvania Troops, 21st Regiment.*
Hunt's (John S.) **Artillery.** See *Union Troops, Regulars, 4th Regiment, Battery L.*
Hunter's (Charles H.) **Infantry.** See *Pennsylvania Troops, 42d Regiment Militia.*
Huntington's (James F.) **Artillery.** See *Ohio Troops, 1st Regiment. Battery H.*
Huntley's (John H.) **Infantry.** See *Maryland Troops, Union, 2d Regiment, P. H. B.*
Hupp's (Abraham) **Artillery.** See *Salem Artillery, post.*
Hurst's (Samuel H.) **Infantry.** See *Ohio Troops. 73d Regiment.*
Hurt's (William B.) **Artillery.** See *Alabama Troops.*
Hutton's (Elihu) **Cavalry.** See *Virginia Troops, Confederate, 20th Regiment.*
Hyman's (Joseph H.) **Infantry.** See *North Carolina Troops, Confederate, 13th Regiment.*
Imboden's (George W.) **Cavalry.** See *Virginia Troops, Confederate, 18th Regiment.*
Iredell's (J. J.) **Infantry.** See *North Carolina Troops, Confederate, 2d Battalion.*
Irish's (Nathaniel) **Artillery.** See *Pennsylvania Troops, Battery F.*
Irvin's (John) **Infantry.** See *Pennsylvania Troops, 149th Regiment.*
Irvine's (William) **Cavalry.** See *New York Troops, 10th Regiment.*
Irwin **Artillery.** See *Sumter Artillery, post, Battery C.*
Jack's (John T.) **Infantry.** See *Pennsylvania Troops, 56th Regiment.*
Jackson's (Allan H.) **Infantry.** See *New York Troops, 134th Regiment.*
Jackson's (Samuel M.) **Infantry.** See *Pennsylvania Troops, 11th Reserves.*
Jackson's (Thomas E.) **Artillery.** See *Virginia Troops, Confederate.*
Jacobs' (William H.) **Infantry.** See *Wisconsin Troops, 26th Regiment.*
Jaehne's (Julius) **Cavalry.** See *Illinois Troops, 16th Regiment.*
Jayne's (Joseph M.) **Infantry.** See *Mississippi Troops, 48th Regiment.*
Jeff. Davis **Artillery.** See *Alabama Troops.*
Jeff. Davis Legion, **Cavalry.** See *Mississippi Troops.*
Jenkins' (David T.) **Infantry.** See *New York Troops, 146th Regiment.*
Jenkins' (Samuel H.) **Infantry.** See *Delaware Troops, 3d Regiment.*
Johns' (Thomas D.) **Infantry.** See *Massachusetts Troops, 7th Regiment.*
Johnson's (Aaron C.) **Artillery.** See *Ohio Troops, 12th Battery.*
Johnson's (Bradley T.) **Infantry.** See *Maryland Troops, Confederate, 1st Battalion.*
Johnson's (Daniel D.) **Infantry.** See *West Virginia Troops, 14th Regiment.*
Johnson's (Dutee) **Heavy Artillery.** See *Rhode Island Troops, 5th Regiment, Battery A.*
Johnson's (George W.) **Infantry.** See *New York Troops, 49th Regiment.*
Johnson's (Marmaduke) **Artillery.** See *Virginia Troops, Confederate.*
Johnston **Artillery.** See *Virginia Troops, Confederate.*
Johnston's (Andrew B.) **Artillery.** See *William G. Crenshaw's Artillery, ante.*
Johnston's (Robert D.) **Infantry.** See *North Carolina Troops, Confederate, 23d Regiment.*
Jones' (Andrew J.) **Heavy Artillery.** See *Pamunkey Heavy Artillery, post.*
Jones' (Archibald F.) **Infantry.** See *Pennsylvania Troops, 53d Regiment.*
Jones' (B. H.) **Infantry.** See *Virginia Troops, Confederate, 60th Regiment.*
Jones' (Charles A.) **Infantry.** See *North Carolina Troops, Union, 1st Regiment (Colored); also Massachusetts Troops, 55th Regiment.**

---

* Temporarily commanding.

Jones' (Edward P.) Infantry. See New York Troops, 125th Regiment.
Jones' (Jesse H.) Infantry. See New York Troops, 60th Regiment.
Jones' (John G.) Infantry. See North Carolina Troops, Confederate, 35th Regiment.
Jones' (Lorenzo J.) Heavy Artillery. See New York Troops, 14th Regiment, Battery D.
Jones' (Noah) Cavalry. See Ohio Troops, 1st Regiment.
Jordan's (John V.) Infantry. See North Carolina Troops, Confederate, 31st Regiment.
Jordan's (Tyler C.) Artillery. See Bedford Artillery, ante.
Jourdan's (James) Infantry. See New York Troops, 158th Regiment.
Joyce's (Robert S.) Artillery. See New York Troops, 28th Battery.
Junior Artillery. See Maryland Troops, Union, Battery A (six months).
Karple's (Henry M.) Infantry. See New York Troops, 52d Regiment.
Keenan's (John B.) Infantry. See Pennsylvania Troops, 11th Regiment.
Keeper's (John V.) Artillery. See West Virginia Troops, Battery B.
Keese's (Oliver, jr.) Infantry. See New York Troops, 118th Regiment.
Keifer's (J. Warren) Infantry. See Ohio Troops, 110th Regiment.
Kelley's (Hugh A.) Cavalry. See Pennsylvania Troops, 20th Regiment.
Kellogg's (Elisha S.) Heavy Artillery. See Connecticut Troops, 2d Regiment.
Kellogg's (Horace) Infantry. See Ohio Troops, 123d Regiment.
Kelly's (Thomas) Infantry. See Pennsylvania Troops, 69th Regiment.
Kelsey's (William) Cavalry. See Maryland Troops, Union, 3d Regiment.
Kemp's (Joseph R.) Infantry. See Pennsylvania Troops.
Kenan's (Thomas S.) Infantry. See North Carolina Troops, Confederate, 43d Regiment.
Kennedy's (John D.) Infantry. See South Carolina Troops, 2d Regiment.
Kester's (John W.) Cavalry. See New Jersey Troops, 1st Regiment.
Ketcham's (John H.) Infantry. See New York Troops, 150th Regiment.
Ketchum's (William A.) Engineers. See New York Troops, 15th Regiment.
Kevill's (Thomas) Artillery. See United Artillery, post.
Key's (J. C. G.) Infantry. See Texas Troops, 4th Regiment.
Kilpatrick's (F. W.) Infantry. See South Carolina Troops, 1st Regiment Volunteers.
King's (J. H.) Infantry. See Alabama Troops, 9th Regiment.
King's (Rufus, jr.) Artillery. See Union Troops, Regulars, 4th Regiment, Battery A.
King and Queen Heavy Artillery. See Virginia Troops, Confederate, 4th Regiment, Battery K.
King William Artillery. See Virginia Troops, Confederate.
Kinzie's (David H.) Artillery. See Union Troops, Regulars, 5th Regiment, Battery K.
Kirkland's (William W.) Infantry. See North Carolina Troops, Confederate, 21st Regiment.
Kirkpatrick's (Thomas J.) Artillery. See Amherst Artillery, ante.
Kitching's (J. Howard) Heavy Artillery. See New York Troops, 6th Regiment.
Kleiser's (Alfred von) Artillery. See New York Troops, 30th Battery.
Knight's (Napoleon B.) Cavalry. See Delaware Troops, 1st Regiment.
Knight's (Walter M.) Artillery. See Rhode Island Troops, 1st Regiment, Battery H.
Knox's (James B.) Infantry. See Pennsylvania Troops, 10th Reserves.
Knox's (Robert T.) Infantry. See Union Troops, Veteran Reserve Corps, 2d Battalion, 50th Company.
Koch's (Charles) Infantry. See New York Troops, 45th Regiment.
Kochersperger's (Charles) Infantry. See Pennsylvania Troops, 71st Regiment.
Kusserow's (Charles) Artillery. See New York Troops, 32d Battery.
Lafayette Cavalry. See Pennsylvania Troops.
Lamar's (John H.) Infantry. See Georgia Troops, 61st Regiment.
Lamar's (T. B.) Infantry. See Florida Troops, 5th Regiment.
Lamb's (William) Heavy Artillery. See North Carolina Troops, Confederate, 2d Regiment.
Lamkin's (James N.) Artillery. See Nelson Artillery, post.

Lamont's (William H.) **Infantry.** See *Pennsylvania Troops, 83d Regiment.*
Lane's (James C.) **Infantry.** See *New York Troops, 102d Regiment.*
Lane's (John R.) **Infantry.** See *North Carolina Troops, Confederate, 26th Regiment.*
Lang's (David) **Infantry.** See *Florida Troops, 8th Regiment.*
Langley's (F. H.) **Infantry.** See *Virginia Troops, Confederate, 1st Regiment.*
Langley's (John F.) **Infantry.** See *New Hampshire Troops, 12th Regiment.*
Lansing's (Jacob H.) **Infantry.** See *New York Troops, 86th Regiment.*
Latham's (Alexander C.) **Artillery.** See *Branch Artillery, ante.*
Latham's (George R.) **Infantry.** See *West Virginia Troops, 2d Regiment.*
Latimer's (Alfred E.) **Infantry.** See *Union Troops, Regulars, 11th Regiment.*
Lay's (Richard G.) **Infantry.** See *Union Troops, Regulars, 3d Regiment.*
Lazelle's (Henry M.) **Cavalry.** See *New York Troops, 16th Regiment.*
Leavitt's (Archibald D.) **Infantry.** See *Maine Troops, 16th Regiment.*
Ledig's (August) **Infantry.** See *Pennsylvania Troops, 75th Regiment.*
Lee Artillery. See *Virginia Troops, Confederate.*
Lee's (Horace C.) **Infantry.** See *Massachusetts Troops, 27th Regiment.*
Leech's (William A.) **Infantry.** See *Pennsylvania Troops, 90th Regiment.*
Le Fort's (George) **Infantry.** See *New York Troops, 73d Regiment.*
Lehmann's (Theodore F.) **Infantry.** See *Pennsylvania Troops, 103d Regiment.*
Leidy's (Asher S.) **Infantry.** See *Pennsylvania Troops, 99th Regiment.*
Lemon's (William) **Infantry.** See *Pennsylvania Troops, 8th Reserves.*
Leonard's (John) **Infantry.** See *New York Troops, 72d Regiment.*
Leonard's (Joseph B.) **Infantry.** See *Massachusetts Troops, 7th Regiment.*
Lessig's (William H.) **Infantry.** See *Pennsylvania Troops, 96th Regiment.*
Lester's (G. A.) **Infantry.** See *Louisiana Troops, 8th Regiment.*
Letcher Artillery. See *Virginia Troops, Confederate.*
Leventhorpe's (Collett) **Infantry.** See *North Carolina Troops, Confederate, 11th Regiment.*
Levi's (John T.) **Artillery.** See *Virginia Troops, Confederate.*
Lewis' (Charles H.) **Infantry.** See *Union Troops, Regulars, 16th Regiment.*
Lewis' (John R.) **Infantry.** See *Vermont Troops, 5th Regiment.*
Lewis' (John W.) **Artillery.** See *Virginia Troops, Confederate.*
Lewis' (William) **Cavalry.** See *Pennsylvania Troops, 5th Regiment.*
Libby's (Edwin) **Infantry.** See *Maine Troops, 4th Regiment.*
Lightfoot's (James N.) **Infantry.** See *Alabama Troops, 6th Regiment.*
Lincoln's (William S.) **Infantry.** See *Massachusetts Troops, 34th Regiment.*
Lindley's (John M.) **Infantry.** See *Indiana Troops, 19th Regiment.*
Lininger's (John C.) **Infantry.** See *Pennsylvania Troops, 2d Battalion.*
Linkons' (B. R.) **Infantry.** See *Virginia Troops, Confederate, 36th Regiment.*
Linton's (John P.) **Infantry.** See *Pennsylvania Troops, 54th Regiment.*
Lipscomb's (T. J.) **Cavalry.** See *South Carolina Troops, 2d Regiment.*
Litchfield's (Allyne C.) **Cavalry.** See *Michigan Troops, 7th Regiment.*
Little's (F. H.) **Infantry.** See *Georgia Troops, 11th Regiment.*
Lockman's (John T.) **Infantry.** See *New York Troops, 119th Regiment.*
Lockwood's (Abram L.) **Infantry.** See *New York Troops, 120th Regiment.*
Lockwood's (Benoni) **Cavalry.** See *Pennsylvania Troops, 6th Regiment.*
Lockwood's (Jonathan H.) **Infantry.** See *West Virginia Troops, 7th Regiment.*
Logie's (William K.) **Infantry.** See *New York Troops, 141st Regiment.*
Long's (Charles H.) **Heavy Artillery.** See *New Hampshire Troops, 1st Battery.*
Long's (John S.) **Infantry.** See *Pennsylvania Troops, 93d Regiment.*
Long's (James W.) **Infantry.** See *Union Troops, Regulars, 2d Regiment.*
Lord's (Newton B.) **Cavalry.** See *New York Troops, 20th Regiment.*
Lord's (William P.) **Cavalry.** See *Delaware Troops, 1st Regiment.*
Lothian's (James A.) **Infantry.** See *Michigan Troops, 26th Regiment.*
Loudoun Rangers, Cavalry. See *Virginia Troops, Union.*

Louisiana Guard, Artillery. See *Louisiana Troops.*
Love's (J. R.) Infantry. See *W. H. Thomas' Legion, post.*
Low's (Thomas) Artillery. See *New York Troops, 23d Battery.*
Lowe's (Samuel D.) Infantry. See *North Carolina Troops, Confederate, 28th Regiment.*
Lowrance's (William L. J.) Infantry. See *North Carolina Troops, Confederate, 34th Regiment.*
Lowry's (Francis M.) Artillery. See *West Virginia Troops, Battery E.*
Lowry's (William M.) Artillery. See *Virginia Troops, Confederate.*
Lowther's (A. A.) Infantry. See *Alabama Troops, 15th Regiment.*
Lumbard's (George W.) Infantry. See *Michigan Troops, 4th Regiment.*
Lumpkin's (Samuel P.) Infantry. See *Georgia Troops, 44th Regiment.*
Lunenburg Heavy Artillery. See *Virginia Troops, Confederate.*
Lurty's (Warren S.) Artillery. See *Virginia Troops, Confederate.*
Lusk's (Isaac M.) Infantry. See *New York Troops, 111th Regiment.*
Lusk's (John A. M.) Artillery. See *Rockbridge Artillery, No. 2, post.*
Lusk's (Thurlow W.) Cavalry. See *Michigan Troops, 1st Regiment.*
Lynch's (William A.) Infantry. See *New York Troops, 42d Regiment.*
Lynchburg Home Guards. See *Virginia Troops, Confederate.*
McAfee's (Lee M.) Infantry. See *North Carolina Troops, Confederate, 49th Regiment.*
McAllister's (Robert) Infantry. See *New Jersey Troops, 11th Regiment.*
McCabe's (George F.) Cavalry. See *Pennsylvania Troops, 13th Regiment.*
McCalmont's (Alfred B.) Infantry. See *Pennsylvania Troops, 142d Regiment.*
McCarthy's (Edward S.) Artillery. See *Richmond Howitzers, 1st Company.*
McCarthy's (Jeremiah) Artillery. See *Pennsylvania Troops, 1st Regiment, Battery E.*
McCartney's (William H.) Artillery. See *Massachusetts Troops, 1st (A) Battery.*
McCaslin's (Maxwell) Infantry. See *West Virginia Troops, 15th Regiment.*
McChesney's (Joseph M.) Infantry. See *North Carolina Troops, Union, 1st Regiment.*
McClanahan's (J. H.) Artillery. See *Virginia Troops, Confederate.*
McClellan's (Samuel A.) Artillery. See *New York Troops, 1st Regiment, Battery G.*
McClennan's (Matthew R.) Infantry. See *Pennsylvania Troops, 138th Regiment.*
McClung's (Hugh L. W.) Artillery. See *Tennessee Troops.*
McComas Artillery. See *Virginia Troops, Confederate.*
McComb's (William) Infantry. See *Tennessee Troops, 14th Regiment.*
McConihe's (Samuel) Infantry. See *New York Troops, 93d Regiment.*
McCreary's (David B.) Infantry. See *Pennsylvania Troops, 145th Regiment.*
McCrone's (Alexander F.) Infantry. See *Patapsco Guards, post.*
McCuen's (Alexander) Infantry. See *Pennsylvania Troops, 72d Regiment.*
McCurdy's (Wilbur G.) Artillery. See *Massachusetts Troops, 7th (G) Battery.*
McDonald's (Alexander J.) Artillery. See *Union Troops, Regulars, 5th Regiment, Battery F.*
McDonough's (Patrick) Infantry. See *Pennsylvania Troops, 2d Reserves.*
McDougall's (Archibald L.) Infantry. See *New York Troops, 123d Regiment.*
MacDougall's (Clinton D.) Infantry. See *New York Troops, 111th Regiment.*
McDowell's (John A.) Infantry. See *North Carolina Troops, Confederate, 1st Regiment.*
McElrath's (Thompson P.) Artillery. See *Union Troops, 5th Regiment.*
McElroy's (John S.) Infantry. See *North Carolina Troops, Confederate, 16th Regiment.*
McElwain's (William S.) Infantry. See *Ohio Troops, 110th Regiment.*
McEvily's (William) Infantry. See *New York Troops, 155th Regiment.*
McGowan's (Thomas S.) Infantry. See *Patapsco Guards, post.*
McGraw's (Joseph) Artillery. See *Purcell Artillery, post.*
McGregor's (William M.) Artillery. See *Virginia Troops, Confederate.*
McIlrath's (James P.) Infantry. See *Ohio Troops, 23d Regiment.*

McIntire's (Samuel B.) **Artillery.** See *Union Troops, Regulars, 2d Regiment, Batteries B and L*.

McIntyre's (James) **Infantry.** See *Pennsylvania Troops, 115th Regiment*.

McIrwin's (Samuel) **Cavalry.** See *New York Troops, 2d Regiment*.

McIvor's (James P.) **Infantry.** See *New York Troops, 170th Regiment*.

McKamy's (J. A.) **Infantry.** See *W. H. Thomas' Legion, post*.

McKay's (William A.) **Heavy Artillery.** See *New York Troops, 2d Regiment*.

McKee's (Samuel A.) **Infantry.** See *Union Troops, Regulars, 2d Regiment*.

McKeen's (H. Boyd) **Infantry.** See *Pennsylvania Troops, 81st Regiment*.

McKethan's (Hector) **Infantry.** See *North Carolina Troops, Confederate, 51st Regiment*.

McKiernan's (James) **Infantry.** See *New Jersey Troops, 7th Regiment*.

McKinley's (Norval) **Infantry.** See *Maryland Troops, Union, 2d Regiment, P. H. B.*

McKnight's (George F.) **Artillery.** See *New York Troops, 12th Battery*.

McKnight's (James) **Artillery.** See *Union Troops, Regulars, 5th Regiment, Battery M*.

McLaughlen's (Napoleon B.) **Infantry.** See *Massachusetts Troops, 1st Regiment*.

McLaughlin's (James H.) **Heavy Artillery.** See *New York Troops, 16th Regiment*.

McMahan's (John) **Cavalry.** See *West Virginia Troops, 2d Regiment*.

McMahon's (James P.) **Infantry.** See *New York Troops, 164th Regiment*.

McMahon's (J. J.) **Infantry.** See *Virginia Troops, Confederate, 63d Regiment*.

McMahon's (John E.) **Infantry.** See *New York Troops, 164th Regiment*.

McMichael's (Richards) **Infantry.** See *Pennsylvania Troops, 53d Regiment*.

McMillan's (Robert) **Infantry.** See *Georgia Troops, 24th Regiment*.

McMullin's (James R.) **Artillery.** See *Ohio Troops, 1st Battery*.

McNary's (William H.) **Infantry.** See *New York Troops, 158th Regiment*.

McNeill's (John H.) **Partisans.** See *Virginia Troops, Confederate*.

MacRae's (William) **Infantry.** See *North Carolina Troops, Confederate, 15th Regiment*.

McVicker's (George W.) **Cavalry.** See *West Virginia Troops, 3d Regiment; also West Virginia Troops, 1st Regiment.*[*]

Macon Artillery. See *Georgia Troops*.

Macon's (Miles C.) **Artillery.** See *Richmond Fayette Artillery, post*.

Macy's (George N.) **Infantry.** See *Massachusetts Troops, 20th Regiment*.

Madill's (Henry J.) **Infantry.** See *Pennsylvania Troops, 141st Regiment*.

Madison Artillery. See *Louisiana Troops*.

Madison Light Artillery. See *Mississippi Troops*.

Manly's (Basil C.) **Artillery.** See *North Carolina Troops, Confederate, 1st Regiment, Battery A.*

Mann's (Daniel P.) **Cavalry.** See *Oneida Cavalry, post*.

Mann's (William D.) **Cavalry.** See *Michigan Troops, 7th Regiment*.

Manning's (Van H.) **Infantry.** See *Arkansas Troops, 3d Regiment*.

Manning's (W. R.) **Infantry.** See *Georgia Troops, 50th Regiment*.

Mansfield's (John) **Infantry.** See *Wisconsin Troops, 2d Regiment*.

Marble's (Frank E.) **Sharpshooters.** See *Union Troops, Volunteers, 1st Regiment*.

Markell's (William L.) **Cavalry.** See *New York Troops, 8th Regiment*.

Markhead's [?] **Cavalry.** Official designation not of record. See —— *Markhead*.

Marshall's (J. K.) **Infantry.** See *North Carolina Troops, Confederate, 52d Regiment*.

Marshall's (J. W.) **Cavalry.** See *Virginia Troops, Confederate, 19th Regiment*.

Martin's (Joseph W.) **Artillery.** See *New York Troops, 6th Battery*.

Martin's (Leonard) **Artillery.** See *Union Troops, Regulars, 5th Regiment, Battery F.*

Martin's (Montgomery) **Infantry.** See *Pennsylvania Troops, 58th Regiment*.

Martin's (S. Taylor) **Artillery.** See *Virginia Troops, Confederate*.

Martin's (William F.) **Infantry.** See *North Carolina Troops, Confederate, 17th Regiment*.

Marye's (Edward A.) **Artillery.** See *Fredericksburg Artillery, ante*.

Marye's (Morton) **Infantry.** See *Virginia Troops, Confederate, 17th Regiment*.

---

*Temporarily commanding.

Maryland Line. See *Maryland Troops, Confederate.*
Mason's (Charles F.) **Artillery.** See *Rhode Island Troops, 1st Regiment, Battery H.*
Mason's (Edwin C.) **Infantry.** See *Maine Troops, 7th Regiment.*
Mason's (Philip D.) **Artillery.** See *Union Troops, Regulars, 1st Regiment, Battery H.*
Massie's (John L.) **Artillery.** See *Fluvanna Artillery, ante.*
Mathews' (J. D.) **Infantry.** See *Georgia Troops, 38th Regiment.*
Matthews Artillery. See *Virginia Troops, Confederate.*
Maurin's (Victor) **Artillery.** See *Donaldsonville Artillery, ante.*
Maury's (R. L.) **Infantry.** See *Virginia Troops, Confederate, 24th Regiment.*
May's (A. J.) **Mounted Rifles.** See *Kentucky Troops, Confederate.*
Mayes' (John) **Cavalry.** See *New York Troops, 3d Regiment.*
Mayo's (Joseph, jr.) **Infantry.** See *Virginia Troops, Confederate, 3d Regiment.*
Mayo's (Robert M.) **Infantry.** See *Virginia Troops, Confederate, 47th Regiment.*
Means' (James C.) **Artillery.** See *West Virginia Troops, Battery F.*
Means' (Samuel C.) **Cavalry.** See *Loudoun Rangers, ante.*
Meikel's (George W.) **Infantry.** See *Indiana Troops, 20th Regiment.*
Mendell's (George H.) **Engineers.** See *Union Troops, Regulars.*
Mercer's (John T.) **Infantry.** See *Georgia Troops, 21st Regiment.*
Merchant's (Charles S.) **Artillery.** See *Union Troops, Regulars, 4th Regiment.*
Merriam's (Gustavus F.) **Heavy Artillery.** See *New York Troops, 5th Regiment.*
Merriam's (Waldo) **Infantry.** See *Massachusetts Troops, 16th Regiment.*
Merrill's (Charles B.) **Infantry.** See *Maine Troops, 17th Regiment.*
Merrill's (Henry P.) **Heavy Artillery.** See *New York Troops, 11th Regiment.*
Merriman's (T. Adams) **Infantry.** See *New York Troops, 92d Regiment.*
Meservey's (Charles C.) **Heavy Artillery.** See *Wisconsin Troops, 1st Regiment, Battery A.*
Metcalf's (Richard) **Artillery.** See *Union Troops, Regulars, 5th Regiment, Battery C.*
Mickley's (James) **Cavalry.** See *Pennsylvania Troops, 21st Regiment.*
Milledge's (John, jr.) **Artillery.** See *Georgia Troops.*
Millen's (John M.) **Cavalry.** See *Georgia Troops, 20th Battalion.*
Miller's (Francis C.) **Infantry.** See *New York Troops, 147th Regiment.*
Miller's (John L.) **Infantry.** See *South Carolina Troops, 12th Regiment.*
Miller's (M. B.) **Artillery.** See *Washington (La.) Artillery, post, 3d Battery.*
Miln's (David I.) **Infantry.** See *New York Troops, 65th Regiment.*
Mindil's (George W.) **Infantry.** See *New Jersey Troops, 33d Regiment.*
Miner's (Milton L.) **Artillery.** See *Indiana Troops, 17th Battery.*
Mink's (Charles E.) **Artillery.** See *New York Troops, 1st Regiment, Battery H.*
Mitchell's (W. L.) **Infantry.** See *North Carolina Troops, Confederate, 22d Regiment.*
Mix's New Cavalry. See *New York Troops, 23d Battalion.*
Mix's (Simon H.) **Cavalry.** See *New York Troops, 3d Regiment.*
Mlotkowski's (Stanislaus) **Artillery.** See *Pennsylvania Troops, Battery A.*
Mobley's (Edward M.) **Infantry.** See *Maryland Troops, Union, 7th Regiment.*
Moesch's (Joseph A.) **Infantry.** See *New York Troops, 83d Regiment.*
Moffett's (C. J.) **Infantry.** See *Georgia Troops, 2d Battalion.*
Moffett's (Samuel A.) **Infantry.** See *New York Troops, 94th Regiment.*
Moffitt's (Stephen) **Infantry.** See *New York Troops, 96th Regiment.*
Monaghan's (William) **Infantry.** See *Louisiana Troops, 6th Regiment.*
Monroe Artillery. See *Virginia Troops, Confederate.*
Montague's (George L.) **Infantry.** See *Massachusetts Troops, 37th Regiment.*
Montague's (Thomas B.) **Heavy Artillery.** See *Virginia Troops, Confederate, 4th Regiment, Battery A.*
Montgomery True Blues, Artillery. See *Alabama Troops.*
Moody's (George V.) **Artillery.** See *Madison Artillery, ante.*
Moody's (William H.) **Infantry.** See *Pennsylvania Troops, 139th Regiment.*
Moor's (Augustus) **Infantry.** See *Ohio Troops, 28th Regiment.*

Moore's (Alexander C.) **Artillery.** See *West Virginia Troops, Battery E.*

Moore's (Alexander D.) **Infantry.** See *North Carolina Troops, Confederate, 66th Regiment.*

Moore's (John W.) **Artillery.** ; See *North Carolina Troops, Confederate, 3d Battalion.*

Moore's (Joseph D.) **Artillery.** See *Virginia Troops, Confederate.*

Moore's (Julian G.) **Artillery.** See *North Carolina Troops, Confederate, 3d Battalion, Battery C.*

Moore's (Roger) **Cavalry.** See *North Carolina Troops, Confederate, 3d Regiment.*

Moore's (William) **Infantry.** See *Pennsylvania Troops, 73d Regiment.*

Moorman's (Marcellus N.) **Artillery.** See *Virginia Troops, Confederate.*

Morgan's (William C.) **Infantry.** See *Maine Troops, 3d Regiment.*

Moroney's (Richard) **Infantry.** See *New York Troops, 69th Regiment.*

Morris Artillery. See *Virginia Troops, Confederate.*

Morris' (Lewis O.) **Heavy Artillery.** See *New York Troops, 7th Regiment.*

Morris' (William E.) **Cavalry.** See *Connecticut Troops, 1st Regiment.*

Morrison's (E. M.) **Infantry.** See *Virginia Troops, Confederate, 15th Regiment.*

Morrison's (Thomas G.) **Infantry.** See *New York Troops, 61st Regiment.*

Morrow's (B. Mortimer) **Cavalry.** See *Pennsylvania Troops, 22d Regiment.*

Morrow's (Henry A.) **Infantry.** See *Michigan Troops, 24th Regiment.*

Morton's (Howard) **Artillery.** See *West Virginia Troops, Battery G.*

Mosby's (John S.) **Cavalry.** See *John S. Mosby.*

Moseley's (Hillery) **Infantry.** See *Mississippi Troops, 42d Regiment.*

Moson's (Richard F.) **Cavalry.** See *Pennsylvania Troops, 21st Regiment.*

Moulton's (Orson) **Infantry.** See *Massachusetts Troops, 25th Regiment.*

Muhlenberg's (Edward D.) **Artillery.** See *Union Troops, Regulars, 4th Regiment, Battery F.*

Munford's (Thomas T.) **Cavalry.** See *Virginia Troops, Confederate, 2d Regiment.*

Murchison's (Kenneth M.) **Infantry.** See *North Carolina Troops, Confederate, 54th Regiment.*

Murphy's (Alexander) **Infantry.** See *Pennsylvania Troops, 49th Regiment Militia.*

Murphy's (Mathew) **Infantry.** See *New York Troops, 182d Regiment.*

Murphy's (Michael C.) **Infantry.** See *New York Troops, 170th Regiment.*

Murray's (Edward) **Heavy Artillery.** See *New York Troops, 5th Regiment.*

Murray's (John B.) **Infantry.** See *New York Troops, 148th Regiment.*

Musser's (John D.) **Infantry.** See *Pennsylvania Troops, 143d Regiment.*

Myers' (William) **Infantry.** See *Ohio Troops, 116th Regiment.*

Nadenbousch's (J. Q. A.) **Infantry.** See *Virginia Troops, Confederate, 2d Regiment.*

Nance's (James D.) **Infantry.** See *South Carolina Troops, 3d Regiment.*

Neblett Heavy Artillery. See *Virginia Troops, Confederate.*

Nelson Artillery. See *Virginia Troops, Confederate.*

Nelson Artillery, No. 2. See *Virginia Troops, Confederate.*

Nelson's (John A.) **Infantry.** See *Union Troops (Colored), 10th Regiment.*

Nethercutt's (John H.) **Infantry.** See *North Carolina Troops, Confederate, 8th Battalion.*

Nevin's (David J.) **Infantry.** See *New York Troops, 62d Regiment.*

Nevin's (John I.) **Infantry.** See *Pennsylvania Troops, 93d Regiment.*

Nevin's (Robert J.) **Artillery.** See *Pennsylvania Troops, Nevin's Battery; also Battery I.*

Newton's (Charles B.) **Heavy Artillery.** See *Massachusetts Troops, 2d Regiment.*

New York 1st Dragoons, Cavalry. See *New York Troops, 19th Regiment.*

New York 2d Militia, Infantry. See *New York Troops, 82d Regiment.*

New York 9th Militia, Infantry. See *New York Troops, 83d Regiment.*

New York 14th Militia, Infantry. See *New York Troops, 81st Regiment.*

New York 20th Militia, Infantry. See *New York Troops, 80th Regiment.*

Nields' (Benjamin) **Artillery.** See *Delaware Troops, 1st Battery.*

Nixon's (Richard) Infantry. See *New York Troops, 99th Regiment.*
Norcom's (Joe) Artillery. See *Washington (La.) Artillery, post, 4th Battery.*
Norfolk Blues, Artillery. See *Virginia Troops, Confederate.*
Norton's (George W.) Artillery. See *Ohio Troops, 1st Regiment, Battery H.*
Nowlen's (Garrett) Infantry. See *Pennsylvania Troops, 116th Regiment.*
O'Connell's (John D.) Infantry. See *Union Troops, Regulars, 14th Regiment.*
Olcott's (Egbert) Infantry. See *New York Troops, 121st Regiment.*
Oley's (John H.) Infantry. See *West Virginia Troops, 8th Regiment.*
Olmstead's (Ralph H.) Cavalry. See *New York Troops, 12th Regiment.*
Onderdonk's (Benjamin F.) Cavalry. See *New York Troops, 7th Regiment.*
O'Neal's (Edward A.) Infantry. See *Alabama Troops, 26th Regiment.*
Oneida Cavalry. See *New York Troops.*
O'Neill's (Henry) Infantry. See *Pennsylvania Troops, 118th Regiment.*
Opp's (Milton) Infantry. See *Pennsylvania Troops, 84th Regiment.*
Orange Artillery. See *Virginia Troops, Confederate.*
Orem's (J. Bailey) Cavalry. See *Maryland Troops, Union, 4th Regiment.*
Orr's (James L.) Infantry. See *South Carolina Troops, 1st Regiment, Rifles.*
Orton's (William H.) Cavalry. See *District of Columbia Troops.*
Orwig's (Thomas G.) Artillery. See *Pennsylvania Troops, 1st Regiment, Battery E.*
Otey Artillery. See *Virginia Troops, Confederate.*
Otey's (Van R.) Infantry. See *Public Guard, Infantry, post.*
Otis' (George H.) Infantry. See *Wisconsin Troops, 2d Regiment.*
Over's (C. Miller) Infantry. See *Pennsylvania Troops, 10th Reserves.*
Owen's (Henry T.) Infantry. See *Virginia Troops, Confederate, 18th Regiment.*
Owen's (Thomas H.) Cavalry. See *Virginia Troops, Confederate, 3d Regiment.*
Owens' (William A.) Infantry. See *North Carolina Troops, Confederate, 53d Regiment.*
Packer's (Warren W.) Infantry. See *Connecticut Troops, 5th Regiment.*
Page's (Powhatan R.) Infantry. See *Virginia Troops, Confederate, 26th Regiment.*
Page's (Richard C. M.) Artillery. See *Morris Artillery, ante.*
Palmer's (Thomas H.) Heavy Artillery. See *Maine Troops, 1st Regiment.*
Palmetto Artillery. See *South Carolina Troops.*
Palmetto Sharpshooters. See *South Carolina Troops.*
Pamunkey Heavy Artillery. See *Virginia Troops, Confederate.*
Paoli's [?] Battalion. Official designation not of record. See —— *Paoli.*
Parham's (William A.) Infantry. See *Virginia Troops, Confederate, 41st Regiment.*
Paris' (Andrew B.) Artillery. See *Staunton Hill Artillery, post.*
Park Artillery. See *Pennsylvania Troops.*
Parker's (Francis M.) Infantry. See *North Carolina Troops, Confederate, 30th Regiment.*
Parker's (N.) Cavalry. See *Kentucky Troops, Confederate, 4th Regiment.*
Parker's (Sewell S.) Infantry. See *Michigan Troops, 26th Regiment.*
Parker's (William W.) Artillery. See *Virginia Troops, Confederate.*
Parnell's (William R.) Cavalry. See *New York Troops, 4th Regiment.*
Parsons' (Joseph B.) Infantry. See *Massachusetts Troops, 10th Regiment.*
Patapsco Guards, Infantry. See *Maryland Troops, Union.*
Pate's (Henry Clay) Cavalry. See *Virginia Troops, Confederate, 5th Regiment.*
Patrick's (John H.) Infantry. See *Ohio Troops, 5th Regiment.*
Patterson's (Edmund Y.) Infantry. See *Pennsylvania Troops, 88th Regiment.*
Patterson's (George M.) Artillery. See *Sumter Artillery, post, Battery B.*
Patterson's (John W.) Infantry. See *Pennsylvania Troops, 102d Regiment.*
Patton's (George S.) Infantry. See *Virginia Troops, Confederate, 22d Regiment.*
Patton's (William) Cavalry. See *Indiana Troops, 3d Regiment.*
Payne's (William H.) Cavalry. See *Virginia Troops, Confederate, 4th Regiment.*
Peale's (Henry) Infantry. See *Connecticut Troops, 18th Regiment.*

Pearson's (Alfred L.) Infantry. See *Pennsylvania Troops, 155th Regiment.*
Pease's (Walter B.) Infantry. See *Union Troops, Regulars, 17th Regiment.*
Peck's (William R.) Infantry. See *Louisiana Troops, 9th Regiment.*
Pee Dee Artillery. See *South Carolina Troops.*
Peeples' (Samuel) Artillery. See *Union Troops, Regulars, 5th Regiment, Battery D.*
Pegram's (Richard G.) Artillery. See *Virginia Troops, Confederate.*
Peirson's (Charles L.) Infantry. See *Massachusetts Troops, 39th Regiment.*
Pendleton's (Edmund) Infantry. See *Louisiana Troops, 15th Regiment.*
Penick's (Nathan) Artillery. See *John W. Lewis' Artillery, ante.*
Penn's (David B.) Infantry. See *Louisiana Troops, 7th Regiment.*
Pennington's (Alexander C. M., jr.) Artillery. See *Union Troops, Regulars, 2d Regiment, Battery M.*
Pennsylvania 1st Rifles, Infantry. See *Pennsylvania Troops, 13th Reserves.*
Penrose's (William H.) Infantry. See *New Jersey Troops, 15th Regiment.*
Perrin's (Abner) Infantry. See *South Carolina Troops, 14th Regiment.*
Perrin's (Walter S.) Artillery. See *Rhode Island Troops, 1st Regiment, Battery B.*
Perry's (Robert C.) Infantry. See *New York Troops, 111th Regiment.*
Perry's (William F.) Infantry. See *Alabama Troops, 44th Regiment.*
Peters' (W. E.) Cavalry. See *Virginia Troops, Confederate, 21st Regiment.*
Petersburg Artillery. See *Virginia Troops, Confederate.*
Pettes' (William H.) Engineers. See *New York Troops, 50th Regiment.*
Phillips' (Charles A.) Artillery. See *Massachusetts Troops, 5th (E) Battery.*
Phillips' (J. J.) Infantry. See *Virginia Troops, Confederate, 9th Regiment.*
Phillips Legion. See *Georgia Troops.*
Pickens' (Samuel B.) Infantry. See *Alabama Troops, 12th Regiment.*
Pierce's (Byron R.) Infantry. See *Michigan Troops, 3d Regiment.*
Pierce's (Francis E.) Infantry. See *New York Troops, 108th Regiment.*
Pierce's (George H.) Heavy Artillery. See *Rhode Island Troops, 5th Regiment, Battery C.*
Pierce's (Lewis B.) Cavalry. See *Pennsylvania Troops, 12th Regiment.*
Pinckard's (L.) Infantry. See *Alabama Troops, 14th Regiment.*
Pingree's (Samuel E.) Infantry. See *Vermont Troops, 3d Regiment.*
Piper's (Alexander) Heavy Artillery. See *New York Troops, 10th Regiment.*
Piper's (James W.) Artillery. See *Union Troops, Regulars, 5th Regiment, Battery E.*
Plater's (John E.) Artillery. See *Chesapeake Artillery, ante.*
Player's (S. T.) Infantry. See *Georgia Troops, 49th Regiment.*
Plympton's (Jonathan F.) Infantry. See *Massachusetts Troops, 19th Regiment.*
Plympton's (Peter W. L.) Infantry. See *Union Troops, Regulars, 7th Regiment.*
Porter's (John C.) Infantry. See *Pennsylvania Troops.*
Porter's (Peter A.) Heavy Artillery. See *New York Troops, 8th Regiment.*
Potter's (Henry L.) Infantry. See *New York Troops, 71st Regiment.*
Potts' (John R.) Artillery. See *Branch Artillery, ante.*
Powell's (Eugene) Infantry. See *Ohio Troops, 66th Regiment.*
Powell's (R. M.) Infantry. See *Texas Troops, 5th Regiment.*
Powers' (Charles J.) Infantry. See *New York Troops, 108th Regiment.*
Powhatan Artillery. See *Virginia Troops, Confederate.*
Pratt's (Franklin A.) Heavy Artillery. See *Connecticut Troops, 1st Regiment, Battery M.*
Preston's (Addison W.) Cavalry. See *Vermont Troops, 1st Regiment.*
Prey's (Gilbert G.) Infantry. See *New York Troops, 104th Regiment.*
Price's (Edward L.) Infantry. See *New York Troops, 145th Regiment.*
Prime's (Nathaniel) Infantry. See *Union Troops, Regulars, 17th Regiment.*
Prince William Cavalry. See *Virginia Troops, Confederate, 4th Regiment.*
Provost Battalion, Infantry. See *Pennsylvania Troops, 1st Battalion.*
Pruyn's (Augustus) Cavalry. See *New York Troops, 4th Regiment.*

Pryor's (W. H.) Infantry. See *Virginia Troops, Confederate, 3d Regiment.*
Public Guard, Infantry. See *Virginia Troops, Confederate.*
Pulaski Artillery. See *Georgia Troops.*
Pulaski Home Guards. See *Virginia Troops, Confederate.*
Pulford's (John) Infantry. See *Michigan Troops, 5th Regiment.*
Purcell Artillery. See *Virginia Troops, Confederate.*
Purdy's (Stephen P.) Cavalry. See *Michigan Troops, 5th Regiment.*
Purnell Legion, Cavalry. See *Maryland Troops, Union.*
Purnell Legion, Infantry. See *Maryland Troops, Union.*
Pye's (Edward) Infantry. See *New York Troops, 95th Regiment.*
Pyles' (L. G.) Infantry. See *Florida Troops, 2d Regiment.*
Quinn's (Timothy) Cavalry. See *New York Troops, 1st Regiment.*
Quirk's (James) Infantry. See *Illinois Troops, 23d Regiment.*
Radcliffe's (James D.) Infantry. See *North Carolina Troops, Confederate, 61st Regiment.*
Rafferty's (Thomas) Infantry. See *New York Troops, 71st Regiment.*
Raine's (Charles I.) Artillery. See *Lee Artillery, ante.*
Ramsay's (John A.) Artillery. See *Rowan Artillery, ante.*
Ramsey's (John) Infantry. See *New Jersey Troops, 8th Regiment.*
Ramsey's (Joseph F.) Infantry. See *Pennsylvania Troops, 1st Battalion.*
Randol's (Alanson M.) Artillery. See *Union Troops, Regulars, 1st Regiment, Batteries E, G, and I.*
Rank's (William D.) Heavy Artillery. See *Pennsylvania Troops, 3d Regiment, Battery H.*
Rankin's (Robert G.) Heavy Artillery. See *North Carolina Troops, Confederate, 1st Battalion, Battery A.*
Rankin's (W. S.) Infantry. See *North Carolina Troops, Confederate, 21st Regiment.*
Ransom's (Alfred) Artillery. See *New York Troops, 23d Battery.*
Ransom's (Dunbar R.) Artillery. See *Union Troops, Regulars, 3d Regiment, Battery C.*
Read's (Edwin W. H.) Infantry. See *Union Troops, Regulars, 8th Regiment.*
Reese's (William J.) Artillery. See *Jeff. Davis Artillery, ante.*
Regan's (Peter C.) Artillery. See *New York Troops, 7th Battery.*
Reichard's (Francis H.) Heavy Artillery. See *Pennsylvania Troops, 3d Regiment, Battery M.*
Reid's (Thomas M.) Infantry. See *New York Troops, 182d Regiment.*
Reilly's (James) Artillery. See *Rowan Artillery, post.*
Reily's (Terrence) Artillery. See *Union Troops, Regulars, 4th Regiment, Battery E.*
Revere's (William H., jr.) Infantry. See *Maryland Troops, Union, 10th Regiment.*
Reynolds' (Gilbert H.) Artillery. See *New York Troops, 1st Regiment, Batteries E and L.*
Reynolds' (John W.) Infantry. See *Pennsylvania Troops, 145th Regiment.*
Reynolds' (Robert W.) Infantry. See *Maryland Troops, Union, 1st Regiment.*
Rhett Artillery. See *Tennessee Troops.*
Rice's (Edmund) Infantry. See *Massachusetts Troops, 19th Regiment.*
Rice's (R. Sidney) Artillery. See *Danville Artillery, ante.*
Rice's (W. G.) Infantry. See *South Carolina Troops, 3d Battalion.*
Rich's (W. W.) Cavalry. See *Phillips Legion, ante.*
Richardson's (James M.) Heavy Artillery. See *Massachusetts Troops, 12th Unattached Company.*
Richardson's (J. B.) Artillery. See *Washington (La.) Artillery, post, 2d Battery.*
Richardson's (J. H.) Cavalry. See *Virginia Troops, Confederate, 39th Battalion.*
Richardson's (John) Infantry. See *Virginia Troops, Confederate, 56th Regiment.*
Richmond Fayette Artillery. See *Virginia Troops, Confederate.*
Richmond Howitzers, Artillery. See *Virginia Troops, Confederate.*

Richmond's (Nathaniel P.) **Cavalry.** See *West Virginia Troops, 1st Regiment.*

Rickards' (William, jr.) **Infantry.** See *Pennsylvania Troops, 29th Regiment.*

Ricketts' (R. Bruce) **Artillery.** See *Pennsylvania Troops, 1st Regiment, Batteries F and G.*

Rider's (Henry W.) **Infantry.** See *New York Troops, 12th Regiment.*

Rigby's (James H.) **Artillery.** See *Maryland Troops, Union, Battery A.*

Riggs' (William J.) **Artillery.** See *New York Troops, 3d Regiment, Battery H.*

Ringgold Artillery. See *Virginia Troops, Confederate.*

Ringgold Cavalry. See *Pennsylvania Troops.*

Ringgold Militia, Artillery. See *George R. Guss' Artillery, ante.*

Ringland's (George S.) **Cavalry.** See *Pennsylvania Troops, 11th Regiment.*

Ripley's (Edward H.) **Infantry.** See *Vermont Troops, 9th Regiment.*

Rittenhouse's (Benjamin F.) **Artillery.** See *Union Troops, Regulars, 5th Regiment, Battery D.*

Rives' (J. Henry) **Artillery.** See *Nelson Artillery, No. 2, ante.*

Roane's (Timothy F.) **Cavalry.** See *West Virginia Troops, 3d Regiment.*

Roath's (Emanuel D.) **Infantry.** See *Pennsylvania Troops, 107th Regiment.*

Roberts' (Joseph) **Heavy Artillery.** See *Pennsylvania Troops, 3d Regiment.*

Roberts' (Samuel) **Infantry.** See *Pennsylvania Troops, 72d Regiment.*

Roberts' (Samuel H.) **Infantry.** See *New York Troops, 139th Regiment.*

Roberts' (W. Dewees) **Cavalry.** See *Pennsylvania Troops, 11th Regiment.*

Robertson's (James E.) **Heavy Artillery.** See *Virginia Troops, Confederate, 20th Battalion.*

Robertson's (John C.) **Heavy Artillery.** See *North Carolina Troops, Confederate, 3d Regiment, Battery F.*

Robertson's (John R.) **Cavalry.** See *Virginia Troops, Confederate, 32d and 42d Battalions.*

Robins' (W. T.) **Cavalry.** See *Virginia Troops, Confederate, 40th and 42d Battalions.*

Robinson's (Oliver O. G.) **Cavalry.** See *Pennsylvania Troops, 3d Regiment.*

Robinson's (O'Neil W., jr.) **Artillery.** See *Maine Troops, 4th Battery.*

Robinson's (Robert A.) **Cavalry.** See *Pennsylvania Troops, 16th Regiment; also Pennsylvania Troops, 4th Regiment.**

Robinson's (W. G.) **Cavalry.** See *North Carolina Troops, Confederate, 2d Regiment.*

Robinson's (William J.) **Infantry.** See *Maryland Troops, Union, 1st Regiment, E. S.*

Robison's (John K.) **Cavalry.** See *Pennsylvania Troops, 16th Regiment.*

Rockbridge Artillery. See *Virginia Troops, Confederate.*

Rockbridge Artillery, No. 2. See *Virginia Troops, Confederate.*

Rockwood's (Theodore H.) **Infantry.** See *Union Troops (Colored), 19th Regiment.*

Rodamour's (Columbus) **Artillery.** See *Ohio Troops, 1st Regiment, Battery K.*

Roder's (John W.) **Artillery.** See *Union Troops, Regulars, 4th Regiment, Battery K.*

Rodgers' (Robert S.) **Infantry.** See *Maryland Troops, Union, 2d Regiment, E. S.*

Rogers' (Edward W.) **Artillery.** See *New York Troops, 19th Battery.*

Rogers' (George T.) **Infantry.** See *Virginia Troops, Confederate, 6th Regiment.*

Rogers' (Horatio, jr.) **Infantry.** See *Rhode Island Troops, 2d Regiment.*

Rogers' (Isaac) **Infantry.** See *Pennsylvania Troops, 110th Regiment.*

Rogers' (Robert E.) **Artillery.** See *New York Troops, 1st Regiment, Battery B.*

Rolfe's (Frank A.) **Heavy Artillery.** See *Massachusetts Troops, 1st Regiment.*

Ronald's (Charles A.) **Infantry.** See *Virginia Troops, Confederate, 4th Regiment.*

Rosney's (Andrew) **Artillery.** See *Pennsylvania Troops, 1st Regiment, Battery D.*

Ross' (George W.) **Infantry.** See *Georgia Troops, 2d Battalion.*

Ross' (Hugh M.) **Artillery.** See *Sumter Artillery, post, Battery A.*

Rosser's (Thomas L.) **Cavalry.** See *Virginia Troops, Confederate, 5th Regiment.*

Rourke's (John) **Artillery.** See *Illinois Troops, 1st Regiment, Battery L.*

Rowan Artillery. See *North Carolina Troops, Confederate.*

---

* Temporarily commanding.

Royer's (Henry) Infantry. See *Pennsylvania Troops, 53d Regiment Militia.*
Royston's (Y. L.) Infantry. See *Alabama Troops, 8th Regiment.*
Ruff's (S. Z.) Infantry. See *Georgia Troops, 18th Regiment.*
Rugg's (Horace P.) Infantry. See *New York Troops, 59th Regiment.*
Ruhl's (Noah G.) Infantry. See *Pennsylvania Troops, 87th Regiment.*
Rumford's (Charles G.) Artillery. See *Delaware Troops, 1st Battery.*
Rush's (George W.) Infantry. See *Georgia Troops, 22d Regiment.*
Rutledge's (Henry M.) Infantry. See *North Carolina Troops, Confederate, 25th Regiment.*
Ryan's (George) Infantry. See *New York Troops, 140th Regiment.*
Ryder's (Patrick) Infantry. See *New York Troops, 88th Regiment.*
Rylander's (J. E.) Infantry. See *Georgia Troops, 10th Battalion.*
Sackett's (William) Cavalry. See *New York Troops, 9th Regiment.*
Sackett's (William H.) Infantry. See *Connecticut Troops, 11th Regiment.*
Salem Artillery. See *Virginia Troops, Confederate.*
Sampson's (Ira B.) Heavy Artillery. See *Massachusetts Troops, 2d Regiment.*
Sanders' (Horace T.) Infantry. See *Wisconsin Troops, 19th Regiment.*
Sanders' (J. C. C.) Infantry. See *Alabama Troops, 11th Regiment.*
Sanderson's (Joseph W.) Heavy Artillery. See *Pennsylvania Troops, 3d Regiment, Battery G.*
Sargent's (Horace B.) Cavalry. See *Massachusetts Troops, 1st Regiment.*
Savage's (James W.) Cavalry. See *New York Troops, 12th Regiment.*
Sawyer's (Edward B.) Cavalry. See *Vermont Troops, 1st Regiment.*
Sawyer's (Franklin) Infantry. See *Ohio Troops, 8th Regiment.*
Sayles' (James A.) Artillery. See *Union Troops, Regulars, 2d Regiment, Battery D.*
Schamberger's (Leander) Heavy Artillery. See *New York Troops, 15th Regiment.*
Scherff's (Martin) Infantry. See *Wisconsin Troops, 19th Regiment.*
Scherrer's (William) Infantry. See *New York Troops, 52d Regiment.*
Schirmer's (Louis) Heavy Artillery. See *New York Troops, 15th Regiment.*
Schoonmaker's (James N.) Cavalry. See *Pennsylvania Troops, 14th Regiment.*
Schoonover's (John) Infantry. See *New Jersey Troops, 11th Regiment.*
Schubert's (Emil) Artillery. See *New York Troops, 9th Battery.*
Schuetz's (John C.) Artillery. See *Michigan Troops, 10th Battery.*
Schulz's (Carl) Artillery. See *Wisconsin Troops, 2d Battery.*
Scott's (Alexander) Infantry. See *West Virginia Troops, 2d Regiment.*
Scott's Nine Hundred, Cavalry. See *New York Troops, 11th Regiment.*
Seaver's (Thomas O.) Infantry. See *Vermont Troops, 3d Regiment.*
Seeley's (Francis W.) Artillery. See *Union Troops, Regulars, 4th Regiment, Battery K.*
Selfridge's (James L.) Infantry. See *Pennsylvania Troops, 46th Regiment.*
Sell's (Benjamin F.) Infantry. See *Ohio Troops, 122d Regiment.*
Sexton's (George A.) Cavalry. See *West Virginia Troops, 3d Regiment.*
Sharra's (Abram) Cavalry. See *Indiana Troops, 1st Regiment.*
Shaw's (H. M.) Infantry. See *North Carolina Troops, Confederate, 8th Regiment.*
Shaw's (James, jr.) Infantry. See *Union Troops (Colored), 7th Regiment.*
Shaw's (John W.) Infantry. See *Ohio Troops, 34th Regiment.*
Sheafer's (Henry J.) Infantry. See *Pennsylvania Troops, 107th Regiment.*
Shears' (George W.) Cavalry. See *Illinois Troops, 12th Regiment.*
Sheffield's (James L.) Infantry. See *Alabama Troops, 48th Regiment.*
Sheldon's (Albert S.) Artillery. See *New York Troops, 1st Regiment, Battery B.*
Shepherd's (Oliver L.) Infantry. See *Union Troops, Regulars, 15th Regiment.*
Sheridan's (Andrew) Infantry. See *Union Troops, Regulars, 3d Regiment.*
Sherwin's (Thomas, jr.) Infantry. See *Massachusetts Troops, 22d Regiment.*
Shingler's (William P.) Cavalry. See *Holcombe Legion, ante.*
Shivers' (W. R.) Infantry. See *Louisiana Troops, 1st Regiment.*
Showalter's (John H.) Infantry. See *West Virginia Troops, 6th Regiment.*

Sides' (Peter) Infantry. See *Pennsylvania Troops, 57th Regiment.*
Simmonds' (Seth J.) Artillery. See *Kentucky Troops, Union.*
Simmons' (Thomas J.) Infantry. See *Georgia Troops, 45th Regiment.*
Simms' (James P.) Infantry. See *Georgia Troops, 53d Regiment.*
Simpson's (Benjamin L.) Infantry. See *Maryland Troops, Union, 9th Regiment.*
Simpson's (John G.) Artillery. See *Pennsylvania Troops, 1st Regiment, Battery A.*
Simpson's (Thomas) Artillery. See *Rhode Island Troops, 1st Regiment, Battery F.*
Sinex's (Joseph H.) Infantry. See *Pennsylvania Troops, 91st Regiment.*
Singeltary's (Thomas C.) Infantry. See *North Carolina Troops, Confederate, 44th Regiment.*
Sisson's (Henry T.) Heavy Artillery. See *Rhode Island Troops, 5th Regiment.*
Skinner's (Frederick G.) Infantry. See *Virginia Troops, Confederate, 1st Regiment.*
Skinner's (James H.) Infantry. See *Virginia Troops, Confederate, 52d Regiment.*
Slaten's (C. W.) Artillery. See *Macon Artillery, ante.*
Slaughter's (P. P.) Infantry. See *Virginia Troops, Confederate, 56th Regiment.*
Sleeper's (J. Henry) Artillery. See *Massachusetts Troops, 10th Battery.*
Slemp's (Campbell) Infantry. See *Virginia Troops, Confederate, 64th Regiment.*
Smith's (Benjamin H., jr.) Artillery. See *Richmond Howitzers, ante, 3d Company.*
Smith's (Charles F.) Infantry. See *New York Troops, 178th Regiment.*
Smith's (Charles H.) Cavalry. See *Maine Troops, 1st Regiment.*
Smith's (C. T.) Cavalry. See *Virginia Troops, Confederate, 36th Battalion.*
Smith's (Frank) Cavalry. See *Ohio Troops, 3d Company.*
Smith's (Frederick F.) Cavalry. See *Virginia Troops, Confederate, 17th Regiment.*
Smith's (George F.) Infantry. See *Pennsylvania Troops, 61st Regiment.*
Smith's (George H.) Infantry. See *Virginia Troops, Confederate, 62d Regiment.*
Smith's (George W. P.) Cavalry. See *Maryland Troops, Union.*
Smith's (Howard M.) Cavalry. See *New York Troops, 19th Regiment.*
Smith's (Jacob) Infantry. See *West Virginia Troops, 14th Regiment.*
Smith's (James E.) Artillery. See *New York Troops, 4th Battery.*
Smith's (James M.) Infantry. See *Georgia Troops, 13th Regiment.*
Smith's (Lewis) Artillery. See *Union Troops, Regulars, 3d Regiment, Battery G.*
Smith's (R. Penn) Infantry. See *Pennsylvania Troops, 71st Regiment.*
Smith's (T.) Infantry. See *Virginia Troops, Confederate, 36th Regiment.*
Smoot's (David L.) Artillery. See *Alexandria Artillery, ante.*
Smyth County Home Guards. See *Virginia Troops, Confederate.*
Smyth's (Thomas A.) Infantry. See *Delaware Troops, 1st Regiment.*
Snider's (Joseph) Cavalry. See *West Virginia Troops, 4th Regiment.*
Snider's (Samuel W.) Cavalry. See *West Virginia Troops, 4th Regiment.*
Snodgrass' (James McK.) Infantry. See *Pennsylvania Troops, 9th Reserves.*
Snow's (Alonzo) Artillery. See *Maryland Troops, Union, Battery B.*
Southerland's (Thomas J.) Artillery. See *North Carolina Troops, Confederate, 1st Regiment, Battery I.*
Southside Artillery. See *Virginia Troops, Confederate.*
Spaulding's (Edwin A.) Infantry. See *Pennsylvania Troops, 141st Regiment.*
Spear's (Ellis) Infantry. See *Maine Troops, 20th Regiment.*
Spear's (Samuel P.) Cavalry. See *Pennsylvania Troops, 11th Regiment.*
Spooner's (Edmund D.) Artillery. See *Union Troops, Regulars, 5th Regiment, Batteries I and L.*
Squires' (C. W.) Artillery. See *Washington (La.) Artillery, post, 1st Battery.*
Stafford Artillery. See *Virginia Troops, Confederate.*
Stafford's (Leroy A.) Infantry. See *Louisiana Troops, 9th Regiment.*
Stable's (James A.) Infantry. See *Pennsylvania Troops, 87th Regiment.*
Stamps' (Timothy H.) Artillery. See *Ringgold Artillery, ante.*
Stanford's (Samuel N.) Cavalry. See *Ohio Troops, 1st Regiment.*
Starr's (James) Cavalry. See *Pennsylvania Troops, 6th Regiment.*

Starr's (Joseph B.) Artillery. See *North Carolina Troops, Confederate*, 13th Battalion, Battery B.

Starr's (William C.) Infantry. See *West Virginia Troops*, 9th Regiment.

State Line. See *Virginia Troops, Confederate*.

Statham's (Charles W.) Artillery. See *Lee Artillery, ante*.

Staunton Artillery. See *Virginia Troops, Confederate*.

Staunton Hill Artillery. See *Virginia Troops, Confederate*.

Staunton's (John F.) Infantry. See *Pennsylvania Troops*, 67th Regiment.

Stedman's (William) Cavalry. See *Ohio Troops*, 6th Regiment.

Steele's (Henry V.) Infantry. See *Michigan Troops*, 26th Regiment.

Steele's (Joseph) Cavalry. See *Pennsylvania Troops*, 2d Regiment.

Steele's (Peter B.) Infantry. See *New York Troops*, 158th Regiment.

Steeple's (John S.) Infantry. See *Pennsylvania Troops*, 88th Regiment.

Stephenson's (Luther, jr.) Infantry. See *Massachusetts Troops*, 32d Regiment.

Sterling's (John W.) Artillery. See *Connecticut Troops*, 2d Battery.

Stetzel's (George) Cavalry. See *Pennsylvania Troops*, 11th Regiment.

Stevens' (Aaron F.) Infantry. See *New Hampshire Troops*, 13th Regiment.

Stevens' (Greenleaf T.) Artillery. See *Maine Troops*, 5th Battery.

Steward's (Ira W.) Artillery. See *New York Troops*, 28th Battery.

Stewart's (Charles H.) Artillery. See *New York Troops*, 3d Regiment.

Stewart's (Gordon A.) Infantry. See *Ohio Troops*, 4th Regiment.

Stewart's (James) Artillery. See *Union Troops, Regulars*, 4th Regiment, Battery B.

Stickney's (James W. H.) Infantry. See *Union Troops, Veteran Reserve Corps*, 2d Battalion.

Stiles' (W. H.) Infantry. See *Georgia Troops*, 60th Regiment.

Stone's (J. M.) Infantry. See *Mississippi Troops*, 2d Regiment.

Stoughton's (Homer R.) Sharpshooters. See *Union Troops, Volunteers*, 2d Regiment.

Stowe's (William A.) Infantry. See *North Carolina Troops, Confederate*, 16th Regiment.

Strang's (John R.) Infantry. See *New York Troops*, 104th Regiment.

Stribling's (Robert M.) Artillery. See *Fauquier Artillery, ante*.

Stricker's (David L.) Infantry. See *Delaware Troops*, 2d Regiment.

Strickler's (Michael B.) Cavalry. See *Pennsylvania Troops*, 20th Regiment.

Stringfield's (W. W.) Infantry. See *W. H. Thomas' Legion, post*.

Strong's (Rollin M.) Infantry. See *Wisconsin Troops*, 19th Regiment.

Sturdivant's (N. A.) Artillery. See *Virginia Troops, Confederate*.

Sturgeon's (James M.) Cavalry. See *New York Troops*, 12th Regiment.

Sudsburg's (Joseph M.) Infantry. See *Maryland Troops, Union*, 3d Regiment.

Summers' (George D.) Infantry. See *Maryland Troops, Union*, 2d Regiment, P. H. B.

Sumter Artillery. See *Georgia Troops*.

Surry Artillery. See *Virginia Troops, Confederate*.

Swain's (James B.) Cavalry. See *New York Troops*, 11th Regiment.

Sweeney's (James W.) Cavalry. See *Virginia Troops, Confederate*, 36th Battalion.

Sweitzer's (Napoleon B.) Cavalry. See *Union Troops, Regulars*, 1st Regiment.

Tabb's (William B.) Infantry. See *Virginia Troops, Confederate*, 59th Regiment.

Taft's (Edward P.) Heavy Artillery. See *New York Troops*, 9th Regiment.

Taft's (Elijah D.) Artillery. See *New York Troops*, 5th Battery.

Talcott's (T. M. R.) Engineers. See *Confederate Troops, Regulars*, 1st Regiment.

Taliaferro's (A. G.) Infantry. See *Virginia Troops, Confederate*, 23d Regiment.

Taliaferro's (V. H.) Cavalry. See *Confederate Troops, Regulars*, 7th Regiment.

Talley's (Jonathan) Artillery. See *Goochland Artillery, ante*.

Talley's (William C.) Infantry. See *Pennsylvania Troops*, 1st Reserves.

Tannatt's (Thomas R.) Heavy Artillery. See *Massachusetts Troops*, 1st Regiment.

Tanner's (William A.) Artillery. See *Courtney Artillery, ante*.

Tappen's (John R.) Infantry. See *New York Troops*, 120th Regiment.

Tapper's (Thomas F. B.) Infantry. See *Pennsylvania Troops, 4th Reserves.*
Tay's (Charles H.) Infantry. See *New Jersey Troops, 10th Regiment.*
Tayloe's (E. P.) Infantry. See *Virginia Troops, Confederate, 22d Battalion.*
Taylor's (Alexander W.) Infantry. See *Pennsylvania Troops, 101st Regiment.*
Taylor's (John P.) Cavalry. ·See *Pennsylvania Troops, 1st Regiment.*
Taylor's (Osmond B.) Artillery. See *Virginia Troops, Confederate.*
Taylor's (W. H.) Infantry. See *Mississippi Troops, 12th Regiment.*
Taylor's (William C. L.) Infantry. See *Indiana Troops, 20th Regiment.*
Tennessee (Confederate) First Cavalry. See *James E. Carter's Cavalry, ante.*
Terrill's (James B.) Infantry. See *Virginia Troops, Confederate, 13th Regiment.*
Terry's (William R.) Infantry. See *Virginia Troops, Confederate, 24th Regiment.*
Tevis' (C. Carroll) Cavalry. See *Maryland Troops, Union, 3d Regiment.*
Theis' (John G.) Artillery. See *West Virginia Troops, Battery C.*
Thoburn's (Joseph) Infantry. See *West Virginia Troops, 1st Regiment.*
Thomas' (Albert F.) Artillery. See *Maine Troops, 2d Battery.*
Thomas' (W. H.) Legion. See *North Carolina Troops, Confederate.*
Thomas' (Winslow M.) Infantry.* See *New York Troops, 149th Regiment.*
Thompson's (Francis W.) Infantry. See *West Virginia Troops, 3d Regiment.*
Thompson's (George W.) Infantry. See *New York Troops, 152d Regiment.*
Thompson's (Henry E.) Cavalry. See *Michigan Troops, 6th Regiment.*
Thompson's (James) Artillery. See *Pennsylvania Troops, Batteries C and F.*
Thompson's (J. B.) Cavalry. See *Virginia Troops, Confederate, 27th Battalion.*
Thompson's (John L.) Cavalry. See *Rhode Island Troops, 1st Regiment.*
Thompson's (William P.) Cavalry. See *Virginia Troops, Confederate, 19th Regiment.*
Thomson's (David) Infantry. See *Ohio Troops, 82d Regiment.*
Thomson's (Thomas) Infantry. See *South Carolina Troops, 2d Regiment, Rifles.*
Thornton's (Thomas R.) Artillery. See *Caroline Artillery, ante.*
Throop's (William A.) Infantry. See *Michigan Troops, 1st Regiment.*
Thruston's (Stephen D.) Infantry. · See *North Carolina Troops, Confederate, 3d Regiment.*
Thurmond's (P. J.) Cavalry. See *Virginia Troops, Confederate.*
Thurmond's (William D.) Cavalry. See *Virginia Troops, Confederate.*
Tice's (Leonard D.) Infantry. See *Vermont Troops, 5th Regiment.*
Tidball's (John C.) Heavy Artillery. See *New York Troops, 4th Regiment.*
Tillery's (Richard C.) Heavy Artillery. See *North Carolina Troops, Confederate, 3d Regiment, Battery F.*
Tinen's (Patrick S.) Infantry. See *Pennsylvania Troops, 69th Regiment.*
Tippin's (Andrew H.) Infantry. See *Pennsylvania Troops, 68th Regiment.*
Tolles' (Samuel) Infantry. See *Connecticut Troops, 15th Regiment.*
Tomlinson's (Abia A.) Infantry. See *West Virginia Troops, 5th Regiment.*
Toon's (Thomas F.) Infantry. See *North Carolina Troops, Confederate, 20th Regiment.*
Touhy's (Thomas) Infantry. See *New York Troops, 63d Regiment.*
Towers' (John R.) Infantry. See *Georgia Troops, 8th Regiment.*
Towers' (Lemuel) Infantry. See *District of Columbia Troops, 1st Regiment.*
Town's (Charles H.) Cavalry. See *Michigan Troops, 1st Regiment.*
Townsend's (Charles) Infantry. See *New York Troops, 106th Regiment.*
Townsend's (Solomon) Cavalry. See *Delaware Troops, 1st Regiment.*
Tracy's (Benjamin F.) Infantry. See *New York Troops, 109th Regiment.*
Trimble's (E.) Cavalry. See *A. J. May's Rifles, ante.*
Tripp's (Porter D.) Infantry. See *Massachusetts Troops, 11th Regiment.*
Troup Artillery. See *Georgia Troops.*
Truefitt's (Henry P., jr.) Infantry. See *Pennsylvania Troops, 119th Regiment.*
Truex's (William S.) Infantry. See *New Jersey Troops, 14th Regiment.*
Tully's (Redmond) Artillery. See *Union Troops, Regulars, 1st Regiment, Battery C.*

---

* Temporarily commanding.

Turley's (John A.) Infantry. See *Ohio Troops, 91st Regiment.*
Turnbull's (Charles N.) Engineers. See *G. H. Mendell's Engineers, ante.*
Turnbull's (John G.) Artillery. See *Union Troops, Regulars, 3d Regiment, Batteries F and K.*
Turney's (Peter) Infantry. See *Tennessee Troops, 1st Regiment, P. A.*
Tyler's (Horatio K.) Artillery. See *Park Artillery, ante.*
Underwood's (Adin B.) Infantry. See *Massachusetts Troops, 33d Regiment.*
United Artillery. See *Virginia Troops, Confederate.*
Upham's (Charles L.) Infantry. See *Connecticut Troops, 15th Regiment.*
Urban's (Casper) Heavy Artillery. See *New York Troops, 5th Regiment.*
Utterback's (Addison W.) Artillery. See *James V. Brooke's Artillery, ante.*
Van de Graaff's (A. S.) Infantry. See *Alabama Troops, 5th Battalion.*
Vandeventer's (Alexander S.) Infantry. See *Virginia Troops, Confederate, 50th Regiment.*
Van Gilder's (Jefferson G.) Cavalry. See *Lafayette Cavalry, ante.*
Van Hook's (J. C.) Infantry. See *North Carolina Troops, Confederate, 50th Regiment.*
Van Ness' (Henry L.) Infantry. See *New York Troops, 67th Regiment.*
Van Voorhis' (Koert S.) Infantry. See *New York Troops, 137th Regiment.*
Vinton's (Harvey H.) Cavalry. See *Michigan Troops, 6th Regiment.*
Voorhes' (George W.) Infantry. See *Ohio Troops, 126th Regiment.*
Vought's (Philip G.) Cavalry. See *New York Troops, 12th Regiment.*
Vredenburgh's (Peter, jr.) Infantry. See *New Jersey Troops, 14th Regiment.*
Waddell's (J. D.) Infantry. See *Georgia Troops, 20th Regiment.*
Waggaman's (Eugene) Infantry. See *Louisiana Troops, 10th Regiment.*
Walbridge's (James H.) Infantry. See *Vermont Troops, 2d Regiment.*
Walcott's (Aaron F.) Artillery. See *Massachusetts Troops, 3d (C) Battery.*
Wales' (John P.) Infantry. See *Union Troops, Regulars, 17th Regiment.*
Walker's (David N.) Artillery. See *Otey Artillery, ante.*
Walker's (Edward J.) Infantry. See *Georgia Troops, 3d Regiment.*
Walker's (Joseph) Infantry. See *Palmetto Sharpshooters, ante.*
Walker's (W. C.) Infantry. See *W. H. Thomas' Legion, ante.*
Walker's (William A.) Infantry. See *Massachusetts Troops, 27th Regiment.*
Walker's (Wilson W.) Infantry. See *Maryland Troops, Union, 2d Regiment, E. S.; also Delaware Troops, 3d Regiment.**
Walkup's (Samuel H.) Infantry. See *North Carolina Troops, Confederate, 48th Regiment.*
Wallace's (George W.) Infantry. See *Union Troops, Regulars, 6th Regiment.*
Wallace's (James) Infantry. See *Maryland Troops, Union, 1st Regiment, E. S.*
Walsh's (James W.) Cavalry. See *Pennsylvania Troops, 3d Regiment.*
Walsh's (Michael) Infantry. See *Union Troops, Veteran Reserve Corps, 1st Battalion, 49th Company.*
Ward's (George) Artillery. See *Madison Light Artillery, ante.*
Ward's (John E.) Infantry. See *Connecticut Troops, 8th Regiment.*
Wardrop's (David W.) Infantry. See *New York Troops, 99th Regiment.*
Waring's (J. F.) Cavalry. See *Jeff. Davis Legion, ante.*
Warner's (James M.) Heavy Artillery. See *Vermont Troops, 1st Regiment.*
Warner's (Lewis D.) Infantry. See *New York Troops, 154th Regiment.*
Warren's (E. T. H.) Infantry. See *Virginia Troops, Confederate, 10th Regiment.*
Warren's (Zenas C.) Artillery. See *New Jersey Troops, 5th Battery.*
Wasden's (Joseph) Infantry. See *Georgia Troops, 22d Regiment.*
Washburn's (James) Infantry. See *Ohio Troops, 116th Regiment.*
Washburne's (A. Livingston) Cavalry. See *New York Troops, 16th Regiment.*
Washington Artillery. See *Louisiana Troops.*
Washington Artillery. See *South Carolina Troops.*

---

* Temporarily commanding.

Washington Cavalry. See *Pennsylvania Troops.*
Washington's (James A.) Infantry. See *North Carolina Troops, Confederate,* 50th *Regiment.*
Waterman's (Richard) Artillery. See *Rhode Island Troops,* 1st *Regiment, Battery C.*
Watkins' (Thomas H.) Cavalry. See *Purnell Legion, Cavalry, ante.*
Watson's (David) Artillery. See *Richmond Howitzers, ante,* 2d *Company.*
Watts' (William) Infantry. See *Virginia Troops, Confederate,* 28th *Regiment.*
Wead's (Frederick F.) Infantry. See *New York Troops,* 98th *Regiment.*
Weaver's (Hanson E.) Infantry. See *Union Troops, Regulars,* 8th *Regiment.*
Webb's (Lewis H.) Artillery. See *North Carolina Troops, Confederate.*
Webb's (Robert F.) Infantry. See *North Carolina Troops, Confederate,* 6th *Regiment.*
Webster's (Edwin H.) Infantry. See *Maryland Troops, Union,* 7th *Regiment.*
Weddle's (Jacob) Infantry. See *West Virginia Troops,* 1st *Regiment.*
Weems' (John B.) Infantry. See *Georgia Troops,* 10th *Regiment.*
Weir's (Gulian V.) Artillery. See *Union Troops, Regulars,* 5th *Regiment,·Battery C.*
Weisiger's (D. A.) Infantry. See *Virginia Troops, Confederate,* 12th *Regiment.*
Welch's (Norval E.) Infantry. See *Michigan Troops,* 16th *Regiment.*
Welling's (Joseph) Heavy Artillery. See *New York Troops,* 9th *Regiment.*
West's (George W.) Infantry. See *Maine Troops,* 17th *Regiment.*
West's (Perry G.) Infantry. See *Exempts' Battalion, ante.*
West's (Robert M.) Artillery. See *Pennsylvania Troops,* 1st *Regiment.*
West's (Rowland R.) Cavalry. See *New York Troops,* 12th *Regiment.*
Weston's (Thomas) Infantry. See *Massachusetts Troops,* 18th *Regiment.*
Wetherill's (John M.) Infantry. See *Pennsylvania Troops,* 82d *Regiment.*
Wetmore's (Oliver, jr.) Heavy Artillery. See *New York Troops,* 13th *Regiment.*
Wharton's (R. W.) Infantry. See *North Carolina Troops, Confederate,* 1st *Battalion.*
Wheeler's (Samuel J.) Cavalry. See *North Carolina Troops, Confederate,* 12th *Battalion.*
Wheeler's (William) Artillery. See *New York Troops,* 13th *Battery.*
Wheelock's (Charles) Infantry. See *New York Troops,* 97th *Regiment.*
Whistler's (Joseph N. G.) Heavy Artillery. See *New York Troops,* 2d *Regiment.*
White's (Amos H.) Cavalry. See *New York Troops,* 5th *Regiment.*
White's (Elijah V.) Cavalry. See *Virginia Troops, Confederate,* 35th *Battalion.*
White's (Robert)·Cavalry. See *Virginia Troops, Confederate,* 41st *Battalion.*
White's (William) Infantry. See *Virginia Troops, Confederate,* 14th *Regiment.*
White's (W. W.) Infantry. See *Georgia Troops,* 7th *Regiment.*
Whitford's (John N.) Infantry. See *North Carolina Troops. Confederate.*
Whiton's (Lyman B.) Heavy Artillery. See *Massachusetts Troops,* 3d *Unattached Company.*
Wickersham's (James P.) Infantry. See *Pennsylvania Troops,* 47th *Regiment Militia.*
Wickham's (Williams C.) Cavalry. See *Virginia Troops, Confederate,* 4th *Regiment.*
Wicks' (Charles H.) Infantry. See *Maryland Troops, Union,* 2d *Regiment, E. S.*
Wiebecke's (Charles) Infantry. See *New Jersey Troops,* 2d *Regiment.*
Wiecker's (Arthur) Artillery. See *New York Troops,* 20th *Battery.*
Wiedrich's (Michael) Artillery· See *New York Troops,* 1st *Regiment, Battery I.*
Willauer's (Seneca G.) Infantry. See *Pennsylvania Troops,* 116th *Regiment.*
Willets' (J. Howard) Infantry. See *New Jersey Troops,* 12th *Regiment.*
Williams' (J. H.) Infantry. See *South Carolina Troops,* 5th *Regiment, State.*
Williams' (J. M.) Infantry. See *Louisiana Troops,* 2d *Regiment.*
Williams' (Samuel J.) Infantry. See *Indiana Troops,* 19th *Regiment.*
Williams' (T. V.) Infantry. See *Virginia Troops, Confederate,* 37th *Regiment.*
Williamson's (Henry V.) Infantry. See *New York Troops,* 83d *Regiment.*
Willis' (Edward) Infantry. See *Georgia Troops,* 12th *Regiment.*
Williston's (Edward B.) Artillery. See *Union Troops.·Regulars,* 2d *Regiment, Battery D.*
Wilson's (James E.) Artillery. See *Union Troops, Regulars,* 2d *Regiment, Battery I.*

Wilson's (John) Infantry. See *New York Troops, 43d Regiment*.

Wilson's (John D.) Artillery   See *Union Troops, Regulars, 1st Regiment, Battery H*.

Wilson's (John W.) Infantry. See *Maryland Troops, Union, 1st Regiment*.

Wilson's (Robert) Infantry. See *New Hampshire Troops, 14th Regiment*.

Wilson's (William R.) Artillery. See *New York Troops, 1st Regiment, Battery F*.

Winegar's (Charles E.) Artillery. See *New York Troops, 1st Regiment, Battery M*.

Wingfield's (John T.) Artillery. See *Sumter Artillery, ante, Battery C*.

Wingfield's (W. L.) Infantry. See *Virginia Troops, Confederate, 28th Regiment*.

Winn's (S. J.) Cavalry. See *Georgia Troops, 16th Battalion*.

Winslow's (Albert H.) Infantry. See *Ohio Troops, 8th Regiment*.

Winslow's (Cleveland) Infantry. See *New York Troops, 5th Regiment (Veteran)*.

Winslow's (George B.) Artillery. See *New York Troops, 1st Regiment, Battery D*.

Wistar's (Joseph W.) Cavalry. See *Pennsylvania Troops, 8th Regiment*.

Witcher's (John S.) Cavalry. See *West Virginia Troops, 3d Regiment*.

Witcher's (V. A.) Cavalry. See *Virginia Troops, Confederate, 34th Battalion*.

Witcher's (William A.) Infantry. See *Virginia Troops, Confederate, 21st Regiment*.

Withers' (Robert E.) Infantry. See *Virginia Troops, Confederate, 18th Regiment*.

Withers' (Robert W.) Infantry. See *Virginia Troops, Confederate, 42d Regiment*.

Woerner's (Christian) Artillery. See *New Jersey Troops, 3d Battery*.

Wolfe's (John P.) Infantry. See *Virginia Troops, Confederate, 51st Regiment*.

Wood's (James, jr.) Infantry. See *New York Troops, 136th Regiment*.

Wood's (J. De Witt) Artillery. See *New York Troops, 33d Battery*.

Woodall's (Daniel) Infantry.* See *New York Troops, 39th Regiment*.

Woodbury's (George T.) Artillery. See *New Jersey Troops, 4th Battery*.

Woodruff's (Carle A.) Artillery. See *Union Troops, Regulars, 2d Regiment, Battery M*.

Woodruff's (Dickinson) Infantry. See *Union Troops, Regulars, 12th Regiment*.

Woodson's (J. G.) Infantry. See *Virginia Troops, Confederate, 19th Regiment*.

Woodward's (George A.) Infantry. See *Pennsylvania Troops, 2d Reserves*.

Woodward's (William H.) Artillery. See *Pennsylvania Troops*.

Woolfolk's (Pichegru, jr.) Artillery. See *Ashland Artillery, ante*.

Woolworth's (Richard H.) Infantry. See *Pennsylvania Troops, 4th Reserves*.

Wooster's (William B.) Infantry. See *Connecticut Troops, 20th Regiment*.

Work's (P. A.) Infantry. See *Texas Troops, 1st Regiment*.

Wright's (G. J.) Cavalry. See *Cobb's Legion, ante*.

Wright's (Levi P.) Heavy Artillery. ·See *Massachusetts Troops, 1st Regiment*.

Wright's (Samuel T.) Artillery. See *Virginia Troops, Confederate*.

Wyatt's (James W.) Artillery. See *Albemarle Artillery, ante*.

Wyndham's (Percy) Cavalry. See *New Jersey Troops, 1st Regiment*.

Wynkoop's (John E.) Cavalry. See *Pennsylvania Troops, 20th Regiment*.

Wythe County Home Guards. See *Virginia Troops, Confederate*.

York's (Zebulon) Infantry. See *Louisiana Troops, 14th Regiment*.

Young's (Edward R.) Artillery. See *Virginia Troops, Confederate*.

Young's (John J.) Artillery. See *Pennsylvania Troops, Battery G*.

Young's (Pierce M. B.) Cavalry. See *Cobb's Legion, ante*.

Zabriskie's (Abram) Infantry. See *New Jersey Troops, 9th Regiment*.

Zell's (T. Elwood) Infantry. See *Pennsylvania Troops, 2d Battalion*.

---

* Temporarily commanding.

INDEX.

Brigades, Divisions, Corps, Armies, and improvised organizations are "Mentioned" under name of commanding officer; State and other organizations under their official designation. (See Alternate Designations, pp. 935-966.)

*Company H served as artillery.

Page.

Georgia Troops. Mentioned—Continued.

Infantry—*Battalions:* **2d,** 685, 900; **3d, Sharpshooters,** 682; **10th,** 403, 690, 851, 906. *Regiments:* **2d,** 683; **3d,** 685, 900; **4th,** 683, 900; **7th, 8th, 9th,** 683; **10th,** 682; **11th,** 683; **12th,** 683, 900; **13th,** 684, 899; **14th,** 686, 901; **15th,** 683; **16th,** 682; **17th,** 683; **18th,** 682; **20th,** 683; **21st,** 683, 900; **22d,** 685, 900; **24th,** 682; **26th, 31st,** 684, 899; **35th,** 686, 901; **38th,** 684, 899; **44th,** 683, 900; **45th,** 686, 901; **48th,** 518, 685, 900; **49th,** 686, 901; **50th, 51st, 53d,** 682; **59th,** 683; **60th,** 684, 899; **61st,** 518, 684, 899.

Miscellaneous—Cobb's Legion, 682, 686, 707, 902, 927; Phillips Legion, 682, 686, 707, 863, 902.

Getchell, Thomas. Mentioned 132, 608

Getty, George W.

  Assignment to command 226

  Correspondence with

    Butler, Benjamin F 453, 543, 569, 572, 576, 581

    Cornog, George T 453

    Foster, John G 199, 403

    Graham, Charles K 572

    Naglee, Henry M 23, 26, 199

    Spear, Samuel P 99, 114

    Stetzel, George 572

    Wetherill, Samuel 403

    Wild, Edward A 542, 543

  Mentioned 57, 107, 142, 184, 194, 226, 230, 240, 267, 406, 470, 524, 618, 619, 624

Getty, G. Thomas. Mentioned 667

Gibbes, W. H. Mentioned 691, 716

Gibboney, John H.

  Correspondence with Samuel Jones 826

  Mentioned 826

Gibbs, Alfred.

  Correspondence with

    King, Rufus 69, 76, 173, 221

    Pleasonton, Alfred 347

  Mentioned 33, 51, 52, 128, 177, 283, 307, 343, 606

Gibbs, Charles W. Mentioned 622

Gibbs, Frank C. Mentioned 124, 157, 604

Gibbs, George C. Mentioned 692, 814, 907

Gibraltar, Steamer. Mentioned 651

Gibson, Augustus A. Mentioned 132, 394, 609

Gibson, J. Catlett. Mentioned 684, 899

Gibson, John A. Mentioned 909

Gibson, Thomas.

  Correspondence with William W. Averell 150, 229, 309

  Mentioned 140, 182, 229

Gibson, William. Mentioned 685, 900

Giddings, Gideon R. Mentioned 118, 123

Giddings, Grotius R. Mentioned 145

Gilbreth, Samuel G. Mentioned 601

Gile, George W. Mentioned 608

Giles, James. Mentioned 682, 812, 908

Gilkyson, Stephen R. Mentioned 602

Gillespie, George L. Correspondence with James C. Duane 200

Gillies, Charles F. Mentioned 615

Page.

Jones, Samuel.

Assignment to command 701

Correspondence with

Adjutant and Inspector General's Office, C. S. A 626,
634, 662, 664, 679, 730, 736, 743, 795, 805, 807, 824, 894, 913

Bowen, H. S. 801

Bowyer, Henry M 735, 744, 822, 875

Bragg, Braxton 799, 807

Bristol, Quartermaster at 875

Browne, William H 663, 801, 874, 878, 879, 881, 891

Buckner, Simon B. 662

Caperton, A. T 851

Claiborne, James R 674, 699

Davis, Jefferson 727, 738, 764

Derrick, Clarence 663

Echols, John 744
750, 751, 756, 775, 778, 785, 789, 791, 795, 796, 799, 822, 834, 852, 856, 870, 891

Ferguson, Milton J 680, 722, 732, 785, 787, 855

French, William H 801

Gibboney, John H 826

Graves, Joseph 875

Hart, William T 717

Imboden, John D 647, 666, 677, 732, 826, 832

Jackson, A. E 678, 680

Jackson, William L 663, 677, 692, 722, 734, 855, 893

Jenkins, Albert G 677

Jones, B. H 734, 782, 804, 826, 855

Kent, Joseph F 666, 733, 787, 822, 826, 875

King, J. Floyd 701

Lee, Robert E 633, 640, 642, 646, 652, 679, 750, 780, 781, 815, 817, 825

McCausland, John 667,
693, 699, 722, 734, 737, 744, 747, 786, 790, 792, 796, 797, 822, 824, 834, 855, 871

McDowell, James 822, 826

Martin, James G 721, 768

Millborough, Va., Agent at 826

Myers, William B 707, 712, 718, 721, 874, 886, 891

Narrows, Va., Operator at 744

Nicholls, Francis T 667, 717, 725, 735, 827, 875

Ordnance Department, C. S. A 732

Patton, George S 634, 664, 693, 699, 722, 733, 734

Preston, Robert T 667, 744

Preston, William 892

Preston, William R 877, 878

Quartermaster-General's Office, C. S. A 782, 797

Ransom, Robert, jr 781, 801, 803, 810, 825, 874, 875, 877

Salem, Va., Operator at 886

Sheffey, J. M 787, 826, 875

Spiller, Frank S 787

Staunton, Va., Commanding Officer at 732

Stringfellow, Charles S 633,
640, 662, 725, 730, 746, 749, 751, 753, 792, 793, 795, 796, 821, 822

Subsistence Department, C. S. A 912

Terrill, George P 668, 712, 735, 822, 827, 875

Wade, James M 713, 735, 797, 822, 827, 829, 875, 876

Page.

Kelley, Benjamin F.—Continued.

 Mentioned 10, 30, 49, 72, 138, 139, 206, 240, 301, 308, 310, 339, 358,

  399, 406, 524, 565, 591, 593–595, 614, 615, 632, 633, 640, 643, 733, 747, 751, 815

 Staff. Announcement of 414

Kelley, Hugh A. Mentioned.................................... 613

Kelley, William B. Mentioned.............................. 415

 For correspondence as A. D. C., see *Jeremiah C. Sullivan.*

Kellogg, Elisha S. Mentioned........................... 133, 609

Kellogg, Horace. Mentioned 140, 615

Kelly, Patrick. Mentioned 120, 600

Kelly, Thomas. Mentioned............................ 120

Kelsey, William. Mentioned.......................... 611

Kelton, John C. For correspondence as A. A. G., see *Army Headquarters.*

Kemp, Joseph R. Mentioned............................ 138, 617

Kemper, James L. Mentioned 682, 741, 764, 765, 811, 847, 904, 905

Kenan, Thomas S. Mentioned 683, 900

Kendrick, E. M. Mentioned............................ 677

Kendrick, William J. For correspondence, see *Virginia, Citizens of.*

Kenly, John R.

 Correspondence with George G. Meade........................... 537

 Mentioned 119, 474, 477, 536, 539, 540, 599

Kennedy, John D. Mentioned............................ 682

Kensel, George A. Mentioned........................... 447, 494

Kent, Joseph F.

 Correspondence with Samuel Jones 666, 733, 787, 822, 826, 875

 Mentioned 668, 712, 787, 797

Kentucky Troops. Mentioned. (Confederate.)

 Cavalry—*Companies:* Fields', 768. *Regiments:* 4th, 813, 824, 909; May's

  Rifles, 813, 909.

 Infantry—*Regiments:* 11th,* 813.

Kentucky Troops. Mentioned. (Union.)

 Artillery, Light—*Batteries:* Simmonds', 139, 616.

Keogh, Myles W.

 Correspondence with Alfred Pleasonton.......................... 377

 Mentioned 378

Ker, George J. Correspondence with Henry M. Naglee..................... 216

Kershaw, Joseph B. Mentioned............................. 682

Kester, John W. Mentioned............................. 588, 589, 606

Ketcham, John H. Mentioned.............................. 127

Ketchum, William A. Mentioned 598

Kevill, Thomas. Mentioned 690, 783, 905

Key, J. C. G. Mentioned 683

Keys, Hugh. Mentioned.................................. 569

Killed and Wounded. See *Confederate Troops* and *Union Troops. Returns of Casualties.*

Kilpatrick, F. W. Mentioned 689

Kilpatrick, Judson.

 Correspondence with

  Custer, George A.................................... 75, 270

  Davies, Henry E., jr 89, 269, 270, 441, 453

  Hall, Josiah 221

  Meade, George G................................. 89, 263

*Also called 10th Kentucky Battalion; afterward 13th Kentucky Cavalry.

Page.

* G. D. Summers' company (F) served as cavalry.

---

*Afterward Battery I, 1st Michigan Light Artillery.
†Afterward Battery K, 1st Michigan Light Artillery.

Page.

Page.

Mosby, John S.
Correspondence with J. E. B. Stuart 931
Mentioned 23, 24, 26, 42, 44, 68, 113, 152,
159, 177, 221, 345, 350, 358, 360, 369, 380, 397, 585, 588, 652, 653, 661, 766, 847
Moseley, E. F. Mentioned 690, 906
Moseley, Hillery. Mentioned 685, 901
Moson, Richard F. Mentioned 137
Mott, Gershom.
Correspondence with
French, William H 327
Prince, Henry 335
Mentioned 122, 333, 339, 602
Moulton, Orson. Mentioned 144, 620
Muhlenberg, Edward D. Mentioned 127
Mulford, John E. Mentioned 268
Mulligan, James A.
Correspondence with Benjamin F. Kelley 264
Mentioned 30, 138, 140, 205, 211, 240, 365, 406, 524, 580, 614, 616
Mundin, Mrs. Mentioned 883
Munford, Thomas T. Mentioned 686, 708, 902
Munitions of War. Supplies of, etc. Communications from
Adjutant-General's Office, U. S. A 14
Adjutant and Inspector General's Office, C. S. A 911
Army Headquarters 8, 13, 589
Benham, Henry W 407
Barnard, John G 393
Bowyer, Thomas M 806
Cole, A. H 655, 657, 715
Custer, George A 448
Early, Jubal A 759
Elzey, Arnold 657, 658
Ewell, Richard S 760
French, S. Bassett 656
Hunt, Henry J 237, 241, 383, 391, 413, 488
Ingalls, Rufus 261, 298, 472, 533
Imboden, John D 913
Jones, Samuel 732, 782
Kilpatrick, Judson 441
Lamar, A. R 911
Lee, Robert E 625, 628, 648, 714, 794, 820, 830, 832, 833, 837, 844, 858, 862, 889, 890
Lee, S. Phillips 353
Meade, George G 85, 332, 407, 408, 420
Navy Department, U. S 353
North Carolina, Governor of 836
Ordnance Department, C. S. A 740
Peck, John J 416
Pendleton, William N 643, 697, 863
Pleasonton, Alfred 382, 404, 418, 448
Quartermaster-General's Office, C. S. A 784
Scammon, Eliakim P 290
Stoneman, George 398, 419, 448
Stuart, J. E. B 62
Subsistence Department, C. S. A 760, 843, 912
Vance, Robert B 836

* 1st Mounted Rifles.

† Also called 69th New York National Guard Artillery.

---

* Also called Wilmington Horse Artillery.
† Also called 59th North Carolina.
‡ Also called 63d North Carolina.

---

* Company L served as cavalry.

---

* Departmental Corps, Department of the Monongahela.

Page.

---

* Consolidated.

† Departmental Corps, Department of the Monongahela.

---

* Consolidated.
† Regiments, etc., designated when practicable.

Virginia Troops. (Confederate.)

Mentioned.

Artillery, Heavy—*Battalions:* 10th, 690, 783, 905; 10th (*Batteries*), B, 783; 18th, 641, 690, 783, 905; 19th, 690, 783, 905; 20th, 641, 690, 783, 905. *Batteries:* Lunenberg, 690, 783, 905; Neblett, 690, 783, 905; Pamunkey, 690, 783, 905. *Regiments:* 4th, 657, 690; 4th (*Batteries*), A, K, 690.

Artillery, Light—*Batteries:* Albemarle, 638, 688, 903; Alexandria, 691, 783, 905; Alleghany, 688, 902; Amherst, 688, 903; Ashland, 687; Bedford, 687; Blount's, 687; Botetourt, 813, 908, 909; Breathed's, 687, 904; Brooke's, 638, 688, 903; Bryan's, 813, 857, 908, 909; Caroline, 691, 783, 905; Charlottesville, 688, 903; Chew's, 687, 816, 904; Courtney, 688, 903; Crenshaw's,* 688, 903; Dabney's, 690; Danville, 688, 903; Davidson's, 757, 813, 909; Fauquier, 687; Fluvanna, 688, 903; Fredericksburg, 688, 903; Goochland, 690, 783, 905; Hampden, 687; Jackson's, 813, 857, 908, 909; Johnson's, 688, 903; Johnston, 690, 783, 905; King William, 688, 902; Lee, 688, 902; Letcher, 688, 903; Levi, 813; Lewis', 688, 903; Lowry's, 813, 909; Lurty's, 857, 908, 909; McClanahan's, 904; McComas, 690, 783, 905; McGregor's, 687, 904; Martin's, 689; Matthews, 690, 783, 905; Monroe, 813, 857, 908, 909; Moore's, 688, 903; Moorman's, 687, 904; Morris, 688, 902; Nelson, 780, 903; Nelson, No. 2, 691, 783, 905; Norfolk Blues, 688, 903; Orange, 688, 902; Otey, 716, 722, 743, 813, 909; Parker's, 637, 687; Pegram's, 689; Petersburg, 64, 692, 906; Powhatan, 688, 903; Purcell, 688, 903; Richmond Fayette, 687, 905; Richmond Howitzers (*Companies*), 1st. 637, 687, 904; 2d, 813, 688, 903; Ringgold, 722, 813, 909; Rockbridge, 688, 903; Rockbridge, No. 2, 638, 688, 903; Salem, 637, 688, 903; Southside, 690, 783, 905; Stafford, 905; Staunton, 637, 688, 903; Staunton Hill, 691, 765, 814, 907; Sturdivant's, 689; Surry, 691, 783, 905; Taylor's, 687; United, 690, 783, 905; Wright's, 689; Young's, 690, 783, 905.

Cavalry—*Battalions:* 27th, 813, 909; 32d, 690, 783; 34th, 556, 732–734, 813, 824, 909; 35th, 42, 107, 152, 253, 340, 380, 687, 707, 902; 36th. 556, 747, 749, 792, 813, 824, 909; 37th, 733, 757, 775, 787, 791, 813, 824, 909; 39th, 899; 40th, 638, 689, 690, 764; 41st, 358, 360, 590, 904, 920, 923; 42d,† 783, 856, 871, 905. *Companies:* McNeill's Partisans, 360, 363, 755; P. J. Thurmond's, 909; W. D. Thurmond's, 909. *Regiments :* 1st, 2d, 3d, 686, 708, 902; 4th, 235, 446, 686, 708, 902; 5th, 152, 660, 686, 708, 902; 6th, 152, 687, 707, 902; 7th, 687, 707, 865, 902;

---

* Afterward Ellett's Battery.
† 32d and 40th Battalions consolidated Sept. 24, 1863, and designated 42d Battalion.

Page.

*Afterward Company L, 2d West Virginia Cavalry.

Lightning Source UK Ltd.
Milton Keynes UK
UKHW02f0717140918
328884UK00014B/1132/P